Student Quick Tips

Use this Student Quick Tips guide for a quick and easy start with McGraw-Hill Connect. You'll get valuable tips on registering, doing assignments, and accessing resources, as well as information about the support center hours.

Getting Started

TIP: To get started in Connect, you will need the following:

- Your instructor's Connect Web Address

  Sample of Connect Web Address:

  http://www.mcgrawhillconnect.com/class/instructorname_section_name

- Connect Access Code

TIP: If you do not have an access code or have not yet secured your tuition funds, you can click "Free Trial" during registration. This trial will provide temporary Connect access (typically three weeks) and will remind you to purchase online access before the end of your trial.

Registration and Sign In

1. Go to the Connect Web Address provided by your instructor
2. Click on **Register Now**
3. Enter your email address

TIP: If you already have a McGraw-Hill account, you will be asked for your password and will not be required to create a new account.

4. Enter a registration code or choose **Buy Online** to purchase access online

(Continued: **Registration and Sign In**)

5. Follow the on-screen directions

TIP: Please choose your Security Question and Answer carefully. We will ask you for this information if you forget your password.

6. When registration is complete, click on **Go to Connect Now**
7. You are now ready to use **Connect**

Trouble Logging In?

- Ensure you are using the same email address you used during registration
- If you have forgotten your password, click on the "Forgot Password?" link at your Instructor's Connect Course Web Address
- When logged into Connect, you can update your account information (e.g. email address, password, and security question/answer) by clicking on the *"My Account"* link located at the top-right corner

Home (Assignments)

TIP: If you are unable to begin an assignment, verify the following:

- The assignment is available (start and due dates)
- That you have not exceeded the maximum number of attempts
- That you have not achieved a score of 100%
- If your assignment contains questions that require manual grading, you will not be able to begin your next attempt until your instructor has graded those questions

(Continued: **Home Assignments**)

TIP: Based on the assignment policy settings established by your Instructor, you may encounter the following limitations when working on your assignment(s):

- Ability to Print Assignment
- Timed assignments – once you begin a "*timed assignment*," the timer will not stop by design

TIP: "*Save & Exit*" vs. "*Submit*" button

- If you are unable to complete your assignment in one sitting, utilize the "*Save & Exit*" button to save your work and complete it at a later time
- Once you have completed your assignment, utilize the "*Submit*" button in order for your assignment to be graded

Library

TIP: The *Library* section of your Connect account provides shortcuts to various resources.

- If you purchased ConnectPlus, you will see an *eBook* link, which can also be accessed from the section information widget of the *Home* tab
- *Recorded Lectures* can be accessed if your instructor is using *Tegrity Campus* to capture lectures. You may also access recorded lectures when taking an assignment by clicking on the projector icon in the navigation bar
- Many McGraw-Hill textbooks offer additional resources such as narrated slides and additional problems, which are accessible through the *Student Resources* link

Reports

TIP: Once you submit your assignment, you can view your available results in the *Reports* tab.

- If you see a dash (-) as your score, your instructor has either delayed or restricted your ability to see the assignment feedback
- Your instructor has the ability to limit the amount of information (e.g. questions, answers, scores) you can view for each submitted assignment

Need More Help?

CONTACT US ONLINE

Visit us at:

www.mcgrawhillconnect.com/support

Browse our support materials including tutorial videos and our searchable Connect knowledge base. If you cannot find an answer to your question, click on "Contact Us" button to send us an email.

GIVE US A CALL

Call us at:

1-800-331-5094

Our live support is available:

Mon-Thurs:	8 am – 11 pm CT
Friday:	8 am – 6 pm CT
Sunday:	6 pm – 11 pm CT

MANAGERIAL ACCOUNTING

FOURTEENTH EDITION

RAY H. GARRISON, D.B.A., CPA
PROFESSOR EMERITUS
BRIGHAM YOUNG UNIVERSITY

ERIC W. NOREEN, PH.D., CMA
PROFESSOR EMERITUS
UNIVERSITY OF WASHINGTON

PETER C. BREWER, PH.D., CPA
MIAMI UNIVERSITY–OXFORD, OHIO

Portland Community College
BA 213

Mc Graw Hill Education

Managerial Accounting, Fourteenth Edition
Portland Community College
BA 213

This book is a McGraw-Hill Learning Solutions textbook and contains select material from *Managerial Accounting*, Fourteenth Edition by Ray H. Garrison, Eric W. Noreen and Peter C. Brewer. Copyright © 2012, 2010, 2008, 2006, 2003, 2000, 1997, 1994, 1991, 1988, 1985, 1982, 1979, 1976 by The McGraw-Hill Companies, Inc. Reprinted with permission of the publisher. Many custom published texts are modified versions or adaptations of our best-selling textbooks. Some adaptations are printed in black and white to keep prices at a minimum, while others are in color.

13 14 15 16 17 18 QVS/QVS 20 19 18 17 16

ISBN-13: 978-0-07-758149-7
ISBN-10: 0-07-758149-0
PART OF:
ISBN-13: 978-0-07-758275-3
ISBN-10: 0-07-758275-6

Learning Solutions Manager: Danielle Meier
Production Editor: Jennifer Pickel
Cover Design: Lou Civitello
Printer/Binder: Quad/Graphics

Dedication

To our families and to our many colleagues who use this book.

About the Authors

Ray H. Garrison is emeritus professor of accounting at Brigham Young University, Provo, Utah. He received his BS and MS degrees from Brigham Young University and his DBA degree from Indiana University.

As a certified public accountant, Professor Garrison has been involved in management consulting work with both national and regional accounting firms. He has published articles in *The Accounting Review, Management Accounting,* and other professional journals. Innovation in the classroom has earned Professor Garrison the Karl G. Maeser Distinguished Teaching Award from Brigham Young University.

Eric W. Noreen has held appointments at institutions in the United States, Europe, and Asia. He is emeritus professor of accounting at the University of Washington.

He received his BA degree from the University of Washington and MBA and PhD degrees from Stanford University. A Certified Management Accountant, he was awarded a Certificate of Distinguished Performance by the Institute of Certified Management Accountants.

Professor Noreen has served as associate editor of *The Accounting Review* and the *Journal of Accounting and Economics*. He has numerous articles in academic journals including: the *Journal of Accounting Research*; *The Accounting Review*; the *Journal of Accounting and Economics*; *Accounting Horizons*; *Accounting, Organizations and Society*; *Contemporary Accounting Research*; the *Journal of Management Accounting Research*; and the *Review of Accounting Studies*.

Professor Noreen has won a number of awards from students for his teaching.

Peter C. Brewer is a professor in the Department of Accountancy at Miami University, Oxford, Ohio. He holds a BS degree in accounting from Penn State University, an MS degree in accounting from the University of Virginia, and a PhD from the University of Tennessee. He has published more than 30 articles in a variety of journals including: *Management Accounting Research*, the *Journal of Information Systems*, *Cost Management*, *Strategic Finance*, the *Journal of Accountancy*, *Issues in Accounting Education*, and the *Journal of Business Logistics*.

Professor Brewer is a member of the editorial board of the *Journal of Accounting Education* and has served on the editorial board of *Issues in Accounting Education*. His article "Putting Strategy into the Balanced Scorecard" won the 2003 International Federation of Accountants' Articles of Merit competition, and his articles "Using Six Sigma to Improve the Finance Function" and "Lean Accounting: What's It All About?" were awarded the Institute of Management Accountants' Lybrand Gold and Silver Medals in 2005 and 2006. He has received Miami University's Richard T. Farmer School of Business Teaching Excellence Award and has been recognized on two occasions by the Miami University Associated Student Government for "making a remarkable commitment to students and their educational development." He is a leading thinker in undergraduate management accounting curriculum innovation and is a frequent presenter at various professional and academic conferences.

Prior to joining the faculty at Miami University, Professor Brewer was employed as an auditor for Touche Ross in the firm's Philadelphia office. He also worked as an internal audit manager for the Board of Pensions of the Presbyterian Church (U.S.A.). He frequently collaborates with companies such as Harris Corporation, Ghent Manufacturing, Cintas, Ethicon Endo-Surgery, Schneider Electric, Lenscrafters, and Fidelity Investments in a consulting or case writing capacity.

Let **Garrison** be Your Guide

It is the *'Bible'* of *Managerial Accounting.*

Mark Motluck, Anderson University

An excellent choice for a first course in managerial accounting.

Steven Huddart, Penn State

Garrison is the gold standard of all accounting texts.

Gene Johnson, Clark College

For centuries, the lighthouse has provided guidance and safe passage for sailors. Similarly, Garrison/Noreen/Brewer has successfully guided millions of students through managerial accounting, helping them sail smoothly through the course.

Decades ago, lighthouses were still being operated manually. In these days of digital transformation, lighthouses are run using automatic lamp changers and other modern devices. In much the same way, Garrison/Noreen/Brewer has evolved over the years. Today, the Garrison book not only guides students—accounting majors and other business majors alike—safely through the course but is enhanced by a number of powerful new tools to augment student learning and increase student motivation. McGraw-Hill's *Connect™ Accounting* offers a number of features to facilitate student learning. Embedded within *Connect Accounting,* our **NEW** intelligent technology, LearnSmart, offers flashcards that personalize the study experience by constantly adapting, emphasizing the concepts a student still needs to master. **NEW** animated, narrated Guided Examples connected to practice exercises within *Connect Accounting* provide a step-by-step walkthrough of a similar exercise, assisting students when they need it most. *Connect Accounting's* **NEW** Self-Quiz and Study provides a study plan that recommends specific readings from the text, supplemental narrated PowerPoints, and practice exercises that will improve students' understanding of each learning objective. Finally, the student library within *Connect* gives students access to additional resources, such as forms for the **NEW** Applying Excel feature, Interactive Presentations for each learning objective, an electronic version of the textbook, and more.

Just as the lighthouse continues to provide reliable guidance to seafarers, the Garrison/Noreen/Brewer book continues its tradition of helping students sail successfully through managerial accounting by always focusing on three important qualities: **relevance, accuracy, and clarity.**

RELEVANCE. Every effort is made to help students relate the concepts in this book to the decisions made by working managers. In the fourteenth edition, the authors have written a new Chapter 1 with the goal of helping all business students better understand why managerial accounting is relevant to their future careers. New and revised In Business boxes throughout the book link chapter concepts to pertinent real-world examples. Service industry references appear throughout the chapter narrative and end-of-chapter material to provide students with relevant context for the material they are learning. The robust *Connect Accounting* technology package is populated with new and exciting tools to help keep students engaged in the learning process. For these reasons and many more, a student reading Garrison should never have to ask "Why am I learning this?"

ACCURACY. The Garrison book continues to set the standard for accurate and reliable material in its fourteenth edition. With each revision, the authors evaluate the book and its supplements in their entirety, working diligently to ensure that the end-of-chapter material, solutions manual, and test bank are consistent, current, and accurate.

CLARITY. Generations of students have praised Garrison for the friendliness and readability of its writing, but that's just the beginning. In the fourteenth edition, the authors have rewritten various chapters with input and guidance from instructors around the country to ensure that teaching and learning from Garrison remains as easy as it can be. In addition, the authors have taken an active role in building out *Connect Accounting*, carefully reviewing its various components to ensure clarity and consistency with the textbook.

The authors' steady focus on these three core elements has led to tremendous results. *Managerial Accounting* has consistently led the market, being used by over two million students and earning a reputation for reliability that other texts aspire to match.

Garrison's *Managerial Accounting* text is one of the best introductory texts available today. It provides students with the tools and information needed to help them successfully learn this material in an interesting and engaging manner. The Garrison text is the only option.

Tracy Campbell Tuttle,
San Diego Mesa Community College

Good service industry materials. The more I read the book, the more I appreciated this information. The homework . . . directed toward service business expands the relevance of the material to the student.

Don Lucy,
Indian River State College

A well-done text that is a pleasure to teach from.

Joseph Gerard,
University of Wisconsin—Whitewater

It's still the best book on the market, and my students continually tell me what a great book it is.

Charles Caliendo,
University of Minnesota

Garrison's

Managerial Accounting includes pedagogical elements that engage and instruct students without cluttering the pages or interrupting student learning. Garrison's key pedagogical tools enhance and support students' understanding of the concepts rather than compete with the narrative for their attention.

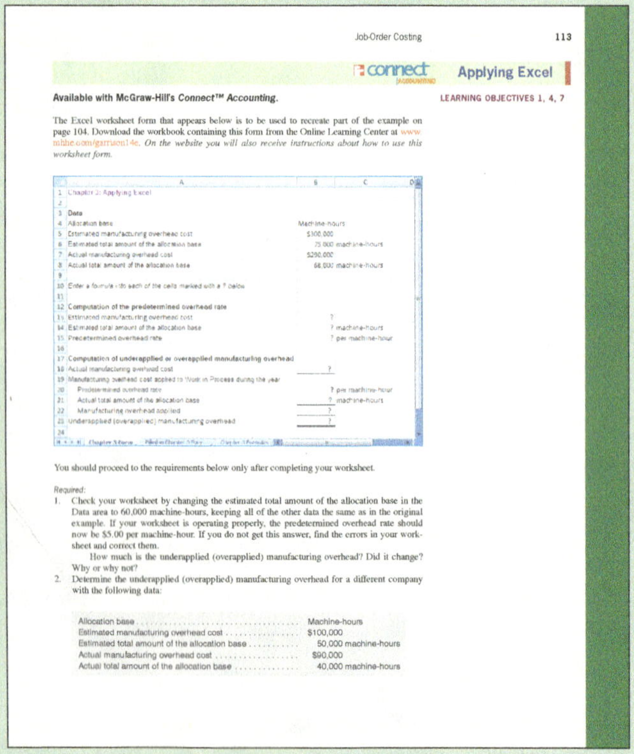

Job-Order Costing 113

connect ACCOUNTING **Applying Excel**

Available with McGraw-Hill's *Connect™ Accounting*.

LEARNING OBJECTIVES 1, 4, 7

The Excel worksheet form that appears below is to be used to recreate part of the example on page 104. Download the workbook containing this form from the Online Learning Center at www.mhhe.com/garrison14e. *On the website you will also receive instructions about how to use this worksheet form.*

	A	B	C
1	Chapter 3: Applying Excel		
2			
3	**Data**		
4	Allocation base	Machine-hours	
5	Estimated manufacturing overhead cost	$300,000	
6	Estimated total amount of the allocation base	75,000	machine-hours
7	Actual manufacturing overhead cost	$290,000	
8	Actual total amount of the allocation base	68,000	machine-hours
9			
10	Enter a formula into each of the cells marked with a ? below		
11			
12	**Computation of the predetermined overhead rate**		
13	Estimated manufacturing overhead cost	?	
14	Estimated total amount of the allocation base	?	machine-hours
15	Predetermined overhead rate	?	per machine-hour
16			
17	**Computation of underapplied or overapplied manufacturing overhead**		
18	Actual manufacturing overhead cost	?	
19	Manufacturing overhead cost applied to Work in Process during the year		
20	Predetermined overhead rate	?	per machine-hour
21	Actual total amount of the allocation base	?	machine-hours
22	Manufacturing overhead applied	?	
23	Underapplied (overapplied) manufacturing overhead	?	
24			

You should proceed to the requirements below only after completing your worksheet.

Required:

1. Check your worksheet by changing the estimated total amount of the allocation base in the Data area to 60,000 machine-hours, keeping all of the other data the same as in the original example. If your worksheet is operating properly, the predetermined overhead rate should now be $5.00 per machine-hour. If you do not get this answer, find the errors in your worksheet and correct them.

   How much is the underapplied (overapplied) manufacturing overhead? Did it change? Why or why not?
2. Determine the underapplied (overapplied) manufacturing overhead for a different company with the following data:

Allocation base	Machine-hours
Estimated manufacturing overhead cost	$100,000
Estimated total amount of the allocation base	50,000 machine-hours
Actual manufacturing overhead cost	$90,000
Actual total amount of the allocation base	40,000 machine-hours

NEW to the fourteenth edition of Garrison!

Applying Excel

This **NEW** and exciting end-of-chapter feature **links the power of Excel with managerial accounting concepts** by illustrating how Excel functionality can be used to better understand accounting data. Applying Excel goes beyond plugging numbers into a template by providing students with an opportunity to build their own Excel worksheets and formulas. Students are then asked "what if" questions in which they analyze not only **how** related pieces of accounting data affect each other but **why** they do. Applying Excel immediately precedes the Exercises in twelve of the fifteen chapters in the book and is also **integrated with McGraw-Hill's *Connect™ Accounting*,** allowing students to practice their skills online with algorithmically generated datasets.

An excellent pedagogical feature that helps further reinforce students' knowledge of key concepts in the text book, while strengthening students' Excel skills that are so important in the work place. This will further enhance an already excellent text.

Marianne L. James, California State University, Los Angeles

[Applying Excel is] an excellent way for students to programmatically develop spreadsheet skills without having to be taught spreadsheet techniques by the instructor. A significant associated benefit is that students gain more exposure to the dynamics of accounting information by working with what-if scenarios.

Earl Godfrey, Gardner–Webb University

Powerful Pedagogy

Opening Vignette

Each chapter opens with a **Business Focus** feature that provides a real-world example for students, allowing them to see how the chapter's information and insights apply to the world outside the classroom. **Learning Objectives** alert students to what they should expect as they progress through the chapter.

Chapter 8

Profit Planning

Planning for a Crisis—Civil War Preservation Trust

BUSINESS FOCUS

The Civil War Preservation Trust (CWPT) is a private, nonprofit organization with 70,000 members that works to preserve the nation's remaining Civil War battlefields—many of which are threatened by commercial development such as shopping centers, houses, industrial parks, and casinos. To forestall development, the CWPT typically purchases the land or development rights to the land. The CWPT has saved over 25,000 acres from development, including, for example, 698 acres of battlefield at Gettysburg.

CWPT's management team was particularly concerned about the budget proposal for 2009, which was to be presented to the board of directors in the fall of 2008. The CWPT is wholly supported by contributions from its members and many of those members had been adversely affected by the ongoing financial crisis that followed the collapse of the subprime mortgage market. Consequently, the funds that would be available for operations in 2009 were particularly difficult to predict. Accordingly, the budget for 2009 contained three variations based on progressively pessimistic economic assumptions. The more pessimistic budgets were called contingent budgets. As 2008 progressed and member contributions declined somewhat from previous levels, CWPT switched to the first contingent budget. This contingent budget required a number of actions to reduce costs including a hiring freeze and a salary freeze, but maintained an aggressive program of protecting battlefield acreage through purchases of land and development rights. Fortunately, the CWPT did not have to switch to the most pessimistic budget—which would have involved layoffs and other extraordinary cost-saving measures.

Instead of reacting in a panic mode to unfavorable developments, CWPT used the budgeting process to carefully plan in advance for a number of possible contingencies. ■

Sources: Communications with James Lighthizer, president, and David Duncan, director of membership and development, Civil War Preservation Trust; and the CWPT website, civilwar.org.

LEARNING OBJECTIVES

After studying Chapter 8, you should be able to:

- LO1 Understand why organizations budget and the processes they use to create budgets.
- LO2 Prepare a sales budget, including a schedule of expected cash collections.
- LO3 Prepare a production budget.
- LO4 Prepare a direct materials budget, including a schedule of expected cash disbursements for purchases of materials.
- LO5 Prepare a direct labor budget.
- LO6 Prepare a manufacturing overhead budget.
- LO7 Prepare a selling and administrative expense budget.
- LO8 Prepare a cash budget.
- LO9 Prepare a budgeted income statement.
- LO10 Prepare a budgeted balance sheet.

335

I like how you engage the reader with the "Business Focus" at the beginning of the chapter.

Kathy Crusto-Way,
Tarrant County College

This textbook speaks to today's student with Excel-based visuals, discussions on hot topics, such as corporate responsibility, and examples from recognizable companies. It also prepares students for business and CPA and CMA examinations.

Alison Jill Brock,
Imperial Valley College

A text the students will enjoy reading.

Ruth W. Epps,
Virginia Commonwealth University

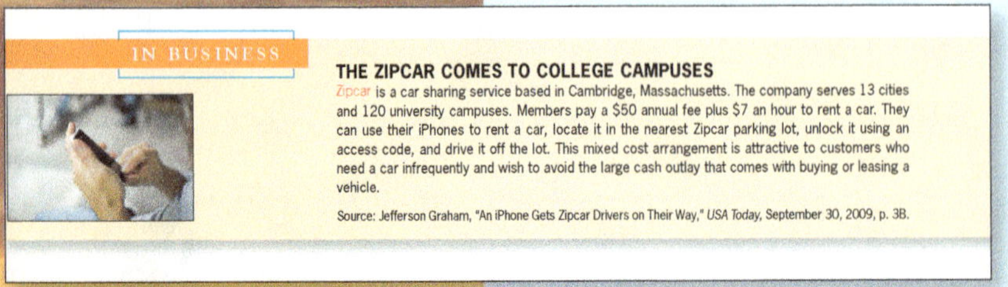

IN BUSINESS

THE ZIPCAR COMES TO COLLEGE CAMPUSES

Zipcar is a car sharing service based in Cambridge, Massachusetts. The company serves 13 cities and 120 university campuses. Members pay a $50 annual fee plus $7 an hour to rent a car. They can use their iPhones to rent a car, locate it in the nearest Zipcar parking lot, unlock it using an access code, and drive it off the lot. This mixed cost arrangement is attractive to customers who need a car infrequently and wish to avoid the large cash outlay that comes with buying or leasing a vehicle.

Source: Jefferson Graham, "An iPhone Gets Zipcar Drivers on Their Way," *USA Today*, September 30, 2009, p. 3B.

In Business Boxes

These helpful boxed features offer a glimpse into how real companies use the managerial accounting concepts discussed within the chapter. Each chapter contains from three to fourteen of these current examples.

I found the text to be thorough and well organized. I was particularly impressed with the numerous real-world examples included in the "in business" boxes to make the topical discussions more meaningful.

Jerry Thorne,
North Carolina
A & T State University

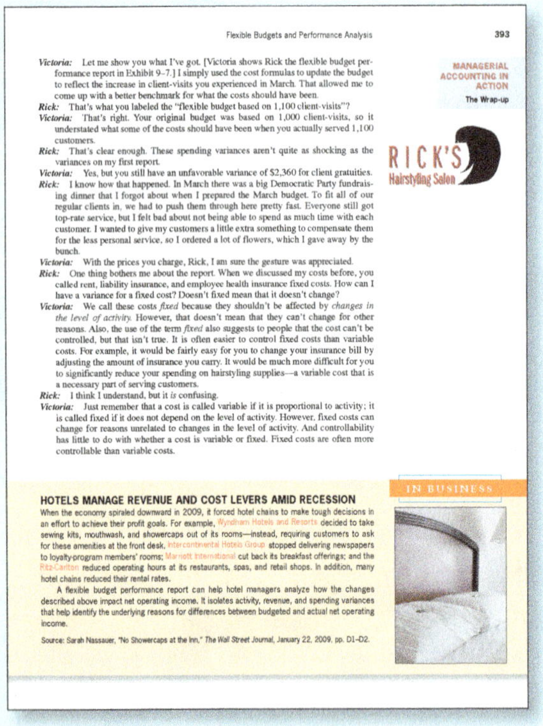

Flexible Budgets and Performance Analysis 393

MANAGERIAL ACCOUNTING IN ACTION

The Wrap-up

Victoria: Let me show you what I've got. [Victoria shows Rick the flexible budget performance report in Exhibit 9–7.] I simply used the cost formulas to update the budget to reflect the increase in client-visits you experienced in March. That allowed me to come up with a better benchmark for what the costs should have been.

Rick: That's what you labeled the "flexible budget based on 1,100 client-visits"?

Victoria: That's right. Your original budget was based on 1,000 client-visits, so it understated what some of the costs should have been when you actually served 1,100 customers.

Rick: That's clear enough. These spending variances aren't quite as shocking as the variances on my first report.

Victoria: Yes, but you still have an unfavorable variance of $2,360 for client gratuities.

Rick: I know how that happened. In March there was a big Democratic Party fundraising dinner that I forgot about when I prepared the March budget. To fit all of our regular clients in, we had to push them through here pretty fast. Everyone still got top-rate service, but I felt bad about not being able to spend as much time with each customer. I wanted to give my customers a little extra something to compensate them for the less personal service, so I ordered a lot of flowers, which I gave away by the bunch.

Victoria: With the prices you charge, Rick, I am sure the gesture was appreciated.

Rick: One thing bothers me about the report. When we discussed my costs before, you called rent, liability insurance, and employee health insurance fixed costs. How can I have a variance for a fixed cost? Doesn't fixed mean that it doesn't change?

Victoria: We call these costs *fixed* because they shouldn't be affected by *changes in the level of activity.* However, that doesn't mean that they can't change for other reasons. Also, the use of the term *fixed* also suggests to people that the cost can't be controlled, but that isn't true. It is often easier to control fixed costs than variable costs. For example, it would be fairly easy for you to change your insurance bill by adjusting the amount of insurance you carry. It would be much more difficult for you to significantly reduce your spending on hairstyling supplies—a variable cost that is a necessary part of serving customers.

Rick: I think I understand, but it *is* confusing.

Victoria: Just remember that a cost is called variable if it is proportional to activity; it is called fixed if it does not depend on the level of activity. However, fixed costs can change for reasons unrelated to changes in the level of activity. And controllability has little to do with whether a cost is variable or fixed. Fixed costs are often more controllable than variable costs.

IN BUSINESS

HOTELS MANAGE REVENUE AND COST LEVERS AMID RECESSION

When the economy spiraled downward in 2009, it forced hotel chains to make tough decisions in an effort to achieve their profit goals. For example, Wyndham Hotels and Resorts decided to take sewing kits, mouthwash, and showercaps out of its rooms—instead, requiring customers to ask for these amenities at the front desk, Intercontinental Hotels Group stopped delivering newspapers to loyalty-program members' rooms; Marriott International cut back its breakfast offerings; and the Ritz-Carlton reduced operating hours at its restaurants, spas, and retail shops. In addition, many hotel chains reduced their rental rates.

A flexible budget performance report can help hotel managers analyze how the changes described above impact net operating income. It isolates activity, revenue, and spending variances that help identify the underlying reasons for differences between budgeted and actual net operating income.

Source: Sarah Nassauer, "No Showercaps at the Inn," *The Wall Street Journal*, January 22, 2009, pp. D1–D2.

Managerial Accounting in Action Vignettes

These vignettes depict cross-functional teams working together in real-life settings, working with the products and services that students recognize from their own lives. Students are shown step-by-step how accounting concepts are implemented in organizations and how these concepts are applied to solve everyday business problems. First, "The Issue" is introduced through a dialogue; the student then walks through the implementation process; finally, "The Wrap-up" summarizes the big picture.

End-of-Chapter Material

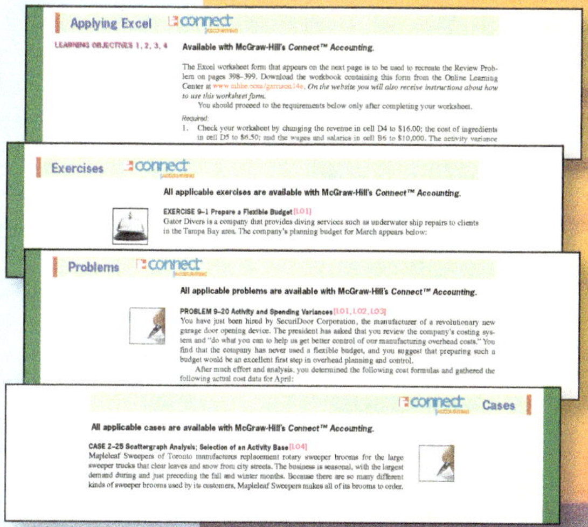

Managerial Accounting has earned a reputation for the best end-of-chapter practice material of any text on the market. Our problem and case material continues to conform to AACSB recommendations and makes a great starting point for class discussions and group projects. When Ray Garrison first wrote *Managerial Accounting,* he started with the end-of-chapter material, then wrote the narrative in support of it. This unique approach to textbook authoring not only ensured consistency between the end-of-chapter material and text content but also underscored Garrison's fundamental belief in the importance of applying theory through practice. It is not enough for students to read, they must also understand. To this day, the guiding principle of that first edition remains, and Garrison's superior end-of-chapter material continues to provide accurate, current, and relevant practice for students.

In this edition, the authors have added a **NEW** end-of-chapter feature called Applying Excel. Applying Excel integrates key course concepts and Excel—a software students will encounter in the workplace, whether they go into accounting or any other business major. With Applying Excel, students not only gain practice working with Excel software, they also learn how Excel can be used to present accounting data and how that data is interrelated. For more information on this exciting new feature, please see page x.

A proven, comprehensive text that effectively covers important managerial accounting topics. [The] end-of-chapter materials are second to none.

Jerry Kreuze,
Western Michigan University

This text is a comprehensive and very readable presentation of essential introductory managerial accounting topics. The end-of-chapter materials are excellent and enhance the chapter material.

Darlene Coarts,
University of Northern Iowa

Garrison's *Managerial Accounting* is one of the most well-written managerial accounting textbooks that I have ever used or reviewed in my 30-year career as a professor of management accounting. The problem material is excellent, the ancillary material is outstanding, and the publisher support is unequaled. The on-line homework system is superior to all that I have used or reviewed.

Olen L. Greer, Missouri State University

This is a tremendously well-organized and written text that is full of real world examples. Complex topics are explained in a simple and yet detailed fashion.

Matt Muller, Adirondack Community College

This is still the best managerial accounting book out there for accounting and non-accounting students!

Alfred C Greenfield, Jr., High Point University

Author-Written Supplements

Unlike other managerial accounting texts, the book's authors write all of the major supplements, ensuring a perfect fit between text and supplements. For more information on *Managerial Accounting's* supplements package, see page xxi.

- Instructor's Manual
- Test bank
- Solutions Manual
- Workbook/Study Guide

Utilizing the Icons

To reflect our service-based economy, the text is replete with examples from service-based businesses. A helpful icon distinguishes service-related examples in the text.

The IFRS icon highlights content that may be affected by the impending change to IFRS and possible convergence between U.S. GAAP and IFRS.

Ethics assignments and examples serve as a reminder that good conduct is vital in business. Icons call out content that relates to ethical behavior for students.

The writing icon denotes problems that require students to use critical thinking as well as writing skills to explain their decisions.

An Excel icon alerts students that spreadsheet templates are available for use with select problems and cases.

New to the Fourteenth Edition

Faculty feedback helps us continue to improve *Managerial Accounting*. In response to reviewer suggestions, the authors have made the following changes to the text:

- A **NEW Applying Excel feature** has been added to Chapters 2–13. Applying Excel gives students the opportunity to practice using Excel formulas to build their own worksheets. They are then asked a series of "what if" questions, all of which illustrate the relationship among various pieces of accounting data. The Applying Excel feature links directly to the concepts introduced in the chapter, providing students with an invaluable opportunity to apply what they have learned using a software they will use throughout their careers, whether they become an accountant or not.
- **Chapter 1** has been completely overhauled to help all business students better understand why managerial accounting is relevant to their future careers.
- **Chapter 2** has been extensively rewritten to include coverage of mixed costs and contribution format income statements. The redundant coverage of the schedule of cost of goods manufactured has been eliminated so that it is now only covered in the Job-Order Costing chapter. The comparison of financial and managerial accounting has been moved to Chapter 1.
- **Chapter 14** This chapter has been completely overhauled to simplify the process of creating a statement of cash flows.
- New **In Business boxes** have been added throughout to provide relevant and updated real-world examples for use in classroom discussion and to support student understanding of key concepts as they read through a chapter.
- The **end-of-chapter practice material** has been updated throughout.

Chapter 1

This chapter has been completely rewritten to better motivate all business students to take an interest in managerial accounting and to appreciate its relevance to their future careers. The new version of Chapter 1 answers three questions: (1) What is Managerial Accounting? (2) Why Does Managerial Accounting Matter to Your Career? and (3) What Skills Do Managers Need to Succeed? It also retains coverage of two topics important to all managers: (1) ethics in business and (2) corporate social responsibility.

Chapter 2

This chapter has been completely revised to achieve three objectives. First, we eliminated redundant coverage of the schedule of cost of goods manufactured, which in previous editions was covered in Chapter 2 as well as the Job-Order Costing chapter. Now this topic is covered only once in the Job-Order Costing chapter using normal costing principles. Second, we moved the coverage of mixed costs, scattergraph plots, and the high-low method from the Cost Behavior chapter to Chapter 2. This enables instructors to introduce cost estimation earlier in the course. The least-squares regression appendix has also been moved from the Cost Behavior chapter to Chapter 2. Third, we moved coverage of traditional and contribution format income statements for merchandising companies from the Cost Behavior chapter to Chapter 2. This enables instructors to introduce contribution format income statements earlier in the course. Using merchandising companies as the initial platform for comparing income statement formats provides an easily understood (student-friendly) introduction to this topic. The more complex arena of manufacturing cost accounting is covered in later chapters such as the Job-Order Costing and Variable Costing chapters. The Cost Behavior chapter has been completely eliminated given that its key learning objectives have been transferred to Chapter 2. The appendix dealing with further classification of labor costs has been moved from Chapter 2 to the Job-Order Costing chapter.

Chapter 3

In this chapter, we adjusted the learning objectives to provide a more logical progression from computing an overhead rate (LO1), to applying overhead cost to jobs (LO2), and then to computing a job cost (LO3). We also added a cost formula approach to computing predetermined overhead rates. We were able to do this because the high-low method is now covered in Chapter 2. We deleted what were formerly learning objectives 1 and 2 from the prior edition of the book and incorporated an exhibit formerly from Chapter 2 that provides a conceptual overview of manufacturing cost flows.

Chapter 6

The coverage of variable and absorption costing has been reorganized so that variable costing is discussed first, followed by absorption costing. Discussing variable costing first (rather than absorption costing) is consistent with the title of the chapter, which focuses on variable costing as a tool for management. The coverage of segmented income statements has been moved from Chapter 12 in the prior edition of the book to this chapter. The common theme that now joins together the chapter's two main topics is the contribution format income statement. The chapter now demonstrates how the contribution format is used for Variable Costing income statements and how it can be used for segmented income statements.

Chapter 10

This chapter's general model for standard cost variance analysis has been reorganized to more clearly integrate with the variance analysis framework introduced in the prior chapter. The prior chapter introduces a framework for computing activity and spending variances within organizations that do not use standard costing. The revised general model in this chapter extends the framework from the prior chapter and explains how it can be used to break down spending variances into quantity and price variances.

Chapter 11

This chapter has been renamed and reorganized. The new title is Performance Measurement in Decentralized Organizations. It is now organized in three main sections. The first section discusses financial performance measures for investment centers. The second section discusses nonfinancial operating performance measures. The third section explains how the balanced scorecard framework can be used to pull together financial and nonfinancial measures into one strategy-driven performance measurement system. Also, the coverage of segmented income statements was moved to an earlier chapter.

Chapter 12

The title of this chapter has been changed from Relevant Costs for Decision Making to Differential Analysis: The Key to Decision Making. This change acknowledges that revenues as well as costs can be relevant to decisions. We have also improved the discussion related to utilization of a constrained resource. The prior edition of the book had one learning objective related to this topic, whereas now we break down the discussion of this topic into two learning objectives. The first learning objective focuses on determining the most profitable use of a constraining resource, and the second learning objective focuses on calculating the value of obtaining more of the constrained resource. We expanded the discussion related to the latter learning objective.

Chapter 14

The chapter has been rewritten to simplify the process of preparing a statement of cash flows. We have added Exhibit 14–4, which succinctly summarizes the main points that students need to understand to prepare a statement of cash flows and revised Exhibit 14–1 so that it provides a more student-friendly definition of operating, investing, and financing activities than in previous editions. We have replaced the worksheet method with an approach that students can use to more efficiently solve end-of-chapter problems and also replaced the two walkthroughs of the Nordstrom example (simplified and full-fledged) with one walkthrough. We have also expanded the discussion related to interpreting the statement of cash flows.

A Market-Leading Book Deserves Market-Leading Technology

McGraw-Hill's *Connect™ Accounting*

McGraw-Hill's *Connect™ Accounting* is an online assignment and assessment solution that connects you with the tools and resources necessary to achieve success through faster learning, more efficient studying, and higher retention of knowledge.

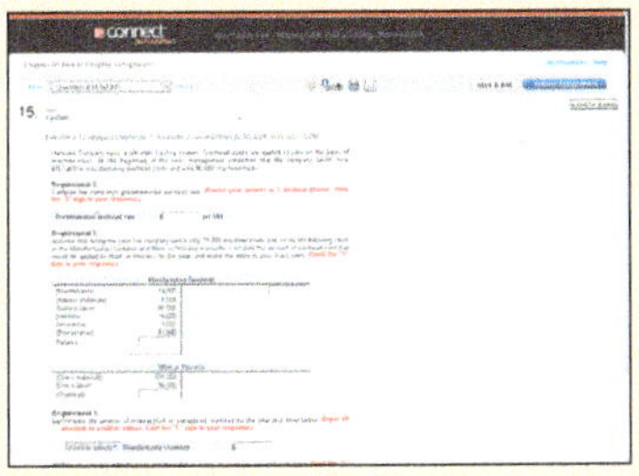

Online Assignments

McGraw-Hill's *Connect Accounting* helps students learn more efficiently by providing feedback and practice material when and where they need it. *Connect Accounting* grades homework automatically and gives immediate feedback on any questions students may have missed.

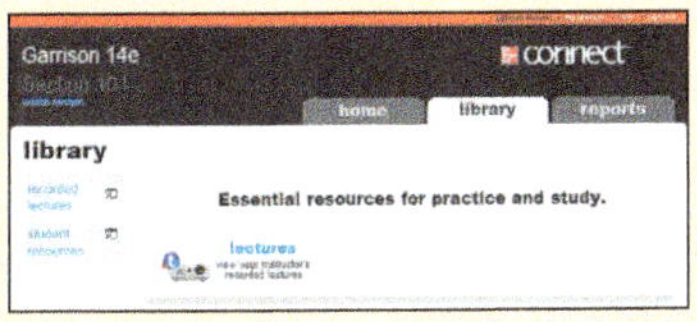

Student Library

The *Connect Accounting* Student Library gives students access to additional resources such as recorded lectures, Self-Quiz and Study practice materials, an eBook, and more.

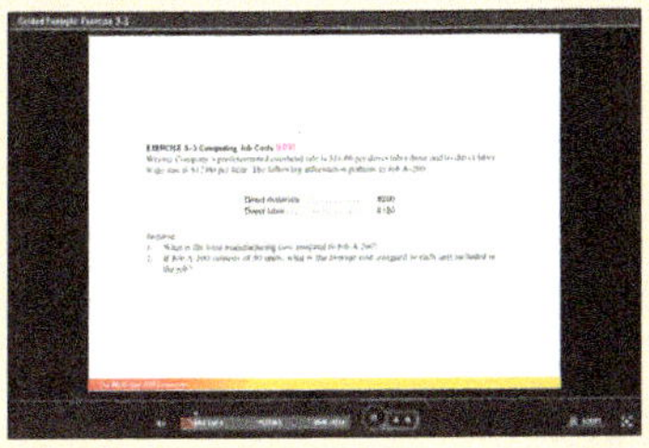

Guided Examples

Guided Examples, embedded within *Connect Accounting*, provide a narrated, animated, step-by-step walkthrough of select exercises similar to those assigned. These short presentations provide reinforcement when students need it most.

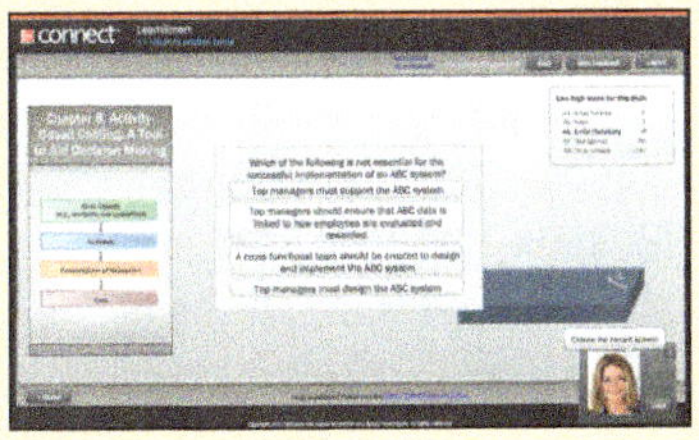

LearnSmart

LearnSmart, an adaptive self-study technology that is housed within *Connect Accounting*, helps students make the best use of their study time. It provides a seamless combination of practice, assessment, and remediation with a focus on the conceptual understanding students will need to succeed in the course. LearnSmart offers intelligent flashcards that personalize the study experience by constantly adapting, emphasizing the concepts the student still needs to master. LearnSmart can be assigned within *Connect* together with quantitative end-of-chapter material to provide comprehensive and balanced homework for students.

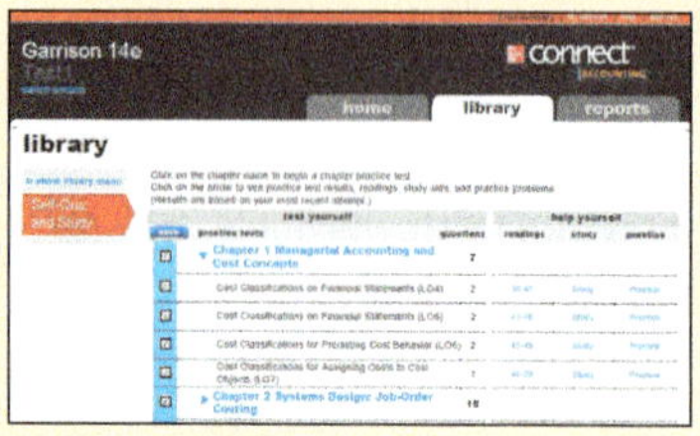

Self-Quiz and Study

Self-Quiz and Study connects students to the learning resources they need to succeed in the course. For each chapter, students can take a practice quiz and immediately see how well they performed. A study plan then recommends specific readings from the text, supplemental study material, and practice exercises that will improve students' understanding and mastery of each learning objective.

Less Managing. More Teaching. Greater Learning.

McGraw-Hill's *Connect Accounting* offers a number of powerful tools and features to make managing assignments easier, so faculty can spend more time teaching. With *Connect Accounting,* students can engage with their coursework anytime, anywhere, making the learning process more accessible and efficient. Please see the previous page for a description of the student tools available within *Connect Accounting.*

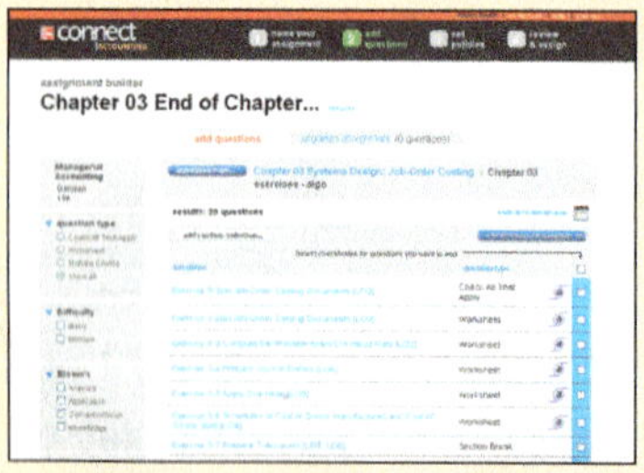

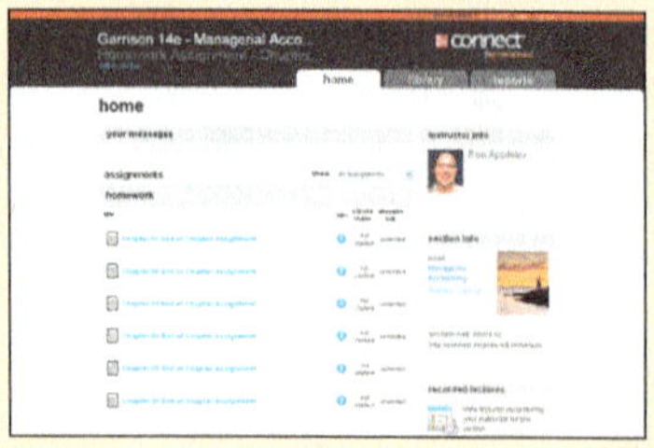

McGraw-Hill's *Connect Accounting* for Instructors

Simple Assignment Management and Smart Grading. With McGraw-Hill's *Connect Accounting*, creating assignments is easier than ever, so you can spend more time teaching and less time managing. *Connect Accounting* enables you to:

- Create and deliver assignments easily with selectable end-of-chapter questions and test bank items.
- Go paperless with the eBook and online submission and grading of student assignments.
- Have assignments scored automatically, giving students immediate feedback on their work and comparisons with correct answers.
- Reinforce classroom concepts with practice tests and instant quizzes.

Instructor Library

The *Connect Accounting* Instructor Library is your repository for additional resources to improve student engagement in and out of class. You can select and use any asset that enhances your lecture. The *Connect Accounting* Instructor Library includes access to:

- Solutions manual
- Instructor's manual
- Test bank
- Instructor PowerPoint® slides
- Transparency masters
- The eBook version of the text

Student Reports

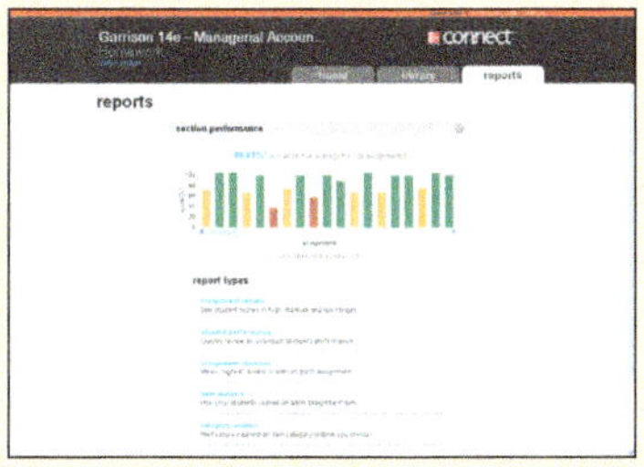

McGraw-Hill's *Connect Accounting* keeps instructors informed about how each student, section, and class is performing, allowing for more productive use of lecture and office hours. The reports tab enables you to:

- View scored work immediately and track individual or group performance with assignment and grade reports.
- Access an instant view of student or class performance relative to learning objectives.
- Collect data and generate reports required by many accreditation organizations, such as AACSB and AICPA.

McGraw-Hill's *Connect™ Plus Accounting*

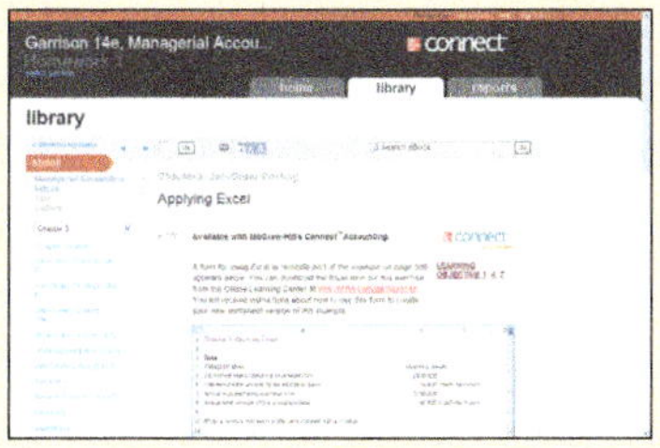

McGraw-Hill reinvents the textbook learning experience for the modern student with *Connect Plus Accounting,* which provides a seamless integration of the eBook and *Connect Accounting. Connect Plus Accounting* provides all of the *Connect Accounting* features, as well as:

- An integrated eBook, allowing for anytime, anywhere access to the textbook.
- Dynamic links between the problems or questions you assign to your students and the location in the eBook where the concept related to that problem or question is covered.
- A powerful search function to pinpoint and connect key concepts in a snap.

For more information about *Connect Accounting*, go to www.mcgrawhillconnect.com, or contact your local McGraw-Hill sales representative.

Tegrity Campus: Lectures 24/7

Tegrity Campus, a new McGraw-Hill company, provides a service that makes class time available 24/7 by automatically capturing every lecture. With a simple one-click start-and-stop process, you capture all computer screens and corresponding audio in a format that is easily searchable, frame by frame. Students can replay any part of any class with easy-to-use browser-based viewing on a PC or Mac, an iPod, or other mobile device.

Educators know that the more students can see, hear, and experience class resources, the better they learn. In fact, studies prove it. Tegrity Campus's unique search feature helps students efficiently find what they need, when they need it, across an entire semester of class recordings. Help turn your students' study time into learning moments immediately supported by your lecture. With Tegrity Campus, you also increase intent listening and class participation by easing students' concerns about note-taking. Lecture Capture will make it more likely you will see students' faces, not the tops of their heads.

To learn more about Tegrity, watch a 2-minute Flash demo at http://tegritycampus.mhhe.com.

Online Course Management

McGraw-Hill Higher Education and Blackboard have teamed up. What does this mean for you?

1. **Your life, simplified.** Now you and your students can access McGraw-Hill's *Connect*™ and Create™ right from within your Blackboard course—all with one single sign-on. Say goodbye to the days of logging in to multiple applications.

2. **Deep integration of content and tools.** Not only do you get single sign-on with *Connect* and Create, you also get deep integration of McGraw-Hill content and content engines right in Blackboard. Whether you're choosing a book for your course or building *Connect* assignments, all the tools you need are right where you want them—inside of Blackboard.

3. **Seamless grade books.** Are you tired of keeping multiple grade books and manually synchronizing grades into Blackboard? We thought so. When a student completes an integrated *Connect* assignment, the grade for that assignment automatically (and instantly) feeds your Blackboard grade center.

4. **A solution for everyone.** Whether your institution is already using Blackboard or you just want to try Blackboard on your own, we have a solution for you. McGraw-Hill and Blackboard can now offer you easy access to industry leading technology and content, whether your campus hosts it, or we do. Be sure to ask your local McGraw-Hill representative for details.

In addition to Blackboard integration, course cartridges for whatever online course management system you use (e.g., WebCT or eCollege) are available for Garrison 14e. Our cartridges are specifically designed to make it easy to navigate and access content online. They are easier than ever to install on the latest version of the course management system available today.

McGraw-Hill/Irwin CARES

At McGraw-Hill/Irwin, we understand that getting the most from new technology can be challenging. That's why our services don't stop after you purchase our book. You can e-mail our Product Specialists 24 hours a day, get product training online, or search our knowledge bank of Frequently Asked Questions on our support Website. For Customer Support, call 800-331-5094 or visit www.mhhe.com/support. One of our Technical Support Analysts will assist you in a timely fashion.

Instructor Supplements

Assurance of Learning Ready

Many educational institutions today are focused on the notion of assurance of learning, an important element of some accreditation standards. *Managerial Accounting,* 14e, is designed specifically to support your assurance of learning initiatives with a simple, yet powerful, solution.

Each test bank question for *Managerial Accounting,* 14e, maps to a specific chapter learning outcome/objective listed in the text. You can use our test bank software, EZ Test, to easily query for learning outcomes/objectives that directly relate to the learning objectives for your course. You can then use the reporting features of EZ Test to aggregate student results in similar fashion, making the collection and presentation of assurance of learning data simple and easy.

AACSB Statement

The McGraw-Hill Companies, Inc., is a proud corporate member of AACSB International. Recognizing the importance and value of AACSB accreditation, we have sought to recognize the curricula guidelines detailed in AACSB standards for business accreditation by connecting selected questions in *Managerial Accounting,* 14e, to the general knowledge and skill guidelines found in the AACSB standards. The statements contained in *Managerial Accounting,* 14e, are provided only as a guide for the users of this text. The AACSB leaves content coverage and assessment clearly within the realm and control of individual schools, the mission of the school, and the faculty. The AACSB does also charge schools with the obligation of doing assessment against their own content and learning goals. While *Managerial Accounting,* 14e, and its teaching package make no claim of any specific AACSB qualification or evaluation, we have, within *Managerial Accounting,* 14e, labeled selected questions according to the six general knowledge and skills areas. The labels or tags within *Managerial Accounting,* 14e, are as indicated. There are, of course, many more within the test bank, the text, and the teaching package which might be used as a "standard" for your course. However, the labeled questions are suggested for your consideration.

McGraw-Hill's *Connect™ Accounting*

McGraw-Hill's *Connect™ Accounting* offers a number of powerful tools and features to make managing your classroom easier. *Connect Accounting* with Garrison 14e offers enhanced features and technology to help both you and your students make the most of your time inside and outside the classroom. See page xvii for more details.

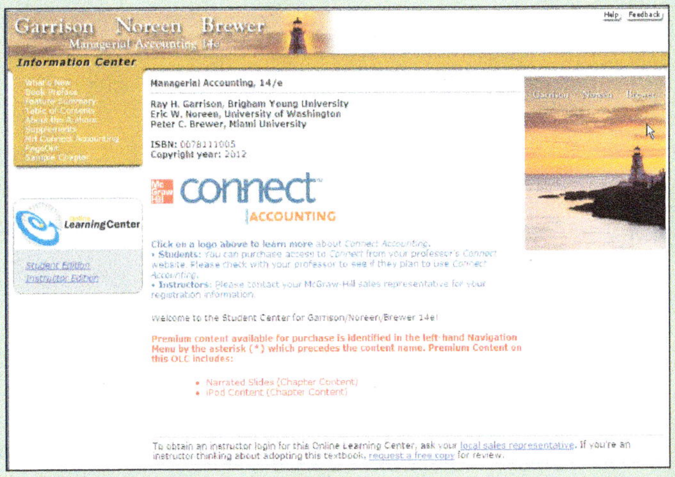

Online Learning Center (www.mhhe.com/garrison14e)

The password protected instructor side of the book's Online Learning Center (OLC) houses all the instructor resources you need to administer your course, including:

- Solutions Manual
- Instructor's Manual
- Test bank
- Instructor PowerPoint slides
- Transparency masters

If you choose to use *Connect Accounting* with Garrison, you will have access to these same resources via the Instructor Library.

Instructor CD-ROM

MHID 0-07-731779-3
ISBN-13 978-0-07-731779-9

Allowing instructors to create a customized multimedia presentation, this all-in-one resource incorporates the Test bank, Instructor PowerPoint slides, Instructor's Manual, and Solutions Manual.

EZ Test

Available on the Instructor's CD, Instructor's OLC, and within the *Connect* Instructor Library.

McGraw-Hill's EZ Test is a flexible electronic testing program. The program allows instructors to create tests from book-specific items. It accommodates a wide range of question types, plus instructors may add their own questions and sort questions by format. EZ Test can also scramble questions and answers for multiple versions of the same test.

Instructor's Manual

Available on the Instructor CD, Instructor's OLC, and within the *Connect* Instructor Library.

Extensive chapter-by-chapter lecture notes help with classroom presentations and contain useful suggestions for presenting key concepts and ideas. This manual is coordinated with the PowerPoint slides, making lesson planning even easier.

Print Test Bank

Volume 1:
MHID 0-07-731782-3
ISBN-13 978-0-07-731782-9

Volume 2:
MHID 0-07-731783-1
ISBN-13 978-0-07-731783-6

Over 2,000 questions are organized by chapter and include true/false, multiple-choice, and problems. The test bank includes worked-out solutions, and all items have been tied to AACSB-AICPA standards and Bloom's Taxonomy categories.

Solutions Manual

Available on the Instructor's CD, Instructor's OLC, and within the *Connect* Instructor Library.

This supplement contains completely worked-out solutions to all assignment material. In addition, the manual contains suggested course outlines and a listing of exercises, problems, and cases scaled according to difficulty and estimated time for completion. Solutions to the NEW Applying Excel feature are housed in the same location as the Solutions Manual and include the completed Excel forms.

Student Supplements

McGraw-Hill's *Connect™ Accounting*

McGraw-Hill's *Connect™ Accounting* helps prepare you for your future by enabling faster learning, more efficient studying, and higher retention of knowledge. See page xvii for more details.

CourseSmart

CourseSmart is a new way to find and buy eTextbooks. At CourseSmart you can save up to 45 percent off the cost of a print textbook, reduce your impact on the environment, and gain access to powerful Web tools for learning. CourseSmart has the largest selection of eTextbooks available anywhere, offering thousands of the most commonly adopted textbooks from a wide variety of higher education publishers. CourseSmart eTextbooks are available in one standard online reader with full text search, notes and highlighting, and e-mail tools for sharing notes between classmates.

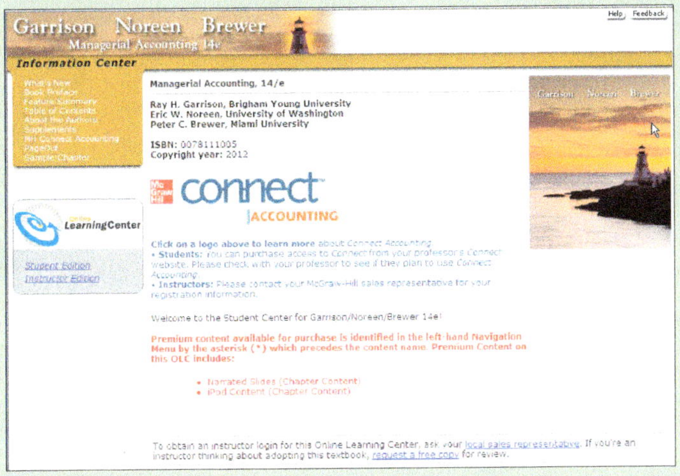

Online Learning Center

www.mhhe.com/garrison14e

The Online Learning Center (OLC) follows *Managerial Accounting* chapter by chapter, offering all kinds of supplementary help for you as you read.

The OLC includes the following resources to help you study more efficiently:

- NEW Applying Excel Forms
- Online Quizzes
- Practice Tests
- Internet Exercises
- Check Figures
- Student PowerPoint slides
- Narrated PowerPoint lectures
- Excel Templates
- iPod Content

If your instructor chooses to use *Connect Accounting* in this course, you will have access to these same resources via the Student Library.

Applying Excel

Forms available on the OLC and in the *Connect* Student Library.

This **NEW and exciting feature** has been added to Chapters 2-13 of the text. Applying Excel gives you the opportunity to build your own Excel worksheet using Excel formulas. You are then asked to answer "what if" questions, all of which illustrate the relationship among various pieces of accounting data. The Applying Excel feature links directly to the concepts introduced in the chapter, providing you with an invaluable opportunity to apply what you have learned utilizing an application you will use throughout your career.

Workbook/Study Guide

MHID: 0-07-731784-X
ISBN-13: 978-0-07-731784-3

This printed study aid provides suggestions for studying chapter material, summarizes essential points in each chapter, and tests your knowledge using self-test questions and exercises.

Working Papers

MHID: 0-07-731785-8
ISBN-13: 978-0-07-731785-0

This printed study aid contains forms that help you organize your solutions to homework problems.

iPod Content

Available on the OLC and in the *Connect* Student Library.

Students can visit the Online Learning Center at www.mhhe.com/garrison14e to download our iPod content. For each chapter of the book they will be able to download narrated lecture presentations, managerial accounting videos, and even self-quizzes designed for use on various versions of iPods. It makes review and study time as easy as putting on earphones.

Check Figures

Available on the OLC and in the *Connect* Student Library.
These provide key answers for selected problems and cases.

Acknowledgments

Suggestions have been received from many of our colleagues throughout the world. Each of those who have offered comments and suggestions has our thanks.

The efforts of many people are needed to develop and improve a text. Among these people are the reviewers and consultants who point out areas of concern, cite areas of strength, and make recommendations for change. In this regard, the following professors provided feedback that was enormously helpful in preparing the fourteenth edition of *Managerial Accounting:*

Helen Adams, *University of Washington*
Akinloye Akindayomi, *University Of Massachusetts–Dartmouth*
David Albrecht, *Bowling Green State University*
Natalie Allen, *Texas A & M University*
Vern Allen, *Central Florida Community College*
Shamir Ally, *DeSales University*
Jane Austin, *Oklahoma City University*
John Babich, *Kankakee Community College*
Ibolya Balog, *Cedar Crest College*
Scottie Barty, *Northern Kentucky University*
Eric Bashaw, *University of Nevada–Las Vegas*
Sharon Bell, *University of North Carolina–Pembroke*
Scott Berube, *University of New Hampshire*
Kelly Blacker, *Mercy College*
Phillip Blanchard, *The University of Arizona*
Charles Blumer, *Saint Charles Community College*
Alison Jill Brock, *Imperial Valley College*
Rada Brooks, *University of California–Berkeley*
Myra Bruegger, *Southeastern Community College*
Georgia Buckles, *Manchester Community College*
Esther Bunn, *Stephen S. Austin State University*
Laurie Burney, *Mississippi State University*
Marci Butterfield, *University of Utah–Salt Lake City*
Charles Caliendo, *University of Minnesota*
Donald Campbell, *Brigham Young University-Idaho*
Tracy Campbell Tuttle, *San Diego Mesa Community College*
Don Campodonico, *Notre Dame de Namur University*
Dana Carpenter, *Madison Area Technical College*
Wanda Causseaux, *Valdosta State University*
David Centers, *Grand Valley State University*
Pamela Champeau, *University of Wisconsin Whitewater*
Valerie Chau, *Palomar College*
Star Ciccio, *Johnson & Wales University*
Richard S. Claire, *Canada College*
Robert Clarke, *Brigham Young University–Idaho*
Curtis Clements, *Abilene Christian University*
Darlene Coarts, *University of Northern Iowa*
Carol Coman, *California Lutheran University*
Jackie Conrecode, *Florida Gulf Coast University*
Debora Constable, *Georgia Perimeter College*
Rita Cook, *University of Delaware*
Wendy Coons, *University of Maine*
Michael Cornick, *Winthrop University*
Deb Cosgrove, *University of Nebraska–Lincoln*
Kathy Crusto-Way, *Tarrant County College*
Robin D'Agati, *Palm Beach State College, Lake Worth*
Patricia Davis, *Keystone College*
Kathleen Davisson, *University of Denver*
Patricia Doherty, *Boston University*
Nina Doherty, *Arkansas Tech University*
Peter Dorff, *Kent State University*
David Doyon, *Southern New Hampshire University*
Emily Drogt, *Grand Valley State University*
Rita Dufour, *Northeast Wisconsin Technical College*
Barbara Durham, *University of Central Florida*
Dean Edmiston, *Emporia State University*
Barb Eide, *University of Wisconsin–Lacrosse*
Rafik Elias, *California State University–Los Angeles*
Richard F. Emery, *Linfield College*
Ruth Epps, *Virginia Commonwealth University*
John Eubanks, *Independence Community College*
Christopher M. Fairchild, *Southeastern University*
Jack Fatica, *Terra Community College*
Christos Fatouros, *Curry College*
Susan Ferguson, *James Madison University*
Jerry Ferry, *University of North Alabama*
Calvin Fink, *Bethune Cookman University*
Virginia Fullwood, *Texas A&M University–Commerce*
Robert Gannon, *Alvernia University*
Joseph Gerard, *University of Wisconsin Whitewater*
Frank Gersich, *Monmouth College*
Hubert Gill, *North Florida*
Jeff Gillespie, *University of Delaware*
Earl Godfrey, *Gardner-Webb University*
Nina Goza, *Arkansas Tech University*
Marina Grau, *HCC–Northwest College*
Alfred C. Greenfield, *Jr., High Point University*
Olen Greer, *Missouri State University*
Steve Groves, *Ivy Tech Community College of Indiana–Kokomo*
Ty Handy, *Vermont Technical College*

Susan Hass, *Simmons College*
Candice Heino, *Anoka Ramsey Community College*
Sueann Hely, *West Kentucky Community & Technical College*
David Henderson, *College of Charleston*
Donna Hetzel, *Western Michigan University–Kalamazoo*
Cynthia Hollenbach, *University of Denver*
Peg Horan, *Wagner College*
Steven Huddart, *Penn State*
George Hunt, *Stephen F Austin State University*
Marianne James, *California State University, Los Angeles*
Gene Johnson, *Clark College*
Bill Joyce, *Minnesota State University–Mankato*
Celina Jozsi, *University of South Florida*
Robert L. Kachur, *Richard Stockton College of New Jersey*
Sue Kattelus, *Michigan State University–East Lansing*
Nancy Kelly, *Middlesex Community College*
Shirly Kleiner, *Johnson County Community College*
Bill Knowles, *University of New Hampshire*
Barbara Kren, *Marquette University*
Jerry Kreuze, *Western Michigan University*
Wikil Kwak, *Nebraska Omaha*
Ron Lazer, *University of Houston–Houston*
Dennis Lopez, *University of Texas–San Antonio*
Don Lucy, *Indian River State College*
Cathy Lumbattis, *Southern Illinois University*
Joseph F. Lupino, *St. Mary's College of California*
Patrick M. Lynch, *Loyola University of New Orleans*
Suneel Maheshwari, *Marshall University*
Linda Malgeri, *Kennesaw State University*
Carol Mannino, *Milwaukee School of Engineering*
Linda Marquis, *Northern Kentucky University*
Melissa Martin, *Arizona State University*
Michele Martinez, *Hillsborough Community College*
Josephine Mathias, *Mercer County Community College*
Annie McGowan, *Texas A&M University*
Michael McLain, *Hampton University*
Heidi Meier, *Cleveland State University*
Edna Mitchell, *Polk State College*
Kim Mollberg, *Minnesota State University–Moorhead*
Shirley Montagne, *Lyndon State College*
Andrew Morgret, *Christian Brothers University*
Jennifer Moriarty, *Hudson Valley Community College*
Mark Motluck, *Anderson University*
Matt Muller, *Adirondack Community College*
Michael Newman, *University of Houston–Houston*
Tracie Nobles, *Austin Community College*
Janet O'Tousa, *University of Notre Dame*
Mehmet Ozbilgin, *Bernard M. Baruch College*
Abbie Gail Parham, *Georgia Southern*
Mary Pearson, *Southern Utah University*
Judy Peterson, *Monmouth College*
Yvonne Phang, *Bernard M. Baruch College*
Jo Ann Pinto, *Montclair State University*
Janice Pitera, *Broome Community College*
Matthew Probst, *Ivy Tech Community College*
Laura Prosser, *Black Hills State University*
Herbert Purick, *Palm Beach State College–Lake Worth*
Marc B. Robinson, *Richard Stockton College of New Jersey*
David Rogers, *Mesa State College*
Lawrence A. Roman, *Cuyahoga Community College*
Luther Ross, *Sr., Central Piedmont Community College*
Amal Said, *University of Toledo*
Rex Schildhouse, *Miramar College*
Nancy Schrumpf, *Parkland College*
Vineeta Sharma, *Florida International University–Miami*
Franklin Shuman, *Utah State University–Logan*
Lakshmy Sivaratnam, *Kansas City Kansas Community College*
Talitha Smith, *Auburn University–Auburn*
Diane Stark, *Phoenix College*
Dennis Stovall, *Grand Valley State University*
Suzy Summers, *Furman University*
Scott Szilagyi, *Fordham University–Bronx*
Rita Taylor, *University of Cincinnati*
Lisa Tekmetarovic, *Truman College*
Teresa Thamer, *Brenau University*
Amanda Thompson-Abbott, *Marshall University*
Jerry Thorne, *North Carolina A&T State University*
Don Trippeer, *SUNY College at Oneonta*
Robin Turner, *Rowan-Cabarrus Community College*
Suneel Udpa, *University of California–Berkeley*
Michael Van Breda, *Southern Methodist University*
Jayaraman Vijayakumar, *Virginia Commonwealth University*
Ron Vogel, *College of Eastern Utah*
David Vyncke, *Scott Community College*
Lorry Wasserman, *University of Portland*
Richard Watson, *University of California–Santa Barbara*
Betsy Wenz, *Indiana University–Kokomo*
Robert Weprin, *Lourdes College*
Gwendolen White, *Ball State University*
Elizabeth Widdison, *University Of Washington*
Janet Woods, *Macon State College*
John Woodward, *Polk State College*
Jia Wu, *University OF Massachusetts–Dartmouth*
Emily Xu, *University of New Hampshire*
Jeff Yu, *Southern Methodist University*
Bert Zarb, *Embry-Riddle Aeronautical University*

We are grateful for the outstanding support from McGraw-Hill. In particular, we would like to thank Stewart Mattson, Editorial Director; Tim Vertovec, Publisher; Donna Dillon, Sponsoring Editor; Emily Hatteberg and Katie Jones, Developmental Editors; Kathleen Klehr, Marketing Manager; Pat Frederickson, Lead Project Manager; Carol Bielski, Production Supervisor; Matthew Baldwin, Lead Designer; Cathy Tepper, Media Project Manager; Allison Souter, Senior Media Project Manager; and Keri Johnson, Photo Research Coordinator.

A special thank you to the following individuals who helped develop the ancillary package: Jon A. Booker and Charles W. Caldwell of Tennessee Technological University, Cynthia J. Rooney of the University of New Mexico, and Susan C. Galbreath of Lipscomb University for crafting the Instructor and Student PowerPoint Slides; Jeannie Folk of the College of DuPage for creating the working papers, online quizzes, online practice exams, and Internet exercises; Patti Lopez of Valencia Community College–East, Aileen Ormiston of Mesa Community College, Christine Denison of Iowa State University, Rebecca Lohmann of Southeast Missouri State University, Kathy Crusto-Way of Tarrant County College–Southeast, Stacy Wade of Western Kentucky University, Deb Cosgrove of University of Nebraska–Lincoln, Chuo-Hsuan Lee of SUNY Plattsburgh, Loretta Manktelow of James Madison University, Xiujun Farrier of Tarrant County College–South, Diane Tanner of the University of North Florida, and Laurie Burney of Mississippi State University for piloting development of our new adaptive, self-study technology, LearnSmart; John Plouffe of California State University–Los Angeles for helping to generate the worked out solutions for the test bank; and Jack Terry of ComSource Associates, Inc., for creating the Excel templates.

Finally, we would like to thank Beth Woods and Helen Roybark for working so hard to ensure an error-free fourteenth edition.

We are grateful to the Institute of Certified Management Accountants for permission to use questions and/or unofficial answers from past Certificate in Management Accounting (CMA) examinations. Likewise, we thank the American Institute of Certified Public Accountants, the Society of Management Accountants of Canada, and the Chartered Institute of Management Accountants (United Kingdom) for permission to use (or to adapt) selected problems from their examinations. These problems bear the notations CPA, SMA, and CIMA respectively.

Ray H. Garrison • Eric Noreen • Peter Brewer

Brief Contents

CONTENTS

Chapter 1

Managerial Accounting: An Overview 1

Chapter 2

Managerial Accounting and Cost Concepts 24

Chapter 3

Job-Order Costing 83

Chapter 4

Process Costing 141

Chapter 5

Cost-Volume-Profit Relationships 183

Chapter 6

Variable Costing and Segment Reporting: Tools for Management 229

Chapter 7

Chapter 8

Chapter 9

Flexible Budgets and Performance Analysis 383

Chapter 10

Standard Costs and Variances 418

Chapter 11

Performance Measurement in Decentralized Organizations 472

Chapter 1

Managerial Accounting: An Overview

BUSINESS FOCUS

Managerial Accounting: It's More Than Just Crunching Numbers

"Creating value through values" is the credo of today's management accountant. It means that management accountants should maintain an unwavering commitment to ethical values while using their knowledge and skills to influence decisions that create value for organizational stakeholders. These skills include managing risks and implementing strategy through planning, budgeting and forecasting, and decision support. Management accountants are strategic business partners who understand the financial and operational sides of the business. They not only report and analyze financial measures, but also nonfinancial measures of process performance and corporate social performance. Think of these responsibilities as profits (financial statements), process (customer focus and satisfaction), people (employee learning and satisfaction), and planet (environmental stewardship). ■

Source: Conversation with Jeff Thomson, president and CEO of the Institute of Management Accountants.

This chapter explains why managerial accounting is important to the future careers of all business students. It begins by answering three questions: (1) What is managerial accounting? (2) Why does managerial accounting matter to your career? and (3) What skills do managers need to succeed? It concludes by discussing two topics important to all managers—the role of ethics in business and corporate social responsibility.

What Is Managerial Accounting?

Many students enrolled in this course will have recently completed an introductory *financial accounting* course. **Financial accounting** is concerned with reporting financial information to external parties, such as stockholders, creditors, and regulators. **Managerial accounting** is concerned with providing information to managers for use within the organization. Exhibit 1–1 summarizes seven key differences between financial and managerial accounting. It recognizes that the fundamental difference between financial and managerial accounting is that financial accounting serves the needs of

EXHIBIT 1–1
Comparison of Financial and Managerial Accounting

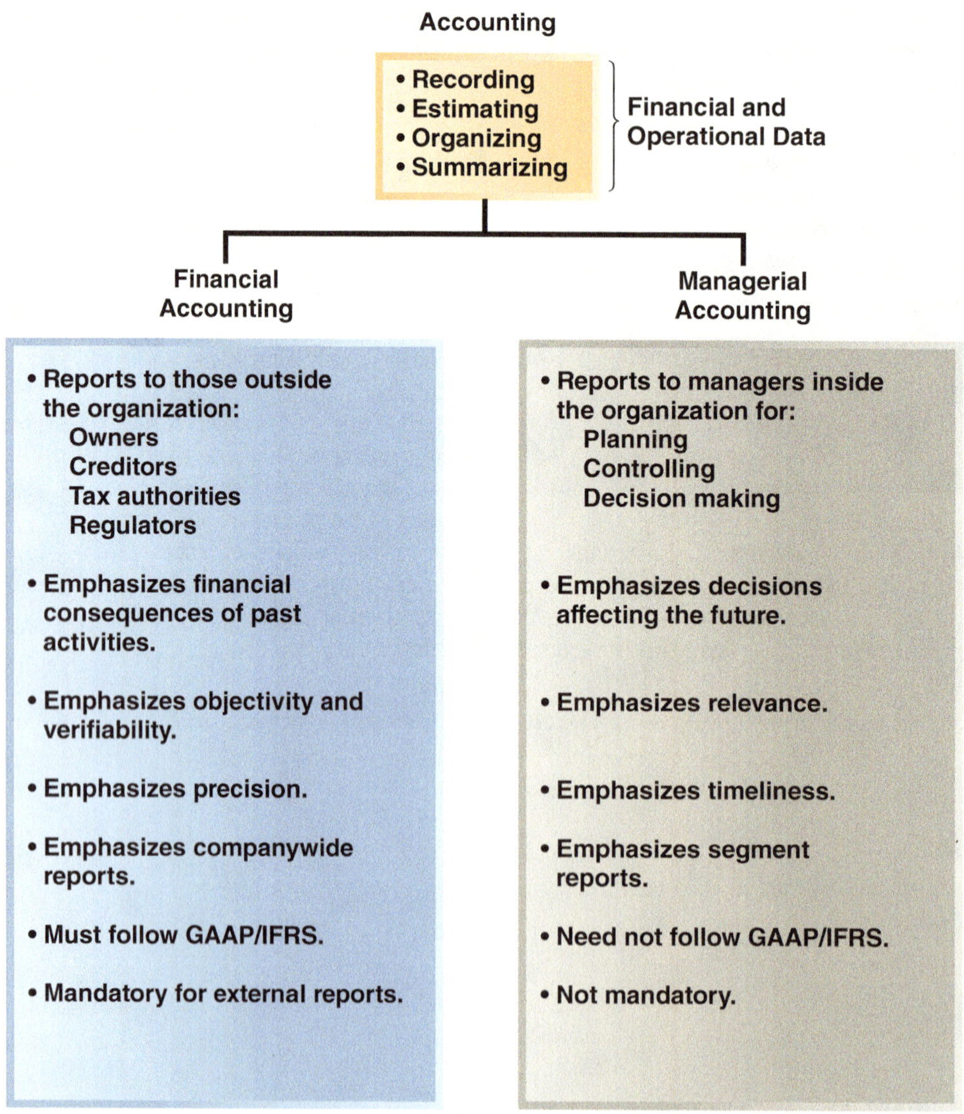

those *outside* the organization, whereas managerial accounting serves the needs of managers employed *inside* the organization. Because of this fundamental difference in users, financial accounting emphasizes the financial consequences of past activities, objectivity and verifiability, precision, and companywide performance, whereas managerial accounting emphasizes decisions affecting the future, relevance, timeliness, and *segment* performance. A **segment** is a part or activity of an organization about which managers would like cost, revenue, or profit data. Examples of business segments include product lines, customer groups (segmented by age, ethnicity, gender, volume of purchases, etc.), geographic territories, divisions, plants, and departments. Finally, financial accounting is mandatory for external reports and it needs to comply with rules, such as generally accepted accounting principles (GAAP) and international financial reporting standards (IFRS), whereas managerial accounting is not mandatory and it does not need to comply with externally imposed rules.

As mentioned in Exhibit 1–1, managerial accounting helps managers perform three vital activities—*planning, controlling,* and *decision making.* **Planning** involves establishing goals and specifying how to achieve them. **Controlling** involves gathering feedback to ensure that the plan is being properly executed or modified as circumstances change. **Decision making** involves selecting a course of action from competing alternatives. Now let's take a closer look at these three pillars of managerial accounting.

Planning

Assume that you work for Procter & Gamble (P&G) and that you are in charge of the company's campus recruiting for all undergraduate business majors. In this example, your planning process would begin by establishing a goal such as: our goal is to recruit the "best and brightest" college graduates. The next stage of the planning process would require specifying how to achieve this goal by answering numerous questions such as:

- How many students do we need to hire in total and from each major?
- What schools do we plan to include in our recruiting efforts?
- Which of our employees will be involved in each school's recruiting activities?
- When will we conduct our interviews?
- How will we compare students to one another to decide who will be extended job offers?
- What salary will we offer our new hires? Will the salaries differ by major?
- How much money can we spend on our recruiting efforts?

As you can see, there are many questions that need to be answered as part of the planning process. Plans are often accompanied by a *budget.* A **budget** is a detailed plan for the future that is usually expressed in formal quantitative terms. As the head of recruiting at P&G, your budget would include two key components. First, you would have to work with other senior managers inside the company to establish a budgeted amount of total salaries that can be offered to all new hires. Second, you would have to create a budget that quantifies how much you intend to spend on your campus recruiting activities.

Controlling

Once you established and started implementing P&G's recruiting plan, you would transition to the control process. This process would involve gathering, evaluating, and responding to feedback to ensure that this year's recruiting process meets expectations. It would also include evaluating the feedback in search of ways to run a more effective recruiting campaign next year. The control process would involve answering questions such as:

- Did we succeed in hiring the planned number of students within each major and at each school?
- Did we lose too many exceptional candidates to competitors?

- Did each of our employees involved in the recruiting process perform satisfactorily?
- Is our method of comparing students to one another working?
- Did the on-campus and office interviews run smoothly?
- Did we stay within our budget in terms of total salary commitments to new hires?
- Did we stay within our budget regarding spending on recruiting activities?

As you can see, there are many questions that need to be answered as part of the control process. When answering these questions your goal would be to go beyond simple yes or no answers in search of the underlying reasons why performance exceeded or failed to meet expectations. Part of the control process includes preparing *performance reports.* A **performance report** compares budgeted data to actual data in an effort to identify and learn from excellent performance and to identify and eliminate sources of unsatisfactory performance. Performance reports can also be used as one of many inputs to help evaluate and reward employees.

Although this example focused on P&G's campus recruiting efforts, we could have described how planning enables FedEx to deliver packages across the globe overnight, or how it helped Apple develop and market the iPad. We could have discussed how the control process helps Pfizer, Eli Lilly, and Abbott Laboratories ensure that their pharmaceutical drugs are produced in conformance with rigorous quality standards, or how Kroger relies on the control process to keep its grocery shelves stocked. We also could have looked at planning and control failures such as BP's massive oil spill in the Gulf of Mexico. In short, all managers (and that probably includes you someday) perform planning and controlling activities.

Decision Making

Perhaps the most basic managerial skill is the ability to make intelligent, data-driven decisions. Broadly speaking, many of those decisions revolve around the following three questions. *What* should we be selling? *Who* should we be serving? *How* should we execute? Exhibit 1–2 provides examples of decisions pertaining to each of these three categories.

The left-hand column of Exhibit 1–2 suggests that every company must make decisions related to the products and services that it sells. For example, each year Procter & Gamble must decide how to allocate its marketing budget across 23 brands that each generates over $1 billion in sales as well as other brands that have promising growth potential. Mattel must decide what new toys to introduce to the market. Southwest Airlines must decide what ticket prices to establish for each of its thousands

EXHIBIT 1–2
Examples of Decisions

What should we be selling?	Who should we be serving?	How should we execute?
What products and services should be the focus of our marketing efforts?	Who should be the focus of our marketing efforts?	How should we supply our parts and services?
What new products and services should we offer?	Who should we start serving?	How should we expand our capacity?
What prices should we charge for our products and services?	Who should pay price premiums or receive price discounts?	How should we reduce our capacity?
What products and services should we discontinue?	Who should we stop serving?	How should we improve our efficiency and effectiveness?

of flights per day. General Motors must decide whether to discontinue certain models of automobiles.

The middle column of Exhibit 1–2 indicates that all companies must make decisions related to the customers that they serve. For example, Sears must decide how to allocate its marketing budget between products that tend to appeal to male versus female customers. FedEx must decide whether to expand its services into new markets across the globe. Hewlett-Packard must decide what price discounts to offer corporate clients that purchase large volumes of its products. A bank must decide whether to discontinue customers that may be unprofitable.

The right-hand column of Exhibit 1–2 shows that companies also make decisions related to how they execute. For example, Boeing must decide whether to rely on outside vendors such as Goodrich, Saab, and Rolls-Royce to manufacture many of the parts used to make its airplanes. Cintas must decide whether to expand its laundering and cleaning capacity in a given geographic region by adding square footage to an existing facility or by constructing an entirely new facility. In an economic downturn, a manufacturer might have to decide whether to eliminate one 8-hour shift at three plants or to close one plant. Finally, all companies have to decide among competing improvement opportunities. For example, a company may have to decide whether to implement a new software system, to upgrade a piece of equipment, or to provide extra training to its employees.

This portion of the chapter has explained that the three pillars of managerial accounting are planning, controlling, and decision making. This book helps prepare you to become an effective manager by explaining how to make intelligent data-driven decisions, how to create financial plans for the future, and how to continually make progress toward achieving goals by obtaining, evaluating, and responding to feedback.

Why Does Managerial Accounting Matter to Your Career?

Many students feel anxious about choosing a major because they are unsure if it will provide a fulfilling career. To reduce these anxieties, we recommend deemphasizing what you cannot control about the future; instead focusing on what you can control right now. More specifically, concentrate on answering the following question: What can you do now to prepare for success in an unknown future career? The best answer is to learn skills that will make it easier for you to adapt to an uncertain future. You need to become adaptable!

Whether you end up working in the United States or abroad, for a large corporation, a small entrepreneurial company, a nonprofit organization, or a governmental entity, you'll need to know how to plan for the future, how to make progress toward achieving goals, and how to make intelligent decisions. In other words, managerial accounting skills are useful in just about any career, organization, and industry. If you commit energy to this course, you'll be making a smart investment in your future—even though you cannot clearly envision it. Next, we will elaborate on this point by explaining how managerial accounting relates to the future careers of business majors and accounting majors.

Business Majors

Exhibit 1–3 provides examples of how planning, controlling, and decision making affect three majors other than accounting—marketing, operations management, and human resource management.

The left-hand column of Exhibit 1–3 describes some planning, controlling, and decision-making applications in the marketing profession. For example, marketing managers make planning decisions related to allocating advertising dollars across various communication mediums and to staffing new sales territories. From a control standpoint, they may closely track sales data to see if a budgeted price cut is generating an anticipated increase in unit

EXHIBIT 1–3
Relating Managerial Accounting to Three Business Majors

	Marketing	Operations Management	Human Resource Management
Planning	How much should we budget for TV, print, and Internet advertising?	How many units should we plan to produce next period?	How much should we plan to spend for occupational safety training?
	How many salespeople should we plan to hire to serve a new territory?	How much should we budget for next period's utility expense?	How much should we plan to spend on employee recruitment advertising?
Controlling	Is the budgeted price cut increasing unit sales as expected?	Did we spend more or less than expected for the units we actually produced?	Is our employee retention rate exceeding our goals?
	Are we accumulating too much inventory during the holiday shopping season?	Are we achieving our goal of reducing the number of defective units produced?	Are we meeting our goal of completing timely performance appraisals?
Decision Making	Should we sell our services as one bundle or sell them separately?	Should we buy a new piece of equipment or upgrade our existing machine?	Should we hire an on-site medical staff to lower our health care costs?
	Should we sell directly to customers or use a distributor?	Should we redesign our manufacturing process to lower inventory levels?	Should we hire temporary workers or full-time employees?

sales, or they may study inventory levels during the holiday shopping season so that they can adjust prices as needed to optimize sales. Marketing managers also make many important decisions such as whether to bundle services together and sell them for one price or to sell each service separately. They may also decide whether to sell products directly to the customer or to sell to a distributor, who then sells to the end consumer.

The middle column of Exhibit 1–3 states that operations managers have to plan how many units to produce to satisfy anticipated customer demand. They also need to budget for operating expenses such as utilities, supplies, and labor costs. In terms of control, they monitor actual spending relative to the budget, and closely watch operational measures such as the number of defects produced relative to the plan. Operations managers make numerous decisions, such as deciding whether to buy a new piece of equipment or upgrade an existing piece of equipment. They also decide whether to invest in redesigning a manufacturing process to reduce inventory levels.

The right-hand column of Exhibit 1–3 explains how human resource managers make a variety of planning decisions, such as budgeting how much to spend on occupational safety training and employee recruitment advertising. They monitor feedback related to numerous management concerns, such as employee retention rates and the timely completion of employee performance appraisals. They also help make many important decisions such as whether to hire on-site medical staff in an effort to lower health care costs, and whether to hire temporary workers or full-time employees in an uncertain economy.

For brevity, Exhibit 1–3 does not include all business majors, such as finance, supply chain management, management information systems, and economics. Can you explain how planning, controlling, and decision-making activities would relate to these majors?

Accounting Majors

Many accounting graduates begin their careers working for public accounting firms that provide a variety of valuable services for their clients. Some of these graduates will build successful and fulfilling careers in the public accounting industry; however, most will leave public accounting at some point to work in other organizations. In fact, the Institute of Management Accountants (IMA) estimates that more than 80% of professional accountants in the United States work in nonpublic accounting environments (www.imanet.org/about_ima/our_mission.aspx).

The public accounting profession has a strong financial accounting orientation. Its most important function is to protect investors and other external parties by assuring them that companies are reporting historical financial results that comply with applicable accounting rules. Managerial accountants also have strong financial accounting skills. For example, they play an important role in helping their organizations design and maintain financial reporting systems that generate reliable financial disclosures. However, the primary role of managerial accountants is to partner with their co-workers within the organization to improve performance.

Given the 80% figure mentioned above, if you are an accounting major there is a very high likelihood that your future will involve working for a nonpublic accounting employer. Your employer will expect you to have strong financial accounting skills, but more importantly, it will expect you to help improve organizational performance by applying the planning, controlling, and decision-making skills that are the foundation of managerial accounting.

IN BUSINESS

A NETWORKING OPPORTUNITY

The Institute of Management Accountants (IMA) is a network of more than 60,000 accounting and finance professionals from over 120 countries. Every year the IMA hosts a student leadership conference that attracts 300 students from over 50 colleges and universities. Guest speakers at past conferences have discussed topics such as leadership, advice for a successful career, how to market yourself in a difficult economy, and excelling in today's multigenerational workforce. One student who attended the conference said, "I liked that I was able to interact with professionals who are in fields that could be potential career paths for me." For more information on this worthwhile networking opportunity, contact the IMA at the phone number and website shown below.

Source: Conversation with Jodi Ryan, the Institute of Management Accountants' Director of Alliances and Student/Academic Communities. (800) 638-4427 or visit its website at www.imanet.org.

Professional Certification—A Smart Investment If you plan to become an accounting major, the Certified Management Accountant (CMA) designation is a globally respected credential (sponsored by the IMA) that will increase your credibility, upward mobility, and compensation. Exhibit 1–4 summarizes the topics covered in the two-part CMA exam. For brevity, we are not going to define all the terms included in this exhibit. Its purpose is simply to emphasize that the CMA exam focuses on the planning, controlling, and decision-making skills that are critically important to nonpublic accounting employers. The CMA's internal management orientation is a complement to the highly respected Certified Public Accountant (CPA) exam that focuses on rule-based compliance—assurance standards, financial accounting standards, business law, and the tax code. Information about becoming a CMA is available on the IMA's website (www.imanet.org) or by calling 1-800-638-4427.

EXHIBIT 1–4
CMA Exam Content Specifications

Part 1 *Financial Planning, Performance, and Control*
- Planning, budgeting, and forecasting
- Performance management
- Cost management
- Internal controls
- Professional ethics

Part 2 *Financial Decision Making*
- Financial statement analysis
- Corporate finance
- Decision analysis and risk management
- Investment decisions
- Professional ethics

IN BUSINESS

HOW'S THE PAY?

The Institute of Management Accountants has created the following table that allows individuals to estimate what their salary would be as a management accountant.

			Your Calculation
Start with this base amount		$72,288	$72,288
If you are top-level management	ADD	$36,591	
OR, if you are entry-level management	SUBTRACT	$23,553	
Number of years in the field ______	TIMES	$700	
If you have an advanced degree.	ADD	$12,216	
If you hold the CMA	ADD	$8,185	
OR, if you hold the CPA	ADD	$11,872	______
Your estimated salary level			______

For example, if you make it to top-level management in 10 years, have an advanced degree and a CMA, your estimated salary would be $136,280 [$72,288 + $36,591 + (10 × 700) + $12,216 + $8,185].

Source: David L. Schroeder, Lee Schiffel, and Kenneth A. Smith, "IMA 2009 Salary Survey," *Strategic Finance*, June 2010, pp. 21–39.

What Skills Do Managers Need to Succeed?

Managers possess a variety of skills that enable them to do their jobs, including strategic management skills, enterprise risk management skills, process management skills, measurement skills, and leadership skills. We will discuss each of these skill sets in turn.

Strategic Management Skills

Successful managers understand that the plans they set forth, the variables they seek to control, and the decisions they make are all influenced by their company's *strategy.* A **strategy** is a "game plan" that enables a company to attract customers by distinguishing itself from competitors. The focal point of a company's strategy should be its target customers. A company can only succeed if it creates a reason for customers to choose it over a competitor. These reasons, or what are more formally called *customer value propositions,* are the essence of strategy.

Customer value propositions tend to fall into three broad categories—*customer intimacy, operational excellence,* and *product leadership.* Companies that adopt a *customer intimacy* strategy are in essence saying to their customers, "You should choose us because we can customize our products and services to meet your individual needs better than our competitors." Ritz-Carlton, Nordstrom, and Virtuoso (a premium service travel agency) rely primarily on a customer intimacy value proposition for their success. Companies that pursue the second customer value proposition, called *operational excellence,* are saying to their target customers, "You should choose us because we deliver products and services faster, more conveniently, and at a lower price than our competitors." Southwest Airlines, Walmart, and Google are examples of companies that succeed first and foremost because of their operational excellence. Companies pursuing the third customer value proposition, called *product leadership,* are saying to their target customers, "You should choose us because we offer higher quality products than our competitors." Apple, BMW, Cisco Systems, and W. L. Gore (the creator of GORE-TEX® fabrics) are examples of companies that succeed because of their product leadership. Although one company may offer its customers a combination of these three customer value propositions, one usually outweighs the other in terms of importance.[1]

IN BUSINESS

A FOUR-YEAR WAITING LIST AT VANILLA BICYCLES

Sacha White started Vanilla Bicycles in Portland, Oregon, in 2001. After eight years in business, he had a four-year backlog of customer orders. He limits his annual production to 40–50 bikes per year that sell for an average of $7,000 each. He uses a silver alloy that costs 20 times as much as brass (which is the industry standard) to join titanium tubes together to form a bike frame. White spends three hours taking a buyer's measurements to determine the exact dimensions of the bike frame. He has resisted expanding production because it would undermine his strategy based on product leadership and customer intimacy. As White said, "If I ended up sacrificing what made Vanilla special just to make more bikes, that wouldn't be worth it to me."

Source: Christopher Steiner, "Heaven on Wheels," *Forbes,* April 13, 2009, p. 75.

Enterprise Risk Management Skills

As a future manager, you need to understand that every business strategy, plan, and decision involves risks. **Enterprise risk management** is a process used by a company to identify those risks and develop responses to them that enable it to be reasonably assured of meeting its goals. The left-hand column of Exhibit 1–5 provides 12 examples of business risks. This list is not exhaustive; rather, its purpose is to illustrate the diverse nature of business risks that companies face. Whether the risks relate to the weather, computer hackers, complying with the law, employee theft, or products harming customers, they all have one thing in common: If the risks are not managed effectively, they can threaten a company's ability to meet its goals.

Once a company identifies its risks, it can respond to them in various ways such as accepting, avoiding, or reducing the risk. Perhaps the most common risk management tactic is to reduce risks by implementing specific controls. The right-hand column of Exhibit 1–5 provides an example of a control that could be implemented to help

[1] These three customer value propositions were defined by Michael Treacy and Fred Wiersema in "Customer Intimacy and Other Value Disciplines," *Harvard Business Review,* Volume 71 Issue 1, pp. 84–93.

EXHIBIT 1–5
Identifying and Controlling Business Risks

Examples of Business Risks	Examples of Controls to Reduce Business Risks
• Intellectual assets being stolen from computer files	• Create firewalls that prohibit computer hackers from corrupting or stealing intellectual property
• Products harming customers	• Develop a formal and rigorous new product testing program
• Losing market share due to the unforeseen actions of competitors	• Develop an approach for legally gathering information about competitors' plans and practices
• Poor weather conditions shutting down operations	• Develop contingency plans for overcoming weather-related disruptions
• A website malfunctioning	• Thoroughly test the website before going "live" on the Internet
• A supplier strike halting the flow of raw materials	• Establish a relationship with two companies capable of providing needed raw materials
• A poorly designed incentive compensation system causing employees to make bad decisions	• Create a balanced set of performance measures that motivates the desired behavior
• Financial statements inaccurately reporting the value of inventory	• Count the physical inventory on hand to make sure that it agrees with the accounting records
• An employee stealing assets	• Segregate duties so that the same employee does not have physical custody of an asset and the responsibility of accounting for it
• An employee accessing unauthorized information	• Create password-protected barriers that prohibit employees from obtaining information not needed to do their jobs
• Inaccurate budget estimates causing excessive or insufficient production	• Implement a rigorous budget review process
• Failing to comply with equal employment opportunity laws	• Create a report that tracks key metrics related to compliance with the laws

reduce each of the risks mentioned in the left-hand column of the exhibit. Although these types of controls cannot completely eliminate risks, companies understand that proactively managing risks is a superior alternative to reacting, perhaps too late, to unfortunate events.

IN BUSINESS

MANAGING THE RISK OF A POWER OUTAGE

Between January and April of 2010, the United States had 35 major power outages. For business owners, these power outages can be costly. For example, a New York night club called the Smoke Jazz and Supper Club lost an estimated $1,500 in revenue when a power outage shut down its on-line reservation system for one night. George Pauli, the owner of Great Embroidery LLC in Mesa, Arizona, estimates that his company has an average of six power outages every year. Since Pauli's sewing machines cannot resume exactly where they leave off when abruptly shut down, each power outage costs him $120 in lost inventory. Pauli decided to buy $700 worth of batteries to keep his sewing machines running during power outages. The batteries paid for themselves in less than one year.

Source: Sarah E. Needleman, "Lights Out Means Lost Sales," *The Wall Street Journal*, July 22, 2010, p. B8.

Process Management Skills

In addition to formulating strategies and controlling risks, managers need to continually improve the *business processes* that serve customers. A **business process** is a series of steps that are followed in order to carry out some task in a business. It is quite common for the linked set of steps comprising a business process to span departmental boundaries. The term *value chain* is often used to describe how an organization's functional departments interact with one another to form business processes. A **value chain,** as shown in Exhibit 1–6, consists of the major business functions that add value to a company's products and services.

Managers frequently use two process management methods that are referred to throughout this book—*lean thinking,* or what is called *Lean Production* in the manufacturing sector, and the *Theory of Constraints.* We will briefly define these management methods now so that you recognize them in later chapters.

EXHIBIT 1–6
Business Functions Making Up the Value Chain

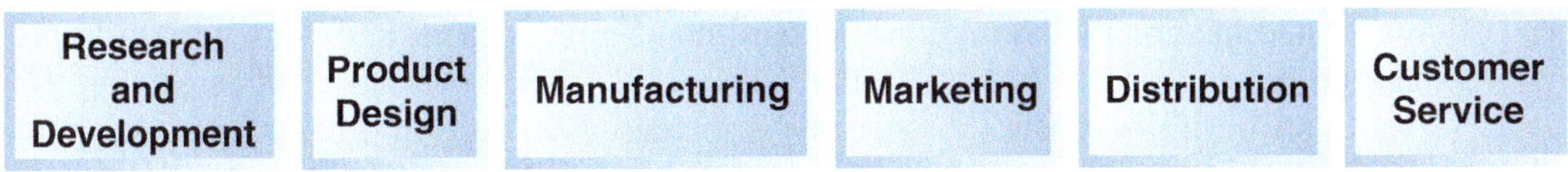

Lean Production

Lean Production is a management approach that organizes resources such as people and machines around the flow of business processes and that only produces units in response to customer orders. It is often called *just-in-time* production (or *JIT*) because products are only manufactured in response to customer orders and they are completed just-in-time to be shipped to customers. Lean thinking differs from traditional manufacturing methods, which organize work departmentally and encourage those departments to maximize their output even if it exceeds customer demand and bloats inventories. Because lean thinking only allows production in response to customer orders, the number of units produced tends to equal the number of units sold, thereby resulting in minimal inventory. The lean approach also results in fewer defects, less wasted effort, and quicker customer response times than traditional production methods.

IN BUSINESS

LEAN SUPPLY CHAIN MANAGEMENT

Tesco, a grocery retailer in Britain, used lean thinking to improve its replenishment process for cola products. Tesco and Britvic (its cola supplier) traced the cola delivery process from "the check-out counter of the grocery store through Tesco's regional distribution center (RDC), Britvic's RDC, the warehouse at the Britvic bottling plant, the filling lines for cola destined for Tesco, and the warehouse of Britvic's can supplier." Each step of the process revealed enormous waste. Tesco implemented numerous changes such as electronically linking its point-of-sale data from its grocery stores to its RDC. This change let customers pace the replenishment process and it helped increase store delivery frequency to every few hours around the clock. Britvic also began delivering cola to Tesco's RDC in wheeled dollies that could be rolled directly into delivery trucks and then to point-of-sale locations in grocery stores.

These changes reduced the total product "touches" from 150 to 50, thereby cutting labor costs. The elapsed time from the supplier's filling line to the customer's cola purchase dropped from 20 days to 5 days. The number of inventory stocking locations declined from five to two, and the supplier's distribution center was eliminated.

Source: Ghostwriter, "Teaching the Big Box New Tricks," *Fortune*, November 14, 2005, pp. 208B–208F.

The Theory of Constraints (TOC) A **constraint** is anything that prevents you from getting more of what you want. Every individual and every organization faces at least one constraint, so it is not difficult to find examples of constraints. You may not have enough time to study thoroughly for every subject *and* to go out with your friends on the weekend, so time is your constraint. United Airlines has only a limited number of loading gates available at its busy Chicago O'Hare hub, so its constraint is loading gates. Vail Resorts has only a limited amount of land to develop as homesites and commercial lots at its ski areas, so its constraint is land.

The **Theory of Constraints (TOC)** is based on the insight that effectively managing the constraint is a key to success. As an example, long waiting periods for surgery are a chronic problem in the National Health Service (NHS), the government-funded provider of health care in the United Kingdom. The diagram in Exhibit 1–7 illustrates a simplified version of the steps followed by a surgery patient. The number of patients who can be processed through each step in a day is indicated in the exhibit. For example, appointments for outpatient visits can be made for as many as 100 referrals from general practitioners in a day.

The constraint, or *bottleneck,* in the system is determined by the step that has the smallest capacity—in this case surgery. The total number of patients processed through the entire system cannot exceed 15 per day—the maximum number of patients who can be treated in surgery. No matter how hard managers, doctors, and nurses try to improve the processing rate elsewhere in the system, they will never succeed in driving down wait lists until the capacity of surgery is increased. In fact, improvements elsewhere in the system—particularly before the constraint—are likely to result in even longer waiting times and more frustrated patients and health care providers. Thus, to be effective, improvement efforts must be focused on the constraint. A business process, such as the process for serving surgery patients, is like a chain. If you want to increase the strength of a chain, what is the most effective way to do this? Should you concentrate your efforts on strengthening the strongest link, all the links, or the weakest link? Clearly, focusing your effort on the weakest link will bring the biggest benefit.

The procedure to follow to strengthen the chain is clear. First, identify the weakest link, which is the constraint. In the case of the NHS, the constraint is surgery. Second, do not place a greater strain on the system than the weakest link can handle—if you do, the chain will break. In the case of the NHS, more referrals than surgery can accommodate lead to unacceptably long waiting lists. Third, concentrate improvement efforts on strengthening the weakest link. In the case of the NHS, this means finding ways to increase the number of surgeries that can be performed in a day. Fourth, if the improvement efforts are successful, eventually the weakest link will improve to the point where it is no longer the weakest link. At that point, the new weakest link (i.e., the new constraint) must be identified, and improvement efforts must be shifted over to that link. This simple sequential process provides a powerful strategy for optimizing business processes.

EXHIBIT 1–7

Processing Surgery Patients at an NHS Facility (simplified)*

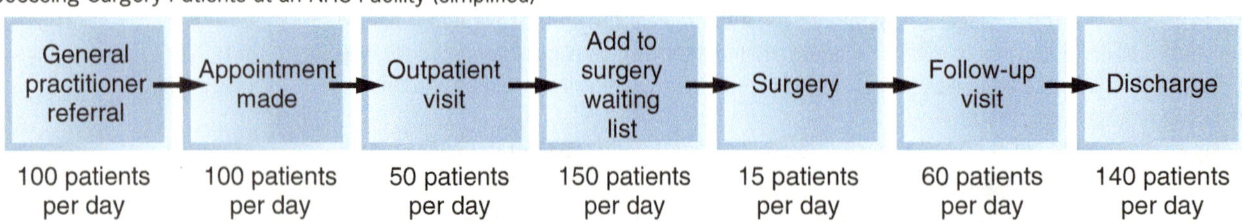

*This diagram originally appeared in the February 1999 issue of the U.K. magazine *Health Management.*

Measurement Skills

When you become a manager you'll need to complement your understanding of strategy, risks, and business processes, with data-driven analysis. If you cannot use measurement skills to provide competent, data-driven answers to challenging questions, then you'll struggle to persuade others to endorse your point-of-view.

The key to being an effective data analyst is to understand that the question you are trying to answer defines what you'll measure and how you'll analyze it. For example, if the question you wish to answer is what net income should my company report to its stockholders, then you'll be measuring and reporting historical financial data that must comply with applicable rules. If you are trying to determine how well your company is serving its customers, then you'll be measuring and analyzing mostly nonfinancial, process-oriented data. If you want to predict whether your company will need to borrow money next year, then your measurement efforts will focus on estimating future cash flows. You have to understand the question first before you can begin measuring and analyzing data.

The primary purpose of this course is to teach you measurement skills that managers use every day to answer the questions described in Exhibit 1–8. Notice that this exhibit is organized by the chapters contained in this book. For example, Chapter 8 teaches you the measurement skills that managers use to answer the question: How should I create a financial plan for next year? Chapters 9 and 10 teach you the measurement skills that managers use to answer the question: How well am I performing relative to my plan? Chapter 7 teaches you measurement skills related to product, service, and customer profitability. Exhibit 1–8 emphasizes that every chapter in this book teaches you measurement and data analysis skills that you'll use throughout your career to plan, control, and make decisions.

EXHIBIT 1–8
Measurement Skills: A Manager's Perspective

Chapter Number	The Key Question from a Manager's Perspective
Chapter 2	What cost classifications do I use for different management purposes?
Chapters 3 & 4	What is the value of our ending inventory and cost of goods sold for external reporting purposes?
Chapter 5	How will my profits change if I change my selling price, sales volume, or costs?
Chapter 6	How should the income statement be presented?
Chapter 7	How profitable is each of our products, services, and customers?
Chapter 8	How should I create a financial plan for next year?
Chapters 9 & 10	How well am I performing relative to my plan?
Chapter 11	What performance measures should we monitor to ensure that we achieve our strategic goals?
Chapter 12	How do I quantify the profit impact of pursuing one course of action versus another?
Chapter 13	How do I make long-term capital investment decisions?
Chapter 14	What cash inflows and outflows explain the change in our cash balance?
Chapter 15	How is our company performing through the eyes of our shareholders, short-term creditors, and long-term creditors?

Leadership Skills

Leadership skills will be critical to your career development for the simple reason that organizations are managed by people, not data and spreadsheets. These people have their own personal interests, insecurities, beliefs, and data-supported conclusions that ensure unanimous support for a given course of action is the exception rather than the rule. Therefore, managers must possess strong leadership skills if they wish to channel their co-workers' efforts toward achieving organizational goals.

To become an effective leader, you'll need to develop six skills. First, you'll need to be technically competent within your area of expertise and knowledgeable of your company's operations outside your functional area of expertise. You cannot lead others (particularly those co-workers outside of your department) if they believe that you are technically incompetent or unfamiliar with how the company actually operates. Second, you must be a person of high integrity. This requires that you not only make ethically grounded decisions yourself, but also that your words and actions help build a culture of organizational integrity. We will have more to say about the importance of ethics shortly. Third, you need to understand how to effectively implement organizational change. People tend to prefer the status quo, so it is often difficult to implement any type of change in a company. To implement change, leaders need to define a vision for the future and be able to motivate and enable others to achieve the vision.

Fourth, leaders need strong communication skills. This includes compelling presentation skills and effective listening skills. They must be able to speak in operational terms and financial terms to communicate effectively with co-workers across the organization. Fifth, leaders must be capable of motivating and mentoring other individuals. As your career evolves, if you cannot advance the skills of your subordinates, then you will not be promoted to jobs that have increasing numbers of people reporting to you. Finally, leaders need to effectively manage team-based decision processes. This requires motivating the team to objectively synthesize data, weigh alternatives, and build consensus around the chosen course of action.

The Importance of Ethics in Business

At the turn of this century, a series of major financial scandals involving Enron, Tyco International, HealthSouth, Adelphia Communications, WorldCom, Global Crossing, Rite Aid, and other companies raised deep concerns about ethics in business. The managers and companies involved in these scandals suffered mightily—from huge fines to jail terms and financial collapse. And the recognition that ethical behavior is absolutely essential for the functioning of our economy led to numerous regulatory changes—some of which we will discuss in a later appendix on corporate governance. But why is ethical behavior so important? This is not a matter of just being "nice." Ethical behavior is the lubricant that keeps the economy running. Without that lubricant, the economy would operate much less efficiently—less would be available to consumers, quality would be lower, and prices would be higher. In other words, without fundamental trust in the integrity of businesses, the economy would operate much less efficiently. James Surowiecki summed up this point as follows:

> [F]lourishing economies require a healthy level of trust in the reliability and fairness of everyday transactions. If you assumed every potential deal was a rip-off or that the products you were buying were probably going to be lemons, then very little business would get done. More important, the costs of the transactions that did take place would be exorbitant because you'd have to do enormous work to investigate each deal and you'd have to rely on the threat of legal action to enforce every contract. For an economy to prosper, what's needed is not a Pollyannaish faith that everyone else has your best interests at

> heart—"caveat emptor" [buyer beware] remains an important truth—but a basic confidence in the promises and commitments that people make about their products and services.[2]

Thus, for the good of everyone—including profit-making companies—it is vitally important that business be conducted within an ethical framework that builds and sustains trust.

The Institute of Management Accountants (IMA) of the United States has adopted an ethical code called the *Statement of Ethical Professional Practice* that describes in some detail the ethical responsibilities of management accountants. Even though the standards were specifically developed for management accountants, they have much broader application.

Code of Conduct for Management Accountants

The IMA's Statement of Ethical Professional Practice consists of two parts that are presented in full in Exhibit 1–9 (page 16). The first part provides general guidelines for ethical behavior. In a nutshell, a management accountant has ethical responsibilities in four broad areas: first, to maintain a high level of professional competence; second, to treat sensitive matters with confidentiality; third, to maintain personal integrity; and fourth, to disclose information in a credible fashion. The second part of the standards specifies what should be done if an individual finds evidence of ethical misconduct. We recommend that you stop at this point and read all of Exhibit 1–9.

The ethical standards provide sound, practical advice for management accountants and managers. Most of the rules in the ethical standards are motivated by a very practical consideration—if these rules were not generally followed in business, then the economy and all of us would suffer. Consider the following specific examples of the consequences of not abiding by the standards:

- Suppose employees could not be trusted with confidential information. Then top managers would be reluctant to distribute such information within the company and, as a result, decisions would be based on incomplete information and operations would deteriorate.
- Suppose employees accepted bribes from suppliers. Then contracts would tend to go to suppliers who pay the highest bribes rather than to the most competent suppliers. Would you like to fly in aircraft whose wings were made by the subcontractor who paid the highest bribe? Would you fly as often? What would happen to the airline industry if its safety record deteriorated due to shoddy workmanship on contracted parts and assemblies?
- Suppose the presidents of companies routinely lied in their annual reports and financial statements. If investors could not rely on the basic integrity of a company's financial statements, they would have little basis for making informed decisions. Suspecting the worst, rational investors would pay less for securities issued by companies and may not be willing to invest at all. As a consequence, companies would have less money for productive investments—leading to slower economic growth, fewer goods and services, and higher prices.

As these examples suggest, if ethical standards were not generally adhered to, everyone would suffer—businesses as well as consumers. Essentially, abandoning ethical standards would lead to a lower standard of living with lower-quality goods and services, less to choose from, and higher prices. In short, following ethical rules such as those in the Statement of Ethical Professional Practice is absolutely essential for the smooth functioning of an advanced market economy.

---

[2] James Surowiecki, "A Virtuous Cycle," *Forbes*, December 23, 2002, pp. 248–256. Reprinted by Permission of Forbes Magazine © 2006 Forbes Inc.

EXHIBIT 1–9
IMA Statement of Ethical Professional Practice

Members of IMA shall behave ethically. A commitment to ethical professional practice includes: overarching principles that express our values, and standards that guide our conduct.

PRINCIPLES

IMA's overarching ethical principles include: Honesty, Fairness, Objectivity, and Responsibility. Members shall act in accordance with these principles and shall encourage others within their organizations to adhere to them.

STANDARDS

A member's failure to comply with the following standards may result in disciplinary action.

I. COMPETENCE

Each member has a responsibility to:
1. Maintain an appropriate level of professional expertise by continually developing knowledge and skills.
2. Perform professional duties in accordance with relevant laws, regulations, and technical standards.
3. Provide decision support information and recommendations that are accurate, clear, concise, and timely.
4. Recognize and communicate professional limitations or other constraints that would preclude responsible judgment or successful performance of an activity.

II. CONFIDENTIALITY

Each member has a responsibility to:
1. Keep information confidential except when disclosure is authorized or legally required.
2. Inform all relevant parties regarding appropriate use of confidential information. Monitor subordinates' activities to ensure compliance.
3. Refrain from using confidential information for unethical or illegal advantage.

III. INTEGRITY

Each member has a responsibility to:
1. Mitigate actual conflicts of interest. Regularly communicate with business associates to avoid apparent conflicts of interest. Advise all parties of any potential conflicts.
2. Refrain from engaging in any conduct that would prejudice carrying out duties ethically.
3. Abstain from engaging in or supporting any activity that might discredit the profession.

IV. CREDIBILITY

Each member has a responsibility to:
1. Communicate information fairly and objectively.
2. Disclose all relevant information that could reasonably be expected to influence an intended user's understanding of the reports, analyses, or recommendations.
3. Disclose delays or deficiencies in information, timeliness, processing, or internal controls in conformance with organization policy and/or applicable law.

RESOLUTION OF ETHICAL CONFLICT

In applying the Standards of Ethical Professional Practice, you may encounter problems identifying unethical behavior or resolving an ethical conflict. When faced with ethical issues, you should follow your organization's established policies on the resolution of such conflict. If these policies do not resolve the ethical conflict, you should consider the following courses of action:
1. Discuss the issue with your immediate supervisor except when it appears that the supervisor is involved. In that case, present the issue to the next level. If you cannot achieve a satisfactory resolution, submit the issue to the next management level. If your immediate superior is the chief executive officer or equivalent, the acceptable reviewing authority may be a group such as the audit committee, executive committee, board of directors, board of trustees, or owners. Contact with levels above the immediate superior should be initiated only with your superior's knowledge, assuming he or she is not involved. Communication of such problems to authorities or individuals not employed or engaged by the organization is not considered appropriate, unless you believe there is a clear violation of the law.
2. Clarify relevant ethical issues by initiating a confidential discussion with an IMA Ethics Counselor or other impartial advisor to obtain a better understanding of possible courses of action.
3. Consult your own attorney as to legal obligations and rights concerning the ethical conflict.

IN BUSINESS

TOYOTA ENCOUNTERS MAJOR PROBLEMS

When Toyota Motor Corporation failed to meet its profit targets, the company set an aggressive goal of reducing the cost of its auto parts by 30%. The quality and safety of the company's automobiles eventually suffered mightily resulting in recalls, litigation, incentive campaigns, and marketing efforts that analysts estimate will cost the company more than $5 billion. The car maker's president, Akio Toyoda, blamed his company's massive quality lapses on an excessive focus on profits and market share. Similarly, Jim Press, Toyota's former top U.S. executive, said the problems were caused by "financially-oriented pirates who didn't have the character to maintain a customer-first focus."

Sources: Yoshio Takahashi, "Toyota Accelerates Its Cost-Cutting Efforts," *The Wall Street Journal*, December 23, 2009, p. B4; Mariko Sanchanta and Yoshio Takahashi, "Toyota's Recall May Top $5 Billion," *The Wall Street Journal*, March 10, 2010, p. B2; and Norihiko Shirouzu, "Toyoda Rues Excessive Profit Focus," *The Wall Street Journal*, March 2, 2010, p. B3.

Corporate Social Responsibility

Companies are responsible for producing financial results that satisfy stockholders. However, they also have a *corporate social responsibility* to serve other stakeholders—such as customers, employees, suppliers, communities, and environmental and human rights advocates—whose interests are tied to the company's performance. **Corporate social responsibility** (CSR) is a concept whereby organizations consider the needs of all stakeholders when making decisions. CSR extends beyond legal compliance to include voluntary actions that satisfy stakeholder expectations. Numerous companies, such as Procter & Gamble, 3M, Eli Lilly and Company, Starbucks, Microsoft, Genentech, Johnson & Johnson, Baxter International, Abbott Laboratories, KPMG, National City Bank, Deloitte, Southwest Airlines, and Caterpillar, prominently describe their corporate social performance on their websites.

Exhibit 1–10 presents examples of corporate social responsibilities that are of interest to six stakeholder groups. Many companies are paying increasing attention to these types of broadly defined responsibilities for four reasons. First, socially responsible investors control more than $2.3 trillion of investment capital. Companies that want access to this capital must excel in terms of their social performance. Second, a growing number of employees want to work for a company that recognizes and responds to its social responsibilities. If companies hope to recruit and retain these highly skilled employees, then they must offer fulfilling careers that serve the needs of broadly defined stakeholders. Third, many customers seek to purchase products and services from socially responsible companies. The Internet enables these customers to readily locate competing products, thereby making it even easier to avoid doing business with undesirable companies. Fourth, nongovernment organizations (NGOs) and activists are more capable than ever of tarnishing a company's reputation by publicizing its environmental or human rights missteps. The Internet has enabled these environmental and human rights advocacy groups to better organize their resources, spread negative information, and take coordinated actions against offending companies.[3]

[3] The insights from this paragraph and many of the examples in Exhibit 1–10 were drawn from Ronald W. Clement, "The Lessons from Stakeholder Theory for U.S. Business Leaders," *Business Horizons*, May/June 2005, pp. 255–264; and Terry Leap and Misty L. Loughry, "The Stakeholder-Friendly Firm," *Business Horizons*, March/April 2004, pp. 27–32.

EXHIBIT 1–10
Examples of Corporate Social Responsibilities

Companies should provide *customers* with:

- Safe, high-quality products that are fairly priced.
- Competent, courteous, and rapid delivery of products and services.
- Full disclosure of product-related risks.
- Easy-to-use information systems for shopping and tracking orders.

Companies and their suppliers should provide *employees* with:

- Safe and humane working conditions.
- Nondiscriminatory treatment and the right to organize and file grievances.
- Fair compensation.
- Opportunities for training, promotion, and personal development.

Companies should provide *suppliers* with:

- Fair contract terms and prompt payments.
- Reasonable time to prepare orders.
- Hassle-free acceptance of timely and complete deliveries.
- Cooperative rather than unilateral actions.

Companies should provide *communities* with:

- Payment of fair taxes.
- Honest information about plans such as plant closings.
- Resources that support charities, schools, and civic activities.
- Reasonable access to media sources.

Companies should provide *stockholders* with:

- Competent management.
- Easy access to complete and accurate financial information.
- Full disclosure of enterprise risks.
- Honest answers to knowledgeable questions.

Companies should provide *environmental and human rights advocates* with:

- Greenhouse gas emissions data.
- Recycling and resource conservation data.
- Child labor transparency.
- Full disclosure of suppliers located in developing countries.

It is important to understand that a company's social performance can impact its financial performance. For example, if a company's poor social performance alienates customers, then its revenues and profits will suffer. This reality explains why companies use enterprise risk management, as previously described, to meet the needs of *all* stakeholders.

IN BUSINESS

SKILL-BASED VOLUNTEERISM GROWS IN POPULARITY

Ernst & Young, a "Big 4" public accounting firm, paid one of its managers to spend 12 weeks in Buenos Aires providing free accounting services to a small publishing company. UPS paid one of its logistics supervisors to help coordinate the Susan G. Komen Breast Cancer Foundation's annual Race for the Cure event. Why are these companies paying their employees to work for other organizations? A survey of 1,800 people ages 13–25 revealed that 79% intend to seek employment with companies that care about contributing to society—underscoring the value of skill-based volunteerism as an employee recruiting and retention tool. Furthermore, enabling employees to apply their skills in diverse business contexts makes them more effective when they return to their regular jobs.

Source: Sarah E. Needleman, "The Latest Office Perk: Getting Paid to Volunteer," *The Wall Street Journal*, April 29, 2008, pp. D1 and D5.

Summary

This chapter defined managerial accounting, explained why it is relevant to business and accounting majors, and described various skills that managers need to do their jobs. It also discussed the importance of ethics in business and corporate social responsibility. The most important goal of this chapter was to help you understand that managerial accounting matters to your future career, regardless of your major. Accounting is the language of business and you'll need to speak this language to communicate effectively with and influence fellow managers.

Glossary

Budget A detailed plan for the future that is usually expressed in formal quantitative terms. (p. 3)

Business process A series of steps that are followed in order to carry out some task in a business. (p. 11)

Constraint Anything that prevents you from getting more of what you want. (p. 12)

Controlling The process of gathering feedback to ensure that a plan is being properly executed or modified as circumstances change. (p. 3)

Corporate social responsibility A concept whereby organizations consider the needs of all stakeholders when making decisions. (p. 17)

Decision making Selecting a course of action from competing alternatives. (p. 3)

Enterprise risk management A process used by a company to identify its risks and develop responses to them that enable it to be reasonably assured of meeting its goals. (p. 9)

Financial accounting The phase of accounting that is concerned with reporting historical financial information to external parties, such as stockholders, creditors, and regulators. (p. 2)

Lean Production A management approach that organizes resources such as people and machines around the flow of business processes and that only produces units in response to customer orders. (p. 11)

Managerial accounting The phase of accounting that is concerned with providing information to managers for use within the organization. (p. 2)

Performance report A report that compares budgeted data to actual data to highlight instances of excellent and unsatisfactory performance. (p. 4)

Planning The process of establishing goals and specifying how to achieve them. (p. 3)

Segment A part or activity of an organization about which managers would like cost, revenue, or profit data. (p. 3)

Strategy A company's "game plan" for attracting customers by distinguishing itself from competitors. (p. 8)

Theory of Constraints A management approach that emphasizes the importance of managing constraints. (p. 12)

Value chain The major business functions that add value to a company's products and services, such as research and development, product design, manufacturing, marketing, distribution, and customer service. (p. 11)

Questions

1–1 How does managerial accounting differ from financial accounting?

1–2 Pick any major television network and describe some planning and control activities that its managers would engage in.

1–3 If you had to decide whether to continue making a component part or to begin buying the part from an overseas supplier, what quantitative and qualitative factors would influence your decision?

1–4 Why do companies prepare budgets?

1–5 Why is managerial accounting relevant to business majors and their future careers?

1–6 Why is managerial accounting relevant to accounting majors and their future careers?

1–7 Pick any large company and describe its strategy using the framework in the chapter.

1–8 Why do management accountants need to understand their company's strategy?
1–9 Pick any large company and describe three risks that it faces and how it responds to those risks.
1–10 Provide three examples of how a company's risks can influence its planning, controlling, and decision-making activities.
1–11 Pick any large company and explain three ways that it could segment its companywide performance.
1–12 Locate the website of any company that publishes a corporate social responsibility report (also referred to as a sustainability report). Describe three nonfinancial performance measures included in the report. Why do you think the company publishes this report?
1–13 Why do companies that implement Lean Production tend to have minimal inventories?
1–14 Why are leadership skills important to managers?
1–15 Why is ethics important to business?

Multiple-choice questions are provided on the text website at www.mhhe.com/garrison14e.

Appendix 1A: Corporate Governance

Effective *corporate governance* enhances stockholders' confidence that a company is being run in their best interests rather than in the interests of top managers. **Corporate governance** is the system by which a company is directed and controlled. If properly implemented, the corporate governance system should provide incentives for the board of directors and top management to pursue objectives that are in the interests of the company's owners and it should provide for effective monitoring of performance.[1]

Unfortunately, history has repeatedly shown that unscrupulous top managers, if unchecked, can exploit their power to defraud stockholders. This unpleasant reality became all too clear in 2001 when the fall of Enron kicked off a wave of corporate scandals. These scandals were characterized by financial reporting fraud and misuse of corporate funds at the very highest levels—including CEOs and CFOs. While this was disturbing in itself, it also indicated that the institutions intended to prevent such abuses weren't working, thus raising fundamental questions about the adequacy of the existing corporate governance system. In an attempt to respond to these concerns, the U.S. Congress passed the most important reform of corporate governance in many decades—*The Sarbanes-Oxley Act of 2002.*

The Sarbanes-Oxley Act of 2002

The **Sarbanes-Oxley Act of 2002** was intended to protect the interests of those who invest in publicly traded companies by improving the reliability and accuracy of corporate financial reports and disclosures. We would like to highlight six key aspects of the legislation.[2]

First, the Act requires that both the CEO and CFO certify in writing that their company's financial statements and accompanying disclosures fairly represent the results of operations—with possible jail time if a CEO or CFO certifies results that they know are false. This creates very powerful incentives for the CEO and CFO to ensure that the financial statements contain no misrepresentations.

Second, the Act established the Public Company Accounting Oversight Board to provide additional oversight over the audit profession. The Act authorizes the Board

[1] This definition of corporate governance was adapted from the 2004 report titled OECD Principles of Corporate Governance published by the Organization for Economic Co-Operation and Development.

[2] A summary of the Sarbanes-Oxley Act of 2002 can be obtained from the American Institute of Certified Public Accountants (AICPA) website http://thecaq.aicpa.org/Resources/Sarbanes+Oxley.

to conduct investigations, to take disciplinary actions against audit firms, and to enact various standards and rules concerning the preparation of audit reports.

Third, the Act places the power to hire, compensate, and terminate the public accounting firm that audits a company's financial reports in the hands of the audit committee of the board of directors. Previously, management often had the power to hire and fire its auditors. Furthermore, the Act specifies that all members of the audit committee must be independent, meaning that they do not have an affiliation with the company they are overseeing, nor do they receive any consulting or advisory compensation from the company.

Fourth, the Act places important restrictions on audit firms. Historically, public accounting firms earned a large part of their profits by providing consulting services to the companies that they audited. This provided the appearance of a lack of independence because a client that was dissatisfied with an auditor's stance on an accounting issue might threaten to stop using the auditor as a consultant. To avoid this possible conflict of interests, the Act prohibits a public accounting firm from providing a wide variety of nonauditing services to an audit client.

Fifth, the Act requires that a company's annual report contain an *internal control report.* Internal controls are put in place by management to provide assurance to investors that financial disclosures are reliable. The report must state that it is management's responsibility to establish and maintain adequate internal controls and it must contain an assessment by management of the effectiveness of its internal control structure. The internal control report is accompanied by an opinion from the company's audit firm as to whether management has maintained effective internal control over its financial reporting process.

Finally, the Act establishes severe penalties of as many as 20 years in prison for altering or destroying any documents that may eventually be used in an official proceeding and as many as 10 years in prison for managers who retaliate against a so-called whistle-blower who goes outside the chain of command to report misconduct. Collectively, these six aspects of the Sarbanes-Oxley Act of 2002 should help reduce the incidence of fraudulent financial reporting.

Internal Control—A Closer Look

Internal control is an important concept for all managers to understand and, although you may not be aware of it, it also plays an important role in your personal life. **Internal control** is a process designed to provide reasonable assurance that objectives are being achieved. For example, one objective for your personal life is to live to a ripe old age. Unfortunately, there are risks that we all encounter that may prohibit us from achieving this objective. For example, we may die prematurely due to a heart attack, a car accident, or a house fire. To reduce the risk of these unfortunate events occurring, we implement controls in our lives. We may exercise regularly and make nutritional food choices to reduce the likelihood of a heart attack. We always wear seat belts and instruct our friends to prohibit us from drinking alcohol and driving a vehicle to reduce the risk of a fatal car crash. We install fire detectors in our homes to reduce the risk of a fatal fire. In short, internal controls are an integral part of our daily lives.

A company uses internal controls to provide reasonable assurance that its financial reports are reliable.[3] Its financial statements may contain intentional or unintentional errors for three reasons. First, the statements may erroneously exclude some transactions. For example, the income statement may fail to include legitimate expenses. Second, the statements may improperly include some transactions. For example, the income statement may include sales revenue that was not earned during the current period. Third, the statements may include transactions that have been recorded erroneously. For example, an expense or sales transaction may be recorded at the wrong amount.

[3] Companies also use internal controls to achieve efficient and effective operations and to ensure compliance with applicable laws and regulations.

Exhibit 1A–1 describes seven types of internal controls that companies use to reduce the risk that these types of errors will occur. Each item in the exhibit is labeled as a *preventive control* and/or a *detective control.* A **preventive control** deters undesirable events from occurring. A **detective control** detects undesirable events that have already occurred. Requiring authorizations for certain types of transactions is a preventive control. For example, companies frequently require that a specific senior manager sign all checks above a particular dollar amount to reduce the risk of an inappropriate cash disbursement. Reconciliations are a detective control. If you have ever compared a bank statement to your checkbook to resolve any discrepancies, then you have performed a type of reconciliation known as a bank reconciliation. This is a detective control because you are seeking to identify any mistakes already made by the bank or existing mistakes in your own records.

Segregation of duties is a preventive control that separates responsibilities for authorizing transactions, recording transactions, and maintaining custody of the related assets. For example, the same employee should not have the ability to authorize inventory purchases, account for those purchases, and manage the inventory storeroom. Physical safeguards prevent unauthorized employees from having access to assets such as inventories and computer equipment. Performance reviews are a detective control performed by employees in supervisory positions to ensure that actual results are reasonable when compared to relevant benchmarks. If actual results unexpectedly deviate from expectations, then it triggers further analysis to determine the root cause of the deviation. Companies maintain records to provide evidence that supports each transaction. For example, companies use serially numbered checks so that they can readily track all of their cash disbursements. Finally, companies use passwords (a preventive control) and access logs (a detective control) to restrict electronic data access as appropriate.

It is important to understand that internal controls cannot guarantee that objectives will be achieved. For example, a person can regularly exercise and eat healthy foods, but this does not guarantee that they will live to a certain age. Similarly, an effective internal control system can provide reasonable assurance that financial statement disclosures are reliable, but it cannot offer guarantees because even a well-designed internal control system can break down. Furthermore, two or more employees may collude to circumvent the control system. Finally, a company's senior leaders may manipulate financial results by intentionally overriding prescribed policies and procedures. This reality highlights the

EXHIBIT 1A–1
Types of Internal Controls for Financial Reporting

Type of Control	Classification	Description
Authorizations	Preventive	Requiring management to formally approve certain types of transactions.
Reconciliations	Detective	Relating data sets to one another to identify and resolve discrepancies.
Segregation of duties	Preventive	Separating responsibilities related to authorizing transactions, recording transactions, and maintaining custody of the related assets.
Physical safeguards	Preventive	Using cameras, locks, and physical barriers to protect assets.
Performance reviews	Detective	Comparing actual performance to various benchmarks to identify unexpected results.
Maintaining records	Detective	Maintaining written and/or electronic evidence to support transactions.
Information systems security	Preventive/Detective	Using controls such as passwords and access logs to ensure appropriate data restrictions.

importance of having senior leaders (including the chief executive officer, the chief financial officer, and the audit committee of the board of directors) who value the importance of effective internal controls and are committed to creating an ethical "tone at the top" of the organization.

Glossary

Corporate governance The system by which a company is directed and controlled. (p. 20)

Detective control A control that detects undesirable events that have already occurred. (p. 22)

Internal control A process designed to provide reasonable assurance that objectives are being achieved. (p. 21)

Preventive control A control that deters undesirable events from occurring. (p. 22)

Sarbanes-Oxley Act of 2002 A law intended to protect the interests of those who invest in publicly traded companies by improving the reliability and accuracy of corporate financial reports and discloures. (p. 20)

Questions

1A–1 Imagine that you are the head coach of a college sports team. One of your most important objectives is to win as many games as possible. Describe some controls that you would implement to help achieve the objective of winning as many games as possible.

1A–2 Perhaps your most important post-graduation objective is to get a job. Describe some control activities that you would pursue to help achieve this objective.

1A–3 Describe some controls that parents use to keep their homes safe for themselves and their children.

Chapter 2

Managerial Accounting and Cost Concepts

LEARNING OBJECTIVES

After studying Chapter 2, you should be able to:

- **LO1** Identify and give examples of each of the three basic manufacturing cost categories.
- **LO2** Distinguish between product costs and period costs and give examples of each.
- **LO3** Understand cost behavior patterns including variable costs, fixed costs, and mixed costs.
- **LO4** Analyze a mixed cost using a scattergraph plot and the high-low method.
- **LO5** Prepare income statements for a merchandising company using the traditional and contribution formats.
- **LO6** Understand the differences between direct and indirect costs.
- **LO7** Understand cost classifications used in making decisions: differential costs, opportunity costs, and sunk costs.
- **LO8** (Appendix 2A) Analyze a mixed cost using a scattergraph plot and the least-squares regression method.
- **LO9** (Appendix 2B) Identify the four types of quality costs and explain how they interact.
- **LO10** (Appendix 2B) Prepare and interpret a quality cost report.

Understanding Costs Aids the Growth of a Billion Dollar Company

BUSINESS FOCUS

In 1986, Women's World of Fitness went bankrupt despite having 14 locations and 50,000 members. The company's owner, Gary Heavin, says the fitness centers contained too many costly amenities such as swimming pools, tanning beds, cardio machines, kid's programs, juice bars, personal trainers, and aerobics classes. As costs escalated, he attempted to increase revenues by offering memberships to men, which alienated his female members. What did Heavin learn from his experience?

In 1992, Heavin founded a new brand of women's fitness centers called Curves. Rather than investing in every conceivable piece of fitness equipment and amenity, Heavin focused on simplicity. He created a simple fitness circuit that uses minimal equipment and is quick and easy for members to complete. Instead of operating almost 24 hours a day, he decided to close his gyms early. Even showers were deemed unnecessary. In short, Heavin eliminated numerous costs that did not provide benefits in the eyes of his customers. With dramatically lower costs, he has been able to maintain his "women only" approach while building a billion dollar company with nearly 10,000 locations worldwide. ■

Source: Alison Stein Wellner, "Gary Heavin Is on a Mission from God," *Inc.* magazine, October 2006, pp. 116–123.

This chapter explains that in managerial accounting the term *cost* is used in many different ways. The reason is that there are many types of costs, and these costs are classified differently according to the immediate needs of management. For example, managers may want cost data to prepare external financial reports, to prepare planning budgets, or to make decisions. Each different use of cost data demands a different classification and definition of costs. For example, the preparation of external financial reports requires the use of historical cost data, whereas decision making may require predictions about future costs. This notion of different costs for different purposes is a critically important aspect of managerial accounting.

General Cost Classifications

We will start our discussion of cost concepts by focusing on manufacturing companies, because they are involved in most of the activities found in other types of organizations. Manufacturing companies such as Texas Instruments, Ford, and DuPont are involved in acquiring raw materials, producing finished goods, marketing, distributing, billing, and almost every other business activity. Therefore, an understanding of costs in a manufacturing company can be very helpful in understanding costs in other types of organizations.

Manufacturing Costs

LEARNING OBJECTIVE 1
Identify and give examples of each of the three basic manufacturing cost categories.

Most manufacturing companies separate manufacturing costs into three broad categories: direct materials, direct labor, and manufacturing overhead. A discussion of each of these categories follows.

Direct Materials The materials that go into the final product are called **raw materials.** This term is somewhat misleading because it seems to imply unprocessed natural resources like wood pulp or iron ore. Actually, raw materials refer to any materials that are used in the final product; and the finished product of one company can become the raw materials of another company. For example, the plastics produced by Du Pont are a raw material used by Hewlett-Packard in its personal computers.

Raw materials may include both *direct* and *indirect materials.* **Direct materials** are those materials that become an integral part of the finished product and whose costs can be conveniently traced to the finished product. This would include, for example, the seats that Airbus purchases from subcontractors to install in its commercial aircraft and the tiny electric motor Panasonic uses in its DVD players.

Sometimes it isn't worth the effort to trace the costs of relatively insignificant materials to end products. Such minor items would include the solder used to make electrical connections in a Sony TV or the glue used to assemble an Ethan Allen chair. Materials such as solder and glue are called **indirect materials** and are included as part of manufacturing overhead, which is discussed later in this section.

Direct Labor **Direct labor** consists of labor costs that can be easily (i.e., physically and conveniently) traced to individual units of product. Direct labor is sometimes called *touch labor* because direct labor workers typically touch the product while it is being made. Examples of direct labor include assembly-line workers at Toyota, carpenters at the home builder KB Home, and electricians who install equipment on aircraft at Bombardier Learjet.

Labor costs that cannot be physically traced to particular products, or that can be traced only at great cost and inconvenience, are termed **indirect labor.** Just like indirect materials, indirect labor is treated as part of manufacturing overhead. Indirect labor includes the labor costs of janitors, supervisors, materials handlers, and night security guards. Although the efforts of these workers are essential, it would be either impractical

IN BUSINESS

IS SENDING JOBS OVERSEAS ALWAYS A GOOD IDEA?

Many companies send jobs from high labor-cost countries such as the United States to lower labor-cost countries such as India and China. But is chasing labor cost savings always the right thing to do? In manufacturing, the answer is no. Typically, total direct labor costs are around 7% to 15% of cost of goods sold. Because direct labor is such a small part of overall costs, the labor savings realized by "offshoring" jobs can easily be overshadowed by a decline in efficiency that occurs simply because production facilities are located farther from the ultimate customers. The increase in inventory carrying costs and obsolescence costs coupled with slower response to customer orders, not to mention foreign currency exchange risks, can more than offset the benefits of employing geographically dispersed low-cost labor.

One manufacturer of casual wear in Los Angeles, California, understands the value of keeping jobs close to home in order to improve performance. The company can fill orders for as many as 160,000 units in 24 hours. In fact, the company carries less than 30 days' inventory and is considering fabricating clothing only after orders are received from customers rather than attempting to forecast what items will sell and making them in advance. How would they do this? The company's entire manufacturing process—including weaving, dyeing, and sewing—is located in downtown Los Angeles, eliminating shipping delays.

Source: Robert Sternfels and Ronald Ritter, "When Offshoring Doesn't Make Sense," *The Wall Street Journal*, October 19, 2004, p. B8.

or impossible to accurately trace their costs to specific units of product. Hence, such labor costs are treated as indirect labor.

Manufacturing Overhead **Manufacturing overhead,** the third element of manufacturing cost, includes all manufacturing costs except direct materials and direct labor. Manufacturing overhead includes items such as indirect materials; indirect labor; maintenance and repairs on production equipment; and heat and light, property taxes, depreciation, and insurance on manufacturing facilities. A company also incurs costs for heat and light, property taxes, insurance, depreciation, and so forth, associated with its selling and administrative functions, but these costs are not included as part of manufacturing overhead. Only those costs associated with *operating the factory* are included in manufacturing overhead.

Various names are used for manufacturing overhead, such as *indirect manufacturing cost, factory overhead,* and *factory burden.* All of these terms are synonyms for *manufacturing overhead.*

Nonmanufacturing Costs

Nonmanufacturing costs are often divided into two categories: (1) *selling costs* and (2) *administrative costs.* **Selling costs** include all costs that are incurred to secure customer orders and get the finished product to the customer. These costs are sometimes called *order-getting* and *order-filling costs.* Examples of selling costs include advertising, shipping, sales travel, sales commissions, sales salaries, and costs of finished goods warehouses.

Administrative costs include all costs associated with the *general management* of an organization rather than with manufacturing or selling. Examples of administrative costs include executive compensation, general accounting, secretarial, public relations, and similar costs involved in the overall, general administration of the organization *as a whole.*

Nonmanufacturing costs are also often called selling, general, and administrative (SG&A) costs or just selling and administrative costs.

Product Costs versus Period Costs

LEARNING OBJECTIVE 2
Distinguish between product costs and period costs and give examples of each.

In addition to classifying costs as manufacturing or nonmanufacturing costs, there are other ways to look at costs. For instance, they can also be classified as either *product costs* or *period costs.* To understand the difference between product costs and period costs, we must first discuss the matching principle from financial accounting.

Generally, costs are recognized as expenses on the income statement in the period that benefits from the cost. For example, if a company pays for liability insurance in advance for two years, the entire amount is not considered an expense of the year in which the payment is made. Instead, one-half of the cost would be recognized as an expense each year. The reason is that both years—not just the first year—benefit from the insurance payment. The unexpensed portion of the insurance payment is carried on the balance sheet as an asset called prepaid insurance.

The *matching principle* is based on the *accrual* concept that *costs incurred to generate a particular revenue should be recognized as expenses in the same period that the revenue is recognized.* This means that if a cost is incurred to acquire or make something that will eventually be sold, then the cost should be recognized as an expense only when the sale takes place—that is, when the benefit occurs. Such costs are called *product costs.*

Product Costs

For financial accounting purposes, **product costs** include all costs involved in acquiring or making a product. In the case of manufactured goods, these costs consist of direct materials, direct labor, and manufacturing overhead. Product costs "attach" to units of product as the goods are purchased or manufactured, and they remain attached as the goods go into inventory awaiting sale. Product costs are initially assigned to an inventory account on the balance sheet. When the goods are sold, the costs are released from inventory as expenses (typically called cost of goods sold) and matched against sales revenue. Because product costs are initially assigned to inventories, they are also known as **inventoriable costs.**

We want to emphasize that product costs are not necessarily treated as expenses in the period in which they are incurred. Rather, as explained above, they are treated as expenses in the period in which the related products *are sold.*

Period Costs

Period costs are all the costs that are not product costs. *All selling and administrative expenses are treated as period costs.* For example, sales commissions, advertising, executive salaries, public relations, and the rental costs of administrative offices are all period costs. Period costs are not included as part of the cost of either purchased or manufactured goods; instead, period costs are expensed on the income statement in the period in which they are incurred using the usual rules of accrual accounting. Keep in mind that the period in which a cost is incurred is not necessarily the period in which cash changes hands. For example, as discussed earlier, the costs of liability insurance are spread across the periods that benefit from the insurance—regardless of the period in which the insurance premium is paid.

Prime Cost and Conversion Cost

Two more cost categories are often used in discussions of manufacturing costs—*prime cost* and *conversion cost.* **Prime cost** is the sum of direct materials cost and direct labor cost. **Conversion cost** is the sum of direct labor cost and manufacturing overhead cost. The term *conversion cost* is used to describe direct labor and manufacturing overhead because these costs are incurred to convert materials into the finished product.

Exhibit 2–1 contains a summary of the cost terms that we have introduced so far.

EXHIBIT 2–1
Summary of Cost Terms

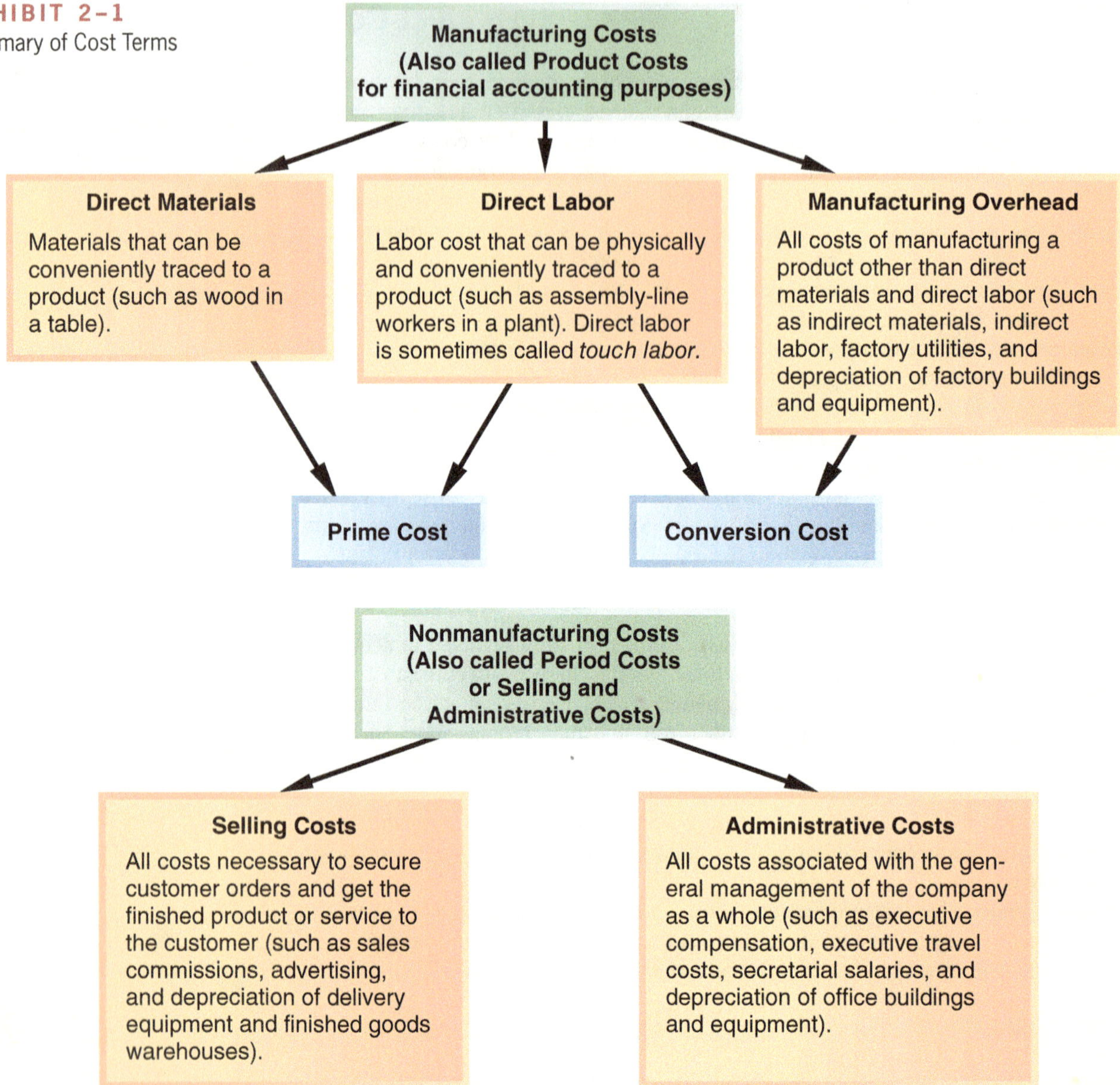

IN BUSINESS

THE CHALLENGES OF MANAGING CHARITABLE ORGANIZATIONS

Charitable organizations, such as Harlem Children's Zone, Sports4Kids, and Citizen Schools, are facing a difficult situation. Many donors—aware of stories involving charities that spent excessively on themselves while losing sight of their mission—have started prohibiting their charity of choice from using donated funds to pay for administrative costs. However, even the most efficient charitable organizations find it difficult to expand without making additions to their infrastructure. For example, Sports4Kids' nationwide expansion of its sports programs drove up administrative costs from 5.6% to 14.7% of its total budget. The organization claims that this cost increase was necessary to build a more experienced management team to oversee the dramatically increased scale of operations.

Many charitable organizations are starting to seek gifts explicitly to fund administrative expenses. Their argument is simple—they cannot do good deeds for other people without incurring such costs.

Source: Rachel Emma Silverman and Sally Beatty, "Save the Children (But Pay the Bills, Too)," *The Wall Street Journal*, December 26, 2006, pp. D1–D2.

Cost Classifications for Predicting Cost Behavior

LEARNING OBJECTIVE 3
Understand cost behavior patterns including variable costs, fixed costs, and mixed costs.

It is often necessary to predict how a certain cost will behave in response to a change in activity. For example, a manager at Qwest, a telephone company, may want to estimate the impact a 5 percent increase in long-distance calls by customers would have on Qwest's total electric bill. **Cost behavior** refers to how a cost reacts to changes in the level of activity. As the activity level rises and falls, a particular cost may rise and fall as well—or it may remain constant. For planning purposes, a manager must be able to anticipate which of these will happen; and if a cost can be expected to change, the manager must be able to estimate how much it will change. To help make such distinctions, costs are often categorized as *variable, fixed,* or *mixed.* The relative proportion of each type of cost in an organization is known as its **cost structure.** For example, an organization might have many fixed costs but few variable or mixed costs. Alternatively, it might have many variable costs but few fixed or mixed costs.

Variable Cost

A **variable cost** varies, in total, in direct proportion to changes in the level of activity. Common examples of variable costs include cost of goods sold for a merchandising company, direct materials, direct labor, variable elements of manufacturing overhead, such as indirect materials, supplies, and power, and variable elements of selling and administrative expenses, such as commissions and shipping costs.[1]

For a cost to be variable, it must be variable *with respect to something.* That "something" is its *activity base.* An **activity base** is a measure of whatever causes the incurrence of a variable cost. An activity base is sometimes referred to as a *cost driver.* Some of the most common activity bases are direct labor-hours, machine-hours, units produced, and units sold. Other examples of activity bases (cost drivers) include the number of miles driven by salespersons, the number of pounds of laundry cleaned by a hotel, the number of calls handled by technical support staff at a software company, and the number of beds occupied in a hospital. *While there are many activity bases within organizations, throughout this textbook, unless stated otherwise, you should assume that the activity base under consideration is the total volume of goods and services provided by the organization. We will specify the activity base only when it is something other than total output.*

IN BUSINESS

COST DRIVERS IN THE ELECTRONICS INDUSTRY

Accenture Ltd. estimates that the U.S. electronics industry spends $13.8 billion annually to rebox, restock, and resell returned products. Conventional wisdom is that customers only return products when they are defective, but the data shows that this explanation only accounts for 5% of customer returns. The biggest cost drivers that cause product returns are that customers often inadvertently buy the wrong products and that they cannot understand how to use the products that they have purchased. Television manufacturer Vizio Inc. has started including more information on its packaging to help customers avoid buying the wrong product. Seagate Technologies is replacing thick instruction manuals with simpler guides that make it easier for customers to begin using their products.

Source: Christopher Lawton, "The War on Returns," *The Wall Street Journal,* May 8, 2008, pp. D1 and D6.

To provide an example of a variable cost, consider Nooksack Expeditions, a small company that provides daylong whitewater rafting excursions on rivers in the North Cascade Mountains. The company provides all of the necessary equipment and experienced

[1] Direct labor costs often can be fixed instead of variable for a variety of reasons. For example, in some countries, such as France, Germany, and Japan, labor regulations and cultural norms may limit management's ability to adjust the labor force in response to changes in activity. In this textbook, always assume that direct labor is a variable cost unless you are explicitly told otherwise.

guides, and it serves gourmet meals to its guests. The meals are purchased from a caterer for $30 a person for a daylong excursion. The behavior of this variable cost, on both a per unit and a total basis, is shown below:

Number of Guests	Cost of Meals per Guest	Total Cost of Meals
250	$30	$7,500
500	$30	$15,000
750	$30	$22,500
1,000	$30	$30,000

While total variable costs change as the activity level changes, it is important to note that a variable cost is constant if expressed on a *per unit* basis. For example, the per unit cost of the meals remains constant at $30 even though the total cost of the meals increases and decreases with activity. The graph on the left-hand side of Exhibit 2–2 illustrates that the total variable cost rises and falls as the activity level rises and falls. At an activity level of 250 guests, the total meal cost is $7,500. At an activity level of 1,000 guests, the total meal cost rises to $30,000.

Fixed Cost

A **fixed cost** is a cost that remains constant, in total, regardless of changes in the level of activity. Examples of fixed costs include straight-line depreciation, insurance, property taxes, rent, supervisory salaries, administrative salaries, and advertising. Unlike variable costs, fixed costs are not affected by changes in activity. Consequently, as the activity level rises and falls, total fixed costs remain constant unless influenced by some outside force, such as a landlord increasing your monthly rental expense. To continue the Nooksack Expeditions example, assume the company rents a building for $500 per month to store its equipment. The total amount of rent paid is the same regardless of the number of guests the company takes on its expeditions during any given month. The concept of a fixed cost is shown graphically on the right-hand side of Exhibit 2–2.

EXHIBIT 2–2
Variable and Fixed Cost Behavior

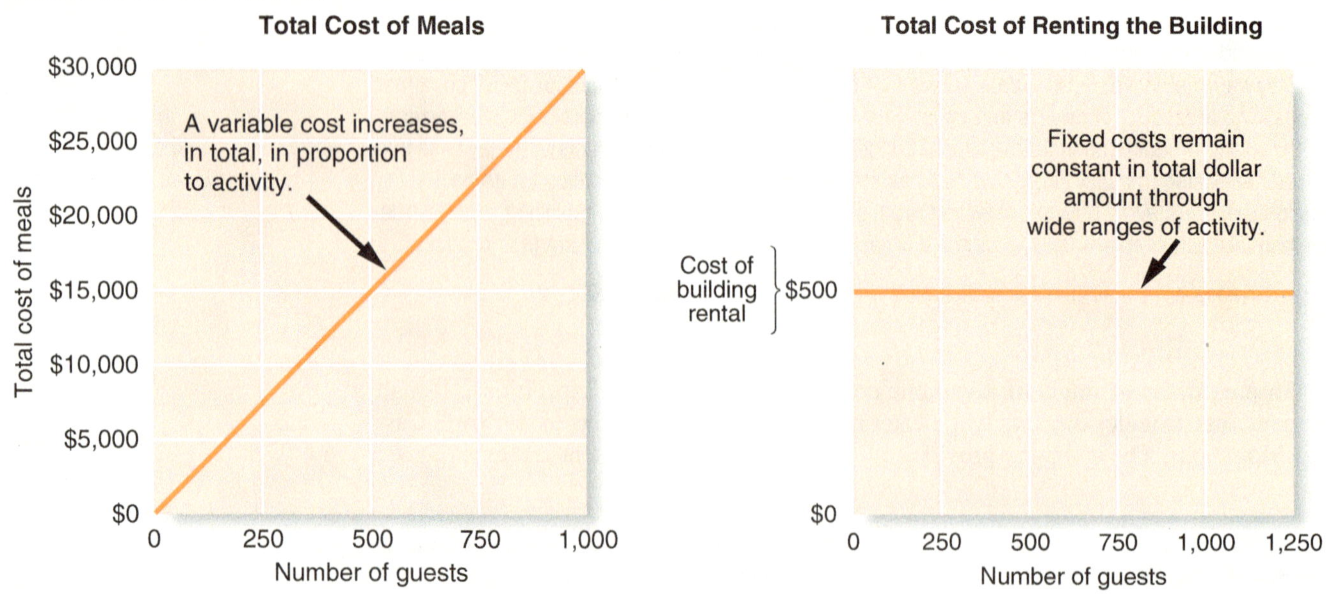

IN BUSINESS

FOOD COSTS AT A LUXURY HOTEL

The Sporthotel Theresa (http://www.theresa.at/), owned and operated by the Egger family, is a four star hotel located in Zell im Zillertal, Austria. The hotel features access to hiking, skiing, biking, and other activities in the Ziller alps as well as its own fitness facility and spa.

Three full meals a day are included in the hotel room charge. Breakfast and lunch are served buffet-style while dinner is a more formal affair with as many as six courses. The chef, Stefan Egger, believes that food costs are roughly proportional to the number of guests staying at the hotel; that is, they are a variable cost. He must order food from suppliers two or three days in advance, but he adjusts his purchases to the number of guests who are currently staying at the hotel and their consumption patterns. In addition, guests make their selections from the dinner menu early in the day, which helps Stefan plan which foodstuffs will be required for dinner. Consequently, he is able to prepare just enough food so that all guests are satisfied and yet waste is held to a minimum.

Source: Conversation with Stefan Egger, chef at the Sporthotel Theresa.

Because total fixed costs remain constant for large variations in the level of activity, the average fixed cost *per unit* becomes progressively smaller as the level of activity increases. If Nooksack Expeditions has only 250 guests in a month, the $500 fixed rental cost would amount to an average of $2 per guest. If there are 1,000 guests, the fixed rental cost would average only 50 cents per guest. The table below illustrates this aspect of the behavior of fixed costs. Note that as the number of guests increase, the average fixed cost per guest drops.

Monthly Rental Cost	Number of Guests	Average Cost per Guest
$500	250	$2.00
$500	500	$1.00
$500	750	$0.67
$500	1,000	$0.50

As a general rule, *we caution against expressing fixed costs on an average per unit basis in internal reports because it creates the false impression that fixed costs are like variable costs and that total fixed costs actually change as the level of activity changes.*

For planning purposes, fixed costs can be viewed as either *committed* or *discretionary.* **Committed fixed costs** represent organizational investments with a *multiyear* planning horizon that can't be significantly reduced even for short periods of time without making fundamental changes. Examples include investments in facilities and equipment, as well as real estate taxes, insurance expenses, and salaries of top management. Even if operations are interrupted or cut back, committed fixed costs remain largely unchanged in the short term because the costs of restoring them later are likely to be far greater than any short-run savings that might be realized. **Discretionary fixed costs** (often referred to as *managed fixed costs*) usually arise from *annual* decisions by management to spend on certain fixed cost items. Examples of discretionary fixed costs include advertising, research, public relations, management development programs, and internships for students. Discretionary fixed costs can be cut for short periods of time with minimal damage to the long-run goals of the organization.

The Linearity Assumption and the Relevant Range

Management accountants ordinarily assume that costs are strictly linear; that is, the relation between cost on the one hand and activity on the other can be represented by a straight line. Economists point out that many costs are actually curvilinear; that is, the

EXHIBIT 2–3
Curvilinear Costs and the Relevant Range

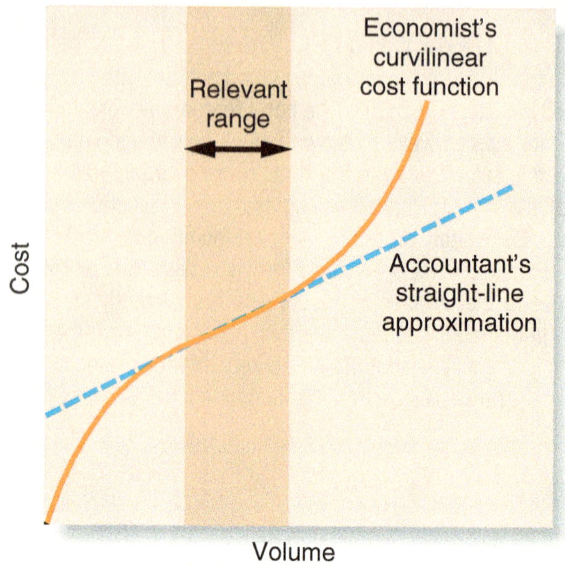

relation between cost and activity is a curve. Nevertheless, even if a cost is not strictly linear, it can be approximated within a narrow band of activity known as the *relevant range* by a straight line as illustrated in Exhibit 2–3. The **relevant range** is the range of activity within which the assumption that cost behavior is strictly linear is reasonably valid. Outside of the relevant range, a fixed cost may no longer be strictly fixed or a variable cost may not be strictly variable. Managers should always keep in mind that assumptions made about cost behavior may be invalid if activity falls outside of the relevant range.

The concept of the relevant range is important in understanding fixed costs. For example, suppose the Mayo Clinic rents a machine for $20,000 per month that tests blood samples for the presence of leukemia cells. Furthermore, suppose that the capacity of the leukemia diagnostic machine is 3,000 tests per month. The assumption that the rent for the diagnostic machine is $20,000 per month is only valid within the relevant range of 0 to 3,000 tests per month. If the Mayo Clinic needed to test 5,000 blood samples per month, then it would need to rent another machine for an additional $20,000 per month. It would be difficult to rent half of a diagnostic machine; therefore, the step pattern depicted in Exhibit 2–4 is typical for such costs. This exhibit shows that the fixed rental expense

EXHIBIT 2–4
Fixed Costs and the Relevant Range

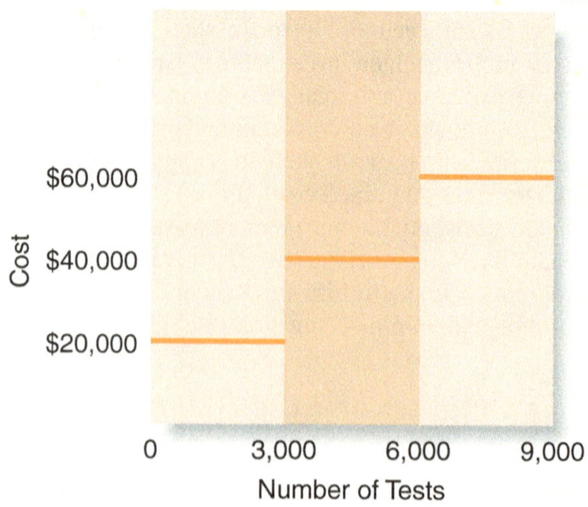

EXHIBIT 2–5
Summary of Variable and Fixed Cost Behavior

	Behavior of the Cost (within the relevant range)	
Cost	In Total	Per Unit
Variable cost	Total variable cost increases and decreases in proportion to changes in the activity level.	Variable cost per unit remains constant.
Fixed cost	Total fixed cost is not affected by changes in the activity level within the relevant range.	Fixed cost per unit decreases as the activity level rises and increases as the activity level falls.

is $20,000 for a relevant range of 0 to 3,000 tests. The fixed rental expense increases to $40,000 within the relevant range of 3,001 to 6,000 tests. The rental expense increases in discrete steps or increments of 3,000 tests, rather than increasing in a linear fashion per test.

This step-oriented cost behavior pattern can also be used to describe other costs, such as some labor costs. For example, salaried employee expenses can be characterized using a step pattern. Salaried employees are paid a fixed amount, such as $40,000 per year, for providing the capacity to work a prespecified amount of time, such as 40 hours per week for 50 weeks a year (= 2,000 hours per year). In this example, the total salaried employee expense is $40,000 within a relevant range of 0 to 2,000 hours of work. The total salaried employee expense increases to $80,000 (or two employees) if the organization's work requirements expand to a relevant range of 2,001 to 4,000 hours of work. Cost behavior patterns such as salaried employees are often called *step-variable costs.* Step-variable costs can often be adjusted quickly as conditions change. Furthermore, the width of the steps for step-variable costs is generally so narrow that these costs can be treated essentially as variable costs for most purposes. The width of the steps for fixed costs, on the other hand, is so wide that these costs should be treated as entirely fixed within the relevant range.

Exhibit 2–5 summarizes four key concepts related to variable and fixed costs. Study it carefully before reading further.

IN BUSINESS

HOW MANY GUIDES?

Majestic Ocean Kayaking, of Ucluelet, British Columbia, is owned and operated by Tracy Morben-Eeftink. The company offers a number of guided kayaking excursions ranging from three-hour tours of the Ucluelet harbor to six-day kayaking and camping trips in Clayoquot Sound. One of the company's excursions is a four-day kayaking and camping trip to The Broken Group Islands in the Pacific Rim National Park. Special regulations apply to trips in the park—including a requirement that one certified guide must be assigned for every five guests or fraction thereof. For example, a trip with 12 guests must have at least three certified guides. Guides are not salaried and are paid on a per-day basis. Therefore, the cost to the company of the guides for a trip is a step-variable cost rather than a fixed cost or a strictly variable cost. One guide is needed for 1 to 5 guests, two guides for 6 to 10 guests, three guides for 11 to 15 guests, and so on.

Sources: Tracy Morben-Eeftink, owner, Majestic Ocean Kayaking. For more information about the company, see www.oceankayaking.com.

Mixed Costs

A **mixed cost** contains both variable and fixed cost elements. Mixed costs are also known as semivariable costs. To continue the Nooksack Expeditions example, the company incurs a mixed cost called fees paid to the state. It includes a license fee of $25,000 per year plus $3 per rafting party paid to the state's Department of Natural Resources. If the

EXHIBIT 2–6
Mixed Cost Behavior

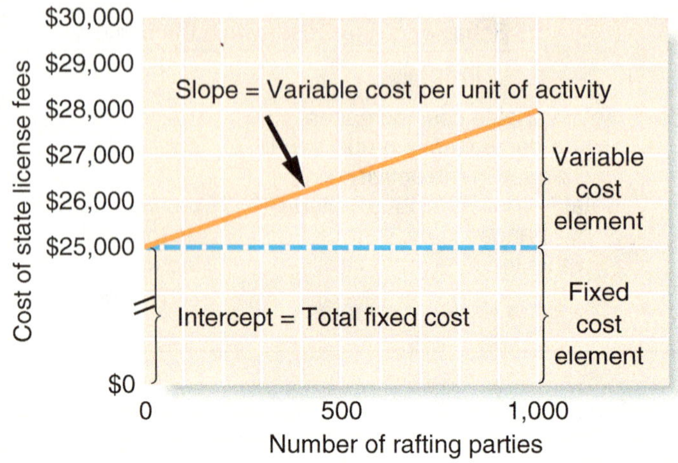

company runs 1,000 rafting parties this year, then the total fees paid to the state would be $28,000, made up of $25,000 in fixed cost plus $3,000 in variable cost. Exhibit 2–6 depicts the behavior of this mixed cost.

Even if Nooksack fails to attract any customers, the company will still have to pay the license fee of $25,000. This is why the cost line in Exhibit 2–6 intersects the vertical cost axis at the $25,000 point. For each rafting party the company organizes, the total cost of the state fees will increase by $3. Therefore, the total cost line slopes upward as the variable cost of $3 per party is added to the fixed cost of $25,000 per year.

Because the mixed cost in Exhibit 2–6 is represented by a straight line, the following equation for a straight line can be used to express the relationship between a mixed cost and the level of activity:

$$Y = a + bX$$

In this equation,

Y = The total mixed cost

a = The total fixed cost (the vertical intercept of the line)

b = The variable cost per unit of activity (the slope of the line)

X = The level of activity

Because the variable cost per unit equals the slope of the straight line, the steeper the slope, the higher the variable cost per unit.

In the case of the state fees paid by Nooksack Expeditions, the equation is written as follows:

$$Y = \$25{,}000 + \$3.00X$$

Y	\$25,000	\$3.00	X
Total mixed cost	Total fixed cost	Variable cost per unit of activity	Activity level

This equation makes it easy to calculate the total mixed cost for any level of activity within the relevant range. For example, suppose that the company expects to organize 800 rafting parties in the next year. The total state fees would be calculated as follows:

$$Y = \$25{,}000 + (\$3.00 \text{ per rafting party} \times 800 \text{ rafting parties})$$
$$= \$27{,}400$$

The Analysis of Mixed Costs

Mixed costs are very common. For example, the overall cost of providing X-ray services to patients at the Harvard Medical School Hospital is a mixed cost. The costs of equipment depreciation and radiologists' and technicians' salaries are fixed, but the costs of X-ray film, power, and supplies are variable. At Southwest Airlines, maintenance costs are a mixed cost. The company incurs fixed costs for renting maintenance facilities and for keeping skilled mechanics on the payroll, but the costs of replacement parts, lubricating oils, tires, and so forth, are variable with respect to how often and how far the company's aircraft are flown.

The fixed portion of a mixed cost represents the minimum cost of having a service *ready and available* for use. The variable portion represents the cost incurred for *actual consumption* of the service, thus it varies in proportion to the amount of service actually consumed.

Managers can use a variety of methods to estimate the fixed and variable components of a mixed cost such as *account analysis,* the *engineering approach,* the *high-low method,* and *least-squares regression analysis.* In **account analysis,** an account is classified as either variable or fixed based on the analyst's prior knowledge of how the cost in the account behaves. For example, direct materials would be classified as variable and a building lease cost would be classified as fixed because of the nature of those costs. The **engineering approach** to cost analysis involves a detailed analysis of what cost behavior should be, based on an industrial engineer's evaluation of the production methods to be used, the materials specifications, labor requirements, equipment usage, production efficiency, power consumption, and so on.

The high-low and least-squares regression methods estimate the fixed and variable elements of a mixed cost by analyzing past records of cost and activity data. We will use an example from Brentline Hospital to illustrate the high-low method calculations and to compare the resulting high-low method cost estimates to those obtained using least-squares regression. Appendix 2A demonstrates how to use Microsoft Excel to perform least-squares regression computations.

Diagnosing Cost Behavior with a Scattergraph Plot

LEARNING OBJECTIVE 4
Analyze a mixed cost using a scattergraph plot and the high-low method.

Assume that Brentline Hospital is interested in predicting future monthly maintenance costs for budgeting purposes. The senior management team believes that maintenance cost is a mixed cost and that the variable portion of this cost is driven by the number of patient-days. Each day a patient is in the hospital counts as one patient-day. The hospital's chief financial officer gathered the following data for the most recent seven-month period:

Month	Activity Level: Patient-Days	Maintenance Cost Incurred
January	5,600	$7,900
February	7,100	$8,500
March	5,000	$7,400
April	6,500	$8,200
May	7,300	$9,100
June	8,000	$9,800
July	6,200	$7,800

The first step in applying the high-low method or the least-squares regression method is to diagnose cost behavior with a scattergraph plot. The scattergraph plot of maintenance costs versus patient-days at Brentline Hospital is shown in Exhibit 2–7. Two things should be noted about this scattergraph:

1. The total maintenance cost, *Y,* is plotted on the vertical axis. Cost is known as the **dependent variable** because the amount of cost incurred during a period depends on

EXHIBIT 2–7
Scattergraph Method of Cost Analysis

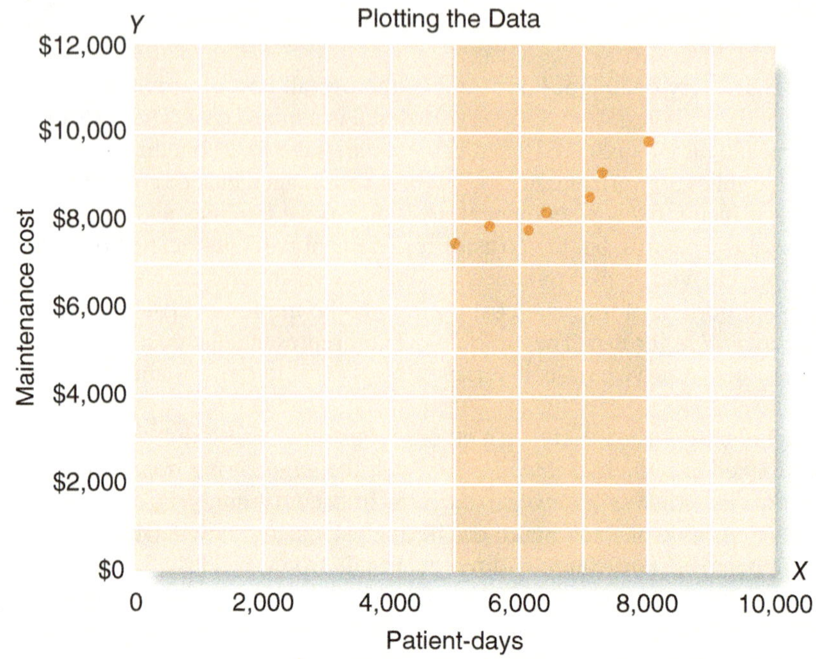

the level of activity for the period. (That is, as the level of activity increases, total cost will also ordinarily increase.)

2. The activity, *X* (patient-days in this case), is plotted on the horizontal axis. Activity is known as the **independent variable** because it causes variations in the cost.

From the scattergraph plot, it is evident that maintenance costs do increase with the number of patient-days in an approximately *linear* fashion. In other words, the points lie more or less along a straight line that slopes upward and to the right. Cost behavior is considered **linear** whenever a straight line is a reasonable approximation for the relation between cost and activity.

Plotting the data on a scattergraph is an essential diagnostic step that should be performed before performing the high-low method or least-squares regression calculations. If the scattergraph plot reveals linear cost behavior, then it makes sense to perform the high-low or least-squares regression calculations to separate the mixed cost into its variable and fixed components. If the scattergraph plot does not depict linear cost behavior, then it makes no sense to proceed any further in analyzing the data.

For example, suppose that Brentline Hospital's management is interested in the relation between the hospital's telephone costs and patient-days. Patients are billed directly for their use of telephones, so those costs do not appear on the hospital's cost records. Rather, management is concerned about the charges for the staff's use of telephones. The data for this cost are plotted in Exhibit 2–8. It is evident from the nonlinear data pattern that while the telephone costs do vary from month to month, they are not related to patient-days. Something other than patient-days is driving the telephone bills. Therefore, it would not make sense to analyze this cost any further by attempting to estimate a variable cost per patient-day for telephone costs. Plotting the data helps diagnose such situations.

Plotting the data on a scattergraph can also reveal nonlinear cost behavior patterns that warrant further data analysis. For example, assume that Brentline Hospital's managers were interested in the relation between total nursing wages and the number of patient-days at the hospital. The permanent, full-time nursing staff can handle up to 7,000 patient-days in a month. Beyond that level of activity, part-time nurses must be called in to help out. The cost and activity data for nurses are plotted on the scattergraph in Exhibit 2–9 (see page 38). Looking at that scattergraph, it is evident that two straight lines would do a much better job of fitting the data than a single straight line. Up to 7,000 patient-days, total nursing wages are essentially a fixed cost. Above 7,000 patient-days, total nursing wages are a

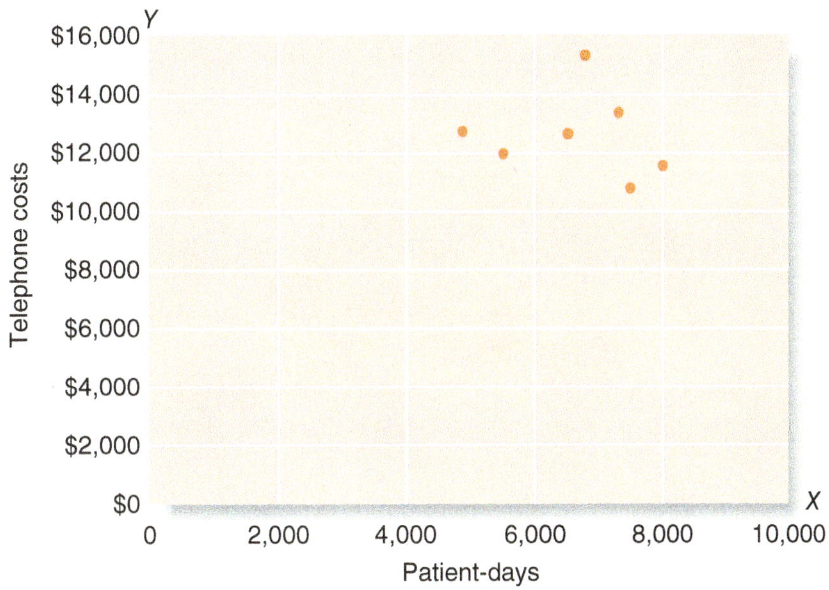

EXHIBIT 2–8
A Diagnostic Scattergraph Plot

mixed cost. This happens because, as previously mentioned, the permanent, full-time nursing staff can handle up to 7,000 patient-days in a month. Above that level, part-time nurses are called in to help, which adds to the cost. Consequently, two straight lines (and two equations) would be used to represent total nursing wages—one for the relevant range of 5,600 to 7,000 patient-days and one for the relevant range of 7,000 to 8,000 patient-days.

IN BUSINESS

OPERATIONS DRIVE COSTS

White Grizzly Adventures is a snowcat skiing and snowboarding company in Meadow Creek, British Columbia, that is owned and operated by Brad and Carole Karafil. The company shuttles 12 guests to the top of the company's steep and tree-covered terrain in a modified snowcat. Guests stay as a group at the company's lodge for a fixed number of days and are provided healthy gourmet meals.

Brad and Carole must decide each year when snowcat operations will begin in December and when they will end in early spring, and how many nonoperating days to schedule between groups of guests for maintenance and rest. These decisions affect a variety of costs. Examples of costs that are fixed and variable with respect to the number of days of operation at White Grizzly include:

Cost	Cost Behavior—Fixed or Variable with Respect to Days of Operation
Property taxes	Fixed
Summer road maintenance and tree clearing	Fixed
Lodge depreciation	Fixed
Snowcat operator and guides	Variable
Cooks and lodge help	Variable
Snowcat depreciation	Variable
Snowcat fuel	Variable
Food*	Variable

*The costs of food served to guests theoretically depend on the number of guests in residence. However, the lodge is almost always filled to its capacity of 12 persons when the snowcat operation is running, so food costs can be considered to be driven by the days of operation.

Source: Brad and Carole Karafil, owners and operators of White Grizzly Adventures, www.whitegrizzly.com.

EXHIBIT 2–9
More than One Relevant Range

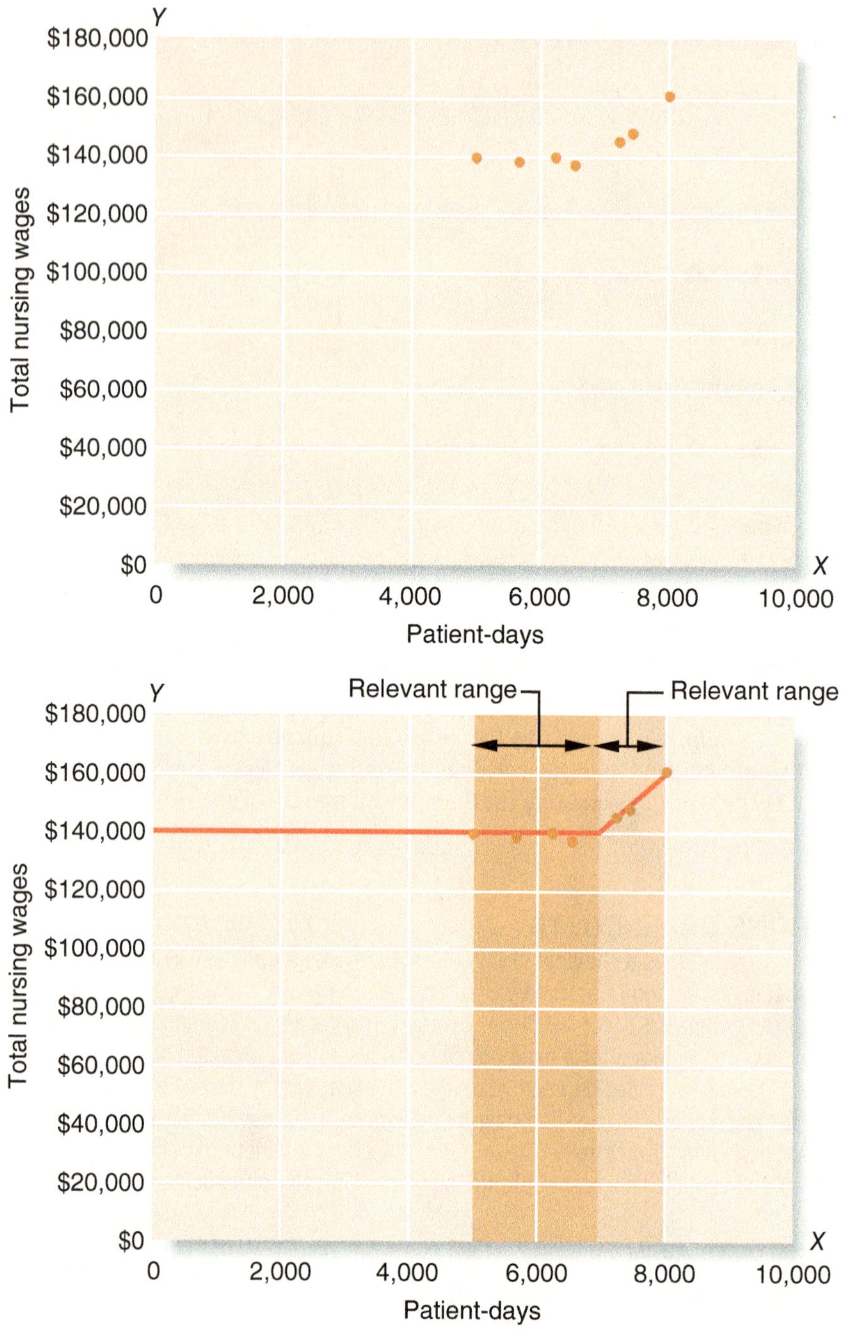

The examples in Exhibits 2–8 and 2–9 illustrate why preparing a scattergraph plot is an essential diagnostic step that should not be overlooked.

The High-Low Method

Assuming that the scattergraph plot indicates a linear relation between cost and activity, the fixed and variable cost elements of a mixed cost can be estimated using the *high-low method* or the *least-squares regression method.* The high-low method is based on the rise-over-run formula for the slope of a straight line. As previously discussed, if the relation between cost and activity can be represented by a straight line, then the slope of the straight line is equal to the variable cost per unit of activity. Consequently, the following formula can be used to estimate the variable cost:

$$\text{Variable cost} = \text{Slope of the line} = \frac{\text{Rise}}{\text{Run}} = \frac{Y_2 - Y_1}{X_2 - X_1}$$

To analyze mixed costs with the **high-low method,** begin by identifying the period with the lowest level of activity and the period with the highest level of activity. The period with the lowest activity is selected as the first point in the above formula and the period with the highest activity is selected as the second point. Consequently, the formula becomes:

$$\text{Variable cost} = \frac{Y_2 - Y_1}{X_2 - X_1} = \frac{\text{Cost at the high activity level} - \text{Cost at the low activity level}}{\text{High activity level} - \text{Low activity level}}$$

or

$$\text{Variable cost} = \frac{\text{Change in cost}}{\text{Change in activity}}$$

Therefore, when the high-low method is used, the variable cost is estimated by dividing the difference in cost between the high and low levels of activity by the change in activity between those two points.

To return to the Brentline Hospital example, using the high-low method, we first identify the periods with the highest and lowest *activity*—in this case, June and March. We then use the activity and cost data from these two periods to estimate the variable cost component as follows:

	Patient-Days	Maintenance Cost Incurred
High activity level (June)	8,000	$9,800
Low activity level (March)	5,000	7,400
Change	3,000	$2,400

$$\text{Variable cost} = \frac{\text{Change in cost}}{\text{Change in activity}} = \frac{\$2{,}400}{3{,}000 \text{ patient-days}} = \$0.80 \text{ per patient-day}$$

Having determined that the variable maintenance cost is 80 cents per patient-day, we can now determine the amount of fixed cost. This is done by taking the total cost at *either* the high or the low activity level and deducting the variable cost element. In the computation below, total cost at the high activity level is used in computing the fixed cost element:

$$\begin{aligned}\text{Fixed cost element} &= \text{Total cost} - \text{Variable cost element} \\ &= \$9{,}800 - (\$0.80 \text{ per patient-day} \times 8{,}000 \text{ patient-days}) \\ &= \$3{,}400\end{aligned}$$

Both the variable and fixed cost elements have now been isolated. The cost of maintenance can be expressed as $3,400 per month plus 80 cents per patient-day or as:

$$Y = \$3{,}400 + \$0.80X$$

↑ Total maintenance cost (Y)

↑ Total patient-days (X)

The data used in this illustration are shown graphically in Exhibit 2–10. Notice that a straight line has been drawn through the points corresponding to the low and high levels

EXHIBIT 2–10
High-Low Method of Cost Analysis

Activity Level	Patient-Days	Maintenance Cost
High	8,000	$9,800
Low	5,000	$7,400

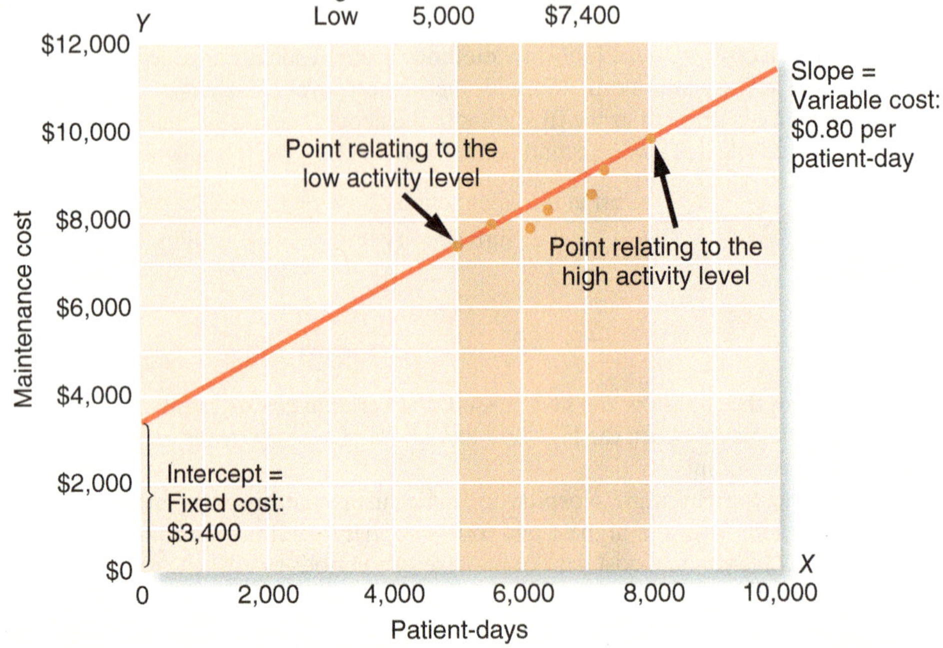

of activity. In essence, that is what the high-low method does—it draws a straight line through those two points.

Sometimes the high and low levels of activity don't coincide with the high and low amounts of cost. For example, the period that has the highest level of activity may not have the highest amount of cost. Nevertheless, the costs at the highest and lowest levels of *activity* are always used to analyze a mixed cost under the high-low method. The reason is that the analyst would like to use data that reflect the greatest possible variation in activity.

The high-low method is very simple to apply, but it suffers from a major (and sometimes critical) defect—it utilizes only two data points. Generally, two data points are not enough to produce accurate results. Additionally, the periods with the highest and lowest activity tend to be unusual. A cost formula that is estimated solely using data from these unusual periods may misrepresent the true cost behavior during normal periods. Such a distortion is evident in Exhibit 2–10. The straight line should probably be shifted down somewhat so that it is closer to more of the data points. For these reasons, least-squares regression will generally be more accurate than the high-low method.

The Least-Squares Regression Method

The **least-squares regression method,** unlike the high-low method, uses all of the data to separate a mixed cost into its fixed and variable components. A *regression line* of the form $Y = a + bX$ is fitted to the data, where a represents the total fixed cost and b represents the variable cost per unit of activity. The basic idea underlying the least-squares regression method is illustrated in Exhibit 2–11 using hypothetical data points. Notice from the exhibit that the deviations from the plotted points to the regression line are measured vertically on the graph. These vertical deviations are called the regression errors. There is nothing mysterious about the least-squares regression method. It simply computes the regression line that minimizes the sum of these squared errors. The formulas that accomplish this are fairly complex and involve numerous calculations, but the principle is simple.

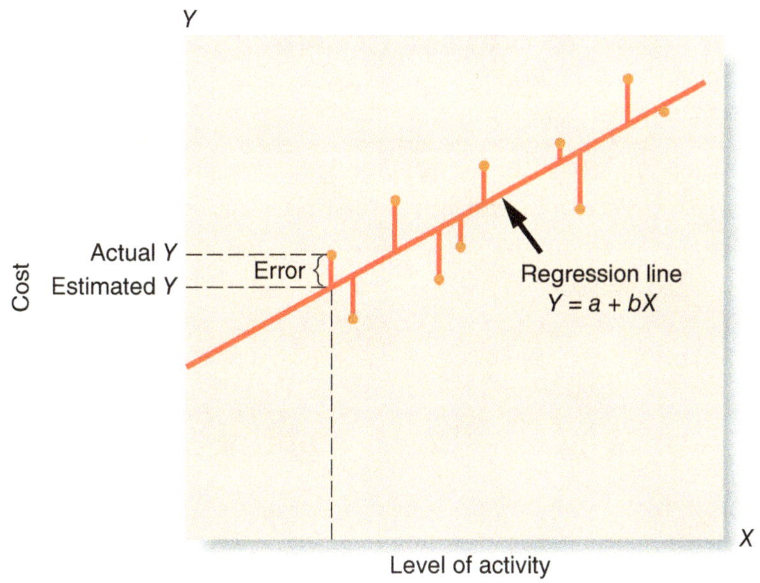

EXHIBIT 2–11
The Concept of Least-Squares Regression

Fortunately, computers are adept at carrying out the computations required by the least-squares regression formulas. The data—the observed values of X and Y—are entered into the computer, and software does the rest. In the case of the Brentline Hospital maintenance cost data, a statistical software package on a personal computer can calculate the following least-squares regression estimates of the total fixed cost (a) and the variable cost per unit of activity (b):

$$a = \$3{,}431$$
$$b = \$0.759$$

Therefore, using the least-squares regression method, the fixed element of the maintenance cost is $3,431 per month and the variable portion is 75.9 cents per patient-day.

In terms of the linear equation $Y = a + bX$, the cost formula can be written as

$$Y = \$3{,}431 + \$0.759X$$

where activity (X) is expressed in patient-days.

Appendix 2A discusses how to use Microsoft Excel to perform least-squares regression calculations. For now, you only need to understand that least-squares regression analysis generally provides more accurate cost estimates than the high-low method because, rather than relying on just two data points, it uses all of the data points to fit a line that minimizes the sum of the squared errors. The table below compares Brentline Hospital's cost estimates using the high-low method and the least-squares regression method:

	High-Low Method	Least-Squares Regression Method
Variable cost estimate per patient-day	$0.800	$0.759
Fixed cost estimate per month	$3,400	$3,431

When the least-squares regression method is used to create a straight line that minimizes the sum of the squared errors, it results in a Y-intercept that is $31 higher than the Y-intercept derived using the high-low method. It also decreases the slope of the straight line resulting in a lower variable cost estimate of $0.759 per patient-day rather than $0.80 per patient-day as derived using the high-low method.

IN BUSINESS

THE ZIPCAR COMES TO COLLEGE CAMPUSES

Zipcar is a car sharing service based in Cambridge, Massachusetts. The company serves 13 cities and 120 university campuses. Members pay a $50 annual fee plus $7 an hour to rent a car. They can use their iPhones to rent a car, locate it in the nearest Zipcar parking lot, unlock it using an access code, and drive it off the lot. This mixed cost arrangement is attractive to customers who need a car infrequently and wish to avoid the large cash outlay that comes with buying or leasing a vehicle.

Source: Jefferson Graham, "An iPhone Gets Zipcar Drivers on Their Way," *USA Today*, September 30, 2009, p. 3B.

Traditional and Contribution Format Income Statements

LEARNING OBJECTIVE 5
Prepare income statements for a merchandising company using the traditional and contribution formats.

In this section of the chapter, we discuss how to prepare traditional and contribution format income statements for a merchandising company.[2] Merchandising companies do not manufacture the products that they sell to customers. For example, Walmart is a merchandising company because it buys finished products from manufacturers and then resells them to end consumers.

The Traditional Format Income Statement

Traditional income statements are prepared primarily for external reporting purposes. The left-hand side of Exhibit 2–12 shows a traditional income statement format for merchandising companies. This type of income statement organizes costs into two categories—cost of goods sold and selling and administrative expenses. Sales minus cost of goods sold equals the *gross margin.* The gross margin minus selling and administrative expenses equals net operating income.

The cost of goods sold reports the *product costs* attached to the merchandise sold during the period. The selling and administrative expenses report all *period costs* that

EXHIBIT 2–12
Comparing Traditional and Contribution Format Income Statements for Merchandising Companies (all numbers are given)

Traditional Format

Sales		$12,000
Cost of goods sold*		6,000
Gross margin		6,000
Selling and administrative expenses:		
Selling	$3,100	
Administrative	1,900	5,000
Net operating income		$ 1,000

Contribution Format

Sales		$12,000
Variable expenses:		
Cost of goods sold	$6,000	
Variable selling	600	
Variable administrative	400	7,000
Contribution margin		5,000
Fixed expenses:		
Fixed selling	2,500	
Fixed administrative	1,500	4,000
Net operating income		$ 1,000

*For a manufacturing company, the cost of goods sold would include some variable costs, such as direct materials, direct labor, and variable overhead, and some fixed costs, such as fixed manufacturing overhead. Income statement formats for manufacturing companies will be explored in greater detail in a subsequent chapter.

[2] Subsequent chapters discuss the cost classifications used on the financial statements of manufacturing companies.

have been expensed as incurred. The cost of goods sold for a merchandising company can be computed directly by multiplying the number of units sold by their unit cost or indirectly using the equation below:

$$\text{Cost of goods sold} = \text{Beginning merchandise inventory} + \text{Purchases} - \text{Ending merchandise inventory}$$

For example, let's assume that the company depicted in Exhibit 2–12 purchased $3,000 of merchandise inventory during the period and had beginning and ending merchandise inventory balances of $7,000 and $4,000, respectively. The equation above could be used to compute the cost of goods sold as follows:

$$\begin{aligned}\text{Cost of goods sold} &= \text{Beginning merchandise inventory} + \text{Purchases} - \text{Ending merchandise inventory}\\ &= \$7{,}000 + \$3{,}000 - \$4{,}000\\ &= \$6{,}000\end{aligned}$$

Although the traditional income statement is useful for external reporting purposes, it has serious limitations when used for internal purposes. It does not distinguish between fixed and variable costs. For example, under the heading "Selling and administrative expenses," both variable administrative costs ($400) and fixed administrative costs ($1,500) are lumped together ($1,900). Internally, managers need cost data organized by cost behavior to aid in planning, controlling, and decision making. The contribution format income statement has been developed in response to these needs.

The Contribution Format Income Statement

The crucial distinction between fixed and variable costs is at the heart of the **contribution approach** to constructing income statements. The unique thing about the contribution approach is that it provides managers with an income statement that clearly distinguishes between fixed and variable costs and therefore aids planning, controlling, and decision making. The right-hand side of Exhibit 2–12 shows a contribution format income statement for merchandising companies.

The contribution approach separates costs into fixed and variable categories, first deducting variable expenses from sales to obtain the *contribution margin.* For a merchandising company, cost of goods sold is a variable cost that gets included in the "Variable expenses" portion of the contribution format income statement. The **contribution margin** is the amount remaining from sales revenues after variable expenses have been deducted. This amount *contributes* toward covering fixed expenses and then toward profits for the period.

The contribution format income statement is used as an internal planning and decision-making tool. Its emphasis on cost behavior aids cost-volume-profit analysis (such as we shall be doing in a subsequent chapter), management performance appraisals, and budgeting. Moreover, the contribution approach helps managers organize data pertinent to numerous decisions such as product-line analysis, pricing, use of scarce resources, and make or buy analysis. All of these topics are covered in later chapters.

Cost Classifications for Assigning Costs to Cost Objects

LEARNING OBJECTIVE 6
Understand the differences between direct and indirect costs.

Costs are assigned to cost objects for a variety of purposes including pricing, preparing profitability studies, and controlling spending. A **cost object** is anything for which cost data are desired—including products, customers, jobs, and organizational subunits. For purposes of assigning costs to cost objects, costs are classified as either *direct* or *indirect.*

Direct Cost

A **direct cost** is a cost that can be easily and conveniently traced to a specified cost object. The concept of direct cost extends beyond just direct materials and direct labor. For example, if Reebok is assigning costs to its various regional and national sales offices, then the salary of the sales manager in its Tokyo office would be a direct cost of that office.

Indirect Cost

An **indirect cost** is a cost that cannot be easily and conveniently traced to a specified cost object. For example, a Campbell Soup factory may produce dozens of varieties of canned soups. The factory manager's salary would be an indirect cost of a particular variety such as chicken noodle soup. The reason is that the factory manager's salary is incurred as a consequence of running the entire factory—it is not incurred to produce any one soup variety. *To be traced to a cost object such as a particular product, the cost must be caused by the cost object.* The factory manager's salary is called a *common cost* of producing the various products of the factory. A **common cost** is a cost that is incurred to support a number of cost objects but cannot be traced to them individually. A common cost is a type of indirect cost.

A particular cost may be direct or indirect, depending on the cost object. While the Campbell Soup factory manager's salary is an *indirect* cost of manufacturing chicken noodle soup, it is a *direct* cost of the manufacturing division. In the first case, the cost object is chicken noodle soup. In the second case, the cost object is the entire manufacturing division.

Cost Classifications for Decision Making

LEARNING OBJECTIVE 7
Understand cost classifications used in making decisions: differential costs, opportunity costs, and sunk costs.

Costs are an important feature of many business decisions. In making decisions, it is essential to have a firm grasp of the concepts *differential cost, opportunity cost,* and *sunk cost.*

Differential Cost and Revenue

Decisions involve choosing between alternatives. In business decisions, each alternative will have costs and benefits that must be compared to the costs and benefits of the other available alternatives. A difference in costs between any two alternatives is known as a **differential cost.** A difference in revenues between any two alternatives is known as **differential revenue.**

A differential cost is also known as an **incremental cost,** although technically an incremental cost should refer only to an increase in cost from one alternative to another; decreases in cost should be referred to as *decremental costs.* Differential cost is a broader term, encompassing both cost increases (incremental costs) and cost decreases (decremental costs) between alternatives.

The accountant's differential cost concept can be compared to the economist's marginal cost concept. In speaking of changes in cost and revenue, the economist uses the terms *marginal cost* and *marginal revenue.* The revenue that can be obtained from selling one more unit of product is called marginal revenue, and the cost involved in producing one more unit of product is called marginal cost. The economist's marginal concept is basically the same as the accountant's differential concept applied to a single unit of output.

Differential costs can be either fixed or variable. To illustrate, assume that Nature Way Cosmetics, Inc., is thinking about changing its marketing method from distribution through retailers to distribution by a network of neighborhood sales representatives. Present costs and revenues are compared to projected costs and revenues in the following table:

	Retailer Distribution (present)	Sales Representatives (proposed)	Differential Costs and Revenues
Revenues (Variable)	$700,000	$800,000	$100,000
Cost of goods sold (Variable)	350,000	400,000	50,000
Advertising (Fixed)	80,000	45,000	(35,000)
Commissions (Variable)	0	40,000	40,000
Warehouse depreciation (Fixed)	50,000	80,000	30,000
Other expenses (Fixed)	60,000	60,000	0
Total expenses	540,000	625,000	85,000
Net operating income	$160,000	$175,000	$ 15,000

According to the above analysis, the differential revenue is $100,000 and the differential costs total $85,000, leaving a positive differential net operating income of $15,000 under the proposed marketing plan.

The decision of whether Nature Way Cosmetics should stay with the present retail distribution or switch to sales representatives could be made on the basis of the net operating incomes of the two alternatives. As we see in the above analysis, the net operating income under the present distribution method is $160,000, whereas the net operating income with sales representatives is estimated to be $175,000. Therefore, using sales representatives is preferred because it would result in $15,000 higher net operating income. Note that we would have arrived at exactly the same conclusion by simply focusing on the differential revenues, differential costs, and differential net operating income, which also show a $15,000 advantage for sales representatives.

In general, only the differences between alternatives are relevant in decisions. Those items that are the same under all alternatives and that are not affected by the decision can be ignored. For example, in the Nature Way Cosmetics example above, the "Other expenses" category, which is $60,000 under both alternatives, can be ignored because it has no effect on the decision. If it were removed from the calculations, the sales representatives would still be preferred by $15,000. This is an extremely important principle in management accounting that we will revisit in later chapters.

Opportunity Cost

Opportunity cost is the potential benefit that is given up when one alternative is selected over another. To illustrate this important concept, consider the following examples:

Example 1 Vicki has a part-time job that pays $200 per week while attending college. She would like to spend a week at the beach during spring break, and her employer has agreed to give her the time off, but without pay. The $200 in lost wages would be an opportunity cost of taking the week off to be at the beach.

Example 2 Suppose that Neiman Marcus is considering investing a large sum of money in land that may be a site for a future store. Rather than invest the funds in land, the company could invest the funds in high-grade securities. The opportunity cost of buying the land is the investment income that could have been realized by purchasing the securities instead.

Example 3 Steve is employed by a company that pays him a salary of $38,000 per year. He is thinking about leaving the company and returning to school. Because returning to school would require that he give up his $38,000 salary, the forgone salary would be an opportunity cost of seeking further education.

Opportunity costs are not usually found in accounting records, but they are costs that must be explicitly considered in every decision a manager makes. Virtually every alternative involves an opportunity cost.

Sunk Cost

A **sunk cost** is a cost *that has already been incurred* and that cannot be changed by any decision made now or in the future. Because sunk costs cannot be changed by any decision, they are not differential costs. And because only differential costs are relevant in a decision, sunk costs should always be ignored.

To illustrate a sunk cost, assume that a company paid $50,000 several years ago for a special-purpose machine. The machine was used to make a product that is now obsolete and is no longer being sold. Even though in hindsight purchasing the machine may have been unwise, the $50,000 cost has already been incurred and cannot be undone. And it would be folly to continue making the obsolete product in a misguided attempt to "recover" the original cost of the machine. In short, the $50,000 originally paid for the machine is a sunk cost that should be ignored in current decisions.

Exhibit 2–13 summarizes the types of cost classifications that we discussed in this chapter. Refer to this exhibit to keep the big picture in mind, which is that *different costs for different purposes* is a critically important concept in management accounting. This chapter discussed four main cost classifications that managers can use for different purposes within organizations.

EXHIBIT 2–13
Summary of Cost Classifications

Purpose of Cost Classification	Cost Classifications

Preparing external financial statements	• Product costs (inventoriable)
	  • Direct materials
	  • Direct labor
	  • Manufacturing overhead
	• Period costs (expensed)
	  • Nonmanufacturing costs
	    • Selling costs
	    • Administrative costs

Predicting cost behavior in response to changes in activity	• Variable cost (proportional to activity) • Fixed cost (constant in total) • Mixed cost (has variable and fixed elements)
Assigning costs to cost objects (e.g., departments or products)	• Direct cost (can be easily traced) • Indirect cost (cannot be easily traced)
Making decisions	• Differential cost (differs between alternatives) • Sunk cost (past cost not affected by a decision) • Opportunity cost (forgone benefit)

Summary

In this chapter, we have discussed ways in which managers classify costs. How the costs will be used—for preparing external reports, predicting cost behavior, assigning costs to cost objects, or decision making—will dictate how the costs are classified.

For external reporting purposes, costs are classified as either product costs or period costs. Product costs are assigned to inventories and are considered assets until the products are sold. At the point of sale, product costs become cost of goods sold on the income statement. In contrast, period costs are taken directly to the income statement as expenses in the period in which they are incurred.

For purposes of predicting how costs will react to changes in activity, costs are classified into three categories—variable, fixed, and mixed. Variable costs, in total, are strictly proportional to activity. The variable cost per unit is constant. Fixed costs, in total, remain the same as the activity level changes within the relevant range. The average fixed cost per unit decreases as the activity level increases. Mixed costs consist of variable and fixed elements and can be expressed in equation form as $Y = a + bX$, where X is the activity, Y is the cost, a is the fixed cost element, and b is the variable cost per unit of activity.

If the relation between cost and activity appears to be linear based on a scattergraph plot, then the variable and fixed components of a mixed cost can be estimated using the high-low method, which implicitly draws a straight line through the points of lowest activity and highest activity, or the least-squares regression method, which uses all of the data points to compute a regression line that minimizes the sum of the squares errors.

The traditional income statement format is used primarily for external reporting purposes. It organizes costs using product and period cost classifications. The contribution format income statement aids decision making because it organizes costs using variable and fixed cost classifications.

For purposes of assigning costs to cost objects such as products or departments, costs are classified as direct or indirect. Direct costs can be conveniently traced to cost objects. Indirect costs cannot be conveniently traced to cost objects.

For purposes of making decisions, the concepts of differential cost and revenue, opportunity cost, and sunk cost are vitally important. Differential costs and revenues are the costs and revenues that differ between alternatives. Opportunity cost is the benefit that is forgone when one alternative is selected over another. Sunk cost is a cost that occurred in the past and cannot be altered. Differential costs and opportunity costs should be carefully considered in decisions. Sunk costs are always irrelevant in decisions and should be ignored.

Review Problem 1: Cost Terms

Many new cost terms have been introduced in this chapter. It will take you some time to learn what each term means and how to properly classify costs in an organization. Consider the following example: Porter Company manufactures furniture, including tables. Selected costs are given below:

1. The tables are made of wood that costs $100 per table.
2. The tables are assembled by workers, at a wage cost of $40 per table.
3. Workers assembling the tables are supervised by a factory supervisor who is paid $38,000 per year.
4. Electrical costs are $2 per machine-hour. Four machine-hours are required to produce a table.
5. The depreciation on the machines used to make the tables totals $10,000 per year. The machines have no resale value and do not wear out through use.
6. The salary of the president of the company is $100,000 per year.
7. The company spends $250,000 per year to advertise its products.
8. Salespersons are paid a commission of $30 for each table sold.
9. Instead of producing the tables, the company could rent its factory space for $50,000 per year.

Required:

Classify these costs according to the various cost terms used in the chapter. *Carefully study the classification of each cost.* If you don't understand why a particular cost is classified the way it is, reread the section of the chapter discussing the particular cost term. The terms *variable cost* and *fixed cost* refer to how costs behave with respect to the number of tables produced in a year.

Solution to Review Problem 1

				Product Cost				
	Variable Cost	Fixed Cost	Period (Selling and Administrative) Cost	Direct Materials	Direct Labor	Manufacturing Overhead	Sunk Cost	Opportunity Cost
1. Wood used in a table ($100 per table)	X			X				
2. Labor cost to assemble a table ($40 per table)	X				X			
3. Salary of the factory supervisor ($38,000 per year)		X				X		
4. Cost of electricity to produce tables ($2 per machine-hour)	X					X		
5. Depreciation of machines used to produce tables ($10,000 per year)		X				X	X*	
6. Salary of the company president ($100,000 per year)		X	X					
7. Advertising expense ($250,000 per year)		X	X					
8. Commissions paid to salespersons ($30 per table sold)	X		X					
9. Rental income forgone on factory space								X†

*This is a sunk cost because the outlay for the equipment was made in a previous period.

†This is an opportunity cost because it represents the potential benefit that is lost or sacrificed as a result of using the factory space to produce tables. Opportunity cost is a special category of cost that is not ordinarily recorded in an organization's accounting records. To avoid possible confusion with other costs, we will not attempt to classify this cost in any other way except as an opportunity cost.

Review Problem 2: High-Low Method

The administrator of Azalea Hills Hospital would like a cost formula linking the administrative costs involved in admitting patients to the number of patients admitted during a month. The Admitting Department's costs and the number of patients admitted during the immediately preceding eight months are given in the following table:

Month	Number of Patients Admitted	Admitting Department Costs
May	1,800	$14,700
June	1,900	$15,200
July	1,700	$13,700
August	1,600	$14,000
September	1,500	$14,300
October	1,300	$13,100
November	1,100	$12,800
December	1,500	$14,600

Required:

1. Use the high-low method to estimate the fixed and variable components of admitting costs.
2. Express the fixed and variable components of admitting costs as a cost formula in the form $Y = a + bX$.

Solution to Review Problem 2

1. The first step in the high-low method is to identify the periods of the lowest and highest activity. Those periods are November (1,100 patients admitted) and June (1,900 patients admitted).

   The second step is to compute the variable cost per unit using those two data points:

Month	Number of Patients Admitted	Admitting Department Costs
High activity level (June)	1,900	$15,200
Low activity level (November)	1,100	12,800
Change	800	$ 2,400

$$\text{Variable cost} = \frac{\text{Change in cost}}{\text{Change in activity}} = \frac{\$2{,}400}{800 \text{ patients admitted}} = \$3 \text{ per patient admitted}$$

The third step is to compute the fixed cost element by deducting the variable cost element from the total cost at either the high or low activity. In the computation below, the high point of activity is used:

$$\begin{aligned}\text{Fixed cost element} &= \text{Total cost} - \text{Variable cost element}\\ &= \$15{,}200 - (\$3 \text{ per patient admitted} \times 1{,}900 \text{ patients admitted})\\ &= \$9{,}500\end{aligned}$$

2. The cost formula is $Y = \$9{,}500 + \$3X$.

Glossary

Account analysis A method for analyzing cost behavior in which an account is classified as either variable or fixed based on the analyst's prior knowledge of how the cost in the account behaves. (p. 35)

Activity base A measure of whatever causes the incurrence of a variable cost. For example, the total cost of X-ray film in a hospital will increase as the number of X-rays taken increases. Therefore, the number of X-rays is the activity base that explains the total cost of X-ray film. (p. 29)

Administrative costs All executive, organizational, and clerical costs associated with the general management of an organization rather than with manufacturing or selling. (p. 26)

Committed fixed costs Investments in facilities, equipment, and basic organizational structure that can't be significantly reduced even for short periods of time without making fundamental changes. (p. 31)

Common cost A cost that is incurred to support a number of cost objects but that cannot be traced to them individually. For example, the wage cost of the pilot of a 747 airliner is a common cost of all of the passengers on the aircraft. Without the pilot, there would be no flight and no passengers. But no part of the pilot's wage is caused by any one passenger taking the flight. (p. 44)

Contribution approach An income statement format that organizes costs by their behavior. Costs are separated into variable and fixed categories rather than being separated into product and period costs for external reporting purposes. (p. 43)

Contribution margin The amount remaining from sales revenues after all variable expenses have been deducted. (p. 43)

Conversion cost Direct labor cost plus manufacturing overhead cost. (p. 27)

Cost behavior The way in which a cost reacts to changes in the level of activity. (p. 29)

Cost object Anything for which cost data are desired. Examples of cost objects are products, customers, jobs, and parts of the organization such as departments or divisions. (p. 43)

Cost structure The relative proportion of fixed, variable, and mixed costs in an organization. (p. 29)

Dependent variable A variable that responds to some causal factor; total cost is the dependent variable, as represented by the letter *Y*, in the equation $Y = a + bX$. (p. 35)

Differential cost A difference in cost between two alternatives. Also see *Incremental cost.* (p. 44)

Differential revenue The difference in revenue between two alternatives. (p. 44)

Direct cost A cost that can be easily and conveniently traced to a specified cost object. (p. 44)

Direct labor Factory labor costs that can be easily traced to individual units of product. Also called *touch labor.* (p. 25)

Direct materials Materials that become an integral part of a finished product and whose costs can be conveniently traced to it. (p. 25)

Discretionary fixed costs Those fixed costs that arise from annual decisions by management to spend on certain fixed cost items, such as advertising and research. (p. 31)

Engineering approach A detailed analysis of cost behavior based on an industrial engineer's evaluation of the inputs that are required to carry out a particular activity and of the prices of those inputs. (p. 35)

Fixed cost A cost that remains constant, in total, regardless of changes in the level of activity within the relevant range. If a fixed cost is expressed on a per unit basis, it varies inversely with the level of activity. (p. 30)

High-low method A method of separating a mixed cost into its fixed and variable elements by analyzing the change in cost between the high and low activity levels. (p. 39)

Incremental cost An increase in cost between two alternatives. Also see *Differential cost.* (p. 44)

Independent variable A variable that acts as a causal factor; activity is the independent variable, as represented by the letter *X*, in the equation $Y = a + bX$. (p. 36)

Indirect cost A cost that cannot be easily and conveniently traced to a specified cost object. (p. 44)

Indirect labor The labor costs of janitors, supervisors, materials handlers, and other factory workers that cannot be conveniently traced to particular products. (p. 25)

Indirect materials Small items of material such as glue and nails that may be an integral part of a finished product, but whose costs cannot be easily or conveniently traced to it. (p. 25)

Inventoriable costs Synonym for product costs. (p. 27)

Least-squares regression method A method of separating a mixed cost into its fixed and variable elements by fitting a regression line that minimizes the sum of the squared errors. (p. 40)

Linear cost behavior Cost behavior is said to be linear whenever a straight line is a reasonable approximation for the relation between cost and activity. (p. 36)

Manufacturing overhead All manufacturing costs except direct materials and direct labor. (p. 26)

Mixed cost A cost that contains both variable and fixed cost elements. (p. 33)

Opportunity cost The potential benefit that is given up when one alternative is selected over another. (p. 45)

Period costs Costs that are taken directly to the income statement as expenses in the period in which they are incurred or accrued. (p. 27)

Prime cost Direct materials cost plus direct labor cost. (p. 27)

Product costs All costs that are involved in acquiring or making a product. In the case of manufactured goods, these costs consist of direct materials, direct labor, and manufacturing overhead. Also see *Inventoriable costs.* (p. 27)

Raw materials Any materials that go into the final product. (p. 25)

Relevant range The range of activity within which assumptions about variable and fixed cost behavior are valid. (p. 32)

Selling costs All costs that are incurred to secure customer orders and get the finished product or service into the hands of the customer. (p. 26)

Sunk cost A cost that has already been incurred and that cannot be changed by any decision made now or in the future. (p. 46)

Variable cost A cost that varies, in total, in direct proportion to changes in the level of activity. A variable cost is constant per unit. (p. 29)

Questions

2–1 What are the three major elements of product costs in a manufacturing company?

2–2 Define the following: (a) direct materials, (b) indirect materials, (c) direct labor, (d) indirect labor, and (e) manufacturing overhead.

2–3 Explain the difference between a product cost and a period cost.

2–4 Distinguish between (*a*) a variable cost, (*b*) a fixed cost, and (*c*) a mixed cost.

2–5 What effect does an increase in volume have on—

a. Unit fixed costs?

b. Unit variable costs?

c. Total fixed costs?

d. Total variable costs?

2–6 Define the following terms: (*a*) cost behavior and (*b*) relevant range.

2–7 What is meant by an *activity base* when dealing with variable costs? Give several examples of activity bases.

2–8 Managers often assume a strictly linear relationship between cost and volume. How can this practice be defended in light of the fact that many costs are curvilinear?

2–9 Distinguish between discretionary fixed costs and committed fixed costs.

2–10 Does the concept of the relevant range apply to fixed costs? Explain.

2–11 What is the major disadvantage of the high-low method?

2–12 Give the general formula for a mixed cost. Which term represents the variable cost? The fixed cost?

2–13 What is meant by the term *least-squares regression?*

2–14 What is the difference between a contribution format income statement and a traditional format income statement?

2–15 What is the contribution margin?

2–16 Define the following terms: differential cost, opportunity cost, and sunk cost.

2–17 Only variable costs can be differential costs. Do you agree? Explain.

Multiple-choice questions are provided on the text website at www.mhhe.com/garrison14e.

connect ACCOUNTING Applying Excel

Available with McGraw-Hill's *Connect™ Accounting.*

LEARNING OBJECTIVE 5

The Excel worksheet form that appears on the next page is to be used to recreate Exhibit 2–12 on page 42. Download the workbook containing this form from the Online Learning Center at www.mhhe.com/garrison14e. *On the website you will also receive instructions about how to use this worksheet form.*

	A	B	C	D
1	Chapter 2: Applying Excel			
2				
3	**Data**			
4	Sales	$12,000		
5	Variable costs:			
6	Cost of goods sold	$6,000		
7	Variable selling	$600		
8	Variable administrative	$400		
9	Fixed costs:			
10	Fixed selling	$2,500		
11	Fixed administrative	$1,500		
12				
13	*Enter a formula into each of the cells marked with a ? below*			
14	**Exhibit 2-12**			
15				
16	**Traditional Format Income Statement**			
17	Sales		?	
18	Cost of goods sold		?	
19	Gross margin		?	
20	Selling and administrative expenses:			
21	Selling	?		
22	Administrative	?	?	
23	Net operating income		?	
24				
25	**Contribution Format Income Statement**			
26	Sales		?	
27	Variable expenses:			
28	Cost of goods sold	?		
29	Variable selling	?		
30	Variable administration	?	?	
31	Contribution margin		?	
32	Fixed expenses:			
33	Fixed selling	?		
34	Fixed administrative	?	?	
35	Net operating income		?	
36				

Chapter 2 Form / Filled in Chapter 2 F

Required:

1. Check your worksheet by changing the variable selling cost in the Data area to $900, keeping all of the other data the same as in Exhibit 2–12. If your worksheet is operating properly, the net operating income under the traditional format income statement and under the contribution format income statement should now be $700 and the contribution margin should now be $4,700. If you do not get these answers, find the errors in your worksheet and correct them.

   How much is the gross margin? Did it change? Why or why not?
2. Suppose that sales are 10% higher as shown below:

Sales	$13,200
Variable costs:	
Cost of goods sold	$6,600
Variable selling	$990
Variable administrative	$440
Fixed costs:	
Fixed selling	$2,500
Fixed administrative	$1,500

   Enter this new data into your worksheet. Make sure that you change all of the data that are different—not just the sales. Print or copy the income statements from your worksheet.

   What happened to the variable costs and to the fixed costs when sales increased by 10%? Why? Did the contribution margin increase by 10%? Why or why not? Did the net operating income increase by 10%? Why or why not?

connect ACCOUNTING

Exercises

All applicable exercises are available with McGraw-Hill's *Connect™ Accounting*.

EXERCISE 2–1 Classifying Manufacturing Costs [LO1]

Your Boat, Inc., assembles custom sailboats from components supplied by various manufacturers. The company is very small and its assembly shop and retail sales store are housed in a Gig Harbor, Washington, boathouse. Below are listed some of the costs that are incurred at the company.

Required:

For each cost, indicate whether it would most likely be classified as direct labor, direct materials, manufacturing overhead, selling, or an administrative cost.

1. The wages of employees who build the sailboats.
2. The cost of advertising in the local newspapers.
3. The cost of an aluminum mast installed in a sailboat.
4. The wages of the assembly shop's supervisor.
5. Rent on the boathouse.
6. The wages of the company's bookkeeper.
7. Sales commissions paid to the company's salespeople.
8. Depreciation on power tools.

EXERCISE 2–2 Classification of Costs as Period or Product Costs [LO2]

Suppose that you have been given a summer job at Fairwings Avionics, a company that manufactures sophisticated radar sets for commercial aircraft. The company, which is privately owned, has approached a bank for a loan to help finance its tremendous growth. The bank requires financial statements before approving such a loan.

Required:

Classify each cost listed below as either a product cost or a period cost for purposes of preparing the financial statements for the bank.

1. The cost of the memory chips used in a radar set.
2. Factory heating costs.
3. Factory equipment maintenance costs.
4. Training costs for new administrative employees.
5. The cost of the solder that is used in assembling the radar sets.
6. The travel costs of the company's salespersons.
7. Wages and salaries of factory security personnel.
8. The cost of air-conditioning executive offices.
9. Wages and salaries in the department that handles billing customers.
10. Depreciation on the equipment in the fitness room used by factory workers.
11. Telephone expenses incurred by factory management.
12. The costs of shipping completed radar sets to customers.
13. The wages of the workers who assemble the radar sets.
14. The president's salary.
15. Health insurance premiums for factory personnel.

EXERCISE 2–3 Fixed and Variable Cost Behavior [LO3]

Koffee Express operates a number of espresso coffee stands in busy suburban malls. The fixed weekly expense of a coffee stand is $1,100 and the variable cost per cup of coffee served is $0.26.

Required:

1. Fill in the following table with your estimates of total costs and average cost per cup of coffee at the indicated levels of activity for a coffee stand. Round off the cost of a cup of coffee to the nearest tenth of a cent.

	Cups of Coffee Served in a Week		
	1,800	1,900	2,000
Fixed cost	?	?	?
Variable cost	?	?	?
Total cost	?	?	?
Average cost per cup of coffee served	?	?	?

2. Does the average cost per cup of coffee served increase, decrease, or remain the same as the number of cups of coffee served in a week increases? Explain.

EXERCISE 2–4 High-Low Method [LO4]

The Edelweiss Hotel in Vail, Colorado, has accumulated records of the total electrical costs of the hotel and the number of occupancy-days over the last year. An occupancy-day represents a room rented out for one day. The hotel's business is highly seasonal, with peaks occurring during the ski season and in the summer.

Month	Occupancy-Days	Electrical Costs
January	2,604	$6,257
February	2,856	$6,550
March	3,534	$7,986
April	1,440	$4,022
May	540	$2,289
June	1,116	$3,591
July	3,162	$7,264
August	3,608	$8,111
September	1,260	$3,707
October	186	$1,712
November	1,080	$3,321
December	2,046	$5,196

Required:

1. Using the high-low method, estimate the fixed cost of electricity per month and the variable cost of electricity per occupancy-day. Round off the fixed cost to the nearest whole dollar and the variable cost to the nearest whole cent.
2. What other factors other than occupancy-days are likely to affect the variation in electrical costs from month to month?

EXERCISE 2–5 Traditional and Contribution Format Income Statements [LO5]

Redhawk, Inc., is a merchandiser that provided the following information:

Number of units sold	10,000
Selling price per unit	$15
Variable selling expense per unit	$2
Variable administrative expense per unit	$1
Total fixed selling expense	$20,000
Total fixed administrative expense	$15,000
Merchandise inventory, beginning balance	$12,000
Merchandise inventory, ending balance	$22,000
Merchandise purchases	$90,000

Required:

1. Prepare a traditional income statement.
2. Prepare a contribution format income statement.

EXERCISE 2–6 Identifying Direct and Indirect Costs [LO6]

The Empire Hotel is a four-star hotel located in downtown Seattle.

Required:

For each of the following costs incurred at the Empire Hotel, indicate whether it would most likely be a direct cost or an indirect cost of the specified cost object by placing an X in the appropriate column.

Cost	Cost Object	Direct Cost	Indirect Cost
Ex. Room service beverages	A particular hotel guest	X	
1. The salary of the head chef	The hotel's restaurant		
2. The salary of the head chef	A particular restaurant customer		
3. Room cleaning supplies	A particular hotel guest		
4. Flowers for the reception desk	A particular hotel guest		
5. The wages of the doorman	A particular hotel guest		
6. Room cleaning supplies	The housecleaning department		
7. Fire insurance on the hotel building	The hotel's gym		
8. Towels used in the gym	The hotel's gym		

EXERCISE 2–7 Differential, Opportunity, and Sunk Costs [LO7]

The Sorrento Hotel is a four-star hotel located in downtown Seattle. The hotel's operations vice president would like to replace the hotel's antiquated computer terminals at the registration desk with attractive state-of-the-art flat-panel displays. The new displays would take less space, would consume less power than the old computer terminals, and would provide additional security since they can only be viewed from a restrictive angle. The new computer displays would not require any new wiring. The hotel's chef believes the funds would be better spent on a new bulk freezer for the kitchen.

Required:

For each of the items below, indicate by placing an X in the appropriate column whether it should be considered a differential cost, an opportunity cost, or a sunk cost in the decision to replace the old computer terminals with new flat-panel displays. If none of the categories apply for a particular item, leave all columns blank.

Item	Differential Cost	Opportunity Cost	Sunk Cost
Ex. Cost of electricity to run the terminals	X		
1. Cost of the new flat-panel displays			
2. Cost of the old computer terminals			
3. Rent on the space occupied by the registration desk . . .			
4. Wages of registration desk personnel			
5. Benefits from a new freezer			
6. Costs of maintaining the old computer terminals			
7. Cost of removing the old computer terminals			
8. Cost of existing registration desk wiring			

EXERCISE 2–8 Cost Behavior; Contribution Format Income Statement [LO3, LO5]

Parker Company manufactures and sells a single product. A partially completed schedule of the company's total and per unit costs over a relevant range of 60,000 to 100,000 units produced and sold each year is given below:

	Units Produced and Sold		
	60,000	80,000	100,000
Total costs:			
Variable costs	$150,000	?	?
Fixed costs	360,000	?	?
Total costs	$510,000	?	?
Cost per unit:			
Variable cost	?	?	?
Fixed cost	?	?	?
Total cost per unit	?	?	?

Required:

1. Complete the schedule of the company's total and unit costs.
2. Assume that the company produces and sells 90,000 units during the year at the selling price of $7.50 per unit. Prepare a contribution format income statement for the year.

EXERCISE 2–9 Cost Classification [LO1, LO2, LO3, LO7]

Several years ago Medex Company purchased a small building adjacent to its manufacturing plant in order to have room for expansion when needed. Since the company had no immediate need for the extra space, the building was rented out to another company for rental revenue of $40,000 per year. The renter's lease will expire next month, and rather than renewing the lease, Medex Company has decided to use the building itself to manufacture a new product.

Direct materials cost for the new product will total $40 per unit. It will be necessary to hire a supervisor to oversee production. Her salary will be $2,500 per month. Workers will be hired to manufacture the new product, with direct labor cost amounting to $18 per unit. Manufacturing operations will occupy all of the building space, so it will be necessary to rent space in a warehouse nearby in order to store finished units of product. The rental cost will be $1,000 per month. In addition, the company will need to rent equipment for use in producing the new product; the rental cost will be $3,000 per month. The company will continue to depreciate the building on a straight-line basis, as in past years. Depreciation on the building is $10,000 per year.

Advertising costs for the new product will total $50,000 per year. Costs of shipping the new product to customers will be $10 per unit. Electrical costs of operating machines will be $2 per unit.

To have funds to purchase materials, meet payrolls, and so forth, the company will have to liquidate some temporary investments. These investments are presently yielding a return of $6,000 per year.

Required:

Prepare an answer sheet with the following column headings:

			Product Cost					
Name of the Cost	Variable Cost	Fixed Cost	Direct Materials	Direct Labor	Manufacturing Overhead	Period (Selling and Administrative) Cost	Opportunity Cost	Sunk Cost

List the different costs associated with the new product decision down the extreme left column (under Name of the Cost). Then place an X under each heading that helps to describe the type of cost involved. There may be X's under several column headings for a single cost. (For example, a cost may be a fixed cost, a period cost, and a sunk cost; you would place an X under each of these column headings opposite the cost.)

EXERCISE 2–10 High-Low Method; Scattergraph Analysis [LO4]

Zerbel Company, a wholesaler of large, custom-built air conditioning units for commercial buildings, has noticed considerable fluctuation in its shipping expense from month to month, as shown below:

Month	Units Shipped	Total Shipping Expense
January	4	$2,200
February	7	$3,100
March	5	$2,600
April	2	$1,500
May	3	$2,200
June	6	$3,000
July	8	$3,600

Required:

1. Prepare a scattergraph using the data given above. Plot cost on the vertical axis and activity on the horizontal axis. Is there an approximately linear relationship between shipping expense and the number of units shipped?

2. Using the high-low method, estimate the cost formula for shipping expense. Draw a straight line through the high and low data points shown in the scattergraph that you prepared in requirement 1. Make sure your line intersects the *Y* axis.
3. Comment on the accuracy of your high-low estimates assuming a least-squares regression analysis estimated the total fixed costs to be $1,010.71 per month and the variable cost to be $317.86 per unit. How would the straight line that you drew in requirement 2 differ from a straight line that minimizes the sum of the squared errors?
4. What factors, other than the number of units shipped, are likely to affect the company's shipping expense? Explain.

EXERCISE 2–11 Traditional and Contribution Format Income Statements [LO5]

Haaki Shop, Inc., is a large retailer of surfboards. The company assembled the information shown below for the quarter ended May 31:

	Amount
Total sales revenue	$800,000
Selling price per surfboard	$400
Variable selling expense per surfboard	$50
Variable administrative expense per surfboard	$20
Total fixed selling expense	$150,000
Total fixed administrative expense	$120,000
Merchandise inventory, beginning balance	$80,000
Merchandise inventory, ending balance	$100,000
Merchandise purchases	$320,000

Required:

1. Prepare a traditional income statement for the quarter ended May 31.
2. Prepare a contribution format income statement for the quarter ended May 31.
3. What was the contribution toward fixed expenses and profits for each surfboard sold during the quarter? (State this figure in a single dollar amount per surfboard.)

EXERCISE 2–12 Cost Behavior; High-Low Method [LO3, LO4]

Speedy Parcel Service operates a fleet of delivery trucks in a large metropolitan area. A careful study by the company's cost analyst has determined that if a truck is driven 120,000 miles during a year, the average operating cost is 11.6 cents per mile. If a truck is driven only 80,000 miles during a year, the average operating cost increases to 13.6 cents per mile.

Required:

1. Using the high-low method, estimate the variable and fixed cost elements of the annual cost of truck operation.
2. Express the variable and fixed costs in the form $Y = a + bX$.
3. If a truck were driven 100,000 miles during a year, what total cost would you expect to be incurred?

EXERCISE 2–13 High-Low Method; Predicting Cost [LO3, LO4]

The number of X-rays taken and X-ray costs over the last nine months in Beverly Hospital are given below:

Month	X-Rays Taken	X-Ray Costs
January	6,250	$28,000
February	7,000	$29,000
March	5,000	$23,000
April	4,250	$20,000
May	4,500	$22,000
June	3,000	$17,000
July	3,750	$18,000
August	5,500	$24,000
September	5,750	$26,000

Required:

1. Using the high-low method, estimate the cost formula for X-ray costs.
2. Using the cost formula you derived above, what X-ray costs would you expect to be incurred during a month in which 4,600 X-rays are taken?
3. Prepare a scattergraph using the data given above. Plot X-ray costs on the vertical axis and the number of X-rays taken on the horizontal axis. Draw a straight line through the two data points that correspond to the high and low levels of activity. Make sure your line intersects the *Y*-axis.
4. Comment on the accuracy of your high-low estimates assuming a least-squares regression analysis estimated the total fixed costs to be $6,529.41 per month and the variable cost to be $3.29 per X-ray taken. How would the straight line that you drew in requirement 3 differ from a straight line that minimizes the sum of the squared errors?
5. Using the least-squares regression estimates given in requirement 4, what X-ray costs would you expect to be incurred during a month in which 4,600 X-rays are taken?

Problems connect ACCOUNTING

All applicable problems are available with McGraw-Hill's *Connect™ Accounting*.

eXcel

PROBLEM 2–14 Contribution Format versus Traditional Income Statement [LO5]

House of Organs, Inc., purchases organs from a well-known manufacturer and sells them at the retail level. The organs sell, on the average, for $2,500 each. The average cost of an organ from the manufacturer is $1,500. The costs that the company incurs in a typical month are presented below:

Costs	Cost Formula
Selling:	
Advertising	$950 per month
Delivery of organs	$60 per organ sold
Sales salaries and commissions	$4,800 per month, plus 4% of sales
Utilities	$650 per month
Depreciation of sales facilities	$5,000 per month
Administrative:	
Executive salaries	$13,500 per month
Depreciation of office equipment	$900 per month
Clerical	$2,500 per month, plus $40 per organ sold
Insurance	$700 per month

During November, the company sold and delivered 60 organs.

Required:

1. Prepare a traditional income statement for November.
2. Prepare a contribution format income statement for November. Show costs and revenues on both a total and a per unit basis down through contribution margin.
3. Refer to the income statement you prepared in (2) above. Why might it be misleading to show the fixed costs on a per unit basis?

PROBLEM 2–15 Identifying Cost Behavior Patterns [LO3]

A number of graphs displaying cost behavior patterns are shown on the next page. The vertical axis on each graph represents total cost and the horizontal axis represents the level of activity (volume).

Required:

1. For each of the following situations, identify the graph that illustrates the cost behavior pattern involved. Any graph may be used more than once.
   a. Electricity bill—a flat fixed charge, plus a variable cost after a certain number of kilowatt-hours are used.

b. City water bill, which is computed as follows:

First 1,000,000 gallons or less	$1,000 flat fee
Next 10,000 gallons	$0.003 per gallon used
Next 10,000 gallons	$0.006 per gallon used
Next 10,000 gallons	$0.009 per gallon used
Etc.	Etc.

c. Depreciation of equipment, where the amount is computed by the straight-line method. When the depreciation rate was established, it was anticipated that the obsolescence factor would be greater than the wear and tear factor.

d. Rent on a factory building donated by the city, where the agreement calls for a fixed fee payment unless 200,000 labor-hours or more are worked, in which case no rent need be paid.

e. Cost of raw materials, where the cost starts at $7.50 per unit and then decreases by 5 cents per unit for each of the first 100 units purchased, after which it remains constant at $2.50 per unit.

f. Salaries of maintenance workers, where one maintenance worker is needed for every 1,000 hours of machine-hours or less (that is, 0 to 1,000 hours requires one maintenance worker, 1,001 to 2,000 hours requires two maintenance workers, etc.).

g. Cost of raw material used.

h. Rent on a factory building donated by the county, where the agreement calls for rent of $100,000 less $1 for each direct labor-hour worked in excess of 200,000 hours, but a minimum rental payment of $20,000 must be paid.

i. Use of a machine under a lease, where a minimum charge of $1,000 is paid for up to 400 hours of machine time. After 400 hours of machine time, an additional charge of $2 per hour is paid up to a maximum charge of $2,000 per period.

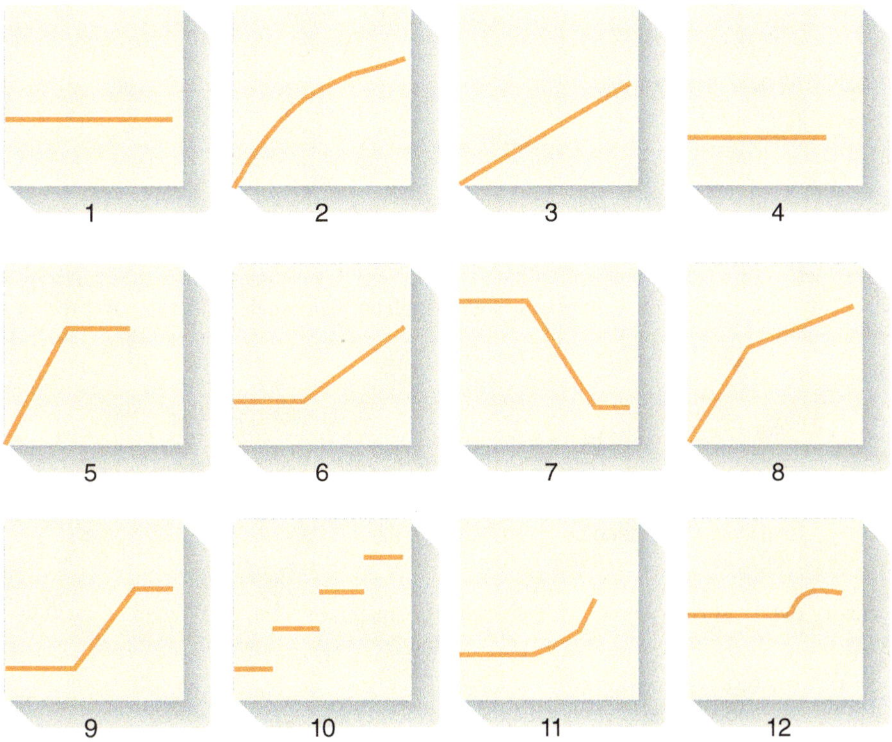

2. How would a knowledge of cost behavior patterns such as those above be of help to a manager in analyzing the cost structure of his or her company?

(CPA, adapted)

PROBLEM 2–16 Variable and Fixed Costs; Subtleties of Direct and Indirect Costs [LO3, LO6]
The Central Area Well-Baby Clinic provides a variety of health services to newborn babies and their parents. The clinic is organized into a number of departments, one of which is the Immunization Center. A number of costs of the clinic and the Immunization Center are listed below.

Example: The cost of polio immunization tablets

a. The salary of the head nurse in the Immunization Center.
b. Costs of incidental supplies consumed in the Immunization Center, such as paper towels.
c. The cost of lighting and heating the Immunization Center.
d. The cost of disposable syringes used in the Immunization Center.
e. The salary of the Central Area Well-Baby Clinic's information systems manager.
f. The costs of mailing letters soliciting donations to the Central Area Well-Baby Clinic.
g. The wages of nurses who work in the Immunization Center.
h. The cost of medical malpractice insurance for the Central Area Well-Baby Clinic.
i. Depreciation on the fixtures and equipment in the Immunization Center.

Required:
For each cost listed above, indicate whether it is a direct or indirect cost of the Immunization Center, whether it is a direct or indirect cost of immunizing particular patients, and whether it is variable or fixed with respect to the number of immunizations administered. Use the form shown below for your answer.

	Direct or Indirect Cost of the Immunization Center		Direct or Indirect Cost of Particular Patients		Variable or Fixed with Respect to the Number of Immunizations Administered	
Item Description	Direct	Indirect	Direct	Indirect	Variable	Fixed
Example: The cost of polio immunization tablets	X		X		X	

PROBLEM 2–17 High-Low Method; Predicting Cost [LO3, LO4]
Echeverria SA is an Argentinian manufacturing company whose total factory overhead costs fluctuate somewhat from year to year according to the number of machine-hours worked in its production facility. These costs (in Argentinian pesos) at high and low levels of activity over recent years are given below:

	Level of Activity	
	Low	High
Machine-hours	60,000	80,000
Total factory overhead costs	274,000 pesos	312,000 pesos

The factory overhead costs above consist of indirect materials, rent, and maintenance. The company has analyzed these costs at the 60,000 machine-hours level of activity as follows:

Indirect materials (variable)	90,000 pesos
Rent (fixed)	130,000
Maintenance (mixed)	54,000
Total factory overhead costs	274,000 pesos

For planning purposes, the company wants to break down the maintenance cost into its variable and fixed cost elements.

Required:

1. Estimate how much of the factory overhead cost of 312,000 pesos at the high level of activity consists of maintenance cost. (Hint: To do this, it may be helpful to first determine how much of the 312,000 pesos cost consists of indirect materials and rent. Think about the behavior of variable and fixed costs.)
2. Using the high-low method, estimate a cost formula for maintenance.
3. What *total* overhead costs would you expect the company to incur at an operating level of 65,000 machine-hours?

PROBLEM 2–18 Cost Behavior; High-Low Method; Contribution Format Income Statement [LO3, LO4, LO5]

eXcel

Frankel Ltd., a British merchandising company, is the exclusive distributor of a product that is gaining rapid market acceptance. The company's revenues and expenses (in British pounds) for the last three months are given below:

Frankel Ltd.
Comparative Income Statements
For the Three Months Ended June 30

	April	May	June
Sales in units	3,000	3,750	4,500
Sales revenue	£420,000	£525,000	£630,000
Cost of goods sold	168,000	210,000	252,000
Gross margin	252,000	315,000	378,000
Selling and administrative expenses:			
Shipping expense	44,000	50,000	56,000
Advertising expense	70,000	70,000	70,000
Salaries and commissions	107,000	125,000	143,000
Insurance expense	9,000	9,000	9,000
Depreciation expense	42,000	42,000	42,000
Total selling and administrative expenses	272,000	296,000	320,000
Net operating income (loss)	£ (20,000)	£ 19,000	£ 58,000

(Note: Frankel Ltd.'s income statement has been recast in the functional format common in the United States. The British currency is the pound, denoted by £.)

Required:

1. Identify each of the company's expenses (including cost of goods sold) as either variable, fixed, or mixed.
2. Using the high-low method, separate each mixed expense into variable and fixed elements. State the cost formula for each mixed expense.
3. Redo the company's income statement at the 4,500-unit level of activity using the contribution format.

PROBLEM 2–19 High-Low and Scattergraph Analysis [LO4]

Sebolt Wire Company heats copper ingots to very high temperatures by placing the ingots in a large heat coil. The heated ingots are then run through a shaping machine that shapes the soft ingot into wire. Due to the long heat-up time, the coil is never turned off. When an ingot is placed in the coil, the temperature is raised to an even higher level, and then the coil is allowed to drop to the "waiting" temperature between ingots. Management needs to know the variable cost of power involved in heating an ingot and the fixed cost of power during "waiting" periods. The following data on ingots processed and power costs are available:

	A	B	C	D
1	Month	Number of Ingots	Power Cost	
2	January	110	$5,500	
3	February	90	$4,500	
4	March	80	$4,400	
5	April	100	$5,000	
6	May	130	$6,000	
7	June	120	$5,600	
8	July	70	$4,000	
9	August	60	$3,200	
10	September	50	$3,400	
11	October	40	$2,400	
12				

Sheet1 Sheet2 Sheet3

Required:

1. Using the high-low method, estimate a cost formula for power cost. Express the formula in the form $Y = a + bX$.
2. Prepare a scattergraph by plotting ingots processed and power cost on a graph. Draw a straight line though the two data points that correspond to the high and low levels of activity. Make sure your line intersects the Y-axis.
3. Comment on the accuracy of your high-low estimates assuming a least-squares regression analysis estimated the total fixed costs to be $1,185.45 per month and the variable cost to be $37.82 per ingot. How would the straight line that you drew in requirement 2 differ from a straight line that minimizes the sum of the squared errors?

PROBLEM 2–20 Ethics and the Manager [LO2]

The top management of General Electronics, Inc., is well known for "managing by the numbers." With an eye on the company's desired growth in overall net profit, the company's CEO (chief executive officer) sets target profits at the beginning of the year for each of the company's divisions. The CEO has stated her policy as follows: "I won't interfere with operations in the divisions. I am available for advice, but the division vice presidents are free to do anything they want so long as they hit the target profits for the year."

In November, Stan Richart, the vice president in charge of the Cellular Telephone Technologies Division, saw that making the current year's target profit for his division was going to be very difficult. Among other actions, he directed that discretionary expenditures be delayed until the beginning of the new year. On December 30, he was angered to discover that a warehouse clerk had ordered $350,000 of cellular telephone parts earlier in December even though the parts weren't really needed by the assembly department until January or February. Contrary to common accounting practice, the General Electronics, Inc., Accounting Policy Manual states that such parts are to be recorded as an expense when delivered. To avoid recording the expense, Mr. Richart asked that the order be canceled, but the purchasing department reported that the parts had already been delivered and the supplier would not accept returns. Because the bill had not yet been paid, Mr. Richart asked the accounting department to correct the clerk's mistake by delaying recognition of the delivery until the bill is paid in January.

Required:

1. Are Mr. Richart's actions ethical? Explain why they are or are not ethical.
2. Do the general management philosophy and accounting policies at General Electronics encourage or discourage ethical behavior? Explain.

PROBLEM 2–21 High-Low Method; Predicting Cost [LO3, LO4]

Golden Company's total overhead cost at various levels of activity are presented below:

Month	Machine-Hours	Total Overhead Cost
March	50,000	$194,000
April	40,000	$170,200
May	60,000	$217,800
June	70,000	$241,600

Assume that the overhead cost above consists of utilities, supervisory salaries, and maintenance. The breakdown of these costs at the 40,000 machine-hour level of activity is as follows:

Utilities (variable)	$ 52,000
Supervisory salaries (fixed)	60,000
Maintenance (mixed)	58,200
Total overhead cost	$170,200

The company wants to break down the maintenance cost into its variable and fixed cost elements.

Required:

1. Estimate how much of the $241,600 of overhead cost in June was maintenance cost. (Hint: To do this, it may be helpful to first determine how much of the $241,600 consisted of utilities and supervisory salaries. Think about the behavior of variable and fixed costs within the relevant range.)
2. Using the high-low method, estimate a cost formula for maintenance.
3. Express the company's total overhead cost in the form $Y = a + bX$.
4. What total overhead cost would you expect to be incurred at an activity level of 45,000 machine-hours?

PROBLEM 2–22 Cost Classification [LO2, LO3, LO6]

Listed below are costs found in various organizations.

1. Depreciation, executive jet.
2. Costs of shipping finished goods to customers.
3. Wood used in manufacturing furniture.
4. Sales manager's salary.
5. Electricity used in manufacturing furniture.
6. Secretary to the company president.
7. Aerosol attachment placed on a spray can produced by the company.
8. Billing costs.
9. Packing supplies for shipping products overseas.
10. Sand used in manufacturing concrete.
11. Supervisor's salary, factory.
12. Executive life insurance.
13. Sales commissions.
14. Fringe benefits, assembly-line workers.
15. Advertising costs.
16. Property taxes on finished goods warehouses.
17. Lubricants for production equipment.

Required:
Prepare an answer sheet with column headings as shown below. For each cost item, indicate whether it would be variable or fixed with respect to the number of units produced and sold; and then whether it would be a selling cost, an administrative cost, or a manufacturing cost. If it is a manufacturing cost, indicate whether it would typically be treated as a direct or indirect cost with respect to units of product. Three sample answers are provided for illustration.

Cost Item	Variable or Fixed	Selling Cost	Administrative Cost	Manufacturing (Product) Cost	
				Direct	Indirect
Direct labor	V			X	
Executive salaries	F		X		
Factory rent	F				X

eXcel

PROBLEM 2–23 High-Low Method; Contribution Format Income Statement [LO4, LO5]
Alden Company has decided to use a contribution format income statement for internal planning purposes. The company has analyzed its expenses and has developed the following cost formulas:

Cost	Cost Formula
Cost of goods sold	$20 per unit sold
Advertising expense	$170,000 per quarter
Sales commissions	5% of sales
Administrative salaries	$80,000 per quarter
Shipping expense	?
Depreciation expense	$50,000 per quarter

Management has concluded that shipping expense is a mixed cost, containing both variable and fixed cost elements. Units sold and the related shipping expense over the last eight quarters are given below:

Quarter	Units Sold	Shipping Expense
Year 1:		
First	16,000	$160,000
Second	18,000	$175,000
Third	23,000	$217,000
Fourth	19,000	$180,000
Year 2:		
First	17,000	$170,000
Second	20,000	$185,000
Third	25,000	$232,000
Fourth	22,000	$208,000

Management would like a cost formula derived for shipping expense so that a budgeted contribution format income statement can be prepared for the next quarter.

Required:
1. Using the high-low method, estimate a cost formula for shipping expense.
2. In the first quarter of Year 3, the company plans to sell 21,000 units at a selling price of $50 per unit. Prepare a contribution format income statement for the quarter.

PROBLEM 2–24 Cost Classification and Cost Behavior [LO2, LO3, LO6]
Heritage Company manufactures a beautiful bookcase that enjoys widespread popularity. The company has a backlog of orders that is large enough to keep production going indefinitely at the plant's full capacity of 4,000 bookcases per year. Annual cost data at full capacity follow:

Direct materials used (wood and glass)	$430,000
Administrative office salaries	$110,000
Factory supervision	$70,000
Sales commissions	$60,000
Depreciation, factory building	$105,000
Depreciation, administrative office equipment	$2,000
Indirect materials, factory	$18,000
Factory labor (cutting and assembly)	$90,000
Advertising	$100,000
Insurance, factory	$6,000
Administrative office supplies (billing)	$4,000
Property taxes, factory	$20,000
Utilities, factory	$45,000

Required:

1. Prepare an answer sheet with the column headings shown below. Enter each cost item on your answer sheet, placing the dollar amount under the appropriate headings. As examples, this has been done already for the first two items in the list above. Note that each cost item is classified in two ways: first, as either variable or fixed with respect to the number of units produced and sold; and second, as either a selling and administrative cost or a product cost. (If the item is a product cost, it should also be classified as either direct or indirect as shown.)

	Cost Behavior		Selling or Administrative	Product Cost	
Cost Item	Variable	Fixed	Cost	Direct	Indirect*
Materials used	$430,000			$430,000	
Administrative office salaries		$110,000	$110,000		

*To units of product.

2. Total the dollar amounts in each of the columns in (1) above. Compute the average product cost per bookcase.
3. Due to a recession, assume that production drops to only 2,000 bookcases per year. Would you expect the average product cost per bookcase to increase, decrease, or remain unchanged? Explain. No computations are necessary.
4. Refer to the original data. The president's next-door neighbor has considered making himself a bookcase and has priced the necessary materials at a building supply store. He has asked the president whether he could purchase a bookcase from the Heritage Company "at cost," and the president has agreed to let him do so.
   a. Would you expect any disagreement between the two men over the price the neighbor should pay? Explain. What price does the president probably have in mind? The neighbor?
   b. Because the company is operating at full capacity, what cost term used in the chapter might be justification for the president to charge the full, regular price to the neighbor and still be selling "at cost"? Explain.

connect ACCOUNTING

Cases

All applicable cases are available with McGraw-Hill's *Connect™ Accounting*.

CASE 2–25 Scattergraph Analysis; Selection of an Activity Base [LO4]

Mapleleaf Sweepers of Toronto manufactures replacement rotary sweeper brooms for the large sweeper trucks that clear leaves and snow from city streets. The business is seasonal, with the largest demand during and just preceding the fall and winter months. Because there are so many different kinds of sweeper brooms used by its customers, Mapleleaf Sweepers makes all of its brooms to order.

The company has been analyzing its overhead accounts to determine fixed and variable components for planning purposes. Below are data for the company's janitorial labor costs over the last nine months. (Cost data are in Canadian dollars.)

	Number of Units Produced	Number of Janitorial Workdays	Janitorial Labor Cost
January	115	21	$3,840
February	109	19	$3,648
March	102	23	$4,128
April	76	20	$3,456
May	69	23	$4,320
June	108	22	$4,032
July	77	16	$2,784
August	71	14	$2,688
September	127	21	$3,840

The number of workdays varies from month to month due to the number of weekdays, holidays, days of vacation, and sick leave taken in the month. The number of units produced in a month varies depending on demand and the number of workdays in the month.

There are two janitors who each work an eight-hour shift each workday. They each can take up to 10 days of paid sick leave each year. Their wages on days they call in sick and their wages during paid vacations are charged to miscellaneous overhead rather than to the janitorial labor cost account.

Required:

1. Plot the janitorial labor cost and units produced on a scattergraph. (Place cost on the vertical axis and units produced on the horizontal axis.)
2. Plot the janitorial labor cost and number of workdays on a scattergraph. (Place cost on the vertical axis and the number of workdays on the horizontal axis.)
3. Which measure of activity—number of units produced or janitorial workdays—should be used as the activity base for explaining janitorial labor cost?

CASE 2–26 Mixed Cost Analysis and the Relevant Range [LO3, LO4]

The Ramon Company is a manufacturer that is interested in developing a cost formula to estimate the fixed and variable components of its monthly manufacturing overhead costs. The company wishes to use machine-hours as its measure of activity and has gathered the data below for this year and last year:

	Last Year		This Year	
Month	Machine-Hours	Overhead Costs	Machine-Hours	Overhead Costs
January	21,000	$84,000	21,000	$86,000
February	25,000	$99,000	24,000	$93,000
March	22,000	$89,500	23,000	$93,000
April	23,000	$90,000	22,000	$87,000
May	20,500	$81,500	20,000	$80,000
June	19,000	$75,500	18,000	$76,500
July	14,000	$70,500	12,000	$67,500
August	10,000	$64,500	13,000	$71,000
September	12,000	$69,000	15,000	$73,500
October	17,000	$75,000	17,000	$72,500
November	16,000	$71,500	15,000	$71,000
December	19,000	$78,000	18,000	$75,000

The company leases all of its manufacturing equipment. The lease arrangement calls for a flat monthly fee up to 19,500 machine-hours. If the machine-hours used exceeds 19,500, then the fee becomes strictly variable with respect to the total number of machine-hours consumed during the month. Lease expense is a major element of overhead cost.

Required:

1. Using the high-low method, estimate a manufacturing overhead cost formula.
2. Prepare a scattergraph using all of the data for the two-year period. Fit a straight line or lines to the plotted points using a ruler. Describe the cost behavior pattern revealed by your scattergraph plot.
3. Assume a least-squares regression analysis using all of the given data points estimated the total fixed costs to be $40,102 and the variable costs to be $2.13 per machine-hour. Do you have any concerns about the accuracy of the high-low estimates that you have computed or the least-squares regression estimates that have been provided?
4. Assume that the company consumes 22,500 machine-hours during a month. Using the high-low method, estimate the total overhead cost that would be incurred at this level of activity. Be sure to consider only the data points contained in the relevant range of activity when performing your computations.
5. Comment on the accuracy of your high-low estimates assuming a least-squares regression analysis using only the data points in the relevant range of activity estimated the total fixed costs to be $10,090 and the variable costs to be $3.53 per machine-hour.

Appendix 2A: Least-Squares Regression Computations

LEARNING OBJECTIVE 8
Analyze a mixed cost using a scattergraph plot and the least-squares regression method.

The least-squares regression method for estimating a linear relationship is based on the equation for a straight line:

$$Y = a + bX$$

As explained in the chapter, least-squares regression selects the values for the intercept *a* and the slope *b* that minimize the sum of the squared errors. The following formulas, which are derived in statistics and calculus texts, accomplish that objective:

$$b = n(\Sigma XY) - \frac{(\Sigma X)(\Sigma Y)}{n(\Sigma X^2) - (\Sigma X)^2}$$

$$a = \frac{(\Sigma Y) - b(\Sigma X)}{n}$$

where:

X = The level of activity (independent variable)
Y = The total mixed cost (dependent variable)
a = The total fixed cost (the vertical intercept of the line)
b = The variable cost per unit of activity (the slope of the line)
n = Number of observations
Σ = Sum across all n observations

Manually performing the calculations required by the formulas is tedious at best. Fortunately, statistical software packages are widely available that perform the calculations automatically. Spreadsheet software, such as Microsoft® Excel, can also be used to do least-squares regression—although it requires a little more work than using a specialized statistical application.

In addition to estimates of the intercept (fixed cost) and slope (variable cost per unit), Excel also provides a statistic called the R^2, which is a measure of "goodness of fit." The R^2 tells us the percentage of the variation in the dependent variable (cost) that is explained by variation in the independent variable (activity). The R^2 varies from 0% to 100%, and the higher the percentage, the better. You should always plot the data in a scattergraph,

EXHIBIT 2A–1
The Least-Squares Regression Worksheet for Brentline Hospital

	A	B	C
1		*Patient*	*Maintenance*
2		*Days*	*Costs*
3	*Month*	*X*	*Y*
4	January	5,600	$7,900
5	February	7,100	$8,500
6	March	5,000	$7,400
7	April	6,500	$8,200
8	May	7,300	$9,100
9	June	8,000	$9,800
10	July	6,200	$7,800
11			
12	Intercept	$3,431	
13	Slope	$0.759	
14	RSQ	$0.90	
15			

Least-squares regression

but it is particularly important to check the data visually when the R^2 is low. A quick look at the scattergraph can reveal that there is little relation between the cost and the activity or that the relation is something other than a simple straight line. In such cases, additional analysis would be required.

To illustrate how Excel can be used to calculate the intercept a, the slope b, and the R^2, we will use the Brentline Hospital data for maintenance costs on page 35. The worksheet in Exhibit 2A–1 contains the data and the calculations.

As you can see, the X values (the independent variable) have been entered in cells B4 through B10. The Y values (the dependent variable) have been entered in cells C4 through C10. The slope, intercept, and R^2 are computed using the Excel functions INTERCEPT, SLOPE, and RSQ. You must specify the range of cells for the Y values and for the X values.

In Exhibit 2A–1, cell B12 contains the formula =INTERCEPT(C4:C10,B4:B10); cell B13 contains the formula =SLOPE(C4:C10,B4:B10); and cell B14 contains the formula = RSQ(C4:C10,B4:B10).

According to the calculations carried out by Excel, the fixed maintenance cost (the intercept) is \$3,431 per month and the variable cost (the slope) is \$0.759 per patient-day. Therefore, the cost formula for maintenance cost is:

$$Y = a + bX$$

$$Y = \$3{,}431 + \$0.759X$$

Note that the R^2 (i.e., RSQ) is 0.90, which is quite good and indicates that 90% of the variation in maintenance costs is explained by the variation in patient-days.

Plotting the data is easy in Excel. Select the range of values that you would like to plot—in this case, cells B4:C10. Then select the Chart Wizard tool on the toolbar and make the appropriate choices in the various dialogue boxes that appear. When you are finished, you should have a scattergraph that looks like the plot in Exhibit 2A–2. Note that the relation between cost and activity is approximately linear, so it is reasonable to fit a straight line to the data as we have implicitly done with the least-squares regression.

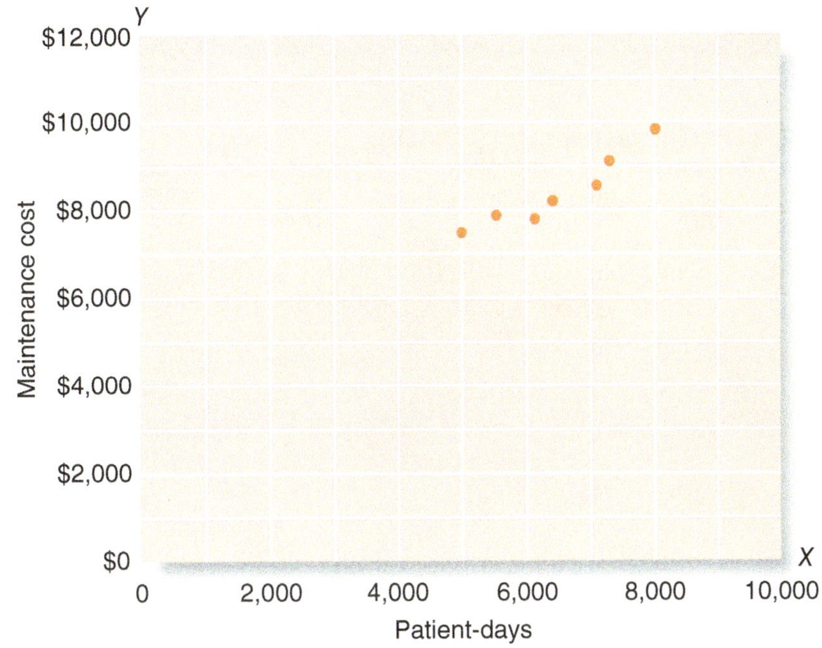

EXHIBIT 2A–2
A Scattergraph Plot of the Brentline Hospital Data

Glossary (Appendix 2A)

R^2 A measure of goodness of fit in least-squares regression analysis. It is the percentage of the variation in the dependent variable that is explained by variation in the independent variable. (p. 67)

connect ACCOUNTING Appendix 2A Exercises and Problems

All applicable exercises and problems are available with McGraw-Hill's *Connect™ Accounting*.

EXERCISE 2A–1 Least-Squares Regression [LO8]

EZ Rental Car offers rental cars in an off-airport location near a major tourist destination in Florida. Management would like to better understand the behavior of the company's costs. One of those costs is the cost of washing cars. The company operates its own car wash facility in which each rental car that is returned is thoroughly cleaned before being released for rental to another customer. Management believes that the costs of operating the car wash should be related to the number of rental returns. Accordingly, the following data have been compiled:

Month	Rental Returns	Car Wash Costs
January	2,310	$10,113
February	2,453	$12,691
March	2,641	$10,905
April	2,874	$12,949
May	3,540	$15,334
June	4,861	$21,455
July	5,432	$21,270
August	5,268	$19,930
September	4,628	$21,860
October	3,720	$18,383
November	2,106	$9,830
December	2,495	$11,081

Required:

Using least-squares regression, estimate the fixed cost and variable cost elements of monthly car wash costs. The fixed cost element should be estimated to the nearest dollar and the variable cost element to the nearest cent.

EXERCISE 2A–2 Least-Squares Regression [LO3, LO8]

One of Varic Company's products goes through a glazing process. The company has observed glazing costs as follows over the last six weeks:

Week	Units Produced	Total Glazing Cost
1	8	$270
2	5	$200
3	10	$310
4	4	$190
5	6	$240
6	9	$290

For planning purposes, the company's management wants to know the amount of variable glazing cost per unit and the total fixed glazing cost per week.

Required:

1. Using the least-squares regression method, estimate the variable and fixed elements of the glazing cost.
2. Express the cost data in (1) above in the form $Y = a + bX$.
3. If the company processes seven units next week, what would be the expected total glazing cost?

PROBLEM 2A–3 Scattergraph; Cost Behavior; Least-Squares Regression Method [LO3, LO8]

Amanda King has just been appointed director of recreation programs for Highland Park, a rapidly growing community in Connecticut. In the past, the city has sponsored a number of softball leagues in the summer months. From the city's cost records, Amanda has found the following total costs associated with the softball leagues over the last five years:

	A	B	C
1	*Number of Leagues*	*Total Cost*	
2	5	$13,000	
3	2	$7,000	
4	4	$10,500	
5	6	$14,000	
6	3	$10,000	
7			

Sheet1 Sheet2 Sheet3

Each league requires its own paid supervisor and paid umpires as well as printed schedules and other copy work. Therefore, Amanda knows that some variable costs are associated with the leagues. She would like to know the amount of variable cost per league and the total fixed cost per year associated with the softball program. This information would help her for planning purposes.

Required:

1. Using the least-squares regression method, estimate the variable cost per league and the total fixed cost per year for the softball program.
2. Express the cost data derived in (1) above in the form $Y = a + bX$.
3. Assume that Amanda would like to expand the softball program during the coming year to involve a total of seven leagues. Compute the expected total cost for the softball program.

Can you see any problem with using the cost formula from (2) above to derive this total cost figure? Explain.

4. Prepare a scattergraph, and fit a line to the plotted points using the cost formula expressed in (2) above.

PROBLEM 2A–4 Least-Squares Regression; Scattergraph; Comparison of Activity Bases [LO3, LO8]

The Hard Rock Mining Company is developing cost formulas for management planning and decision-making purposes. The company's cost analyst has concluded that utilities cost is a mixed cost, and he is attempting to find a base with which the cost might be closely correlated. The controller has suggested that tons mined might be a good base to use in developing a cost formula. The production superintendent disagrees; she thinks that direct labor-hours would be a better base. The cost analyst has decided to try both bases and has assembled the following information:

Quarter	Tons Mined	Direct Labor-Hours	Utilities Cost
Year 1:			
First	15,000	5,000	$50,000
Second	11,000	3,000	$45,000
Third	21,000	4,000	$60,000
Fourth	12,000	6,000	$75,000
Year 2:			
First	18,000	10,000	$100,000
Second	25,000	9,000	$105,000
Third	30,000	8,000	$85,000
Fourth	28,000	11,000	$120,000

Required:

1. Using tons mined as the independent (*X*) variable:
   a. Determine a cost formula for utilities cost using the least-squares regression method.
   b. Prepare a scattergraph and plot the tons mined and utilities cost. (Place cost on the vertical axis and tons mined on the horizontal axis.) Fit a straight line to the plotted points using the cost formula determined in (*a*) above.
2. Using direct labor-hours as the independent (*X*) variable, repeat the computations in (*a*) and (*b*) above.
3. Would you recommend that the company use tons mined or direct labor-hours as a base for planning utilities cost?

CASE 2A–5 Analysis of Mixed Costs in a Pricing Decision [LO3, LO8]

Jasmine Lee owns a catering company that serves food and beverages at exclusive parties and business functions. Lee's business is seasonal, with a heavy schedule during the summer months and holidays and a lighter schedule at other times.

One of the major events that Lee's customers request is a cocktail party. She offers a standard cocktail party and has estimated the cost per guest for this party as follows:

Food and beverages	$17.00
Labor (0.5 hour @ $10.00 per hour)	5.00
Overhead (0.5 hour @ $18.63 per hour)	9.32
Total cost per guest	$31.32

This standard cocktail party lasts three hours and Lee hires one worker for every six guests, which is one-half hour of labor per guest. These workers are hired only as needed and are paid only for the hours they actually work.

Lee ordinarily charges $45 per guest. She is confident about her estimates of the costs of food and beverages and labor, but is not as comfortable with the estimate of overhead cost. The $18.63

overhead cost per labor-hour was determined by dividing total overhead expenses for the last 12 months by total labor-hours for the same period. Monthly data concerning overhead costs and labor-hours appear below:

Month	Labor Hours	Overhead Expenses
January	1,500	$ 44,000
February	1,680	47,200
March	1,800	48,000
April	2,520	51,200
May	2,700	53,600
June	3,300	56,800
July	3,900	59,200
August	4,500	61,600
September	4,200	60,000
October	2,700	54,400
November	1,860	49,600
December	3,900	58,400
Total	34,560	$644,000

Lee has received a request to bid on a 120-guest fund-raising cocktail party to be given next month by an important local charity. (The party would last the usual three hours.) She would like to win this contract because the guest list for this charity event includes many prominent individuals that she would like to land as future clients. Lee is confident that these potential customers would be favorably impressed by her company's services at the charity event.

Required:

1. Prepare a scattergraph plot that puts labor-hours on the *X*-axis and overhead expenses on the *Y*-axis. What insights are revealed by your scattergraph?
2. Use the least-squares regression method to estimate the fixed and variable components of overhead expenses.
3. Estimate the contribution to profit of a standard 120-guest cocktail party if Lee charges her usual price of $45 per guest. (In other words, by how much would her overall profit increase?)
4. How low could Lee bid for the charity event, in terms of a price per guest, and still not lose money on the event itself?
5. The individual who is organizing the charity's fund-raising event has indicated that he has already received a bid under $42 from another catering company. Do you think Lee should bid below her normal $45 per guest price for the charity event? Why or why not?

(CMA, adapted)

Appendix 2B: Cost of Quality

A company may have a product with a high-quality design that uses high-quality components, but if the product is poorly assembled or has other defects, the company will have high warranty repair costs and dissatisfied customers. People who are dissatisfied with a product are unlikely to buy the product again. They often tell others about their bad experiences. This is the worst possible sort of advertising. To prevent such problems, companies expend a great deal of effort to reduce defects. The objective is to have high *quality of conformance.*

Quality of Conformance

A product that meets or exceeds its design specifications and is free of defects that mar its appearance or degrade its performance is said to have high **quality of conformance.** Note that if an economy car is free of defects, it can have a quality of conformance that is just as high as a defect-free luxury car. The purchasers of economy cars cannot expect their cars to be as opulently equipped as luxury cars, but they can and do expect them to be free of defects.

Preventing, detecting, and dealing with defects causes costs that are called *quality costs* or the *cost of quality.* The use of the term *quality cost* is confusing to some people. It does not refer to costs such as using a higher-grade leather to make a wallet or using 14K gold instead of gold-plating in jewelry. Instead, the term **quality cost** refers to all of the costs that are incurred to prevent defects or that result from defects in products.

LEARNING OBJECTIVE 9
Identify the four types of quality costs and explain how they interact.

Quality costs can be broken down into four broad groups. Two of these groups—known as *prevention costs* and *appraisal costs*—are incurred in an effort to keep defective products from falling into the hands of customers. The other two groups of costs—known as *internal failure costs* and *external failure costs*—are incurred because defects occur despite efforts to prevent them. Examples of specific costs involved in each of these four groups are given in Exhibit 2B–1.

Several things should be noted about the quality costs shown in the exhibit. First, quality costs don't relate to just manufacturing; rather, they relate to all the activities in a company from initial research and development (R&D) through customer service. Second, the number of costs associated with quality is very large; total quality cost can be very high unless management gives this area special attention. Finally, the costs in the four groupings are quite different. We will now look at each of these groupings more closely.

Prevention Costs

Generally, the most effective way to manage quality costs is to avoid having defects in the first place. It is much less costly to prevent a problem from ever happening than it is to find and correct the problem after it has occurred. **Prevention costs** support activities whose purpose is to reduce the number of defects.

EXHIBIT 2B–1
Typical Quality Costs

Prevention Costs	Internal Failure Costs
Systems development	Net cost of scrap
Quality engineering	Net cost of spoilage
Quality training	Rework labor and overhead
Quality circles	Reinspection of reworked products
Statistical process control activities	Retesting of reworked products
Supervision of prevention activities	Downtime caused by quality problems
Quality data gathering, analysis, and reporting	Disposal of defective products
Quality improvement projects	Analysis of the cause of defects in production
Technical support provided to suppliers	Re-entering data because of keying errors
Audits of the effectiveness of the quality system	Debugging software errors
Appraisal Costs	**External Failure Costs**
Test and inspection of incoming materials	Cost of field servicing and handling complaints
Test and inspection of in-process goods	Warranty repairs and replacements
Final product testing and inspection	Repairs and replacements beyond the warranty period
Supplies used in testing and inspection	Product recalls
Supervision of testing and inspection activities	Liability arising from defective products
Depreciation of test equipment	Returns and allowances arising from quality problems
Maintenance of test equipment	Lost sales arising from a reputation for poor quality
Plant utilities in the inspection area	
Field testing and appraisal at customer site	

Note from Exhibit 2B–1 that prevention costs include activities relating to quality circles and statistical process control. **Quality circles** consist of small groups of employees that meet on a regular basis to discuss ways to improve quality. Both management and workers are included in these circles. Quality circles are widely used and can be found in manufacturing companies, utilities, health care organizations, banks, and many other organizations.

Statistical process control is a technique that is used to detect whether a process is in or out of control. An out-of-control process results in defective units and may be caused by a miscalibrated machine or some other factor. In statistical process control, workers use charts to monitor the quality of units that pass through their workstations. With these charts, workers can quickly spot processes that are out of control and that are creating defects. Problems can be immediately corrected and further defects prevented rather than waiting for an inspector to catch the defects later.

Note also from the list of prevention costs in Exhibit 2B–1 that some companies provide technical support to their suppliers as a way of preventing defects. Particularly in just-in-time (JIT) systems, such support to suppliers is vital. In a JIT system, parts are delivered from suppliers just in time and in just the correct quantity to fill customer orders. There are no parts stockpiles. If a defective part is received from a supplier, the part cannot be used and the order for the ultimate customer cannot be filled on time. Hence, every part received from a supplier must be free of defects. Consequently, companies that use JIT often require that their suppliers use sophisticated quality control programs such as statistical process control and that their suppliers certify that they will deliver parts and materials that are free of defects.

Appraisal Costs

Any defective parts and products should be caught as early as possible in the production process. **Appraisal costs,** which are sometimes called *inspection costs,* are incurred to identify defective products *before* the products are shipped to customers. Unfortunately, performing appraisal activities doesn't keep defects from happening again, and most managers now realize that maintaining an army of inspectors is a costly (and ineffective) approach to quality control. Therefore, employees are increasingly being asked to be responsible for their own quality control. This approach, along with designing products to be easy to manufacture properly, allows quality to be built into products rather than relying on inspection to get the defects out.

Internal Failure Costs

Failure costs are incurred when a product fails to conform to its design specifications. Failure costs can be either internal or external. **Internal failure costs** result from identifying defects before they are shipped to customers. These costs include scrap, rejected products, reworking of defective units, and downtime caused by quality problems. In some companies, as little as 10% of the company's products make it through the production process without rework of some kind. Of course, the more effective a company's appraisal activities, the greater the chance of catching defects internally and the greater the level of internal failure costs. This is the price that is paid to avoid incurring external failure costs, which can be devastating.

External Failure Costs

External failure costs result when a defective product is delivered to a customer. As shown in Exhibit 2B–1, external failure costs include warranty repairs and replacements, product recalls, liability arising from legal action against a company, and lost sales arising from a reputation for poor quality. Such costs can decimate profits.

In the past, some managers have taken the attitude, "Let's go ahead and ship everything to customers, and we'll take care of any problems under the warranty." This attitude generally results in high external failure costs, customer ill will, and declining market share and profits.

Distribution of Quality Costs

Quality costs for some companies range between 10% and 20% of total sales, whereas experts say that these costs should be more in the 2% to 4% range. How does a company reduce its total quality cost? The answer lies in how the quality costs are distributed. Refer to the graph in Exhibit 2B–2, which shows total quality costs as a function of the quality of conformance.

The graph shows that when the quality of conformance is low, total quality cost is high and that most of this cost consists of costs of internal and external failure. A low quality of conformance means that a high percentage of units are defective and hence the company has high failure costs. However, as a company spends more and more on prevention and appraisal, the percentage of defective units drops. This results in lower internal and external failure costs. Ordinarily, total quality cost drops rapidly as the quality of conformance increases. Thus, a company can reduce its total quality cost by focusing its efforts on prevention and appraisal. The cost savings from reduced defects usually swamp the costs of the additional prevention and appraisal efforts.

The graph in Exhibit 2B–2 has been drawn so that the total quality cost is minimized when the quality of conformance is less than 100%. However, some experts contend that the total quality cost is not minimized until the quality of conformance is 100% and there are no defects. Indeed, many companies have found that the total quality costs seem to keep dropping even when the quality of conformance approaches 100% and defect rates get as low as 1 in a million units. Others argue that total quality cost eventually increases as the quality of conformance increases. However, in most companies this does not seem to happen until the quality of conformance is very close to 100% and defect rates are very close to zero.

EXHIBIT 2B–2
Effect of Quality Costs on Quality of Conformance

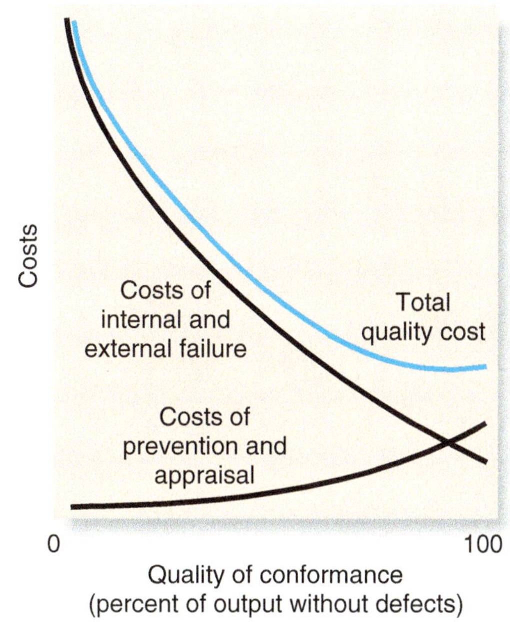

As a company's quality program becomes more refined and as its failure costs begin to fall, prevention activities usually become more effective than appraisal activities. Appraisal can only find defects, whereas prevention can eliminate them. The best way to prevent defects from happening is to design processes that reduce the likelihood of defects and to continually monitor processes using statistical process control methods.

Quality Cost Reports

LEARNING OBJECTIVE 10
Prepare and interpret a quality cost report.

As an initial step in quality improvement programs, companies often construct a *quality cost report* that provides an estimate of the financial consequences of the company's current level of defects. A **quality cost report** details the prevention costs, appraisal costs, and costs of internal and external failures that arise from the company's current quality control efforts. Managers are often shocked by the magnitude of these costs. A typical quality cost report is shown in Exhibit 2B–3.

EXHIBIT 2B–3
Quality Cost Report

Ventura Company
Quality Cost Report
For Years 1 and 2

	Year 1		Year 2	
	Amount	Percent*	Amount	Percent*
Prevention costs:				
Systems development	$ 270,000	0.54%	$ 400,000	0.80%
Quality training	130,000	0.26%	210,000	0.42%
Supervision of prevention activities	40,000	0.08%	70,000	0.14%
Quality improvement projects	210,000	0.42%	320,000	0.64%
Total prevention cost	650,000	1.30%	1,000,000	2.00%
Appraisal costs:				
Inspection	560,000	1.12%	600,000	1.20%
Reliability testing	420,000	0.84%	580,000	1.16%
Supervision of testing and inspection	80,000	0.16%	120,000	0.24%
Depreciation of test equipment	140,000	0.28%	200,000	0.40%
Total appraisal cost	1,200,000	2.40%	1,500,000	3.00%
Internal failure costs:				
Net cost of scrap	750,000	1.50%	900,000	1.80%
Rework labor and overhead	810,000	1.62%	1,430,000	2.86%
Downtime due to defects in quality	100,000	0.20%	170,000	0.34%
Disposal of defective products	340,000	0.68%	500,000	1.00%
Total internal failure cost	2,000,000	4.00%	3,000,000	6.00%
External failure costs:				
Warranty repairs	900,000	1.80%	400,000	0.80%
Warranty replacements	2,300,000	4.60%	870,000	1.74%
Allowances	630,000	1.26%	130,000	0.26%
Cost of field servicing	1,320,000	2.64%	600,000	1.20%
Total external failure cost	5,150,000	10.30%	2,000,000	4.00%
Total quality cost	$9,000,000	18.00%	$7,500,000	15.00%

*As a percentage of total sales. In each year sales totaled $50,000,000.

Several things should be noted from the data in the exhibit. First, Ventura Company's quality costs are poorly distributed in both years, with most of the costs due to either internal failure or external failure. The external failure costs are particularly high in Year 1 in comparison to other costs.

Second, note that the company increased its spending on prevention and appraisal activities in Year 2. As a result, internal failure costs went up in that year (from $2 million in Year 1 to $3 million in Year 2), but external failure costs dropped sharply (from $5.15 million in Year 1 to only $2 million in Year 2). Because of the increase in appraisal activity in Year 2, more defects were caught inside the company before they were shipped to customers. This resulted in more cost for scrap, rework, and so forth, but saved huge amounts in warranty repairs, warranty replacements, and other external failure costs.

Third, note that as a result of greater emphasis on prevention and appraisal, *total* quality cost decreased in Year 2. As continued emphasis is placed on prevention and appraisal in future years, total quality cost should continue to decrease. That is, future increases in prevention and appraisal costs should be more than offset by decreases in failure costs. Moreover, appraisal costs should also decrease as more effort is placed into prevention.

Quality Cost Reports in Graphic Form

As a supplement to the quality cost report shown in Exhibit 2B–3, companies frequently prepare quality cost information in graphic form. Graphic presentations include pie charts, bar graphs, trend lines, and so forth. The data for Ventura Company from Exhibit 2B–3 are presented in bar graph form in Exhibit 2B–4.

The first bar graph in Exhibit 2B–4 is scaled in terms of dollars of quality cost, and the second is scaled in terms of quality cost as a percentage of sales. In both graphs, the data are "stacked" upward. That is, appraisal costs are stacked on top of prevention costs, internal failure costs are stacked on top of the sum of prevention costs plus appraisal costs, and so forth. The percentage figures in the second graph show that total quality cost equals 18% of sales in Year 1 and 15% of sales in Year 2, the same as reported earlier in Exhibit 2B–3.

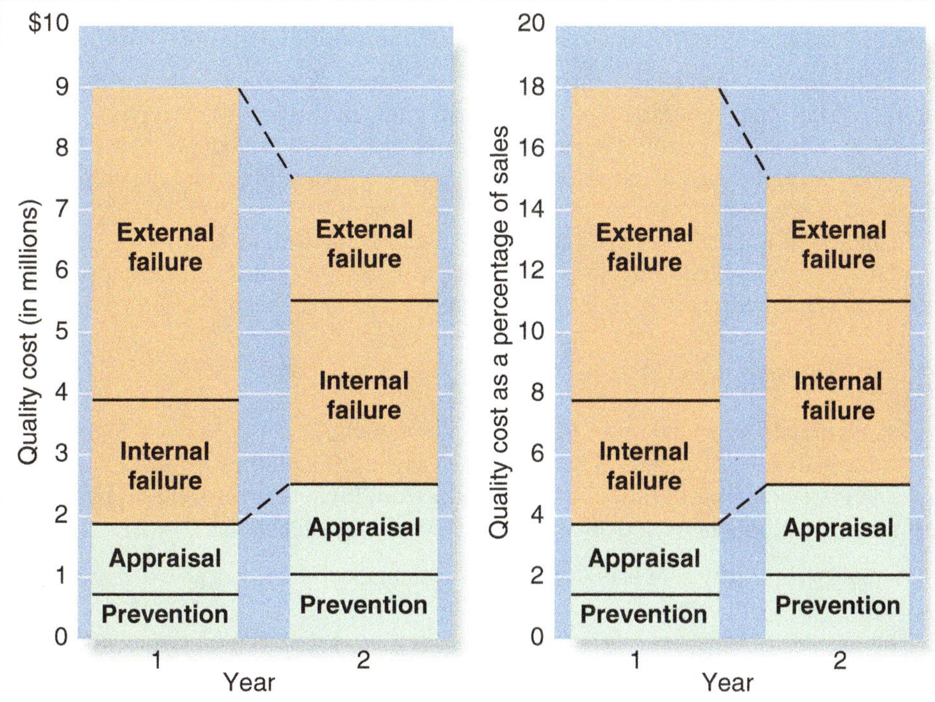

EXHIBIT 2B–4
Quality Cost Reports in Graphic Form

Data in graphic form help managers to see trends more clearly and to see the magnitude of the various costs in relation to each other. Such graphs are easily prepared using computer graphics and spreadsheet applications.

Uses of Quality Cost Information

A quality cost report has several uses. First, quality cost information helps managers see the financial significance of defects. Managers usually are not aware of the magnitude of their quality costs because these costs cut across departmental lines and are not normally tracked and accumulated by the cost system. Thus, when first presented with a quality cost report, managers often are surprised by the amount of cost attributable to poor quality.

Second, quality cost information helps managers identify the relative importance of the quality problems faced by their companies. For example, the quality cost report may show that scrap is a major quality problem or that the company is incurring huge warranty costs. With this information, managers have a better idea of where to focus their efforts.

Third, quality cost information helps managers see whether their quality costs are poorly distributed. In general, quality costs should be distributed more toward prevention and appraisal activities and less toward failures.

Counterbalancing these uses, three limitations of quality cost information should be recognized. First, simply measuring and reporting quality costs does not solve quality problems. Problems can be solved only by taking action. Second, results usually lag behind quality improvement programs. Initially, total quality cost may even increase as quality control systems are designed and installed. Decreases in quality costs may not begin to occur until the quality program has been in effect for some time. And third, the most important quality cost, lost sales arising from customer ill will, is usually omitted from the quality cost report because it is difficult to estimate.

Typically, during the initial years of a quality improvement program, the benefits of compiling a quality cost report outweigh the costs and limitations of the reports. As managers gain experience in balancing prevention and appraisal activities, the need for quality cost reports often diminishes.

International Aspects of Quality

Many of the tools used in quality management today were developed in Japan after World War II. In statistical process control, Japanese companies borrowed heavily from the work of W. Edwards Deming. However, Japanese companies are largely responsible for quality circles, JIT, the idea that quality is everyone's responsibility, and the emphasis on prevention rather than on inspection.

In the 1980s, quality reemerged as a pivotal factor in the market. Many companies now find that it is impossible to effectively compete without a very strong quality program in place. This is particularly true of companies that wish to compete in the European market.

The ISO 9000 Standards

The International Organization for Standardization (ISO), based in Geneva, Switzerland, has established quality control guidelines known as the **ISO 9000 standards.** Many companies and organizations in Europe will buy only from ISO 9000-certified suppliers. This means that the suppliers must demonstrate to a certifying agency that:

1. A quality control system is in use, and the system clearly defines an expected level of quality.
2. The system is fully operational and is backed up with detailed documentation of quality control procedures.
3. The intended level of quality is being achieved on a sustained, consistent basis.

The key to receiving certification under the ISO 9000 standards is documentation. It's one thing for a company to say that it has a quality control system in operation, but it's quite a different thing to be able to document the steps in that system. Under ISO 9000, this documentation must be so detailed and precise that if all the employees in a company were suddenly replaced, the new employees could use the documentation to make the product exactly as it was made by the old employees. Even companies with good quality control systems find that it takes up to two years of painstaking work to develop this detailed documentation. But companies often find that compiling this documentation results in improvements in their quality systems.

The ISO 9000 standards have become an international measure of quality. Although the standards were developed to control the quality of goods sold in European countries, they have become widely accepted elsewhere as well. Companies in the United States that export to Europe often expect their own suppliers to comply with ISO 9000 standards because these exporters must document the quality of the materials going into their products as part of their own ISO 9000 certification.

The ISO program for certification of quality management programs is not limited to manufacturing companies. The American Institute of Certified Public Accountants was the first professional membership organization in the United States to win recognition under an ISO certification program.

Summary (Appendix 2B)

Defects cause costs, which can be classified into prevention costs, appraisal costs, internal failure costs, and external failure costs. Prevention costs are incurred to keep defects from happening. Appraisal costs are incurred to ensure that defective products, once made, are not shipped to customers. Internal failure costs are incurred as a consequence of detecting defective products before they are shipped to customers. External failure costs are the consequences (in terms of repairs, servicing, and lost future business) of delivering defective products to customers. Most experts agree that management effort should be focused on preventing defects. Small investments in prevention can lead to dramatic reductions in appraisal costs and costs of internal and external failure.

Quality costs are summarized on a quality cost report. This report shows the types of quality costs being incurred and their significance and trends. The report helps managers understand the importance of quality costs, spot problem areas, and assess the way in which the quality costs are distributed.

Glossary (Appendix 2B)

Appraisal costs Costs that are incurred to identify defective products before the products are shipped to customers. (p. 74)

External failure costs Costs that are incurred when a product or service that is defective is delivered to a customer. (p. 74)

Internal failure costs Costs that are incurred as a result of identifying defective products before they are shipped to customers. (p. 74)

ISO 9000 standards Quality control requirements issued by the International Organization for Standardization that relate to products sold in European countries. (p. 78)

Prevention costs Costs that are incurred to keep defects from occurring. (p. 73)

Quality circles Small groups of employees that meet on a regular basis to discuss ways of improving quality. (p. 74)

Quality cost Costs that are incurred to prevent defective products from falling into the hands of customers or that are incurred as a result of defective units. (p. 73)

Quality cost report A report that details prevention costs, appraisal costs, and the costs of internal and external failures. (p. 76)

Quality of conformance The degree to which a product or service meets or exceeds its design specifications and is free of defects or other problems that mar its appearance or degrade its performance. (p. 72)

Statistical process control A charting technique used to monitor the quality of work being done in a workstation for the purpose of immediately correcting any problems. (p. 74)

Appendix 2B Exercises and Problems connect ACCOUNTING

All applicable exercises and problems are available with McGraw-Hill's *Connect™ Accounting.*

EXERCISE 2B–1 Using Quality Management Terms [LO9]

Listed below are terms relating to quality management.

Appraisal costs	Quality circles
Quality cost report	Prevention costs
Quality	External failure costs
Internal failure costs	Quality of conformance

Choose the term or terms that most appropriately complete the following statements. The terms can be used more than once. (Note that a blank can hold more than one word.)

1. When a product or service does not conform to customer expectations in terms of features or performance, it is viewed as being poor in ________________.
2. A product or service will have a low ________________ if it does not function the way its designers intended, or if it has many defects as a result of sloppy manufacture.
3. A company incurs ________________ and ________________ in an effort to keep poor quality of conformance from occurring.
4. A company incurs ________________ and ________________ because poor quality of conformance has occurred.
5. Of the four groups of costs associated with quality of conformance, ________________ are generally the most damaging to a company.
6. Inspection, testing, and other costs incurred to keep defective products from being shipped to customers are known as ________________.
7. ________________ are incurred in an effort to eliminate poor product design, defective manufacturing practices, and the providing of substandard service.
8. The costs relating to defects, rejected products, and downtime caused by quality problems are known as ________________.
9. When a product that is defective in some way is delivered to a customer, then ___________ are incurred.
10. Over time, a company's total quality costs should decrease if it redistributes its quality costs by placing its greatest emphasis on ________________ and ________________.
11. In many companies, small groups of employees, known as ________________, meet on a regular basis to discuss ways to improve the quality of output.
12. The way to ensure that management is aware of the costs associated with quality is to summarize such costs on a ________________.

EXERCISE 2B–2 Classification of Quality Costs [LO9]

A number of activities that are part of a company's quality control system are listed below:

a. Repairs of goods still under warranty.
b. Customer returns due to defects.
c. Statistical process control.
d. Disposal of spoiled goods.
e. Maintaining testing equipment.
f. Inspecting finished goods.
g. Downtime caused by quality problems.
h. Debugging errors in software.
i. Recalls of defective products.
j. Training quality engineers.
k. Re-entering data due to typing errors.
l. Inspecting materials received from suppliers.
m. Audits of the quality system.
n. Supervision of testing personnel.
o. Rework labor.

Required:

1. Classify the costs associated with each of these activities into one of the following categories: prevention cost, appraisal cost, internal failure cost, or external failure cost.

2. Which of the four types of costs listed in (1) above are incurred to keep poor quality of conformance from occurring? Which of the four types of costs are incurred because poor quality of conformance has occurred?

PROBLEM 2B–3 Quality Cost Report [LO9, LO10]

Yedder Enterprises was a pioneer in designing and producing precision surgical lasers. Yedder's product was brilliantly designed, but the manufacturing process was neglected by management with a consequence that quality problems have been chronic. When customers complained about defective units, Yedder would simply send out a repairperson or replace the defective unit with a new one. Recently, several competitors came out with similar products without Yedder's quality problems, and as a consequence Yedder's sales have declined.

To rescue the situation, Yedder embarked on an intensive campaign to strengthen its quality control at the beginning of the current year. These efforts met with some success—the downward slide in sales was reversed, and sales grew from $95 million last year to $100 million this year. To help monitor the company's progress, costs relating to quality and quality control were compiled for last year and for the first full year of the quality campaign this year. The costs, which do not include the lost sales due to a reputation for poor quality, appear below:

	Costs (in thousands)	
	Last Year	This Year
Product recalls	$3,500	$600
Systems development	$120	$680
Inspection	$1,700	$2,770
Net cost of scrap	$800	$1,300
Supplies used in testing	$30	$40
Warranty repairs	$3,300	$2,800
Rework labor	$1,400	$1,600
Statistical process control	$0	$270
Customer returns of defective goods	$3,200	$200
Cost of testing equipment	$270	$390
Quality engineering	$1,080	$1,650
Downtime due to quality problems	$600	$1,100

Required:

1. Prepare a quality cost report for both this year and last year. Carry percentage computations to two decimal places.
2. Prepare a bar graph showing the distribution of the various quality costs by category.
3. Prepare a written evaluation to accompany the reports you have prepared in (1) and (2) above. This evaluation should discuss the distribution of quality costs in the company, changes in the distribution over the last year, and any other information you believe would be useful to management.

PROBLEM 2B–4 Analyzing a Quality Cost Report [LO10]

Bergen, Inc., produces telephone equipment at its Georgia plant. In recent years, the company's market share has been eroded by stiff competition from Asian and European competitors. Price and product quality are the two key areas in which companies compete in this market.

Two years ago, Jerry Holman, Bergen's president, decided to devote more resources to improving product quality after learning that his company's products had been ranked fourth in quality in a survey of telephone equipment users. He believed that Bergen could no longer afford to ignore the importance of product quality. Holman set up a task force that he headed to implement a formal quality improvement program. Included on this task force were representatives from engineering, sales, customer service, production, and accounting. This broad representation was needed because Holman believed that this was a companywide program, and that all employees should share the responsibility for its success.

After the first meeting of the task force, Sheila Haynes, manager of sales, asked Tony Reese, production manager, what he thought of the proposed program. Reese replied, "I have reservations. Quality is too abstract to be attaching costs to it and then to be holding you and me responsible for cost improvements. I like to work with goals that I can see and count! I'm nervous about having my annual bonus based on a decrease in quality costs; there are too many variables that we have no control over."

Bergen's quality improvement program has now been in operation for two years. The company's most recent quality cost report is shown below.

Bergen, Inc. Quality Cost Report (in thousands)	Year 1	Year 2
Prevention costs:		
Machine maintenance	$ 215	$ 160
Training suppliers	5	15
Design reviews	20	95
Total prevention cost	240	270
Appraisal costs:		
Incoming inspection	45	22
Final testing	160	94
Total appraisal cost	205	116
Internal failure costs:		
Rework	120	62
Scrap	68	40
Total internal failure cost	188	102
External failure costs:		
Warranty repairs	69	23
Customer returns	262	80
Total external failure cost	331	103
Total quality cost	$ 964	$ 591
Total production cost	$4,120	$4,510

As they were reviewing the report, Haynes asked Reese what he now thought of the quality improvement program. "The work is really moving through the production department," Reese replied. "We used to spend time helping the customer service department solve their problems, but they are leaving us alone these days. I have no complaints so far, and I'm relieved to see that the new quality improvement hasn't adversely affected our bonuses. I'm anxious to see if it increases our bonuses in the future."

Required:

1. By analyzing the company's quality cost report, determine if Bergen, Inc.'s quality improvement program has been successful. *List specific evidence to support your answer.* Show percentage figures in two ways: first, as a percentage of total production cost; and second, as a percentage of total quality cost. Carry all computations to one decimal place.
2. Discuss why Tony Reese's current reaction to the quality improvement program is more favorable than his initial reaction.
3. Jerry Holman believed that the quality improvement program was essential and that Bergen, Inc., could no longer afford to ignore the importance of product quality. Discuss how Bergen, Inc., could measure the opportunity cost of not implementing the quality improvement program.

(CMA, adapted)

Chapter 3

Job-Order Costing

Two Former College Students Succeeding as Entrepreneurs

BUSINESS FOCUS

When the University of Dayton athletic department needed 2,000 customized T-shirts to give away at its first home basketball game of the year, it chose University Tees to provide the shirts. A larger competitor could have been chosen, but University Tees won the order because of its fast customer response time, low price, and high quality.

University Tees is a small business that was started in February 2003 by two Miami University seniors—Joe Haddad and Nick Dadas (see the company's website at www.universitytees.com). The company creates the artwork for customized T-shirts and then relies on carefully chosen suppliers to manufacture the product.

Accurately calculating the cost of each potential customer order is critically important to University Tees because the company needs to be sure that the price exceeds the cost associated with satisfying the order. The costs include the cost of the T-shirts themselves, printing costs (which vary depending on the quantity of shirts produced and the number of colors printed per shirt), silk screen costs (which also vary depending on the number of colors included in a design), shipping costs, and the artwork needed to create a design. The company also takes into account its competitors' pricing strategies when developing its own prices. ■

Source: Conversation with Joe Haddad, cofounder of University Tees.

LEARNING OBJECTIVES

After studying Chapter 3, you should be able to:

LO1 Compute a predetermined overhead rate.

LO2 Apply overhead cost to jobs using a predetermined overhead rate.

LO3 Compute the total cost and average cost per unit of a job.

LO4 Understand the flow of costs in a job-order costing system and prepare appropriate journal entries to record costs.

LO5 Use T-accounts to show the flow of costs in a job-order costing system.

LO6 Prepare schedules of cost of goods manufactured and cost of goods sold and an income statement.

LO7 Compute underapplied or overapplied overhead cost and prepare the journal entry to close the balance in Manufacturing Overhead to the appropriate accounts.

LO8 (Appendix 3A) Understand the implications of basing the predetermined overhead rate on activity at capacity rather than on estimated activity for the period.

LO9 (Appendix 3B) Properly account for labor costs associated with idle time, overtime, and fringe benefits.

Understanding how products and services are costed is vital to managers because the way in which these costs are determined can have a substantial impact on reported profits, as well as on key management decisions.

A managerial costing system should provide cost data to help managers plan, control, and make decisions. Nevertheless, external financial reporting and tax reporting requirements often heavily influence how costs are accumulated and summarized on managerial reports. This is true of product costing. In this chapter we use *absorption costing* to determine product costs. In **absorption costing,** all manufacturing costs, both fixed and variable, are assigned to units of product—units are said to *fully absorb manufacturing costs.* In later chapters we look at alternatives to absorption costing such as variable costing and activity-based costing.

Most countries—including the United States—require some form of absorption costing for both external financial reports and for tax reports. In addition, the vast majority of companies throughout the world also use absorption costing in their management reports. Because absorption costing is the most common approach to product costing throughout the world, we discuss it first and then discuss the alternatives in subsequent chapters.

Job-Order Costing—An Overview

Under absorption costing, product costs include all manufacturing costs. Some manufacturing costs, such as direct materials, can be directly traced to particular products. For example, the cost of the airbags installed in a Toyota Camry can be easily traced to that particular auto. But what about manufacturing costs like factory rent? Such costs do not change from month to month, whereas the number and variety of products made in the factory may vary dramatically from one month to the next. Because these costs remain unchanged from month to month regardless of what products are made, they are clearly not caused by—and cannot be directly traced to—any particular product. Therefore, these types of costs are assigned to products and services by averaging across time and across products. The type of production process influences how this averaging is done.

Job-order costing is used in situations where many *different* products are produced each period. For example, a Levi Strauss clothing factory would typically make many different types of jeans for both men and women during a month. A particular order might consist of 1,000 boot-cut men's blue denim jeans, style number A312. This order of 1,000 jeans is called a *job.* In a job-order costing system, costs are traced and allocated to jobs and then the costs of the job are divided by the number of units in the job to arrive at an average cost per unit.

Other examples of situations where job-order costing would be used include large-scale construction projects managed by Bechtel International, commercial aircraft produced by Boeing, greeting cards designed and printed by Hallmark, and airline meals prepared by LSG SkyChefs. All of these examples are characterized by diverse outputs. Each Bechtel project is unique and different from every other—the company may be simultaneously constructing a dam in Zaire and a bridge in Indonesia. Likewise, each airline orders a different type of meal from LSG SkyChefs' catering service.

Job-order costing is also used extensively in service industries. For example, hospitals, law firms, movie studios, accounting firms, advertising agencies, and repair shops all use a variation of job-order costing to accumulate costs. Although the detailed example of job-order costing provided in the following section deals with a manufacturing company, the same basic concepts and procedures are used by many service organizations.

IN BUSINESS

IS THIS REALLY A JOB?

VBT Bicycling Vacations of Bristol, Vermont, offers deluxe bicycling vacations in the United States, Canada, Europe, and other locations throughout the world. For example, the company offers a 10-day tour of the Puglia region of Italy—the "heel of the boot." The tour price includes international airfare, 10 nights of lodging, most meals, use of a bicycle, and ground transportation as needed. Each tour is led by at least two local tour leaders, one of whom rides with the guests along the tour route. The other tour leader drives a "sag wagon" that carries extra water, snacks, and bicycle repair equipment and is available for a shuttle back to the hotel or up a hill. The sag wagon also transports guests' luggage from one hotel to another.

Each specific tour can be considered a job. For example, Giuliano Astore and Debora Trippetti, two natives of Puglia, led a VBT tour with 17 guests over 10 days in late April. At the end of the tour, Giuliano submitted a report, a sort of job cost sheet, to VBT headquarters. This report detailed the on the ground expenses incurred for this specific tour, including fuel and operating costs for the van, lodging costs for the guests, the costs of meals provided to guests, the costs of snacks, the cost of hiring additional ground transportation as needed, and the wages of the tour leaders. In addition to these costs, some costs are paid directly by VBT in Vermont to vendors. The total cost incurred for the tour is then compared to the total revenue collected from guests to determine the gross profit for the tour.

Sources: Giuliano Astore and Gregg Marston, President, VBT Bicycling Vacations. For more information about VBT, see www.vbt.com.

Job-Order Costing—An Example

To introduce job-order costing, we will follow a specific job as it progresses through the manufacturing process. This job consists of two experimental couplings that Yost Precision Machining has agreed to produce for Loops Unlimited, a manufacturer of roller coasters. Couplings connect the cars on the roller coaster and are a critical component in the performance and safety of the ride. Before we begin our discussion, recall from the previous chapter that companies generally classify manufacturing costs into three broad categories: (1) direct materials, (2) direct labor, and (3) manufacturing overhead. As we study the operation of a job-order costing system, we will see how each of these three types of costs is recorded and accumulated.

MANAGERIAL ACCOUNTING IN ACTION
The Issue

Yost Precision Machining is a small company in Michigan that specializes in fabricating precision metal parts that are used in a variety of applications ranging from deep-sea exploration vehicles to the inertial triggers in automobile air bags. The company's top managers gather every morning at 8:00 A.M. in the company's conference room for the daily planning meeting. Attending the meeting this morning are: Jean Yost, the company's president; David Cheung, the marketing manager; Debbie Turner, the production manager; and Marc White, the company controller. The president opened the meeting:

YOST Precision Machining

Jean: The production schedule indicates we'll be starting Job 2B47 today. Isn't that the special order for experimental couplings, David?

David: That's right. That's the order from Loops Unlimited for two couplings for their new roller coaster ride for Magic Mountain.

Debbie: Why only two couplings? Don't they need a coupling for every car?

David: Yes. But this is a completely new roller coaster. The cars will go faster and will be subjected to more twists, turns, drops, and loops than on any other existing roller coaster. To hold up under these stresses, Loops Unlimited's engineers completely redesigned the cars and couplings. They want us to make just two of these new couplings for testing purposes. If the design works, then we'll have the inside track on the order to supply couplings for the whole ride.

EXHIBIT 3–1
Materials Requisition Form

Materials Requistion Number	14873	Date	March 2
Job Number to Be Charged	2B47		
Department	Milling		

Description	Quantity	Unit Cost	Total Cost
M46 Housing	2	$124	$248
G7 Connector	4	$103	412
			$660

Jean: We agreed to take on this initial order at our cost just to get our foot in the door. Marc, will there be any problem documenting our cost so we can get paid?

Marc: No problem. The contract with Loops stipulates that they will pay us an amount equal to our cost of goods sold. With our job-order costing system, I can tell you the cost on the day the job is completed.

Jean: Good. Is there anything else we should discuss about this job at this time? No? Well then let's move on to the next item of business.

Measuring Direct Materials Cost

The blueprints submitted by Loops Unlimited indicate that each experimental coupling will require three parts that are classified as direct materials: two G7 Connectors and one M46 Housing. Each coupling requires two connectors and one housing, so to make two couplings, four connectors and two housings are required. This is a custom product that is being made for the first time, but if this were one of the company's standard products, it would have an established *bill of materials.* A **bill of materials** is a document that lists the type and quantity of each type of direct material needed to complete a unit of product.

When an agreement has been reached with the customer concerning the quantities, prices, and shipment date for the order, a *production order* is issued. The Production Department then prepares a *materials requisition form* similar to the form in Exhibit 3–1. The **materials requisition form** is a document that specifies the type and quantity of materials to be drawn from the storeroom and identifies the job that will be charged for the cost of the materials. The form is used to control the flow of materials into production and also for making entries in the accounting records.

The Yost Precision Machining materials requisition form in Exhibit 3–1 shows that the company's Milling Department has requisitioned two M46 Housings and four G7 Connectors for the Loops Unlimited job, which has been designated as Job 2B47.

Job Cost Sheet

After a production order has been issued, the Accounting Department's job-order costing software system automatically generates a *job cost sheet* like the one presented in Exhibit 3–2. A **job cost sheet** records the materials, labor, and manufacturing overhead costs charged to that job.

EXHIBIT 3–2
Job Cost Sheet

JOB COST SHEET

Job Number	2B47	Date Initiated	March 2
Department	Milling	Date Completed	
Item	Special order coupling	Units Completed	
For Stock			

Direct Materials		Direct Labor			Manufacturing Overhead		
Req. No.	Amount	Ticket	Hours	Amount	Hours	Rate	Amount
14873	$660	843	5	$45			

Cost Summary		Units Shipped		
Direct Materials	$	Date	Number	Balance
Direct Labor	$			
Manufacturing Overhead	$			
Total Cost	$			
Unit Product Cost	$			

After direct materials are issued, the cost of these materials are automatically recorded on the job cost sheet. Note from Exhibit 3–2, for example, that the $660 cost for direct materials shown earlier on the materials requisition form has been charged to Job 2B47 on its job cost sheet. The requisition number 14873 from the materials requisition form appears on the job cost sheet to make it easier to identify the source document for the direct materials charge.

Measuring Direct Labor Cost

Direct labor consists of labor charges that are easily traced to a particular job. Labor charges that cannot be easily traced directly to any job are treated as part of manufacturing overhead. As discussed in the previous chapter, this latter category of labor costs is called *indirect labor* and includes tasks such as maintenance, supervision, and cleanup.

Today many companies rely on computerized systems (rather than paper and pencil) to maintain employee *time tickets.* A completed **time ticket** is an hour-by-hour summary of the employee's activities throughout the day. One computerized approach to creating time tickets uses bar codes to capture data. Each employee and each job has a unique bar code. When beginning work on a job, the employee scans three bar codes using a handheld device much like the bar code readers at grocery store checkout stands. The first bar code indicates that a job is being started; the second is the unique bar code on the employee's identity badge; and the third is the unique bar code of the job itself. This information is fed automatically via an electronic network to a computer that notes the time and records all of the data. When the task is completed, the employee scans a bar code indicating the task is complete, the bar code on his or her identity badge, and the bar code attached to the job. This information is relayed to the computer that again notes the

EXHIBIT 3–3
Employee Time Ticket

Time Ticket No.	843	Date	March 3
Employee	Mary Holden	Station	4

Started	Ended	Time Completed	Rate	Amount	Job Number
7:00	12:00	5.0	$9	$45	2B47
12:30	2:30	2.0	9	18	2B50
2:30	3:30	1.0	9	9	Maintenance
Totals		8.0		$72	

time, and a time ticket, such as the one shown in Exhibit 3–3, is automatically prepared. Because all of the source data is already in computer files, the labor costs can be automatically posted to job cost sheets. For example, Exhibit 3–3 shows $45 of direct labor cost related to Job 2B47. This amount is automatically posted to the job cost sheet shown in Exhibit 3–2. The time ticket in Exhibit 3–3 also shows $9 of indirect labor costs related to performing maintenance. This cost is treated as part of manufacturing overhead and does not get posted on a job cost sheet.

IN BUSINESS

BUCKING THE TREND: USING PEOPLE INSTEAD OF MACHINES

For decades, overhead costs have been going up and labor costs have been going down as companies have replaced people with machines. However, at the French automaker Renault, the exact opposite has been happening with its no-frills vehicle called the Logan. The Logan was intentionally stripped of costly elements and unnecessary technology so that the car could be sold for $6,000 in emerging Eastern European markets. The car's simplified design enables Renault's manufacturing plant in Romania to assemble the car almost entirely with people instead of robots. The monthly pay for a line worker at Renault's Romanian plant is $324 versus an average of more than $4,700 per worker in Western European countries. Thanks in part to low-cost labor, Logan's production costs are estimated to be just $1,089 per unit.

The Logan is finding buyers not only in emerging markets but also in more advanced Western European nations where customers have been clamoring for the car. Renault expects sales for the Logan to climb to one million vehicles—adding $341 million to its profits.

Source: Gail Edmondson and Constance Faivre d'Arcier, "Got 5,000 Euros? Need a New Car?" *BusinessWeek*, July 4, 2005, p. 49.

LEARNING OBJECTIVE 1
Compute a predetermined overhead rate.

Computing Predetermined Overhead Rates

Recall that product costs include manufacturing overhead as well as direct materials and direct labor. Therefore, manufacturing overhead also needs to be recorded on the job cost sheet. However, assigning manufacturing overhead to a specific job involves some difficulties. There are three reasons for this:

1. Manufacturing overhead is an *indirect cost.* This means that it is either impossible or difficult to trace these costs to a particular product or job.

2. Manufacturing overhead consists of many different items ranging from the grease used in machines to the annual salary of the production manager.
3. Because of the fixed costs in manufacturing overhead, total manufacturing overhead costs tend to remain relatively constant from one period to the next even though the number of units produced can fluctuate widely. Consequently, the average cost per unit will vary from one period to the next.

Given these problems, allocation is used to assign overhead costs to products. Allocation is accomplished by selecting an *allocation base* that is common to all of the company's products and services. An **allocation base** is a measure such as direct labor-hours (DLH) or machine-hours (MH) that is used to assign overhead costs to products and services. The most widely used allocation bases in manufacturing are direct labor-hours, direct labor cost, machine-hours and (where a company has only a single product) units of product.

Manufacturing overhead is commonly assigned to products using *a predetermined overhead rate.* The **predetermined overhead rate** is computed by dividing the total estimated manufacturing overhead cost for the period by the estimated total amount of the allocation base as follows:

$$\text{Predetermined overhead rate} = \frac{\text{Estimated total manufacturing overhead cost}}{\text{Estimated total amount of the allocation base}}$$

The predetermined overhead rate is computed before the period begins using a four-step process. The first step is to estimate the total amount of the allocation base (the denominator) that will be required for next period's estimated level of production. The second step is to estimate the total fixed manufacturing overhead cost for the coming period and the variable manufacturing overhead cost per unit of the allocation base. The third step is to use the cost formula shown below to estimate the total manufacturing overhead cost (the numerator) for the coming period:

$$Y = a + bX$$

Where,

Y = The estimated total manufacturing overhead cost
a = The estimated total fixed manufacturing overhead cost
b = The estimated variable manufacturing overhead cost per unit of the allocation base
X = The estimated total amount of the allocation base

The fourth step is to compute the predetermined overhead rate. Notice, the estimated amount of the allocation base is determined before estimating the total manufacturing overhead cost. This needs to be done because total manufacturing overhead cost includes variable overhead costs that depend on the amount of the allocation base.

Applying Manufacturing Overhead

LEARNING OBJECTIVE 2
Apply overhead cost to jobs using a predetermined overhead rate.

To repeat, the predetermined overhead rate is computed *before* the period begins. The predetermined overhead rate is then used to apply overhead cost to jobs throughout the period. The process of assigning overhead cost to jobs is called **overhead application.** The formula for determining the amount of overhead cost to apply to a particular job is:

$$\begin{array}{c}\text{Overhead applied to}\\\text{a particular job}\end{array} = \begin{array}{c}\text{Predetermined}\\\text{overhead rate}\end{array} \times \begin{array}{c}\text{Amount of the allocation}\\\text{base incurred by the job}\end{array}$$

For example, if the predetermined overhead rate is $8 per direct labor-hour, then $8 of overhead cost is *applied* to a job for each direct labor-hour incurred on the job. When the allocation base is direct labor-hours, the formula becomes:

$$\begin{array}{c}\text{Overhead applied to}\\\text{a particular job}\end{array} = \begin{array}{c}\text{Predetermined}\\\text{overhead rate}\end{array} \times \begin{array}{c}\text{Actual direct labor-hours}\\\text{charged to the job}\end{array}$$

Manufacturing Overhead—A Closer Look

To illustrate the steps involved in computing and using a predetermined overhead rate, let's return to Yost Precision Machining and make the following assumptions. In step one, the company estimated that 40,000 direct labor-hours would be required to support the production planned for the year. In step two, it estimated \$220,000 of total fixed manufacturing overhead cost for the coming year and \$2.50 of variable manufacturing overhead cost per direct labor-hour. Given these assumptions, in step three the company used the cost formula shown below to estimate its total manufacturing overhead cost for the year:

$$Y = a + bX$$

$$Y = \$220{,}000 + (\$2.50 \text{ per direct labor-hour} \times 40{,}000 \text{ direct labor-hours})$$

$$Y = \$220{,}000 + \$100{,}000$$

$$Y = \$320{,}000$$

In step four, Yost Precision Machining computed its predetermined overhead rate for the year of \$8 per direct labor-hour as shown below:

$$\text{Predetermined overhead rate} = \frac{\text{Estimated total manufacturing overhead cost}}{\text{Estimated total amount of the allocation base}}$$

$$= \frac{\$320{,}000}{40{,}000 \text{ direct labor-hours}}$$

$$= \$8 \text{ per direct labor-hour}$$

The job cost sheet in Exhibit 3–4 indicates that 27 direct labor-hours (i.e., DLHs) were charged to Job 2B47. Therefore, a total of \$216 of manufacturing overhead cost would be applied to the job:

$$\begin{array}{c}\text{Overhead applied to} \\ \text{Job 2B47}\end{array} = \begin{array}{c}\text{Predetermined} \\ \text{overhead rate}\end{array} \times \begin{array}{c}\text{Actual direct labor-hours} \\ \text{charged to Job 2B47}\end{array}$$

$$= \$8 \text{ per DLH} \times 27 \text{ DLHs}$$

$$= \$216 \text{ of overhead applied to Job 2B47}$$

This amount of overhead has been entered on the job cost sheet in Exhibit 3–4. Note that this is *not* the actual amount of overhead caused by the job. Actual overhead costs are *not* assigned to jobs—if that could be done, the costs would be direct costs, not overhead. The overhead assigned to the job is simply a share of the total overhead that was estimated at the beginning of the year. A **normal cost system,** which we have been describing, applies overhead to jobs by multiplying a predetermined overhead rate by the actual amount of the allocation base incurred by the jobs.

The Need for a Predetermined Rate

Instead of using a predetermined rate based on estimates, why not base the overhead rate on the *actual* total manufacturing overhead cost and the *actual* total amount of the allocation base incurred on a monthly, quarterly, or annual basis? If an actual rate is computed monthly or quarterly, seasonal factors in overhead costs or in the allocation base can produce fluctuations in the overhead rate. For example, the costs of heating and cooling a factory in Illinois will be highest in the winter and summer months and lowest in the spring and fall. If the overhead rate is recomputed at the end of each month or each quarter based on actual costs and activity, the overhead rate would go up in the winter and summer and down in the spring and fall. As a result, two identical jobs, one completed in the winter and one completed in the spring, would be assigned different manufacturing overhead costs. Many managers believe that such fluctuations in product costs serve

EXHIBIT 3–4
A Completed Job Cost Sheet

JOB COST SHEET

Job Number	2B47	Date Initiated	March 2
Department	Milling	Date Completed	March 8
Item	Special order coupling		
For Stock		Units Completed	2

Direct Materials		Direct Labor			Manufacturing Overhead		
Req. No.	Amount	Ticket	Hours	Amount	Hours	Rate	Amount
14873	$ 660	843	5	$ 45	27	$8/DLH	$216
14875	506	846	8	60			
14912	238	850	4	21			
	$1,404	851	10	54			
			27	$180			

Cost Summary		Units Shipped		
		Date	Number	Balance
Direct Materials	$ 1,404	March 8	—	2
Direct Labor	$ 180			
Manufacturing Overhead	$ 216			
Total Product Cost	$ 1,800			
Unit Product Cost	$ 900*			

*$1,800 ÷ 2 units = $900 per unit.

no useful purpose. To avoid such fluctuations, actual overhead rates could be computed on an annual or less-frequent basis. However, if the overhead rate is computed annually based on the actual costs and activity for the year, the manufacturing overhead assigned to any particular job would not be known until the end of the year. For example, the cost of Job 2B47 at Yost Precision Machining would not be known until the end of the year, even though the job will be completed and shipped to the customer in March. For these reasons, most companies use predetermined overhead rates rather than actual overhead rates in their cost accounting systems.

Choice of an Allocation Base for Overhead Cost

Ideally, the allocation base in the predetermined overhead rate should *drive* the overhead cost. A **cost driver** is a factor, such as machine-hours, beds occupied, computer time, or flight-hours, that causes overhead costs. If the base in the predetermined overhead rate does not "drive" overhead costs, product costs will be distorted. For example, if direct labor-hours is used to allocate overhead, but in reality overhead has little to do with direct labor-hours, then products with high direct labor-hour requirements will be overcosted.

Most companies use direct labor-hours or direct labor cost as the allocation base for manufacturing overhead. In the past, direct labor accounted for up to 60% of the cost of many products, with overhead cost making up only a portion of the remainder. This situation has changed for two reasons. First, sophisticated automated equipment has taken over functions that used to be performed by direct labor workers. Because the costs of acquiring and maintaining such equipment are classified as overhead, this increases overhead while decreasing direct labor. Second, products are becoming more sophisticated and complex and are changed more frequently. This increases the need for highly skilled indirect workers such as engineers. As a result of these two trends, direct labor has decreased relative to overhead as a component of product costs.

In companies where direct labor and overhead costs have been moving in opposite directions, it would be difficult to argue that direct labor "drives" overhead costs. Accordingly, managers in some companies use *activity-based costing* principles to redesign their cost accounting systems. Activity-based costing is designed to more accurately reflect the demands that products, customers, and other cost objects make on overhead resources. The activity-based approach is discussed in more detail in Chapter 7.

Although direct labor may not be an appropriate allocation base in some industries, in others it continues to be a significant driver of manufacturing overhead. Indeed, most manufacturing companies in the United States continue to use direct labor as the primary or secondary allocation base for manufacturing overhead. The key point is that the allocation base used by the company should really drive, or cause, overhead costs, and direct labor is not always the most appropriate allocation base.

IN BUSINESS

REDUCING HEALTH-DAMAGING BEHAVIORS

Cianbro is an industrial construction company headquartered in Pittsfield, Maine, whose goal is "To be the healthiest company in America." It introduced a corporate wellness program to attack employee behaviors that drive up health-care costs. The table below summarizes the number of employees in five health risk categories as of 2003 and 2005. The decreases in the number of employees in these high-risk categories are evidence that the wellness program was effective in helping employees make positive lifestyle changes. This should result in reduced health-care costs for the company.

	Number of Employees		
Health Risk Category	January 2003	March 2005	Decrease
Obesity	432	353	79
High cholesterol	637	515	122
Tobacco use	384	274	110
Inactivity	354	254	100
High blood pressure	139	91	48

Source: Cianbro, WELCOA's *Absolute Advantage* Magazine, 2006.

LEARNING OBJECTIVE 3
Compute the total cost and average cost per unit of a job.

Computation of Unit Costs

With the application of Yost Precision Machining's $216 of manufacturing overhead to the job cost sheet in Exhibit 3–4, the job cost sheet is complete except for two final steps. First, the totals for direct materials, direct labor, and manufacturing overhead are transferred to the Cost Summary section of the job cost sheet and added together to obtain the total cost for the job.[1] Then the total product cost ($1,800) is divided by the number of units (2) to obtain the unit product cost ($900). This unit product cost information is used for valuing unsold units in ending inventory and for determining cost of goods sold. As indicated earlier, *this unit product cost is an average cost and should not be interpreted as the cost that would actually be incurred if another unit were produced.* The incremental cost of an additional unit is something less than the average unit cost of $900 because much of the actual overhead costs would not change if another unit were produced.

[1] Notice, we are assuming that Job 2B47 required direct materials and direct labor beyond the charges shown in Exhibits 3–1 and 3–3.

In the 8:00 A.M. daily planning meeting on March 9, Jean Yost, the president of Yost Precision Machining, once again drew attention to Job 2B47, the experimental couplings:

Jean: I see Job 2B47 is completed. Let's get those couplings shipped immediately to Loops Unlimited so they can get their testing program under way. Marc, how much are we going to bill Loops for those two units?

Marc: Because we agreed to sell the experimental couplings at cost, we will be charging Loops Unlimited just $900 a unit.

Jean: Fine. Let's hope the couplings work out and we make some money on the big order later.

MANAGERIAL ACCOUNTING IN ACTION

The Wrap-up

YOST Precision Machining

IN BUSINESS

ONE-OF-A-KIND MASTERPIECE

In a true job-order costing environment, every job is unique. For example, Purdey manufactures 80–90 shotguns per year with each gun being a specially commissioned one-of-a-kind masterpiece. The prices start at $110,000 because every detail is custom built, engraved, assembled, and polished by a skilled craftsman. The hand engraving can take months to complete and may add as much as $100,000 to the price. The guns are designed to shoot perfectly straight and their value increases over time even with heavy use. One Purdey gun collector said "when I shoot my Purdeys I feel like an orchestra conductor waving my baton."

Source: Eric Arnold, "Aim High," *Forbes*, December 28, 2009, p. 86.

Job-Order Costing—The Flow of Costs

LEARNING OBJECTIVE 4
Understand the flow of costs in a job-order costing system and prepare appropriate journal entries to record costs.

We are now ready to discuss the flow of costs through a job-order costing system. Exhibit 3–5 provides a conceptual overview of these cost flows. It highlights the fact that *product costs* flow through inventories on the balance sheet and then on to cost of goods sold in the income statement. More specifically, raw materials purchases are recorded in the *Raw Materials* inventory account. **Raw materials** include any materials that go into the final product. When raw materials are used in production, their costs are transferred to the *Work in Process* inventory account as direct materials.[2] **Work in process** consists of units of product that are only partially complete and will require further work before they are ready for sale to the customer. Notice that direct labor costs are added directly to Work in Process—they do not flow through Raw Materials inventory. Manufacturing overhead costs are applied to Work in Process by multiplying the predetermined overhead rate by the actual quantity of the allocation base consumed by each job.[3] When goods are completed, their costs are transferred from Work in Process to *Finished Goods.* **Finished goods** consist of completed units of product that have not yet been sold to customers. The amount transferred from Work in Process to Finished Goods is referred to as the *cost of goods manufactured.* The **cost of goods manufactured** includes the manufacturing costs associated with the goods that were finished during the period. As goods are sold, their costs are transferred from Finished Goods to Cost of Goods Sold. At this point, the various costs required to make the product are finally recorded as an expense. Until that point, these costs are in inventory accounts on the balance sheet. Period costs (or selling and administrative expenses) do not flow through inventories on the balance sheet. They are recorded as expenses on the income statement in the period incurred.

[2] Indirect material costs are accounted for as part of manufacturing overhead.

[3] For simplicity, Exhibit 3–5 assumes that Cost of Goods Sold does not need to be adjusted as discussed later in the chapter.

EXHIBIT 3–5
Cost Flows and Classifications in a Manufacturing Company

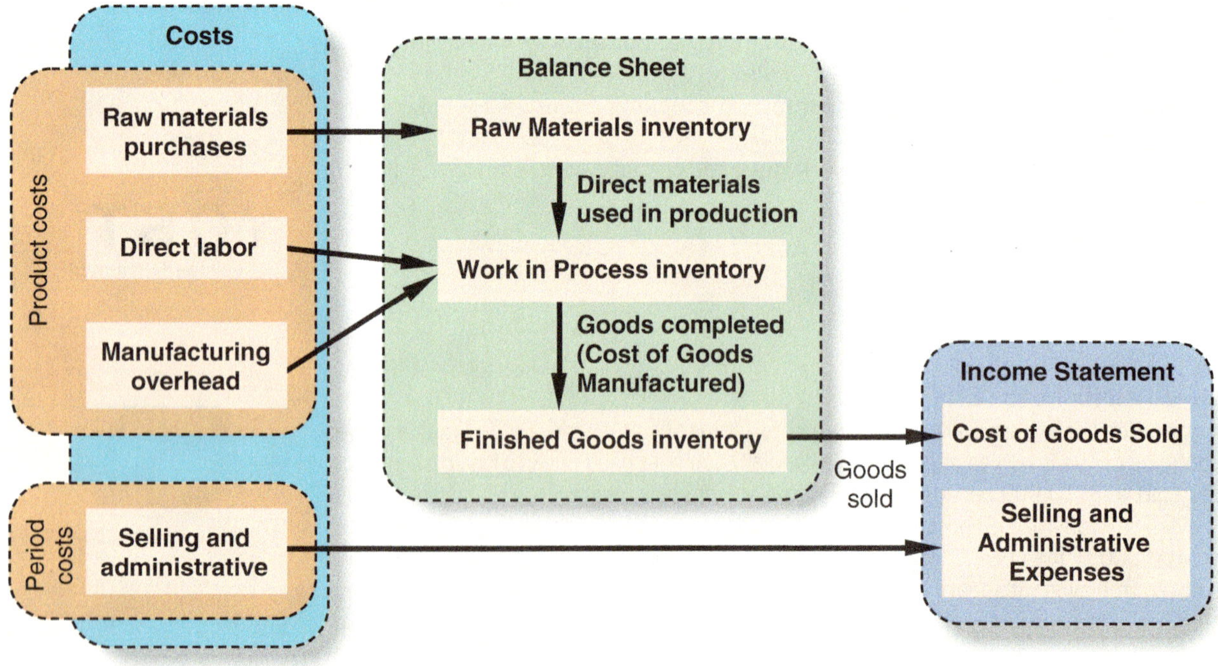

To illustrate the cost flows through a company's general ledger, we will consider a single month's activity at Ruger Corporation, a producer of gold and silver commemorative medallions. Ruger Corporation has two jobs in process during April, the first month of its fiscal year. Job A, a special minting of 1,000 gold medallions commemorating the invention of motion pictures, was started during March. By the end of March, $30,000 in manufacturing costs had been recorded for the job. Job B, an order for 10,000 silver medallions commemorating the fall of the Berlin Wall, was started in April.

The Purchase and Issue of Materials

On April 1, Ruger Corporation had $7,000 in raw materials on hand. During the month, the company purchased on account an additional $60,000 in raw materials. The purchase is recorded in journal entry (1) below:

(1)

Raw Materials	60,000	
Accounts Payable		60,000

As explained in the previous chapter, Raw Materials is an asset account. Thus, when raw materials are purchased, they are initially recorded as an asset—not as an expense.

Issue of Direct and Indirect Materials

During April, $52,000 in raw materials were requisitioned from the storeroom for use in production. These raw materials included $50,000 of direct and $2,000 of indirect materials. Entry (2) records issuing the materials to the production departments.

(2)

Work in Process	50,000	
Manufacturing Overhead	2,000	
Raw Materials		52,000

The materials charged to Work in Process represent direct materials for specific jobs. These costs are also recorded on the appropriate job cost sheets. This point is illustrated in Exhibit 3–6, where $28,000 of the $50,000 in direct materials is charged to Job A's cost sheet and the remaining $22,000 is charged to Job B's cost sheet. (In this example, all data are presented in summary form and the job cost sheet is abbreviated.)

The $2,000 charged to Manufacturing Overhead in entry (2) represents indirect materials. Observe that the Manufacturing Overhead account is separate from the Work in Process account. The purpose of the Manufacturing Overhead account is to accumulate all manufacturing overhead costs as they are incurred during a period.

Before leaving Exhibit 3–6, we need to point out one additional thing. Notice from the exhibit that the job cost sheet for Job A contains a beginning balance of $30,000. We stated earlier that this balance represents the cost of work done during March that has been carried forward to April. Also note that the Work in Process account contains the same $30,000 balance. Thus, the Work in Process account summarizes all of the costs appearing on the job cost sheets of the jobs that are in process. Job A was the only job in process at the beginning of April, so the beginning balance in the Work in Process account equals Job A's beginning balance of $30,000.

Labor Cost

In April, the employee time tickets included $60,000 recorded for direct labor and $15,000 for indirect labor. The following entry summarizes these costs:

(3)

Work in Process	60,000	
Manufacturing Overhead	15,000	
Salaries and Wages Payable		75,000

Only the direct labor cost of $60,000 is added to the Work in Process account. At the same time that direct labor costs are added to Work in Process, they are also added to the individual job cost sheets, as shown in Exhibit 3–7. During April, $40,000 of direct labor cost was charged to Job A and the remaining $20,000 was charged to Job B.

The labor costs charged to Manufacturing Overhead ($15,000) represent the indirect labor costs of the period, such as supervision, janitorial work, and maintenance.

EXHIBIT 3–6
Raw Materials Cost Flows

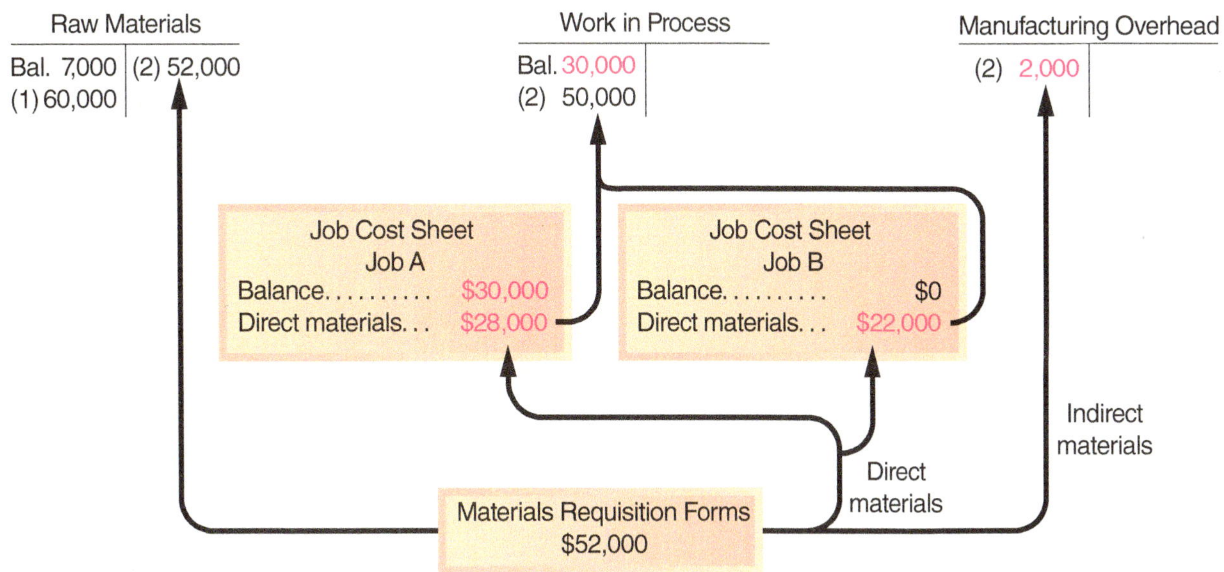

EXHIBIT 3–7
Labor Cost Flows

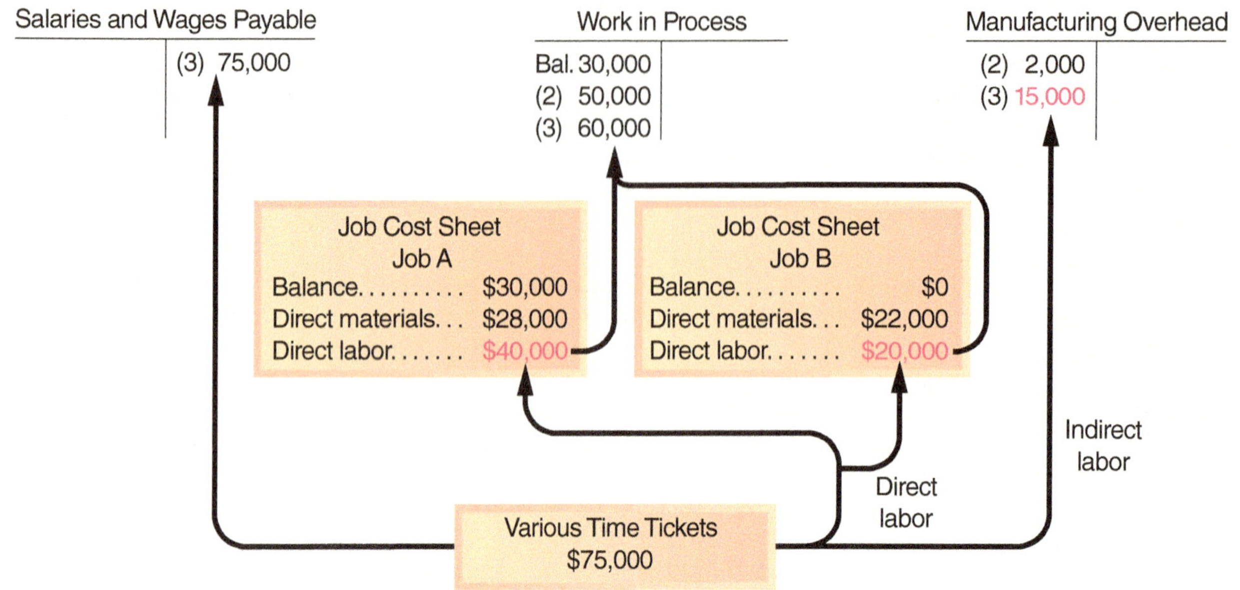

Manufacturing Overhead Costs

Recall that all manufacturing costs other than direct materials and direct labor are classified as manufacturing overhead costs. These costs are entered directly into the Manufacturing Overhead account as they are incurred. To illustrate, assume that Ruger Corporation incurred the following general factory costs during April:

Utilities (heat, water, and power)	$21,000
Rent on factory equipment	16,000
Miscellaneous factory overhead costs	3,000
Total	$40,000

The following entry records the incurrence of these costs:

(4)

Manufacturing Overhead	40,000	
Accounts Payable*		40,000

*Accounts such as Cash may also be credited

In addition, assume that during April, Ruger Corporation recognized $13,000 in accrued property taxes and that $7,000 in prepaid insurance expired on factory buildings and equipment. The following entry records these items:

(5)

Manufacturing Overhead	20,000	
Property Taxes Payable		13,000
Prepaid Insurance		7,000

Finally, assume that the company recognized $18,000 in depreciation on factory equipment during April. The following entry records the accrual of this depreciation:

(6)

Manufacturing Overhead	18,000	
Accumulated Depreciation		18,000

In short, manufacturing overhead costs are recorded directly into the Manufacturing Overhead account as they are incurred.

Applying Manufacturing Overhead

Because actual manufacturing costs are charged to the Manufacturing Overhead control account rather than to Work in Process, how are manufacturing overhead costs assigned to Work in Process? The answer is, by means of the predetermined overhead rate. Recall from our discussion earlier in the chapter that a predetermined overhead rate is established at the beginning of each year. The rate is calculated by dividing the estimated total manufacturing overhead cost for the year by the estimated total amount of the allocation base (measured in machine-hours, direct labor-hours, or some other base). The predetermined overhead rate is then used to apply overhead costs to jobs. For example, if machine-hours is the allocation base, overhead cost is applied to each job by multiplying the predetermined overhead rate by the number of machine-hours charged to the job.

To illustrate, assume that Ruger Corporation's predetermined overhead rate is $6 per machine-hour. Also assume that during April, 10,000 machine-hours were worked on Job A and 5,000 machine-hours were worked on Job B (a total of 15,000 machine-hours). Thus, $90,000 in overhead cost ($6 per machine-hour × 15,000 machine-hours = $90,000) would be applied to Work in Process. The following entry records the application of Manufacturing Overhead to Work in Process:

(7)

Work in Process	90,000	
Manufacturing Overhead		90,000

The flow of costs through the Manufacturing Overhead account is shown in Exhibit 3–8. The actual overhead costs on the debit side in the Manufacturing Overhead account in Exhibit 3–8 are the costs that were added to the account in entries (2)–(6). Observe that recording these actual overhead costs [entries (2)–(6)] and the application of overhead to Work in Process [entry (7)] represent two separate and entirely distinct processes.

The Concept of a Clearing Account

The Manufacturing Overhead account operates as a clearing account. As we have noted, actual factory overhead costs are debited to the account as they are incurred throughout the year. When a job is completed (or at the end of an accounting period), overhead cost is applied to the job using the predetermined overhead rate, and Work in Process is debited and Manufacturing Overhead is credited. This sequence of events is illustrated below:

Manufacturing Overhead (a clearing account)

Actual overhead costs are charged to this account as they are incurred throughout the period.	Overhead is applied to Work in Process using the predetermined overhead rate.

As we emphasized earlier, the predetermined overhead rate is based entirely on estimates of what the level of activity and overhead costs are *expected* to be, and it is established before the year begins. As a result, the overhead cost applied during a year will almost certainly turn out to be more or less than the actual overhead cost incurred. For example, notice from Exhibit 3–8 that Ruger Corporation's actual overhead costs for the period are $5,000 greater than the overhead cost that has been applied to Work in Process, resulting in a $5,000 debit balance in the Manufacturing Overhead account. We will reserve discussion of what to do with this $5,000 balance until later in the chapter.

For the moment, we can conclude from Exhibit 3–8 that the cost of a completed job consists of the actual direct materials cost of the job, the actual direct labor cost of the job, and the manufacturing overhead cost *applied* to the job. Pay particular attention to the following subtle but important point: *Actual overhead costs are not*

EXHIBIT 3–8
The Flow of Costs in Overhead Application

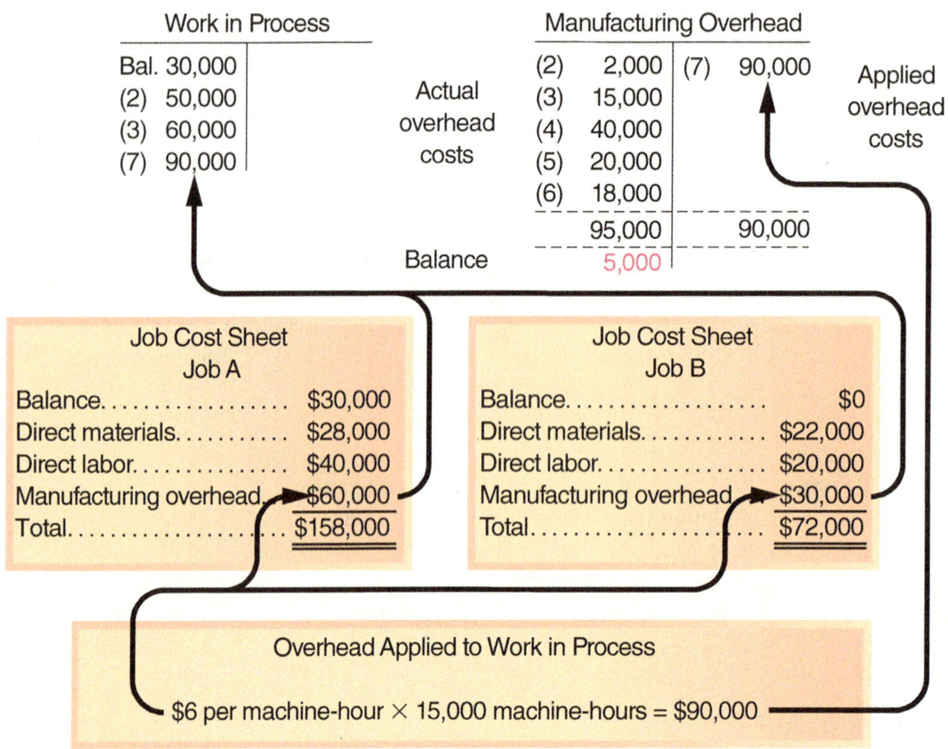

charged to jobs; actual overhead costs do not appear on the job cost sheet nor do they appear in the Work in Process account. Only the applied overhead cost, based on the predetermined overhead rate, appears on the job cost sheet and in the Work in Process account.

Nonmanufacturing Costs

In addition to manufacturing costs, companies also incur selling and administrative costs. These costs should be treated as period expenses and charged directly to the income statement. *Nonmanufacturing costs should not go into the Manufacturing Overhead account.* To illustrate the correct treatment of nonmanufacturing costs, assume that Ruger Corporation incurred $30,000 in selling and administrative salary costs during April. The following entry summarizes the accrual of those salaries:

(8)

Salaries Expense	30,000	
Salaries and Wages Payable		30,000

Assume that depreciation on office equipment during April was $7,000. The entry is as follows:

(9)

Depreciation Expense	7,000	
Accumulated Depreciation		7,000

Pay particular attention to the difference between this entry and entry (6) where we recorded depreciation on factory equipment. In journal entry (6), depreciation on factory equipment was debited to Manufacturing Overhead and is therefore a product cost. In journal entry (9) above, depreciation on office equipment is debited to Depreciation Expense. Depreciation on office equipment is a period expense rather than a product cost.

Finally, assume that advertising was $42,000 and that other selling and administrative expenses in April totaled $8,000. The following entry records these items:

(10)

Advertising Expense	42,000	
Other Selling and Administrative Expense	8,000	
Accounts Payable*		50,000

*Other accounts, such as Cash may be credited.

The amounts in entries (8) through (10) are recorded directly into expense accounts—they have no effect on product costs. The same will be true of any other selling and administrative expenses incurred during April, including sales commissions, depreciation on sales equipment, rent on office facilities, insurance on office facilities, and related costs.

Cost of Goods Manufactured

When a job has been completed, the finished output is transferred from the production departments to the finished goods warehouse. By this time, the accounting department will have charged the job with direct materials and direct labor cost, and manufacturing overhead will have been applied using the predetermined overhead rate. A transfer of costs is made within the costing system that *parallels* the physical transfer of goods to the finished goods warehouse. The costs of the completed job are transferred out of the Work in Process account and into the Finished Goods account. The sum of all amounts transferred between these two accounts represents the cost of goods manufactured for the period.

In the case of Ruger Corporation, assume that Job A was completed during April. The following entry transfers the cost of Job A from Work in Process to Finished Goods:

(11)

Finished Goods	158,000	
Work in Process		158,000

The $158,000 represents the completed cost of Job A, as shown on the job cost sheet in Exhibit 3–8. Because Job A was the only job completed during April, the $158,000 also represents the cost of goods manufactured for the month.

Job B was not completed by the end of the month, so its cost will remain in the Work in Process account and carry over to the next month. If a balance sheet is prepared at the end of April, the cost accumulated thus far on Job B will appear as the asset "Work in Process inventory."

Cost of Goods Sold

As finished goods are shipped to customers, their accumulated costs are transferred from the Finished Goods account to the Cost of Goods Sold account. If an entire job is shipped at one time, then the entire cost appearing on the job cost sheet is transferred to the Cost of Goods Sold account. In most cases, however, only a portion of the units involved in a particular job will be immediately sold. In these situations, the unit product cost must be used to determine how much product cost should be removed from Finished Goods and charged to Cost of Goods Sold.

For Ruger Corporation, we will assume 750 of the 1,000 gold medallions in Job A were shipped to customers by the end of the month for total sales revenue of $225,000. Because 1,000 units were produced and the total cost of the job from the job cost sheet was $158,000, the unit product cost was $158. The following journal entries would record the sale (all sales were on account):

(12)

Accounts Receivable	225,000	
Sales		225,000

(13)

Cost of Goods Sold	118,500	
Finished Goods		118,500
(750 units × $158 per unit = $118,500)		

LEARNING OBJECTIVE 5
Use T-accounts to show the flow of costs in a job-order costing system.

Entry (13) completes the flow of costs through the job-order costing system. To pull the entire Ruger Corporation example together, journal entries (1) through (13) are summarized in Exhibit 3–9. The flow of costs through the accounts is presented in T-account form in Exhibit 3–10.

EXHIBIT 3–9
Summary of Ruger Corporation Journal Entries

	Debit	Credit
(1)		
Raw Materials	60,000	
Accounts Payable		60,000
(2)		
Work in Process	50,000	
Manufacturing Overhead	2,000	
Raw Materials		52,000
(3)		
Work in Process	60,000	
Manufacturing Overhead	15,000	
Salaries and Wages Payable		75,000
(4)		
Manufacturing Overhead	40,000	
Accounts Payable		40,000
(5)		
Manufacturing Overhead	20,000	
Property Taxes Payable		13,000
Prepaid Insurance		7,000
(6)		
Manufacturing Overhead	18,000	
Accumulated Depreciation		18,000
(7)		
Work in Process	90,000	
Manufacturing Overhead		90,000
(8)		
Salaries Expense	30,000	
Salaries and Wages Payable		30,000
(9)		
Depreciation Expense	7,000	
Accumulated Depreciation		7,000
(10)		
Advertising Expense	42,000	
Other Selling and Administrative Expense	8,000	
Accounts Payable		50,000
(11)		
Finished Goods	158,000	
Work in Process		158,000
(12)		
Accounts Receivable	225,000	
Sales		225,000
(13)		
Cost of Goods Sold	118,500	
Finished Goods		118,500

EXHIBIT 3–10
Summary of Cost Flows—Ruger Corporation

Accounts Receivable

Bal.	XX		
(12)	225,000		

Prepaid Insurance

Bal.	XX		
		(5)	7,000

Raw Materials

Bal.	7,000	(2)	52,000
(1)	60,000		
Bal.	15,000		

Work in Process

Bal.	30,000	(11)	158,000
(2)	50,000		
(3)	60,000		
(7)	90,000		
Bal.	72,000		

Finished Goods

Bal.	10,000	(13)	118,500
(11)	158,000		
Bal.	49,500		

Accumulated Depreciation

		Bal.	XX
		(6)	18,000
		(9)	7,000

Manufacturing Overhead

(2)	2,000	(7)	90,000
(3)	15,000		
(4)	40,000		
(5)	20,000		
(6)	18,000		
	95,000		90,000
Bal.	5,000		

Accounts Payable

		Bal.	XX
		(1)	60,000
		(4)	40,000
		(10)	50,000

Salaries and Wages Payable

		Bal.	XX
		(3)	75,000
		(8)	30,000

Property Taxes Payable

		Bal.	XX
		(5)	13,000

Capital Stock

		Bal.	XX

Retained Earnings

		Bal.	XX

Sales

		(12)	225,000

Cost of Goods Sold

(13)	118,500		

Salaries Expense

(8)	30,000		

Depreciation Expense

(9)	7,000		

Advertising Expense

(10)	42,000		

Other Selling and Administrative Expense

(10)	8,000		

Explanation of entries:

(1) Raw materials purchased.
(2) Direct and indirect materials issued into production.
(3) Direct and indirect factory labor cost incurred.
(4) Utilities and other factory costs incurred.
(5) Property taxes and insurance incurred on the factory.
(6) Depreciation recorded on factory assets.
(7) Overhead cost applied to Work in Process.
(8) Administrative salaries expense incurred.
(9) Depreciation recorded on office equipment.
(10) Advertising and other selling and administrative expense incurred.
(11) Cost of goods manufactured transferred to finished goods.
(12) Sale of Job A recorded.
(13) Cost of goods sold recorded for Job A.

Schedules of Cost of Goods Manufactured and Cost of Goods Sold

LEARNING OBJECTIVE 6
Prepare schedules of cost of goods manufactured and cost of goods sold and an income statement.

This section uses the Ruger Corporation example to explain how to prepare schedules of cost of goods manufactured and cost of goods sold as well as an income statement. The **schedule of cost of goods manufactured** contains three elements of product costs—direct materials, direct labor, and manufacturing overhead—and it summarizes the portions of those costs that remain in ending Work in Process inventory and that are transferred out of Work in Process into Finished Goods. The **schedule of cost of goods sold** also contains three elements of product costs—direct materials, direct labor, and manufacturing overhead—and it summarizes the portions of those costs that remain in ending Finished Goods inventory and that are transferred out of Finished Goods into Cost of Goods Sold.

Exhibit 3–11 presents Ruger Corporation's schedules of cost of goods manufactured and cost of goods sold. We want to draw your attention to three key aspects of the schedule of cost of goods manufactured. First, three amounts are always added together—direct materials used in production ($50,000), direct labor ($60,000), and manufacturing overhead applied to work in process ($90,000)—to yield the total manufacturing costs ($200,000). Notice, the direct materials used in production ($50,000) is included in total manufacturing costs instead of raw material purchases ($60,000). The direct materials used in production will usually differ from the amount of raw material purchases when the raw materials inventory balance changes or indirect materials are withdrawn from raw materials inventory. Second, the amount of manufacturing overhead applied to Work in Process ($90,000) is computed by multiplying the predetermined overhead rate by the actual amount of the allocation base recorded on all jobs. *The actual manufacturing overhead costs incurred during the period are not added to the Work in Process account.* Third, total manufacturing costs ($200,000) plus beginning Work in Process inventory ($30,000)

EXHIBIT 3–11
Schedules of Cost of Goods Manufactured and Cost of Goods Sold

Cost of Goods Manufactured		
Direct materials:		
Raw materials inventory, beginning	$ 7,000	
Add: Purchases of raw materials	60,000	
Total raw materials available	67,000	
Deduct: Raw materials inventory, ending	15,000	
Raw materials used in production	52,000	
Deduct: Indirect materials included in manufacturing overhead	2,000	$ 50,000
Direct labor		60,000
Manufacturing overhead applied to work in process		90,000
Total manufacturing costs		200,000
Add: Beginning work in process inventory		30,000
		230,000
Deduct: Ending work in process inventory		72,000
Cost of goods manufactured		$158,000
Cost of Goods Sold		
Finished goods inventory, beginning		$ 10,000
Add: Cost of goods manufactured		158,000
Cost of goods available for sale		168,000
Deduct: Finished goods inventory, ending		49,500
Unadjusted cost of goods sold		118,500
Add: Underapplied overhead		5,000
Adjusted cost of goods sold		$123,500

*Note that the underapplied overhead is added to cost of goods sold. If overhead were overapplied, it would be deducted from cost of goods sold.

EXHIBIT 3–12
Income Statement

Ruger Corporation Income Statement For the Month Ending April 30		
Sales		$225,000
Cost of goods sold ($118,500 + $5,000)		123,500
Gross margin		101,500
Selling and administrative expenses:		
Salaries expense	$30,000	
Depreciation expense	7,000	
Advertising expense	42,000	
Other expense	8,000	87,000
Net operating income		$ 14,500

minus ending Work in Process inventory ($72,000) equals the cost of goods manufactured ($158,000). The cost of goods manufactured represents the cost of the goods completed during the period and transferred from Work in Process to Finished Goods.

The schedule of cost of goods sold shown in Exhibit 3–11 relies on the following equation to compute the unadjusted cost of goods sold:

$$\text{Unadjusted cost of goods sold} = \text{Beginning finished goods inventory} + \text{Cost of goods manufactured} - \text{Ending finished goods inventory}$$

The beginning finished goods inventory ($10,000) plus the cost of goods manufactured ($158,000) equals the cost of goods available for sale ($168,000). The cost of goods available for sale ($168,000) minus the ending finished goods inventory ($49,500) equals the unadjusted cost of goods sold ($118,500). Finally, the unadjusted cost of goods sold ($118,500) plus the underapplied overhead ($5,000) equals adjusted cost of goods sold ($123,500). The next section of the chapter takes a closer look at why cost of goods sold needs to be adjusted for the amount of underapplied or overapplied overhead

Exhibit 3–12 presents Ruger Corporation's income statement for April. Observe that the cost of goods sold on this statement is carried over from Exhibit 3–11. The selling and administrative expenses (which total $87,000) did not flow through the schedules of cost of goods manufactured and cost of goods sold. Journal entries 8–10 (page 100) show that these items were immediately debited to expense accounts rather than being debited to inventory accounts.

Underapplied and Overapplied Overhead—A Closer Look

LEARNING OBJECTIVE 7
Compute underapplied or overapplied overhead cost and prepare the journal entry to close the balance in Manufacturing Overhead to the appropriate accounts.

This section explains how to compute underapplied and overapplied overhead and how to dispose of any balance remaining in the Manufacturing Overhead account at the end of a period.

Computing Underapplied and Overapplied Overhead

Because the predetermined overhead rate is established before the period begins and is based entirely on estimated data, the overhead cost applied to Work in Process will generally differ from the amount of overhead cost actually incurred. In the case of Ruger Corporation, for example, the predetermined overhead rate of $6 per hour was used to apply $90,000 of overhead cost to Work in Process, whereas actual overhead costs for April proved to be $95,000 (see Exhibit 3–8). The difference between the overhead cost applied to Work in Process and the actual overhead costs of a period is called either **underapplied** or **overapplied overhead.** For Ruger Corporation, overhead was underapplied by

$5,000 because the applied cost ($90,000) was $5,000 less than the actual cost ($95,000). If the situation had been reversed and the company had applied $95,000 in overhead cost to Work in Process while incurring actual overhead costs of only $90,000, then the overhead would have been overapplied.

What is the cause of underapplied or overapplied overhead? Basically, the method of applying overhead to jobs using a predetermined overhead rate assumes that actual overhead costs will be proportional to the actual amount of the allocation base incurred during the period. If, for example, the predetermined overhead rate is $6 per machine-hour, then it is assumed that actual overhead costs incurred will be $6 for every machine-hour that is actually worked. There are at least two reasons why this may not be true. First, much of the overhead often consists of fixed costs that do not change as the number of machine-hours incurred goes up or down. Second, spending on overhead items may or may not be under control. If individuals who are responsible for overhead costs do a good job, those costs should be less than were expected at the beginning of the period. If they do a poor job, those costs will be more than expected.

To illustrate these concepts, suppose that two companies—Turbo Crafters and Black & Howell—have prepared the following estimated data for the coming year:

	Turbo Crafters	Black & Howell
Allocation base	Machine-hours	Direct materials cost
Estimated manufacturing overhead cost (a)	$300,000	$120,000
Estimated total amount of the allocation base (b)	75,000 machine-hours	$80,000 direct materials cost
Predetermined overhead rate (a) ÷ (b)	$4 per machine-hour	150% of direct materials cost

Note that when the allocation base is dollars (such as direct materials cost in the case of Black & Howell) the predetermined overhead rate is expressed as a percentage of the allocation base. When dollars are divided by dollars, the result is a percentage.

Now assume that because of unexpected changes in overhead spending and in demand for the companies' products, the *actual* overhead cost and the actual activity recorded during the year in each company are as follows:

	Turbo Crafters	Black & Howell
Actual manufacturing overhead cost	$290,000	$130,000
Actual total amount of the allocation base	68,000 machine-hours	$90,000 direct materials cost

For each company, note that the actual data for both cost and the allocation base differ from the estimates used in computing the predetermined overhead rate. This results in underapplied and overapplied overhead as follows:

	Turbo Crafters	Black & Howell
Actual manufacturing overhead cost	$290,000	$130,000
Manufacturing overhead cost applied to Work in Process during the year:		
Predetermined overhead rate (a)	$4 per machine-hour	150% of direct materials cost
Actual total amount of the allocation base (b)	68,000 machine-hours	$90,000 direct materials cost
Manufacturing overhead applied (a) × (b)	$272,000	$135,000
Underapplied (overapplied) manufacturing overhead	$18,000	$(5,000)

For Turbo Crafters, the amount of overhead cost applied to Work in Process ($272,000) is less than the actual overhead cost for the year ($290,000). Therefore, overhead is underapplied.

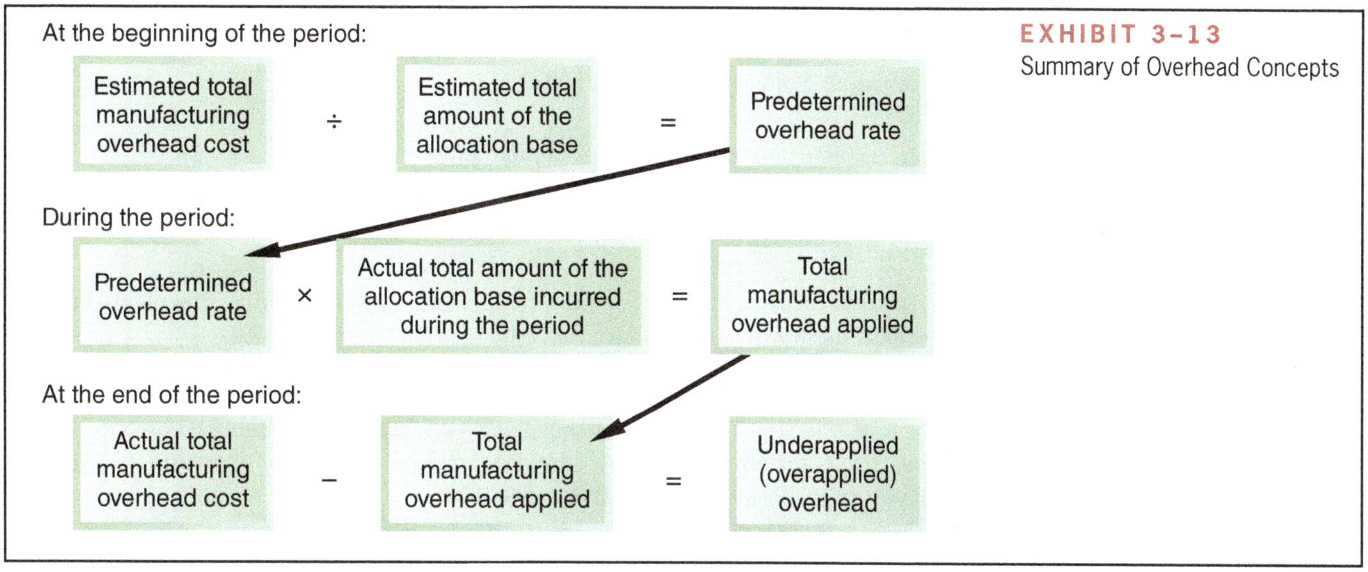

EXHIBIT 3–13
Summary of Overhead Concepts

For Black & Howell, the amount of overhead cost applied to Work in Process ($135,000) is greater than the actual overhead cost for the year ($130,000), so overhead is overapplied.

A summary of these concepts is presented in Exhibit 3–13.

Disposition of Underapplied or Overapplied Overhead Balances

If we return to the Ruger Corporation example and look at the Manufacturing Overhead T-account in Exhibit 3–10, you will see that there is a debit balance of $5,000. Remember that debit entries to the account represent actual overhead costs incurred, whereas credit entries represent overhead costs applied to jobs. In this case, the actual overhead costs incurred exceeded the overhead costs applied to jobs by $5,000—hence, the debit balance of $5,000. This may sound familiar. We just discussed in the previous section the fact that the overhead costs incurred ($95,000) exceeded the overhead costs applied ($90,000), and that the difference is called underapplied overhead. These are just two ways of looking at the same thing. If there is a *debit* balance in the Manufacturing Overhead account of X dollars, then the overhead is *underapplied* by X dollars. On the other hand, if there is a *credit* balance in the Manufacturing Overhead account of Y dollars, then the overhead is *overapplied* by Y dollars. What do we do with the balance in the Manufacturing Overhead account at the end of the accounting period?

The underapplied or overapplied balance remaining in the Manufacturing Overhead account at the end of a period is treated in one of two ways:

1. Closed out to Cost of Goods Sold.
2. Allocated among the Work in Process, Finished Goods, and Cost of Goods Sold accounts in proportion to the overhead applied during the current period in ending balances.

Closed Out to Cost of Goods Sold

Closing out the balance in Manufacturing Overhead to Cost of Goods Sold is simpler than the allocation method. In the Ruger Corporation example, the entry to close the $5,000 of underapplied overhead to Cost of Goods Sold is:

(14)

Cost of Goods Sold	5,000	
Manufacturing Overhead		5,000

Note that because the Manufacturing Overhead account has a debit balance, Manufacturing Overhead must be credited to close out the account. This has the effect of increasing Cost of Goods Sold for April to $123,500:

Unadjusted cost of goods sold [from entry (13)]	$118,500
Add underapplied overhead [entry (14)]	5,000
Adjusted cost of goods sold	$123,500

After this adjustment has been made, Ruger Corporation's income statement for April will appear as shown earlier in Exhibit 3–12.

Note that this adjustment makes sense. The unadjusted cost of goods sold is based on the amount of manufacturing overhead applied to jobs, not the manufacturing overhead costs actually incurred. Because overhead was underapplied, not enough cost was applied to jobs. Hence, the cost of goods sold was understated. Adding the underapplied overhead to the cost of goods sold corrects this understatement.

Allocated between Accounts Allocation of underapplied or overapplied overhead between Work in Process, Finished Goods, and Cost of Goods Sold is more accurate than closing the entire balance into Cost of Goods Sold. This allocation assigns overhead costs to where they would have gone had the estimates included in the predetermined overhead rate matched the actual amounts.

Had Ruger Corporation chosen to allocate the underapplied overhead among the inventory accounts and Cost of Goods Sold, it would first be necessary to determine the amount of overhead that had been applied during April to each of the accounts. The computations would have been as follows:

Overhead applied in work in process inventory, April 30 (Job B) . . .	$30,000	33.33%
Overhead applied in finished goods inventory, April 30		
Job A: ($60,000/1,000 units = $60 per unit) × 250 units	15,000	16.67%
Overhead applied in cost of goods sold, April		
Job A: ($60,000/1,000 units = $60 per unit) × 750 units	45,000	50.00%
Total overhead applied	$90,000	100.00%

Based on the above percentages, the underapplied overhead (i.e., the debit balance in Manufacturing Overhead) would be allocated as shown in the following journal entry:

Work in Process (33.33% × $5,000)	1,666.50	
Finished Goods (16.67% × $5,000)	833.50	
Cost of Goods Sold (50.00% × $5,000)	2,500.00	
Manufacturing Overhead		5,000.00

Note that the first step in the allocation process was to determine the amount of overhead applied in each of the accounts. For Finished Goods, for example, the total amount of overhead applied to Job A, $60,000, was divided by the total number of units in Job A, 1,000 units, to arrive at the average overhead applied of $60 per unit. Because 250 units from Job A were still in ending finished goods inventory, the amount of overhead applied in the Finished Goods Inventory account was $60 per unit multiplied by 250 units or $15,000 in total.

If overhead had been overapplied, the entry above would have been just the reverse, because a credit balance would have existed in the Manufacturing Overhead account.

Which Method Should Be Used for Disposing of Underapplied or Overapplied Overhead?

The allocation method is generally considered more accurate than simply closing out the underapplied or overapplied overhead to Cost of Goods Sold. However, the allocation method is more complex. We will always specify which method you are to use in problem assignments.

A General Model of Product Cost Flows

Exhibit 3–14 presents a T-account model of the flow of costs in a product costing system. This model can be very helpful in understanding how production costs flow through a costing system and finally end up as Cost of Goods Sold on the income statement.

Multiple Predetermined Overhead Rates

Our discussion in this chapter has assumed that there is a single predetermined overhead rate for an entire factory called a **plantwide overhead rate.** This is a fairly common practice—particularly in smaller companies. But in larger companies, *multiple predetermined overhead rates* are often used. In a **multiple predetermined overhead rate** system each production department may have its own predetermined overhead rate. Such a system, while more complex, is more accurate because it can reflect differences across departments in how overhead costs are incurred. For example, in departments that are relatively labor intensive overhead might be allocated based on direct labor-hours and in departments that are relatively machine intensive overhead might be allocated based on machine-hours. When multiple predetermined overhead rates are used, overhead is applied in each department according to its own overhead rate as jobs proceed through the department.

EXHIBIT 3–14
A General Model of Cost Flows

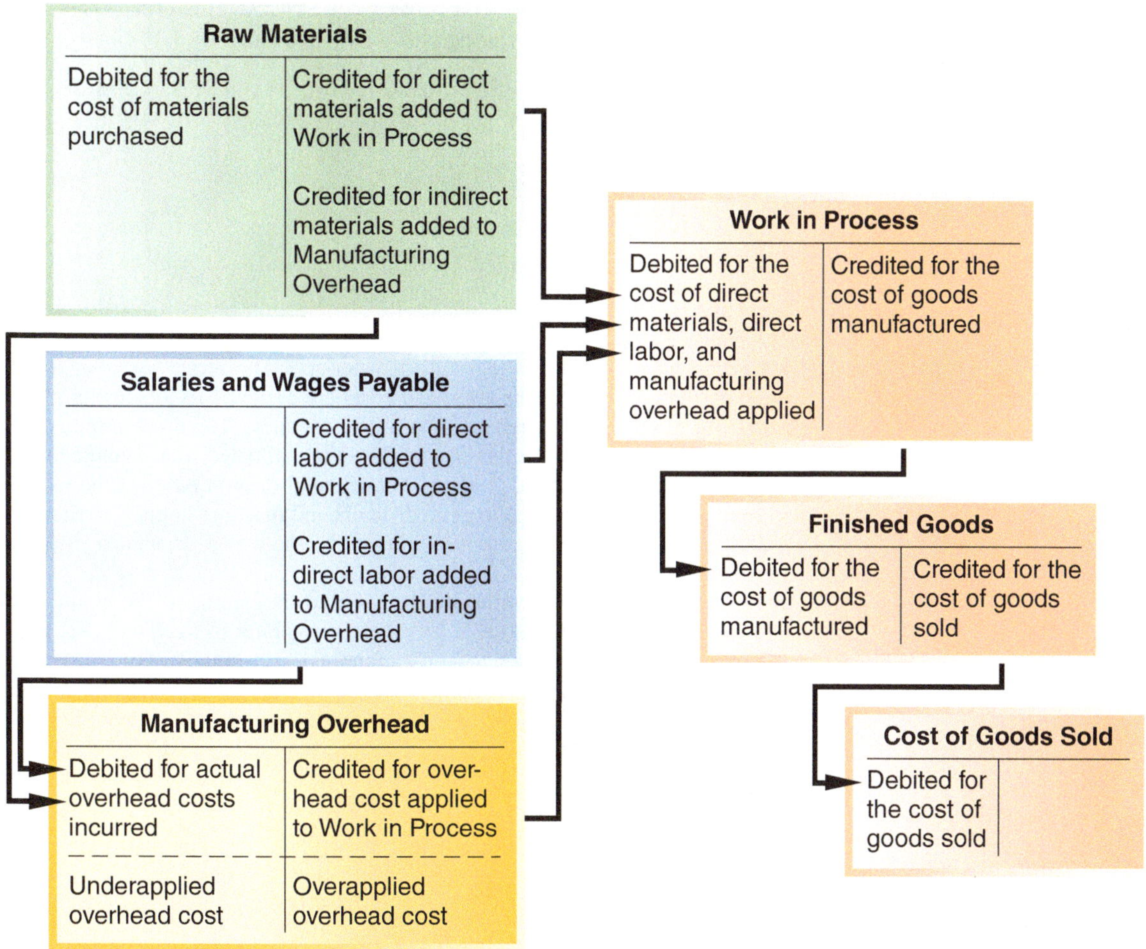

Job-Order Costing in Service Companies

Job-order costing is used in service organizations such as law firms, movie studios, hospitals, and repair shops, as well as in manufacturing companies. In a law firm, for example, each client is a "job," and the costs of that job are accumulated day by day on a job cost sheet as the client's case is handled by the firm. Legal forms and similar inputs represent the direct materials for the job; the time expended by attorneys is like direct labor; and the costs of secretaries and legal aids, rent, depreciation, and so forth, represent the overhead.

In a movie studio such as Columbia Pictures, each film produced by the studio is a "job," and costs of direct materials (costumes, props, film, etc.) and direct labor (actors, directors, and extras) are charged to each film's job cost sheet. A share of the studio's overhead costs, such as utilities, depreciation of equipment, wages of maintenance workers, and so forth, is also charged to each film.

In sum, job-order costing is a versatile and widely used costing method that may be encountered in virtually any organization that provides diverse products or services.

IN BUSINESS

MANAGING JOB COSTS IN A SERVICE BUSINESS

IBM has created a software program called Professional Marketplace to match IBM employees with client needs. "Using Marketplace, IBM consultants working for customers can search through 100 job classifications and 10,000 skills, figuring out who inside IBM is available, where they are located and roughly how much it costs the company to use them." Thus far, the results have been encouraging. IBM has reduced its reliance on outside contractors by 5% to 7% and its consultants spend more of their time in billable work. Furthermore, IBM's senior consultants can search across the globe for available employees with particular niche skills with the click of a mouse instead of having to rely on numerous time-consuming phone calls and emails.

Source: Charles Forelle, "IBM Tool Deploys Employees Efficiently," *The Wall Street Journal*, July 14, 2005, p. B3.

Summary

Job-order costing is used in situations where the organization offers many different products or services, such as in furniture manufacturing, hospitals, and legal firms. Materials requisition forms and labor time tickets are used to assign direct materials and direct labor costs to jobs in a job-order costing system. Manufacturing overhead costs are assigned to jobs using a predetermined overhead rate. All of the costs are recorded on a job cost sheet. The predetermined overhead rate is determined before the period begins by dividing the estimated total manufacturing overhead cost for the period by the estimated total amount of the allocation base for the period. The most frequently used allocation bases are direct labor-hours and machine-hours. Overhead is applied to jobs by multiplying the predetermined overhead rate by the actual amount of the allocation base recorded for the job.

Because the predetermined overhead rate is based on estimates, the actual overhead cost incurred during a period may be more or less than the amount of overhead cost applied to production. Such a difference is referred to as underapplied or overapplied overhead. The underapplied or overapplied overhead for a period can be either closed out to Cost of Goods Sold or allocated between Work in Process, Finished Goods, and Cost of Goods Sold. When overhead is underapplied, manufacturing overhead costs have been understated and therefore inventories and/or expenses must be adjusted upwards. When overhead is overapplied, manufacturing overhead costs have been overstated and therefore inventories and/or expenses must be adjusted downwards.

Review Problem: Job-Order Costing

Hogle Corporation is a manufacturer that uses job-order costing. On January 1, the beginning of its fiscal year, the company's inventory balances were as follows:

Raw materials	$20,000
Work in process	$15,000
Finished goods	$30,000

The company applies overhead cost to jobs on the basis of machine-hours worked. For the current year, the company's predetermined overhead rate was based on a cost formula that estimated $450,000 of total manufacturing overhead for an estimated activity level of 75,000 machine-hours. The following transactions were recorded for the year:

a. Raw materials were purchased on account, $410,000.
b. Raw materials were requisitioned for use in production, $380,000 ($360,000 direct materials and $20,000 indirect materials).
c. The following costs were accrued for employee services: direct labor, $75,000; indirect labor, $110,000; sales commissions, $90,000; and administrative salaries, $200,000.
d. Sales travel costs were $17,000.
e. Utility costs in the factory were $43,000.
f. Advertising costs were $180,000.
g. Depreciation was recorded for the year, $350,000 (80% relates to factory operations, and 20% relates to selling and administrative activities).
h. Insurance expired during the year, $10,000 (70% relates to factory operations, and the remaining 30% relates to selling and administrative activities).
i. Manufacturing overhead was applied to production. Due to greater than expected demand for its products, the company worked 80,000 machine-hours on all jobs during the year.
j. Goods costing $900,000 to manufacture according to their job cost sheets were completed during the year.
k. Goods were sold on account to customers during the year for a total of $1,500,000. The goods cost $870,000 to manufacture according to their job cost sheets.

Required:

1. Prepare journal entries to record the preceding transactions.
2. Post the entries in (1) above to T-accounts (don't forget to enter the beginning balances in the inventory accounts).
3. Is Manufacturing Overhead underapplied or overapplied for the year? Prepare a journal entry to close any balance in the Manufacturing Overhead account to Cost of Goods Sold. Do not allocate the balance between ending inventories and Cost of Goods Sold.
4. Prepare an income statement for the year.

Solution to Review Problem

		Debit	Credit
1.	*a.* Raw Materials	410,000	
	Accounts Payable		410,000
	b. Work in Process	360,000	
	Manufacturing Overhead	20,000	
	Raw Materials		380,000
	c. Work in Process	75,000	
	Manufacturing Overhead	110,000	
	Sales Commissions Expense	90,000	
	Administrative Salaries Expense	200,000	
	Salaries and Wages Payable		475,000
	d. Sales Travel Expense	17,000	
	Accounts Payable		17,000
	e. Manufacturing Overhead	43,000	
	Accounts Payable		43,000
	f. Advertising Expense	180,000	
	Accounts Payable		180,000
	g. Manufacturing Overhead	280,000	
	Depreciation Expense	70,000	
	Accumulated Depreciation		350,000

		Debit	Credit
h.	Manufacturing Overhead	7,000	
	Insurance Expense	3,000	
	Prepaid Insurance		10,000

i. The predetermined overhead rate for the year is computed as follows:

$$\text{Predetermined overhead rate} = \frac{\text{Estimated total manufacturing overhead cost}}{\text{Estimated total amount of the allocation base}}$$

$$= \frac{\$450{,}000}{75{,}000 \text{ machine-hours}}$$

$$= \$6 \text{ per machine-hour}$$

Based on the 80,000 machine-hours actually worked during the year, the company applied \$480,000 in overhead cost to production: \$6 per machine-hour × 80,000 machine-hours = \$480,000. The following entry records this application of overhead cost:

		Debit	Credit
	Work in Process	480,000	
	Manufacturing Overhead		480,000
j.	Finished Goods	900,000	
	Work in Process		900,000
k.	Accounts Receivable	1,500,000	
	Sales		1,500,000
	Cost of Goods Sold	870,000	
	Finished Goods		870,000

2.

Accounts Receivable

	Debit		Credit
(k)	1,500,000		

Prepaid Insurance

	Debit		Credit
		(h)	10,000

Raw Materials

	Debit		Credit
Bal.	20,000	(b)	380,000
(a)	410,000		
Bal.	50,000		

Work in Process

	Debit		Credit
Bal.	15,000	(j)	900,000
(b)	360,000		
(c)	75,000		
(i)	480,000		
Bal.	30,000		

Finished Goods

	Debit		Credit
Bal.	30,000	(k)	870,000
(j)	900,000		
Bal.	60,000		

Manufacturing Overhead

	Debit		Credit
(b)	20,000	(i)	480,000
(c)	110,000		
(e)	43,000		
(g)	280,000		
(h)	7,000		
	460,000		480,000
		Bal.	20,000

Accumulated Depreciation

	Debit		Credit
		(g)	350,000

Accounts Payable

	Debit		Credit
		(a)	410,000
		(d)	17,000
		(e)	43,000
		(f)	180,000

Salaries and Wages Payable

	Debit		Credit
		(c)	475,000

Sales

	Debit		Credit
		(k)	1,500,000

Cost of Goods Sold

	Debit		Credit
(k)	870,000		

Sales Commissions Expense

	Debit		Credit
(c)	90,000		

Administrative Salaries Expense

	Debit		Credit
(c)	200,000		

Sales Travel Expense

	Debit		Credit
(d)	17,000		

Advertising Expense

	Debit		Credit
(f)	180,000		

Depreciation Expense

	Debit		Credit
(g)	70,000		

Insurance Expense

	Debit		Credit
(h)	3,000		

3. Manufacturing overhead is overapplied for the year. The entry to close it out to Cost of Goods Sold is as follows:

Manufacturing Overhead	20,000	
Cost of Goods Sold		20,000

4.

Hogle Corporation Income Statement For the Year Ended December 31		
Sales		$1,500,000
Cost of goods sold ($870,000 − $20,000)		850,000
Gross margin		650,000
Selling and administrative expenses:		
Sales commissions expense	$ 90,000	
Administrative salaries expense	200,000	
Sales travel expense	17,000	
Advertising expense	180,000	
Depreciation expense	70,000	
Insurance expense	3,000	560,000
Net operating income		$ 90,000

Glossary

Absorption costing A costing method that includes all manufacturing costs—direct materials, direct labor, and both variable and fixed manufacturing overhead—in the cost of a product. (p. 84)

Allocation base A measure of activity such as direct labor-hours or machine-hours that is used to assign costs to cost objects. (p. 89)

Bill of materials A document that shows the quantity of each type of direct material required to make a product. (p. 86)

Cost driver A factor, such as machine-hours, beds occupied, computer time, or flight-hours, that causes overhead costs. (p. 91)

Cost of goods manufactured The manufacturing costs associated with the goods that were finished during the period. (p. 93)

Finished goods Units of product that have been completed but not yet sold to customers. (p. 93)

Job cost sheet A form that records the materials, labor, and manufacturing overhead costs charged to a job. (p. 86)

Job-order costing A costing system used in situations where many different products, jobs, or services are produced each period. (p. 84)

Materials requisition form A document that specifies the type and quantity of materials to be drawn from the storeroom and that identifies the job that will be charged for the cost of those materials. (p. 86)

Multiple predetermined overhead rates A costing system with multiple overhead cost pools and a different predetermined overhead rate for each cost pool, rather than a single predetermined overhead rate for the entire company. Each production department may be treated as a separate overhead cost pool. (p. 107)

Normal cost system A costing system in which overhead costs are applied to a job by multiplying a predetermined overhead rate by the actual amount of the allocation base incurred by the job. (p. 90)

Overapplied overhead A credit balance in the Manufacturing Overhead account that occurs when the amount of overhead cost applied to Work in Process exceeds the amount of overhead cost actually incurred during a period. (p. 103)

Overhead application The process of charging manufacturing overhead cost to job cost sheets and to the Work in Process account. (p. 89)

Plantwide overhead rate A single predetermined overhead rate that is used throughout a plant. (p. 107)

Predetermined overhead rate A rate used to charge manufacturing overhead cost to jobs that is established in advance for each period. It is computed by dividing the estimated total manufacturing overhead cost for the period by the estimated total amount of the allocation base for the period. (p. 89)

Raw materials Any materials that go into the final product. (p. 93)

Schedule of cost of goods manufactured A schedule that contains three elements of product costs—direct materials, direct labor, and manufacturing overhead—and that summarizes the portions of those costs that remain in ending Work in Process inventory and that are transferred out of Work in Process into Finished Goods. (p. 102)

Schedule of cost of goods sold A schedule that contains three elements of product costs—direct materials, direct labor, and manufacturing overhead—and that summarizes the portions of those costs that remain in ending Finished Goods inventory and that are transferred out of Finished Goods into Cost of Goods Sold. (p. 102)

Time ticket A document that is used to record the amount of time an employee spends on various activities. (p. 87)

Underapplied overhead A debit balance in the Manufacturing Overhead account that occurs when the amount of overhead cost actually incurred exceeds the amount of overhead cost applied to Work in Process during a period. (p. 103)

Work in process Units of product that are only partially complete and will require further work before they are ready for sale to the customer. (p. 93)

Questions

3–1 Why aren't actual manufacturing overhead costs traced to jobs just as direct materials and direct labor costs are traced to jobs?

3–2 Explain the four-step process used to compute a predetermined overhead rate.

3–3 What is the purpose of the job cost sheet in a job-order costing system?

3–4 Explain how a sales order, a production order, a materials requisition form, and a labor time ticket are involved in producing and costing products.

3–5 Explain why some production costs must be assigned to products through an allocation process.

3–6 Why do companies use predetermined overhead rates rather than actual manufacturing overhead costs to apply overhead to jobs?

3–7 What factors should be considered in selecting a base to be used in computing the predetermined overhead rate?

3–8 If a company fully allocates all of its overhead costs to jobs, does this guarantee that a profit will be earned for the period?

3–9 What account is credited when overhead cost is applied to Work in Process? Would you expect the amount applied for a period to equal the actual overhead costs of the period? Why or why not?

3–10 What is underapplied overhead? Overapplied overhead? What disposition is made of these amounts at the end of the period?

3–11 Provide two reasons why overhead might be underapplied in a given year.

3–12 What adjustment is made for underapplied overhead on the schedule of cost of goods sold? What adjustment is made for overapplied overhead?

3–13 What is a plantwide overhead rate? Why are multiple overhead rates, rather than a plantwide overhead rate, used in some companies?

3–14 What happens to overhead rates based on direct labor when automated equipment replaces direct labor?

Multiple-choice questions are provided on the text website at www.mhhe.com/garrison14e.

Applying Excel

LEARNING OBJECTIVES 1, 4, 7

Available with McGraw-Hill's *Connect™ Accounting*.

The Excel worksheet form that appears below is to be used to recreate part of the example on page 104. Download the workbook containing this form from the Online Learning Center at www.mhhe.com/garrison14e. *On the website you will also receive instructions about how to use this worksheet form.*

	A	B	C
1	Chapter 3: Applying Excel		
2			
3	Data		
4	Allocation base	Machine-hours	
5	Estimated manufacturing overhead cost	$300,000	
6	Estimated total amount of the allocation base	75,000	machine-hours
7	Actual manufacturing overhead cost	$290,000	
8	Actual total amount of the allocation base	68,000	machine-hours
9			
10	*Enter a formula into each of the cells marked with a ? below*		
11			
12	**Computation of the predetermined overhead rate**		
13	Estimated manufacturing overhead cost	?	
14	Estimated total amount of the allocation base	?	machine-hours
15	Predetermined overhead rate	?	per machine-hour
16			
17	**Computation of underapplied or overapplied manufacturing overhead**		
18	Actual manufacturing overhead cost	?	
19	Manufacturing overhead cost applied to Work in Process during the year:		
20	Predetermined overhead rate	?	per machine-hour
21	Actual total amount of the allocation base	?	machine-hours
22	Manufacturing overhead applied	?	
23	Underapplied (overapplied) manufacturing overhead	?	
24			

Chapter 3 Form | Filled in Chapter 3 Form | Chapter 3 Formulas

You should proceed to the requirements below only after completing your worksheet.

Required:

1. Check your worksheet by changing the estimated total amount of the allocation base in the Data area to 60,000 machine-hours, keeping all of the other data the same as in the original example. If your worksheet is operating properly, the predetermined overhead rate should now be $5.00 per machine-hour. If you do not get this answer, find the errors in your worksheet and correct them.

   How much is the underapplied (overapplied) manufacturing overhead? Did it change? Why or why not?
2. Determine the underapplied (overapplied) manufacturing overhead for a different company with the following data:

Allocation base	Machine-hours
Estimated manufacturing overhead cost	$100,000
Estimated total amount of the allocation base	50,000 machine-hours
Actual manufacturing overhead cost	$90,000
Actual total amount of the allocation base	40,000 machine-hours

3. What happens to the underapplied (overapplied) manufacturing overhead from part (2) if the estimated total amount of the allocation base is changed to 40,000 machine-hours and everything else remains the same? Why is the amount of underapplied (overapplied) manufacturing overhead different from part (2)?
4. Change the estimated total amount of the allocation base back to 50,000 machine-hours so that the data looks exactly like it did in part (2). Now change the actual manufacturing overhead cost to $100,000. What is the underapplied (overapplied) manufacturing overhead now? Why is the amount of underapplied (overapplied) manufacturing overhead different from part (2)?

Exercises

connect ACCOUNTING

All applicable exercises are available with McGraw-Hill's *Connect™ Accounting.*

EXERCISE 3–1 Compute the Predetermined Overhead Rate [LO1]

Logan Products computes its predetermined overhead rate annually on the basis of direct labor-hours. At the beginning of the year, it estimated that 40,000 direct labor-hours would be required for the period's estimated level of production. The company also estimated $466,000 of fixed manufacturing overhead expenses for the coming period and variable manufacturing overhead of $3.00 per direct labor-hour. Logan's actual manufacturing overhead for the year was $713,400 and its actual total direct labor was 41,000 hours.

Required:

Compute the company's predetermined overhead rate for the year.

EXERCISE 3–2 Apply Overhead [LO2]

Westan Corporation uses a predetermined overhead rate of $23.10 per direct labor-hour. This predetermined rate was based on a cost formula that estimated $277,200 of total manufacturing overhead for an estimated activity level of 12,000 direct labor-hours.

The company incurred actual total manufacturing overhead costs of $266,000 and 12,600 total direct labor-hours during the period.

Required:

Determine the amount of manufacturing overhead that would have been applied to all jobs during the period.

EXERCISE 3–3 Computing Job Costs [LO3]

Weaver Company's predetermined overhead rate is $18.00 per direct labor-hour and its direct labor wage rate is $12.00 per hour. The following information pertains to Job A-200:

Direct materials	$200
Direct labor	$120

Required:

1. What is the total manufacturing cost assigned to Job A-200?
2. If Job A-200 consists of 50 units, what is the average cost assigned to each unit included in the job?

EXERCISE 3–4 Prepare Journal Entries [LO4]

Kirkaid Company recorded the following transactions for the just completed month.

a. $86,000 in raw materials were purchased on account.
b. $84,000 in raw materials were requisitioned for use in production. Of this amount, $72,000 was for direct materials and the remainder was for indirect materials.

c. Total labor wages of $108,000 were incurred. Of this amount, $105,000 was for direct labor and the remainder was for indirect labor.
d. Additional manufacturing overhead costs of $197,000 were incurred.

Required:
Record the above transactions in journal entries.

EXERCISE 3–5 Prepare T-Accounts [LO5, LO7]
Granger Products recorded the following transactions for the just completed month. The company had no beginning inventories.

a. $75,000 in raw materials were purchased for cash.
b. $73,000 in raw materials were requisitioned for use in production. Of this amount, $67,000 was for direct materials and the remainder was for indirect materials.
c. Total labor wages of $152,000 were incurred and paid. Of this amount, $134,000 was for direct labor and the remainder was for indirect labor.
d. Additional manufacturing overhead costs of $126,000 were incurred and paid.
e. Manufacturing overhead costs of $178,000 were applied to jobs using the company's predetermined overhead rate.
f. All of the jobs in progress at the end of the month were completed and shipped to customers.
g. Any underapplied or overapplied overhead for the period was closed out to Cost of Goods Sold.

Required:
1. Post the above transactions to T-accounts.
2. Determine the cost of goods sold for the period.

EXERCISE 3–6 Schedules of Cost of Goods Manufactured and Cost of Goods Sold [LO6]
Parmitan Corporation has provided the following data concerning last month's manufacturing operations.

Purchases of raw materials	$53,000
Indirect materials included in manufacturing overhead	$8,000
Direct labor	$62,000
Manufacturing overhead applied to work in process	$41,000
Underapplied overhead	$8,000

	Beginning	Ending
Inventories:		
Raw materials	$24,000	$6,000
Work in process	$41,000	$38,000
Finished goods	$86,000	$93,000

Required:
1. Prepare a schedule of cost of goods manufactured for the month.
2. Prepare a schedule of cost of goods sold for the month.

EXERCISE 3–7 Underapplied and Overapplied Overhead [LO7]
Cretin Enterprises uses a predetermined overhead rate of $21.40 per direct labor-hour. This predetermined rate was based on a cost formula that estimated $171,200 of total manufacturing overhead for an estimated activity level of 8,000 direct labor-hours.

The company incurred actual total manufacturing overhead costs of $172,500 and 8,250 total direct labor-hours during the period.

Required:
1. Determine the amount of underapplied or overapplied manufacturing overhead for the period.
2. Assuming that the entire amount of the underapplied or overapplied overhead is closed out to cost of goods sold, what would be the effect of the underapplied or overapplied overhead on the company's gross margin for the period?

EXERCISE 3–8 Schedules of Cost of Goods Manufactured and Cost of Goods Sold; Income Statement [LO6]

The following data from the just completed year are taken from the accounting records of Eccles Company:

Sales	$643,000
Direct labor cost	$90,000
Raw material purchases	$132,000
Selling expenses	$100,000
Administrative expenses	$43,000
Manufacturing overhead applied to work in process	$210,000
Actual manufacturing overhead costs	$220,000

Inventories:	Beginning of Year	End of Year
Raw materials	$8,000	$10,000
Work in process	$5,000	$20,000
Finished goods	$70,000	$25,000

Required:

1. Prepare a schedule of cost of goods manufactured. Assume all raw materials used in production were direct materials.
2. Prepare a schedule of cost of goods sold.
3. Prepare an income statement.

EXERCISE 3–9 Apply Overhead to a Job [LO2]

Winston Company applies overhead cost to jobs on the basis of direct labor cost. Job X, which was started and completed during the current period, shows charges of $18,000 for direct materials, $10,000 for direct labor, and $15,000 for overhead on its job cost sheet. Job Q, which is still in process at year-end, shows charges of $20,000 for direct materials, and $8,000 for direct labor.

Required:

Should any overhead cost be added to Job Q at year-end? If so, how much? Explain.

EXERCISE 3–10 Applying Overhead; Computing Unit Product Cost [LO2, LO3]

A company assigns overhead cost to completed jobs on the basis of 120% of direct labor cost. The job cost sheet for Job 413 shows that $12,000 in direct materials has been used on the job and that $8,000 in direct labor cost has been incurred. A total of 200 units were produced in Job 413.

Required:

What is the total manufacturing cost assigned to Job 413? What is the unit product cost for Job 413?

EXERCISE 3–11 Journal Entries and T-Accounts [LO2, LO4, LO5]

Foley Company uses a job-order costing system. The following data relate to the month of October, the first month of the company's fiscal year:

a. Raw materials purchased on account, $210,000.
b. Raw materials issued to production, $190,000 (80% direct and 20% indirect).
c. Direct labor cost incurred, $49,000; and indirect labor cost incurred, $21,000.
d. Depreciation recorded on factory equipment, $105,000.
e. Other manufacturing overhead costs incurred during October, $130,000 (credit Accounts Payable).
f. The company applies manufacturing overhead cost to production on the basis of $4 per machine-hour. A total of 75,000 machine-hours were recorded for October.
g. Production orders costing $510,000 according to their job cost sheets were completed during October and transferred to Finished Goods.
h. Production orders that had cost $450,000 to complete according to their job cost sheets were shipped to customers during the month. These goods were sold on account at 50% above cost.

Required:

1. Prepare journal entries to record the information given above.
2. Prepare T-accounts for Manufacturing Overhead and Work in Process. Post the relevant information above to each account. Compute the ending balance in each account, assuming that Work in Process has a beginning balance of $35,000.

EXERCISE 3–12 Computing Predetermined Overhead Rates and Job Costs [LO1, LO2, LO3, LO7]

Kody Corporation uses a job-order costing system with a plantwide overhead rate based on machine-hours. At the beginning of the year, the company made the following estimates:

Machine-hours required to support estimated production	150,000
Fixed manufacturing overhead cost	$750,000
Variable manufacturing overhead cost per machine-hour	$4.00

Required:

1. Compute the predetermined overhead rate.
2. During the year Job 500 was started and completed. The following information was available with respect to this job:

Direct materials requisitioned	$350
Direct labor cost	$230
Machine-hours used	30

   Compute the total manufacturing cost assigned to Job 500.
3. During the year the company worked a total of 147,000 machine-hours on all jobs and incurred actual manufacturing overhead costs of $1,325,000. What is the amount of underapplied or overapplied overhead for the year? If this amount were closed out entirely to Cost of Goods Sold, would the journal entry increase or decrease net operating income?

EXERCISE 3–13 Applying Overhead; Cost of Goods Manufactured [LO2, LO6, LO7]

The following cost data relate to the manufacturing activities of Black Company during the just completed year:

Manufacturing overhead costs:	
Property taxes, factory	$3,000
Utilities, factory	5,000
Indirect labor	10,000
Depreciation, factory	24,000
Insurance, factory	6,000
Total actual manufacturing overhead costs	$48,000
Other costs incurred:	
Purchases of raw materials	$32,000
Direct labor cost	$40,000
Inventories:	
Raw materials, beginning	$8,000
Raw materials, ending	$7,000
Work in process, beginning	$6,000
Work in process, ending	$7,500

The company uses a predetermined overhead rate to apply overhead cost to jobs. The rate for the year was $5 per machine-hour; a total of 10,000 machine-hours was recorded for the year. All raw materials ultimately become direct materials—none are classified as indirect materials.

Required:

1. Compute the amount of underapplied or overapplied overhead cost for the year.
2. Prepare a schedule of cost of goods manufactured for the year.

EXERCISE 3–14 Varying Predetermined Overhead Rates [LO1, LO2, LO3]

Javadi Company makes a single product that is subject to wide seasonal variations in demand. The company uses a job-order costing system and computes predetermined overhead rates on a quarterly basis using the number of units to be produced as the allocation base. Its estimated costs, by quarter, for the coming year are given below:

	Quarter			
	First	Second	Third	Fourth
Direct materials	$240,000	$120,000	$ 60,000	$180,000
Direct labor	96,000	48,000	24,000	72,000
Manufacturing overhead	228,000	204,000	192,000	?
Total manufacturing costs (a)	$564,000	$372,000	$276,000	$?
Number of units to be produced (b)	80,000	40,000	20,000	60,000
Estimated unit product cost (a) ÷ (b)	$7.05	$9.30	$13.80	?

Management finds the variation in quarterly unit product costs to be confusing and difficult to work with. It has been suggested that the problem lies with manufacturing overhead because it is the largest element of total manufacturing cost. Accordingly, you have been asked to find a more appropriate way of assigning manufacturing overhead cost to units of product.

Required:

1. Using the high-low method, estimate the fixed manufacturing overhead cost per quarter and the variable manufacturing overhead cost per unit. Create a cost formula to estimate the total manufacturing overhead cost for the fourth quarter. Compute the total manufacturing cost and unit product cost for the fourth quarter.
2. What is causing the estimated unit product cost to fluctuate from one quarter to the next?
3. How would you recommend stabilizing the company's unit product cost? Support your answer with computations that adapt the cost formula you created in requirement 1.

EXERCISE 3–15 Departmental Overhead Rates [LO1, LO2, LO3]

Diewold Company has two departments, Milling and Assembly. The company uses a job-order costing system and computes a predetermined overhead rate in each department. The Milling Department bases its rate on machine-hours, and the Assembly Department bases its rate on direct labor-hours. At the beginning of the year, the company made the following estimates:

	Department	
	Milling	Assembly
Direct labor-hours	8,000	80,000
Machine-hours	60,000	3,000
Total fixed manufacturing overhead cost	$390,000	$500,000
Variable manufacturing overhead per machine-hour	$2.00	—
Variable manufacturing overhead per direct labor-hour	—	$3.75

Required:

1. Compute the predetermined overhead rate to be used in each department.
2. Assume that the overhead rates you computed in (1) above are in effect. The job cost sheet for Job 407, which was started and completed during the year, showed the following:

	Department	
	Milling	Assembly
Direct labor-hours	5	20
Machine-hours	90	4
Materials requisitioned	$800	$370
Direct labor cost	$45	$160

Compute the total manufacturing cost assigned to Job 407.

3. Would you expect substantially different amounts of overhead cost to be charged to some jobs if the company used a plantwide overhead rate based on direct labor-hours instead of using departmental rates? Explain. No computations are necessary.

EXERCISE 3–16 Applying Overhead; Journal Entries; Disposition of Underapplied or Overapplied Overhead [LO4, LO5, LO7]

The following information is taken from the accounts of FasGrow Company. The entries in the T-accounts are summaries of the transactions that affected those accounts during the year.

Manufacturing Overhead

	Debit		Credit
(a)	380,000	(b)	410,000
		Bal.	30,000

Work in Process

	Debit		Credit
Bal.	105,000	(c)	760,000
	210,000		
	115,000		
(b)	410,000		
Bal.	80,000		

Finished Goods

	Debit		Credit
Bal.	160,000	(d)	820,000
(c)	760,000		
Bal.	100,000		

Cost of Goods Sold

	Debit		Credit
(d)	820,000		

The overhead that had been applied to production during the year is distributed among the ending balances in the accounts as follows:

Work in Process, ending	$32,800
Finished Goods, ending	41,000
Cost of Goods Sold	336,200
Overhead applied	$410,000

For example, of the $80,000 ending balance in Work in Process, $32,800 was overhead that had been applied during the year.

Required:

1. Identify the reasons for entries (a) through (d).
2. Assume that the company closes any balance in the Manufacturing Overhead account directly to Cost of Goods Sold. Prepare the necessary journal entry.
3. Assume instead that the company allocates any balance in the Manufacturing Overhead account to the other accounts in proportion to the overhead applied during the year that is in the ending balance in each account. Prepare the necessary journal entry, with supporting computations.

EXERCISE 3–17 Applying Overhead; T-Accounts; Journal Entries [LO1, LO2, LO4, LO5, LO7]

Medusa Products uses a job-order costing system. Overhead costs are applied to jobs on the basis of machine-hours. At the beginning of the year, management estimated that 85,000 machine-hours would be required for the period's estimated level of production. The company also estimated $106,250 of fixed manufacturing overhead expenses for the coming period and variable manufacturing overhead of $0.75 per machine-hour.

Required:

1. Compute the company's predetermined overhead rate.

2. Assume that during the year the company actually works only 80,000 machine-hours and incurs the following costs in the Manufacturing Overhead and Work in Process accounts:

Manufacturing Overhead		
(Utilities)	14,000	?
(Insurance)	9,000	
(Maintenance)	33,000	
(Indirect materials)	7,000	
(Indirect labor)	65,000	
(Depreciation)	40,000	

Work in Process		
(Direct materials)	530,000	
(Direct labor)	85,000	
(Overhead)	?	

Copy the data in the T-accounts above onto your answer sheet. Compute the amount of overhead cost that would be applied to Work in Process for the year, and make the entry in your T-accounts.

3. Compute the amount of underapplied or overapplied overhead for the year, and show the balance in your Manufacturing Overhead T-account. Prepare a journal entry to close out the balance in this account to Cost of Goods Sold.
4. Explain why the manufacturing overhead was underapplied or overapplied for the year.

EXERCISE 3–18 Plantwide and Departmental Overhead Rates; Job Costs [LO1, LO2, LO3]

Smithson Company uses a job-order costing system and has two manufacturing departments—Molding and Fabrication. The company provided the following estimates at the beginning of the year:

	Molding	Fabrication	Total
Machine-hours	20,000	30,000	50,000
Fixed manufacturing overhead costs	$800,000	$300,000	$1,100,000
Variable manufacturing overhead per machine-hour	$5.00	$5.00	

During the year, the company had no beginning or ending inventories and it started, completed, and sold only two jobs—Job D-75 and Job C-100. It provided the following information related to those two jobs:

Job D-75:	Molding	Fabrication	Total
Direct materials cost	$375,000	$325,000	$700,000
Direct labor cost	$200,000	$160,000	$360,000
Machine-hours	15,000	5,000	20,000

Job C-100:	Molding	Fabrication	Total
Direct materials cost	$300,000	$250,000	$550,000
Direct labor cost	$175,000	$225,000	$400,000
Machine-hours	5,000	25,000	30,000

Smithson had no overapplied or underapplied manufacturing overhead during the year.

Required:

1. Assume Smithson uses a plantwide overhead rate based on machine-hours.
   a. Compute the predetermined plantwide overhead rate.
   b. Compute the total manufacturing costs assigned to Job D-75 and Job C-100.
   c. If Smithson establishes bid prices that are 150% of total manufacturing costs, what bid price would it have established for Job D-75 and Job C-100?
   d. What is Smithson's cost of goods sold for the year?

2. Assume Smithson uses departmental overhead rates based on machine-hours.
   a. Compute the predetermined departmental overhead rates.
   b. Compute the total manufacturing costs assigned to Job D-75 and Job C-100.
   c. If Smithson establishes bid prices that are 150% of total manufacturing costs, what bid price would it have established for Job D-75 and Job C-100?
   d. What is Smithson's cost of goods sold for the year?
3. What managerial insights are revealed by the computations that you performed in this problem? (Hint: Do the cost of goods sold amounts that you computed in requirements 1 and 2 differ from one another? Do the bid prices that you computed in requirements 1 and 2 differ from one another? Why?)

EXERCISE 3–19 Applying Overhead; Journal Entries; T-Accounts [LO1, LO2, LO3, LO4, LO5]

Custom Metal Works produces castings and other metal parts to customer specifications. The company uses a job-order costing system and applies overhead costs to jobs on the basis of machine-hours. At the beginning of the year, the company used a cost formula to estimate that it would incur $4,320,000 in manufacturing overhead cost at an activity level of 576,000 machine-hours.

The company had no work in process at the beginning of the year. The company spent the entire month of January working on one large order—Job 382, which was an order for 8,000 machined parts. Cost data for January follow:

a. Raw materials purchased on account, $315,000.
b. Raw materials requisitioned for production, $270,000 (80% direct and 20% indirect).
c. Labor cost incurred in the factory, $190,000, of which $80,000 was direct labor and $110,000 was indirect labor.
d. Depreciation recorded on factory equipment, $63,000.
e. Other manufacturing overhead costs incurred, $85,000 (credit Accounts Payable).
f. Manufacturing overhead cost was applied to production on the basis of 40,000 machine-hours actually worked during January.
g. The completed job was moved into the finished goods warehouse on January 31 to await delivery to the customer. (In computing the dollar amount for this entry, remember that the cost of a completed job consists of direct materials, direct labor, and *applied* overhead.)

Required:

1. Prepare journal entries to record items (a) through (f) above. Ignore item (g) for the moment.
2. Prepare T-accounts for Manufacturing Overhead and Work in Process. Post the relevant items from your journal entries to these T-accounts.
3. Prepare a journal entry for item (g) above.
4. Compute the unit product cost that will appear on the job cost sheet for Job 382.

EXERCISE 3–20 Applying Overhead in a Service Company [LO1, LO2, LO3]

Pearson Architectural Design began operations on January 2. The following activity was recorded in the company's Work in Process account for the first month of operations:

Work in Process

Costs of subcontracted work	90,000	To completed projects	570,000
Direct staff costs	200,000		
Studio overhead	320,000		

Pearson Architectural Design is a service firm, so the names of the accounts it uses are different from the names used in manufacturing companies. Costs of Subcontracted Work is comparable to Direct Materials; Direct Staff Costs is the same as Direct Labor; Studio Overhead is the same as Manufacturing Overhead; and Completed Projects is the same as Finished Goods. Apart from the difference in terms, the accounting methods used by the company are identical to the methods used by manufacturing companies.

Pearson Architectural Design uses a job-order costing system and applies studio overhead to Work in Process on the basis of direct staff costs. At the end of January, only one job was still in process. This job (the Krimmer Corporation Headquarters project) had been charged with $13,500 in direct staff costs.

Required:

1. Compute the predetermined overhead rate that was in use during January.
2. Complete the following job cost sheet for the partially completed Krimmer Corporation Headquarters project.

Job Cost Sheet Krimmer Corporation Headquarters Project As of January 31	
Costs of subcontracted work	$?
Direct staff costs	?
Studio overhead	?
Total cost to January 31	$?

Problems

Connect ACCOUNTING

All applicable problems are available with McGraw-Hill's *Connect™ Accounting*.

PROBLEM 3–21 Predetermined Overhead Rate; Disposition of Underapplied or Overapplied Overhead [LO1, LO7]

Savallas Company is highly automated and uses computers to control manufacturing operations. The company uses a job-order costing system and applies manufacturing overhead cost to products on the basis of computer-hours. The following estimates were used in preparing the predetermined overhead rate at the beginning of the year:

Computer-hours	85,000
Fixed manufacturing overhead cost	$1,275,000
Variable manufacturing overhead per computer-hour	$3.00

During the year, a severe economic recession resulted in cutting back production and a buildup of inventory in the company's warehouse. The company's cost records revealed the following actual cost and operating data for the year:

Computer-hours	60,000
Manufacturing overhead cost	$1,350,000
Inventories at year-end:	
Raw materials	$400,000
Work in process	$160,000
Finished goods	$1,040,000
Cost of goods sold	$2,800,000

Required:

1. Compute the company's predetermined overhead rate for the year.
2. Compute the underapplied or overapplied overhead for the year.
3. Assume the company closes any underapplied or overapplied overhead directly to Cost of Goods Sold. Prepare the appropriate entry.
4. Assume that the company allocates any underapplied or overapplied overhead to Work in Process, Finished Goods, and Cost of Goods Sold on the basis of the amount of overhead applied during the year that remains in each account at the end of the year. These amounts are $43,200 for Work in Process, $280,800 for Finished Goods, and $756,000 for Cost of Goods Sold. Prepare the journal entry to show the allocation.
5. How much higher or lower will net operating income be for the year if the underapplied or overapplied overhead is allocated rather than closed directly to Cost of Goods Sold?

PROBLEM 3–22 Schedules of Cost of Goods Manufactured and Cost of Goods Sold; Income Statement [LO6]

Valenko Company provided the following account balances for the year ended December 31 (all raw materials are used in production as direct materials):

Selling expenses	$215,000
Purchases of raw materials	$260,000
Direct labor	?
Administrative expenses	$160,000
Manufacturing overhead applied to work in process	$340,000
Total actual manufacturing overhead costs	$350,000

Inventory balances at the beginning and end of the year were as follows:

	Beginning of Year	End of Year
Raw materials	$50,000	$40,000
Work in process	?	$33,000
Finished goods	$30,000	?

The total manufacturing costs for the year were $675,000; the cost of goods available for sale totaled $720,000; the unadjusted cost of goods sold totaled $665,000; and the net operating income was $35,000. The company's overapplied or underapplied overhead is closed entirely to cost of goods sold.

Required:

Prepare schedules of cost of goods manufactured and cost of goods sold and an income statement. (Hint: Prepare the income statement and schedule of cost of goods sold first followed by the schedule of cost of goods manufactured.)

PROBLEM 3–23 T-Account Analysis of Cost Flows [LO1, LO5, LO6, LO7]

Selected T-accounts for Rolm Company are given below for the just completed year:

Raw Materials

Bal. 1/1	30,000	Credits	?
Debits	420,000		
Bal. 12/31	60,000		

Manufacturing Overhead

Debits	385,000	Credits	?

Work in Process

Bal. 1/1	70,000	Credits	810,000
Direct materials	320,000		
Direct labor	110,000		
Overhead	400,000		
Bal. 12/31	?		

Factory Wages Payable

Debits	179,000	Bal. 1/1	10,000
		Credits	175,000
		Bal. 12/31	6,000

Finished Goods

Bal. 1/1	40,000	Credits	?
Debits	?		
Bal. 12/31	130,000		

Cost of Goods Sold

Debits	?		

Required:

1. What was the cost of raw materials put into production during the year?
2. How much of the materials in (1) above consisted of indirect materials?
3. How much of the factory labor cost for the year consisted of indirect labor?
4. What was the cost of goods manufactured for the year?
5. What was the cost of goods sold for the year (before considering underapplied or overapplied overhead)?
6. If overhead is applied to production on the basis of direct materials cost, what rate was in effect during the year?
7. Was manufacturing overhead underapplied or overapplied? By how much?
8. Compute the ending balance in the Work in Process inventory account. Assume that this balance consists entirely of goods started during the year. If $32,000 of this balance is direct materials cost, how much of it is direct labor cost? Manufacturing overhead cost?

eXcel

PROBLEM 3–24 Schedule of Cost of Goods Manufactured; Overhead Analysis [LO1, LO2, LO3, LO6, LO7]

The Pacific Manufacturing Company operates a job-order costing system and applies overhead cost to jobs on the basis of direct labor cost. Its predetermined overhead rate was based on a cost formula that estimated $126,000 of manufacturing overhead for an estimated allocation base of $84,000 direct labor dollars. The company has provided the following data in the form of an Excel worksheet:

	A	B	C	D
1		*Beginning*	*Ending*	
2	Raw Materials	$21,000	$16,000	
3	Work in Process	$44,000	$40,000	
4	Finished Goods	$68,000	$60,000	
5				
6	*The following actual costs were incurred during the year*			
7	Purchase of raw materials (all direct)		$133,000	
8	Direct labor cost		$80,000	
9	Manufacturing overhead costs:			
10	Insurance, factory		$7,000	
11	Depreciation of equipment		$18,000	
12	Indirect labor		$42,000	
13	Property taxes		$9,000	
14	Maintenance		$11,000	
15	Rent, building		$36,000	
16				
17				

Sheet1 Sheet2 Sheet3

Required:

1. *a.* Compute the predetermined overhead rate for the year.
   b. Compute the amount of underapplied or overapplied overhead for the year.
2. Prepare a schedule of cost of goods manufactured for the year. Assume all raw materials are used in production as direct materials.
3. Compute the unadjusted cost of goods sold for the year. (Do not include any underapplied or overapplied overhead in your cost of goods sold figure.) What options are available for disposing of underapplied or overapplied overhead?
4. Job 137 was started and completed during the year. What price would have been charged to the customer if the job required $3,200 in materials and $4,200 in direct labor cost, and the company priced its jobs at 40% above the job's cost according to the accounting system?
5. Direct labor made up $8,000 of the $40,000 ending Work in Process inventory balance. Supply the information missing below:

Direct materials	$?
Direct labor	8,000
Manufacturing overhead	?
Work in process inventory	$40,000

PROBLEM 3–25 Journal Entries; T-Accounts; Financial Statements [LO1, LO2, LO3, LO4, LO5, LO6, LO7]

eXcel

Southworth Company uses a job-order costing system and applies manufacturing overhead cost to jobs on the basis of the cost of direct materials used in production. Its predetermined overhead rate was based on a cost formula that estimated $248,000 of manufacturing overhead for an estimated allocation base of $155,000 direct material dollars. The following transactions took place during the year (all purchases and services were acquired on account):

a. Raw materials purchased, $142,000.
b. Raw materials requisitioned for use in production (all direct materials), $150,000.
c. Utility bills incurred in the factory, $21,000.
d. Costs for salaries and wages were incurred as follows:

Direct labor	$216,000
Indirect labor	$90,000
Selling and administrative salaries	$145,000

e. Maintenance costs incurred in the factory, $15,000.
f. Advertising costs incurred, $130,000.
g. Depreciation recorded for the year, $50,000 (90% relates to factory assets, and the remainder relates to selling and administrative assets).
h. Rental cost incurred on buildings, $90,000 (80% of the space is occupied by the factory, and 20% is occupied by sales and administration).
i. Miscellaneous selling and administrative costs incurred, $17,000.
j. Manufacturing overhead cost was applied to jobs, $ __?__.
k. Cost of goods manufactured for the year, $590,000.
l. Sales for the year (all on account) totaled $1,000,000. These goods cost $600,000 according to their job cost sheets.

The balances in the inventory accounts at the beginning of the year were as follows:

Raw Materials	$18,000
Work in Process	$24,000
Finished Goods	$35,000

Required:

1. Prepare journal entries to record the above data.
2. Post your entries to T-accounts. (Don't forget to enter the opening inventory balances above.) Determine the ending balances in the inventory accounts and in the Manufacturing Overhead account.
3. Prepare a schedule of cost of goods manufactured.
4. Prepare a journal entry to close any balance in the Manufacturing Overhead account to Cost of Goods Sold. Prepare a schedule of cost of goods sold.
5. Prepare an income statement for the year.
6. Job 218 was one of the many jobs started and completed during the year. The job required $3,600 in direct materials and 400 hours of direct labor time at a rate of $11 per hour. If the job contained 500 units and the company billed at 75% above the unit product cost on the job cost sheet, what price per unit would have been charged to the customer?

PROBLEM 3–26 Multiple Departments; Applying Overhead [LO1, LO2, LO3, LO7]

eXcel

WoodGrain Technology makes home office furniture from fine hardwoods. The company uses a job-order costing system and predetermined overhead rates to apply manufacturing overhead cost to jobs. The predetermined overhead rate in the Preparation Department is based on machine-hours, and the rate in the Fabrication Department is based on direct labor-hours. At the beginning of the year, the company's management made the following estimates for the year:

	Department	
	Preparation	Fabrication
Machine-hours	80,000	21,000
Direct labor-hours	35,000	50,000
Direct materials cost	$190,000	$400,000
Direct labor cost	$280,000	$530,000
Fixed manufacturing overhead cost	$256,000	$520,000
Variable manufacturing overhead per machine-hour	$2.00	—
Variable manufacturing overhead per direct labor-hour	—	$4.00

Job 127 was started on April 1 and completed on May 12. The company's cost records show the following information concerning the job:

	Department	
	Preparation	Fabrication
Machine-hours	350	70
Direct labor-hours	80	130
Direct materials cost	$940	$1,200
Direct labor cost	$710	$980

Required:

1. Compute the predetermined overhead rate used during the year in the Preparation Department. Compute the rate used in the Fabrication Department.
2. Compute the total overhead cost applied to Job 127.
3. What would be the total cost recorded for Job 127? If the job contained 25 units, what would be the unit product cost?
4. At the end of the year, the records of WoodGrain Technology revealed the following *actual* cost and operating data for all jobs worked on during the year:

	Department	
	Preparation	Fabrication
Machine-hours	73,000	24,000
Direct labor-hours	30,000	54,000
Direct materials cost	$165,000	$420,000
Manufacturing overhead cost	$390,000	$740,000

What was the amount of underapplied or overapplied overhead in each department at the end of the year?

PROBLEM 3–27 Comprehensive Problem [LO1, LO2, LO4, LO5, LO6, LO7]

Sovereign Millwork, Ltd., produces reproductions of antique residential moldings at a plant located in Manchester, England. Because there are hundreds of products, some of which are made only to order, the company uses a job-order costing system. On July 1, the start of the company's fiscal year, inventory account balances were as follows:

Raw Materials	£10,000
Work in Process	£4,000
Finished Goods	£8,000

The company applies overhead cost to jobs on the basis of machine-hours. Its predetermined overhead rate for the fiscal year starting July 1 was based on a cost formula that estimated £99,000 of manufacturing overhead for an estimated activity level of 45,000 machine-hours. During the year, the following transactions were completed:

a. Raw materials purchased on account, £160,000.
b. Raw materials requisitioned for use in production, £140,000 (materials costing £120,000 were chargeable directly to jobs; the remaining materials were indirect).
c. Costs for employee services were incurred as follows:

Direct labor	£90,000
Indirect labor	£60,000
Sales commissions	£20,000
Administrative salaries	£50,000

d. Prepaid insurance expired during the year, £18,000 (£13,000 of this amount related to factory operations, and the remainder related to selling and administrative activities).
e. Utility costs incurred in the factory, £10,000.
f. Advertising costs incurred, £15,000.
g. Depreciation recorded on equipment, £25,000. (£20,000 of this amount was on equipment used in factory operations; the remaining £5,000 was on equipment used in selling and administrative activities.)
h. Manufacturing overhead cost was applied to jobs, £?. (The company recorded 50,000 machine-hours of operating time during the year.)
i. Goods that had cost £310,000 to manufacture according to their job cost sheets were completed.
j. Sales (all on account) to customers during the year totaled £498,000. These goods had cost £308,000 to manufacture according to their job cost sheets.

Required:

1. Prepare journal entries to record the transactions for the year.
2. Prepare T-accounts for inventories, Manufacturing Overhead, and Cost of Goods Sold. Post relevant data from your journal entries to these T-accounts (don't forget to enter the opening balances in your inventory accounts). Compute an ending balance in each account.
3. Is Manufacturing Overhead underapplied or overapplied for the year? Prepare a journal entry to close any balance in the Manufacturing Overhead account to Cost of Goods Sold.
4. Prepare an income statement for the year. (Do not prepare a schedule of cost of goods manufactured; all of the information needed for the income statement is available in the journal entries and T-accounts you have prepared.)

PROBLEM 3–28 Cost Flows; T-Accounts; Income Statement [LO1, LO2, LO5, LO6, LO7]
Fantastic Props, Inc., designs and fabricates movie props such as mock-ups of star-fighters and cybernetic robots. The company's balance sheet as of January 1, the beginning of the current year, appears below:

Fantastic Props, Inc. Balance Sheet January 1		
Assets		
Current assets:		
Cash		$ 15,000
Accounts receivable		40,000
Inventories:		
Raw materials	$ 25,000	
Work in process	30,000	
Finished goods (props awaiting shipment)	45,000	100,000
Prepaid insurance		5,000
Total current assets		160,000
Buildings and equipment	500,000	
Less accumulated depreciation	210,000	290,000
Total assets		$450,000
Liabilities and Stockholders' Equity		
Accounts payable		$ 75,000
Capital stock	$250,000	
Retained earnings	125,000	375,000
Total liabilities and stockholders' equity		$450,000

Because each prop is a unique design and may require anything from a few hours to a month or more to complete, Fantastic Props uses a job-order costing system. Overhead in the fabrication shop is charged to props on the basis of direct labor cost. The company's predetermined overhead rate for the year is based on a cost formula that estimated $80,000 in manufacturing overhead for an estimated allocation base of $100,000 direct labor dollars. The following transactions were recorded during the year:

a. Raw materials, such as wood, paints, and metal sheeting, were purchased on account, $80,000.
b. Raw materials were issued to production, $90,000; $5,000 of this amount was for indirect materials.
c. Payroll costs incurred and paid: direct labor, $120,000; indirect labor, $30,000; and selling and administrative salaries, $75,000.
d. Fabrication shop utilities costs incurred, $12,000.
e. Depreciation recorded for the year, $30,000 ($5,000 on selling and administrative assets; $25,000 on fabrication shop assets).
f. Prepaid insurance expired, $4,800 ($4,000 related to fabrication shop operations, and $800 related to selling and administrative activities).
g. Shipping expenses incurred, $40,000.
h. Other manufacturing overhead costs incurred, $17,000 (credit Accounts Payable).
i. Manufacturing overhead was applied to production. Overhead is applied on the basis of direct labor cost.
j. Movie props that cost $310,000 to produce according to their job cost sheets were completed.
k. Sales for the year totaled $450,000 and were all on account. The total cost to produce these movie props was $300,000 according to their job cost sheets.
l. Collections on account from customers, $445,000.
m. Payments on account to suppliers, $150,000.

Required:

1. Prepare a T-account for each account on the company's balance sheet, and enter the beginning balances.

2. Make entries directly into the T-accounts for transactions (a) through (m). Create new T-accounts as needed. Determine an ending balance for each T-account.
3. Was manufacturing overhead underapplied or overapplied for the year? Assume that the company allocates any overhead balance between the Work in Process, Finished Goods, and Cost of Goods Sold accounts. Prepare a journal entry to show the allocation. (Round allocation percentages to one decimal place.)
4. Prepare an income statement for the year. (Do not prepare a schedule of cost of goods manufactured; all of the information needed for the income statement is available in the T-accounts.)

Cases

connect ACCOUNTING

All applicable cases are available with McGraw-Hill's *Connect™ Accounting*.

CASE 3–29 Plantwide versus Departmental Overhead Rates; Underapplied or Overapplied Overhead [LO1, LO2, LO3, LO7]

"Don't tell me we've lost another bid!" exclaimed Sandy Kovallas, president of Lenko Products, Inc. "I'm afraid so," replied Doug Martin, the operations vice president. "One of our competitors underbid us by about $10,000 on the Hastings job." "I just can't figure it out," said Kovallas. "It seems we're either too high to get the job or too low to make any money on half the jobs we bid anymore. What's happened?"

Lenko Products manufactures specialized goods to customers' specifications and operates a job-order costing system. Manufacturing overhead cost is applied to jobs on the basis of direct labor cost. The following estimates were made at the beginning of the year:

	Department			
	Cutting	Machining	Assembly	Total Plant
Direct labor	$300,000	$200,000	$400,000	$900,000
Manufacturing overhead	$540,000	$800,000	$100,000	$1,440,000

Jobs require varying amounts of work in the three departments. The Hastings job, for example, would have required manufacturing costs in the three departments as follows:

	Department			
	Cutting	Machining	Assembly	Total Plant
Direct materials	$12,000	$900	$5,600	$18,500
Direct labor	$6,500	$1,700	$13,000	$21,200
Manufacturing overhead	?	?	?	?

The company uses a plantwide overhead rate to apply manufacturing overhead cost to jobs.

Required:

1. Assuming the use of a plantwide overhead rate:
   a. Compute the rate for the current year.
   b. Determine the amount of manufacturing overhead cost that would have been applied to the Hastings job.
2. Suppose that instead of using a plantwide overhead rate, the company had used a separate predetermined overhead rate in each department. Under these conditions:
   a. Compute the rate for each department for the current year.
   b. Determine the amount of manufacturing overhead cost that would have been applied to the Hastings job.
3. Explain the difference between the manufacturing overhead that would have been applied to the Hastings job using the plantwide rate in question 1(b) and using the departmental rates in question 2(b).

4. Assume that it is customary in the industry to bid jobs at 150% of total manufacturing cost (direct materials, direct labor, and applied overhead). What was the company's bid price on the Hastings job? What would the bid price have been if departmental overhead rates had been used to apply overhead cost?
5. At the end of the year, the company assembled the following *actual* cost data relating to all jobs worked on during the year:

	Department			
	Cutting	Machining	Assembly	Total Plant
Direct materials.	$760,000	$90,000	$410,000	$1,260,000
Direct labor	$320,000	$210,000	$340,000	$870,000
Manufacturing overhead.	$560,000	$830,000	$92,000	$1,482,000

Compute the underapplied or overapplied overhead for the year (*a*) assuming that a plantwide overhead rate is used, and (*b*) assuming that departmental overhead rates are used.

CASE 3–30 Ethics and the Manager [LO1, LO2, LO7]

Cristin Madsen has recently been transferred to the Appliances Division of Solequin Corporation. Shortly after taking over her new position as divisional controller, she was asked to develop the division's predetermined overhead rate for the upcoming year. The accuracy of the rate is important because it is used throughout the year and any overapplied or underapplied overhead is closed out to Cost of Goods Sold at the end of the year. Solequin Corporation uses direct labor-hours in all of its divisions as the allocation base for manufacturing overhead.

To compute the predetermined overhead rate, Cristin divided her estimate of the total manufacturing overhead for the coming year by the production manager's estimate of the total direct labor-hours for the coming year. She took her computations to the division's general manager for approval but was quite surprised when he suggested a modification in the base. Her conversation with the general manager of the Appliances Division, Lance Jusic, went like this:

Madsen: Here are my calculations for next year's predetermined overhead rate. If you approve, we can enter the rate into the computer on January 1 and be up and running in the job-order costing system right away this year.

Jusic: Thanks for coming up with the calculations so quickly, and they look just fine. There is, however, one slight modification I would like to see. Your estimate of the total direct labor-hours for the year is 110,000 hours. How about cutting that to about 105,000 hours?

Madsen: I don't know if I can do that. The production manager says she will need about 110,000 direct labor-hours to meet the sales projections for next year. Besides, there are going to be over 108,000 direct labor-hours during the current year and sales are projected to be higher next year.

Jusic: Cristin, I know all of that. I would still like to reduce the direct labor-hours in the base to something like 105,000 hours. You probably don't know that I had an agreement with your predecessor as divisional controller to shave 5% or so off the estimated direct labor-hours every year. That way, we kept a reserve that usually resulted in a big boost to net operating income at the end of the fiscal year in December. We called it our Christmas bonus. Corporate headquarters always seemed as pleased as punch that we could pull off such a miracle at the end of the year. This system has worked well for many years, and I don't want to change it now.

Required:

1. Explain how shaving 5% off the estimated direct labor-hours in the base for the predetermined overhead rate usually results in a big boost in net operating income at the end of the fiscal year.
2. Should Cristin Madsen go along with the general manager's request to reduce the direct labor-hours in the predetermined overhead rate computation to 105,000 direct labor-hours?

Appendix 3A: The Predetermined Overhead Rate and Capacity

LEARNING OBJECTIVE 8
Understand the implications of basing the predetermined overhead rate on activity at capacity rather than on estimated activity for the period.

Companies typically base their predetermined overhead rates on the estimated, or budgeted, amount of the allocation base for the upcoming period. This is the method that is used in the chapter, but it is a practice that has come under severe criticism.[1] The criticism centers on how fixed manufacturing overhead costs are handled under this traditional approach. As we shall see, the critics argue that, in general, too much fixed manufacturing overhead cost is applied to products. To focus on this issue, we will make two simplifying assumptions in this appendix: (1) we will consider only fixed manufacturing overhead; and (2) we will assume that the actual fixed manufacturing overhead at the end of the period is the same as the estimated, or budgeted, fixed manufacturing overhead at the beginning of the period. Neither of these assumptions is entirely realistic. Ordinarily, some manufacturing overhead is variable and even fixed costs can differ from what was expected at the beginning of the period, but making those assumptions enables us to focus on the primary issues the critics raise.

An example will help us to understand the controversy. Prahad Corporation manufactures music CDs for local recording studios. The company's CD duplicating machine is capable of producing a new CD every 10 seconds from a master CD. The company leases the CD duplicating machine for $180,000 per year, and this is the company's only manufacturing overhead cost. With allowances for setups and maintenance, the machine is theoretically capable of producing up to 900,000 CDs per year. However, due to weak retail sales of CDs, the company's commercial customers are unlikely to order more than 600,000 CDs next year. The company uses machine time as the allocation base for applying manufacturing overhead to CDs. These data are summarized below:

Prahad Corporation Data	
Total manufacturing overhead cost	$180,000 per year
Allocation base—machine time per CD	10 seconds per CD
Capacity	900,000 CDs per year
Budgeted output for next year	600,000 CDs

If Prahad follows common practice and computes its predetermined overhead rate using estimated or budgeted figures, then its predetermined overhead rate for next year would be $0.03 per second of machine time computed as follows:

$$\text{Predetermined overhead rate} = \frac{\text{Estimated total manufacturing overhead cost}}{\text{Estimated total amount of the allocation base}}$$

$$= \frac{\$180{,}000}{600{,}000 \text{ CDs} \times 10 \text{ seconds per CD}}$$

$$= \$0.03 \text{ per second}$$

Because each CD requires 10 seconds of machine time, each CD will be charged for $0.30 of overhead cost.

Critics charge that there are two problems with this procedure. First, if predetermined overhead rates are based on budgeted activity and overhead includes significant

[1] Institute of Management Accountants, *Measuring the Cost of Capacity: Statements on Management Accounting, Number 4Y,* Montvale, NJ; Thomas Klammer, ed., *Capacity Measurement and Improvement: A Manager's Guide to Evaluating and Optimizing Capacity Productivity* (Chicago: CAM-I, Irwin Professional Publishing); and C. J. McNair, "The Hidden Costs of Capacity," *The Journal of Cost Management* (Spring 1994), pp. 12–24.

fixed costs, then the unit product costs will fluctuate depending on the budgeted level of activity for the period. For example, if the budgeted output for the year was only 300,000 CDs, the predetermined overhead rate would be \$0.06 per second of machine time or \$0.60 per CD rather than \$0.30 per CD. In general, if budgeted output falls, the overhead cost per unit will increase; it will appear that the CDs cost more to make. Managers may then be tempted to increase prices at the worst possible time—just as demand is falling.

Second, critics charge that under the traditional approach, products are charged for resources that they don't use. When the fixed costs of capacity are spread over estimated activity, the units that are produced must shoulder the costs of unused capacity. That is why the applied overhead cost per unit increases as the level of activity falls. The critics argue that products should be charged only for the capacity that they use; they should not be charged for the capacity they don't use. This can be accomplished by basing the predetermined overhead rate on capacity as follows:

$$\text{Predetermined overhead rate based on capacity} = \frac{\text{Estimated total manufacturing overhead cost at capacity}}{\text{Estimated total amount of the allocation base at capacity}}$$

$$= \frac{\$180{,}000}{900{,}000 \text{ CDs} \times 10 \text{ seconds per CD}}$$

$$= \$0.02 \text{ per second}$$

It is important to realize that the numerator in this predetermined overhead rate is the estimated total manufacturing overhead cost *at capacity.* In general, the numerator in a predetermined overhead rate is the estimated total manufacturing overhead cost for the level of activity in the denominator. Ordinarily, the estimated total manufacturing overhead cost *at capacity* will be larger than the estimated total manufacturing overhead cost *at the estimated level of activity.* The estimated level of activity in this case was 600,000 CDs (or 6 million seconds of machine time), whereas capacity is 900,000 CDs (or 9 million seconds of machine time). The estimated total manufacturing overhead cost at 600,000 CDs was \$180,000. This also happens to be the estimated total manufacturing overhead cost at 900,000 CDs, but that only happens because we have assumed that the manufacturing overhead is entirely fixed. If manufacturing overhead contained any variable element, the total manufacturing overhead would be larger at 900,000 CDs than at 600,000 CDs and, in that case, the predetermined overhead rate should reflect that fact.

At any rate, returning to the computation of the predetermined overhead rate based on capacity, the predetermined overhead rate is \$0.02 per second and so the overhead cost applied to each CD would be \$0.20. This charge is constant and would not be affected by the level of activity during a period. If output falls, the charge would still be \$0.20 per CD.

This method will almost certainly result in underapplied overhead. If actual output at Prahad Corporation is 600,000 CDs, then only \$120,000 of overhead cost would be applied to products (\$0.20 per CD × 600,000 CDs). Because the actual overhead cost is \$180,000, overhead would be underapplied by \$60,000. Because we are assuming that manufacturing overhead is entirely fixed and that actual manufacturing overhead equals the manufacturing overhead as estimated at the beginning of the year, the underapplied overhead represents the cost of unused capacity. In other words, if there had been no unused capacity, there would have been no underapplied overhead. The critics suggest that the underapplied overhead that results from unused capacity should be separately disclosed on the income statement as the Cost of Unused Capacity—a period expense. Disclosing this cost as a lump sum on the income statement, rather than burying it in Cost of Goods Sold or ending inventories, makes it much more visible to managers. An example of such an income statement appears below:

Prahad Corporation Income Statement For the Year Ended December 31		
Sales[1]		$1,200,000
Cost of goods sold[2]		1,080,000
Gross margin		120,000
Other expenses:		
Cost of unused capacity[3]	$60,000	
Selling and administrative expenses[4]	90,000	150,000
Net operating loss		($ 30,000)

[1] Assume sales of 600,000 CDs at $2 per CD.
[2] Assume the unit product cost of the CDs is $1.80, including $0.20 for manufacturing overhead.
[3] See the calculations in the text on the prior page. Underapplied overhead is $60,000.
[4] Assume selling and administrative expenses total $90,000.

Note that the cost of unused capacity is prominently displayed on this income statement.

Official pronouncements do not prohibit basing predetermined overhead rates on capacity for external reports.[2] Nevertheless, basing the predetermined overhead rate on estimated or budgeted activity is a long-established practice in industry, and some managers and accountants may object to the large amounts of underapplied overhead that would often result from using capacity to determine predetermined overhead rates. And some may insist that the underapplied overhead be allocated among Cost of Goods Sold and ending inventories—which would defeat the purpose of basing the predetermined overhead rate on capacity.

IN BUSINESS

RESOURCE CONSUMPTION ACCOUNTING

Clopay Plastic Products Company, headquartered in Cincinnati, Ohio, recently implemented a pilot application of a German cost accounting system known in the United States as Resource Consumption Accounting (RCA). One of the benefits of RCA is that it uses the estimated total amount of the allocation base at capacity to calculate overhead rates and to assign costs to cost objects. This makes idle capacity visible to managers who can react to this information by either growing sales or taking steps to reduce the amount and cost of available capacity. It also ensures that products are only charged for the resources used to produce them.

Clopay's old cost system spread all of the company's manufacturing overhead costs over the units produced. So, if Clopay's senior managers decided to discontinue what appeared to be an unprofitable product, the unit costs of the remaining products would increase as the fixed overhead costs of the newly idled capacity were spread over the remaining products.

Source: B. Douglas Clinton and Sally A. Webber, "Here's Innovation in Management Accounting with Resource Consumption Accounting," *Strategic Finance*, October 2004, pp. 21–26.

[2] Institute of Management Accountants, *Measuring the Cost of Capacity*, pp. 46–47.

Appendix 3A Exercises and Problems

connect ACCOUNTING

All applicable exercises and problems are available with McGraw-Hill's *Connect™ Accounting*.

EXERCISE 3A–1 Overhead Rates and Capacity Issues [LO1, LO2, LO7, LO8]

Estate Pension Services helps clients to set up and administer pension plans that are in compliance with tax laws and regulatory requirements. The firm uses a job-order costing system in which overhead is applied to clients' accounts on the basis of professional staff hours charged to the accounts. Data concerning two recent years appear below:

	2010	2011
Estimated professional staff hours to be charged to clients' accounts	2,400	2,250
Estimated overhead cost	$144,000	$144,000
Professional staff hours available	3,000	3,000

"Professional staff hours available" is a measure of the capacity of the firm. Any hours available that are not charged to clients' accounts represent unused capacity. All of the firm's overhead is fixed.

Required:

1. Jennifer Miyami is an established client whose pension plan was set up many years ago. In both 2010 and 2011, only five hours of professional staff time were charged to Ms. Miyami's account. If the company bases its predetermined overhead rate on the estimated overhead cost and the estimated professional staff hours to be charged to clients, how much overhead cost would have been applied to Ms. Miyami's account in 2010? In 2011?
2. Suppose that the company bases its predetermined overhead rate on the estimated overhead cost and the estimated professional staff hours to be charged to clients as in (1) above. Also suppose that the actual professional staff hours charged to clients' accounts and the actual overhead costs turn out to be exactly as estimated in both years. By how much would the overhead be underapplied or overapplied in 2010? In 2011?
3. Refer back to the data concerning Ms. Miyami in (1) above. If the company bases its predetermined overhead rate on the professional staff hours available, how much overhead cost would have been applied to Ms. Miyami's account in 2010? In 2011?
4. Suppose that the company bases its predetermined overhead rate on the professional staff hours available as in (3) above. Also, suppose that the actual professional staff hours charged to clients' accounts and the actual overhead costs turn out to be exactly as estimated in both years. By how much would the overhead be underapplied or overapplied in 2010? In 2011?

EXERCISE 3A–2 Overhead Rate Based on Capacity [LO8]

Wixis Cabinets makes custom wooden cabinets for high-end stereo systems from specialty woods. The company uses a job-order costing system. The capacity of the plant is determined by the capacity of its constraint, which is time on the automated bandsaw that makes finely beveled cuts in wood according to the preprogrammed specifications of each cabinet. The bandsaw can operate up to 180 hours per month. The estimated total manufacturing overhead at capacity is $14,760 per month. The company bases its predetermined overhead rate on capacity, so its predetermined overhead rate is $82 per hour of bandsaw use.

The results of a recent month's operations appear below:

Sales	$43,740
Beginning inventories	$0
Ending inventories	$0
Direct materials	$5,350
Direct labor (all variable)	$8,860
Manufacturing overhead incurred	$14,220
Selling and administrative expense	$8,180
Actual hours of bandsaw use	150

Required:

1. Prepare an income statement following the example in Appendix 3A in which any underapplied overhead is directly recorded on the income statement as an expense.
2. Why is overhead ordinarily underapplied when the predetermined overhead rate is based on capacity?

PROBLEM 3A–3 Predetermined Overhead Rate and Capacity [LO1, LO2, LO7, LO8]

Skid Road Recording, Inc., is a small audio recording studio located in Seattle. The company handles work for advertising agencies—primarily for radio ads—and has a few singers and bands as clients. Skid Road Recording handles all aspects of recording from editing to making a digital master from which CDs can be copied. The competition in the audio recording industry in Seattle has always been tough, but it has been getting even tougher over the last several years. The studio has been losing customers to newer studios that are equipped with more up-to-date equipment and that are able to offer very attractive prices and excellent service. Summary data concerning the last two years of operations follow:

	2010	2011
Estimated hours of studio service	1,000	750
Estimated studio overhead cost	$90,000	$90,000
Actual hours of studio service provided	900	600
Actual studio overhead cost incurred	$90,000	$90,000
Hours of studio service at capacity	1,800	1,800

The company applies studio overhead to recording jobs on the basis of the hours of studio service provided. For example, 30 hours of studio time were required to record, edit, and master the *Slug Fest* music CD for a local band. All of the studio overhead is fixed, and the actual overhead cost incurred was exactly as estimated at the beginning of the year in both 2010 and 2011.

Required:

1. Skid Road Recording computes its predetermined overhead rate at the beginning of each year based on the estimated studio overhead and the estimated hours of studio service for the year. How much overhead would have been applied to the *Slug Fest* job if it had been done in 2010? In 2011? By how much would overhead have been underapplied or overapplied in 2010? In 2011?
2. The president of Skid Road Recording has heard that some companies in the industry have changed to a system of computing the predetermined overhead rate at the beginning of each year based on the hours of studio service that could be provided at capacity. He would like to know what effect this method would have on job costs. How much overhead would have been applied using this method to the *Slug Fest* job if it had been done in 2010? In 2011? By how much would overhead have been underapplied or overapplied in 2010 using this method? In 2011?
3. How would you interpret the underapplied or overapplied overhead that results from using studio hours at capacity to compute the predetermined overhead rate?
4. What fundamental business problem is Skid Road Recording facing? Which method of computing the predetermined overhead rate is likely to be more helpful in facing this problem? Explain.

CASE 3A–4 Ethics; Predetermined Overhead Rate and Capacity [LO2, LO7, LO8]

Melissa Ostwerk, the new controller of TurboDrives, Inc., has just returned from a seminar on the choice of the activity level in the predetermined overhead rate. Even though the subject did not sound exciting at first, she found that there were some important ideas presented that should get a hearing at her company. After returning from the seminar, she arranged a meeting with the production manager, Jan Kingman, and the assistant production manager, Lonny Chan.

Melissa: I ran across an idea that I wanted to check out with both of you. It's about the way we compute predetermined overhead rates.

Jan: We're all ears.

Melissa: We compute the predetermined overhead rate by dividing the estimated total factory overhead for the coming year, which is all a fixed cost, by the estimated total units produced for the coming year.

Lonny: We've been doing that as long as I've been with the company.

Jan: And it has been done that way at every other company I've worked at, except at most places they divide by direct labor-hours.

Melissa: We use units because it is simpler and we basically make one product with minor variations. But, there's another way to do it. Instead of basing the overhead rate on the estimated total units produced for the coming year, we could base it on the total units produced at capacity.

Lonny: Oh, the Marketing Department will love that. It will drop the costs on all of our products. They'll go wild over there cutting prices.

Melissa: That is a worry, but I wanted to talk to both of you first before going over to Marketing.

Jan: Aren't you always going to have a lot of underapplied overhead?

Melissa: That's correct, but let me show you how we would handle it. Here's an example based on our budget for next year.

Budgeted (estimated) production	80,000 units
Budgeted sales	80,000 units
Capacity	100,000 units
Selling price	$70 per unit
Variable manufacturing cost	$18 per unit
Total manufacturing overhead cost (all fixed)	$2,000,000
Selling and administrative expenses (all fixed)	$1,950,000
Beginning inventories	$0

Traditional approach to computing the predetermined overhead rate:

$$\text{Predetermined overhead rate} = \frac{\text{Estimated total manufacturing overhead cost}}{\text{Estimated total amount of the allocation base}}$$

$$= \frac{\$2,000,000}{80,000 \text{ units}} = \$25 \text{ per unit}$$

Budgeted Income Statement		
Revenue (80,000 units × $70 per unit)		$5,600,000
Cost of goods sold:		
Variable manufacturing (80,000 units × $18 per unit)	$1,440,000	
Manufacturing overhead applied (80,000 units × $25 per unit)	2,000,000	3,440,000
Gross margin		2,160,000
Selling and administrative expenses		1,950,000
Net operating income		$ 210,000

New approach to computing the predetermined overhead rate using capacity in the denominator:

$$\text{Predetermined overhead rate} = \frac{\text{Estimated total manufacturing overhead cost at capacity}}{\text{Estimated total amount of the allocation base at capacity}}$$

$$= \frac{\$2,000,000}{100,000 \text{ units}} = \$20 \text{ per unit}$$

Budgeted Income Statement		
Revenue (80,000 units × $70 per unit)		$5,600,000
Cost of goods sold:		
Variable manufacturing (80,000 units × $18 per unit)	$1,440,000	
Manufacturing overhead applied (80,000 units × $20 per unit)	1,600,000	3,040,000
Gross margin		2,560,000
Cost of unused capacity [(100,000 units − 80,000 units) × $20 per unit]		400,000
Selling and administrative expenses		1,950,000
Net operating income		$ 210,000

Jan: Whoa!! I don't think I like the looks of that "Cost of unused capacity." If that thing shows up on the income statement, someone from headquarters is likely to come down here looking for some people to lay off.

Lonny: I'm worried about something else, too. What happens when sales are not up to expectations? Can we pull the "hat trick"?

Melissa: I'm sorry, I don't understand.

Jan: Lonny's talking about something that happens fairly regularly. When sales are down and profits look like they are going to be lower than the president told the owners they were going to be, the president comes down here and asks us to deliver some more profits.

Lonny: And we pull them out of our hat.

Jan: Yeah, we just increase production until we get the profits we want.

Melissa: I still don't understand. You mean you increase sales?

Jan: Nope, we increase production. We're the production managers, not the sales managers.

Melissa: I get it. Because you have produced more, the sales force has more units it can sell.

Jan: Nope, the marketing people don't do a thing. We just build inventories and that does the trick.

Required:

In all of the questions below, assume that the predetermined overhead rate under the traditional method is $25 per unit, and under the new method it is $20 per unit. Also, assume that under the traditional method any underapplied or overapplied overhead is taken directly to the income statement as an adjustment to Cost of Goods Sold.

1. Suppose actual production is 80,000 units. Compute the net operating incomes that would be realized under the traditional and new methods if actual sales are 75,000 units and everything else turns out as expected.
2. How many units would have to be produced under each of the methods in order to realize the budgeted net operating income of $210,000 if actual sales are 75,000 units and everything else turns out as expected?
3. What effect does the new method based on capacity have on the volatility of net operating income?
4. Will the "hat trick" be easier or harder to perform if the new method based on capacity is used?
5. Do you think the "hat trick" is ethical?

Appendix 3B: Further Classification of Labor Costs

LEARNING OBJECTIVE 9
Properly account for labor costs associated with idle time, overtime, and fringe benefits.

Idle time, overtime, and fringe benefits associated with direct labor workers pose particular problems in accounting for labor costs. Are these costs a part of the costs of direct labor or are they something else?

Idle Time

Machine breakdowns, materials shortages, power failures, and the like result in idle time. The labor costs incurred during idle time may be treated as a manufacturing overhead cost rather than as a direct labor cost. This approach spreads such costs over all the production of a period rather than just the jobs that happen to be in process when breakdowns or other disruptions occur.

To give an example of how the cost of idle time may be handled, assume that a press operator earns \$12 per hour. If the press operator is paid for a normal 40-hour workweek but is idle for 3 hours during a given week due to breakdowns, labor cost would be allocated as follows:

Direct labor (\$12 per hour × 37 hours)	\$444
Manufacturing overhead (idle time: \$12 per hour × 3 hours)	36
Total cost for the week	\$480

Overtime Premium

The overtime premium paid to factory workers (direct labor as well as indirect labor) is usually considered to be part of manufacturing overhead and is not assigned to any particular order. At first glance this may seem strange because overtime is always spent working on some particular order. Why not charge that order for the overtime cost? The reason is that it would be considered unfair and arbitrary to charge an overtime premium against a particular order simply because the order *happened* to fall on the tail end of the daily production schedule.

To illustrate, assume that two batches of goods, order A and order B, each take three hours to complete. The production run on order A is scheduled early in the day, but the production run on order B is scheduled late in the afternoon. By the time the run on order B is completed, two hours of overtime have been logged. The necessity to work overtime was a result of the fact that total production exceeded the regular time available. Order B was no more responsible for the overtime than was order A. Therefore, managers feel that all production should share in the premium charge that resulted. This is considered a more equitable way of handling overtime premium because it doesn't penalize one run simply because it happens to occur late in the day.

Let us again assume that a press operator in a plant earns \$12 per hour. She is paid time and a half for overtime (time in excess of 40 hours a week). During a given week, she works 45 hours and has no idle time. Her labor cost for the week would be allocated as follows:

Direct labor (\$12 per hour × 45 hours)	\$540
Manufacturing overhead (overtime premium: \$6 per hour × 5 hours)	30
Total cost for the week	\$570

Observe from this computation that only the overtime premium of \$6 per hour is charged to the overhead account—*not* the entire \$18 earned for each hour of overtime work (\$12 regular rate per hour × 1.5 hours = \$18).

Labor Fringe Benefits

Labor fringe benefits are made up of employment-related costs paid by the employer and include the costs of insurance programs, retirement plans, various supplemental unemployment benefits, and hospitalization plans. The employer also pays the employer's share of Social Security, Medicare, workers' compensation, federal employment tax, and state unemployment insurance. These costs often add up to as much as 30% to 40% of base pay.

Many companies treat all such costs as indirect labor by adding them to manufacturing overhead. Other companies treat the portion of fringe benefits that relates to direct labor as additional direct labor cost. This approach is conceptually superior because the fringe benefits provided to direct labor workers clearly represent an added cost of their services.

Appendix 3B Exercises and Problems

All applicable exercises and problems are available with McGraw-Hill's *Connect™ Accounting.*

EXERCISE 3B–1 Allocations of the Cost of Idle Time [LO9]

Chris Shannon is employed by Acme Company and is paid $18 per hour. Last week she worked 36 hours assembling one of the company's products and was idle 4 hours due to material shortages. Acme's employees are engaged at their workstations for a normal 40-hour week.

Required:

Allocate Ms. Shannon's earnings for the week between direct labor and manufacturing overhead.

EXERCISE 3B–2 Allocations of Overtime Pay [LO9]

Barry DeJay operates a stamping machine on the assembly line of Clinton Manufacturing Company. Last week Mr. DeJay worked 46 hours. His basic wage rate is $16 per hour, with time and a half for overtime (time worked in excess of 40 hours per week).

Required:

Allocate Mr. DeJay's earnings for the week between direct labor and manufacturing overhead.

EXERCISE 3B–3 Classification of Overtime Cost [LO9]

Several weeks ago you called Jiffy Plumbing Company to have some routine repair work done on the plumbing system in your home. The plumber came about two weeks later, at four o'clock in the afternoon, and spent two hours completing your repair work. When you received your bill from the company, it contained a $75 charge for labor—$30 for the first hour and $45 for the second.

When questioned about the difference in hourly rates, the company's service manager explained that the higher rate for the second hour contained a charge for an "overtime premium," because the union required that plumbers be paid time and a half for any work in excess of eight hours per day. The service manager further explained that the company was working overtime to "catch up a little" on its backlog of work orders, but still needed to maintain a "decent" profit margin on the plumbers' time.

Required:

1. Do you agree with the company's computation of the labor charge on your job?
2. The company pays its plumbers $20 per hour for the first eight hours worked in a day and $30 per hour for any additional time worked. Show how the cost of the plumber's time for the day (nine hours) should be allocated between direct labor and general overhead on the company's books.
3. Under what circumstances might the company be justified in charging an overtime premium for repair work on your home?

EXERCISE 3B–4 Classification of Labor Costs [LO9]

Fred Austin is employed by White Company where he assembles a component part for one of the company's products. Fred is paid $12 per hour for regular time, and he is paid time and a half (i.e., $18 per hour) for all work in excess of 40 hours per week.

Required:

1. Assume that during a given week Fred is idle for two hours due to machine breakdowns and that he is idle for four more hours due to material shortages. No overtime is recorded for the week. Allocate Fred's wages for the week between direct labor and manufacturing overhead.
2. Assume that during a following week Fred works a total of 50 hours. He has no idle time for the week. Allocate Fred's wages for the week between direct labor and manufacturing overhead.
3. Fred's company provides an attractive package of fringe benefits for its employees. This package includes a retirement program and a health insurance program. Explain two ways that the company could handle the costs of its direct laborers' fringe benefits in its cost records.

PROBLEM 3B–5 Classification of Labor Costs [LO9]

Lynn Bjorland is employed by Southern Laboratories and is directly involved in preparing the company's leading antibiotic drug. Lynn's basic wage rate is $24 per hour. The company pays its employees time and a half (i.e., $36 per hour) for any work in excess of 40 hours per week.

Required:

1. Suppose that in a given week Lynn works 45 hours. Compute Lynn's total wages for the week. How much of this cost would the company allocate to direct labor? To manufacturing overhead?
2. Suppose in another week that Lynn works 50 hours but is idle for 4 hours during the week due to equipment breakdowns. Compute Lynn's total wages for the week. How much of this amount would be allocated to direct labor? To manufacturing overhead?
3. Southern Laboratories has an attractive package of fringe benefits that costs the company $8 for each hour of employee time (either regular time or overtime). During a particular week, Lynn works 48 hours but is idle for 3 hours due to material shortages. Compute Lynn's total wages and fringe benefits for the week. If the company treats all fringe benefits as part of manufacturing overhead cost, how much of Lynn's wages and fringe benefits for the week would be allocated to direct labor? To manufacturing overhead?
4. Refer to the data in (3) above. If the company treats that part of fringe benefits relating to direct labor as added direct labor cost, how much of Lynn's wages and fringe benefits for the week will be allocated to direct labor? To manufacturing overhead?

Process Costing

Costing the "Quicker-Picker-Upper"

BUSINESS FOCUS

If you have ever spilled milk, there is a good chance that you used Bounty paper towels to clean up the mess. Procter & Gamble (P&G) manufactures Bounty in two main processing departments—Paper Making and Paper Converting. In the Paper Making Department, wood pulp is converted into paper and then spooled into 2,000 pound rolls. In the Paper Converting Department, two of the 2,000 pound rolls of paper are simultaneously unwound into a machine that creates a two-ply paper towel that is decorated, perforated, and embossed to create texture. The large sheets of paper towels that emerge from this process are wrapped around a cylindrical cardboard core measuring eight feet in length. Once enough sheets wrap around the core, the eight foot roll is cut into individual rolls of Bounty that are sent down a conveyor to be wrapped, packed, and shipped.

In this type of manufacturing environment, costs cannot be readily traced to individual rolls of Bounty; however, given the homogeneous nature of the product, the total costs incurred in the Paper Making Department can be spread uniformly across its output of 2,000 pound rolls of paper. Similarly, the total costs incurred in the Paper Converting Department (including the cost of the 2,000 pound rolls that are transferred in from the Paper Making Department) can be spread uniformly across the number of cases of Bounty produced.

P&G uses a similar costing approach for many of its products such as Tide, Crest toothpaste, and Pringles. ■

Source: Conversation with Brad Bays, formerly a Procter & Gamble financial executive.

LEARNING OBJECTIVES

After studying Chapter 4, you should be able to:

- **LO1** Record the flow of materials, labor, and overhead through a process costing system.
- **LO2** Compute the equivalent units of production using the weighted-average method.
- **LO3** Compute the cost per equivalent unit using the weighted-average method.
- **LO4** Assign costs to units using the weighted-average method.
- **LO5** Prepare a cost reconciliation report.
- **LO6** (Appendix 4A) Compute the equivalent units of production using the FIFO method.
- **LO7** (Appendix 4A) Compute the cost per equivalent unit using the FIFO method.
- **LO8** (Appendix 4A) Assign costs to units using the FIFO method.
- **LO9** (Appendix 4A) Prepare a cost reconciliation report using the FIFO method.
- **LO10** (Appendix 4B) Allocate service department costs to operating departments using the direct method.
- **LO11** (Appendix 4B) Allocate service department costs to operating departments using the step-down method.

Job-order costing and process costing are two common methods for determining unit product costs. As explained in the previous chapter, job-order costing is used when many different jobs or products are worked on each period. Examples of industries that use job-order costing include furniture manufacturing, special-order printing, shipbuilding, and many types of service organizations.

By contrast, **process costing** is used most commonly in industries that convert raw materials into homogeneous (i.e., uniform) products, such as bricks, soda, or paper, on a continuous basis. Examples of companies that would use process costing include Reynolds Aluminum (aluminum ingots), Scott Paper (toilet paper), General Mills (flour), Exxon (gasoline and lubricating oils), Coppertone (sunscreens), and Kellogg's (breakfast cereals). In addition, process costing is sometimes used in companies with assembly operations. A form of process costing may also be used in utilities that produce gas, water, and electricity.

Our purpose in this chapter is to explain how product costing works in a process costing system.

Comparison of Job-Order and Process Costing

In some ways process costing is very similar to job-order costing, and in some ways it is very different. In this section, we focus on these similarities and differences to provide a foundation for the detailed discussion of process costing that follows.

Similarities between Job-Order and Process Costing

Much of what you learned in the previous chapter about costing and cost flows applies equally well to process costing in this chapter. We are not throwing out all that we have learned about costing and starting from "scratch" with a whole new system. The similarities between job-order and process costing can be summarized as follows:

1. Both systems have the same basic purposes—to assign material, labor, and manufacturing overhead costs to products and to provide a mechanism for computing unit product costs.
2. Both systems use the same basic manufacturing accounts, including Manufacturing Overhead, Raw Materials, Work in Process, and Finished Goods.
3. The flow of costs through the manufacturing accounts is basically the same in both systems.

As can be seen from this comparison, much of the knowledge that you have already acquired about costing is applicable to a process costing system. Our task now is to refine and extend your knowledge to process costing.

Differences between Job-Order and Process Costing

There are three differences between job-order and process costing. First, process costing is used when a company produces a continuous flow of units that are indistinguishable from one another. Job-order costing is used when a company produces many different jobs that have unique production requirements. Second, under process costing, it makes no sense to try to identify materials, labor, and overhead costs with a particular customer order (as we did with job-order costing) because each order is just one of many that are filled from a continuous flow of virtually identical units from the production line. Accordingly, process costing accumulates costs by department (rather than by order) and assigns these costs uniformly to all units that pass through the department during a period. Job cost sheets (which we used for job-order costing) are not used to accumulate

EXHIBIT 4–1
Differences between Job-Order and Process Costing

Job-Order Costing	Process Costing
1. Many different jobs are worked on during each period, with each job having different production requirements.	1. A single product is produced either on a continuous basis or for long periods of time. All units of product are identical.
2. Costs are accumulated by individual job.	2. Costs are accumulated by department.
3. Unit costs are computed *by job* on the job cost sheet.	3. Unit costs are computed *by department.*

costs. Third, process costing systems compute unit costs by department. This differs from job-order costing where unit costs are computed by job on the job cost sheet. Exhibit 4–1 summarizes the differences just described.

Cost Flows in Process Costing

Before going through a detailed example of process costing, it will be helpful to see how, in a general way, manufacturing costs flow through a process costing system.

Processing Departments

A **processing department** is an organizational unit where work is performed on a product and where materials, labor, or overhead costs are added to the product. For example, a Nalley's potato chip factory might have three processing departments—one for preparing potatoes, one for cooking, and one for inspecting and packaging. A brick factory might have two processing departments—one for mixing and molding clay into brick form and one for firing the molded brick. Some products and services may go through a number of processing departments, while others may go through only one or two. Regardless of the number of processing departments, they all have two essential features. First, the activity in the processing department is performed uniformly on all of the units passing through it. Second, the output of the processing department is homogeneous; in other words, all of the units produced are identical.

Products in a process costing environment, such as bricks or potato chips, typically flow in sequence from one department to another as in Exhibit 4–2.

EXHIBIT 4–2
Sequential Processing Departments

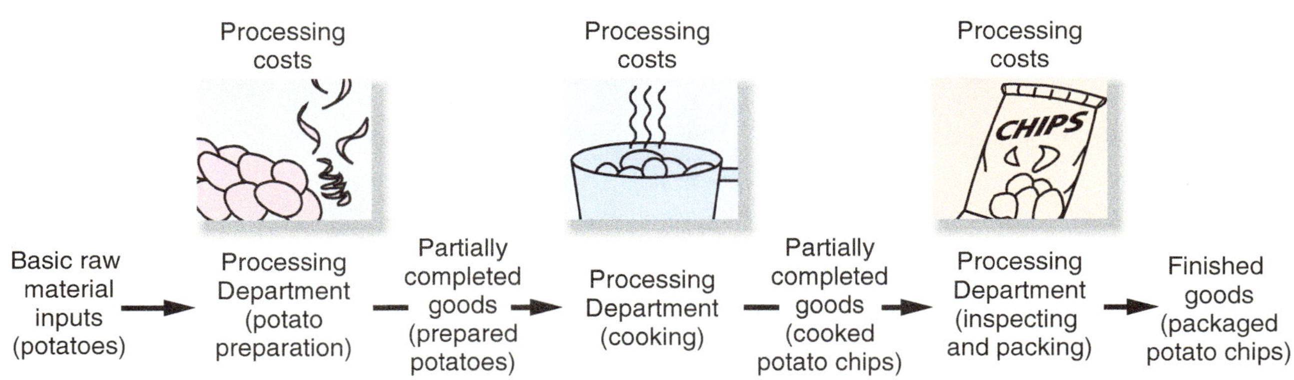

IN BUSINESS

MONKS MAKE A LIVING SELLING BEER

The Trappist monks of St. Sixtus monastery in Belgium have been brewing beer since 1839. Customers must make an appointment with the monastery to buy a maximum of two 24-bottle cases per month. The scarce and highly prized beer sells for more than $15 per 11-ounce bottle.

The monk's brewing ingredients include water, malt, hops, sugar, and yeast. The sequential steps of the beer-making process include grinding and crushing the malt grain, brewing by adding water to the crushed malt, filtering to separate a liquid called wort from undissolved grain particles, boiling to sterilize the wort (including adding sugar to increase the density of the wort), fermentation by adding yeast to convert sugar into alcohol and carbon dioxide, storage where the beer is aged for at least three weeks, and bottling where more sugar and yeast are added to enable two weeks of additional fermentation in the bottle.

Unlike growth-oriented for-profit companies, the monastery has not expanded its production capacity since 1946, seeking instead to sell just enough beer to sustain the monks' modest lifestyle.

Source: John W. Miller, "Trappist Command: Thou Shalt Not Buy Too Much of Our Beer," *The Wall Street Journal*, November 29, 2007, pp. A1 and A14.

The Flow of Materials, Labor, and Overhead Costs

Cost accumulation is simpler in a process costing system than in a job-order costing system. In a process costing system, instead of having to trace costs to hundreds of different jobs, costs are traced to only a few processing departments.

A T-account model of materials, labor, and overhead cost flows in a process costing system is shown in Exhibit 4–3. Several key points should be noted from this exhibit. First, note that a separate Work in Process account is maintained for *each processing department*. In contrast, in a job-order costing system the entire company may

EXHIBIT 4–3
T-Account Model of Process Costing Flows

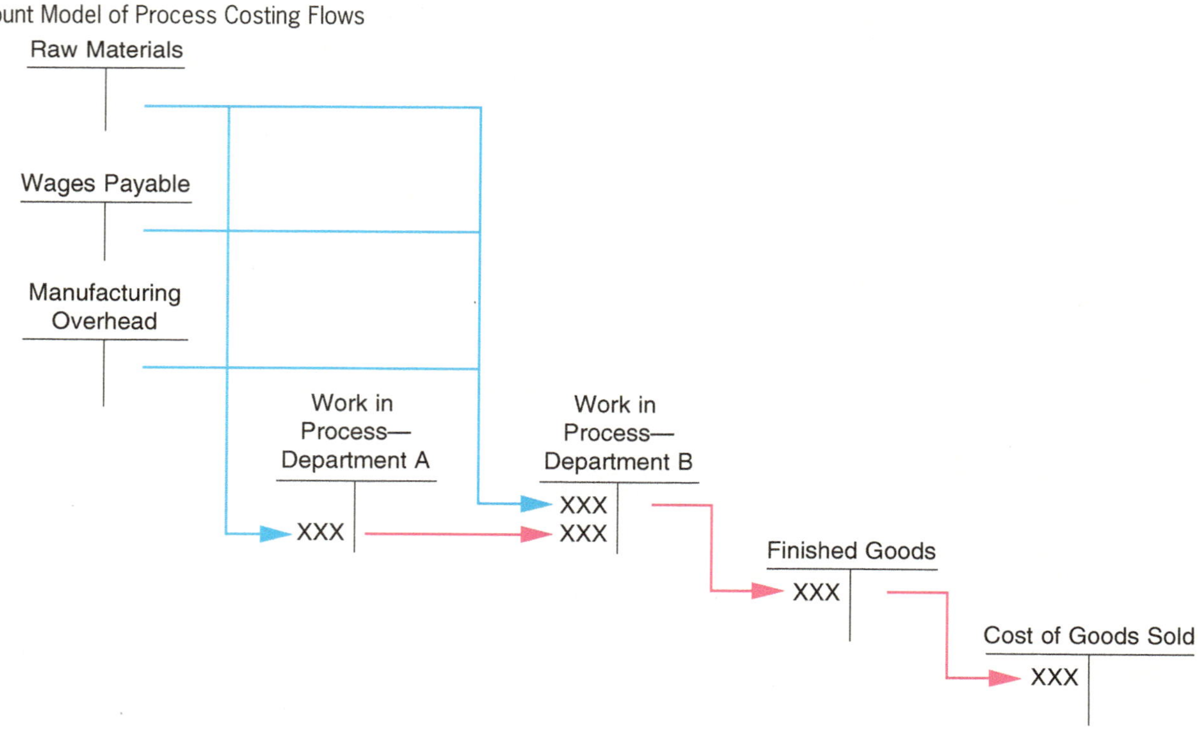

have only one Work in Process account. Second, note that the completed production of the first processing department (Department A in the exhibit) is transferred to the Work in Process account of the second processing department (Department B). After further work in Department B, the completed units are then transferred to Finished Goods. (In Exhibit 4–3, we show only two processing departments, but a company can have many processing departments.)

Finally, note that materials, labor, and overhead costs can be added in *any* processing department—not just the first. Costs in Department B's Work in Process account consist of the materials, labor, and overhead costs incurred in Department B plus the costs attached to partially completed units transferred in from Department A (called transferred-in costs).

Materials, Labor, and Overhead Cost Entries

LEARNING OBJECTIVE 1
Record the flow of materials, labor, and overhead through a process costing system.

To complete our discussion of cost flows in a process costing system, in this section we show journal entries relating to materials, labor, and overhead costs at Megan's Classic Cream Soda, a company that has two processing departments—Formulating and Bottling. In the Formulating Department, ingredients are checked for quality and then mixed and injected with carbon dioxide to create bulk cream soda. In the Bottling Department, bottles are checked for defects, filled with cream soda, capped, visually inspected again for defects, and then packed for shipping.

Materials Costs

As in job-order costing, materials are drawn from the storeroom using a materials requisition form. Materials can be added in any processing department, although it is not unusual for materials to be added only in the first processing department, with subsequent departments adding only labor and overhead costs.

At Megan's Classic Cream Soda, some materials (i.e., water, flavors, sugar, and carbon dioxide) are added in the Formulating Department and some materials (i.e., bottles, caps, and packing materials) are added in the Bottling Department. The journal entry to record the materials used in the first processing department, the Formulating Department, is as follows:

Work in Process—Formulating	XXX	
Raw Materials		XXX

The journal entry to record the materials used in the second processing department, the Bottling Department, is as follows:

Work in Process—Bottling	XXX	
Raw Materials		XXX

Labor Costs

In process costing, labor costs are traced to departments—not to individual jobs. The following journal entry records the labor costs in the Formulating Department at Megan's Classic Cream Soda:

Work in Process—Formulating	XXX	
Salaries and Wages Payable		XXX

A similar entry would be made to record labor costs in the Bottling Department.

Overhead Costs

In process costing, as in job-order costing, predetermined overhead rates are usually used. Manufacturing overhead cost is applied according to the amount of the allocation base that is incurred in the department. The following journal entry records the overhead cost applied in the Formulating Department:

Work in Process—Formulating	XXX	
Manufacturing Overhead		XXX

A similar entry would be made to apply manufacturing overhead costs in the Bottling Department.

Completing the Cost Flows Once processing has been completed in a department, the units are transferred to the next department for further processing, as illustrated in the T-accounts in Exhibit 4–3. The following journal entry transfers the cost of partially completed units from the Formulating Department to the Bottling Department:

Work in Process—Bottling	XXX	
Work in Process—Formulating		XXX

After processing has been completed in the Bottling Department, the costs of the completed units are transferred to the Finished Goods inventory account:

Finished Goods	XXX	
Work in Process—Bottling		XXX

Finally, when a customer's order is filled and units are sold, the cost of the units is transferred to Cost of Goods Sold:

Cost of Goods Sold	XXX	
Finished Goods		XXX

To summarize, the cost flows between accounts are basically the same in a process costing system as they are in a job-order costing system. The only difference at this point is that in a process costing system each department has a separate Work in Process account.

IN BUSINESS

THE DIFFERENCE BETWEEN LABOR RATES AND LABOR COST

The emergence of China as a global competitor has increased the need for managers to understand the difference between labor rates and labor cost. Labor rates reflect the amount paid to employees per hour or month. Labor costs measure the employee compensation paid per unit of output. For example, Tenneco has plants in Shanghai, China, and Litchfield, Michigan, that both manufacture exhaust systems for automobiles. The monthly labor rate per employee at the Shanghai plant ranges from $210–$250, whereas the same figure for the Litchfield plant ranges from $1,880–$4,064. A naïve interpretation of these labor rates would be to automatically assume that the Shanghai plant is the lower labor cost facility. A wiser comparison of the two plants' labor costs would account for the fact that the Litchfield plant produced 1.4 million exhaust systems in 2005 compared to 400,000 units at the Shanghai plant, while having only 20% more employees than the Shanghai plant.

Source: Alex Taylor III, "A Tale of Two Factories," *Fortune*, September 18, 2006, pp. 118–126.

We now turn our attention to Double Diamond Skis, a company that manufactures a high-performance deep-powder ski, and that uses process costing to determine its unit product costs. The company's production process is illustrated in Exhibit 4–4. Skis go through a sequence of five processing departments, starting with the Shaping and Milling Department and ending with the Finishing and Pairing Department. The basic idea in process costing is to add together all of the costs incurred in a department during a period and then to spread those costs uniformly across the units processed in that department during that period. As we shall see, applying this simple idea involves a few complications.

Equivalent Units of Production

After materials, labor, and overhead costs have been accumulated in a department, the department's output must be determined so that unit product costs can be computed. The difficulty is that a department usually has some partially completed units in its ending

EXHIBIT 4–4
The Production Process at Double Diamond Skis*

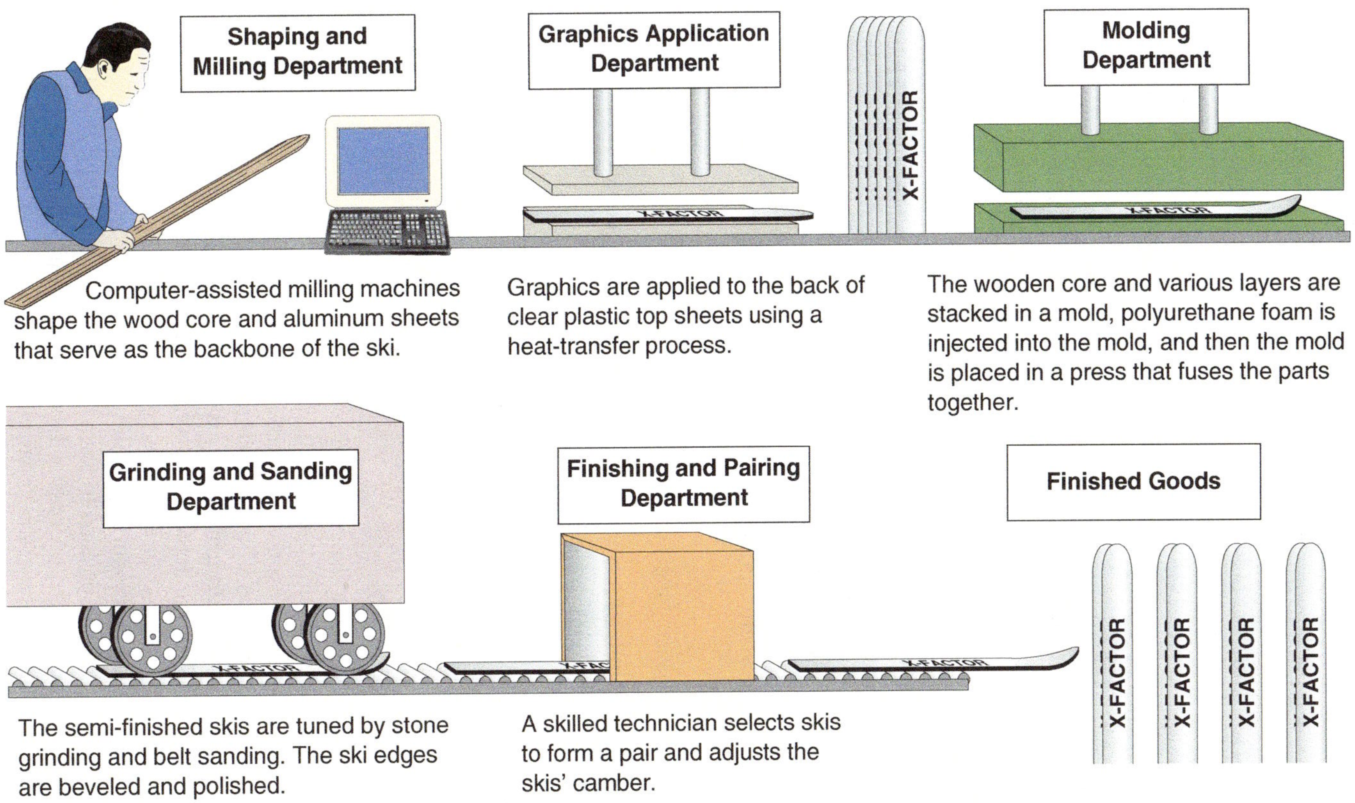

*Adapted from Bill Gout, Jesse James Doquilo, and Studio M D, "Capped Crusaders," *Skiing,* October 1993, pp. 138–144.

inventory. It does not seem reasonable to count these partially completed units as equivalent to fully completed units when counting the department's output. Therefore, these partially completed units are translated into an *equivalent* number of fully completed units. In process costing, this translation is done using the following formula:

Equivalent units = Number of partially completed units × Percentage completion

As the formula states, **equivalent units** is the product of the number of partially completed units and the percentage completion of those units with respect to the processing in the department. Roughly speaking, the equivalent units is the number of complete units that could have been obtained from the materials and effort that went into the partially complete units.

For example, suppose the Molding Department at Double Diamond has 500 units in its ending work in process inventory that are 60% complete with respect to processing in the department. These 500 partially complete units are equivalent to 300 fully complete units (500 × 60% = 300). Therefore, the ending work in process inventory contains 300 equivalent units. These equivalent units are added to any units completed during the period to determine the department's output for the period—called the *equivalent units of production.*

Equivalent units of production for a period can be computed in different ways. In this chapter, we discuss the *weighted-average method.* In Appendix 4A, we discuss the *FIFO method.* The **FIFO method** of process costing is a method in which equivalent units and unit costs relate only to work done during the current period. In contrast, the **weighted-average method** blends together units and costs from the current period with units and costs from the prior period. In the weighted-average method, the **equivalent units of production** for a department are the number of units transferred to the next department (or to finished goods) plus the equivalent units in the department's ending work in process inventory.

Weighted-Average Method

LEARNING OBJECTIVE 2
Compute the equivalent units of production using the weighted-average method.

Under the weighted-average method, a department's equivalent units are computed as follows:

Weighted-Average Method
(a separate calculation is made for each cost category in each processing department)

Equivalent units of production = Units transferred to the next department or to finished goods + Equivalent units in ending work in process inventory

Note that the computation of the equivalent units of production involves adding the number of units transferred out of the department to the equivalent units in the department's ending inventory. There is no need to compute the equivalent units for the units transferred out of the department—they are 100% complete with respect to the work done in that department or they would not be transferred out. In other words, each unit transferred out of the department is counted as one equivalent unit.

Consider the Shaping and Milling Department at Double Diamond. This department uses computerized milling machines to precisely shape the wooden core and metal sheets that will be used to form the backbone of the ski. (See Exhibit 4–4 for an overview of the production process at Double Diamond.) The activity shown at the top of the next page took place in the department in May.

Note the use of the term *conversion* in the table on the next page. **Conversion cost,** as defined in an earlier chapter, is direct labor cost plus manufacturing overhead cost. In process costing, conversion cost is often treated as a single element of product cost.

Note that the beginning work in process inventory was 55% complete with respect to materials costs and 30% complete with respect to conversion costs. This means that 55% of the materials costs required to complete the units in the department had

Shaping and Milling Department	Units	Percent Complete Materials	Percent Complete Conversion
Beginning work in process	200	55%	30%
Units started into production during May	5,000		
Units completed during May and transferred to the next department	4,800	100%*	100%*
Ending work in process	400	40%	25%

*We always assume that units transferred out of a department are 100% complete with respect to the processing done in that department.

already been incurred. Likewise, 30% of the conversion costs required to complete the units had already been incurred.

Two equivalent unit figures must be computed—one for materials and one for conversion. These computations are shown in Exhibit 4–5.

Note that the computations in Exhibit 4–5 ignore the fact that the units in the beginning work in process inventory were partially complete. For example, the 200 units in beginning inventory were already 30% complete with respect to conversion costs. Nevertheless, the weighted-average method is concerned only with the 4,900 equivalent units that are in ending inventories and in units transferred to the next department; it is not concerned with the fact that the beginning inventory was already partially complete. In other words, the 4,900 equivalent units computed using the weighted-average method include work that was accomplished in prior periods. This is a key point concerning the weighted-average method and it is easy to overlook.

Exhibit 4–6 provides another way of looking at the computation of equivalent units of production. This exhibit depicts the equivalent units computation for conversion costs. Study it carefully before going on.

EXHIBIT 4–5
Equivalent Units of Production: Weighted-Average Method

Shaping and Milling Department	Materials	Conversion
Units transferred to the next department	4,800	4,800
Ending work in process:		
Materials: 400 units × 40% complete	160	
Conversion: 400 units × 25% complete		100
Equivalent units of production	4,960	4,900

IN BUSINESS

CUTTING CONVERSION COSTS

Cemex SA, the world's third largest cement maker, owns 54 plants. Each of these plants consumes 800 tons of fuel a day heating kilns to 2,700 degrees Fahrenheit. Consequently, energy costs account for 40% of the company's overall conversion costs. Historically, Cemex relied exclusively on coal to heat its kilns; however, faced with soaring coal prices and shrinking profits, the company desperately needed a cheaper fuel. Cemex turned its attention to an oil industry waste product called *petroleum coke* that burns hotter than coal and costs half as much. The company spent about $150 million to convert its kilns to burn petroleum coke. Overall, Cemex has cut its energy bills by 17%, helping it earn higher profit margins than its biggest rivals.

Source: John Lyons, "Expensive Energy? Burn Other Stuff, One Firm Decides," *The Wall Street Journal*, September 1, 2004, pp. A1 and A8.

EXHIBIT 4–6
Visual Perspective of Equivalent Units of Production

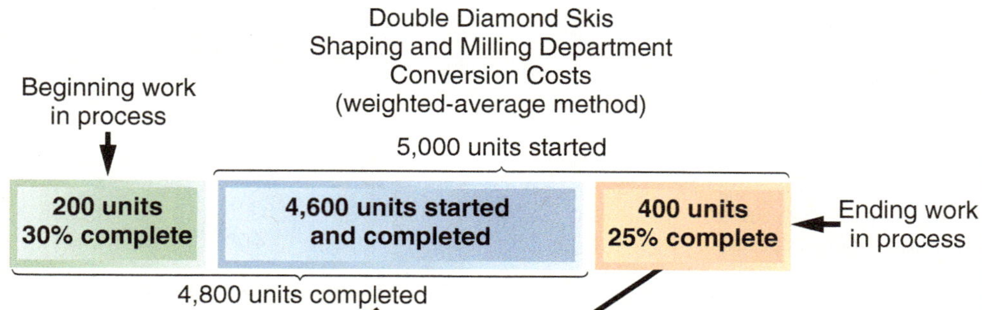

Units completed and transferred to next department	4,800
Ending work in process: 400 units × 25%	100
Equivalent units of production	4,900

Compute and Apply Costs

LEARNING OBJECTIVE 3
Compute the cost per equivalent unit using the weighted-average method.

In the last section we computed the equivalent units of production for materials and for conversion at Double Diamond Skis. In this section we will compute the cost per equivalent unit for materials and for conversion. We will then use these costs to value ending work in process and finished goods inventories. Exhibit 4–7 displays all of the data concerning May's operations in the Shaping and Milling Department that we will need to complete these tasks.

Cost per Equivalent Unit—Weighted-Average Method

In the weighted-average method, the cost per equivalent unit is computed as follows:

Weighted-Average Method
(a separate calculation is made for each cost category in each processing department)

$$\text{Cost per equivalent unit} = \frac{\text{Cost of beginning work in process inventory} + \text{Cost added during the period}}{\text{Equivalent units of production}}$$

EXHIBIT 4–7
Shaping and Milling Department Data for May Operations

Work in process, beginning:	
Units in process	200
Completion with respect to materials	55%
Completion with respect to conversion	30%
Costs in the beginning inventory:	
Materials cost	$ 9,600
Conversion cost	5,575
Total cost in the beginning inventory	$15,175
Units started into production during the period	5,000
Units completed and transferred out	4,800
Costs added to production during the period:	
Materials cost	$368,600
Conversion cost	350,900
Total cost added in the department	$719,500
Work in process, ending:	
Units in process	400
Completion with respect to materials	40%
Completion with respect to conversion	25%

Note that the numerator is the sum of the cost of beginning work in process inventory and of the cost added during the period. Thus, the weighted-average method blends together costs from the prior and current periods. That is why it is called the weighted-average method; it averages together units and costs from both the prior and current periods.

The costs per equivalent unit for materials and for conversion are computed below for the Shaping and Milling Department for May:

Shaping and Milling Department
Costs per Equivalent Unit

	Materials	Conversion
Cost of beginning work in process inventory	$ 9,600	$ 5,575
Costs added during the period	368,600	350,900
Total cost (a)	$378,200	$356,475
Equivalent units of production (see the computations in the previous section) (b)	4,960	4,900
Cost per equivalent unit (a) ÷ (b)	$76.25	$72.75

Applying Costs—Weighted-Average Method

LEARNING OBJECTIVE 4
Assign costs to units using the weighted-average method.

The costs per equivalent unit are used to value units in ending inventory and units that are transferred to the next department. For example, each unit transferred out of Double Diamond's Shaping and Milling Department to the Graphics Application Department, as depicted in Exhibit 4–4, will carry with it a cost of $149.00 ($76.25 for materials cost and $72.75 for conversion cost). Because 4,800 units were transferred out in May to the next department, the total cost assigned to those units would be $715,200 (= 4,800 units × $149.00 per unit).

A complete accounting of the costs of both ending work in process inventory and the units transferred out appears below:

Shaping and Milling Department
Costs of Ending Work in Process Inventory and the Units Transferred Out

	Materials	Conversion	Total
Ending work in process inventory:			
Equivalent units of production (materials: 400 units × 40% complete; conversion: 400 units × 25% complete) (a)	160	100	
Cost per equivalent unit (see above) (b)	$76.25	$72.75	
Cost of ending work in process inventory (a) × (b)	$12,200	$7,275	$19,475
Units completed and transferred out:			
Units transferred to the next department (a)	4,800	4,800	
Cost per equivalent unit (see above) (b)	$76.25	$72.75	
Cost of units transferred out (a) × (b)	$366,000	$349,200	$715,200

In each case, the equivalent units are multiplied by the cost per equivalent unit to determine the cost assigned to the units. This is done for each cost category—in this case, materials and conversion. The equivalent units for the units completed and transferred out are simply the number of units transferred to the next department because they would not have been transferred unless they were complete.

LEARNING OBJECTIVE 5
Prepare a cost reconciliation report.

Cost Reconciliation Report

The costs assigned to ending work in process inventory and to the units transferred out reconcile with the costs we started with in Exhibit 4–7 as shown below:

Shaping and Milling Department Cost Reconciliation	
Costs to be accounted for:	
Cost of beginning work in process inventory (Exhibit 4–7)	$ 15,175
Costs added to production during the period (Exhibit 4–7)	719,500
Total cost to be accounted for	$734,675
Costs accounted for as follows:	
Cost of ending work in process inventory (see page 151)	$ 19,475
Cost of units transferred out (see page 151)	715,200
Total cost accounted for	$734,675

The $715,200 cost of the units transferred to the next department, Graphics Application, will be accounted for in that department as "costs transferred in." It will be treated in the process costing system as just another category of costs like materials or conversion costs. The only difference is that the costs transferred in will always be 100% complete with respect to the work done in the Graphics Applications Department. Costs are passed on from one department to the next in this fashion, until they reach the last processing department, Finishing and Pairing. When the products are completed in this last department, their costs are transferred to finished goods.

Operation Costing

The costing systems discussed in Chapters 3 and 4 represent the two ends of a continuum. On one end is job-order costing, which is used by companies that produce many different products in one facility. On the other end is process costing, which is used by companies that produce homogeneous products in large quantities. Between these two extremes there are many hybrid systems that include characteristics of both job-order and process costing. One of these hybrids is called *operation costing.*

Operation costing is used in situations where products have some common characteristics and some individual characteristics. Shoes, for example, have common characteristics in that all styles involve cutting and sewing that can be done on a repetitive basis, using the same equipment and following the same basic procedures. Shoes also have individual characteristics—some are made of expensive leathers and others may be made using inexpensive synthetic materials. In a situation such as this, where products have some common characteristics but also must be processed individually, operation costing may be used to determine product costs.

As mentioned above, operation costing is a hybrid system that employs aspects of both job-order and process costing. Products are typically processed in batches when operation costing is used, with each batch charged for its own specific materials. In this sense, operation costing is similar to job-order costing. However, labor and overhead costs are accumulated by operation or by department, and these costs are assigned to units as in process costing. If shoes are being produced, each shoe is charged the same per unit conversion cost, regardless of the style involved, but it is charged with its specific materials cost. Thus, the company is able to distinguish between styles in terms of materials, but it is able to employ the simplicity of a process costing system for labor and overhead costs.

Examples of other products for which operation costing may be used include electronic equipment (such as semiconductors), textiles, clothing, and jewelry (such as rings, bracelets, and medallions). Products of this type are typically produced in batches, but they can vary considerably from model to model or from style to style in terms of the cost of materials.

Summary

Process costing is used in situations where homogeneous products or services are produced on a continuous basis. Costs flow through the manufacturing accounts in basically the same way in a process costing system as in a job-order costing system. However, costs are accumulated by department rather than by job in process costing.

In process costing, the equivalent units of production must be determined for each cost category in each department. Under the weighted-average method, the equivalent units of production equals the number of units transferred out to the next department or to finished goods plus the equivalent units in ending work in process inventory. The equivalent units in ending inventory equals the product of the number of partially completed units in ending work in process inventory and their percentage of completion with respect to the specific cost category.

Under the weighted-average method, the cost per equivalent unit for a specific cost category is computed by adding the cost of beginning work in process inventory and the cost added during the period and then dividing the result by the equivalent units of production. The cost per equivalent unit is then used to value the ending work in process inventory and the units transferred out to the next department or to finished goods.

The cost reconciliation report reconciles the cost of beginning inventory and the costs added to production during the period to the cost of ending inventory and the cost of units transferred out.

Costs are transferred from one department to the next until the last processing department. At that point, the cost of completed units is transferred to finished goods.

Review Problem: Process Cost Flows and Costing Units

Luxguard Home Paint Company produces exterior latex paint, which it sells in one-gallon containers. The company has two processing departments—Base Fab and Finishing. White paint, which is used as a base for all the company's paints, is mixed from raw ingredients in the Base Fab Department. Pigments are then added to the basic white paint, the pigmented paint is squirted under pressure into one-gallon containers, and the containers are labeled and packed for shipping in the Finishing Department. Information relating to the company's operations for April follows:

a. Issued raw materials for use in production: Base Fab Department, $851,000; and Finishing Department, $629,000.
b. Incurred direct labor costs: Base Fab Department, $330,000; and Finishing Department, $270,000.
c. Applied manufacturing overhead cost: Base Fab Department, $665,000; and Finishing Department, $405,000.
d. Transferred basic white paint from the Base Fab Department to the Finishing Department, $1,850,000.
e. Transferred paint that had been prepared for shipping from the Finishing Department to Finished Goods, $3,200,000.

Required:

1. Prepare journal entries to record items (a) through (e) above.
2. Post the journal entries from (1) above to T-accounts. The balance in the Base Fab Department's Work in Process account on April 1 was $150,000; the balance in the Finishing Department's Work in Process account was $70,000. After posting entries to the T-accounts, find the ending balance in each department's Work in Process account.
3. Determine the cost of ending work in process inventories and of units transferred out of the Base Fab Department in April. The following additional information is available regarding production in the Base Fab Department during April:

Production data:	
Units (gallons) in process, April 1: materials 100% complete; labor and overhead 60% complete	30,000
Units (gallons) started into production during April	420,000
Units (gallons) completed and transferred to the Finishing Department	370,000
Units (gallons) in process, April 30: materials 50% complete; labor and overhead 25% complete	80,000
Cost data:	
Work in process inventory, April 1:	
Materials	$ 92,000
Labor	21,000
Overhead	37,000
Total cost of work in process	$ 150,000
Cost added during April:	
Materials	$ 851,000
Labor	330,000
Overhead	665,000
Total cost added during April	$1,846,000

4. Prepare a cost reconciliation report for April.

Solution to Review Problem

1.

		Debit	Credit
a.	Work in Process—Base Fab Department	851,000	
	Work in Process—Finishing Department	629,000	
	Raw Materials		1,480,000
b.	Work in Process—Base Fab Department	330,000	
	Work in Process—Finishing Department	270,000	
	Salaries and Wages Payable		600,000
c.	Work in Process—Base Fab Department	665,000	
	Work in Process—Finishing Department	405,000	
	Manufacturing Overhead		1,070,000
d.	Work in Process—Finishing Department	1,850,000	
	Work in Process—Base Fab Department		1,850,000
e.	Finished Goods	3,200,000	
	Work in Process—Finishing Department		3,200,000

2.

Raw Materials

Bal.	XXX	(a)	1,480,000

Salaries and Wages Payable

		(b)	600,000

Work in Process—Base Fab Department

Bal.	150,000	(d)	1,850,000
(a)	851,000		
(b)	330,000		
(c)	665,000		
Bal.	146,000		

Manufacturing Overhead

(Various actual costs)		(c)	1,070,000

Work in Process—Finishing Department

Bal.	70,000	(e)	3,200,000
(a)	629,000		
(b)	270,000		
(c)	405,000		
(d)	1,850,000		
Bal.	24,000		

Finished Goods

Bal.	XXX		
(e)	3,200,000		

3. First, we must compute the equivalent units of production for each cost category:

Base Fab Department Equivalent Units of Production	Materials	Labor	Overhead
Units transferred to the next department	370,000	370,000	370,000
Ending work in process inventory (materials: 80,000 units × 50% complete; labor: 80,000 units × 25% complete; overhead: 80,000 units × 25% complete)	40,000	20,000	20,000
Equivalent units of production	410,000	390,000	390,000

Then we must compute the cost per equivalent unit for each cost category:

Base Fab Department Costs per Equivalent Unit	Materials	Labor	Overhead
Costs:			
Cost of beginning work in process inventory	$ 92,000	$ 21,000	$ 37,000
Costs added during the period	851,000	330,000	665,000
Total cost (a)	$943,000	$351,000	$702,000
Equivalent units of production (b)	410,000	390,000	390,000
Cost per equivalent unit (a) ÷ (b)	$2.30	$0.90	$1.80

The costs per equivalent unit can then be applied to the units in ending work in process inventory and the units transferred out as follows:

Base Fab Department Costs of Ending Work in Process Inventory and the Units Transferred Out	Materials	Labor	Overhead	Total
Ending work in process inventory:				
Equivalent units of production	40,000	20,000	20,000	
Cost per equivalent unit	$2.30	$0.90	$1.80	
Cost of ending work in process inventory	$92,000	$18,000	$36,000	$146,000
Units completed and transferred out:				
Units transferred to the next department	370,000	370,000	370,000	
Cost per equivalent unit	$2.30	$0.90	$1.80	
Cost of units completed and transferred out . . .	$851,000	$333,000	$666,000	$1,850,000

4.

Base Fab Department Cost Reconciliation	
Costs to be accounted for:	
Cost of beginning work in process inventory	$ 150,000
Costs added to production during the period	1,846,000
Total cost to be accounted for	$1,996,000
Costs accounted for as follows:	
Cost of ending work in process inventory	$ 146,000
Cost of units transferred out	1,850,000
Total cost accounted for	$1,996,000

Glossary

Conversion cost Direct labor cost plus manufacturing overhead cost. (p. 148)

Equivalent units The product of the number of partially completed units and their percentage of completion with respect to a particular cost. Equivalent units are the number of complete whole units that could be obtained from the materials and effort contained in partially completed units. (p. 148)

Equivalent units of production (weighted-average method) The units transferred to the next department (or to finished goods) during the period plus the equivalent units in the department's ending work in process inventory. (p. 148)

FIFO method A process costing method in which equivalent units and unit costs relate only to work done during the current period. (p. 148)

Operation costing A hybrid costing system used when products have some common characteristics and some individual characteristics. (p. 152)

Process costing A costing method used when essentially homogeneous products are produced on a continuous basis. (p. 142)

Processing department An organizational unit where work is performed on a product and where materials, labor, or overhead costs are added to the product. (p. 143)

Weighted-average method A process costing method that blends together units and costs from both the current and prior periods. (p. 148)

Questions

4–1 Under what conditions would it be appropriate to use a process costing system?

4–2 In what ways are job-order and process costing similar?

4–3 Why is cost accumulation simpler in a process costing system than it is in a job-order costing system?

4–4 How many Work in Process accounts are maintained in a company that uses process costing?

4–5 Assume that a company has two processing departments—Mixing followed by Firing. Prepare a journal entry to show a transfer of work in process from the Mixing Department to the Firing Department.

4–6 Assume that a company has two processing departments—Mixing followed by Firing. Explain what costs might be added to the Firing Department's Work in Process account during a period.

4–7 What is meant by the term *equivalent units of production* when the weighted-average method is used?

4–8 Watkins Trophies, Inc., produces thousands of medallions made of bronze, silver, and gold. The medallions are identical except for the materials used in their manufacture. What costing system would you advise the company to use?

Multiple-choice questions are provided on the text website at www.mhhe.com/garrison14e.

connect ACCOUNTING **Applying Excel**

Available with McGraw-Hill's *Connect™ Accounting.*

LEARNING OBJECTIVES 2, 3, 4, 5

The Excel worksheet form that appears below is to be used to recreate the extended example on pages 150–152. Download the workbook containing this form from the Online Learning Center at www.mhhe.com/garrison14e. *On the website you will also receive instructions about how to use this worksheet form.*

	A	B	C	D	E
1	Chapter 4: Applying Excel				
2					
3	Data				
4	Work in process, beginning:				
5	Units in process	200			
6	Completion with respect to materials	55%			
7	Completion with respect to conversion	30%			
8	Costs in the beginning inventory:				
9	Materials cost	$9,600			
10	Conversion cost	$5,575			
11	Units started into production during the period	5,000			
12	Costs added to production during the period:				
13	Materials cost	$368,600			
14	Conversion cost	$350,900			
15	Work in process, ending:				
16	Units in process	400			
17	Completion with respect to materials	40%			
18	Completion with respect to conversion	25%			
19					
20	*Enter a formula into each of the cells marked with a ? below*				
21					
22	**Weighted Average method:**				
23					
24	***Equivalent Units of Production***				
25		Materials	Conversion		
26	Units transferred to the next department	?	?		
27	Ending work in process:				
28	Materials	?			
29	Conversion		?		
30	Equivalent units of production	?	?		
31					
32	***Costs per Equivalent Unit***				
33		Materials	Conversion		
34	Cost of beginning work in process inventory	?	?		
35	Costs added during the period	?	?		
36	Total cost	?	?		
37	Equivalent units of production	?	?		
38	Cost per equivalent unit	?	?		
39					
40	***Costs of Ending Work in Process Inventory and the Units Transferred Out***				
41		Materials	Conversion	Total	
42	Ending work in process inventory:				
43	Equivalent units of production	?	?		
44	Cost per equivalent unit	?	?		
45	Cost of ending work in process inventory	?	?	?	
46					
47	Units completed and transferred out:				
48	Units transferred to the next department	?	?		
49	Cost per equivalent unit	?	?		
50	Cost of units transferred out	?	?	?	
51					
52	***Cost Reconciliation***				
53	Costs to be accounted for:				
54	Cost of beginning work in process inventory	?			
55	Costs added to production during the period	?			
56	Total cost to be accounted for	?			
57	Costs to be accounted for as follows:				
58	Cost of ending work in process inventory	?			
59	Cost of units transferred out	?			
60	Total cost accounted for	?			
61					

Chapter 4 Form / Filled in Chapter 4 Form / Chapt

You should proceed to the requirements below only after completing your worksheet.

Required:

1. Check your worksheet by changing the beginning work in process inventory to 100 units, the units started into production during the period to 2,500 units, and the units in ending work in process inventory to 200 units, keeping all of the other data the same as in the original example. If your worksheet is operating properly, the cost per equivalent unit for materials should now be $152.50 and the cost per equivalent unit for conversion should be $145.50. If you do not get these answers, find the errors in your worksheet and correct them.

   How much is the total cost of the units transferred out? Did it change? Why or why not?

2. Enter the following data from a different company into your worksheet:

Work in process, beginning:	
Units in process	200
Completion with respect to materials	100%
Completion with respect to conversion	20%
Costs in the beginning inventory:	
Materials cost	$2,000
Conversion cost	$800
Units started into production during the period	1,800
Costs added to production during the period:	
Materials cost	$18,400
Conversion cost	$38,765
Work in process, ending:	
Units in process	100
Completion with respect to materials	100%
Completion with respect to conversion	30%

What is the cost of the units transferred out?

3. What happens to the cost of the units transferred out in part (2) above if the percentage completion with respect to conversion for the beginning inventory is changed from 20% to 40% and everything else remains the same? What happens to the cost per equivalent unit for conversion? Explain.

Exercises

connect ACCOUNTING

All applicable exercises are available with McGraw-Hill's *Connect™ Accounting*.

EXERCISE 4–1 Process Costing Journal Entries [LO1]

Arizona Brick Corporation produces bricks in two processing departments—Molding and Firing. Information relating to the company's operations in March follows:

a. Raw materials were issued for use in production: Molding Department, $28,000; and Firing Department, $5,000.
b. Direct labor costs were incurred: Molding Department, $18,000; and Firing Department, $5,000.
c. Manufacturing overhead was applied: Molding Department, $24,000; and Firing Department, $37,000.
d. Unfired, molded bricks were transferred from the Molding Department to the Firing Department. According to the company's process costing system, the cost of the unfired, molded bricks was $67,000.
e. Finished bricks were transferred from the Firing Department to the finished goods warehouse. According to the company's process costing system, the cost of the finished bricks was $108,000.
f. Finished bricks were sold to customers. According to the company's process costing system, the cost of the finished bricks sold was $106,000.

Required:

Prepare journal entries to record items (a) through (f) above.

EXERCISE 4–2 Computation of Equivalent Units—Weighted-Average Method [LO2]

Lindex Company uses a process costing system. The following data are available for one department for October:

		Percent Completed	
	Units	Materials	Conversion
Work in process, October 1	50,000	90%	60%
Work in process, October 31	30,000	70%	50%

The department started 390,000 units into production during the month and transferred 410,000 completed units to the next department.

Required:

Compute the equivalent units of production for October, assuming that the company uses the weighted-average method of accounting for units and costs.

EXERCISE 4–3 Cost Per Equivalent Unit—Weighted-Average Method [LO3]

Billinstaff Industries uses the weighted-average method in its process costing system. Data for the Assembly Department for May appear below:

	Materials	Labor	Overhead
Work in process, May 1	$14,550	$23,620	$118,100
Cost added during May	$88,350	$14,330	$71,650
Equivalent units of production	1,200	1,100	1,100

Required:

1. Compute the cost per equivalent unit for materials, for labor, and for overhead.
2. Compute the total cost per equivalent whole unit.

EXERCISE 4–4 Applying Costs to Units—Weighted-Average Method [LO4]

Data concerning a recent period's activity in the Prep Department, the first processing department in a company that uses process costing, appear below:

	Materials	Conversion
Equivalent units of production in ending work in process	300	100
Cost per equivalent unit	$31.56	$9.32

A total of 1,300 units were completed and transferred to the next processing department during the period.

Required:

Compute the cost of the units transferred to the next department during the period and the cost of ending work in process inventory.

EXERCISE 4–5 Cost Reconciliation Report—Weighted-Average Method [LO5]

Lech-Zurs Bakerie Corporation uses a process costing system. The Baking Department is one of the processing departments in its apple strudel manufacturing facility. In July in the Baking Department, the cost of beginning work in process inventory was $4,830, the cost of ending work in process inventory was $1,120, and the cost added to production was $25,650.

Required:

Prepare a cost reconciliation report for the Baking Department for July.

EXERCISE 4–6 Equivalent Units and Cost per Equivalent Unit—Weighted-Average Method [LO2, LO3]

Kalox, Inc., manufactures an antacid product that passes through two departments. Data for May for the first department follow:

	Gallons	Materials	Labor	Overhead
Work in process, May 1	80,000	$68,600	$30,000	$48,000
Gallons started in process	760,000			
Gallons transferred out	790,000			
Work in process, May 31	50,000			
Cost added during May		$907,200	$370,000	$592,000

The beginning work in process inventory was 80% complete with respect to materials and 75% complete with respect to labor and overhead. The ending work in process inventory was 60% complete with respect to materials and 20% complete with respect to labor and overhead.

Required:

Assume that the company uses the weighted-average method of accounting for units and costs.

1. Compute the equivalent units for May's activity for the first department.
2. Determine the costs per equivalent unit for May.

EXERCISE 4–7 Comprehensive Exercise; Second Production Department—Weighted-Average Method [LO2, LO3, LO4, LO5]

Papyrutech Corporation produces fine papers in three production departments—Pulping, Drying, and Finishing. In the Pulping Department, raw materials such as wood fiber and rag cotton are mechanically and chemically treated to separate their fibers. The result is a thick slurry of fibers. In the Drying Department, the wet fibers transferred from the Pulping Department are laid down on porous webs, pressed to remove excess liquid, and dried in ovens. In the Finishing Department, the dried paper is coated, cut, and spooled onto reels. The company uses the weighted-average method in its process costing system. Data for October for the Drying Department follow:

		Percent Completed	
	Units	Pulping	Conversion
Work in process inventory, October 1	4,000	100%	60%
Work in process inventory, October 31	6,000	100%	75%
Pulping cost in work in process inventory, October 1			$1,500
Conversion cost in work in process inventory, October 1			$400
Units transferred to the next production department			146,000
Pulping cost added during October			$59,300
Conversion cost added during October			$22,100

No materials are added in the Drying Department. Pulping cost represents the costs of the wet fibers transferred in from the Pulping Department. Wet fiber is processed in the Drying Department in batches; each unit in the above table is a batch, and one batch of wet fibers produces a set amount of dried paper that is passed on to the Finishing Department.

Required:

1. Determine the equivalent units for October for pulping and conversion.
2. Compute the costs per equivalent unit for October for pulping and conversion.
3. Determine the total cost of ending work in process inventory and the total cost of units transferred to the Finishing Department in October.
4. Prepare a cost reconciliation report for the Drying Department for October.

EXERCISE 4–8 Process Costing Journal Entries [LO1]

Schneider Brot is a bread-baking company located in Aachen, Germany, near the Dutch border. The company uses a process costing system for its single product—a popular pumpernickel bread. Schneider Brot has two processing departments—Mixing and Baking. The T-accounts below show the flow of costs through the two departments in April (all amounts are in the currency euros):

Work in Process—Mixing

Balance 4/1	10,000	Transferred out	760,000
Direct materials	330,000		
Direct labor	260,000		
Overhead	190,000		

Work in Process—Baking

Balance 4/1	20,000	Transferred out	980,000
Transferred in	760,000		
Direct labor	120,000		
Overhead	90,000		

Required:

Prepare journal entries showing the flow of costs through the two processing departments during April.

EXERCISE 4–9 Cost Assignment; Cost Reconciliation—Weighted-Average Method [LO2, LO4, LO5]
Kenton Industrial Corporation uses the weighted-average method in its process costing system. During April, the Baker Assembly Department completed its processing of 18,000 units and transferred them to the next department. The cost of beginning inventory and the costs added during April amounted to $855,000 in total. The ending inventory in April consisted of 1,500 units, which were 90% complete with respect to materials and 40% complete with respect to labor and overhead. The costs per equivalent unit for the month were as follows:

	Materials	Labor	Overhead
Cost per equivalent unit	$24.00	$7.00	$14.00

Required:
1. Compute the equivalent units of materials, labor, and overhead in the ending inventory for the month.
2. Compute the cost of ending inventory and of the units transferred to the next department for April.
3. Prepare a cost reconciliation for April. (Note: You will not be able to break the cost to be accounted for into the cost of beginning inventory and costs added during the month.)

EXERCISE 4–10 Equivalent Units—Weighted-Average Method [LO2]
Societe Clemeau, a company located in Lyons, France, manufactures cement for the construction industry. Data relating to the kilograms of cement processed through the Mixing Department, the first department in the production process, are provided below for May:

		Percent Completed	
	Kilograms of Cement	Materials	Conversion
Work in process, May 1	80,000	80%	20%
Work in process, May 31	50,000	40%	10%
Started into production during May	300,000		

Required:
1. Compute the number of kilograms of cement completed and transferred out of the Mixing Department during May.
2. Compute the equivalent units of production for materials and for conversion for May.

EXERCISE 4–11 Equivalent Units and Cost per Equivalent Unit—Weighted-Average Method [LO2, LO3, LO4]
Solex Company produces a high-quality insulation material that passes through two production processes. Data for June for the first process follow:

	Units	Completion with Respect to Materials	Completion with Respect to Conversion
Work in process inventory, June 1	60,000	75%	40%
Work in process inventory, June 30	40,000	50%	25%

Materials cost in work in process inventory, June 1	$56,600
Conversion cost in work in process inventory, June 1	$14,900
Units started into production	280,000
Units transferred to the next process	300,000
Materials cost added during June	$385,000
Conversion cost added during June	$214,500

Required:
1. Assume that the company uses the weighted-average method of accounting for units and costs. Determine the equivalent units for June for the first process.

2. Compute the costs per equivalent unit for June for the first process.
3. Determine the total cost of ending work in process inventory and the total cost of units transferred to the next process in June.

EXERCISE 4–12 Equivalent Units—Weighted-Average Method [LO2]

Gulf Fisheries, Inc., processes tuna for various distributors. Two departments are involved—Cleaning and Packing. Data relating to pounds of tuna processed in the Cleaning Department during May are given below:

		Percent Completed	
	Pounds of Tuna	Materials	Labor and Overhead
Work in process, May 1	30,000	100%	55%
Work in process, May 31	20,000	100%	90%

*Labor and overhead only.

A total of 480,000 pounds of tuna were started into processing during May. All materials are added at the beginning of processing in the Cleaning Department.

Required:

Compute the equivalent units for May for both materials and labor and overhead assuming that the company uses the weighted-average method of accounting for units.

Problems

connect ACCOUNTING

All applicable problems are available with McGraw-Hill's *Connect™ Accounting*.

PROBLEM 4–13 Comprehensive Problem Weighted-Average Method [LO2, LO3, LO4, LO5]

The PVC Company manufactures a high-quality plastic pipe that goes through three processing stages prior to completion.

Information on work in the first department, Cooking, is given below for May:

Production data:	
Pounds in process, May 1: materials 100% complete; conversion 90% complete	70,000
Pounds started into production during May	350,000
Pounds completed and transferred to the next department	?
Pounds in process, May 31: materials 75% complete; conversion 25% complete	40,000
Cost data:	
Work in process inventory, May 1:	
Materials cost	$86,000
Conversion cost	$36,000
Cost added during May:	
Materials cost	$447,000
Conversion cost	$198,000

The company uses the weighted-average method.

Required:

1. Compute the equivalent units of production.
2. Compute the costs per equivalent unit for the month.
3. Determine the cost of ending work in process inventory and of the units transferred out to the next department.
4. Prepare a cost reconciliation report for the month.

PROBLEM 4–14 Comprehensive Problem—Weighted-Average Method [LO2, LO3, LO4, LO5]
Honeybutter, Inc., manufactures a product that goes through two departments prior to completion—the Mixing Department followed by the Packaging Department. The following information is available about work in the first department, the Mixing Department, during June.

	A	B	C	D
1			*Percent Completed*	
2		*Units*	*Materials*	*Conversion*
3	Work in process, beginning	70,000	70%	40%
4	Started into production	460,000		
5	Completed and transferred out	450,000		
6	Work in process, ending	80,000	75%	25%
7				
8			*Materials*	*Conversion*
9	Work in process, beginning		$36,550	$13,500
10	Cost added during June		$391,850	$287,300
11				
12				

Required:
Assume that the company uses the weighted-average method.
1. Determine the equivalent units for June for the Mixing Department.
2. Compute the costs per equivalent unit for June for the Mixing Department.
3. Determine the total cost of ending work in process inventory and the total cost of units transferred to the Packaging Department.
4. Prepare a cost reconciliation report for the Mixing Department for June.

PROBLEM 4–15 Analysis of Work in Process T-account—Weighted-Average Method [LO1, LO2, LO3, LO4]

eXcel

Brady Products manufactures a silicone paste wax that goes through three processing departments—Cracking, Blending, and Packing. All raw materials are introduced at the start of work in the Cracking Department. The Work in Process T-account for the Cracking Department for a recent month is given below:

Work in Process—Cracking Department

Inventory, May 1	63,700	Completed and transferred to the Blending Department	?
Materials	397,600		
Conversion	187,600		
Inventory, May 31	?		

The May 1 work in process inventory consisted of 35,000 pounds with $43,400 in materials cost and $20,300 in conversion cost. The May 1 work in process inventory was 100% complete with respect to materials and 80% complete with respect to conversion. During May, 280,000 pounds were started into production. The May 31 inventory consisted of 45,000 pounds that were 100% complete with respect to materials and 60% complete with respect to conversion. The company uses the weighted-average method to account for units and costs.

Required:

1. Determine the equivalent units of production for May.
2. Determine the costs per equivalent unit for May.
3. Determine the cost of the units completed and transferred to the Blending Department during May.

PROBLEM 4–16 Cost Flows [LO1]

Nature's Way, Inc., keeps one of its production facilities busy making a perfume called Essence de la Vache. The perfume goes through two processing departments: Blending and Bottling.

The following incomplete Work in Process account is provided for the Blending Department for March:

Work in Process—Blending

March 1 balance	32,800	Completed and transferred	
Materials	147,600	to Bottling (760,000 ounces)	?
Direct labor	73,200		
Overhead	481,000		
March 31 balance	?		

The $32,800 beginning inventory in the Blending Department consisted of the following elements: materials, $8,000; direct labor, $4,000; and overhead applied, $20,800.

Costs incurred during March in the Bottling Department were: materials used, $45,000; direct labor, $17,000; and overhead cost applied to production, $108,000.

Required:

1. Prepare journal entries to record the costs incurred in both the Blending Department and Bottling Department during March. Key your entries to items (a) through (g) below:
   a. Raw materials were issued for use in production.
   b. Direct labor costs were incurred.
   c. Manufacturing overhead costs for the entire factory were incurred, $596,000. (Credit Accounts Payable and use a single Manufacturing Overhead control account for the entire factory.)
   d. Manufacturing overhead was applied to production using a predetermined overhead rate.
   e. Units that were complete with respect to processing in the Blending Department were transferred to the Bottling Department, $722,000.
   f. Units that were complete with respect to processing in the Bottling Department were transferred to Finished Goods, $920,000.
   g. Completed units were sold on account for $1,400,000. The cost of goods sold was $890,000.
2. Post the journal entries from (1) above to T-accounts. The following account balances existed at the beginning of March. (The beginning balance in the Blending Department's Work in Process account is given above.)

Raw Materials	$198,600
Work in Process—Bottling Department	$49,000
Finished Goods	$20,000

After posting the entries to the T-accounts, find the ending balances in the inventory accounts and the manufacturing overhead account.

PROBLEM 4–17 Comprehensive Problem; Second Production Department—Weighted-Average Method [LO2, LO3, LO4, LO5]

Bohemian Links Inc. produces sausages in three production departments—Mixing, Casing and Curing, and Packaging. In the Mixing Department, meats are prepared and ground and then mixed with spices. The spiced meat mixture is then transferred to the Casing and Curing Department, where the mixture is force-fed into casings and then hung and cured in climate-controlled smoking chambers. In the Packaging Department, the cured sausages are sorted, packed, and labeled. The company uses the weighted-average method in its process costing system. Data for April for the Casing and Curing Department follow:

	Units	Percent Completed		
		Mixing	Materials	Conversion
Work in process inventory, April 1	1	100%	60%	50%
Work in process inventory, April 30	1	100%	20%	10%

	Mixing	Materials	Conversion
Work in process inventory, April 1	$1,640	$26	$105
Cost added during April	$94,740	$8,402	$61,197

Mixing cost represents the costs of the spiced meat mixture transferred in from the Mixing Department. The spiced meat mixture is processed in the Casing and Curing Department in batches; each unit in the above table is a batch, and one batch of spiced meat mixture produces a set amount of sausages that are passed on to the Packaging Department. During April, 60 batches (i.e., units) were completed and transferred to the Packaging Department.

Required:

1. Determine the equivalent units for April for mixing, materials, and conversion. Do not round off your computations.
2. Compute the costs per equivalent unit for April for mixing, materials, and conversion.
3. Determine the total cost of ending work in process inventory and the total cost of units transferred to the Packaging Department in April.
4, Prepare a cost reconciliation report for the Casing and Curing Department for April.

PROBLEM 4–18 Interpreting a Report—Weighted-Average Method [LO2, LO3, LO4]

Bell Computers, Ltd., located in Liverpool, England, assembles a standardized personal computer from parts it purchases from various suppliers. The production process consists of several steps, starting with assembly of the "mother" circuit board, which contains the central processing unit. This assembly takes place in the CPU Assembly Department. The company recently hired a new accountant who prepared the following report for the department for May using the weighted-average method:

Units to be accounted for:	
Work in process, May 1: materials 90% complete; conversion 80% complete	5,000
Started into production	29,000
Total units	34,000
Units accounted for as follows:	
Transferred to next department	30,000
Work in process, May 31: materials 75% complete; conversion 50% complete	4,000
Total units	34,000

Cost Reconciliation	
Cost to be accounted for:	
Work in process, May 1	£ 13,400
Cost added in the department	87,800
Total cost to be accounted for	£101,200
Cost accounted for as follows:	
Work in process, May 31	£ 8,200
Transferred to next department	93,000
Total cost accounted for	£101,200

The company's management would like some additional information about May's operation in the CPU Assembly Department. (The currency in England is the pound, which is denoted by the symbol £.)

Required:

1. How many units were started and completed during May?
2. What were the equivalent units for May for materials and conversion costs?
3. What were the costs per equivalent unit for May? The following additional data are available concerning the department's costs:

	Materials	Conversion	Total
Work in process, May 1	£9,000	£4,400	£13,400
Costs added during May	£57,000	£30,800	£87,800

4. Verify the accountant's ending work in process inventory figure (£8,200) given in the report.
5. The new manager of the CPU Assembly Department was asked to estimate the incremental cost of processing an additional 1,000 units through the department. He took the unit cost for an equivalent whole unit you computed in (3) above and multiplied this figure by 1,000. Will this method yield a valid estimate of incremental cost? Explain.

Cases

All applicable cases are available with McGraw-Hill's *Connect™ Accounting.*

CASE 4–19 Ethics and the Manager; Understanding the Impact of Percentage Completion on Profit [LO2, LO3, LO4]

Thad Kostowski and Carol Lee are production managers in the Appliances Division of Mesger Corporation, which has several dozen plants scattered in locations throughout the world. Carol manages the plant located in Kansas City, Missouri, while Thad manages the plant in Roseville, Oregon. Production managers are paid a salary and get an additional bonus equal to 10% of their base salary if the entire division meets or exceeds its target profits for the year. The bonus is determined in March after the company's annual report has been prepared and issued to stockholders.

Late in February, Carol received a phone call from Thad that went like this:

Thad: How's it going, Carol?

Carol: Fine, Thad. How's it going with you?

Thad: Great! I just got the preliminary profit figures for the division for last year and we are within $62,500 of making the year's target profits. All we have to do is to pull a few strings, and we'll be over the top!

Carol: What do you mean?

Thad: Well, one thing that would be easy to change is your estimate of the percentage completion of your ending work in process inventories.

Carol: I don't know if I should do that, Thad. Those percentage completion numbers are supplied by Jean Jackson, my lead supervisor. I have always trusted her to provide us with good estimates. Besides, I have already sent the percentage completion figures to the corporate headquarters.

Thad: You can always tell them there was a mistake. Think about it, Carol. All of us managers are doing as much as we can to pull this bonus out of the hat. You may not want the bonus check, but the rest of us sure could use it.

The final processing department in Carol's production facility began the year with no work in process inventories. During the year, 270,000 units were transferred in from the prior processing department and 250,000 units were completed and sold. Costs transferred in from the prior department totaled $49,221,000. No materials are added in the final processing department. A total of $16,320,000 of conversion cost was incurred in the final processing department during the year.

Required:

1. Jean Jackson estimated that the units in ending inventory in the final processing department were 25% complete with respect to the conversion costs of the final processing department. If this estimate of the percentage completion is used, what would be the cost of goods sold for the year?
2. Does Thad Kostowski want the estimated percentage completion to be increased or decreased? Explain why.

3. What percentage completion figure would result in increasing the reported net operating income by $62,500 over the net operating income that would be reported if the 25% figure were used?
4. Do you think Carol Lee should go along with the request to alter estimates of the percentage completion? Why or why not?

CASE 4–20 Second Department—Weighted-Average Method [LO2, LO3, LO4]

eXcel

Durall Company manufactures a plastic gasket that is used in automobile engines. The gaskets go through three processing departments: Mixing, Forming, and Stamping. The company's accountant (who is very inexperienced) has prepared a summary of production and costs for the Forming Department for October as follows:

Forming Department costs:	
Work in process inventory, October 1, 8,000 units: materials 100% complete; conversion 7/8 complete	$ 22,420*
Costs transferred in from the Mixing Department	81,480
Material added during October (added when processing is 50% complete in the Forming Department)	27,600
Conversion costs added during October	96,900
Total departmental costs	$228,400
Forming Department costs assigned to:	
Units completed and transferred to the Stamping Department, 100,000 units at $2.284 each	$228,400
Work in process inventory, October 31, 5,000 units: conversion 2/5 complete	—
Total departmental costs assigned	$228,400

*Consists of cost transferred in, $8,820; materials cost, $3,400; and conversion costs, $10,200.

After mulling over the data above, Durall's president commented, "I can't understand what's happening here. Despite a concentrated effort at cost reduction, our unit cost actually went up in the Forming Department last month. With that kind of performance, year-end bonuses are out of the question for the people in that department."

The company uses the weighted-average method in its process costing.

Required:

1. Prepare a report for the Forming Department for October showing how much cost should have been assigned to the units completed and transferred to the Stamping Department and to the ending work in process inventory.
2. Explain to the president why the unit cost appearing on the report prepared by the accountant is so high.

Appendix 4A: FIFO Method

The FIFO method of process costing differs from the weighted-average method in two ways: (1) the computation of equivalent units, and (2) the way in which costs of beginning inventory are treated. The FIFO method is generally considered more accurate than the weighted-average method, but it is more complex. The complexity is not a problem for computers, but the FIFO method is a little more difficult to understand and to learn than the weighted-average method.

LEARNING OBJECTIVE 6
Compute the equivalent units of production using the FIFO method.

Equivalent Units—FIFO Method

The computation of equivalent units under the FIFO method differs from the computation under the weighted-average method in two ways.

First, the "units transferred out" is divided into two parts. One part consists of the units from the beginning inventory that were completed and transferred out, and the other part consists of the units that were both *started* and *completed* during the current period.

Second, full consideration is given to the amount of work expended during the current period on units in the *beginning* work in process inventory as well as on units in the ending inventory. Thus, under the FIFO method, both beginning and ending inventories are converted to an equivalent units basis. For the beginning inventory, the equivalent units represent the work done to *complete* the units; for the ending inventory, the equivalent units represent the work done to bring the units to a stage of partial completion at the end of the period (the same as with the weighted-average method).

The formula for computing the equivalent units of production under the FIFO method is more complex than under the weighted-average method:

FIFO Method
(a separate calculation is made for each cost category in each processing department)

Equivalent units of production = Equivalent units to complete beginning work in process inventory*
+ Units started and completed during the period
+ Equivalent units in ending work in process inventory

*Equivalent units to complete beginning work in process inventory = Units in beginning work in process inventory × (100% − Percentage completion of beginning work in process inventory)

Or, the equivalent units of production can also be determined as follows:

Equivalent units of production = Units transferred out
+ Equivalent units in ending work in process inventory
− Equivalent units in beginning work in process inventory

To illustrate the FIFO method, refer again to the data for the Shaping and Milling Department at Double Diamond Skis. The department completed and transferred 4,800 units to the Graphics Application Department during May. Because 200 of these units came from the beginning inventory, the Shaping and Milling Department must have started and completed 4,600 units during May. The 200 units in the beginning inventory were 55% complete with respect to materials and only 30% complete with respect to conversion costs when the month started. Thus, to complete these units the department must have added another 45% of materials costs (100% − 55% = 45%) and another 70% of conversion costs (100% − 30% = 70%). Following this line of reasoning, the equivalent units for the department for May would be computed as shown in Exhibit 4A–1.

Comparison of Equivalent Units of Production under the Weighted-Average and FIFO Methods

Stop at this point and compare the data in Exhibit 4A–1 with the data in Exhibit 4–5 in the chapter, which shows the computation of equivalent units under the weighted-average method. Also refer to Exhibit 4A–2, which compares the two methods.

The essential difference between the two methods is that the weighted-average method blends work and costs from the prior period with work and costs in the current

EXHIBIT 4A-1
Equivalent Units of Production: FIFO Method

	Materials	Conversion
To complete beginning work in process:		
Materials: 200 units × (100% − 55%)*	90	
Conversion: 200 units × (100% − 30%)*		140
Units started and completed during the period	4,600†	4,600†
Ending work in process:		
Materials: 400 units × 40% complete	160	
Conversion: 400 units × 25% complete		100
Equivalent units of production	4,850	4,840

*This is the work needed to complete the units in beginning inventory.
†5,000 units started − 400 units in ending work in process = 4,600 units started and completed. This can also be computed as 4,800 units completed and transferred to the next department − 200 units in beginning work in process inventory. The FIFO method assumes that the units in beginning inventory are finished first.

EXHIBIT 4A-2
Visual Perspective of Equivalent Units of Production

Double Diamond Skis
Shaping and Milling Department
Conversion Costs

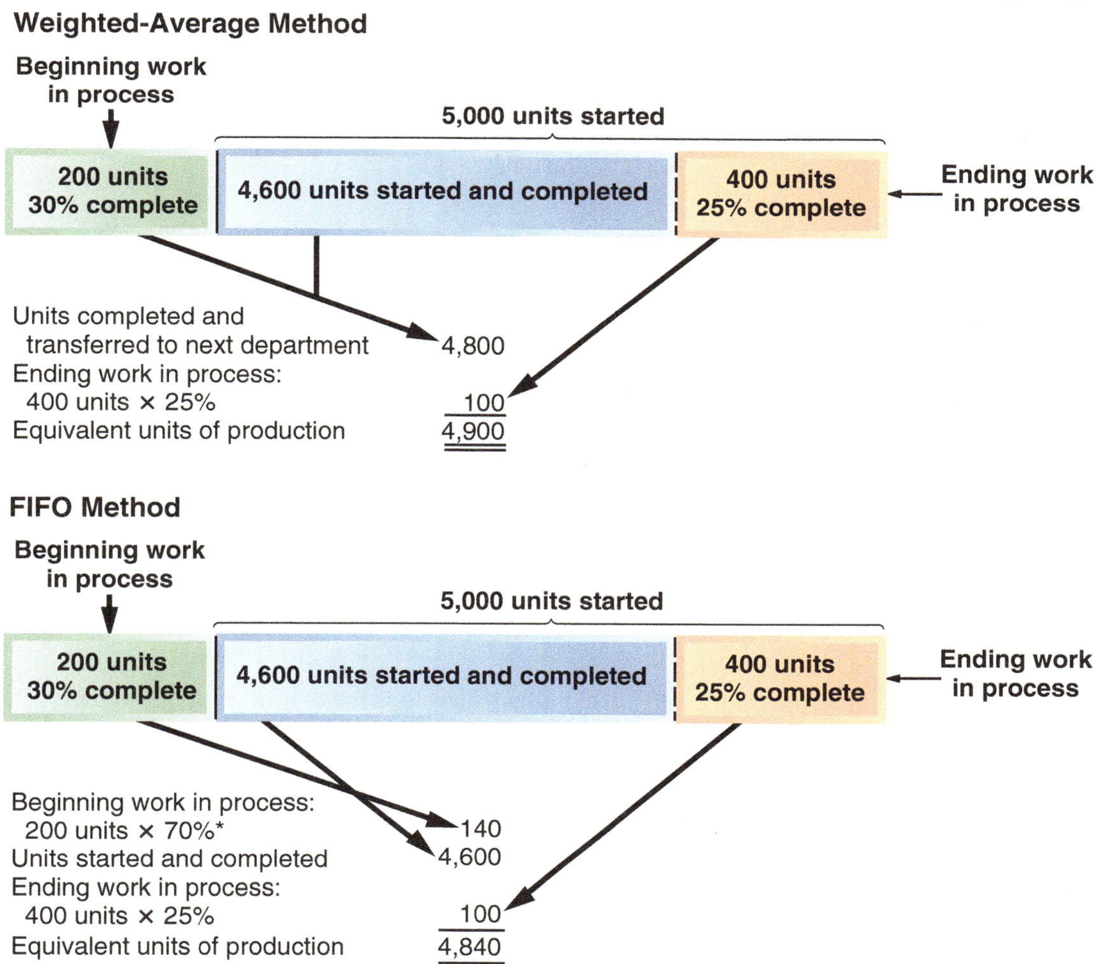

* 100% – 30% = 70%. This 70% represents the work needed to complete the units in the beginning inventory.

period, whereas the FIFO method separates the two periods. To see this more clearly, consider the following reconciliation of the two calculations of equivalent units:

Shaping and Milling Department	Materials	Conversion
Equivalent units—weighted-average method	4,960	4,900
Less equivalent units in beginning inventory:		
200 units × 55%	110	
200 units × 30%		60
Equivalent units of production—FIFO method	4,850	4,840

From the above, it is evident that the FIFO method removes the equivalent units that were already in beginning inventory from the equivalent units as defined using the weighted-average method. Thus, the FIFO method isolates the equivalent units that are due to work performed during the current period. The weighted-average method blends together the equivalent units already in beginning inventory with the equivalent units that are due to work performed in the current period.

Cost per Equivalent Unit—FIFO Method

LEARNING OBJECTIVE 7
Compute the cost per equivalent unit using the FIFO method.

In the FIFO method, the cost per equivalent unit is computed as follows:

FIFO Method
(a separate calculation is made for each cost category in each processing department)

$$\text{Cost per equivalent unit} = \frac{\text{Cost added during the period}}{\text{Equivalent units of production}}$$

Unlike the weighted-average method, in the FIFO method the cost per equivalent unit is based only on the costs incurred in the department in the current period.

The costs per equivalent unit for materials and for conversion are computed below for the Shaping and Milling Department for May:

Shaping and Milling Department
Costs per Equivalent Unit—FIFO method

	Materials	Conversion
Cost added during the period (a)	$368,600	$350,900
Equivalent units of production (b)	4,850	4,840
Cost per equivalent unit (a) ÷ (b)	$76.00	$72.50

Applying Costs—FIFO Method

LEARNING OBJECTIVE 8
Assign costs to units using the FIFO method.

The costs per equivalent unit are used to value units in ending inventory and units that are transferred to the next department. For example, each unit transferred out of the Shaping and Milling Department to the Graphics Application Department will carry with it a cost of $148.50—$76.00 for materials cost and $72.50 for conversion cost. Because 4,800 units were transferred out in May to the next department, the total cost assigned to those units would be $712,800 (4,800 units × $148.50 per unit).

A complete accounting of the costs of both ending work in process inventory and the units transferred out appears on the next page. It is more complicated than the weighted-average method. This is because the cost of the units transferred out consists of three separate components: (1) the cost of beginning work in process inventory; (2) the cost to complete the units in beginning work in process inventory; and (3) the cost of units started and completed during the period.

Shaping and Milling Department Costs of Ending Work in Process Inventory and Units Transferred Out—FIFO Method			
	Materials	Conversion	Total
Ending work in process inventory:			
Equivalent units of production (see Exhibit 4A–1) (a)	160	100	
Cost per equivalent unit (see page 170) (b)	$76.00	$72.50	
Cost of ending work in process inventory (a) × (b)	$12,160	$7,250	$19,410
Units transferred out:			
Cost in beginning work in process inventory	$9,600	$5,575	$15,175
Cost to complete the units in beginning work in process inventory:			
Equivalent units of production required to complete the units in beginning inventory (see Exhibit 4A–1) (a)	90	140	
Cost per equivalent unit (see page 170) (b)	$76.00	$72.50	
Cost to complete the units in beginning inventory (a) × (b)	$6,840	$10,150	$16,990
Cost of units started and completed this period:			
Units started and completed this period (see Exhibit 4A–1) (a)	4,600	4,600	
Cost per equivalent unit (see page 170) (b)	$76.00	$72.50	
Cost of units started and completed this period (a) × (b)	$349,600	$333,500	$683,100
Total cost of units transferred out			$715,265

Again, note that the cost of the units transferred out consists of three distinct components—the cost of beginning work in process inventory, the cost to complete the units in beginning inventory, and the cost of units started and completed during the period. This is a major difference between the weighted-average and FIFO methods.

Cost Reconciliation Report—FIFO Method

LEARNING OBJECTIVE 9
Prepare a cost reconciliation report using the FIFO method.

The costs assigned to ending work in process inventory and to the units transferred out reconcile with the costs we started with in Exhibit 4–7 as shown below:

Shaping and Milling Department Cost Reconciliation	
Costs to be accounted for:	
Cost of beginning work in process inventory (Exhibit 4–7)	$ 15,175
Costs added to production during the period (Exhibit 4–7)	719,500
Total cost to be accounted for	$734,675
Costs accounted for as follows:	
Cost of ending work in process inventory (see above)	$ 19,410
Cost of units transferred out (see above)	715,265
Total cost accounted for	$734,675

The $715,265 cost of the units transferred to the next department, Graphics Application, will be accounted for in that department as "costs transferred in." As in the weighted-average method, this cost will be treated in the process costing system as just another category of costs, like materials or conversion costs. The only difference is that the costs transferred in will always be 100% complete with respect to the work done in the Graphics Applications Department. Costs are passed on from one department to the next in this fashion, until they reach the last processing department, Finishing and Pairing. When the products are completed in this last department, their costs are transferred to finished goods.

A Comparison of Costing Methods

In most situations, the weighted-average and FIFO methods will produce very similar unit costs. If there never are any ending inventories, the two methods will produce identical results. The reason for this is that without any ending inventories, no costs can be carried forward into the next period and the weighted-average method will base unit costs on just the current period's costs—just as in the FIFO method. If there *are* ending inventories, either erratic input prices or erratic production levels would also be required to generate much of a difference in unit costs under the two methods. This is because the weighted-average method will blend the unit costs from the prior period with the unit costs of the current period. Unless these unit costs differ greatly, the blending will not make much difference.

Nevertheless, from the standpoint of cost control, the FIFO method is superior to the weighted-average method. Current performance should be evaluated based on costs of the current period only but the weighted-average method mixes costs of the current period with costs of the prior period. Thus, under the weighted-average method, the manager's apparent performance in the current period is influenced by what happened in the prior period. This problem does not arise under the FIFO method because the FIFO method makes a clear distinction between costs of prior periods and costs incurred during the current period. For the same reason, the FIFO method also provides more up-to-date cost data for decision-making purposes.

On the other hand, the weighted-average method is simpler to apply than the FIFO method, but computers can handle the additional calculations with ease once they have been appropriately programmed.

Appendix 4A Exercises and Problems

connect ACCOUNTING

All applicable exercises and problems are available with McGraw-Hill's *Connect™ Accounting.*

EXERCISE 4A–1 Computation of Equivalent Units—FIFO Method [LO6]

Refer to the data for Lindex Company in Exercise 4–2.

Required:

Compute the equivalent units of production for October assuming that the company uses the FIFO method for accounting for units and costs.

EXERCISE 4A–2 Cost per Equivalent Unit—FIFO Method [LO7]

Resprin Company uses the FIFO method in its process costing system. Data for the Assembly Department for May appear below:

	Materials	Labor	Overhead
Cost added during May	$82,560	$52,920	$132,300
Equivalent units of production	16,000	14,000	14,000

Required:

Compute the cost per equivalent unit for materials, for labor, for overhead, and in total.

EXERCISE 4A–3 Applying Costs to Units—FIFO Method [LO8]
Data concerning a recent period's activity in the Mixing Department, the first processing department in a company that uses process costing, appear below:

	Materials	Conversion
Cost of work in process inventory at the beginning of the period	$2,700	$380
Equivalent units of production in the ending work in process inventory	800	200
Equivalent units of production required to complete the beginning work in process inventory	400	700
Cost per equivalent unit for the period	$4.40	$1.30

A total of 8,000 units were completed and transferred to the next processing department during the period. Beginning work in process inventory consisted of 1,000 units and ending work in process inventory consisted of 2,000 units.

Required:
Using the FIFO method, compute the cost of the units transferred to the next department during the period and the cost of ending work in process inventory.

EXERCISE 4A–4 Cost Reconciliation Report—FIFO Method [LO9]
Kippinger Baking Corporation uses a process costing system in its large-scale baking operations. The Mixing Department is one of the company's processing departments. In the Mixing Department in August, the cost of beginning work in process inventory was $4,230, the cost of ending work in process inventory was $3,870, and the cost added to production was $46,320.

Required:
Prepare a cost reconciliation report for the Mixing Department for August.

EXERCISE 4A–5 Equivalent Units—FIFO Method [LO6]
Refer to the data for Gulf Fisheries, Inc., in Exercise 4–12.

Required:
Compute the equivalent units for May for the Cleaning Department, assuming that the company uses the FIFO method of accounting for units.

EXERCISE 4A–6 Equivalent Units—FIFO Method [LO6]
Refer to the data for Societe Clemeau in Exercise 4–10.

Required:
1. Compute the number of kilograms of cement completed and transferred out of the Mixing Department during May.
2. Compute the equivalent units of production for materials and for conversion for May.

EXERCISE 4A–7 Equivalent Units and Cost per Equivalent Unit—FIFO Method [LO6, LO7]
Refer to the data for Kalox, Inc., in Exercise 4–6.

Required:
Assume that the company uses the FIFO method of accounting for units and costs.
1. Compute the equivalent units for May's activity for the first processing department.
2. Determine the costs per equivalent unit for May.

EXERCISE 4A–8 Computation of Equivalent Units—FIFO Method [LO6]

QualCon, Inc., produces wine bottles for vintners in a process that starts in the Melt and Mold Department. Data concerning that department's operations in the most recent period appear below:

Beginning work in process:	
Units in process	400
Stage of completion with respect to materials	75%
Stage of completion with respect to conversion	25%
Units started into production during the month	42,600
Units completed and transferred out	42,500
Ending work in process:	
Units in process	500
Stage of completion with respect to materials	80%
Stage of completion with respect to conversion	30%

Required:

QualCon uses the FIFO method in its process costing system. Compute the equivalent units of production for the period for the Melt and Mold Department.

EXERCISE 4A–9 Equivalent Units; Applying Costs—FIFO Method [LO6, LO7, LO8]

Krollon Company uses the FIFO method in its process costing system. The following data are for the most recent month of operations in one of the company's processing departments:

Units in beginning inventory	400		
Units started into production	4,300		
Units in ending inventory	300		
Units transferred to the next department	4,400		
		Materials	Conversion
Percentage completion of beginning inventory		70%	30%
Percentage completion of ending inventory		80%	40%

According to the company's costing system, the cost of beginning inventory was $7,886, of which $4,897 was for materials and the remainder was for conversion cost. The costs added during the month amounted to $181,652. The costs per equivalent unit for the month were:

	Materials	Conversion
Cost per equivalent unit	$18.20	$23.25

Required:

1. Compute the total cost per equivalent unit for the month.
2. Compute the equivalent units of material and of conversion costs in the ending inventory.
3. Compute the equivalent units of material and of conversion costs that were required to complete the beginning inventory.
4. Determine the number of units started and completed during the month.
5. Determine the costs of ending inventory and units transferred out.

PROBLEM 4A–10 Equivalent Units; Applying Costs—FIFO Method [LO6, LO7, LO8, LO9]

Reutter Company manufactures a single product and uses process costing. The company's product goes through two processing departments, Etching and Wiring. The following activity was recorded in the Etching Department during July:

Production data:	
Units in process, July 1: materials 60% complete; conversion 30% complete	60,000
Units started into production	510,000
Units in process, July 31: materials 80% complete; conversion 40% complete	70,000
Cost data:	
Work in process inventory, July 1:	
Materials cost	$27,000
Conversion cost	$13,000
Cost added during July:	
Materials cost	$468,000
Conversion cost	$357,000

Materials are added at several stages during the etching process. The company uses the FIFO method.

Required:

1. Determine the equivalent units for July for the Etching Department.
2. Compute the costs per equivalent unit for July for the Etching Department.
3. Determine the total cost of ending work in process inventory and the total cost of units transferred to the next process for the Etching Department in July.
4. Prepare a cost reconciliation report for the Etching Department for July.

PROBLEM 4A–11 Equivalent Units, Cost per Equivalent Unit, Applying Costs—FIFO Method [LO6, LO7, LO8, LO9]

Refer to the data for the Mixing Department in Honeybutter, Inc., in Problem 4–14. Assume that the company uses the FIFO method rather than the weighted-average method in its process costing system.

Required:

1. Determine the equivalent units for June for the Mixing Department.
2. Compute the costs per equivalent unit for June for the Mixing Department.
3. Determine the total cost of ending work in process inventory and the total cost of units transferred to the next process for the Mixing Department in June.
4. Prepare a cost reconciliation report for the Mixing Department for June.

CASE 4A–12 Second Department—FIFO Method [LO6, LO7, LO8]

Refer to the data for Durall Company in Case 4–20. Assume that the company uses the FIFO method in its process costing system.

Required:

1. Prepare a report for the Forming Department for October showing how much cost should have been assigned to the units completed and transferred to the Stamping Department and to the ending work in process inventory.
2. Assume that in order to remain competitive, the company undertook a major cost-cutting program during October. Would the effects of this cost-cutting program tend to show up more under the weighted-average method or under the FIFO method? Explain your answer.

Appendix 4B: Service Department Allocations

Most large organizations have both *operating departments* and *service departments.* The central purposes of the organization are carried out in the operating departments. In contrast, service departments do not directly engage in operating activities. Instead, they provide services or assistance to the operating departments. Examples of operating departments include the Surgery Department at Mt. Sinai Hospital, the Geography Department at the University of Washington, the Marketing Department at Allstate Insurance Company, and production departments at manufacturers such as Mitsubishi, Hewlett-Packard, and Michelin. In process costing, the processing departments are all operating departments. Examples of service departments include Cafeteria, Internal Auditing, Human Resources, Cost Accounting, and Purchasing.

The overhead costs of operating departments commonly include allocations of costs from the service departments. To the extent that service department costs are classified as production costs, they should be included in unit product costs and thus, must be allocated to operating departments in a process costing system.

Three approaches are used to allocate the costs of service departments to other departments: the direct method, the step-down method, and the reciprocal method. These three methods are discussed in the following sections. However, before getting into the details of these methods, we will discuss *interdepartmental services.*

Interdepartmental Services Many service departments provide services to each other, as well as to operating departments. For example, the Cafeteria Department provides meals for all employees, including those assigned to other service departments, as well as to employees of the operating departments. In turn, the Cafeteria Department may receive services from other service departments, such as from Custodial Services or from Personnel. Services provided between service departments are known as *interdepartmental* or *reciprocal services.*

Direct Method

LEARNING OBJECTIVE 10
Allocate service department costs to operating departments using the direct method.

The *direct method* is the simplest of the three cost allocation methods. It ignores the services provided by a service department to other service departments (e.g., interdepartmental services) and allocates all service department costs directly to operating departments. Even if a service department (such as Personnel) provides a large amount of service to another service department (such as the cafeteria), no allocations are made between the two departments. Rather, all costs are allocated *directly* to the operating departments, bypassing the other service departments; hence, the term *direct method.*

For an example of the direct method, consider Mountain View Hospital, which has two service departments and two operating departments as shown below. The hospital allocates its Hospital Administration costs on the basis of employee-hours and its Custodial Services costs on the basis of square feet occupied.

	Service Departments		Operating Departments		
	Hospital Administration	Custodial Services	Laboratory	Patient Care	Total
Departmental costs before allocation	$360,000	$90,000	$261,000	$689,000	$1,400,000
Employee hours	12,000	6,000	18,000	30,000	66,000
Space occupied—square feet	10,000	200	5,000	45,000	60,200

EXHIBIT 4B–1
Direct Method of Allocation

	Service Departments		Operating Departments		
	Hospital Administration	Custodial Services	Laboratory	Patient Care	Total
Departmental costs before allocation	$360,000	$90,000	$261,000	$689,000	$1,400,000
Allocation:					
Hospital Administration costs (18⁄48, 30⁄48)*	(360,000)		135,000	225,000	
Custodial Services costs (5⁄50, 45⁄50)†		(90,000)	9,000	81,000	
Total cost after allocation	$ 0	$ 0	$405,000	$995,000	$1,400,000

*Based on the employee-hours in the two operating departments, which are 18,000 hours + 30,000 hours = 48,000 hours.
†Based on the square feet occupied by the two operating departments, which is 5,000 square feet + 45,000 square feet = 50,000 square feet.

The direct method of allocating the hospital's service department costs to the operating departments is shown in Exhibit 4B–1. Several things should be noted in this exhibit. First, the employee-hours of the Hospital Administration Department and the Custodial Services Department are ignored when allocating the costs of Hospital Administration using the direct method. *Under the direct method, any of the allocation base attributable to the service departments themselves is ignored; only the amount of the allocation base attributable to the operating departments is used in the allocation.* Note that the same rule is used when allocating the costs of the Custodial Services Department. Even though the Hospital Administration and Custodial Services departments occupy some space, this is ignored when the Custodial Services costs are allocated. Finally, note that after all allocations have been completed, all of the service department costs are contained in the two operating departments.

Although the direct method is simple, it is less accurate than the other methods because it ignores interdepartmental services.

Step-Down Method

LEARNING OBJECTIVE 11
Allocate service department costs to operating departments using the step-down method.

Unlike the direct method, the *step-down method* provides for allocation of a service department's costs to other service departments, as well as to operating departments. The step-down method is sequential. The sequence typically begins with the department that provides the greatest amount of service to other service departments. After its costs have been allocated, the process continues, step by step, ending with the department that provides the least amount of services to other service departments. This step procedure is illustrated in Exhibit 4B–2.

Exhibit 4B–3 shows the details of the step-down method. Note the following three key points about these allocations. First, under Allocation in Exhibit 4B–3, you see two allocations, or steps. In the first step, the costs of Hospital Administration are allocated to another service department (Custodial Services) as well as to the operating departments. In contrast to the direct method, the allocation base for Hospital Administration costs now includes the employee-hours for Custodial Services as well as for the operating departments. However, the allocation base still excludes the employee-hours for Hospital Administration itself. *In both the direct and step-down methods, any amount of the allocation base attributable to the service department whose cost is being allocated is always ignored.* Second, looking again at Exhibit 4B–3, note that in the second step under the Allocation heading, the cost of Custodial Services is allocated to the two operating departments, and none of the cost is allocated to Hospital Administration even though Hospital Administration occupies space in the building. *In the step-down method,*

EXHIBIT 4B–2
Graphic Illustration—Step-Down Method

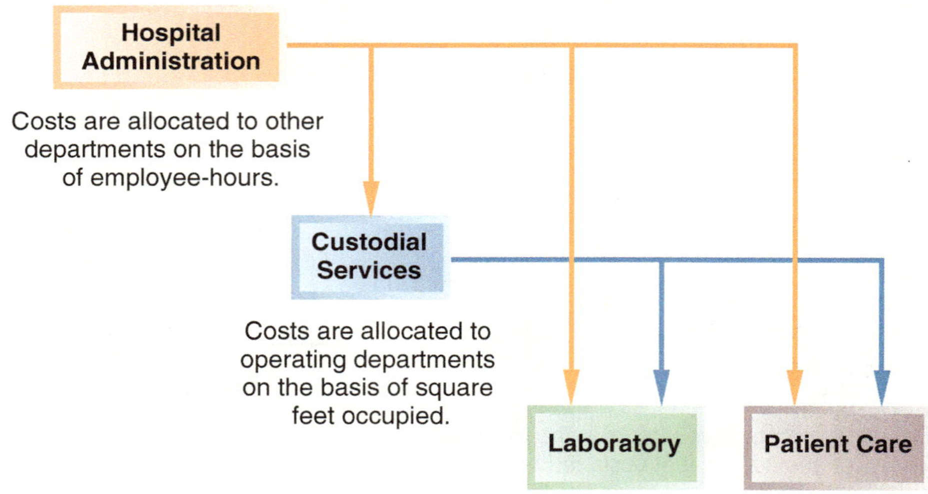

any amount of the allocation base that is attributable to a service department whose cost has already been allocated is ignored. After a service department's costs have been allocated, costs of other service departments are not reallocated back to it. Third, note that the cost of Custodial Services allocated to other departments in the second step ($130,000) in Exhibit 4B–3 includes the costs of Hospital Administration that were allocated to Custodial Services in the first step in Exhibit 4B–3.

Reciprocal Method

The *reciprocal method* gives full recognition to interdepartmental services. Under the step-down method only partial recognition of interdepartmental services is possible. The step-down method always allocates costs forward—never backward. The reciprocal method, by contrast, allocates service department costs in *both* directions. Thus, because Custodial Services in the prior example provides services for Hospital Administration, part of Custodial Services' costs will be allocated *back* to Hospital Administration if the reciprocal method is used. At the same time, part of Hospital Administration's costs will be allocated *forward* to Custodial Services. Reciprocal allocation requires the use of simultaneous linear equations and is beyond the scope of this book. Examples of the reciprocal method can be found in more advanced cost accounting texts.

EXHIBIT 4B–3
Step-Down Method of Allocation

	Service Departments		Operating Departments		
	Hospital Administration	Custodial Services	Laboratory	Patient Care	Total
Departmental costs before allocation	$360,000	$ 90,000	$261,000	$ 689,000	$1,400,000
Allocation:					
Hospital Administration costs (6/54, 18/54, 30/54)*	(360,000)	40,000	120,000	200,000	
Custodial Services costs (5/50, 45/50)†		(130,000)	13,000	117,000	
Total cost after allocation	$ 0	$ 0	$394,000	$1,006,000	$1,400,000

*Based on the employee-hours in Custodial Services and the two operating departments, which are 6,000 hours + 18,000 hours + 30,000 hours = 54,000 hours.
†As in Exhibit 4B–1, this allocation is based on the square feet occupied by the two operating departments.

Appendix 4B Exercises and Problems

All applicable exercises and problems are available with McGraw-Hill's *Connect™ Accounting.*

EXERCISE 4B–1 Direct Method [LO10]

Ignatius College has provided the following data to be used in its service department cost allocations:

	Service Departments		Operating Departments	
	Administration	Physical Plant Services	Undergraduate Programs	Graduate Programs
Departmental costs before allocations	$2,070,000	$720,000	$23,650,000	$2,980,000
Student credit-hours			40,000	5,000
Space occupied in square feet	30,000	5,000	250,000	50,000

Required:

Using the direct method, allocate the costs of the service departments to the two operating departments. Allocate the costs of the Administration Department on the basis of student credit-hours and the costs of the Physical Plant Services Department on the basis of space occupied.

EXERCISE 4B–2 Step-Down Method [LO11]

University District Co-op, a whole foods grocery and coffee shop, has provided the following data to be used in its service department cost allocations:

	Service Departments		Operating Departments	
	Administration	Building Services	Groceries	Coffee Shop
Departmental costs before allocations	$200,000	$60,000	$3,860,000	$340,000
Employee-hours	480	320	2,720	160
Space occupied in square feet	800	1,200	9,500	500

Required:

Using the step-down method, allocate the costs of the service departments to the two operating departments. Allocate the costs of the Administration Department first on the basis of employee-hours and then the costs of the Building Services Department on the basis of space occupied.

EXERCISE 4B–3 Step-Down Method [LO11]

Arbon Company has three service departments and two operating departments. Selected data concerning the five departments are presented below:

	Service Departments			Operating Departments		
	Administrative	Janitorial	Equipment Maintenance	Prep	Finishing	Total
Costs	$84,000	$67,800	$36,000	$256,100	$498,600	$942,500
Number of employees	80	60	240	600	300	1,280
Square feet of space occupied	3,000	12,000	10,000	20,000	70,000	115,000
Machine-hours				10,000	30,000	40,000

The company allocates service department costs by the step-down method in the following order: Administrative (number of employees), Janitorial (space occupied), and Equipment Maintenance (machine-hours).

Required:
Using the step-down method, allocate the service department costs to the operating departments.

EXERCISE 4B–4 Direct Method [LO10]
Refer to the data for Arbon Company in Exercise 4B–3.

Required:
Assuming that the company uses the direct method rather than the step-down method to allocate service department costs, how much cost would be assigned to each operating department?

PROBLEM 4B–5 Step-Down Method [LO11]
Pleasant View Hospital has three service departments—Food Services, Administrative Services, and X-ray Services. The costs of these departments are allocated by the step-down method, using the allocation bases and in the order shown below:

Service Department	Costs Incurred	Base for Allocation
Food Services	Variable	Meals served
	Fixed	Peak-period needs
Administrative Services	Variable	Files processed
	Fixed	10% X-ray Services, 20% Outpatient Clinic, 30% OB Care, and 40% General Hospital
X-ray Services	Variable	X-rays taken
	Fixed	Peak-period needs

Estimated cost and operating data for all departments in the hospital for the forthcoming month are presented in the following table:

	Food Services	Admin. Services	X-Ray Services	Outpatient Clinic	OB Care	General Hospital	Total
Variable costs	$ 73,150	$ 6,800	$38,100	$11,700	$ 14,850	$ 53,400	$198,000
Fixed costs	48,000	33,040	59,520	26,958	99,738	344,744	612,000
Total costs	$121,150	$39,840	$97,620	$38,658	$114,588	$398,144	$810,000
Meals served		1,000	500		7,000	30,000	38,500
Percent of peak-period Food Services needs		2%	1%		17%	80%	100%
Files processed			1,500	3,000	900	12,000	17,400
X-rays taken				1,200	350	8,400	9,950
Percent of peak-period X-ray Services needs				13%	3%	84%	100%

All billing in the hospital is done through the Outpatient Clinic, OB Care, or General Hospital. The hospital's administrator wants the costs of the three service departments allocated to these three billing centers.

Required:
Prepare the cost allocation desired by the hospital administrator. Include under each billing center the direct costs of the center as well as the costs allocated from the service departments.

PROBLEM 4B–6 Step-Down Method versus Direct Method; Predetermined Overhead Rates [LO10, LO11]
Petah, Ltd., of Tel Aviv, Israel, has budgeted costs in its various departments as follows for the coming year:

Factory Administration	₪ 540,000
Custodial Services	137,520
Personnel	57,680
Maintenance.	90,400
Stamping—overhead	752,600
Assembly—overhead	351,800
Total overhead cost	₪1,930,000

The Israeli currency is the shekel, denoted by ₪. The company allocates service department costs to other departments, *in the order listed below.*

	Number of Employees	Total Labor-Hours	Square Meters of Space Occupied	Direct Labor-Hours	Machine-Hours
Factory Administration	22	—	5,000	—	—
Custodial Services	8	6,000	2,000	—	—
Personnel	10	10,000	3,000	—	—
Maintenance	50	44,000	10,000	—	—
Stamping—overhead	80	60,000	70,000	40,000	140,000
Assembly—overhead	120	180,000	20,000	160,000	20,000
	290	300,000	110,000	200,000	160,000

Stamping and Assembly are operating departments; the other departments are service departments. Factory Administration is allocated on the basis of labor-hours; Custodial Services on the basis of square meters occupied; Personnel on the basis of number of employees; and Maintenance on the basis of machine-hours.

Required:

1. Allocate service department costs to consuming departments by the step-down method. Then compute predetermined overhead rates in the operating departments, using a machine-hours basis in Stamping and a direct labor-hours basis in Assembly.
2. Repeat (1) above, this time using the direct method. Again, compute predetermined overhead rates in Stamping and Assembly.
3. Assume that the company doesn't bother with allocating service department costs but simply computes a single plantwide overhead rate based on total overhead costs (both service department and operating department costs) divided by total direct labor-hours. Compute the plantwide overhead rate.
4. Suppose a job requires machine and labor time as follows:

	Machine-Hours	Direct Labor-Hours
Stamping Department	190	25
Assembly Department	10	75
Total hours	200	100

Using the overhead rates computed in (1), (2), and (3) above, compute the amount of overhead cost that would be assigned to the job if the overhead rates were developed using the step-down method, the direct method, and the plantwide method. (Round allocations to the nearest whole shekel.)

CASE 4B–7 Step-Down Method versus Direct Method [LO10, LO11]

"I can't understand what's happening here," said Mike Holt, president of Severson Products, Inc. "We always seem to bid too high on jobs that require a lot of labor time in the Finishing Department, and we always seem to get every job we bid on that requires a lot of machine time in the Milling Department. Yet we don't seem to be making much money on those Milling Department jobs. I wonder if the problem is in our overhead rates."

Severson Products manufactures high-quality wood products to customers' specifications. Some jobs take a large amount of machine work in the Milling Department, and other jobs take a large amount of hand finishing work in the Finishing Department. In addition to the Milling and Finishing departments, the company has three service departments. The costs of these service departments are allocated to other departments *in the order listed on the following page.* (For each service department, use the most appropriate allocation base.)

	Total Labor-Hours	Square Feet of Space Occupied	Number of Employees	Machine-Hours	Direct Labor-Hours
Cafeteria	16,000	12,000	25		
Custodial Services	9,000	3,000	40		
Machinery Maintenance	15,000	10,000	60		
Milling	30,000	40,000	100	160,000	20,000
Finishing	100,000	20,000	300	40,000	70,000
	170,000	85,000	525	200,000	90,000

Budgeted overhead costs in each department for the current year are as follows:

Cafeteria	$ 320,000*
Custodial Services	65,400
Machinery Maintenance	93,600
Milling	416,000
Finishing	166,000
Total budgeted cost	$1,061,000

*This represents the amount of cost subsidized by the company.

Because of its simplicity, the company has always used the direct method to allocate service department costs to the two operating departments.

Required:

1. Using the step-down method, allocate service department costs to the consuming departments. Then compute predetermined overhead rates in the operating departments for the current year using machine-hours as the allocation base in the Milling Department and direct labor-hours as the allocation base in the Finishing Department.
2. Repeat (1) above, this time using the direct method. Again compute predetermined overhead rates in the Milling and Finishing Departments.
3. Assume that during the current year the company bids on a job that requires machine and labor time as follows:

	Machine-Hours	Direct Labor-Hours
Milling Department	2,000	1,600
Finishing Department	800	13,000
Total hours	2,800	14,600

a. Determine the amount of overhead that would be assigned to the job if the company used the overhead rates developed in (1) above. Then determine the amount of overhead that would be assigned to the job if the company used the overhead rates developed in (2) above.

b. Explain to the president why the step-down method provides a better basis for computing predetermined overhead rates than the direct method.

Chapter 5

Cost-Volume-Profit Relationships

LEARNING OBJECTIVES

After studying Chapter 5, you should be able to:

- **LO1** Explain how changes in activity affect contribution margin and net operating income.
- **LO2** Prepare and interpret a cost-volume-profit (CVP) graph and a profit graph.
- **LO3** Use the contribution margin ratio (CM ratio) to compute changes in contribution margin and net operating income resulting from changes in sales volume.
- **LO4** Show the effects on net operating income of changes in variable costs, fixed costs, selling price, and volume.
- **LO5** Determine the level of sales needed to achieve a desired target profit.
- **LO6** Determine the break-even point.
- **LO7** Compute the margin of safety and explain its significance.
- **LO8** Compute the degree of operating leverage at a particular level of sales and explain how it can be used to predict changes in net operating income.
- **LO9** Compute the break-even point for a multiproduct company and explain the effects of shifts in the sales mix on contribution margin and the break-even point.

BUSINESS FOCUS

Moreno Turns Around the Los Angeles Angels

When Arturo Moreno bought Major League Baseball's Los Angeles Angels in 2003, the team was drawing 2.3 million fans and losing $5.5 million per year. Moreno immediately cut prices to attract more fans and increase profits. In his first spring training game, he reduced the price of selected tickets from $12 to $6. By increasing attendance, Moreno understood that he would sell more food and souvenirs. He dropped the price of draft beer by $2 and cut the price of baseball caps from $20 to $7.

The Angels now consistently draw about 3.4 million fans per year. This growth in attendance helped double stadium sponsorship revenue to $26 million, and it motivated the Fox Sports Network to pay the Angels $500 million to broadcast all of its games for the next ten years. Since Moreno bought the Angels, annual revenues have jumped from $127 million to $212 million, and the team's operating loss of $5.5 million has been transformed to a profit of $10.3 million. ■

Source: Matthew Craft, "Moreno's Math," *Forbes*, May 11, 2009, pp. 84–87.

Cost-volume-profit (CVP) analysis is a powerful tool that helps managers understand the relationships among cost, volume, and profit. CVP analysis focuses on how profits are affected by the following five factors:

1. Selling prices.
2. Sales volume.
3. Unit variable costs.
4. Total fixed costs.
5. Mix of products sold.

Because CVP analysis helps managers understand how profits are affected by these key factors, it is a vital tool in many business decisions. These decisions include what products and services to offer, what prices to charge, what marketing strategy to use, and what cost structure to maintain. To help understand the role of CVP analysis in business decisions, consider the case of Acoustic Concepts, Inc., a company founded by Prem Narayan.

MANAGERIAL ACCOUNTING IN ACTION

The Issue

Prem, who was a graduate student in engineering at the time, started Acoustic Concepts to market a radical new speaker he had designed for automobile sound systems. The speaker, called the Sonic Blaster, uses an advanced microprocessor and proprietary software to boost amplification to awesome levels. Prem contracted with a Taiwanese electronics manufacturer to produce the speaker. With seed money provided by his family, Prem placed an order with the manufacturer and ran advertisements in auto magazines.

The Sonic Blaster was an almost immediate success, and sales grew to the point that Prem moved the company's headquarters out of his apartment and into rented quarters in a nearby industrial park. He also hired a receptionist, an accountant, a sales manager, and a small sales staff to sell the speakers to retail stores. The accountant, Bob Luchinni, had worked for several small companies where he had acted as a business advisor as well as accountant and bookkeeper. The following discussion occurred soon after Bob was hired:

Prem: Bob, I've got a lot of questions about the company's finances that I hope you can help answer.

Bob: We're in great shape. The loan from your family will be paid off within a few months.

Prem: I know, but I am worried about the risks I've taken on by expanding operations. What would happen if a competitor entered the market and our sales slipped? How far could sales drop without putting us into the red? Another question I've been trying to resolve is how much our sales would have to increase to justify the big marketing campaign the sales staff is pushing for.

Bob: Marketing always wants more money for advertising.

Prem: And they are always pushing me to drop the selling price on the speaker. I agree with them that a lower price will boost our sales volume, but I'm not sure the increased volume will offset the loss in revenue from the lower price.

Bob: It sounds like these questions are all related in some way to the relationships among our selling prices, our costs, and our volume. I shouldn't have a problem coming up with some answers.

Prem: Can we meet again in a couple of days to see what you have come up with?

Bob: Sounds good. By then I'll have some preliminary answers for you as well as a model you can use for answering similar questions in the future.

The Basics of Cost-Volume-Profit (CVP) Analysis

Bob Luchinni's preparation for his forthcoming meeting with Prem begins with the contribution income statement. The contribution income statement emphasizes the behavior of costs and therefore is extremely helpful to managers in judging the impact on profits of changes in selling price, cost, or volume. Bob will base his analysis on the following contribution income statement he prepared last month:

Acoustic Concepts, Inc.
Contribution Income Statement
For the Month of June

	Total	Per Unit
Sales (400 speakers)	$100,000	$250
Variable expenses	60,000	150
Contribution margin	40,000	$100
Fixed expenses	35,000	
Net operating income	$ 5,000	

Notice that sales, variable expenses, and contribution margin are expressed on a per unit basis as well as in total on this contribution income statement. The per unit figures will be very helpful to Bob in some of his calculations. Note that this contribution income statement has been prepared for management's use inside the company and would not ordinarily be made available to those outside the company.

Contribution Margin

LEARNING OBJECTIVE 1
Explain how changes in activity affect contribution margin and net operating income.

Contribution margin is the amount remaining from sales revenue after variable expenses have been deducted. Thus, it is the amount available to cover fixed expenses and then to provide profits for the period. Notice the sequence here—contribution margin is used *first* to cover the fixed expenses, and then whatever remains goes toward profits. If the contribution margin is not sufficient to cover the fixed expenses, then a loss occurs for the period. To illustrate with an extreme example, assume that Acoustic Concepts sells only one speaker during a particular month. The company's income statement would appear as follows:

Contribution Income Statement
Sales of 1 Speaker

	Total	Per Unit
Sales (1 speaker)	$ 250	$250
Variable expenses	150	150
Contribution margin	100	$100
Fixed expenses	35,000	
Net operating loss	$(34,900)	

For each additional speaker the company sells during the month, $100 more in contribution margin becomes available to help cover the fixed expenses. If a second speaker is sold, for example, then the total contribution margin will increase by $100 (to a total of $200) and the company's loss will decrease by $100, to $34,800:

Contribution Income Statement
Sales of 2 Speakers

	Total	Per Unit
Sales (2 speakers)	$ 500	$250
Variable expenses	300	150
Contribution margin	200	$100
Fixed expenses	35,000	
Net operating loss	$(34,800)	

If enough speakers can be sold to generate $35,000 in contribution margin, then all of the fixed expenses will be covered and the company will *break even* for the month—that is, it will show neither profit nor loss but just cover all of its costs. To reach the break-even point, the company will have to sell 350 speakers in a month because each speaker sold yields $100 in contribution margin:

Contribution Income Statement
Sales of 350 Speakers

	Total	Per Unit
Sales (350 speakers)	$87,500	$250
Variable expenses	52,500	150
Contribution margin	35,000	$100
Fixed expenses	35,000	
Net operating income	$ 0	

Computation of the break-even point is discussed in detail later in the chapter; for the moment, note that the **break-even point** is the level of sales at which profit is zero.

Once the break-even point has been reached, net operating income will increase by the amount of the unit contribution margin for each additional unit sold. For example, if 351 speakers are sold in a month, then the net operating income for the month will be $100 because the company will have sold 1 speaker more than the number needed to break even:

Contribution Income Statement
Sales of 351 Speakers

	Total	Per Unit
Sales (351 speakers)	$87,750	$250
Variable expenses	52,650	150
Contribution margin	35,100	$100
Fixed expenses	35,000	
Net operating income	$ 100	

If 352 speakers are sold (2 speakers above the break-even point), the net operating income for the month will be $200. If 353 speakers are sold (3 speakers above the break-even point), the net operating income for the month will be $300, and so forth. To estimate the profit at any sales volume above the break-even point, multiply the number of units sold in excess of the break-even point by the unit contribution margin. The result represents the anticipated profits for the period. Or, to estimate the effect of a planned increase in sales on profits, simply multiply the increase in units sold by the unit contribution margin. The result will be the expected increase in profits. To illustrate, if Acoustic Concepts is currently selling 400 speakers per month and plans to increase sales to 425 speakers per month, the anticipated impact on profits can be computed as follows:

Increased number of speakers to be sold	25
Contribution margin per speaker	× $100
Increase in net operating income	$2,500

These calculations can be verified as follows:

	Sales Volume			
	400 Speakers	425 Speakers	Difference (25 Speakers)	Per Unit
Sales (@ $250 per speaker)	$100,000	$106,250	$6,250	$250
Variable expenses (@ $150 per speaker)	60,000	63,750	3,750	150
Contribution margin	40,000	42,500	2,500	$100
Fixed expenses	35,000	35,000	0	
Net operating income	$ 5,000	$ 7,500	$2,500	

To summarize, if sales are zero, the company's loss would equal its fixed expenses. Each unit that is sold reduces the loss by the amount of the unit contribution margin. Once the break-even point has been reached, each additional unit sold increases the company's profit by the amount of the unit contribution margin.

CVP Relationships in Equation Form

The contribution format income statement can be expressed in equation form as follows:

$$\text{Profit} = (\text{Sales} - \text{Variable expenses}) - \text{Fixed expenses}$$

For brevity, we use the term *profit* to stand for net operating income in equations.

When a company has only a *single* product, as at Acoustic Concepts, we can further refine the equation as follows:

$$\text{Sales} = \text{Selling price per unit} \times \text{Quantity sold} = P \times Q$$

$$\text{Variable expenses} = \text{Variable expenses per unit} \times \text{Quantity sold} = V \times Q$$

$$\text{Profit} = (P \times Q - V \times Q) - \text{Fixed expenses}$$

We can do all of the calculations of the previous section using this simple equation. For example, on the previous page we computed that the net operating income (profit) at sales of 351 speakers would be $100. We can arrive at the same conclusion using the above equation as follows:

$$\begin{aligned}
\text{Profit} &= (P \times Q - V \times Q) - \text{Fixed expenses}\\
\text{Profit} &= (\$250 \times 351 - \$150 \times 351) - \$35{,}000\\
&= (\$250 - \$150) \times 351 - \$35{,}000\\
&= (\$100) \times 351 - \$35{,}000\\
&= \$35{,}100 - \$35{,}000 = \$100
\end{aligned}$$

It is often useful to express the simple profit equation in terms of the unit contribution margin (Unit CM) as follows:

$$\text{Unit CM} = \text{Selling price per unit} - \text{Variable expenses per unit} = P - V$$

$$\text{Profit} = (P \times Q - V \times Q) - \text{Fixed expenses}$$

$$\text{Profit} = (P - V) \times Q - \text{Fixed expenses}$$

$$\text{Profit} = \text{Unit CM} \times Q - \text{Fixed expenses}$$

We could also have used this equation to determine the profit at sales of 351 speakers as follows:

$$\begin{aligned} \text{Profit} &= \text{Unit CM} \times Q - \text{Fixed expenses} \\ &= \$100 \times 351 - \$35{,}000 \\ &= \$35{,}100 - \$35{,}000 = \$100 \end{aligned}$$

For those who are comfortable with algebra, the quickest and easiest approach to solving the problems in this chapter may be to use the simple profit equation in one of its forms.

CVP Relationships in Graphic Form

LEARNING OBJECTIVE 2
Prepare and interpret a cost-volume-profit (CVP) graph and a profit graph.

The relationships among revenue, cost, profit, and volume are illustrated on a **cost-volume-profit (CVP) graph.** A CVP graph highlights CVP relationships over wide ranges of activity. To help explain his analysis to Prem Narayan, Bob Luchinni prepared a CVP graph for Acoustic Concepts.

Preparing the CVP Graph

In a CVP graph (sometimes called a *break-even chart*), unit volume is represented on the horizontal (X) axis and dollars on the vertical (Y) axis. Preparing a CVP graph involves the three steps depicted in Exhibit 5–1:

1. Draw a line parallel to the volume axis to represent total fixed expense. For Acoustic Concepts, total fixed expenses are $35,000.
2. Choose some volume of unit sales and plot the point representing total expense (fixed and variable) at the sales volume you have selected. In Exhibit 5–1, Bob Luchinni chose a volume of 600 speakers. Total expense at that sales volume is:

Fixed expense	$ 35,000
Variable expense (600 speakers × $150 per speaker)	90,000
Total expense	$125,000

After the point has been plotted, draw a line through it back to the point where the fixed expense line intersects the dollars axis.

EXHIBIT 5–1
Preparing the CVP Graph

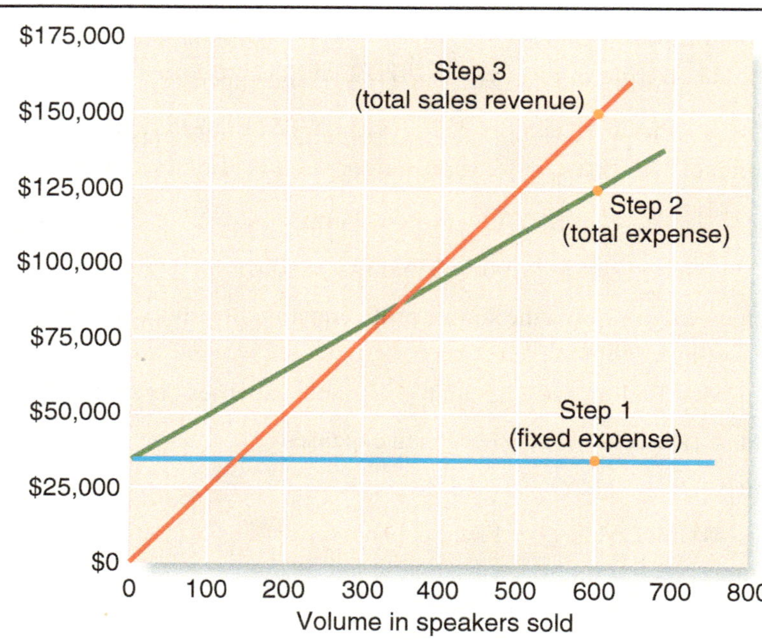

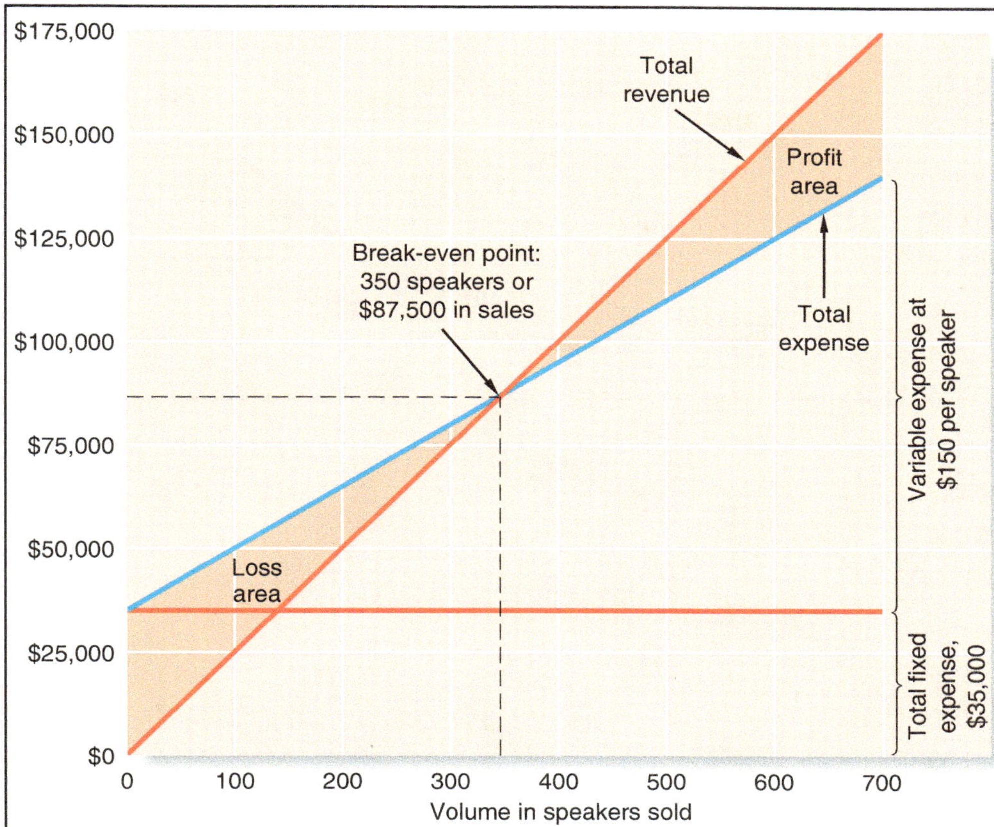

EXHIBIT 5–2
The Completed CVP Graph

3. Again choose some sales volume and plot the point representing total sales dollars at the activity level you have selected. In Exhibit 5–1, Bob Luchinni again chose a volume of 600 speakers. Sales at that volume total $150,000 (600 speakers × $250 per speaker). Draw a line through this point back to the origin.

The interpretation of the completed CVP graph is given in Exhibit 5–2. The anticipated profit or loss at any given level of sales is measured by the vertical distance between the total revenue line (sales) and the total expense line (variable expense plus fixed expense).

The break-even point is where the total revenue and total expense lines cross. The break-even point of 350 speakers in Exhibit 5–2 agrees with the break-even point computed earlier.

As discussed earlier, when sales are below the break-even point—in this case, 350 units—the company suffers a loss. Note that the loss (represented by the vertical distance between the total expense and total revenue lines) gets bigger as sales decline. When sales are above the break-even point, the company earns a profit and the size of the profit (represented by the vertical distance between the total revenue and total expense lines) increases as sales increase.

An even simpler form of the CVP graph, which we call a profit graph, is presented in Exhibit 5–3. That graph is based on the following equation:

$$\text{Profit} = \text{Unit CM} \times Q - \text{Fixed expenses}$$

In the case of Acoustic Concepts, the equation can be expressed as:

$$\text{Profit} = \$100 \times Q - \$35{,}000$$

EXHIBIT 5–3
The Profit Graph

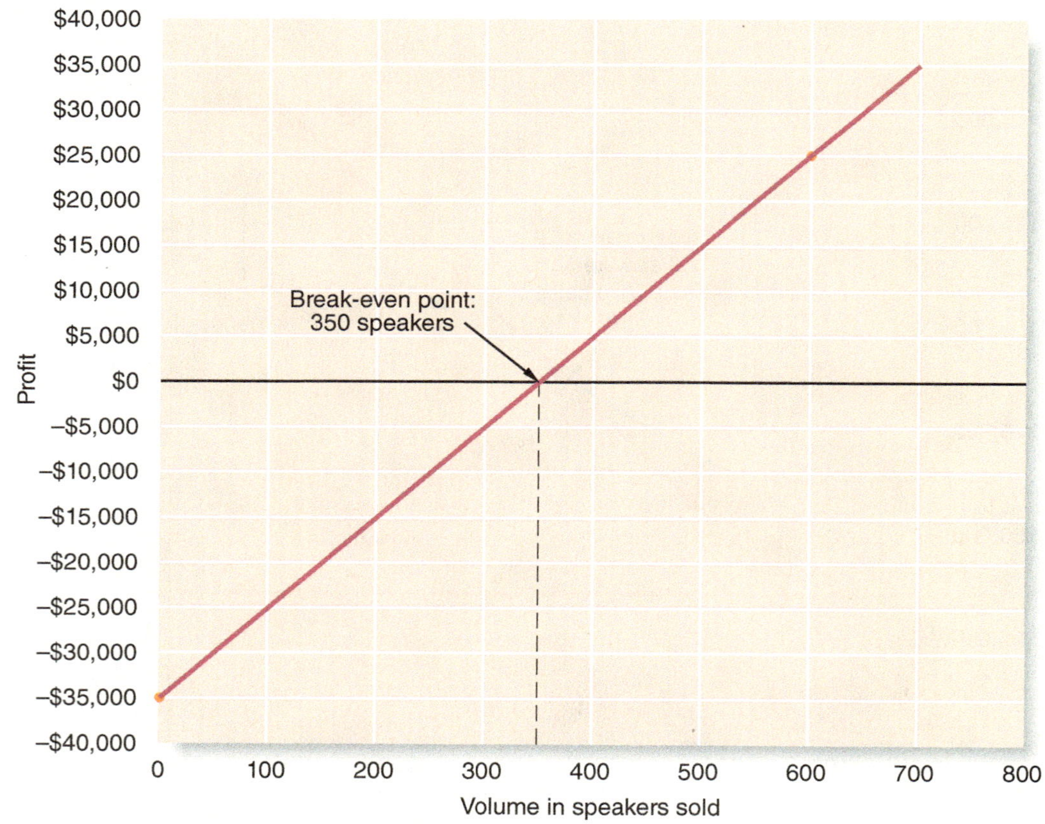

Because this is a linear equation, it plots as a single straight line. To plot the line, compute the profit at two different sales volumes, plot the points, and then connect them with a straight line. For example, when the sales volume is zero (i.e., $Q = 0$), the profit is $-\$35{,}000$ ($= \$100 \times 0 - \$35{,}000$). When Q is 600, the profit is \$25,000 ($= \$100 \times 600 - \$35{,}000$). These two points are plotted in Exhibit 5–3 and a straight line has been drawn through them.

The break-even point on the profit graph is the volume of sales at which profit is zero and is indicated by the dashed line on the graph. Note that the profit steadily increases to the right of the break-even point as the sales volume increases and that the loss becomes steadily worse to the left of the break-even point as the sales volume decreases.

Contribution Margin Ratio (CM Ratio)

LEARNING OBJECTIVE 3
Use the contribution margin ratio (CM ratio) to compute changes in contribution margin and net operating income resulting from changes in sales volume.

In the previous section, we explored how cost-volume-profit relationships can be visualized. In this section, we show how the *contribution margin ratio* can be used in cost-volume-profit calculations. As the first step, we have added a column to Acoustic Concepts' contribution format income statement in which sales revenues, variable expenses, and contribution margin are expressed as a percentage of sales:

	Total	Per Unit	Percent of Sales
Sales (400 speakers)	$100,000	$250	100%
Variable expenses	60,000	150	60%
Contribution margin	40,000	$100	40%
Fixed expenses	35,000		
Net operating income	$ 5,000		

The contribution margin as a percentage of sales is referred to as the **contribution margin ratio (CM ratio).** This ratio is computed as follows:

$$\text{CM ratio} = \frac{\text{Contribution margin}}{\text{Sales}}$$

For Acoustic Concepts, the computations are:

$$\text{CM ratio} = \frac{\text{Total contribution margin}}{\text{Total sales}} = \frac{\$40{,}000}{\$100{,}000} = 40\%$$

In a company such as Acoustic Concepts that has only one product, the CM ratio can also be computed on a per unit basis as follows:

$$\text{CM ratio} = \frac{\text{Unit contribution margin}}{\text{Unit selling price}} = \frac{\$100}{\$250} = 40\%$$

The CM ratio shows how the contribution margin will be affected by a change in total sales. Acoustic Concepts' CM ratio of 40% means that for each dollar increase in sales, total contribution margin will increase by 40 cents ($1 sales × CM ratio of 40%). Net operating income will also increase by 40 cents, assuming that fixed costs are not affected by the increase in sales. Generally, the effect of a change in sales on the contribution margin is expressed in equation form as:

$$\text{Change in contribution margin} = \text{CM ratio} \times \text{Change in sales}$$

As this illustration suggests, *the impact on net operating income of any given dollar change in total sales can be computed by applying the CM ratio to the dollar change.* For example, if Acoustic Concepts plans a $30,000 increase in sales during the coming month, the contribution margin should increase by $12,000 ($30,000 increase in sales × CM ratio of 40%). As we noted above, net operating income will also increase by $12,000 if fixed costs do not change. This is verified by the following table:

	Sales Volume			Percent of Sales
	Present	Expected	Increase	
Sales	$100,000	$130,000	$30,000	100%
Variable expenses	60,000	78,000*	18,000	60%
Contribution margin	40,000	52,000	12,000	40%
Fixed expenses	35,000	35,000	0	
Net operating income	$ 5,000	$ 17,000	$12,000	

*$130,000 expected sales ÷ $250 per unit = 520 units. 520 units × $150 per unit = $78,000.

The relation between profit and the CM ratio can also be expressed using the following equation:

$$\text{Profit} = \text{CM ratio} \times \text{Sales} - \text{Fixed expenses}^{1}$$

For example, at sales of $130,000, the profit is expected to be $17,000 as shown below:

$$\begin{aligned}\text{Profit} &= \text{CM ratio} \times \text{Sales} - \text{Fixed expenses}\\ &= 0.40 \times \$130{,}000 - \$35{,}000\\ &= \$52{,}000 - \$35{,}000 = \$17{,}000\end{aligned}$$

[1] This equation can be derived using the basic profit equation and the definition of the CM ratio as follows:

$$\text{Profit} = (\text{Sales} - \text{Variable expenses}) - \text{Fixed expenses}$$

$$\text{Profit} = \text{Contribution margin} - \text{Fixed expenses}$$

$$\text{Profit} = \frac{\text{Contribution margin}}{\text{Sales}} \times \text{Sales} - \text{Fixed expenses}$$

$$\text{Profit} = \text{CM ratio} \times \text{Sales} - \text{Fixed expenses}$$

Again, if you are comfortable with algebra, this approach will often be quicker and easier than constructing contribution format income statements.

The CM ratio is particularly valuable in situations where the dollar sales of one product must be traded off against the dollar sales of another product. In this situation, products that yield the greatest amount of contribution margin per dollar of sales should be emphasized.

Some Applications of CVP Concepts

LEARNING OBJECTIVE 4
Show the effects on net operating income of changes in variable costs, fixed costs, selling price, and volume.

Bob Luchinni, the accountant at Acoustic Concepts, wanted to demonstrate to the company's president Prem Narayan how the concepts developed on the preceding pages can be used in planning and decision making. Bob gathered the following basic data:

	Per Unit	Percent of Sales
Selling price	$250	100%
Variable expenses	150	60%
Contribution margin	$100	40%

Recall that fixed expenses are $35,000 per month. Bob Luchinni will use these data to show the effects of changes in variable costs, fixed costs, sales price, and sales volume on the company's profitability in a variety of situations.

Before proceeding further, however, we need to introduce another concept—the *variable expense ratio.* The **variable expense ratio** is the ratio of variable expenses to sales. It can be computed by dividing the total variable expenses by the total sales, or in a single product analysis, it can be computed by dividing the variable expenses per unit by the unit selling price. In the case of Acoustic Concepts, the variable expense ratio is 0.60; that is, variable expense is 60% of sales. Expressed as an equation, the definition of the variable expense ratio is:

$$\text{Variable expense ratio} = \frac{\text{Variable expenses}}{\text{Sales}}$$

This leads to a useful equation that relates the CM ratio to the variable expense ratio as follows:

$$\text{CM ratio} = \frac{\text{Contribution margin}}{\text{Sales}}$$

$$\text{CM ratio} = \frac{\text{Sales} - \text{Variable expenses}}{\text{Sales}}$$

$$\text{CM ratio} = 1 - \text{Variable expense ratio}$$

Change in Fixed Cost and Sales Volume

Acoustic Concepts is currently selling 400 speakers per month at $250 per speaker for total monthly sales of $100,000. The sales manager feels that a $10,000 increase in the monthly advertising budget would increase monthly sales by $30,000 to a total of 520 units. Should the advertising budget be increased? The table on the next page shows the financial impact of the proposed change in the monthly advertising budget.

	Current Sales	Sales with Additional Advertising Budget	Difference	Percent of Sales
Sales	$100,000	$130,000	$30,000	100%
Variable expenses	60,000	78,000*	18,000	60%
Contribution margin	40,000	52,000	12,000	40%
Fixed expenses	35,000	45,000†	10,000	
Net operating income	$ 5,000	$ 7,000	$ 2,000	

*520 units × $150 per unit = $78,000.
†$35,000 + additional $10,000 monthly advertising budget = $45,000.

Assuming no other factors need to be considered, the increase in the advertising budget should be approved because it would increase net operating income by $2,000. There are two shorter ways to arrive at this solution. The first alternative solution follows:

Alternative Solution 1

Expected total contribution margin:	
$130,000 × 40% CM ratio	$52,000
Present total contribution margin:	
$100,000 × 40% CM ratio	40,000
Incremental contribution margin	12,000
Change in fixed expenses:	
Less incremental advertising expense	10,000
Increased net operating income	$ 2,000

Because in this case only the fixed costs and the sales volume change, the solution can also be quickly derived as follows:

Alternative Solution 2

Incremental contribution margin:	
$30,000 × 40% CM ratio	$12,000
Less incremental advertising expense	10,000
Increased net operating income	$ 2,000

Notice that this approach does not depend on knowledge of previous sales. Also note that it is unnecessary under either shorter approach to prepare an income statement. Both of the alternative solutions involve **incremental analysis**—they consider only the revenue, cost, and volume that will change if the new program is implemented. Although in each case a new income statement could have been prepared, the incremental approach is simpler and more direct and focuses attention on the specific changes that would occur as a result of the decision.

Change in Variable Costs and Sales Volume Refer to the original data. Recall that Acoustic Concepts is currently selling 400 speakers per month. Prem is considering the use of higher-quality components, which would increase variable costs (and thereby reduce the contribution margin) by $10 per speaker. However, the sales manager predicts that using higher-quality components would increase sales to 480 speakers per month. Should the higher-quality components be used?

The $10 increase in variable costs would decrease the unit contribution margin by $10—from $100 down to $90.

Solution

Expected total contribution margin with higher-quality components:	
480 speakers × $90 per speaker	$43,200
Present total contribution margin:	
400 speakers × $100 per speaker	40,000
Increase in total contribution margin	$ 3,200

According to this analysis, the higher-quality components should be used. Because fixed costs would not change, the $3,200 increase in contribution margin shown above should result in a $3,200 increase in net operating income.

IN BUSINESS

GROWING SALES AT AMAZON.COM

Amazon.com was deciding between two tactics for growing sales and profits. The first approach was to invest in television advertising. The second approach was to offer free shipping on larger orders. To evaluate the first option, Amazon.com invested in television ads in two markets—Minneapolis, Minnesota, and Portland, Oregon. The company quantified the profit impact of this choice by subtracting the increase in fixed advertising costs from the increase in contribution margin. The profit impact of television advertising paled in comparison to the free "super saver shipping" program, which the company introduced on orders over $99. In fact, the free shipping option proved to be so popular and profitable that within two years Amazon.com dropped its qualifying threshold to $49 and then again to a mere $25. At each stage of this progression, Amazon.com used cost-volume-profit analysis to determine whether the extra volume from liberalizing the free shipping offer more than offset the associated increase in shipping costs.

Source: Rob Walker, "Because 'Optimism is Essential,' " *Inc.* magazine, April 2004 pp. 149–150.

Change in Fixed Cost, Sales Price, and Sales Volume Refer to the original data and recall again that Acoustic Concepts is currently selling 400 speakers per month. To increase sales, the sales manager would like to cut the selling price by $20 per speaker and increase the advertising budget by $15,000 per month. The sales manager believes that if these two steps are taken, unit sales will increase by 50% to 600 speakers per month. Should the changes be made?

A decrease in the selling price of $20 per speaker would decrease the unit contribution margin by $20 down to $80.

Solution

Expected total contribution margin with lower selling price:	
600 speakers × $80 per speaker	$48,000
Present total contribution margin:	
400 speakers × $100 per speaker	40,000
Incremental contribution margin	8,000
Change in fixed expenses:	
Less incremental advertising expense	15,000
Reduction in net operating income	$ (7,000)

According to this analysis, the changes should not be made. The $7,000 reduction in net operating income that is shown above can be verified by preparing comparative income statements as shown on the next page.

	Present 400 Speakers per Month		Expected 600 Speakers per Month		
	Total	Per Unit	Total	Per Unit	Difference
Sales	$100,000	$250	$138,000	$230	$38,000
Variable expenses	60,000	150	90,000	150	30,000
Contribution margin	40,000	$100	48,000	$ 80	8,000
Fixed expenses	35,000		50,000*		15,000
Net operating income (loss)	$ 5,000		$ (2,000)		$ (7,000)

*35,000 + Additional monthly advertising budget of $15,000 = $50,000.

Change in Variable Cost, Fixed Cost, and Sales Volume Refer to Acoustic Concepts' original data. As before, the company is currently selling 400 speakers per month. The sales manager would like to pay salespersons a sales commission of $15 per speaker sold, rather than the flat salaries that now total $6,000 per month. The sales manager is confident that the change would increase monthly sales by 15% to 460 speakers per month. Should the change be made?

Solution Changing the sales staff's compensation from salaries to commissions would affect both fixed and variable expenses. Fixed expenses would decrease by $6,000, from $35,000 to $29,000. Variable expenses per unit would increase by $15, from $150 to $165, and the unit contribution margin would decrease from $100 to $85.

Expected total contribution margin with sales staff on commissions:	
460 speakers × $85 per speaker	$39,100
Present total contribution margin:	
400 speakers × $100 per speaker	40,000
Decrease in total contribution margin	(900)
Change in fixed expenses:	
Add salaries avoided if a commission is paid	6,000
Increase in net operating income	$ 5,100

According to this analysis, the changes should be made. Again, the same answer can be obtained by preparing comparative income statements:

	Present 400 Speakers per Month		Expected 460 Speakers per Month		
	Total	Per Unit	Total	Per Unit	Difference
Sales	$100,000	$250	$115,000	$250	$15,000
Variable expenses	60,000	150	75,900	165	15,900
Contribution margin	40,000	$100	39,100	$ 85	900
Fixed expenses	35,000		29,000		(6,000)*
Net operating income	$ 5,000		$ 10,100		$ 5,100

*Note: A *reduction* in fixed expenses has the effect of *increasing* net operating income.

Change in Selling Price Refer to the original data where Acoustic Concepts is currently selling 400 speakers per month. The company has an opportunity to make a bulk sale of 150 speakers to a wholesaler if an acceptable price can be negotiated. This sale would not disturb the company's regular sales and would not affect the company's total fixed expenses. What price per speaker should be quoted to the wholesaler if Acoustic Concepts is seeking a profit of $3,000 on the bulk sale?

Solution

Variable cost per speaker	$150
Desired profit per speaker:	
$3,000 ÷ 150 speakers	20
Quoted price per speaker	$170

Notice that fixed expenses are not included in the computation. This is because fixed expenses are not affected by the bulk sale, so all of the additional contribution margin increases the company's profits.

IN BUSINESS

MANAGING RISK IN THE BOOK PUBLISHING INDUSTRY

Greenleaf Book Group is a book publishing company in Austin, Texas, that attracts authors who are willing to pay publishing costs and forgo up-front advances in exchange for a larger royalty rate on each book sold. For example, assume a typical publisher prints 10,000 copies of a new book that it sells for $12.50 per unit. The publisher pays the author an advance of $20,000 to write the book and then incurs $60,000 of expenses to market, print, and edit the book. The publisher also pays the author a 20% royalty (or $2.50 per unit) on each book sold above 8,000 units. In this scenario, the publisher must sell 6,400 books to break even (= $80,000 in fixed costs ÷ $12.50 per unit). If all 10,000 copies are sold, the author earns $25,000 (= $20,000 advance + 2,000 copies × $2.50) and the publisher earns $40,000 (= $125,000 − $60,000 − $20,000 − $5,000).

Greenleaf alters the financial arrangement described above by requiring the author to assume the risk of poor sales. It pays the author a 70% royalty on all units sold (or $8.75 per unit), but the author forgoes the $20,000 advance and pays Greenleaf $60,000 to market, print, and edit the book. If the book flops, the author fails to recover her production costs. If all 10,000 units are sold, the author earns $27,500 (= $10,000 units × $8.75 − $60,000) and Greenleaf earns $37,500 (= 10,000 units × ($12.50 − $8.75)).

Source: Christopher Steiner, "Book It," *Forbes*, September 7, 2009, p. 58.

Target Profit and Break-Even Analysis

Target profit analysis and break-even analysis are used to answer questions such as how much would we have to sell to make a profit of $10,000 per month or how much would we have to sell to avoid incurring a loss?

Target Profit Analysis

LEARNING OBJECTIVE 5
Determine the level of sales needed to achieve a desired target profit.

Target profit analysis is one of the key uses of CVP analysis. In **target profit analysis,** we estimate what sales volume is needed to achieve a specific target profit. For example, suppose that Prem Narayan of Acoustic Concepts would like to know what sales would have to be to attain a target profit of $40,000 per month. To answer this question, we can proceed using the equation method or the formula method.

The Equation Method We can use a basic profit equation to find the sales volume required to attain a target profit. In the case of Acoustic Concepts, the company has only one product so we can use the contribution margin form of the equation. Remembering that the target profit is \$40,000, the unit contribution margin is \$100, and the fixed expense is \$35,000, we can solve as follows:

$$\begin{aligned} \text{Profit} &= \text{Unit CM} \times Q - \text{Fixed expense} \\ \$40{,}000 &= \$100 \times Q - \$35{,}000 \\ \$100 \times Q &= \$40{,}000 + \$35{,}000 \\ Q &= (\$40{,}000 + \$35{,}000) \div \$100 \\ Q &= 750 \end{aligned}$$

Thus, the target profit can be achieved by selling 750 speakers per month.

The Formula Method The formula method is a short-cut version of the equation method. Note that in the next to the last line of the above solution, the sum of the target profit of \$40,000 and the fixed expense of \$35,000 is divided by the unit contribution margin of \$100. In general, in a single-product situation, we can compute the sales volume required to attain a specific target profit using the following formula:

$$\text{Unit sales to attain the target profit} = \frac{\text{Target profit} + \text{Fixed expenses}^{2}}{\text{Unit CM}}$$

In the case of Acoustic Concepts, the formula yields the following answer:

$$\begin{aligned} \text{Unit sales to attain the target profit} &= \frac{\text{Target profit} + \text{Fixed expenses}}{\text{Unit CM}} \\ &= \frac{\$40{,}000 + \$35{,}000}{\$100} \\ &= 750 \end{aligned}$$

Note that this is the same answer we got when we used the equation method—and it always will be. The formula method simply skips a few steps in the equation method.

Target Profit Analysis in Terms of Sales Dollars Instead of unit sales, we may want to know what dollar sales are needed to attain the target profit. We can get this answer using several methods. First, we could solve for the unit sales to attain the target profit using the equation method or the formula method and then multiply the result by the selling price. In the case of Acoustic Concepts, the required sales volume using this approach would be computed as 750 speakers × \$250 per speaker or \$187,500 in total sales.

We can also solve for the required sales volume to attain the target profit of \$40,000 at Acoustic Concepts using the basic equation stated in terms of the contribution margin ratio:

$$\begin{aligned} \text{Profit} &= \text{CM ratio} \times \text{Sales} - \text{Fixed expenses} \\ \$40{,}000 &= 0.40 \times \text{Sales} - \$35{,}000 \\ 0.40 \times \text{Sales} &= \$40{,}000 + \$35{,}000 \\ \text{Sales} &= (\$40{,}000 + \$35{,}000) \div 0.40 \\ \text{Sales} &= \$187{,}500 \end{aligned}$$

[2] This equation can be derived as follows:

$$\begin{aligned} \text{Profit} &= \text{Unit CM} \times Q - \text{Fixed expenses} \\ \text{Target profit} &= \text{Unit CM} \times Q - \text{Fixed expenses} \\ \text{Unit CM} \times Q &= \text{Target profit} + \text{Fixed expenses} \\ Q &= (\text{Target profit} + \text{Fixed expenses}) \div \text{Unit CM} \end{aligned}$$

Note that in the next to the last line of the previous solution, the sum of the target profit of \$40,000 and the fixed expense of \$35,000 is divided by the contribution margin ratio of 0.40. In general, we can compute dollar sales to attain a target profit as follows:

$$\text{Dollar sales to attain a target profit} = \frac{\text{Target profit} + \text{Fixed expenses}^{3}}{\text{CM ratio}}$$

At Acoustic Concepts, the formula yields the following answer:

$$\begin{aligned}\text{Dollar sales to attain a target profit} &= \frac{\text{Target profit} + \text{Fixed expenses}}{\text{CM ratio}}\\ &= \frac{\$40{,}000 + \$35{,}000}{0.40}\\ &= \$187{,}500\end{aligned}$$

Again, you get exactly the same answer whether you use the equation method or just use the formula.

In companies with multiple products, sales volume is more conveniently expressed in terms of total sales dollars than in terms of unit sales. The contribution margin ratio approach to target profit analysis is particularly useful for such companies.

Break-Even Analysis

LEARNING OBJECTIVE 6
Determine the break-even point.

Earlier in the chapter we defined the break-even point as the level of sales at which the company's profit is zero. What we call *break-even analysis* is really just a special case of target profit analysis in which the target profit is zero. We can use either the equation method or the formula method to solve for the break-even point, but for brevity we will illustrate just the formula method. The equation method works exactly like it did in target profit analysis. The only difference is that the target profit is zero in break-even analysis.

Break-Even in Unit Sales

In a single product situation, recall that the formula for the unit sales to attain a specific target profit is:

$$\text{Unit sales to attain the target profit} = \frac{\text{Target profit} + \text{Fixed expenses}}{\text{Unit CM}}$$

To compute the unit sales to break even, all we have to do is to set the target profit to zero in the above equation as follows:

$$\text{Unit sales to break even} = \frac{\$0 + \text{Fixed expenses}}{\text{Unit CM}}$$

$$\text{Unit sales to break even} = \frac{\text{Fixed expenses}}{\text{Unit CM}}$$

In the case of Acoustic Concepts, the break-even point can be computed as follows:

$$\begin{aligned}\text{Unit sales to break even} &= \frac{\text{Fixed expenses}}{\text{Unit CM}}\\ &= \frac{\$35{,}000}{\$100}\\ &= 350\end{aligned}$$

Thus, as we determined earlier in the chapter, Acoustic Concepts breaks even at sales of 350 speakers per month.

---

[3] This equation can be derived as follows:

$$\begin{aligned}\text{Profit} &= \text{CM ratio} \times \text{Sales} - \text{Fixed expenses}\\ \text{Target profit} &= \text{CM ratio} \times \text{Sales} - \text{Fixed expenses}\\ \text{CM ratio} \times \text{Sales} &= \text{Target profit} + \text{Fixed expenses}\\ \text{Sales} &= (\text{Target profit} + \text{Fixed expenses}) \div \text{CM ratio}\end{aligned}$$

Break-Even in Sales Dollars We can find the break-even point in sales dollars using several methods. First, we could solve for the break-even point in unit sales using the equation method or the formula method and then multiply the result by the selling price. In the case of Acoustic Concepts, the break-even point in sales dollars using this approach would be computed as 350 speakers × $250 per speaker or $87,500 in total sales.

We can also solve for the break-even point in sales dollars at Acoustic Concepts using the basic profit equation stated in terms of the contribution margin ratio or we can use the formula for the target profit. Again, for brevity, we will use the formula.

$$\text{Dollar sales to attain a target profit} = \frac{\text{Target profit} + \text{Fixed expenses}}{\text{CM ratio}}$$

$$\text{Dollar sales to break even} = \frac{\$0 + \text{Fixed expenses}}{\text{CM ratio}}$$

$$\text{Dollar sales to break even} = \frac{\text{Fixed expenses}}{\text{CM ratio}}$$

The break-even point at Acoustic Concepts would be computed as follows:

$$\begin{aligned}\text{Dollar sales to break even} &= \frac{\text{Fixed expenses}}{\text{CM ratio}}\\ &= \frac{\$35{,}000}{0.40}\\ &= \$87{,}500\end{aligned}$$

IN BUSINESS

COST OVERRUNS INCREASE THE BREAK-EVEN POINT

When Airbus launched the A380 555-seat jetliner in 2000, the company said it would need to sell 250 units to break even on the project. By 2006, Airbus was admitting that more than $3 billion of cost overruns had raised the project's break-even point to 420 airplanes. Although Airbus has less than 170 orders for the A380, the company remains optimistic that it will sell 751 units over the next 20 years. Given that Airbus rival Boeing predicts the total market size for all airplanes with more than 400 seats will not exceed 990 units, it remains unclear if Airbus will ever break even on its investment in the A380 aircraft.

Source: Daniel Michaels, "Embattled Airbus Lifts Sales Target for A380 to Profit," *The Wall Street Journal*, October 20, 2006, p. A6.

The Margin of Safety

LEARNING OBJECTIVE 7
Compute the margin of safety and explain its significance.

The **margin of safety** is the excess of budgeted or actual sales dollars over the break-even volume of sales dollars. It is the amount by which sales can drop before losses are incurred. The higher the margin of safety, the lower the risk of not breaking even and incurring a loss. The formula for the margin of safety is:

$$\text{Margin of safety in dollars} = \text{Total budgeted (or actual) sales} - \text{Break-even sales}$$

The margin of safety can also be expressed in percentage form by dividing the margin of safety in dollars by total dollar sales:

$$\text{Margin of safety percentage} = \frac{\text{Margin of safety in dollars}}{\text{Total budgeted (or actual) sales in dollars}}$$

The calculation of the margin of safety for Acoustic Concepts is:

Sales (at the current volume of 400 speakers) (a)	$100,000
Break-even sales (at 350 speakers)	87,500
Margin of safety in dollars (b)	$ 12,500
Margin of safety percentage, (b) ÷ (a)	12.5%

This margin of safety means that at the current level of sales and with the company's current prices and cost structure, a reduction in sales of $12,500, or 12.5%, would result in just breaking even.

In a single-product company like Acoustic Concepts, the margin of safety can also be expressed in terms of the number of units sold by dividing the margin of safety in dollars by the selling price per unit. In this case, the margin of safety is 50 speakers ($12,500 ÷ $250 per speaker = 50 speakers).

IN BUSINESS

COMPUTING MARGIN OF SAFETY FOR A SMALL BUSINESS

Sam Calagione owns Dogfish Head Craft Brewery, a microbrewery in Rehobeth Beach, Delaware. He charges distributors as much as $100 per case for his premium beers such as World Wide Stout. The high-priced microbrews bring in $800,000 in operating income on revenue of $7 million. Calagione reports that his raw ingredients and labor costs for one case of World Wide Stout are $30 and $16, respectively. Bottling and packaging costs are $6 per case. Gas and electric costs are about $10 per case.

If we assume that World Wide Stout is representative of all Dogfish microbrews, then we can compute the company's margin of safety in five steps. First, variable cost as a percentage of sales is 62% [($30 + $16 + $6 + $10)/$100]. Second, the contribution margin ratio is 38% (1 − 0.62). Third, Dogfish's total fixed cost is $1,860,000 [($7,000,000 × 0.38) − $800,000]. Fourth, the break-even point in sales dollars is $4,894,737 ($1,860,000/0.38). Fifth, the margin of safety is $2,105,263 ($7,000,000 − $4,894,737).

Source: Patricia Huang, "Château Dogfish," *Forbes*, February 28, 2005, pp. 57–59.

MANAGERIAL ACCOUNTING IN ACTION
The Wrap-up

Prem Narayan and Bob Luchinni met to discuss the results of Bob's analysis.

Prem: Bob, everything you have shown me is pretty clear. I can see what impact the sales manager's suggestions would have on our profits. Some of those suggestions are quite good and others are not so good. I am concerned that our margin of safety is only 50 speakers. What can we do to increase this number?

Bob: Well, we have to increase total sales or decrease the break-even point or both.

Prem: And to decrease the break-even point, we have to either decrease our fixed expenses or increase our unit contribution margin?

Bob: Exactly.

Prem: And to increase our unit contribution margin, we must either increase our selling price or decrease the variable cost per unit?

Bob: Correct.

Prem: So what do you suggest?

Bob: Well, the analysis doesn't tell us which of these to do, but it does indicate we have a potential problem here.

Prem: If you don't have any immediate suggestions, I would like to call a general meeting next week to discuss ways we can work on increasing the margin of safety. I think everyone will be concerned about how vulnerable we are to even small downturns in sales.

CVP Considerations in Choosing a Cost Structure

Cost structure refers to the relative proportion of fixed and variable costs in an organization. Managers often have some latitude in trading off between these two types of costs. For example, fixed investments in automated equipment can reduce variable labor costs. In this section, we discuss the choice of a cost structure. We also introduce the concept of *operating leverage.*

Cost Structure and Profit Stability

Which cost structure is better—high variable costs and low fixed costs, or the opposite? No single answer to this question is possible; each approach has its advantages. To show what we mean, refer to the contribution format income statements given below for two blueberry farms. Bogside Farm depends on migrant workers to pick its berries by hand, whereas Sterling Farm has invested in expensive berry-picking machines. Consequently, Bogside Farm has higher variable costs, but Sterling Farm has higher fixed costs:

	Bogside Farm		Sterling Farm	
	Amount	Percent	Amount	Percent
Sales	$100,000	100%	$100,000	100%
Variable expenses	60,000	60%	30,000	30%
Contribution margin	40,000	40%	70,000	70%
Fixed expenses	30,000		60,000	
Net operating income	$ 10,000		$ 10,000	

Which farm has the better cost structure? The answer depends on many factors, including the long-run trend in sales, year-to-year fluctuations in the level of sales, and the attitude of the owners toward risk. If sales are expected to exceed $100,000 in the future, then Sterling Farm probably has the better cost structure. The reason is that its CM ratio is higher, and its profits will therefore increase more rapidly as sales increase. To illustrate, assume that each farm experiences a 10% increase in sales without any increase in fixed costs. The new income statements would be as follows:

	Bogside Farm		Sterling Farm	
	Amount	Percent	Amount	Percent
Sales	$110,000	100%	$110,000	100%
Variable expenses	66,000	60%	33,000	30%
Contribution margin	44,000	40%	77,000	70%
Fixed expenses	30,000		60,000	
Net operating income	$ 14,000		$ 17,000	

Sterling Farm has experienced a greater increase in net operating income due to its higher CM ratio even though the increase in sales was the same for both farms.

What if sales drop below $100,000? What are the farms' break-even points? What are their margins of safety? The computations needed to answer these questions are shown below using the formula method:

	Bogside Farm	Sterling Farm
Fixed expenses	$ 30,000	$ 60,000
Contribution margin ratio	÷ 0.40	÷ 0.70
Dollar sales to break even	$ 75,000	$ 85,714
Total current sales (a)	$100,000	$100,000
Break-even sales	75,000	85,714
Margin of safety in sales dollars (b)	$ 25,000	$ 14,286
Margin of safety percentage (b) ÷ (a)	25.0%	14.3%

Bogside Farm's margin of safety is greater and its contribution margin ratio is lower than Sterling Farm. Therefore, Bogside Farm is less vulnerable to downturns than Sterling Farm. Due to its lower contribution margin ratio, Bogside Farm will not lose contribution margin as rapidly as Sterling Farm when sales decline. Thus, Bogside Farm's profit will be less volatile. We saw earlier that this is a drawback when sales increase, but it provides more protection when sales drop. And because its break-even point is lower, Bogside Farm can suffer a larger sales decline before losses emerge.

To summarize, without knowing the future, it is not obvious which cost structure is better. Both have advantages and disadvantages. Sterling Farm, with its higher fixed costs and lower variable costs, will experience wider swings in net operating income as sales fluctuate, with greater profits in good years and greater losses in bad years. Bogside Farm, with its lower fixed costs and higher variable costs, will enjoy greater profit stability and will be more protected from losses during bad years, but at the cost of lower net operating income in good years.

Operating Leverage

LEARNING OBJECTIVE 8
Compute the degree of operating leverage at a particular level of sales and explain how it can be used to predict changes in net operating income.

A lever is a tool for multiplying force. Using a lever, a massive object can be moved with only a modest amount of force. In business, *operating leverage* serves a similar purpose. **Operating leverage** is a measure of how sensitive net operating income is to a given percentage change in dollar sales. Operating leverage acts as a multiplier. If operating leverage is high, a small percentage increase in sales can produce a much larger percentage increase in net operating income.

Operating leverage can be illustrated by returning to the data for the two blueberry farms. We previously showed that a 10% increase in sales (from $100,000 to $110,000 in each farm) results in a 70% increase in the net operating income of Sterling Farm (from $10,000 to $17,000) and only a 40% increase in the net operating income of Bogside Farm (from $10,000 to $14,000). Thus, for a 10% increase in sales, Sterling Farm experiences a much greater percentage increase in profits than does Bogside Farm. Therefore, Sterling Farm has greater operating leverage than Bogside Farm.

The **degree of operating leverage** at a given level of sales is computed by the following formula:

$$\text{Degree of operating leverage} = \frac{\text{Contribution margin}}{\text{Net operating income}}$$

The degree of operating leverage is a measure, at a given level of sales, of how a percentage change in sales volume will affect profits. To illustrate, the degree of operating leverage for the two farms at $100,000 sales would be computed as follows:

$$\text{Bogside Farm: } \frac{\$40{,}000}{\$10{,}000} = 4$$

$$\text{Sterling Farm: } \frac{\$70{,}000}{\$10{,}000} = 7$$

Because the degree of operating leverage for Bogside Farm is 4, the farm's net operating income grows four times as fast as its sales. In contrast, Sterling Farm's net operating income grows seven times as fast as its sales. Thus, if sales increase by 10%, then we can expect the net operating income of Bogside Farm to increase by four times this amount, or by 40%, and the net operating income of Sterling Farm to increase by seven times this amount, or by 70%. In general, this relation between the percentage change in sales and the percentage change in net operating income is given by the following formula:

$$\text{Percentage change in net operating income} = \text{Degree of operating leverage} \times \text{Percentage change in sales}$$

$$\text{Bogside Farm: Percentage change in net operating income} = 4 \times 10\% = 40\%$$

$$\text{Sterling Farm: Percentage change in net operating income} = 7 \times 10\% = 70\%$$

What is responsible for the higher operating leverage at Sterling Farm? The only difference between the two farms is their cost structure. If two companies have the same total revenue and same total expense but different cost structures, then the company with the higher proportion of fixed costs in its cost structure will have higher operating leverage. Referring back to the original example on page 201, when both farms have sales of $100,000 and total expenses of $90,000, one-third of Bogside Farm's costs are fixed but two-thirds of Sterling Farm's costs are fixed. As a consequence, Sterling's degree of operating leverage is higher than Bogside's.

The degree of operating leverage is not a constant; it is greatest at sales levels near the break-even point and decreases as sales and profits rise. The following table shows the degree of operating leverage for Bogside Farm at various sales levels. (Data used earlier for Bogside Farm are shown in color.)

Sales	$75,000	$80,000	$100,000	$150,000	$225,000
Variable expenses	45,000	48,000	60,000	90,000	135,000
Contribution margin (a)	30,000	32,000	40,000	60,000	90,000
Fixed expenses	30,000	30,000	30,000	30,000	30,000
Net operating income (b)	$ 0	$ 2,000	$ 10,000	$ 30,000	$ 60,000
Degree of operating leverage, (a) ÷ (b)	∞	16	4	2	1.5

Thus, a 10% increase in sales would increase profits by only 15% (10% × 1.5) if sales were previously $225,000, as compared to the 40% increase we computed earlier at the $100,000 sales level. The degree of operating leverage will continue to decrease the farther the company moves from its break-even point. At the break-even point, the degree of operating leverage is infinitely large ($30,000 contribution margin ÷ $0 net operating income = ∞).

IN BUSINESS

THE DANGERS OF A HIGH DEGREE OF OPERATING LEVERAGE

In recent years, computer chip manufacturers have poured more than $75 billion into constructing new manufacturing facilities to meet the growing demand for digital devices such as iPhones and Blackberrys. Because 70% of the costs of running these facilities are fixed, a sharp drop in customer demand forces these companies to choose between two undesirable options. They can slash production levels and absorb large amounts of unused capacity costs, or they can continue producing large volumes of output in spite of shrinking demand, thereby flooding the market with excess supply and lowering prices. Either choice distresses investors who tend to shy away from computer chip makers in economic downturns.

Source: Bruce Einhorn, "Chipmakers on the Edge," *BusinessWeek*, January 5, 2009, pp. 30–31.

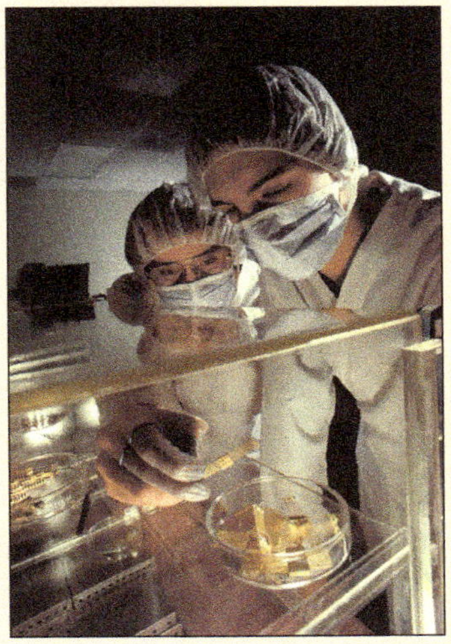

The degree of operating leverage can be used to quickly estimate what impact various percentage changes in sales will have on profits, without the necessity of preparing detailed income statements. As shown by our examples, the effects of operating leverage can be dramatic. If a company is near its break-even point, then even small percentage increases in sales can yield large percentage increases in profits. *This explains why management will often work very hard for only a small increase in sales volume.* If the degree of operating leverage is 5, then a 6% increase in sales would translate into a 30% increase in profits.

Structuring Sales Commissions

Companies usually compensate salespeople by paying them a commission based on sales, a salary, or a combination of the two. Commissions based on sales dollars can lead to lower profits. To illustrate, consider Pipeline Unlimited, a producer of surfing equipment. Salespersons sell the company's products to retail sporting goods stores throughout North America and the Pacific Basin. Data for two of the company's surfboards, the XR7 and Turbo models, appear below:

	Model	
	XR7	Turbo
Selling price	$695	$749
Variable expenses	344	410
Contribution margin	$351	$339

Which model will salespeople push hardest if they are paid a commission of 10% of sales revenue? The answer is the Turbo because it has the higher selling price and hence the larger commission. On the other hand, from the standpoint of the company, profits will be greater if salespeople steer customers toward the XR7 model because it has the higher contribution margin.

To eliminate such conflicts, commissions can be based on contribution margin rather than on selling price. If this is done, the salespersons will want to sell the mix of products that maximizes contribution margin. Providing that fixed costs are not affected by the sales mix, maximizing the contribution margin will also maximize the company's profit.[4] In effect, by maximizing their own compensation, salespersons will also maximize the company's profit.

IN BUSINESS

AN ALTERNATIVE APPROACH TO SALES COMMISSIONS

Thrive Networks, located in Concord, Massachusetts, used to pay its three salesmen based on individually earned commissions. This system seemed to be working fine as indicated by the company's sales growth from $2.7 million in 2002 to $3.6 million in 2003. However, the company felt there was a better way to motivate and compensate its salesmen. It pooled commissions across the three salesmen and compensated them collectively. The new approach was designed to build teamwork and leverage each salesman's individual strengths. Jim Lippie, the director of business development, was highly skilled at networking and generating sales leads. John Barrows, the sales director, excelled at meeting with prospective clients and producing compelling proposals. Nate Wolfson, the CEO and final member of the sales team, was the master at closing the deal. The new approach has worked so well that Wolfson plans to use three-person sales teams in his offices nationwide.

Source: Cara Cannella, "Kill the Commissions," *Inc.* Magazine, August 2004, p. 38.

Sales Mix

LEARNING OBJECTIVE 9
Compute the break-even point for a multiproduct company and explain the effects of shifts in the sales mix on contribution margin and the break-even point.

Before concluding our discussion of CVP concepts, we need to consider the impact of changes in *sales mix* on a company's profit.

[4] This also assumes the company has no production constraint. If it does, the sales commissions should be modified. See the Profitability Appendix at the end of the book.

The Definition of Sales Mix

The term **sales mix** refers to the relative proportions in which a company's products are sold. The idea is to achieve the combination, or mix, that will yield the greatest profits. Most companies have many products, and often these products are not equally profitable. Hence, profits will depend to some extent on the company's sales mix. Profits will be greater if high-margin rather than low-margin items make up a relatively large proportion of total sales.

Changes in the sales mix can cause perplexing variations in a company's profits. A shift in the sales mix from high-margin items to low-margin items can cause total profits to decrease even though total sales may increase. Conversely, a shift in the sales mix from low-margin items to high-margin items can cause the reverse effect—total profits may increase even though total sales decrease. It is one thing to achieve a particular sales volume; it is quite another to sell the most profitable mix of products.

IN BUSINESS

WALMART ATTEMPTS TO SHIFT ITS SALES MIX

Almost 130 million customers shop at Walmart's 3,200 U.S. stores each week. However, less than half of them shop the whole store—choosing to buy only low-margin basics while skipping higher-margin departments such as apparel. In an effort to shift its sales mix toward higher-margin merchandise, Walmart has reduced spending on advertising and plowed the money into remodeling the clothing departments within its stores. The company hopes this remodeling effort will entice its customers to add clothing to their shopping lists while bypassing the apparel offerings of competitors such as Kohl's and Target.

Source: Robert Berner, "Fashion Emergency at Walmart," *BusinessWeek*, July 31, 2006, p. 67.

Sales Mix and Break-Even Analysis

If a company sells more than one product, break-even analysis is more complex than discussed to this point. The reason is that different products will have different selling prices, different costs, and different contribution margins. Consequently, the break-even point depends on the mix in which the various products are sold. To illustrate, consider Virtual Journeys Unlimited, a small company that imports DVDs from France. At present, the company sells two DVDs: the Le Louvre DVD, a tour of the famous art museum in Paris; and the Le Vin DVD, which features the wines and wine-growing regions of France. The company's September sales, expenses, and break-even point are shown in Exhibit 5–4.

As shown in the exhibit, the break-even point is $60,000 in sales, which was computed by dividing the company's fixed expenses of $27,000 by its overall CM ratio of 45%. However, this is the break-even only if the company's sales mix does not change. Currently, the Le Louvre DVD is responsible for 20% and the Le Vin DVD for 80% of the company's dollar sales. Assuming this sales mix does not change, if total sales are $60,000, the sales of the Le Louvre DVD would be $12,000 (20% of $60,000) and the sales of the Le Vin DVD would be $48,000 (80% of $60,000). As shown in Exhibit 5–4, at these levels of sales, the company would indeed break even. But $60,000 in sales represents the break-even point for the company only if the sales mix does not change. *If the sales mix changes, then the break-even point will also usually change.* This is illustrated by the results for October in which the sales mix shifted away from the more profitable Le Vin DVD (which has a 50% CM ratio) toward the less profitable Le Louvre CD (which has a 25% CM ratio). These results appear in Exhibit 5–5.

EXHIBIT 5–4
Multiproduct Break-Even Analysis

Virtual Journeys Unlimited
Contribution Income Statement
For the Month of September

	Le Louvre DVD		Le Vin DVD		Total	
	Amount	Percent	Amount	Percent	Amount	Percent
Sales	$20,000	100%	$80,000	100%	$100,000	100%
Variable expenses	15,000	75%	40,000	50%	55,000	55%
Contribution margin	$ 5,000	25%	$40,000	50%	45,000	45%
Fixed expenses					27,000	
Net operating income					$ 18,000	

Computation of the break-even point:

$$\frac{\text{Fixed expenses}}{\text{Overall CM ratio}} = \frac{\$27{,}000}{0.45} = \$60{,}000$$

Verification of the break-even point:

	Le Louvre DVD	Le Vin DVD	Total
Current dollar sales	$20,000	$80,000	$100,000
Percentage of total dollar sales	20%	80%	100%
Sales at the break-even point	$12,000	$48,000	$60,000

	Le Louvre DVD		Le Vin DVD		Total	
	Amount	Percent	Amount	Percent	Amount	Percent
Sales	$12,000	100%	$48,000	100%	$ 60,000	100%
Variable expenses	9,000	75%	24,000	50%	33,000	55%
Contribution margin	$ 3,000	25%	$24,000	50%	27,000	45%
Fixed expenses					27,000	
Net operating income					$ 0	

EXHIBIT 5–5
Multiproduct Break-Even Analysis: A Shift in Sales Mix (see Exhibit 5–4)

Virtual Journeys Unlimited
Contribution Income Statement
For the Month of October

	Le Louvre DVD		Le Vin DVD		Total	
	Amount	Percent	Amount	Percent	Amount	Percent
Sales	$80,000	100%	$20,000	100%	$100,000	100%
Variable expenses	60,000	75%	10,000	50%	70,000	70%
Contribution margin	$20,000	25%	$10,000	50%	30,000	30%
Fixed expenses					27,000	
Net operating income					$ 3,000	

Computation of the break-even point:

$$\frac{\text{Fixed expenses}}{\text{Overall CM ratio}} = \frac{\$27{,}000}{0.30} = \$90{,}000$$

Although sales have remained unchanged at $100,000, the sales mix is exactly the reverse of what it was in Exhibit 5–4, with the bulk of the sales now coming from the less profitable Le Louvre DVD. Notice that this shift in the sales mix has caused both the overall CM ratio and total profits to drop sharply from the prior month even though total sales are the same. The overall CM ratio has dropped from 45% in September to only 30% in October, and net operating income has dropped from $18,000 to only $3,000. In addition, with the drop in the overall CM ratio, the company's break-even point is no longer $60,000 in sales. Because the company is now realizing less average contribution margin per dollar of sales, it takes more sales to cover the same amount of fixed costs. Thus, the break-even point has increased from $60,000 to $90,000 in sales per year.

In preparing a break-even analysis, an assumption must be made concerning the sales mix. Usually the assumption is that it will not change. However, if the sales mix is expected to change, then this must be explicitly considered in any CVP computations.

Assumptions of CVP Analysis

A number of assumptions commonly underlie CVP analysis:

1. Selling price is constant. The price of a product or service will not change as volume changes.
2. Costs are linear and can be accurately divided into variable and fixed elements. The variable element is constant per unit, and the fixed element is constant in total over the entire relevant range.
3. In multiproduct companies, the sales mix is constant.
4. In manufacturing companies, inventories do not change. The number of units produced equals the number of units sold.

While these assumptions may be violated in practice, the results of CVP analysis are often "good enough" to be quite useful. Perhaps the greatest danger lies in relying on simple CVP analysis when a manager is contemplating a large change in volume that lies outside of the relevant range. For example, a manager might contemplate increasing the level of sales far beyond what the company has ever experienced before. However, even in these situations the model can be adjusted as we have done in this chapter to take into account anticipated changes in selling prices, fixed costs, and the sales mix that would otherwise violate the assumptions mentioned above. For example, in a decision that would affect fixed costs, the change in fixed costs can be explicitly taken into account as illustrated earlier in the chapter in the Acoustic Concepts example on pages 192–195.

Summary

CVP analysis is based on a simple model of how profits respond to prices, costs, and volume. This model can be used to answer a variety of critical questions such as what is the company's break-even volume, what is its margin of safety, and what is likely to happen if specific changes are made in prices, costs, and volume.

A CVP graph depicts the relationships between unit sales on the one hand and fixed expenses, variable expenses, total expenses, total sales, and profits on the other hand. The profit graph is simpler than the CVP graph and shows how profits depend on sales. The CVP and profit graphs are useful for developing intuition about how costs and profits respond to changes in sales.

The contribution margin ratio is the ratio of the total contribution margin to total sales. This ratio can be used to quickly estimate what impact a change in total sales would have on net operating income. The ratio is also useful in break-even analysis.

Target profit analysis is used to estimate how much sales would have to be to attain a specified target profit. The unit sales required to attain the target profit can be estimated by dividing the sum of the target profit and fixed expense by the unit contribution margin. Break-even analysis is a special case of target profit analysis that is used to estimate how much sales would have to be to just break even. The unit sales required to break even can be estimated by dividing the fixed expense by the unit contribution margin.

The margin of safety is the amount by which the company's current sales exceeds break-even sales.

The degree of operating leverage allows quick estimation of what impact a given percentage change in sales would have on the company's net operating income. The higher the degree of operating leverage, the greater is the impact on the company's profits. The degree of operating leverage is not constant—it depends on the company's current level of sales.

The profits of a multiproduct company are affected by its sales mix. Changes in the sales mix can affect the break-even point, margin of safety, and other critical factors.

Review Problem: CVP Relationships

Voltar Company manufactures and sells a specialized cordless telephone for high electromagnetic radiation environments. The company's contribution format income statement for the most recent year is given below:

	Total	Per Unit	Percent of Sales
Sales (20,000 units)	$1,200,000	$60	100%
Variable expenses	900,000	45	? %
Contribution margin	300,000	$15	? %
Fixed expenses	240,000		
Net operating income	$ 60,000		

Management is anxious to increase the company's profit and has asked for an analysis of a number of items.

Required:

1. Compute the company's CM ratio and variable expense ratio.
2. Compute the company's break-even point in both units and sales dollars. Use the equation method.
3. Assume that sales increase by $400,000 next year. If cost behavior patterns remain unchanged, by how much will the company's net operating income increase? Use the CM ratio to compute your answer.
4. Refer to the original data. Assume that next year management wants the company to earn a profit of at least $90,000. How many units will have to be sold to meet this target profit?
5. Refer to the original data. Compute the company's margin of safety in both dollar and percentage form.
6. *a.* Compute the company's degree of operating leverage at the present level of sales.
   b. Assume that through a more intense effort by the sales staff, the company's sales increase by 8% next year. By what percentage would you expect net operating income to increase? Use the degree of operating leverage to obtain your answer.
   c. Verify your answer to (*b*) by preparing a new contribution format income statement showing an 8% increase in sales.
7. In an effort to increase sales and profits, management is considering the use of a higher-quality speaker. The higher-quality speaker would increase variable costs by $3 per unit, but management could eliminate one quality inspector who is paid a salary of $30,000 per year. The sales manager estimates that the higher-quality speaker would increase annual sales by at least 20%.
   a. Assuming that changes are made as described above, prepare a projected contribution format income statement for next year. Show data on a total, per unit, and percentage basis.
   b. Compute the company's new break-even point in both units and dollars of sales. Use the formula method.
   c. Would you recommend that the changes be made?

Solution to Review Problem

1.

$$\text{CM ratio} = \frac{\text{Unit contribution margin}}{\text{Unit selling price}} = \frac{\$15}{\$60} = 25\%$$

$$\text{Variable expense ratio} = \frac{\text{Variable expense}}{\text{Selling price}} = \frac{\$45}{\$60} = 75\%$$

2.

$$\text{Profit} = \text{Unit CM} \times Q - \text{Fixed expenses}$$

$$\$0 = (\$60 - \$45) \times Q - \$240{,}000$$

$$\$15Q = \$240{,}000$$

$$Q = \$240{,}000 \div \$15$$

$$Q = 16{,}000 \text{ units; or at \$60 per unit, \$960,000}$$

3.

Increase in sales	$400,000
Multiply by the CM ratio	× 25%
Expected increase in contribution margin	$100,000

Because the fixed expenses are not expected to change, net operating income will increase by the entire $100,000 increase in contribution margin computed above.

4. Equation method:

$$\text{Profit} = \text{Unit CM} \times Q - \text{Fixed expenses}$$

$$\$90{,}000 = (\$60 - \$45) \times Q - \$240{,}000$$

$$\$15Q = \$90{,}000 + \$240{,}000$$

$$Q = \$330{,}000 \div \$15$$

$$Q = 22{,}000 \text{ units}$$

Formula method:

$$\frac{\text{Unit sales to attain}}{\text{the target profit}} = \frac{\text{Target profit} + \text{Fixed expenses}}{\text{Contribution margin per unit}} = \frac{\$90{,}000 + \$240{,}000}{\$15 \text{ per unit}} = 22{,}000 \text{ units}$$

5.

$$\text{Margin of safety in dollars} = \text{Total sales} - \text{Break-even sales}$$

$$= \$1{,}200{,}000 - \$960{,}000 = \$240{,}000$$

$$\text{Margin of safety percentage} = \frac{\text{Margin of safety in dollars}}{\text{Total sales}} = \frac{\$240{,}000}{\$1{,}200{,}000} = 20\%$$

6. *a.*

$$\text{Degree of operating leverage} = \frac{\text{Contribution margin}}{\text{Net operating income}} = \frac{\$300{,}000}{\$60{,}000} = 5$$

b.

Expected increase in sales	8%
Degree of operating leverage	× 5
Expected increase in net operating income	40%

c. If sales increase by 8%, then 21,600 units (20,000 × 1.08 = 21,600) will be sold next year. The new contribution format income statement would be as follows:

	Total	Per Unit	Percent of Sales
Sales (21,600 units)	$1,296,000	$60	100%
Variable expenses	972,000	45	75%
Contribution margin	324,000	$15	25%
Fixed expenses	240,000		
Net operating income	$ 84,000		

Thus, the $84,000 expected net operating income for next year represents a 40% increase over the $60,000 net operating income earned during the current year:

$$\frac{\$84{,}000 - \$60{,}000}{\$60{,}000} = \frac{\$24{,}000}{\$60{,}000} = 40\% \text{ increase}$$

Note from the income statement on the prior page that the increase in sales from 20,000 to 21,600 units has increased *both* total sales and total variable expenses.

7. *a.* A 20% increase in sales would result in 24,000 units being sold next year: 20,000 units × 1.20 = 24,000 units.

	Total	Per Unit	Percent of Sales
Sales (24,000 units)	$1,440,000	$60	100%
Variable expenses	1,152,000	48*	80%
Contribution margin	288,000	$12	20%
Fixed expenses	210,000†		
Net operating income	$ 78,000		

*$45 + $3 = $48; $48 ÷ $60 = 80%.
†$240,000 − $30,000 = $210,000.

Note that the change in per unit variable expenses results in a change in both the per unit contribution margin and the CM ratio.

b.

$$\text{Unit sales to break even} = \frac{\text{Fixed expenses}}{\text{Unit contribution margin}}$$

$$= \frac{\$210{,}000}{\$12 \text{ per unit}} = 17{,}500 \text{ units}$$

$$\text{Dollar sales to break even} = \frac{\text{Fixed expenses}}{\text{CM ratio}}$$

$$= \frac{\$210{,}000}{0.20} = \$1{,}050{,}000$$

c. Yes, based on these data, the changes should be made. The changes increase the company's net operating income from the present $60,000 to $78,000 per year. Although the changes also result in a higher break-even point (17,500 units as compared to the present 16,000 units), the company's margin of safety actually becomes greater than before:

$$\text{Margin of safety in dollars} = \text{Total sales} - \text{Break-even sales}$$

$$= \$1{,}440{,}000 - \$1{,}050{,}000 = \$390{,}000$$

As shown in (5) on the prior page, the company's present margin of safety is only $240,000. Thus, several benefits will result from the proposed changes.

Glossary

Break-even point The level of sales at which profit is zero. (p. 186)

Contribution margin ratio (CM ratio) A ratio computed by dividing contribution margin by dollar sales. (p. 191)

Cost-volume-profit (CVP) graph A graphical representation of the relationships between an organization's revenues, costs, and profits on the one hand and its sales volume on the other hand. (p. 188)

Degree of operating leverage A measure, at a given level of sales, of how a percentage change in sales will affect profits. The degree of operating leverage is computed by dividing contribution margin by net operating income. (p. 202)

Incremental analysis An analytical approach that focuses only on those costs and revenues that change as a result of a decision. (p. 193)

Margin of safety The excess of budgeted or actual dollar sales over the break-even dollar sales. (p. 199)

Operating leverage A measure of how sensitive net operating income is to a given percentage change in dollar sales. (p. 202)

Sales mix The relative proportions in which a company's products are sold. Sales mix is computed by expressing the sales of each product as a percentage of total sales. (p. 205)

Target profit analysis Estimating what sales volume is needed to achieve a specific target profit. (p. 196)

Variable expense ratio A ratio computed by dividing variable expenses by dollar sales (p. 192)

Questions

5–1 What is meant by a product's contribution margin ratio? How is this ratio useful in planning business operations?

5–2 Often the most direct route to a business decision is an incremental analysis. What is meant by an *incremental analysis?*

5–3 In all respects, Company A and Company B are identical except that Company A's costs are mostly variable, whereas Company B's costs are mostly fixed. When sales increase, which company will tend to realize the greatest increase in profits? Explain.

5–4 What is meant by the term *operating leverage?*

5–5 What is meant by the term *break-even point?*

5–6 In response to a request from your immediate supervisor, you have prepared a CVP graph portraying the cost and revenue characteristics of your company's product and operations. Explain how the lines on the graph and the break-even point would change if (*a*) the selling price per unit decreased, (*b*) fixed cost increased throughout the entire range of activity portrayed on the graph, and (*c*) variable cost per unit increased.

5–7 What is meant by the margin of safety?

5–8 What is meant by the term *sales mix?* What assumption is usually made concerning sales mix in CVP analysis?

5–9 Explain how a shift in the sales mix could result in both a higher break-even point and a lower net income.

Multiple-choice questions are provided on the text website at www.mhhe.com/garrison14e.

connect ACCOUNTING

Applying Excel

LEARNING OBJECTIVES 6, 7, 8

Available with McGraw-Hill's *Connect™ Accounting.*

The Excel worksheet form that appears on the next page is to be used to recreate portions of the Review Problem on pages 208–210. Download the workbook containing this form from the Online Learning Center at www.mhhe.com/garrison14e. *On the website you will also receive instructions about how to use this worksheet form.*

	A	B	C	D
1	Chapter 5: Applying Excel			
2				
3	**Data**			
4	Unit sales	20,000	units	
5	Selling price per unit	$60	per unit	
6	Variable expenses per unit	$45	per unit	
7	Fixed expenses	$240,000		
8				
9	*Enter a formula into each of the cells marked with a ? below*			
10	**Review Problem: CVP Relationships**			
11				
12	***Compute the CM ratio and variable expense ratio***			
13	Selling price per unit	?	per unit	
14	Variable expenses per unit	?	per unit	
15	Contribution margin per unit	?	per unit	
16				
17	CM ratio	?		
18	Variable expense ratio	?		
19				
20	***Compute the break-even***			
21	Break-even in unit sales	?	units	
22	Break-even in dollar sales	?		
23				
24	***Compute the margin of safety***			
25	Margin of safety in dollars	?		
26	Margin of safety percentage	?		
27				
28	***Compute the degree of operating leverage***			
29	Sales	?		
30	Variable expenses	?		
31	Contribution margin	?		
32	Fixed expenses	?		
33	Net operating income	?		
34				
35	Degree of operating leverage	?		
36				

Chapter 5 Form | Filled in Chapter 5 Form

You should proceed to the requirements below only after completing your worksheet.

Required:

1. Check your worksheet by changing the fixed expenses to $270,000. If your worksheet is operating properly, the degree of operating leverage should be 10. If you do not get this answer, find the errors in your worksheet and correct them. How much is the margin of safety percentage? Did it change? Why or why not?
2. Enter the following data from a different company into your worksheet:

Unit sales	10,000 units
Selling price per unit	$120 per unit
Variable expenses per unit	$72 per unit
Fixed expenses	$420,000

   What is the margin of safety percentage? What is the degree of operating leverage?
3. Using the degree of operating leverage and without changing anything in your worksheet, calculate the percentage change in net operating income if unit sales increase by 15%.

4. Confirm the calculations you made in part (3) above by increasing the unit sales in your worksheet by 15%. What is the new net operating income and by what percentage did it increase?
5. Thad Morgan, a motorcycle enthusiast, has been exploring the possibility of relaunching the Western Hombre brand of cycle that was popular in the 1930s. The retro-look cycle would be sold for $10,000 and at that price, Thad estimates 600 units would be sold each year. The variable cost to produce and sell the cycles would be $7,500 per unit. The annual fixed cost would be $1,200,000.
   a. What would be the break-even unit sales, the margin of safety in dollars, and the degree of operating leverage?
   b. Thad is worried about the selling price. Rumors are circulating that other retro brands of cycles may be revived. If so, the selling price for the Western Hombre would have to be reduced to $9,000 to compete effectively. In that event, Thad would also reduce fixed expenses by $300,000 by reducing advertising expenses, but he still hopes to sell 600 units per year. Do you think this is a good plan? Explain. Also, explain the degree of operating leverage that appears on your worksheet.

connect ACCOUNTING Exercises

All applicable exercises are available with McGraw-Hill's *Connect™ Accounting*.

EXERCISE 5–1 Preparing a Contribution Format Income Statement [LO1]
Wheeler Corporation's most recent income statement follows:

	Total	Per Unit
Sales (8,000 units)	$208,000	$26.00
Variable expenses	144,000	18.00
Contribution margin	64,000	$ 8.00
Fixed expenses	56,000	
Net operating income	$ 8,000	

Required:
Prepare a new contribution format income statement under each of the following conditions (consider each case independently):
1. The sales volume increases by 50 units.
2. The sales volume declines by 50 units.
3. The sales volume is 7,000 units.

EXERCISE 5–2 Prepare a Cost-Volume-Profit (CVP) Graph [LO2]
Katara Enterprises distributes a single product whose selling price is $36 and whose variable expense is $24 per unit. The company's monthly fixed expense is $12,000.

Required:
1. Prepare a cost-volume-profit graph for the company up to a sales level of 2,000 units.
2. Estimate the company's break-even point in unit sales using your cost-volume-profit graph.

EXERCISE 5–3 Prepare a Profit Graph [LO2]
Capricio Enterprises distributes a single product whose selling price is $19 and whose variable expense is $15 per unit. The company's fixed expense is $12,000 per month.

Required:
1. Prepare a profit graph for the company up to a sales level of 4,000 units.
2. Estimate the company's break-even point in unit sales using your profit graph.

EXERCISE 5–4 Computing and Using the CM Ratio [LO3]
Last month when Harrison Creations, Inc., sold 40,000 units, total sales were $300,000, total variable expenses were $240,000, and fixed expenses were $45,000.

Required:
1. What is the company's contribution margin (CM) ratio?
2. Estimate the change in the company's net operating income if it were to increase its total sales by $1,500.

EXERCISE 5–5 Changes in Variable Costs, Fixed Costs, Selling Price, and Volume [LO4]
Data for Herron Corporation are shown below:

	Per Unit	Percent of Sales
Selling price	$75	100%
Variable expenses	45	60%
Contribution margin	$30	40%

Fixed expenses are $75,000 per month and the company is selling 3,000 units per month.

Required:
1. The marketing manager believes that an $8,000 increase in the monthly advertising budget would increase monthly sales by $15,000. Should the advertising budget be increased?
2. Refer to the original data. Management is considering using higher-quality components that would increase the variable cost by $3 per unit. The marketing manager believes that the higher-quality product would increase sales by 15% per month. Should the higher-quality components be used?

EXERCISE 5–6 Compute the Level of Sales Required to Attain a Target Profit [LO5]
Liman Corporation has a single product whose selling price is $140 and whose variable expense is $60 per unit. The company's monthly fixed expense is $40,000.

Required:
1. Using the equation method, solve for the unit sales that are required to earn a target profit of $6,000.
2. Using the formula method, solve for the dollar sales that are required to earn a target profit of $8,000.

EXERCISE 5–7 Compute the Break-Even Point [LO6]
Maxson Products distributes a single product, a woven basket whose selling price is $8 and whose variable cost is $6 per unit. The company's monthly fixed expense is $5,500.

Required:
1. Solve for the company's break-even point in unit sales using the equation method.
2. Solve for the company's break-even point in sales dollars using the equation method and the CM ratio.
3. Solve for the company's break-even point in unit sales using the formula method.
4. Solve for the company's break-even point in sales dollars using formula method and the CM ratio.

EXERCISE 5–8 Compute the Margin of Safety [LO7]
Mohan Corporation is a distributor of a sun umbrella used at resort hotels. Data concerning next month's budget appear below:

Selling price	$25 per unit
Variable expenses	$15 per unit
Fixed expenses	$8,500 per month
Unit sales	1,000 units per month

Required:

1. Compute the company's margin of safety.
2. Compute the company's margin of safety as a percentage of its sales.

EXERCISE 5–9 Compute and Use the Degree of Operating Leverage [LO8]

Eneliko Company installs home theater systems. The company's most recent monthly contribution format income statement appears below:

	Amount	Percent of Sales
Sales	$120,000	100%
Variable expenses	84,000	70%
Contribution margin	36,000	30%
Fixed expenses	24,000	
Net operating income	$ 12,000	

Required:

1. Compute the company's degree of operating leverage.
2. Using the degree of operating leverage, estimate the impact on net operating income of a 10% increase in sales.
3. Verify your estimate from part (2) above by constructing a new contribution format income statement for the company assuming a 10% increase in sales.

EXERCISE 5–10 Compute the Break-Even Point for a Multiproduct Company [LO9]

Lucky Products markets two computer games: Predator and Runway. A contribution format income statement for a recent month for the two games appears below:

	Predator	Runway	Total
Sales	$100,000	$50,000	$150,000
Variable expenses	25,000	5,000	30,000
Contribution margin	$ 75,000	$45,000	120,000
Fixed expenses			90,000
Net operating income			$ 30,000

Required:

1. Compute the overall contribution margin (CM) ratio for the company.
2. Compute the overall break-even point for the company in sales dollars.
3. Verify the overall break-even point for the company by constructing a contribution format income statement showing the appropriate levels of sales for the two products.

EXERCISE 5–11 Break-Even Analysis; Target Profit; Margin of Safety; CM Ratio [LO1, LO3, LO5, LO6, LO7]

Pringle Company distributes a single product. The company's sales and expenses for a recent month follow:

	Total	Per Unit
Sales	$600,000	$40
Variable expenses	420,000	28
Contribution margin	180,000	$12
Fixed expenses	150,000	
Net operating income	$ 30,000	

Required:

1. What is the monthly break-even point in units sold and in sales dollars?
2. Without resorting to computations, what is the total contribution margin at the break-even point?
3. How many units would have to be sold each month to earn a target profit of $18,000? Use the formula method. Verify your answer by preparing a contribution format income statement at the target level of sales.
4. Refer to the original data. Compute the company's margin of safety in both dollar and percentage terms.
5. What is the company's CM ratio? If monthly sales increase by $80,000 and there is no change in fixed expenses, by how much would you expect monthly net operating income to increase?

EXERCISE 5–12 Break-Even and Target Profit Analysis [LO4, LO5, LO6]

Reveen Products sells camping equipment. One of the company's products, a camp lantern, sells for $90 per unit. Variable expenses are $63 per lantern, and fixed expenses associated with the lantern total $135,000 per month.

Required:

1. Compute the company's break-even point in number of lanterns and in total sales dollars.
2. If the variable expenses per lantern increase as a percentage of the selling price, will it result in a higher or a lower break-even point? Why? (Assume that the fixed expenses remain unchanged.)
3. At present, the company is selling 8,000 lanterns per month. The sales manager is convinced that a 10% reduction in the selling price will result in a 25% increase in the number of lanterns sold each month. Prepare two contribution format income statements, one under present operating conditions, and one as operations would appear after the proposed changes. Show both total and per unit data on your statements.
4. Refer to the data in (3) above. How many lanterns would have to be sold at the new selling price to yield a minimum net operating income of $72,000 per month?

EXERCISE 5–13 Break-Even Analysis and CVP Graphing [LO2, LO4, LO6]

Chi Omega Sorority is planning its annual Riverboat Extravaganza. The Extravaganza committee has assembled the following expected costs for the event:

Dinner (per person)	$7
Favors and program (per person)	$3
Band	$1,500
Tickets and advertising	$700
Riverboat rental	$4,800
Floorshow and strolling entertainers	$1,000

The committee members would like to charge $30 per person for the evening's activities.

Required:

1. Compute the break-even point for the Extravaganza (in terms of the number of persons that must attend).
2. Assume that only 250 persons attended the Extravaganza last year. If the same number attend this year, what price per ticket must be charged to break even?
3. Refer to the original data ($30 ticket price per person). Prepare a CVP graph for the Extravaganza from zero tickets up to 600 tickets sold.

EXERCISE 5–14 Multiproduct Break-Even Analysis [LO9]

Okabee Enterprises is the distributor for two products, Model A100 and Model B900. Monthly sales and the contribution margin ratios for the two products follow:

	Product		
	Model A100	Model B900	Total
Sales	$700,000	$300,000	$1,000,000
Contribution margin ratio	60%	70%	?

The company's fixed expenses total $598,500 per month.

Required:

1. Prepare a contribution format income statement for the company as a whole.
2. Compute the break-even point for the company based on the current sales mix.
3. If sales increase by $50,000 per month, by how much would you expect net operating income to increase? What are your assumptions?

EXERCISE 5–15 Operating Leverage [LO4, LO8]

Superior Door Company sells prehung doors to home builders. The doors are sold for $60 each. Variable costs are $42 per door, and fixed costs total $450,000 per year. The company is currently selling 30,000 doors per year.

Required:

1. Prepare a contribution format income statement for the company at the present level of sales and compute the degree of operating leverage.
2. Management is confident that the company can sell 37,500 doors next year (an increase of 7,500 doors, or 25%, over current sales). Compute the following:
   a. The expected percentage increase in net operating income for next year.
   b. The expected net operating income for next year. (Do not prepare an income statement; use the degree of operating leverage to compute your answer.)

EXERCISE 5–16 Break-Even and Target Profit Analysis [LO3, LO4, LO5, LO6]

Super Sales Company is the exclusive distributor for a revolutionary bookbag. The product sells for $60 per unit and has a CM ratio of 40%. The company's fixed expenses are $360,000 per year. The company plans to sell 17,000 bookbags this year.

Required:

1. What are the variable expenses per unit?
2. Using the equation method:
   a. What is the break-even point in units and in sales dollars?
   b. What sales level in units and in sales dollars is required to earn an annual profit of $90,000?
   c. Assume that through negotiation with the manufacturer the Super Sales Company is able to reduce its variable expenses by $3 per unit. What is the company's new break-even point in units and in sales dollars?
3. Repeat (2) above using the formula method.

EXERCISE 5–17 Using a Contribution Format Income Statement [LO1, LO4]
Porter Company's most recent contribution format income statement is shown below:

	Total	Per Unit
Sales (30,000 units)	$150,000	$5
Variable expenses	90,000	3
Contribution margin	60,000	$2
Fixed expenses	50,000	
Net operating income	$ 10,000	

Required:
Prepare a new contribution format income statement under each of the following conditions (consider each case independently):

1. The number of units sold increases by 15%.
2. The selling price decreases by 50 cents per unit, and the number of units sold increases by 20%.
3. The selling price increases by 50 cents per unit, fixed expenses increase by $10,000, and the number of units sold decreases by 5%.
4. Variable expenses increase by 20 cents per unit, the selling price increases by 12%, and the number of units sold decreases by 10%.

EXERCISE 5–18 Missing Data; Basic CVP Concepts [LO1, LO9]
Fill in the missing amounts in each of the eight case situations below. Each case is independent of the others. (Hint: One way to find the missing amounts would be to prepare a contribution format income statement for each case, enter the known data, and then compute the missing items.)

a. Assume that only one product is being sold in each of the four following case situations:

Case	Units Sold	Sales	Variable Expenses	Contribution Margin per Unit	Fixed Expenses	Net Operating Income (Loss)
1	9,000	$270,000	$162,000	?	$90,000	?
2	?	$350,000	?	$15	$170,000	$40,000
3	20,000	?	$280,000	$6	?	$35,000
4	5,000	$160,000	?	?	$82,000	$(12,000)

b. Assume that more than one product is being sold in each of the four following case situations:

Case	Sales	Variable Expenses	Average Contribution Margin (Percent)	Fixed Expenses	Net Operating Income (Loss)
1	$450,000	?	40%	?	$65,000
2	$200,000	$130,000	?	$60,000	?
3	?	?	80%	$470,000	$90,000
4	$300,000	$90,000	?	?	$(15,000)

Problems

All applicable problems are available with McGraw-Hill's *Connect™ Accounting*.

PROBLEM 5–19 Basic CVP Analysis; Graphing [LO1, LO2, LO4, LO6]
Shirts Unlimited operates a chain of shirt stores that carry many styles of shirts that are all sold at the same price. To encourage sales personnel to be aggressive in their sales efforts, the company pays a substantial sales commission on each shirt sold. Sales personnel also receive a small basic salary.

The following worksheet contains cost and revenue data for Store 36. These data are typical of the company's many outlets:

	A	B	C
1		*Per Shirt*	
2	Selling price	$ 40.00	
3			
4	Variable expenses:		
5	Invoice cost	$ 18.00	
6	Sales commission	7.00	
7	Total variable expenses	$ 25.00	
8			
9		*Annual*	
10	Fixed expenses:		
11	Rent	$ 80,000	
12	Advertising	150,000	
13	Salaries	70,000	
14	Total fixed expenses	$ 300,000	
15			
16			

The company has asked you, as a member of its planning group, to assist in some basic analysis of its stores and company policies.

Required:

1. Calculate the annual break-even point in dollar sales and in unit sales for Store 36.
2. Prepare a CVP graph showing cost and revenue data for Store 36 from zero shirts up to 30,000 shirts sold each year. Clearly indicate the break-even point on the graph.
3. If 19,000 shirts are sold in a year, what would be Store 36's net operating income or loss?
4. The company is considering paying the store manager of Store 36 an incentive commission of $3 per shirt (in addition to the salespersons' commissions). If this change is made, what will be the new break-even point in dollar sales and in unit sales?
5. Refer to the original data. As an alternative to (4) above, the company is considering paying the store manager a $3 commission on each shirt sold in excess of the break-even point. If this change is made, what will be the store's net operating income or loss if 23,500 shirts are sold in a year?
6. Refer to the original data. The company is considering eliminating sales commissions entirely in its stores and increasing fixed salaries by $107,000 annually.
   a. If this change is made, what will be the new break-even point in dollar sales and in unit sales in Store 36?
   b. Would you recommend that the change be made? Explain.

PROBLEM 5–20 Basics of CVP Analysis; Cost Structure [LO1, LO3, LO4, LO5, LO6]
Memofax, Inc., produces memory enhancement kits for fax machines. Sales have been very erratic, with some months showing a profit and some months showing a loss. The company's contribution format income statement for the most recent month is given below:

Sales (13,500 units at $20 per unit)	$270,000
Variable expenses	189,000
Contribution margin	81,000
Fixed expenses	90,000
Net operating loss	$ (9,000)

Required:
1. Compute the company's CM ratio and its break-even point in both units and dollars.
2. The sales manager feels that an $8,000 increase in the monthly advertising budget, combined with an intensified effort by the sales staff, will result in a $70,000 increase in monthly sales. If the sales manager is right, what will be the effect on the company's monthly net operating income or loss? (Use the incremental approach in preparing your answer.)
3. Refer to the original data. The president is convinced that a 10% reduction in the selling price, combined with an increase of $35,000 in the monthly advertising budget, will double unit sales. What will the new contribution format income statement look like if these changes are adopted?
4. Refer to the original data. The company's advertising agency thinks that a new package would help sales. The new package being proposed would increase packaging costs by $0.60 per unit. Assuming no other changes, how many units would have to be sold each month to earn a profit of $4,500?
5. Refer to the original data. By automating, the company could slash its variable expenses in half. However, fixed costs would increase by $118,000 per month.
   a. Compute the new CM ratio and the new break-even point in both units and dollars.
   b. Assume that the company expects to sell 20,000 units next month. Prepare two contribution format income statements, one assuming that operations are not automated and one assuming that they are.
   c. Would you recommend that the company automate its operations? Explain.

PROBLEM 5–21 Basic CVP Analysis [LO1, LO3, LO4, LO6, LO8]
Stratford Company distributes a lightweight lawn chair that sells for $15 per unit. Variable expenses are $6 per unit, and fixed expenses total $180,000 annually.

Required:
Answer the following independent questions:
1. What is the product's CM ratio?
2. Use the CM ratio to determine the break-even point in sales dollars.
3. The company estimates that sales will increase by $45,000 during the coming year due to increased demand. By how much should net operating income increase?
4. Assume that the operating results for last year were as follows:

Sales	$360,000
Variable expenses	144,000
Contribution margin	216,000
Fixed expenses	180,000
Net operating income	$ 36,000

   a. Compute the degree of operating leverage at the current level of sales.
   b. The president expects sales to increase by 15% next year. By how much should net operating income increase?
5. Refer to the original data. Assume that the company sold 28,000 units last year. The sales manager is convinced that a 10% reduction in the selling price, combined with a $70,000 increase in advertising expenditures, would increase annual unit sales by 50%. Prepare two contribution format income statements, one showing the results of last year's operations and one showing what the results of operations would be if these changes were made. Would you recommend that the company do as the sales manager suggests?

6. Refer to the original data. Assume again that the company sold 28,000 units last year. The president feels that it would be unwise to change the selling price. Instead, he wants to increase the sales commission by $2 per unit. He thinks that this move, combined with some increase in advertising, would double annual unit sales. By how much could advertising be increased with profits remaining unchanged? Do not prepare an income statement; use the incremental analysis approach.

PROBLEM 5–22 Sales Mix; Multiproduct Break-Even Analysis [LO9]
Marlin Company, a wholesale distributor, has been operating for only a few months. The company sells three products—sinks, mirrors, and vanities. Budgeted sales by product and in total for the coming month are shown below:

	Product							
	Sinks		Mirrors		Vanities		Total	
Percentage of total sales	48%		20%		32%		100%	
Sales	$240,000	100%	$100,000	100%	$160,000	100%	$500,000	100%
Variable expenses	72,000	30%	80,000	80%	88,000	55%	240,000	48%
Contribution margin	$168,000	70%	$ 20,000	20%	$ 72,000	45%	260,000	52%
Fixed expenses							223,600	
Net operating income							$ 36,400	

$$\text{Dollar sales to break-even} = \frac{\text{Fixed expenses}}{\text{CM ratio}} = \frac{\$223{,}600}{0.52} = \$430{,}000$$

As shown by these data, net operating income is budgeted at $36,400 for the month, and break-even sales at $430,000.

Assume that actual sales for the month total $500,000 as planned. Actual sales by product are: sinks, $160,000; mirrors, $200,000; and vanities, $140,000.

Required:

1. Prepare a contribution format income statement for the month based on actual sales data. Present the income statement in the format shown above.
2. Compute the break-even point in sales dollars for the month, based on your actual data.
3. Considering the fact that the company met its $500,000 sales budget for the month, the president is shocked at the results shown on your income statement in (1) above. Prepare a brief memo for the president explaining why both the operating results and the break-even point in sales dollars are different from what was budgeted.

PROBLEM 5–23 Sales Mix; Break-Even Analysis; Margin of Safety [LO7, LO9]
Puleva Milenario SA, a company located in Toledo, Spain, manufactures and sells two models of luxuriously finished cutlery—Alvaro and Bazan. Present revenue, cost, and unit sales data for the two products appear below. All currency amounts are stated in terms of euros, which are indicated by the symbol €.

	Alvaro	Bazan
Selling price per unit	€4.00	€6.00
Variable expenses per unit	€2.40	€1.20
Number of units sold monthly	200 units	80 units

Fixed expenses are €660 per month.

Required:

1. Assuming the sales mix above, do the following:
   a. Prepare a contribution format income statement showing both euro and percent columns for each product and for the company as a whole.
   b. Compute the break-even point in euros for the company as a whole and the margin of safety in both euros and percent of sales.
2. The company has developed another product, Cano, that the company plans to sell for €8 each. At this price, the company expects to sell 40 units per month of the product. The variable expense would be €6 per unit. The company's fixed expenses would not change.

a. Prepare another contribution format income statement, including sales of Cano (sales of the other two products would not change).

b. Compute the company's new break-even point in euros for the company as a whole and the new margin of safety in both euros and percent of sales.

3. The president of the company was puzzled by your analysis. He did not understand why the break-even point has gone up even though there has been no increase in fixed expenses and the addition of the new product has increased the total contribution margin. Explain to the president what has happened.

PROBLEM 5–24 Sales Mix; Multiproduct Break-Even Analysis [LO9]

Topper Sports, Inc., produces high-quality sports equipment. The company's Racket Division manufactures three tennis rackets—the Standard, the Deluxe, and the Pro—that are widely used in amateur play. Selected information on the rackets is given below:

	Standard	Deluxe	Pro
Selling price per racket	$40.00	$60.00	$90.00
Variable expenses per racket:			
Production	$22.00	$27.00	$31.50
Selling (5% of selling price)	$2.00	$3.00	$4.50

All sales are made through the company's own retail outlets. The Racket Division has the following fixed costs:

	Per Month
Fixed production costs	$120,000
Advertising expense	100,000
Administrative salaries	50,000
Total	$270,000

Sales, in units, over the past two months have been as follows:

	Standard	Deluxe	Pro	Total
April	2,000	1,000	5,000	8,000
May	8,000	1,000	3,000	12,000

Required:

1. Prepare contribution format income statements for April and May. Use the following headings:

	Standard		Deluxe		Pro		Total	
	Amount	Percent	Amount	Percent	Amount	Percent	Amount	Percent
Sales								
Etc.								

Place the fixed expenses only in the Total column. Do not show percentages for the fixed expenses.

2. Upon seeing the income statements in (1) above, the president stated, "I can't believe this! We sold 50% more rackets in May than in April, yet profits went down. It's obvious that costs are out of control in that division." What other explanation can you give for the drop in net operating income?
3. Compute the Racket Division's break-even point in dollar sales for April.
4. Without doing any calculations, explain whether the break-even point would be higher or lower with May's sales mix than with April's sales mix.
5. Assume that sales of the Standard racket increase by $20,000. What would be the effect on net operating income? What would be the effect if Pro racket sales increased by $20,000? Do not prepare income statements; use the incremental analysis approach in determining your answer.

PROBLEM 5–25 Break-Even Analysis; Pricing [LO1, LO4, LO6]
Detmer Holdings AG of Zurich, Switzerland, has just introduced a new fashion watch for which the company is trying to find an optimal selling price. Marketing studies suggest that the company can increase sales by 5,000 units for each SFr2 per unit reduction in the selling price. (SFr2 denotes 2 Swiss francs.) The company's present selling price is SFr90 per unit, and variable expenses are SFr60 per unit. Fixed expenses are SFr840,000 per year. The present annual sales volume (at the SFr90 selling price) is 25,000 units.

Required:

1. What is the present yearly net operating income or loss?
2. What is the present break-even point in units and in Swiss franc sales?
3. Assuming that the marketing studies are correct, what is the *maximum* profit that the company can earn yearly? At how many units and at what selling price per unit would the company generate this profit?
4. What would be the break-even point in units and in Swiss franc sales using the selling price you determined in (3) above (i.e., the selling price at the level of maximum profits)? Why is this break-even point different from the break-even point you computed in (2) above?

PROBLEM 5–26 Changes in Cost Structure; Break-Even Analysis; Operating Leverage; Margin of Safety [LO4, LO6, LO7, LO8]
Frieden Company's contribution format income statement for the most recent month is given below:

Sales (40,000 units)	$800,000
Variable expenses	560,000
Contribution margin	240,000
Fixed expenses	192,000
Net operating income	$ 48,000

The industry in which Frieden Company operates is quite sensitive to cyclical movements in the economy. Thus, profits vary considerably from year to year according to general economic conditions. The company has a large amount of unused capacity and is studying ways of improving profits.

Required:

1. New equipment has come on the market that would allow Frieden Company to automate a portion of its operations. Variable expenses would be reduced by $6 per unit. However, fixed expenses would increase to a total of $432,000 each month. Prepare two contribution format income statements, one showing present operations and one showing how operations would appear if the new equipment is purchased. Show an Amount column, a Per Unit column, and a Percent column on each statement. Do not show percentages for the fixed expenses.
2. Refer to the income statements in (1) above. For both present operations and the proposed new operations, compute (*a*) the degree of operating leverage, (*b*) the break-even point in dollars, and (*c*) the margin of safety in both dollar and percentage terms.
3. Refer again to the data in (1) above. As a manager, what factor would be paramount in your mind in deciding whether to purchase the new equipment? (Assume that ample funds are available to make the purchase.)
4. Refer to the original data. Rather than purchase new equipment, the marketing manager argues that the company's marketing strategy should be changed. Instead of paying sales commissions, which are included in variable expenses, the marketing manager suggests that salespersons be paid fixed salaries and that the company invest heavily in advertising. The marketing manager claims that this new approach would increase unit sales by 50% without any change in selling price; the company's new monthly fixed expenses would be $240,000; and its net operating income would increase by 25%. Compute the break-even point in dollar sales for the company under the new marketing strategy. Do you agree with the marketing manager's proposal?

PROBLEM 5–27 Interpretive Questions on the CVP Graph [LO2, LO6]
A CVP graph, as illustrated on the next page, is a useful technique for showing relationships among an organization's costs, volume, and profits.

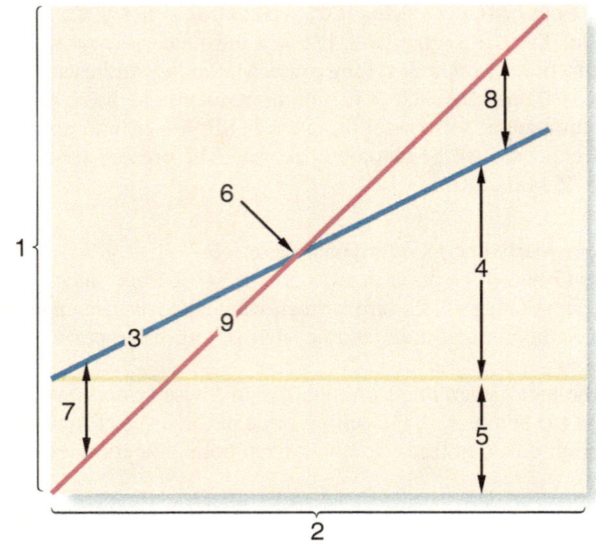

Required:

1. Identify the numbered components in the CVP graph.
2. State the effect of each of the following actions on line 3, line 9, and the break-even point. For line 3 and line 9, state whether the action will cause the line to:

   Remain unchanged.
   Shift upward.
   Shift downward.
   Have a steeper slope (i.e., rotate upward).
   Have a flatter slope (i.e., rotate downward).
   Shift upward *and* have a steeper slope.
   Shift upward *and* have a flatter slope.
   Shift downward *and* have a steeper slope.
   Shift downward *and* have a flatter slope.

   In the case of the break-even point, state whether the action will cause the break-even point to:

   Remain unchanged.
   Increase.
   Decrease.
   Probably change, but the direction is uncertain.

   Treat each case independently.

   x. *Example.* Fixed costs are increased by $20,000 each period.
   Answer (see choices above): Line 3: Shift upward.
   Line 9: Remain unchanged.
   Break-even point: Increase.

   a. The unit selling price is decreased from $30 to $27.
   b. The per unit variable costs are increased from $12 to $15.
   c. The total fixed costs are reduced by $40,000.
   d. Five thousand fewer units are sold during the period than were budgeted.
   e. Due to purchasing a robot to perform a task that was previously done by workers, fixed costs are increased by $25,000 per period, and variable costs are reduced by $8 per unit.
   f. As a result of a decrease in the cost of materials, both unit variable costs and the selling price are decreased by $3.
   g. Advertising costs are increased by $50,000 per period, resulting in a 10% increase in the number of units sold.
   h. Due to paying salespersons a commission rather than a flat salary, fixed costs are reduced by $21,000 per period, and unit variable costs are increased by $6.

PROBLEM 5–28 Graphing; Incremental Analysis; Operating Leverage [LO2, LO4, LO5, LO6, LO8]

Teri Hall has recently opened Sheer Elegance, Inc., a store specializing in fashionable stockings. Ms. Hall has just completed a course in managerial accounting, and she believes that she can apply certain aspects of the course to her business. She is particularly interested in adopting the cost-volume-profit (CVP) approach to decision making. Thus, she has prepared the following analysis:

Sales price per pair of stockings	$2.00
Variable expense per pair of stockings	0.80
Contribution margin per pair of stockings	$1.20
Fixed expense per year:	
Building rental	$12,000
Equipment depreciation	3,000
Selling	30,000
Administrative	15,000
Total fixed expense	$60,000

Required:

1. How many pairs of stockings must be sold to break even? What does this represent in total dollar sales?
2. Prepare a CVP graph or a profit graph for the store from zero pairs up to 70,000 pairs of stockings sold each year. Indicate the break-even point on the graph.
3. How many pairs of stockings must be sold to earn a $9,000 target profit for the first year?
4. Ms. Hall now has one full-time and one part-time salesperson working in the store. It will cost her an additional $8,000 per year to convert the part-time position to a full-time position. Ms. Hall believes that the change would bring in an additional $20,000 in sales each year. Should she convert the position? Use the incremental approach. (Do not prepare an income statement.)
5. Refer to the original data. Actual operating results for the first year are as follows:

Sales	$125,000
Variable expenses	50,000
Contribution margin	75,000
Fixed expenses	60,000
Net operating income	$ 15,000

   a. What is the store's degree of operating leverage?
   b. Ms. Hall is confident that with some effort she can increase sales by 20% next year. What would be the expected percentage increase in net operating income? Use the degree of operating leverage concept to compute your answer.

PROBLEM 5–29 Various CVP Questions: Break-Even Point; Cost Structure; Target Sales [LO1, LO3, LO4, LO5, LO6, LO8]

Tyrene Products manufactures recreational equipment. One of the company's products, a skateboard, sells for $37.50. The skateboards are manufactured in an antiquated plant that relies heavily on direct labor workers. Thus, variable costs are high, totaling $22.50 per skateboard of which 60% is direct labor cost.

Over the past year the company sold 40,000 skateboards, with the following operating results:

Sales (40,000 skateboards)	$1,500,000
Variable expenses	900,000
Contribution margin	600,000
Fixed expenses	480,000
Net operating income	$ 120,000

Management is anxious to maintain and perhaps even improve its present level of income from the skateboards.

Required:

1. Compute (*a*) the CM ratio and the break-even point in skateboards, and (*b*) the degree of operating leverage at last year's level of sales.
2. Due to an increase in labor rates, the company estimates that variable costs will increase by \$3 per skateboard next year. If this change takes place and the selling price per skateboard remains constant at \$37.50, what will be the new CM ratio and the new break-even point in skateboards?
3. Refer to the data in (2) above. If the expected change in variable costs takes place, how many skateboards will have to be sold next year to earn the same net operating income, \$120,000, as last year?
4. Refer again to the data in (2) above. The president has decided that the company may have to raise the selling price of its skateboards. If Tyrene Products wants to maintain *the same CM ratio as last year*, what selling price per skateboard must it charge next year to cover the increased labor costs?
5. Refer to the original data. The company is considering the construction of a new, automated plant. The new plant would slash variable costs by 40%, but it would cause fixed costs to increase by 90%. If the new plant is built, what would be the company's new CM ratio and new break-even point in skateboards?
6. Refer to the data in (5) above.
   a. If the new plant is built, how many skateboards will have to be sold next year to earn the same net operating income, \$120,000, as last year?
   b. Assume that the new plant is constructed and that next year the company manufactures and sells 40,000 skateboards (the same number as sold last year). Prepare a contribution format income statement, and compute the degree of operating leverage.
   c. If you were a member of top management, would you have been in favor of constructing the new plant? Explain.

PROBLEM 5–30 Break-Even and Target Profit Analysis [LO5, LO6]

The Marbury Stein Shop sells steins from all parts of the world. The owner of the shop, Clint Marbury, is thinking of expanding his operations by hiring college students, on a commission basis, to sell steins at the local college. The steins will bear the school emblem.

These steins must be ordered from the manufacturer three months in advance, and because of the unique emblem of each college, they cannot be returned. The steins would cost Marbury \$15 each with a minimum order of 200 steins. Any additional steins would have to be ordered in increments of 50.

Because Marbury's plan would not require any additional facilities, the only costs associated with the project would be the cost of the steins and the cost of sales commissions. The selling price of the steins would be \$30 each. Marbury would pay the students a commission of \$6 for each stein sold.

Required:

1. To make the project worthwhile in terms of his own time, Marbury would require a \$7,200 profit for the first six months of the venture. What level of sales in units and dollars would be required to attain this target net operating income? Show all computations.
2. Assume that the venture is undertaken and an order is placed for 200 steins. What would be Marbury's break-even point in units and in sales dollars? Show computations, and explain the reasoning behind your answer.

PROBLEM 5–31 Changes in Fixed and Variable Costs; Break-Even and Target Profit Analysis [LO4, LO5, LO6]

Novelties, Inc., produces and sells highly faddish products directed toward the preteen market. A new product has come onto the market that the company is anxious to produce and sell. Enough capacity exists in the company's plant to produce 30,000 units each month. Variable expenses to manufacture and sell one unit would be \$1.60, and fixed expenses would total \$40,000 per month.

The Marketing Department predicts that demand for the product will exceed the 30,000 units that the company is able to produce. Additional production capacity can be rented from another company at a fixed expense of \$2,000 per month. Variable expenses in the rented facility would total \$1.75 per unit, due to somewhat less efficient operations than in the main plant. The product would sell for \$2.50 per unit.

Required:

1. Compute the monthly break-even point for the new product in units and in total dollar sales.
2. How many units must be sold each month to make a monthly profit of $9,000?
3. If the sales manager receives a bonus of 15 cents for each unit sold in excess of the break-even point, how many units must be sold each month to earn a return of 25% on the monthly investment in fixed expenses?

connect ACCOUNTING **Cases**

All applicable cases are available with McGraw-Hill's *Connect™ Accounting*.

CASE 5–32 Cost Structure; Break-Even Point; Target Profits [LO4, LO5, LO6]

Marston Corporation manufactures disposable thermometers that are sold to hospitals through a network of independent sales agents located in the United States and Canada. These sales agents sell a variety of products to hospitals in addition to Marston's disposable thermometer. The sales agents are currently paid an 18% commission on sales, and this commission rate was used when Marston's management prepared the following budgeted absorption income statement for the upcoming year.

Marston Corporation Budgeted Income Statement		
Sales		$30,000,000
Cost of goods sold:		
Variable	$17,400,000	
Fixed	2,800,000	20,200,000
Gross margin		9,800,000
Selling and administrative expenses:		
Commissions	5,400,000	
Fixed advertising expense	800,000	
Fixed administrative expense	3,200,000	9,400,000
Net operating income		$ 400,000

Since the completion of the above statement, Marston's management has learned that the independent sales agents are demanding an increase in the commission rate to 20% of sales for the upcoming year. This would be the third increase in commissions demanded by the independent sales agents in five years. As a result, Marston's management has decided to investigate the possibility of hiring its own sales staff to replace the independent sales agents.

Marston's controller estimates that the company will have to hire eight salespeople to cover the current market area, and the total annual payroll cost of these employees will be about $700,000, including fringe benefits. The salespeople will also be paid commissions of 10% of sales. Travel and entertainment expenses are expected to total about $400,000 for the year. The company will also have to hire a sales manager and support staff whose salaries and fringe benefits will come to $200,000 per year. To make up for the promotions that the independent sales agents had been running on behalf of Marston, management believes that the company's budget for fixed advertising expenses should be increased by $500,000.

Required:

1. Assuming sales of $30,000,000, construct a budgeted contribution format income statement for the upcoming year for each of the following alternatives:
   a. The independent sales agents' commission rate remains unchanged at 18%.
   b. The independent sales agents' commission rate increases to 20%.
   c. The company employs its own sales force.
2. Calculate Marston Corporation's break-even point in sales dollars for the upcoming year assuming the following:
   a. The independent sales agents' commission rate remains unchanged at 18%.
   b. The independent sales agents' commission rate increases to 20%.
   c. The company employs its own sales force.

3. Refer to your answer to (1)(b) above. If the company employs its own sales force, what volume of sales would be necessary to generate the net operating income the company would realize if sales are $30,000,000 and the company continues to sell through agents (at a 20% commission rate)?
4. Determine the volume of sales at which net operating income would be equal regardless of whether Marston Corporation sells through agents (at a 20% commission rate) or employs its own sales force.
5. Prepare a graph on which you plot the profits for both of the following alternatives.
   a. The independent sales agents' commission rate increases to 20%.
   b. The company employs its own sales force.
   On the graph, use total sales revenue as the measure of activity.
6. Write a memo to the president of Marston Corporation in which you make a recommendation as to whether the company should continue to use independent sales agents (at a 20% commission rate) or employ its own sales force. Fully explain the reasons for your recommendation in the memo.

(CMA, adapted)

CASE 5–33 Break-Evens for Individual Products in a Multiproduct Company [LO6, LO9]

Jasmine Park encountered her boss, Rick Gompers, at the pop machine in the lobby. Rick is the vice president of marketing at Down South Lures Corporation. Jasmine was puzzled by some calculations she had been doing, so she asked him:

Jasmine: "Rick, I'm not sure how to go about answering the questions that came up at the meeting with the president yesterday."

Rick: "What's the problem?"

Jasmine: "The president wanted to know the break even for each of the company's products, but I am having trouble figuring them out."

Rick: "I'm sure you can handle it, Jasmine. And, by the way, I need your analysis on my desk tomorrow morning at 8:00 A.M. sharp so I can look at it before the follow-up meeting at 9:00."

Down South Lures makes three fishing lures in its manufacturing facility in Alabama. Data concerning these products appear below.

	Frog	Minnow	Worm
Normal annual sales volume	100,000	200,000	300,000
Unit selling price	$2.00	$1.40	$0.80
Variable cost per unit	$1.20	$0.80	$0.50

Total fixed expenses for the entire company are $282,000 per year. All three products are sold in highly competitive markets, so the company is unable to raise its prices without losing unacceptable numbers of customers. The company has no work in process or finished goods inventories due to an extremely effective lean manufacturing system.

Required:

1. What is the company's overall break-even point in total sales dollars?
2. Of the total fixed costs of $282,000, $18,000 could be avoided if the Frog lure product were dropped, $96,000 if the Minnow lure product were dropped, and $60,000 if the Worm lure product were dropped. The remaining fixed expenses of $108,000 consist of common fixed costs such as administrative salaries and rent on the factory building that could be avoided only by going out of business entirely.
   a. What is the break-even point in units for each product?
   b. If the company sells exactly the break-even quantity of each product, what will be the overall profit of the company? Explain this result.

Chapter 6

Variable Costing and Segment Reporting: Tools for Management

BUSINESS FOCUS

IBM's $2.5 Billion Investment in Technology

When it comes to state-of-the-art in automation, IBM's $2.5 billion semiconductor manufacturing facility in East Fishkill, New York, is tough to beat. The plant uses wireless networks, 600 miles of cable, and more than 420 servers to equip itself with what IBM claims is more computing power than NASA uses to launch a space shuttle.

Each batch of 25 wafers (one wafer can be processed into 1,000 computer chips) travels through the East Fishkill plant's manufacturing process without ever being touched by human hands. A computer system "looks at orders and schedules production runs . . . adjusts schedules to allow for planned maintenance and . . . feeds vast reams of production data into enterprise-wide management and financial-reporting systems." The plant can literally run itself as was the case a few years ago when a snowstorm hit and everyone went home while the automated system continued to manufacture computer chips until it ran out of work.

In a manufacturing environment such as this, labor costs are insignificant and fixed overhead costs are huge. There is a strong temptation to build inventories and increase profits without increasing sales. How can this be done you ask? It would seem logical that producing more units would have no impact on profits unless the units were sold, right? Wrong! As we will discover in this chapter, absorption costing—the most widely used method of determining product costs—can artificially increase profits by increasing the quantity of units produced. ■

Source: Ghostwriter, "Big Blue's $2.5 Billion Sales Tool," *Fortune*, September 19, 2005, pp. 316F–316J.

LEARNING OBJECTIVES

After studying Chapter 6, you should be able to:

LO1 Explain how variable costing differs from absorption costing and compute unit product costs under each method.

LO2 Prepare income statements using both variable and absorption costing.

LO3 Reconcile variable costing and absorption costing net operating incomes and explain why the two amounts differ.

LO4 Prepare a segmented income statement that differentiates traceable fixed costs from common fixed costs and use it to make decisions.

This chapter describes two applications of the contribution format income statements that were introduced in Chapters 2 and 5. First, it explains how manufacturing companies can prepare *variable costing* income statements, which rely on the contribution format, for internal decision making purposes. The variable costing approach will be contrasted with *absorption costing* income statements, which were discussed in Chapter 3 and are generally used for external reports. Ordinarily, variable costing and absorption costing produce different net operating income figures, and the difference can be quite large. In addition to showing how these two methods differ, we will describe the advantages of variable costing for internal reporting purposes and we will show how management decisions can be affected by the costing method chosen.

Second, the chapter explains how the contribution format can be used to prepare segmented income statements. In addition to companywide income statements, managers need to measure the profitability of individual *segments* of their organizations. A **segment** is a part or activity of an organization about which managers would like cost, revenue, or profit data. This chapter explains how to create contribution format income statements that report profit data for business segments, such as divisions, individual stores, geographic regions, customers, and product lines.

Overview of Variable and Absorption Costing

LEARNING OBJECTIVE 1
Explain how variable costing differs from absorption costing and compute unit product costs under each method.

As you begin to read about variable and absorption costing income statements in the coming pages, focus your attention on three key concepts. First, both income statement formats include product costs and period costs, although they define these cost classifications differently. Second, variable costing income statements are grounded in the contribution format. They categorize expenses based on cost behavior—variable costs are reported separately from fixed costs. Absorption costing income statements ignore variable and fixed cost distinctions. Third, as mentioned in the paragraph above, variable and absorption costing net operating income figures often differ from one another. The reason for these differences always relates to the fact the variable costing and absorption costing income statements account for fixed manufacturing overhead differently. *Pay very close attention to the two different ways that variable costing and absorption costing account for fixed manufacturing overhead.*

Variable Costing

Under **variable costing,** only those manufacturing costs that vary with output are treated as product costs. This would usually include direct materials, direct labor, and the variable portion of manufacturing overhead. Fixed manufacturing overhead is not treated as a product cost under this method. Rather, fixed manufacturing overhead is treated as a period cost and, like selling and administrative expenses, it is expensed in its entirety each period. Consequently, the cost of a unit of product in inventory or in cost of goods sold under the variable costing method does not contain any fixed manufacturing overhead cost. Variable costing is sometimes referred to as *direct costing* or *marginal costing.*

Absorption Costing

As discussed in Chapter 3, **absorption costing** treats *all* manufacturing costs as product costs, regardless of whether they are variable or fixed. The cost of a unit of product under the absorption costing method consists of direct materials, direct labor, and *both* variable and fixed manufacturing overhead. Thus, absorption costing allocates a portion of fixed

EXHIBIT 6–1
Variable Costing versus Absorption Costing

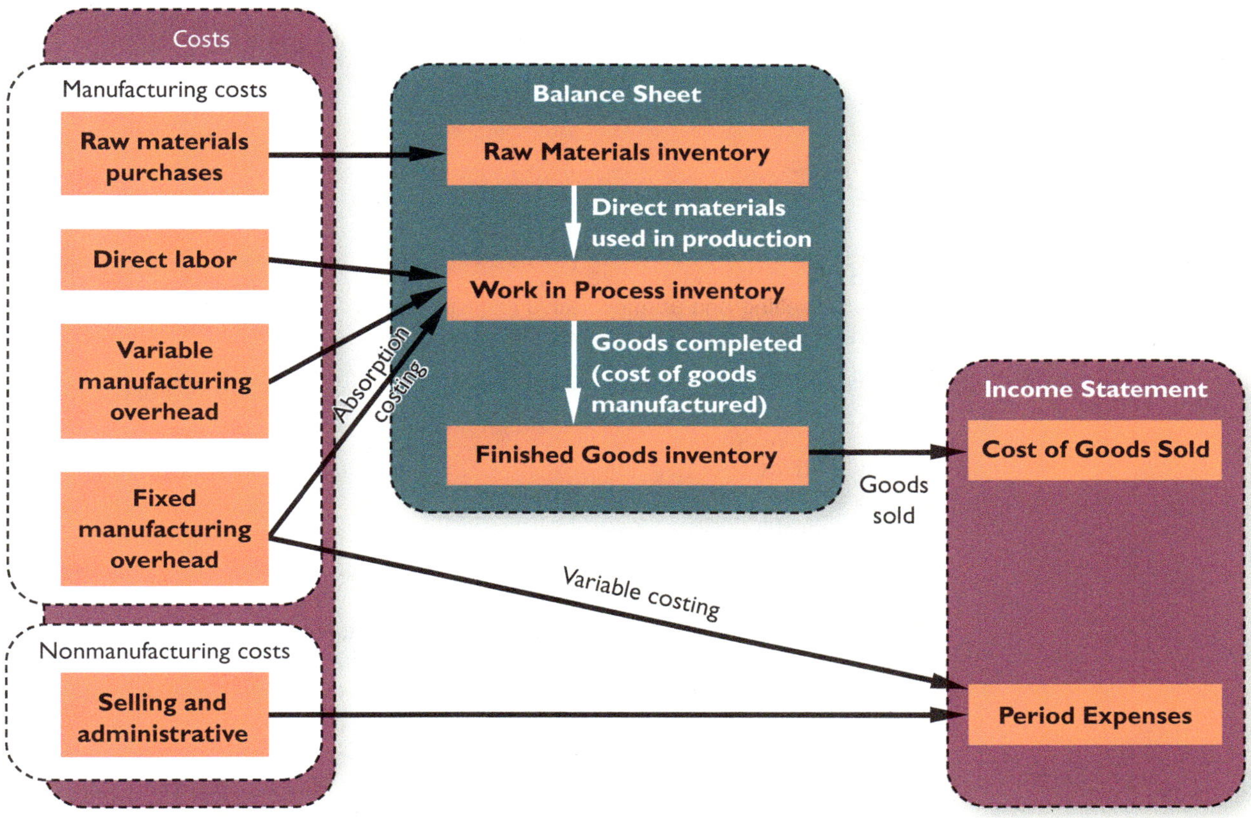

manufacturing overhead cost to each unit of product, along with the variable manufacturing costs. Because absorption costing includes all manufacturing costs in product costs, it is frequently referred to as the *full cost* method.

Selling and Administrative Expenses

Selling and administrative expenses are never treated as product costs, regardless of the costing method. Thus, under absorption and variable costing, variable and fixed selling and administrative expenses are always treated as period costs and are expensed as incurred.

Summary of Differences The essential difference between variable costing and absorption costing, as illustrated in Exhibit 6–1, is how each method accounts for fixed manufacturing overhead costs—all other costs are treated the same under the two methods. In absorption costing, fixed manufacturing overhead costs are included as part of the costs of work in process inventories. When units are completed, these costs are transferred to finished goods and only when the units are sold do these costs flow through to the income statement as part of cost of goods sold. In variable costing, fixed manufacturing overhead costs are considered to be period costs—just like selling and administrative costs—and are taken immediately to the income statement as period expenses.

Variable and Absorption Costing—An Example

To illustrate the difference between variable costing and absorption costing, consider Weber Light Aircraft, a company that produces light recreational aircraft. Data concerning the company's operations appear below:

	Per Aircraft		Per Month
Selling price	$100,000		
Direct materials	$19,000		
Direct labor	$5,000		
Variable manufacturing overhead	$1,000		
Fixed manufacturing overhead			$70,000
Variable selling and administrative expenses	$10,000		
Fixed selling and administrative expenses			$20,000
	January	**February**	**March**
Beginning inventory	0	0	1
Units produced	1	2	4
Units sold	1	1	5
Ending inventory	0	1	0

As you review the data above, it is important to realize that for the months of January, February, and March, the selling price per aircraft, variable cost per aircraft, and total monthly fixed expenses never change. The only variables that change in this example are the number of units produced (January = 1 unit produced; February = 2 units produced; March = 4 units produced) and the number of units sold (January = 1 unit sold; February = 1 unit sold; March = 5 units sold).

We will first construct the company's variable costing income statements for January, February, and March. Then we will show how the company's net operating income would be determined for the same months using absorption costing.

Variable Costing Contribution Format Income Statement

LEARNING OBJECTIVE 2
Prepare income statements using both variable and absorption costing.

To prepare the company's variable costing income statements for January, February, and March we begin by computing the unit product cost. Under variable costing, product costs consist solely of variable production costs. At Weber Light Aircraft, the variable production cost per unit is $25,000, determined as follows:

Variable Costing Unit Product Cost	
Direct materials	$19,000
Direct labor	5,000
Variable manufacturing overhead	1,000
Variable costing unit product cost	$25,000

Since each month's variable production cost is $25,000 per aircraft, the variable costing cost of goods sold for all three months can be easily computed as follows:

Variable Costing Cost of Goods Sold	January	February	March
Variable production cost (a)	$25,000	$25,000	$25,000
Units sold (b)	1	1	5
Variable cost of goods sold (a) × (b)	$25,000	$25,000	$125,000

And the company's total selling and administrative expense would be derived as follows:

Selling and Administrative Expenses	January	February	March
Variable selling and administrative expense (@ $10,000 per unit sold)	$10,000	$10,000	$50,000
Fixed selling and administrative expense	20,000	20,000	20,000
Total selling and administrative expense	$30,000	$30,000	$70,000

Putting it all together, the variable costing income statements would appear as shown in Exhibit 6–2. Notice, the contribution format has been used in these income statements. Also, the monthly fixed manufacturing overhead costs ($70,000) have been recorded as a period expense in the month incurred.

EXHIBIT 6–2
Variable Costing Income Statements

Variable Costing Contribution Format Income Statements	January	February	March
Sales	$100,000	$100,000	$500,000
Variable expenses:			
Variable cost of goods sold	25,000	25,000	125,000
Variable selling and administrative expense	10,000	10,000	50,000
Total variable expenses	35,000	35,000	175,000
Contribution margin	65,000	65,000	325,000
Fixed expenses:			
Fixed manufacturing overhead	70,000	70,000	70,000
Fixed selling and administrative expense	20,000	20,000	20,000
Total fixed expenses	90,000	90,000	90,000
Net operating income (loss)	$ (25,000)	$ (25,000)	$235,000

A simple method for understanding how Weber Light Aircraft computed its variable costing net operating income figures is to focus on the contribution margin per aircraft sold, which is computed as follows:

Contribution Margin per Aircraft Sold		
Selling price per aircraft		$100,000
Variable production cost per aircraft	$25,000	
Variable selling and administrative expense per aircraft	10,000	35,000
Contribution margin per aircraft		$ 65,000

The variable costing net operating income for each period can always be computed by multiplying the number of units sold by the contribution margin per unit and then subtracting total fixed costs. For Weber Light Aircraft these computations would appear as follows:

	January	February	March
Number of aircraft sold	1	1	5
Contribution margin per aircraft	× $65,000	× $65,000	× $65,000
Total contribution margin	$65,000	$65,000	$325,000
Total fixed expenses	90,000	90,000	90,000
Net operating income (loss)	$(25,000)	$(25,000)	$235,000

Notice, January and February have the same net operating loss. This occurs because one aircraft was sold in each month and, as previously mentioned, the selling price per aircraft, variable cost per aircraft, and total monthly fixed expenses remain constant.

Absorption Costing Income Statement

As we begin the absorption costing portion of the example, remember that the only reason absorption costing income differs from variable costing is that the methods account for fixed manufacturing overhead differently. Under absorption costing, fixed manufacturing overhead is included in product costs. In variable costing, fixed manufacturing overhead is not included in product costs and instead is treated as a period expense just like selling and administrative expenses.

The first step in preparing Weber's absorption costing income statements for January, February, and March, is to determine the company's unit product costs for each month as follows[1]:

Absorption Costing Unit Product Cost	January	February	March
Direct materials	$19,000	$19,000	$19,000
Direct labor	5,000	5,000	5,000
Variable manufacturing overhead	1,000	1,000	1,000
Fixed manufacturing overhead ($70,000 ÷ 1 unit produced in January; $70,000 ÷ 2 units produced in February; $70,000 ÷ 4 units produced in March)	70,000	35,000	17,500
Absorption costing unit product cost	$95,000	$60,000	$42,500

Notice that in each month, Weber's fixed manufacturing overhead cost of $70,000 is divided by the number of units produced to determine the fixed manufacturing overhead cost per unit.

Given these unit product costs, the company's absorption costing net operating income in each month would be determined as shown in Exhibit 6–3.

The sales for all three months in Exhibit 6–3 are the same as the sales shown in the variable costing income statements. The January cost of goods sold consists of one unit produced during January at a cost of $95,000 according to the absorption costing system. The February cost of goods sold consists of one unit produced during February at a cost of $60,000 according to the absorption costing system. The March cost of goods sold ($230,000) consists of one unit produced during February at an absorption cost of $60,000 plus four units produced in March with a total absorption cost of $170,000 (= 4 units produced × $42,500 per unit). The selling and administrative expenses equal the amounts reported in the variable costing income statements; however they are reported as one amount rather than being separated into variable and fixed components.

EXHIBIT 6–3
Absorption Costing Income Statements

Absorption Costing Income Statements	January	February	March
Sales	$100,000	$100,000	$500,000
Cost of goods sold ($95,000 × 1 unit; $60,000 × 1 unit; $60,000 × 1 unit + $42,500 × 4 units)	95,000	60,000	230,000
Gross margin	5,000	40,000	270,000
Selling and administrative expenses	30,000	30,000	70,000
Net operating income (loss)	$(25,000)	$ 10,000	$200,000

[1] For simplicity, we assume in this section that an actual costing system is used in which actual costs are spread over the units produced during the period. If a predetermined overhead rate were used, the analysis would be similar, but more complex.

Note that even though sales were exactly the same in January and February and the cost structure did not change, net operating income was $35,000 higher in February than in January under absorption costing. This occurs because one aircraft produced in February is not sold until March. This aircraft has $35,000 of fixed manufacturing overhead attached to it that was incurred in February, but will not be recorded as part of cost of goods sold until March.

Contrasting the variable costing and absorption costing income statements in Exhibits 6–2 and 6–3, note that net operating income is the same in January under variable costing and absorption costing, but differs in the other two months. We will discuss this in some depth shortly. Also note that the format of the variable costing income statement differs from the absorption costing income statement. An absorption costing income statement categorizes costs by function—manufacturing versus selling and administrative. All of the manufacturing costs flow through the absorption costing cost of goods sold and all of the selling and administrative costs are listed separately as period expenses. In contrast, in the contribution approach, costs are categorized according to how they behave. All of the variable expenses are listed together and all of the fixed expenses are listed together. The variable expenses category includes manufacturing costs (i.e., variable cost of goods sold) as well as selling and administrative expenses. The fixed expenses category also includes both manufacturing costs and selling and administrative expenses.

IN BUSINESS

THE BEHAVIORAL SIDE OF CALCULATING UNIT PRODUCT COSTS

In 2004, Andreas STIHL, a manufacturer of chain saws and other landscaping products, asked its U.S. subsidiary, STIHL Inc., to replace its absorption costing income statements with the variable costing approach. From a computer systems standpoint, the change was not disruptive because STIHL used an enterprise system called SAP that accommodates both absorption and variable costing. However, from a behavioral standpoint, STIHL felt the change could be very disruptive. For example, STIHL's senior managers were keenly aware that the variable costing approach reported lower unit product costs than the absorption costing approach. Given this reality, the sales force might be inclined to erroneously conclude that each product had magically become more profitable, thereby justifying ill-advised price reductions. Because of behavioral concerns such as this, STIHL worked hard to teach its employees how to interpret a variable costing income statement.

Source: Carl S. Smith, "Going for GPK: STIHL Moves Toward This Costing System in the United States," *Strategic Finance*, April 2005, pp. 36–39.

Reconciliation of Variable Costing with Absorption Costing Income

LEARNING OBJECTIVE 3
Reconcile variable costing and absorption costing net operating incomes and explain why the two amounts differ.

As noted earlier, variable costing and absorption costing net operating incomes may not be the same. In the case of Weber Light Aircraft, the net operating incomes are the same in January, but differ in the other two months. These differences occur because under absorption costing some fixed manufacturing overhead is capitalized in inventories (i.e., included in product costs) rather than currently expensed on the income statement. If inventories increase during a period, under absorption costing some of the fixed manufacturing overhead of the current period will be *deferred* in ending inventories. For example, in February two aircraft were produced and each carried with it $35,000 (= $70,000 ÷ 2 aircraft produced) in fixed manufacturing overhead. Since only one aircraft was sold, $35,000 of this fixed manufacturing overhead was on February's absorption costing income statement as part of cost of goods sold, but $35,000 would have been on the balance sheet as part of finished goods inventories. In contrast, under variable costing *all* of the $70,000 of fixed manufacturing overhead appeared on the February income statement as a period expense. Consequently, net operating income was higher under absorption costing than under variable costing by $35,000 in February. This was reversed in March when four units were produced, but five were sold. In March, under absorption costing $105,000 of fixed manufacturing overhead was included in cost of goods sold ($35,000 for the unit produced in February and sold in March plus $17,500 for each of the four units produced and sold in March), but only $70,000 was recognized as a period expense under variable costing. Hence, the net operating income in March was $35,000 lower under absorption costing than under variable costing.

In general, when the units produced exceed unit sales and hence inventories increase, net operating income is higher under absorption costing than under variable costing. This occurs because some of the fixed manufacturing overhead of the period is *deferred* in inventories under absorption costing. In contrast, when unit sales exceed the units produced and hence inventories decrease, net operating income is lower under absorption costing than under variable costing. This occurs because some of the fixed manufacturing overhead of previous periods is *released* from inventories under absorption costing. When the units produced and unit sales are equal, no change in inventories occurs and absorption costing and variable costing net operating incomes are the same.[2]

Variable costing and absorption costing net operating incomes can be reconciled by determining how much fixed manufacturing overhead was deferred in, or released from, inventories during the period:

Fixed Manufacturing Overhead Deferred in, or Released from, Inventories under Absorption Costing

	January	February	March
Fixed manufacturing overhead in beginning inventories	$0	$ 0	$ 35,000
Fixed manufacturing overhead in ending inventories	0	35,000	0
Fixed manufacturing overhead deferred in (released from) inventories	$0	$35,000	$(35,000)

The reconciliation would then be reported as shown in Exhibit 6–4:

EXHIBIT 6–4
Reconciliation of Variable Costing and Absorption Costing Net Operating Incomes

Reconciliation of Variable Costing and Absorption Costing Net Operating Incomes

	January	February	March
Variable costing net operating income (loss)	$(25,000)	$(25,000)	$235,000
Add (deduct) fixed manufacturing overhead deferred in (released from) inventory under absorption costing	0	35,000	(35,000)
Absorption costing net operating income (loss) . . .	$(25,000)	$ 10,000	$200,000

Again note that the difference between variable costing net operating income and absorption costing net operating income is entirely due to the amount of fixed manufacturing overhead that is deferred in, or released from, inventories during the period

[2] These general statements about the relation between variable costing and absorption costing net operating income assume LIFO is used to value inventories. Even when LIFO is not used, the general statements tend to be correct. Although U.S. GAAP allows LIFO and FIFO inventory flow assumptions, International Financial Reporting Standards do not allow a LIFO inventory flow assumption.

EXHIBIT 6–5
Comparative Income Effects—Absorption and Variable Costing

Relation between Production and Sales for the Period	Effect on Inventories	Relation between Absorption and Variable Costing Net Operating Incomes
Units produced = Units sold	No change in inventories	Absorption costing net operating income = Variable costing net operating income
Units produced > Units sold	Inventories increase	Absorption costing net operating income > Variable costing net operating income*
Units produced < Units sold	Inventories decrease	Absorption costing net operating income < Variable costing net operating income†

*Net operating income is higher under absorption costing because fixed manufacturing overhead cost is *deferred* in inventory under absorption costing as inventories increase.
†Net operating income is lower under absorption costing because fixed manufacturing overhead cost is *released* from inventory under absorption costing as inventories decrease.

under absorption costing. Changes in inventories affect absorption costing net operating income—they do not affect variable costing net operating income, providing that variable manufacturing costs per unit are stable.

The reasons for differences between variable and absorption costing net operating incomes are summarized in Exhibit 6–5. When the units produced equal the units sold, as in January for Weber Light Aircraft, absorption costing net operating income will equal variable costing net operating income. This occurs because when production equals sales, all of the fixed manufacturing overhead incurred in the current period flows through to the income statement under both methods. For companies that use Lean Production, the number of units produced tends to equal the number of units sold. This occurs because goods are produced in response to customer orders, thereby eliminating finished goods inventories and reducing work in process inventory to almost nothing. So, when a company uses Lean Production differences in variable costing and absorption costing net operating income will largely disappear.

When the units produced exceed the units sold, absorption costing net operating income will exceed variable costing net operating income. This occurs because inventories have increased; therefore, under absorption costing some of the fixed manufacturing overhead incurred in the current period is deferred in ending inventories on the balance sheet, whereas under variable costing all of the fixed manufacturing overhead incurred in the current period flows through to the income statement. In contrast, when the units produced are less than the units sold, absorption costing net operating income will be less than variable costing net operating income. This occurs because inventories have decreased; therefore, under absorption costing fixed manufacturing overhead that had been deferred in inventories during a prior period flows through to the current period's income statement together with all of the fixed manufacturing overhead incurred during the current period. Under variable costing, just the fixed manufacturing overhead of the current period flows through to the income statement.

IN BUSINESS

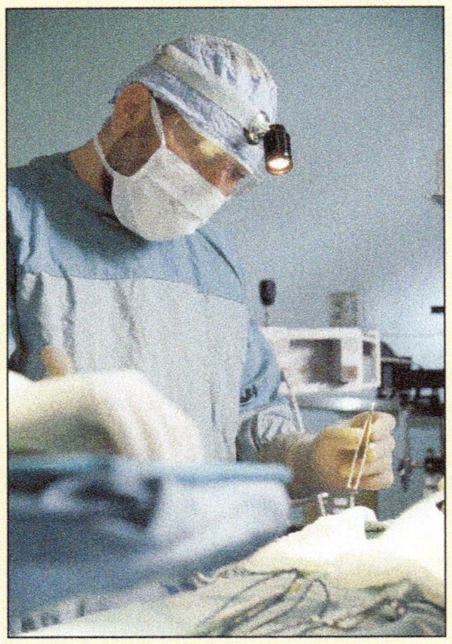

LEAN MANUFACTURING SHRINKS INVENTORIES

Conmed, a surgical device maker in Utica, New York, switched to lean manufacturing by replacing its assembly lines with U-shaped production cells. It also started producing only enough units to satisfy customer demand rather than producing as many units as possible and storing them in warehouses. The company calculated that its customers use one of its disposable surgical devices every 90 seconds, so that is precisely how often it produces a new unit. Its assembly area for fluid-injection devices used to occupy 3,300 square feet of space and contained $93,000 worth of parts. Now the company produces its fluid-injection devices in 660 square feet of space while maintaining only $6,000 of parts inventory.

When Conmed adopted lean manufacturing, it substantially reduced its finished goods inventories. What impact do you think this initial reduction in inventories may have had on net operating income? Why?

Source: Pete Engardio, "Lean and Mean Gets Extreme," *BusinessWeek,* March 23 and 30, 2009, pp. 60–62.

Advantages of Variable Costing and the Contribution Approach

Variable costing, together with the contribution approach, offers appealing advantages for internal reports. This section discusses four of those advantages.

Enabling CVP Analysis

CVP analysis requires that we break costs down into their fixed and variable components. Because variable costing income statements categorize costs as fixed and variable, it is much easier to use this income statement format to perform CVP analysis than attempting to use the absorption costing format, which mixes together fixed and variable costs.

Moreover, absorption costing net operating income may or may not agree with the results of CVP analysis. For example, let's suppose that you are interested in computing the sales that would be necessary to generate a target profit of $235,000 at Weber Light Aircraft. A CVP analysis based on the January variable costing income statement from Exhibit 6–2 would proceed as follows:

Sales (a)	$100,000
Contribution margin (b)	$65,000
Contribution margin ratio (b) ÷ (a)	65%
Total fixed expenses	$90,000

$$\text{Dollar sales to attain target profit} = \frac{\text{Target profit} + \text{Fixed expenses}}{\text{CM ratio}}$$

$$= \frac{\$235{,}000 + \$90{,}000}{0.65} = \$500{,}000$$

Thus, a CVP analysis based on the January variable costing income statement predicts that the net operating income would be $235,000 when sales are $500,000. And indeed, the net operating income under variable costing *is* $235,000 when the sales are $500,000 in March. However, the net operating income under absorption costing is *not* $235,000 in March, even though the sales are $500,000. Why is this? The reason is that under absorption costing, net operating income can be distorted by changes in inventories. In March, inventories decreased, so some of the fixed manufacturing overhead that had been deferred in February's ending inventories was released to the March income statement, resulting in a net operating income that is $35,000 lower than the $235,000 predicted by CVP analysis. If inventories had increased in March, the opposite would have occurred—the absorption costing net operating income would have been higher than the $235,000 predicted by CVP analysis.

Explaining Changes in Net Operating Income

The variable costing income statements in Exhibit 6–2 are clear and easy to understand. All other things the same, when sales go up, net operating income goes up. When sales go down, net operating income goes down. When sales are constant, net operating income is constant. The number of unit produced does not affect net operating income.

Absorption costing income statements can be confusing and are easily misinterpreted. Look again at the absorption costing income statements in Exhibit 6–3; a manager might wonder why net operating income went up from January to February even though sales were exactly the same. Was it a result of lower selling costs, more efficient operations, or was it some other factor? In fact, it was simply because the number of units produced exceeded the number of units sold in February and so some of the fixed manufacturing overhead costs were deferred in inventories in that month. These costs have not gone away—they will eventually flow through to the income statement in a later period when inventories go down. There is no way to tell this from the absorption costing income statements.

To avoid mistakes when absorption costing is used, readers of financial statements should be alert to changes in inventory levels. Under absorption costing, if inventories increase, fixed manufacturing overhead costs are deferred in inventories, which in turn increases net operating income. If inventories decrease, fixed manufacturing overhead costs are released from inventories, which in turn decreases net operating income. Thus, when absorption costing is used, fluctuations in net operating income can be due to changes in inventories rather than to changes in sales.

Supporting Decision Making

The variable costing method correctly identifies the additional variable costs that will be incurred to make one more unit. It also emphasizes the impact of fixed costs on profits. The total amount of fixed manufacturing costs appears explicitly on the income statement, highlighting that the whole amount of fixed manufacturing costs must be covered for the company to be truly profitable. In the Weber Light Aircraft example, the variable costing income statements correctly report that the cost of producing another unit is $25,000 and they explicitly recognize that $70,000 of fixed manufactured overhead must be covered to earn a profit.

Under absorption costing, fixed manufacturing overhead costs appear to be variable with respect to the number of units sold, but they are not. For example, in January, the absorption unit product cost at Weber Light Aircraft is $95,000, but the variable portion of this cost is only $25,000. The fixed overhead costs of $70,000 are commingled with variable production costs, thereby obscuring the impact of fixed overhead costs on profits. Because absorption unit product costs are stated on a per unit basis, managers may mistakenly believe that if another unit is produced, it will cost the company $95,000. But of course it would not. The cost of producing another unit would be only $25,000. Misinterpreting absorption unit product costs as variable can lead to many problems, including inappropriate pricing decisions and decisions to drop products that are in fact profitable.

Adapting to the Theory of Constraints

The Theory of Constraints (TOC), which was introduced in Chapter 1, suggests that the key to improving a company's profits is managing its constraints. For reasons that will be discussed in a later chapter, this requires careful identification of each product's variable costs. Consequently, companies involved in TOC use a form of variable costing.

Variable costing income statements require one adjustment to support the TOC approach. Direct labor costs need to be removed from variable production costs and reported as part of the fixed manufacturing costs that are entirely expensed in the period incurred. The TOC treats direct labor costs as a fixed cost for three reasons. First, even though direct labor workers may be paid on an hourly basis, many companies have a commitment—sometimes enforced by labor contracts or by law—to guarantee workers a minimum number of paid hours. Second, direct labor is not usually the constraint; therefore, there is no reason to increase it. Hiring more direct labor workers would increase costs without increasing the output of saleable products and services. Third, TOC emphasizes continuous improvement to maintain competitiveness. Without committed and enthusiastic employees, sustained continuous improvement is virtually impossible. Because layoffs often have devastating effects on employee morale, managers involved in TOC are extremely reluctant to lay off employees.

For these reasons, most managers in TOC companies regard direct labor as a committed-fixed cost rather than a variable cost. Hence, in the modified form of variable costing used in TOC companies, direct labor is not usually classified as a product cost.

Segmented Income Statements and the Contribution Approach

LEARNING OBJECTIVE 4
Prepare a segmented income statement that differentiates traceable fixed costs from common fixed costs and use it to make decisions.

In the remainder of the chapter, we'll learn how to use the contribution approach to construct income statements for business segments. These segmented income statements are useful for analyzing the profitability of segments, making decisions, and measuring the performance of segment managers.

Traceable and Common Fixed Costs and the Segment Margin

You need to understand three new terms to prepare segmented income statements using the contribution approach—*traceable fixed cost, common fixed cost,* and *segment margin.*

A **traceable fixed cost** of a segment is a fixed cost that is incurred because of the existence of the segment—if the segment had never existed, the fixed cost would not have been incurred; and if the segment were eliminated, the fixed cost would disappear. Examples of traceable fixed costs include the following:

- The salary of the Fritos product manager at PepsiCo is a *traceable* fixed cost of the Fritos business segment of PepsiCo.
- The maintenance cost for the building in which Boeing 747s are assembled is a *traceable* fixed cost of the 747 business segment of Boeing.
- The liability insurance at Disney World is a *traceable* fixed cost of the Disney World business segment of the Disney Corporation.

A **common fixed cost** is a fixed cost that supports the operations of more than one segment, but is not traceable in whole or in part to any one segment. Even if a segment were entirely eliminated, there would be no change in a true common fixed cost. For example:

- The salary of the CEO of General Motors is a *common* fixed cost of the various divisions of General Motors.
- The cost of heating a Safeway or Kroger grocery store is a *common* fixed cost of the store's various departments—groceries, produce, bakery, meat, etc.

- The cost of the receptionist's salary at an office shared by a number of doctors is a *common* fixed cost of the doctors. The cost is traceable to the office, but not to individual doctors.

To prepare a segmented income statement, variable expenses are deducted from sales to yield the contribution margin for the segment. The contribution margin tells us what happens to profits as volume changes—holding a segment's capacity and fixed costs constant. The contribution margin is especially useful in decisions involving temporary uses of capacity such as special orders. These types of decisions often involve only variable costs and revenues—the two components of contribution margin.

The **segment margin** is obtained by deducting the traceable fixed costs of a segment from the segment's contribution margin. It represents the margin available after a segment has covered all of its own costs. *The segment margin is the best gauge of the long-run profitability of a segment* because it includes only those costs that are caused by the segment. If a segment can't cover its own costs, then that segment probably should be dropped (unless it has important side effects on other segments). Notice, common fixed costs are not allocated to segments.

From a decision-making point of view, the segment margin is most useful in major decisions that affect capacity such as dropping a segment. By contrast, as we noted earlier, the contribution margin is most useful in decisions involving short-run changes in volume, such as pricing special orders that involve temporary use of existing capacity.

IN BUSINESS

HAS THE INTERNET KILLED CATALOGS?

Smith & Hawken, an outdoor-accessories retailer, has experienced growing Internet sales and declining catalog sales. These trends seem consistent with conventional wisdom, which suggests that the Internet will make catalogs obsolete. Yet, Smith & Hawken, like many retailers with growing Internet sales, has no plans to discontinue its catalogs. In fact, the total number of catalogs mailed in the United States by all companies has jumped from 16.6 billion in 2002 to 19.2 billion in 2005. Why?

Catalog shoppers and Internet shoppers are not independent customer segments. Catalog shoppers frequently choose to complete their sales transactions online rather than placing telephone orders. This explains why catalogs remain a compelling marketing medium even though catalog sales are declining for many companies. If retailers separately analyze catalog sales and Internet sales, they may discontinue the catalogs segment while overlooking the adverse impact of this decision on Internet segment margins.

Source: Louise Lee, "Catalogs, Catalogs, Everywhere," *BusinessWeek*, December 4, 2006, pp. 32–34.

Identifying Traceable Fixed Costs

The distinction between traceable and common fixed costs is crucial in segment reporting because traceable fixed costs are charged to segments and common fixed costs are not. In an actual situation, it is sometimes hard to determine whether a cost should be classified as traceable or common.

The general guideline is to treat as traceable costs *only those costs that would disappear over time if the segment itself disappeared.* For example, if one division within a company were sold or discontinued, it would no longer be necessary to pay that division manager's salary. Therefore the division manager's salary would be classified as a traceable fixed cost of the division. On the other hand, the president of the company undoubtedly would continue to be paid even if one of many divisions was dropped. In fact, he or she might even be paid more if dropping the division was a good idea. Therefore, the president's salary is common to the company's divisions and should not be charged to them.

When assigning costs to segments, the key point is to resist the temptation to allocate costs (such as depreciation of corporate facilities) that are clearly common and that will continue regardless of whether the segment exists or not. *Any allocation of common costs to segments reduces the value of the segment margin as a measure of long-run segment profitability and segment performance.*

Traceable Costs Can Become Common Costs

Fixed costs that are traceable to one segment may be a common cost of another segment. For example, United Airlines might want a segmented income statement that shows the segment margin for a particular flight from Chicago to Paris further broken down into first-class, business-class, and economy-class segment margins. The airline must pay a substantial landing fee at Charles DeGaulle airport in Paris. This fixed landing fee is a traceable cost of the flight, but it is a common cost of the first-class, business-class, and economy-class segments. Even if the first-class cabin is empty, the entire landing fee must be paid. So the landing fee is not a traceable cost of the first-class cabin. But on the other hand, paying the fee is necessary in order to have any first-class, business-class, or economy-class passengers. So the landing fee is a common cost of these three classes.

Segmented Income Statements—An Example

ProphetMax, Inc., is a rapidly growing computer software company. Exhibit 6–6 shows its variable costing income statement for the most recent month. As the company has grown, its senior managers have asked for segmented income statements that could be used to make decisions and evaluate managerial performance. ProphetMax's controller responded by creating examples of contribution format income statements segmented by the company's divisions, product lines, and sales channels. She created Exhibit 6–7 to explain that ProphetMax's profits can be segmented into its two divisions—the Business Products Division and the Consumer Products Division. The Consumer Products Division's profits can be further segmented into the Clip Art and Computer Games product lines. Finally, the Computer Games product line's profits (within the Consumer Products Division) can be segmented into the Online and Retail Stores sales channels.

IN BUSINESS

COMPUTING SEGMENT MARGINS HELPS AN ENTREPRENEUR

In 2001, Victoria Pappas Collection, a small company specializing in women's sportswear, reported a net loss of $280,000 on sales of $1 million. When the company's founder, Vickie Giannukos, segmented her company's income statement into the six markets that she was serving, the results were revealing. The Dallas and Atlanta markets generated $825,000 of sales and incurred $90,000 of traceable fixed costs. The other four markets combined produced $175,000 of sales and also incurred $90,000 of traceable fixed costs. Given the average contribution margin ratio of 38%, the Dallas and Atlanta markets earned a segment margin of $223,500 [($825,000 × 38%) − $90,000] while the other four markets combined incurred a loss of $23,500 [($175,000 × 38%) − $90,000].

Vicky had made a common mistake—she chased every possible dollar of sales without knowing if her efforts were profitable. Based on her segmented income statements, she discontinued operations in three cities and hired a new sales representative in Los Angeles. She decided to focus on growing sales in Dallas and Atlanta while deferring expansion into new markets until it could be done profitably.

Source: Norm Brodsky, "The Thin Red Line," *Inc.* Magazine, January 2004, pp. 49–52.

EXHIBIT 6–6
ProphetMax, Inc. Variable Costing Income Statement

ProphetMax, Inc. Variable Costing Income Statement	
Sales	$500,000
Variable expenses:	
Variable cost of goods sold	180,000
Other variable expenses	50,000
Total variable expenses	230,000
Contribution margin	270,000
Fixed expenses	255,000
Net operating income	$ 15,000

EXHIBIT 6–7
ProphetMax, Inc.: Examples of Business Segments

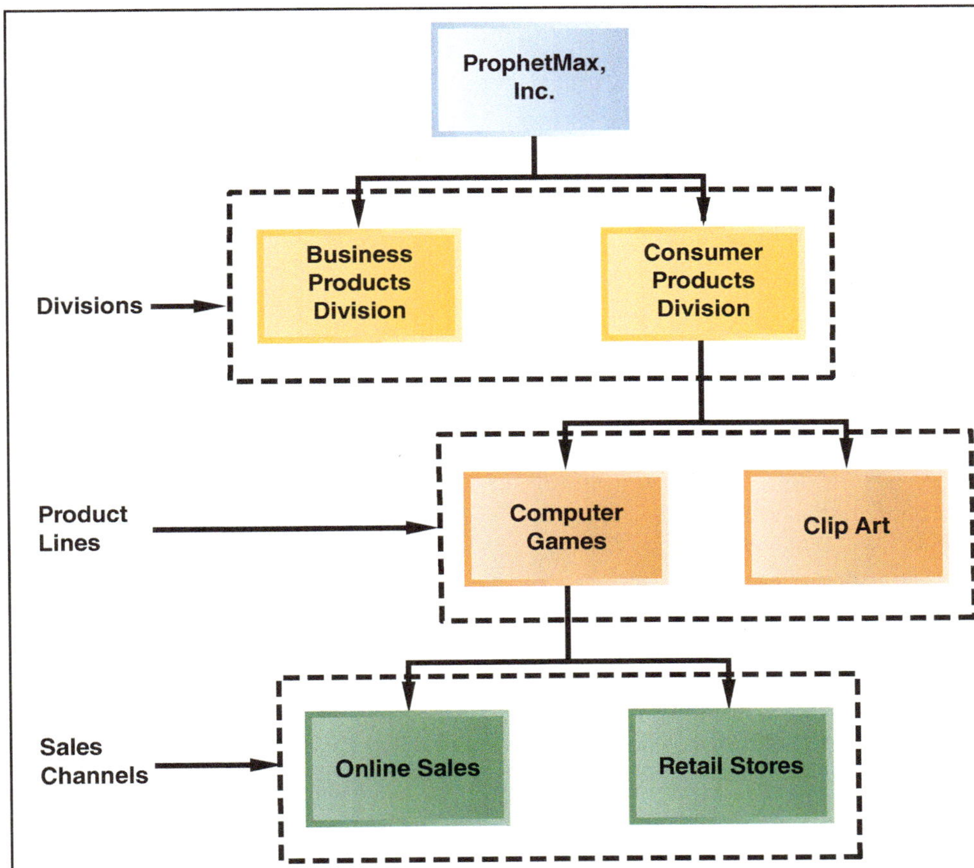

Levels of Segmented Income Statements

Exhibit 6–8, on the next page, contains the controller's segmented income statements for the segments depicted in Exhibit 6–7. The contribution format income statement for the entire company appears at the very top of the exhibit under the column labeled Total Company. Notice, the net operating income shown in this column ($15,000) is the same as the net operating income shown in Exhibit 6–6. Immediately to the right of the Total Company column are two columns—one for each of the two divisions. We can see that the Business Products Division's traceable fixed expenses are $90,000 and the Consumer Products Division's are $80,000. These $170,000 of traceable fixed expenses (as shown in the Total Company column) plus the $85,000 of common fixed expenses not traceable to individual divisions equals ProphetMax's total fixed expenses ($255,000) as shown in Exhibit 6–6. We can also see that the Business Products Division's segment margin is $60,000 and the Consumer

EXHIBIT 6–8
ProphetMax, Inc.—Segmented Income Statements in the Contribution Format

Segments Defined as Divisions

	Total Company	Divisions: Business Products Division	Divisions: Consumer Products Division
Sales	$500,000	$300,000	$200,000
Variable expenses:			
Variable cost of goods sold	180,000	120,000	60,000
Other variable expenses	50,000	30,000	20,000
Total variable expenses	230,000	150,000	80,000
Contribution margin	270,000	150,000	120,000
Traceable fixed expenses	170,000	90,000	80,000
Divisional segment margin	100,000	$ 60,000	$ 40,000
Common fixed expenses not traceable to individual divisions	85,000		
Net operating income	$ 15,000		

Segments Defined as Product Lines of the Consumer Products Division

	Consumer Products Division	Product Line: Clip Art	Product Line: Computer Games
Sales	$200,000	$75,000	$125,000
Variable expenses:			
Variable cost of goods sold	60,000	20,000	40,000
Other variable expenses	20,000	5,000	15,000
Total variable expenses	80,000	25,000	55,000
Contribution margin	120,000	50,000	70,000
Traceable fixed expenses	70,000	30,000	40,000
Product-line segment margin	50,000	$20,000	$ 30,000
Common fixed expenses not traceable to individual product lines	10,000		
Divisional segment margin	$ 40,000		

Segments Defined as Sales Channels for One Product Line, Computer Games, of the Consumer Products Division

	Computer Games	Sales Channels: Online Sales	Sales Channels: Retail Stores
Sales	$125,000	$100,000	$25,000
Variable expenses:			
Variable cost of goods sold	40,000	32,000	8,000
Other variable expenses	15,000	5,000	10,000
Total variable expenses	55,000	37,000	18,000
Contribution margin	70,000	63,000	7,000
Traceable fixed expenses	25,000	15,000	10,000
Sales-channel segment margin	45,000	$ 48,000	$ (3,000)
Common fixed expenses not traceable to individual sales channels	15,000		
Product-line segment margin	$ 30,000		

Products Division's is $40,000. These segment margins show the company's divisional managers how much each of their divisions is contributing to the company's profits.

The middle portion of Exhibit 6–8 further segments the Consumer Products Division into its two product lines, Clip Art and Computer Games. The dual nature of some fixed costs can be seen in this portion of the exhibit. Notice, in the top portion of Exhibit 6–8 when segments are defined as divisions, the Consumer Products Division has $80,000 in traceable fixed expenses. However, when we drill down to the product lines (in the middle portion of the exhibit), only $70,000 of the $80,000 cost that was traceable to the Consumer Products Division is traceable to the product lines. The other $10,000 becomes a common fixed cost of the two product lines of the Consumer Products Division.

Why would $10,000 of traceable fixed costs become a common fixed cost when the division is divided into product lines? The $10,000 is the monthly depreciation expense on a machine that is used to encase products in tamper-proof packages for the consumer market. The depreciation expense is a traceable cost of the Consumer Products Division as a whole, but it is a common cost of the division's two product lines. Even if one of the product lines were discontinued entirely, the machine would still be used to wrap the remaining products. Therefore, none of the depreciation expense can really be traced to individual products.

The $70,000 traceable fixed cost of the product lines consists of the costs of product specific advertising. A total of $30,000 was spent on advertising clip art and $40,000 was spent on advertising computer games. Clearly, these costs can be traced to the individual product lines.

Segmented Income Statements and Decision Making

The bottom portion of Exhibit 6–8 can be used to illustrate how segmented income statements support decision making. It further segments the Computer Games product line into its two sales channels, Online Sales and Retail Stores. The Online Sales segment has a segment margin of $48,000 and the Retail Stores segment has a segment margin of $(3,000). Let's assume that ProphetMax wants to know the profit impact of discontinuing the sale of computer games through its Retail Stores sales channel. The company believes that online sales of its computer games will increase 10% if it discontinues the Retail Stores sales channel. It also believes that the Business Products Division and Clip Art product line will be unaffected by this decision. How would you compute the profit impact of this decision?

The first step is to calculate the profit impact of the Retail Stores sales channel disappearing. If this sales channel disappears, we assume its sales, variable expenses, and traceable fixed expenses would all disappear. The quickest way to summarize these financial impacts is to focus on the Retail Stores' segment margin. In other words, if the Retail Stores sales channel disappears, then its segment margin of a loss of $3,000 would also disappear. This would increase ProphetMax's net operating income by $3,000. The second step is to calculate the profit impact of increasing online sales of computer games by 10%. To perform this calculation, we assume that the Online Sales total traceable fixed expenses ($15,000) remain constant and its contribution margin ratio remains constant at 63% (= $63,000 ÷ $100,000). If online sales increase $10,000 (= $100,000 × 10%), then the Online Sales segment's contribution margin will increase by $6,300 (= $10,000 × 63%). The overall profit impact of discontinuing the Retail Stores sales channel can be summarized as follows:

Avoidance of the retail segment's loss	$3,000
Online Sales additional contribution margin	6,300
Increase in ProphetMax's net operating income	$9,300

Segmented Income Statements—Common Mistakes

All of the costs attributable to a segment—and only those costs—should be assigned to the segment. Unfortunately, companies often make mistakes when assigning costs to segments. They omit some costs, inappropriately assign traceable fixed costs, and arbitrarily allocate common fixed costs.

Omission of Costs

The costs assigned to a segment should include all costs attributable to that segment from the company's entire value chain. All of these functions, from research and development, through product design, manufacturing, marketing, distribution, and customer service, are required to bring a product or service to the customer and generate revenues.

However, only manufacturing costs are included in product costs under absorption costing, which is widely regarded as required for external financial reporting. To avoid having to maintain two costing systems and to provide consistency between internal and external reports, many companies also use absorption costing for their internal reports such as segmented income statements. As a result, such companies omit from their profitability analysis part or all of the "upstream" costs in the value chain, which consist of research and development and product design, and the "downstream" costs, which consist of marketing, distribution, and customer service. Yet these nonmanufacturing costs are just as essential in determining product profitability as are the manufacturing costs. These upstream and downstream costs, which are usually included in selling and administrative expenses on absorption costing income statements, can represent half or more of the total costs of an organization. If either the upstream or downstream costs are omitted in profitability analysis, then the product is undercosted and management may unwittingly develop and maintain products that in the long run result in losses.

Inappropriate Methods for Assigning Traceable Costs among Segments

In addition to omitting costs, many companies do not correctly handle traceable fixed expenses on segmented income statements. First, they do not trace fixed expenses to segments even when it is feasible to do so. Second, they use inappropriate allocation bases to allocate traceable fixed expenses to segments.

Failure to Trace Costs Directly Costs that can be traced directly to a specific segment should be charged directly to that segment and should not be allocated to other segments. For example, the rent for a branch office of an insurance company should be charged directly to the branch office rather than included in a companywide overhead pool and then spread throughout the company.

Inappropriate Allocation Base Some companies use arbitrary allocation bases to allocate costs to segments. For example, some companies allocate selling and administrative expenses on the basis of sales revenues. Thus, if a segment generates 20% of total company sales, it would be allocated 20% of the company's selling and administrative expenses as its "fair share." This same basic procedure is followed if cost of goods sold or some other measure is used as the allocation base.

Costs should be allocated to segments for internal decision-making purposes only when the allocation base actually drives the cost being allocated (or is very highly correlated with the real cost driver). For example, sales should be used to allocate selling and administrative expenses only if a 10% increase in sales will result in a 10% increase in selling and administrative expenses. To the extent that selling and administrative expenses are not driven by sales volume, these expenses will be improperly allocated—with a disproportionately high percentage of the selling and administrative expenses assigned to the segments with the largest sales.

Arbitrarily Dividing Common Costs among Segments

The third business practice that leads to distorted segment costs is the practice of assigning nontraceable costs to segments. For example, some companies allocate the common costs of the corporate headquarters building to products on segment reports. However, in a multiproduct company, no single product is likely to be responsible for any significant amount of this cost. Even if a product were eliminated entirely, there would usually be no significant effect on any of the costs of the corporate headquarters building. In short, there is no cause-and-effect relation between the cost of the corporate headquarters building and the existence of any one product. As a consequence, any allocation of the cost of the corporate headquarters building to the products must be arbitrary.

Common costs like the costs of the corporate headquarters building are necessary, of course, to have a functioning organization. The practice of arbitrarily allocating common costs to segments is often justified on the grounds that "someone" has to "cover the common costs." While it is undeniably true that a company must cover its common costs to earn a profit, arbitrarily allocating common costs to segments does not ensure that this will happen. In fact, adding a share of common costs to the real costs of a segment may make an otherwise profitable segment appear to be unprofitable. If a manager eliminates the apparently unprofitable segment, the real traceable costs of the segment will be saved, but its revenues will be lost. And what happens to the common fixed costs that were allocated to the segment? They don't disappear; they are reallocated to the remaining segments of the company. That makes all of the remaining segments appear to be less profitable—possibly resulting in dropping other segments. The net effect will be to reduce the overall profits of the company and make it even more difficult to "cover the common costs."

Additionally, common fixed costs are not manageable by the manager to whom they are arbitrarily allocated; they are the responsibility of higher-level managers. When common fixed costs are allocated to managers, they are held responsible for those costs even though they cannot control them.

IN BUSINESS

MANAGING PRODUCT INNOVATION AT GOOGLE

Marissa Mayer, Google's vice president for search products and user experience, believes that the company's future success hinges on innovation. She encourages risk-taking and readily acknowledges that 60–80% of the company's new products will fail. However, creating an organizational culture that embraces failure also helps produce the new product introductions that should sustain the company's future sales growth. Google's senior managers can use segmented income statements to identify the unprofitable products that should be discontinued and to track the performance of thriving new product innovations.

Source: Ben Elgin, "So Much Fanfare, So Few Hits," *BusinessWeek*, July 10, 2006, pp. 26–29.

Income Statements—An External Reporting Perspective

Companywide Income Statements

Practically speaking, absorption costing is required for external reports according to U.S. generally accepted accounting principles (GAAP).[3] Furthermore, International Financial Reporting Standards (IFRS) explicitly require companies to use absorption costing. Probably because of the cost and possible confusion of maintaining two separate costing systems—one for external reporting and one for internal reporting—most companies use absorption costing for their external and internal reports.

[3] The Financial Accounting Standards Board (FASB) has created a single source of authoritative nongovernmental U.S. generally accepted accounting principles (GAAP) called the FASB Accounting Standards Codification (FASB codification). Although the FASB codification does not explicitly disallow variable costing, it does explicitly prohibit companies from excluding all manufacturing overhead costs from product costs. It also provides an in-depth discussion of fixed overhead allocation to products, thereby implying that absorption costing is required for external reports. Although some companies expense significant elements of fixed manufacturing costs on their external reports, practically speaking, U.S. GAAP requires absorption costing for external reports.

With all of the advantages of the contribution approach, you may wonder why the absorption approach is used at all. While the answer is partly due to adhering to tradition, absorption costing is also attractive to many accountants and managers because they believe it better matches costs with revenues. Advocates of absorption costing argue that *all* manufacturing costs must be assigned to products in order to properly match the costs of producing units of product with their revenues when they are sold. The fixed costs of depreciation, taxes, insurance, supervisory salaries, and so on, are just as essential to manufacturing products as are the variable costs.

Advocates of variable costing argue that fixed manufacturing costs are not really the costs of any particular unit of product. These costs are incurred to have the *capacity* to make products during a particular period and will be incurred even if nothing is made during the period. Moreover, whether a unit is made or not, the fixed manufacturing costs will be exactly the same. Therefore, variable costing advocates argue that fixed manufacturing costs are not part of the costs of producing a particular unit of product, and thus, the matching principle dictates that fixed manufacturing costs should be charged to the current period.

Segmented Financial Information

U.S. GAAP and IFRS require that publicly traded companies include segmented financial and other data in their annual reports and that the segmented reports prepared for external users *must use the same methods and definitions that the companies use in internal segmented reports that are prepared to aid in making operating decisions.* This is a very unusual stipulation because companies are not ordinarily required to report the same data to external users that are used for internal decision-making purposes. This requirement creates incentives for publicly traded companies to avoid using the contribution format for internal segmented reports. Segmented contribution format income statements contain vital information that companies are often very reluctant to release to the public (and hence competitors). In addition, this requirement creates problems in reconciling internal and external reports.

IN BUSINESS

3M REPORTS SEGMENTED PROFITABILITY TO SHAREHOLDERS

In 2009, 3M Company reported segmented profitability to its shareholders by product lines and geographic areas. A portion of the company's segmented information is summarized below (all numbers are in millions):

	Net Sales	Net Operating Income
Product Lines:		
Industrial and transportation	$7,116	$1,238
Health care	$4,294	$1,350
Consumer and office	$3,471	$748
Safety, security, and protection services	$3,180	$745
Display and graphics	$3,132	$590
Electro and communications	$2,276	$322
Geographic Areas:		
United States	$8,509	$1,640
Asia Pacific	$6,120	$1,528
Europe, Middle East and Africa	$5,972	$1,003
Latin America and Canada	$2,516	$631

3M's annual report does not report the gross margins or contribution margins for its business segments. Why do you think this is the case?

Source: 3M Company, 2009 Annual Report.

Summary

Variable and absorption costing are alternative methods of determining unit product costs. Under variable costing, only those manufacturing costs that vary with output are treated as product costs. This includes direct materials, variable overhead, and ordinarily direct labor. Fixed manufacturing overhead is treated as a period cost and it is expensed on the income statement as incurred. By contrast, absorption costing treats fixed manufacturing overhead as a product cost, along with direct materials, direct labor, and variable overhead. Under both costing methods, selling and administrative expenses are treated as period costs and they are expensed on the income statement as incurred.

Because absorption costing treats fixed manufacturing overhead as a product cost, a portion of fixed manufacturing overhead is assigned to each unit as it is produced. If units of product are unsold at the end of a period, then the fixed manufacturing overhead cost attached to those units is carried with them into the inventory account and deferred to a future period. When these units are later sold, the fixed manufacturing overhead cost attached to them is released from the inventory account and charged against income as part of cost of goods sold. Thus, under absorption costing, it is possible to defer a portion of the fixed manufacturing overhead cost from one period to a future period through the inventory account.

Unfortunately, this shifting of fixed manufacturing overhead cost between periods can cause erratic fluctuations in net operating income and can result in confusion and unwise decisions. To guard against mistakes when they interpret income statement data, managers should be alert to changes in inventory levels or unit product costs during the period.

Segmented income statements provide information for evaluating the profitability and performance of divisions, product lines, sales territories, and other segments of a company. Under the contribution approach, variable costs and fixed costs are clearly distinguished from each other and only those costs that are traceable to a segment are assigned to the segment. A cost is considered traceable to a segment only if the cost is caused by the segment and could be avoided by eliminating the segment. Fixed common costs are not allocated to segments. The segment margin consists of revenues, less variable expenses, less traceable fixed expenses of the segment.

Review Problem 1: Contrasting Variable and Absorption Costing

Dexter Corporation produces and sells a single product, a wooden hand loom for weaving small items such as scarves. Selected cost and operating data relating to the product for two years are given below:

Selling price per unit	$50
Manufacturing costs:	
Variable per unit produced:	
Direct materials	$11
Direct labor	$6
Variable manufacturing overhead	$3
Fixed manufacturing overhead per year	$120,000
Selling and administrative expenses:	
Variable per unit sold	$4
Fixed per year	$70,000

	Year 1	Year 2
Units in beginning inventory	0	2,000
Units produced during the year	10,000	6,000
Units sold during the year	8,000	8,000
Units in ending inventory	2,000	0

Required:

1. Assume the company uses absorption costing.
   a. Compute the unit product cost in each year.
   b. Prepare an income statement for each year.

2. Assume the company uses variable costing.
   a. Compute the unit product cost in each year.
   b. Prepare an income statement for each year.
3. Reconcile the variable costing and absorption costing net operating incomes.

Solution to Review Problem 1

1. *a.* Under absorption costing, all manufacturing costs, variable and fixed, are included in unit product costs:

	Year 1	Year 2
Direct materials	$11	$11
Direct labor	6	6
Variable manufacturing overhead	3	3
Fixed manufacturing overhead		
($120,000 ÷ 10,000 units)	12	
($120,000 ÷ 6,000 units)		20
Absorption costing unit product cost	$32	$40

b. The absorption costing income statements follow:

	Year 1	Year 2
Sales (8,000 units × $50 per unit)	$400,000	$400,000
Cost of goods sold (8,000 units × $32 per unit); (2,000 units × $32 per unit) + (6,000 units × $40 per unit)	256,000	304,000
Gross margin	144,000	96,000
Selling and administrative expenses (8,000 units × $4 per unit + $70,000)	102,000	102,000
Net operating income (loss)	$ 42,000	$ (6,000)

2. *a.* Under variable costing, only the variable manufacturing costs are included in unit product costs:

	Year 1	Year 2
Direct materials	$11	$11
Direct labor	6	6
Variable manufacturing overhead	3	3
Variable costing unit product cost	$20	$20

b. The variable costing income statements follow:

	Year 1		Year 2	
Sales (8,000 units × $50 per unit)		$400,000		$400,000
Variable expenses:				
Variable cost of goods sold (8,000 units × $20 per unit)	$160,000		$160,000	
Variable selling and administrative expenses (8,000 units × $4 per unit)	32,000	192,000	32,000	192,000
Contribution margin		208,000		208,000
Fixed expenses:				
Fixed manufacturing overhead	120,000		120,000	
Fixed selling and administrative expenses	70,000	190,000	70,000	190,000
Net operating income		$ 18,000		$ 18,000

3. The reconciliation of the variable and absorption costing net operating incomes follows:

	Year 1	Year 2
Variable costing net operating income	$18,000	$18,000
Add fixed manufacturing overhead costs deferred in inventory under absorption costing (2,000 units × $12 per unit)	24,000	
Deduct fixed manufacturing overhead costs released from inventory under absorption costing (2,000 units × $12 per unit)		(24,000)
Absorption costing net operating income (loss)	$42,000	$ (6,000)

Review Problem 2: Segmented Income Statements

The business staff of the law firm Frampton, Davis & Smythe has constructed the following report which breaks down the firm's overall results for last month into two business segments—family law and commercial law:

	Total	Family Law	Commercial Law
Revenues from clients	$1,000,000	$400,000	$600,000
Variable expenses	220,000	100,000	120,000
Contribution margin	780,000	300,000	480,000
Traceable fixed expenses	670,000	280,000	390,000
Segment margin	110,000	20,000	90,000
Common fixed expenses	60,000	24,000	36,000
Net operating income (loss)	$ 50,000	$ (4,000)	$ 54,000

However, this report is not quite correct. The common fixed expenses such as the managing partner's salary, general administrative expenses, and general firm advertising have been allocated to the two segments based on revenues from clients.

Required:

1. Redo the segment report, eliminating the allocation of common fixed expenses. Would the firm be better off financially if the family law segment were dropped? (Note: Many of the firm's commercial law clients also use the firm for their family law requirements such as drawing up wills.)
2. The firm's advertising agency has proposed an ad campaign targeted at boosting the revenues of the family law segment. The ad campaign would cost $20,000, and the advertising agency claims that it would increase family law revenues by $100,000. The managing partner of Frampton, Davis & Smythe believes this increase in business could be accommodated without any increase in fixed expenses. Estimate the effect this ad campaign would have on the family law segment margin and on the firm's overall net operating income.

Solution to Review Problem 2

1. The corrected segmented income statement appears below:

	Total	Family Law	Commercial Law
Revenues from clients	$1,000,000	$400,000	$600,000
Variable expenses	220,000	100,000	120,000
Contribution margin	780,000	300,000	480,000
Traceable fixed expenses	670,000	280,000	390,000
Segment margin	110,000	$ 20,000	$ 90,000
Common fixed expenses	60,000		
Net operating income	$ 50,000		

No, the firm would not be financially better off if the family law practice were dropped. The family law segment is covering all of its own costs and is contributing $20,000 per month to covering the common fixed expenses of the firm. While the segment margin for family law is much lower than for commercial law, it is still profitable. Moreover, family law may be a service that the firm must provide to its commercial clients in order to remain competitive.

2. The ad campaign can be estimated to increase the family law segment margin by $55,000 as follows:

Increased revenues from clients	$100,000
Family law contribution margin ratio ($300,000 ÷ $400,000)	× 75%
Incremental contribution margin	$ 75,000
Less cost of the ad campaign	20,000
Increased segment margin	$ 55,000

Because there would be no increase in fixed expenses (including common fixed expenses), the increase in overall net operating income is also $55,000.

Glossary

Absorption costing A costing method that includes all manufacturing costs—direct materials, direct labor, and both variable and fixed manufacturing overhead—in unit product costs. (p. 230)

Common fixed cost A fixed cost that supports more than one business segment, but is not traceable in whole or in part to any one of the business segments. (p. 240)

Segment Any part or activity of an organization about which managers seek cost, revenue, or profit data. (p. 230)

Segment margin A segment's contribution margin less its traceable fixed costs. It represents the margin available after a segment has covered all of its own traceable costs. (p. 241)

Traceable fixed cost A fixed cost that is incurred because of the existence of a particular business segment and that would be eliminated if the segment were eliminated. (p. 240)

Variable costing A costing method that includes only variable manufacturing costs—direct materials, direct labor, and variable manufacturing overhead—in unit product costs. (p. 230)

Questions

6–1 What is the basic difference between absorption costing and variable costing?

6–2 Are selling and administrative expenses treated as product costs or as period costs under variable costing?

6–3 Explain how fixed manufacturing overhead costs are shifted from one period to another under absorption costing.

6–4 What are the arguments in favor of treating fixed manufacturing overhead costs as product costs?

6–5 What are the arguments in favor of treating fixed manufacturing overhead costs as period costs?

6–6 If the units produced and unit sales are equal, which method would you expect to show the higher net operating income, variable costing or absorption costing? Why?

6–7 If the units produced exceed unit sales, which method would you expect to show the higher net operating income, variable costing or absorption costing? Why?

6–8 If fixed manufacturing overhead costs are released from inventory under absorption costing, what does this tell you about the level of production in relation to the level of sales?

6–9 Under absorption costing, how is it possible to increase net operating income without increasing sales?

6–10 How does Lean Production reduce or eliminate the difference in reported net operating income between absorption and variable costing?

6–11 What is a segment of an organization? Give several examples of segments.

6–12 What costs are assigned to a segment under the contribution approach?

6–13 Distinguish between a traceable cost and a common cost. Give several examples of each.

6–14 Explain how the segment margin differs from the contribution margin.

6–15 Why aren't common costs allocated to segments under the contribution approach?

6–16 How is it possible for a cost that is traceable to a segment to become a common cost if the segment is divided into further segments?

Multiple-choice questions are provided on the text website at www.mhhe.com/garrison14e.

connect ACCOUNTING

Applying Excel

Available with McGraw-Hill's *Connect™ Accounting*.

LEARNING OBJECTIVE 2

The Excel worksheet form that appears below is to be used to recreate portions of Review Problem 1 on pages 249–251. Download the workbook containing this form from the Online Learning Center at www.mhhe.com/garrison14e. *On the website you will also receive instructions about how to use this worksheet form.*

	A	B	C	D	E	F
1	Chapter 6: Applying Excel					
2						
3	Data					
4	Selling price per unit	$50				
5	Manufacturing costs:					
6	Variable per unit produced:					
7	Direct materials	$11				
8	Direct labor	$6				
9	Variable manufacturing overhead	$3				
10	Fixed manufacturing overhead per year	$120,000				
11	Selling and administrative expenses					
12	Variable per unit sold	$4				
13	Fixed per year	$70,000				
14						
15		Year 1	Year 2			
16	Units in beginning inventory	0				
17	Units produced during the year	10,000	6,000			
18	Units sold during the year	8,000	8,000			
19						
20	*Enter a formula into each of the cells marked with a ? below*					
21	**Review Problem 1: Contrasting Variable and Absorption Costing**					
22						
23	*Compute the Ending Inventory*					
24		Year 1	Year 2			
25	Units in beginning inventory	0	?			
26	Units produced during the year	?	?			
27	Units sold during the year	?	?			
28	Units in ending inventory	?	?			
29						
30	*Compute the Absorption Costing Unit Product Cost*					
31		Year 1	Year 2			
32	Direct materials	?	?			
33	Direct labor	?	?			
34	Variable manufacturing overhead	?	?			
35	Fixed manufacturing overhead	?	?			
36	Absorption costing unit product cost	?	?			
37						
38	*Construct the Absorption Costing Income Statement*					
39		Year 1	Year 2			
40	Sales	?	?			
41	Cost of goods sold	?	?			
42	Gross margin	?	?			
43	Selling and administrative expenses	?	?			
44	Net operating income	?	?			
45						
46	*Compute the Variable Costing Unit Product Cost*					
47		Year 1	Year 2			
48	Direct materials	?	?			
49	Direct labor	?	?			
50	Variable manufacturing overhead	?	?			
51	Variable costing unit product cost	?	?			
52						
53	*Construct the Variable Costing Income Statement*					
54		Year 1		Year 2		
55	Sales		?		?	
56	Variable expenses:					
57	Variable cost of goods sold	?		?		
58	Variable selling and administrative expenses	?	?	?	?	
59	Contribution margin		?		?	
60	Fixed expenses:					
61	Fixed manufacturing overhead	?		?		
62	Fixed selling and administrative expenses	?	?	?	?	
63	Net operating income		?		?	
64						

Chapter 6 Form / Filled in Chapter 6 Form / Chapter 6

You should proceed to the requirements below only after completing your worksheet.

Required:

1. Check your worksheet by changing the units sold in the Data to 6,000 for Year 2. The cost of goods sold under absorption costing for Year 2 should now be $240,000. If it isn't, check cell C41. The formula in this cell should be =IF(C26<C27,C26*C36+(C27-C26)*B36,C27*C36).] If your worksheet is operating properly, the net operating income under both absorption costing and variable costing should be $(34,000) for Year 2. That is, the loss in Year 2 is $34,000 under both systems. If you do not get these answers, find the errors in your worksheet and correct them.

   Why is the absorption costing net operating income now equal to the variable costing net operating income in Year 2?
2. Enter the following data from a different company into your worksheet:

Data		
Selling price per unit	$75	
Manufacturing costs:		
Variable per unit produced:		
Direct materials	$12	
Direct labor	$5	
Variable manufacturing overhead	$7	
Fixed manufacturing overhead per year	$150,000	
Selling and administrative expenses:		
Variable per unit sold	$1	
Fixed per year	$60,000	
	Year 1	Year 2
Units in beginning inventory	0	
Units produced during the year	15,000	10,000
Units sold during the year	12,000	12,000

   Is the net operating income under variable costing different in Year 1 and Year 2? Why or why not? Explain the relation between the net operating income under absorption costing and variable costing in Year 1. Explain the relation between the net operating income under absorption costing and variable costing in Year 2.
3. At the end of Year 1, the company's board of directors set a target for Year 2 of net operating income of $500,000 under absorption costing. If this target is met, a hefty bonus would be paid to the CEO of the company. Keeping everything else the same from part (2) above, change the units produced in Year 2 to 50,000 units. Would this change result in a bonus being paid to the CEO? Do you think this change would be in the best interests of the company? What is likely to happen in Year 3 to the absorption costing net operating income if sales remain constant at 12,000 units per year?

Exercises

All applicable exercises are available with McGraw-Hill's *Connect™ Accounting*.

EXERCISE 6–1 Variable and Absorption Costing Unit Product Costs [LO1]
Shastri Bicycle of Mumbai, India, produces an inexpensive, yet rugged, bicycle for use on the city's crowded streets that it sells for 500 rupees. (Indian currency is denominated in rupees, denoted by R.) Selected data for the company's operations last year follow:

Units in beginning inventory	0
Units produced	10,000
Units sold	8,000
Units in ending inventory	2,000
Variable costs per unit:	
Direct materials	R120
Direct labor	R140
Variable manufacturing overhead	R50
Variable selling and administrative	R20
Fixed costs:	
Fixed manufacturing overhead	R600,000
Fixed selling and administrative	R400,000

Required:
1. Assume that the company uses absorption costing. Compute the unit product cost for one bicycle.
2. Assume that the company uses variable costing. Compute the unit product cost for one bicycle.

EXERCISE 6–2 Variable Costing Income Statement; Explanation of Difference in Net Operating Income [LO2]

Refer to the data in Exercise 6–1 for Shastri Bicycle. The absorption costing income statement prepared by the company's accountant for last year appears below:

Sales	R4,000,000
Cost of goods sold	2,960,000
Gross margin	1,040,000
Selling and administrative expense	560,000
Net operating income	R 480,000

Required:
1. Determine how much of the ending inventory consists of fixed manufacturing overhead cost deferred in inventory to the next period.
2. Prepare an income statement for the year using variable costing. Explain the difference in net operating income between the two costing methods.

EXERCISE 6–3 Reconciliation of Absorption and Variable Costing Net Operating Incomes [LO3]

High Tension Transformers, Inc., manufactures heavy-duty transformers for electrical switching stations. The company uses variable costing for internal management reports and absorption costing for external reports to shareholders, creditors, and the government. The company has provided the following data:

	Year 1	Year 2	Year 3
Inventories:			
Beginning (units)	180	150	160
Ending (units)	150	160	200
Variable costing net operating income	$292,400	$269,200	$251,800

The company's fixed manufacturing overhead per unit was constant at $450 for all three years.

Required:

1. Determine each year's absorption costing net operating income. Present your answer in the form of a reconciliation report.
2. In Year 4, the company's variable costing net operating income was $240,200 and its absorption costing net operating income was $267,200. Did inventories increase or decrease during Year 4? How much fixed manufacturing overhead cost was deferred or released from inventory during Year 4?

EXERCISE 6–4 Basic Segmented Income Statement [LO4]

Caltec, Inc., produces and sells recordable CD and DVD packs. Revenue and cost information relating to the products follow:

	Product	
	CD	DVD
Selling price per pack	$8.00	$25.00
Variable expenses per pack	$3.20	$17.50
Traceable fixed expenses per year	$138,000	$45,000

Common fixed expenses in the company total $105,000 annually. Last year the company produced and sold 37,500 CD packs and 18,000 DVD packs.

Required:

Prepare a contribution format income statement for the year segmented by product lines.

EXERCISE 6–5 Deducing Changes in Inventories [LO3]

Ferguson Products Inc., a manufacturer, reported $130 million in sales and a loss of $25 million in its absorption costing income statement provided to shareholders. According to a CVP analysis prepared for management, the company's break-even point is $120 million in sales.

Required:

Assuming that the CVP analysis is correct, is it likely that the company's inventory level increased, decreased, or remained unchanged during the year? Explain.

EXERCISE 6–6 Inferring Costing Method; Unit Product Cost [LO1]

Amcor, Inc., incurs the following costs to produce and sell a single product.

Variable costs per unit:	
Direct materials	$10
Direct labor	$5
Variable manufacturing overhead	$2
Variable selling and administrative expenses	$4
Fixed costs per year:	
Fixed manufacturing overhead	$90,000
Fixed selling and administrative expenses	$300,000

During the last year, 30,000 units were produced and 25,000 units were sold. The Finished Goods inventory account at the end of the year shows a balance of $85,000 for the 5,000 unsold units.

Required:

1. Is the company using absorption costing or variable costing to cost units in the Finished Goods inventory account? Show computations to support your answer.
2. Assume that the company wishes to prepare financial statements for the year to issue to its stockholders.
   a. Is the $85,000 figure for Finished Goods inventory the correct amount to use on these statements for external reporting purposes? Explain.
   b. At what dollar amount *should* the 5,000 units be carried in inventory for external reporting purposes?

EXERCISE 6–7 Variable and Absorption Costing Unit Product Costs and Income Statements [LO1, LO2]

Maxwell Company manufactures and sells a single product. The following costs were incurred during the company's first year of operations:

Variable costs per unit:	
Manufacturing:	
Direct materials	$18
Direct labor	$7
Variable manufacturing overhead	$2
Variable selling and administrative	$2
Fixed costs per year:	
Fixed manufacturing overhead	$200,000
Fixed selling and administrative expenses	$110,000

During the year, the company produced 20,000 units and sold 16,000 units. The selling price of the company's product is $50 per unit.

Required:

1. Assume that the company uses absorption costing:
   a. Compute the unit product cost.
   b. Prepare an income statement for the year.
2. Assume that the company uses variable costing:
   a. Compute the unit product cost.
   b. Prepare an income statement for the year.
3. The company's controller believes that the company should have set last year's selling price at $51 instead of $50 per unit. She estimates the company could have sold 15,000 units at a price of $51 per unit, thereby increasing the company's gross margin by $2,000 and its net operating income by $4,000. Assuming the controller's estimates are accurate, do you think the price increase would have been a good idea?

EXERCISE 6–8 Segmented Income Statement [LO4]

Michaels Company segments its income statement into its East and West Divisions. The company's overall sales, contribution margin ratio, and net operating income are $600,000, 50%, and $50,000, respectively. The West Division's contribution margin and contribution margin ratio are $150,000 and 75%, respectively. The East Division's segment margin is $70,000. The company has $60,000 of common fixed costs that cannot be traced to either division.

Required:

Prepare an income statement for Michaels Company that uses the contribution format and is segmented by divisions. In addition, for the company as a whole and for each segment, show each item on the segmented income statements as a percent of sales.

EXERCISE 6–9 Variable Costing Unit Product Cost and Income Statement; Break-Even [LO1, LO2]
CompuDesk, Inc., makes an oak desk specially designed for personal computers. The desk sells for $200. Data for last year's operations follow:

Units in beginning inventory	0
Units produced	10,000
Units sold	9,000
Units in ending inventory	1,000
Variable costs per unit:	
Direct materials	$ 60
Direct labor	30
Variable manufacturing overhead	10
Variable selling and administrative	20
Total variable cost per unit	$120
Fixed costs:	
Fixed manufacturing overhead	$300,000
Fixed selling and administrative	450,000
Total fixed costs	$750,000

Required:

1. Assume that the company uses variable costing. Compute the unit product cost for one computer desk.
2. Assume that the company uses variable costing. Prepare a contribution format income statement for the year.
3. What is the company's break-even point in terms of units sold?

EXERCISE 6–10 Absorption Costing Unit Product Cost and Income Statement [LO1, LO2]
Refer to the data in Exercise 6–9 for CompuDesk. Assume in this exercise that the company uses absorption costing.

Required:

1. Compute the unit product cost for one computer desk.
2. Prepare an income statement.

EXERCISE 6–11 Segmented Income Statement [LO4]
Bovine Company, a wholesale distributor of DVDs, has been experiencing losses for some time, as shown by its most recent monthly contribution format income statement below:

Sales	$1,500,000
Variable expenses	588,000
Contribution margin	912,000
Fixed expenses	945,000
Net operating loss	$ (33,000)

In an effort to isolate the problem, the president has asked for an income statement segmented by geographic market. Accordingly, the Accounting Department has developed the following data:

	Geographic Market		
	South	Central	North
Sales	$400,000	$600,000	$500,000
Variable expenses as a percentage of sales	52%	30%	40%
Traceable fixed expenses	$240,000	$330,000	$200,000

Required:

1. Prepare a contribution format income statement segmented by geographic market, as desired by the president.
2. The company's sales manager believes that sales in the Central geographic market could be increased by 15% if monthly advertising were increased by $25,000. Would you recommend the increased advertising? Show computations to support your answer.

EXERCISE 6–12 Variable and Absorption Costing Unit Product Costs and Income Statements [LO1, LO2, LO3]

Fletcher Company manufactures and sells one product. The following information pertains to each of the company's first two years of operations:

Variable costs per unit:	
Manufacturing:	
Direct materials	$20
Direct labor	$12
Variable manufacturing overhead	$4
Variable selling and administrative	$3
Fixed costs per year:	
Fixed manufacturing overhead	$200,000
Fixed selling and administrative expenses	$80,000

During its first year of operations, Fletcher produced 50,000 units and sold 40,000 units. During its second year of operations, it produced 40,000 units and sold 50,000 units. The selling price of the company's product is $50 per unit.

Required:

1. Assume the company uses variable costing:
   a. Compute the unit product cost for year 1 and year 2.
   b. Prepare an income statement for year 1 and year 2.
2. Assume the company uses absorption costing:
   a. Compute the unit product cost for year 1 and year 2.
   b. Prepare an income statement for year 1 and year 2.
3. Explain the difference between variable costing and absorption costing net operating income in year 1. Also, explain why the two net operating incomes differ in year 2.

EXERCISE 6–13 Variable Costing Income Statement; Reconciliation [LO2, LO3]

Morey Company has just completed its first year of operations. The company's absorption costing income statement for the year appears below:

Morey Company Income Statement	
Sales (40,000 units at $33.75 per unit)	$1,350,000
Cost of goods sold (40,000 units × $21 per unit)	840,000
Gross margin	510,000
Selling and administrative expenses	420,000
Net operating income	$ 90,000

The company's selling and administrative expenses consist of $300,000 per year in fixed expenses and $3 per unit sold in variable expenses. The company's $21 per unit product cost given above is computed as follows:

Direct materials	$10
Direct labor	4
Variable manufacturing overhead	2
Fixed manufacturing overhead ($250,000 ÷ 50,000 units)	5
Absorption costing unit product cost	$21

Required:
1. Redo the company's income statement in the contribution format using variable costing.
2. Reconcile any difference between the net operating income on your variable costing income statement and the net operating income on the absorption costing income statement.

EXERCISE 6–14 Working with a Segmented Income Statement [LO4]
Marple Associates is a consulting firm that specializes in information systems for construction and landscaping companies. The firm has two offices—one in Houston and one in Dallas. The firm classifies the direct costs of consulting jobs as variable costs. A segmented contribution format income statement for the company's most recent year is given below:

	Total Company		Office: Houston		Office: Dallas	
Sales	$750,000	100.0%	$150,000	100%	$600,000	100%
Variable expenses	405,000	54.0	45,000	30	360,000	60
Contribution margin	345,000	46.0	105,000	70	240,000	40
Traceable fixed expenses	168,000	22.4	78,000	52	90,000	15
Office segment margin	177,000	23.6	$ 27,000	18%	$150,000	25%
Common fixed expenses not traceable to offices	120,000	16.0				
Net operating income	$ 57,000	7.6%				

Required:
1. By how much would the company's net operating income increase if Dallas increased its sales by $75,000 per year? Assume no change in cost behavior patterns.
2. Refer to the original data. Assume that sales in Houston increase by $50,000 next year and that sales in Dallas remain unchanged. Assume no change in fixed costs.
   a. Prepare a new segmented income statement for the company using the above format. Show both amounts and percentages.
   b. Observe from the income statement you have prepared that the CM ratio for Houston has remained unchanged at 70% (the same as in the above data) but that the segment margin ratio has changed. How do you explain the change in the segment margin ratio?

EXERCISE 6–15 Working with a Segmented Income Statement [LO4]
Refer to the data in Exercise 6–14. Assume that Dallas' sales by major market are as follows:

	Dallas		Market: Construction Clients		Market: Landscaping Clients	
Sales	$600,000	100%	$400,000	100%	$200,000	100%
Variable expenses	360,000	60	260,000	65	100,000	50
Contribution margin	240,000	40	140,000	35	100,000	50
Traceable fixed expenses	72,000	12	20,000	5	52,000	26
Market segment margin	168,000	28	$120,000	30%	$ 48,000	24%
Common fixed expenses not traceable to markets	18,000	3				
Office segment margin	$150,000	25%				

The company would like to initiate an intensive advertising campaign in one of the two markets during the next month. The campaign would cost $8,000. Marketing studies indicate that such a campaign would increase sales in the construction market by $70,000 or increase sales in the landscaping market by $60,000.

Required:
1. In which of the markets would you recommend that the company focus its advertising campaign? Show computations to support your answer.
2. In Exercise 6–14, Dallas shows $90,000 in traceable fixed expenses. What happened to the $90,000 in this exercise?

Problems

All applicable problems are available with McGraw-Hill's *Connect™ Accounting*.

PROBLEM 6–16 Variable and Absorption Costing Unit Product Costs and Income Statements; Explanation of Difference in Net Operating Income [LO1, LO2, LO3]
Wiengot Antennas, Inc., produces and sells a unique type of TV antenna. The company has just opened a new plant to manufacture the antenna, and the following cost and revenue data have been provided for the first month of the plant's operation in the form of a worksheet.

	A	B	C
1	Beginning inventory	0	
2	Units produced	40,000	
3	Units sold	35,000	
4	Selling price per unit	$60	
5			
6	Selling and administrative expenses:		
7	Variable per unit	$2	
8	Fixed (total)	$560,000	
9	Manufacturing costs		
10	Direct materials cost per unit	$15	
11	Direct labor cost per unit	$7	
12	Variable manufacturing overhead cost per unit	$2	
13	Fixed manufacturing overhead cost (total)	$640,000	
14			

Sheet1 Sheet2 Sheet3

Because the new antenna is unique in design, management is anxious to see how profitable it will be and has asked that an income statement be prepared for the month.

Required:

1. Assume that the company uses absorption costing.
   a. Determine the unit product cost.
   b. Prepare an income statement for the month.
2. Assume that the company uses variable costing.
   a. Determine the unit product cost.
   b. Prepare a contribution format income statement for the month.
3. Explain the reason for any difference in the ending inventory balances under the two costing methods and the impact of this difference on reported net operating income.

PROBLEM 6–17 Variable and Absorption Costing Unit Product Costs and Income Statements [LO1, LO2]
Nickelson Company manufactures and sells one product. The following information pertains to each of the company's first three years of operations:

Variable costs per unit:	
Manufacturing:	
Direct materials	$25
Direct labor	$16
Variable manufacturing overhead	$5
Variable selling and administrative	$2
Fixed costs per year:	
Fixed manufacturing overhead	$300,000
Fixed selling and administrative expenses	$180,000

During its first year of operations Nickelson produced 60,000 units and sold 60,000 units. During its second year of operations it produced 75,000 units and sold 50,000 units. In its third year, Nickelson produced 40,000 units and sold 65,000 units. The selling price of the company's product is $56 per unit.

Required:
1. Compute the company's break-even point in units sold.
2. Assume the company uses variable costing:
   a. Compute the unit product cost for year 1, year 2, and year 3.
   b. Prepare an income statement for year 1, year 2, and year 3.
3. Assume the company uses absorption costing:
   a. Compute the unit product cost for year 1, year 2, and year 3.
   b. Prepare an income statement for year 1, year 2, and year 3.
4. Compare the net operating income figures that you computed in requirements 2 and 3 to the break-even point that you computed in requirement 1. Which net operating income figures seem counterintuitive? Why?

eXcel

PROBLEM 6–18 Variable Costing Income Statement; Reconciliation [LO2, LO3]

During Denton Company's first two years of operations, the company reported absorption costing net operating income as follows:

	Year 1	Year 2
Sales (@ $50 per unit)	$1,000,000	$1,500,000
Cost of goods sold (@ $34 per unit)	680,000	1,020,000
Gross margin	320,000	480,000
Selling and administrative expenses*	310,000	340,000
Net operating income	$ 10,000	$ 140,000

*$3 per unit variable; $250,000 fixed each year.

The company's $34 unit product cost is computed as follows:

Direct materials	$ 8
Direct labor	10
Variable manufacturing overhead	2
Fixed manufacturing overhead ($350,000 ÷ 25,000 units)	14
Absorption costing unit product cost	$34

Production and cost data for the two years are given below:

	Year 1	Year 2
Units produced	25,000	25,000
Units sold	20,000	30,000

Required:
1. Prepare a variable costing contribution format income statement for each year.
2. Reconcile the absorption costing and variable costing net operating income figures for each year.

PROBLEM 6–19 Segment Reporting and Decision Making [LO4]

The most recent monthly contribution format income statement for Reston Company is given below:

Reston Company Income Statement For the Month Ended May 31		
Sales	$900,000	100.0%
Variable expenses	408,000	45.3
Contribution margin	492,000	54.7
Fixed expenses	465,000	51.7
Net operating income	$ 27,000	3.0%

Management is disappointed with the company's performance and is wondering what can be done to improve profits. By examining sales and cost records, you have determined the following:

a. The company is divided into two sales territories—Central and Eastern. The Central Territory recorded $400,000 in sales and $208,000 in variable expenses during May. The remaining sales and variable expenses were recorded in the Eastern Territory. Fixed expenses of $160,000 and $130,000 are traceable to the Central and Eastern Territories, respectively. The rest of the fixed expenses are common to the two territories.

b. The company is the exclusive distributor for two products—Awls and Pows. Sales of Awls and Pows totaled $100,000 and $300,000, respectively, in the Central Territory during May. Variable expenses are 25% of the selling price for Awls and 61% for Pows. Cost records show that $60,000 of the Central Territory's fixed expenses are traceable to Awls and $54,000 to Pows, with the remainder common to the two products.

Required:

1. Prepare contribution format segmented income statements, first showing the total company broken down between sales territories and then showing the Central Territory broken down by product line. In addition, for the company as a whole and for each segment, show each item on the segmented income statements as a percent of sales.
2. Look at the statement you have prepared showing the total company segmented by sales territory. What points revealed by this statement should be brought to management's attention?
3. Look at the statement you have prepared showing the Central Territory segmented by product lines. What points revealed by this statement should be brought to management's attention?

PROBLEM 6–20 Comprehensive Problem with Labor Fixed [LO1, LO2, LO3]

Advance Products, Inc., has just organized a new division to manufacture and sell specially designed tables using select hardwoods for personal computers. The division's monthly costs are shown in the schedule below:

Manufacturing costs:	
Variable costs per unit:	
Direct materials	$86
Variable manufacturing overhead	$4
Fixed manufacturing overhead costs (total)	$240,000
Selling and administrative costs:	
Variable	15% of sales
Fixed (total)	$160,000

Advance Products regards all of its workers as full-time employees and the company has a long-standing no-layoff policy. Furthermore, production is highly automated. Accordingly, the company includes its labor costs in its fixed manufacturing overhead. The tables sell for $250 each.

During the first month of operations, the following activity was recorded:

Units produced	4,000
Units sold	3,200

Required:

1. Compute the unit product cost under:
   a. Absorption costing.
   b. Variable costing.
2. Prepare an income statement for the month using absorption costing.
3. Prepare a contribution format income statement for the month using variable costing.
4. Assume that the company must obtain additional financing. As a member of top management, which of the statements that you have prepared in (2) and (3) above would you prefer to take with you to negotiate with the bank? Why?
5. Reconcile the absorption costing and variable costing net operating incomes in (2) and (3) above.

PROBLEM 6–21 Prepare and Reconcile Variable Costing Statements [LO1, LO2, LO3]

Linden Company manufactures and sells a single product. Cost data for the product follow:

Variable costs per unit:	
Direct materials	$ 6
Direct labor	12
Variable factory overhead	4
Variable selling and administrative	3
Total variable costs per unit	$25
Fixed costs per month:	
Fixed manufacturing overhead	$240,000
Fixed selling and administrative	180,000
Total fixed cost per month	$420,000

The product sells for $40 per unit. Production and sales data for May and June, the first two months of operations, are as follows:

	Units Produced	Units Sold
May	30,000	26,000
June	30,000	34,000

Income statements prepared by the accounting department, using absorption costing, are presented below:

	May	June
Sales	$1,040,000	$1,360,000
Cost of goods sold	780,000	1,020,000
Gross margin	260,000	340,000
Selling and administrative expenses	258,000	282,000
Net operating income	$ 2,000	$ 58,000

Required:

1. Determine the unit product cost under:
   a. Absorption costing.
   b. Variable costing.
2. Prepare contribution format variable costing income statements for May and June.
3. Reconcile the variable costing and absorption costing net operating incomes.
4. The company's Accounting Department has determined the break-even point to be 28,000 units per month, computed as follows:

$$\frac{\text{Fixed cost per month}}{\text{Unit contribution margin}} = \frac{\$420{,}000}{\$15 \text{ per unit}} = 28{,}000 \text{ units}$$

Upon receiving this figure, the president commented, "There's something peculiar here. The controller says that the break-even point is 28,000 units per month. Yet we sold only 26,000 units in

May, and the income statement we received showed a $2,000 profit. Which figure do we believe?" Prepare a brief explanation of what happened on the May income statement.

PROBLEM 6–22 Absorption and Variable Costing; Production Constant, Sales Fluctuate [LO1, LO2, LO3]

Sandi Scott obtained a patent on a small electronic device and organized Scott Products, Inc., to produce and sell the device. During the first month of operations, the device was very well received on the market, so Ms. Scott looked forward to a healthy profit. For this reason, she was surprised to see a loss for the month on her income statement. This statement was prepared by her accounting service, which takes great pride in providing its clients with timely financial data. The statement follows:

Scott Products, Inc. Income Statement		
Sales (40,000 units)		$200,000
Variable expenses:		
Variable cost of goods sold	$80,000	
Variable selling and administrative expenses	30,000	110,000
Contribution margin		90,000
Fixed expenses:		
Fixed manufacturing overhead	75,000	
Fixed selling and administrative expenses	20,000	95,000
Net operating loss		$ (5,000)

Ms. Scott is discouraged over the loss shown for the month, particularly because she had planned to use the statement to encourage investors to purchase stock in the new company. A friend, who is a CPA, insists that the company should be using absorption costing rather than variable costing. He argues that if absorption costing had been used, the company would probably have reported a profit for the month.

Selected cost data relating to the product and to the first month of operations follow:

Units produced	50,000
Units sold	40,000
Variable costs per unit:	
Direct materials	$1.00
Direct labor	$0.80
Variable manufacturing overhead	$0.20
Variable selling and administrative expenses	$0.75

Required:

1. Complete the following:
   a. Compute the unit product cost under absorption costing.
   b. Redo the company's income statement for the month using absorption costing.
   c. Reconcile the variable and absorption costing net operating income (loss) figures.
2. Was the CPA correct in suggesting that the company really earned a "profit" for the month? Explain.
3. During the second month of operations, the company again produced 50,000 units but sold 60,000 units. (Assume no change in total fixed costs.)
   a. Prepare a contribution format income statement for the month using variable costing.
   b. Prepare an income statement for the month using absorption costing.
   c. Reconcile the variable costing and absorption costing net operating incomes.

PROBLEM 6–23 Restructuring a Segmented Income Statement [LO4]

Brabant NV of the Netherlands is a wholesale distributor of Dutch cheeses that it sells throughout the European Community. Unfortunately, the company's profits have been declining, which has caused considerable concern. To help understand the condition of the company, the managing director of the company has requested that the monthly income statement be segmented by sales territory. Accordingly, the company's accounting department has prepared the following statement for March, the most recent month. (The Dutch currency is the euro which is designated by €.)

	Sales Territory		
	Southern Europe	Middle Europe	Northern Europe
Sales	€300,000	€800,000	€700,000
Territorial expenses (traceable):			
Cost of goods sold	93,000	240,000	315,000
Salaries	54,000	56,000	112,000
Insurance	9,000	16,000	14,000
Advertising	105,000	240,000	245,000
Depreciation	21,000	32,000	28,000
Shipping	15,000	32,000	42,000
Total territorial expenses	297,000	616,000	756,000
Territorial income (loss) before corporate expenses	3,000	184,000	(56,000)
Corporate expenses:			
Advertising (general)	15,000	40,000	35,000
General administrative	20,000	20,000	20,000
Total corporate expenses	35,000	60,000	55,000
Net operating income (loss)	€(32,000)	€124,000	€(111,000)

Cost of goods sold and shipping expenses are both variable; other costs are all fixed. Brabant NV purchases cheeses at auction and from farmers' cooperatives, and it distributes them in the three territories listed above. Each of the three sales territories has its own manager and sales staff. The cheeses vary widely in profitability; some have a high margin and some have a low margin. (Certain cheeses, after having been aged for long periods, are the most expensive and carry the highest margins.)

Required:

1. List any disadvantages or weaknesses that you see to the statement format illustrated above.
2. Explain the basis that is apparently being used to allocate the corporate expenses to the territories. Do you agree with these allocations? Explain.
3. Prepare a new segmented contribution format income statement for May. Show a Total column as well as data for each territory. In addition, for the company as a whole and for each sales territory, show each item on the segmented income statement as a percent of sales.
4. Analyze the statement that you prepared in (3) above. What points that might help to improve the company's performance would you bring to management's attention?

PROBLEM 6–24 Incentives Created by Absorption Costing; Ethics and the Manager [LO2]

Aristotle Constantinos, the manager of DuraProducts' Australian Division, is trying to set the production schedule for the last quarter of the year. The Australian Division had planned to sell 100,000 units during the year, but current projections indicate sales will be only 78,000 units in total. By September 30 the following activity had been reported:

	Units
Inventory, January 1	0
Production	72,000
Sales	60,000
Inventory, September 30	12,000

Demand has been soft, and the sales forecast for the last quarter is only 18,000 units.

The division can rent warehouse space to store up to 30,000 units. The division should maintain a minimum inventory level of at least 1,500 units. Mr. Constantinos is aware that production must be at least 6,000 units per quarter in order to retain a nucleus of key employees. Maximum production capacity is 45,000 units per quarter.

Due to the nature of the division's operations, fixed manufacturing overhead is a major element of product cost.

Required:

1. Assume that the division is using variable costing. How many units should be scheduled for production during the last quarter of the year? (The basic formula for computing the required production for a period in a company is: Expected sales + Desired ending inventory − Beginning inventory = Required production.) Show computations and explain your answer. Will the number of units scheduled for production affect the division's reported profit for the year? Explain.
2. Assume that the division is using absorption costing and that the divisional manager is given an annual bonus based on the division's net operating income. If Mr. Constantinos wants to maximize his division's net operating income for the year, how many units should be scheduled for production during the last quarter? [See the formula in (1) above.] Explain.
3. Identify the ethical issues involved in the decision Mr. Constantinos must make about the level of production for the last quarter of the year.

PROBLEM 6–25 Prepare and Interpret Statements; Changes in Both Sales and Production; Lean Production [LO1, LO2, LO3]

Memotec, Inc., manufactures and sells a unique electronic part. Operating results for the first three years of activity were as follows (absorption costing basis):

	Year 1	Year 2	Year 3
Sales	$1,000,000	$800,000	$1,000,000
Cost of goods sold	800,000	560,000	850,000
Gross margin	200,000	240,000	150,000
Selling and administrative expenses	170,000	150,000	170,000
Net operating income (loss)	$ 30,000	$ 90,000	$ (20,000)

Sales dropped by 20% during Year 2 due to the entry of several foreign competitors into the market. Memotec had expected sales to remain constant at 50,000 units for the year; production was set at 60,000 units in order to build a buffer of protection against unexpected spurts in demand. By the start of Year 3, management could see that spurts in demand were unlikely and that the inventory was excessive. To work off the excessive inventories, Memotec cut back production during Year 3, as shown below:

	Year 1	Year 2	Year 3
Production in units	50,000	60,000	40,000
Sales in units	50,000	40,000	50,000

Additional information about the company follows:

a. The company's plant is highly automated. Variable manufacturing costs (direct materials, direct labor, and variable manufacturing overhead) total only $4 per unit, and fixed manufacturing overhead costs total $600,000 per year.
b. Fixed manufacturing overhead costs are applied to units of product on the basis of each year's production. That is, a new fixed overhead rate is computed each year.
c. Variable selling and administrative expenses are $2 per unit sold. Fixed selling and administrative expenses total $70,000 per year.
d. The company uses a FIFO inventory flow assumption.

Memotec's management can't understand why profits tripled during Year 2 when sales dropped by 20%, and why a loss was incurred during Year 3 when sales recovered to previous levels.

Required:

1. Prepare a contribution format variable costing income statement for each year.
2. Refer to the absorption costing income statements on the previous page.
   a. Compute the unit product cost in each year under absorption costing. (Show how much of this cost is variable and how much is fixed.)
   b. Reconcile the variable costing and absorption costing net operating incomes for each year.
3. Refer again to the absorption costing income statements. Explain why net operating income was higher in Year 2 than it was in Year 1 under the absorption approach, in light of the fact that fewer units were sold in Year 2 than in Year 1.
4. Refer again to the absorption costing income statements. Explain why the company suffered a loss in Year 3 but reported a profit in Year 1, although the same number of units was sold in each year.
5. *a.* Explain how operations would have differed in Year 2 and Year 3 if the company had been using Lean Production with the result that ending inventory was zero.
   b. If Lean Production had been in use during Year 2 and Year 3, and the predetermined overhead rate is based on 50,000 units per year, what would the company's net operating income (or loss) have been in each year under absorption costing? Explain the reason for any differences between these income figures and the figures reported by the company in the statements on the previous page.

PROBLEM 6–26 Segmented Income Statements [LO4]

Vega Foods, Inc., has recently purchased a small mill that it intends to operate as one of its subsidiaries. The newly acquired mill has three products that it offers for sale—wheat cereal, pancake mix, and flour. Each product sells for $10 per package. Materials, labor, and other variable production costs are $3.00 per bag of wheat cereal, $4.20 per bag of pancake mix, and $1.80 per bag of flour. Sales commissions are 10% of sales for any product. All other costs are fixed.

The mill's income statement for the most recent month is given below:

		Product Line		
	Total Company	Wheat Cereal	Pancake Mix	Flour
Sales	$600,000	$200,000	$300,000	$100,000
Expenses:				
Materials, labor, and other	204,000	60,000	126,000	18,000
Sales commissions	60,000	20,000	30,000	10,000
Advertising	123,000	48,000	60,000	15,000
Salaries	66,000	34,000	21,000	11,000
Equipment depreciation	30,000	10,000	15,000	5,000
Warehouse rent	12,000	4,000	6,000	2,000
General administration	90,000	30,000	30,000	30,000
Total expenses	585,000	206,000	288,000	91,000
Net operating income (loss)	$ 15,000	$ (6,000)	$ 12,000	$ 9,000

The following additional information is available about the company:

a. The same equipment is used to mill and package all three products. In the above income statement, equipment depreciation has been allocated on the basis of sales dollars. An analysis of equipment usage indicates that it is used 40% of the time to make wheat cereal, 50% of the time to make pancake mix, and 10% of the time to make flour.

b. All three products are stored in the same warehouse. In the above income statement, the warehouse rent has been allocated on the basis of sales dollars. The warehouse contains 24,000 square feet of space, of which 8,000 square feet are used for wheat cereal, 14,000 square feet are used for pancake mix, and 2,000 square feet are used for flour. The warehouse space costs the company $0.50 per square foot per month to rent.

c. The general administration costs relate to the administration of the company as a whole. In the above income statement, these costs have been divided equally among the three product lines.

d. All other costs are traceable to the product lines.

Vega Foods' management is anxious to improve the mill's 2.5% margin on sales.

Required:

1. Prepare a new contribution format segmented income statement for the month. Adjust the allocation of equipment depreciation and warehouse rent as indicated by the additional information provided.
2. After seeing the income statement in the main body of the problem, management has decided to eliminate the wheat cereal because it is not returning a profit, and to focus all available resources on promoting the pancake mix.
   a. Based on the statement you have prepared, do you agree with the decision to eliminate the wheat cereal? Explain.
   b. Based on the statement you have prepared, do you agree with the decision to focus all available resources on promoting the pancake mix? Assume that an ample market is available for all three products. (Hint: compute the contribution margin ratio for each product.)

connect ACCOUNTING Cases

All applicable cases are available with McGraw-Hill's *Connect™ Accounting*.

CASE 6–27 Variable and Absorption Costing Unit Product Costs and Income Statements [LO1, LO2]
O'Donnell Company manufactures and sells one product. The following information pertains to each of the company's first three years of operations:

Variable costs per unit:	
Manufacturing	
Direct materials	$30
Direct labor	$18
Variable manufacturing overhead	$6
Variable selling and administrative	$4
Fixed costs per year:	
Fixed manufacturing overhead	$600,000
Fixed selling and administrative expenses	$180,000

During its first year of operations, O'Donnell produced 100,000 units and sold 80,000 units. During its second year of operations, it produced 75,000 units and sold 90,000 units. In its third year, O'Donnell produced 80,000 units and sold 75,000 units. The selling price of the company's product is $70 per unit.

Required:

1. Assume the company uses variable costing and a FIFO inventory flow assumption (FIFO means first-in first-out. In other words, it assumes that the oldest units in inventory are sold first):
   a. Compute the unit product cost for year 1, year 2, and year 3.
   b. Prepare an income statement for year 1, year 2, and year 3.
2. Assume the company uses variable costing and a LIFO inventory flow assumption (LIFO means last-in first-out. In other words, it assumes that the newest units in inventory are sold first):
   a. Compute the unit product cost for year 1, year 2, and year 3.
   b. Prepare an income statement for year 1, year 2, and year 3.
3. Assume the company uses absorption costing and a FIFO inventory flow assumption (FIFO means first-in first-out. In other words, it assumes that the oldest units in inventory are sold first):
   a. Compute the unit product cost for year 1, year 2, and year 3.
   b. Prepare an income statement for year 1, year 2, and year 3.
4. Assume the company uses absorption costing and a LIFO inventory flow assumption (LIFO means last-in first-out. In other words, it assumes that the newest units in inventory are sold first):
   a. Compute the unit product cost for year 1, year 2, and year 3.
   b. Prepare an income statement for year 1, year 2, and year 3.

CASE 6–28 Service Organization; Segment Reporting [LO4]

The American Association of Acupuncturists is a professional association for acupuncturists that has 10,000 members. The association operates from a central headquarters but has local chapters throughout North America. The association's monthly journal, *American Acupuncture,* features recent developments in the field. The association also publishes special reports and books, and it sponsors courses that qualify members for the continuing professional education credit required by state certification boards. The association's statement of revenues and expenses for the current year is presented below:

American Association of Acupuncturists Statement of Revenues and Expenses For the Year Ended December 31	
Revenues	$970,000
Expenses:	
Salaries	440,000
Occupancy costs	120,000
Distributions to local chapters	210,000
Printing	82,000
Mailing	24,000
Continuing education instructors' fees	60,000
General and administrative	27,000
Total expenses	963,000
Excess of revenues over expenses	$ 7,000

The board of directors of the association has requested that you construct a segmented income statement that shows the financial contribution of each of the association's four major programs—membership service, journal, books and reports, and continuing education. The following data have been gathered to aid you:

a. Membership dues are $60 per year, of which $15 covers a one-year subscription to the association's journal. The other $45 pays for general membership services.

b. One-year subscriptions to *American Acupuncture* are sold to nonmembers and libraries at $20 per subscription. A total of 1,000 of these subscriptions were sold last year. In addition to subscriptions, the journal generated $50,000 in advertising revenues. The costs per journal subscription, for members as well as nonmembers, were $4 for printing and $1 for mailing.

c. A variety of technical reports and professional books were sold for a total of $70,000 during the year. Printing costs for these materials totaled $25,000, and mailing costs totaled $8,000.

d. The association offers a number of continuing education courses. The courses generated revenues of $230,000 last year.

e. Salary costs and space occupied by each program and the central staff are as follows:

	Salaries	Space Occupied (square feet)
Membership services	$170,000	3,000
Journal	60,000	1,000
Books and reports	40,000	1,000
Continuing education	50,000	2,000
Central staff	120,000	3,000
Total	$440,000	10,000

f. The $120,000 in occupancy costs incurred last year includes $20,000 in rental cost for a portion of the warehouse used by the Membership Services program for storage purposes. The association has a flexible rental agreement that allows it to pay rent only on the warehouse space it uses.

g. Printing costs other than for journal subscriptions and for books and reports related to Continuing Education.

h. Distributions to local chapters are for general membership services.

i. General and administrative expenses include costs relating to overall administration of the association as a whole. The association's central staff does some mailing of materials for general administrative purposes.
j. The expenses that can be traced or assigned to the central staff, as well as any other expenses that are not traceable to the programs, will be treated as common costs. It is not necessary to distinguish between variable and fixed costs.

Required:

1. Prepare a contribution format segmented income statement for the American Association of Acupuncturists for last year. This statement should show the segment margin for each program as well as results for the association as a whole.
2. Give arguments for and against allocating all costs of the association to the four programs.

(CMA, adapted)

Chapter 7

Activity-Based Costing: A Tool to Aid Decision Making

LEARNING OBJECTIVES

After studying Chapter 7, you should be able to:

LO1 Understand activity-based costing and how it differs from a traditional costing system.

LO2 Assign costs to cost pools using a first-stage allocation.

LO3 Compute activity rates for cost pools.

LO4 Assign costs to a cost object using a second-stage allocation.

LO5 Use activity-based costing to compute product and customer margins.

LO6 (Appendix 7A) Prepare an action analysis report using activity-based costing data and interpret the report.

LO7 (Appendix 7B) Use activity-based costing techniques to compute unit product costs for external reports.

Managing Product Complexity

BUSINESS FOCUS

Managers often understand that increasing the variety of raw material inputs used in their products increases costs. For example, General Mills studied its 50 varieties of Hamburger Helper and concluded that it could lower costs by discontinuing half of them without alienating customers. Seagate studied seven varieties of its computer hard drives and found that only 2% of their parts could be shared by more than one hard drive. The engineers fixed the problem by redesigning the hard drives so that they used more common component parts. Instead of using 61 types of screws to make the hard drives, the engineers reduced the number of screws needed to 19. Eventually all Seagate products were designed so that 75% of their component parts were shared with other product lines.

Activity-based costing systems quantify the increase in costs, such as procurement costs, material handling costs, and assembly costs that are caused by inefficient product designs and other factors. ■

Sources: Mina Kimes, "Cereal Cost Cutters," *Fortune*, November 10, 2008, p. 24; Erika Brown, "Drive Fast, Drive Hard," *Forbes*, January 9, 2006, pp. 92–96.

This chapter introduces the concept of *activity-based costing* which has been embraced by a wide variety of organizations including Charles Schwab, Citigroup, Lowe's, Coca-Cola, Conco Food Service, Banta Foods, J&B Wholesale, Fairchild Semiconductor, Assan Aluminum, Sysco Foods, Fisher Scientific International, and Peregrine Outfitters. **Activity-based costing (ABC)** is a costing method that is designed to provide managers with cost information for strategic and other decisions that potentially affect capacity and therefore "fixed" as well as variable costs. Activity-based costing is ordinarily used as a supplement to, rather than as a replacement for, a company's usual costing system. Most organizations that use activity-based costing have two costing systems—the official costing system that is used for preparing external financial reports and the activity-based costing system that is used for internal decision making and for managing activities.

This chapter focuses primarily on ABC applications in manufacturing to provide a contrast with the material presented in earlier chapters. More specifically, Chapters 3 and 4 focused on traditional absorption costing systems used by manufacturing companies to calculate unit product costs for the purpose of valuing inventories and determining cost of goods sold for external financial reports. In contrast, this chapter explains how manufacturing companies can use activity-based costing rather than traditional methods to calculate unit product costs for the purposes of managing overhead and making decisions. Chapter 6 had a similar purpose. That chapter focused on how to use variable costing to aid decisions that do not affect fixed costs. This chapter extends that idea to show how activity-based costing can be used to aid decisions that potentially affect fixed costs as well as variable costs.

Activity-Based Costing: An Overview

LEARNING OBJECTIVE 1
Understand activity-based costing and how it differs from a traditional costing system.

As stated above, traditional absorption costing is designed to provide data for external financial reports. In contrast, activity-based costing is designed to be used for internal decision making. As a consequence, activity-based costing differs from traditional cost accounting in three ways. In activity-based costing:

1. Nonmanufacturing as well as manufacturing costs may be assigned to products, but only on a cause-and-effect basis.
2. Some manufacturing costs may be excluded from product costs.
3. Numerous overhead cost pools are used, each of which is allocated to products and other cost objects using its own unique measure of activity.

Each of these departures from traditional cost accounting practice will be discussed in turn.

Nonmanufacturing Costs and Activity-Based Costing

In traditional cost accounting, only manufacturing costs are assigned to products. Selling and administrative expenses are treated as period expenses and are not assigned to products. However, many of these nonmanufacturing costs are also part of the costs of selling, distributing, and servicing specific products. For example, commissions paid to salespersons, shipping costs, and warranty repair costs can be easily traced to individual products. In this chapter, we will use the term *overhead* to refer to nonmanufacturing costs as well as to indirect manufacturing costs. In activity-based costing, products are assigned all of the overhead costs—nonmanufacturing as well as manufacturing—that they can reasonably be supposed to have caused. In essence, we will be determining the entire cost of a product rather than just its manufacturing cost. The focus in Chapters 3 and 4 was on determining just the manufacturing cost of a product.

Manufacturing Costs and Activity-Based Costing

In traditional cost accounting systems, *all* manufacturing costs are assigned to products—even manufacturing costs that are not caused by the products. For example, in Chapter 3 we learned that a predetermined plantwide overhead rate is computed by dividing *all* budgeted manufacturing overhead costs by a measure of budgeted activity such as direct labor-hours. This approach spreads *all* manufacturing overhead costs across products based on each product's direct labor-hour usage. In contrast, activity-based costing systems purposely do not assign two types of manufacturing overhead costs to products.

Manufacturing overhead includes costs such as the factory security guard's wages, the plant controller's salary, and the cost of supplies used by the plant manager's secretary. These types of costs are assigned to products in a traditional absorption costing system even though they are totally unaffected by which products are made during a period. In contrast, activity-based costing systems do not arbitrarily assign these types of costs, which are called *organization-sustaining* costs, to products. Activity-based costing treats these types of costs as period expenses rather than product costs.

Additionally, in a traditional absorption costing system, the costs of unused, or idle, capacity are assigned to products. If the budgeted level of activity declines, the overhead rate and unit product costs increase as the increasing costs of idle capacity are spread over a smaller base. In contrast, in activity-based costing, products are only charged for the costs of the capacity they use—not for the costs of capacity they don't use. This provides more stable unit product costs and is consistent with the goal of assigning to products only the costs of the resources that they use.[1]

Cost Pools, Allocation Bases, and Activity-Based Costing

Throughout the 19th century and most of the 20th century, cost system designs were simple and satisfactory. Typically, either one plantwide overhead cost pool or a number of departmental overhead cost pools were used to assign overhead costs to products. The plantwide and departmental approaches always had one thing in common—they relied on allocation bases such as direct labor-hours and machine-hours for allocating overhead costs to products. In the labor-intensive production processes of many years ago, direct labor was the most common choice for an overhead allocation base because it represented a large component of product costs, direct labor-hours were closely tracked, and many managers believed that direct labor-hours, the total volume of units produced, and overhead costs were highly correlated. (Three variables, such as direct labor-hours, the total volume of units produced, and overhead costs, are highly correlated if they tend to move together.) Given that most companies at the time were producing a very limited variety of products that required similar resources to produce, allocation bases such as direct labor-hours, or even machine-hours, worked fine because, in fact, there was probably little difference in the overhead costs attributable to different products.

Then conditions began to change. As a percentage of total cost, direct labor began declining and overhead began increasing. Many tasks previously done by direct laborers were being performed by automated equipment—a component of overhead. Companies began creating new products and services at an ever-accelerating rate that differed in volume, batch size, and complexity. Managing and sustaining this product diversity required investing in many more overhead resources, such as production schedulers and product design engineers, that had no obvious connection to direct labor-hours or machine-hours. In this new environment, continuing to rely exclusively on a limited number of overhead cost pools and traditional allocation bases posed the risk that reported unit product costs would be distorted and, therefore, misleading when used for decision-making purposes.

[1] Appendix 3A discusses how the costs of idle capacity can be accounted for as a period cost in an income statement. This treatment highlights the cost of idle capacity rather than burying it in inventory and cost of goods sold. The procedures laid out in this chapter for activity-based costing have the same end effect.

Activity-based costing, thanks to advances in technology that make more complex cost systems feasible, provides an alternative to the traditional plantwide and departmental approaches to defining cost pools and selecting allocation bases. The activity-based approach has appeal in today's business environment because it uses more cost pools and unique measures of activity to better understand the costs of managing and sustaining product diversity.

In activity-based costing, an **activity** is any event that causes the consumption of overhead resources. An **activity cost pool** is a "bucket" in which costs are accumulated that relate to a single activity measure in the ABC system. An **activity measure** is an allocation base in an activity-based costing system. The term *cost driver* is also used to refer to an activity measure because the activity measure should "drive" the cost being allocated. The two most common types of activity measures are *transaction drivers* and *duration drivers.* **Transaction drivers** are simple counts of the number of times an activity occurs, such as the number of bills sent out to customers. **Duration drivers** measure the amount of time required to perform an activity, such as the time spent preparing individual bills for customers. In general, duration drivers are more accurate measures of resource consumption than transaction drivers, but they take more effort to record. For that reason, transaction drivers are often used in practice.

IN BUSINESS

GASTRONOMIC COST DRIVERS AT THE CLUB MED—BORA BORA

The Club Med—Bora Bora of Tahiti is a resort owned and operated by the French company Club Med. Most guests buy all-inclusive packages that include lodging, participation in the resort's many activities, a full range of beverages, and sumptuous buffet meals. The resort's guests come from around the world including Asia, North America, South America, and Europe. The international nature of the club's guests poses challenges for the kitchen staff—for example, Japanese breakfasts feature miso soup, stewed vegetables in soy sauce, and rice porridge whereas Germans are accustomed to cold cuts, cheese, and bread for breakfast. Moreover, the number of guests varies widely from 300 in the high season to 20 in the low season. The chefs in the kitchen must ensure that food in the correct quantities and variety are available to please the club's varied clientele. To make this possible, a report is prepared each day that lists how many Japanese guests, German guests, French guests, Polish guests, U.S. guests, and so forth, are currently registered. This information helps the chefs prepare the appropriate quantities of specialized foods. In essence, costs in the kitchen are driven not by the number of guests alone, but by how many guests are Japanese, how many German, how many French, and so on. The costs are driven by multiple drivers.

Source: Conversation with Dominique Tredano, Chef de Village (i.e., general manager), Club Med—Bora, Bora. For information about Club Med, see www.clubmed.com.

Traditional cost systems rely exclusively on allocation bases that are driven by the volume of production. On the other hand, activity-based costing defines five levels of activity—unit-level, batch-level, product-level, customer-level, and organization-sustaining—that largely do *not* relate to the volume of units produced. The costs and corresponding activity measures for unit-level activities do relate to the volume of units produced; however, the remaining categories do not. These levels are described as follows:[2]

1. **Unit-level activities** are performed each time a unit is produced. The costs of unit-level activities should be proportional to the number of units produced. For example, providing power to run processing equipment would be a unit-level activity because power tends to be consumed in proportion to the number of units produced.
2. **Batch-level activities** are performed each time a batch is handled or processed, regardless of how many units are in the batch. For example, tasks such as placing

[2] Robin Cooper, "Cost Classification in Unit-Based and Activity-Based Manufacturing Cost Systems," *Journal of Cost Management,* Fall 1990, pp. 4–14.

purchase orders, setting up equipment, and arranging for shipments to customers are batch-level activities. They are incurred once for each batch (or customer order). Costs at the batch level depend on the number of batches processed rather than on the number of units produced, the number of units sold, or other measures of volume. For example, the cost of setting up a machine for batch processing is the same regardless of whether the batch contains one or thousands of items.

3. **Product-level activities** relate to specific products and typically must be carried out regardless of how many batches are run or units of product are produced or sold. For example, activities such as designing a product, advertising a product, and maintaining a product manager and staff are all product-level activities.
4. **Customer-level activities** relate to specific customers and include activities such as sales calls, catalog mailings, and general technical support that are not tied to any specific product.
5. **Organization-sustaining activities** are carried out regardless of which customers are served, which products are produced, how many batches are run, or how many units are made. This category includes activities such as heating the factory, cleaning executive offices, providing a computer network, arranging for loans, preparing annual reports to shareholders, and so on.

Many companies throughout the world continue to base overhead allocations on direct labor-hours or machine-hours. In situations where overhead costs and direct labor-hours are highly correlated or in situations where the goal of the overhead allocation process is to prepare external financial reports, this practice makes sense. However, if plantwide overhead costs do not move in tandem with plantwide direct labor-hours or machine-hours, product costs will be distorted—with the potential of distorting decisions made within the company.

IN BUSINESS

DINING IN THE CANYON

Western River Expeditions (www.westernriver.com) runs river rafting trips on the Colorado, Green, and Salmon rivers. One of its most popular trips is a six-day trip down the Grand Canyon, which features famous rapids such as Crystal and Lava Falls as well as the awesome scenery accessible only from the bottom of the Grand Canyon. The company runs trips of one or two rafts, each of which carries two guides and up to 18 guests. The company provides all meals on the trip, which are prepared by the guides.

In terms of the hierarchy of activities, a guest can be considered as a unit and a raft as a batch. In that context, the wages paid to the guides are a batch-level cost because each raft requires two guides regardless of the number of guests in the raft. Each guest is given a mug to use during the trip and to take home at the end of the trip as a souvenir. The cost of the mug is a unit-level cost because the number of mugs given away is strictly proportional to the number of guests on a trip.

What about the costs of food served to guests and guides—is this a unit-level cost, a batch-level cost, a product-level cost, or an organization-sustaining cost? At first glance, it might be thought that food costs are a unit-level cost—the greater the number of guests, the higher the food costs. However, that is not quite correct. Standard menus have been created for each day of the trip. For example, the first night's menu might consist of shrimp cocktail, steak, cornbread, salad, and cheesecake. The day before a trip begins, all of the food needed for the trip is taken from the central warehouse and packed in modular containers. It isn't practical to finely adjust the amount of food for the actual number of guests planned to be on a trip—most of the food comes prepackaged in large lots. For example, the shrimp cocktail menu may call for two large bags of frozen shrimp per raft and that many bags will be packed regardless of how many guests are expected on the raft. Consequently, the costs of food are not a unit-level cost that varies with the number of guests actually on a trip. Instead, the costs of food are a batch-level cost.

Source: Conversations with Western River Expeditions personnel.

Designing an Activity-Based Costing (ABC) System

There are three essential characteristics of a successful activity-based costing implementation. First, top managers must strongly support the ABC implementation because their leadership is instrumental in properly motivating all employees to embrace the need to change. Second, top managers should ensure that ABC data is linked to how people are evaluated and rewarded. If employees continue to be evaluated and rewarded using traditional (non-ABC) cost data, they will quickly get the message that ABC is not important and they will abandon it. Third, a cross-functional team should be created to design and implement the ABC system. The team should include representatives from each area that will use ABC data, such as the marketing, production, engineering, and accounting departments. These cross-functional employees possess intimate knowledge of many parts of an organization's operations that is necessary for designing an effective ABC system. Furthermore, tapping the knowledge of cross-functional managers lessens their resistance to ABC because they feel included in the implementation process. Time after time, when accountants have attempted to implement an ABC system on their own without top-management support and cross-functional involvement, the results have been ignored.

IN BUSINESS

IMPLEMENTING ACTIVITY-BASED COSTING IN CHINA

Xu Ji Electric Company is publicly traded on China's Shen Zhen Stock Exchange. From 2001–2003, it successfully implemented an activity-based costing (ABC) system because top-level managers continuously supported the new system—particularly during a challenging phase when the ABC software encountered problems. The ABC adoption was also aided by Xu Ji's decision to drive the implementation using a top-down approach, which is aligned with the company's cultural norm of deferring to and supporting the hierarchical chain of command.

Xu Ji's experience is similar to Western ABC implementations that have consistently recognized the necessity of top-level management support. However, contrary to Xu Ji's experience, many Western managers do not readily support the top-down implementation of new management innovations in their organizations. They prefer to be involved in the decision-making processes that introduce change into their organizations.

Source: Lana Y.J. Liu and Fei Pan, "The Implementation of Activity-Based Costing in China: An Innovation Action Research Approach," *The British Accounting Review* 39, 2007, pp. 249–264.

MANAGERIAL ACCOUNTING IN ACTION
The Issue

Classic Brass, Inc., makes two main product lines for luxury yachts—standard stanchions and custom compass housings. The president of the company, John Towers, recently attended a management conference at which activity-based costing was discussed. Following the conference, he called a meeting of the company's top managers to discuss what he had learned. Attending the meeting were production manager Susan Richter, the marketing manager Tom Olafson, and the accounting manager Mary Goodman. He began the conference by distributing the company's income statement that Mary Goodman had prepared a few hours earlier (see Exhibit 7–1):

John: Well, it's official. Our company has sunk into the red for the first time in its history—a loss of $1,250.

Tom: I don't know what else we can do! Given our successful efforts to grow sales of the custom compass housings, I was expecting to see a boost to our bottom line, not a net loss. Granted, we have been losing even more bids than usual for standard stanchions because of our recent price increase, but . . .

John: Do you think our prices for standard stanchions are too high?

Tom: No, I don't think our prices are too high. I think our competitors' prices are too low. In fact, I'll bet they are pricing below their cost.

EXHIBIT 7–1
Classic Brass Income Statement

Classic Brass
Income Statement
Year Ended December 31, 2011

Sales		$3,200,000
Cost of goods sold:		
Direct materials	$ 975,000	
Direct labor	351,250	
Manufacturing overhead*	1,000,000	2,326,250
Gross margin		873,750
Selling and administrative expenses:		
Shipping expenses	65,000	
General administrative expenses	510,000	
Marketing expenses	300,000	875,000
Net operating loss		$ (1,250)

*The company's traditional cost system allocates manufacturing overhead to products using a plantwide overhead rate and machine-hours as the allocation base. Inventory levels did not change during the year.

Susan: Why would our competitors price below their cost?

Tom: They are out to grab market share.

Susan: What good is more market share if they are losing money on every unit sold?

John: I think Susan has a point. Mary, what is your take on this?

Mary: If our competitors are pricing standard stanchions below cost, shouldn't they be losing money rather than us? If our company is the one using accurate information to make informed decisions while our competitors are supposedly clueless, then why is our "bottom line" taking a beating? Unfortunately, I think we may be the ones shooting in the dark, not our competitors.

John: Based on what I heard at the conference that I just attended, I am inclined to agree. One of the presentations at the conference dealt with activity-based costing. As the speaker began describing the usual insights revealed by activity-based costing systems, I was sitting in the audience getting an ill feeling in my stomach.

Mary: Honestly John, I have been claiming for years that our existing cost system is okay for external reporting, but it is dangerous to use it for internal decision making. It sounds like you are on board now, right?

John: Yes.

Mary: Well then, how about if all of you commit the time and energy to help me build a fairly simple activity-based costing system that may shed some light on the problems we are facing?

John: Let's do it. I want each of you to appoint one of your top people to a special "ABC team" to investigate how we cost products.

Like most other ABC implementations, the ABC team decided that its new ABC system would supplement, rather than replace, the existing cost accounting system, which would continue to be used for external financial reports. The new ABC system would be used to prepare special reports for management decisions such as bidding on new business.

The accounting manager drew the chart appearing in Exhibit 7–2 to explain the general structure of the ABC model to her team members. Cost objects such as products generate activities. For example, a customer order for a custom compass housing requires the activity of preparing a production order. Such an activity consumes resources. A production order uses a sheet of paper and takes time to fill out. And consumption of resources causes costs. The greater the number of sheets used to fill out production orders and the greater the amount of time devoted to filling out such orders, the greater the cost. Activity-based costing attempts to trace through these relationships to identify how products and customers affect costs.

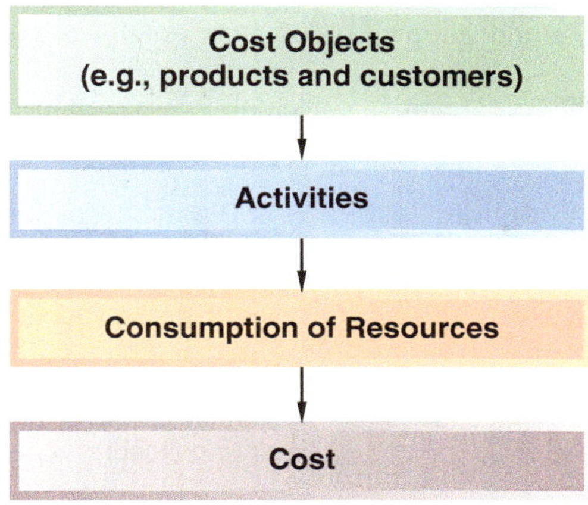

EXHIBIT 7–2
The Activity-Based Costing Model

As in most other companies, the ABC team at Classic Brass felt that the company's traditional cost accounting system adequately measured the direct materials and direct labor costs of products because these costs are directly traced to products. Therefore, the ABC study would be concerned solely with the other costs of the company—manufacturing overhead and selling and administrative costs.

The team felt it was important to carefully plan how it would go about implementing the new ABC system at Classic Brass. Accordingly, it broke down the implementation process into five steps:

Steps for Implementing Activity-Based Costing:

1. Define activities, activity cost pools, and activity measures.
2. Assign overhead costs to activity cost pools.
3. Calculate activity rates.
4. Assign overhead costs to cost objects using the activity rates and activity measures.
5. Prepare management reports.

Step 1: Define Activities, Activity Cost Pools, and Activity Measures

The first major step in implementing an ABC system is to identify the activities that will form the foundation for the system. This can be difficult and time-consuming and involves a great deal of judgment. A common procedure is for the individuals on the ABC implementation team to interview people who work in overhead departments and ask them to describe their major activities. Ordinarily, this results in a very long list of activities.

The length of such lists of activities poses a problem. On the one hand, the greater the number of activities tracked in the ABC system, the more accurate the costs are likely to be. On the other hand, a complex system involving large numbers of activities is costly to design, implement, maintain, and use. Consequently, the original lengthy list of activities is usually reduced to a handful by combining similar activities. For example, several actions may be involved in handling and moving raw materials—from receiving raw materials on the loading dock to sorting them into the appropriate bins in the storeroom. All of these activities might be combined into a single activity called material handling.

When combining activities in an ABC system, activities should be grouped together at the appropriate level. Batch-level activities should not be combined with unit-level activities or product-level activities with batch-level activities and so on. In general, it is best to combine only those activities that are highly correlated with each other within a level. For example, the number of customer orders received is likely to be highly correlated with the number of completed customer orders shipped, so these two batch-level activities (receiving and shipping orders) can usually be combined with little loss of accuracy.

At Classic Brass, the ABC team, in consultation with top managers, selected the following *activity cost pools* and *activity measures:*

Activity Cost Pools at Classic Brass	
Activity Cost Pool	Activity Measure
Customer orders	Number of customer orders
Product design	Number of product designs
Order size	Machine-hours
Customer relations	Number of active customers
Other	Not applicable

The *Customer Orders* cost pool will be assigned all costs of resources that are consumed by taking and processing customer orders, including costs of processing paperwork and any costs involved in setting up machines for specific orders. The activity measure for this cost pool is the number of customer orders received. This is a batch-level activity because each order generates work that occurs regardless of whether the order is for one unit or 1,000 units.

The *Product Design* cost pool will be assigned all costs of resources consumed by designing products. The activity measure for this cost pool is the number of products designed. This is a product-level activity because the amount of design work on a new product does not depend on the number of units ultimately ordered or batches ultimately run.

The *Order Size* cost pool will be assigned all costs of resources consumed as a consequence of the number of units produced, including the costs of miscellaneous factory supplies, power to run machines, and some equipment depreciation. This is a unit-level activity because each unit requires some of these resources. The activity measure for this cost pool is machine-hours.

The *Customer Relations* cost pool will be assigned all costs associated with maintaining relations with customers, including the costs of sales calls and the costs of entertaining customers. The activity measure for this cost pool is the number of customers the company has on its active customer list. The Customer Relations cost pool represents a customer-level activity.

The *Other* cost pool will be assigned all overhead costs that are not associated with customer orders, product design, the size of the orders, or customer relations. These costs mainly consist of organization-sustaining costs and the costs of unused, idle capacity. These costs *will not* be assigned to products because they represent resources that are *not* consumed by products.

It is unlikely that any other company would use exactly the same activity cost pools and activity measures that were selected by Classic Brass. Because of the amount of judgment involved, the number and definitions of the activity cost pools and activity measures used by companies vary considerably.

The Mechanics of Activity-Based Costing

LEARNING OBJECTIVE 2
Assign costs to cost pools using a first-stage allocation.

Step 2: Assign Overhead Costs to Activity Cost Pools

Exhibit 7–3 shows the annual overhead costs (both manufacturing and nonmanufacturing) that Classic Brass intends to assign to its activity cost pools. Notice the data in the exhibit are organized by department (e.g., Production, General Administrative, and Marketing). This is because the data have been extracted from the company's general ledger. General ledgers usually classify costs within the departments where the costs

EXHIBIT 7–3
Annual Overhead Costs (Both Manufacturing and Nonmanufacturing) at Classic Brass

Production Department:		
Indirect factory wages	$500,000	
Factory equipment depreciation	300,000	
Factory utilities	120,000	
Factory building lease	80,000	$1,000,000
General Administrative Department:		
Administrative wages and salaries	400,000	
Office equipment depreciation	50,000	
Administrative building lease	60,000	510,000
Marketing Department:		
Marketing wages and salaries	250,000	
Selling expenses	50,000	300,000
Total overhead cost		$1,810,000

are incurred. For example, salaries, supplies, rent, and so forth incurred in the marketing department are charged to that department. The functional orientation of the general ledger mirrors the presentation of costs in the absorption income statement in Exhibit 7–1. In fact, you'll notice the total costs for the Production Department in Exhibit 7–3 ($1,000,000) equal the total manufacturing overhead costs from the income statement in Exhibit 7–1. Similarly, the total costs for the General Administrative and Marketing Departments in Exhibit 7–3 ($510,000 and $300,000) equal the marketing and general and administrative expenses shown in Exhibit 7–1.

Three costs included in the income statement in Exhibit 7–1—direct materials, direct labor, and shipping—are excluded from the costs shown in Exhibit 7–3. The ABC team purposely excluded these costs from Exhibit 7–3 because the existing cost system can accurately trace direct materials, direct labor, and shipping costs to products. There is no need to incorporate these direct costs in the activity-based allocations of indirect costs.

Classic Brass's activity-based costing system will divide the nine types of overhead costs in Exhibit 7–3 among its activity cost pools via an allocation process called *first-stage allocation.* The **first-stage allocation** in an ABC system is the process of assigning functionally organized overhead costs derived from a company's general ledger to the activity cost pools.

First-stage allocations are usually based on the results of interviews with employees who have first-hand knowledge of the activities. For example, Classic Brass needs to allocate $500,000 of indirect factory wages to its five activity cost pools. These allocations will be more accurate if the employees who are classified as indirect factory workers (e.g., supervisors, engineers, and quality inspectors) are asked to estimate what percentage of their time is spent dealing with customer orders, with product design, with processing units of product (i.e., order size), and with customer relations. These interviews are conducted with considerable care. Those who are interviewed must thoroughly understand what the activities encompass and what is expected of them in the interview. In addition, departmental managers are typically interviewed to determine how the nonpersonnel costs should be distributed across the activity cost pools. For example, the Classic Brass production manager would be interviewed to determine how the $300,000 of factory equipment depreciation (shown in Exhibit 7–3) should be allocated to the activity cost pools. The key question that the production manager would need to answer is "What percentage of the available machine capacity is consumed by each activity such as the number of customer orders or the number of units processed (i.e., size of orders)?"

IN BUSINESS

ABC HELPS A DAIRY UNDERSTAND ITS COSTS

Kemps LLC, headquartered in Minneapolis, Minnesota, produces dairy products such as milk, yogurt, and ice cream. The company implemented an ABC system that helped managers understand the impact of product and customer diversity on profit margins. The ABC model "captured differences in how the company entered orders from customers (customer phone call, salesperson call, fax, truck-driver entry, EDI, or Internet), how it packaged orders (full stacks of six cases, individual cases, or partial break-pack cases for small orders), how it delivered orders (commercial carriers or its own fleet, including route miles), and time spent by the driver at each customer location."

Kemps' ABC system helped the company acquire a large national customer because it identified "the specific manufacturing, distribution, and order handling costs associated with serving this customer." The ability to provide the customer with accurate cost information built a trusting relationship that distinguished Kemps from other competitors. Kemps also used its ABC data to transform unprofitable customers into profitable ones. For example, one customer agreed to accept a 13% price increase, to eliminate two low-volume products, and to begin placing full truckload orders rather than requiring partial truckload shipments, thereby lowering Kemps' costs by $150,000 per year.

Source: Robert S. Kaplan and Steven R. Anderson, "Time-Driven Activity-Based Costing," *Harvard Business Review*, November 2004, pp. 131–139.

The results of the interviews at Classic Brass are displayed in Exhibit 7–4. For example, factory equipment depreciation is distributed 20% to Customer Orders, 60% to Order Size, and 20% to the Other cost pool. The resource in this instance is machine time. According to the estimates made by the production manager, 60% of the total available machine time was used to actually process units to fill orders. This percentage is entered in the Order Size column. Each customer order requires setting up, which also requires machine time. This activity consumes 20% of the total available machine time and is entered under the Customer Orders column. The remaining 20% of available machine time represents idle time and is entered under the Other column.

Exhibit 7–4 and many of the other exhibits in this chapter are presented in the form of Excel spreadsheets. All of the calculations required in activity-based costing can be done by hand. Nevertheless, setting up an activity-based costing system on a spreadsheet or using special ABC software can save a lot of work—particularly in situations involving many activity cost pools and in organizations that periodically update their ABC systems.

We will not go into the details of how all of the percentages in Exhibit 7–4 were determined. However, note that 100% of the factory building lease has been assigned to the Other cost pool. Classic Brass has a single production facility. It has no plans to expand or to sublease any excess space. The cost of this production facility is treated as an organization-sustaining cost because there is no way to avoid even a portion of this cost if a particular product or customer were to be dropped. (Remember that organization-sustaining costs are assigned to the Other cost pool and are not allocated to products.) In contrast, some companies have separate facilities for manufacturing specific products. The costs of these separate facilities could be directly traced to the specific products.

Once the percentage distributions in Exhibit 7–4 have been established, it is easy to allocate costs to the activity cost pools. The results of this first-stage allocation are displayed in Exhibit 7–5. Each cost is allocated across the activity cost pools by multiplying it by the percentages in Exhibit 7–4. For example, the indirect factory wages of $500,000 are multiplied by the 25% entry under Customer Orders in Exhibit 7–4 to arrive at the $125,000 entry under Customer Orders in Exhibit 7–5. Similarly, the indirect factory wages of $500,000 are multiplied by the 40% entry under Product Design in Exhibit 7–4 to arrive at the $200,000 entry under Product Design in Exhibit 7–5. All of the entries in Exhibit 7–5 are computed in this way.

EXHIBIT 7–4
Results of Interviews: Distribution of Resource Consumption across Activity Cost Pools

	Activity Cost Pools					
	Customer Orders	Product Design	Order Size	Customer Relations	Other	Totals
Production Department:						
Indirect factory wages	25%	40%	20%	10%	5%	100%
Factory equipment depreciation	20%	0%	60%	0%	20%	100%
Factory utilities	0%	10%	50%	0%	40%	100%
Factory building lease	0%	0%	0%	0%	100%	100%
General Administrative Department:						
Administrative wages and salaries	15%	5%	10%	30%	40%	100%
Office equipment depreciation	30%	0%	0%	25%	45%	100%
Administrative building lease	0%	0%	0%	0%	100%	100%
Marketing Department:						
Marketing wages and salaries	22%	8%	0%	60%	10%	100%
Selling expenses	10%	0%	0%	70%	20%	100%

EXHIBIT 7–5
First-Stage Allocations to Activity Cost Pools

	Activity Cost Pools					
	Customer Orders	Product Design	Order Size	Customer Relations	Other	Totals
Production Department:						
Indirect factory wages	$ 125,000	$ 200,000	$ 100,000	$ 50,000	$ 25,000	$ 500,000
Factory equipment depreciation	60,000	0	180,000	0	60,000	300,000
Factory utilities	0	12,000	60,000	0	48,000	120,000
Factory building lease	0	0	0	0	80,000	80,000
General Administrative Department:						
Administrative wages and salaries	60,000	20,000	40,000	120,000	160,000	400,000
Office equipment depreciation	15,000	0	0	12,500	22,500	50,000
Administrative building lease	0	0	0	0	60,000	60,000
Marketing Department:						
Marketing wages and salaries	55,000	20,000	0	150,000	25,000	250,000
Selling expenses	5,000	0	0	35,000	10,000	50,000
Total	$ 320,000	$ 252,000	$ 380,000	$ 367,500	$ 490,500	$ 1,810,000

Exhibit 7–4 shows that Customer Orders consume 25% of the resources represented by the $500,000 of indirected factory wages.

$25\% \times \$500{,}000 = \$125{,}000$

Other entries in the table are computed in a similar fashion.

Now that the first-stage allocations to the activity cost pools have been completed, the next step is to compute the activity rates.

Step 3: Calculate Activity Rates

LEARNING OBJECTIVE 3
Compute activity rates for cost pools.

The activity rates that will be used for assigning overhead costs to products and customers are computed in Exhibit 7–6. The ABC team determined the total activity for each cost pool that would be required to produce the company's present product mix and to serve its present customers. These numbers are listed in Exhibit 7–6. For example, the ABC team found that 400 new product designs are required each year to serve the company's present customers. The activity rates are computed by dividing the *total* cost for each activity by its *total* activity. For example, the $320,000 total annual cost for the Customer Orders cost pool (which was computed in Exhibit 7–5) is divided by the total of 1,000 customer orders per year to arrive at the activity rate of $320 per customer order. Similarly, the $252,000 *total* cost for the Product Design cost pool is divided by the *total* number of designs (i.e., 400 product designs) to determine the activity rate of $630 per design. Note that an activity rate is not computed for the Other category of costs. This is because the *Other* cost pool consists of organization-sustaining costs and costs of idle capacity that are not allocated to products and customers.

The rates in Exhibit 7–6 indicate that *on average* a customer order consumes resources that cost $320; a product design consumes resources that cost $630; a unit of product consumes resources that cost $19 per machine-hour; and maintaining relations with a customer consumes resources that cost $1,470. Note that these are *average* figures. Some members of the ABC design team at Classic Brass argued that it would be unfair to charge all new products the same $630 product design cost regardless of how much design time they actually require. After discussing the pros and cons, the team concluded that it would not be worth the effort at the present time to keep track of actual design time spent on each new product. They felt that the benefits of increased accuracy would not be great enough to justify the higher cost of implementing and maintaining the more detailed costing system. Similarly, some team members were uncomfortable assigning the same $1,470 cost to each customer. Some customers are undemanding—ordering standard products well in advance of their needs. Others are very demanding and consume large amounts of marketing and administrative staff time. These are generally customers who order customized products, who tend to order at the last minute, and who change their minds. While everyone agreed with this observation, the data that would be required to measure individual customers' demands on resources were not currently available. Rather than delay implementation of the ABC system, the team decided to defer such refinements to a later date.

Before proceeding further, it would be helpful to get a better idea of the overall process of assigning costs to products and other cost objects in an ABC system. Exhibit 7–7 provides

EXHIBIT 7–6
Computation of Activity Rates

	A	B	C	D	E	F
1	*Activity Cost Pools*	*(a)* *Total Cost**	*(b)* *Total Activity*		*(a) ÷ (b)* *Activity Rate*	
2	Customer orders	$320,000	1,000	orders	$320	per order
3	Product design	$252,000	400	designs	$630	per design
4	Order size	$380,000	20,000	MHs	$19	per MH
5	Customer relations	$367,500	250	customers	$1,470	per customer
6	Other	$490,500	Not applicable		Not applicable	
7						
8	*From Exhibit 7-5.					
9						

Exhibit 7-4 | Exhibit 7-5 | Exhibit 7-6 | Exhibit 7-8

EXHIBIT 7–7
The Activity-Based Costing Model at Classic Brass

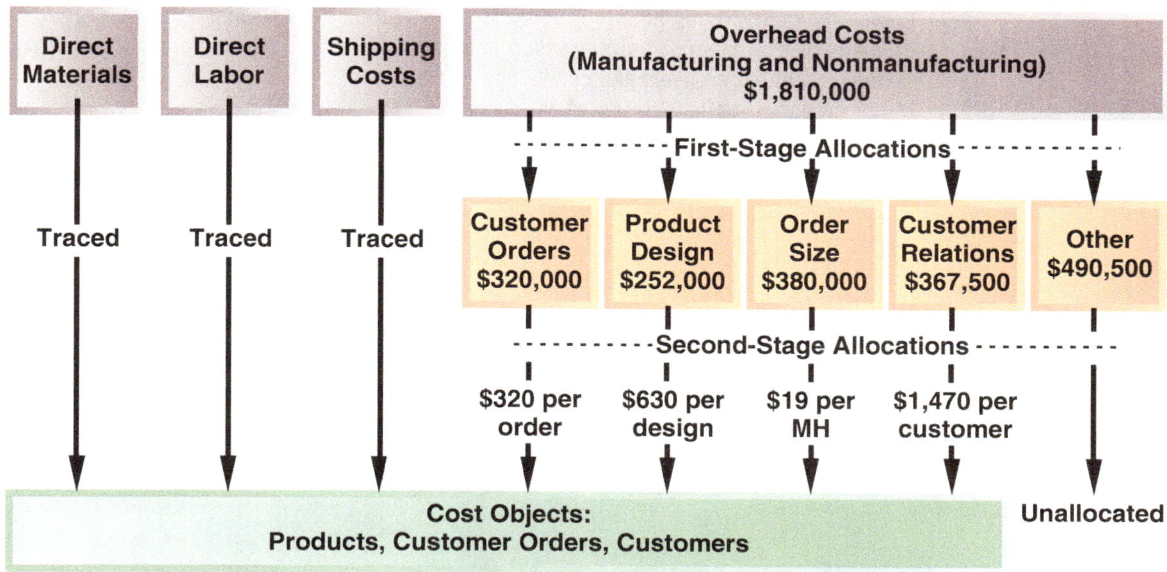

a visual perspective of the ABC system at Classic Brass. We recommend that you carefully go over this exhibit. In particular, note that the Other category, which contains organization-sustaining costs and costs of idle capacity, is not allocated to products or customers.

Step 4: Assign Overhead Costs to Cost Objects

LEARNING OBJECTIVE 4
Assign costs to a cost object using a second-stage allocation.

The fourth step in the implementation of activity-based costing is called *second-stage allocation.* In the **second-stage allocation,** activity rates are used to apply overhead costs to products and customers. First, we will illustrate how to assign costs to products followed by an example of how to assign costs to customers.

The data needed by the ABC team to assign overhead costs to Classic Brass's two products—standard stanchions and custom compass housings—are as follows:

Standard Stanchions

1. This product line does not require any new design resources.
2. 30,000 units were ordered during the year, comprising 600 separate orders.
3. Each stanchion requires 35 minutes of machine time for a total of 17,500 machine-hours.

Custom Compass Housings

1. This is a custom product that requires new design resources.
2. There were 400 orders for custom compass housings. Orders for this product are placed separately from orders for standard stanchions.
3. There were 400 custom designs prepared. One custom design was prepared for each order.
4. Because some orders were for more than one unit, a total of 1,250 custom compass housings were produced during the year. A custom compass housing requires an average of 2 machine-hours for a total of 2,500 machine-hours.

Notice, 600 customer orders were placed for standard stanchions and 400 customer orders were placed for custom compass housings, for a total of 1,000 customer orders. All 400 product designs related to custom compass housings; none related to standard stanchions. Producing 30,000 standard stanchions required 17,500 machine-hours and

IN BUSINESS

HOW MUCH DOES IT COST TO HANDLE A PIECE OF LUGGAGE?

It costs an airline about $15 to carry a piece of checked luggage from one destination another. The activity "transporting luggage" consists of numerous sub-activities such as tagging bags, sorting them, placing them on carts, transporting bags planeside, loading them into the airplane, and delivering them to carousels and connecting flights.

A variety of employees invest a portion of their labor hours "transporting luggage" including ground personnel, check-in agents, service clerks, baggage service managers, and maintenance workers. In total, labor costs comprise $9 per bag. Airlines also spend millions of dollars on baggage equipment, sorting systems, carts, tractors, and conveyors, as well as rental costs related to bag rooms, carousels, and offices. They also pay to deliver misplaced bags to customers' homes and to compensate customers for lost bags that are never found. These expenses add up to about $4 per bag. The final expense related to transporting luggage is fuel costs, which average about $2 per bag.

Many major airlines are charging $15 each way for one checked bag and $25 each way for a second checked bag. United Airlines expects to collect $275 million annually for its first and second bag fees.

Source: Scott McCartney, "What It Costs an Airline to Fly Your Luggage," *The Wall Street Journal*, November 25, 2008, p. D1 and D8.

producing 1,250 custom compass housings required 2,500 machine-hours, for a total of 20,000 machine-hours.

Exhibit 7–8 illustrates how overhead costs are assigned to the standard stanchions and custom compass housings. For example, the exhibit shows that $192,000 of overhead costs are assigned from the Customer Orders activity cost pool to the standard stanchions ($320 per order × 600 orders). Similarly, $128,000 of overhead costs are assigned from the Customer Orders activity cost pool to the custom compass housings ($320 per

EXHIBIT 7–8
Assigning Overhead Costs to Products

	A	B	C	D	E	F
1	**Overhead Cost for the Standard Stanchions**					
2	*Activity Cost Pools*	*(a) Activity Rate**		*(b) Activity*		*(a) × (b) ABC Cost*
3	Customer orders	$320	per order	600	orders	$ 192,000
4	Product design	$630	per design	0	designs	0
5	Order size	$19	per MH	17,500	MHs	332,500
6	Total					$ 524,500
7						
8	**Overhead Cost for the Custom Compass Housing**					
9	*Activity Cost Pools*	*(a) Activity Rate**		*(b) Activity*		*(a) × (b) ABC Cost*
10	Customer orders	$320	per order	400	orders	$ 128,000
11	Product design	$630	per design	400	designs	252,000
12	Order size	$19	per MH	2,500	MHs	47,500
13	Total					$ 427,500
14						
15	*From Exhibit 7-6.					
16						

Exhibit 7-6 | Exhibit 7-8 | Exhibit 7-9 | Ex

order × 400 orders). The Customer Orders cost pool contained a total of $320,000 (see Exhibit 7–5 or 7–6) and this total amount has been assigned to the two products ($192,000 + $128,000 = $320,000).

Exhibit 7–8 shows that a total of $952,000 of overhead costs is assigned to Classic Brass's two product lines—$524,500 to standard stanchions and $427,500 to custom compass housings. This amount is less than the $1,810,000 of overhead costs included in the ABC system. Why? The total amount of overhead assigned to products does not match the total amount of overhead cost in the ABC system because the ABC team purposely did not assign the $367,500 of Customer Relations and $490,500 of Other costs to products. The Customer Relations activity is a customer-level activity and the Other activity is an organization-sustaining activity—neither activity is caused by products. As shown below, when the Customer Relations and Other activity costs are added to the $952,000 of overhead costs assigned to products, the total is $1,810,000.

	Standard Stanchions	Custom Compass Housings	Total
Overhead Costs Assigned to Products			
Customer orders	$192,000	$128,000	$ 320,000
Product design	0	252,000	252,000
Order size	332,500	47,500	380,000
Subtotal	$524,500	$427,500	952,000
Overhead Costs not Assigned to Products			
Customer relations			367,500
Other			490,500
Subtotal			858,000
Total overhead cost			$1,810,000

Next, we describe another example of second-stage allocation—assigning activity costs to customers. The data needed by Classic Brass to assign overhead costs to one of its customers—Windward Yachts—are as follows:

Windward Yachts

1. The company placed a total of three orders.
   a. Two orders were for 150 standard stanchions per order.
   b. One order was for a single custom compass housing unit.
2. A total of 177 machine-hours were used to fulfill the three customer orders.
   a. The 300 standard stanchions required 175 machine-hours.
   b. The custom compass housing required 2 machine-hours.
3. Windward Yachts is one of 250 customers served by Classic Brass.

Exhibit 7–9 illustrates how the ABC system assigns overhead costs to this customer. As shown in Exhibit 7–9, the ABC team calculated that $6,423 of overhead costs should be assigned to Windward Yachts. The exhibit shows that Windward Yachts is assigned $960 ($320 per order × 3 orders) of overhead costs from the Customer Orders activity cost pool; $630 ($630 per design × 1 design) from the Product Design cost pool; $3,363 ($19 per machine-hour × 177 machine-hours) from the Order Size cost pool; and $1,470 ($1,470 per customer × 1 customer) from the Customer Relations cost pool.

EXHIBIT 7–9
Assigning Overhead Costs to Customers

	A	B	C	D	E	F
1	**Overhead Cost for Windward Yachts**					
2						
3	*Activity Cost Pools*		*(a)* *Activity Rate**		*(b)* *Activity*	*(a) × (b)* *ABC Cost*
4	Customer orders	$320	per order	3	orders	$ 960
5	Product design	$630	per design	1	designs	630
6	Order size	$19	per MH	177	MHs	3,363
7	Customer relations	$1,470	per customer	1	customer	1,470
8	Total overhead cost assigned to customer					$ 6,423
9						
10	*From Exhibit 7-6.					
11						

Exhibit 7-9 / Exhibit 7-10 / Exhibit 7-10 (2) / Exhib

With second-stage allocations complete, the ABC design team was ready to turn its attention to creating reports that would help explain the company's first ever net operating loss.

Step 5: Prepare Management Reports

LEARNING OBJECTIVE 5
Use activity-based costing to compute product and customer margins.

The most common management reports prepared with ABC data are product and customer profitability reports. These reports help companies channel their resources to their most profitable growth opportunities while at the same time highlighting products and customers that drain profits. We begin by illustrating a product profitability report followed by a customer profitability report.

The Classic Brass ABC team realized that the profit from a product, also called the *product margin*, is a function of the product's sales and the direct and indirect costs that the product causes. The ABC cost allocations shown in Exhibit 7–8 only summarize each product's indirect (i.e., overhead) costs. Therefore, to compute a product's profit (i.e., product margin), the design team needed to gather each product's sales and direct costs in addition to the overhead costs previously computed. The pertinent sales and direct cost data for each product are shown below. Notice the numbers in the total column agree with the income statement in Exhibit 7–1.

	Standard Stanchions	Custom Compass Housings	Total
Sales	$2,660,000	$540,000	$3,200,000
Direct costs:			
Direct materials	$905,500	$69,500	$975,000
Direct labor	$263,750	$87,500	$351,250
Shipping	$60,000	$5,000	$65,000

Having gathered the above data, the design team created the product profitability report shown in Exhibit 7–10. The report revealed that standard stanchions are profitable, with a positive product margin of $906,250, whereas the custom compass housings are unprofitable, with a negative product margin of $49,500. Keep in mind that the product profitability report purposely does not include the costs in the Customer Relations and Other activity cost pools. These costs, which total $858,000, were excluded from the

EXHIBIT 7–10
Product Margins—Activity-Based Costing

	A	B	C	D	E	F
1	**Product Margins—Activity-Based Costing**					
2		*Standard Stanchions*			*Custom Compass Housings*	
3	Sales		$ 2,660,000			$ 540,000
4	Costs:					
5	Direct materials	$ 905,500			$ 69,500	
6	Direct labor	263,750			87,500	
7	Shipping	60,000			5,000	
8	Customer orders (from Exhibit 7-8)	192,000			128,000	
9	Product design (from Exhibit 7-8)	-			252,000	
10	Order size (from Exhibit 7-8)	332,500			47,500	
11	Total cost		1,753,750			589,500
12	Product margin		$ 906,250			$ (49,500)
13						

Exhibit 7-10 / Exhibit 7-10 (2) / Exhibit 7-11 / Exhibit 7-1

report because they are not caused by the products. Customer Relations costs are caused by customers, not products. The Other costs are organization-sustaining costs and unused capacity costs that are not caused by any particular product.

The product margins can be reconciled with the company's net operating loss as follows:

	Standard Stanchions	Custom Compass Housings	Total
Sales (See Exhibit 7–10)	$2,660,000	$540,000	$3,200,000
Total costs (See Exhibit 7–10)	1,753,750	589,500	2,343,250
Product margins (See Exhibit 7–10)	$ 906,250	$ (49,500)	856,750
Overhead costs not assigned to products:			
Customer relations			367,500
Other			490,500
Total			858,000
Net operating loss			$ (1,250)

Next, the design team created a customer profitability report for Windward Yachts. Similar to the product profitability report, the design team needed to gather data concerning sales to Windward Yachts and the direct material, direct labor, and shipping costs associated with those sales. Those data are presented below:

	Windward Yachts
Sales	$11,350
Direct costs:	
Direct material costs	$2,123
Direct labor costs	$1,900
Shipping costs	$205

IN BUSINESS

IS ACTIVITY-BASED COSTING STILL BEING USED?

Researchers surveyed 348 managers to determine which costing methods their companies use. The table below shows the percentage of respondents whose companies use the various costing methods to assign departmental costs to cost objects such as products.

	Departments						
Costing Method	Research and Development	Product and Process Design	Production	Sales and Marketing	Distribution	Customer Service	Shared Services
Activity-based	13.0%	14.7%	18.3%	17.3%	17.2%	21.8%	23.0%
Standard[1]	17.6%	20.7%	42.0%	18.1%	28.4%	18.5%	23.0%
Normal[2]	4.6%	8.6%	9.9%	7.9%	6.0%	8.1%	5.6%
Actual[3]	23.1%	25.0%	23.7%	23.6%	26.7%	16.9%	15.9%
Other	1.9%	0.9%	0.0%	0.8%	0.9%	1.6%	2.4%
Not allocated	39.8%	30.2%	6.1%	32.3%	20.7%	33.1%	30.2%

[1]Standard costing is used for the variance computations in Chapter 10.
[2]Normal costing is used for the job-order costing computations in Chapter 3.
[3]Actual costing is used to create the absorption and variable costing income statements in Chapter 6.

The results show that 18.3% of respondents use ABC to allocate production costs to cost objects and 42% use standard costing for the same purpose. ABC is used by at least 13% of respondents within all functional departments across the value chain. Many companies do not allocate nonproduction costs to cost objects.

Source: William O. Stratton, Denis Desroches, Raef Lawson, and Toby Hatch, "Activity-Based Costing: Is It Still Relevant?" *Management Accounting Quarterly*, Spring 2009, pp. 31–40.

Using these data and the data from Exhibit 7–9, the design team created the customer profitability report shown in Exhibit 7–11. The report revealed that the customer margin for Windward Yachts is $699. A similar report could be prepared for each of Classic

EXHIBIT 7–11
Customer Margin—Activity-Based Costing

	A	B	C
1	**Customer Margin—Activity-Based Costing**		
2		*Windward Yachts*	
3	Sales		$ 11,350
4	Costs:		
5	Direct materials	$ 2,123	
6	Direct labor	1,900	
7	Shipping	205	
8	Customer orders (from Exhibit 7-9)	960	
9	Product design (from Exhibit 7-9)	630	
10	Order size (from Exhibit 7-9)	3,363	
11	Customer relations (from Exhibit 7-9)	1,470	10,651
12	Customer margin		$ 699
13			

Exhibit 7-11 | Exhibit 7-12 | Exhib

Brass's 250 customers, thereby enabling the company to cultivate relationships with its most profitable customers, while taking steps to reduce the negative impact of unprofitable customers.

Comparison of Traditional and ABC Product Costs

The ABC team used a two-step process to compare its traditional and ABC product costs. First, the team reviewed the product margins reported by the traditional cost system. Then, it contrasted the differences between the traditional and ABC product margins.

Product Margins Computed Using the Traditional Cost System

Classic Brass's traditional cost system assigns only manufacturing costs to products—this includes direct materials, direct labor, and manufacturing overhead. Selling and administrative costs are not assigned to products. Exhibit 7–12 shows the product margins reported by Classic Brass's traditional cost system. We will explain how these margins were calculated in three steps. First, the sales and direct materials and direct labor cost data are the same numbers used by the ABC team to prepare Exhibit 7–10. In other words, the traditional cost system and the ABC system treat these three pieces of revenue and cost data identically.

Second, the traditional cost system uses a plantwide overhead rate to assign manufacturing overhead costs to products. The numerator for the plantwide overhead rate is \$1,000,000, which is the total amount of manufacturing overhead shown on the income statement in Exhibit 7–1. The footnote in Exhibit 7–1 mentions that the traditional cost system uses machine-hours to assign manufacturing overhead costs to products. The Order Size activity in Exhibit 7–6 used 20,000 machine-hours as its level of activity. These same 20,000 machine-hours would be used in the denominator of the plantwide overhead rate, which is computed as follows:

$$\text{Plantwide overhead rate} = \frac{\text{Total estimated manufacturing overhead}}{\text{Total estimated machine-hours}}$$

$$= \frac{\$1{,}000{,}000}{20{,}000 \text{ machine-hours}}$$

$$= \$50 \text{ per machine-hour}$$

Because 17,500 machine-hours were worked on standard stanchions, this product line is assigned \$875,000 (17,500 machine-hours × \$50 per machine-hour) of manufacturing overhead cost. Similarly, the custom compass housings required 2,500 machine-hours, so this product line is assigned \$125,000 (2,500 machine-hours × \$50 per machine-hour) of manufacturing overhead cost. The sales of each product minus its cost of goods sold equals the product margin of \$615,750 for standard stanchions and \$258,000 for custom compass housings.

Notice, the net operating loss of \$1,250 shown in Exhibit 7–12 agrees with the loss reported in the income statement in Exhibit 7–1 and with the loss shown in the table beneath Exhibit 7–10. The company's *total* sales, *total* costs, and its resulting net operating loss are the same regardless of whether you are looking at the absorption income statement in Exhibit 7–1, the ABC product profitability analysis depicted on page 289, or the traditional product profitability analysis in Exhibit 7–12. Although the "total pie" remains constant across the traditional and ABC systems, what differs is how the pie is divided between the two product lines. The traditional product margin calculations suggest that standard stanchions are generating a product margin of \$615,750 and the custom compass housings a product margin of \$258,000. However, these product margins differ

EXHIBIT 7–12
Product Margins—Traditional Costing System

	A	B	C	D	E	F	G	H	I
1	**Product Margins—Traditional Cost System**								
2		*Standard Stanchions*			*Custom Compass Housings*			*Total*	
3	Sales		$2,660,000			$ 540,000			$3,200,000
4	Cost of goods sold:								
5	Direct materials	$ 905,500			$ 69,500			$ 975,000	
6	Direct labor	263,750			87,500			351,250	
7	Manufacturing overhead	875,000	2,044,250		125,000	282,000		1,000,000	2,326,250
8	Product margin		$ 615,750			$ 258,000			873,750
9	Selling and administrative								875,000
10	Net operating loss								$ (1,250)
11									

Exhibit 7-10 (2) / Exhibit 7-11 / **Exhibit 7-12** / Exhibit 7-13 / Exhibit 7A-1

from the ABC product margins reported in Exhibit 7–10. Indeed, the traditional cost system is sending misleading signals to Classic Brass's managers about each product's profitability. Let's explain why.

The Differences between ABC and Traditional Product Costs

The changes in product margins caused by switching from the traditional cost system to the activity-based costing system are shown below:

	Standard Stanchions	Custom Compass Housings
Product margins—traditional	$615,750	$ 258,000
Product margins—ABC	906,250	(49,500)
Change in reported product margins	$290,500	$(307,500)

The traditional cost system overcosts the standard stanchions and consequently reports an artificially low product margin for this product. The switch to an activity-based view of product profitability increases the product margin on standard stanchions by $290,500. In contrast, the traditional cost system undercosts the custom compass housings and reports an artificially high product margin for this product. The switch to activity-based costing decreases the product margin on custom compass housings by $307,500.

The reasons for the change in reported product margins between the two costing methods are revealed in Exhibit 7–13. The top portion of the exhibit shows each product's direct and indirect cost assignments as reported by the traditional cost system in Exhibit 7–12. For example, Exhibit 7–13 includes the following costs for standard stanchions: direct materials, $905,500; direct labor, $263,750; and manufacturing overhead, $875,000. Each of these costs corresponds with those reported in Exhibit 7–12. Notice, the selling and administrative costs of $875,000 are purposely not allocated to products because these costs are considered to be period costs. Similarly, the bottom portion of Exhibit 7–13 summarizes the direct and indirect cost assignments as reported by the activity-based costing system in Exhibit 7–10. The only new information in Exhibit 7–13 is shown in the two columns of percentages. The first column of percentages shows the percentage of each cost assigned to standard stanchions. For example, the $905,500 of direct materials cost traced to standard stanchions is 92.9% of the company's total direct materials cost of $975,000. The second column of percentages does the same thing for custom compass housings.

EXHIBIT 7–13
A Comparison of Traditional and Activity-Based Cost Assignments

	Standard Stanchions		Custom Compass Housings		
Traditional Cost System	(a) Amount	(a) ÷ (c) %	(b) Amount	(b) ÷ (c) %	(c) Total
Direct materials	$ 905,500	92.9%	$ 69,500	7.1%	$ 975,000
Direct labor	263,750	75.1%	87,500	24.9%	351,250
Manufacturing overhead	875,000	87.5%	125,000	12.5%	1,000,000
Total cost assigned to products	$2,044,250		$282,000		2,326,250
Selling and administrative					875,000
Total cost					$3,201,250
Activity-Based Costing System					
Direct costs:					
Direct materials	$ 905,500	92.9%	$ 69,500	7.1%	$ 975,000
Direct labor	263,750	75.1%	87,500	24.9%	351,250
Shipping	60,000	92.3%	5,000	7.7%	65,000
Indirect costs:					
Customer orders	192,000	60.0%	128,000	40.0%	320,000
Product design	0	0.0%	252,000	100.0%	252,000
Order size	332,500	87.5%	47,500	12.5%	380,000
Total cost assigned to products	$1,753,750		$589,500		2,343,250
Costs not assigned to products:					
Customer relations					367,500
Other					490,500
Total cost					$3,201,250

There are three reasons why the traditional and activity-based costing systems report different product margins. First, Classic Brass's traditional cost system allocates all manufacturing overhead costs to products. This forces both products to absorb all manufacturing overhead costs regardless of whether they actually consumed the costs that were allocated to them. The ABC system does not assign the manufacturing overhead costs consumed by the Customer Relations activity to products because these costs are caused by customers, not specific products. It also does not assign the manufacturing overhead costs included in the Other activity to products because these organization-sustaining and unused capacity costs are not caused by any particular product. From an ABC point of view, assigning these costs to products is inherently arbitrary and counterproductive.

Second, Classic Brass's traditional cost system allocates all of the manufacturing overhead costs using a volume-related allocation base—machine-hours—that may or may not reflect what actually causes the costs. In other words, in the traditional system, 87.5% of each manufacturing overhead cost is implicitly assigned to standard stanchions and 12.5% is assigned to custom compass housings. For example, the traditional cost system inappropriately assigns 87.5% of the costs of the Customer Orders activity (a batch-level activity) to standard stanchions even though the ABC system revealed that standard stanchions caused only 60% of these costs. Conversely, the traditional cost system assigns only 12.5% of these costs to custom compass housings even though this product caused 40% of these costs. Similarly, the traditional cost system assigns 87.5% of the costs of the Product Design activity (a product-level activity) to standard stanchions even though the standard stanchions caused none (0%) of these costs. All (100%) of the costs of the Product Design activity, rather than just 12.5%, should be assigned to custom compass housings. The result is that traditional cost systems overcost high-volume products (such as the standard stanchions) and undercost low-volume products (such as the custom compass housings) because they assign batch-level and product-level costs using volume-related allocation bases.

The third reason the product margins differ between the two cost systems is that the ABC system assigns the nonmanufacturing overhead costs caused by products to those products on a cause-and-effect basis. The traditional cost system disregards these costs because they are classified as period costs. The ABC system directly traces shipping costs to products and includes the nonmanufacturing overhead costs caused by products in the activity cost pools that are assigned to products.

The ABC design team presented the results of its work in a meeting attended by all of the top managers of Classic Brass, including the president John Towers, the production manager Susan Richter, the marketing manager Tom Olafson, and the accounting manager Mary Goodman. The ABC team brought with them copies of the chart showing the ABC design (Exhibit 7–7), and the table comparing the traditional and ABC cost assignments (Exhibit 7–13). After the formal presentation by the ABC team, the following discussion took place:

MANAGERIAL ACCOUNTING IN ACTION
The Wrap-Up

John: I would like to personally thank the ABC team for all of the work they have done and for an extremely interesting presentation. I am now beginning to wonder about a lot of the decisions we have made in the past using our old cost accounting system. According to the ABC analysis, we had it all backwards. We are losing money on the custom products and making a fistful on the standard products.

Mary: I have to admit that I had no idea that the Product Design work for custom compass housings was so expensive! I knew burying these costs in our plantwide overhead rate was penalizing standard stanchions, but I didn't understand the magnitude of the problem.

Susan: I never did believe we were making a lot of money on the custom jobs. You ought to see all of the problems they create for us in production.

Tom: I hate to admit it, but the custom jobs always seem to give us headaches in marketing, too.

John: If we are losing money on custom compass housings, why not suggest to our customers that they go elsewhere for that kind of work?

Tom: Wait a minute, we would lose a lot of sales.

Susan: So what, we would save a lot more costs.

Mary: Maybe yes, maybe no. Some of the costs would not disappear if we were to drop the custom business.

Tom: Like what?

Mary: Well Tom, I believe you said that about 10% of your time is spent dealing with new products. As a consequence, 10% of your salary was allocated to the Product Design cost pool. If we were to drop all of the products requiring design work, would you be willing to take a 10% pay cut?

Tom: I trust you're joking.

Mary: Do you see the problem? Just because 10% of your time is spent on custom products doesn't mean that the company would save 10% of your salary if the custom products were dropped. Before we take a drastic action like dropping the custom products, we should identify which costs are really relevant.

John: I think I see what you are driving at. We wouldn't want to drop a lot of products only to find that our costs really haven't changed much. It is true that dropping the products would free up resources like Tom's time, but we had better be sure we have some good use for those resources *before* we take such an action.

As this discussion among the managers of Classic Brass illustrates, caution should be exercised before taking action based on an ABC analysis such as the one shown in Exhibits 7–10 and 7–11. The product and customer margins computed in these exhibits are a useful starting point for further analysis, but managers need to know what costs are really affected before taking any action such as dropping a product or customer or changing the prices of products or services. Appendix 7A shows how an *action analysis report* can be constructed to help managers make such decisions. An **action analysis report** provides more detail about costs and how they might adjust to changes in activity than the ABC analysis presented in Exhibits 7–10 and 7–11.

IN BUSINESS

COMPARING ACTIVITY-BASED AND TRADITIONAL PRODUCT COSTS

Airco Heating and Air Conditioning (Airco), located in Van Buren, Arkansas, implemented an ABC system to better understand the profitability of its products. The ABC system assigned $4,458,605 of overhead costs to eight activities as follows:

Activity Cost Pool	Total Cost	Total Activity	Activity Rate
Machines	$ 435,425	73,872 machine-hours	$5.89
Data record maintenance	132,597	14 products administered	$9,471.21
Material handling	1,560,027	16,872 products	$92.46
Product changeover	723,338	72 setup hours	$10,046.36
Scheduling	24,877	2,788 production runs	$8.92
Raw material receiving	877,107	2,859 receipts	$306.79
Product shipment	561,014	13,784,015 miles	$0.04
Customer service	144,220	2,533 customer contacts	$56.94
Total	$4,458,605		

Airco's managers were surprised by the fact that 55% [($1,560,027 + $877,107) ÷ $4,458,605] of its overhead resources were consumed by the material handling and raw material receiving activities. They responded by reducing the raw material and part transport distances within the facility. In addition, they compared the traditional and ABC product margin percentages (computed by dividing each product's margin by the sales of the product) for the company's seven product lines of air conditioners as summarized below:

	Product						
	5-Ton	6-Ton	7.5-Ton	10-Ton	12.5-Ton	15-Ton	20-Ton
Traditional product margin %	−20%	4%	40%	−4%	20%	42%	70%
ABC product margin %	−15%	−8%	50%	1%	−6%	40%	69%

In response to the ABC data, Airco decided to explore the possibility of raising prices on 5-ton, 6-ton, and 12.5-ton air conditioners while at the same time seeking to reduce overhead consumption by these products.

Source: Copyright 2004 from Heather Nachtmann and Mohammad Hani Al-Rifai, "An Application of Activity-Based Costing in the Air Conditioner Manufacturing Industry," *The Engineering Economist* 49, Issue 3, 2004, pp. 221–236. Reproduced by permission of Taylor & Francis Group, LLC, www.taylorandfrancis.com.

Targeting Process Improvements

Activity-based costing can also be used to identify activities that would benefit from process improvements. When used in this way, activity-based costing is often called *activity-based management.* Basically, **activity-based management** involves focusing on activities to eliminate waste, decrease processing time, and reduce defects. Activity-based management is used in organizations as diverse as manufacturing companies, hospitals, and the U.S. Marine Corps.

The first step in any improvement program is to decide what to improve. The Theory of Constraints approach discussed in Chapter 1 is a powerful tool for targeting the area in an organization whose improvement will yield the greatest benefit. Activity-based management provides another approach. The activity rates computed in activity-based costing can provide valuable clues concerning where there is waste and opportunity for improvement. For example, looking at the activity rates in Exhibit 7–6, managers at Classic Brass may conclude that $320 to process a customer order is far too expensive for an activity that adds no value to the product. As a consequence, they may target their process improvement efforts toward the Customer Orders activity.

Benchmarking is another way to leverage the information in activity rates. **Benchmarking** is a systematic approach to identifying the activities with the greatest room for improvement. It is based on comparing the performance in an organization with the performance of other, similar organizations known for their outstanding performance. If a particular part of the organization performs far below the world-class standard, managers will be likely to target that area for improvement.

IN BUSINESS

PROCESS IMPROVEMENTS HELP NURSES

Providence Portland Medical Center (PPMC) used ABC to improve one of the most expensive and error-prone processes within its nursing units—ordering, distributing, and administering medications to patients. To the surprise of everyone involved, the ABC data showed that "medication-related activities made up 43% of the nursing unit's total operating costs." The ABC team members knew that one of the root causes of this time-consuming process was the illegibility of physician orders that are faxed to the pharmacy. Replacing the standard fax machine with a much better $5,000 machine virtually eliminated unreadable orders and decreased follow-up telephone calls by more than 90%—saving the hospital $500,000 per year. In total, the ABC team generated improvement ideas that offered $1 million of net savings in redeployable resources. "This amount translates to additional time that nurses and pharmacists can spend on direct patient care."

Source: "How ABC Analysis Will Save PPMC Over $1 Million a Year," *Financial Analysis, Planning & Reporting,* November 2003, pp. 6–10.

Activity-Based Costing and External Reports

Although activity-based costing generally provides more accurate product costs than traditional costing methods, it is infrequently used for external reports for a number of reasons.[3] First, external reports are less detailed than internal reports prepared for decision making. On the external reports, individual product costs are not reported. Cost of goods sold and inventory valuations are disclosed, but they are not broken down by product. If

[3] Appendix 7B illustrates how a variation of activity-based costing can be used to develop product costs for external reports.

some products are undercosted and some are overcosted, the errors tend to offset each other when the product costs are added together.

Second, it is often very difficult to make changes in a company's accounting system. The official cost accounting systems in most large companies are usually embedded in complex computer programs that have been modified in-house over the course of many years. It is extremely difficult to make changes in such computer programs without causing numerous bugs.

Third, an ABC system such as the one described in this chapter does not conform to generally accepted accounting principles (GAAP). As discussed in Chapters 2, 3, and 4, product costs computed for external reports must include all of the manufacturing costs and only manufacturing costs; but in an ABC system as described in this chapter, product costs exclude some manufacturing costs and include some nonmanufacturing costs. It is possible to adjust the ABC data at the end of the period to conform to GAAP, but that requires more work.

Fourth, auditors are likely to be uncomfortable with allocations that are based on interviews with the company's personnel. Such subjective data can be easily manipulated by management to make earnings and other key variables look more favorable.

For all of these reasons, most companies confine their ABC efforts to special studies for management, and they do not attempt to integrate activity-based costing into their formal cost accounting systems.

The Limitations of Activity-Based Costing

Implementing an activity-based costing system is a major project that requires substantial resources. And once implemented, an activity-based costing system is more costly to maintain than a traditional costing system—data concerning numerous activity measures must be periodically collected, checked, and entered into the system. The benefits of increased accuracy may not outweigh these costs.

Activity-based costing produces numbers, such as product margins, that are at odds with the numbers produced by traditional costing systems. But managers are accustomed to using traditional costing systems to run their operations and traditional costing systems are often used in performance evaluations. Essentially, activity-based costing changes the rules of the game. It is a fact of human nature that changes in organizations, particularly those that alter the rules of the game, inevitably face resistance. This underscores the importance of top management support and the full participation of line managers, as well as the accounting staff, in any activity-based costing initiative. If activity-based costing is viewed as an accounting initiative that does not have the full support of top management, it is doomed to failure.

In practice, most managers insist on fully allocating all costs to products, customers, and other costing objects in an activity-based costing system—including the costs of idle capacity and organization-sustaining costs. This results in overstated costs and understated margins and mistakes in pricing and other critical decisions.

Activity-based costing data can easily be misinterpreted and must be used with care when used in making decisions. Costs assigned to products, customers, and other cost objects are only *potentially* relevant. Before making any significant decisions using activity-based costing data, managers must identify which costs are really relevant for the decision at hand. See Appendix 7A for more details.

As discussed in the previous section, reports generated by the best activity-based costing systems do not conform to external reporting requirements. Consequently, an organization involved in activity-based costing should have two cost systems—one for internal use and one for preparing external reports. This is costlier than maintaining just one system and may cause confusion about which system is to be believed and relied on.

IN BUSINESS

A CRITICAL PERSPECTIVE OF ABC

Marconi is a Portuguese telecommunications company that encountered problems with its ABC system. The company's production managers felt that 23% of the costs included in the system were common costs that should not be allocated to products and that allocating these costs to products was not only inaccurate, but also irrelevant to their operational cost reduction efforts. Furthermore, Marconi's front-line workers resisted the ABC system because they felt it might be used to weaken their autonomy and to justify downsizing, outsourcing, and work intensification. They believed that ABC created a "turkeys queuing for Christmas syndrome" because they were expected to volunteer information to help create a cost system that could eventually lead to their demise. These two complications created a third problem—the data necessary to build the ABC cost model was provided by disgruntled and distrustful employees. Consequently, the accuracy of the data was questionable at best. In short, Marconi's experiences illustrate some of the challenges that complicate real-world ABC implementations.

Source: Maria Major and Trevor Hopper, "Managers Divided: Implementing ABC in a Portuguese Telecommunications Company," *Management Accounting Research*, June 2005, pp. 205–229.

Summary

Traditional cost accounting methods suffer from several defects that can result in distorted costs for decision-making purposes. All manufacturing costs—even those that are not caused by any specific product—are allocated to products. Nonmanufacturing costs that are caused by products are not assigned to products. And finally, traditional methods tend to place too much reliance on unit-level allocation bases such as direct labor and machine-hours. This results in overcosting high-volume products and undercosting low-volume products and can lead to mistakes when making decisions.

Activity-based costing estimates the costs of the resources consumed by cost objects such as products and customers. The activity-based costing approach assumes that cost objects generate activities that in turn consume costly resources. Activities form the link between costs and cost objects. Activity-based costing is concerned with overhead—both manufacturing overhead and selling and administrative overhead. The accounting for direct labor and direct materials is usually the same under traditional and ABC costing methods.

To build an ABC system, companies typically choose a small set of activities that summarize much of the work performed in overhead departments. Associated with each activity is an activity cost pool. To the extent possible, overhead costs are directly traced to these activity cost pools. The remaining overhead costs are allocated to the activity cost pools in the first-stage allocation. Interviews with managers often form the basis for these allocations.

An activity rate is computed for each cost pool by dividing the costs assigned to the cost pool by the measure of activity for the cost pool. Activity rates provide useful information to managers concerning the costs of performing overhead activities. A particularly high cost for an activity may trigger efforts to improve the way the activity is carried out in the organization.

In the second-stage allocation, activity rates are used to apply costs to cost objects such as products and customers. The costs computed under activity-based costing are often quite different from the costs generated by a company's traditional cost accounting system. While the ABC system is almost certainly more accurate, managers should nevertheless exercise caution before making decisions based on the ABC data. Some of the costs may not be avoidable and hence would not be relevant.

Review Problem: Activity-Based Costing

Ferris Corporation makes a single product—a fire-resistant commercial filing cabinet—that it sells to office furniture distributors. The company has a simple ABC system that it uses for internal decision making. The company has two overhead departments whose costs are listed on the following page:

Manufacturing overhead	$500,000
Selling and administrative overhead	300,000
Total overhead costs	$800,000

The company's ABC system has the following activity cost pools and activity measures:

Activity Cost Pool	Activity Measure
Assembling units	Number of units
Processing orders	Number of orders
Supporting customers	Number of customers
Other	Not applicable

Costs assigned to the "Other" activity cost pool have no activity measure; they consist of the costs of unused capacity and organization-sustaining costs—neither of which are assigned to orders, customers, or the product.

Ferris Corporation distributes the costs of manufacturing overhead and selling and administrative overhead to the activity cost pools based on employee interviews, the results of which are reported below:

Distribution of Resource Consumption Across Activity Cost Pools					
	Assembling Units	Processing Orders	Supporting Customers	Other	Total
Manufacturing overhead	50%	35%	5%	10%	100%
Selling and administrative overhead	10%	45%	25%	20%	100%
Total activity	1,000 units	250 orders	100 customers		

Required:

1. Perform the first-stage allocation of overhead costs to the activity cost pools as in Exhibit 7–5.
2. Compute activity rates for the activity cost pools as in Exhibit 7–6.
3. OfficeMart is one of Ferris Corporation's customers. Last year, OfficeMart ordered filing cabinets four different times. OfficeMart ordered a total of 80 filing cabinets during the year. Construct a table as in Exhibit 7–9 showing the overhead costs attributable to OfficeMart.
4. The selling price of a filing cabinet is $595. The cost of direct materials is $180 per filing cabinet, and direct labor is $50 per filing cabinet. What is the customer margin of OfficeMart? See Exhibit 7–11 for an example of how to complete this report.

Solution to Review Problem

1. The first-stage allocation of costs to the activity cost pools appears below:

	Activity Cost Pools				
	Assembling Units	Processing Orders	Supporting Customers	Other	Total
Manufacturing overhead	$250,000	$175,000	$ 25,000	$ 50,000	$500,000
Selling and administrative overhead	30,000	135,000	75,000	60,000	300,000
Total cost	$280,000	$310,000	$100,000	$110,000	$800,000

2. The activity rates for the activity cost pools are:

Activity Cost Pools	(a) Total Cost	(b) Total Activity	(a) ÷ (b) Activity Rate
Assembling units	$280,000	1,000 units	$280 per unit
Processing orders	$310,000	250 orders	$1,240 per order
Supporting customers	$100,000	100 customers	$1,000 per customer

3. The overhead cost attributable to OfficeMart would be computed as follows:

Activity Cost Pools	(a) Activity Rate	(b) Activity	(a) × (b) ABC Cost
Assembling units	$280 per unit	80 units	$22,400
Processing orders	$1,240 per order	4 orders	$4,960
Supporting customers	$1,000 per customer	1 customer	$1,000

4. The customer margin can be computed as follows:

Sales ($595 per unit × 80 units)		$47,600
Costs:		
Direct materials ($180 per unit × 80 units)	$14,400	
Direct labor ($50 per unit × 80 units)	4,000	
Assembling units (above)	22,400	
Processing orders (above)	4,960	
Supporting customers (above)	1,000	46,760
Customer margin		$ 840

Glossary

Action analysis report A report showing what costs have been assigned to a cost object, such as a product or customer, and how difficult it would be to adjust the cost if there is a change in activity. (p. 295)

Activity An event that causes the consumption of overhead resources in an organization. (p. 275)

Activity-based costing (ABC) A costing method based on activities that is designed to provide managers with cost information for strategic and other decisions that potentially affect capacity and therefore fixed as well as variable costs. (p. 273)

Activity-based management (ABM) A management approach that focuses on managing activities as a way of eliminating waste and reducing delays and defects. (p. 296)

Activity cost pool A "bucket" in which costs are accumulated that relate to a single activity measure in an activity-based costing system. (p. 275)

Activity measure An allocation base in an activity-based costing system; ideally, a measure of the amount of activity that drives the costs in an activity cost pool. (p. 275)

Batch-level activities Activities that are performed each time a batch of goods is handled or processed, regardless of how many units are in the batch. The amount of resource consumed depends on the number of batches run rather than on the number of units in the batch. (p. 275)

Benchmarking A systematic approach to identifying the activities with the greatest potential for improvement. (p. 296)

Customer-level activities Activities that are carried out to support customers, but that are not related to any specific product. (p. 276)

Duration driver A measure of the amount of time required to perform an activity. (p. 275)

First-stage allocation The process by which overhead costs are assigned to activity cost pools in an activity-based costing system. (p. 281)

Organization-sustaining activities Activities that are carried out regardless of which customers are served, which products are produced, how many batches are run, or how many units are made. (p. 276)

Product-level activities Activities that relate to specific products that must be carried out regardless of how many units are produced and sold or batches run. (p. 276)

Second-stage allocation The process by which activity rates are used to apply costs to products and customers in activity-based costing. (p. 285)

Transaction driver A simple count of the number of times an activity occurs. (p. 275)

Unit-level activities Activities that are performed each time a unit is produced. (p. 275)

Questions

7–1 In what fundamental ways does activity-based costing differ from traditional costing methods such as job-order costing as described in Chapter 3?

7–2 Why is direct labor a poor base for allocating overhead in many companies?

7–3 Why are top management support and cross-functional involvement crucial when attempting to implement an activity-based costing system?

7–4 What are unit-level, batch-level, product-level, customer-level, and organization-sustaining activities?

7–5 What types of costs should not be assigned to products in an activity-based costing system?

7–6 Why are there two stages of allocation in activity-based costing?

7–7 Why is the first stage of the allocation process in activity-based costing often based on interviews?

7–8 When activity-based costing is used, why do manufacturing overhead costs often shift from high-volume products to low-volume products?

7–9 How can the activity rates (i.e., cost per activity) for the various activities be used to target process improvements?

7–10 Why is the activity-based costing described in this chapter unacceptable for external financial reports?

Multiple-choice questions are provided on the text website at www.mhhe.com/garrison14e.

connect ACCOUNTING Applying Excel

Available with McGraw-Hill's *Connect™ Accounting.*

LEARNING OBJECTIVES 1, 2, 3, 4

The Excel worksheet form that appears on the next page is to be used to recreate the Review Problem on pages 298–300. Download the workbook containing this form from the Online Learning Center at www.mhhe.com/garrison14e. *On the website you will also receive instructions about how to use this worksheet form.*

	A	B	C	D	E	F	G
1	Chapter 7: Applying Excel						
2							
3	**Data**						
4	Manufacturing overhead	$500,000					
5	Selling and administrative overhead	$300,000					
6							
7		*Assembling Units*	*Processing Orders*	*Supporting Customers*	*Other*		
8	Manufacturing overhead	50%	35%	5%	10%		
9	Selling and administrative overhead	10%	45%	25%	20%		
10	Total activity	1,000	250	100			
11		units	orders	customers			
12							
13	OfficeMart orders:						
14	Customers	1	customer				
15	Orders	4	orders				
16	Number of filing cabinets ordered in total	80	units				
17	Selling price	$595					
18	Direct materials	$180					
19	Direct labor	$50					
20							
21	*Enter a formula into each of the cells marked with a ? below*						
22	**Review Problem: Activity-Based Costing**						
23							
24	***Perform the first stage allocations***						
25		*Assembling Units*	*Processing Orders*	*Supporting Customers*	*Other*	*Total*	
26	Manufacturing overhead	?	?	?	?	?	
27	Selling and administrative overhead	?	?	?	?	?	
28	Total cost	?	?	?	?	?	
29							
30	***Compute the activity rates***						
31	*Activity Cost Pools*	*Total Cost*	*Total Activity*		*Activity Rate*		
32	Assembling units	?	?	units	?	per unit	
33	Processing orders	?	?	orders	?	per order	
34	Supporting customers	?	?	customers	?	per customer	
35							
36	***Compute the overhead cost attributable to the OfficeMart orders***						
37	*Activity Cost Pools*	*Activity Rate*		*Activity*		*ABC Cost*	
38	Assembling units	?	per unit	?	units	?	
39	Processing orders	?	per order	?	orders	?	
40	Supporting customers	?	per customer	?	customer	?	
41							
42	***Determine the customer margin for the OfficeMart orders under Activity-Based Costing***						
43	Sales		?				
44	Costs:						
45	Direct materials	?					
46	Direct labor	?					
47	Unit-related overhead	?					
48	Order-related overhead	?					
49	Customer-related overhead	?	?				
50	Customer margin		?				
51							
52	***Determine the product margin for the OfficeMart orders under a traditional cost system***						
53	Manufacturing overhead	?					
54	Total activity	?	units				
55	Manufacturing overhead per unit	?	per unit				
56							
57	Sales		?				
58	Costs:						
59	Direct materials	?					
60	Direct labor	?					
61	Manufacturing overhead	?	?				
62	Traditional costing product margin		?				
63							

Chapter 7 Form | Filled in Chapter 7 Form | Chapter 7 Formulas

You should proceed to the requirements below only after completing your worksheet.

Required:

1. Check your worksheet by doubling the units ordered in cell B16 to 160. The customer margin under activity-based costing should now be $7,640 and the traditional costing product margin should be $(21,600). If you do not get these results, find the errors in your worksheet and correct them.
   a. Why has the customer margin under activity-based costing more than doubled when the number of units ordered is doubled?
   b. Why has the traditional costing product margin exactly doubled from a loss of $10,800 to a loss of $21,600?
   c. Which costing system, activity-based costing or traditional costing, provides a more accurate picture of what happens to profits as the number of units ordered increases? Explain.
2. Let's assume that OfficeMart places different orders next year, purchasing higher-end filing cabinets more frequently, but in smaller quantities per order. Enter the following data into your worksheet:

Data				
Manufacturing overhead	$500,000			
Selling and administrative overhead	$300,000			
	Assembling Units	Processing Orders	Supporting Customers	Other
Manufacturing overhead	50%	35%	5%	10%
Selling and administrative overhead	10%	45%	25%	20%
Total activity	1,000 units	250 orders	100 customers	
OfficeMart orders:				
Customers	1 customer			
Orders	20 orders			
Total number of filing cabinets ordered	80 units			
Selling price	$795			
Direct materials	$185			
Direct labor	$90			

   a. What is the customer margin under activity-based costing?
   b. What is the product margin under the traditional cost system?
   c. Explain why the profitability picture looks much different now than it did when OfficeMart was ordering less expensive filing cabinets less frequently, but in larger quantities per order.
3. Using the data you entered in part (2), change the percentage of selling and administrative overhead attributable to processing orders from 45% to 30% and the percentage attributable to supporting customers from 25% to 40%. That portion of the worksheet should look like this:

	Assembling Units	Processing Orders	Supporting Customers	Other
Manufacturing overhead	50%	35%	5%	10%
Selling and administrative overhead	10%	30%	40%	20%
Total activity	1,000 units	250 orders	100 customers	

a. Relative to the results from part (2), what has happened to the customer margin under activity-based costing? Why?

b. Relative to the results from part (2), what has happened to the product margin under the traditional cost system? Why?

Exercises connect ACCOUNTING

All applicable exercises are available with McGraw-Hill's *Connect™ Accounting.*

EXERCISE 7–1 ABC Cost Hierarchy [LO1]

The following activities occur at Greenwich Corporation, a company that manufactures a variety of products.

a. Various individuals manage the parts inventories.
b. A clerk in the factory issues purchase orders for a job.
c. The personnel department trains new production workers.
d. The factory's general manager meets with other department heads such as marketing to coordinate plans.
e. Direct labor workers assemble products.
f. Engineers design new products.
g. The materials storekeeper issues raw materials to be used in jobs.
h. The maintenance department performs periodic preventive maintenance on general-use equipment.

Required:

Classify each of the activities above as either a unit-level, batch-level, product-level, or organization-sustaining activity.

EXERCISE 7–2 First-Stage Allocation [LO2]

VaultOnWheels Corporation operates a fleet of armored cars that make scheduled pickups and deliveries for its customers in the Phoenix area. The company is implementing an activity-based costing system that has four activity cost pools: Travel, Pickup and Delivery, Customer Service, and Other. The activity measures are miles for the Travel cost pool, number of pickups and deliveries for the Pickup and Delivery cost pool, and number of customers for the Customer Service cost pool. The Other cost pool has no activity measure because it is an organization-sustaining activity. The following costs will be assigned using the activity-based costing system:

Driver and guard wages	$ 840,000
Vehicle operating expense	270,000
Vehicle depreciation	150,000
Customer representative salaries and expenses	180,000
Office expenses	40,000
Administrative expenses	340,000
Total cost	$1,820,000

The distribution of resource consumption across the activity cost pools is as follows:

	Travel	Pickup and Delivery	Customer Service	Other	Totals
Driver and guard wages	40%	45%	10%	5%	100%
Vehicle operating expense	75%	5%	0%	20%	100%
Vehicle depreciation	70%	10%	0%	20%	100%
Customer representative salaries and expenses	0%	0%	85%	15%	100%
Office expenses	0%	25%	35%	40%	100%
Administrative expenses	0%	5%	55%	40%	100%

Required:
Complete the first-stage allocations of costs to activity cost pools as illustrated in Exhibit 7–5.

EXERCISE 7–3 Compute Activity Rates [LO3]

As You Like It Gardening is a small gardening service that uses activity-based costing to estimate costs for pricing and other purposes. The proprietor of the company believes that costs are driven primarily by the size of customer lawns, the size of customer garden beds, the distance to travel to customers, and the number of customers. In addition, the costs of maintaining garden beds depends on whether the beds are low-maintenance beds (mainly ordinary trees and shrubs) or high-maintenance beds (mainly flowers and exotic plants). Accordingly, the company uses the five activity cost pools listed below:

Activity Cost Pool	Activity Measure
Caring for lawn	Square feet of lawn
Caring for garden beds—low maintenance	Square feet of low-maintenance beds
Caring for garden beds—high maintenance	Square feet of high-maintenance beds
Travel to jobs	Miles
Customer billing and service	Number of customers

The company has already completed its first-stage allocations of costs. The company's annual costs and activities are summarized as follows:

Activity Cost Pool	Estimated Overhead Cost	Expected Activity
Caring for lawn	$77,400	180,000 square feet of lawn
Caring for garden beds—low maintenance	$30,000	24,000 square feet of low-maintenance beds
Caring for garden beds—high maintenance	$57,600	18,000 square feet of high-maintenance beds
Travel to jobs	$4,200	15,000 miles
Customer billing and service	$8,700	30 customers

Required:
Compute the activity rate for each of the activity cost pools.

EXERCISE 7–4 Second-Stage Allocation [LO4]

Larner Corporation is a diversified manufacturer of industrial goods. The company's activity-based costing system contains the following six activity cost pools and activity rates:

Activity Cost Pool	Activity Rates
Supporting direct labor	$7.00 per direct labor-hour
Machine processing	$3.00 per machine-hour
Machine setups	$40.00 per setup
Production orders	$160.00 per order
Shipments	$120.00 per shipment
Product sustaining	$800.00 per product

Activity data have been supplied for the following products:

	Total Expected Activity	
	J78	W52
Direct labor-hours	1,000	40
Machine-hours	3,200	30
Machine setups	5	1
Production orders	5	1
Shipments	10	1
Product sustaining	1	1

Required:
Determine the total overhead cost that would be assigned to each of the products listed above in the activity-based costing system.

EXERCISE 7–5 Product and Customer Profitability Analysis [LO4, LO5]
Updraft Systems, Inc., makes paragliders for sale through specialty sporting goods stores. The company has a standard paraglider model, but also makes custom-designed paragliders. Management has designed an activity-based costing system with the following activity cost pools and activity rates:

Activity Cost Pool	Activity Rate
Supporting direct labor	$18 per direct labor-hour
Order processing	$192 per order
Custom designing	$261 per custom design
Customer service	$426 per customer

Management would like an analysis of the profitability of a particular customer, Eagle Wings, which has ordered the following products over the last 12 months:

	Standard Model	Custom Design
Number of gliders	10	2
Number of orders	1	2
Number of custom designs	0	2
Direct labor-hours per glider	28.50	32.00
Selling price per glider	$1,650	$2,300
Direct materials cost per glider	$462	$576

The company's direct labor rate is $19 per hour.

Required:
Using the company's activity-based costing system, compute the customer margin of Eagle Wings.

EXERCISE 7–6 Second-Stage Allocation to an Order [LO4]
Transvaal Mining Tools Ltd. of South Africa makes specialty tools used in the mining industry. The company uses an activity-based costing system for internal decision-making purposes. The company has four activity cost pools as listed below:

Activity Cost Pool	Activity Measure	Activity Rate
Order size	Number of direct labor-hours	R17.60 per direct labor-hour*
Customer orders	Number of customer orders	R360 per customer order
Product testing	Number of testing hours	R79 per testing hour
Selling	Number of sales calls	R1,494 per sales call

*(The currency in South Africa is the rand, denoted here by R.)

The managing director of the company would like information concerning the cost of a recently completed order for hard-rock drills. The order required 150 direct labor-hours, 18 hours of product testing, and three sales calls.

Required:
Prepare a report summarizing the overhead costs assigned to the order for hard-rock drills. What is the total overhead cost assigned to the order?

EXERCISE 7–7 First-Stage Allocations [LO2]

The operations vice president of First Bank of Eagle, Kristin Wu, has been interested in investigating the efficiency of the bank's operations. She has been particularly concerned about the costs of handling routine transactions at the bank and would like to compare these costs at the bank's various branches. If the branches with the most efficient operations can be identified, their methods can be studied and then replicated elsewhere. While the bank maintains meticulous records of wages and other costs, there has been no attempt thus far to show how those costs are related to the various services provided by the bank. Ms. Wu has asked your help in conducting an activity-based costing study of bank operations. In particular, she would like to know the cost of opening an account, the cost of processing deposits and withdrawals, and the cost of processing other customer transactions.

The Avon branch of First Bank of Eagle has submitted the following cost data for last year:

Teller wages	$150,000
Assistant branch manager salary . . .	70,000
Branch manager salary	85,000
Total	$305,000

Virtually all of the other costs of the branch—rent, depreciation, utilities, and so on—are organization-sustaining costs that cannot be meaningfully assigned to individual customer transactions such as depositing checks.

In addition to the cost data above, the employees of the Avon branch have been interviewed concerning how their time was distributed last year across the activities included in the activity-based costing study. The results of those interviews appear below:

	Distribution of Resource Consumption Across Activities				
	Opening Accounts	Processing Deposits and Withdrawals	Processing Other Customer Transactions	Other Activities	Totals
Teller wages	0%	75%	15%	10%	100%
Assistant branch manager salary	10%	15%	25%	50%	100%
Branch manager salary	0%	0%	20%	80%	100%

Required:

Prepare the first-stage allocation for Ms. Wu as illustrated in Exhibit 7–5.

EXERCISE 7–8 Computing and Interpreting Activity Rates [LO3]

(This exercise is a continuation of Exercise 7–7; it should be assigned *only* if Exercise 7–7 is also assigned.) The manager of the Avon branch of First Bank of Eagle has provided the following data concerning the transactions of the branch during the past year:

Activity	Total Activity at the Avon Branch
Opening accounts	200 accounts opened
Processing deposits and withdrawals	50,000 deposits and withdrawals
Processing other customer transactions . . .	1,000 other customer transactions

The lowest costs reported by other branches for these activities are displayed below:

Activity	Lowest Cost among All First Bank of Eagle Branches
Opening accounts	$24.35 per account opened
Processing deposits and withdrawals	$2.72 per deposit or withdrawal
Processing other customer transactions	$48.90 per other customer transaction

Required:

1. Using the first-stage allocation from Exercise 7–7 and the above data, compute the activity rates for the activity-based costing system. (Use Exhibit 7–6 as a guide.) Round all computations to the nearest whole cent.
2. What do these results suggest to you concerning operations at the Avon branch?

EXERCISE 7–9 Customer Profitability Analysis [LO3, LO4, LO5]

Med Max buys surgical supplies from a variety of manufacturers and then resells and delivers these supplies to hundreds of hospitals. Med Max sets its prices for all hospitals by marking up its cost of goods sold to those hospitals by 5%. For example, if a hospital buys supplies from Med Max that had cost Med Max $100 to buy from manufacturers, Med Max would charge the hospital $105 to purchase these supplies.

For years, Med Max believed that the 5% markup covered its selling and administrative expenses and provided a reasonable profit. However, in the face of declining profits Med Max decided to implement an activity-based costing system to help improve its understanding of customer profitability. The company broke its selling and administrative expenses into five activities as shown below:

Activity Cost Pool	Activity Measure	Total Cost	Total Activity
Customer deliveries	Number of deliveries	$ 400,000	5,000 deliveries
Manual order processing	Number of manual orders	300,000	4,000 orders
Electronic order processing	Number of electronic orders	200,000	12,500 orders
Line item picking	Number of line items picked	500,000	400,000 line items
Other organization-sustaining costs	NA	600,000	
Total selling and administrative expenses		$2,000,000	

Med Max gathered the data below for two of the many hospitals that it serves—City General and County General (both hospitals purchased a total quantity of medical supplies that had cost Med Max $30,000 to buy from its manufacturers):

	Activity	
Activity Measure	City General	County General
Number of deliveries	10	20
Number of manual orders	0	40
Number of electronic orders	10	0
Number of line items picked	100	260

Required:

1. Compute the total revenue that Med Max would receive from City General and County General.
2. Compute the activity rate for each activity cost pool.
3. Compute the total activity costs that would be assigned to City General and County General.
4. Compute Med Max's customer margin for City General and County General. (Hint: Do not overlook the $30,000 cost of goods sold that Med Max incurred serving each hospital.)
5. Describe the purchasing behaviors that are likely to characterize Med Max's least profitable customers.

EXERCISE 7–10 Activity Measures [LO1]

Various activities at Morales Corporation, a manufacturing company, are listed below. Each activity has been classified as unit-level, batch-level, product-level, customer-level, or organization-sustaining.

	Activity	Activity Classification	Examples of Activity Measures
a.	Materials are moved from the receiving dock to the assembly area by a material-handling crew	Batch-level	
b.	Direct labor workers assemble various products	Unit-level	
c.	Diversity training is provided to all employees in the company	Organization-sustaining	
d.	A product is designed by a cross-functional team	Product-level	
e.	Equipment is set up to process a batch	Batch-level	
f.	A customer is billed for all products delivered during the month	Customer-level	

Required:

Complete the table by providing an example of an activity measure for each activity.

EXERCISE 7–11 Comprehensive Activity-Based Costing Exercise [LO2, LO3, LO4, LO5]

Silicon Optics has supplied the following data for use in its activity-based costing system:

Overhead Costs	
Wages and salaries	$350,000
Other overhead costs	200,000
Total overhead costs	$550,000

Activity Cost Pool	Activity Measure	Total Activity
Direct labor support	Number of direct labor-hours	10,000 DLHs
Order processing	Number of orders	500 orders
Customer support	Number of customers	100 customers
Other	This is an organization-sustaining activity	Not applicable

	Distribution of Resource Consumption Across Activities				
	Direct Labor Support	Order Processing	Customer Support	Other	Total
Wages and salaries	30%	35%	25%	10%	100%
Other overhead costs	25%	15%	20%	40%	100%

During the year, Silicon Optics completed an order for a special optical switch for a new customer, Indus Telecom. This customer did not order any other products during the year. Data concerning that order follow:

Data Concerning the Indus Telecom Order	
Selling price	$295 per unit
Units ordered	100 units
Direct materials	$264 per unit
Direct labor-hours	0.5 DLH per unit
Direct labor rate	$25 per DLH

Required:

1. Using Exhibit 7–5 as a guide, prepare a report showing the first-stage allocations of overhead costs to the activity cost pools.
2. Using Exhibit 7–6 as a guide, compute the activity rates for the activity cost pools.
3. Prepare a report showing the overhead costs for the order from Indus Telecom, including customer support costs.
4. Using Exhibit 7–11 as a guide, prepare a report showing the customer margin for Indus Telecom.

EXERCISE 7–12 Computing ABC Product Costs [LO3, LO4]

Performance Products Corporation makes two products, titanium Rims and Posts. Data regarding the two products follow:

	Direct Labor-Hours per Unit	Annual Production
Rims	0.40	20,000 units
Posts.	0.20	80,000 units

Additional information about the company follows:

a. Rims require $17 in direct materials per unit, and Posts require $10.
b. The direct labor wage rate is $16 per hour.
c. Rims are more complex to manufacture than Posts, and they require special equipment.
d. The ABC system has the following activity cost pools:

	A	B	C	D	E
1		*Estimated*		*Activity*	
2	*Activity Cost Pool (and activity measure)*	*Overhead Cost*	*Rims*	*Posts*	*Total*
3	Machine setups (number of setups)	$21,600	100	80	180
4	Special processing (machine-hours)	$180,000	4,000	0	4,000
5	General factory (direct labor-hours)	$288,000	8,000	16,000	24,000

Required:

1. Compute the activity rate for each activity cost pool.
2. Determine the unit cost of each product according to the ABC system, including direct materials and direct labor.

EXERCISE 7–13 Second-Stage Allocation and Margin Calculations [LO4, LO5]

Theatre Seating, Inc., makes high-quality adjustable seats for theaters. The company's activity-based costing system has four activity cost pools, which are listed below along with their activity measures and activity rates:

Activity Cost Pool	Activity Measure	Activity Rate
Supporting direct labor	Number of direct labor-hours	$12 per direct labor-hour
Batch processing	Number of batches	$96 per batch
Order processing	Number of orders	$284 per order
Customer service	Number of customers	$2,620 per customer

The company just completed a single order from CineMax Entertainment Corporation for 2,400 custom seats. The order was produced in four batches. Each seat required 0.8 direct labor-hours. The selling price was $137.95 per seat, the direct materials cost was $112.00 per seat, and the direct labor cost was $14.40 per seat. This was the only order from CineMax Entertainment for the year.

Required:

Using Exhibit 7–11 as a guide, prepare a report showing the customer margin on sales to CineMax Entertainment for the year.

EXERCISE 7–14 Cost Hierarchy [LO1]

Green Glider Corporation makes golf carts that it sells directly to golf courses throughout the world. Several basic models are available, which are modified to suit the needs of each particular golf course. A golf course located in the Pacific Northwest, for example, would typically specify that its golf carts come equipped with retractable rain-proof covers. In addition, each customer (i.e., golf course) customizes its golf carts with its own color scheme and logo. The company typically makes all of the golf carts for a customer before starting work on the next customer's golf carts. A number of activities carried out at Green Glider Corporation are listed below:

a. The purchasing department orders the specific color of paint specified by the customer from the company's supplier.
b. A steering wheel is installed in a golf cart.
c. An outside attorney draws up a new generic sales contract for the company limiting Green Glider's liability in case of accidents that involve its golf carts.
d. The company's paint shop makes a stencil for a customer's logo.
e. A sales representative visits an old customer to check on how the company's golf carts are working out and to try to make a new sale.
f. The accounts receivable department prepares the bill for a completed order.
g. Electricity is used to heat and light the factory and the administrative offices.
h. A golf cart is painted.
i. The company's engineer modifies the design of a model to eliminate a potential safety problem.
j. The marketing department has a catalogue printed and then mails copies to golf course managers.
k. Completed golf carts are individually tested on the company's test track.
l. A new model golf cart is shipped to the leading golfing trade magazine to be evaluated for the magazine's annual rating of golf carts.

Required:

Classify each of the costs or activities above as unit-level, batch-level, product-level, customer-level, or organization-sustaining. In this case, customers are golf courses, products are models of the golf cart, a batch is a specific order from a customer, and units are individual golf carts.

EXERCISE 7–15 Calculating and Interpreting Activity-Based Costing Data [LO3, LO4]

Sven's Cookhouse is a popular restaurant located on Lake Union in Seattle. The owner of the restaurant has been trying to better understand costs at the restaurant and has hired a student intern to conduct an activity-based costing study. The intern, in consultation with the owner, identified three major activities. She then completed the first-stage allocations of costs to the activity cost pools, using data from last month's operations. The results appear below:

Activity Cost Pool	Activity Measure	Total Cost	Total Activity
Serving a party of diners	Number of parties served	$12,000	5,000 parties
Serving a diner	Number of diners served	$90,000	12,000 diners
Serving a drink	Number of drinks ordered	$26,000	10,000 drinks

The above costs include all of the costs of the restaurant except for organization-sustaining costs such as rent, property taxes, and top-management salaries. A group of diners who ask to sit at the same table are counted as a party. Some costs, such as the costs of cleaning linen, are the same whether one person is at a table or the table is full. Other costs, such as washing dishes, depend on the number of diners served.

Prior to the activity-based costing study, the owner knew very little about the costs of the restaurant. He knew that the total cost for the month (including organization-sustaining costs) was $180,000 and that 12,000 diners had been served. Therefore, the average cost per diner was $15.

Required:

1. According to the activity-based costing system, what is the total cost of serving each of the following parties of diners?

  a. A party of four diners who order three drinks in total.
  b. A party of two diners who do not order any drinks.
  c. A lone diner who orders two drinks.

2. Convert the total costs you computed in (1) above to costs per diner. In other words, what is the average cost per diner for serving each of the following parties?
   a. A party of four diners who order three drinks in total.
   b. A party of two diners who do not order any drinks.
   c. A lone diner who orders two drinks.
3. Why do the costs per diner for the three different parties differ from each other and from the overall average cost of $15.00 per diner?

Problems

connect ACCOUNTING

All applicable problems are available with McGraw-Hill's *Connect™ Accounting.*

PROBLEM 7–16 Second-Stage Allocations and Product Margins [LO4, LO5]

AnimPix, Inc., is a small company that creates computer-generated animations for films and television. Much of the company's work consists of short commercials for television, but the company also does realistic computer animations for special effects in movies.

The young founders of the company have become increasingly concerned with the economics of the business—particularly because many competitors have sprung up recently in the local area. To help understand the company's cost structure, an activity-based costing system has been designed. Three major activities are carried out in the company: animation concept, animation production, and contract administration. The animation concept activity is carried out at the contract proposal stage when the company bids on projects. This is an intensive activity that involves individuals from all parts of the company in creating storyboards and prototype stills to be shown to the prospective client. After the client has accepted a project, the animation goes into production and contract administration begins. Technical staff do almost all of the work involved in animation production, whereas the administrative staff is largely responsible for contract administration. The activity cost pools and their activity measures and rates are listed below:

Activity Cost Pool	Activity Measure	Activity Rate
Animation concept	Number of proposals	$6,000 per proposal
Animation production	Minutes of animation	$7,700 per minute of animation
Contract administration	Number of contracts	$6,600 per contract

These activity rates include all of the costs of the company, except for the costs of idle capacity and organization-sustaining costs. There are no direct labor or direct materials costs.

Preliminary analysis using these activity rates has indicated that the local commercials segment of the market may be unprofitable. This segment is highly competitive. Producers of local commercials may ask several companies like AnimPix to bid, which results in an unusually low ratio of accepted contracts to bids. Furthermore, the animation sequences tend to be much shorter for local commercials than for other work. Because animation work is billed at standard rates according to the running time of the completed animation, the revenues from these short projects tend to be below average. Data concerning activity in the local commercials market appear below:

Activity Measure	Local Commercials
Number of proposals	20
Minutes of animation	12
Number of contracts	8

The total sales for local commercials amounted to $240,000.

Required:

1. Determine the cost of serving the local commercials market.
2. Prepare a report showing the margin earned serving the local commercials market. (Remember, this company has no direct materials or direct labor costs.)
3. What would you recommend to management concerning the local commercials market?

PROBLEM 7–17 Comparing Traditional and Activity-Based Product Margins [LO1, LO3, LO4, LO5]

Precision Manufacturing Inc. (PMI) makes two types of industrial component parts—the EX300 and the TX500. An absorption costing income statement for the most recent period is shown below:

Precision Manufacturing Inc. Income Statement	
Sales	$1,700,000
Cost of goods sold	1,200,000
Gross margin	500,000
Selling and administrative expenses	550,000
Net operating loss	$ (50,000)

PMI produced and sold 60,000 units of EX300 at a price of $20 per unit and 12,500 units of TX500 at a price of $40 per unit. The company's traditional cost system allocates manufacturing overhead to products using a plantwide overhead rate and direct labor dollars as the allocation base. Additional information relating to the company's two product lines is shown below:

	EX300	TX500	Total
Direct materials	$366,325	$162,550	$ 528,875
Direct labor	$120,000	$42,500	162,500
Manufacturing overhead			508,625
Cost of goods sold			$1,200,000

The company has created an activity-based costing system to evaluate the profitability of its products. PMI's ABC implementation team concluded that $50,000 and $100,000 of the company's advertising expenses could be directly traced to EX300 and TX500, respectively. The remainder of the selling and administrative expenses was organization-sustaining in nature. The ABC team also distributed the company's manufacturing overhead to four activities as shown below:

Activity Cost Pool (and Activity Measure)	Manufacturing Overhead	Activity		
		EX300	TX500	Total
Machining (machine-hours)	$198,250	90,000	62,500	152,500
Setups (setup hours)	150,000	75	300	375
Product-sustaining (number of products)	100,000	1	1	2
Other (organization-sustaining costs)	60,375	NA	NA	NA
Total manufacturing overhead cost	$508,625			

Required:

1. Using Exhibit 7–12 as a guide, compute the product margins for the EX300 and TX500 under the company's traditional costing system.
2. Using Exhibit 7–10 as a guide, compute the product margins for EX300 and TX500 under the activity-based costing system.
3. Using Exhibit 7–13 as a guide, prepare a quantitative comparison of the traditional and activity-based cost assignments. Explain why the traditional and activity-based cost assignments differ.

PROBLEM 7–18 Comparing Traditional and Activity-Based Product Margins [LO1, LO3, LO4, LO5]
Rocky Mountain Corporation makes two types of hiking boots—Xactive and the Pathbreaker. Data concerning these two product lines appear below:

	Xactive	Pathbreaker
Selling price per unit	$127.00	$89.00
Direct materials per unit	$64.80	$51.00
Direct labor per unit	$18.20	$13.00
Direct labor-hours per unit	1.4 DLHs	1.0 DLHs
Estimated annual production and sales	25,000 units	75,000 units

The company has a traditional costing system in which manufacturing overhead is applied to units based on direct labor-hours. Data concerning manufacturing overhead and direct labor-hours for the upcoming year appear below:

Estimated total manufacturing overhead	$2,200,000
Estimated total direct labor-hours	110,000 DLHs

Required:

1. Using Exhibit 7–12 as a guide, compute the product margins for the Xactive and the Pathbreaker products under the company's traditional costing system.
2. The company is considering replacing its traditional costing system with an activity-based costing system that would assign its manufacturing overhead to the following four activity cost pools (the Other cost pool includes organization-sustaining costs and idle capacity costs):

Activities and Activity Measures	Estimated Overhead Cost	Expected Activity		
		Xactive	Pathbreaker	Total
Supporting direct labor (direct labor-hours)	$ 797,500	35,000	75,000	110,000
Batch setups (setups)	680,000	250	150	400
Product sustaining (number of products)	650,000	1	1	2
Other	72,500	NA	NA	NA
Total manufacturing overhead cost	$2,200,000			

   Using Exhibit 7–10 as a guide, compute the product margins for the Xactive and the Pathbreaker products under the activity-based costing system.
3. Using Exhibit 7–13 as a guide, prepare a quantitative comparison of the traditional and activity-based cost assignments. Explain why the traditional and activity-based cost assignments differ.

PROBLEM 7–19 Activity-Based Costing and Bidding on Jobs [LO2, LO3, LO4]
Denny Asbestos Removal Company removes potentially toxic asbestos insulation and related products from buildings. The company's estimator has been involved in a long-simmering dispute with the on-site work supervisors. The on-site supervisors claim that the estimator does not adequately distinguish between routine work such as removal of asbestos insulation around heating pipes in older homes and nonroutine work such as removing asbestos-contaminated ceiling plaster in industrial buildings. The on-site supervisors believe that nonroutine work is far more expensive than routine work and should bear higher customer charges. The estimator sums up his position in this way: "My job is to measure the area to be cleared of asbestos. As directed by top management, I simply multiply the square footage by $4,000 per thousand square feet to determine the bid price. Since our average cost is only $3,000 per thousand square feet, that leaves enough cushion to take

care of the additional costs of nonroutine work that shows up. Besides, it is difficult to know what is routine or nonroutine until you actually start tearing things apart."

To shed light on this controversy, the company initiated an activity-based costing study of all of its costs. Data from the activity-based costing system follow:

Activity Cost Pool	Activity Measure	Total Activity
Removing asbestos	Thousands of square feet	500 thousand square feet
Estimating and job setup	Number of jobs	200 jobs*
Working on nonroutine jobs . . .	Number of nonroutine jobs	25 nonroutine jobs
Other (organization-sustaining and idle capacity costs)	None	Not applicable

*The total number of jobs includes nonroutine jobs as well as routine jobs. Nonroutine jobs as well as routine jobs require estimating and setup work.

Costs for the Year	
Wages and salaries	$ 200,000
Disposal fees	600,000
Equipment depreciation	80,000
On-site supplies	60,000
Office expenses	190,000
Licensing and insurance	370,000
Total cost	$1,500,000

	Distribution of Resource Consumption Across Activities				
	Removing Asbestos	Estimating and Job Setup	Working on Nonroutine Jobs	Other	Total
Wages and salaries	40%	10%	35%	15%	100%
Disposal fees	70%	0%	30%	0%	100%
Equipment depreciation	50%	0%	40%	10%	100%
On-site supplies	55%	15%	20%	10%	100%
Office expenses	10%	40%	30%	20%	100%
Licensing and insurance	50%	0%	40%	10%	100%

Required:

1. Using Exhibit 7–5 as a guide, perform the first-stage allocation of costs to the activity cost pools.
2. Using Exhibit 7–6 as a guide, compute the activity rates for the activity cost pools.
3. Using the activity rates you have computed, determine the total cost and the average cost per thousand square feet of each of the following jobs according to the activity-based costing system.
   a. A routine 2,000-square-foot asbestos removal job.
   b. A routine 4,000-square-foot asbestos removal job.
   c. A nonroutine 2,000-square-foot asbestos removal job.
4. Given the results you obtained in (3) above, do you agree with the estimator that the company's present policy for bidding on jobs is adequate?

eXcel

PROBLEM 7–20 Evaluating the Profitability of Services [LO2, LO3, LO4, LO5]

Gore Range Carpet Cleaning is a family-owned business in Eagle-Vail, Colorado. For its services, the company has always charged a flat fee per hundred square feet of carpet cleaned. The current fee is $22.95 per hundred square feet. However, there is some question about whether the company is actually making any money on jobs for some customers—particularly those located on more remote ranches that require considerable travel time. The owner's daughter, home for the summer from college, has suggested investigating this question using activity-based costing. After some discussion, a simple system consisting of four activity cost pools seemed to be adequate. The activity cost pools and their activity measures appear below:

Activity Cost Pool	Activity Measure	Activity for the Year
Cleaning carpets	Square feet cleaned (00s)	10,000 hundred square feet
Travel to jobs	Miles driven	50,000 miles
Job support	Number of jobs	1,800 jobs
Other (organization-sustaining and idle capacity costs)	None	Not applicable

The total cost of operating the company for the year is $340,000, which includes the following costs:

Wages	$140,000
Cleaning supplies	25,000
Cleaning equipment depreciation	10,000
Vehicle expenses	30,000
Office expenses	60,000
President's compensation	75,000
Total cost	$340,000

Resource consumption is distributed across the activities as follows:

	Distribution of Resource Consumption Across Activities				
	Cleaning Carpets	Travel to Jobs	Job Support	Other	Total
Wages	75%	15%	0%	10%	100%
Cleaning supplies	100%	0%	0%	0%	100%
Cleaning equipment depreciation	70%	0%	0%	30%	100%
Vehicle expenses	0%	80%	0%	20%	100%
Office expenses	0%	0%	60%	40%	100%
President's compensation	0%	0%	30%	70%	100%

Job support consists of receiving calls from potential customers at the home office, scheduling jobs, billing, resolving issues, and so on.

Required:

1. Using Exhibit 7–5 as a guide, prepare the first-stage allocation of costs to the activity cost pools.
2. Using Exhibit 7–6 as a guide, compute the activity rates for the activity cost pools.
3. The company recently completed a 6 hundred square-foot carpet-cleaning job at the Lazy Bee Ranch—a 52-mile round-trip from the company's offices in Eagle-Vail. Compute the cost of this job using the activity-based costing system.
4. The revenue from the Lazy Bee Ranch was $137.70 (6 hundred square-feet at $22.95 per hundred square feet). Using Exhibit 7–11 as a guide, prepare a report showing the margin from this job.
5. What do you conclude concerning the profitability of the Lazy Bee Ranch job? Explain.
6. What advice would you give the president concerning pricing jobs in the future?

Appendix 7A: ABC Action Analysis

LEARNING OBJECTIVE 6
Prepare an action analysis report using activity-based costing data and interpret the report.

A conventional ABC analysis, such as the one presented in Exhibits 7–10 and 7–11 in the chapter, has several important limitations. Referring back to Exhibit 7–10, recall that the custom compass housings show a negative product margin of $49,500. Because of this apparent loss, managers were considering dropping this product. However, as the discussion among the managers revealed, it is unlikely that all of the $589,500 cost of the product would be avoided if it were dropped. Some of these costs would continue even if the product were totally eliminated. *Before* taking action, it is vital to identify which costs would be avoided and which costs would continue. Only those costs that can be avoided are relevant in the decision. Moreover, many of the costs are managed costs that would require explicit management action to eliminate. If the custom compass housings product line were eliminated, the direct materials cost would be avoided without any explicit management action—the materials simply wouldn't be ordered. On the other hand, if the custom compass housings were dropped, explicit management action would be required to eliminate the salaries of overhead workers that are assigned to this product.

Simply shifting these managed costs to other products would not solve anything. These costs would have to be eliminated or the resources *shifted to the constraint* to have any benefit to the company. While eliminating the cost is obviously beneficial, redeploying the resources is only beneficial if the resources are shifted to the constraint in the process. If the resources are redeployed to a work center that is not a constraint, it would increase the excess capacity in that work center—which has no direct benefit to the company.

In addition, if some overhead costs need to be eliminated as a result of dropping a product, specific managers must be held responsible for eliminating those costs or the reductions are unlikely to occur. If no one is specifically held responsible for eliminating the costs, they will almost certainly continue to be incurred. Without external pressure, managers usually avoid cutting costs in their areas of responsibility. The action analysis report developed in this appendix is intended to help top managers identify what costs are relevant in a decision and to place responsibility for the elimination of those costs on the appropriate managers.

Activity Rates—Action Analysis Report

Constructing an action analysis report begins with the results of the first-stage allocation, which is reproduced as Exhibit 7A–1 (page 318). In contrast to the conventional ABC analysis covered in the chapter, the calculation of the activity rates for an action analysis report is a bit more involved. In addition to computing an overall activity rate for each activity cost pool, an activity rate is computed for each cell in Exhibit 7A–1. The computations of activity rates for the action analysis are carried out in Exhibit 7A–2 (page 318). For example, the $125,000 cost of indirect factory wages for the Customer Orders cost pool is divided by the total activity for that cost pool—1,000 orders—to arrive at the activity rate of $125 per customer order for indirect factory wages. Similarly, the $200,000 cost of indirect factory wages for the Product Design cost pool is divided by the total activity for that cost pool—400 designs—to arrive at the activity rate of $500 per design for indirect factory wages. Note that the totals at the bottom of Exhibit 7A–2 agree with the overall activity rates in Exhibit 7–6 in the chapter. Exhibit 7A–2, which shows the activity rates for the action analysis report, contains more detail than Exhibit 7–6, which contains the activity rates for the conventional ABC analysis.

EXHIBIT 7A–1
First-Stage Allocations to Activity Cost Pools

	Customer Orders	Product Design	Order Size	Customer Relations	Other	Total
	Activity Cost Pools					
Production Department:						
Indirect factory wages	$ 125,000	$ 200,000	$ 100,000	$ 50,000	$ 25,000	$ 500,000
Factory equipment depreciation	60,000	0	180,000	0	60,000	300,000
Factory utilities	0	12,000	60,000	0	48,000	120,000
Factory building lease	0	0	0	0	80,000	80,000
General Administrative Department:						
Administrative wages and salaries	60,000	20,000	40,000	120,000	160,000	400,000
Office equipment depreciation	15,000	0	0	12,500	22,500	50,000
Administrative building lease	0	0	0	0	60,000	60,000
Marketing Department:						
Marketing wages and salaries	55,000	20,000	0	150,000	25,000	250,000
Selling expenses	5,000	0	0	35,000	10,000	50,000
Total cost	$ 320,000	$ 252,000	$ 380,000	$ 367,500	$ 490,500	$ 1,810,000

EXHIBIT 7A–2
Computation of the Activity Rates for the Action Analysis Report

	Customer Orders	Product Design	Order Size	Customer Relations	Other
	Activity Cost Pools				
Total activity	1,000 orders	400 product designs	20,000 machine-hours	250 active customers	Not applicable*
Production Department:					
Indirect factory wages	$ 125	$ 500	$ 5	$ 200	
Factory equipment depreciation	60	0	9	0	
Factory utilities	0	30	3	0	
Factory building lease	0	0	0	0	
General Administrative Department:					
Administrative wages and salaries	60	50	2	480	
Office equipment depreciation	15	0	0	50	
Administrative building lease	0	0	0	0	
Marketing Department:					
Marketing wages and salaries	55	50	0	600	
Selling expenses	5	0	0	140	
Total (conventional ABC analysis)	$ 320	$ 630	$ 19	$ 1,470	

*Activity rates are not computed for the Other cost pool since these costs will not be allocated further.

$125,000 ÷ 1,000 orders = $125 per order.

Other entries in the table are computed similarly.

Assignment of Overhead Costs to Products—Action Analysis Report

Computing the overhead costs to be assigned to products for an action analysis report also involves more detail than for a conventional ABC analysis. The computations for Classic Brass are carried out in Exhibit 7A–3. For example, the activity rate of $125 per customer order for indirect factory wages is multiplied by 600 orders for the standard stanchions to arrive at the cost of $75,000 for indirect factory wages in Exhibit 7A–3. Instead

EXHIBIT 7A–3
Action Analysis Cost Matrices

Action Analysis Cost Matrix for Standard Stanchions

	Customer Orders	Product Design	Order Size	Customer Relations	Total
	Activity Cost Pools				
Total activity for stanchions	600 orders	product designs	17,500 machine-hours	Not applicable	
Production Department:					
Indirect factory wages	$ 75,000	$ 0	$ 87,500		$ 162,500
Factory equipment depreciation	36,000	0	157,500		193,500
Factory utilities	0	0	52,500		52,500
Factory building lease	0	0	0		0
General Administrative Department:					
Administrative wages and salaries	36,000	0	35,000		71,000
Office equipment depreciation	9,000	0	0		9,000
Administrative building lease	0	0	0		0
Marketing Department:					
Marketing wages and salaries	33,000	0	0		33,000
Selling expenses	3,000	0	0		3,000
Total (conventional ABC analysis)	$ 192,000	$ 0	$ 332,500		$ 524,500

From Exhibit 7A–2, the activity rate for indirect factory wages for the Customer Orders cost pool is $125 per order.

$125 per order × 600 orders = $75,000

Other entries in the table are computed in a similar way.

Action Analysis Cost Matrix for the Custom Compass Housings

	Customer Orders	Product Design	Order Size	Customer Relations	Total
	Activity Cost Pools				
Total activity for custom compass housings	400 order	400 product design	2,500 machine-hours	Not applicable	
Production Department:					
Indirect factory wages	$ 50,000	$ 200,000	$ 12,500		$ 262,500
Factory equipment depreciation	24,000	0	22,500		46,500
Factory utilities	0	12,000	7,500		19,500
Factory building lease	0	0	0		0
General Administrative Department:					
Administrative wages and salaries	24,000	20,000	5,000		49,000
Office equipment depreciation	6,000	0	0		6,000
Administrative building lease	0	0	0		0
Marketing Department:					
Marketing wages and salaries	22,000	20,000	0		42,000
Selling expenses	2,000	0	0		2,000
Total (conventional ABC analysis)	$ 128,000	$ 252,000	$ 47,500		$ 427,500

From Exhibit 7A–2, the activity rate for indirect factory wages for the Customer Orders cost pool is $125 per order.

$125 per order × 400 orders = $50,000

Other entries in the table are computed in a similar way.

of just a single cost number for each cost pool as in the conventional ABC analysis, we now have an entire cost matrix showing much more detail. Note that the column totals for the cost matrix in Exhibit 7A–3 agree with the ABC costs for standard stanchions in Exhibit 7–8. Indeed, the conventional ABC analysis of Exhibit 7–10 can be easily constructed using the column totals at the bottom of the cost matrices in Exhibit 7A–3. In contrast, the action analysis report will be based on the row totals at the right of the cost matrices in Exhibit 7A–3. In addition, the action analysis report will include a simple color-coding scheme that will help managers identify how easily the various costs can be adjusted.

Ease of Adjustment Codes

The ABC team constructed Exhibit 7A–4 to aid managers in the use of the ABC data. In this exhibit, each cost has been assigned an *ease of adjustment code*—Green, Yellow, or Red. The **ease of adjustment code** reflects how easily the cost could be adjusted to changes in activity.[4] "Green" costs are those costs that would adjust more or less automatically to changes in activity without any action by managers. For example, direct materials costs would adjust to changes in orders without any action being taken by managers. If a customer does not order stanchions, the direct materials for the stanchions would not be required and would not be ordered. "Yellow" costs are those costs that could be adjusted in response to changes in activity, but such adjustments require management action; the adjustment is not automatic. The ABC team believes, for example, that direct labor costs should be included in the Yellow category. Managers must make difficult decisions and take explicit action to increase or decrease, in aggregate, direct labor costs—particularly because the company has a no lay-off policy. "Red" costs are costs that could be adjusted to changes in activity only with a great deal of difficulty, and the adjustment would require management action. The building leases fall into this category because it would be very difficult and expensive to break the leases.

The Action Analysis View of the ABC Data

Looking at Exhibit 7A–3, the totals on the right-hand side of the table indicate that the $427,500 of overhead cost for the custom compass housings consists of $262,500 of indirect factory wages, $46,500 of factory equipment depreciation, and so on. These data

EXHIBIT 7A–4
Ease of Adjustment Codes

Green: *Costs that adjust automatically to changes in activity without management action.*

Direct materials
Shipping costs

Yellow: *Costs that could, in principle, be adjusted to changes in activity, but management action would be required.*

Direct labor
Indirect factory wages
Factory utilities
Administrative wages and salaries
Office equipment depreciation
Marketing wages and salaries
Selling expenses

Red: *Costs that would be very difficult to adjust to changes in activity and management action would be required.*

Factory equipment depreciation
Factory building lease
Administrative building lease

[4] The idea of using colors to code how easily costs can be adjusted was suggested to us at a seminar put on by Boeing and by an article by Alfred King, "Green Dollars and Blue Dollars: The Paradox of Cost Reduction," *Journal of Cost Management*, Fall 1993, pp. 44–52.

	A	B	C
1	**Custom Compass Housings**		
2	Sales (from Exhibit 7-10)		$ 540,000
3			
4	Green costs:		
5	Direct materials (from Exhibit 7-10)	$ 69,500	
6	Shipping (from Exhibit 7-10)	5,000	74,500
7	Green margin		465,500
8			
9	Yellow costs:		
10	Direct labor (from Exhibit 7-10)	87,500	
11	Indirect factory wages (from Exhibit 7A-3)	262,500	
12	Factory utilities (from Exhibit 7A-3)	19,500	
13	Administrative wages and salaries (from Exhibit 7A-3)	49,000	
14	Office equipment depreciation (from Exhibit 7A-3)	6,000	
15	Marketing wages and salaries (from Exhibit 7A-3)	42,000	
16	Selling expenses (from Exhibit 7A-3)	2,000	468,500
17	Yellow margin		(3,000)
18			
19	Red costs:		
20	Factory equipment depreciation (from Exhibit 7A-3)	46,500	
21	Factory building lease (from Exhibit 7A-3)	0	
22	Administrative building lease (from Exhibit 7A-3)	0	46,500
23	Red margin		$ (49,500)
24			

Exhibit 7A-3B | **Exhibit 7A-5** | Activity rates

EXHIBIT 7A–5
Action Analysis of Custom Compass Housings: Activity-Based Costing System

are displayed in Exhibit 7A–5, which shows an action analysis of the custom compass housings product. An action analysis report shows what costs have been assigned to the cost object, such as a product or customer, and how difficult it would be to adjust the cost if there is a change in activity. Note that the Red margin at the bottom of Exhibit 7A–5, ($49,500), is exactly the same as the product margin for the custom compass housings in Exhibit 7–10 in the chapter.

The cost data in the action analysis in Exhibit 7A–5 are arranged by the color coded ease of adjustment. All of the Green costs—those that adjust more or less automatically to changes in activity—appear together at the top of the list of costs. These costs total $74,500 and are subtracted from the sales of $540,000 to yield a Green margin of $465,500. The same procedure is followed for the Yellow and Red costs. This action analysis indicates what costs would have to be cut and how difficult it would be to cut them if the custom compass housings product were dropped. Prior to making any decision about dropping products, the managers responsible for the costs must agree to either eliminate the resources represented by those costs or to transfer the resources to an area in the organization that really needs the resources—namely, a constraint. If managers do not make such a commitment, it is likely that the costs would continue to be incurred. As a result, the company would lose the sales from the products without really eliminating the costs.

MANAGERIAL ACCOUNTING IN ACTION
The Wrap-Up

After the action analysis was prepared by the ABC team, top management at Classic Brass met once again to review the results of the ABC analysis.

John: When we last met, we had discussed the advisability of discontinuing the custom compass housings product line. I understand that the ABC team has done some additional analysis to help us in making this decision.

Mary: That's right. The action analysis report we put together indicates how easy it would be to adjust each cost and where specific cost savings would have to come from if we were to drop the custom compass housings.

John: What's this red margin at the bottom of the action analysis? Isn't that a product margin?

Mary: Yes, it is. However, we call it a red margin because we should stop and think very, very carefully before taking any actions based on that margin.

John: Why is that?

Mary: As an example, we subtracted the costs of factory equipment depreciation to arrive at that red margin. We doubt that we could avoid any of that cost if we were to drop custom orders. We use the same machines on custom orders that we use on standard products. The factory equipment has no resale value, and it does not wear out through use.

John: What about this yellow margin?

Mary: Yellow means proceed with a great deal of caution. To get to the yellow margin we deducted from sales numerous costs that could be adjusted only if the managers involved are willing to eliminate resources or shift them to the constraint.

John: If I understand the yellow margin correctly, the apparent loss of $3,000 on the custom compass housings is the result of the indirect factory wages of $262,500.

Susan: Right, that's basically the wages of our design engineers.

John: I am uncomfortable with the idea of laying off any of our designers for numerous reasons. So where does that leave us?

Mary: What about raising prices on our custom products?

Tom: We should be able to do that. We have been undercutting the competition to make sure that we won bids on custom work because we thought it was a very profitable thing to do.

John: Why don't we just charge directly for design work?

Tom: Some of our competitors already do that. However, I don't think we would be able to charge enough to cover our design costs.

John: Can we do anything to make our design work more efficient so it costs us less? I'm not going to lay anyone off, but if we make the design process more efficient, we could lower the charge for design work and spread those costs across more customers.

Susan: That may be possible. I'll form a process improvement team to look at it.

John: Let's get some benchmark data on design costs. If we set our minds to it, I'm sure we can be world class in no time.

Susan: Okay. Mary, will you help with the benchmark data?

Mary: Sure.

John: Let's meet again in about a week to discuss our progress. Is there anything else on the agenda for today?

The points raised in the preceding discussion are extremely important. By measuring the resources consumed by products (and other cost objects), an ABC system provides a much better basis for decision making than a traditional cost accounting system that spreads overhead costs around without much regard for what might be causing the overhead. A well-designed ABC system provides managers with estimates of potentially relevant costs that can be a very useful starting point for management analysis.

Summary (Appendix 7A)

The action analysis report illustrated in this appendix is a valuable addition to the ABC toolkit. An action analysis report provides more information for decision making than a conventional ABC analysis. The action analysis report makes it clear where costs would have to be adjusted in the organization as a result of an action. In a conventional ABC analysis, a cost such as $320 for processing an order represents costs from many parts of the organization. If an order is dropped, there will be little pressure to actually eliminate the $320 cost unless it is clear where the costs are incurred and which managers would be responsible for reducing the cost. In contrast, an action analysis report traces the costs to where they are incurred in the organization and makes it much easier to assign responsibility to managers for reducing costs. In addition, an action analysis report provides information concerning how easily a cost can be adjusted. Costs that cannot be adjusted are not relevant in a decision.

Exhibit 7A–6 summarizes all of the steps required to create both an action analysis report as illustrated in this appendix and an activity analysis as shown in the chapter.

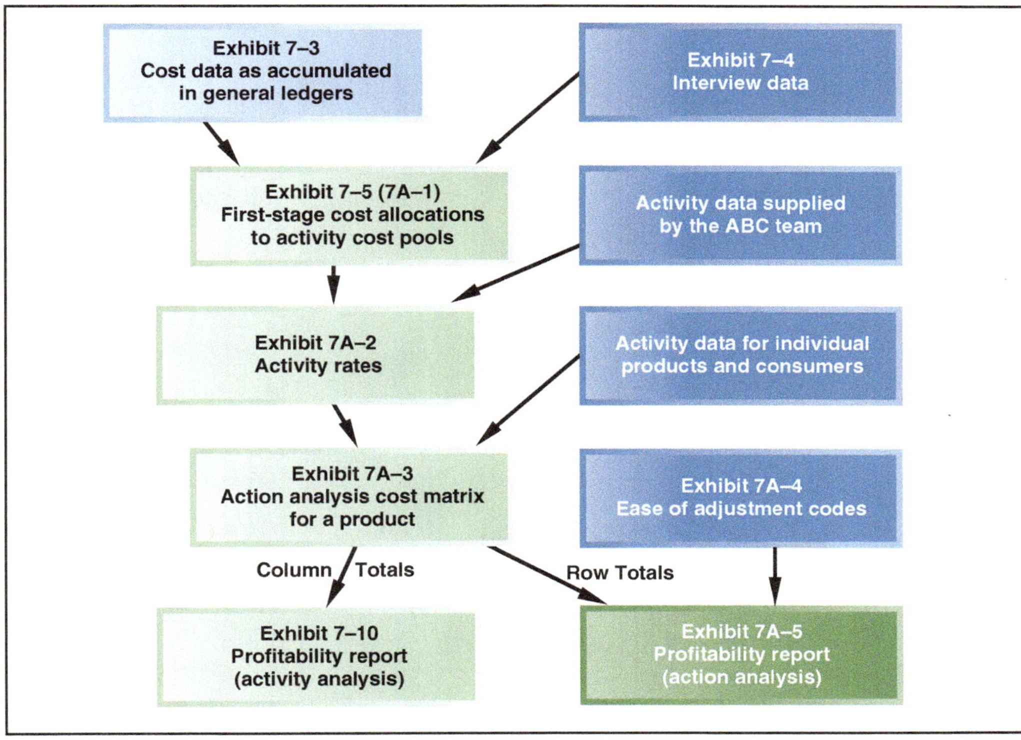

EXHIBIT 7A–6
Summary of the Steps to Produce an Action Analysis Report

Review Problem: Activity Analysis Report

Refer to the data for Ferris Corporation in the Review Problem at the end of the chapter on pages 298–300.

Required:

1. Compute activity rates for Ferris Corporation as in Exhibit 7A–2.
2. Using Exhibit 7A–3 as a guide, construct a table showing the overhead costs for the OfficeMart orders described in requirement (3) of the Review Problem at the end of the chapter.
3. The management of Ferris Corporation has assigned ease of adjustment codes to costs as follows:

Cost	Ease of Adjustment Code
Direct materials	Green
Direct labor	Yellow
Manufacturing overhead	Yellow
Selling and administrative overhead	Red

Using Exhibit 7A–5 as a guide, prepare an action analysis of the OfficeMart orders.

Solution to Review Problem

1. The activity rates for the activity cost pools are:

	Assembling Units	Processing Orders	Supporting Customers
Total activity	1,000 units	250 orders	100 customers
Manufacturing overhead	$250	$ 700	$ 250
Selling and administrative overhead	30	540	750
Total	$280	$1,240	$1,000

2. The overhead cost for the four orders of a total of 80 filing cabinets would be computed as follows:

	Assembling Units	Processing Orders	Supporting Customers	Total
Activity	80 units	4 orders	1 customer	
Manufacturing overhead	$20,000	$2,800	$ 250	$23,050
Selling and administrative overhead	2,400	2,160	750	5,310
Total	$22,400	$4,960	$1,000	$28,360

3. The action analysis report is:

Sales		$47,600
Green costs:		
Direct materials	$14,400	14,400
Green margin		33,200
Yellow costs:		
Direct labor	4,000	
Manufacturing overhead	23,050	27,050
Yellow margin		6,150
Red costs:		
Selling and administrative overhead	5,310	5,310
Red margin		$ 840

Glossary (Appendix 7A)

Ease of adjustment codes Costs are coded as Green, Yellow, or Red—depending on how easily the cost could be adjusted to changes in activity. "Green" costs adjust automatically to changes in activity. "Yellow" costs could be adjusted in response to changes in activity, but such adjustments require management action; the adjustment is not automatic. "Red" costs could be adjusted to changes in activity only with a great deal of difficulty and would require management action. (p. 320)

Appendix 7A Exercises and Problems

All applicable exercises and problems are available with McGraw-Hill's *Connect™ Accounting*.

EXERCISE 7A–1 Preparing an Action Analysis Report [LO6]

Pro Golf Corporation produces private label golf clubs for pro shops throughout North America. The company uses activity-based costing to evaluate the profitability of serving its customers. This analysis is based on categorizing the company's costs as follows, using the ease of adjustment color coding scheme described in Appendix 7A:

	Ease of Adjustment Code
Direct materials	Green
Direct labor	Yellow
Indirect labor	Yellow
Factory equipment depreciation	Red
Factory administration	Red
Selling and administrative wages and salaries	Red
Selling and administrative depreciation	Red
Marketing expenses	Yellow

Management would like to evaluate the profitability of a particular customer—the Peregrine Golf Club of Eagle, Colorado. Over the last 12 months this customer submitted one order for 80 golf clubs that had to be produced in two batches due to differences in product labeling requested by the customer. Summary data concerning the order appear below:

Number of clubs	80
Number of orders	1
Number of batches	2
Direct labor-hours per club	0.3
Selling price per club	$48.00
Direct materials cost per club	$25.40
Direct labor rate per hour	$21.50

A cost analyst working in the controller's office at the company has already produced the action analysis cost matrix for the Peregrine Golf Club that follows:

Action Analysis Cost Matrix for Peregrine Golf Club

	Activity Cost Pools				
	Volume	Batch Processing	Order Processing	Customer Service	Total
Activity	24 direct labor-hours	2 batches	1 order	1 customer	
Manufacturing overhead:					
Indirect labor	$ 33.60	$51.60	$ 4.80	$ 0.00	$ 90.00
Factory equipment depreciation	105.60	0.80	0.00	0.00	106.40
Factory administration	16.80	0.60	14.00	231.00	262.40
Selling and administrative overhead:					
Wages and salaries	12.00	0.00	38.00	386.00	436.00
Depreciation	0.00	0.00	5.00	25.00	30.00
Marketing expenses	115.20	0.00	57.00	368.00	540.20
Total	$283.20	$53.00	$118.80	$1,010.00	$1,465.00

Required:

Prepare an action analysis report showing the profitability of the Peregrine Golf Club. Include direct materials and direct labor costs in the report. Use Exhibit 7A–5 as a guide for organizing the report.

EXERCISE 7A–2 Second-Stage Allocation Using the Action Analysis Approach [LO4, LO6]

This exercise should be assigned in conjunction with Exercise 7–6.

The results of the first-stage allocation of the activity-based costing system at Transvaal Mining Tools Ltd., in which the activity rates were computed, appear below:

	Order Size	Customer Orders	Product Testing	Selling
Manufacturing overhead:				
Indirect labor	R 9.60	R 231.00	R 36.00	R 0.00
Factory depreciation	7.00	0.00	18.00	0.00
Factory utilities	0.20	0.00	1.00	0.00
Factory administration	0.00	46.00	24.00	12.00
Selling and administrative:				
Wages and salaries	0.80	72.00	0.00	965.00
Depreciation	0.00	11.00	0.00	36.00
Taxes and insurance	0.00	0.00	0.00	49.00
Selling expenses	0.00	0.00	0.00	432.00
Total overhead cost	R 17.60	R 360.00	R 79.00	R 1,494.00

Required:

1. Using Exhibit 7A–3 as a guide, prepare a report showing the overhead cost of the order for hard-rock drills discussed in Exercise 7–6. What is the total overhead cost of the order?
2. Explain the two different perspectives this report gives to managers concerning the nature of the overhead costs involved in the order. (Hint: Look at the row and column totals of the report you have prepared.)

EXERCISE 7A–3 Second-Stage Allocations and Margin Calculations Using the Action Analysis Approach [LO4, LO6]

Refer to the data for Theatre Seating, Inc., in Exercise 7–13 and the following additional details concerning the activity rates:

	Activity Rates			
	Supporting Direct Labor	Batch Processing	Order Processing	Customer Service
Manufacturing overhead:				
Indirect labor	$ 1.80	$72.00	$ 18.00	$ 0.00
Factory equipment depreciation . . .	7.35	3.25	0.00	0.00
Factory administration	2.10	7.00	28.00	268.00
Selling and administrative:				
Wages and salaries	0.50	13.00	153.00	1,864.00
Depreciation	0.00	0.75	6.00	26.00
Marketing expenses	0.25	0.00	79.00	462.00
Total activity rate	$12.00	$96.00	$284.00	$2,620.00

Management has provided their ease of adjustment codes for purposes of preparing action analyses.

	Ease of Adjustment Codes
Direct materials	Green
Direct labor	Yellow
Manufacturing overhead:	
Indirect labor	Yellow
Factory equipment depreciation	Red
Factory administration	Red
Selling and administrative:	
Wages and salaries	Red
Depreciation	Red
Marketing expenses	Yellow

Required:

Using Exhibit 7A–5 as a guide, prepare an action analysis report for CineMax Entertainment similar to those prepared for products.

EXERCISE 7A–4 Comprehensive Activity-Based Costing Exercise [LO2, LO3, LO4, LO6]

Refer to the data for Silicon Optics in Exercise 7–11.

Required:

1. Using Exhibit 7A–1 as a guide, prepare a report showing the first-stage allocations of overhead costs to the activity cost pools.
2. Using Exhibit 7A–2 as a guide, compute the activity rates for the activity cost pools.
3. Using Exhibit 7A–3 as a guide, prepare a report showing the overhead costs for the order from Indus Telecom including customer support costs.
4. Using Exhibit 7–11 as a guide, prepare a report showing the customer margin for Indus Telecom.
5. Using Exhibit 7A–5 as a guide, prepare an action analysis report showing the customer margin for Indus Telecom. Direct materials should be coded as a Green cost, direct labor and wages and salaries as Yellow costs, and other overhead costs as a Red cost.
6. What action, if any, do you recommend as a result of the above analyses?

PROBLEM 7A–5 Second-Stage Allocations and Product Margins [LO4, LO6]

Refer to the data for AnimPix, Inc., in Problem 7–16. In addition, the company has provided the following details concerning its activity rates:

	Activity Rates		
	Animation Concept	Animation Production	Contract Administration
Technical staff salaries	$3,500	$5,000	$1,800
Animation equipment depreciation	600	1,500	0
Administrative wages and salaries	1,400	200	4,600
Supplies costs	300	600	100
Facility costs	200	400	100
Total	$6,000	$7,700	$6,600

Management has provided the following ease of adjustment codes for the various costs:

	Ease of Adjustment Code
Technical staff salaries	Red
Animation equipment depreciation	Red
Administrative wages and salaries	Yellow
Supplies costs	Green
Facility costs	Red

These codes created some controversy. In particular, some administrators objected to coding their own salaries Yellow, while the technical staff salaries were coded Red. However, the founders of the firm overruled these objections by pointing out that "our technical staff is our most valuable asset. Good animators are extremely difficult to find, and they would be the last to go if we had to cut back."

Required:

1. Using Exhibit 7A–3 as a guide, determine the cost of the local commercials market. (Think of the local commercials market as a product.)
2. Using Exhibit 7A–5 as a guide, prepare an action analysis report concerning the local commercials market. (This company has no direct materials or direct labor costs.)
3. What would you recommend to management concerning the local commercials market?

Appendix 7B: Using a Modified Form of Activity-Based Costing to Determine Product Costs for External Reports

LEARNING OBJECTIVE 7
Use activity-based costing techniques to compute unit product costs for external reports.

This chapter has emphasized using activity-based costing information in internal decisions. However, a modified form of activity-based costing can also be used to develop product costs for external financial reports. For this purpose, product costs include all manufacturing overhead costs—including organization-sustaining costs and the costs of idle capacity—and exclude all nonmanufacturing costs, even costs that are clearly caused by the products.

The simplest absorption costing systems as described in Chapter 3 assign manufacturing overhead costs to products using a single factory-wide predetermined overhead rate based on direct labor-hours or machine-hours. When activity-based costing is used to assign manufacturing overhead costs to products, a predetermined overhead rate is computed for each activity cost pool. An example will make this difference clear.

Maxtar Industries manufactures high-quality smoker/barbecue units. The company has two product lines—Premium and Standard. The company has traditionally applied manufacturing overhead costs to these products using a plantwide predetermined overhead rate based on direct labor-hours. Exhibit 7B–1 details how the unit product costs of the two product lines are computed using the company's traditional costing system. The unit product cost of the Premium product line is $71.60 and the unit product cost of the Standard product line is $53.70 according to this traditional costing system.

Maxtar Industries has recently experimented with an activity-based costing approach for determining its unit product costs for external reporting purposes. The company's activity-based costing system has three activity cost pools: (1) supporting direct labor; (2) setting up machines; and (3) parts administration. The top of Exhibit 7B–2 displays basic data concerning these activity cost pools. Note that the total estimated overhead cost in

EXHIBIT 7B–1
Maxtar Industries' Traditional Costing System

Basic Data

Total estimated manufacturing overhead cost	$1,520,000
Total estimated direct labor-hours	400,000 DLHs

	Premium	Standard
Direct materials per unit	$40.00	$30.00
Direct labor per unit	$24.00	$18.00
Direct labor-hours per unit	2.0 DLHs	1.5 DLHs
Units produced	50,000 units	200,000 units

Computation of the Predetermined Overhead Rate

$$\text{Predetermined overhead rate} = \frac{\text{Total estimated manufacturing overhead}}{\text{Total estimated amount of the allocation base}}$$

$$= \frac{\$1{,}520{,}000}{400{,}000\text{ DLHs}} = \$3.80\text{ per DLH}$$

Traditional Unit Product Costs

	Premium	Standard
Direct materials	$40.00	$30.00
Direct labor	24.00	18.00
Manufacturing overhead (2.0 DLHs × $3.80 per DLH; 1.5 DLHs × $3.80 per DLH)	7.60	5.70
Unit product cost	$71.60	$53.70

EXHIBIT 7B–2
Maxtar Industries' Activity-Based Costing System

Basic Data

Activities and Activity Measures	Estimated Overhead Cost	Expected Activity: Premium	Standard	Total
Supporting direct labor (DLHs)	$ 800,000	100,000	300,000	400,000
Setting up machines (setups)	480,000	600	200	800
Parts administration (part types)	240,000	140	60	200
Total manufacturing overhead cost . . .	$1,520,000			

Computation of Activity Rates

Activities	(a) Estimated Overhead Cost	(b) Total Expected Activity	(a) ÷ (b) Activity Rate
Supporting direct labor	$800,000	400,000 DLHs	$2 per DLH
Setting up machines	$480,000	800 setups	$600 per setup
Parts administration	$240,000	200 part types	$1,200 per part type

Assigning Overhead Costs to Products

Overhead Cost for the Premium Product

Activity Cost Pools	(a) Activity Rate	(b) Activity	(a) × (b) ABC Cost
Supporting direct labor . . .	$2 per DLH	100,000 DLHs	$200,000
Setting up machines	$600 per setup	600 setups	360,000
Parts administration	$1,200 per part type	140 part types	168,000
Total			$728,000

Overhead Cost for the Standard Product

Activity Cost Pools	(a) Activity Rate	(b) Activity	(a) × (b) ABC Cost
Supporting direct labor	$2 per DLH	300,000 DLHs	$600,000
Setting up machines	$600 per setup	200 setups	120,000
Parts administration	$1,200 per part type	60 part types	72,000
Total			$792,000

Activity-Based Costing Product Costs

	Premium	Standard
Direct materials	$40.00	$30.00
Direct labor	24.00	18.00
Manufacturing overhead ($728,000 ÷ 50,000 units; $792,000 ÷ 200,000 units)	14.56	3.96
Unit product cost	$78.56	$51.96

these three costs pools, $1,520,000, agrees with the total estimated overhead cost in the company's traditional costing system. The company's activity-based costing system simply provides an alternative way to allocate the company's manufacturing overhead across the two products.

The activity rates for the three activity cost pools are computed in the second table in Exhibit 7B–2. For example, the total cost in the "setting up machines" activity cost pool, $480,000, is divided by the total activity associated with that cost pool, 800 setups, to determine the activity rate of $600 per setup.

The activity rates are used to allocate overhead costs to the two products in the third table in Exhibit 7B–2. For example, the activity rate for the "setting up machines" activity cost pool, $600 per setup, is multiplied by the Premium product line's 600 setups to determine the $360,000 machine setup cost allocated to the Premium product line.

The table at the bottom of Exhibit 7B–2 displays the overhead costs per unit and the activity-based costing unit product costs. The overhead cost per unit is determined by dividing the total overhead cost by the number of units produced. For example, the Premium product line's total overhead cost of $728,000 is divided by 50,000 units to determine the $14.56 overhead cost per unit. Note that the unit product costs differ from those computed using the company's traditional costing system in Exhibit 7B–1. Because the activity-based costing system contains both a batch-level (setting up machines) and a product-level (parts administration) activity cost pool, the unit product costs under activity-based costing follow the usual pattern in which overhead costs are shifted from the high-volume to the low-volume product. The unit product cost of the Standard product line, the high-volume product, has gone down from $53.70 under the traditional costing system to $51.96 under activity-based costing. In contrast, the unit product cost of the Premium product line, the low-volume product, has increased from $71.60 under the traditional costing system to $78.56 under activity-based costing. Instead of arbitrarily assigning most of the costs of setting up machines and of parts administration to the high-volume product, the activity-based costing system more accurately assigns these costs to the two products.

Appendix 7B Exercises and Problems

All applicable exercises and problems are available with McGraw-Hill's *Connect™ Accounting*.

EXERCISE 7B–1 Activity-Based Costing Product Costs for External Reports [LO7]

Pryad Corporation makes ultra-lightweight backpacking tents. Data concerning the company's two product lines appear below:

	Deluxe	Standard
Direct materials per unit	$60.00	$45.00
Direct labor per unit	$9.60	$7.20
Direct labor-hours per unit	0.8 DLHs	0.6 DLHs
Estimated annual production	10,000 units	70,000 units

The company has a traditional costing system in which manufacturing overhead is applied to units based on direct labor-hours. Data concerning manufacturing overhead and direct labor-hours for the upcoming year appear below:

Estimated total manufacturing overhead	$290,000
Estimated total direct labor-hours	50,000 DLHs

Required:

1. Determine the unit product costs of the Deluxe and Standard products under the company's traditional costing system.

2. The company is considering replacing its traditional costing system for determining unit product costs for external reports with an activity-based costing system. The activity-based costing system would have the following three activity cost pools:

Activities and Activity Measures	Estimated Overhead Cost	Expected Activity		
		Deluxe	Standard	Total
Supporting direct labor (direct labor-hours) . . .	$150,000	8,000	42,000	50,000
Batch setups (setups)	60,000	200	50	250
Safety testing (tests)	80,000	80	20	100
Total manufacturing overhead cost	$290,000			

Determine the unit product costs of the Deluxe and Standard products under the activity-based costing system.

EXERCISE 7B–2 Activity-Based Costing Product Costs for External Reports [LO7]

Kunkel Company makes two products and uses a traditional costing system in which a single plantwide predetermined overhead rate is computed based on direct labor-hours. Data for the two products for the upcoming year follow:

	Mercon	Wurcon
Direct materials cost per unit . . .	$10.00	$8.00
Direct labor cost per unit	$3.00	$3.75
Direct labor-hours per unit	0.20	0.25
Number of units produced	10,000	40,000

These products are customized to some degree for specific customers.

Required:

1. The company's manufacturing overhead costs for the year are expected to be $336,000. Using the company's traditional costing system, compute the unit product costs for the two products.
2. Management is considering an activity-based costing system in which half of the overhead would continue to be allocated on the basis of direct labor-hours and half would be allocated on the basis of engineering design time. The Mercon product is expected to need 4,000 engineering design hours and the Wurcon product is also expected to need 4,000 engineering design hours. Compute the unit product costs for the two products using the proposed ABC system.
3. Explain why the unit product costs differ between the two systems.

PROBLEM 7B–3 Activity-Based Costing as an Alternative to Traditional Product Costing [LO7]

Rehm Company manufactures a product that is available in both a deluxe model and a regular model. The company has manufactured the regular model for years. The deluxe model was introduced several years ago to tap a new segment of the market. Since introduction of the deluxe model, the company's profits have steadily declined, and management has become increasingly concerned about the accuracy of its costing system. Sales of the deluxe model have been increasing rapidly.

Manufacturing overhead is assigned to products on the basis of direct labor-hours. For the current year, the company has estimated that it will incur $6,000,000 in manufacturing overhead cost and produce 15,000 units of the deluxe model and 120,000 units of the regular model. The deluxe model requires 1.6 hours of direct labor time per unit, and the regular model requires 0.8 hours. Material and labor costs per unit are as follows:

	Model	
	Deluxe	Regular
Direct materials	$154	$112
Direct labor	$16	$8

Required:

1. Using direct labor-hours as the base for assigning manufacturing overhead cost to products, compute the predetermined overhead rate. Using this rate and other data from the problem, determine the unit product cost of each model.
2. Management is considering using activity-based costing to apply manufacturing overhead costs to products for external financial reports. The activity-based costing system would have the following four activity cost pools:

Activity Cost Pool	Activity Measure	Estimated Overhead Costs
Purchase orders	Number of purchase orders	$ 252,000
Scrap/rework orders	Number of scrap/rework orders	648,000
Product testing	Number of tests	1,350,000
Machine related	Machine-hours	3,750,000
Total overhead cost		$6,000,000

Activity Measure	Expected Activity		
	Deluxe	Regular	Total
Number of purchase orders	400	800	1,200
Number of scrap/rework orders	500	400	900
Number of tests	6,000	9,000	15,000
Machine-hours	20,000	30,000	50,000

Using Exhibit 7–6 as a guide, compute the predetermined overhead rates (i.e., activity rates) for each of the four activity cost pools.

3. Using the predetermined overhead rates computed in part (2) above, do the following:
   a. Compute the total amount of manufacturing overhead cost that would be applied to each model using the activity-based costing system. After these totals have been computed, determine the amount of manufacturing overhead cost per unit for each model.
   b. Compute the unit product cost of each model (materials, labor, and manufacturing overhead).
4. From the data you have developed in (1) through (3) above, identify factors that may account for the company's declining profits.

PROBLEM 7B–4 Activity-Based Costing as an Alternative to Traditional Product Costing [LO7]

Erte, Inc., manufactures two models of high-pressure steam valves, the XR7 model and the ZD5 model. Data regarding the two products follow:

Product	Direct Labor-Hours	Annual Production	Total Direct Labor-Hours
XR7	0.2 DLHs per unit	20,000 units	4,000 DLHs
ZD5	0.4 DLHs per unit	40,000 units	16,000 DLHs
			20,000 DLHs

Additional information about the company follows:

a. Product XR7 requires $35 in direct materials per unit, and product ZD5 requires $25.
b. The direct labor rate is $20 per hour.
c. The company has always used direct labor-hours as the base for applying manufacturing overhead cost to products. Manufacturing overhead totals $1,480,000 per year.

d. Product XR7 is more complex to manufacture than product ZD5 and requires the use of a special milling machine.
e. Because of the special work required in (d) above, the company is considering the use of activity-based costing to apply overhead cost to products. Three activity cost pools have been identified and the first-stage allocations have been completed. Data concerning these activity cost pools appear below:

Activity Cost Pool	Activity Measure	Estimated Total Cost	Estimated Total Activity XR7	ZD5	Total
Machine setups	Number of setups	$ 180,000	150	100	250
Special milling	Machine-hours	300,000	1,000	0	1,000
General factory	Direct labor-hours	1,000,000	4,000	16,000	20,000
		$1,480,000			

Required:
1. Assume that the company continues to use direct labor-hours as the base for applying overhead cost to products.
   a. Compute the predetermined overhead rate.
   b. Determine the unit product cost of each product.
2. Assume that the company decides to use activity-based costing to apply overhead cost to products.
   a. Compute the activity rate for each activity cost pool. Also, compute the amount of overhead cost that would be applied to each product.
   b. Determine the unit product cost of each product.
3. Explain why overhead cost shifted from the high-volume product to the low-volume product under activity-based costing.

CASE 7B–5 Activity-Based Costing as an Alternative to Traditional Product Costing [LO7]

Coffee Bean, Inc. (CBI), is a processor and distributor of a variety of blends of coffee. The company buys coffee beans from around the world and roasts, blends, and packages them for resale. CBI currently has 40 different coffees that it sells to gourmet shops in one-pound bags. The major cost of the coffee is raw materials. However, the company's predominantly automated roasting, blending, and packing process requires a substantial amount of manufacturing overhead. The company uses relatively little direct labor.

Some of CBI's coffees are very popular and sell in large volumes, while a few of the newer blends have very low volumes. CBI prices its coffee at manufacturing cost plus a markup of 30%. If CBI's prices for certain coffees are significantly higher than market, adjustments are made to bring CBI's prices more into alignment with the market because customers are somewhat price conscious.

For the coming year, CBI's budget includes estimated manufacturing overhead cost of $3,000,000. CBI assigns manufacturing overhead to products on the basis of direct labor-hours. The expected direct labor cost totals $600,000, which represents 50,000 hours of direct labor time. Based on the sales budget and expected raw materials costs, the company will purchase and use $6,000,000 of raw materials (mostly coffee beans) during the year.

The expected costs for direct materials and direct labor for one-pound bags of two of the company's coffee products appear below.

	Mona Loa	Malaysian
Direct materials	$4.20	$3.20
Direct labor (0.025 hours per bag)	$0.30	$0.30

CBI's controller believes that the company's traditional costing system may be providing misleading cost information. To determine whether or not this is correct, the controller has prepared an analysis of the year's expected manufacturing overhead costs, as shown in the following table:

Activity Cost Pool	Activity Measure	Expected Activity for the Year	Expected Cost for the Year
Purchasing	Purchase orders	1,710 orders	$ 513,000
Material handling	Number of setups	1,800 setups	720,000
Quality control	Number of batches	600 batches	144,000
Roasting	Roasting hours	96,100 roasting hours	961,000
Blending	Blending hours	33,500 blending hours	402,000
Packaging	Packaging hours	26,000 packaging hours	260,000
Total manufacturing overhead cost			$3,000,000

Data regarding the expected production of Mona Loa and Malaysian coffee are presented below.

	Mona Loa	Malaysian
Expected sales	100,000 pounds	2,000 pounds
Batch size	10,000 pounds	500 pounds
Setups	3 per batch	3 per batch
Purchase order size	20,000 pounds	500 pounds
Roasting time per 100 pounds	1.0 hour	1.0 hour
Blending time per 100 pounds	0.5 hour	0.5 hour
Packaging time per 100 pounds	0.1 hour	0.1 hour

Required:

1. Using direct labor-hours as the base for assigning manufacturing overhead cost to products, do the following:
   a. Determine the predetermined overhead rate that will be used during the year.
   b. Determine the unit product cost of one pound of Mona Loa coffee and one pound of Malaysian coffee.
2. Using activity-based costing as the basis for assigning manufacturing overhead cost to products, do the following:
   a. Determine the total amount of manufacturing overhead cost assigned to the Mona Loa coffee and to the Malaysian coffee for the year.
   b. Using the data developed in (2a) above, compute the amount of manufacturing overhead cost per pound of Mona Loa coffee and Malaysian coffee. Round all computations to the nearest whole cent.
   c. Determine the unit product cost of one pound of Mona Loa coffee and one pound of Malaysian coffee.
3. Write a brief memo to the president of CBI explaining what you have found in (1) and (2) above and discussing the implications to the company of using direct labor as the base for assigning manufacturing overhead cost to products.

(CMA, adapted)

Profit Planning

Planning for a Crisis—Civil War Preservation Trust

BUSINESS FOCUS

The Civil War Preservation Trust (CWPT) is a private, nonprofit organization with 70,000 members that works to preserve the nation's remaining Civil War battlefields—many of which are threatened by commercial development such as shopping centers, houses, industrial parks, and casinos. To forestall development, the CWPT typically purchases the land or development rights to the land. The CWPT has saved over 25,000 acres from development, including, for example, 698 acres of battlefield at Gettysburg.

CWPT's management team was particularly concerned about the budget proposal for 2009, which was to be presented to the board of directors in the fall of 2008. The CWPT is wholly supported by contributions from its members and many of those members had been adversely affected by the ongoing financial crisis that followed the collapse of the subprime mortgage market. Consequently, the funds that would be available for operations in 2009 were particularly difficult to predict. Accordingly, the budget for 2009 contained three variations based on progressively pessimistic economic assumptions. The more pessimistic budgets were called contingent budgets. As 2008 progressed and member contributions declined somewhat from previous levels, CWPT switched to the first contingent budget. This contingent budget required a number of actions to reduce costs including a hiring freeze and a salary freeze, but maintained an aggressive program of protecting battlefield acreage through purchases of land and development rights. Fortunately, the CWPT did not have to switch to the most pessimistic budget—which would have involved layoffs and other extraordinary cost-saving measures.

Instead of reacting in a panic mode to unfavorable developments, CWPT used the budgeting process to carefully plan in advance for a number of possible contingencies. ■

Sources: Communications with James Lighthizer, president, and David Duncan, director of membership and development, Civil War Preservation Trust; and the CWPT website, civilwar.org.

LEARNING OBJECTIVES

After studying Chapter 8, you should be able to:

- **LO1** Understand why organizations budget and the processes they use to create budgets.
- **LO2** Prepare a sales budget, including a schedule of expected cash collections.
- **LO3** Prepare a production budget.
- **LO4** Prepare a direct materials budget, including a schedule of expected cash disbursements for purchases of materials.
- **LO5** Prepare a direct labor budget.
- **LO6** Prepare a manufacturing overhead budget.
- **LO7** Prepare a selling and administrative expense budget.
- **LO8** Prepare a cash budget.
- **LO9** Prepare a budgeted income statement.
- **LO10** Prepare a budgeted balance sheet.

In this chapter, we focus on the steps taken by businesses to achieve their planned levels of profits—a process called *profit planning.* Profit planning is accomplished by preparing a number of budgets that together form an integrated business plan known as the *master budget.* The master budget is an essential management tool that communicates management's plans throughout the organization, allocates resources, and coordinates activities.

The Basic Framework of Budgeting

LEARNING OBJECTIVE 1
Understand why organizations budget and the processes they use to create budgets.

A **budget** is a detailed plan for the future that is usually expressed in formal quantitative terms. Individuals sometimes create household budgets that balance their income and expenditures for food, clothing, housing, and so on while providing for some savings. Once the budget is established, actual spending is compared to the budget to make sure the plan is being followed. Companies use budgets in a similar way, although the amount of work and underlying details far exceed a personal budget.

Budgets are used for two distinct purposes—*planning* and *control.* **Planning** involves developing goals and preparing various budgets to achieve those goals. **Control** involves gathering feedback to ensure that the plan is being properly executed or modified as circumstances change. To be effective, a good budgeting system must provide for both planning and control. Good planning without effective control is a waste of time and effort.

Advantages of Budgeting

Organizations realize many benefits from budgeting, including:

1. Budgets *communicate* management's plans throughout the organization.
2. Budgets force managers to *think about* and *plan* for the future. In the absence of the necessity to prepare a budget, many managers would spend all of their time dealing with day-to-day emergencies.
3. The budgeting process provides a means of *allocating resources* to those parts of the organization where they can be used most effectively.
4. The budgeting process can uncover potential *bottlenecks* before they occur.
5. Budgets *coordinate* the activities of the entire organization by *integrating* the plans of its various parts. Budgeting helps to ensure that everyone in the organization is pulling in the same direction.
6. Budgets define goals and objectives that can serve as *benchmarks* for evaluating subsequent performance.

IN BUSINESS

EXECUTING STRATEGY WITH BUDGETS

Robert DeMartini, the CEO of New Balance, set a goal of tripling his company's revenues to $3 billion in four years. He tripled the company's annual advertising budget and doubled its consumer research budget in an effort to attract more young customers. These decisions represented a strategic shift for New Balance, which usually spends less than $20 million per year in advertising compared to competitors such as Nike and Adidas, which annually invest $184 million and $80 million, respectively.

One reason companies prepare budgets is to allocate resources across departments in a manner that supports strategic priorities. DeMartini used the budget to send a clear signal that his marketing department was expected to play a huge role in achieving the company's revenue growth targets. As time progresses, he will compare the company's actual revenue growth from young consumers to the marketing department's expenditures to see if his strategy is working or requires adjustment.

Source: Stephanie Kang, "New Balance Steps up Marketing Drive," *The Wall Street Journal,* March 21, 2008, p. B3.

Responsibility Accounting

Most of what we say in this chapter and in the next three chapters is concerned with *responsibility accounting.* The basic idea underlying **responsibility accounting** is that a manager should be held responsible for those items—and *only* those items—that the manager can actually control to a significant extent. Each line item (i.e., revenue or cost) in the budget is the responsibility of a manager who is held responsible for subsequent deviations between budgeted goals and actual results. In effect, responsibility accounting *personalizes* accounting information by holding individuals responsible for revenues and costs. This concept is central to any effective profit planning and control system. Someone must be held responsible for each cost or else no one will be responsible and the cost will inevitably grow out of control.

What happens if actual results do not measure up to the budgeted goals? The manager is not necessarily penalized. However, the manager should take the initiative to correct any unfavorable discrepancies, should understand the source of significant favorable or unfavorable discrepancies, and should be prepared to explain the reasons for discrepancies to higher management. The point of an effective responsibility accounting system is to make sure that nothing "falls through the cracks," that the organization reacts quickly and appropriately to deviations from its plans, and that the organization learns from the feedback it gets by comparing budgeted goals to actual results. The point is *not* to penalize individuals for missing targets.

IN BUSINESS

NEW YORK CITY MAYOR BENEFITS FROM BUDGETS

Michael Bloomberg, the mayor of New York City, makes annual budget presentations to his fellow elected officials, the city council, and the media. Historically, the city's mayors had delegated these types of presentations to one of their budget directors; however, Bloomberg believes that by investing his time in explaining the factors influencing the city's economy, his constituents will gain a better understanding of his fiscal priorities. This, in turn, helps improve his negotiations with the city council and his relationships with various advocacy groups. The mayor also makes his entire budget available online so that New Yorkers can scrutinize budgeting details, such as the cost of running specific government agencies.

Source: Tom Lowry, "The CEO Mayor," *BusinessWeek*, June 25, 2007, pp. 58–64.

Choosing a Budget Period

Operating budgets ordinarily cover a one-year period corresponding to the company's fiscal year. Many companies divide their budget year into four quarters. The first quarter is then subdivided into months, and monthly budgets are developed. The last three quarters may be carried in the budget as quarterly totals only. As the year progresses, the figures for the second quarter are broken down into monthly amounts, then the third-quarter figures are broken down, and so forth. This approach has the advantage of requiring periodic review and reappraisal of budget data throughout the year.

Continuous or *perpetual budgets* are sometimes used. A **continuous** or **perpetual budget** is a 12-month budget that rolls forward one month (or quarter) as the current month (or quarter) is completed. In other words, one month (or quarter) is added to the end of the budget as each month (or quarter) comes to a close. This approach keeps managers focused at least one year ahead so that they do not become too narrowly focused on short-term results.

In this chapter, we will look at one-year operating budgets. However, using basically the same techniques, operating budgets can be prepared for periods that extend over many years. It may be difficult to accurately forecast sales and other data much beyond

EXHIBIT 8–1
The Initial Flow of Budget Data in a Participative Budgeting System

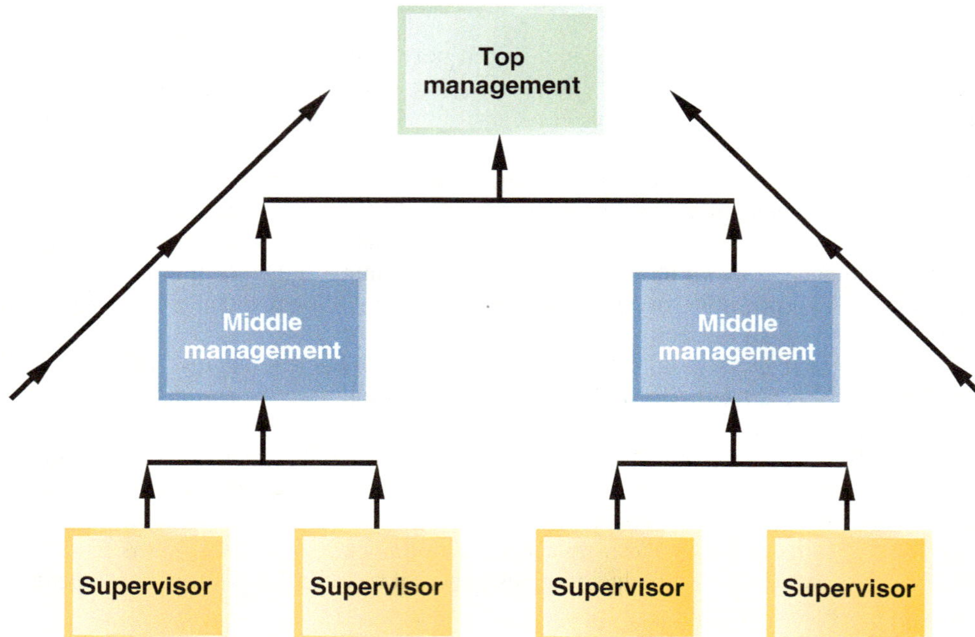

The initial flow of budget data in a participative budgeting system is from lower levels of responsibility to higher levels of responsibility. Each person with responsibility for cost control will prepare his or her own budget estimates and submit them to the next higher level of management. These estimates are reviewed and consolidated as they move upward in the organization.

a year, but even rough estimates can be invaluable in uncovering potential problems and opportunities that would otherwise be overlooked.

The Self-Imposed Budget

The success of a budget program is largely determined by the way a budget is developed. Oftentimes, the budget is imposed from above, with little participation by lower-level managers. However, in the most successful budget programs, managers actively participate in preparing their own budgets. Imposing expectations from above and then penalizing employees who do not meet those expectations will generate resentment rather than cooperation and commitment. In fact, many managers believe that being empowered to create their own *self-imposed budgets* is the most effective method of budget preparation. A **self-imposed budget** or **participative budget,** as illustrated in Exhibit 8–1, is a budget that is prepared with the full cooperation and participation of managers at all levels.

Self-imposed budgets have a number of advantages:

1. Individuals at all levels of the organization are recognized as members of the team whose views and judgments are valued by top management.
2. Budget estimates prepared by front-line managers are often more accurate and reliable than estimates prepared by top managers who have less intimate knowledge of markets and day-to-day operations.
3. Motivation is generally higher when individuals participate in setting their own goals than when the goals are imposed from above. Self-imposed budgets create commitment.
4. A manager who is not able to meet a budget that has been imposed from above can always say that the budget was unrealistic and impossible to meet. With a self-imposed budget, this excuse is not available.

One important limitation of self-imposed budgeting is that lower-level managers may allow too much *budgetary slack.* Because the manager who creates the budget will be held accountable for actual results that deviate from the budget, the manager will have a natural tendency to submit a budget that is easy to attain (i.e., the manager will build slack into the budget). For this reason, budgets prepared by lower-level managers should be scrutinized by higher levels of management. Questionable items should be discussed and modified as appropriate. Without such a review, self-imposed budgets may be too slack, resulting in suboptimal performance.

As these comments suggest, all levels in the organization should work together to produce the budget. Lower-level managers are more familiar with day-to-day operations than top managers. Top managers should have a more strategic perspective than lower-level managers. Each level of responsibility in an organization should contribute its unique knowledge and perspective in a cooperative effort to develop an integrated budget. Nevertheless, a self-imposed approach to setting budgets works best when all managers understand the organization's strategy. Otherwise, the budgets proposed by the lower-level managers will lack coherent direction. In later chapters, we discuss in greater detail how a company can go about formulating its strategy and communicating it throughout the organization.

Unfortunately, most companies do not follow the budgeting process we have described. Typically, top managers initiate the budgeting process by issuing profit targets. Lower-level managers are directed to prepare budgets that meet those targets. The difficulty is that the targets set by top managers may be unrealistically high or may allow too much slack. If the targets are too high and employees know they are unrealistic, motivation will suffer. If the targets allow too much slack, waste will occur. Unfortunately, top managers are often not in a position to know whether the targets are appropriate. Admittedly, a self-imposed budgeting system may lack sufficient strategic direction and lower-level managers may be tempted to build slack into their budgets. Nevertheless, because of the motivational advantages of self-imposed budgets, top managers should be cautious about imposing inflexible targets from above.

Human Factors in Budgeting

The success of a budget program also depends on the degree to which top management accepts the budget program as a vital part of the company's activities and the way in which top management uses budgeted data.

If a budget program is to be successful, it must have the complete acceptance and support of the persons who occupy key management positions. If lower or middle managers sense that top management is lukewarm about budgeting, or if they sense that top management simply tolerates budgeting as a necessary evil, then their own attitudes will reflect a similar lack of enthusiasm. Budgeting is hard work, and if top management is not enthusiastic about and committed to the budget program, then it is unlikely that anyone else in the organization will be either.

In administering the budget program, it is particularly important that top management not use the budget to pressure or blame employees. Using budgets in such negative ways will breed hostility, tension, and mistrust rather than cooperation and productivity. Unfortunately, the budget is too often used as a pressure device and excessive emphasis is placed on "meeting the budget" under all circumstances. Rather than being used as a weapon, the budget should be used as a positive instrument to assist in establishing goals, measuring operating results, and isolating areas that need attention.

The human aspects of budgeting are extremely important. The remainder of the chapter deals with technical aspects of budgeting, but do not lose sight of the human aspects. The purpose of the budget is to motivate people and to coordinate their efforts. This purpose is undermined if managers become preoccupied with the technical aspects, or if the budget is used in a rigid and inflexible manner to control people.

How challenging should budget targets be? Some experts argue that budget targets should be very challenging and should require managers to stretch to meet goals. Even the most capable managers may have to scramble to meet such a "stretch budget" and they may not always succeed. In practice, most companies set their budget targets at a "highly achievable" level. A highly achievable budget may be challenging, but it can almost always be met by competent managers exerting reasonable effort.

Bonuses based on meeting and exceeding budgets are often a key element of management compensation. Typically, no bonus is paid unless the budget is met. The bonus often increases when the budget target is exceeded, but the bonus is usually capped out at some level. For obvious reasons, managers who have such a bonus plan or whose performance is evaluated based on meeting budget targets usually prefer to be evaluated based on highly achievable budgets rather than on stretch budgets. Moreover, highly achievable budgets may help build a manager's confidence and generate greater commitment to the budget. And finally, highly achievable budgets may result in less undesirable behavior at the end of budgetary periods by managers who are intent on earning their bonuses.

IN BUSINESS

BIASING FORECASTS

A manager's compensation is often tied to the budget. Typically, no bonus is paid unless a minimum performance hurdle such as 80% of the budget target is attained. Once that hurdle is passed, the manager's bonus increases until a cap is reached. That cap is often set at 120% of the budget target.

This common method of tying a manager's compensation to the budget has some serious negative side effects. For example, a marketing manager for a big beverage company intentionally grossly understated demand for the company's products for an upcoming major holiday so that the budget target for revenues would be low and easy to beat. Unfortunately, the company tied its production to this biased forecast and ran out of products to sell during the height of the holiday selling season.

As another example, near the end of the year another group of managers announced a price increase of 10% effective January 2 of the following year. Why would they do this? By announcing this price increase, managers hoped that customers would order before the end of the year, helping managers meet their sales targets for the current year. Sales in the following year would, of course, drop. What trick would managers pull to meet their sales targets next year in the face of this drop in demand?

Sources: Michael C. Jensen, "Corporate Budgeting Is Broken—Let's Fix It," *Harvard Business Review*, November 2001; and Michael C. Jensen, "Why Pay People to Lie?" *The Wall Street Journal*, January 8, 2001, p. A32.

The Budget Committee

A standing **budget committee** is usually responsible for overall policy relating to the budget program and for coordinating the preparation of the budget itself. This committee may consist of the president; vice presidents in charge of various functions such as sales, production, and purchasing; and the controller. Difficulties and disputes relating to the budget are resolved by the budget committee. In addition, the budget committee approves the final budget.

Disputes can (and do) erupt over budget matters. Because budgets allocate resources, the budgeting process determines to a large extent which departments get more resources and which get less. Also, the budget sets the benchmarks used to evaluate managers and their departments. Therefore, it should not be surprising that managers take the budgeting process very seriously and invest considerable energy and emotion in ensuring that their interests, and those of their departments, are protected. Because of this, the budgeting process can easily degenerate into interoffice arguments in which the ultimate goal of working together toward common goals is forgotten.

Running a successful budgeting program that avoids interoffice battles requires considerable interpersonal skills in addition to purely technical skills. But even the best interpersonal skills will fail if, as discussed earlier, top management uses the budget process to inappropriately pressure employees or to assign blame.

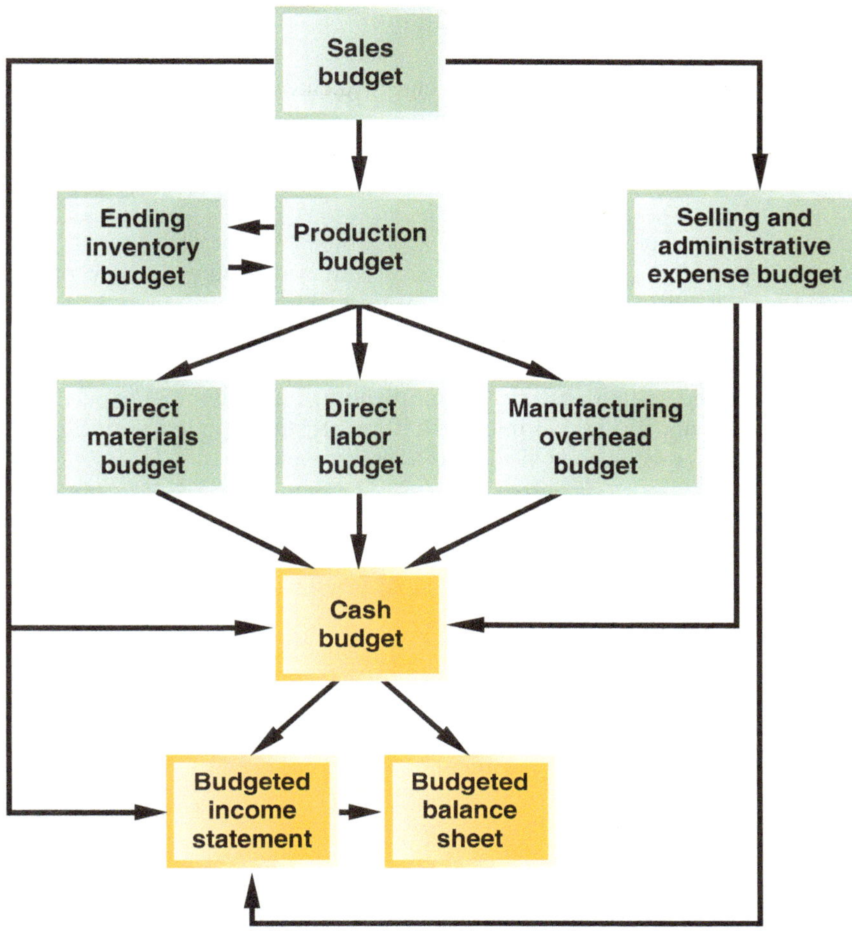

EXHIBIT 8–2
The Master Budget Interrelationships

The Master Budget: An Overview

The **master budget** consists of a number of separate but interdependent budgets that formally lay out the company's sales, production, and financial goals. The master budget culminates in a cash budget, a budgeted income statement, and a budgeted balance sheet. Exhibit 8–2 provides an overview of the various parts of the master budget and how they are related.

The first step in the budgeting process is the preparation of the **sales budget,** which is a detailed schedule showing the expected sales for the budget period. An accurate sales budget is the key to the entire budgeting process. As illustrated in Exhibit 8–2, all other parts of the master budget depend on the sales budget. If the sales budget is inaccurate, the rest of the budget will be inaccurate. The sales budget is based on the company's sales forecast, which may require the use of sophisticated mathematical models and statistical tools. We will not go into the details of how sales forecasts are made. This is a subject that is most appropriately covered in marketing courses.

The sales budget helps determine how many units need to be produced. Thus, the production budget is prepared after the sales budget. The production budget in turn is used to determine the budgets for manufacturing costs including the direct materials budget, the direct labor budget, and the manufacturing overhead budget. These budgets are then combined with data from the sales budget and the selling and administrative expense budget to determine the *cash budget.* A **cash budget** is a detailed plan showing how cash resources will be acquired and used. Observe from Exhibit 8–2 that all of the operating budgets have an impact on the cash budget. After the cash budget is prepared, the budgeted income statement and then the budgeted balance sheet can be prepared.

Preparing the Master Budget

MANAGERIAL ACCOUNTING IN ACTION
The Issue

Tom Wills is the majority stockholder and chief executive officer of Hampton Freeze, Inc., a company he started in 2010. The company makes premium popsicles using only natural ingredients and featuring exotic flavors such as tangy tangerine and minty mango. The company's business is highly seasonal, with most of the sales occurring in spring and summer.

In 2011, the company's second year of operations, a major cash crunch in the first and second quarters almost forced the company into bankruptcy. In spite of this cash crunch, 2011 turned out to be a very successful year in terms of both cash flow and net income. Partly as a result of that harrowing experience, Tom decided toward the end of 2011 to hire a professional financial manager. Tom interviewed several promising candidates for the job and settled on Larry Giano, who had considerable experience in the packaged foods industry. In the job interview, Tom questioned Larry about the steps he would take to prevent a recurrence of the 2011 cash crunch:

Tom: As I mentioned earlier, we are going to end 2011 with a very nice profit. What you may not know is that we had some very big financial problems this year.
Larry: Let me guess. You ran out of cash sometime in the first or second quarter.
Tom: How did you know?
Larry: Most of your sales are in the second and third quarter, right?
Tom: Sure, everyone wants to buy popsicles in the spring and summer, but nobody wants them when the weather turns cold.
Larry: So you don't have many sales in the first quarter?
Tom: Right.
Larry: And in the second quarter, which is the spring, you are producing like crazy to fill orders?
Tom: Sure.
Larry: Do your customers, the grocery stores, pay you the day you make your deliveries?
Tom: Are you kidding? Of course not.
Larry: So in the first quarter, you don't have many sales. In the second quarter, you are producing like crazy, which eats up cash, but you aren't paid by your customers until long after you have paid your employees and suppliers. No wonder you had a cash problem. I see this pattern all the time in food processing because of the seasonality of the business.
Tom: So what can we do about it?
Larry: The first step is to predict the magnitude of the problem before it occurs. If we can predict early in the year what the cash shortfall is going to be, we can go to the bank and arrange for credit before we really need it. Bankers tend to be leery of panicky people who show up begging for emergency loans. They are much more likely to make the loan if you look like you are in control of the situation.
Tom: How can we predict the cash shortfall?
Larry: You can put together a cash budget. While you're at it, you might as well do a master budget. You'll find it is well worth the effort.
Tom: I don't like budgets. They are too confining. My wife budgets everything at home, and I can't spend what I want.
Larry: Can I ask a personal question?
Tom: What?
Larry: Where did you get the money to start this business?
Tom: Mainly from our family's savings. I get your point. We wouldn't have had the money to start the business if my wife hadn't been forcing us to save every month.

Larry: Exactly. I suggest you use the same discipline in your business. It is even more important here because you can't expect your employees to spend your money as carefully as you would.

With the full backing of Tom Wills, Larry Giano set out to create a master budget for the company for the year 2012. In his planning for the budgeting process, Larry drew up the following list of documents that would be a part of the master budget:

1. A sales budget, including a schedule of expected cash collections.
2. A production budget (a merchandise purchases budget would be used in a merchandising company).
3. A direct materials budget, including a schedule of expected cash disbursements for purchases of materials.
4. A direct labor budget.
5. A manufacturing overhead budget.
6. An ending finished goods inventory budget.
7. A selling and administrative expense budget.
8. A cash budget.
9. A budgeted income statement.
10. A budgeted balance sheet.

Larry felt it was important to have everyone's cooperation in the budgeting process, so he asked Tom to call a companywide meeting to explain the budgeting process. At the meeting there was initially some grumbling, but Tom was able to convince nearly everyone of the necessity for planning and getting better control over spending. It helped that the cash crisis earlier in the year was still fresh in everyone's minds. As much as some people disliked the idea of budgets, they liked their jobs more.

In the months that followed, Larry worked closely with all of the managers involved in the master budget, gathering data from them and making sure that they understood and fully supported the parts of the master budget that would affect them. In subsequent years, Larry hoped to turn the whole budgeting process over to the managers and to take a more advisory role.

The interdependent documents that Larry Giano prepared for Hampton Freeze are Schedules 1 through 10 of the company's master budget. In this section, we will study these schedules.

The Sales Budget

LEARNING OBJECTIVE 2
Prepare a sales budget, including a schedule of expected cash collections.

The sales budget is the starting point in preparing the master budget. As shown earlier in Exhibit 8–2, all other items in the master budget, including production, purchases, inventories, and expenses, depend on it.

The sales budget is constructed by multiplying budgeted unit sales by the selling price. Schedule 1 contains the quarterly sales budget for Hampton Freeze for the year 2012. Notice from the schedule that the company plans to sell 100,000 cases of popsicles during the year, with sales peaking in the third quarter.

A schedule of expected cash collections, such as the one that appears in the bottom portion of Schedule 1, is prepared after the sales budget. This schedule will be needed later to prepare the cash budget. Cash collections consist of collections on credit sales made to customers in prior periods plus collections on sales made in the current budget period. At Hampton Freeze, all sales are on credit; furthermore, experience has shown that 70% of sales are collected in the quarter in which the sale is made and the remaining 30% are collected in the following quarter. For example, 70% of the first quarter sales of \$200,000 (or \$140,000) is collected during the first quarter and 30% (or \$60,000) is collected during the second quarter.

SCHEDULE 1

	A	B	C	D	E	F
1		**Hampton Freeze, Inc.**				
2		**Sales Budget**				
3		**For the Year Ended December 31, 2012**				
4						
5		*Quarter*				
6		*1*	*2*	*3*	*4*	*Year*
7	Budgeted sales in cases	10,000	30,000	40,000	20,000	100,000
8	Selling price per case	$ 20.00	$ 20.00	$ 20.00	$ 20.00	$ 20.00
9	Total sales	$200,000	$600,000	$800,000	$400,000	$ 2,000,000
10						
11	Percentage of sales collected in the period of the sale			70%		
12	Percentage of sales collected in the period after the sale			30%		
13		70%	30%			
14		**Schedule of Expected Cash Collections**				
15	Accounts receivable, beginning balance[1]	$ 90,000				$ 90,000
16	First-quarter sales[2]	140,000	$ 60,000			200,000
17	Second-quarter sales[3]		420,000	$ 180,000		600,000
18	Third-quarter sales[4]			560,000	$ 240,000	800,000
19	Fourth-quarter sales[5]	-	-	-	280,000	280,000
20	Total cash collections[6]	$230,000	$480,000	$740,000	$520,000	$ 1,970,000

Schedule 1 | Schedule 2 | Schedule 3 | Schedule 4 | Schedule 5 | Sch

[1]Cash collections from last year's fourth-quarter sales. See the beginning-of-year balance sheet on page 357.
[2]$200,000 × 70%; $200,000 × 30%.
[3]$600,000 × 70%; $600,000 × 30%.
[4]$800,000 × 70%; $800,000 × 30%.
[5]$400,000 × 70%.
[6]Uncollected fourth-quarter sales ($120,000) appear as accounts receivable on the company's end-of-year budgeted balance sheet (see Schedule 10 on page 358).

IN BUSINESS

THE IMPORTANCE OF SALES RISK MANAGEMENT

David Flynn founded Amistad Media Group in 1994 to help companies market themselves to growing Hispanic communities in places such as Nebraska, Kansas, and North Carolina. While Amistad's sales steadily grew to a peak of $49 million in 2003, its customer base had not grown much in nine years. In fact, just two companies generated the bulk of Amistad's sales—Novamex and the U.S. Army. When the U.S. Army dropped Amistad as a supplier in 2005, the company's sales plummeted and it was bankrupt by 2006.

Amistad's demise highlights the importance of evaluating a company's sales forecast not only in terms of dollars, but also in terms of the number of customers served. Small companies in particular should seek to diversify their customer base, thereby reducing the risk that losing one or two customers will put them out of business.

Source: Patrick Cliff, "Adios to a Pioneering Hispanic Marketing Firm," *Inc.* Magazine, May, 2006, p. 34.

The Production Budget

LEARNING OBJECTIVE 3
Prepare a production budget.

The production budget is prepared after the sales budget. The **production budget** lists the number of units that must be produced to satisfy sales needs and to provide for the desired ending inventory. Production needs can be determined as follows:

Budgeted unit sales	XXXX
Add desired ending inventory of finished goods	XXXX
Total needs	XXXX
Less beginning inventory of finished goods	XXXX
Required production	XXXX

Note that production requirements are influenced by the desired level of the ending inventory. Inventories should be carefully planned. Excessive inventories tie up funds and create storage problems. Insufficient inventories can lead to lost sales or last-minute, high-cost production efforts. At Hampton Freeze, management believes that an ending inventory equal to 20% of the next quarter's sales strikes the appropriate balance.

Schedule 2 contains the production budget for Hampton Freeze. The first row in the production budget contains the budgeted sales, which have been taken directly from the sales budget (Schedule 1). The total needs for the first quarter are determined by adding together the budgeted sales of 10,000 cases for the quarter and the desired ending inventory of 6,000 cases. As discussed above, the ending inventory is intended to provide some cushion in the event that problems develop in production or sales increase unexpectedly. Because the budgeted sales for the second quarter are 30,000 cases and management would like the ending inventory in each quarter to equal 20% of the following quarter's sales, the desired ending inventory for the first quarter is 6,000 cases (20% of 30,000 cases). Consequently, the total needs for the first quarter are 16,000 cases. However, because the company already has 2,000 cases in beginning inventory, only 14,000 cases need to be produced in the first quarter.

Pay particular attention to the Year column to the right of the production budget in Schedule 2. In some cases (e.g., budgeted sales, total needs, and required production), the amount listed for the year is the sum of the quarterly amounts for the item. In other cases

SCHEDULE 2

Hampton Freeze, Inc.
Production Budget
For the Year Ended December 31, 2012

	Quarter 1	Quarter 2	Quarter 3	Quarter 4	Year
Budgeted sales in cases (Schedule 1)	10,000	30,000	40,000	20,000	100,000
Add desired ending inventory of finished goods*	6,000	8,000	4,000	3,000	3,000
Total needs	16,000	38,000	44,000	23,000	103,000
Less beginning inventory of finished goods†	2,000	6,000	8,000	4,000	2,000
Required production in cases	14,000	32,000	36,000	19,000	101,000

(Annotations: 20% of next quarter's sales; the Quarter 4 ending inventory of 3,000 is Assumed.)

Schedule 2 | Schedule 3 | Schedule 4 | Schedule 5 | Schedule 6

*Twenty percent of the next quarter's sales. The ending inventory of 3,000 cases is assumed.
†The beginning inventory in each quarter is the same as the prior quarter's ending inventory.

(e.g., desired ending inventory of finished goods and beginning inventory of finished goods), the amount listed for the year is not simply the sum of the quarterly amounts. From the standpoint of the entire year, the beginning finished goods inventory is the same as the beginning finished goods inventory for the first quarter—it is *not* the sum of the beginning finished goods inventories for all quarters. Similarly, from the standpoint of the entire year, the ending finished goods inventory is the same as the ending finished goods inventory for the fourth quarter—it is *not* the sum of the ending finished goods inventories for all four quarters. It is important to pay attention to such distinctions in all of the schedules that follow.

Inventory Purchases—Merchandising Company

Hampton Freeze prepares a production budget because it is a *manufacturing* company. If it were a *merchandising* company, instead it would prepare a **merchandise purchases budget** showing the amount of goods to be purchased from suppliers during the period.

The format of the merchandise purchases budget is shown below:

Budgeted cost of goods sold	XXXXX
Add desired ending merchandise inventory	XXXXX
Total needs	XXXXX
Less beginning merchandise inventory	XXXXX
Required purchases	XXXXX

A merchandising company would prepare a merchandise purchases budget such as the one above for each item carried in stock. The merchandise purchases budget can be expressed in dollars (as shown above) or in units. The top line of a merchandise purchases budget based on units would say Budgeted unit sales instead of Budgeted cost of goods sold.

The Direct Materials Budget

LEARNING OBJECTIVE 4
Prepare a direct materials budget, including a schedule of expected cash disbursements for purchases of materials.

A direct materials budget is prepared after the production requirements have been computed. The **direct materials budget** details the raw materials that must be purchased to fulfill the production budget and to provide for adequate inventories. The required purchases of raw materials are computed as follows:

Required production in units of finished goods	XXXXX
Raw materials required per unit of finished goods	XXXXX
Raw materials needed to meet the production schedule	XXXXX
Add desired ending raw materials inventory	XXXXX
Total raw material needs	XXXXX
Less beginning raw materials inventory	XXXXX
Raw materials to be purchased	XXXXX
Unit cost of raw materials	XXXXX
Cost of raw materials to be purchased	XXXXX

Schedule 3 contains the direct materials budget for Hampton Freeze. The only raw material included in that budget is high fructose sugar, which is the major ingredient in popsicles other than water. The remaining raw materials are relatively insignificant and are included in variable manufacturing overhead. As with finished goods, management

SCHEDULE 3

Hampton Freeze, Inc.
Direct Materials Budget
For the Year Ended December 31, 2012

	Quarter 1	Quarter 2	Quarter 3	Quarter 4	Year
Required production in cases (Schedule 2)	14,000	32,000	36,000	19,000	101,000
Raw materials needed per case (pounds)	15	15	15	15	15
Raw materials needed to meet production	210,000	480,000	540,000	285,000	1,515,000
Add desired ending raw materials inventory[1]	48,000	54,000	28,500	22,500	22,500
Total raw material needs	258,000	534,000	568,500	307,500	1,537,500
Less beginning raw materials inventory	21,000	48,000	54,000	28,500	21,000
Raw materials to be purchased	237,000	486,000	514,500	279,000	1,516,500
Cost of raw materials per pound	$ 0.20	$ 0.20	$ 0.20	$ 0.20	$ 0.20
Cost of raw materials to be purchased	$47,400	$97,200	$102,900	$55,800	$ 303,300

Assumed (Year ending inventory, 22,500); 10% (each quarter's ending inventory is 10% of the next quarter's production needs)

Percentage of purchases paid for in the period of the purchase	50%
Percentage of purchases paid for in the period after purchase	50%

Schedule of Expected Cash Disbursements for Materials

	Quarter 1	Quarter 2	Quarter 3	Quarter 4	Year
Accounts payable, beginning balance[2]	$25,800				$ 25,800
First-quarter purchases[3]	23,700	$23,700			47,400
Second-quarter purchases[4]		48,600	$ 48,600		97,200
Third-quarter purchases[5]			51,450	$51,450	102,900
Fourth-quarter purchases[6]	-	-	-	27,900	27,900
Total cash disbursements for materials	$49,500	$72,300	$100,050	$79,350	$ 301,200

[1]Ten percent of the next quarter's production needs. For example, the second-quarter production needs are 480,000 pounds. Therefore, the desired ending inventory for the first quarter would be 10% × 480,000 pounds = 48,000 pounds. The ending inventory of 22,500 pounds for the fourth quarter is assumed.

[2]Cash payments for last year's fourth-quarter material purchases. See the beginning-of-year balance sheet on page 357.

[3]$47,400 × 50%; $47,400 × 50%.

[4]$97,200 × 50%; $97,200 × 50%.

[5]$102,900 × 50%; $102,900 × 50%.

[6]$55,800 × 50%. Unpaid fourth-quarter purchases ($27,900) appear as accounts payable on the company's end-of-year budgeted balance sheet (see Schedule 10 on page 358).

would like to maintain some inventories of raw materials to act as a cushion. In this case, management would like to maintain ending inventories of sugar equal to 10% of the following quarter's production needs.

The first line in the direct materials budget contains the required production for each quarter, which is taken directly from the production budget (Schedule 2). Looking at the first quarter, because the production schedule calls for production of 14,000 cases of popsicles and each case requires 15 pounds of sugar, the total production needs are 210,000 pounds of sugar (14,000 cases × 15 pounds per case). In addition, management wants to have ending inventories of 48,000 pounds of sugar, which is 10% of the following quarter's needs of 480,000 pounds. Consequently, the total needs are 258,000 pounds (210,000 pounds for the current quarter's production plus 48,000 pounds for the desired ending inventory). However, because the company already has

21,000 pounds in beginning inventory, only 237,000 pounds of sugar (258,000 pounds − 21,000 pounds) will need to be purchased. Finally, the cost of the raw materials purchases is determined by multiplying the amount of raw material to be purchased by its unit cost. In this case, because 237,000 pounds of sugar need to be purchased during the first quarter and sugar costs $0.20 per pound, the total cost will be $47,400 (237,000 pounds × $0.20 per pound).

As with the production budget, the amounts listed under the Year column are not always the sum of the quarterly amounts. The desired ending raw materials inventory for the year is the same as the desired ending raw materials inventory for the fourth quarter. Likewise, the beginning raw materials inventory for the year is the same as the beginning raw materials inventory for the first quarter.

The direct materials budget (or the merchandise purchases budget for a merchandising company) is usually accompanied by a schedule of expected cash disbursements for raw materials (or merchandise purchases). This schedule is needed to prepare the overall cash budget. Disbursements for raw materials (or merchandise purchases) consist of payments for purchases on account in prior periods plus any payments for purchases in the current budget period. Schedule 3 contains such a schedule of cash disbursements for Hampton Freeze.

Ordinarily, companies do not immediately pay their suppliers. At Hampton Freeze, the policy is to pay for 50% of purchases in the quarter in which the purchase is made and 50% in the following quarter, so while the company intends to purchase $47,400 worth of sugar in the first quarter, the company will only pay for half, $23,700, in the first quarter and the other half will be paid in the second quarter. The company will also pay $25,800 in the first quarter for sugar that was purchased on account in the previous quarter, but not yet paid for. This is the beginning balance in the accounts payable. Therefore, the total cash disbursements for sugar in the first quarter are $49,500—the $25,800 payment for sugar acquired in the previous quarter plus the $23,700 payment for sugar acquired during the first quarter.

The Direct Labor Budget

LEARNING OBJECTIVE 5
Prepare a direct labor budget.

The **direct labor budget** shows the direct labor-hours required to satisfy the production budget. By knowing in advance how much labor time will be needed throughout the budget year, the company can develop plans to adjust the labor force as the situation requires. Companies that neglect to budget run the risk of facing labor shortages or having to hire and lay off workers at awkward times. Erratic labor policies lead to insecurity, low morale, and inefficiency.

The direct labor budget for Hampton Freeze is shown in Schedule 4. The first line in the direct labor budget consists of the required production for each quarter, which is taken directly from the production budget (Schedule 2). The direct labor requirement for each quarter is computed by multiplying the number of units to be produced in that quarter by the number of direct labor-hours required to make a unit. For example, 14,000 cases are to be produced in the first quarter and each case requires 0.40 direct labor-hour, so a total of 5,600 direct labor-hours (14,000 cases × 0.40 direct labor-hour per case) will be required in the first quarter. The direct labor requirements can then be translated into budgeted direct labor costs. How this is done will depend on the company's labor policy. In Schedule 4, Hampton Freeze has assumed that the direct labor force will be adjusted as the work requirements change from quarter to quarter. In that case, the direct labor cost is computed by simply multiplying the direct labor-hour requirements by the direct labor rate per hour. For example, the direct labor cost in the first quarter is $84,000 (5,600 direct labor-hours × $15 per direct labor-hour).

However, many companies have employment policies or contracts that prevent them from laying off and rehiring workers as needed. Suppose, for example, that Hampton Freeze has 25 workers who are classified as direct labor, but each of them is guaranteed at least 480 hours of pay each quarter at a rate of $15 per hour. In that case, the minimum direct labor cost for a quarter would be as follows:

25 workers × 480 hours per worker × $15 per hour = $180,000

SCHEDULE 4

Hampton Freeze, Inc.
Direct Labor Budget
For the Year Ended December 31, 2012

	Quarter 1	Quarter 2	Quarter 3	Quarter 4	Year
Required production in cases (Schedule 2)	14,000	32,000	36,000	19,000	101,000
Direct labor-hours per case	0.40	0.40	0.40	0.40	0.40
Total direct labor-hours needed	5,600	12,800	14,400	7,600	40,400
Direct labor cost per hour	$ 15.00	$ 15.00	$ 15.00	$ 15.00	$ 15.00
Total direct labor cost*	$ 84,000	$ 192,000	$ 216,000	$ 114,000	$ 606,000

*This schedule assumes that the direct labor workforce will be fully adjusted to the total direct labor-hours needed each quarter.

Note that in this case the direct labor costs for the first and fourth quarters would have to be increased to $180,000.

IN BUSINESS

MANAGING LABOR COSTS IN A DIFFICULT ECONOMY

When the economy sours, many companies choose to lay off employees. While this tactic lowers costs in the short run, it also lowers the morale and productivity of retained employees, sacrifices the institutional knowledge possessed by terminated employees, and increases future recruiting and training costs. Hypertherm Inc. has not fired a permanent employee since its founding in 1968, instead responding to economic hardship by eliminating overtime, cutting temporary staff, delaying capital investments, shifting cross-trained employees to new job responsibilities, and implementing a four-day work week. Hypertherm's employees regularly share their process improvement ideas with the company because they know if they eliminate non–value-added portions of their job responsibilities the company will redeploy them rather than eliminate non–value-added labor costs by firing them.

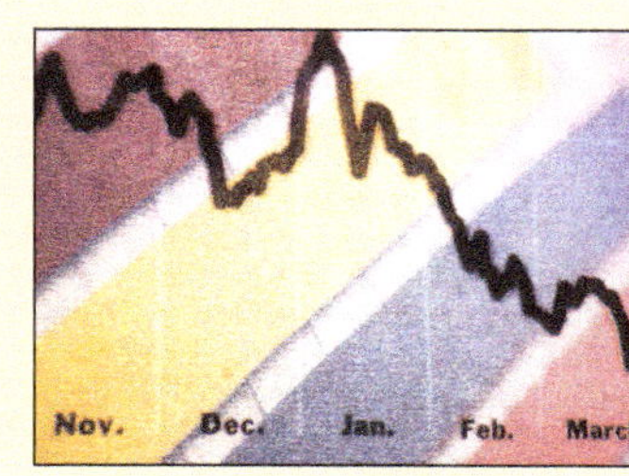

Source: Cari Tuna, "Some Firms Cut Costs Without Resorting to Layoffs," *The Wall Street Journal*, December 15, 2008, p. B4.

The Manufacturing Overhead Budget

LEARNING OBJECTIVE 6
Prepare a manufacturing overhead budget.

The **manufacturing overhead budget** lists all costs of production other than direct materials and direct labor. Schedule 5 shows the manufacturing overhead budget for Hampton Freeze. At Hampton Freeze, manufacturing overhead is separated into variable and fixed components. The variable component is $4 per direct labor-hour and the fixed component is $60,600 per quarter. Because the variable component of manufacturing overhead depends on direct labor, the first line in the manufacturing overhead budget consists of the budgeted direct labor-hours from the direct labor budget (Schedule 4). The budgeted direct labor-hours in each quarter are multiplied by the variable rate to determine the variable component of manufacturing overhead. For example, the variable manufacturing overhead for the first quarter is $22,400 (5,600 direct labor-hours × $4.00 per direct labor-hour). This is added to the fixed manufacturing overhead for the quarter to determine the total manufacturing overhead for the quarter of $83,000 ($22,400 + $60,600).

A few words about fixed costs and the budgeting process are in order. In most cases, fixed costs are the costs of supplying capacity to make products, process purchase orders, handle customer calls, and so on. The amount of capacity that will be required depends

SCHEDULE 5

	A	B	C	D	E	F
1	Hampton Freeze, Inc.					
2	Manufacturing Overhead Budget					
3	For the Year Ended December 31, 2012					
4						
5		Quarter				
6		1	2	3	4	Year
7	Budgeted direct labor-hours (Schedule 4)	5,600	12,800	14,400	7,600	40,400
8	Variable manufacturing overhead rate	$ 4.00	$ 4.00	$ 4.00	$ 4.00	$ 4.00
9	Variable manufacturing overhead	$ 22,400	$ 51,200	$ 57,600	$ 30,400	$ 161,600
10	Fixed manufacturing overhead	60,600	60,600	60,600	60,600	242,400
11	Total manufacturing overhead	83,000	111,800	118,200	91,000	404,000
12	Less depreciation	15,000	15,000	15,000	15,000	60,000
13	Cash disbursements for manufacturing overhead	$ 68,000	$ 96,800	$ 103,200	$ 76,000	$ 344,000
14						
15	Total manufacturing overhead (a)					$ 404,000
16	Budgeted direct labor-hours (b)					40,400
17	Predetermined overhead rate for the year (a)÷(b)					$ 10.00
18						

Schedule 1 / Schedule 2 / Schedule 3 / Schedule 4 / **Schedule 5** / Schedule

on the expected level of activity for the period. If the expected level of activity is greater than the company's current capacity, then fixed costs may have to be increased. Or, if the expected level is appreciably below the company's current capacity, then it may be desirable to decrease fixed costs if possible. However, once the level of the fixed costs has been determined in the budget, the costs really are fixed. The time to adjust fixed costs is during the budgeting process. An activity-based costing system can help to determine the appropriate level of fixed costs at budget time by answering questions like, "How many clerks will we need to process the anticipated number of purchase orders next year?" For simplicity, in all of the budgeting examples in this book assume that the appropriate levels of fixed costs have already been determined.

The last line of Schedule 5 for Hampton Freeze shows the budgeted cash disbursements for manufacturing overhead. Because some of the overhead costs are not cash outflows, the total budgeted manufacturing overhead costs must be adjusted to determine the cash disbursements for manufacturing overhead. At Hampton Freeze, the only significant noncash manufacturing overhead cost is depreciation, which is $15,000 per quarter. These noncash depreciation charges are deducted from the total budgeted manufacturing overhead to determine the expected cash disbursements. Hampton Freeze pays all overhead costs involving cash disbursements in the quarter incurred. Note that the company's predetermined overhead rate for the year is $10 per direct labor-hour, which is determined by dividing the total budgeted manufacturing overhead for the year by the total budgeted direct labor-hours for the year.

The Ending Finished Goods Inventory Budget

After completing Schedules 1–5, Larry Giano had all of the data he needed to compute unit product costs. This computation was needed for two reasons: first, to determine cost of goods sold on the budgeted income statement; and second, to value ending inventories. The cost of unsold units is computed on the **ending finished goods inventory budget.**

Larry Giano considered using variable costing to prepare Hampton Freeze's budget statements, but he decided to use absorption costing instead because the bank would very likely require absorption costing. He also knew that it would be easy to convert the absorption costing financial statements to a variable costing basis later. At this point, the primary concern was to determine what financing, if any, would be required in 2012 and then to arrange for that financing from the bank.

SCHEDULE 6

Hampton Freeze, Inc.						
Ending Finished Goods Inventory Budget						
(absorption costing basis)						
For the Year Ended December 31, 2012						
Item	*Quantity*		*Cost*		*Total*	
Production cost per case:						
Direct materials	15.00	pounds	$ 0.20	per pound	$	3.00
Direct labor	0.40	hours	$15.00	per hour		6.00
Manufacturing overhead	0.40	hours	$10.00	per hour		4.00
Unit product cost					$	13.00
Budgeted finished goods inventory:						
Ending finished goods inventory in cases (Schedule 2)						3,000
Unit product cost (see above)					$	13.00
Ending finished goods inventory in dollars						$39,000

The unit product cost computations are shown in Schedule 6. For Hampton Freeze, the absorption costing unit product cost is $13 per case of popsicles—consisting of $3 of direct materials, $6 of direct labor, and $4 of manufacturing overhead. The manufacturing overhead is applied to units of product at the rate of $10 per direct labor-hour. The budgeted carrying cost of the ending inventory is $39,000.

The Selling and Administrative Expense Budget

LEARNING OBJECTIVE 7
Prepare a selling and administrative expense budget.

The **selling and administrative expense budget** lists the budgeted expenses for areas other than manufacturing. In large organizations, this budget would be a compilation of many smaller, individual budgets submitted by department heads and other persons responsible for selling and administrative expenses. For example, the marketing manager would submit a budget detailing the advertising expenses for each budget period.

Schedule 7 contains the selling and administrative expense budget for Hampton Freeze. Like the manufacturing overhead budget, the selling and administrative expense budget is divided into variable and fixed cost components. In the case of Hampton Freeze, the variable selling and administrative expense is $1.80 per case. Consequently, budgeted sales in cases for each quarter are entered at the top of the schedule. These data are taken from the sales budget (Schedule 1). The budgeted variable selling and administrative expenses are determined by multiplying the budgeted cases sold by the variable selling and administrative expense per case. For example, the budgeted variable selling and administrative expense for the first quarter is $18,000 (10,000 cases × $1.80 per case). The fixed selling and administrative expenses (all given data) are then added to the variable selling and administrative expenses to arrive at the total budgeted selling and administrative expenses. Finally, to determine the cash disbursements for selling and administrative items, the total budgeted selling and administrative expense is adjusted by subtracting any noncash selling and administrative expenses (in this case, just depreciation).[1]

[1] Other adjustments might need to be made for differences between cash flows on the one hand and revenues and expenses on the other hand. For example, if property taxes are paid twice a year in installments of $8,000 each, the expense for property tax would have to be "backed out" of the total budgeted selling and administrative expenses and the cash installment payments added to the appropriate quarters to determine the cash disbursements. Similar adjustments might also need to be made in the manufacturing overhead budget. We generally ignore these complications in this chapter.

SCHEDULE 7

Hampton Freeze, Inc.
Selling and Administrative Expense Budget
For the Year Ended December 31, 2012

	Quarter 1	Quarter 2	Quarter 3	Quarter 4	Year
Budgeted sales in cases (Schedule 1)	10,000	30,000	40,000	20,000	100,000
Variable selling and administrative expense per case	$ 1.80	$ 1.80	$ 1.80	$ 1.80	$ 1.80
Variable selling and administrative expense	$ 18,000	$ 54,000	$ 72,000	$ 36,000	$180,000
Fixed selling and administrative expenses:					
Advertising	20,000	20,000	20,000	20,000	80,000
Executive salaries	55,000	55,000	55,000	55,000	220,000
Insurance	10,000	10,000	10,000	10,000	40,000
Property taxes	4,000	4,000	4,000	4,000	16,000
Depreciation	10,000	10,000	10,000	10,000	40,000
Total fixed selling and administrative expenses	99,000	99,000	99,000	99,000	396,000
Total selling and administrative expenses	117,000	153,000	171,000	135,000	576,000
Less depreciation	10,000	10,000	10,000	10,000	40,000
Cash disbursements for selling and administrative expenses	$107,000	$143,000	$161,000	$125,000	$536,000

IN BUSINESS

CANON INVESTS IN RESEARCH AND DEVELOPMENT

When Canon Inc., the world's leading digital camera manufacturer, prepares the research and development (R&D) portion of its selling and administrative expense budget, the focus is on making long-run investments to grow sales rather than cutting costs to maximize short-run profits. In 2005, Canon spent 8% of its sales on R&D while many of its competitors spent 6% to 7.5% of their sales on R&D. Canon's CEO Fujio Mitarai described his company's R&D philosophy by saying "we have to plant the seeds for the next decade and beyond." Indeed, Canon's seeds have blossomed as the company has secured more than 17,000 patents since 1995—second only to IBM. Canon's commitment to R&D helps explain why its digital cameras are delivering healthy earnings at a time when many of its competitors are losing money.

Source: Ian Rowley, Hiroko Tashiro, and Louise Lee, "Canon: Combat-Ready," *BusinessWeek*, September 5, 2005, pp. 48–49.

The Cash Budget

LEARNING OBJECTIVE 8
Prepare a cash budget.

As illustrated in Exhibit 8–2, the cash budget combines much of the data developed in the preceding steps. It is a good idea to review Exhibit 8–2 to get the big picture firmly in your mind before moving on.

The cash budget is composed of four major sections:

1. The receipts section.
2. The disbursements section.
3. The cash excess or deficiency section.
4. The financing section.

The receipts section lists all of the cash inflows, except from financing, expected during the budget period. Generally, the major source of receipts is from sales.

IN BUSINESS

MISMATCHED CASH FLOWS—CLIMBING THE HILLS AND VALLEYS

The Washington Trails Association (WTA) is a private, nonprofit organization primarily concerned with protecting and maintaining hiking trails in the state of Washington. Some 2,000 WTA volunteer workers donate more than 80,000 hours per year maintaining trails in rugged landscapes on federal, state, and private lands. The organization is supported by membership dues, voluntary contributions, grants, and some contract work for government.

The organization's income and expenses are erratic—although somewhat predictable—over the course of the year as shown in the chart below. Expenses tend to be highest in the spring and summer when most of the trail maintenance work is done. However, income spikes in December well after the expenses have been incurred. With cash outflows running ahead of cash inflows for much of the year, it is very important for the WTA to carefully plan its cash budget and to maintain adequate cash reserves to be able to pay its bills.

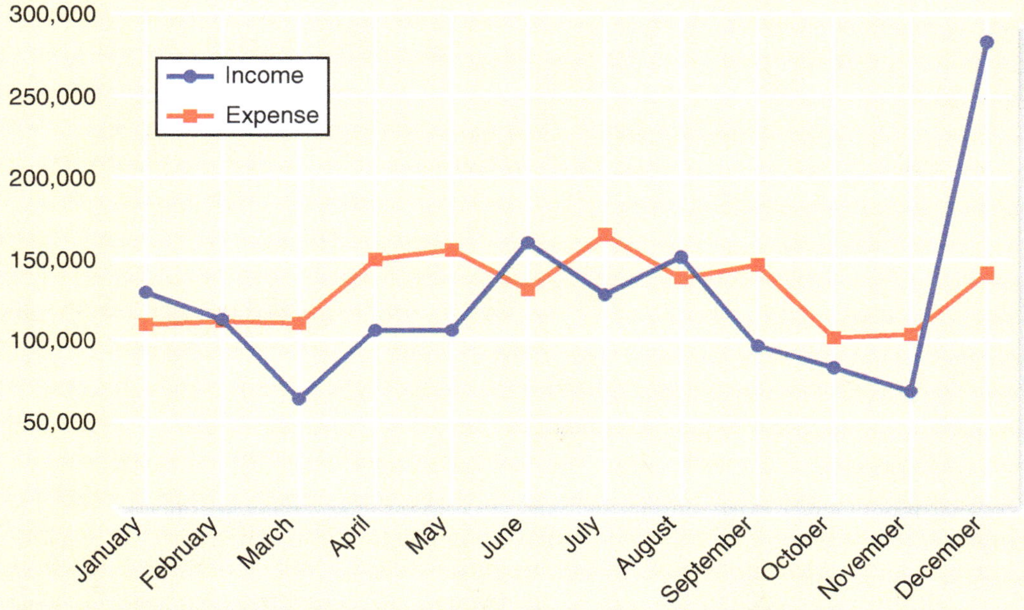

Note: Total income and total expense are approximately equal over the course of the year.

Sources: Conversation with Elizabeth Lunney, President of the Washington Trails Association; WTA documents; and the WTA website www.wta.org.

The disbursements section summarizes all cash payments that are planned for the budget period. These payments include raw materials purchases, direct labor payments, manufacturing overhead costs, and so on, as contained in their respective budgets. In addition, other cash disbursements such as equipment purchases and dividends are listed.

The cash excess or deficiency section is computed as follows:

Cash balance, beginning	XXXX
Add receipts	XXXX
Total cash available	XXXX
Less disbursements	XXXX
Excess (deficiency) of cash available over disbursements	XXXX

SCHEDULE 8

Hampton Freeze, Inc.
Cash Budget
For the Year Ended December 31, 2012

			Quarter				
		Schedule	1	2	3	4	Year
7	Cash balance, beginning		$ 42,500	$ 36,000	$ 33,900	$ 165,650	$ 42,500
8	Add receipts:						
9	Collections from customers	1	230,000	480,000	740,000	520,000	1,970,000
10	Total cash available		272,500	516,000	773,900	685,650	2,012,500
11	Less disbursements:						
12	Direct materials	3	49,500	72,300	100,050	79,350	301,200
13	Direct labor	4	84,000	192,000	216,000	114,000	606,000
14	Manufacturing overhead	5	68,000	96,800	103,200	76,000	344,000
15	Selling and administrative	7	107,000	143,000	161,000	125,000	536,000
16	Equipment purchases		50,000	40,000	20,000	20,000	130,000
17	Dividends		8,000	8,000	8,000	8,000	32,000
18	Total disbursements		366,500	552,100	608,250	422,350	1,949,200
19	Excess (deficiency) of cash available over disbursements		(94,000)	(36,100)	165,650	263,300	63,300
20	Financing:						
21	Borrowings (at the beginnings of quarters)		130,000	70,000	-	-	200,000
22	Repayments (at end of the year)		-	-	-	(200,000)	(200,000)
23	Interest		-	-	-	(21,900)	(21,900)
24	Total financing		130,000	70,000	-	(221,900)	(21,900)
25	Cash balance, ending		$ 36,000	$ 33,900	$ 165,650	$ 41,400	$ 41,400

Schedule 6 | Schedule 7 | Schedule 8 | Schedule 9 | Schedule 10

If a cash deficiency exists during any budget period, the company will need to borrow funds. If there is a cash excess during any budget period, funds borrowed in previous periods can be repaid or the excess funds can be invested.

The financing section details the borrowings and repayments projected to take place during the budget period. It also lists interest payments that will be due on money borrowed.[2]

The cash balances at both the beginning and end of the year may be adequate even though a serious cash deficit occurs at some point during the year. Consequently, the cash budget should be broken down into time periods that are short enough to capture major fluctuations in cash balances. While a monthly cash budget is most common, some organizations budget cash on a weekly or even daily basis. Larry Giano has prepared a quarterly cash budget for Hampton Freeze that can be further refined as necessary. This budget appears in Schedule 8. The cash budget builds on the earlier schedules and on additional data that are provided below:

- The beginning cash balance is $42,500.
- Management plans to spend $130,000 during the year on equipment purchases: $50,000 in the first quarter; $40,000 in the second quarter; $20,000 in the third quarter; and $20,000 in the fourth quarter.
- The board of directors has approved cash dividends of $8,000 per quarter.
- Management would like to have a cash balance of at least $30,000 at the beginning of each quarter for contingencies.

[2] The format for the statement of cash flows, which is discussed in a later chapter, may also be used for the cash budget.

- Hampton Freeze has an agreement with a local bank that allows the company to borrow in increments of $10,000 at the beginning of each quarter, up to a total loan balance of $250,000. The interest rate on these loans is 1% per month, and for simplicity, we will assume that interest is not compounded. The company would, as far as it is able, repay the loan plus accumulated interest at the end of the year.

The cash budget is prepared one quarter at a time, starting with the first quarter. Larry began the cash budget by entering the beginning balance of cash for the first quarter of $42,500—a number that is given on the previous page. Receipts—in this case, just the $230,000 in cash collections from customers—are added to the beginning balance to arrive at the total cash available of $272,500. Because the total disbursements are $366,500 and the total cash available is only $272,500, there is a shortfall of $94,000. Because management would like to have a beginning cash balance of at least $30,000 for the second quarter, the company will need to borrow at least $124,000.

Required Borrowings at the Beginning of the First Quarter	
Desired ending cash balance	$ 30,000
Plus deficiency of cash available over disbursements	94,000
Minimum required borrowings	$124,000

Recall that the bank requires that loans be made in increments of $10,000. Because Hampton Freeze needs to borrow at least $124,000, it will have to borrow $130,000.

The second quarter of the cash budget is handled similarly. Note that the ending cash balance for the first quarter is brought forward as the beginning cash balance for the second quarter. Also note that additional borrowing is required in the second quarter because of the continued cash shortfall.

Required Borrowings at the Beginning of the Second Quarter	
Desired ending cash balance	$30,000
Plus deficiency of cash available over disbursements	36,100
Minimum required borrowings	$66,100

Again, recall that the bank requires that loans be made in increments of $10,000. Because Hampton Freeze needs to borrow at least $66,100 at the beginning of the second quarter, the company will have to borrow $70,000 from the bank.

In the third quarter, the cash flow situation improves dramatically and the excess of cash available over disbursements is $165,650. Therefore, the company will end the quarter with ample cash and no further borrowing is necessary.

At the end of the fourth quarter, the loan and accumulated interest must be repaid. The accumulated interest can be computed as follows:

Interest on $130,000 borrowed at the beginning of the first quarter:	
$130,000 × 0.01 per month × 12 months*	$15,600
Interest on $70,000 borrowed at the beginning of the second quarter:	
$70,000 × 0.01 per month × 9 months*	6,300
Total interest accrued to the end of the fourth quarter	$21,900

*Simple, rather than compounded, interest is assumed for simplicity.

Note that the loan repayment of $200,000 ($130,000 + $70,000) appears in the financing section for the fourth quarter along with the interest payment of $21,900 computed above.

As with the production and raw materials budgets, the amounts under the Year column in the cash budget are not always the sum of the amounts for the four quarters. In particular, the beginning cash balance for the year is the same as the beginning cash balance for the first quarter and the ending cash balance for the year is the same as the ending cash balance for the fourth quarter. Also note the beginning cash balance in any quarter is the same as the ending cash balance for the previous quarter.

IN BUSINESS

NEW INSPECTIONS PINCH CASH FLOWS

Herald Metal and Plastic Works is a Chinese toy manufacturer that produces Star Wars action figures and G.I. Joes for Hasbro Inc. in the United States. The company used to ship its toys to America immediately after they rolled off the production line. However, this changed when American consumers discovered that some Chinese companies were using poisonous lead-based paint in their manufacturing processes. The Chinese government now requires toy manufacturers to store finished goods in warehouses for anywhere from three weeks to two months until its inspectors certify them for export.

Herald Metal and Plastic Works borrows money from lenders to buy raw materials and pay laborers to make its toys. The company is struggling to repay its loans because the government's inspection process delays cash receipts from customers.

Source: Chi-Chu Tschang, "Bottlenecks in Toyland," *BusinessWeek*, October 15, 2007, p. 52.

The Budgeted Income Statement

LEARNING OBJECTIVE 9
Prepare a budgeted income statement.

A budgeted income statement can be prepared from the data developed in Schedules 1–8. *The budgeted income statement is one of the key schedules in the budget process.* It shows the company's planned profit and serves as a benchmark against which subsequent company performance can be measured.

Schedule 9 contains the budgeted income statement for Hampton Freeze.

SCHEDULE 9

Hampton Freeze, Inc.
Budgeted Income Statement
For the Year Ended December 31, 2012

	Schedules	
Sales	1	$ 2,000,000
Cost of goods sold*	1,6	1,300,000
Gross margin		700,000
Selling and administrative expenses	7	576,000
Net operating Income		124,000
Interest expense	8	21,900
Net Income		$ 102,100

Schedule 8 | Schedule 9 | Schedule 10

*100,000 cases sold × $13 per case = $1,300,000.

The Budgeted Balance Sheet

LEARNING OBJECTIVE 10
Prepare a budgeted balance sheet.

The budgeted balance sheet is developed using data from the balance sheet from the beginning of the budget period and data contained in the various schedules. Hampton Freeze's budgeted balance sheet is presented in Schedule 10. Some of the data on the budgeted balance sheet have been taken from the company's previous end-of-year balance sheet for 2011 which appears below:

Hampton Freeze, Inc.
Balance Sheet
December 31, 2011

Assets		
Current assets:		
Cash	$ 42,500	
Accounts receivable	90,000	
Raw materials inventory (21,000 pounds)	4,200	
Finished goods inventory (2,000 cases)	26,000	
Total current assets		$162,700
Plant and equipment:		
Land	80,000	
Buildings and equipment	700,000	
Accumulated depreciation	(292,000)	
Plant and equipment, net		488,000
Total assets		$650,700
Liabilities and Stockholders' Equity		
Current liabilities:		
Accounts payable (raw materials)		$ 25,800
Stockholders' equity:		
Common stock, no par	$175,000	
Retained earnings	449,900	
Total stockholders' equity		624,900
Total liabilities and stockholders' equity		$650,700

After completing the master budget, Larry Giano took the documents to Tom Wills, chief executive officer of Hampton Freeze, for his review.

MANAGERIAL ACCOUNTING IN ACTION
The Wrap-up

Larry: Here's the budget. Overall, the net income is excellent, and the net cash flow for the entire year is positive.

Tom: Yes, but I see on this cash budget that we have the same problem with negative cash flows in the first and second quarters that we had last year.

Larry: That's true. I don't see any way around that problem. However, there is no doubt in my mind that if you take this budget to the bank today, they'll approve an open line of credit that will allow you to borrow enough to make it through the first two quarters without any problem.

Tom: Are you sure? They didn't seem very happy to see me last year when I came in for an emergency loan.

Larry: Did you repay the loan on time?

Tom: Sure.

Larry: I don't see any problem. You won't be asking for an emergency loan this time. The bank will have plenty of warning. And with this budget, you have a solid plan that shows when and how you are going to pay off the loan. Trust me, they'll go for it.

SCHEDULE 10

	A	B	C	D	E
1	**Hampton Freeze, Inc.**				
2	**Budgeted Balance Sheet**				
3	**December 31, 2012**				
4					
5	*Assets*				
6	Current assets:				
7	Cash	$ 41,400	(a)		
8	Accounts receivable	120,000	(b)		
9	Raw materials inventory	4,500	(c)		
10	Finished goods inventory	39,000	(d)		
11	Total current assets			$ 204,900	
12	Plant and equipment:				
13	Land	80,000	(e)		
14	Buildings and equipment	830,000	(f)		
15	Accumulated depreciation	(392,000)	(g)		
16	Plant and equipment, net			518,000	
17	Total assets			$ 722,900	
18					
19	*Liabilities and Stockholders' Equity*				
20	Current liabilities:				
21	Accounts payable (raw materials)			$ 27,900	(h)
22	Stockholders' equity:				
23	Common stock, no par	$ 175,000	(i)		
24	Retained earnings	520,000	(j)		
25	Total stockholders' equity			695,000	
26	Total liabilities and stockholders' equity			$ 722,900	
27					

Schedule 9 | **Schedule 10**

Explanation of December 31, 2012, balance sheet figures:

(a) The ending cash balance, as projected by the cash budget in Schedule 8.

(b) Thirty percent of fourth-quarter sales, from Schedule 1 ($400,000 × 30% = $120,000).

(c) From Schedule 3, the ending raw materials inventory will be 22,500 pounds. This material costs $0.20 per pound. Therefore, the ending inventory in dollars will be 22,500 pounds × $0.20 per pound = $4,500.

(d) From Schedule 6.

(e) From the December 31, 2011, balance sheet (no change).

(f) The December 31, 2011, balance sheet indicated a balance of $700,000. During 2012, $130,000 of additional equipment will be purchased (see Schedule 8), bringing the December 31, 2012, balance to $830,000.

(g) The December 31, 2011, balance sheet indicated a balance of $292,000. During 2012, $100,000 of depreciation will be taken ($60,000 on Schedule 5 and $40,000 on Schedule 7), bringing the December 31, 2012, balance to $392,000.

(h) One-half of the fourth-quarter raw materials purchases, from Schedule 3.

(i) From the December 31, 2011, balance sheet (no change).

(j)

December 31, 2011, balance	$449,900
Add net income, from Schedule 9	102,100
	552,000
Deduct dividends paid, from Schedule 8	32,000
December 31, 2012, balance	$520,000

IN BUSINESS

MOVING BEYOND EXCEL TO THE WEB

While research shows that two-thirds of U.S. companies still rely on Microsoft Excel for their budgeting process, some companies are evolving to a more technologically advanced approach. For example, Hendrick Motorsports has vaulted to the top of the NASCAR racing circuit thanks in part to its new budgeting process. Scott Lampe, Hendrick's CFO, discarded Excel in favor of Forecaster, a web-based budgeting program. He commented "with a spreadsheet, you can build the model the way you want it . . . The problem is, only you understand that model. Then you have to explain it to everyone, one at a time." The web-based approach enables Lampe to involve his crew chiefs, chassis guys, and engine guys in the budgeting process.

The Facilities & Operations (F&O) Business Office of the Battelle, Pacific Northwest National Laboratory has over 130 budget activities—each of which requires the preparation of an annual budget. In 2001, F&O replaced its spreadsheet-driven budget with a web-based approach. The new system enables F&O "management and their support staff to directly input their business plan and budget requests, eliminating the need for central business planning and budgeting staff to upload the numerous budget requests and subsequent changes." The web-based budgeting system saves F&O personnel more than 500 hours that were previously spent preparing Excel spreadsheets and uploading data.

Sources: John Goff, "In The Fast Lane," *CFO*, December 2004, pp. 53–58; Peter T. Smith, Craig A. Goranson, and Mary F. Astley, "Intranet Budgeting Does the Trick," *Strategic Finance*, May 2003, pp. 30–33.

Summary

This chapter describes the budgeting process and shows how the various operating budgets relate to each other. The sales budget is the foundation for profit planning. Once the sales budget has been set, the production budget and the selling and administrative expense budget can be prepared because they depend on how many units are to be sold. The production budget determines how many units are to be produced, so after it is prepared, the various manufacturing cost budgets can be prepared. All of these budgets feed into the cash budget and the budgeted income statement and balance sheet. The parts of the master budget are connected in many ways. For example, the schedule of expected cash collections, which is completed in connection with the sales budget, provides data for both the cash budget and the budgeted balance sheet.

The material in this chapter is just an introduction to budgeting and profit planning. In later chapters, we will see how budgets are used to control day-to-day operations and how they are used in performance evaluation.

Review Problem: Budget Schedules

Mynor Corporation manufactures and sells a seasonal product that has peak sales in the third quarter. The following information concerns operations for Year 2—the coming year—and for the first two quarters of Year 3:

a. The company's single product sells for $8 per unit. Budgeted sales in units for the next six quarters are as follows (all sales are on credit):

	Year 2 Quarter				Year 3 Quarter	
	1	2	3	4	1	2
Budgeted unit sales	40,000	60,000	100,000	50,000	70,000	80,000

b. Sales are collected in the following pattern: 75% in the quarter the sales are made, and the remaining 25% in the following quarter. On January 1, Year 2, the company's balance sheet showed $65,000 in accounts receivable, all of which will be collected in the first quarter of the year. Bad debts are negligible and can be ignored.
c. The company desires an ending finished goods inventory at the end of each quarter equal to 30% of the budgeted unit sales for the next quarter. On December 31, Year 1, the company had 12,000 units on hand.
d. Five pounds of raw materials are required to complete one unit of product. The company requires ending raw materials inventory at the end of each quarter equal to 10% of the following quarter's production needs. On December 31, Year 1, the company had 23,000 pounds of raw materials on hand.
e. The raw material costs $0.80 per pound. Raw material purchases are paid for in the following pattern: 60% paid in the quarter the purchases are made, and the remaining 40% paid in the following quarter. On January 1, Year 2, the company's balance sheet showed $81,500 in accounts payable for raw material purchases, all of which will be paid for in the first quarter of the year.

Required:

Prepare the following budgets and schedules for the year, showing both quarterly and total figures:

1. A sales budget and a schedule of expected cash collections.
2. A production budget.
3. A direct materials budget and a schedule of expected cash payments for purchases of materials.

Solution to Review Problem

1. The sales budget is prepared as follows:

	Year 2 Quarter				
	1	2	3	4	Year
Budgeted unit sales	40,000	60,000	100,000	50,000	250,000
Selling price per unit	× $8	× $8	× $8	× $8	× $8
Total sales	$320,000	$480,000	$800,000	$400,000	$2,000,000

Based on the budgeted sales above, the schedule of expected cash collections is prepared as follows:

	Year 2 Quarter				
	1	2	3	4	Year
Accounts receivable, beginning balance	$ 65,000				$ 65,000
First-quarter sales ($320,000 × 75%, 25%)	240,000	$ 80,000			320,000
Second-quarter sales ($480,000 × 75%, 25%)		360,000	$120,000		480,000
Third-quarter sales ($800,000 × 75%, 25%)			600,000	$200,000	800,000
Fourth-quarter sales ($400,000 × 75%)				300,000	300,000
Total cash collections	$305,000	$440,000	$720,000	$500,000	$1,965,000

2. Based on the sales budget in units, the production budget is prepared as follows:

	Year 2 Quarter					Year 3 Quarter	
	1	2	3	4	Year	1	2
Budgeted unit sales	40,000	60,000	100,000	50,000	250,000	70,000	80,000
Add desired ending finished goods inventory*	18,000	30,000	15,000	21,000†	21,000	24,000	
Total needs	58,000	90,000	115,000	71,000	271,000	94,000	
Less beginning finished goods inventory	12,000	18,000	30,000	15,000	12,000	21,000	
Required production	46,000	72,000	85,000	56,000	259,000	73,000	

*30% of the following quarter's budgeted sales in units.
†30% of the budgeted Year 3 first-quarter sales.

3. Based on the production budget, raw materials will need to be purchased during the year as follows:

	Year 2 Quarter					Year 3 Quarter
	1	2	3	4	Year 2	1
Required production (units)	46,000	72,000	85,000	56,000	259,000	73,000
Raw materials needed per unit (pounds)	× 5	× 5	× 5	× 5	× 5	× 5
Production needs (pounds)	230,000	360,000	425,000	280,000	1,295,000	365,000
Add desired ending inventory of raw materials (pounds)*	36,000	42,500	28,000	36,500†	36,500	
Total needs (pounds)	266,000	402,500	453,000	316,500	1,331,500	
Less beginning inventory of raw materials (pounds)	23,000	36,000	42,500	28,000	23,000	
Raw materials to be purchased (pounds)	243,000	366,500	410,500	288,500	1,308,500	
Cost of raw materials per pound	× $0.80	× $0.80	× $0.80	× $0.80	× $0.80	
Cost of raw materials to be purchased	$194,400	$293,200	$328,400	$230,800	$1,046,800	

*10% of the following quarter's production needs in pounds.
†10% of the Year 3 first-quarter production needs in pounds.

Based on the raw material purchases above, expected cash payments are computed as follows:

	Year 2 Quarter				
	1	2	3	4	Year 2
Accounts payable, beginning balance	$ 81,500				$ 81,500
First-quarter purchases ($194,400 × 60%, 40%)	116,640	$ 77,760			194,400
Second-quarter purchases ($293,200 × 60%, 40%)		175,920	$117,280		293,200
Third-quarter purchases ($328,400 × 60%, 40%)			197,040	$131,360	328,400
Fourth-quarter purchases ($230,800 × 60%)				138,480	138,480
Total cash disbursements	$198,140	$253,680	$314,320	$269,840	$1,035,980

Glossary

Budget A detailed plan for the future that is usually expressed in formal quantitative terms. (p. 336)

Budget committee A group of key managers who are responsible for overall budgeting policy and for coordinating the preparation of the budget. (p. 340)

Cash budget A detailed plan showing how cash resources will be acquired and used over a specific time period. (p. 341)

Continuous budget A 12-month budget that rolls forward one month as the current month is completed. (p. 337)

Control The process of gathering feedback to ensure that a plan is being properly executed or modified as circumstances change. (p. 336)

Direct labor budget A detailed plan that shows the direct labor-hours required to fulfill the production budget. (p. 348)

Direct materials budget A detailed plan showing the amount of raw materials that must be purchased to fulfill the production budget and to provide for adequate inventories. (p. 346)

Ending finished goods inventory budget A budget showing the dollar amount of unsold finished goods inventory that will appear on the ending balance sheet. (p. 350)

Manufacturing overhead budget A detailed plan showing the production costs, other than direct materials and direct labor, that will be incurred over a specified time period. (p. 349)

Master budget A number of separate but interdependent budgets that formally lay out the company's sales, production, and financial goals and that culminates in a cash budget, budgeted income statement, and budgeted balance sheet. (p. 341)

Merchandise purchases budget A detailed plan used by a merchandising company that shows the amount of goods that must be purchased from suppliers during the period. (p. 346)

Participative budget See *Self-imposed budget.* (p. 338)

Perpetual budget See *Continuous budget.* (p. 337)

Planning Developing goals and preparing budgets to achieve those goals. (p. 336)

Production budget A detailed plan showing the number of units that must be produced during a period in order to satisfy both sales and inventory needs. (p. 344)

Responsibility accounting A system of accountability in which managers are held responsible for those items of revenue and cost—and only those items—over which they can exert significant control. The managers are held responsible for differences between budgeted and actual results. (p. 337)

Sales budget A detailed schedule showing expected sales expressed in both dollars and units. (p. 341)

Self-imposed budget A method of preparing budgets in which managers prepare their own budgets. These budgets are then reviewed by higher-level managers, and any issues are resolved by mutual agreement. (p. 338)

Selling and administrative expense budget A detailed schedule of planned expenses that will be incurred in areas other than manufacturing during a budget period. (p. 351)

Questions

8–1 What is a budget? What is budgetary control?

8–2 Discuss some of the major benefits to be gained from budgeting.

8–3 What is meant by the term *responsibility accounting?*

8–4 What is a master budget? Briefly describe its contents.

8–5 Why is the sales forecast the starting point in budgeting?

8–6 "As a practical matter, planning and control mean exactly the same thing." Do you agree? Explain.

8–7 Describe the flow of budget data in an organization. Who are the participants in the budgeting process, and how do they participate?

8–8 What is a self-imposed budget? What are the major advantages of self-imposed budgets? What caution must be exercised in their use?

8–9 How can budgeting assist a company in planning its workforce staffing levels?

8–10 "The principal purpose of the cash budget is to see how much cash the company will have in the bank at the end of the year." Do you agree? Explain.

Multiple-choice questions are provided on the text website at www.mhhe.com/garrison14e.

Applying Excel connect ACCOUNTING

LEARNING OBJECTIVES 2, 3, 4

Available with McGraw-Hill's *Connect™ Accounting.*

The Excel worksheet form that appears on the next page is to be used to recreate the Review Problem on pages 359–361. Download the workbook containing this form from the Online Learning Center at www.mhhe.com/garrison14e. *On the website you will also receive instructions about how to use this worksheet form.*

	A	B	C	D	E	F	G	H	I
1	Chapter 8: Applying Excel								
2									
3	Data		Year 2 Quarter			Year 3 Quarter			
4		1	2	3	4	1	2		
5	Budgeted unit sales	40,000	60,000	100,000	50,000	70,000	80,000		
6									
7	• Selling price per unit	$8	per unit						
8	• Accounts receivable, beginning balance	$65,000							
9	• Sales collected in the quarter sales are made	75%							
10	• Sales collected in the quarter after sales are made	25%							
11	• Desired ending finished goods inventory is	30%	of the budgeted unit sales of the next quarter						
12	• Finished goods inventory, beginning	12,000	units						
13	• Raw materials required to produce one unit	5	pounds						
14	• Desired ending inventory of raw materials is	10%	of the next quarter's production needs						
15	• Raw materials inventory, beginning	23,000	pounds						
16	• Raw material costs	$0.80	per pound						
17	• Raw materials purchases are paid	60%	in the quarter the purchases are made						
18	and	40%	in the quarter following purchase						
19	• Accounts payable for raw materials, beginning balance	$81,500							
20									
21	*Enter a formula into each of the cells marked with a ? below*								
22	**Review Problem: Budget Schedules**								
23									
24	***Construct the sales budget***		Year 2 Quarter			Year 3 Quarter			
25		1	2	3	4	1	2		
26	Budgeted unit sales	?	?	?	?	?	?		
27	Selling price per unit	?	?	?	?	?	?		
28	Total sales	?	?	?	?	?	?		
29									
30	***Construct the schedule of expected cash collections***		Year 2 Quarter						
31		1	2	3	4	Year			
32	Accounts receivable, beginning balance	?				?			
33	First-quarter sales	?	?			?			
34	Second-quarter sales		?	?		?			
35	Third-quarter sales			?	?	?			
36	Fourth-quarter sales				?	?			
37	Total cash collections	?	?	?	?	?			
38									
39	***Construct the production budget***		Year 2 Quarter				Year 3 Quarter		
40		1	2	3	4	Year	1	2	
41	Budgeted unit sales	?	?	?	?	?	?	?	
42	Add desired finished goods inventory	?	?	?	?	?	?		
43	Total needs	?	?	?	?	?	?		
44	Less beginning inventory	?	?	?	?	?	?		
45	Required production	?	?	?	?	?	?		
46									
47	***Construct the raw materials purchases budget***		Year 2 Quarter				Year 3 Quarter		
48		1	2	3	4	Year	1		
49	Required production (units)	?	?	?	?	?	?		
50	Raw materials required to produce one unit	?	?	?	?	?	?		
51	Production needs (pounds)	?	?	?	?	?	?		
52	Add desired ending inventory of raw materials (pounds)	?	?	?	?	?			
53	Total needs (pounds)	?	?	?	?	?			
54	Less beginning inventory of raw materials (pounds)	?	?	?	?	?			
55	Raw materials to be purchased	?	?	?	?	?			
56	Cost of raw materials per pound	?	?	?	?	?			
57	Cost of raw materials to be purchased	?	?	?	?	?			
58									
59	***Construct the schedule of expected cash payments***		Year 2 Quarter						
60		1	2	3	4	Year			
61	Accounts payable, beginning balance	?				?			
62	First-quarter purchases	?	?			?			
63	Second-quarter purchases		?	?		?			
64	Third-quarter purchases			?	?	?			
65	Fourth-quarter purchases				?	?			
66	Total cash disbursements	?	?	?	?	?			
67									

Chapter 8 Form | Filled in Chapter 8 Form | Chapter 8 Formulas | Chapter 8 Requirement

You should proceed to the requirements below only after completing your worksheet.

Required:

1. Check your worksheet by changing the budgeted unit sales in Quarter 2 of Year 2 in cell C5 to 75,000 units. The total expected cash collections for the year should now be $2,085,000. If you do not get this answer, find the errors in your worksheet and correct them. Have the total cash disbursements for the year changed? Why or why not?
2. The company has just hired a new marketing manager who insists that unit sales can be dramatically increased by dropping the selling price from $8 to $7. The marketing manager would like to use the following projections in the budget:

Data	Year 2 Quarter				Year 3 Quarter	
	1	2	3	4	1	2
Budgeted unit sales	50,000	70,000	120,000	80,000	90,000	100,000
Selling price per unit	$7 per unit					

a. What are the total expected cash collections for the year under this revised budget?
b. What is the total required production for the year under this revised budget?
c. What is the total cost of raw materials to be purchased for the year under this revised budget?
d. What are the total expected cash disbursements for raw materials for the year under this revised budget?
e. After seeing this revised budget, the production manager cautioned that due to the current production constraint, a complex milling machine, the plant can produce no more than 90,000 units in any one quarter. Is this a potential problem? If so, what can be done about it?

Exercises

All applicable exercises are available with McGraw-Hill's *Connect™ Accounting.*

EXERCISE 8–1 Schedule of Expected Cash Collections [LO2]
Midwest Products is a wholesale distributor of leaf rakes. Thus, peak sales occur in August of each year as shown in the company's sales budget for the third quarter, given below:

	July	August	September	Total
Budgeted sales (all on account)	$600,000	$900,000	$500,000	$2,000,000

From past experience, the company has learned that 20% of a month's sales are collected in the month of sale, another 70% are collected in the month following sale, and the remaining 10% are collected in the second month following sale. Bad debts are negligible and can be ignored. May sales totaled $430,000, and June sales totaled $540,000.

Required:

1. Prepare a schedule of expected cash collections from sales, by month and in total, for the third quarter.
2. Assume that the company will prepare a budgeted balance sheet as of September 30. Compute the accounts receivable as of that date.

EXERCISE 8–2 Production Budget [LO3]
Crystal Telecom has budgeted the sales of its innovative mobile phone over the next four months as follows:

	Sales in Units
July	30,000
August	45,000
September	60,000
October	50,000

The company is now in the process of preparing a production budget for the third quarter. Past experience has shown that end-of-month finished goods inventories must equal 10% of the next month's sales. The inventory at the end of June was 3,000 units.

Required:
Prepare a production budget for the third quarter showing the number of units to be produced each month and for the quarter in total.

EXERCISE 8–3 Direct Materials Budget [LO4]
Micro Products, Inc., has developed a very powerful electronic calculator. Each calculator requires three small "chips" that cost $2 each and are purchased from an overseas supplier. Micro Products has prepared a production budget for the calculator by quarters for Year 2 and for the first quarter of Year 3, as shown below:

	Year 2				Year 3
	First	Second	Third	Fourth	First
Budgeted production, in calculators	60,000	90,000	150,000	100,000	80,000

The chip used in production of the calculator is sometimes hard to get, so it is necessary to carry large inventories as a precaution against stockouts. For this reason, the inventory of chips at the end of a quarter must equal 20% of the following quarter's production needs. A total of 36,000 chips will be on hand to start the first quarter of Year 2.

Required:
Prepare a direct materials budget for chips, by quarter and in total, for Year 2. At the bottom of your budget, show the dollar amount of purchases for each quarter and for the year in total.

EXERCISE 8–4 Direct Labor Budget [LO5]
The production manager of Junnen Corporation has submitted the following forecast of units to be produced for each quarter of the upcoming fiscal year.

	1st Quarter	2nd Quarter	3rd Quarter	4th Quarter
Units to be produced	5,000	4,400	4,500	4,900

Each unit requires 0.40 direct labor-hours and direct labor-hour workers are paid $11 per hour.

Required:
1. Construct the company's direct labor budget for the upcoming fiscal year, assuming that the direct labor workforce is adjusted each quarter to match the number of hours required to produce the forecasted number of units produced.
2. Construct the company's direct labor budget for the upcoming fiscal year, assuming that the direct labor workforce is *not* adjusted each quarter. Instead, assume that the company's direct labor workforce consists of permanent employees who are guaranteed to be paid for at least 1,800 hours of work each quarter. If the number of required direct labor-hours is less than this number, the workers are paid for 1,800 hours anyway. Any hours worked in excess of 1,800 hours in a quarter are paid at the rate of 1.5 times the normal hourly rate for direct labor.

EXERCISE 8–5 Manufacturing Overhead Budget [LO6]
The direct labor budget of Krispin Corporation for the upcoming fiscal year includes the following budgeted direct labor-hours.

	1st Quarter	2nd Quarter	3rd Quarter	4th Quarter
Budgeted direct labor-hours	5,000	4,800	5,200	5,400

The company's variable manufacturing overhead rate is $1.75 per direct labor-hour and the company's fixed manufacturing overhead is $35,000 per quarter. The only noncash item included in fixed manufacturing overhead is depreciation, which is $15,000 per quarter.

Required:

1. Construct the company's manufacturing overhead budget for the upcoming fiscal year.
2. Compute the company's manufacturing overhead rate (including both variable and fixed manufacturing overhead) for the upcoming fiscal year. Round off to the nearest whole cent.

EXERCISE 8–6 Selling and Administrative Expense Budget [LO7]

The budgeted unit sales of Haerve Company for the upcoming fiscal year are provided below:

	1st Quarter	2nd Quarter	3rd Quarter	4th Quarter
Budgeted unit sales	12,000	14,000	11,000	10,000

The company's variable selling and administrative expenses per unit are $2.75. Fixed selling and administrative expenses include advertising expenses of $12,000 per quarter, executive salaries of $40,000 per quarter, and depreciation of $16,000 per quarter. In addition, the company will make insurance payments of $6,000 in the 2nd Quarter and $6,000 in the 4th Quarter. Finally, property taxes of $6,000 will be paid in the 3rd Quarter.

Required:

Prepare the company's selling and administrative expense budget for the upcoming fiscal year.

EXERCISE 8–7 Cash Budget [LO8]

Forest Outfitters is a retailer that is preparing its budget for the upcoming fiscal year. Management has prepared the following summary of its budgeted cash flows:

	1st Quarter	2nd Quarter	3rd Quarter	4th Quarter
Total cash receipts	$340,000	$670,000	$410,000	$470,000
Total cash disbursements	$530,000	$450,000	$430,000	$480,000

The company's beginning cash balance for the upcoming fiscal year will be $50,000. The company requires a minimum cash balance of $30,000 and may borrow any amount needed from a local bank at a quarterly interest rate of 3%. The company may borrow any amount at the beginning of any quarter and may repay its loans, or any part of its loans, at the end of any quarter. Interest payments are due on any principal at the time it is repaid.

Required:

Prepare the company's cash budget for the upcoming fiscal year.

EXERCISE 8–8 Budgeted Income Statement [LO9]

Seattle Cat is the wholesale distributor of a small recreational catamaran sailboat. Management has prepared the following summary data to use in its annual budgeting process:

Budgeted unit sales	380
Selling price per unit	$1,850
Cost per unit	$1,425
Variable selling and administrative expenses (per unit)	$85
Fixed selling and administrative expenses (per year)	$105,000
Interest expense for the year	$11,000

Required:

Prepare the company's budgeted income statement using an absorption income statement format as shown in Schedule 9.

EXERCISE 8–9 Budgeted Balance Sheet [LO10]

The management of Academic Copy, a photocopying center located on University Avenue, has compiled the following data to use in preparing its budgeted balance sheet for next year:

	Ending Balances
Cash	?
Accounts receivable	$6,500
Supplies inventory	$2,100
Equipment	$28,000
Accumulated depreciation	$9,000
Accounts payable	$1,900
Common stock	$4,000
Retained earnings	?

The beginning balance of retained earnings was $21,000, net income is budgeted to be $8,600, and dividends are budgeted to be $3,500.

Required:

Prepare the company's budgeted balance sheet.

EXERCISE 8–10 Sales and Production Budgets [LO2, LO3]

The marketing department of Graber Corporation has submitted the following sales forecast for the upcoming fiscal year.

	1st Quarter	2nd Quarter	3rd Quarter	4th Quarter
Budgeted unit sales	16,000	15,000	14,000	15,000

The selling price of the company's product is $22.00 per unit. Management expects to collect 75% of sales in the quarter in which the sales are made, 20% in the following quarter, and 5% of sales are expected to be uncollectible. The beginning balance of accounts receivable, all of which is expected to be collected in the first quarter, is $66,000.

The company expects to start the first quarter with 3,200 units in finished goods inventory. Management desires an ending finished goods inventory in each quarter equal to 20% of the next quarter's budgeted sales. The desired ending finished goods inventory for the fourth quarter is 3,400 units.

Required:

1. Prepare the company's sales budget and schedule of expected cash collections.
2. Prepare the company's production budget for the upcoming fiscal year.

EXERCISE 8–11 Direct Materials and Direct Labor Budgets [LO4, LO5]

The production department of Priston Company has submitted the following forecast of units to be produced by quarter for the upcoming fiscal year.

	1st Quarter	2nd Quarter	3rd Quarter	4th Quarter
Units to be produced	6,000	7,000	8,000	5,000

In addition, the beginning raw materials inventory for the 1st Quarter is budgeted to be 3,600 pounds and the beginning accounts payable for the 1st Quarter is budgeted to be $11,775.

Each unit requires three pounds of raw material that costs $2.50 per pound. Management desires to end each quarter with a raw materials inventory equal to 20% of the following quarter's production needs. The desired ending inventory for the 4th Quarter is 3,700 pounds. Management plans to pay for 70% of raw material purchases in the quarter acquired and 30% in the following quarter. Each unit requires 0.50 direct labor-hours and direct labor-hour workers are paid $12 per hour.

Required:

1. Prepare the company's direct materials budget and schedule of expected cash disbursements for purchases of materials for the upcoming fiscal year.
2. Prepare the company's direct labor budget for the upcoming fiscal year, assuming that the direct labor workforce is adjusted each quarter to match the number of hours required to produce the forecasted number of units produced.

EXERCISE 8–12 Direct Labor and Manufacturing Overhead Budgets [LO5, LO6]

The Production Department of Harveton Corporation has submitted the following forecast of units to be produced by quarter for the upcoming fiscal year.

	1st Quarter	2nd Quarter	3rd Quarter	4th Quarter
Units to be produced	16,000	15,000	14,000	15,000

Each unit requires 0.80 direct labor-hours and direct labor-hour workers are paid $11.50 per hour.

In addition, the variable manufacturing overhead rate is $2.50 per direct labor-hour. The fixed manufacturing overhead is $90,000 per quarter. The only noncash element of manufacturing overhead is depreciation, which is $34,000 per quarter.

Required:

1. Prepare the company's direct labor budget for the upcoming fiscal year, assuming that the direct labor workforce is adjusted each quarter to match the number of hours required to produce the forecasted number of units produced.
2. Prepare the company's manufacturing overhead budget.

EXERCISE 8–13 Production and Direct Materials Budgets [LO3, LO4]

Tonga Toys manufactures and distributes a number of products to retailers. One of these products, Playclay, requires three pounds of material A135 in the manufacture of each unit. The company is now planning raw materials needs for the third quarter—July, August, and September. Peak sales of Playclay occur in the third quarter of each year. To keep production and shipments moving smoothly, the company has the following inventory requirements:

a. The finished goods inventory on hand at the end of each month must be equal to 5,000 units plus 30% of the next month's sales. The finished goods inventory on June 30 is budgeted to be 17,000 units.

b. The raw materials inventory on hand at the end of each month must be equal to one-half of the following month's production needs for raw materials. The raw materials inventory on June 30 for material A135 is budgeted to be 64,500 pounds.

c. The company maintains no work in process inventories.

A sales budget for Playclay for the last six months of the year follows.

	Budgeted Sales in Units
July	40,000
August	50,000
September	70,000
October	35,000
November	20,000
December	10,000

Required:

1. Prepare a production budget for Playclay for the months July, August, September, and October.
2. Examine the production budget that you prepared. Why will the company produce more units than it sells in July and August and less units than it sells in September and October?
3. Prepare a direct materials budget showing the quantity of material A135 to be purchased for July, August, and September and for the quarter in total.

EXERCISE 8–14 Schedules of Expected Cash Collections and Disbursements; Income Statement; Balance Sheet [LO2, LO4, LO9, LO10]

Colerain Corporation is a merchandising company that is preparing a profit plan for the third quarter of the calendar year. The company's balance sheet as of June 30 is shown below:

Colerain Corporation Balance Sheet June 30	
Assets	
Cash	$ 80,000
Accounts receivable	126,000
Inventory	52,000
Plant and equipment, net of depreciation	200,000
Total assets	$458,000
Liabilities and Stockholders' Equity	
Accounts payable	$ 61,100
Common stock	300,000
Retained earnings	96,900
Total liabilities and stockholders' equity	$458,000

Colerain's managers have made the following additional assumptions and estimates:

1. Estimated sales for July, August, September, and October will be $200,000, $220,000, 210,000, and $230,000, respectively.
2. All sales are on credit and all credit sales are collected. Each month's credit sales are collected 30% in the month of sale and 70% in the month following the sale. All of the accounts receivable at June 30 will be collected in July.
3. Each month's ending inventory must equal 40% of the cost of next month's sales. The cost of goods sold is 65% of sales. The company pays for 50% of its merchandise purchases in the month of the purchase and the remaining 50% in the month following the purchase. All of the accounts payable at June 30 will be paid in July.
4. Monthly selling and administrative expenses are always $65,000. Each month $5,000 of this total amount is depreciation expense and the remaining $60,000 relates to expenses that are paid in the month they are incurred.
5. The company does not plan to borrow money or pay or declare dividends during the quarter ended September 30. The company does not plan to issue any common stock or repurchase its own stock during the quarter ended September 30.

Required:

1. Prepare a schedule of expected cash collections for July, August, and September. Also compute total cash collections for the quarter ended September 30th.
2. *a.* Prepare a merchandise purchases budget for July, August, and September. Also compute total merchandise purchases for the quarter ended September 30th.

   b. Prepare a schedule of expected cash disbursements for merchandise purchases for July, August, and September. Also compute total cash disbursements for merchandise purchases for the quarter ended September 30th.
3. Prepare an income statement for the quarter ended September 30th. Use the absorption format shown in Schedule 9.
4. Prepare a balance sheet as of September 30th.

EXERCISE 8–15 Cash Budget Analysis [LO8]

A cash budget, by quarters, is shown on the following page for a retail company (000 omitted). The company requires a minimum cash balance of $5,000 to start each quarter.

	Quarter				
	1	2	3	4	Year
Cash balance, beginning	$ 9	$?	$?	$?	$?
Add collections from customers	?	?	125	?	391
Total cash available	85	?	?	?	?
Less disbursements:					
Purchases of inventory	40	58	?	32	?
Operating expenses	?	42	54	?	180
Equipment purchases	10	8	8	?	36
Dividends	2	2	2	2	?
Total disbursements	?	110	?	?	?
Excess (deficiency) of cash available over disbursements	(3)	?	30	?	?
Financing:					
Borrowings	?	20	—	—	?
Repayments (including interest)*	—	—	(?)	(7)	(?)
Total financing	?	?	?	?	?
Cash balance, ending	$?	$?	$?	$?	$?

*Interest will total $4,000 for the year.

Required:
Fill in the missing amounts in the table above.

Problems

All applicable problems are available with McGraw-Hill's *Connect™ Accounting*.

PROBLEM 8–16 Schedules of Expected Cash Collections and Disbursements [LO2, LO4, LO8]
Calgon Products, a distributor of organic beverages, needs a cash budget for September. The following information is available:

a. The cash balance at the beginning of September is $9,000.
b. Actual sales for July and August and expected sales for September are as follows:

	July	August	September
Cash sales	$ 6,500	$ 5,250	$ 7,400
Sales on account	20,000	30,000	40,000
Total sales	$26,500	$35,250	$47,400

Sales on account are collected over a three-month period as follows: 10% collected in the month of sale, 70% collected in the month following sale, and 18% collected in the second month following sale. The remaining 2% is uncollectible.

c. Purchases of inventory will total $25,000 for September. Twenty percent of a month's inventory purchases are paid for during the month of purchase. The accounts payable remaining from August's inventory purchases total $16,000, all of which will be paid in September.
d. Selling and administrative expenses are budgeted at $13,000 for September. Of this amount, $4,000 is for depreciation.

e. Equipment costing $18,000 will be purchased for cash during September, and dividends totaling $3,000 will be paid during the month.
f. The company maintains a minimum cash balance of $5,000. An open line of credit is available from the company's bank to bolster the cash balance as needed.

Required:
1. Prepare a schedule of expected cash collections for September.
2. Prepare a schedule of expected cash disbursements for inventory purchases for September.
3. Prepare a cash budget for September. Indicate in the financing section any borrowing that will be needed during September. Assume that any interest will not be paid until the following month.

PROBLEM 8–17 Cash Budget with Supporting Schedules [LO2, LO4, LO8]

Janus Products, Inc., is a merchandising company that sells binders, paper, and other school supplies. The company is planning its cash needs for the third quarter. In the past, Janus Products has had to borrow money during the third quarter to support peak sales of back-to-school materials, which occur during August. The following information has been assembled to assist in preparing a cash budget for the quarter:
a. Budgeted monthly absorption costing income statements for July–October are as follows:

	July	August	September	October
Sales	$40,000	$70,000	$50,000	$45,000
Cost of goods sold	24,000	42,000	30,000	27,000
Gross margin	16,000	28,000	20,000	18,000
Selling and administrative expenses:				
Selling expense	7,200	11,700	8,500	7,300
Administrative expense*	5,600	7,200	6,100	5,900
Total selling and administratire expenses	12,800	18,900	14,600	13,200
Net operating income	$ 3,200	$ 9,100	$ 5,400	$ 4,800

*Includes $2,000 depreciation each month.

b. Sales are 20% for cash and 80% on credit.
c. Credit sales are collected over a three-month period with 10% collected in the month of sale, 70% in the month following sale, and 20% in the second month following sale. May sales totaled $30,000, and June sales totaled $36,000.
d. Inventory purchases are paid for within 15 days. Therefore, 50% of a month's inventory purchases are paid for in the month of purchase. The remaining 50% is paid in the following month. Accounts payable for inventory purchases at June 30 total $11,700.
e. The company maintains its ending inventory levels at 75% of the cost of the merchandise to be sold in the following month. The merchandise inventory at June 30 is $18,000.
f. Land costing $4,500 will be purchased in July.
g. Dividends of $1,000 will be declared and paid in September.
h. The cash balance on June 30 is $8,000; the company must maintain a cash balance of at least this amount at the end of each month.
i. The company has an agreement with a local bank that allows it to borrow in increments of $1,000 at the beginning of each month, up to a total loan balance of $40,000. The interest rate on these loans is 1% per month, and for simplicity, we will assume that interest is not compounded. The company would, as far as it is able, repay the loan plus accumulated interest at the end of the quarter.

Required:
1. Prepare a schedule of expected cash collections for July, August, and September and for the quarter in total.
2. Prepare the following for merchandise inventory:

   a. A merchandise purchases budget for July, August, and September.
   b. A schedule of expected cash disbursements for merchandise purchases for July, August, and September and for the quarter in total.
3. Prepare a cash budget for July, August, and September and for the quarter in total.

PROBLEM 8–18 Cash Budget with Supporting Schedules; Changing Assumptions [LO2, LO4, LO8]
Refer to the data for Janus Products, Inc., in Problem 8–17. The company's president is interested in knowing how reducing inventory levels and collecting accounts receivable sooner will impact the cash budget. He revises the cash collection and ending inventory assumptions as follows:

1. Sales continue to be 20% for cash and 80% on credit. However, credit sales from July, August, and September are collected over a three-month period with 25% collected in the month of sale, 60% collected in the month following sale, and 15% in the second month following sale. Credit sales from May and June are collected during the third quarter using the collection percentages specified in Problem 8–17.
2. The company maintains its ending inventory levels for July, August, and September at 25% of the cost of merchandise to be sold in the following month. The merchandise inventory at June 30 remains $18,000 and accounts payable for inventory purchases at June 30 remains $11,700.

All other information from Problem 8–17 that is not referred to above remains the same.

Required:
1. Using the president's new assumptions in (1) above, prepare a schedule of expected cash collections for July, August, and September and for the quarter in total.
2. Using the president's new assumptions in (2) above, prepare the following for merchandise inventory:
   a. A merchandise purchases budget for July, August, and September.
   b. A schedule of expected cash disbursements for merchandise purchases for July, August, and September and for the quarter in total.
3. Using the president's new assumptions, prepare a cash budget for July, August, September, and for the quarter in total.
4. Prepare a brief memorandum for the president explaining how his revised assumptions affect the cash budget.

PROBLEM 8–19 Integration of Sales, Production, and Direct Materials Budgets [LO2, LO3, LO4]
Crydon, Inc., manufactures an advanced swim fin for scuba divers. Management is now preparing detailed budgets for the third quarter, July through September, and has assembled the following information to assist in preparing the budget:

a. The Marketing Department has estimated sales as follows for the remainder of the year (in pairs of swim fins):
   The selling price of the swim fins is $50 per pair.

July	6,000	October	4,000
August	7,000	November	3,000
September	5,000	December	3,000

b. All sales are on account. Based on past experience, sales are expected to be collected in the following pattern:

   40% in the month of sale
   50% in the month following sale
   10% uncollectible

   The beginning accounts receivable balance (excluding uncollectible amounts) on July 1 will be $130,000.
c. The company maintains finished goods inventories equal to 10% of the following month's sales. The inventory of finished goods on July 1 will be 600 pairs.

d. Each pair of swim fins requires 2 pounds of geico compound. To prevent shortages, the company would like the inventory of geico compound on hand at the end of each month to be equal to 20% of the following month's production needs. The inventory of geico compound on hand on July 1 will be 2,440 pounds.
e. Geico compound costs $2.50 per pound. Crydon pays for 60% of its purchases in the month of purchase; the remainder is paid for in the following month. The accounts payable balance for geico compound purchases will be $11,400 on July 1.

Required:
1. Prepare a sales budget, by month and in total, for the third quarter. (Show your budget in both pairs of swim fins and dollars.) Also prepare a schedule of expected cash collections, by month and in total, for the third quarter.
2. Prepare a production budget for each of the months July through October.
3. Prepare a direct materials budget for geico compound, by month and in total, for the third quarter. Also prepare a schedule of expected cash disbursements for geico compound, by month and in total, for the third quarter.

PROBLEM 8–20 Cash Budget; Income Statement; Balance Sheet [LO2, LO4, LO8, LO9, LO10]
The balance sheet of Phototec, Inc., a distributor of photographic supplies, as of May 31 is given below:

Phototec, Inc. Balance Sheet May 31	
Assets	
Cash	$ 8,000
Accounts receivable	72,000
Inventory	30,000
Buildings and equipment, net of depreciation	500,000
Total assets	$610,000
Liabilities and Stockholders' Equity	
Accounts payable	$ 90,000
Note payable	15,000
Capital stock	420,000
Retained earnings	85,000
Total liabilities and stockholders' equity	$610,000

The company is in the process of preparing a budget for June and has assembled the following data:
a. Sales are budgeted at $250,000 for June. Of these sales, $60,000 will be for cash; the remainder will be credit sales. One-half of a month's credit sales are collected in the month the sales are made, and the remainder is collected the following month. All of the May 31 accounts receivable will be collected in June.
b. Purchases of inventory are expected to total $200,000 during June. These purchases will all be on account. Forty percent of all inventory purchases are paid for in the month of purchase; the remainder are paid in the following month. All of the May 31 accounts payable to suppliers will be paid during June.
c. The June 30 inventory balance is budgeted at $40,000.
d. Selling and administrative expenses for June are budgeted at $51,000, exclusive of depreciation. These expenses will be paid in cash. Depreciation is budgeted at $2,000 for the month.
e. The note payable on the May 31 balance sheet will be paid during June. The company's interest expense for June (on all borrowing) will be $500, which will be paid in cash.
f. New warehouse equipment costing $9,000 will be purchased for cash during June.
g. During June, the company will borrow $18,000 from its bank by giving a new note payable to the bank for that amount. The new note will be due in one year.

Required:
1. Prepare a cash budget for June. Support your budget with a schedule of expected cash collections from sales and a schedule of expected cash disbursements for inventory purchases.
2. Prepare a budgeted income statement for June. Use the absorption costing income statement format as shown in Schedule 9.
3. Prepare a budgeted balance sheet as of June 30.

PROBLEM 8–21 Schedule of Expected Cash Collections; Cash Budget [LO2, LO8]

Natural Care Corp., a distributor of natural cosmetics, is ready to begin its third quarter, in which peak sales occur. The company has requested a $60,000, 90-day loan from its bank to help meet cash requirements during the quarter. Because Natural Care has experienced difficulty in paying off its loans in the past, the bank's loan officer has asked the company to prepare a cash budget for the quarter. In response to this request, the following data have been assembled:

a. On July 1, the beginning of the third quarter, the company will have a cash balance of $43,000.

b. Actual sales for the last two months and budgeted sales for the third quarter follow (all sales are on account):

May (actual)	$360,000
June (actual)	$280,000
July (budgeted)	$350,000
August (budgeted)	$420,000
September (budgeted)	$360,000

Past experience shows that 25% of a month's sales are collected in the month of sale, 70% in the month following sale, and 2% in the second month following sale. The remainder is uncollectible.

c. Budgeted merchandise purchases and budgeted expenses for the third quarter are given below:

	July	August	September
Merchandise purchases	$170,000	$155,000	$165,000
Salaries and wages	$70,000	$70,000	$65,000
Advertising	$80,000	$90,000	$100,000
Rent payments	$30,000	$30,000	$30,000
Depreciation	$40,000	$40,000	$40,000

Merchandise purchases are paid in full during the month following purchase. Accounts payable for merchandise purchases on June 30, which will be paid during July, total $160,000.

d. Equipment costing $25,000 will be purchased for cash during July.

e. In preparing the cash budget, assume that the $60,000 loan will be made in July and repaid in September. Interest on the loan will total $2,000.

Required:

1. Prepare a schedule of expected cash collections for July, August, and September and for the quarter in total.
2. Prepare a cash budget, by month and in total, for the third quarter.
3. If the company needs a minimum cash balance of $20,000 to start each month, can the loan be repaid as planned? Explain.

PROBLEM 8–22 Behavioral Aspects of Budgeting; Ethics and the Manager [LO1]

Granger Stokes, managing partner of the venture capital firm of Halston and Stokes, was dissatisfied with the top management of PrimeDrive, a manufacturer of computer disk drives. Halston and Stokes had invested $20 million in PrimeDrive, and the return on their investment had been unsatisfactory for several years. In a tense meeting of the board of directors of PrimeDrive, Stokes exercised his firm's rights as the major equity investor in PrimeDrive and fired PrimeDrive's chief executive officer (CEO). He then quickly moved to have the board of directors of PrimeDrive appoint himself as the new CEO.

Stokes prided himself on his hard-driving management style. At the first management meeting, he asked two of the managers to stand and fired them on the spot, just to show everyone who was in control of the company. At the budget review meeting that followed, he ripped up the departmental budgets that had been submitted for his review and yelled at the managers for their "wimpy, do nothing targets." He then ordered everyone to submit new budgets calling for at least a 40% increase in sales volume and announced that he would not accept excuses for results that fell below budget.

Keri Kalani, an accountant working for the production manager at PrimeDrive, discovered toward the end of the year that her boss had not been scrapping defective disk drives that had been returned by customers. Instead, he had been shipping them in new cartons to other customers to avoid booking losses. Quality control had deteriorated during the year as a result of the push for increased volume, and returns of defective TRX drives were running as high as 15% of the new drives shipped. When she confronted her boss with her discovery, he told her to mind her own business. And then, to justify his actions, he said, "All of us managers are finding ways to hit Stokes's targets."

Required:

1. Is Granger Stokes using budgets as a planning and control tool?
2. What are the behavioral consequences of the way budgets are being used at PrimeDrive?
3. What, if anything, do you think Keri Kalani should do?

(CMA, adapted)

PROBLEM 8–23 Schedule of Expected Cash Collections; Cash Budget [LO2, LO8]

Jodi Horton, president of the retailer Crestline Products, has just approached the company's bank with a request for a $30,000, 90-day loan. The purpose of the loan is to assist the company in acquiring inventories in support of peak April sales. Because the company has had some difficulty in paying off its loans in the past, the loan officer has asked for a cash budget to help determine whether the loan should be made. The following data are available for the months April–June, during which the loan will be used:

a. On April 1, the start of the loan period, the cash balance will be $26,000. Accounts receivable on April 1 will total $151,500, of which $141,000 will be collected during April and $7,200 will be collected during May. The remainder will be uncollectible.
b. Past experience shows that 20% of a month's sales are collected in the month of sale, 75% in the month following sale, and 4% in the second month following sale. The other 1% represents bad debts that are never collected. Budgeted sales and expenses for the three-month period follow:

	April	May	June
Sales (all on account)	$200,000	$300,000	$250,000
Merchandise purchases	$120,000	$180,000	$150,000
Payroll.	$9,000	$9,000	$8,000
Lease payments	$15,000	$15,000	$15,000
Advertising	$70,000	$80,000	$60,000
Equipment purchases	$8,000	—	—
Depreciation	$10,000	$10,000	$10,000

c. Merchandise purchases are paid in full during the month following purchase. Accounts payable for merchandise purchases on March 31, which will be paid during April, total $108,000.
d. In preparing the cash budget, assume that the $30,000 loan will be made in April and repaid in June. Interest on the loan will total $1,200.

Required:

1. Prepare a schedule of expected cash collections for April, May, and June and for the three months in total.
2. Prepare a cash budget, by month and in total, for the three-month period.
3. If the company needs a minimum cash balance of $20,000 to start each month, can the loan be repaid as planned? Explain.

PROBLEM 8–24 Cash Budget with Supporting Schedules [LO2, LO4, LO7, LO8]

The president of Univax, Inc., has just approached the company's bank seeking short-term financing for the coming year, Year 2. Univax is a distributor of commercial vacuum cleaners. The bank has stated that the loan request must be accompanied by a detailed cash budget that shows the quarters in which financing will be needed, as well as the amounts that will be needed and the quarters in which repayments can be made.

To provide this information for the bank, the president has directed that the following data be gathered from which a cash budget can be prepared:

a. Budgeted sales and merchandise purchases for Year 2, as well as actual sales and purchases for the last quarter of Year 1, are as follows:

	A	B	C
1			
2		*Sales*	*Merchandise Purchases*
3	Year 1:		
4	Fourth quarter actual	$300,000	$180,000
5	Year 2:		
6	First quarter estimated	$400,000	$260,000
7	Second quarter estimated	$500,000	$310,000
8	Third quarter estimated	$600,000	$370,000
9	Fourth quarter estimated	$480,000	$240,000
10			

b. The company typically collects 33% of a quarter's sales before the quarter ends and another 65% in the following quarter. The remainder is uncollectible. This pattern of collections is now being experienced in the actual data for the Year 1 fourth quarter.

c. Some 20% of a quarter's merchandise purchases are paid for within the quarter. The remainder is paid in the following quarter.

d. Selling and administrative expenses for Year 2 are budgeted at $90,000 per quarter plus 12% of sales. Of the fixed amount, $20,000 each quarter is depreciation.

e. The company will pay $10,000 in cash dividends each quarter.

f. Land purchases will be made as follows during the year: $80,000 in the second quarter and $48,500 in the third quarter.

g. The Cash account contained $20,000 at the end of Year 1. The company must maintain a minimum cash balance of at least $18,000.

h. The company has an agreement with a local bank that allows the company to borrow in increments of $10,000 at the beginning of each quarter, up to a total loan balance of $100,000. The interest rate on these loans is 1% per month, and for simplicity, we will assume that interest is not compounded. The company would, as far as it is able, repay the loan plus accumulated interest at the end of the year.

i. At present, the company has no loans outstanding.

Required:

1. Prepare the following, by quarter and in total, for Year 2:
   a. A schedule of expected cash collections on sales.
   b. A schedule of expected cash disbursements for merchandise purchases.
2. Compute the expected cash disbursements for selling and administrative expenses, by quarter and in total, for Year 2.
3. Prepare a cash budget by quarter and in total for Year 2.

PROBLEM 8–25 Behavioral Aspects of Budgeting [LO1]

Five years ago, Jack Cadence left his position at a large company to start Advanced Technologies Co. (ATC), a software design company. ATC's first product was a unique software package that seamlessly integrates networked PCs. Robust sales of this initial product permitted the company to begin development of other software products and to hire additional personnel. The staff at ATC quickly grew from three people working out of Cadence's basement to over 70 individuals working in leased spaces at an industrial park. Continued growth led Cadence to hire seasoned marketing, distribution, and production managers and an experienced accountant, Bill Cross.

Recently, Cadence decided that the company had become too large to run on an informal basis and that a formalized planning and control program centered around a budget was necessary. Cadence asked the accountant, Bill Cross, to work with him in developing the initial budget for ATC.

Cadence forecasted sales revenues based on his projections for both the market growth for the initial software and successful completion of new products. Cross used this data to construct the master budget for the company, which he then broke down into departmental budgets. Cadence and Cross met a number of times over a three-week period to hammer out the details of the budgets.

When Cadence and Cross were satisfied with their work, the various departmental budgets were distributed to the department managers with a cover letter explaining ATC's new budgeting system. The letter requested everyone's assistance in working together to achieve the budget objectives.

Several of the department managers were displeased with how the budgeting process was undertaken. In discussing the situation among themselves, they felt that some of the budget projections were overly optimistic and not realistically attainable.

Required:

1. How does the budgeting process Cadence and Cross used at ATC differ from recommended practice?
2. What are the behavioral implications of the way Cadence and Cross went about preparing the master budget?

(CMA, adapted)

PROBLEM 8–26 Completing a Master Budget [LO2, LO4, LO7, LO8, LO9, LO10]

The following data relate to the operations of Picanuy Corporation, a wholesale distributor of consumer goods:

Current assets as of December 31:	
Cash	$6,000
Accounts receivable	$36,000
Inventory	$9,800
Buildings and equipment, net	$110,885
Accounts payable	$32,550
Capital stock	$100,000
Retained earnings	$30,135

a. The gross margin is 30% of sales. (In other words, cost of goods sold is 70% of sales.)

b. Actual and budgeted sales data are as follows:

December (actual)	$60,000
January	$70,000
February	$80,000
March	$85,000
April	$55,000

c. Sales are 40% for cash and 60% on credit. Credit sales are collected in the month following sale. The accounts receivable at December 31 are the result of December credit sales.

d. Each month's ending inventory should equal 20% of the following month's budgeted cost of goods sold.

e. One-quarter of a month's inventory purchases is paid for in the month of purchase; the other three-quarters is paid for in the following month. The accounts payable at December 31 are the result of December purchases of inventory.

f. Monthly expenses are as follows: commissions, $12,000; rent, $1,800; other expenses (excluding depreciation), 8% of sales. Assume that these expenses are paid monthly. Depreciation is $2,400 for the quarter and includes depreciation on new assets acquired during the quarter.

g. Equipment will be acquired for cash: $3,000 in January and $8,000 in February.

h. Management would like to maintain a minimum cash balance of $5,000 at the end of each month. The company has an agreement with a local bank that allows the company to borrow in increments of $1,000 at the beginning of each month, up to a total loan balance of $50,000. The interest rate on these loans is 1% per month, and for simplicity, we will assume that interest is not compounded. The company would, as far as it is able, repay the loan plus accumulated interest at the end of the quarter.

Required:

Using the data above:

1. Complete the following schedule:

Schedule of Expected Cash Collections

	January	February	March	Quarter
Cash sales	$28,000			
Credit sales	36,000			
Total collections	$64,000			

2. Complete the following:

Merchandise Purchases Budget	January	February	March	Quarter
Budgeted cost of goods sold	$49,000*			
Add desired ending inventory	11,200†			
Total needs	60,200			
Less beginning inventory	9,800			
Required purchases	$50,400			

*$70,000 sales × 70% = $49,000.
†$80,000 × 70% × 20% = $11,200.

Schedule of Expected Cash Disbursements—Merchandise Purchases	January	February	March	Quarter
December purchases	$32,550*			$32,550
January purchases	12,600	$37,800		50,400
February purchases				
March purchases				
Total disbursements	$45,150			

*Beginning balance of the accounts payable.

3. Complete the following schedule:

Schedule of Expected Cash Disbursements—Selling and Administrative Expenses	January	February	March	Quarter
Commissions	$12,000			
Rent	1,800			
Other expenses	5,600			
Total disbursements	$19,400			

4. Complete the following cash budget:

Cash Budget	January	February	March	Quarter
Cash balance, beginning	$ 6,000			
Add cash collections	64,000			
Total cash available	70,000			
Less cash disbursements:				
For inventory	45,150			
For operating expenses	19,400			
For equipment	3,000			
Total cash disbursements	67,550			
Excess (deficiency) of cash	2,450			
Financing				
Etc.				

5. Prepare an absorption costing income statement, similar to the one shown in Schedule 9 in the chapter, for the quarter ended March 31.
6. Prepare a balance sheet as of March 31.

PROBLEM 8–27 Completing a Master Budget [LO2, LO4, LO7, LO8, LO9, LO10]
Nordic Company, a merchandising company, prepares its master budget on a quarterly basis. The following data have been assembled to assist in preparation of the master budget for the second quarter.

a. As of March 31 (the end of the prior quarter), the company's balance sheet showed the following account balances:

Cash	$ 9,000	
Accounts receivable	48,000	
Inventory	12,600	
Buildings and equipment (net)	214,100	
Accounts payable		$ 18,300
Capital stock		190,000
Retained earnings		75,400
	$283,700	$283,700

b. Actual sales for March and budgeted sales for April–July are as follows:

March (actual)	$60,000
April	$70,000
May	$85,000
June	$90,000
July	$50,000

c. Sales are 20% for cash and 80% on credit. All payments on credit sales are collected in the month following the sale. The accounts receivable at March 31 are a result of March credit sales.

d. The company's gross margin percentage is 40% of sales. (In other words, cost of goods sold is 60% of sales.)

e. Monthly selling and administrative expenses are budgeted as follows: salaries and wages, $7,500 per month; shipping, 6% of sales; advertising, $6,000 per month; other expenses, 4% of sales. Depreciation, including depreciation on new assets acquired during the quarter, will be $6,000 for the quarter.

f. Each month's ending inventory should equal 30% of the following month's cost of goods sold.

g. Half of a month's inventory purchases are paid for in the month of purchase and half in the following month.

h. Equipment purchases during the quarter will be as follows: April, $11,500; and May, $3,000.

i. Dividends totaling $3,500 will be declared and paid in June.

j. Management wants to maintain a minimum cash balance of $8,000. The company has an agreement with a local bank that allows the company to borrow in increments of $1,000 at the beginning of each month, up to a total loan balance of $20,000. The interest rate on these loans is 1% per month, and for simplicity, we will assume that interest is not compounded. The company would, as far as it is able, repay the loan plus accumulated interest at the end of the quarter.

Required:

Using the data above, complete the following statements and schedules for the second quarter:

1. Schedule of expected cash collections:

	April	May	June	Total
Cash sales	$14,000			
Credit sales	48,000			
Total collections	$62,000			

2. *a.* Merchandise purchases budget:

	April	May	June	Total
Budgeted cost of goods sold	$42,000*	$51,000		
Add desired ending inventory	15,300†			
Total needs	57,300			
Less beginning inventory	12,600			
Required purchases	$44,700			

*$70,000 sales × 60% = $42,000.

†$51,000 × 30% = $15,300.

b. Schedule of expected cash disbursements for merchandise purchases:

	April	May	June	Total
For March purchases	$18,300			$18,300
For April purchases	22,350	$22,350		44,700
For May purchases				
For June purchases				
Total cash disbursements for purchases	$40,650			

3. Schedule of expected cash disbursements for selling and administrative expenses:

	April	May	June	Total
Salaries and wages	$ 7,500			
Shipping	4,200			
Advertising	6,000			
Other expenses	2,800			
Total cash disbursements for selling and administrative expenses	$20,500			

4. Cash budget:

	April	May	June	Total
Cash balance, beginning	$ 9,000			
Add cash collections	62,000			
Total cash available	71,000			
Less cash disbursements:				
For inventory purchases	40,650			
For selling and administrative expenses	20,500			
For equipment purchases	11,500			
For dividends	—			
Total cash disbursements	72,650			
Excess (deficiency) of cash	(1,650)			
Financing				
Etc.				

5. Prepare an absorption costing income statement for the quarter ending June 30 as shown in Schedule 9 in the chapter.
6. Prepare a balance sheet as of June 30.

Cases

All applicable cases are available with McGraw-Hill's *Connect™ Accounting*.

CASE 8–28 Evaluating a Company's Budget Procedures [LO1]

Tom Emory and Jim Morris strolled back to their plant from the administrative offices of Ferguson & Son Manufacturing Company. Tom is manager of the machine shop in the company's factory; Jim is manager of the equipment maintenance department.

The men had just attended the monthly performance evaluation meeting for plant department heads. These meetings had been held on the third Tuesday of each month since Robert Ferguson, Jr., the president's son, had become plant manager a year earlier.

As they were walking, Tom Emory spoke: "Boy, I hate those meetings! I never know whether my department's accounting reports will show good or bad performance. I'm beginning to expect the worst. If the accountants say I saved the company a dollar, I'm called 'Sir,' but if I spend even a little too much—boy, do I get in trouble. I don't know if I can hold on until I retire."

Tom had just been given the worst evaluation he had ever received in his long career with Ferguson & Son. He was the most respected of the experienced machinists in the company. He had been with Ferguson & Son for many years and was promoted to supervisor of the machine shop when the company expanded and moved to its present location. The president (Robert Ferguson, Sr.) had often stated that the company's success was due to the high-quality work of machinists like Tom. As supervisor, Tom stressed the importance of craftsmanship and told his workers that he wanted no sloppy work coming from his department.

When Robert Ferguson, Jr., became the plant manager, he directed that monthly performance comparisons be made between actual and budgeted costs for each department. The departmental budgets were intended to encourage the supervisors to reduce inefficiencies and to seek cost reduction opportunities. The company controller was instructed to have his staff "tighten" the budget slightly whenever a department attained its budget in a given month; this was done to reinforce the plant manager's desire to reduce costs. The young plant manager often stressed the importance of continued progress toward attaining the budget; he also made it known that he kept a file of these performance reports for future reference when he succeeded his father.

Tom Emory's conversation with Jim Morris continued as follows:

Emory: I really don't understand. We've worked so hard to meet the budget, and the minute we do so they tighten it on us. We can't work any faster and still maintain quality. I think my men are ready to quit trying. Besides, those reports don't tell the whole story. We always seem to be interrupting the big jobs for all those small rush orders. All that setup and machine adjustment time is killing us. And quite frankly, Jim, you were no help. When our hydraulic press broke down last month, your people were nowhere to be found. We had to take it apart ourselves and got stuck with all that idle time.

Morris: I'm sorry about that, Tom, but you know my department has had trouble making budget, too. We were running well behind at the time of that problem, and if we'd spent a day on that old machine, we would never have made it up. Instead we made the scheduled inspections of the forklift trucks because we knew we could do those in less than the budgeted time.

Emory: Well, Jim, at least you have some options. I'm locked into what the scheduling department assigns to me and you know they're being harassed by sales for those special orders. Incidentally, why didn't your report show all the supplies you guys wasted last month when you were working in Bill's department?

Morris: We're not out of the woods on that deal yet. We charged the maximum we could to other work and haven't even reported some of it yet.

Emory: Well, I'm glad you have a way of avoiding the pressure. The accountants seem to know everything that's happening in my department, sometimes even before I do. I thought all that budget and accounting stuff was supposed to help, but it just gets me into trouble. It's all a big pain. I'm trying to put out quality work; they're trying to save pennies.

Required:

1. Identify the problems that exist in Ferguson & Son Manufacturing Company's budgetary control system and explain how the problems are likely to reduce the effectiveness of the system.
2. Explain how Ferguson & Son Manufacturing Company's budgetary control system could be revised to improve its effectiveness.

(CMA, adapted)

CASE 8–29 Master Budget with Supporting Schedules [LO2, LO4, LO8, LO9, LO10]

You have just been hired as a management trainee by Cravat Sales Company, a nationwide distributor of a designer's silk ties. The company has an exclusive franchise on the distribution of the ties, and sales have grown so rapidly over the last few years that it has become necessary to add new members to the management team. You have been given responsibility for all planning and budgeting. Your first assignment is to prepare a master budget for the next three months, starting April 1. You are anxious to make a favorable impression on the president and have assembled the information below.

The company desires a minimum ending cash balance each month of $10,000. The ties are sold to retailers for $8 each. Recent and forecasted sales in units are as follows:

January (actual)	20,000	June	60,000
February (actual)	24,000	July	40,000
March (actual)	28,000	August	36,000
April	35,000	September	32,000
May	45,000		

The large buildup in sales before and during June is due to Father's Day. Ending inventories are supposed to equal 90% of the next month's sales in units. The ties cost the company $5 each.

Purchases are paid for as follows: 50% in the month of purchase and the remaining 50% in the following month. All sales are on credit, with no discount, and payable within 15 days. The company has found, however, that only 25% of a month's sales are collected by month-end. An additional 50% is collected in the following month, and the remaining 25% is collected in the second month following sale. Bad debts have been negligible.

The company's monthly selling and administrative expenses are given below:

Variable:	
Sales commissions	$1 per tie
Fixed:	
Wages and salaries	$22,000
Utilities	$14,000
Insurance	$1,200
Depreciation	$1,500
Miscellaneous	$3,000

All selling and administrative expenses are paid during the month, in cash, with the exception of depreciation and insurance expired. Land will be purchased during May for $25,000 cash. The company declares dividends of $12,000 each quarter, payable in the first month of the following quarter. The company's balance sheet at March 31 is given below:

Assets	
Cash	$ 14,000
Accounts receivable ($48,000 February sales; $168,000 March sales)	216,000
Inventory (31,500 units)	157,500
Prepaid insurance	14,400
Fixed assets, net of depreciation	172,700
Total assets	$574,600
Liabilities and Stockholders' Equity	
Accounts payable	$ 85,750
Dividends payable	12,000
Capital stock	300,000
Retained earnings	176,850
Total liabilities and stockholders' equity	$574,600

The company has an agreement with a bank that allows it to borrow in increments of $1,000 at the beginning of each month, up to a total loan balance of $150,000. The interest rate on these loans is 1% per month, and for simplicity, we will assume that interest is not compounded. At the end of the quarter, the company would pay the bank all of the accumulated interest on the loan and as much of the loan as possible (in increments of $1,000), while still retaining at least $10,000 in cash.

Required:

Prepare a master budget for the three-month period ending June 30. Include the following detailed budgets:

1. *a.* A sales budget by month and in total.
   b. A schedule of expected cash collections from sales, by month and in total.
   c. A merchandise purchases budget in units and in dollars. Show the budget by month and in total.
   d. A schedule of expected cash disbursements for merchandise purchases, by month and in total.
2. A cash budget. Show the budget by month and in total.
3. A budgeted income statement for the three-month period ending June 30. Use the contribution approach.
4. A budgeted balance sheet as of June 30.

Chapter 9

Flexible Budgets and Performance Analysis

BUSINESS FOCUS

The Inevitability of Forecasting Errors

While companies derive numerous benefits from planning for the future, they must be able to respond when actual results deviate from the plan. For example, just two months after telling Wall Street analysts that it would break even for the first quarter of 2005, General Motors (GM) acknowledged that its actual sales were far less than its original forecast and the company would lose $850 million in the quarter. For the year, GM acknowledged that projected earnings would be 80% lower than previously indicated. The company's stock price dropped by $4.71.

When a company's plans deviate from its actual results, managers need to understand the reasons for the deviations. How much is caused by the fact that actual sales differ from budgeted sales? How much is caused by the actions of managers? In the case of GM, the actual level of sales is far less than the budget, so some actual costs are likely to be less than originally budgeted. These lower costs do not signal managerial effectiveness. This chapter explains how to analyze the sources of discrepancies between budgeted and actual results. ■

Source: Alex Taylor III, "GM Hits the Skids," *Fortune*, April 4, 2005, pp. 71–74.

LEARNING OBJECTIVES

After studying Chapter 9, you should be able to:

- **LO1** Prepare a flexible budget.
- **LO2** Prepare a report showing activity variances.
- **LO3** Prepare a report showing revenue and spending variances.
- **LO4** Prepare a performance report that combines activity variances and revenue and spending variances.
- **LO5** Prepare a flexible budget with more than one cost driver.
- **LO6** Understand common errors made in preparing performance reports based on budgets and actual results.

In the last chapter we explored how budgets are developed before a period begins. Budgeting involves a lot of time and effort and the results of the budgeting process should not be shoved into a filing cabinet and forgotten. To be useful, budgets should provide guidance in conducting actual operations and should be part of the performance evaluation process. However, managers need to be very careful about how budgets are used. In government, budgets often establish how much will be spent, and indeed, spending more than was budgeted may be a criminal offense. That is not true in other organizations. In for-profit organizations, actual spending will rarely be the same as the spending that was budgeted at the beginning of the period. The reason is that the actual level of activity (such as unit sales) will rarely be the same as the budgeted activity; therefore, many actual costs and revenues will naturally differ from what was budgeted. Should a manager be penalized for spending 10% more than budgeted for a variable cost like direct materials if unit sales are 10% higher than budgeted? Of course not. In this chapter we will explore how budgets can be adjusted so that meaningful comparisons to actual costs can be made.

Flexible Budgets

Characteristics of a Flexible Budget

LEARNING OBJECTIVE 1
Prepare a flexible budget.

The budgets that we explored in the last chapter were *planning budgets.* A **planning budget** is prepared before the period begins and is valid for only the planned level of activity. A static planning budget is suitable for planning but is inappropriate for evaluating how well costs are controlled. If the actual level of activity differs from what was planned, it would be misleading to compare actual costs to the static, unchanged planning budget. If activity is higher than expected, variable costs should be higher than expected; and if activity is lower than expected, variable costs should be lower than expected.

Flexible budgets take into account how changes in activity affect costs. A **flexible budget** is an estimate of what revenues and costs should have been, given the actual level of activity for the period. When a flexible budget is used in performance evaluation, actual costs are compared to what the costs *should have been for the actual level of activity during the period* rather than to the static planning budget. This is a very important distinction. If adjustments for the level of activity are not made, it is very difficult to interpret discrepancies between budgeted and actual costs.

IN BUSINESS

WHY DO COMPANIES NEED FLEXIBLE BUDGETS?

The difficulty of accurately predicting future financial performance can be readily understood by reading the annual report of any publicly traded company. For example Nucor Corporation, a steel manufacturer headquartered in Charlotte, North Carolina, cites numerous reasons why its actual results may differ from expectations, including the following: (1) the supply and cost of raw materials, electricity, and natural gas may change unexpectedly; (2) the market demand for steel products may change; (3) competitive pressures from imports and substitute materials may intensify; (4) uncertainties regarding the global economy may affect customer demand; (5) changes to U.S. and foreign trade policy may alter current importing and exporting practices; and (6) new government regulations could significantly increase environmental compliance costs. Each of these factors could cause static budget revenues and/or costs to differ from actual results.

Source: Nucor Corporation 2004 annual report, p. 3.

EXHIBIT 9–1
Planning Budget

Rick's Hairstyling Planning Budget For the Month Ended March 31	
Budgeted client-visits (q)	1,000
Revenue (180.00q$)	$180,000
Expenses:	
Wages and salaries ($65,000 + 37.00q$)	102,000
Hairstyling supplies (1.50q$)	1,500
Client gratuities (4.10q$)	4,100
Electricity ($1,500 + 0.10q$)	1,600
Rent ($28,500)	28,500
Liability insurance ($2,800)	2,800
Employee health insurance ($21,300)	21,300
Miscellaneous ($1,200 + 0.20q$)	1,400
Total expense	163,200
Net operating income	$ 16,800

Deficiencies of the Static Planning Budget

To illustrate the difference between a static planning budget and a flexible budget, consider Rick's Hairstyling, an upscale hairstyling salon located in Beverly Hills that is owned and managed by Rick Manzi. The salon has very loyal customers—many of whom are associated with the film industry. Recently Rick has been attempting to get better control of his revenues and costs, and at the urging of his accounting and business adviser, Victoria Kho, he has begun to prepare monthly budgets. Victoria Kho is an accountant in independent practice who specializes in small service-oriented businesses like Rick's Hairstyling.

At the end of February, Rick prepared the March budget that appears in Exhibit 9–1. Rick believes that the number of customers served in a month is the best way to measure the overall level of activity in his salon. He refers to these visits as client-visits. A customer who comes into the salon and has his or her hair styled is counted as one client-visit.

Note that the term *revenue* is used in the planning budget rather than *sales.* We use the term revenue throughout the chapter because some organizations have sources of revenue other than sales. For example, donations, as well as sales, are counted as revenue in nonprofit organizations.

Rick has identified eight major categories of costs—wages and salaries, hairstyling supplies, client gratuities, electricity, rent, liability insurance, employee health insurance, and miscellaneous. Client gratuities consist of flowers, candies, and glasses of champagne that Rick gives to his customers while they are in the salon.

Working with Victoria, Rick had already estimated a cost formula for each cost. For example, they determined that the cost formula for electricity should be $1,500 + 0.10q$, where q equals the number of client-visits. In other words, electricity is a mixed cost with a $1,500 fixed element and a $0.10 per client-visit variable element. Once the budgeted level of activity was set at 1,000 client-visits, it was easy to compute the budgeted amount for each line item in the budget. For example, using the cost formula, the budgeted cost for electricity was set at $1,600 (= $1,500 + $0.10 × 1,000).

At the end of March, Rick found that his actual profit was $21,230 as shown in the income statement in Exhibit 9–2. It is important to realize that the actual results are *not* determined by plugging the actual number of client-visits into the revenue and cost formulas. The formulas are simply estimates of what the revenues and costs should be for a given level of activity. What actually happens usually differs from what is supposed to happen.

Referring back to Exhibit 9–1, the budgeted net operating income was $16,800, so the actual profit was substantially higher than planned at the beginning of the month. This

EXHIBIT 9–2
Actual Results—Income Statement

Rick's Hairstyling Income Statement For the Month Ended March 31	
Actual client-visits	1,100
Revenue	$194,200
Expenses:	
Wages and salaries	106,900
Hairstyling supplies	1,620
Client gratuities	6,870
Electricity	1,550
Rent	28,500
Liability insurance	2,800
Employee health insurance	22,600
Miscellaneous	2,130
Total expense	172,970
Net operating income	$ 21,230

was, of course, good news, but Rick wanted to know more. Business was up by 10%—the salon had 1,100 client-visits instead of the budgeted 1,000 client-visits. Could this alone explain the higher net income? The answer is no. An increase in net operating income of 10% would have resulted in net operating income of only $18,480 (= 1.1 × $16,800), not the $21,230 actually earned during the month. What is responsible for this better outcome? Higher prices? Lower costs? Something else? Whatever the cause, Rick would like to know the answer and then hopefully repeat the same performance next month.

In an attempt to analyze what happened in March, Rick prepared the report comparing actual to budgeted costs that appears in Exhibit 9–3. Note that most of the variances in this report are labeled unfavorable (U) rather than favorable (F) even though net operating income was actually higher than expected. For example, wages and salaries show an unfavorable variance of $4,900 because the budget called for wages and salaries of $102,000, whereas the actual wages and salaries expense was $106,900. The problem with the report, as Rick immediately realized, is that it compares revenues and costs at one level of activity (1,000 client-visits) to revenues and costs at a different level of activity (1,100 client-visits). This is like comparing apples to oranges. Because Rick had 100 more client-visits than expected, some of his costs should be higher than budgeted. From Rick's standpoint, the increase in activity was good and should be counted as a favorable variance, but the increase in activity has an apparently negative impact on most of the costs in the report. Rick knew that something would have to be done to make the report more meaningful, but he was unsure of what to do. So he made an appointment to meet with Victoria Kho to discuss the next step.

MANAGERIAL ACCOUNTING IN ACTION
The Issue

RICK'S Hairstyling Salon

Victoria: How is the budgeting going?
Rick: Pretty well. I didn't have any trouble putting together the budget for March. I also prepared a report comparing the actual results for March to the budget, but that report isn't giving me what I really want to know.
Victoria: Because your actual level of activity didn't match your budgeted activity?
Rick: Right. I know the level of activity shouldn't affect my fixed costs, but we had more client-visits than I had expected and that had to affect my other costs.
Victoria: So you want to know whether the higher actual costs are justified by the higher level of activity?
Rick: Precisely.
Victoria: If you leave your reports and data with me, I can work on it later today, and by tomorrow I'll have a report to show you.

EXHIBIT 9–3
Comparison of Static Planning Budget to Actual Results

Rick's Hairstyling
Comparison of Planning Budget to Actual Results
For the Month Ended March 31

	Planning Budget	Actual Results	Variances
Client-visits	1,000	1,100	
Revenue	$180,000	$194,200	$14,200 F
Expenses:			
Wages and salaries	102,000	106,900	4,900 U
Hairstyling supplies	1,500	1,620	120 U
Client gratuities	4,100	6,870	2,770 U
Electricity	1,600	1,550	50 F
Rent	28,500	28,500	0
Liability insurance	2,800	2,800	0
Employee health insurance	21,300	22,600	1,300 U
Miscellaneous	1,400	2,130	730 U
Total expense	163,200	172,970	9,770 U
Net operating income	$ 16,800	$ 21,230	$ 4,430 F

How a Flexible Budget Works

A flexible budget approach recognizes that a budget can be adjusted to show what costs *should be* for the actual level of activity. To illustrate how flexible budgets work, Victoria prepared the report in Exhibit 9–4 that shows what the *revenues and costs should have been given the actual level of activity* in March. Preparing the report is straightforward. The cost formula for each cost is used to estimate what the cost should have been for 1,100 client-visits—the actual level of activity for March. For example, using the cost formula $1,500 + $0.10*q*, the cost of electricity in March *should have been* $1,610 (= $1,500 + $0.10 × 1,100).

We can see from the flexible budget that the net operating income in March *should have been* $30,510, but recall from Exhibit 9–2 that the net operating income was actually only $21,230. The results are not as good as we thought. Why? We will answer that question shortly.

EXHIBIT 9–4
Flexible Budget Based on Actual Activity

Rick's Hairstyling
Flexible Budget
For the Month Ended March 31

Actual client-visits (*q*)	1,100
Revenue ($180.00*q*)	$198,000
Expenses:	
Wages and salaries ($65,000 + $37.00*q*)	105,700
Hairstyling supplies ($1.50*q*)	1,650
Client gratuities ($4.10*q*)	4,510
Electricity ($1,500 + $0.10*q*)	1,610
Rent ($28,500)	28,500
Liability insurance ($2,800)	2,800
Employee health insurance ($21,300)	21,300
Miscellaneous ($1,200 + $0.20*q*)	1,420
Total expense	167,490
Net operating income	$ 30,510

To summarize to this point, Rick had budgeted for a profit of $16,800. The actual profit was quite a bit higher—$21,230. However, given the amount of business in March, the profit should have been even higher—$30,510. What are the causes of these discrepancies? Rick would certainly like to build on the positive factors, while working to reduce the negative factors. But what are they?

Flexible Budget Variances

To answer Rick's questions concerning the discrepancies between budgeted and actual costs, we will need to break down the variances shown in Exhibit 9–3 into two types of variances—activity variances and revenue and spending variances. We do that in the next two sections.

Activity Variances

LEARNING OBJECTIVE 2
Prepare a report showing activity variances.

Part of the discrepancy between the budgeted profit and the actual profit is due to the fact that the actual level of activity in March was higher than expected. How much of this discrepancy was due to this single factor? The report in Exhibit 9–5 is designed to answer this question. In that report, the planning budget from the beginning of the period is compared to the flexible budget based on the actual level of activity for the period. The planning budget shows what should have happened at the budgeted level of activity whereas the flexible budget shows what should have happened at the actual level of activity. Therefore, the differences between the planning budget and the flexible budget show what should have happened solely because the actual level of activity differed from what had been expected.

For example, the budget based on 1,000 client-visits shows revenue of $180,000 (= $180 per client-visit × 1,000 client-visits). The flexible budget based on 1,100 client-visits shows revenue of $198,000 (= $180 per client-visit × 1,100 client-visits). Because the salon had 100 more client-visits than anticipated in the budget, actual revenue should

EXHIBIT 9–5
Activity Variances from Comparing the Planning Budget to the Flexible Budget Based on Actual Activity

Rick's Hairstyling
Activity Variances
For the Month Ended March 31

	Planning Budget	Flexible Budget	Activity Variances
Client-visits	1,000	1,100	
Revenue ($180.00*q*)	$180,000	$198,000	$18,000 F
Expenses:			
Wages and salaries ($65,000 + $37.00*q*)	102,000	105,700	3,700 U
Hairstyling supplies ($1.50*q*)	1,500	1,650	150 U
Client gratuities ($4.10*q*)	4,100	4,510	410 U
Electricity ($1,500 + $0.10*q*)	1,600	1,610	10 U
Rent ($28,500)	28,500	28,500	0
Liability insurance ($2,800)	2,800	2,800	0
Employee health insurance ($21,300)	21,300	21,300	0
Miscellaneous ($1,200 + $0.20*q*)	1,400	1,420	20 U
Total expense	163,200	167,490	4,290 U
Net operating income	$ 16,800	$ 30,510	$13,710 F

have been higher than budgeted revenue by $18,000 (= $198,000 − $180,000). This activity variance is shown on the report as $18,000 F (favorable). Similarly, the budget based on 1,000 client-visits shows electricity costs of $1,600 (= $1,500 + $0.10 per client-visit × 1,000 client-visits). The flexible budget based on 1,100 client-visits shows electricity costs of $1,610 (= $1,500 + $0.10 per client-visit × 1,100 client-visits). Because the salon had 100 more client-visits than anticipated in the budget, actual electricity costs should have been higher than budgeted costs by $10 (= $1,610 − $1,600). The activity variance for electricity is shown on the report as $10 U (unfavorable). Note that in this case, the label "unfavorable" may be a little misleading. Costs *should* be $10 higher for electricity simply because business was up by 100 client-visits; therefore, is this variance really unfavorable if it was a necessary cost of serving more customers? For reasons such as this, we would like to caution you against assuming that unfavorable variances always indicate bad performance and favorable variances always indicate good performance.

Because all of the variances on this report are solely due to the difference in the level of activity between the planning budget from the beginning of the period and the actual level of activity, they are called **activity variances.** For example, the activity variance for revenue is $18,000 F, the activity variance for electricity is $10 U, and so on. The most important activity variance appears at the very bottom of the report; namely, the $13,710 F (favorable) variance for net operating income. This variance says that because activity was higher than expected in the planning budget, the net operating income should have been $13,710 higher. We caution against placing too much emphasis on any other single variance in this report. As we have said above, one would expect some costs to be higher as a consequence of more business. It is misleading to think of these unfavorable variances as indicative of poor performance.

On the other hand, the favorable activity variance for net operating income is important. Let's explore this variance a bit more thoroughly. First, as we have already noted, activity was up by 10%, but the flexible budget indicates that net operating income should have increased much more than 10%. A 10% increase in net operating income from the $16,800 in the planning budget would result in net operating income of $18,480 (= 1.1 × $16,800); however, the flexible budget shows much higher net operating income of $30,510. Why? The short answer is: Because of the presence of fixed costs. When we apply the 10% increase to the budgeted net operating income to estimate the profit at the higher level of activity, we implicitly assume that the revenues and *all* of the costs increase by 10%. But they do not. Note that when the activity level increases by 10%, three of the costs—rent, liability insurance, and employee health insurance—do not increase at all. These are all purely fixed costs. So while sales do increase by 10%, these costs do not increase. This results in net operating income increasing by more than 10%. A similar effect occurs with the mixed costs which contain fixed cost elements—wages and salaries, electricity, and miscellaneous. While sales increase by 10%, these mixed costs increase by less than 10%, resulting in an overall increase in net operating income of more than 10%. Because of the existence of fixed costs, net operating income does not change in proportion to changes in the level of activity. There is a leverage effect. The percentage changes in net operating income are ordinarily larger than the percentage increases in activity.

Revenue and Spending Variances

LEARNING OBJECTIVE 3
Prepare a report showing revenue and spending variances.

In the last section we answered the question "What impact did the change in activity have on our revenues, costs, and profit?" In this section we will answer the question "How well did we control our revenues, our costs, and our profit?"

Recall that the flexible budget based on the actual level of activity in Exhibit 9–4 shows what *should have happened given the actual level of activity.* If we compare this flexible budget to actual results, we compare what should have happened to what actually happened. This is done in Exhibit 9–6.

EXHIBIT 9–6
Revenue and Spending Variances from Comparing the Flexible Budget to the Actual Results

Rick's Hairstyling
Revenue and Spending Variances
For the Month Ended March 31

	Flexible Budget	Actual Results	Revenue and Spending Variances
Client-visits	1,100	1,100	
Revenue ($180.00*q*)	$198,000	$194,200	$3,800 U
Expenses:			
Wages and salaries ($65,000 + $37.00*q*)	105,700	106,900	1,200 U
Hairstyling supplies ($1.50*q*)	1,650	1,620	30 F
Client gratuities ($4.10*q*)	4,510	6,870	2,360 U
Electricity ($1,500 + $0.10*q*)	1,610	1,550	60 F
Rent ($28,500)	28,500	28,500	0
Liability insurance ($2,800)	2,800	2,800	0
Employee health insurance ($21,300)	21,300	22,600	1,300 U
Miscellaneous ($1,200 + $0.20*q*)	1,420	2,130	710 U
Total expense	167,490	172,970	5,480 U
Net operating income	$ 30,510	$ 21,230	$9,280 U

Focusing first on revenue, the flexible budget indicates that, given the actual level of activity, revenue should have been $198,000. However, actual revenue totaled $194,200. Consequently, revenue was $3,800 less than it should have been, given the actual number of client-visits for the month. This discrepancy is labeled as a $3,800 U (unfavorable) variance and is called a *revenue variance.* A **revenue variance** is the difference between what the total revenue should have been, given the actual level of activity for the period, and the actual total revenue. If actual revenue exceeds what the revenue should have been, the variance is labeled favorable. If actual revenue is less than what the revenue should have been, the variance is labeled unfavorable. Why would actual revenue be less than or more than it should have been, given the actual level of activity? Basically, the

IN BUSINESS

STATE OF THE UNION SPEECH HURTS CORPORATE JET INDUSTRY

In December 2008, Detroit auto executives flew private corporate jets to Washington D.C. to plead for billions of taxpayer dollars to save their companies. The public outcry was loud and clear: How could companies on the verge of bankruptcy afford to transport their executives in private corporate jets? One month later President Obama's State of the Union speech included criticism of CEOs who "disappear on a private jet."

The impact of these events on the corporate jet manufacturing industry was swift and severe. Dassault Aviation had 27 more order cancellations than new orders in the first quarter of 2009. Cessna Aircraft had 92 first-quarter order cancellations and laid off 42% of its workforce. Approximately 3,100 jets flooded the resale market compared to 1,800 jets for resale in the first quarter of the prior year. The CEO of Cessna and the president of Gulfstream Aerospace went to the White House in May 2009 to seek an end to the rhetoric that was destroying their sales.

These facts illustrate how an activity variance can be affected by uncontrollable events. The actual first-quarter sales at these companies were substantially lower than their budgeted sales due to reasons that they could not foresee or control.

Source: Carol Matlack, "Public Flak Grounds Private Jets," *BusinessWeek*, June 8, 2009, p. 13.

revenue variance is favorable if the average selling price is greater than expected; it is unfavorable if the average selling price is less than expected. This could happen for a variety of reasons including a change in selling price, a different mix of products sold, a change in the amount of discounts given, poor accounting controls, and so on.

Focusing next on costs, the flexible budget indicates that electricity costs should have been $1,610 for the 1,100 client-visits in March. However, the actual electricity cost was $1,550. Because the cost was $60 less than we would have expected for the actual level of activity during the period, it is labeled as a favorable variance, $60 F. This is an example of a *spending variance*. By definition, a **spending variance** is the difference between how much a cost should have been, given the actual level of activity, and the actual amount of the cost. If the actual cost is greater than what the cost should have been, the variance is labeled as unfavorable. If the actual cost is less than what the cost should have been, the variance is labeled as favorable. Why would a cost have a favorable or unfavorable variance? There are many possible explanations including paying a higher price for inputs than should have been paid, using too many inputs for the actual level of activity, a change in technology, and so on. In the next chapter we will delve into this topic in greater detail.

Note from Exhibit 9–6 that the overall net operating income variance is $9,280 U (unfavorable). This means that given the actual level of activity for the period, the net operating income was $9,280 lower than it should have been. There are a number of reasons for this. The most prominent is the unfavorable revenue variance of $3,800. Next in line is the $2,360 unfavorable variance for client gratuities. Looking at this in another way, client gratuities were more than 50% larger than they should have been according to the flexible budget. This is a variance that Rick would almost certainly want to investigate further. Rick may directly control the client gratuities himself. If not, he may want to know who authorized the additional expenditures. Why were they so large? Was more given away than usual? If so, why? Were more expensive gratuities given to clients? If so, why? Note that this unfavorable variance is not necessarily a bad thing. It is possible, for example, that more lavish use of gratuities led to the 10% increase in client-visits.

A Performance Report Combining Activity and Revenue and Spending Variances

LEARNING OBJECTIVE 4
Prepare a performance report that combines activity variances and revenue and spending variances.

Exhibit 9–7 displays a performance report that combines the activity variances (from Exhibit 9–5) with the revenue and spending variances (from Exhibit 9–6). The report brings together information from those two earlier exhibits in a way that makes it easier to interpret what happened during the period. The format of this report is a bit different from the format of the previous reports in that the variances appear between the amounts being compared rather than after them. For example, the activity variances appear between the planning budget amounts and the flexible budget amounts. In Exhibit 9–5, the activity variances appeared after the planning budget and the flexible budget.

Note two numbers in particular in the performance report—the activity variance for net operating income of $13,710 F (favorable) and the overall revenue and spending variance for net operating income of $9,280 U (unfavorable). It is worth repeating what those two numbers mean. The $13,710 favorable activity variance occurred because actual activity (1,100 client-visits) was greater than the budgeted level of activity (1,000 client-visits). The $9,280 unfavorable overall revenue and spending variance occurred because the profit was not as large as it should have been for the actual level of activity for the period. These two different variances mean very different things and call for different types of actions. To generate a favorable activity variance for net operating income, managers must take actions to increase client-visits. To generate a favorable overall revenue and spending variance, managers must take actions to protect selling prices, increase operating efficiency, and reduce the prices of inputs.

The performance report in Exhibit 9–7 provides much more useful information to managers than the simple comparison of budgeted to actual results in Exhibit 9–3. In Exhibit 9–3, the effects of changes in activity were jumbled together with the effects of

EXHIBIT 9–7
Performance Report Combining Activity Variances with Revenue and Spending Variances

Rick's Hairstyling
Flexible Budget Performance Report
For the Month Ended March 31

	(1) Planning Budget	Activity Variances (2) – (1)	(2) Flexible Budget	Revenue and Spending Variances (3) – (2)	(3) Actual Results
Client-visits	1,000		1,100		1,100
Revenue ($180.00*q*)	$180,000	$18,000 F	$198,000	$3,800 U	$194,200
Expenses:					
Wages and salaries ($65,000 + $37.00*q*)	102,000	3,700 U	105,700	1,200 U	106,900
Hairstyling supplies ($1.50*q*)	1,500	150 U	1,650	30 F	1,620
Client gratuities ($4.10*q*)	4,100	410 U	4,510	2,360 U	6,870
Electricity ($1,500 + $0.10*q*)	1,600	10 U	1,610	60 F	1,550
Rent ($28,500)	28,500	0	28,500	0	28,500
Liability insurance ($2,800)	2,800	0	2,800	0	2,800
Empoloyee health insurance ($21,300)	21,300	0	21,300	1,300 U	22,600
Miscellaneous ($1,200 + $0.20*q*)	1,400	20 U	1,420	710 U	2,130
Total expense	163,200	4,290 U	167,490	5,480 U	172,970
Net operating income	$ 16,800	$13,710 F	$ 30,510	$9,280 U	$ 21,230

how well prices were controlled and operations were managed. The performance report in Exhibit 9–7 clearly separates these effects, allowing managers to take a much more focused approach in evaluating operations.

To get a better idea of how the performance report accomplishes this task, look at hairstyling supplies in the performance report. In the planning budget, this cost was $1,500, whereas the actual cost for the period was $1,620. In the comparison of the planning budget to actual results in Exhibit 9–3, this difference is shown as an unfavorable variance of $120. Exhibit 9–3 uses a static planning budget approach that compares actual costs at one level of activity to budgeted costs at a different level of activity. As we said before, this is like comparing apples to oranges. This variance is actually a mixture of two very different effects. This becomes clear in the performance report in Exhibit 9–7. The difference between the budgeted amount and the actual results is composed of two different variances—an unfavorable activity variance of $150 and a favorable spending variance of $30. The activity variance occurs because activity was greater than anticipated in the planning budget, which naturally resulted in a higher total cost for this variable cost. The favorable spending variance occurred because less was spent on hairstyling supplies than one would have expected, given the actual level of activity for the month.

The flexible budget performance report in Exhibit 9–7 provides a more valid assessment of performance than simply comparing static planning budget costs to actual costs because actual costs are compared to what costs should have been at the actual level of activity. In other words, apples are compared to apples. When this is done, we see that the spending variance for hairstyling supplies is $30 F (favorable) rather than $120 U (unfavorable) as it was in the original static planning budget performance report (see Exhibit 9–3). In some cases, as with hairstyling supplies in Rick's report, an unfavorable static planning budget variance may be transformed into a favorable revenue or spending variance when an increase in activity is properly taken into account. The following discussion took place the next day at Rick's salon.

MANAGERIAL ACCOUNTING IN ACTION
The Wrap-up

Victoria: Let me show you what I've got. [Victoria shows Rick the flexible budget performance report in Exhibit 9–7.] I simply used the cost formulas to update the budget to reflect the increase in client-visits you experienced in March. That allowed me to come up with a better benchmark for what the costs should have been.

Rick: That's what you labeled the "flexible budget based on 1,100 client-visits"?

Victoria: That's right. Your original budget was based on 1,000 client-visits, so it understated what some of the costs should have been when you actually served 1,100 customers.

Rick: That's clear enough. These spending variances aren't quite as shocking as the variances on my first report.

Victoria: Yes, but you still have an unfavorable variance of $2,360 for client gratuities.

Rick: I know how that happened. In March there was a big Democratic Party fundraising dinner that I forgot about when I prepared the March budget. To fit all of our regular clients in, we had to push them through here pretty fast. Everyone still got top-rate service, but I felt bad about not being able to spend as much time with each customer. I wanted to give my customers a little extra something to compensate them for the less personal service, so I ordered a lot of flowers, which I gave away by the bunch.

Victoria: With the prices you charge, Rick, I am sure the gesture was appreciated.

Rick: One thing bothers me about the report. When we discussed my costs before, you called rent, liability insurance, and employee health insurance fixed costs. How can I have a variance for a fixed cost? Doesn't fixed mean that it doesn't change?

Victoria: We call these costs *fixed* because they shouldn't be affected by *changes in the level of activity*. However, that doesn't mean that they can't change for other reasons. Also, the use of the term *fixed* also suggests to people that the cost can't be controlled, but that isn't true. It is often easier to control fixed costs than variable costs. For example, it would be fairly easy for you to change your insurance bill by adjusting the amount of insurance you carry. It would be much more difficult for you to significantly reduce your spending on hairstyling supplies—a variable cost that is a necessary part of serving customers.

Rick: I think I understand, but it *is* confusing.

Victoria: Just remember that a cost is called variable if it is proportional to activity; it is called fixed if it does not depend on the level of activity. However, fixed costs can change for reasons unrelated to changes in the level of activity. And controllability has little to do with whether a cost is variable or fixed. Fixed costs are often more controllable than variable costs.

IN BUSINESS

HOTELS MANAGE REVENUE AND COST LEVERS AMID RECESSION

When the economy spiraled downward in 2009, it forced hotel chains to make tough decisions in an effort to achieve their profit goals. For example, Wyndham Hotels and Resorts decided to take sewing kits, mouthwash, and showercaps out of its rooms—instead, requiring customers to ask for these amenities at the front desk. Intercontinental Hotels Group stopped delivering newspapers to loyalty-program members' rooms; Marriott International cut back its breakfast offerings; and the Ritz-Carlton reduced operating hours at its restaurants, spas, and retail shops. In addition, many hotel chains reduced their rental rates.

A flexible budget performance report can help hotel managers analyze how the changes described above impact net operating income. It isolates activity, revenue, and spending variances that help identify the underlying reasons for differences between budgeted and actual net operating income.

Source: Sarah Nassauer, "No Showercaps at the Inn," *The Wall Street Journal*, January 22, 2009, pp. D1–D2.

Performance Reports in Nonprofit Organizations

The performance reports in nonprofit organizations are basically the same as the performance reports we have considered so far—with one prominent difference. Nonprofit organizations usually receive a significant amount of funding from sources other than sales. For example, universities receive their funding from sales (i.e., tuition charged to students), from endowment income and donations, and—in the case of public universities—from state appropriations. This means that, like costs, the revenue in governmental and nonprofit organizations may consist of both fixed and variable elements. For example, the Seattle Opera Company's revenue in a recent year consisted of grants and donations of \$12,719,000 and ticket sales of \$8,125,000 (or about \$75.35 per ticket sold). Consequently, the revenue formula for the opera can be written as:

$$\text{Revenue} = \$12{,}719{,}000 + \$75.35q$$

where q is the number of tickets sold. In other respects, the performance report for the Seattle Opera and other nonprofit organizations would be similar to the performance report in Exhibit 9–7.

Performance Reports in Cost Centers

Performance reports are often prepared for organizations that do not have any source of outside revenue. In particular, in a large organization a performance report may be prepared for each department—including departments that do not sell anything to outsiders. For example, a performance report is very commonly prepared for production departments in manufacturing companies. Such reports should be prepared using the same principles we have discussed and should look very much like the performance report in Exhibit 9–7—with the exception that revenue, and consequently net operating income, will not appear on the report. Because the managers in these departments are responsible for costs, but not revenues, they are often called *cost centers.*

Flexible Budgets with Multiple Cost Drivers

LEARNING OBJECTIVE 5
Prepare a flexible budget with more than one cost driver.

At Rick's Hairstyling, we have thus far assumed that there is only one cost driver—the number of client-visits. However, in the activity-based costing chapter, we found that more than one cost driver might be needed to adequately explain all of the costs in an organization. For example, some of the costs at Rick's Hairstyling probably depend more on the number of hours that the salon is open for business than the number of client-visits. Specifically, most of Rick's employees are paid salaries, but some are paid on an hourly basis. None of the employees is paid on the basis of the number of customers actually served. Consequently, the cost formula for wages and salaries would be more accurate if it were stated in terms of the hours of operation rather than the number of client-visits. The cost of electricity is even more complex. Some of the cost is fixed—the heat must be kept at some minimum level even at night when the salon is closed. Some of the cost depends on the number of client-visits—the power consumed by hair dryers depends on the number of customers served. Some of the cost depends on the number of hours the salon is open—the costs of lighting the salon and heating it to a comfortable temperature. Consequently, the cost formula for electricity would be more accurate if it were stated in terms of both the number of client-visits and the hours of operation rather than just on the number of client-visits.

Exhibit 9–8 shows a flexible budget in which these changes have been made. In that flexible budget, two cost drivers are listed—client-visits and hours of operation—where q_1 refers to client-visits and q_2 refers to hours of operation. For example, wages and salaries depend on the hours of operation and its cost formula is $\$65{,}000 + \$220q_2$. Because

EXHIBIT 9–8
Flexible Budget Based on More than One Cost Driver

Rick's Hairstyling
Flexible Budget
For the Month Ended March 31

Actual client-visits (q_1)	1,100
Actual hours of operation (q_2)	185
Revenue (180.00q_1$)	$198,000
Expenses:	
Wages and salaries ($65,000 + 220q_2$)	105,700
Hairstyling supplies (1.50q_1$)	1,650
Client gratuities (4.10q_1$)	4,510
Electricity ($390 + 0.10q_1$ + 6.00q_2$)	1,610
Rent ($28,500)	28,500
Liability insurance ($2,800)	2,800
Employee health insurance ($21,300)	21,300
Miscellaneous ($1,200 + 0.20q_1$)	1,420
Total expense	167,490
Net operating income	$ 30,510

the salon actually operated 185 hours, the flexible budget amount for wages and salaries is $105,700 (= $65,000 + $220 × 185). The electricity cost depends on both client-visits and the hours of operation and its cost formula is $390 + 0.10q_1$ + 6.00q_2$. Because the actual number of client-visits was 1,100 and the salon actually operated for 185 hours, the flexible budget amount for electricity is $1,610 (= $390 + $0.10 × 1,100 + $6.00 × 185).

This revised flexible budget based on both client-visits and hours of operation can be used exactly like we used the earlier flexible budget based on just client-visits to compute activity variances as in Exhibit 9–5, revenue and spending variances as in Exhibit 9–6, and a performance report as in Exhibit 9–7. The difference is that because the cost formulas based on more than one cost driver are more accurate than the cost formulas based on just one cost driver, the variances will also be more accurate.

IN BUSINESS

HOSPITALS TURN TO FLEXIBLE BUDGETS

Mary Wilkes, a senior managing director with Phase 2 Consulting, says that hospitals may have to pay as much as $300,000 to install a flexible budgeting system, but the investment should readily pay for itself by enabling "more efficient use of hospital resources, particularly when it comes to labor." One of the keys to creating an effective flexible budgeting system is to recognize the existence of multiple cost drivers. Many hospitals frequently use patient volume as a cost driver when preparing flexible budgets; however, other variables can influence revenues and costs. For example, the percentage of patients covered by private insurance, Medicaid, or Medicare, as well as the proportion of uninsured patients all influence revenues and costs. A flexible budgeting system that incorporates patient volume and these other variables will be more accurate than one based solely on patient volume.

Source: Paul Barr, "Flexing Your Budget," *Modern Healthcare*, September 12, 2005, pp. 24–26.

Some Common Errors

LEARNING OBJECTIVE 6
Understand common errors made in preparing performance reports based on budgets and actual results.

We started this chapter by discussing the need for managers to understand the difference between what was expected to happen—formalized by the planning budget—and what actually happened. To meet this need, we developed a flexible budget that allowed us to isolate activity variances and revenue and spending variances. Unfortunately, this approach is not always followed in practice—resulting in misleading and difficult-to-interpret reports. The most common errors in preparing performance reports are to implicitly assume that all costs are fixed or to implicitly assume that all costs are variable. These erroneous assumptions lead to inaccurate benchmarks and incorrect variances.

We have already discussed one of these errors—assuming that all costs are fixed. This is the error that is made when static planning budget costs are compared to actual costs without any adjustment for the actual level of activity. Such a comparison appeared in Exhibit 9–3. For convenience, the comparison of budgeted to actual revenues and costs is repeated in Exhibit 9–9. Looking at that exhibit, note that the budgeted cost of hairstyling supplies of $1,500 is directly compared to the actual cost of $1,620, resulting in an unfavorable variance of $120. But this comparison only makes sense if the cost of hairstyling supplies is fixed. If the cost of hairstyling supplies isn't fixed (and indeed it is not), one would *expect* the cost to go up because of the increase in activity over the budget. Comparing static planning budget costs to actual costs only makes sense if the cost is fixed. If the cost isn't fixed, it needs to be adjusted for any change in activity that occurs during the period.

The other common error when comparing budgets to actual results is to assume that all costs are variable. A report that makes this error appears in Exhibit 9–10. The variances in this report are computed by comparing actual results to the amounts in the second numerical column where *all* of the budget items have been inflated by 10%—the percentage by which activity increased. This is a perfectly valid adjustment to make if an item is strictly variable—like sales and hairstyling supplies. It is *not* a valid adjustment if the item contains any fixed element. Take, for example, rent. If the salon serves 10% more customers in a given month, would you expect the rent to increase by 10%? The answer is no. Ordinarily, the rent is fixed in advance and does not depend on the volume of business. Therefore, the amount shown in the second numerical column of $31,350 is incorrect, which leads to the erroneous favorable variance of $2,850. In fact, the actual rent paid was exactly equal to the budgeted rent, so there should be no variance at all on a valid report.

EXHIBIT 9–9
Faulty Analysis Comparing Budgeted Amounts to Actual Amounts (Implicitly Assumes All Income Statement Items Are Fixed)

Rick's Hairstyling
For the Month Ended March 31

	Planning Budget	Actual Results	Variances
Client-visits	1,000	1,100	
Revenue	$180,000	$194,200	$14,200 F
Expenses:			
Wages and salaries	102,000	106,900	4,900 U
Hairstyling supplies	1,500	1,620	120 U
Client gratuities	4,100	6,870	2,770 U
Electricity	1,600	1,550	50 F
Rent	28,500	28,500	0
Liability insurance	2,800	2,800	0
Employee health insurance	21,300	22,600	1,300 U
Miscellaneous	1,400	2,130	730 U
Total expense	163,200	172,970	9,770 U
Net operating income	$ 16,800	$ 21,230	$ 4,430 F

EXHIBIT 9–10
Faulty Analysis That Assumes All Budget Items Are Variable

Rick's Hairstyling
For the Month Ended March 31

	(1) Planning Budget	(2) Planning Budget × (1,100/1,000)	(3) Actual Results	Variances (3) − (2)
Client-visits	1,000		1,100	
Revenue	$180,000	$198,000	$194,200	$3,800 U
Expenses:				
Wages and salaries	102,000	112,200	106,900	5,300 F
Hairstyling supplies	1,500	1,650	1,620	30 F
Client gratuities	4,100	4,510	6,870	2,360 U
Electricity	1,600	1,760	1,550	210 F
Rent	28,500	31,350	28,500	2,850 F
Liability insurance	2,800	3,080	2,800	280 F
Employee health insurance	21,300	23,430	22,600	830 F
Miscellaneous	1,400	1,540	2,130	590 U
Total expense	163,200	179,520	172,970	6,550 F
Net operating income	$ 16,800	$ 18,480	$ 21,230	$2,750 F

IN BUSINESS

KNOW YOUR COSTS

Understanding the difference between fixed and variable costs can be critical. Kennard T. Wing, of OMG Center for Collaborative Learning, reports that a large health care system made the mistake of classifying all of its costs as variable. As a consequence, when volume dropped, managers felt that costs should be cut proportionately and more than 1,000 people were laid off—even though "the workload of most of them had no direct relation to patient volume. The result was that morale of the survivors plummeted and within a year the system was scrambling to replace not only those it had let go, but many others who had quit. The point is, the accounting systems we design and implement really do affect management decisions in significant ways. A system built on a bad model of the business will either not be used or, if used, will lead to bad decisions."

Source: Kennard T. Wing, "Using Enhanced Cost Models in Variance Analysis for Better Control and Decision Making," *Management Accounting Quarterly*, Winter 2000, pp. 27–35.

Summary

Directly comparing static planning budget revenues and costs to actual revenues and costs can easily lead to erroneous conclusions. Actual revenues and costs differ from budgeted revenues and costs for a variety of reasons, but one of the biggest is a change in the level of activity. One would expect actual revenues and costs to increase or decrease as the activity level increases or decreases. Flexible budgets enable managers to isolate the various causes of the differences between budgeted and actual costs.

A flexible budget is a budget that is adjusted to the actual level of activity. It is the best estimate of what revenues and costs should have been, given the actual level of activity during the period. The flexible budget can be compared to the budget from the beginning of the period or to the actual results.

When the flexible budget is compared to the budget from the beginning of the period, activity variances are the result. An activity variance shows how a revenue or cost should have changed in response to the difference between budgeted and actual activity.

When the flexible budget is compared to actual results, revenue and spending variances are the result. A favorable revenue variance indicates that revenue was larger than should have been expected, given the actual level of activity. An unfavorable revenue variance indicates that revenue was less than it should have been, given the actual level of activity. A favorable spending variance indicates that the cost was less than expected, given the actual level of activity. An unfavorable spending variance indicates that the cost was greater than it should have been, given the actual level of activity.

A flexible budget performance report combines the activity variances and the revenue and spending variances on one report.

Common errors in comparing budgeted costs to actual costs are to assume all costs are fixed or to assume all costs are variable. If all costs are assumed to be fixed, the variances for variable and mixed costs will be incorrect. If all costs are assumed to be variable, the variances for fixed and mixed costs will be incorrect. The variance for a cost will only be correct if the actual behavior of the cost is used to develop the flexible budget benchmark.

Review Problem: Variance Analysis Using a Flexible Budget

Harrald's Fish House is a family-owned restaurant that specializes in Scandinavian-style seafood. Data concerning the restaurant's monthly revenues and costs appear below (q refers to the number of meals served):

	Formula
Revenue	16.50q$
Cost of ingredients	6.25q$
Wages and salaries	$10,400
Utilities	$800 + 0.20q$
Rent	$2,200
Miscellaneous	$600 + 0.80q$

Required:

1. Prepare the restaurant's planning budget for April assuming that 1,800 meals are served.
2. Assume that 1,700 meals were actually served in April. Prepare a flexible budget for this level of activity.
3. The actual results for April appear below. Prepare a flexible budget performance report for the restaurant for April.

Revenue	$27,920
Cost of ingredients	$11,110
Wages and salaries	$10,130
Utilities	$1,080
Rent	$2,200
Miscellaneous	$2,240

Solution to Review Problem

1. The planning budget for April appears below:

Harrald's Fish House Planning Budget For the Month Ended April 30	
Budgeted meals served (q)	1,800
Revenue (16.50q$)	$29,700
Expenses:	
Cost of ingredients (6.25q$)	11,250
Wages and salaries ($10,400)	10,400
Utilities ($800 + 0.20q$)	1,160
Rent ($2,200)	2,200
Miscellaneous ($600 + 0.80q$)	2,040
Total expense	27,050
Net operating income	$ 2,650

2. The flexible budget for April appears below:

Harrald's Fish House Flexible Budget For the Month Ended April 30	
Actual meals served (q)	1,700
Revenue (\$16.50q)	\$28,050
Expenses:	
Cost of ingredients (\$6.25q)	10,625
Wages and salaries (\$10,400)	10,400
Utilities (\$800 + \$0.20q)	1,140
Rent (\$2,200)	2,200
Miscellaneous (\$600 + \$0.80q)	1,960
Total expense	26,325
Net operating income	\$ 1,725

3. The flexible budget performance report for April appears below:

Harrald's Fish House
Flexible Budget Performance Report
For the Month Ended April 30

	(1) Planning Budget	Activity Variances (2) − (1)	(2) Flexible Budget	Revenue and Spending Variances (3) − (2)	(3) Actual Results
Meals served	1,800		1,700		1,700
Revenue (\$16.50q)	\$29,700	\$1,650 U	\$28,050	\$130 U	\$27,920
Expenses:					
Cost of ingredients (\$6.25q)	11,250	625 F	10,625	485 U	11,110
Wages and salaries (\$10,400)	10,400	0	10,400	270 F	10,130
Utilities (\$800 + \$0.20q)	1,160	20 F	1,140	60 F	1,080
Rent (\$2,200)	2,200	0	2,200	0	2,200
Miscellaneous (\$600 + \$0.80q)	2,040	80 F	1,960	280 U	2,240
Total expense	27,050	725 F	26,325	435 U	26,760
Net operating income	\$ 2,650	\$ 925 U	\$ 1,725	\$565 U	\$ 1,160

Glossary

Activity variance The difference between a revenue or cost item in the static planning budget and the same item in the flexible budget. An activity variance is due solely to the difference between the level of activity assumed in the planning budget and the actual level of activity used in the flexible budget. (p. 389)

Flexible budget A report showing estimates of what revenues and costs should have been, given the actual level of activity for the period. (p. 384)

Planning budget A budget created at the beginning of the budgeting period that is valid only for the planned level of activity. (p. 384)

Revenue variance The difference between how much the revenue should have been, given the actual level of activity, and the actual revenue for the period. A favorable (unfavorable) revenue variance occurs because the revenue is higher (lower) than expected, given the actual level of activity for the period. (p. 390)

Spending variance The difference between how much a cost should have been, given the actual level of activity, and the actual amount of the cost. A favorable (unfavorable) spending variance occurs because the cost is lower (higher) than expected, given the actual level of activity for the period. (p. 391)

Questions

9–1 What is a static planning budget?
9–2 What is a flexible budget and how does it differ from a static planning budget?
9–3 What are some of the possible reasons that actual results may differ from what had been budgeted at the beginning of a period?
9–4 Why is it difficult to interpret a difference between how much expense was budgeted and how much was actually spent?
9–5 What is an activity variance and what does it mean?
9–6 What is a revenue variance and what does it mean?
9–7 What is a spending variance and what does it mean?
9–8 What does a flexible budget performance report do that a simple comparison of budgeted to actual results does not do?
9–9 How does a flexible budget based on two cost drivers differ from a flexible budget based on a single cost driver?
9–10 What assumption is implicitly made about cost behavior when a static planning budget is directly compared to actual results? Why is this assumption questionable?
9–11 What assumption is implicitly made about cost behavior when all of the items in a static planning budget are adjusted in proportion to a change in activity? Why is this assumption questionable?

Multiple-choice questions are provided on the text website at www.mhhe.com/garrison14e.

Applying Excel

connect ACCOUNTING

LEARNING OBJECTIVES 1, 2, 3, 4

Available with McGraw-Hill's *Connect™ Accounting*.

The Excel worksheet form that appears on the next page is to be used to recreate the Review Problem on pages 398–399. Download the workbook containing this form from the Online Learning Center at www.mhhe.com/garrison14e. *On the website you will also receive instructions about how to use this worksheet form.*

You should proceed to the requirements below only after completing your worksheet.

Required:

1. Check your worksheet by changing the revenue in cell D4 to \$16.00; the cost of ingredients in cell D5 to \$6.50; and the wages and salaries in cell B6 to \$10,000. The activity variance for net operating income should now be \$850 U and the spending variance for total expenses should be \$410 U. If you do not get these answers, find the errors in your worksheet and correct them.
   a. What is the activity variance for revenue? Explain this variance.
   b. What is the spending variance for the cost of ingredients? Explain this variance.

	A	B	C	D	E	F	G	H
1	Chapter 9: Applying Excel							
2								
3	**Data**							
4	Revenue			$16.50 q				
5	Cost of ingredients			$6.25 q				
6	Wages and salaries	$10,400						
7	Utilities	$800	+	$0.20 q				
8	Rent	$2,200						
9	Miscellaneous	$600	+	$0.80 q				
10								
11	Actual results:							
12	Revenue	$27,920						
13	Cost of ingredients	$11,110						
14	Wages and salaries	$10,130						
15	Utilities	$1,080						
16	Rent	$2,200						
17	Miscellaneous	$2,240						
18								
19	Planning budget activity	1,800 meals served						
20	Actual activity	1,700 meals served						
21								
22	*Enter a formula into each of the cells marked with a ? below*							
23	**Review Problem: Variance Analysis Using a Flexible Budget**							
24								
25	***Construct a flexible budget performance report***							
26–29		*Planning Budget*	*Activity Variances*		*Flexible Budget*	*Revenue and Spending Variances*		*Actual Results*
30	Meals served	?			?			?
31	Revenue	?	?		?	?		?
32	Expenses:							
33	Cost of ingredients	?	?		?	?		?
34	Wages and salaries	?	?		?	?		?
35	Utilities	?	?		?	?		?
36	Rent	?	?		?	?		?
37	Miscellaneous	?	?		?	?		?
38	Total expenses	?	?		?	?		?
39	Net operating income	?	?		?	?		?
40								

Chapter 9 Form | Filled in Chapter 9 Form | Chapter 9 Formulas

2. Revise the data in your worksheet to reflect the results for the following year:

Data				
Revenue			$16.50	q
Cost of ingredients			$6.25	q
Wages and salaries	$10,400			
Utilities	$800	+	$0.20	q
Rent	$2,200			
Miscellaneous	$600	+	$0.80	q
Actual results:				
Revenue	$28,900			
Cost of ingredients	$11,300			
Wages and salaries	$10,300			
Utilities	$1,120			
Rent	$2,300			
Miscellaneous	$2,020			
Planning budget activity	1,700	meals served		
Actual activity	1,800	meals served		

Using the flexible budget performance report, briefly evaluate the company's performance for the year and indicate where attention should be focused.

Exercises

All applicable exercises are available with McGraw-Hill's *Connect™ Accounting*.

EXERCISE 9–1 Prepare a Flexible Budget [LO1]

Gator Divers is a company that provides diving services such as underwater ship repairs to clients in the Tampa Bay area. The company's planning budget for March appears below:

Gator Divers Planning Budget For the Month Ended March 31	
Budgeted diving-hours (q)	200
Revenue (380.00q$)	$76,000
Expenses:	
Wages and salaries ($12,000 + 130.00q$)	38,000
Supplies (5.00q$)	1,000
Equipment rental ($2,500 + 26.00q$)	7,700
Insurance ($4,200)	4,200
Miscellaneous ($540 + 1.50q$)	840
Total expense	51,740
Net operating income	$24,260

Required:

During March, the company's activity was actually 190 diving-hours. Prepare a flexible budget for that level of activity.

EXERCISE 9–2 Prepare a Report Showing Activity Variances [LO2]

Air Meals is a company that prepares in-flight meals for airlines in its kitchen located next to the local airport. The company's planning budget for December appears below:

Air Meals Planning Budget For the Month Ended December 31	
Budgeted meals (q)	20,000
Revenue (3.80q$)	$76,000
Expenses:	
Raw materials (2.30q$)	46,000
Wages and salaries ($6,400 + 0.25q$)	11,400
Utilities ($2,100 + 0.05q$)	3,100
Facility rent ($3,800)	3,800
Insurance ($2,600)	2,600
Miscellaneous ($700 + 0.10q$)	2,700
Total expense	69,600
Net operating income	$ 6,400

In December, 21,000 meals were actually served. The company's flexible budget for this level of activity is as follows:

Air Meals Flexible Budget For the Month Ended December 31	
Budgeted meals (*q*)	21,000
Revenue ($3.80*q*)	$79,800
Expenses:	
Raw materials ($2.30*q*)	48,300
Wages and salaries ($6,400 + $0.25*q*)	11,650
Utilities ($2,100 + $0.05*q*)	3,150
Facility rent ($3,800)	3,800
Insurance ($2,600)	2,600
Miscellaneous ($700 + $0.10*q*)	2,800
Total expense	72,300
Net operating income	$ 7,500

Required:

1. Prepare a report showing the company's activity variances for December.
2. Which of the activity variances should be of concern to management? Explain.

EXERCISE 9–3 Prepare a Report Showing Revenue and Spending Variances [LO3]

Olympia Bivalve farms and sells oysters in the Pacific Northwest. The company harvested and sold 7,000 pounds of oysters in July. The company's flexible budget for July appears below:

Olympia Bivalve Flexible Budget For the Month Ended July 31	
Actual pounds (*q*)	7,000
Revenue ($4.20*q*)	$29,400
Expenses:	
Packing supplies ($0.40*q*)	2,800
Oyster bed maintenance ($3,600)	3,600
Wages and salaries ($2,540 + $0.50*q*)	6,040
Shipping ($0.75*q*)	5,250
Utilities ($1,260)	1,260
Other ($510 + $0.05*q*)	860
Total expense	19,810
Net operating income	$ 9,590

The actual results for July appear below:

Olympia Bivalve Income Statement For the Month Ended July 31	
Actual pounds	7,000
Revenue	$28,600
Expenses:	
Packing supplies	2,970
Oyster bed maintenance	3,460
Wages and salaries	6,450
Shipping	4,980
Utilities	1,070
Other	1,480
Total expense	20,410
Net operating income	$ 8,190

Required:
Prepare a report showing the company's revenue and spending variances for July.

EXERCISE 9–4 Prepare a Flexible Budget Performance Report [LO4]
Mt. Hood Air offers scenic overflights of Mt. Hood and the Columbia River gorge. Data concerning the company's operations in August appear below:

Mt. Hood Air
Operating Data
For the Month Ended August 31

	Planning Budget	Flexible Budget	Actual Results
Flights (*q*)	50	52	52
Revenue ($360.00*q*)	$18,000	$18,720	$16,980
Expenses:			
Wages and salaries ($3,800 + $92.00*q*)	8,400	8,584	8,540
Fuel ($34.00*q*)	1,700	1,768	1,930
Airport fees ($870 + $35.00*q*)	2,620	2,690	2,690
Aircraft depreciation ($11.00*q*)	550	572	572
Office expenses ($230 + $1.00*q*)	280	282	450
Total expense	13,550	13,896	14,182
Net operating income	$ 4,450	$ 4,824	$ 2,798

The company measures its activity in terms of flights. Customers can buy individual tickets for overflights or hire an entire plane for an overflight at a discount.

Required:
1. Prepare a flexible budget performance report for August.
2. Which of the variances should be of concern to management? Explain.

EXERCISE 9–5 Prepare a Flexible Budget with More Than One Cost Driver [LO5]
Icicle Bay Tours operates day tours of coastal glaciers in Alaska on its tour boat the Emerald Glacier. Management has identified two cost drivers—the number of cruises and the number of passengers—that it uses in its budgeting and performance reports. The company publishes a schedule of day cruises that it may supplement with special sailings if there is sufficient demand. Up to 80 passengers can be accommodated on the tour boat. Data concerning the company's cost formulas appear below:

	Fixed Cost per Month	Cost per Cruise	Cost per Passenger
Vessel operating costs	$6,800	$475.00	$3.50
Advertising	$2,700		
Administrative costs	$5,800	$36.00	$1.80
Insurance	$3,600		

For example, vessel operating costs should be $6,800 per month plus $475.00 per cruise plus $3.50 per passenger. The company's sales should average $28.00 per passenger. The company's planning budget for August is based on 58 cruises and 3,200 passengers.

Required:
Prepare the company's planning budget for August.

EXERCISE 9–6 Analyze a Performance Report [LO6]
The Exterminator Inc. provides on-site residential pest extermination services. The company has several mobile teams who are dispatched from a central location in company-owned trucks. The company uses the number of jobs to measure activity. At the beginning of May, the company

budgeted for 200 jobs, but the actual number of jobs turned out to be 208. A report comparing the budgeted revenues and costs to the actual revenues and costs appears below:

The Exterminator Inc.
Variance Report
For the Month Ended May 31

	Planning Budget	Actual Results	Variances
Jobs	200	208	
Revenue	$37,000	$36,400	$600 U
Expenses:			
Mobile team operating costs	16,900	17,060	160 U
Exterminating supplies	4,000	4,350	350 U
Advertising	900	1,040	140 U
Dispatching costs	2,700	2,340	360 F
Office rent	2,300	2,300	0
Insurance	3,600	3,600	0
Total expense	30,400	30,690	290 U
Net operating income	$ 6,600	$ 5,710	$890 U

Required:
Is the above variance report useful for evaluating how well revenues and costs were controlled during May? Why or why not?

EXERCISE 9–7 Critique a Variance Report [LO6]

Refer to the data for The Exterminator Inc. in Exercise 9–6. A management intern has suggested that the budgeted revenues and costs should be adjusted for the actual level of activity in May before they are compared to the actual revenues and costs. Because the actual level of activity was 4% higher than budgeted, the intern suggested that all budgeted revenues and costs should be adjusted upward by 4%. A report comparing the budgeted revenues and costs, with this adjustment, to the actual revenues and costs appears below:

The Exterminator Inc.
Variance Report
For the Month Ended May 31

	Adjusted Planning Budget	Actual Results	Variances
Jobs	208	208	
Revenue	$38,480	$36,400	$2,080 U
Expenses:			
Mobile team operating costs	17,576	17,060	516 F
Exterminating supplies	4,160	4,350	190 U
Advertising	936	1,040	104 U
Dispatching costs	2,808	2,340	468 F
Office rent	2,392	2,300	92 F
Insurance	3,744	3,600	144 F
Total expense	31,616	30,690	926 F
Net operating income	$ 6,864	$ 5,710	$1,154 U

Required:
Is the above variance report useful for evaluating how well revenues and costs were controlled during May? Why or why not?

EXERCISE 9–8 Flexible Budgets and Activity Variances [LO1, LO2]
Harold's Roof Repair has provided the following data concerning its costs:

	Fixed Cost per Month	Cost per Repair-Hour
Wages and salaries	$21,380	$15.80
Parts and supplies		$7.50
Equipment depreciation	$2,740	$0.60
Truck operating expenses.	$5,820	$1.90
Rent	$4,650	
Administrative expenses.	$3,870	$0.70

For example, wages and salaries should be $21,380 plus $15.80 per repair-hour. The company expected to work 2,500 repair-hours in June, but actually worked 2,400 repair-hours. The company expects its sales to be $43.50 per repair-hour.

Required:
Prepare a report showing the company's activity variances for June.

EXERCISE 9–9 Flexible Budget [LO1]
Auto Lavage is a Canadian company that owns and operates a large automatic carwash facility near Quebec. The following table provides data concerning the company's costs:

	Fixed Cost per Month	Cost per Car Washed
Cleaning supplies.		$0.70
Electricity	$1,400	$0.10
Maintenance.		$0.30
Wages and salaries.	$4,700	$0.40
Depreciation	$8,300	
Rent.	$2,100	
Administrative expenses.	$1,800	$0.05

For example, electricity costs are $1,400 per month plus $0.10 per car washed. The company expects to wash 8,000 cars in October and to collect an average of $5.90 per car washed.

Required:
Prepare the company's planning budget for October.

EXERCISE 9–10 Flexible Budget [LO1]
Refer to the data for Auto Lavage in Exercise 9–9. The company actually washed 8,100 cars in October.

Required:
Prepare the company's flexible budget for October.

EXERCISE 9–11 Prepare a Report Showing Activity Variances [LO2]
Refer to the data for Auto Lavage in Exercise 9–9. The actual operating results for October appear below:

Auto Lavage Income Statement For the Month Ended October 31	
Actual cars washed	8,100
Revenue	$49,300
Expenses:	
Cleaning supplies	6,100
Electricity	2,170
Maintenance	2,640
Wages and salaries.	8,260
Depreciation	8,300
Rent	2,300
Administrative expenses	2,100
Total expense	31,870
Net operating income	$17,430

Required:
Prepare a report showing the company's activity variances for October.

EXERCISE 9–12 Prepare a Report Showing Revenue and Spending Variances [LO3]
Refer to the data for Auto Lavage in Exercises 9–9 and 9–11.

Required:
Prepare a report showing the company's revenue and spending variances for October.

EXERCISE 9–13 Prepare a Flexible Budget Performance Report [LO4]
Refer to the data for Auto Lavage in Exercises 9–9 and 9–11.

Required:
Prepare a flexible budget performance report that shows the company's activity variances and revenue and spending variances for October.

EXERCISE 9–14 Flexible Budget [LO1]
Pierr Manufacturing Inc. has provided the following information concerning its manufacturing costs:

	Fixed Cost per Month	Cost per Machine-Hour
Direct materials		$5.70
Direct labor	$42,800	
Supplies		$0.20
Utilities	$1,600	$0.15
Depreciation	$14,900	
Insurance	$11,400	

For example, utilities should be $1,600 per month plus $0.15 per machine-hour. The company expects to work 4,000 machine-hours in July. Note that the company's direct labor is a fixed cost.

Required:
Prepare the company's planning budget for manufacturing costs for July.

EXERCISE 9–15 Critique a Report; Prepare a Performance Report [LO1, LO4, LO6]
Wings Flight School offers flying lessons at a small municipal airport. The school's owner and manager has been attempting to evaluate performance and control costs using a variance report that compares the planning budget to actual results. A recent variance report appears below:

Wings Flight School Variance Report For the Month Ended August 31			
	Planning Budget	Actual Results	Variances
Lessons	200	210	
Revenue	$45,000	$47,300	$2,300 F
Expenses:			
Instructor wages	12,400	12,910	510 U
Aircraft depreciation	11,400	11,970	570 U
Fuel	4,200	5,150	950 U
Maintenance	3,270	3,470	200 U
Ground facility expenses	2,440	2,350	90 F
Administration	4,410	4,340	70 F
Total expense	38,120	40,190	2,070 U
Net operating income	$ 6,880	$ 7,110	$ 230 F

After several months of using such variance reports, the owner has become frustrated. For example, she is quite confident that instructor wages were very tightly controlled in August, but the report shows an unfavorable variance.

The planning budget was developed using the following formulas, where q is the number of lessons sold:

Revenue	$225q$
Instructor wages	$62q$
Aircraft depreciation	$57q$
Fuel	$21q$
Maintenance	$670 + $13q$
Ground facility expenses	$1,640 + $4q$
Administration	$4,210 + $1q$

Required:

1. Should the owner feel frustrated with the variance reports? Explain.
2. Prepare a flexible budget performance report for the school for August.
3. Evaluate the school's performance for August.

EXERCISE 9–16 Working with More Than One Cost Driver [LO4, LO5]

The Toque Cooking Academy runs short cooking courses at its small campus. Management has identified two cost drivers that it uses in its budgeting and performance reports—the number of courses and the total number of students. For example, the school might run four courses in a month and have a total of 60 students enrolled in those four courses. Data concerning the company's cost formulas appear below:

	Fixed Cost per month	Cost per Course	Cost per Student
Instructor wages		$2,980	
Classroom supplies			$310
Utilities	$1,230	$85	
Campus rent	$5,100		
Insurance	$2,340		
Administrative expenses	$3,940	$46	$7

For example, administrative expenses should be $3,940 per month plus $46 per course plus $7 per student. The company's sales should average $850 per student.

The actual operating results for October appear below:

	Actual
Revenue	$48,100
Instructor wages	$11,200
Classroom supplies	$18,450
Utilities	$1,980
Campus rent	$5,100
Insurance	$2,480
Administrative expenses	$3,970

Required:

1. The Toque Cooking Academy expects to run four courses with a total of 60 students in October. Prepare the company's planning budget for this level of activity.
2. The school actually ran four courses with a total of 58 students in October. Prepare the company's flexible budget for this level of activity.
3. Prepare a flexible budget performance report that shows both activity variances and revenue and spending variances for October.

EXERCISE 9–17 Flexible Budgets and Revenue and Spending Variances [LO1, LO3]

Gelato Supremo is a popular neighborhood gelato shop. The company has provided the following data concerning its operations:

	Fixed Element per Month	Variable Element per Liter	Actual Total for July
Revenue		$13.50	$69,420
Raw materials		$5.10	$26,890
Wages	$4,800	$1.20	$11,200
Utilities	$1,860	$0.15	$2,470
Rent	$3,150		$3,150
Insurance	$1,890		$1,890
Miscellaneous	$540	$0.15	$1,390

While gelato is sold by the cone or cup, the shop measures its activity in terms of the total number of liters of gelato sold. For example, wages should be $4,800 plus $1.20 per liter of gelato sold, and the actual wages for July were $11,200. Gelato Supremo expected to sell 5,000 liters in July, but actually sold 4,900 liters.

Required:

Prepare a report showing Gelato Supremo revenue and spending variances for July.

EXERCISE 9–18 Flexible Budget Performance Report [LO1, LO4]

AirAssurance Corporation provides on-site air quality testing services. The company has provided the following data concerning its operations:

	Fixed Component per Month	Variable Component per Job	Actual Total for March
Revenue		$275	$24,750
Technician wages	$8,600		$8,450
Mobile lab operating expenses	$4,900	$29	$7,960
Office expenses	$2,700	$3	$2,850
Advertising expenses	$1,580		$1,650
Insurance	$2,870		$2,870
Miscellaneous expenses	$960	$2	$465

The company uses the number of jobs as its measure of activity. For example, mobile lab operating expenses should be $4,900 plus $29 per job, and the actual mobile lab operating expenses for March were $7,960.

The company expected to work 100 jobs in March, but actually worked 98 jobs.

Required:

Prepare a flexible budget performance report showing AirAssurance Corporation's activity variances and revenue and spending variances for March.

EXERCISE 9–19 Flexible Budget Performance Report in a Cost Center [LO1, LO4]

Triway Packaging Corporation manufactures and sells a wide variety of packaging products. Performance reports are prepared monthly for each department. The planning budget and flexible budget for the Production Department are based on the following formulas, where q is the number of direct labor-hours worked in a month:

Direct labor	16.30q$
Indirect labor	$4,300 + 1.80q$
Utilities	$5,600 + 0.70q$
Supplies	$1,400 + 0.30q$
Equipment depreciation	$18,600 + 2.80q$
Factory rent	$8,300
Property taxes	$2,800
Factory administration	$13,400 + 0.90q$

The actual costs incurred in November in the Production Department are listed below:

	Actual Cost Incurred in November
Direct labor	$63,520
Indirect labor	$10,680
Utilities	$8,790
Supplies	$2,810
Equipment depreciation	$29,240
Factory rent	$8,700
Property taxes	$2,800
Factory administration	$16,230

Required:

1. The company had budgeted for an activity level of 4,000 labor-hours in November. Prepare the Production Department's planning budget for the month.
2. The company actually worked 3,800 labor-hours in November. Prepare the Production Department's flexible budget for the month.
3. Prepare the Production Department's flexible budget performance report for November, including both the activity and spending variances.
4. What aspects of the flexible budget performance report should be brought to management's attention? Explain.

Problems

connect ACCOUNTING

All applicable problems are available with McGraw-Hill's *Connect™ Accounting*.

PROBLEM 9–20 Activity and Spending Variances [LO1, LO2, LO3]

You have just been hired by SecuriDoor Corporation, the manufacturer of a revolutionary new garage door opening device. The president has asked that you review the company's costing system and "do what you can to help us get better control of our manufacturing overhead costs." You find that the company has never used a flexible budget, and you suggest that preparing such a budget would be an excellent first step in overhead planning and control.

After much effort and analysis, you determined the following cost formulas and gathered the following actual cost data for April:

	Cost Formula	Actual Cost in April
Utilities	$16,500 plus $0.15 per machine-hour	$21,300
Maintenance	$38,600 plus $1.80 per machine-hour	$68,400
Supplies	$0.50 per machine-hour	$9,800
Indirect labor	$94,300 plus $1.20 per machine-hour	$119,200
Depreciation	$68,000	$69,700

During April, the company worked 18,000 machine-hours and produced 12,000 units. The company had originally planned to work 20,000 machine-hours during April.

Required:

1. Prepare a report showing the activity variances for April. Explain what these variances mean.
2. Prepare a report showing the spending variances for April. Explain what these variances mean.

PROBLEM 9–21 More Than One Cost Driver [LO4, LO5]

Verona Pizza is a small neighborhood pizzeria that has a small area for in-store dining as well offering takeout and free home delivery services. The pizzeria's owner has determined that the shop has two major cost drivers—the number of pizzas sold and the number of deliveries made. Data concerning the pizzeria's costs appear below:

	Fixed Cost per Month	Cost per Pizza	Cost per Delivery
Pizza ingredients		$4.20	
Kitchen staff	$5,870		
Utilities	$590	$0.10	
Delivery person			$2.90
Delivery vehicle	$610		$1.30
Equipment depreciation	$384		
Rent	$1,790		
Miscellaneous	$710	$0.05	

In October, the pizzeria budgeted for 1,500 pizzas at an average selling price of $13.00 per pizza and for 200 deliveries.

Data concerning the pizzeria's operations in October appear below:

	Actual Results
Pizzas	1,600
Deliveries	180
Revenue	$21,340
Pizza ingredients	$6,850
Kitchen staff	$5,810
Utilities	$875
Delivery person	$522
Delivery vehicle	$982
Equipment depreciation	$384
Rent	$1,790
Miscellaneous	$778

Required:

1. Prepare a flexible budget performance report that shows both activity variances and revenue and spending variances for the pizzeria for October.
2. Explain the activity variances.

PROBLEM 9–22 Performance Report for a Nonprofit Organization [LO1, LO4, LO6]

The KGV Blood Bank, a private charity partly supported by government grants, is located on the Caribbean island of St. Lucia. The blood bank has just finished its operations for September, which was a particularly busy month due to a powerful hurricane that hit neighboring islands causing many injuries. The hurricane largely bypassed St. Lucia, but residents of St. Lucia willingly donated their blood to help people on other islands. As a consequence, the blood bank collected and processed over 20% more blood than had been originally planned for the month.

A report prepared by a government official comparing actual costs to budgeted costs for the blood bank appears on the following page. (The currency on St. Lucia is the East Caribbean dollar.) Continued support from the government depends on the blood bank's ability to demonstrate control over its costs.

KGV Blood Bank Cost Control Report For the Month Ended September 30	Planning Budget	Actual Results	Variances
Liters of blood collected	600	780	
Medical supplies	$ 7,110	$ 9,252	$2,142 U
Lab tests	8,610	10,782	2,172 U
Equipment depreciation	1,900	2,100	200 U
Rent	1,500	1,500	0
Utilities	300	324	24 U
Administration	14,310	14,575	265 U
Total expense	$33,730	$38,533	$4,803 U

The managing director of the blood bank was very unhappy with this report, claiming that his costs were higher than expected due to the emergency on the neighboring islands. He also pointed out that the additional costs had been fully covered by payments from grateful recipients on the other islands. The government official who prepared the report countered that all of the figures had been submitted by the blood bank to the government; he was just pointing out that actual costs were a lot higher than promised in the budget.

The following cost formulas were used to construct the planning budget:

Medical supplies	$11.85q
Lab tests	$14.35q
Equipment depreciation	$1,900
Rent	$1,500
Utilities	$300
Administration	$13,200 + $1.85q

Required:

1. Prepare a new performance report for September using the flexible budget approach.
2. Do you think any of the variances in the report you prepared should be investigated? Why?

PROBLEM 9–23 Critiquing a Variance Report; Preparing a Performance Report [LO1, LO4, LO6]

Several years ago, Shipley Corporation developed a comprehensive budgeting system for profit planning and control purposes. While departmental supervisors have been happy with the system, the factory manager has expressed considerable dissatisfaction with the information being generated by the system.

A typical departmental cost report for a recent period follows:

	A	B	C	D	E
1	Assembly Department				
2	Cost Report				
3	For the Month Ended March 31				
4					
5		Planning Budget	Actual Results	Variances	
6	Machine-hours	30,000	25,000		
7					
8	Variable costs:				
9	Supplies	$ 6,000	$ 5,400	$ 600 F	
10	Scrap	15,000	14,000	1,000 F	
11	Indirect materials	52,500	47,000	5,500 F	
12	Fixed costs:				
13	Wages and salaries	60,000	61,900	1,900 U	
14	Equipment depreciation	90,000	90,000	-	
15	Total cost	$ 223,500	$ 218,300	$ 5,200 F	
16					

Sheet1 Sheet2 Sheet3

After receiving a copy of this cost report, the supervisor of the Assembly Department stated, "These reports are super. It makes me feel really good to see how well things are going in my department. I can't understand why those people upstairs complain so much about the reports."

For the last several years, the company's marketing department has chronically failed to meet the sales goals expressed in the company's monthly budgets.

Required:

1. The company's president is uneasy about the cost reports and would like you to evaluate their usefulness to the company.
2. What changes, if any, should be made in the reports to give better insight into how well departmental supervisors are controlling costs?
3. Prepare a new performance report for the quarter, incorporating any changes you suggested in question (2) above.
4. How well were costs controlled in the Assembly Department in March?

PROBLEM 9–24 Critiquing a Cost Report; Preparing a Performance Report [LO1, LO4, LO6]

Sue Jaski, supervisor of the Karaki Corporation's Machining Department, was visibly upset after being reprimanded for her department's poor performance over the prior month. The department's cost control report is given below:

Karaki Corporation—Machining Department
Cost Control Report
For the Month Ended June 30

	Planning Budget	Actual Results	Variances
Machine-hours	40,000	42,000	
Direct labor wages	$70,000	$71,400	$1,400 U
Supplies	20,000	21,300	1,300 U
Maintenance	20,100	20,100	0
Utilities	18,800	19,000	200 U
Supervision	41,000	41,000	0
Depreciation	67,000	67,000	0
Total	$236,900	$239,800	$2,900 U

"I just can't understand all the red ink," Jaski complained to the supervisor of another department. "When the boss called me in, I thought he was going to give me a pat on the back because I know for a fact that my department worked more efficiently last month than it has ever worked before. Instead, he tore me apart. I thought for a minute that it might be over the supplies that were stolen out of our warehouse last month. But they only amounted to a couple of hundred dollars, and just look at this report. Everything is unfavorable."

Direct labor wages and supplies are variable costs; supervision and depreciation are fixed costs; and maintenance and utilities are mixed costs. The fixed component of the budgeted maintenance cost is $12,100; the fixed component of the budgeted utilities cost is $12,800.

Required:

1. Evaluate the company's cost control report and explain why the variances were all unfavorable.
2. Prepare a performance report that will help Ms. Jaski's superiors assess how well costs were controlled in the Machining Department.

PROBLEM 9–25 Critiquing a Report; Preparing a Performance Budget [LO1, LO4, LO6]

Facilitator Corp. is a company that acts as a facilitator in tax-favored real estate swaps. Such swaps, known as 1031 exchanges, permit participants to avoid some or all of the capital gains taxes that would otherwise be due. The bookkeeper for the company has been asked to prepare a report for the company to help its owner/manager analyze performance. The first such report appears below:

Facilitator Corp
Analysis of Revenues and Costs
For the Month Ended May 31

	Planning Budget Unit Revenues and Costs	Actual Unit Revenues and Costs	Variances
Exchanges completed	20	25	
Revenue	$550	$500	$50 U
Expenses:			
Legal and search fees	155	161	6 U
Office expenses	209	172	37 F
Equipment depreciation	30	24	6 F
Rent	75	60	15 F
Insurance	15	12	3 F
Total expense	484	429	55 F
Net operating income	$ 66	$ 71	$ 5 F

Note that the revenues and costs in the above report are *unit* revenues and costs. For example, the average office expense is $209 per exchange completed on the planning budget; whereas, the average actual office expense is $172 per exchange completed.

Legal and search fees is a variable cost; office expenses is a mixed cost; and equipment depreciation, rent, and insurance are fixed costs. In the planning budget, the fixed component of office expenses was $4,100.

All of the company's revenues come from fees collected when an exchange is completed.

Required:

1. Evaluate the report prepared by the bookkeeper.
2. Prepare a performance report that would help the owner/manager assess the performance of the company in May.
3. Using the report you created, evaluate the performance of the company in May.

Cases

All applicable cases are available with McGraw-Hill's *Connect™ Accounting*.

CASE 9–26 Ethics and the Manager [LO3]

Lance Prating is the controller of the Colorado Springs manufacturing facility of Prudhom Enterprises, Inc. The annual cost control report is one of the many reports that must be filed with corporate headquarters and is due at corporate headquarters shortly after the beginning of the New Year. Prating does not like putting work off to the last minute, so just before Christmas he prepared a preliminary draft of the cost control report. Some adjustments would later be required for transactions that occur between Christmas and New Year's Day. A copy of the preliminary draft report, which Prating completed on December 21, follows:

Colorado Springs Manufacturing Facility Cost Control Report December 21 Preliminary Draft			
	Flexible Budget	Actual Results	Spending Variances
Labor-hours	9,000	9,000	
Direct labor	$162,000	$164,600	$2,600 U
Power	2,700	2,950	250 U
Supplies	28,800	29,700	900 U
Equipment depreciation	226,500	228,300	1,800 U
Supervisory salaries	189,000	187,300	1,700 F
Insurance	23,000	23,000	0
Industrial engineering	160,000	154,000	6,000 F
Factory building lease	46,000	46,000	0
Total expense	$838,000	$835,850	$2,150 F

Tab Kapp, the general manager at the Colorado Springs facility, asked to see a copy of the preliminary draft report. Prating carried a copy of the report to Kapp's office where the following discussion took place:

Kapp: Wow! Almost all of the variances on the report are unfavorable. The only favorable variances are for supervisory salaries and industrial engineering. How did we have an unfavorable variance for depreciation?

Prating: Do you remember that milling machine that broke down because the wrong lubricant was used by the machine operator?

Kapp: Yes.

Prating: We couldn't fix it. We had to scrap the machine and buy a new one.

Kapp: This report doesn't look good. I was raked over the coals last year when we had just a few unfavorable variances.

Prating: I'm afraid the final report is going to look even worse.

Kapp: Oh?

Prating: The line item for industrial engineering on the report is for work we hired Sanchez Engineering to do for us. The original contract was for $160,000, but we asked them to do some additional work that was not in the contract. We have to reimburse Sanchez Engineering for the costs of that additional work. The $154,000 in actual costs that appears on the preliminary draft report reflects only their billings up through December 21. The last bill they had sent us was on November 28, and they completed the project just last week. Yesterday I got a call from Mary Jurney over at Sanchez and she said they would be sending us a final bill for the project before the end of the year. The total bill, including the reimbursements for the additional work, is going to be . . .

Kapp: I am not sure I want to hear this.

Prating: $176,000

Kapp: Ouch!

Prating: The additional work added $16,000 to the cost of the project.

Kapp: I can't turn in a report with an overall unfavorable variance! They'll kill me at corporate headquarters. Call up Mary at Sanchez and ask her not to send the bill until after the first of the year. We have to have that $6,000 favorable variance for industrial engineering on the report.

Required:

What should Lance Prating do? Explain.

CASE 9–27 Critiquing a Report; Preparing Spending Variances [LO3, LO5, LO6]

Farrar University offers an extensive continuing education program in many cities throughout the state. For the convenience of its faculty and administrative staff and to save costs, the university operates a motor pool. The motor pool operated with 20 vehicles until February, when an additional automobile was acquired at the request of the university administration. The motor pool furnishes gasoline, oil, and other supplies for its automobiles. A mechanic does routine maintenance and minor repairs. Major repairs are performed at a nearby commercial garage. Each year, the supervisor of the motor pool prepares an annual budget, which is reviewed by the university and approved after suitable modifications.

The following cost control report shows actual operating costs for March of the current year compared to one-twelfth of the annual budget.

Farrar University Motor Pool Cost Control Report For the Month Ended March 31	Annual Budget	Monthly Budget (1/12 of Annual Budget)	March Actual	(Over) Under Budget
Miles	600,000	50,000	58,000	
Autos	20	20	21	
Gasoline	$ 96,000	$ 8,000	$ 8,970	$ (970)
Oil, minor repairs, parts	30,000	2,500	2,840	(340)
Outside repairs	9,600	800	980	(180)
Insurance	18,000	1,500	1,625	(125)
Salaries and benefits	103,320	8,610	8,610	0
Vehicle depreciation	48,000	4,000	4,200	(200)
Total	$304,920	$25,410	$27,225	$(1,815)

The annual budget was based on the following assumptions:

a. $0.16 per mile for gasoline.
b. $0.05 per mile for oil, minor repairs, and parts.
c. $480 per automobile per year for outside repairs.
d. $900 per automobile per year for insurance.
e. $8,610 per month for salaries and benefits.
f. $2,400 per automobile per year for depreciation.

The supervisor of the motor pool is unhappy with the report, claiming it paints an unfair picture of the motor pool's performance.

Required:

1. Prepare a new performance report for March based on a flexible budget that shows spending variances.
2. What are the deficiencies in the original cost control report? How does the report that you prepared in part (1) above overcome these deficiencies?

(CMA, adapted)

CASE 9–28 Performance Report with More Than One Cost Driver [LO4, LO5]

The Munchkin Theater is a nonprofit organization devoted to staging plays for children. The theater has a very small full-time professional administrative staff. Through a special arrangement with the actors' union, actors and directors rehearse without pay and are paid only for actual performances.

The costs from the current year's planning budget appear below. The Munchkin Theater had tentatively planned to put on five different productions with a total of 60 performances. For example, one of the productions was *Peter Rabbit,* which had five performances.

The Munchkin Theater Costs from the Planning Budget For the Year Ended December 31	
Budgeted number of productions	5
Budgeted number of performances	60
Actors' and directors' wages	$144,000
Stagehands' wages	27,000
Ticket booth personnel and ushers' wages	10,800
Scenery, costumes, and props	43,000
Theater hall rent	45,000
Printed programs	10,500
Publicity	13,000
Administrative expenses	43,200
Total	$336,500

Some of the costs vary with the number of productions, some with the number of performances, and some are fixed and depend on neither the number of productions nor the number of performances. The costs of scenery, costumes, props, and publicity vary with the number of productions. It doesn't make any difference how many times *Peter Rabbit* is performed, the cost of the scenery is the same. Likewise, the cost of publicizing a play with posters and radio commercials is the same whether there are 10, 20, or 30 performances of the play. On the other hand, the wages of the actors, directors, stagehands, ticket booth personnel, and ushers vary with the number of performances. The greater the number of performances, the higher the wage costs will be. Similarly, the costs of renting the hall and printing the programs will vary with the number of performances. Administrative expenses are more difficult to pin down, but the best estimate is that approximately 75% of the budgeted costs are fixed, 15% depend on the number of productions staged, and the remaining 10% depend on the number of performances.

After the beginning of the year, the board of directors of the theater authorized changing the theater's program to four productions and a total of 64 performances. Actual costs were higher than the costs from the planning budget. (Grants from donors and ticket sales were also correspondingly higher, but are not shown here.) Data concerning the actual costs appear below:

The Munchkin Theater Actual Costs For the Year Ended December 31	
Actual number of productions	4
Actual number of performances	64
Actors' and directors' wages	$148,000
Stagehands' wages	28,600
Ticket booth personnel and ushers' wages	12,300
Scenery, costumes, and props	39,300
Theater hall rent	49,600
Printed programs	10,950
Publicity	12,000
Administrative expenses	41,650
Total	$342,400

Required:

1. Prepare a flexible budget for The Munchkin Theater based on the actual activity of the year.
2. Prepare a flexible budget performance report for the year that shows both activity variances and spending variances.
3. If you were on the board of directors of the theater, would you be pleased with how well costs were controlled during the year? Why or why not?
4. The cost formulas provide figures for the average cost per production and average cost per performance. How accurate do you think these figures would be for predicting the cost of a new production or of an additional performance of a particular production?

Chapter 10

Standard Costs and Variances

Managing Materials and Labor

LEARNING OBJECTIVES

After studying Chapter 10, you should be able to:

LO1 Compute the direct materials quantity and price variances and explain their significance.

LO2 Compute the direct labor efficiency and rate variances and explain their significance.

LO3 Compute the variable manufacturing overhead efficiency and rate variances and explain their significance.

LO4 (Appendix 10A) Compute and interpret the fixed overhead volume and budget variances.

LO5 (Appendix 10B) Prepare journal entries to record standard costs and variances.

BUSINESS FOCUS

Schneider Electric's Oxford, Ohio, plant manufactures *busways* that transport electricity from its point of entry into a building to remote locations throughout the building. The plant's managers pay close attention to direct material costs because they are more than half of the plant's total manufacturing costs. To help control scrap rates for direct materials such as copper, steel, and aluminum, the accounting department prepares direct materials quantity variances. These variances compare the standard quantity of direct materials that should have been used to make a product (according to computations by the plant's engineers) to the amount of direct materials that were actually used. Keeping a close eye on these differences helps to identify and deal with the causes of excessive scrap, such as an inadequately trained machine operator, poor quality raw material inputs, or a malfunctioning machine.

Because direct labor is also a significant component of the plant's total manufacturing costs, the management team daily monitors the direct labor efficiency variance. This variance compares the standard amount of labor time allowed to make a product to the actual amount of labor time used. When idle workers cause an unfavorable labor efficiency variance, managers temporarily move workers from departments with slack to departments with a backlog of work to be done. ■

Source: Author's conversation with Doug Taylor, plant controller, Schneider Electric's Oxford, Ohio, plant.

In the last chapter, we investigated flexible budget variances. These variances provide feedback concerning how well an organization performed in relation to its budget. The impact on profit of a change in the level of activity is captured in the overall net operating income activity variance. The revenue and spending variances indicate how well revenues and costs were controlled—given the actual level of activity. In the case of many of the spending variances, we can get even more detail about how well costs were controlled. For example, at Rick's Hairstyling, an unfavorable spending variance for hairstyling supplies could be due to using too many supplies or to paying too much for the supplies, or some combination of the two. It would be useful to separate those two different effects, particularly if different people are responsible for using the supplies and for purchasing them. In this chapter, we will learn how that can be done for some costs; basically, we will decompose spending variances into two parts—a part that measures how well resources were used and a part that measures how well the acquisition prices of those resources were controlled.

Companies in highly competitive industries like Federal Express, Southwest Airlines, Dell, and Toyota must be able to provide high-quality goods and services at low cost. If they do not, their customers will buy from more efficient competitors. Stated in the starkest terms, managers must obtain inputs such as raw materials and electricity at the lowest possible prices and must use them as effectively as possible—while maintaining or increasing the quality of what they sell. If inputs are purchased at prices that are too high or more input is used than is really necessary, higher costs will result.

How do managers control the prices that are paid for inputs and the quantities that are used? They could examine every transaction in detail, but this obviously would be an inefficient use of management time. For many companies, the answer to this control problem lies at least partially in standard costs.

Standard Costs—Setting the Stage

A *standard* is a benchmark or "norm" for measuring performance. Standards are found everywhere. Your doctor evaluates your weight using standards for individuals of your age, height, and gender. The food we eat in restaurants is prepared using standardized recipes. The buildings we live in conform to standards set in building codes. Standards are also widely used in managerial accounting where they relate to the *quantity* and *cost* (or acquisition price) of inputs used in manufacturing goods or providing services.

Quantity and price standards are set for each major input such as raw materials and labor time. *Quantity standards* specify how much of an input should be used to make a product or provide a service. *Price standards* specify how much should be paid for each unit of the input. Actual quantities and actual costs of inputs are compared to these standards. If either the quantity or the cost of inputs departs significantly from the standards, managers investigate the discrepancy to find the cause of the problem and eliminate it. This process is called **management by exception.**

In our daily lives, we often operate in a management by exception mode. Consider what happens when you sit down in the driver's seat of your car. You put the key in the ignition, you turn the key, and your car starts. Your expectation (standard) that the car will start is met; you do not have to open the car hood and check the battery, the connecting cables, the fuel lines, and so on. If you turn the key and the car does not start, then you have a discrepancy (variance). Your expectations are not met, and you need to investigate why. Note that even if the car starts after a second try, it still would be wise to investigate. The fact that the expectation was not met should be viewed as an opportunity to uncover the cause of the problem rather than as simply an annoyance. If the underlying cause is not discovered and corrected, the problem may recur and become much worse.

This basic approach to identifying and solving problems is the essence of the *variance analysis cycle,* which is illustrated in Exhibit 10–1. The cycle begins with the preparation of standard cost performance reports in the accounting department. These reports

EXHIBIT 10–1
The Variance Analysis Cycle

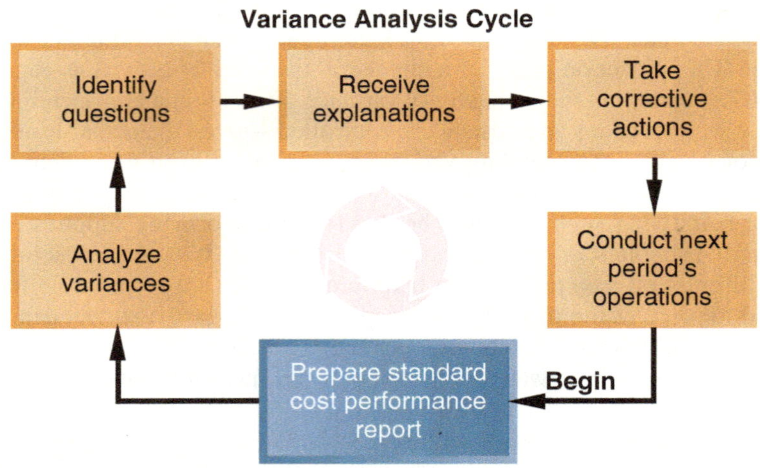

highlight the *variances,* which are the differences between actual results and what should have occurred according to the standards. The variances raise questions. Why did this variance occur? Why is this variance larger than it was last period? The significant variances are investigated to discover their root causes. Corrective actions are taken. And then next period's operations are carried out. The cycle begins again with the preparation of a new standard cost performance report for the latest period. The emphasis should be on highlighting problems, finding their root causes, and then taking corrective action. The goal is to improve operations—not to assign blame.

Who Uses Standard Costs?

Manufacturing, service, food, and not-for-profit organizations all make use of standards to some extent. Auto service centers like Firestone and Sears, for example, often set specific labor time standards for the completion of certain tasks, such as installing a carburetor or doing a valve job, and then measure actual performance against these standards. Fast-food outlets such as McDonald's have exacting standards for the quantity of meat going into a sandwich, as well as standards for the cost of the meat. Hospitals have standard costs for food, laundry, and other items, as well as standard time allowances for certain routine activities, such as laboratory tests. In short, you are likely to run into standard costs in virtually any line of business.

Manufacturing companies often have highly developed standard costing systems in which standards for direct materials, direct labor, and overhead are created for each product. A **standard cost card** shows the standard quantities and costs of the inputs required to produce a unit of a specific product. In the following section, we provide an example of a standard cost card.

Setting Standard Costs

Standards should be designed to encourage efficient *future* operations, not just a repetition of *past* operations that may or may not have been efficient. Standards tend to fall into one of two categories—either ideal or practical.

Ideal standards can be attained only under the best circumstances. They allow for no machine breakdowns or other work interruptions, and they call for a level of effort that can be attained only by the most skilled and efficient employees working at peak effort 100% of the time. Some managers feel that such standards spur continual improvement. These managers argue that even though employees know they will rarely meet the standard, it is a constant reminder of the need for ever-increasing efficiency and effort. Few organizations use ideal standards. Most managers feel that ideal standards tend to discourage even the most diligent workers. Moreover, variances from ideal standards are difficult to interpret. Large variances from the ideal are normal and it is therefore difficult to "manage by exception."

Practical standards are standards that are "tight but attainable." They allow for normal machine downtime and employee rest periods, and they can be attained through reasonable, though highly efficient, efforts by the average worker. Variances from practical standards typically signal a need for management attention because they represent deviations that fall outside of normal operating conditions. Furthermore, practical standards can serve multiple purposes. In addition to signaling abnormal conditions, they can also be used in forecasting cash flows and in planning inventory. By contrast, ideal standards cannot be used for these purposes because they do not allow for normal inefficiencies and result in unrealistic forecasts.

Throughout the remainder of this chapter, we will assume that practical rather than ideal standards are in use.

MANAGERIAL ACCOUNTING IN ACTION

The Issue

Colonial Pewter Company

The Colonial Pewter Company was organized a year ago. The company's only product is an elaborate reproduction of an eighteenth century pewter bookend. The bookend is made largely by hand, using traditional metalworking tools. Consequently, the manufacturing process is labor intensive and requires a high level of skill.

Colonial Pewter has recently expanded its workforce to take advantage of unexpected demand for the bookends as gifts. The company started with a small cadre of experienced pewter workers but has had to hire less experienced workers as a result of the expansion. The president of the company, J. D. Wriston, has called a meeting to discuss production problems. Attending the meeting are Tom Kuchel, the production manager; Janet Warner, the purchasing manager; and Terry Sherman, the corporate controller.

J. D.: I've got a feeling that we aren't getting the production we should out of our new people.

Tom: Give us a chance. Some of the new people have been with the company for less than a month.

Janet: Let me add that production seems to be wasting an awful lot of material—particularly pewter. That stuff is very expensive.

Tom: What about the shipment of defective pewter that you bought—the one with the iron contamination? That caused us major problems.

Janet: How was I to know it was off-grade? Besides, it was a great deal.

J. D.: Calm down everybody. Let's get the facts before we start attacking each other.

Tom: I agree. The more facts the better.

J. D.: Okay, Terry, it's your turn. Facts are the controller's department.

Terry: I'm afraid I can't provide the answers off the top of my head, but if you give me about a week I can set up a system that can routinely answer questions relating to worker productivity, material waste, and input prices.

J. D.: Let's mark it on our calendars.

Setting Direct Materials Standards

Terry Sherman's first task was to prepare price and quantity standards for the company's only significant raw material, pewter ingots. The **standard price per unit** for direct materials should reflect the final, delivered cost of the materials. After consulting with purchasing manager Janet Warner, Terry set the standard price of pewter at $4.00 per pound.

The **standard quantity per unit** for direct materials should reflect the amount of material required for each unit of finished product as well as an allowance for unavoidable waste.[1] After consulting with the production manager, Tom Kuchel, Terry set the quantity standard for pewter at 3.0 pounds per pair of bookends.

[1] Although allowances for waste, spoilage, and rejects are often built into standards, this practice is often criticized because it contradicts the zero defects goal that underlies many process improvement programs. If allowances for waste, spoilage, and rejects are built into the standard cost, those allowances should be periodically reviewed and reduced over time to reflect improved processes, better training, and better equipment.

IN BUSINESS

SKYROCKETING TRANSPORTATION COSTS AFFECT DIRECT MATERIALS STANDARDS

Direct materials price standards should reflect the final delivered cost of the materials. Given increases in the costs of shipping raw materials across oceans, many companies have increased their price standards. For example, the average cost to rent a ship to transport raw materials from Brazil to China has increased from $65,000 to $180,000. In some instances, shipping costs now exceed the cost of the cargo itself. It costs about $88 to ship a ton of iron ore from Brazil to Asia; however, the iron ore itself only costs $60 per ton.

Source: Robert Guy Matthews, "Ship Shortage Pushes Up Prices of Raw Materials," *The Wall Street Journal*, October 22, 2007, pp. A1 and A12.

Once Terry established the price and quantity standards he computed the standard cost of material per unit of the finished product as follows:

3.0 pounds per unit × $4.00 per pound = $12.00 per unit

This $12.00 cost will appear on the product's standard cost card.

Setting Direct Labor Standards

Direct labor price and quantity standards are usually expressed in terms of a labor rate and labor-hours. The **standard rate per hour** for direct labor should include hourly wages, employment taxes, and fringe benefits. Using wage records and in consultation with the production manager, Terry Sherman determined the standard rate per direct labor-hour to be $22.00.

Many companies prepare a single standard rate per hour for all employees in a department. This standard rate reflects the expected "mix" of workers, even though the actual wage rates may vary somewhat from individual to individual due to differing skills or seniority.

The standard direct labor time required to complete a unit of product (called the **standard hours per unit**) is perhaps the single most difficult standard to determine. One approach is to break down each task into elemental body movements (such as reaching, pushing, and turning over). Published tables of standard times for such movements can be used to estimate the total time required to complete the task. Another approach is for an industrial engineer to do a time and motion study, actually clocking the time required for each task. As stated earlier, the standard time should include allowances for breaks, personal needs of employees, cleanup, and machine downtime.

After consulting with the production manager, Terry set the standard for direct labor time at 0.50 direct labor-hours per pair of bookends.

Once Terry established the rate and time standards, he computed the standard direct labor cost per unit of product as follows:

0.50 direct labor-hours per unit × $22.00 per direct labor-hour = $11.00 per unit

This $11.00 per unit standard direct labor cost appears along with direct materials on the standard cost card for a pair of pewter bookends.

Setting Variable Manufacturing Overhead Standards

As with direct labor, the price and quantity standards for variable manufacturing overhead are usually expressed in terms of rate and hours. The rate represents *the variable portion of the predetermined overhead rate* discussed in the job-order costing

Inputs	(1) Standard Quantity or Hours	(2) Standard Price or Rate	Standard Cost (1) × (2)
Direct materials	3.0 pounds	$4.00 per pound	$12.00
Direct labor	0.50 hours	$22.00 per hour	11.00
Variable manufacturing overhead	0.50 hours	$6.00 per hour	3.00
Total standard cost per unit			$26.00

EXHIBIT 10–2
Standard Cost Card—Variable Manufacturing Costs

chapter; the hours relate to the activity base that is used to apply overhead to units of product (usually machine-hours or direct labor-hours). At Colonial Pewter, the variable portion of the predetermined overhead rate is $6.00 per direct labor-hour. Therefore, Terry computed the standard variable manufacturing overhead cost per unit as follows:

0.50 direct labor-hours per unit × $6.00 per direct labor-hour = $3.00 per unit

This $3.00 per unit cost for variable manufacturing overhead appears along with direct materials and direct labor on the standard cost card in Exhibit 10–2. Observe that the **standard cost per unit** for variable manufacturing overhead is computed the same way as for direct materials or direct labor—the standard quantity allowed per unit of the output is multiplied by the standard price. In this case, the standard quantity is expressed as 0.5 direct labor-hours per unit and the standard price (or rate) is expressed as $6.00 per direct labor-hour.

Using Standards in Flexible Budgets

The standard costs of $12.00 per unit for materials, $11.00 per unit for direct labor, and $3.00 per unit for variable manufacturing overhead can be used to compute activity and spending variances as described in the previous chapter. To illustrate, Colonial Pewter's flexible budget performance report for June is shown in Exhibit 10–3. Notice, the report includes an activity variance and a spending variance for direct materials, direct labor, and variable overhead. This performance report is based on the following data:

Originally budgeted output in June	2,100 units
Actual output in June	2,000 units
Actual direct materials cost in June*	$24,700
Actual direct labor cost in June	$22,680
Actual variable manufacturing overhead cost in June	$7,140

*There were no beginning or ending inventories of raw materials in June; all materials purchased were used.

For example, the direct labor cost for the planning budget in Exhibit 10–3 is $23,100 (= $11.00 per unit × 2,100 units).

While the performance report in Exhibit 10–3 is useful, it would be even more useful if the spending variances could be broken down into their price-related and quantity-related components. For example, the direct materials spending variance in the report is $700 unfavorable. This means that, given the actual level of production for the period, direct materials costs were too high by $700—at least according to the standard costs. Was this due to higher than expected prices for materials? Or was it due to too much material being used? The standard cost variances we will be discussing in the rest of the chapter are designed to answer these questions.

EXHIBIT 10–3
Flexible Budget Performance Report for Manufacturing Costs

Colonial Pewter
Flexible Budget Performance Report—Manufacturing Costs Only
For the Month Ended June 30

	Planning Budget	Activity Variances	Flexible Budget	Spending Variances	Actual Results
Bookends produced (q)	2,100		2,000		2,000
Direct materials (12.00q$)	$25,200	$1,200 F	$24,000	$700 U	$24,700
Direct labor (11.00q$)	$23,100	$1,100 F	$22,000	$680 U	$22,680
Variable manufacturing overhead (3.00q$)	$6,300	$300 F	$6,000	$1,140 U	$7,140

A General Model for Standard Cost Variance Analysis

The basic idea in standard cost variance analysis is to decompose spending variances from the flexible budget into two elements—one due to the amount of the input that is used and the other due to the price paid for the input. Using too much of the input results in an unfavorable quantity variance. Paying too much for the input results in an unfavorable price variance. A **quantity variance** is the difference between how much of an input was actually used and how much should have been used and is stated in dollar terms using the standard price of the input. A **price variance** is the difference between the actual price of an input and its standard price, multiplied by the actual amount of the input purchased.

Why are standards separated into two categories—quantity and price? Quantity variances and price variances usually have different causes. In addition, different managers are usually responsible for buying and for using inputs. For example, in the case of a raw material, a purchasing manager is responsible for its price. However, the production manager is responsible for the amount of the raw material actually used to make products. As we shall see, setting up separate quantity and price standards allows us to better separate the responsibilities of these two managers. It also allows us to prepare more timely reports. The purchasing manager's tasks are completed when the material is delivered for use in the factory. A performance report for the purchasing manager can be prepared at that point. However, the production manager's responsibilities have just begun at that point. A performance report for the production manager must be delayed until production is completed and it is known how much raw material was used in the final product. Therefore, it is important to clearly distinguish between deviations from price standards (the responsibility of the purchasing manager) and deviations from quantity standards (the responsibility of the production manager).

Exhibit 10–4 presents a general model that can be used to decompose the spending variance for a variable cost into a *quantity variance* and a *price variance.* Column (1) in this exhibit corresponds with the Flexible Budget column in Exhibit 10–3. Column (3) corresponds with the Actual Results column in Exhibit 10–3. Column (2) has been inserted into Exhibit 10–4 to enable separating the spending variance into a quantity variance and a price variance.

Three things should be noted from Exhibit 10–4. First, a quantity variance and a price variance can be computed for each of the three variable cost elements—direct materials, direct labor, and variable manufacturing overhead—even though the variances have different names. For example, a price variance is called a *materials price variance* in the case of direct materials but a *labor rate variance* in the case of direct labor and a *variable overhead rate variance* in the case of variable manufacturing overhead.

EXHIBIT 10–4
A General Model for Standard Cost Variance Analysis—Variable Manufacturing Costs

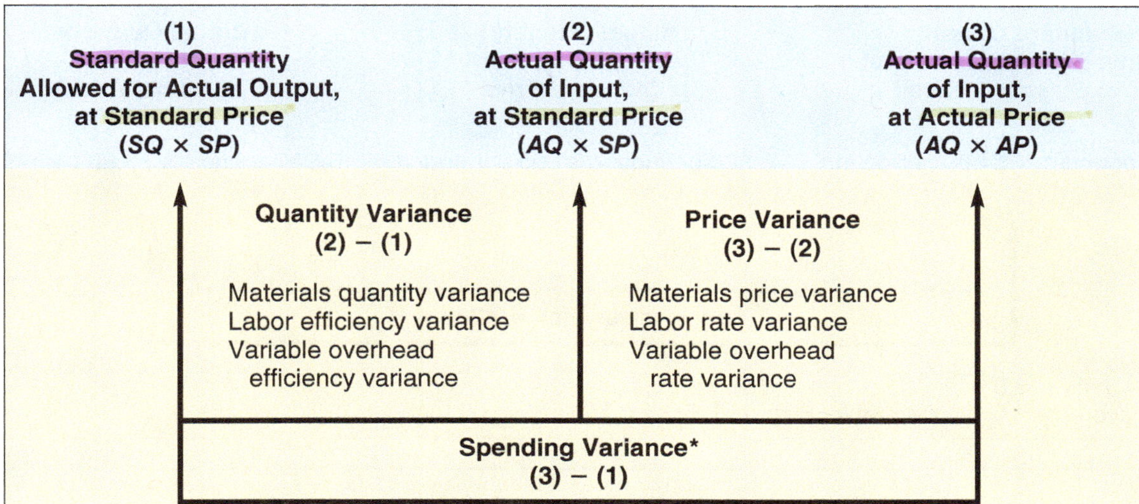

*In the case of materials, the materials quantity variance and the materials price variance do not sum to the spending variance when the amount purchased differs from the amount used in production. This exception will be covered later in the chapter.

Second, the quantity variance—regardless of what it is called—is computed in exactly the same way regardless of whether one is dealing with direct materials, direct labor, or variable manufacturing overhead. The same is true of the price variance.

Third, the input is the actual quantity of direct materials or direct labor purchased; the output is the good production of the period, expressed in terms of the *standard quantity* (or the *standard hours) allowed for the actual output* (see column 1 in Exhibit 10–4). The **standard quantity allowed** or **standard hours allowed** means the amount of an input *that should have been used* to produce the actual output of the period. This could be more or less than the actual amount of the input, depending on the efficiency or inefficiency of operations. The standard quantity allowed is computed by multiplying the actual output in units by the standard input allowed per unit of output.

With this general model as the foundation, we will now calculate Colonial Pewter's quantity and price variances.

Using Standard Costs—Direct Materials Variances

LEARNING OBJECTIVE 1
Compute the direct materials quantity and price variances and explain their significance.

After determining Colonial Pewter Company's standard costs for direct materials, direct labor, and variable manufacturing overhead, Terry Sherman's next step was to compute the company's variances for June. As discussed in the preceding section, variances are computed by comparing standard costs to actual costs. Terry referred to the standard cost card in Exhibit 10–2 that shows the standard cost of direct materials was computed as follows:

$$3.0 \text{ pounds per unit} \times \$4.00 \text{ per pound} = \$12.00 \text{ per unit}$$

Colonial Pewter's records for June showed that 6,500 pounds of pewter were purchased at a cost of $3.80 per pound, for a total cost of $24,700. All of the material purchased was

EXHIBIT 10–5
Standard Cost Variance Analysis—Direct Materials
(Note: The quantity of materials purchased equals the quantity used in production.)

(1) Standard Quantity Allowed for Actual Output, at Standard Price (*SQ* × *SP*)	(2) Actual Quantity of Input, at Standard Price (*AQ* × *SP*)	(3) Actual Quantity of Input, at Actual Price (*AQ* × *AP*)
6,000 pounds* × \$4.00 per pound = \$24,000	6,500 pounds × \$4.00 per pound = \$26,000	6,500 pounds × \$3.80 per pound = \$24,700

Quantity variance = \$2,000 U

Price variance = \$1,300 F

Spending variance = \$700 U

*2,000 units × 3.0 pounds per unit = 6,000 pounds.
F = Favorable; U = Unfavorable.

used during June to manufacture 2,000 pairs of pewter bookends.[2] Using these data and the standard costs from Exhibit 10–2, Terry computed the quantity and price variances shown in Exhibit 10–5.

The variances in Exhibit 10–5 are based on three different total costs—\$24,000, \$26,000, and \$24,700. The first, \$24,000, refers to how much should have been spent on pewter to produce the actual output of 2,000 units. The standards call for 3 pounds of pewter per unit. Because 2,000 units were produced, 6,000 pounds of pewter should have been used. This is referred to as the *standard quantity allowed for the actual output.* If this 6,000 pounds of pewter had been purchased at the standard price of \$4.00 per pound, the company would have spent \$24,000. This is the amount that appears in the company's flexible budget for the month.

The third total cost figure, \$24,700, is the actual amount paid for the actual amount of pewter purchased. The difference between the \$24,700 actually spent and the amount that should have been spent, \$24,000, is the spending variance for the month of \$700. This variance is unfavorable (denoted by U) because the amount that was actually spent exceeded the amount that should have been spent.

The second total cost figure, \$26,000, is the key that allows us to decompose the spending variance into two distinct elements—one due to quantity and one due to price. It represents how much the company should have spent if it had purchased the actual amount of input, 6,500 pounds, at the standard price of \$4.00 a pound rather than the actual price of \$3.80 a pound.

The Materials Quantity Variance

Using the \$26,000 total cost figure in column (2), we can make two comparisons—one with the total cost of \$24,000 in column (1) and one with the total cost of \$24,700 in column (3). The difference between the \$24,000 in column (1) and the \$26,000 in column (2) is the quantity variance of \$2,000, which is labeled as unfavorable (denoted by U).

[2] Throughout this section, we assume zero beginning and ending inventories of materials and that all materials purchased during a period are used during that period. The more general case in which there are beginning and ending inventories of materials and materials are not necessarily used during the period in which they are purchased is considered later in the chapter.

To understand this quantity variance, note that the actual amount of pewter used in production was 6,500 pounds. However, the standard amount of pewter allowed for the actual output is 6,000 pounds. Therefore, too much pewter was used to produce the actual output—by a total of 500 pounds. To express this in dollar terms, the 500 pounds is multiplied by the standard price of $4.00 per pound to yield the quantity variance of $2,000. Why is the standard price of the pewter, rather than the actual price, used in this calculation? The production manager is ordinarily responsible for the quantity variance. If the actual price were used in the calculation of the quantity variance, the production manager would be held responsible for the efficiency or inefficiency of the purchasing manager. Apart from being unfair, fruitless arguments between the production manager and purchasing manager would occur every time the actual price of an input was above its standard price. To avoid these arguments, the standard price is used when computing the quantity variance. The quantity variance in Exhibit 10–5 is labeled unfavorable (U) because more pewter was used to produce the actual output than the standard allows. A quantity variance is labeled favorable (F) if the actual quantity is less than the standard quantity.

The Materials Price Variance

The difference between the $26,000 in column (2) and the $24,700 in column (3) is the price variance of $1,300, which is labeled as favorable (denoted by F).

To understand the price variance, note that the $3.80 per pound price paid for the pewter is $0.20 less than the $4.00 per pound standard price allowed for the pewter. Because 6,500 pounds were purchased, the total amount of the variance is $1,300 (= $0.20 per pound × 6,500 pounds). This variance is labeled favorable (F) because the actual purchase price was less than the standard purchase price. A price variance is labeled unfavorable (U) if the actual purchase price exceeds the standard purchase price.

The computations in Exhibit 10–5 reflect the fact that all of the material purchased during June was also used during June. If the amount of material purchased differs from the amount that is used, the computation of the price variance is a bit different. This slight complication is covered at the end of this chapter.

IN BUSINESS

DIRECT MATERIAL PURCHASES: A RISK MANAGEMENT PERSPECTIVE

Shenzhen Hepalink manufactures heparin, a blood-thinning medication that is injected directly into the bloodstream of some surgical patients. The company relies on suppliers to extract its raw material, called crude heparin, from the intestines of slaughtered pigs. The harvesting of crude heparin is susceptible to contamination if the process is improperly managed and monitored. For example, Baxter International recently recalled tainted heparin that some people believe caused illnesses, allergic reactions, and deaths in some patients in the United States and Germany.

Shenzhen Hepalink strives to reduce contamination risks by buying crude heparin only from Chinese government-regulated slaughterhouses instead of rural unregulated slaughterhouses. The company also maintains quality assurance laboratories on each supplier's premises to ensure compliance with applicable rules. These safeguards increase Shenzhen Hepalink's raw materials cost, but they also reduce the risk of contaminated heparin eventually being injected into a patient's bloodstream.

Source: Gordon Fairclough, "How a Heparin Maker in China Tackles Risks," *The Wall Street Journal*, March 10, 2009, pp. B1 and B5.

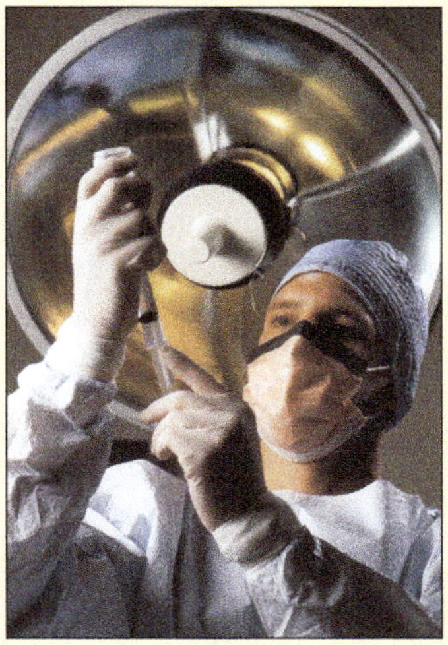

Materials Quantity Variance—A Closer Look

The **materials quantity variance** measures the difference between the quantity of materials used in production and the quantity that should have been used according to the standard. Although the variance is concerned with the physical usage of materials, as shown in Exhibit 10–5, it is generally stated in dollar terms to help gauge its importance. The formula for the materials quantity variance is as follows:

$$\text{Materials quantity variance} = (AQ \times SP) - (SQ \times SP)$$

Actual quantity used — Standard price — Standard quantity allowed for actual output

The formula can be factored as follows:

$$\text{Materials quantity variance} = (AQ - SQ)SP$$

Using the data from Exhibit 10–5 in the formula, we have the following:

$$\text{SQ} = 2{,}000 \text{ units} \times 3.0 \text{ pounds per unit} = 6{,}000 \text{ pounds.}$$

$$\text{Materials quantity variance} = (6{,}500 \text{ pounds} - 6{,}000 \text{ pounds}) \times \$4.00 \text{ per pound}$$
$$= \$2{,}000 \text{ U}$$

The answer, of course, is the same as that shown in Exhibit 10–5.

Variance reports are often presented in the form of a table. An excerpt from Colonial Pewter's variance report is shown below along with the production manager's explanation for the materials quantity variance.

Colonial Pewter Company
Variance Report—Production Department

Type of Material	(1) Standard Price	(2) Actual Quantity	(3) Standard Quantity Allowed	(4) Difference in Quantity (2) − (3)	Total Quantity Variance (1) × (4)	Explanation
Pewter	$4.00	6,500 pounds	6,000 pounds	500 pounds	$2,000 U	Low-quality materials unsuitable for production.

F = Favorable; U = Unfavorable.

It is best to isolate the materials quantity variance when materials are used in production. Materials are drawn for the number of units to be produced, according to the standard bill of materials for each unit. Any additional materials are usually drawn with an excess materials requisition slip, which differs from the normal requisition slips. This procedure calls attention to the excessive usage of materials *while production is still in process* and provides an opportunity to correct any developing problem.

Excessive materials usage can result from many factors, including faulty machines, inferior materials quality, untrained workers, and poor supervision. Generally speaking, it is the responsibility of the production department to see that material usage is kept in line with standards. There may be times, however, when the *purchasing* department is responsible for an unfavorable materials quantity variance. For example, if the purchasing department buys inferior materials at a lower price, the materials may be unsuitable for use and may result in excessive waste. Thus, purchasing rather than production would be responsible for the quantity variance. At Colonial Pewter, the production manager, Tom Kuchel, claimed on the Production Department's Performance Report that low-quality materials were the cause of the unfavorable materials quantity variance for June.

Materials Price Variance—A Closer Look

A **materials price variance** measures the difference between what is paid for a given quantity of materials and what should have been paid according to the standard. From Exhibit 10–5, this difference can be expressed by the following formula:

$$\text{Materials price variance} = (AQ \times AP) - (AQ \times SP)$$

where AQ = Actual quantity purchased, AP = Actual price, SP = Standard price

The formula can be factored as follows:

$$\text{Materials price variance} = AQ(AP - SP)$$

Using the data from Exhibit 10–5 in this formula, we have the following:

Materials price variance = 6,500 pounds ($3.80 per pound − $4.00 per pound) = $1,300 F

Notice that the answer is the same as that shown in Exhibit 10–5. Also note that when using this formula approach, a negative variance is always labeled as favorable (F) and a positive variance is always labeled as unfavorable (U). This will be true of all variance formulas in this chapter.

An excerpt from Colonial Pewter's variance report is shown below along with the purchasing manager's explanation for the materials price variance.

Colonial Pewter Company
Variance Report—Purchasing Department

Item Purchased	(1) Quantity Purchased	(2) Actual Price	(3) Standard Price	(4) Difference in Price (2) − (3)	Total Price Variance (1) × (4)	Explanation
Pewter	6,500 pounds	$3.80	$4.00	$0.20	$1,300 F	Bargained for an especially good price.

F = Favorable; U = Unfavorable.

Isolation of Variances Variances should be isolated and brought to the attention of management as quickly as possible so that problems can be promptly identified and corrected. The most significant variances should be viewed as "red flags"; an exception has occurred that requires explanation by the responsible manager and perhaps follow-up effort. The performance report itself may contain explanations for the variances, as illustrated above. In the case of Colonial Pewter Company, the purchasing manager said that the favorable price variance resulted from bargaining for an especially good price.

Responsibility for the Variance Who is responsible for the materials price variance? Generally speaking, the purchasing manager has control over the price paid for goods and is therefore responsible for the materials price variance. Many factors influence the prices paid for goods including how many units are ordered, how the order is delivered, whether the order is a rush order, and the quality of materials purchased. If any of these factors deviates from what was assumed when the standards were set, a price variance can result. For example, purchasing second-grade materials rather than top-grade materials may result in a favorable price variance because the lower-grade materials may be less costly. However, we should keep in mind that the lower-grade materials may create production problems.

IN BUSINESS

MANAGING MATERIALS PRICE VARIANCES

When Tata Motors lost $110 million in 2000, the company's executives mandated a 10% reduction in costs. Tata's purchasing managers responded by using reverse auctions to buy raw materials. Reverse auctions require suppliers to bid against one another for the right to sell raw material inputs to Tata Motors. The supplier who places the lowest bid wins the contract. Tata's purchasing managers have used 750 reverse auctions a year to lower the company's average purchase prices by 7%. While this practice produces favorable purchase price variances and higher profits in the short run, these benefits may eventually be offset by greater scrap, rework, warranty repairs, customer complaints, and lost sales.

Source: Robyn Meredith, "The Next People's Car," *Forbes*, April 16, 2007, pp. 70–74.

However, someone other than the purchasing manager could be responsible for a materials price variance. For example, due to production problems beyond the purchasing manager's control, the purchasing manager may have to use express delivery. In these cases, the production manager should be held responsible for the resulting price variances.

A word of caution is in order. Variance analysis should not be used to assign blame. The emphasis should be on *supporting* the line managers and *assisting* them in meeting the goals that they have participated in setting for the company. In short, the emphasis should be positive rather than negative. Excessive dwelling on what has already happened, particularly in terms of trying to find someone to blame, can destroy morale and kill any cooperative spirit.

Using Standard Costs—Direct Labor Variances

LEARNING OBJECTIVE 2
Compute the direct labor efficiency and rate variances and explain their significance.

Terry Sherman's next step in determining Colonial Pewter's variances for June was to compute the direct labor variances for the month. Recall from Exhibit 10–2 that the standard direct labor cost per unit of product is $11, computed as follows:

$$0.50 \text{ hours per unit} \times \$22.00 \text{ per hour} = \$11.00 \text{ per unit}$$

During June, the company paid its direct labor workers $22,680, including payroll taxes and fringe benefits, for 1,050 hours of work. This was an average of $21.60 per hour. Using these data and the standard costs from Exhibit 10–2, Terry computed the direct labor efficiency and rate variances that appear in Exhibit 10–6.

Notice that the column headings in Exhibit 10–6 are the same as those used in the prior two exhibits, except that in Exhibit 10–6 the terms *hours* and *rate* are used in place of the terms *quantity* and *price.*

Labor Efficiency Variance—A Closer Look

The **labor efficiency variance** attempts to measure the productivity of direct labor. No variance is more closely watched by management because it is widely believed that increasing direct labor productivity is vital to reducing costs. The formula for the labor efficiency variance is expressed as follows:

$$\text{Labor efficiency variance} = (AH \times SR) - (SH \times SR)$$

where AH = Actual hours; SR = Standard rate; SH = Standard hours allowed for actual output

EXHIBIT 10–6
Standard Cost Variance Analysis—Direct Labor

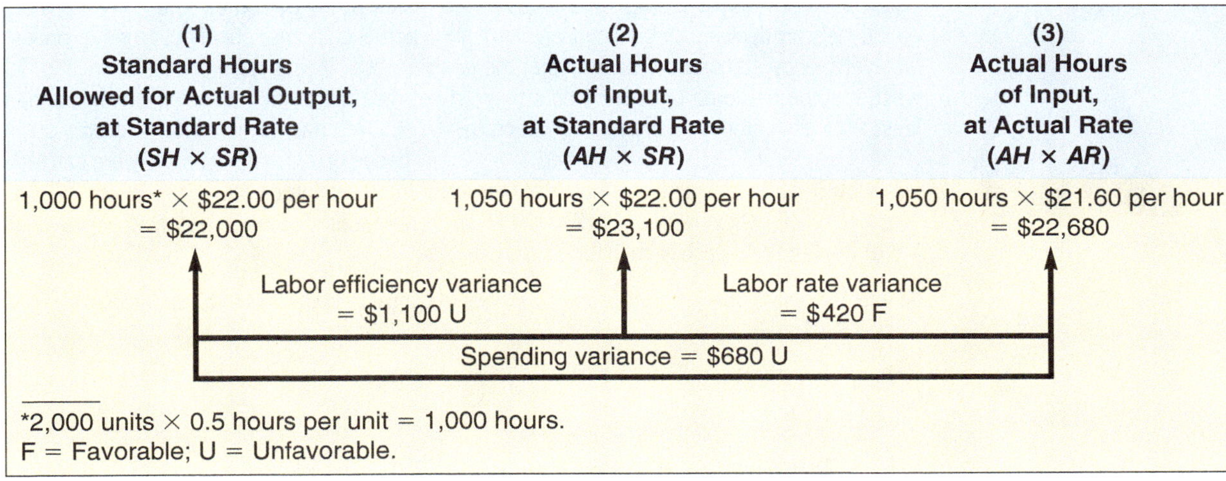

The formula can be factored as follows:

$$\text{Labor efficiency variance} = (AH - SH)SR$$

Using the data from Exhibit 10–6 in the formula, we have the following:

$$SH = 2{,}000 \text{ units} \times 0.5 \text{ hours per unit} = 1{,}000 \text{ hours.}$$

$$\text{Labor efficiency variance} = (1{,}050 \text{ hours} - 1{,}000 \text{ hours})\ \$22.00 \text{ per hour} = \$1{,}100 \text{ U}$$

Possible causes of an unfavorable labor efficiency variance include poorly trained or motivated workers; poor quality materials, requiring more labor time; faulty equipment, causing breakdowns and work interruptions; poor supervision of workers; and inaccurate standards. The managers in charge of production would usually be responsible for control of the labor efficiency variance. However, the purchasing manager could be held responsible if the purchase of poor-quality materials resulted in excessive labor processing time.

Another important cause of an unfavorable labor efficiency variance may be insufficient demand for the company's products. Managers in some companies argue that it is difficult, and perhaps unwise, to constantly adjust the workforce in response to changes in the amount of work that needs to be done. In such companies, the direct labor workforce is essentially fixed in the short run. If demand is insufficient to keep everyone busy, workers are not laid off and an unfavorable labor efficiency variance will often be recorded.

If customer orders are insufficient to keep the workers busy, the work center manager has two options—either accept an unfavorable labor efficiency variance or build inventory.[3] A central lesson of Lean Production is that building inventory with no immediate prospect of sale is a bad idea. Excessive inventory—particularly work in process inventory—leads to high defect rates, obsolete goods, and inefficient operations. As a consequence, when the workforce is basically fixed in the short term, managers must be

[3] For further discussion, see Eliyahu M. Goldratt and Jeff Cox, *The Goal*, 2nd rev. ed. (Croton-on-Hudson, NY: North River Press, 1992).

IN BUSINESS

CASHIERS FACE THE STOPWATCH

Operations Workforce Optimization (OWO) writes software that uses engineered labor standards to determine how long it should take a cashier to check out a customer. The software measures an employee's productivity by continuously comparing actual customer checkout times to pre-established labor efficiency standards. For example, the cashiers at Meijer, a regional retailer located in the Midwest, may be demoted or terminated if they do not meet or exceed labor efficiency standards for at least 95% of customers served. In addition to Meijer, OWO has attracted other clients such as Gap, Limited Brands, Office Depot, Nike, and Toys "R" Us, based on claims that its software can reduce labor costs by 5–15%. The software has also attracted the attention of the United Food and Commercial Workers Union, which represents 27,000 Meijer employees. The union has filed a grievance against Meijer related to its cashier monitoring system.

Source: Vanessa O'Connell, "Stores Count Seconds to Cut Labor Costs," *The Wall Street Journal*, November 17, 2008, pp. A1–A15.

cautious about how labor efficiency variances are used. Some experts advocate eliminating labor efficiency variances in such situations—at least for the purposes of motivating and controlling workers on the shop floor.

Labor Rate Variance—A Closer Look

As explained earlier, the price variance for direct labor is commonly called the **labor rate variance.** This variance measures any deviation from standard in the average hourly rate paid to direct labor workers. The formula for the labor rate variance is expressed as follows:

$$\text{Labor rate variance} = (AH \times AR) - (AH \times SR)$$

Actual hours (AH) · Actual rate (AR) · Standard rate (SR)

The formula can be factored as follows:

$$\text{Labor rate variance} = AH(AR - SR)$$

Using the data from Exhibit 10–6 in the formula, the labor rate variance can be computed as follows:

$$\text{Labor rate variance} = 1{,}050 \text{ hours } (\$21.60 \text{ per hour} - \$22.00 \text{ per hour}) = \$420\text{ F}$$

In most companies, the wage rates paid to workers are quite predictable. Nevertheless, rate variances can arise because of the way labor is used. Skilled workers with high hourly rates of pay may be given duties that require little skill and call for lower hourly rates of pay. This will result in an unfavorable labor rate variance because the actual hourly rate of pay will exceed the standard rate specified for the particular task. In contrast, a favorable rate variance would result when workers who are paid at a rate lower than specified in the standard are assigned to the task. However, the lower-paid workers may not be as efficient. Finally, overtime work at premium rates will result in an unfavorable rate variance if the overtime premium is charged to the direct labor account.

Who is responsible for controlling the labor rate variance? Because labor rate variances generally arise as a result of how labor is used, production supervisors are usually responsible for seeing that labor rate variances are kept under control.

Using Standard Costs—Variable Manufacturing Overhead Variances

LEARNING OBJECTIVE 3
Compute the variable manufacturing overhead efficiency and rate variances and explain their significance.

The final step in Terry Sherman's analysis of Colonial Pewter's variances for June was to compute the variable manufacturing overhead variances. The variable portion of manufacturing overhead can be analyzed using the same basic formulas that we used to analyze direct materials and direct labor. Recall from Exhibit 10–2 that the standard variable manufacturing overhead is $3.00 per unit of product, computed as follows:

$$0.5 \text{ hours per unit} \times \$6.00 \text{ per hour} = \$3.00 \text{ per unit}$$

Colonial Pewter's cost records showed that the total actual variable manufacturing overhead cost for June was $7,140. Recall from the earlier discussion of the direct labor variances that 1,050 hours of direct labor time were recorded during the month and that the company produced 2,000 pairs of bookends. Terry's analysis of this overhead data appears in Exhibit 10–7.

Notice the similarities between Exhibits 10–6 and 10–7. These similarities arise from the fact that direct labor-hours are being used as the base for allocating overhead cost to units of product; thus, the same hourly figures appear in Exhibit 10–7 for variable manufacturing overhead as in Exhibit 10–6 for direct labor. The main difference between the two exhibits is in the standard hourly rate being used, which in this company is much lower for variable manufacturing overhead than for direct labor.

Manufacturing Overhead Variances—A Closer Look

The formula for the **variable overhead efficiency variance** is expressed as follows:

$$\text{Variable overhead efficiency variance} = (AH \times SR) - (SH \times SR)$$

Actual hours; Standard rate; Standard hours allowed for actual output

EXHIBIT 10–7
Standard Cost Variance Analysis—Variable Manufacturing Overhead

(1) Standard Hours Allowed for Actual Output, at Standard Rate (*SH* × *SR*)	(2) Actual Hours of Input, at Standard Rate (*AH* × *SR*)	(3) Actual Hours of Input, at Actual Rate (*AH* × *AR*)
1,000 hours* × $6.00 per hour = $6,000	1,050 hours × $6.00 per hour = $6,300	1,050 hours × $6.80 per hour† = $7,140

Variable overhead efficiency variance = $300 U (between (1) and (2))

Variable overhead rate variance = $840 U (between (2) and (3))

Spending Variance = $1,140 U

*2,000 units × 0.5 hours per unit = 1,000 hours.
†$7,140 ÷ 1,050 hours = $6.80 per hour.
F = Favorable; U = Unfavorable.

This formula can be factored as follows:

$$\text{Variable overhead efficiency variance} = (AH - SH)SR$$

Again using the data from Exhibit 10–7, the variance can be computed as follows:

$$SH = 2{,}000 \text{ units} \times 0.5 \text{ hours per unit} = 1{,}000 \text{ hours}$$

$$\text{Variable overhead efficiency variance} = (1{,}050 \text{ hours} - 1{,}000 \text{ hours})\ \$6.00 \text{ per hour}$$
$$= \$300 \text{ U}$$

The formula for the **variable overhead rate variance** is expressed as follows:

$$\text{Variable overhead rate variance} = (AH \times AR) - (AH \times SR)$$

Actual hours — Actual rate — Standard rate

This formula can be factored as follows:

$$\text{Variable overhead rate variance} = AH(AR - SR)$$

Using the data from Exhibit 10–7 in the formula, the variable overhead rate variance can be computed as follows:

$$AR = \$7{,}140 \div 1{,}050 \text{ hours} = \$6.80 \text{ per hour}$$

$$\text{Variable overhead rate variance} = 1{,}050 \text{ hours } (\$6.80 \text{ per hour} - \$6.00 \text{ per hour})$$
$$= \$840 \text{ U}$$

The interpretation of the variable overhead variances is not as clear as the direct materials and direct labor variances. In particular, the variable overhead efficiency variance is exactly the same as the direct labor efficiency variance except for one detail—the rate that is used to translate the variance into dollars. In both cases, the variance is the difference between the actual hours worked and the standard hours allowed for the actual output. In the case of the direct labor efficiency variance, this difference is multiplied by the direct labor rate. In the case of the variable overhead efficiency variance, this difference is multiplied by the variable overhead rate. So when direct labor is used as the base for overhead, whenever the direct labor efficiency variance is favorable, the variable overhead efficiency variance will be favorable. And whenever the direct labor efficiency variance is unfavorable, the variable overhead efficiency variance will be unfavorable. Indeed, the variable overhead efficiency variance really doesn't tell us anything about how efficiently overhead resources were used. It depends solely on how efficiently direct labor was used.

MANAGERIAL ACCOUNTING IN ACTION

The Wrap-up

In preparation for the scheduled meeting to discuss his analysis of Colonial Pewter's standard costs and variances, Terry distributed Exhibits 10–2 through 10–7 to the management group of Colonial Pewter. This included J. D. Wriston, the president of the company; Tom Kuchel, the production manager; and Janet Warner, the purchasing manager. J. D. Wriston opened the meeting with the following question:

J. D.: Terry, I think I understand the report you distributed, but just to make sure, would you mind summarizing the highlights of what you found?

Colonial Pewter Company

Terry: As you can see, the biggest problems are the unfavorable materials quantity variance of $2,000 and the unfavorable labor efficiency variance of $1,100.

J. D.: Tom, you're the production boss. What do you think is causing the unfavorable labor efficiency variance?

Tom: It has to be the new production workers. Our experienced workers shouldn't have much problem meeting the standard of half an hour per unit. We all knew that there would be some inefficiency for a while as we brought new people on board. My plan for overcoming the problem is to pair up each of the new guys with one of our old-timers and have them work together for a while. It would slow down our older guys a bit, but I'll bet the unfavorable variance disappears and our new workers would learn a lot.

J. D.: Sounds good. Now, what about that $2,000 unfavorable materials quantity variance?

Terry: Tom, are the new workers generating a lot of scrap?

Tom: Yeah, I guess so.

J. D.: I think that could be part of the problem. Can you do anything about it?

Tom: I can watch the scrap closely for a few days to see where it's being generated. If it is the new workers, I can have the old-timers work with them on the problem when I team them up.

J. D.: Janet, the favorable materials price variance of $1,300 isn't helping us if it is contributing to the unfavorable materials quantity and labor efficiency variances. Let's make sure that our raw material purchases conform to our quality standards.

Janet: Fair enough.

J. D.: Good. Let's reconvene in a few weeks to see what has happened. Hopefully, we can get those unfavorable variances under control.

An Important Subtlety in the Materials Variances

Most companies compute the materials price variance when materials are purchased rather than when they are used in production. There are two reasons for this practice. First, delaying the computation of the price variance until the materials are used would result in less timely variance reports. Second, computing the price variance when the materials are purchased allows materials to be carried in the inventory accounts at their standard cost. This greatly simplifies bookkeeping. (See Appendix 10B at the end of the chapter for an explanation of how the bookkeeping works in a standard costing system.)

The equations presented earlier that define the direct materials quantity and price variances are correct and are reproduced below:

$$\text{Materials quantity variance} = (AQ \times SP) - (SQ \times SP)$$

AQ: Actual quantity ***used***; SP: Standard price; SQ: Standard quantity allowed for the actual output

$$\text{Materials price variance} = (AQ \times AP) - (AQ \times SP)$$

AQ: Actual quantity ***purchased***; AP: Actual price; SP: Standard price

Carefully note that the materials quantity variance is based on the actual quantity *used,* whereas the materials price variance is based on the actual quantity *purchased.* This is a subtle, but important, distinction. It didn't matter in the earlier example because the amount purchased (6,500 pounds of pewter) was the same as the amount used (again, 6,500 pounds of pewter). It *does* matter when the quantity purchased differs from the quantity used.

To illustrate, assume that during June Colonial Pewter purchased 7,000 pounds of materials at $3.80 per pound instead of 6,500 pounds as assumed earlier in the chapter. In this case, the quantity and price variances for direct materials would be computed as shown below:

$$\text{Materials quantity variance} = (AQ\ used \times SP) - (SQ \times SP)$$

$$= (6{,}500 \text{ pounds} \times \$4.00 \text{ per pound}) - (6{,}000 \text{ pounds} \times \$4.00 \text{ per pound})$$

$$= (6{,}500 \text{ pounds} - 6{,}000 \text{ pounds}) \times \$4.00 \text{ per pound}$$

$$= \$2{,}000\ \text{U}$$

$$\text{Materials price variance} = (AQ\ purchased \times AP) - (AQ\ purchased \times SP)$$

$$= (7{,}000 \text{ pounds} \times \$3.80 \text{ per pound}) - (7{,}000 \text{ pounds} \times \$4.00 \text{ per pound})$$

$$= 7{,}000 \text{ pounds} \times (\$3.80 \text{ per pound} - \$4.00 \text{ per pound})$$

$$= \$1{,}400\ \text{F}$$

This distinction between the actual quantity purchased and actual quantity used is perhaps clearer in Exhibit 10–8.

Note that the format of Exhibit 10–8 differs from the format of Exhibit 10–5—both of which are used to compute the direct materials variances. *Exhibit 10–8 can always be used to compute the direct materials variances. Exhibit 10–5 can only be used to compute the direct materials variances when the amount purchased equals the amount used.*

In Exhibit 10–8, the computation of the quantity variance is based on the actual input used whereas the computation of the price variance is based on the amount of the input purchased. Column (2) of Exhibit 10–8 contains two different total costs for this reason. When the quantity variance is computed, the total cost used from column (2) is $26,000—which is the cost of the actual input *used,* evaluated at the standard price. When the price variance is computed, the total cost used from column (2) is $28,000—which is the cost of the input *purchased,* evaluated at the standard price.

Note that the price variance is computed on the entire amount of material purchased (7,000 pounds), whereas the quantity variance is computed only on the amount of materials used in production during the month (6,500 pounds). What about the other 500 pounds of material that were purchased during the period, but that have not yet been used? When those materials are used in future periods, a quantity variance will be computed. However, a price variance will not be computed when the materials are finally used because the price variance was computed when the materials were purchased.

Finally, because the quantity variance is based on the amount used whereas the price variance is based on the amount purchased, the two variances do not generally

EXHIBIT 10–8
Standard Cost Variance Analysis—Direct Materials
(Note: The quantity of materials purchased does not equal the quantity used in production.)

(1) Standard Quantity Allowed for Actual Output, at Standard Price (*SQ* × *SP*)	(2) Actual Quantity of Input, at Standard Price (*AQ* × *SP*)	(3) Actual Quantity of Input, at Actual Price (*AQ* × *AP*)
6,000 pounds* × $4.00 per pound = $24,000	6,500 Pounds × $4.00 per pound = $26,000	7,000 pounds × $3.80 per pound = $26,600

Quantity variance = $2,000 U

7,000 pounds × $4.00 per pound = $28,000

Price variance = $1,400 F

In this case, the quantity variance and the price variance do not sum to the spending variance because the price variance is based on the quantity purchased whereas the quantity variance is based on the quantity used in production, and the two numbers differ.

*2,000 units × 3.0 pounds per unit = 6,000 pounds.
F = Favorable; U = Unfavorable.

sum to the spending variance from the flexible budget, which is wholly based on the amount used.

We would like to repeat that the variance formulas and Exhibit 10–8 can always be used. *However, Exhibit 10–5 can only be used in the special case when the quantity of materials purchased equals the quantity of materials used!*

Variance Analysis and Management by Exception

Variance analysis and performance reports are important elements of *management by exception,* which is an approach that emphasizes focusing on those areas of responsibility where goals and expectations are not being met.

The budgets and standards discussed in this chapter and in the preceding chapter reflect management's plans. If all goes according to plan, there will be little difference between actual results and the results that would be expected according to the budgets and standards. If this happens, managers can concentrate on other issues. However, if actual results do not conform to the budget and to standards, the performance reporting system sends a signal to managers that an "exception" has occurred. This signal is in the form of a variance from the budget or standards.

However, are all variances worth investigating? The answer is no. Differences between actual results and what was expected will almost always occur. If every variance were investigated, management would waste a great deal of time tracking down nickel-and-dime differences. Variances may occur for a variety of reasons—only some of

EXHIBIT 10–9
A Statistical Control Chart

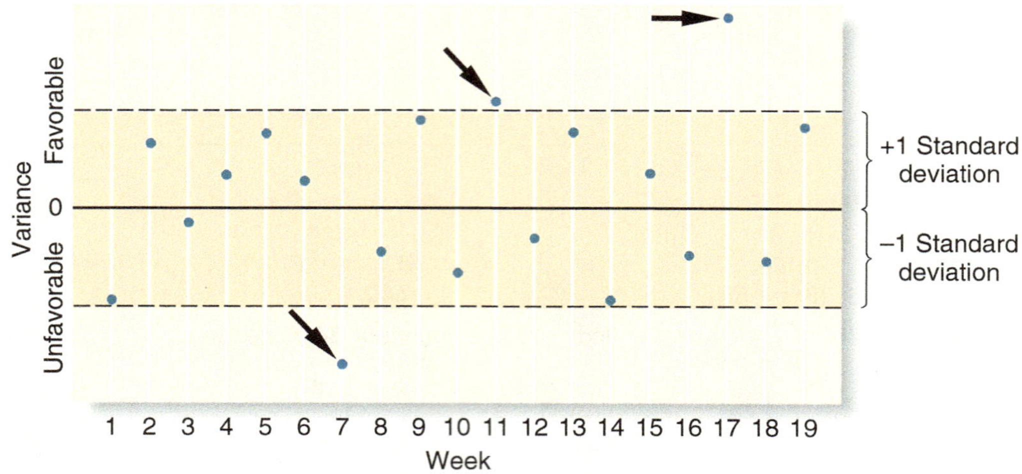

which are significant and worthy of management's attention. For example, hotter-than-normal weather in the summer may result in higher-than-expected electrical bills for air conditioning. Or, workers may work slightly faster or slower on a particular day. Because of unpredictable random factors, one can expect that virtually every cost category will produce a variance of some kind.

How should managers decide which variances are worth investigating? One clue is the size of the variance. A variance of $5 is probably not big enough to warrant attention, whereas a variance of $5,000 might well be worth tracking down. Another clue is the size of the variance relative to the amount of spending. A variance that is only 0.1% of spending on an item is likely to be well within the bounds one would normally expect due to random factors. On the other hand, a variance of 10% of spending is much more likely to be a signal that something is wrong.

A more dependable approach is to plot variance data on a statistical control chart, such as illustrated in Exhibit 10–9. The basic idea underlying a statistical control chart is that some random fluctuations in variances from period to period are normal. A variance should only be investigated when it is unusual relative to that normal level of random fluctuation. Typically, the standard deviation of the variances is used as the measure of the normal level of fluctuations. A rule of thumb is adopted such as "investigate all variances that are more than *X* standard deviations from zero." In the control chart in Exhibit 10–9, *X* is 1.0. That is, the rule of thumb in this company is to investigate all variances that are more than one standard deviation in either direction (favorable or unfavorable) from zero. This means that the variances in weeks 7, 11, and 17 would have been investigated, but none of the others.

What value of *X* should be chosen? The bigger the value of *X*, the wider the band of acceptable variances that would not be investigated. Thus, the bigger the value of *X*, the less time will be spent tracking down variances, but the more likely it is that a real out-of-control situation will be overlooked. Ordinarily, if *X* is selected to be 1.0, roughly 30% of all variances will trigger an investigation even though there is no real problem. If *X* is set at 1.5, the figure drops to about 13%. If *X* is set at 2.0, the figure drops all the way to about 5%. Don't forget, however, that selecting a big value of *X* will result not only in fewer false alarms but also in a higher probability that a real problem will be overlooked.

In addition to watching for unusually large variances, the pattern of the variances should be monitored. For example, a run of steadily mounting variances should trigger an investigation even though none of the variances is large enough by itself to warrant investigation.

International Uses of Standard Costs

Standard costs are used by companies throughout the world. One study found that three-fourths of the companies surveyed in the United Kingdom, two-thirds of the companies surveyed in Canada, and 40% of the companies surveyed in Japan used standard cost systems.[4]

Standard costs were first introduced in Japan after World War II, with Nippon Electronics Company (NEC) being one of the first Japanese companies to adopt standard costs for all of its products. Many other Japanese companies followed NEC's lead and developed standard cost systems. The ways in which these standard costs are used in Japan—and also in the other countries cited above—are shown in Exhibit 10–10.

Over time, the pattern of use shown in Exhibit 10–10 may change, but at present managers can expect to encounter standard costs in most industrialized nations. Moreover, the most important uses are for cost management and budgetary planning purposes.

EXHIBIT 10–10
Uses of Standard Costs in Four Countries

	United States	United Kingdom	Canada	Japan
Cost management	1*	2	2	1
Budgetary planning and control†	2	3	1	3
Pricing decisions	3	1	3	2
Financial statement preparation	4	4	4	4

*The numbers 1 through 4 denote importance of use of standard costing systems, from greatest to least.
†Includes management planning.
Source: Compiled from data in a study by Shin'ichi Inoue, "Comparative Studies of Recent Development of Cost Management Problems in U.S.A., U.K., Canada, and Japan," Research Paper No. 29, Kagawa University, p. 20.

Evaluation of Controls Based on Standard Costs

Advantages of Standard Costs

Standard cost systems have a number of advantages.

1. Standard costs are a key element in a management by exception approach. If costs conform to the standards, managers can focus on other issues. When costs are significantly outside the standards, managers are alerted that problems may exist that require attention. This approach helps managers focus on important issues.
2. Standards that are viewed as reasonable by employees can promote economy and efficiency. They provide benchmarks that individuals can use to judge their own performance.
3. Standard costs can greatly simplify bookkeeping. Instead of recording actual costs for each job, the standard costs for direct materials, direct labor, and overhead can be charged to jobs.
4. Standard costs fit naturally in an integrated system of "responsibility accounting." The standards establish what costs should be, who should be responsible for them, and whether actual costs are under control.

[4] Shin'ichi Inoue, "Comparative Studies of Recent Development of Cost Management Problems in U.S.A., U.K., Canada, and Japan," Research Paper No. 29, Kagawa University, p. 17. The study included 95 United States companies, 52 United Kingdom companies, 82 Canadian companies, and 646 Japanese companies.

Potential Problems with the Use of Standard Costs

The improper use of standard costs can present a number of potential problems.

1. Standard cost variance reports are usually prepared on a monthly basis and often are released days or even weeks after the end of the month. As a consequence, the information in the reports may be so outdated that it is almost useless. Timely, frequent reports that are approximately correct are better than infrequent reports that are very precise but out of date by the time they are released. Some companies are now reporting variances and other key operating data daily or even more frequently.

2. If managers are insensitive and use variance reports as a club, morale may suffer. Employees should receive positive reinforcement for work well done. Management by exception, by its nature, tends to focus on the negative. If variances are used as a club, subordinates may be tempted to cover up unfavorable variances or take actions that are not in the best interests of the company to make sure the variances are favorable. For example, workers may put on a crash effort to increase output at the end of the month to avoid an unfavorable labor efficiency variance. In the rush to produce more output, quality may suffer.
3. Labor quantity standards and efficiency variances make two important assumptions. First, they assume that the production process is labor-paced; if labor works faster, output will go up. However, output in many companies is not determined by how fast labor works; rather, it is determined by the processing speed of machines. Second, the computations assume that labor is a variable cost. However, direct labor may be essentially fixed. If labor is fixed, then an undue emphasis on labor efficiency variances creates pressure to build excess inventories.
4. In some cases, a "favorable" variance can be as bad or worse than an "unfavorable" variance. For example, McDonald's has a standard for the amount of hamburger meat that should be in a Big Mac. A "favorable" variance would mean that less meat was used than the standard specifies. The result is a substandard Big Mac and possibly a dissatisfied customer.
5. Too much emphasis on meeting the standards may overshadow other important objectives such as maintaining and improving quality, on-time delivery, and customer satisfaction. This tendency can be reduced by using supplemental performance measures that focus on these other objectives.
6. Just meeting standards may not be sufficient; continual improvement may be necessary to survive in a competitive environment. For this reason, some companies focus on the trends in the standard cost variances—aiming for continual improvement rather than just meeting the standards. In other companies, engineered standards are replaced either by a rolling average of actual costs, which is expected to decline, or by very challenging target costs.

In sum, managers should exercise considerable care when using a standard cost system. It is particularly important that managers go out of their way to focus on the positive, rather than just on the negative, and to be aware of possible unintended consequences.

Summary

A standard is a benchmark, or "norm," for measuring performance. Standards are set for both the quantity and the cost of inputs needed to manufacture goods or to provide services. Quantity standards indicate how much of an input, such as labor time or raw materials, should be used to make a product or provide a service. Cost standards indicate what the cost of the input should be.

Standards are normally set so that they can be attained by reasonable, though highly efficient, efforts. Such "practical" standards are believed to positively motivate employees.

When standards are compared to actual performance, the difference is referred to as a *variance.* Variances are computed and reported to management on a regular basis for both the quantity and the price elements of direct materials, direct labor, and variable overhead. Quantity variances are computed by taking the difference between the actual amount of the input used and the amount of input that is allowed for the actual output, and then multiplying the result by the standard price of the input. Price variances are computed by taking the difference between actual and standard prices and multiplying the result by the amount of input purchased.

Not all variances require management attention. Only unusual or particularly significant variances should be investigated—otherwise a great deal of time would be spent investigating unimportant matters. Additionally, it should be emphasized that the point of the investigation should not be to find someone to blame. The point of the investigation is to pinpoint the problem so that it can be fixed and operations improved.

Traditional standard cost variance reports are often supplemented with other performance measures. Overemphasis on standard cost variances may lead to problems in other critical areas such as product quality, inventory levels, and on-time delivery.

Review Problem: Standard Costs

Xavier Company produces a single product. Variable manufacturing overhead is applied to products on the basis of direct labor-hours. The standard costs for one unit of product are as follows:

Direct material: 6 ounces at $0.50 per ounce	$ 3.00
Direct labor: 0.6 hours at $30.00 per hour	18.00
Variable manufacturing overhead: 0.6 hours at $10.00 per hour	6.00
Total standard variable cost per unit	$27.00

During June, 2,000 units were produced. The costs associated with June's operations were as follows:

Material purchased: 18,000 ounces at $0.60 per ounce	$10,800
Material used in production: 14,000 ounces	—
Direct labor: 1,100 hours at $30.50 per hour	$33,550
Variable manufacturing overhead costs incurred	$12,980

Required:

Compute the direct materials, direct labor, and variable manufacturing overhead variances.

Solution to Review Problem

Direct Materials Variances

Standard Quantity Allowed for Actual Output, at Standard Price (*SQ* × *SP*)	Actual Quantity of Input at Standard Price (*AQ* × *SP*)	Actual Quantity of Input, at Actual Price (*AQ* × *AP*)
12,000 ounces* × $0.50 per ounce = $6,000	14,000 ounces × $0.50 per ounce = $7,000	18,000 ounces × $0.60 per pound = $10,800

Quantity variance = $1,000 U

18,000 ounces × $0.50 per ounce = $9,000

Price variance = $1,800 U

*2,000 units × 6 ounces per unit = 12,000 ounces.

Using the formulas in the chapter, the same variances would be computed as follows:

$$\text{Materials quantity variance} = (AQ - SQ)SP$$

$$(14{,}000 \text{ ounces} - 12{,}000 \text{ ounces})\ \$0.50 \text{ per ounce} = \$1{,}000\ \text{U}$$

$$\text{Materials price variance} = AQ(AP - SP)$$

$$18{,}000 \text{ ounces } (\$0.60 \text{ per ounce} - \$0.50 \text{ per ounce}) = \$1{,}800\ \text{U}$$

Direct Labor Variances

Standard Hours Allowed for Actual Output, at Standard Rate (*SH* × *SR*)	Actual Hours of Input, at Standard Rate (*AH* × *SR*)	Actual Hours of Input, at Actual Rate (*AH* × *AR*)
1,200 hours* × $30.00 per hour = $36,000	1,100 hours × $30.00 per hour = $33,000	1,100 hours × $30.50 per hour = $33,550

Labor efficiency variance = $3,000 F

Labor rate variance = $550 U

Spending variance = $2,450 F

*2,000 units × 0.6 hours per unit = 1,200 hours.
F = Favorable; U = Unfavorable.

Using the formulas in the chapter, the same variances can be computed as follows:

$$\begin{aligned}\text{Labor efficiency variance} &= (AH \times SR) - (SH \times SR)\\ &= (1{,}100 \text{ hours} \times \$30.00 \text{ per hour}) - (1{,}200 \text{ hours} \times \$30.00 \text{ per hour})\\ &= (1{,}100 \text{ hours} - 1{,}200 \text{ hours}) \times \$30.00 \text{ per hour}\\ &= \$3{,}000\ \text{F}\end{aligned}$$

$$\begin{aligned}\text{Labor rate variance} &= (AH \times AR) - (AH \times SR)\\ &= (1{,}100 \text{ hours} \times \$30.00 \text{ per hour}) - (1{,}100 \text{ hours} \times \$30.50 \text{ per hour})\\ &= 1{,}100 \text{ hours} \times (\$30.00 \text{ per hour} - \$30.50 \text{ per hour})\\ &= \$550\ \text{U}\end{aligned}$$

Variable Manufacturing Overhead Variances

Standard Hours Allowed for Actual Output, at Standard Rate (*SH* × *SR*)	Actual Hours of Input, at Standard Rate (*AH* × *SR*)	Actual Hours of Input, at Actual Rate (*AH* × *AR*)
1,200 hours* × $10.00 per hour = $12,000	1,100 hours × $10.00 per hour = $11,000	1,100 hours × $11.80 per hour† = $12,980

Variable overhead effciency variance = $1,000 F

Variable overhead rate variance = $1,980 U

Spending variance = $980 U

*2,000 units × 0.6 hours per unit = 1,200 hours.
†$12,980 ÷ 1,100 hours = $11.80 per hour.
F = Favorable; U = Unfavorable.

Using the formulas in the chapter, the same variances can be computed as follows:

$$\text{Variable overhead efficiency variance} = (AH \times SR) - (SH \times SR)$$
$$= (1{,}100 \text{ hours} \times \$10.00 \text{ per hour}) - (1{,}200 \text{ hours} \times \$10.00 \text{ per hour})$$
$$= (1{,}100 \text{ hours} - 1{,}200 \text{ hours}) \times \$10.00 \text{ per hour}$$
$$= \$1{,}000 \text{ F}$$

$$\text{Variable overhead rate variance} = (AH \times AR) - (AH \times SR)$$
$$= (1{,}100 \text{ hours} \times \$10.00 \text{ per hour}) - (1{,}100 \text{ hours} \times \$11.80 \text{ per hour})$$
$$= 1{,}100 \text{ hours} \times (\$10.00 \text{ per hour} - \$11.80 \text{ per hour})$$
$$= \$1{,}980 \text{ U}$$

Glossary

Ideal standards Standards that assume peak efficiency at all times. (p. 420)

Labor efficiency variance The difference between the actual hours taken to complete a task and the standard hours allowed for the actual output, multiplied by the standard hourly labor rate. (p. 430)

Labor rate variance The difference between the actual hourly labor rate and the standard rate, multiplied by the number of hours worked during the period. (p. 432)

Management by exception A management system in which standards are set for various activities, with actual results compared to these standards. Significant deviations from standards are flagged as exceptions. (p. 419)

Materials price variance The difference between the actual unit price paid for an item and the standard price, multiplied by the quantity purchased. (p. 429)

Materials quantity variance The difference between the actual quantity of materials used in production and the standard quantity allowed for the actual output, multiplied by the standard price per unit of materials. (p. 427)

Practical standards Standards that allow for normal machine downtime and other work interruptions and that can be attained through reasonable, though highly efficient, efforts by the average worker. (p. 421)

Price variance A variance that is computed by taking the difference between the actual price and the standard price and multiplying the result by the actual quantity of the input. (p. 424)

Quantity variance A variance that is computed by taking the difference between the actual quantity of the input used and the amount of the input that should have been used for the actual level of output and multiplying the result by the standard price of the input. (p. 424)

Standard cost card A detailed listing of the standard amounts of inputs and their costs that are required to produce one unit of a specific product. (p. 420)

Standard cost per unit The standard quantity allowed of an input per unit of a specific product, multiplied by the standard price of the input. (p. 423)

Standard hours allowed The time that should have been taken to complete the period's output. It is computed by multiplying the actual number of units produced by the standard hours per unit. (p. 425)

Standard hours per unit The amount of direct labor time that should be required to complete a single unit of product, including allowances for breaks, machine downtime, cleanup, rejects, and other normal inefficiencies. (p. 422)

Standard price per unit The price that should be paid for an input. (p. 421)

Standard quantity allowed The amount of an input that should have been used to complete the period's actual output. It is computed by multiplying the actual number of units produced by the standard quantity per unit. (p. 425)

Standard quantity per unit The amount of an input that should be required to complete a single unit of product, including allowances for normal waste, spoilage, rejects, and other normal inefficiencies. (p. 421)

Standard rate per hour The labor rate that should be incurred per hour of labor time, including employment taxes and fringe benefits. (p. 422)

Variable overhead efficiency variance The difference between the actual level of activity (direct labor-hours, machine-hours, or some other base) and the standard activity allowed, multiplied by the variable part of the predetermined overhead rate. (p. 433)

Variable overhead rate variance The difference between the actual variable overhead cost incurred during a period and the standard cost that should have been incurred based on the actual activity of the period. (p. 434)

Questions

10–1 What is a quantity standard? What is a price standard?

10–2 Distinguish between ideal and practical standards.

10–3 What is meant by the term *management by exception?*

10–4 Why are separate price and quantity variances computed?

10–5 Who is generally responsible for the materials price variance? The materials quantity variance? The labor efficiency variance?

10–6 The materials price variance can be computed at what two different points in time? Which point is better? Why?

10–7 If the materials price variance is favorable but the materials quantity variance is unfavorable, what might this indicate?

10–8 Should standards be used to identify who to blame for problems?

10–9 "Our workers are all under labor contracts; therefore, our labor rate variance is bound to be zero." Discuss.

10–10 What effect, if any, would you expect poor-quality materials to have on direct labor variances?

10–11 If variable manufacturing overhead is applied to production on the basis of direct labor-hours and the direct labor efficiency variance is unfavorable, will the variable overhead efficiency variance be favorable or unfavorable, or could it be either? Explain.

10–12 What is a statistical control chart, and how is it used?

10–13 Why can undue emphasis on labor efficiency variances lead to excess work in process inventories?

Multiple-choice questions are provided on the text website at www.mhhe.com/garrison14e.

Applying Excel connect ACCOUNTING

LEARNING OBJECTIVES 1, 2, 3

Available with McGraw-Hill's *Connect™ Accounting*.

The Excel worksheet form that appears on the next page is to be used to recreate the main example in the text on pages 423–433. Download the workbook containing this form from the Online Learning Center at www.mhhe.com/garrison14e. *On the website you will also receive instructions about how to use this worksheet form.*

You should proceed to the requirements below only after completing your worksheet.

Required:

1. Check your worksheet by changing the direct materials standard quantity in cell B6 to 2.9 pounds, the direct labor quantity standard quantity in cell B7 to 0.6 hours, and the variable

	A	B	C	D	E	F
1	Chapter 10: Applying Excel					
2						
3	**Data**					
4	***Exhibit 10-2: Standard Cost Card***					
5	*Inputs*	*Standard Quantity*		*Standard Price*		
6	Direct materials	3.0 pounds		$4.00 per pound		
7	Direct labor	0.50 hours		$22.00 per hour		
8	Variable manufacturing overhead	0.50 hours		$6.00 per hour		
9						
10	Actual results:					
11	Actual output	2,000 units				
12	Actual variable manufacturing overhead cost	$7,140				
13		*Actual Quantity*		*Actual price*		
14	Actual direct materials cost	6,500 pounds		$3.80 per pound		
15	Actual direct labor cost	1,050 hours		$21.60 per hour		
16						
17	*Enter a formula into each of the cells marked with a ? below*					
18	**Main Example: Chapter 10**					
19						
20	***Exhibit 10-5: Standard Cost Variance Analysis–Direct Materials***					
21	Standard Quantity Allowed for the Actual Output, at Standard Price	? pounds ×		? per pound =		?
22	Actual Quantity of Input, at Standard Price	? pounds ×		? per pound =		?
23	Actual Quantity of Input, at Actual Price	? pounds ×		? per pound =		?
24	Direct materials variances:					
25	Materials quantity variance	?				
26	Materials price variance	?				
27	Materials spending variance	?				
28						
29	***Exhibit 10-6: Standard Cost Variance Analysis–Direct Labor***					
30	Standard Hours Allowed for the Actual Output, at Standard Rate	? hours ×		? per hour =		?
31	Actual Hours of Input, at Standard Rate	? hours ×		? per hour =		?
32	Actual Hours of Input, at Actual Rate	? hours ×		? per hour =		?
33	Direct labor variances:					
34	Labor efficiency variance	?				
35	Labor rate variance	?				
36	Labor spending variance	?				
37						
38	***Exhibit 10-7: Standard Cost Variance Analysis–Variable Manufacturing Overhead***					
39	Standard Hours Allowed for the Actual Output, at Standard Rate	? hours ×		? per hour =		?
40	Actual Hours of Input, at Standard Rate	? hours ×		? per hour =		?
41	Actual Hours of Input, at Actual Rate	? hours ×		? per hour =		?
42	Variable overhead variances:					
43	Variable overhead efficiency variance	?				
44	Variable overhead rate variance	?				
45	Variable overhead spending variance	?				
46						

Chapter 10 Form | Filled in Chapter 10 Form | Chapter 10 Formulas

manufacturing overhead in cell B8 to 0.6 hours. The materials spending variance should now be $1,500 U, the labor spending variance should now be $3,720 F, and the variable overhead spending variance should now be $60 F. If you do not get these answers, find the errors in your worksheet and correct them.

a. What is the materials quantity variance? Explain this variance.

b. What is the labor rate variance? Explain this variance.

2. Revise the data in your worksheet to reflect the results for the subsequent period:

Data Exhibit 10–2: Standard Cost Card		
Inputs	Standard Quantity	Standard Price
Direct materials	3.0 pounds	$4.00 per pound
Direct labor	0.50 hours	$22.00 per hour
Variable manufacturing overhead	0.50 hours	$6.00 per hour
Actual results:		
Actual output	2,100 units	
Actual variable manufacturing overhead cost	$5,100	
	Actual Quantity	Actual price
Actual direct materials cost	6,350 pounds	$4.10 per pound
Actual direct labor cost	1,020 hours	$22.10 per hour

a. What is the materials quantity variance? What is the materials price variance?
b. What is the labor efficiency variance? What is the labor rate variance?
c. What is the variable overhead efficiency variance? What is the variable overhead rate variance?

Exercises connect ACCOUNTING

All applicable exercises are available with McGraw-Hill's *Connect™ Accounting*.

EXERCISE 10–1 Material Variances [LO1]

Harmon Household Products, Inc., manufactures a number of consumer items for general household use. One of these products, a chopping board, requires an expensive hardwood. During a recent month, the company manufactured 4,000 chopping boards using 11,000 board feet of hardwood. The hardwood cost the company $18,700.

The company's standards for one chopping board are 2.5 board feet of hardwood, at a cost of $1.80 per board foot.

Required:

1. According to the standards, what cost for wood should have been incurred to make 4,000 chopping blocks? How much greater or less is this than the cost that was incurred?
2. Break down the difference computed in (1) above into a materials price variance and a materials quantity variance.

EXERCISE 10–2 Direct Labor Variances [LO2]

AirMeals, Inc., prepares in-flight meals for a number of major airlines. One of the company's products is stuffed cannelloni with roasted pepper sauce, fresh baby corn, and spring salad. During the most recent week, the company prepared 6,000 of these meals using 1,150 direct labor-hours. The company paid these direct labor workers a total of $11,500 for this work, or $10 per hour.

According to the standard cost card for this meal, it should require 0.20 direct labor-hours at a cost of $9.50 per hour.

Required:

1. According to the standards, what direct labor cost should have been incurred to prepare 6,000 meals? How much does this differ from the actual direct labor cost?
2. Break down the difference computed in (1) above into a labor rate variance and a labor efficiency variance.

EXERCISE 10–3 Variable Overhead Variances [LO3]

Order Up, Inc., provides order fulfillment services for dot.com merchants. The company maintains warehouses that stock items carried by its dot.com clients. When a client receives an order from a customer, the order is forwarded to Order Up, which pulls the item from storage, packs it, and ships it to the customer. The company uses a predetermined variable overhead rate based on direct labor-hours.

In the most recent month, 140,000 items were shipped to customers using 5,800 direct labor-hours. The company incurred a total of $15,950 in variable overhead costs.

According to the company's standards, 0.04 direct labor-hours are required to fulfill an order for one item and the variable overhead rate is $2.80 per direct labor-hour.

Required:

1. According to the standards, what variable overhead cost should have been incurred to fill the orders for the 140,000 items? How much does this differ from the actual variable overhead cost?
2. Break down the difference computed in (1) above into a variable overhead rate variance and a variable overhead efficiency variance.

EXERCISE 10–4 Labor and Variable Manufacturing Overhead Variances [LO2, LO3]

Hollowell Audio, Inc., manufactures military-specification compact discs. The company uses standards to control its costs. The labor standards that have been set for one disc are as follows:

Standard Hours	Standard Rate per Hour	Standard Cost
6 minutes	$24.00	$2.40

During July, 2,125 hours of direct labor time were required to make 20,000 discs. The direct labor cost totaled $49,300 for the month.

Required:

1. According to the standards, what direct labor cost should have been incurred to make the 20,000 discs? By how much does this differ from the cost that was incurred?
2. Break down the difference in cost from (1) above into a labor rate variance and a labor efficiency variance.
3. The budgeted variable manufacturing overhead rate is $16.00 per direct labor-hour. During July, the company incurred $39,100 in variable manufacturing overhead cost. Compute the variable overhead rate and efficiency variances for the month.

EXERCISE 10–5 Working Backwards from Labor Variances [LO2]

The Worldwide Credit Card, Inc., uses standards to control the labor time involved in opening mail from card holders and recording the enclosed remittances. Incoming mail is gathered into batches, and a standard time is set for opening and recording each batch. The labor standards relating to one batch are as follows:

	Standard Hours	Standard Rate	Standard Cost
Per batch	1.25	$12.00	$15.00

The record showing the time spent last week in opening batches of mail has been misplaced. However, the batch supervisor recalls that 168 batches were received and opened during the week, and the controller recalls the following variance data relating to these batches:

Total labor spending variance	$330 U
Labor rate variance	$150 F

Required:

1. Determine the number of actual labor-hours spent opening batches during the week.
2. Determine the actual hourly rate paid to employees for opening batches last week.

(Hint: A useful way to proceed would be to work from known to unknown data either by using the variance formulas or by using the columnar format shown in Exhibit 10–6.)

EXERCISE 10–6 Material and Labor Variances [LO1, LO2]

Sonne Company produces a perfume called Whim. The direct materials and direct labor standards for one bottle of Whim are given below:

	Standard Quantity or Hours	Standard Price or Rate	Standard Cost
Direct materials	7.2 ounces	$2.50 per ounce	$18.00
Direct labor	0.4 hours	$10.00 per hour	$4.00

During the most recent month, the following activity was recorded:

a. Twenty thousand ounces of material were purchased at a cost of $2.40 per ounce.
b. All of the material was used to produce 2,500 bottles of Whim.
c. Nine hundred hours of direct labor time were recorded at a total labor cost of $10,800.

Required:

1. Compute the direct materials price and quantity variances for the month.
2. Compute the direct labor rate and efficiency variances for the month.

EXERCISE 10–7 Material Variances [LO1]

Refer to the data in Exercise 10–6. Assume that instead of producing 2,500 bottles of Whim during the month, the company produced only 2,000 bottles using 16,000 ounces of material. (The rest of the material purchased remained in raw materials inventory.)

Required:

Compute the direct materials price and quantity variances for the month.

EXERCISE 10–8 Material and Labor Variances [LO1, LO2]

Topper Toys has developed a new toy called the Brainbuster. The company has a standard cost system to help control costs and has established the following standards for the Brainbuster toy:

Direct materials: 8 diodes per toy at $0.30 per diode
Direct labor: 0.6 hours per toy at $14.00 per hour

During August, the company produced 5,000 Brainbuster toys. Production data on the toy for August follow:

Direct materials: 70,000 diodes were purchased at a cost of $0.28 per diode. 20,000 of these diodes were still in inventory at the end of the month.
Direct labor: 3,200 direct labor-hours were worked at a cost of $48,000.

Required:

1. Compute the following variances for August:
   a. Direct materials price and quantity variances.
   b. Direct labor rate and efficiency variances.
2. Prepare a brief explanation of the possible causes of each variance.

Problems

connect ACCOUNTING

All applicable problems are available with McGraw-Hill's *Connect™ Accounting.*

PROBLEM 10–9 Comprehensive Variance Analysis [LO1, LO2, LO3]

Portland Company's Ironton Plant produces precast ingots for industrial use. Carlos Santiago, who was recently appointed general manager of the Ironton Plant, has just been handed the plant's contribution format income statement for October. The statement is shown below:

	Budgeted	Actual
Sales (5,000 ingots)	$250,000	$250,000
Variable expenses:		
Variable cost of goods sold*	80,000	96,390
Variable selling expenses	20,000	20,000
Total variable expenses	100,000	116,390
Contribution margin	150,000	133,610
Fixed expenses:		
Manufacturing overhead	60,000	60,000
Selling and administrative	75,000	75,000
Total fixed expenses	135,000	135,000
Net operating income (loss)	$ 15,000	$ (1,390)

*Contains direct materials, direct labor, and variable manufacturing overhead.

Mr. Santiago was shocked to see the loss for the month, particularly because sales were exactly as budgeted. He stated, "I sure hope the plant has a standard cost system in operation. If it doesn't, I won't have the slightest idea of where to start looking for the problem."

The plant does use a standard cost system, with the following standard variable cost per ingot:

	Standard Quantity or Hours	Standard Price or Rate	Standard Cost
Direct materials	4.0 pounds	$2.50 per pound	$10.00
Direct labor	0.6 hours	$9.00 per hour	5.40
Variable manufacturing overhead	0.3 hours*	$2.00 per hour	0.60
Total standard variable cost			$16.00

*Based on machine-hours.

During October the plant produced 5,000 ingots and incurred the following costs:

a. Purchased 25,000 pounds of materials at a cost of $2.95 per pound. There were no raw materials in inventory at the beginning of the month.
b. Used 19,800 pounds of materials in production. (Finished goods and work in process inventories are insignificant and can be ignored.)
c. Worked 3,600 direct labor-hours at a cost of $8.70 per hour.
d. Incurred a total variable manufacturing overhead cost of $4,320 for the month. A total of 1,800 machine-hours was recorded.

It is the company's policy to close all variances to cost of goods sold on a monthly basis.

Required:

1. Compute the following variances for October:
   a. Direct materials price and quantity variances.
   b. Direct labor rate and efficiency variances.
   c. Variable overhead rate and efficiency variances.
2. Summarize the variances that you computed in (1) above by showing the net overall favorable or unfavorable variance for October. What impact did this figure have on the company's income statement?
3. Pick out the two most significant variances that you computed in (1) above. Explain to Mr. Santiago possible causes of these variances.

PROBLEM 10–10 Variance Analysis in a Hospital [LO1, LO2, LO3]

"What's going on in that lab?" asked Derek Warren, chief administrator for Cottonwood Hospital, as he studied the prior month's reports. "Every month the lab teeters between a profit and a loss. Are we going to have to increase our lab fees again?"

"We can't," replied Lois Ankers, the controller. "We're getting *lots* of complaints about the last increase, particularly from the insurance companies and governmental health units. They're now paying only about 80% of what we bill. I'm beginning to think the problem is on the cost side."

To determine if lab costs are in line with other hospitals, Mr. Warren has asked you to evaluate the costs for the past month. Ms. Ankers has provided you with the following information:

a. Two basic types of tests are performed in the lab—smears and blood tests. During the past month, 2,700 smears and 900 blood tests were performed in the lab.
b. Small glass plates are used in both types of tests. During the past month, the hospital purchased 16,000 plates at a cost of $38,400. This cost is net of a 4% purchase discount. A total of 2,000 of these plates were unused at the end of the month; no plates were on hand at the beginning of the month.
c. During the past month, 1,800 hours of labor time were used in performing smears and blood tests. The cost of this labor time was $18,450.
d. The lab's variable overhead cost last month totaled $11,700.

Cottonwood Hospital has never used standard costs. By searching industry literature, however, you have determined the following nationwide averages for hospital labs:

Plates: Three plates are required per lab test. These plates cost $2.50 each and are disposed of after the test is completed.

Labor: Each smear should require 0.3 hours to complete, and each blood test should require 0.6 hours to complete. The average cost of this lab time is $12 per hour.

Overhead: Overhead cost is based on direct labor-hours. The average rate of variable overhead is $6 per hour.

Required:

1. Compute the materials price variance for the plates purchased last month, and compute a materials quantity variance for the plates used last month.
2. For labor cost in the lab:
   a. Compute a labor rate variance and a labor efficiency variance.
   b. In most hospitals, three-fourths of the workers in the lab are certified technicians and one-fourth are assistants. In an effort to reduce costs, Cottonwood Hospital employs only one-half certified technicians and one-half assistants. Would you recommend that this policy be continued? Explain.
3. Compute the variable overhead rate and efficiency variances. Is there any relation between the variable overhead efficiency variance and the labor efficiency variance? Explain.

PROBLEM 10-11 Basic Variance Analysis [LO1, LO2, LO3]

Barberry, Inc., manufactures a product called Fruta. The company uses a standard cost system and has established the following standards for one unit of Fruta:

	A	B	C	D	E	F
1		*Standard Quantity*		*Standard Price or Rate*		*Standard Cost*
2	Direct materials	1.5	pounds	$6.00	per pound	$ 9.00
3	Direct labor	0.6	hours	$12.00	per hour	7.20
4	Variable manufacturing overhead	0.6	hours	$2.50	per hour	1.50
5						$ 17.70
6						

Sheet1 Sheet2 Sheet3

During June, the company recorded this activity related to production of Fruta:

a. The company produced 3,000 units during June.
b. A total of 8,000 pounds of material were purchased at a cost of $46,000.
c. There was no beginning inventory of materials; however, at the end of the month, 2,000 pounds of material remained in ending inventory.
d. The company employs 10 persons to work on the production of Fruta. During June, they worked an average of 160 hours at an average rate of $12.50 per hour.
e. Variable manufacturing overhead is assigned to Fruta on the basis of direct labor-hours. Variable manufacturing overhead costs during June totaled $3,600.

The company's management is anxious to determine the efficiency of Fruta production activities.

Required:

1. For direct materials:
   a. Compute the price and quantity variances.
   b. The materials were purchased from a new supplier who is anxious to enter into a long-term purchase contract. Would you recommend that the company sign the contract? Explain.
2. For labor employed in the production of Fruta:
   a. Compute the rate and efficiency variances.
   b. In the past, the 10 persons employed in the production of Fruta consisted of 4 senior workers and 6 assistants. During June, the company experimented with 5 senior workers and 5 assistants. Would you recommend that the new labor mix be continued? Explain.
3. Compute the variable overhead rate and efficiency variances. What relation can you see between this efficiency variance and the labor efficiency variance?

PROBLEM 10–12 Basic Variance Analysis; the Impact of Variances on Unit Costs [LO1, LO2, LO3]

Landers Company manufactures a number of products. The standards relating to one of these products are shown below, along with actual cost data for May.

	Standard Cost per Unit		Actual Cost per Unit
Direct materials:			
Standard: 1.80 feet at $3.00 per foot	$ 5.40		
Actual: 1.75 feet at $3.20 per foot			$ 5.60
Direct labor:			
Standard: 0.90 hours at $18.00 per hour	16.20		
Actual: 0.95 hours at $17.40 per hour			16.53
Variable overhead:			
Standard: 0.90 hours at $5.00 per hour	4.50		
Actual: 0.95 hours at $4.60 per hour			4.37
Total cost per unit	$26.10		$26.50
Excess of actual cost over standard cost per unit		$0.40	

The production superintendent was pleased when he saw this report and commented: "This $0.40 excess cost is well within the 2 percent limit management has set for acceptable variances. It's obvious that there's not much to worry about with this product."

Actual production for the month was 12,000 units. Variable overhead cost is assigned to products on the basis of direct labor-hours. There were no beginning or ending inventories of materials.

Required:

1. Compute the following variances for May:
   a. Materials price and quantity variances.
   b. Labor rate and efficiency variances.
   c. Variable overhead rate and efficiency variances.
2. How much of the $0.40 excess unit cost is traceable to each of the variances computed in (1) above.
3. How much of the $0.40 excess unit cost is traceable to apparent inefficient use of labor time?
4. Do you agree that the excess unit cost is not of concern?

PROBLEM 10–13 Materials and Labor Variances; Computations from Incomplete Data [LO1, LO2]

Topaz Company makes one product and has set the following standards for materials and labor:

	Direct Materials	Direct Labor
Standard quantity or hours per unit	? pounds	2.5 hours
Standard price or rate	? per pound	$9.00 per hour
Standard cost per unit	?	$22.50

During the past month, the company purchased 6,000 pounds of direct materials at a cost of $16,500. All of this material was used in the production of 1,400 units of product. Direct labor cost totaled $28,500 for the month. The following variances have been computed:

Materials quantity variance	$1,200 U
Total materials spending variance	$300 F
Labor efficiency variance	$4,500 F

Required:

1. For direct materials:
   a. Compute the standard price per pound for materials.
   b. Compute the standard quantity allowed for materials for the month's production.
   c. Compute the standard quantity of materials allowed per unit of product.
2. For direct labor:
   a. Compute the actual direct labor cost per hour for the month.
   b. Compute the labor rate variance.

(Hint: In completing the problem, it may be helpful to move from known to unknown data either by using the variance formulas or by using the columnar format shown in Exhibits 10–5 and 10–6.)

eXcel

PROBLEM 10–14 Comprehensive Variance Analysis [LO1, LO2, LO3]
Vitalite, Inc., produces a number of products, including a body-wrap kit. Standard variable costs relating to a single kit are given below:

	Standard Quantity or Hours	Standard Price or Rate	Standard Cost
Direct materials	?	$6 per yard	$?
Direct labor	?	?	?
Variable manufacturing overhead	?	$2 per direct labor-hour	?
Total standard cost per kit			$42

During August, 500 kits were manufactured and sold. Selected information relating to the month's production is given below:

	Materials Used	Direct Labor	Variable Manufacturing Overhead
Total standard cost*	?	$8,000	$1,600
Actual costs incurred	$10,000	?	$1,620
Materials price variance	?		
Materials quantity variance	$600 U		
Labor rate variance		?	
Labor efficiency variance		?	
Variable overhead rate variance			?
Variable overhead efficiency variance			?

*For the month's production.

The following additional information is available for August's production of kits:

Actual direct labor-hours	900
Difference between standard and actual cost per kit produced during August	$0.14 U

Required:
1. What was the total standard cost of the materials used during August?
2. How many yards of material are required at standard per kit?
3. What was the materials price variance for August if there were no beginning or ending inventories of materials?
4. What is the standard direct labor rate per hour?
5. What was the labor rate variance for August? The labor efficiency variance?
6. What was the variable overhead rate variance for August? The variable overhead efficiency variance?
7. Complete the standard cost card for one kit shown at the beginning of the problem.

eXcel

PROBLEM 10–15 Comprehensive Variance Analysis [LO1, LO2, LO3]
Helix Company produces several products in its factory, including a karate robe. The company uses a standard cost system to assist in the control of costs. According to the standards that have

been set for the robes, the factory should work 780 direct labor-hours each month and produce 1,950 robes. The standard costs associated with this level of production are as follows:

	Total	Per Unit of Product
Direct materials	$35,490	$18.20
Direct labor	$7,020	3.60
Variable manufacturing overhead (based on direct labor-hours)	$2,340	1.20
		$23.00

During April, the factory worked only 760 direct labor-hours and produced 2,000 robes. The following actual costs were recorded during the month:

	Total	Per Unit of Product
Direct materials (6,000 yards)	$36,000	$18.00
Direct labor	$7,600	3.80
Variable manufacturing overhead	$3,800	1.90
		$23.70

At standard, each robe should require 2.8 yards of material. All of the materials purchased during the month were used in production.

Required:

Compute the following variances for April:

1. The materials price and quantity variances.
2. The labor rate and efficiency variances.
3. The variable manufacturing overhead rate and efficiency variances.

PROBLEM 10–16 Multiple Products, Materials, and Processes [LO1, LO2]

Monte Rosa Corporation produces two products, Alpha8s and Zeta9s, which pass through two operations, Sintering and Finishing. Each of the products uses two raw materials, X342 and Y561. The company uses a standard cost system, with the following standards for each product (on a per unit basis):

	Raw Material		Standard Labor Time	
Product	X342	Y561	Sintering	Finishing
Alpha8	1.8 kilos	2.0 liters	0.20 hours	0.80 hours
Zeta9	3.0 kilos	4.5 liters	0.35 hours	0.90 hours

Information relating to materials purchased and materials used in production during May follows:

Material	Purchases	Purchase Cost	Standard Price	Used in Production
X342	14,000 kilos	$51,800	$3.50 per kilo	8,500 kilos
Y561	15,000 liters	$19,500	$1.40 per liter	13,000 liters

The following additional information is available:

a. The company recognizes price variances when materials are purchased.
b. The standard labor rate is $20.00 per hour in Sintering and $19.00 per hour in Finishing.
c. During May, 1,200 direct labor-hours were worked in Sintering at a total labor cost of $27,000, and 2,850 direct labor-hours were worked in Finishing at a total labor cost of $59,850.
d. Production during May was 1,500 Alpha8s and 2,000 Zeta9s.

Required:

1. Prepare a standard cost card for each product, showing the standard cost of direct materials and direct labor.
2. Compute the materials quantity and price variances for each material.
3. Compute the direct labor efficiency and rate variances for each operation.

Case connect ACCOUNTING

All applicable cases are available with McGraw-Hill's *Connect™ Accounting*.

CASE 10–17 Working Backwards from Variance Data [LO1, LO2, LO3]

You have recently accepted a position with Lorthen Inc. As part of your duties, you review the variances that are reported for each period and make a presentation to the company's executive committee.

Earlier this morning you received the variances for one of the company's major products for the most recent period. After reviewing the variances and organizing the data for your presentation, you accidentally placed the material on top of some papers that were going to the shredder. In the middle of lunch you suddenly realized your mistake and dashed to the shredding room. There you found the operator busily feeding your pages through the machine. You managed to pull only part of one page from the feeding chute, which contains the following information:

Standard Cost Card	
Direct materials, 2.0 meters at $16.00 per meter	$32.00
Direct labor, 1.0 hours at $15.00 per hour.	$15.00
Variable overhead, 1.0 hours at $9.00 per hour	$9.00

	Total Standard Cost	Quantity or Efficiency Variance	Price or Rate Variance
Direct materials	$608,000	$32,000 U	$11,600 F
Direct labor	$285,000	$15,000 U	$4,000 U
Variable overhead	$171,000	Ruined by shredder	$4,000 F

The standard for variable overhead is based on direct labor-hours. All of the materials purchased during the period were used in production.

At lunch your supervisor said how pleased she was with your work and that she was looking forward to your presentation that afternoon. You realize that to avoid looking like a bungling fool you must somehow generate the necessary "backup" data for the variances before the executive committee meeting starts in one hour.

Required:

1. How many units were produced during the period?
2. How many meters of direct materials were purchased and used in production?
3. What was the actual cost per meter of material?
4. How many actual direct labor-hours were worked during the period?
5. What was the actual rate per direct labor-hour?
6. How much actual variable manufacturing overhead cost was incurred during the period?

Appendix 10A: Predetermined Overhead Rates and Overhead Analysis in a Standard Costing System

LEARNING OBJECTIVE 4
Compute and interpret the fixed overhead volume and budget variances.

In this appendix, we will investigate how the predetermined overhead rates that we discussed in the job-order costing chapter earlier in the book can be used in a standard costing system. Throughout this appendix, we assume that an absorption costing system is used in which *all* manufacturing costs—both fixed and variable—are included in product costs.

EXHIBIT 10A–1
MicroDrive Corporation Data

Budgeted production	25,000 motors
Standard machine-hours per motor	2 machine-hours per motor
Budgeted machine-hours (2 machine-hours per motor × 25,000 motors)	50,000 machine-hours
Actual production	20,000 motors
Standard machine-hours allowed for the actual production (2 machine-hours per motor × 20,000 motors)	40,000 machine-hours
Actual machine-hours.	42,000 machine-hours
Budgeted variable manufacturing overhead . . .	$75,000
Budgeted fixed manufacturing overhead	$300,000
Total budgeted manufacturing overhead	$375,000
Actual variable manufacturing overhead	$71,000
Actual fixed manufacturing overhead	$308,000
Total actual manufacturing overhead	$379,000

Predetermined Overhead Rates

The data in Exhibit 10A–1 pertain to MicroDrive Corporation, a company that produces miniature electric motors. Note that the company budgeted for 50,000 machine-hours based on production of 25,000 motors. At this level of activity, the budgeted variable manufacturing overhead was $75,000 and the budgeted fixed manufacturing overhead was $300,000.

Recall from the job-order costing chapter that the following formula is used to set the predetermined overhead rate at the beginning of the period:

$$\text{Predetermined overhead rate} = \frac{\text{Estimated total manufacturing overhead cost}}{\text{Estimated total amount of the allocation base}}$$

The estimated total amount of the allocation base in the formula for the predetermined overhead rate is called the **denominator activity.**

As discussed in the job-order costing chapter, once the predetermined overhead rate has been determined, it remains unchanged throughout the period, even if the actual level of activity differs from what was estimated. Consequently, the amount of overhead applied to each unit of product is the same regardless of when it is produced during the period.

MicroDrive Corporation uses budgeted machine-hours as its denominator activity in the predetermined overhead rate. Consequently, the company's predetermined overhead rate would be computed as follows:

$$\text{Predetermined overhead rate} = \frac{\$375{,}000}{50{,}000 \text{ MHs}} = \$7.50 \text{ per MH}$$

This predetermined overhead rate can be broken down into its variable and fixed components as follows:

$$\text{Variable componenet of the predetermined overhead rate} = \frac{\$75{,}000}{50{,}000 \text{ MHs}} = \$1.50 \text{ per MH}$$

$$\text{Fixed component of the predetermined overhead rate} = \frac{\$300{,}000}{50{,}000 \text{ MHs}} = \$6.00 \text{ per MH}$$

For every standard machine-hour recorded, work in process is charged with $7.50 of manufacturing overhead, of which $1.50 represents variable manufacturing overhead and

$6.00 represents fixed manufacturing overhead. In total, MicroDrive Corporation would apply $300,000 of overhead to work in process as shown below:

$$\text{Overhead applied} = \frac{\text{Predetermined}}{\text{overhead rate}} \times \frac{\text{Standard hours allowed}}{\text{for the actual output}}$$

$$= \$7.50 \text{ per machine-hour} \times 40{,}000 \text{ machine-hours}$$

$$= \$300{,}000$$

Overhead Application in a Standard Cost System

To understand fixed overhead variances, we first have to understand how overhead is applied to work in process in a standard cost system. Recall that in the job-order costing chapter we applied overhead to work in process on the basis of the actual level of activity. This procedure was correct because at the time we were dealing with a normal cost system.[1] However, we are now dealing with a standard cost system. In such a system, overhead is applied to work in process on the basis of the *standard hours allowed for the actual output of the period* rather than on the basis of the actual number of hours worked. Exhibit 10A–2 illustrates this point. In a standard cost system, every unit of a particular product is charged with the same amount of overhead cost, regardless of how much time the unit actually requires for processing.

EXHIBIT 10A–2
Applied Overhead Costs: Normal Cost System versus Standard Cost System

Normal Cost System — Manufacturing Overhead		Standard Cost System — Manufacturing Overhead	
Actual overhead costs incurred.	Applied overhead costs: Actual hours × Predetermined overhead rate.	Actual overhead costs incurred.	Applied overhead costs: Standard hours allowed for actual output × Predetermined overhead rate.
Underapplied or overapplied overhead		Underapplied or overapplied overhead	

Budget Variance

Two fixed manufacturing overhead variances are computed in a standard costing system—a *budget variance* and a *volume variance.* These variances are computed in Exhibit 10A–3. The **budget variance** is simply the difference between the actual fixed manufacturing overhead and the budgeted fixed manufacturing overhead for the period. The formula is:

$$\text{Budget variance} = \text{Actual fixed overhead} - \text{Budgeted fixed overhead}$$

If the actual fixed overhead cost exceeds the budgeted fixed overhead cost, the budget variance is labeled unfavorable. If the actual fixed overhead cost is less than the budgeted fixed overhead cost, the budget variance is labeled favorable.

Applying the formula to the MicroDrive Corporation data, the budget variance is computed as follows:

$$\text{Budget variance} = \$308{,}000 - \$300{,}000 = \$8{,}000 \text{ U}$$

[1] Normal cost systems are discussed on page 90 in the job-order costing chapter.

EXHIBIT 10A–3
Fixed Overhead Variances

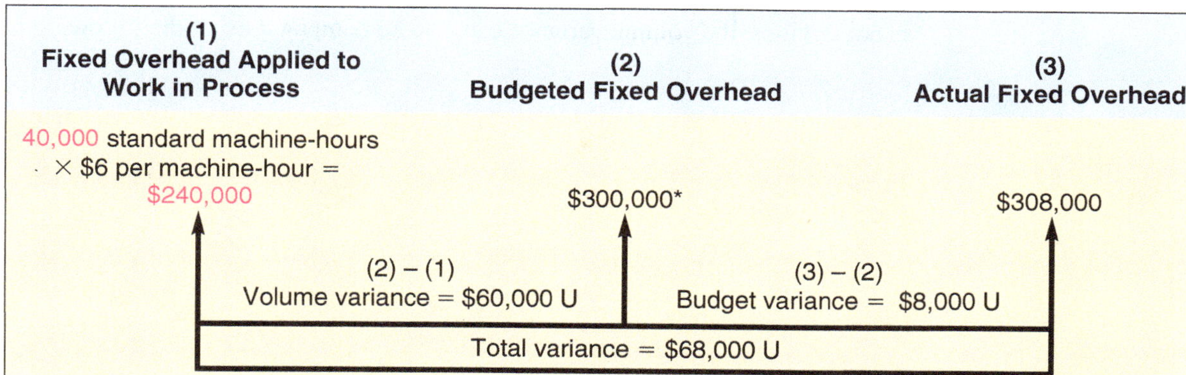

*As originally budgeted (see Exhibit 10A–1). This amount can also be expressed as 50,000 denominator machine-hours × $6 per machine-hour = $300,000.
F = Favorable; U = Unfavorable.

According to the budget, the fixed manufacturing overhead should have been $300,000, but it was actually $308,000. Because the actual cost exceeds the budget by $8,000, the variance is labeled as unfavorable; however, this label does not automatically signal ineffective managerial performance. For example, this variance may be the result of waste and inefficiency, or it may be due to an unforeseen yet prudent investment in fixed overhead resources that improves product quality or manufacturing cycle efficiency.

Volume Variance

The **volume variance** is defined by the following formula:

$$\text{Volume variance} = \begin{array}{c}\text{Budgeted fixed}\\ \text{overhead}\end{array} - \begin{array}{c}\text{Fixed overhead applied}\\ \text{to work in process}\end{array}$$

When the budgeted fixed manufacturing overhead exceeds the fixed manufacturing overhead applied to work in process, the volume variance is labeled as unfavorable. When the budgeted fixed manufacturing overhead is less than the fixed manufacturing overhead applied to work in process, the volume variance is labeled as favorable. As we shall see, caution is advised when interpreting this variance.

To understand the volume variance, we need to understand how fixed manufacturing overhead is applied to work in process in a standard costing system. As discussed earlier, fixed manufacturing overhead is applied to work in process on the basis of the standard hours allowed for the actual output of the period. In the case of MicroDrive Corporation, the company produced 20,000 motors and the standard for each motor is 2 machine-hours. Therefore, the standard hours allowed for the actual output is 40,000 machine-hours (= 20,000 motors × 2 machine-hours). As shown in Exhibit 10A–3, the predetermined fixed manufacturing overhead rate of $6.00 per machine-hour is multiplied by the 40,000 standard machine-hours allowed for the actual output to arrive at $240,000 of fixed manufacturing overhead applied to work in process. Another way to think of this is that the standard for each motor is 2 machine-hours. Because the predetermined fixed manufacturing overhead rate is $6.00 per machine-hour, each motor is assigned $12.00 (= 2 machine-hours × $6.00 per machine-hour) of fixed manufacturing overhead. Consequently, a total of $240,000 of fixed manufacturing overhead is applied to the 20,000 motors that are actually produced. Under either explanation, the volume variance according to the formula is:

$$\text{Volume variance} = \$300{,}000 - \$240{,}000 = \$60{,}000\text{ U}$$

The key to interpreting the volume variance is to understand that it depends on the difference between the hours used in the denominator to compute the predetermined overhead rate and the standard hours allowed for the actual output of the period. While it is not obvious, the volume variance can also be computed using the following formula:

$$\text{Volume variance} = \text{Fixed component of the predetermined overhead rate} \times \left(\text{Denominator hours} - \text{Standard hours allowed for the actual output}\right)$$

In the case of MicroDrive Corporation, the volume variance can be computed using this formula as follows:

$$\begin{aligned}\text{Volume variance} &= \frac{\$6.00 \text{ per}}{\text{machine-hour}} \times \left(\frac{50{,}000}{\text{machine-hours}} - \frac{40{,}000}{\text{machine-hours}}\right)\\ &= \$6.00 \text{ per machine-hour} \times (10{,}000 \text{ machine-hours})\\ &= \$60{,}000\ \text{U}\end{aligned}$$

Note that this agrees with the volume variance computed using the earlier formula.

Focusing on this new formula, if the denominator hours exceed the standard hours allowed for the actual output, the volume variance is unfavorable. If the denominator hours are less than the standard hours allowed for the actual output, the volume variance is favorable. Stated differently, the volume variance is unfavorable if the actual level of activity is less than expected. The volume variance is favorable if the actual level of activity is greater than expected. It is important to note that the volume variance does not measure overspending or underspending. A company should incur the same dollar amount of fixed overhead cost regardless of whether the period's activity was above or below the planned (denominator) level.

The volume variance is often viewed as a measure of the utilization of facilities. If the standard hours allowed for the actual output are greater than (less than) the denominator hours, it signals efficient (inefficient) usage of facilities. However, other measures of utilization—such as the percentage of capacity utilized—are easier to compute and understand. Perhaps a better interpretation of the volume variance is that it is the error that occurs when the level of activity is incorrectly estimated and the costing system assumes fixed costs behave as if they are variable. This interpretation may be clearer in the next section that graphically analyses the fixed manufacturing overhead variances.

Graphic Analysis of Fixed Overhead Variances

Exhibit 10A–4 shows a graphic analysis that offers insights into the fixed overhead budget and volume variances. As shown in the graph, fixed overhead cost is applied to work in process at the predetermined rate of $6.00 for each standard hour of activity. (The applied-cost line is the upward-sloping line on the graph.) Because a denominator level of 50,000 machine-hours was used in computing the $6.00 rate, the applied-cost line crosses the budget-cost line at exactly 50,000 machine-hours. If the denominator hours and the standard hours allowed for the actual output are the same, there is no volume variance. It is only when the standard hours differ from the denominator hours that a volume variance arises.

In MicroDrive's case, the standard hours allowed for the actual output (40,000 hours) are less than the denominator hours (50,000 hours). The result is an unfavorable volume variance because less cost was applied to production than was originally budgeted. If the situation had been reversed and the standard hours allowed for the actual output had exceeded the denominator hours, then the volume variance on the graph would have been favorable.

Cautions in Fixed Overhead Analysis

A volume variance for fixed overhead arises because when applying the costs to work in process, we act *as if* the fixed costs are variable. The graph in Exhibit 10A–4 illustrates this point. Notice from the graph that fixed overhead costs are applied to work in process at a rate of $6 per hour *as if* they are variable. Treating these costs as if they are variable

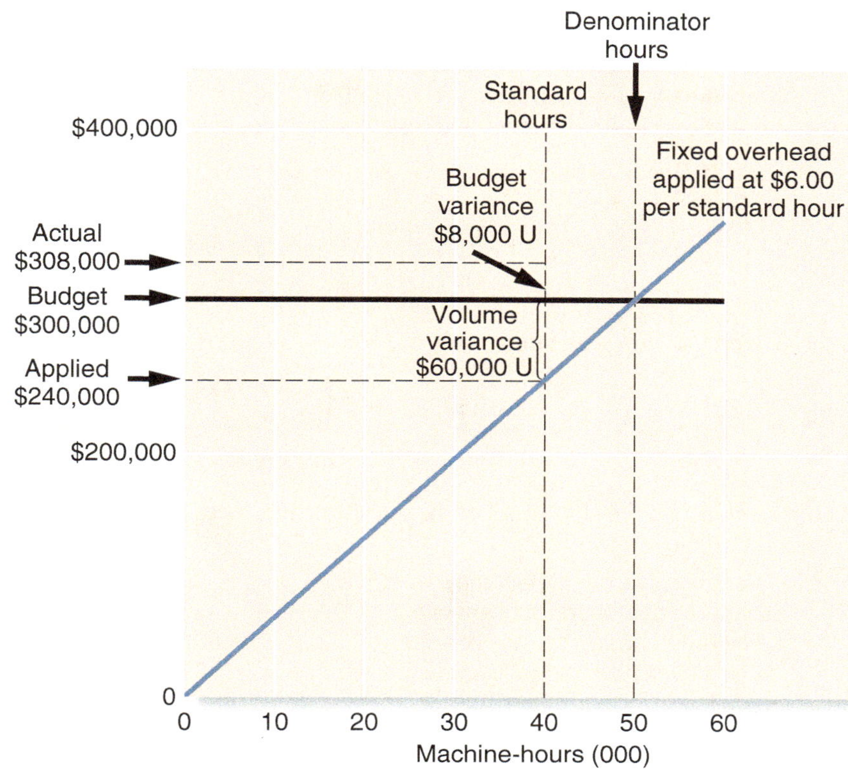

EXHIBIT 10A–4
Graphic Analysis of Fixed Overhead Variances

is necessary for product costing purposes, but some real dangers lurk here. Managers can easily be misled into thinking that fixed costs are *in fact* variable.

Keep clearly in mind that fixed overhead costs come in large chunks. Expressing fixed costs on a unit or per hour basis, though necessary for product costing for external reports, is artificial. Increases or decreases in activity in fact have no effect on total fixed costs within the relevant range of activity. Even though fixed costs are expressed on a unit or per hour basis, they are *not* proportional to activity. In a sense, the volume variance is the error that occurs as a result of treating fixed costs as variable costs in the costing system.

Reconciling Overhead Variances and Underapplied or Overapplied Overhead

In a standard cost system, the underapplied or overapplied overhead for a period equals the sum of the overhead variances. To see this, we will return to the MicroDrive Corporation example.

As discussed earlier, in a standard cost system, overhead is applied to work in process on the basis of the standard hours allowed for the actual output of the period. The following table shows how the underapplied or overapplied overhead for MicroDrive is computed.

Predetermined overhead rate (a)	$7.50 per machine-hour
Standard hours allowed for the actual output [Exhibit 10A–1] (b)	40,000 machine-hours
Manufacturing overhead applied (a) × (b)	$300,000
Actual manufacturing overhead [Exhibit 10A–1]	$379,000
Manufacturing overhead underapplied or overapplied	$79,000 underapplied

We have already computed the budget variance and the volume variance for this company. We will also need to compute the variable manufacturing overhead variances. The data for these computations are contained in Exhibit 10A–1. Recalling the formulas for the variable manufacturing overhead variances from earlier in this chapter, we can compute the variable overhead efficiency and rate variances as follows:

$$\text{Variable overhead efficiency variance} = (AH \times SR) - (SH \times SR)$$
$$= (\$63{,}000) - \left(\begin{matrix}40{,}000\\ \text{machine-hours}\end{matrix} \times \begin{matrix}\$1.50 \text{ per}\\ \text{machine-hour}\end{matrix}\right)$$
$$= \$63{,}000 - \$60{,}000 = \$3{,}000 \text{ U}$$

$$\text{Variable overhead rate variance} = (AH \times AR) - (AH \times SR)$$
$$= (\$71{,}000) - \left(\begin{matrix}42{,}000\\ \text{machine-hours}\end{matrix} \times \begin{matrix}\$1.50 \text{ per}\\ \text{machine-hour}\end{matrix}\right)$$
$$= \$71{,}000 - \$63{,}000 = \$8{,}000 \text{ U}$$

We can now compute the sum of all of the overhead variances as follows:

Variable overhead efficiency variance	$ 3,000 U
Variable overhead rate variance	8,000 U
Fixed overhead volume variance	60,000 U
Fixed overhead budget variance	8,000 U
Total of the overhead variances	$79,000 U

Note that the total of the overhead variances is $79,000, which equals the underapplied overhead of $79,000. In general, if the overhead is underapplied, the total of the standard cost overhead variances is unfavorable. If the overhead is overapplied, the total of the standard cost overhead variances is favorable.

Glossary

Budget variance The difference between the actual fixed overhead costs and the budgeted fixed overhead costs for the period. (p. 456)

Denominator activity The level of activity used to compute the predetermined overhead rate. (p. 455)

Volume variance The variance that arises whenever the standard hours allowed for the actual output of a period are different from the denominator activity level that was used to compute the predetermined overhead rate. It is computed by multiplying the fixed component of the predetermined overhead rate by the difference between the denominator hours and the standard hours allowed for the actual output. (p. 457)

Appendix 10A Exercises and Problems

connect ACCOUNTING

All applicable exercises and problems are available with McGraw-Hill's *Connect™ Accounting*.

EXERCISE 10A–1 Applying Overhead in a Standard Costing System [LO4]

Mosbach Corporation has a standard cost system in which it applies overhead to products based on the standard direct labor-hours allowed for the actual output of the period. Data concerning the most recent year are as follows:

Variable overhead cost per direct labor-hour	$3.50
Total fixed overhead cost per year	$600,000
Budgeted standard direct labor-hours (denominator level of activity)	80,000
Actual direct labor-hours	84,000
Standard direct labor-hours allowed for the actual output	82,000

Required:

1. Compute the predetermined overhead rate for the year.
2. Determine the amount of overhead that would be applied to the output of the period.

EXERCISE 10A–2 Fixed Overhead Variances [LO4]

Lusive Corporation has a standard cost system in which it applies overhead to products based on the standard direct labor-hours allowed for the actual output of the period. Data concerning the most recent year appear below:

Total budgeted fixed overhead cost for the year	$400,000
Actual fixed overhead cost for the year	$394,000
Budgeted standard direct labor-hours (denominator level of activity)	50,000
Actual direct labor-hours	51,000
Standard direct labor-hours allowed for the actual output	48,000

Required:

1. Compute the fixed portion of the predetermined overhead rate for the year.
2. Compute the fixed overhead budget and volume variances.

EXERCISE 10A–3 Fixed Overhead Variances [LO4]

Selected operating information on three different companies for a recent period is given below:

	Company		
	X	Y	Z
Full-capacity direct labor-hours	20,000	9,000	10,000
Budgeted direct labor-hours*	19,000	8,500	8,000
Actual direct labor-hours	19,500	8,000	9,000
Standard direct labor-hours allowed for actual output	18,500	8,250	9,500

*Denominator activity for computing the predetermined overhead rate.

Required:

For each company, state whether the volume variance would be favorable or unfavorable and explain why.

EXERCISE 10A–4 Relations Among Fixed Overhead Variances [LO4]

Selected information relating to the fixed overhead costs of Westwood Company for the most recent year is given below:

Activity:	
Number of units produced	9,500
Standard machine-hours allowed per unit	2
Denominator activity (machine-hours)	20,000
Costs:	
Actual fixed overhead costs incurred	$79,000
Budget variance	$1,000 F

Overhead cost is applied to products on the basis of standard machine-hours.

Required:
1. What was the fixed portion of the predetermined overhead rate?
2. What were the standard machine-hours allowed for the period's production?
3. What was the volume variance?

EXERCISE 10A–5 Predetermined Overhead Rates [LO4]

Operating at a normal level of 24,000 direct labor-hours per year, Trone Company produces 8,000 units of product. The direct labor wage rate is $12.60 per hour. Two pounds of raw materials go into each unit of product at a cost of $4.20 per pound. Variable manufacturing overhead should be $1.60 per standard direct labor-hour. Fixed manufacturing overhead should be $84,000 per year.

Required:
1. Using 24,000 direct labor-hours as the denominator activity, compute the predetermined overhead rate and break it down into fixed and variable elements.
2. Complete the standard cost card below for one unit of product:

Direct materials, 2 pounds at $4.20 per pound	$8.40
Direct labor, ?	?
Variable manufacturing overhead, ?	?
Fixed manufacturing overhead, ?	?
Total standard cost per unit	$?

EXERCISE 10A–6 Predetermined Overhead Rate; Overhead Variances [LO3, LO4]

Weller Company's variable manufacturing overhead should be $1.05 per standard machine-hour and its fixed manufacturing overhead should be $24,800 per month. The following information is available for a recent month:

a. The denominator activity of 8,000 machine-hours was chosen to compute the predetermined overhead rate.
b. At the 8,000 standard machine-hours level of activity, the company should produce 3,200 units of product.
c. The company's actual operating results were as follows:

Number of units produced	3,500
Actual machine-hours	8,500
Actual variable manufacturing overhead cost	$9,860
Actual fixed manufacturing overhead cost	$25,100

Required:
1. Compute the predetermined overhead rate and break it down into variable and fixed cost elements.
2. What were the standard hours allowed for the year's actual output?
3. Compute the variable overhead rate and efficiency variances and the fixed overhead budget and volume variances.

EXERCISE 10A–7 Using Fixed Overhead Variances [LO4]

The standard cost card for the single product manufactured by Prince Company is given below:

Standard Cost Card—Per Unit	
Direct materials, 3.5 feet at $4.00 per foot	$14.00
Direct labor, 0.8 direct labor-hours at $18.00 per direct labor-hour	14.40
Variable overhead, 0.8 direct labor-hours at $2.50 per direct labor-hour	2.00
Fixed overhead, 0.8 direct labor-hours at $6.00 per direct labor-hour	4.80
Total standard cost per unit	$35.20

Last year, the company produced 10,000 units of product and worked 8,200 actual direct labor-hours. Manufacturing overhead cost is applied to production on the basis of direct labor-hours. Selected data relating to the company's fixed manufacturing overhead cost for the year are shown below:

Fixed Overhead Applied to Work in Process	Budgeted Fixed Overhead	Actual Fixed Overhead
_?_ hours × \$6 per hour = \$_?_	?	\$45,600
Volume variance = \$3,000 F		Budget variance = \$?_

Required:

1. What were the standard hours allowed for the year's production?
2. What was the amount of budgeted fixed overhead cost for the year?
3. What was the budget variance for the year?
4. What denominator activity level did the company use in setting the predetermined overhead rate for the year?

PROBLEM 10A–8 Comprehensive Standard Cost Variances [LO1, LO2, LO3, LO4]

"It certainly is nice to see that small variance on the income statement after all the trouble we've had lately in controlling manufacturing costs," said Linda White, vice president of Molina Company. "The \$12,250 overall manufacturing variance reported last period is well below the 3% limit we have set for variances. We need to congratulate everybody on a job well done."

The company produces and sells a single product. The standard cost card for the product follows:

Standard Cost Card—Per Unit	
Direct materials, 4 yards at \$3.50 per yard	\$14.00
Direct labor, 1.5 direct labor-hours at \$12.00 per direct labor-hour	18.00
Variable overhead, 1.5 direct labor-hours at \$2.00 per direct labor-hour	3.00
Fixed overhead, 1.5 direct-labor hours at \$6.00 per direct labor-hour	9.00
Standard cost per unit	\$44.00

The following additional information is available for the year just completed:

a. The company manufactured 20,000 units of product during the year.
b. A total of 78,000 yards of material was purchased during the year at a cost of \$3.75 per yard. All of this material was used to manufacture the 20,000 units. There were no beginning or ending inventories for the year.
c. The company worked 32,500 direct labor-hours during the year at a cost of \$11.80 per hour.
d. Overhead cost is applied to products on the basis of standard direct labor-hours. Data relating to manufacturing overhead costs follow:

Denominator activity level (direct labor-hours)	25,000
Budgeted fixed overhead costs	\$150,000
Actual fixed overhead costs	\$148,000
Actual variable overhead costs	\$68,250

Required:

1. Compute the direct materials price and quantity variances for the year.
2. Compute the direct labor rate and efficiency variances for the year.

3. For manufacturing overhead, compute the following:
   a. The variable overhead rate and efficiency variances for the year.
   b. The fixed overhead budget and volume variances for the year.
4. Total the variances you have computed, and compare the net amount with the $12,250 mentioned by the vice president. Do you agree that everyone should be congratulated for a job well done? Explain.

PROBLEM 10A–9 Selection of a Denominator; Overhead Analysis; Standard Cost Card [LO3, LO4]
Scott Company's variable manufacturing overhead should be $2.50 per standard direct labor-hour and fixed manufacturing overhead should be $320,000 per year.

The company produces a single product that requires 2.5 direct labor-hours to complete. The direct labor wage rate is $20 per hour. Three yards of raw material are required for each unit of product, at a cost of $5 per yard.

Demand for the company's product differs widely from year to year. Expected activity for this year is 50,000 direct labor-hours; normal activity is 40,000 direct labor-hours per year.

Required:

1. Assume that the company chooses 40,000 direct labor-hours as the denominator level of activity. Compute the predetermined overhead rate, breaking it down into fixed and variable cost components.
2. Assume that the company chooses 50,000 direct labor-hours as the denominator level of activity. Repeat the computations in (1) above.
3. Complete two standard cost cards as outlined below.

Denominator Activity: 40,000 DLHs	
Direct materials, 3 yards at $5 per yard	$15.00
Direct labor, ?	?
Variable manufacturing overhead, ?	?
Fixed manufacturing overhead, ?	?
Total standard cost per unit	$?

Denominator Activity: 50,000 DLHs	
Direct materials, 3 yards at $5 per yard	$15.00
Direct labor, ?	?
Variable manufacturing overhead, ?	?
Fixed manufacturing overhead, ?	?
Total standard cost per unit	$?

4. Assume that 48,000 actual hours are worked during the year, and that 18,500 units are produced. Actual manufacturing overhead costs for the year are as follows:

Variable manufacturing overhead cost	$124,800
Fixed manufacturing overhead cost	321,700
Total manufacturing overhead cost	$446,500

   a. Compute the standard hours allowed for the year's actual output.
   b. Compute the missing items from the Manufacturing Overhead account below. Assume that the company uses 40,000 direct labor-hours (normal activity) as the denominator activity figure in computing overhead rates, as you have used in (1) above.

Manufacturing Overhead

Actual costs	446,500	?
	?	?

c. Analyze your underapplied or overapplied overhead balance in terms of variable overhead rate and efficiency variances and fixed overhead budget and volume variances.

5. Looking at the variances that you have computed, what appears to be the major disadvantage of using normal activity rather than expected actual activity as a denominator in computing the predetermined overhead rate? What advantages can you see to offset this disadvantage?

PROBLEM 10A–10 Applying Overhead; Overhead Variances [LO3, LO4]

Highland Shortbread, Ltd., of Aberdeen, Scotland, produces a single product and uses a standard cost system to help control costs. Manufacturing overhead is applied to production on the basis of standard machine-hours. According to the company's flexible budget, the following overhead costs should be incurred at an activity level of 18,000 machine-hours (the denominator activity level chosen for the year):

Variable manufacturing overhead cost	£ 31,500
Fixed manufacturing overhead cost	72,000
Total manufacturing overhead cost	£103,500

During the year, the following operating results were recorded:

Actual machine-hours worked	15,000
Standard machine-hours allowed	16,000
Actual variable manufacturing overhead cost incurred	£26,500
Actual fixed manufacturing overhead cost incurred	£70,000

At the end of the year, the company's Manufacturing Overhead account contained the following data:

Manufacturing Overhead

Actual costs	96,500	Applied costs	92,000
	4,500		

Management would like to determine the cause of the £4,500 underapplied overhead.

Required:

1. Compute the predetermined overhead rate for the year. Break it down into variable and fixed cost elements.
2. Show how the £92,000 "Applied costs" figure in the Manufacturing Overhead account was computed.
3. Analyze the £4,500 underapplied overhead figure in terms of the variable overhead rate and efficiency variances and the fixed overhead budget and volume variances.
4. Explain the meaning of each variance that you computed in (3) above.

PROBLEM 10A–11 Applying Overhead; Overhead Variances [LO3, LO4]

Wymont Company produces a single product that requires a large amount of labor time. Overhead cost is applied on the basis of standard direct labor-hours. Variable manufacturing overhead should be $2.00 per standard direct labor-hour and fixed manufacturing overhead should be $180,000 per year.

The company's product requires 4 feet of direct material that has a standard cost of $3.00 per foot. The product requires 1.5 hours of direct labor time. The standard labor rate is $12.00 per hour.

During the year, the company had planned to operate at a denominator activity level of 30,000 direct labor-hours and to produce 20,000 units of product. Actual activity and costs for the year were as follows:

Number of units produced	22,000
Actual direct labor-hours worked	35,000
Actual variable manufacturing overhead cost incurred	$63,000
Actual fixed manufacturing overhead cost incurred	$181,000

Required:

1. Compute the predetermined overhead rate for the year. Break the rate down into variable and fixed components.
2. Prepare a standard cost card for the company's product; show the details for all manufacturing costs on your standard cost card.
3. *a.* Compute the standard direct labor-hours allowed for the year's production.
   b. Complete the following Manufacturing Overhead T-account for the year:

Manufacturing Overhead	
?	?
?	?

4. Determine the reason for the underapplied or overapplied overhead from (3) above by computing the variable overhead rate and efficiency variances and the fixed overhead budget and volume variances.
5. Suppose the company had chosen 36,000 direct labor-hours as the denominator activity rather than 30,000 hours. State which, if any, of the variances computed in (4) above would have changed, and explain how the variance(s) would have changed. No computations are necessary.

eXcel

PROBLEM 10A–12 Comprehensive Standard Cost Variances [LO1, LO2, LO3, LO4]

Dresser Company uses a standard cost system and sets predetermined overhead rates on the basis of direct labor-hours. The following data are taken from the company's budget for the current year:

Denominator activity (direct labor-hours)	9,000
Variable manufacturing overhead cost at 9,000 direct labor-hours	$34,200
Fixed manufacturing overhead cost	$63,000

The standard cost card for the company's only product is given below:

Direct materials, 4 pounds at $2.60 per pound	$10.40
Direct labor, 2 direct labor-hours at $9.00 per hour	18.00
Overhead, 2 direct labor-hours at $10.80 per hour	21.60
Standard cost per unit	$50.00

During the year, the company produced 4,800 units of product and incurred the following costs:

Materials purchased, 30,000 pounds at $2.50 per pound	$75,000
Materials used in production (in pounds)	20,000
Direct labor cost incurred, 10,000 direct labor-hours at $8.60 per direct labor-hour	$86,000
Variable manufacturing overhead cost incurred	$35,900
Fixed manufacturing overhead cost incurred	$64,800

Required:

1. Redo the standard cost card in a clearer, more usable format by detailing the variable and fixed overhead cost elements.
2. Prepare an analysis of the variances for materials and labor for the year.
3. Prepare an analysis of the variances for variable and fixed overhead for the year.
4. What effect, if any, does the choice of a denominator activity level have on standard unit costs? Is the volume variance a controllable variance from a spending point of view? Explain.

Appendix 10B: Journal Entries to Record Variances

LEARNING OBJECTIVE 5
Prepare journal entries to record standard costs and variances.

Although standard costs and variances can be computed and used by management without being formally entered into the accounting records, many organizations prefer to make formal journal entries. Formal entry tends to give variances a greater emphasis than informal, off-the-record computations. This emphasis signals management's desire to keep costs within the limits that have been set. In addition, formal use of standard costs simplifies the bookkeeping process enormously. Inventories and cost of goods sold can be valued at their standard costs—eliminating the need to keep track of the actual cost of each unit.

Direct Materials Variances

To illustrate the journal entries needed to record standard cost variances, we will return to the data contained in the review problem at the end of the chapter. The entry to record the purchase of direct materials would be as follows:

Raw Materials (18,000 ounces at $0.50 per ounce)	9,000	
Materials Price Variance (18,000 ounces at $0.10 per ounce U)	1,800	
Accounts Payable (18,000 ounces at $0.60 per ounce)		10,800

Notice that the price variance is recognized when purchases are made, rather than when materials are actually used in production and that the materials are carried in the inventory account at standard cost. As direct materials are later drawn from inventory and used in production, the quantity variance is isolated as follows:

Work in Process (12,000 ounces at $0.50 per ounce)	6,000	
Materials Quantity Variance (2,000 ounces U at $0.50 per ounce)	1,000	
Raw Materials (14,000 ounces at $0.50 per ounce)		7,000

Thus, direct materials are added to the Work in Process account at the standard cost of the materials that should have been used to produce the actual output.

Notice that both the price variance and the quantity variance above are unfavorable and are debit entries. If either of these variances had been favorable, it would have appeared as a credit entry.

Direct Labor Variances

Referring again to the cost data in the review problem at the end of the chapter, the journal entry to record the incurrence of direct labor cost would be:

Work in Process (1,200 hours at $30.00 per hour)	36,000	
Labor Rate Variance (1,100 hours at $0.50 U)	550	
Labor Efficiency Variance (100 hours F at $30.00 per hour)		3,000
Wages Payable (1,100 hours at $30.50 per hour)		33,550

Thus, as with direct materials, direct labor costs enter into the Work in Process account at standard, both in terms of the rate and in terms of the hours allowed for the actual production of the period. Note that the unfavorable labor efficiency variance is a debit entry whereas the favorable labor rate variance is a credit entry.

Cost Flows in a Standard Cost System

The flow of costs through the company's accounts are illustrated in Exhibit 10B–1. Note that entries into the various inventory accounts are made at standard cost—not actual cost. The differences between actual and standard costs are entered into special accounts that

EXHIBIT 10B–1
Cost Flows in a Standard Cost System*

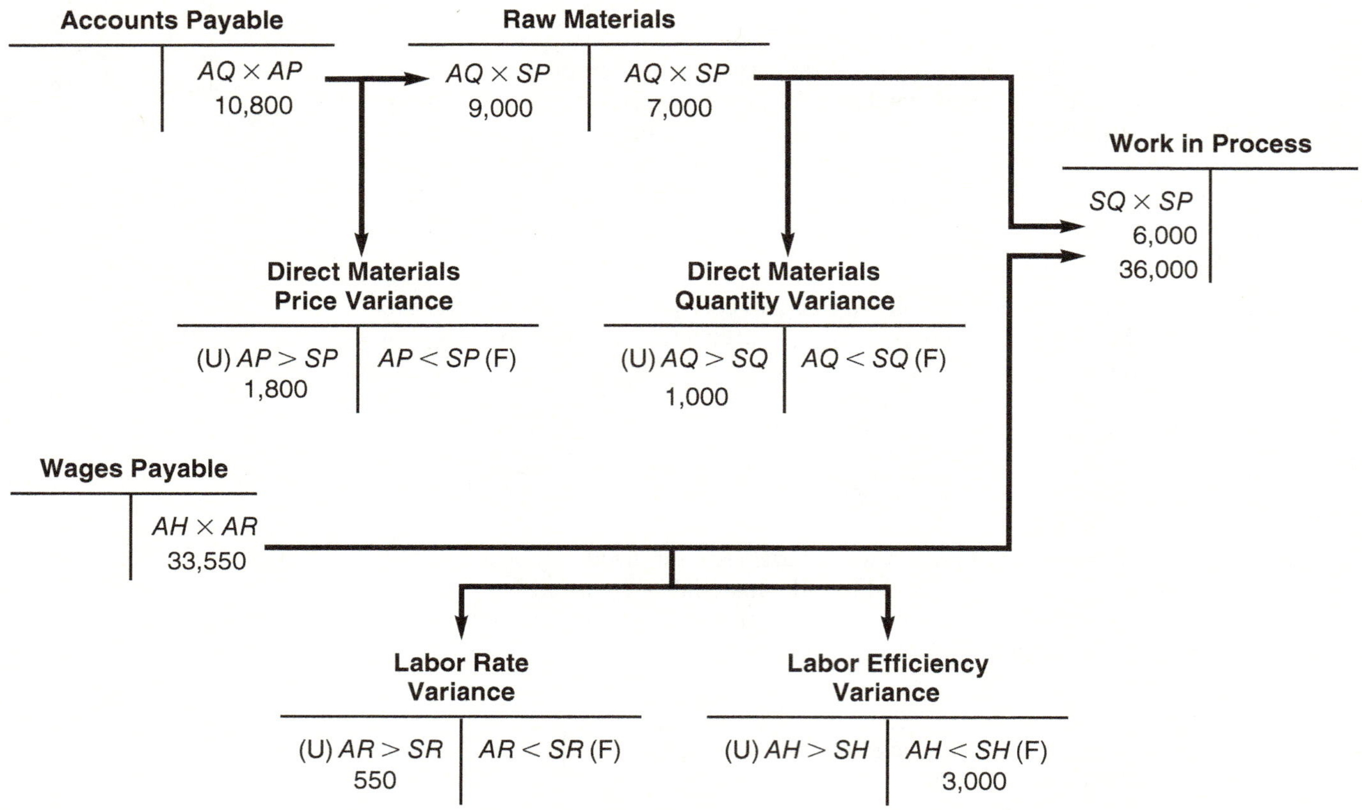

*The authors would like to thank Professor Rick French for suggesting this exhibit.

accumulate the various standard cost variances. Ordinarily, these standard cost variance accounts are closed out to Cost of Goods Sold at the end of the period. Unfavorable variances increase Cost of Goods Sold, and favorable variances decrease Cost of Goods Sold.

Appendix 10B Exercises and Problems

All applicable exercises and problems are available with McGraw-Hill's *Connect™ Accounting*.

EXERCISE 10B–1 Recording Variances in the General Ledger [LO5]

Kinkel Corporation makes a product with the following standard costs for direct material and direct labor:

Direct material: 1.50 meters at $5.40 per meter	$8.10
Direct labor: 0.25 hours at $14.00 per hour	$3.50

During the most recent month, 8,000 units were produced. The costs associated with the month's production of this product were as follows:

Material purchased: 15,000 meters at $5.60 per meter	$84,000
Material used in production: 11,900 meters	—
Direct labor: 1,950 hours at $14.20 per hour	$27,690

The standard cost variances for direct material and direct labor are:

Materials price variance: 15,000 meters at $0.20 per meter U	$3,000 U
Materials quantity variance: 100 meters at $5.40 per meter F	$540 F
Labor rate variance: 1,950 hours at $0.20 per hour U	$390 U
Labor efficiency variance: 50 hours at $14.00 per hour F.	$700 F

Required:

1. Prepare the journal entry to record the purchase of materials on account for the month.
2. Prepare the journal entry to record the use of materials for the month.
3. Prepare the journal entry to record the incurrence of direct labor cost for the month.

EXERCISE 10B–2 Material and Labor Variances; Journal Entries [LO1, LO2, LO5]
Aspen Products, Inc., began production of a new product on April 1. The company uses a standard cost system and has established the following standards for one unit of the new product:

	Standard Quantity or Hours	Standard Price or Rate	Standard Cost
Direct materials.	3.5 feet	$6.00 per foot	$21.00
Direct labor	0.4 hours	$10.00 per hour	$4.00

During April, the following activity was recorded regarding the new product:

a. Purchased 7,000 feet of material at a cost of $5.75 per foot.
b. Used 6,000 feet of material to produce 1,500 units of the new product.
c. Worked 725 direct labor-hours on the new product at a cost of $8,120.

Required:

1. For direct materials:
   a. Compute the direct materials price and quantity variances.
   b. Prepare journal entries to record the purchase of materials and the use of materials in production.
2. For direct labor:
   a. Compute the direct labor rate and efficiency variances.
   b. Prepare journal entries to record the incurrence of direct labor cost for the month.
3. Post the entries you have prepared to the T-accounts below:

Raw Materials	
?	?
Bal. ?	

Accounts Payable	
	40,250

Materials Price Variance	

Wages Payable	
	8,120

Materials Quantity Variance	

Labor Rate Variance	

Work in Process	
Materials used ?	
Labor cost ?	

Labor Efficiency Variance	

PROBLEM 10B–3 Comprehensive Variance Analysis with Incomplete Data; Journal Entries [LO1, LO2, LO3, LO5]

Topline Surf Boards manufactures a single product. The standard cost of one unit of this product is as follows:

Direct materials: 6 feet at $1.00 per foot	$ 6.00
Direct labor: 1 hour at $4.50 per hour	4.50
Variable manufacturing overhead: 1 hour at $3.00 per hour	3.00
Total standard variable cost per unit	$13.50

During October, 6,000 units were produced. Selected data relating to the month's production follow:

Material purchased: 60,000 feet at $0.95 per foot	$57,000
Material used in production: 38,000 feet	—
Direct labor: __?__ hours at $ __?__ per hour	$27,950
Variable manufacturing overhead cost incurred	$20,475
Variable manufacturing overhead efficiency variance	$1,500 U

There was no beginning inventory of raw materials. The variable manufacturing overhead rate is based on direct labor-hours.

Required:

1. For direct materials:
   a. Compute the price and quantity variances for October.
   b. Prepare journal entries to record activity for October.
2. For direct labor:
   a. Compute the rate and efficiency variances for October.
   b. Prepare a journal entry to record labor activity for October.
3. For variable manufacturing overhead:
   a. Compute the spending variance for October, and verify the efficiency variance given above.
   b. If manufacturing overhead is applied to production on the basis of direct labor-hours, is it possible to have a favorable direct labor efficiency variance and an unfavorable variable overhead efficiency variance? Explain.
4. State possible causes of each variance that you have computed.

PROBLEM 10B–4 Comprehensive Variance Analysis; Journal Entries [LO1, LO2, LO3, LO5]

Vermont Mills, Inc., is a large producer of men's and women's clothing. The company uses standard costs for all of its products. The standard costs and actual costs for a recent period are given below for one of the company's product lines (per unit of product):

	Standard Cost	Actual Cost
Direct materials:		
Standard: 4.0 yards at $3.60 per yard	$14.40	
Actual: 4.4 yards at $3.35 per yard		$14.74
Direct labor:		
Standard: 1.6 hours at $4.50 per hour	7.20	
Actual: 1.4 hours at $4.85 per hour		6.79
Variable manufacturing overhead:		
Standard: 1.6 hours at $1.80 per hour	2.88	
Actual: 1.4 hours at $2.15 per hour		3.01
Total cost per unit	$24.48	$24.54

During this period, the company produced 4,800 units of product. A comparison of standard and actual costs for the period on a total cost basis is given below:

Actual costs: 4,800 units at $24.54	$117,792
Standard costs: 4,800 units at $24.48	117,504
Difference in cost—unfavorable	$ 288

There was no inventory of materials on hand to start the period. During the period, 21,120 yards of materials were purchased and used in production.

Required:

1. For direct materials:
    a. Compute the price and quantity variances for the period.
    b. Prepare journal entries to record all activity relating to direct materials for the period.
2. For direct labor:
    a. Compute the rate and efficiency variances.
    b. Prepare a journal entry to record the incurrence of direct labor cost for the period.
3. Compute the variable manufacturing overhead rate and efficiency variances.
4. On seeing the $288 total cost variance, the company's president stated, "This variance of $288 is only 0.2% of the $117,504 standard cost for the period. It's obvious that our costs are well under control." Do you agree? Explain.
5. State possible causes of each variance that you have computed.

Case

All applicable cases are available with McGraw-Hill's *Connect™ Accounting*.

CASE 10B–5 Ethics and the Manager; Rigging Standards [LO5]

Stacy Cummins, the newly hired controller at Merced Home Products, Inc., was disturbed by what she had discovered about the standard costs at the Home Security Division. In looking over the past several years of quarterly earnings reports at the Home Security Division, she noticed that the first-quarter earnings were always poor, the second-quarter earnings were slightly better, the third-quarter earnings were again slightly better, and the fourth quarter always ended with a spectacular performance in which the Home Security Division managed to meet or exceed its target profit for the year. She also was concerned to find letters from the company's external auditors to top management warning about an unusual use of standard costs at the Home Security Division.

When Ms. Cummins ran across these letters, she asked the assistant controller, Gary Farber, if he knew what was going on at the Home Security Division. Gary said that it was common knowledge in the company that the vice president in charge of the Home Security Division, Preston Lansing, had rigged the standards at his division in order to produce the same quarterly earnings pattern every year. According to company policy, variances are taken directly to the income statement as an adjustment to cost of goods sold.

Favorable variances have the effect of increasing net operating income, and unfavorable variances have the effect of decreasing net operating income. Lansing had rigged the standards so that there were always large favorable variances. Company policy was a little vague about when these variances have to be reported on the divisional income statements. While the intent was clearly to recognize variances on the income statement in the period in which they arise, nothing in the company's accounting manuals actually explicitly required this. So for many years, Lansing had followed a practice of saving up the favorable variances and using them to create a nice smooth pattern of earnings growth in the first three quarters, followed by a big "Christmas present" of an extremely good fourth quarter. (Financial reporting regulations forbid carrying variances forward from one year to the next on the annual audited financial statements, so all of the variances must appear on the divisional income statement by the end of the year.)

Ms. Cummins was concerned about these findings and attempted to bring up the subject with the president of Merced Home Products but was told that "we all know what Lansing's doing, but as long as he continues to turn in such good reports, don't bother him." When Ms. Cummins asked if the board of directors was aware of the situation, the president somewhat testily replied, "Of course they are aware."

Required:

1. How did Preston Lansing probably "rig" the standard costs—are the standards set too high or too low? Explain.
2. Should Preston Lansing be permitted to continue his practice of managing reported earnings?
3. What should Stacy Cummins do in this situation?

Chapter 11

Performance Measurement in Decentralized Organizations

LEARNING OBJECTIVES

After studying Chapter 11, you should be able to:

LO1 Compute return on investment (ROI) and show how changes in sales, expenses, and assets affect ROI.

LO2 Compute residual income and understand its strengths and weaknesses.

LO3 Compute delivery cycle time, throughput time, and manufacturing cycle efficiency (MCE).

LO4 Understand how to construct and use a balanced scorecard.

LO5 (Appendix 11A) Determine the range, if any, within which a negotiated transfer price should fall.

LO6 (Appendix 11B) Charge operating departments for services provided by service departments.

Sony Attempts to Rebound

BUSINESS FOCUS

In the past, Sony has delighted customers with its Walkman, the Trinitron TV, the PlayStation, and the CD. However, in the digital media era Sony has lost ground to many better-managed competitors such as Microsoft, Apple, Sharp, and Nokia. Sony is attempting to rebound by discontinuing unprofitable segments such as Aibo, a line of robotic pets; Qualia, a line of boutique electronics; 1,220 cosmetic salons; and 18 Maxim de Paris restaurants. In addition, the company has closed nine plants, sold $705 million worth of assets, and eliminated 5,700 jobs.

The next step for Sony is to improve communications across its remaining business units. For example, at one point Sony had three business units unknowingly competing against one another by developing their own digital music players. Sony's challenge is to encourage decentralized decision making to spur product innovation, while centralizing control of communications across the company so that engineers do not create competing or incompatible products. ■

Source: Marc Gunther, "The Welshman, the Walkman, and the Salarymen," *Fortune*, June 12, 2006, pp. 70–83.

Except in very small organizations, top managers must delegate some decisions. For example, the CEO of the Hyatt Hotel chain cannot be expected to decide whether a particular hotel guest at the Hyatt Hotel on Maui should be allowed to check out later than the normal checkout time. Instead, employees at Maui are authorized to make this decision. As in this example, managers in large organizations have to delegate some decisions to those who are at lower levels in the organization.

Decentralization in Organizations

In a **decentralized organization,** decision-making authority is spread throughout the organization rather than being confined to a few top executives. As noted above, out of necessity all large organizations are decentralized to some extent. Organizations do differ, however, in the extent to which they are decentralized. In strongly centralized organizations, decision-making authority is reluctantly delegated to lower-level managers who have little freedom to make decisions. In strongly decentralized organizations, even the lowest-level managers are empowered to make as many decisions as possible. Most organizations fall somewhere between these two extremes.

Advantages and Disadvantages of Decentralization

The major advantages of decentralization include:

1. By delegating day-to-day problem solving to lower-level managers, top management can concentrate on bigger issues, such as overall strategy.
2. Empowering lower-level managers to make decisions puts the decision-making authority in the hands of those who tend to have the most detailed and up-to-date information about day-to-day operations.
3. By eliminating layers of decision making and approvals, organizations can respond more quickly to customers and to changes in the operating environment.
4. Granting decision-making authority helps train lower-level managers for higher-level positions.
5. Empowering lower-level managers to make decisions can increase their motivation and job satisfaction.

The major disadvantages of decentralization include:

1. Lower-level managers may make decisions without fully understanding the big picture.
2. If lower-level managers make their own decisions independently of each other, coordination may be lacking.
3. Lower-level managers may have objectives that clash with the objectives of the entire organization.[1] For example, a manager may be more interested in increasing the size of his or her department, leading to more power and prestige, than in increasing the department's effectiveness.

---

[1] Similar problems exist with top-level managers as well. The shareholders of the company delegate their decision-making authority to the top managers. Unfortunately, top managers may abuse that trust by rewarding themselves and their friends too generously, spending too much company money on palatial offices, and so on. The issue of how to ensure that top managers act in the best interests of the company's owners continues to challenge experts. To a large extent, the owners rely on performance evaluation using return on investment and residual income measures, as discussed later in the chapter, and on bonuses and stock options. The stock market is also an important disciplining mechanism. If top managers squander the company's resources, the price of the company's stock will almost surely fall—resulting in a loss of prestige, bonuses, and possibly a job. And, of course, particularly outrageous self-dealing may land a CEO in court, as recent events have demonstrated.

4. Spreading innovative ideas may be difficult in a decentralized organization. Someone in one part of the organization may have a terrific idea that would benefit other parts of the organization, but without strong central direction the idea may not be shared with, and adopted by, other parts of the organization.

IN BUSINESS

DECENTRALIZATION: A DELICATE BALANCE

Decentralization has its advantages and disadvantages. Bed Bath & Beyond, a specialty retailer, benefits from allowing its local store managers to choose 70% of their store's merchandise based on local customer tastes. For example, the company's Manhattan stores stock wall paint, but its suburban stores do not because home improvement giants in the suburbs, such as Home Depot, meet this customer need.

On the other hand, Nestle, the Swiss consumer food products company, has been working to overcome glaring inefficiencies resulting from its decentralized management structure. For example, in Switzerland "each candy and ice cream factory was ordering its own sugar. Moreover, different factories were using different names for the identical grade of sugar, making it almost impossible for bosses at headquarters to track costs." Nestle hopes to significantly reduce costs and simplify recordkeeping by centralizing its raw materials purchases.

Sources: Nanette Byrnes, "What's Beyond for Bed Bath & Beyond?" *BusinessWeek*, January 19, 2004, pp. 44–50; and Carol Matlack, "Nestle Is Starting to Slim Down at Last," *BusinessWeek*, October 27, 2003, pp. 56–57.

Responsibility Accounting

Decentralized organizations need *responsibility accounting systems* that link lower-level managers' decision-making authority with accountability for the outcomes of those decisions. The term **responsibility center** is used for any part of an organization whose manager has control over and is accountable for cost, profit, or investments. The three primary types of responsibility centers are *cost centers, profit centers,* and *investment centers.*

Cost, Profit, and Investment Centers

Cost Center The manager of a **cost center** has control over costs, but not over revenue or the use of investment funds. Service departments such as accounting, finance, general administration, legal, and personnel are usually classified as cost centers. In addition, manufacturing facilities are often considered to be cost centers. The managers of cost centers are expected to minimize costs while providing the level of products and services demanded by other parts of the organization. For example, the manager of a manufacturing facility would be evaluated at least in part by comparing actual costs to how much costs should have been for the actual level of output during the period. Standard cost variances and flexible budget variances, such as those discussed in earlier chapters, are often used to evaluate cost center performance.

Profit Center The manager of a **profit center** has control over both costs and revenue, but not over the use of investment funds. For example, the manager in charge of a Six Flags amusement park would be responsible for both the revenues and costs, and hence the profits, of the amusement park, but may not have control over major investments in the park. Profit center managers are often evaluated by comparing actual profit to targeted or budgeted profit.

IN BUSINESS

RESPONSIBILITY ACCOUNTING: A CHINESE PERSPECTIVE

For years Han Dan Iron and Steel Company was under Chinese government control. During this period, the company's management accounting system focused on complying with government mandates rather than responding to the market. As a market-oriented economy began to emerge, the company realized that its management accounting system was obsolete. Managers were preoccupied with meeting production quotas imposed by the government rather than controlling costs and meeting profit targets or encouraging productivity improvements. To remedy this situation, the company implemented what it called a *responsibility cost control system* that (1) set cost and profit targets, (2) assigned target costs to responsibility center managers, (3) evaluated the performance of responsibility center managers based on their ability to meet the targets, and (4) provided incentives to improve productivity.

Source: Z. Jun Lin and Zengbiao Yu, "Responsibility Cost Control System in China: A Case of Management Accounting Application," *Management Accounting Research*, December 2002, pp. 447–467.

Investment Center The manager of an **investment center** has control over cost, revenue, and investments in operating assets. For example, General Motors' vice president of manufacturing in North America would have a great deal of discretion over investments in manufacturing—such as investing in equipment to produce more fuel-efficient engines. Once General Motors' top-level managers and board of directors approve the vice president's investment proposals, he is held responsible for making them pay off. As discussed in the next section, investment center managers are often evaluated using return on investment (ROI) or residual income measures.

Evaluating Investment Center Performance—Return on Investment

LEARNING OBJECTIVE 1
Compute return on investment (ROI) and show how changes in sales, expenses, and assets affect ROI.

An investment center is responsible for earning an adequate return on investment. The following two sections present two methods for evaluating this aspect of an investment center's performance. The first method, covered in this section, is called *return on investment* (ROI). The second method, covered in the next section, is called *residual income.*

The Return on Investment (ROI) Formula

Return on investment (ROI) is defined as net operating income divided by average operating assets:

$$\text{ROI} = \frac{\text{Net operating income}}{\text{Average operating assets}}$$

The higher a business segment's return on investment (ROI), the greater the profit earned per dollar invested in the segment's operating assets.

Net Operating Income and Operating Assets Defined

Note that *net operating income,* rather than net income, is used in the ROI formula. **Net operating income** is income before interest and taxes and is sometimes referred to as EBIT (earnings before interest and taxes). Net operating income is used in the formula because the base (i.e., denominator) consists of *operating assets.* To be consistent, we use net operating income in the numerator.

Operating assets include cash, accounts receivable, inventory, plant and equipment, and all other assets held for operating purposes. Examples of assets that are not included in operating assets (i.e., examples of nonoperating assets) include land held for future use, an investment in another company, or a building rented to someone else. These assets are not held for operating purposes and therefore are excluded from operating assets. The operating assets base used in the formula is typically computed as the average of the operating assets between the beginning and the end of the year.

Most companies use the net book value (i.e., acquisition cost less accumulated depreciation) of depreciable assets to calculate average operating assets. This approach has drawbacks. An asset's net book value decreases over time as the accumulated depreciation increases. This decreases the denominator in the ROI calculation, thus increasing ROI. Consequently, ROI mechanically increases over time. Moreover, replacing old depreciated equipment with new equipment increases the book value of depreciable assets and decreases ROI. Hence, using net book value in the calculation of average operating assets results in a predictable pattern of increasing ROI over time as accumulated depreciation grows and discourages replacing old equipment with new, updated equipment. An alternative to using net book value is the gross cost of the asset, which ignores accumulated depreciation. Gross cost stays constant over time because depreciation is ignored; therefore, ROI does not grow automatically over time, and replacing a fully depreciated asset with a comparably priced new asset will not adversely affect ROI.

Nevertheless, most companies use the net book value approach to computing average operating assets because it is consistent with their financial reporting practices of recording the net book value of assets on the balance sheet and including depreciation as an operating expense on the income statement. In this text, we will use the net book value approach unless a specific exercise or problem directs otherwise.

Understanding ROI

The equation for ROI, net operating income divided by average operating assets, does not provide much help to managers interested in taking actions to improve their ROI. It only offers two levers for improving performance—net operating income and average operating assets. Fortunately, ROI can also be expressed in terms of **margin** and **turnover** as follows:

$$\text{ROI} = \text{Margin} \times \text{Turnover}$$

where

$$\text{Margin} = \frac{\text{Net operating income}}{\text{Sales}}$$

and

$$\text{Turnover} = \frac{\text{Sales}}{\text{Average operating assets}}$$

Note that the sales terms in the margin and turnover formulas cancel out when they are multiplied together, yielding the original formula for ROI stated in terms of net operating income and average operating assets. So either formula for ROI will give the same answer. However, the margin and turnover formulation provides some additional insights.

Margin and turnover are important concepts in understanding how a manager can affect ROI. All other things the same, margin is ordinarily improved by increasing selling prices, reducing operating expenses, or increasing unit sales. Increasing selling prices and reducing operating expenses both increase net operating income and therefore margin. Increasing unit sales also ordinarily increases the margin because of operating leverage. As discussed in a previous chapter, because of operating leverage, a given percentage increase in unit sales usually leads to an even larger percentage increase in net operating income. Therefore, an increase in unit sales ordinarily has the effect of increasing margin. Some managers tend to focus too much on margin and ignore turnover. However,

IN BUSINESS

J. CREW PULLS THE ROI LEVERS

J. Crew has adopted an interesting strategy for improving its ROI. The company has started selling "super-premium products—such as $1,500 cashmere coats and $1,500 beaded tunics—in limited editions, sometimes no more than 100 pieces nationwide." The intentional creation of scarcity causes many items to sell out within weeks as shoppers snatch them up before they are gone for good.

This strategy is helping boost J. Crew's ROI in two ways. First, the company earns higher margins on premium-priced products where customer demand dramatically exceeds supply. Second, the company is slashing its inventories because such small quantities of each item are purchased from suppliers. While J. Crew sacrifices some sales from customers who would have purchased sold out items, the overall effect on profits has been favorable. "Tighter inventories mean that J. Crew is no longer putting reams of clothes on sale, a move that kills profit margins and trains shoppers to wait for discounts. At one point . . . half of J. Crew's clothing sold at a discount. Today only a small percentage of it does."

Source: Julia Boorstin, "Mickey Drexler's Second Coming," *Fortune*, May 2, 2005, pp. 101–104.

turnover incorporates a crucial area of a manager's responsibility—the investment in operating assets. Excessive funds tied up in operating assets (e.g., cash, accounts receivable, inventories, plant and equipment, and other assets) depress turnover and lower ROI. In fact, excessive operating assets can be just as much of a drag on ROI as excessive operating expenses, which depress margin.

Many actions involve combinations of changes in sales, expenses, and operating assets. For example, a manager may make an investment in (i.e., increase) operating assets to reduce operating expenses or increase sales. Whether the net effect is favorable or not is judged in terms of its overall impact on ROI.

For example, suppose that the Montvale Burger Grill expects the following operating results next month:

Sales	$100,000
Operating expenses	$90,000
Net operating income	$10,000
Average operating assets	$50,000

The expected return on investment (ROI) for the month is computed as follows:

$$\text{ROI} = \frac{\text{Net operating income}}{\text{Sales}} \times \frac{\text{Sales}}{\text{Average operating assets}}$$

$$= \frac{\$10{,}000}{\$100{,}000} \times \frac{\$100{,}000}{\$50{,}000}$$

$$= 10\% \times 2 = 20\%$$

Suppose that the manager of the Montvale Burger Grill is considering investing $2,000 in a state-of-the-art soft-serve ice cream machine that can dispense a number of different flavors. This new machine would boost sales by $4,000, but would require additional operating expenses of $1,000. Thus, net operating income would increase by $3,000, to $13,000. The new ROI would be:

$$\text{ROI} = \frac{\text{Net operating income}}{\text{Sales}} \times \frac{\text{Sales}}{\text{Average operating assets}}$$

$$= \frac{\$13{,}000}{\$104{,}000} \times \frac{\$104{,}000}{\$52{,}000}$$

$$= 12.5\% \times 2 = 25\% \text{ (as compared to 20\% originally)}$$

EXHIBIT 11–1
Elements of Return on Investment (ROI)

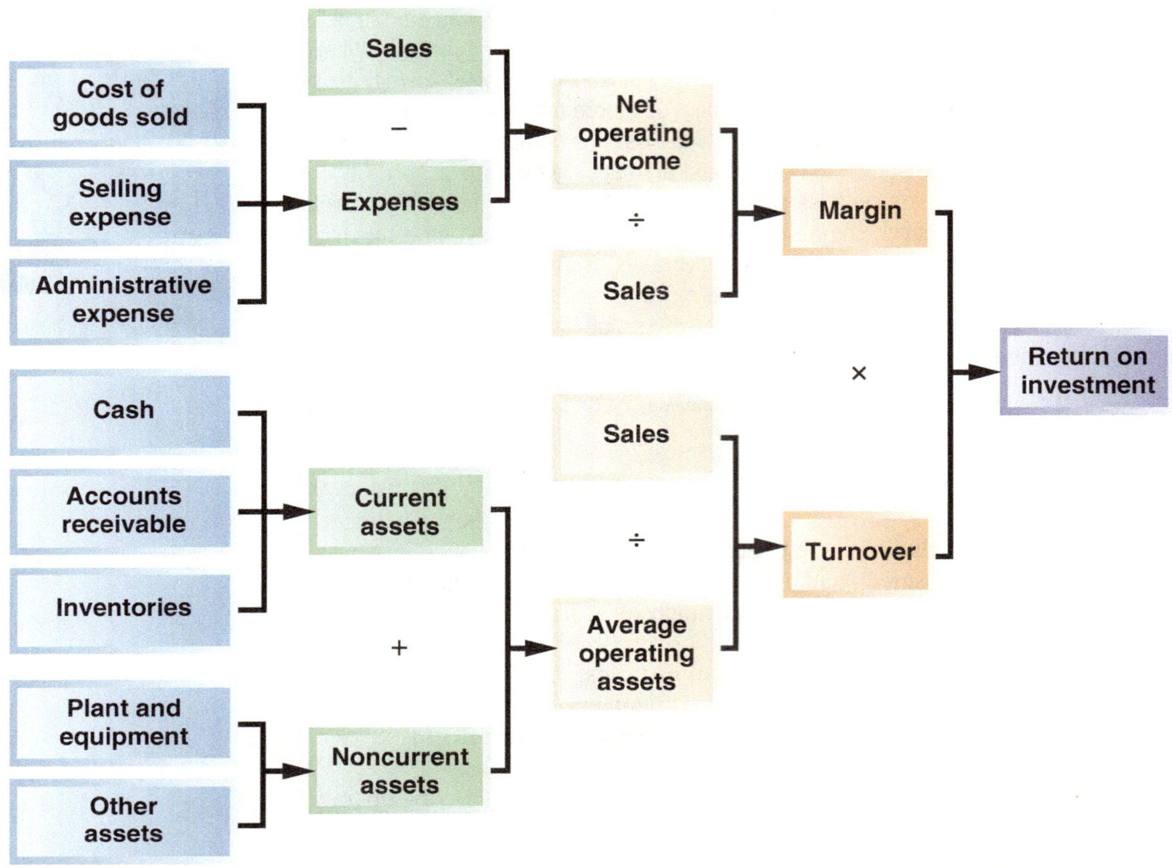

In this particular example, the investment increases ROI, but that will not always happen.

E.I. du Pont de Nemours and Company (better known as DuPont) pioneered the use of ROI and recognized the importance of looking at both margin and turnover in assessing a manager's performance. ROI is now widely used as the key measure of investment center performance. ROI reflects in a single figure many aspects of the manager's responsibilities. It can be compared to the returns of other investment centers in the organization, the returns of other companies in the industry, and to the past returns of the investment center itself. DuPont also developed the diagram that appears in Exhibit 11–1. This exhibit helps managers understand how they can improve ROI.

IN BUSINESS

MICROSOFT MANAGES IN AN ECONOMIC DOWNTURN

Microsoft responded to tough economic times by lowering its prices, thereby accepting lower margins per unit sold in exchange for higher turnover. For example, Microsoft lowered the price of its Office software from $150 to $100 (after promotional discounts) and realized a 415% increase in unit sales. In China, the company combated huge piracy problems by dropping the price of Office to $29, resulting in an 800% increase in sales. Microsoft established a selling price of $200 for its Windows 7 PC operating system, which was $40 less than the price the company charged for its predecessor Vista PC operating system.

Source: Peter Burrows, "Microsoft's Aggressive New Pricing Strategy," *BusinessWeek*, July 27, 2009, p. 51.

Criticisms of ROI

Although ROI is widely used in evaluating performance, it is subject to the following criticisms:

1. Just telling managers to increase ROI may not be enough. Managers may not know how to increase ROI; they may increase ROI in a way that is inconsistent with the company's strategy; or they may take actions that increase ROI in the short run but harm the company in the long run (such as cutting back on research and development). This is why ROI is best used as part of a balanced scorecard, as discussed later in this chapter. A balanced scorecard can provide concrete guidance to managers, making it more likely that their actions are consistent with the company's strategy and reducing the likelihood that they will boost short-run performance at the expense of long-term performance.
2. A manager who takes over a business segment typically inherits many committed costs over which the manager has no control. These committed costs may be relevant in assessing the performance of the business segment as an investment but they make it difficult to fairly assess the performance of the manager.
3. As discussed in the next section, a manager who is evaluated based on ROI may reject investment opportunities that are profitable for the whole company but would have a negative impact on the manager's performance evaluation.

Residual Income

LEARNING OBJECTIVE 2
Compute residual income and understand its strengths and weaknesses.

Residual income is another approach to measuring an investment center's performance. **Residual income** is the net operating income that an investment center earns above the minimum required return on its operating assets. In equation form, residual income is calculated as follows:

$$\text{Residual income} = \text{Net operating income} - \left(\text{Average operating assets} \times \text{Minimum required rate of return}\right)$$

Economic Value Added (EVA®) is an adaptation of residual income that has been adopted by many companies.[2] Under EVA, companies often modify their accounting principles in various ways. For example, funds used for research and development are often treated as investments rather than as expenses.[3] These complications are best dealt with in a more advanced course; in this text we will not draw any distinction between residual income and EVA.

When residual income or EVA is used to measure performance, the objective is to maximize the total amount of residual income or EVA, not to maximize ROI. This is an important distinction. If the objective were to maximize ROI, then every company should divest all of its products except the single product with the highest ROI.

A wide variety of organizations have embraced some version of residual income or EVA, including Bausch & Lomb, Best Buy, Boise Cascade, Coca-Cola, Dun and Bradstreet, Eli Lilly, Federated Mogul, Georgia-Pacific, Guidant Corporation, Hershey Foods, Husky Injection Molding, J.C. Penney, Kansas City Power & Light, Olin, Quaker Oats,

---

[2] The basic idea underlying residual income and economic value added has been around for over 100 years. In recent years, economic value added has been popularized and trademarked by the consulting firm Stern, Stewart & Co.

[3] Over 100 different adjustments could be made for deferred taxes, LIFO reserves, provisions for future liabilities, mergers and acquisitions, gains or losses due to changes in accounting rules, operating leases, and other accounts, but most companies make only a few. For further details, see John O'Hanlon and Ken Peasnell, "Wall Street's Contribution to Management Accounting: the Stern Stewart EVA® Financial Management System," *Management Accounting Research* 9, 1998, pp. 421–444.

Silicon Valley Bank, Sprint, Toys R Us, Tupperware, and the United States Postal Service. In addition, financial institutions such as Credit Suisse First Boston now use EVA—and its allied concept, market value added—to evaluate potential investments in other companies.

For purposes of illustration, consider the following data for an investment center—the Ketchikan Division of Alaskan Marine Services Corporation.

Alaskan Marine Services Corporation Ketchikan Division Basic Data for Performance Evaluation	
Average operating assets	$100,000
Net operating income	$20,000
Minimum required rate of return	15%

Alaskan Marine Services Corporation has long had a policy of using ROI to evaluate its investment center managers, but it is considering switching to residual income. The controller of the company, who is in favor of the change to residual income, has provided the following table that shows how the performance of the division would be evaluated under each of the two methods:

Alaskan Marine Services Corporation
Ketchikan Division

	Alternative Performance Measures	
	ROI	Residual Income
Average operating assets (a)	$100,000	$100,000
Net operating income (b)	$20,000	$20,000
ROI, (b) ÷ (a)	20%	
Minimum required return (15% × $100,000)		15,000
Residual income		$ 5,000

The reasoning underlying the residual income calculation is straightforward. The company is able to earn a rate of return of at least 15% on its investments. Because the company has invested $100,000 in the Ketchikan Division in the form of operating assets, the company should be able to earn at least $15,000 (15% × $100,000) on this investment. Because the Ketchikan Division's net operating income is $20,000, the residual income above and beyond the minimum required return is $5,000. If residual income is adopted as the performance measure to replace ROI, the manager of the Ketchikan Division would be evaluated based on the growth in residual income from year to year.

Motivation and Residual Income

One of the primary reasons why the controller of Alaskan Marine Services Corporation would like to switch from ROI to residual income relates to how managers view new investments under the two performance measurement schemes. The residual income approach encourages managers to make investments that are profitable for the entire company but that would be rejected by managers who are evaluated using the ROI formula.

To illustrate this problem with ROI, suppose that the manager of the Ketchikan Division is considering purchasing a computerized diagnostic machine to aid in servicing marine diesel engines. The machine would cost $25,000 and is expected to generate additional operating income of $4,500 a year. From the standpoint of the company, this would be a good investment because it promises a rate of return of 18% ($4,500 ÷ $25,000), which exceeds the company's minimum required rate of return of 15%.

If the manager of the Ketchikan Division is evaluated based on residual income, she would be in favor of the investment in the diagnostic machine as shown below:

Alaskan Marine Services Corporation
Ketchikan Division
Performance Evaluated Using Residual Income

	Present	New Project	Overall
Average operating assets	$100,000	$25,000	$125,000
Net operating income	$20,000	$4,500	$24,500
Minimum required return	15,000	3,750*	18,750
Residual income	$ 5,000	$ 750	$ 5,750

*$25,000 × 15% = $3,750.

Because the project would increase the residual income of the Ketchikan Division by $750, the manager would choose to invest in the new diagnostic machine.

Now suppose that the manager of the Ketchikan Division is evaluated based on ROI. The effect of the diagnostic machine on the division's ROI is computed below:

Alaskan Marine Services Corporation
Ketchikan Division
Performance Evaluated Using ROI

	Present	New Project	Overall
Average operating assets (a)	$100,000	$25,000	$125,000
Net operating income (b)	$20,000	$4,500	$24,500
ROI, (b) ÷ (a)	20%	18%	19.6%

The new project reduces the division's ROI from 20% to 19.6%. This happens because the 18% rate of return on the new diagnostic machine, while above the company's 15% minimum required rate of return, is below the division's current ROI of 20%. Therefore, the new diagnostic machine would decrease the division's ROI even though it would be a good investment from the standpoint of the company as a whole. If the manager of the division is evaluated based on ROI, she will be reluctant to even propose such an investment.

Generally, a manager who is evaluated based on ROI will reject any project whose rate of return is below the division's current ROI even if the rate of return on the project is above the company's minimum required rate of return. In contrast, managers who are evaluated using residual income will pursue any project whose rate of return is above the minimum required rate of return because it will increase their residual income. Because it is in the best interests of the company as a whole to accept any project whose rate of return is above the minimum required rate of return, managers who are evaluated based on residual income will tend to make better decisions concerning investment projects than managers who are evaluated based on ROI.

Divisional Comparison and Residual Income

The residual income approach has one major disadvantage. It can't be used to compare the performance of divisions of different sizes. Larger divisions often have more residual income than smaller divisions, not necessarily because they are better managed but simply because they are bigger.

As an example, consider the following residual income computations for the Wholesale Division and the Retail Division of Sisal Marketing Corporation:

	Wholesale Division	Retail Division
Average operating assets (a)	$1,000,000	$250,000
Net operating income	$120,000	$40,000
Minimum required return: 10% × (a)	100,000	25,000
Residual income	$ 20,000	$15,000

Observe that the Wholesale Division has slightly more residual income than the Retail Division, but that the Wholesale Division has $1,000,000 in operating assets as compared to only $250,000 in operating assets for the Retail Division. Thus, the Wholesale Division's greater residual income is probably due to its larger size rather than the quality of its management. In fact, it appears that the smaller division may be better managed because it has been able to generate nearly as much residual income with only one-fourth as much in operating assets. When comparing investment centers, it is probably better to focus on the percentage change in residual income from year to year rather than on the absolute amount of the residual income.

Operating Performance Measures

LEARNING OBJECTIVE 3
Compute delivery cycle time, throughput time, and manufacturing cycle efficiency (MCE).

In addition to financial performance measures, organizations use many nonfinancial performance measures. While financial measures pick up the *results* of what people in the organization do, they do not measure what *drives* organizational performance. For example, activity and revenue variances pick up the results of efforts aimed at increasing sales, but they do not measure the actions that actually drive sales such as improving quality, exposing more potential customers to the product, filling customer orders on time, and so on. Consequently, many organizations use a variety of nonfinancial performance measures in addition to financial measures. In this section we will discuss three examples of such measures that are critical to success in many organizations—delivery cycle time, throughput time, and manufacturing cycle efficiency. Note that while these examples focus on manufacturers, very similar measures can be used by any service organization that experiences a delay between receiving a customer request and responding to that request.

Delivery Cycle Time

The amount of time from when a customer order is received to when the completed order is shipped is called **delivery cycle time.** This time is clearly a key concern to many customers, who would like the delivery cycle time to be as short as possible. Cutting the delivery cycle time may give a company a key competitive advantage—and may be necessary for survival.

Throughput (Manufacturing Cycle) Time

The amount of time required to turn raw materials into completed products is called **throughput time,** or *manufacturing cycle time.* The relation between the delivery cycle time and the throughput (manufacturing cycle) time is illustrated in Exhibit 11–2.

EXHIBIT 11–2
Delivery Cycle Time and Throughput (Manufacturing Cycle) Time

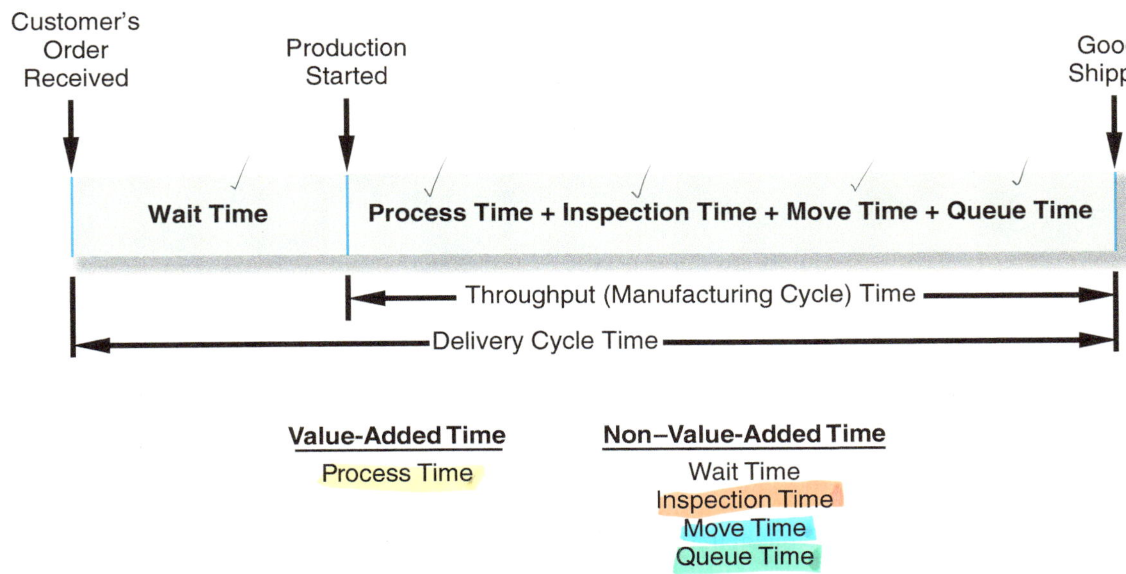

As shown in Exhibit 11–2, the throughput time, or manufacturing cycle time, is made up of process time, inspection time, move time, and queue time. *Process time* is the amount of time work is actually done on the product. *Inspection time* is the amount of time spent ensuring that the product is not defective. *Move time* is the time required to move materials or partially completed products from workstation to workstation. *Queue time* is the amount of time a product spends waiting to be worked on, to be moved, to be inspected, or to be shipped.

As shown at the bottom of Exhibit 11–2, only one of these four activities adds value to the product—process time. The other three activities—inspecting, moving, and queuing—add no value and should be eliminated as much as possible.

Manufacturing Cycle Efficiency (MCE)

Through concerted efforts to eliminate the *non–value-added* activities of inspecting, moving, and queuing, some companies have reduced their throughput time to only a fraction of previous levels. In turn, this has helped to reduce the delivery cycle time from months to only weeks or hours. Throughput time, which is considered to be a key measure in delivery performance, can be put into better perspective by computing the **manufacturing cycle efficiency (MCE).** The MCE is computed by relating the value-added time to the throughput time. The formula is:

$$\text{MCE} = \frac{\text{Value-added time (Process time)}}{\text{Throughput (manufacturing cycle) time}}$$

Any non-value-added time results in an MCE of less than 1. An MCE of 0.5, for example, would mean that half of the total production time consists of inspection, moving, and similar non–value-added activities. In many manufacturing companies, the MCE is less than 0.1 (10%), which means that 90% of the time a unit is in process is spent on activities that do not add value to the product. Monitoring the MCE helps companies to reduce non–value-added activities and thus get products into the hands of customers more quickly and at a lower cost.

Example To provide an example of these measures, consider the following data for Novex Company:

Novex Company keeps careful track of the time to complete customer orders. During the most recent quarter, the following average times were recorded per order:

	Days
Wait time	17.0
Inspection time	0.4
Process time	2.0
Move time	0.6
Queue time	5.0

Goods are shipped as soon as production is completed.

Required:

1. Compute the throughput time.
2. Compute the manufacturing cycle efficiency (MCE).
3. What percentage of the production time is spent in non–value-added activities?
4. Compute the delivery cycle time.

Solution

1. Throughput time = Process time + Inspection time + Move time + Queue time
= 2.0 days + 0.4 days + 0.6 days + 5.0 days
= 8.0 days

IN BUSINESS

LEAN OPERATING PERFORMANCE MEASURES

Watlow Electric Manufacturing Company implemented *lean accounting* to support its lean manufacturing methods. The company stopped providing standard cost variance reports to operating managers because the information was generated too late (at the end of each month) and it could not be understood by frontline employees. Instead, the company began reporting daily and hourly process-oriented measures that helped frontline workers improve performance.

Examples of lean operating performance measures are shown in the table below:

Measure	Description of Measure
On-time delivery percentage	Measures the percentage of orders that customers would define as being delivered on time.
Day-by-the-hour	Measures the quantity of production on an hourly basis to ensure that it is synchronized with customer demand.
First time through percentage	Measures the percentage of completed units that are free of defects.
Number of accidents and injuries . . .	Measures the number of accidents and injuries on the manufacturing floor.
5S audit	Measures the cell workers' ability to keep their work area organized and clean.

Note: 5S stands for Sort, Straighten, Shine, Standardize, and Sustain

Sources: Jan Brosnahan, "Unleash the Power of Lean Accounting," *Journal of Accountancy*, July 2008, pp. 60–66; and Brian Maskell and Frances Kennedy, "Why Do We Need Lean Accounting and How Does It Work?" *Journal of Corporate Accounting and Finance*, March/April 2007, pp. 59–73.

2. Only process time represents value-added time; therefore, MCE would be computed as follows:

$$\text{MCE} = \frac{\text{Value-added time}}{\text{Throughput time}} = \frac{2.0 \text{ days}}{8.0 \text{ days}}$$
$$= 0.25$$

Thus, once put into production, a typical order is actually being worked on only 25% of the time.

3. Because the MCE is 25%, 75% (100% − 25%) of total production time is spent in non–value-added activities.
4. Delivery cycle time = Wait time + Throughput time
= 17.0 days + 8.0 days
= 25.0 days

Balanced Scorecard

LEARNING OBJECTIVE 4
Understand how to construct and use a balanced scorecard.

Financial measures, such as ROI and residual income, and operating measures, such as those discussed in the previous section, may be included in a *balanced scorecard.* A **balanced scorecard** consists of an integrated set of performance measures that are derived from and support a company's strategy. A strategy is essentially a theory about how to achieve the organization's goals. For example, Southwest Airlines' strategy is to offer an *operational excellence* customer value proposition that has three key components—low ticket prices, convenience, and reliability. The company operates only one type of aircraft, the Boeing 737, to reduce maintenance and training costs and simplify scheduling. It further reduces costs by not offering meals, seat assignments, or baggage transfers and by booking a large portion of its passenger revenue over the Internet. Southwest also uses point-to-point flights rather than the hub-and-spoke approach of its larger competitors, thereby providing customers convenient, nonstop service to their final destination. Because Southwest serves many less-congested airports such as Chicago Midway, Burbank, Manchester, Oakland, and Providence, it offers quicker passenger check-ins and reliable departures, while maintaining high asset utilization (i.e., the company's average gate turnaround time of 25 minutes enables it to function with fewer planes and gates). Overall, the company's strategy has worked. At a time when Southwest Airlines' larger competitors are struggling, it continues to earn substantial profits.

Under the balanced scorecard approach, top management translates its strategy into performance measures that employees can understand and influence. For example, the amount of time passengers have to wait in line to have their baggage checked might be a performance measure for the supervisor in charge of the Southwest Airlines check-in counter at the Burbank airport. This performance measure is easily understood by the supervisor, and can be improved by the supervisor's actions.

Common Characteristics of Balanced Scorecards

Performance measures used in the balanced scorecard approach tend to fall into the four groups illustrated in Exhibit 11–3: financial, customer, internal business processes, and learning and growth. Internal business processes are what the company does in an attempt to satisfy customers. For example, in a manufacturing company, assembling a product is an internal business process. In an airline, handling baggage is an internal business process. The idea underlying these groupings (as indicated by the vertical arrows in Exhibit 11–3) is that learning is necessary to improve internal business processes; improving business processes is necessary to improve customer satisfaction; and improving customer satisfaction is necessary to improve financial results.

Note that the emphasis in Exhibit 11–3 is on *improvement*—not on just attaining some specific objective such as profits of $10 million. In the balanced scorecard approach, continual improvement is encouraged. If an organization does not continually improve, it will eventually lose out to competitors that do.

EXHIBIT 11–3
From Strategy to Performance Measures: The Balanced Scorecard

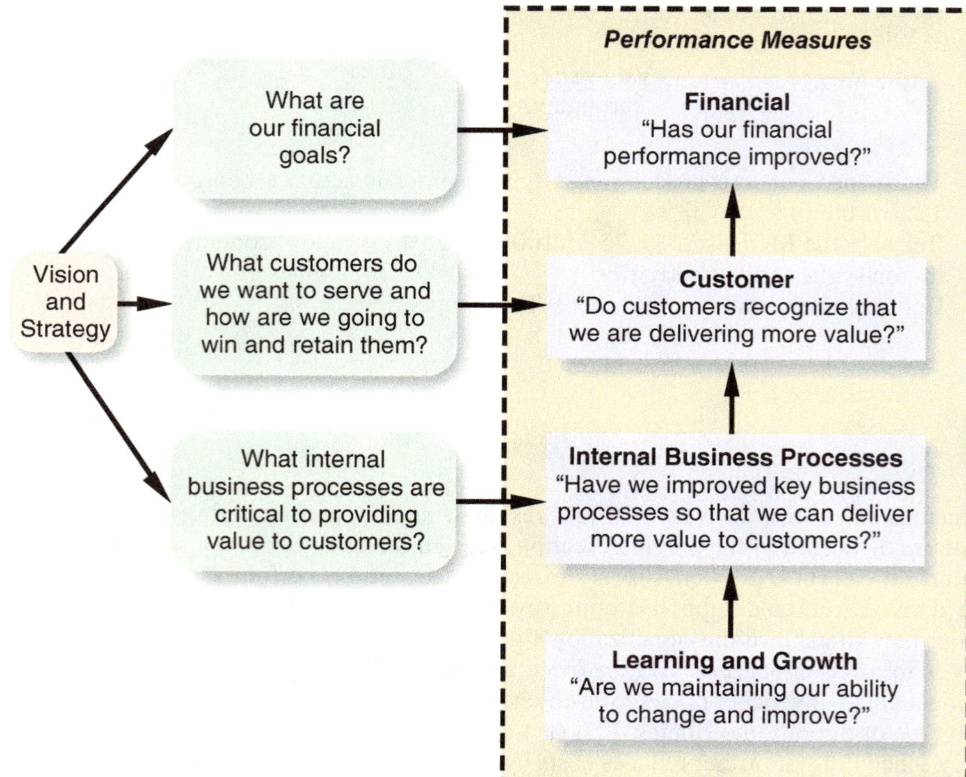

IN BUSINESS

WHY DO COMPANIES FAIL TO EXECUTE THEIR STRATEGIES?

Robert Paladino served as the vice president and global leader of the Telecommunications and Utility Practice for the Balanced Scorecard Collaborative—a consulting organization that works with companies to implement balanced scorecards. He offers four reasons why nine out of ten organizations fail to execute their business strategies.

First, only 5% of a company's workforce understands their organization's strategy. Paladino commented "if employees don't understand the strategic objectives, then they could be focused on closing the wrong performance gaps." Second, 85% of management teams spend less than one hour per month discussing strategy. Managers cannot effectively implement strategies if they do not spend enough time talking about them. Third, 60% of organizations do not link their budgets to strategy. The inevitable result is that companies pursue "financial strategies that differ from or, worse, may be in conflict with their business and customer quality strategies." Finally, only 25% of managers have their incentives linked to strategy. Thus, most managers are working to maximize their compensation by improving strategically misguided metrics.

Paladino says the balanced scorecard overcomes these four barriers because it helps employees focus their actions on executing organizational strategies.

Source: Robert E. Paladino, "Balanced Forecasts Drive Value," *Strategic Finance*, January 2005, pp. 37–42.

Financial performance measures appear at the top of Exhibit 11–3. Ultimately, most companies exist to provide financial rewards to owners. There are exceptions. Some companies—for example, The Body Shop—may have loftier goals such as providing environmentally friendly products to consumers. However, even nonprofit organizations must generate enough financial resources to stay in operation.

However, for several reasons, financial performance measures are not sufficient in themselves—they should be integrated with nonfinancial measures in a well-designed balanced scorecard. First, financial measures are lag indicators that report on the results of past actions. In contrast, nonfinancial measures of key success drivers such as customer satisfaction are leading indicators of future financial performance. Second, top managers are ordinarily responsible for the financial performance measures—not lower-level managers. The supervisor in charge of checking in passengers can be held responsible for how long passengers have to wait in line. However, this supervisor cannot reasonably be held responsible for the entire company's profit. That is the responsibility of the airline's top managers.

Exhibit 11–4 lists some examples of performance measures that can be found on the balanced scorecards of companies. However, few companies, if any, would use all of these performance measures, and almost all companies would add other performance measures. Managers should carefully select performance measures for their own company's balanced scorecard, keeping the following points in mind. First and foremost, the performance measures should be consistent with, and follow from, the company's strategy. If the performance measures are not consistent with the company's strategy, people will find themselves working at cross-purposes. Second, the performance measures should be understandable and controllable to a significant extent by those being evaluated. Third, the scorecard should not have too many performance measures. This can lead to a lack of focus and confusion.

While the entire organization will have an overall balanced scorecard, each responsible individual will have his or her own personal scorecard as well. This scorecard should consist of items the individual can personally influence that relate directly to the performance measures on the overall balanced scorecard. The performance measures on this personal scorecard should not be overly influenced by actions taken by others in the company or by events that are outside of the individual's control. And, focusing on the performance measure should not lead an individual to take actions that are counter to the organization's objectives.

With those broad principles in mind, we will now take a look at how a company's strategy affects its balanced scorecard.

IN BUSINESS

MEASURING CUSTOMER LOYALTY

Bain & Company consultant Fred Reichheld recommends measuring customer loyalty with one question—"On a scale of 0 to 10, how likely is it that you would recommend us to your friends and colleagues?" Customers who choose a score of 9 or 10 are labeled promoters. Those who choose a score of 0 to 6 are categorized as detractors, while those who select 7 or 8 are deemed passively satisfied. The net promoter score measures the difference between the percentages of customers who are promoters and detractors. Reichheld's research suggests that changes in a company's net promoter score correlate with (or move in tandem with) changes in its sales.

General Electric's Healthcare Division used net promoter scores to determine 20% of its managers' bonuses. The metric was eventually rolled out to all General Electric divisions. Other adopters of the net promoter score include American Express, consulting firm BearingPoint, and software maker Intuit.

Source: Jean McGregor, "Would You Recommend Us?" *BusinessWeek*, January 30, 2006, p. 94.

A Company's Strategy and the Balanced Scorecard

Returning to the performance measures in Exhibit 11–3, each company must decide which customers to target and what internal business processes are crucial to attracting and retaining those customers. Different companies, having different strategies, will

EXHIBIT 11–4
Examples of Performance Measures for Balanced Scorecards

Customer Perspective	
Performance Measure	Desired Change
Customer satisfaction as measured by survey results	+
Number of customer complaints	−
Market share	+
Product returns as a percentage of sales	−
Percentage of customers retained from last period	+
Number of new customers	+

Internal Business Processes Perspective	
Performance Measure	Desired Change
Percentage of sales from new products	+
Time to introduce new products to market	−
Percentage of customer calls answered within 20 seconds	+
On-time deliveries as a percentage of all deliveries	+
Work in process inventory as a percentage of sales	−
Unfavorable standard cost variances	−
Defect-free units as a percentage of completed units	+
Delivery cycle time	−
Throughput time	−
Manufacturing cycle efficiency	+
Quality costs	−
Setup time	−
Time from call by customer to repair of product	−
Percent of customer complaints settled on first contact	+
Time to settle a customer claim	−

Learning and Growth Perspective	
Performance Measure	Desired Change
Suggestions per employee	+
Employee turnover	−
Hours of in-house training per employee	+

target different customers with different kinds of products and services. Take the automobile industry as an example. BMW stresses engineering and handling; Volvo, safety; Jaguar, luxury detailing; and Honda, reliability. Because of these differences in emphasis, a one-size-fits-all approach to performance measurement won't work even within this one industry. Performance measures must be tailored to the specific strategy of each company.

Suppose, for example, that Jaguar's strategy is to offer distinctive, richly finished luxury automobiles to wealthy individuals who prize handcrafted, individualized products. To deliver this customer intimacy value proposition to its wealthy target customers, Jaguar might create such a large number of options for details, such as leather seats, interior and exterior color combinations, and wooden dashboards, that each car becomes virtually one of a kind. For example, instead of just offering tan or blue leather seats in standard cowhide, the company may offer customers the choice of an almost infinite palette of colors in any of a number of different exotic leathers. For such a system to work effectively, Jaguar would have to be able to deliver a completely customized car within a reasonable amount of time—and without incurring more cost for this customization than the customer is willing to pay. Exhibit 11–5 suggests how Jaguar might reflect this strategy in its balanced scorecard.

If the balanced scorecard is correctly constructed, the performance measures should be linked together on a cause-and-effect basis. Each link can then be read as a hypothesis in the form "If we improve this performance measure, then this other performance measure should also improve." Starting from the bottom of Exhibit 11–5, we can read the links between performance measures as follows. If employees acquire the skills to install new options more effectively, then the company can offer more options and the options can be installed in less time. If more options are available and they are installed in less time, then customer surveys should show greater satisfaction with the range of options available. If customer satisfaction improves, then the number of cars sold should increase. In addition, if customer satisfaction improves, the company should be able to maintain or increase its selling prices, and if the time to install options decreases, the

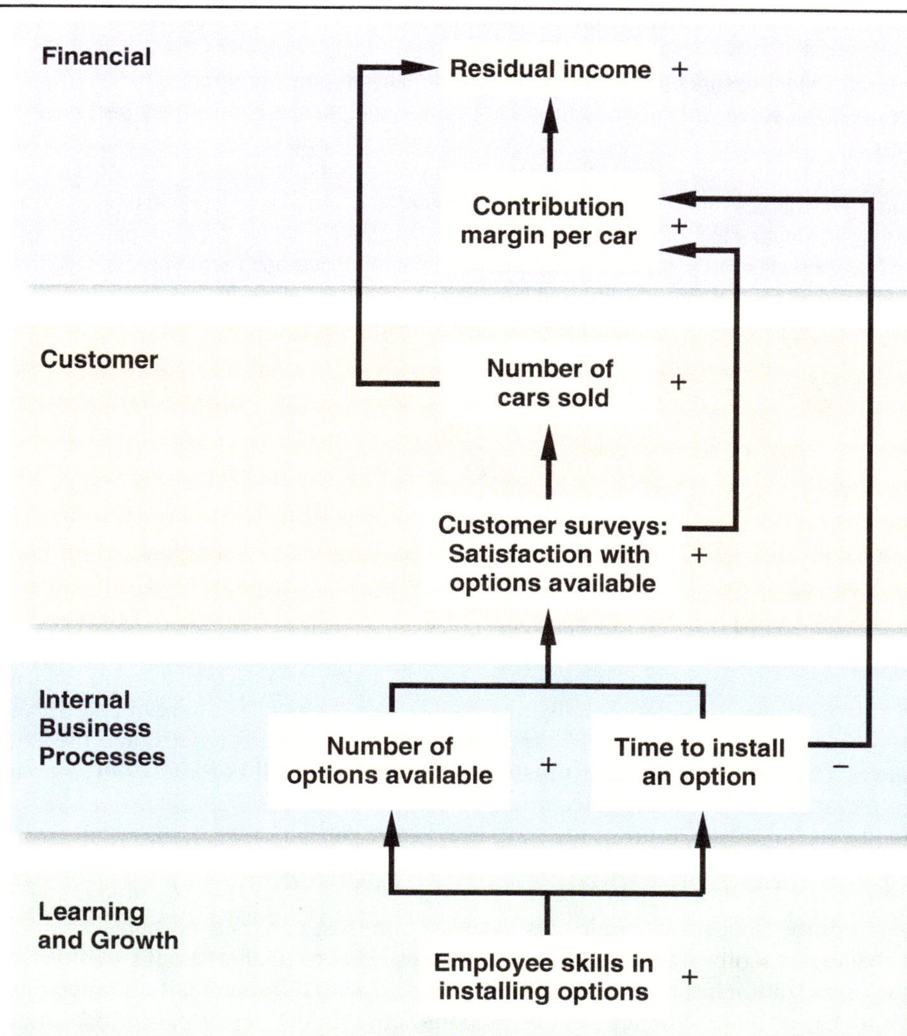

EXHIBIT 11–5
A Possible Strategy at Jaguar and the Balanced Scorecard

costs of installing the options should decrease. Together, this should result in an increase in the contribution margin per car. If the contribution margin per car increases and more cars are sold, the result should be an increase in residual income.

In essence, the balanced scorecard lays out a theory of how the company can take concrete actions to attain its desired outcomes (financial, in this case). The strategy laid out in Exhibit 11–5 seems plausible, but it should be regarded as only a theory. For example, if the company succeeds in increasing the number of options available and in decreasing the time required to install options and yet there is no increase in customer satisfaction, the number of cars sold, the contribution margin per car, or residual income, the strategy would have to be reconsidered. One of the advantages of the balanced scorecard is that it continually tests the theories underlying management's strategy. If a strategy is not working, it should become evident when some of the predicted effects (i.e., more car sales) don't occur. Without this feedback, the organization may drift on indefinitely with an ineffective strategy based on faulty assumptions.

IN BUSINESS

THE WELLNESS SCORECARD

Towers Watson estimates that America's average annual health care spending per employee now exceeds $10,000, up from $5,386 in 2002. However, companies that have implemented high-performing corporate wellness programs have annual health care costs that are $1,800 per employee less than other organizations. These high-performing companies create and track wellness performance measures as an important part of managing their programs.

The wellness scorecard is one framework for measuring corporate wellness performance. It has four categories of measures—attitudes, participation, physical results, and financial results—that are connected on a cause-and-effect basis. If employee attitudes toward the company's wellness program improve, then it should increase the rate of employee participation in wellness activities. If employees increase their participation rates, then it should produce physical results, such as lower obesity rates, lower incidents of diabetes, and increased smoking cessation rates. These physical improvements should produce positive financial results for the company, such as lower medical, pharmaceutical, and disability disbursements.

Sources: Towers Perrin, "2010 Health Care Cost Survey," www.towerswatson.com; and Peter C. Brewer, Angela Gallo, and Melanie R. Smith, "Getting Fit with Corporate Wellness Programs," *Strategic Finance*, May 2010, pp. 27–33.

The balanced scorecard has been embraced by a wide variety of organizations including Bank of Tokyo-Mitsubishi UFJ, Brigham & Women's Hospital, KeyCorp, Chilectra, China Resources Microelectronics, Delta Dental of Kansas, Gerdau Acominas, Korea East-West Power, Luxfer Gas Cylinders, Marriott Vacation Club International, Metro de Madrid, National Federation of Coffee Growers of Colombia, Sprint Nextel, Best Buy, Ingersoll Rand, Serono, Tennessee Valley Authority, Royal Canadian Mounted Police, Crown Castle International, Ricoh Corporation, Mobistar, Hilton Hotels, and the United States Postal Service. It has been estimated that about half of all Fortune 1000 companies have implemented a balanced scorecard.

Tying Compensation to the Balanced Scorecard

Incentive compensation for employees, such as bonuses, can, and probably should, be tied to balanced scorecard performance measures. However, this should be done only after the organization has been successfully managed with the scorecard for some time—perhaps a year or more. Managers must be confident that the performance measures are reliable, sensible, understood by those who are being evaluated, and not easily manipulated. As Robert Kaplan and David Norton, the originators of the balanced scorecard

IN BUSINESS

SUSTAINABILITY AND THE BALANCED SCORECARD

The Sustainable Investment Research Analyst Network (SIRAN) studied changes in the sustainability reporting practices of the Standard & Poor's (S&P) 100 companies from 2005 to 2007. Eighty-six of the S&P 100 companies had corporate sustainability websites as of 2007, an increase of 48% since 2005. Forty-nine of the S&P 100 companies published sustainability reports in 2007, up 26% from 2005.

Graham Hubbard, a professor at the University of Adelaide, recommends incorporating sustainability reporting into the balanced scorecard by adding two categories of measures related to social performance and environmental performance. Social performance measures focus on a company's philanthropic investments, community service, and employee safety and satisfaction. Environmental measures focus on a company's energy and water use per unit of output and its waste generation and disposal performance.

Sources: Ghostwriter, "Rise in Sustainability Reporting by S&P 100 Companies," *Business and the Environment with ISO14000 Updates*, October 2008, pp. 5–6; and Graham Hubbard, "Measuring Organizational Performance: Beyond the Triple Bottom Line," *Business Strategy and the Environment*, March 2009, pp. 177–191.

concept point out, "compensation is such a powerful lever that you have to be pretty confident that you have the right measures and have good data for the measures before making the link."[4]

Advantages of Timely and Graphic Feedback

Whatever performance measures are used, they should be reported on a frequent and timely basis. For example, data about defects should be reported to the responsible managers at least once a day so that action can be quickly taken if an unusual number of defects occurs. In the most advanced companies, any defect is reported *immediately,* and its cause is tracked down before any more defects occur. Another common characteristic of the performance measures under the balanced scorecard approach is that managers focus on *trends* in the performance measures over time. The emphasis is on progress and *improvement* rather than on meeting any specific standard.

IN BUSINESS

CORPORATE GOVERNANCE AND THE BALANCED SCORECARD

Historically, the board of directors of First Commonwealth Financial Corporation of Pennsylvania had only been given access to financial measures that were required for regulatory purposes. In the aftermath of corporate scandals such as Enron, Tyco, and WorldCom, the board decided to improve its oversight of the corporation by creating a balanced scorecard that not only helped ensure regulatory compliance but that also included forward-looking information about the company's strategy execution.

The board's scorecard had four main perspectives—learning and growth, internal, stakeholder, and financial. The internal perspective included three main processes—performance oversight, executive enhancement, and compliance and communication. For performance oversight, the board created measures related to approving strategies and overseeing execution and approving and monitoring funding for strategic initiatives. The executive enhancement measures focused on evaluating and rewarding executive performance and overseeing succession planning for key positions. The compliance and communication measures related to ensuring clear and reliable corporate disclosures and actively monitoring risk and regulatory compliance.

Source: Robert S. Kaplan and Michael Nagel, "First Commonwealth Financial Corporation," *Harvard Business School Publishing*, 2003, pp. 1–30.

[4] Lori Calabro, "On Balance: A CFO Interview," *CFO,* February 2001, pp. 73–78.

Summary

For purposes of evaluating performance, business units are classified as cost centers, profit centers, and investment centers. Cost and profit centers are commonly evaluated using standard cost and flexible budget variances as discussed in prior chapters. Investment centers are evaluated using the techniques discussed in this chapter.

Return on investment (ROI) and residual income and its cousin EVA are widely used to evaluate the performance of investment centers. ROI suffers from the underinvestment problem—managers are reluctant to invest in projects that would decrease their ROI but whose returns exceed the company's required rate of return. The residual income and EVA approaches solve this problem by giving managers full credit for any returns in excess of the company's required rate of return.

A balanced scorecard is an integrated system of performance measures designed to support an organization's strategy. The various measures in a balanced scorecard should be linked on a plausible cause-and-effect basis from the very lowest level up through the organization's ultimate objectives. The balanced scorecard is essentially a theory about how specific actions taken by various people in the organization will further the organization's objectives. The theory should be viewed as tentative and subject to change if the actions do not in fact result in improvements in the organization's financial and other goals. If the theory changes, then the performance measures on the balanced scorecard should also change. The balanced scorecard is a dynamic measurement system that evolves as an organization learns more about what works and what doesn't work and refines its strategy accordingly.

Review Problem: Return on Investment (ROI) and Residual Income

The Magnetic Imaging Division of Medical Diagnostics, Inc., has reported the following results for last year's operations:

Sales	$25 million
Net operating income	$3 million
Average operating assets	$10 million

Required:

1. Compute the Magnetic Imaging Division's margin, turnover, and ROI.
2. Top management of Medical Diagnostics, Inc., has set a minimum required rate of return on average operating assets of 25%. What is the Magnetic Imaging Division's residual income for the year?

Solution to Review Problem

1. The required calculations follow:

$$\text{Margin} = \frac{\text{Net operating income}}{\text{Sales}} = \frac{\$3{,}000{,}000}{\$25{,}000{,}000} = 12\%$$

$$\text{Turnover} = \frac{\text{Sales}}{\text{Average operating assets}} = \frac{\$25{,}000{,}000}{\$10{,}000{,}000} = 2.5$$

$$\text{ROI} = \text{Margin} \times \text{Turnover} = 12\% \times 2.5 = 30\%$$

2. The Magnetic Imaging Division's residual income is computed as follows:

Average operating assets	$10,000,000
Net operating income	$3,000,000
Minimum required return (25% × $10,000,000)	2,500,000
Residual income	$ 500,000

Glossary

Balanced scorecard An integrated set of performance measures that are derived from and support the organization's strategy. (p. 485)

Cost center A business segment whose manager has control over cost but has no control over revenue or investments in operating assets. (p. 474)

Decentralized organization An organization in which decision-making authority is not confined to a few top executives but rather is spread throughout the organization. (p. 473)

Delivery cycle time The elapsed time from receipt of a customer order to when the completed goods are shipped to the customer. (p. 482)

Economic Value Added (EVA) A concept similar to residual income in which a variety of adjustments may be made to GAAP financial statements for performance evaluation purposes. (p. 479)

Investment center A business segment whose manager has control over cost, revenue, and investments in operating assets. (p. 475)

Manufacturing cycle efficiency (MCE) Process (value-added) time as a percentage of throughput time. (p. 483)

Margin Net operating income divided by sales. (p. 476)

Net operating income Income before interest and income taxes have been deducted. (p. 475)

Operating assets Cash, accounts receivable, inventory, plant and equipment, and all other assets held for operating purposes. (p. 476)

Profit center A business segment whose manager has control over cost and revenue but has no control over investments in operating assets. (p. 474)

Residual income The net operating income that an investment center earns above the minimum required return on its operating assets. (p. 479)

Responsibility center Any business segment whose manager has control over costs, revenues, or investments in operating assets. (p. 474)

Return on investment (ROI) Net operating income divided by average operating assets. It also equals margin multiplied by turnover. (p. 475)

Throughput time The amount of time required to turn raw materials into completed products. (p. 482)

Turnover Sales divided by average operating assets. (p. 476)

Questions

11–1 What is meant by the term *decentralization?*

11–2 What benefits result from decentralization?

11–3 Distinguish between a cost center, a profit center, and an investment center.

11–4 What is meant by the terms *margin* and *turnover* in ROI calculations?

11–5 What is meant by residual income?

11–6 In what way can the use of ROI as a performance measure for investment centers lead to bad decisions? How does the residual income approach overcome this problem?

11–7 What is the difference between delivery cycle time and throughput time? What four elements make up throughput time? What elements of throughput time are value-added and what elements are non–value-added?

11–8 What does a manufacturing cycle efficiency (MCE) of less than 1 mean? How would you interpret an MCE of 0.40?

11–9 Why do the measures used in a balanced scorecard differ from company to company?

11–10 Why does the balanced scorecard include financial performance measures as well as measures of how well internal business processes are doing?

Multiple-choice questions are provided on the text website at www.mhhe.com/garrison14e.

Applying Excel

LEARNING OBJECTIVES 1, 2

Available with McGraw-Hill's *Connect™ Accounting*.

The Excel worksheet form that appears below is to be used to recreate the Review Problem in the text on pages 492–493. Download the workbook containing this form from the Online Learning Center at www.mhhe.com/garrison14e. *On the website you will also receive instructions about how to use this worksheet form.*

	A	B	C	D	E
1	Chapter 11: Applying Excel				
2					
3	**Data**				
4	Sales	$25,000,000			
5	Net operating income	$3,000,000			
6	Average operating assets	$10,000,000			
7	Minimum required rate of return	25%			
8					
9	*Enter a formula into each of the cells marked with a ? below*				
10	**Review Problem: Return on Investment (ROI) and Residual Income**				
11					
12	***Compute the ROI***				
13	Margin	?			
14	Turnover	?			
15	ROI	?			
16					
17	***Compute the residual income***				
18	Average operating assets	?			
19	Net operating income	?			
20	Minimum required return	?			
21	Residual income	?			
22					

Chapter 11 Form | Filled in Chapter 11 Form

You should proceed to the requirements below only after completing your worksheet.

Required:

1. Check your worksheet by changing the average operating assets in cell B6 to $8,000,000. The ROI should now be 38% and the residual income should now be $1,000,000. If you do not get these answers, find the errors in your worksheet and correct them.

   Explain why the ROI and the residual income both increase when the average operating assets decrease.

2. Revise the data in your worksheet as follows:

Data	
Sales	$1,200
Net operating income	$72
Average operating assets	$500
Minimum required rate of return	15%

a. What is the ROI?
b. What is the residual income?
c. Explain the relationship between the ROI and the residual income?

connect ACCOUNTING Exercises

All applicable exercises are available with McGraw-Hill's *Connect™ Accounting*.

EXERCISE 11–1 Compute the Return on Investment (ROI) [LO1]

Tundra Services Company, a division of a major oil company, provides various services to the operators of the North Slope oil field in Alaska. Data concerning the most recent year appear below:

Sales	$18,000,000
Net operating income	$5,400,000
Average operating assets	$36,000,000

Required:
1. Compute the margin for Tundra Services Company.
2. Compute the turnover for Tundra Services Company.
3. Compute the return on investment (ROI) for Tundra Services Company.

EXERCISE 11–2 Residual Income [LO2]

Midlands Design Ltd. of Manchester, England, is a company specializing in providing design services to residential developers. Last year the company had net operating income of £400,000 on sales of £2,000,000. The company's average operating assets for the year were £2,200,000 and its minimum required rate of return was 16%. (The currency in the United Kingdom is the pound, denoted by £.)

Required:
Compute the company's residual income for the year.

EXERCISE 11–3 Measures of Internal Business Process Performance [LO3]

Lipex, Ltd., of Birmingham, England, is interested in cutting the amount of time between when a customer places an order and when the order is completed. For the first quarter of the year, the following data were reported:

Inspection time	0.5 days
Process time	2.8 days
Wait time	16.0 days
Queue time	4.0 days
Move time	0.7 days

Required:
1. Compute the throughput time.
2. Compute the manufacturing cycle efficiency (MCE) for the quarter.
3. What percentage of the throughput time was spent in non–value-added activities?
4. Compute the delivery cycle time.
5. If by using Lean Production all queue time can be eliminated in production, what will be the new MCE?

EXERCISE 11–4 Creating a Balanced Scorecard [LO4]

Mason Paper Company (MPC) manufactures commodity grade papers for use in computer printers and photocopiers. MPC has reported net operating losses for the last two years due to intense price pressure from much larger competitors. The MPC management team—including Kristen Townsend (CEO), Mike Martinez (vice president of Manufacturing), Tom Andrews (vice president of Marketing), and Wendy Chen (CFO)—is contemplating a change in strategy to save the company from impending bankruptcy. Excerpts from a recent management team meeting are shown below:

Townsend: As we all know, the commodity paper manufacturing business is all about economies of scale. The largest competitors with the lowest cost per unit win. The limited capacity of our older machines prohibits us from competing in the high-volume commodity paper grades. Furthermore, expanding our capacity by acquiring a new paper-making machine is out of the question given the extraordinarily high price tag. Therefore, I propose that we abandon cost reduction as a strategic goal and instead pursue manufacturing flexibility as the key to our future success.

Chen: Manufacturing flexibility? What does that mean?

Martinez: It means we have to abandon our "crank out as many tons of paper as possible" mentality. Instead, we need to pursue the low-volume business opportunities that exist in the nonstandard, specialized paper grades. To succeed in this regard, we'll need to improve our flexibility in three ways. First, we must improve our ability to switch between paper grades. Right now, we require an average of four hours to change over to another paper grade. Timely customer deliveries are a function of changeover performance. Second, we need to expand the range of paper grades that we can manufacture. Currently, we can only manufacture three paper grades. Our customers must perceive that we are a "one-stop shop" that can meet all of their paper grade needs. Third, we will need to improve our yields (e.g., tons of acceptable output relative to total tons processed) in the nonstandard paper grades. Our percentage of waste within these grades will be unacceptably high unless we do something to improve our processes. Our variable costs will go through the roof if we cannot increase our yields!

Chen: Wait just a minute! These changes are going to destroy our equipment utilization numbers!

Andrews: You're right Wendy; however, equipment utilization is not the name of the game when it comes to competing in terms of flexibility. Our customers don't care about our equipment utilization. Instead, as Mike just alluded to, they want just-in-time delivery of smaller quantities of a full range of paper grades. If we can shrink the elapsed time from order placement to order delivery and expand our product offerings, it will increase sales from current customers and bring in new customers. Furthermore, we will be able to charge a premium price because of the limited competition within this niche from our cost-focused larger competitors. Our contribution margin per ton should drastically improve!

Martinez: Of course, executing the change in strategy will not be easy. We'll need to make a substantial investment in training because ultimately it is our people who create our flexible manufacturing capabilities.

Chen: If we adopt this new strategy, it is definitely going to impact how we measure performance. We'll need to create measures that motivate our employees to make decisions that support our flexibility goals.

Townsend: Wendy, you hit the nail right on the head. For our next meeting, could you pull together some potential measures that support our new strategy?

Required:

1. Contrast MPC's previous manufacturing strategy with its new manufacturing strategy.
2. Generally speaking, why would a company that changes its strategic goals need to change its performance measurement system as well? What are some examples of measures that would have been appropriate for MPC prior to its change in strategy? Why would those measures fail to support MPC's new strategy?
3. Construct a balanced scorecard that would support MPC's new manufacturing strategy. Use arrows to show the causal links between the performance measures and show whether the performance measure should increase or decrease over time. Feel free to create measures that may not be specifically mentioned in the chapter, but nonetheless make sense given the strategic goals of the company.
4. What hypotheses are built into MPC's balanced scorecard? Which of these hypotheses do you believe are most questionable and why?

EXERCISE 11–5 Cost-Volume-Profit Analysis and Return on Investment (ROI) [LO1]
Images.com is a small Internet retailer of high-quality posters. The company has $800,000 in operating assets and fixed expenses of $160,000 per year. With this level of operating assets and fixed expenses, the company can support sales of up to $5 million per year. The company's contribution margin ratio is 10%, which means that an additional dollar of sales results in additional contribution margin, and net operating income, of 10 cents.

Required:

1. Complete the following table showing the relationship between sales and return on investment (ROI).

Sales	Net Operating Income	Average Operating Assets	ROI
$4,500,000	$290,000	$800,000	?
$4,600,000	?	$800,000	?
$4,700,000	?	$800,000	?
$4,800,000	?	$800,000	?
$4,900,000	?	$800,000	?
$5,000,000	?	$800,000	?

2. What happens to the company's return on investment (ROI) as sales increase? Explain.

EXERCISE 11–6 Effects of Changes in Sales, Expenses, and Assets on ROI [LO1]
BusServ.com Corporation provides business-to-business services on the Internet. Data concerning the most recent year appear below:

Sales	$8,000,000
Net operating income	$800,000
Average operating assets	$3,200,000

Required:
Consider each question below independently. Carry out all computations to two decimal places.

1. Compute the company's return on investment (ROI).
2. The entrepreneur who founded the company is convinced that sales will increase next year by 150% and that net operating income will increase by 400%, with no increase in average operating assets. What would be the company's ROI?
3. The Chief Financial Officer of the company believes a more realistic scenario would be a $2 million increase in sales, requiring an $800,000 increase in average operating assets, with a resulting $250,000 increase in net operating income. What would be the company's ROI in this scenario?

EXERCISE 11–7 Contrasting Return on Investment (ROI) and Residual Income [LO1, LO2]
Rains Nickless Ltd. of Australia has two divisions that operate in Perth and Darwin. Selected data on the two divisions follow:

	Division	
	Perth	Darwin
Sales	$9,000,000	$20,000,000
Net operating income	$630,000	$1,800,000
Average operating assets	$3,000,000	$10,000,000

Required:

1. Compute the return on investment (ROI) for each division.
2. Assume that the company evaluates performance using residual income and that the minimum required rate of return for any division is 16%. Compute the residual income for each division.

3. Is the Darwin Division's greater residual income an indication that it is better managed? Explain.

EXERCISE 11–8 Return on Investment (ROI) and Residual Income Relations [LO1, LO2]

A family friend has asked your help in analyzing the operations of three anonymous companies operating in the same service sector industry. Supply the missing data in the table below:

	Company		
	A	B	C
Sales	$400,000	$750,000	$600,000
Net operating income	$?	$ 45,000	$?
Average operating assets	$160,000	?	$150,000
Return on investment (ROI)	20%	18%	?
Minimum required rate of return:			
Percentage	15%	?	12%
Dollar amount	$?	$ 50,000	$?
Residual income	$?	$?	$ 6,000

EXERCISE 11–9 Evaluating New Investments Using Return on Investment (ROI) and Residual Income [LO1, LO2]

Selected sales and operating data for three divisions of three different companies are given below:

	Division A	Division B	Division C
Sales	$6,000,000	$10,000,000	$8,000,000
Average operating assets	$1,500,000	$5,000,000	$2,000,000
Net operating income	$300,000	$900,000	$180,000
Minimum required rate of return	15%	18%	12%

Required:

1. Compute the return on investment (ROI) for each division, using the formula stated in terms of margin and turnover.
2. Compute the residual income for each division.
3. Assume that each division is presented with an investment opportunity that would yield a rate of return of 17%.
   a. If performance is being measured by ROI, which division or divisions will probably accept the opportunity? Reject? Why?
   b. If performance is being measured by residual income, which division or divisions will probably accept the opportunity? Reject? Why?

EXERCISE 11–10 Computing and Interpreting Return on Investment (ROI) [LO1]

Selected operating data on the two divisions of York Company are given below:

	Division	
	Eastern	Western
Sales	$1,000,000	$1,750,000
Average operating assets	$500,000	$500,000
Net operating income	$90,000	$105,000
Property, plant, and equipment	$250,000	$200,000

Required:

1. Compute the rate of return for each division using the return on investment (ROI) formula stated in terms of margin and turnover.
2. Which divisional manager seems to be doing the better job? Why?

EXERCISE 11–11 Creating a Balanced Scorecard [LO4]

Ariel Tax Services prepares tax returns for individual and corporate clients. As the company has gradually expanded to 10 offices, the founder, Max Jacobs, has begun to feel as though he is losing control of operations. In response to this concern, he has decided to implement a performance measurement system that will help control current operations and facilitate his plans of expanding to 20 offices.

Jacobs describes the keys to the success of his business as follows:

"Our only real asset is our people. We must keep our employees highly motivated and we must hire the 'cream of the crop.' Interestingly, employee morale and recruiting success are both driven by the same two factors—compensation and career advancement. In other words, providing superior compensation relative to the industry average coupled with fast-track career advancement opportunities keeps morale high and makes us a very attractive place to work. It drives a high rate of job offer acceptances relative to job offers tendered."

"Hiring highly qualified people and keeping them energized ensures operational success, which in our business is a function of productivity, efficiency, and effectiveness. Productivity boils down to employees being billable rather than idle. Efficiency relates to the time required to complete a tax return. Finally, effectiveness is critical to our business in the sense that we cannot tolerate errors. Completing a tax return quickly is meaningless if the return contains errors."

"Our growth depends on acquiring new customers through word-of-mouth from satisfied repeat customers. We believe that our customers come back year after year because they value error-free, timely, and courteous tax return preparation. Common courtesy is an important aspect of our business! We call it service quality, and it all ties back to employee morale in the sense that happy employees treat their clients with care and concern."

"While sales growth is obviously important to our future plans, growth without a corresponding increase in profitability is useless. Therefore, we understand that increasing our profit margin is a function of cost-efficiency as well as sales growth. Given that payroll is our biggest expense, we must maintain an optimal balance between staffing levels and the revenue being generated. As I alluded to earlier, the key to maintaining this balance is employee productivity. If we can achieve cost-efficient sales growth, we should eventually have 20 profitable offices!"

Required:

1. Create a balanced scorecard for Ariel Tax Services. Link your scorecard measures using the framework from Exhibit 11–5. Indicate whether each measure is expected to increase or decrease. Feel free to create measures that may not be specifically mentioned in the chapter, but make sense given the strategic goals of the company.
2. What hypotheses are built into the balanced scorecard for Ariel Tax Services? Which of these hypotheses do you believe are most questionable and why?
3. Discuss the potential advantages and disadvantages of implementing an internal business process measure called *total dollar amount of tax refunds generated.* Would you recommend using this measure in Ariel's balanced scorecard?
4. Would it be beneficial to attempt to measure each office's individual performance with respect to the scorecard measures that you created? Why or why not?

EXERCISE 11–12 Effects of Changes in Profits and Assets on Return on Investment (ROI) [LO1]

The Abs Shoppe is a regional chain of health clubs. The managers of the clubs, who have authority to make investments as needed, are evaluated based largely on return on investment (ROI). The Abs Shoppe reported the following results for the past year:

Sales	$800,000
Net operating income	$16,000
Average operating assets	$100,000

Required:

The following questions are to be considered independently. Carry out all computations to two decimal places.

1. Compute the club's return on investment (ROI).
2. Assume that the manager of the club is able to increase sales by $80,000 and that as a result net operating income increases by $6,000. Further assume that this is possible without any increase in operating assets. What would be the club's return on investment (ROI)?
3. Assume that the manager of the club is able to reduce expenses by $3,200 without any change in sales or operating assets. What would be the club's return on investment (ROI)?
4. Assume that the manager of the club is able to reduce operating assets by $20,000 without any change in sales or net operating income. What would be the club's return on investment (ROI)?

EXERCISE 11–13 Return on Investment (ROI) Relations [LO1]
Provide the missing data in the following table:

	Division		
	Fab	Consulting	IT
Sales.	$800,000	$?	$?
Net operating income.	$ 72,000	$?	$40,000
Average operating assets.	$?	$130,000	$?
Margin.	?	4%	8%
Turnover	?	5	?
Return on investment (ROI)	18%	?	20%

Problems

connect ACCOUNTING

All applicable problems are available with McGraw-Hill's *Connect™ Accounting*.

eXcel

PROBLEM 11–14 Return on Investment (ROI) and Residual Income [LO1, LO2]
"I know headquarters wants us to add that new product line," said Fred Halloway, manager of Kirsi Products' East Division. "But I want to see the numbers before I make a move. Our division's return on investment (ROI) has led the company for three years, and I don't want any letdown."

Kirsi Products is a decentralized wholesaler with four autonomous divisions. The divisions are evaluated on the basis of ROI, with year-end bonuses given to divisional managers who have the highest ROI. Operating results for the company's East Division for last year are given below:

Sales	$21,000,000
Variable expenses	13,400,000
Contribution margin.	7,600,000
Fixed expenses	5,920,000
Net operating income	$ 1,680,000
Divisional operating assets	$ 5,250,000

The company had an overall ROI of 18% last year (considering all divisions). The company's East Division has an opportunity to add a new product line that would require an investment of $3,000,000. The cost and revenue characteristics of the new product line per year would be as follows:

Sales	$9,000,000
Variable expenses	65% of sales
Fixed expenses	$2,520,000

Required:

1. Compute the East Division's ROI for last year; also compute the ROI as it would appear if the new product line is added.

2. If you were in Fred Halloway's position, would you accept or reject the new product line? Explain.
3. Why do you suppose headquarters is anxious for the East Division to add the new product line?
4. Suppose that the company's minimum required rate of return on operating assets is 15% and that performance is evaluated using residual income.
   a. Compute the East Division's residual income for last year; also compute the residual income as it would appear if the new product line is added.
   b. Under these circumstances, if you were in Fred Halloway's position would you accept or reject the new product line? Explain.

PROBLEM 11–15 Comparison of Performance Using Return on Investment (ROI) [LO1]

Comparative data on three companies in the same service industry are given below:

	Company		
	A	B	C
Sales	$4,000,000	$1,500,000	$?
Net operating income	$ 560,000	$ 210,000	$?
Average operating assets	$2,000,000	?	$3,000,000
Margin	?	?	3.5%
Turnover	?	?	2
Return on investment (ROI)	?	7%	?

Required:
1. What advantages are there to breaking down the ROI computation into two separate elements, margin and turnover?
2. Fill in the missing information above, and comment on the relative performance of the three companies in as much detail as the data permit. Make *specific recommendations* about how to improve the ROI.

(Adapted from National Association of Accountants, *Research Report No. 35,* p. 34)

PROBLEM 11–16 Measures of Internal Business Process Performance [LO3]

MacIntyre Fabrications, Ltd., of Aberdeen, Scotland, has recently begun a continuous improvement campaign in conjunction with a move toward Lean Production. Management has developed new performance measures as part of this campaign. The following operating data have been gathered over the last four months:

	Month			
	1	2	3	4
Throughput time	?	?	?	?
Manufacturing cycle efficiency	?	?	?	?
Delivery cycle time	?	?	?	?
Percentage of on-time deliveries	72%	73%	78%	85%
Total sales (units)	10,540	10,570	10,550	10,490

Management would like to know the company's throughput time, manufacturing cycle efficiency, and delivery cycle time. The data to compute these measures have been gathered and appear below:

	Month			
	1	2	3	4
Move time per unit, in days	0.5	0.5	0.4	0.5
Process time per unit, in days	0.6	0.5	0.5	0.4
Wait time per order before start of production, in days	9.6	8.7	5.3	4.7
Queue time per unit, in days	3.6	3.6	2.6	1.7
Inspection time per unit, in days	0.7	0.7	0.4	0.3

Required:

1. For each month, compute the following:
   a. The throughput time.
   b. The manufacturing cycle efficiency (MCE).
   c. The delivery cycle time.
2. Using the performance measures given in the problem and those you computed in (1) above, identify whether the trend over the four months is generally favorable, generally unfavorable, or mixed. What areas apparently require improvement and how might they be improved?
3. Refer to the move time, process time, and so forth, given for month 4.
   a. Assume that in month 5 the move time, process time, and so forth, are the same as for month 4, except that through the implementation of Lean Production, the company is able to completely eliminate the queue time during production. Compute the new throughput time and MCE.
   b. Assume that in month 6 the move time, process time, and so forth, are the same as for month 4, except that the company is able to completely eliminate both the queue time during production and the inspection time. Compute the new throughput time and MCE.

PROBLEM 11–17 Building a Balanced Scorecard [LO4]

Deer Creek ski resort was for many years a small, family-owned resort serving day skiers from nearby towns. Deer Creek was recently acquired by Mountain Associates, a major ski resort operator with destination resorts in several western states. The new owners have plans to upgrade the resort into a destination resort for vacationers staying for a week or more. As part of this plan, the new owners would like to make major improvements in the Lynx Lair Lodge, the resort's on-the-hill fast-food restaurant. The menu at the Lodge is very limited—hamburgers, hot dogs, chili, tuna fish sandwiches, french fries, and packaged snacks. The previous owners of the resort had felt no urgency to upgrade the food service at the Lodge because there is little competition. If skiers want lunch on the mountain, the only alternatives are the Lynx Lair Lodge or a brown bag lunch brought from home.

As part of the deal when acquiring Deer Creek, Mountain Associates agreed to retain all of the current employees of the resort. The manager of the Lodge, while hardworking and enthusiastic, has very little experience in the restaurant business. The manager is responsible for selecting the menu, finding and training employees, and overseeing daily operations. The kitchen staff prepares food and washes dishes. The dining room staff takes orders, serves as cashiers, and cleans the dining room area.

Shortly after taking over Deer Creek, management of Mountain Associates held a day-long meeting with all of the employees of the Lynx Lair Lodge to discuss the future of the ski resort and management's plans for the Lodge. At the end of this meeting, top management and Lodge employees created a balanced scorecard for the Lodge that would help guide operations for the coming ski season. Almost everyone who participated in the meeting seemed to be enthusiastic about the scorecard and management's plans for the Lodge.

The following performance measures were included on the balanced scorecard for the Lynx Lair Lodge:

- Customer satisfaction with service, as measured by customer surveys.
- Total Lynx Lair Lodge profit.
- Dining area cleanliness, as rated by a representative from Mountain Associates management.
- Average time to prepare an order.
- Customer satisfaction with menu choices, as measured by surveys.
- Average time to take an order.
- Percentage of kitchen staff completing institutional cooking course at the local community college.
- Sales.
- Percentage of dining room staff completing hospitality course at the local community college.
- Number of menu items.

Mountain Associates will pay for the costs of staff attending courses at the local community college.

Required:

1. Using the above performance measures, construct a balanced scorecard for the Lynx Lair Lodge. Use Exhibit 11–5 as a guide. Use arrows to show causal links and indicate with a + or − whether the performance measure should increase or decrease.
2. What hypotheses are built into the balanced scorecard for the Lynx Lair Lodge? Which of these hypotheses do you believe are most questionable? Why?
3. How will management know if one of the hypotheses underlying the balanced scorecard is false?

PROBLEM 11–18 Return on Investment (ROI) and Residual Income [LO1, LO2]
Financial data for Bridger, Inc., for last year are as follows:

Bridger, Inc. Balance Sheet	Beginning Balance	Ending Balance
Assets		
Cash	$ 125,000	$ 130,000
Accounts receivable	340,000	480,000
Inventory	570,000	490,000
Plant and equipment, net	845,000	820,000
Investment in Brier Company	400,000	430,000
Land (undeveloped)	250,000	250,000
Total assets	$2,530,000	$2,600,000
Liabilities and Stockholders' Equity		
Accounts payable	$ 380,000	$ 340,000
Long-term debt	1,000,000	1,000,000
Stockholders' equity	1,150,000	1,260,000
Total liabilities and stockholders' equity	$2,530,000	$2,600,000

Bridger, Inc. Income Statement		
Sales		$4,180,000
Operating expenses		3,553,000
Net operating income		627,000
Interest and taxes:		
Interest expense	$120,000	
Tax expense	200,000	320,000
Net income		$ 307,000

The company paid dividends of $197,000 last year. The "Investment in Brier Company" on the balance sheet represents an investment in the stock of another company.

Required:

1. Compute the company's margin, turnover, and return on investment (ROI) for last year.
2. The board of directors of Bridger, Inc., has set a minimum required return of 20%. What was the company's residual income last year?

PROBLEM 11–19 Perverse Effects of Some Performance Measures [LO4]

There is often more than one way to improve a performance measure. Unfortunately, some of the actions taken by managers to make their performance look better may actually harm the organization. For example, suppose the marketing department is held responsible only for increasing the performance measure "total revenues." Increases in total revenues may be achieved by working harder and smarter, but they can also usually be achieved by simply cutting prices. The increase in volume from cutting prices almost always results in greater total revenues; however, it does not always lead to greater total profits. Those who design performance measurement systems need to keep in mind that managers who are under pressure to perform may take actions to improve performance measures that have negative consequences elsewhere.

Required:

For each of the following situations, describe actions that managers might take to show improvement in the performance measure but which do not actually lead to improvement in the organization's overall performance.

1. Concerned with the slow rate at which new products are brought to market, top management of a consumer electronics company introduces a new performance measure—speed-to-market. The research and development department is given responsibility for this performance measure, which measures the average amount of time a product is in development before it is released to the market for sale.

2. The CEO of a telephone company has been under public pressure from city officials to fix the large number of public pay phones that do not work. The company's repair people complain that the problem is vandalism and damage caused by theft of coins from coin boxes—particularly in high-crime areas in the city. The CEO says she wants the problem solved and has pledged to city officials that there will be substantial improvement by the end of the year. To ensure that this is done, she makes the managers in charge of installing and maintaining pay phones responsible for increasing the percentage of public pay phones that are fully functional.
3. A manufacturing company has been plagued by the chronic failure to ship orders to customers by the promised date. To solve this problem, the production manager has been given the responsibility of increasing the percentage of orders shipped on time. When a customer calls in an order, the production manager and the customer agree to a delivery date. If the order is not completed by that date, it is counted as a late shipment.
4. Concerned with the productivity of employees, the board of directors of a large multinational corporation has dictated that the manager of each subsidiary will be held responsible for increasing the revenue per employee of his or her subsidiary.

eXcel

PROBLEM 11–20 Return on Investment (ROI) Analysis [LO1]
The contribution format income statement for Westex, Inc., for its most recent period is given below:

	A	B	C	D
1			*Total*	*Unit*
2	Sales		$1,000,000	$50.00
3	Variable expenses		600,000	30.00
4	Contribution margin		400,000	20.00
5	Fixed expenses		320,000	16.00
6	Net operating income		80,000	4.00
7	Income taxes @	40%	32,000	1.60
8	Net income		$ 48,000	$ 2.40
9				

Sheet1 Sheet2 Sheet3

The company had average operating assets of $500,000 during the period.

Required:
1. Compute the company's return on investment (ROI) for the period using the ROI formula stated in terms of margin and turnover.

For each of the following questions, indicate whether the margin and turnover will increase, decrease, or remain unchanged as a result of the events described, and then compute the new ROI figure. Consider each question separately, starting in each case from the original ROI computed in (1) above.

2. The company achieves a cost savings of $10,000 per period by using less costly materials.
3. Using Lean Production, the company is able to reduce the average level of inventory by $100,000. (The released funds are used to pay off bank loans.)
4. Sales are increased by $100,000; operating assets remain unchanged.
5. The company issues bonds and uses the proceeds to purchase $125,000 in machinery and equipment at the beginning of the period. Interest on the bonds is $15,000 per period. Sales remain unchanged. The new, more efficient equipment reduces production costs by $5,000 per period.
6. The company invests $180,000 of cash (received on accounts receivable) in a plot of land that is to be held for possible future use as a plant site.
7. Obsolete inventory carried on the books at a cost of $20,000 is scrapped and written off as a loss.

PROBLEM 11–21 Creating Balanced Scorecards that Support Different Strategies [LO4]
The Midwest Consulting Group (MCG) helps companies build balanced scorecards. As part of its marketing efforts, MCG conducts an annual balanced scorecard workshop for prospective clients. As MCG's newest employee, your boss has asked you to participate in this year's workshop by explaining to attendees how a company's strategy determines the measures that are appropriate for its balanced scorecard. Your boss has provided you with the excerpts below from the annual reports of two current MCG clients. She has asked you to use these excerpts in your portion of the workshop.

Excerpt from Applied Pharmaceuticals' annual report:

> The keys to our business are consistent and timely new product introductions and manufacturing process integrity. The new product introduction side of the equation is a function of research and development (R&D) yield (e.g., the number of marketable drug compounds created relative to the total number of potential compounds pursued). We seek to optimize our R&D yield and first-to-market capability by investing in state-of-the-art technology, hiring the highest possible percentage of the "best and the brightest" engineers that we pursue, and providing world-class training to those engineers. Manufacturing process integrity is all about establishing world-class quality specifications and then relentlessly engaging in prevention and appraisal activities to minimize defect rates. Our customers must have an awareness of, and respect for, our brand image of being "first to market and first in quality." If we deliver on this pledge to our customers, then our financial goal of increasing our return on stockholders' equity should take care of itself.

Excerpt from Destination Resorts International's annual report:

> Our business succeeds or fails based on the quality of the service that our front-line employees provide to customers. Therefore, it is imperative that we strive to maintain high employee morale and minimize employee turnover. In addition, it is critical that we train our employees to use technology to create one seamless worldwide experience for our repeat customers. Once an employee enters a customer preference (e.g., provide two extra pillows in the room, deliver fresh brewed coffee to the room at 8:00 A.M., etc.) into our database, our worldwide workforce strives to ensure that a customer will never need to repeat it at any of our destination resorts. If we properly train and retain a motivated workforce, we should see continuous improvement in our percentage of error-free repeat customer check-ins, the time taken to resolve customer complaints, and our independently assessed room cleanliness. This in turn should drive improvement in our customer retention, which is the key to meeting our revenue growth goals.

Required:

1. Based on the excerpts above, compare and contrast the strategies of Applied Pharmaceuticals and Destination Resorts International.
2. Select balanced scorecard measures for each company and link the scorecard measures using the framework from Exhibit 11–5. Use arrows to show the causal links between the performance measures and show whether the performance measure should increase or decrease over time. Feel free to create measures that may not be specifically mentioned in the chapter, but nonetheless make sense given the strategic goals of each company.
3. What hypotheses are built into each balanced scorecard? Why do the hypotheses differ between the two companies?

PROBLEM 11–22 Internal Business Process Performance Measures [LO3]

Exeter Corporation has recently begun a continuous improvement campaign. As a consequence, there have been many changes in operating procedures. Progress has been slow, particularly in trying to develop new performance measures for the factory.

Management has been gathering the following data over the past four months:

	Month			
	1	2	3	4
Quality control measures:				
Customer complaints as a percentage of units sold . . .	1.4%	1.3%	1.1%	1.0%
Warranty claims as a percentage of units sold	2.3%	2.1%	2.0%	1.8%
Defects as a percentage of units produced	4.6%	4.2%	3.7%	3.4%
Material control measures:				
Scrap as a percentage of total cost	3.2%	2.9%	3.0%	2.7%
Machine performance measures:				
Percentage of machine availability	80%	82%	81%	79%
Use as a percentage of availability	75%	73%	71%	70%
Average setup time (hours)	2.7	2.5	2.5	2.6
Delivery performance measures:				
Throughput time	?	?	?	?
Manufacturing cycle efficiency	?	?	?	?
Delivery cycle time	?	?	?	?
Percentage of on-time deliveries	84%	87%	91%	95%

The president has attended conferences at which the importance of throughput time, manufacturing cycle efficiency, and delivery cycle time were stressed, but no one at the company is sure how they are computed. The data to compute these measures have been gathered and appear below:

	Month			
	1	2	3	4
Wait time per order before start of production, in days	16.7	15.2	12.3	9.6
Inspection time per unit, in days	0.1	0.3	0.6	0.8
Process time per unit, in days	0.6	0.6	0.6	0.6
Queue time per unit, in days	5.6	5.7	5.6	5.7
Move time per unit, in days	1.4	1.3	1.3	1.4

Required:

1. For each month, compute the following operating performance measures:
   a. Throughput time.
   b. Manufacturing cycle efficiency (MCE).
   c. Delivery cycle time.
2. Using the performance measures given in the problem and those you computed in (1) above, do the following:
   a. Identify areas where the company seems to be improving.
   b. Identify areas where the company seems to be deteriorating or stagnating.
   c. Explain why you think some specific areas are improving while others are not.
3. Refer to the move time, process time, and so forth, given above for month 4.
   a. Assume that in month 5 the move time, process time, and so forth, are the same as for month 4, except that through the implementation of Lean Production, the company is able to completely eliminate the queue time during production. Compute the new throughput time and MCE.
   b. Assume that in month 6 the move time, process time, and so forth, are the same as for month 4, except that the company is able to completely eliminate both the queue time during production and the inspection time. Compute the new throughput time and MCE.

Case

All applicable cases are available with McGraw-Hill's *Connect™ Accounting*.

CASE 11–23 Balanced Scorecard [LO4]

Weierman Department Store is located in the downtown area of a medium-sized city in the American Midwest. While the store had been profitable for many years, it is facing increasing competition from large national chains that have set up stores in the city's suburbs. Recently, the downtown area has been undergoing revitalization, and the owners of Weierman Department Store are somewhat optimistic that profitability can be restored.

In an attempt to accelerate the return to profitability, the management of Weierman Department Store is in the process of designing a balanced scorecard for the company. Management believes the company should focus on two key problems. First, customers are taking longer and longer to pay the bills they incur on the department store's charge card, and they have far more bad debts than are normal for the industry. If this problem were solved, the company would have more cash to make much needed renovations. Investigation has revealed that much of the problem with late payments and unpaid bills is apparently due to disputed bills that are the result of incorrect charges on the customer bills. These incorrect charges usually occur because salesclerks enter data incorrectly on the charge account slip. Second, the company has been incurring large losses on unsold seasonal apparel. Such items are ordinarily resold at a loss to discount stores that specialize in such distress items.

The meeting in which the balanced scorecard approach was discussed was disorganized and ineffectively led—possibly because no one other than one of the vice presidents had read anything about how to put a balanced scorecard together. Nevertheless, a number of potential performance measures were suggested by various managers. These potential performance measures are:

Performance measures suggested by various managers:

- Total sales revenue.
- Percentage of salesclerks trained to correctly enter data on charge account slips.
- Customer satisfaction with accuracy of charge account bills from monthly customer survey.
- Sales per employee.
- Travel expenses for buyers for trips to fashion shows.
- Average age of accounts receivables.
- Courtesy shown by junior staff members to senior staff members based on surveys of senior staff.
- Unsold inventory at the end of the season as a percentage of total cost of sales.
- Sales per square foot of floor space.
- Percentage of suppliers making just-in-time deliveries.
- Quality of food in the staff cafeteria based on staff surveys.
- Written-off accounts receivables (bad debts) as a percentage of sales.
- Percentage of charge account bills containing errors.
- Percentage of employees who have attended the city's cultural diversity workshop.
- Total profit.
- Profit per employee.

Required:

1. As someone with more knowledge of the balanced scorecard than almost anyone else in the company, you have been asked to build an integrated balanced scorecard. In your scorecard, use only performance measures suggested by the managers above. You do not have to use all of the performance measures suggested by the managers, but you should build a balanced scorecard that reveals a strategy for dealing with the problems with accounts receivable and with unsold merchandise. Construct the balanced scorecard following the format used in Exhibit 11–5. Do not be particularly concerned with whether a specific performance measure falls within the learning and growth, internal business process, customer, or financial perspective. However, clearly show the causal links between the performance measures with arrows and whether the performance measures should show increases or decreases.
2. Assume that the company adopts your balanced scorecard. After operating for a year, there are improvements in some performance measures but not in others. What should management do next?
3. *a.* Suppose that customers express greater satisfaction with the accuracy of their charge account bills, but the performance measures for the average age of accounts receivable and for bad debts do not improve. Explain why this might happen.

   b. Suppose that the performance measures for the average age of accounts receivable, bad debts, and unsold inventory improve, but total profits do not. Explain why this might happen. Assume in your answer that the explanation lies within the company.

Appendix 11A: Transfer Pricing

Divisions in a company often supply goods and services to other divisions within the same company. For example, the truck division of Toyota supplies trucks to other Toyota divisions to use in their operations. When the divisions are evaluated based on their profit, ROI, or residual income, a price must be established for such a transfer—otherwise, the division that produces the good or service will receive no credit. The price in such a situation is called a *transfer price*. A **transfer price** is the price charged when one segment of a company provides goods or services to another segment of the same company. For example, most companies in the oil industry, such as Shell, have petroleum refining and retail sales divisions that are evaluated on the basis of ROI or residual income. The petroleum refining division processes crude oil into gasoline, kerosene, lubricants, and other end products. The retail sales division takes gasoline and other products from the refining division and sells them through the company's chain of service stations. Each product has a price for transfers within the company. Suppose the transfer price for gasoline is $0.80 a gallon. Then the refining division gets credit for $0.80 a gallon of revenue on its segment report and the retailing division must deduct $0.80 a gallon as an expense on its segment report. Clearly, the refining division would like the transfer price to be as high as possible, whereas the retailing division would like the transfer price to be as low as possible. However, the transaction has no direct effect on the entire company's reported profit. It is like taking money out of one pocket and putting it into the other.

Managers are intensely interested in how transfer prices are set because they can have a dramatic effect on the reported profitability of their divisions. Three common approaches are used to set transfer prices:

1. Allow the managers involved in the transfer to negotiate the transfer price.
2. Set transfer prices at cost using either variable cost or full (absorption) cost.
3. Set transfer prices at the market price.

We will consider each of these transfer pricing methods in turn, beginning with negotiated transfer prices. Throughout the discussion, keep in mind that *the fundamental objective in setting transfer prices is to motivate the managers to act in the best interests of the overall company.* In contrast, **suboptimization** occurs when managers do not act in the best interests of the overall company or even in the best interests of their own division.

Negotiated Transfer Prices

LEARNING OBJECTIVE 5
Determine the range, if any, within which a negotiated transfer price should fall.

A **negotiated transfer price** results from discussions between the selling and buying divisions. Negotiated transfer prices have several important advantages. First, this approach preserves the autonomy of the divisions and is consistent with the spirit of decentralization. Second, the managers of the divisions are likely to have much better information about the potential costs and benefits of the transfer than others in the company.

When negotiated transfer prices are used, the managers who are involved in a proposed transfer within the company meet to discuss the terms and conditions of the transfer. They may decide not to go through with the transfer, but if they do, they must agree to a transfer price. Generally speaking, we cannot predict what transfer price they will agree to. However, we can confidently predict two things: (1) the selling division will agree to the transfer only if its profits increase as a result of the transfer, and (2) the buying division will agree to the transfer only if its profits also increase as a result of the transfer. This may seem obvious, but it is an important point.

Clearly, if the transfer price is below the selling division's cost, the selling division will incur a loss on the transaction and it will refuse to agree to the transfer. Likewise, if the transfer price is set too high, it will be impossible for the buying division to make any profit on the transferred item. For any given proposed transfer, the transfer price has both a lower limit (determined by the situation of the selling division) and an upper limit (determined by the situation of the buying division). The actual transfer price agreed to by the two division managers can fall anywhere between those two limits. These limits determine the **range of acceptable transfer prices**—the range of transfer prices within which the profits of both divisions participating in a transfer would increase.

An example will help us to understand negotiated transfer prices. Harris & Louder, Ltd., owns fast-food restaurants and snack food and beverage manufacturers in the United Kingdom. One of the restaurants, Pizza Maven, serves a variety of beverages along with pizzas. One of the beverages is ginger beer, which is served on tap. Harris & Louder has just purchased a new division, Imperial Beverages, that produces ginger beer. The managing director of Imperial Beverages has approached the managing director of Pizza Maven about purchasing Imperial Beverages' ginger beer to sell at Pizza Maven restaurants rather than its usual brand of ginger beer. Managers at Pizza Maven agree that the quality of Imperial Beverages' ginger beer is comparable to the quality of their regular brand. It is just a question of price. The basic facts are as follows (the currency in this example is pounds, denoted here as £):

Imperial Beverages:	
Ginger beer production capacity per month	10,000 barrels
Variable cost per barrel of ginger beer	£8 per barrel
Fixed costs per month	£70,000
Selling price of Imperial Beverages ginger beer on the outside market	£20 per barrel
Pizza Maven:	
Purchase price of regular brand of ginger beer . .	£18 per barrel
Monthly consumption of ginger beer	2,000 barrels

The Selling Division's Lowest Acceptable Transfer Price The selling division, Imperial Beverages, will be interested in a proposed transfer only if its profit increases. Clearly, the transfer price must not fall below the variable cost per barrel of £8. In addition, if Imperial Beverages does not have sufficient capacity to fill the Pizza Maven order while supplying its regular customers, then it would have to sacrifice some of its regular sales. Imperial Beverages would expect to be compensated for the contribution margin on any lost sales. In sum, if the transfer has no effect on fixed costs, then from the selling division's standpoint, the transfer price must cover both the variable costs of producing the transferred units and any opportunity costs from lost sales.

Seller's perspective:

$$\text{Transfer price} \geq \text{Variable cost per unit} + \frac{\text{Total contribution margin on lost sales}}{\text{Number of units transferred}}$$

The Buying Division's Highest Acceptable Transfer Price The buying division, Pizza Maven, will be interested in a transfer only if its profit increases. In cases like this where a buying division has an outside supplier, the buying division's decision is simple. Buy from the inside supplier if the price is less than the price offered by the outside supplier.

Purchaser's perspective:

$$\text{Transfer price} \leq \text{Cost of buying from outside supplier}$$

Or, if an outside supplier does not exist:

$$\text{Transfer price} \leq \text{Profit to be earned per unit sold (not including the transfer price)}$$

We will consider several different hypothetical situations and see what the range of acceptable transfer prices would be in each situation.

Selling Division with Idle Capacity Suppose that Imperial Beverages has sufficient idle capacity to satisfy Pizza Maven's demand for ginger beer without sacrificing sales of ginger beer to its regular customers. To be specific, let's suppose that Imperial Beverages is selling only 7,000 barrels of ginger beer a month on the outside market. That leaves unused capacity of 3,000 barrels a month—more than enough to satisfy Pizza Maven's requirement of 2,000 barrels a month. What range of transfer prices, if any, would make both divisions better off with the transfer of 2,000 barrels a month?

1. The selling division, Imperial Beverages, will be interested in the transfer only if:

$$\text{Transfer price} \geq \text{Variable cost per unit} + \frac{\text{Total contribution margin on lost sales}}{\text{Number of units transferred}}$$

Because Imperial Beverages has enough idle capacity, there are no lost outside sales. And because the variable cost per unit is £8, the lowest acceptable transfer price for the selling division is £8.

$$\text{Transfer price} \geq £8 + \frac{£0}{2{,}000} = £8$$

2. The buying division, Pizza Maven, can buy similar ginger beer from an outside vendor for £18. Therefore, Pizza Maven would be unwilling to pay more than £18 per barrel for Imperial Beverages' ginger beer.

$$\text{Transfer price} \leq \text{Cost of buying from outside supplier} = £18$$

3. Combining the requirements of both the selling division and the buying division, the acceptable range of transfer prices in this situation is:

$$£8 \leq \text{Transfer price} \leq £18$$

Assuming that the managers understand their own businesses and that they are cooperative, they should be able to agree on a transfer price within this range.

Selling Division with No Idle Capacity

Suppose that Imperial Beverages has *no* idle capacity; it is selling 10,000 barrels of ginger beer a month on the outside market at £20 per barrel. To fill the order from Pizza Maven, Imperial Beverages would have to divert 2,000 barrels from its regular customers. What range of transfer prices, if any, would make both divisions better off transferring the 2,000 barrels within the company?

1. The selling division, Imperial Beverages, will be interested in the transfer only if:

$$\text{Transfer price} \geq \frac{\text{Variable cost}}{\text{per unit}} + \frac{\text{Total contribution margin on lost sales}}{\text{Number of units transferred}}$$

Because Imperial Beverages has no idle capacity, there *are* lost outside sales. The contribution margin per barrel on these outside sales is £12 (£20 − £8).

$$\text{Transfer price} \geq £8 + \frac{(£20 - £8) \times 2{,}000}{2{,}000} = £8 + (£20 - £8) = £20$$

Thus, as far as the selling division is concerned, the transfer price must at least cover the revenue on the lost sales, which is £20 per barrel. This makes sense because the cost of producing the 2,000 barrels is the same whether they are sold on the inside market or on the outside. The only difference is that the selling division loses the revenue of £20 per barrel if it transfers the barrels to Pizza Maven.

2. As before, the buying division, Pizza Maven, would be unwilling to pay more than the £18 per barrel it is already paying for similar ginger beer from its regular supplier.

$$\text{Transfer price} \leq \text{Cost of buying from outside supplier} = £18$$

3. Therefore, the selling division would insist on a transfer price of at least £20. But the buying division would refuse any transfer price above £18. It is impossible to satisfy both division managers simultaneously; there can be no agreement on a transfer price and no transfer will take place. Is this good? The answer is yes. From the standpoint of the entire company, the transfer doesn't make sense. Why give up sales of £20 to save costs of £18?

Basically, the transfer price is a mechanism for dividing between the two divisions any profit the entire company earns as a result of the transfer. If the company as a whole loses money on the transfer, there will be no profit to divide up, and it will be impossible for the two divisions to come to an agreement. On the other hand, if the company as a whole makes money on the transfer, there will be a profit to share, and it will always be possible for the two divisions to find a mutually agreeable transfer price that increases the profits of both divisions. If the pie is bigger, it is always possible to divide it up in such a way that everyone has a bigger piece.

Selling Division Has Some Idle Capacity

Suppose now that Imperial Beverages is selling 9,000 barrels of ginger beer a month on the outside market. Pizza Maven can only sell one kind of ginger beer on tap. It cannot buy 1,000 barrels from Imperial

Beverages and 1,000 barrels from its regular supplier; it must buy all of its ginger beer from one source.

To fill the entire 2,000-barrel a month order from Pizza Maven, Imperial Beverages would have to divert 1,000 barrels from its regular customers who are paying £20 per barrel. The other 1,000 barrels can be made using idle capacity. What range of transfer prices, if any, would make both divisions better off transferring the 2,000 barrels within the company?

1. As before, the selling division, Imperial Beverages, will insist on a transfer price that at least covers its variable cost and opportunity cost:

$$\text{Transfer price} \geq \begin{matrix}\text{Variable cost}\\ \text{per unit}\end{matrix} + \frac{\text{Total contribution margin on lost sales}}{\text{Number of units transferred}}$$

   Because Imperial Beverages does not have enough idle capacity to fill the entire order for 2,000 barrels, there *are* lost outside sales. The contribution margin per barrel on the 1,000 barrels of lost outside sales is £12 (£20 − £8).

$$\text{Transfer price} \geq £8 + \frac{(£20 - £8) \times 1{,}000}{2{,}000} = £8 + £6 = £14$$

   Thus, as far as the selling division is concerned, the transfer price must cover the variable cost of £8 plus the average opportunity cost of lost sales of £6.

2. As before, the buying division, Pizza Maven, would be unwilling to pay more than the £18 per barrel it pays its regular supplier.

$$\text{Transfer price} \leq \text{Cost of buying from outside suppliers} = £18$$

3. Combining the requirements for both the selling and buying divisions, the range of acceptable transfer prices is:

$$£14 \leq \text{Transfer price} \leq £18$$

   Again, assuming that the managers understand their own businesses and that they are cooperative, they should be able to agree on a transfer price within this range.

No Outside Supplier If Pizza Maven has no outside supplier for the ginger beer, the highest price the buying division would be willing to pay depends on how much the buying division expects to make on the transferred units—excluding the transfer price. If, for example, Pizza Maven expects to earn £30 per barrel of ginger beer after paying its own expenses, then it should be willing to pay up to £30 per barrel to Imperial Beverages. Remember, however, that this assumes Pizza Maven cannot buy ginger beer from other sources.

Evaluation of Negotiated Transfer Prices As discussed earlier, if a transfer within the company would result in higher overall profits for the company, there is always a range of transfer prices within which both the selling and buying division would also have higher profits if they agree to the transfer. Therefore, if the managers understand their own businesses and are cooperative, then they should always be able to agree on a transfer price if it is in the best interests of the company that they do so.

Unfortunately, not all managers understand their own businesses and not all managers are cooperative. As a result, negotiations often break down even when it would be in the managers' own best interests to come to an agreement. Sometimes that is the fault of the way managers are evaluated. If managers are pitted against each other rather than against their own past performance or reasonable benchmarks, a noncooperative atmosphere is almost guaranteed. Nevertheless, even with the best performance evaluation system, some people by nature are not cooperative.

Given the disputes that often accompany the negotiation process, many companies rely on some other means of setting transfer prices. Unfortunately, as we will see below, all of the alternatives to negotiated transfer prices have their own serious drawbacks.

Transfers at the Cost to the Selling Division

Many companies set transfer prices at either the variable cost or full (absorption) cost incurred by the selling division. Although the cost approach to setting transfer prices is relatively simple to apply, it has some major defects.

First, the use of cost—particularly full cost—as a transfer price can lead to bad decisions and thus suboptimization. Return to the example involving the ginger beer. The full cost of ginger beer can never be less than £15 per barrel (£8 per barrel variable cost + £7 per barrel fixed cost at capacity). What if the cost of buying the ginger beer from an outside supplier is less than £15—for example, £14 per barrel? If the transfer price were set at full cost, then Pizza Maven would never want to buy ginger beer from Imperial Beverages because it could buy its ginger beer from an outside supplier at a lower price. However, from the standpoint of the company as a whole, ginger beer should be transferred from Imperial Beverages to Pizza Maven whenever Imperial Beverages has idle capacity. Why? Because when Imperial Beverages has idle capacity, it only costs the company £8 in variable cost to produce a barrel of ginger beer, but it costs £14 per barrel to buy from outside suppliers.

Second, if cost is used as the transfer price, the selling division will never show a profit on any internal transfer. The only division that shows a profit is the division that makes the final sale to an outside party.

Third, cost-based prices do not provide incentives to control costs. If the actual costs of one division are simply passed on to the next, there is little incentive for anyone to work to reduce costs. This problem can be overcome by using standard costs rather than actual costs for transfer prices.

Despite these shortcomings, cost-based transfer prices are often used in practice. Advocates argue that they are easily understood and convenient to use.

Transfers at Market Price

Some form of competitive **market price** (i.e., the price charged for an item on the open market) is sometimes advocated as the best approach to the transfer pricing problem—particularly if transfer price negotiations routinely become bogged down.

The market price approach is designed for situations in which there is an *outside market* for the transferred product or service; the product or service is sold in its present form to outside customers. If the selling division has no idle capacity, the market price is the correct choice for the transfer price. This is because, from the company's perspective, the real cost of the transfer is the opportunity cost of the lost revenue on the outside sale. Whether the item is transferred internally or sold on the outside market, the production costs are exactly the same. If the market price is used as the transfer price, the selling division manager will not lose anything by making the transfer, and the buying division manager will get the correct signal about how much it really costs the company for the transfer to take place.

While the market price works well when the selling division has no idle capacity, difficulties occur when the selling division has idle capacity. Recalling once again the ginger beer example, the outside market price for the ginger beer produced by Imperial Beverages is £20 per barrel. However, Pizza Maven can purchase all of the ginger beer it wants from outside suppliers for £18 per barrel. Why would Pizza Maven ever buy from Imperial Beverages if Pizza Maven is forced to pay Imperial Beverages' market price? In some market price-based transfer pricing schemes, the transfer price would be lowered to £18, the outside vendor's market price, and Pizza Maven would be directed to buy from Imperial Beverages as long as Imperial Beverages is willing to sell. This scheme can work reasonably well, but a drawback is that managers at Pizza Maven will regard the cost of ginger beer as £18 rather than the £8, which is the real cost to the company when the selling division has idle capacity. Consequently, the managers of Pizza Maven will make pricing and other decisions based on an incorrect cost.

Unfortunately, none of the possible solutions to the transfer pricing problem are perfect—not even market-based transfer prices.

Divisional Autonomy and Suboptimization

The principles of decentralization suggest that companies should grant managers autonomy to set transfer prices and to decide whether to sell internally or externally. It may be very difficult for top managers to accept this principle when their subordinate managers are about to make a suboptimal decision. However, if top management intervenes, the purposes of decentralization are defeated. Furthermore, to impose the correct transfer price, top managers would have to know details about the buying and selling divisions' outside market, variable costs, and capacity utilization. The whole premise of decentralization is that local managers have access to better information for operational decisions than top managers at corporate headquarters.

Of course, if a division manager consistently makes suboptimal decisions, the performance of the division will suffer. The offending manager's compensation will be adversely affected and promotion will become less likely. Thus, a performance evaluation system based on divisional profits, ROI, or residual income provides some built-in checks and balances. Nevertheless, if top managers wish to create a culture of autonomy and independent profit responsibility, they must allow their subordinate managers to control their own destiny—even to the extent of granting their managers the right to make mistakes.

International Aspects of Transfer Pricing

The objectives of transfer pricing change when a multinational corporation is involved and the goods and services being transferred cross international borders. In this context, the objectives of international transfer pricing focus on minimizing taxes, duties, and foreign exchange risks, along with enhancing a company's competitive position and improving its relations with foreign governments. Although domestic objectives such as managerial motivation and divisional autonomy are always important, they often become secondary when international transfers are involved. Companies will focus instead on charging a transfer price that reduces its total tax bill or that strengthens a foreign subsidiary.

For example, charging a low transfer price for parts shipped to a foreign subsidiary may reduce customs duty payments as the parts cross international borders, or it may help the subsidiary to compete in foreign markets by keeping the subsidiary's costs low. On the other hand, charging a high transfer price may help a multinational corporation draw profits out of a country that has stringent controls on foreign remittances, or it may allow a multinational corporation to shift income from a country that has high income tax rates to a country that has low rates.

Review Problem: Transfer Pricing

Situation A

Collyer Products, Inc., has a Valve Division that manufactures and sells a standard valve:

Capacity in units	100,000
Selling price to outside customers	$30
Variable costs per unit	$16
Fixed costs per unit (based on capacity)	$9

The company has a Pump Division that could use this valve in one of its pumps. The Pump Division is currently purchasing 10,000 valves per year from an overseas supplier at a cost of $29 per valve.

Required:

1. Assume that the Valve Division has enough idle capacity to handle all of the Pump Division's needs. What is the acceptable range, if any, for the transfer price between the two divisions?

2. Assume that the Valve Division is selling all of the valves that it can produce to outside customers. What is the acceptable range, if any, for the transfer price between the two divisions?
3. Assume again that the Valve Division is selling all of the valves that it can produce to outside customers. Also assume that \$3 in variable expenses can be avoided on transfers within the company, due to reduced selling costs. What is the acceptable range, if any, for the transfer price between the two divisions?

Solution to Situation A

1. Because the Valve Division has idle capacity, it does not have to give up any outside sales to take on the Pump Division's business. Applying the formula for the lowest acceptable transfer price from the viewpoint of the selling division, we get:

$$\text{Transfer price} \geq \frac{\text{Variable cost}}{\text{per unit}} + \frac{\text{Total contribution margin on lost sales}}{\text{Number of units transferred}}$$

$$\text{Transfer price} \geq \$16 + \frac{\$0}{10{,}000} = \$16$$

The Pump Division would be unwilling to pay more than \$29, the price it is currently paying an outside supplier for its valves. Therefore, the transfer price must fall within the range:

$$\$16 \leq \text{Transfer price} \leq \$29$$

2. Because the Valve Division is selling all of the valves that it can produce on the outside market, it would have to give up some of these outside sales to take on the Pump Division's business. Thus, the Valve Division has an opportunity cost, which is the total contribution margin on lost sales:

$$\text{Transfer price} \geq \frac{\text{Variable cost}}{\text{per unit}} + \frac{\text{Total contribution margin on lost sales}}{\text{Number of units transferred}}$$

$$\text{Transfer price} \geq \$16 + \frac{(\$30 - \$16) \times 10{,}000}{10{,}000} = \$16 + \$14 = \$30$$

Because the Pump Division can purchase valves from an outside supplier at only \$29 per unit, no transfers will be made between the two divisions.
3. Applying the formula for the lowest acceptable transfer price from the viewpoint of the selling division, we get:

$$\text{Transfer price} \geq \frac{\text{Variable cost}}{\text{per unit}} + \frac{\text{Total contribution margin on lost sales}}{\text{Number of units transferred}}$$

$$\text{Transfer price} \geq (\$16 - \$3) + \frac{(\$30 - \$16) \times 10{,}000}{10{,}000} = \$13 + \$14 = \$27$$

In this case, the transfer price must fall within the range:

$$\$27 \leq \text{Transfer price} \leq \$29$$

Situation B

Refer to the original data in situation A above. Assume that the Pump Division needs 20,000 special high-pressure valves per year. The Valve Division's variable costs to manufacture and ship the special valve would be \$20 per unit. To produce these special valves, the Valve Division would have to reduce its production and sales of regular valves from 100,000 units per year to 70,000 units per year.

Required:

As far as the Valve Division is concerned, what is the lowest acceptable transfer price?

Solution to Situation B

To produce the 20,000 special valves, the Valve Division will have to give up sales of 30,000 regular valves to outside customers. Applying the formula for the lowest acceptable transfer price from the viewpoint of the selling division, we get:

$$\text{Transfer price} \geq \frac{\text{Variable cost}}{\text{per unit}} + \frac{\text{Total contribution margin on lost sales}}{\text{Number of units transferred}}$$

$$\text{Transfer price} \geq \$20 + \frac{(\$30 - \$16) \times 30{,}000}{20{,}000} = \$20 + \$21 = \$41$$

Glossary (Appendix 11A)

Market price The price charged for an item on the open market. (p. 512)
Negotiated transfer price A transfer price agreed on between buying and selling divisions. (p. 508)
Range of acceptable transfer prices The range of transfer prices within which the profits of both the selling division and the buying division would increase as a result of a transfer. (p. 508)
Suboptimization An overall level of profits that is less than a segment or a company is capable of earning. (p. 508)
Transfer price The price charged when one division or segment provides goods or services to another division or segment of an organization. (p. 507)

connect ACCOUNTING Appendix 11A Exercises and Problems

All applicable exercises and problems are available with McGraw-Hill's *Connect™ Accounting*.

EXERCISE 11A–1 Transfer Pricing Situations [LO5]
In each of the cases below, assume that Division X has a product that can be sold either to outside customers or to Division Y of the same company for use in its production process. The managers of the divisions are evaluated based on their divisional profits.

	Case A	Case B
Division X:		
Capacity in units	100,000	100,000
Number of units being sold to outside customers	100,000	80,000
Selling price per unit to outside customers	$50	$35
Variable costs per unit	$30	$20
Fixed costs per unit (based on capacity)	$8	$6
Division Y:		
Number of units needed for production	20,000	20,000
Purchase price per unit now being paid to an outside supplier	$47	$34

Required:
1. Refer to the data in case A above. Assume that $3 per unit in variable selling costs can be avoided on intracompany sales. If the managers are free to negotiate and make decisions on their own, will a transfer take place? If so, within what range will the transfer price fall? Explain.
2. Refer to the data in case B above. In this case, there will be no savings in variable selling costs on intracompany sales. If the managers are free to negotiate and make decisions on their own, will a transfer take place? If so, within what range will the transfer price fall? Explain.

EXERCISE 11A–2 Transfer Pricing from Viewpoint of the Entire Company [LO5]
Division A manufactures picture tubes for TVs. The tubes can be sold either to Division B of the same company or to outside customers. Last year, the following activity was recorded in Division A:

Selling price per tube	$175
Variable cost per tube	$130
Number of tubes:	
Produced during the year	20,000
Sold to outside customers	16,000
Sold to Division B	4,000

Sales to Division B were at the same price as sales to outside customers. The tubes purchased by Division B were used in a TV set manufactured by that division. Division B incurred $300 in additional variable cost per TV and then sold the TVs for $600 each.

Required:

1. Prepare income statements for last year for Division A, Division B, and the company as a whole.
2. Assume that Division A's manufacturing capacity is 20,000 tubes per year. Next year, Division B wants to purchase 5,000 tubes from Division A, rather than only 4,000 tubes as in last year. (Tubes of this type are not available from outside sources.) From the standpoint of the company as a whole, should Division A sell the 1,000 additional tubes to Division B, or should it continue to sell them to outside customers? Explain.

EXERCISE 11A–3 Transfer Pricing Basics [LO5]

Nelcro Company's Electrical Division produces a high-quality transformer. Sales and cost data on the transformer follow:

Selling price per unit on the outside market	$40
Variable costs per unit	$21
Fixed costs per unit (based on capacity)	$9
Capacity in units	60,000

Nelcro Company has a Motor Division that would like to begin purchasing this transformer from the Electrical Division. The Motor Division is currently purchasing 10,000 transformers each year from another company at a cost of $38 per transformer. Nelcro Company evaluates its division managers on the basis of divisional profits.

Required:

1. Assume that the Electrical Division is now selling only 50,000 transformers each year to outside customers.
   a. From the standpoint of the Electrical Division, what is the lowest acceptable transfer price for transformers sold to the Motor Division?
   b. From the standpoint of the Motor Division, what is the highest acceptable transfer price for transformers acquired from the Electrical Division?
   c. If left free to negotiate without interference, would you expect the division managers to voluntarily agree to the transfer of 10,000 transformers from the Electrical Division to the Motor Division? Why or why not?
   d. From the standpoint of the entire company, should a transfer take place? Why or why not?
2. Assume that the Electrical Division is now selling all of the transformers it can produce to outside customers.
   a. From the standpoint of the Electrical Division, what is the lowest acceptable transfer price for transformers sold to the Motor Division?
   b. From the standpoint of the Motor Division, what is the highest acceptable transfer price for transformers acquired from the Electrical Division?
   c. If left free to negotiate without interference, would you expect the division managers to voluntarily agree to the transfer of 10,000 transformers from the Electrical Division to the Motor Division? Why or why not?
   d. From the standpoint of the entire company, should a transfer take place? Why or why not?

PROBLEM 11A–4 Market-Based Transfer Price [LO5]

Damico Company's Board Division manufactures an electronic control board that is widely used in high-end DVD players. The cost per control board is as follows:

Variable cost per board	$120
Fixed cost per board*	30
Total cost per board	$150

*Based on a capacity of 800,000 boards per year.

Part of the Board Division's output is sold to outside manufacturers of DVD players, and part is sold to Damico Company's Consumer Products Division, which produces a DVD player under the Damico name. The Board Division charges a selling price of $190 per control board for all sales, both internally and externally.

The costs, revenues, and net operating income associated with the Consumer Products Division's DVD player are given below:

Selling price per player		$580
Variable costs per player:		
Cost of the control board	$190	
Variable cost of other parts	230	
Total variable costs		420
Contribution margin		160
Fixed costs per player*		85
Net operating income per player		$ 75

*Based on a capacity of 200,000 DVD players per year.

The Consumer Products Division has an order from an overseas distributor for 5,000 DVD players. The distributor wants to pay only $400 per DVD player.

Required:

1. Assume that the Consumer Products Division has enough idle capacity to fill the 5,000-unit order. Is the division likely to accept the $400 price, or to reject it? Explain.
2. Assume that both the Board Division and the Consumer Products Division have idle capacity. Under these conditions, would rejecting the $400 price be advantageous for the company as a whole, or would it result in the loss of potential profits? Show computations to support your answer.
3. Assume that the Board Division is operating at capacity and could sell all of its control boards to outside manufacturers of DVD players. Assume, however, that the Consumer Products Division has enough idle capacity to fill the 5,000-unit order. Under these conditions, compute the profit impact to the Consumer Products Division of accepting the order at the $400 price.
4. What conclusions do you draw concerning the use of market price as a transfer price in intracompany transactions?

PROBLEM 11A–5 Basic Transfer Pricing [LO5]

In cases 1-3 below, assume that Division A has a product that can be sold either to Division B of the same company or to outside customers. The managers of both divisions are evaluated based on their own division's return on investment (ROI). The managers are free to decide if they will participate in any internal transfers. All transfer prices are negotiated. Treat each case independently.

	Case			
	1	2	3	4
Division A:				
Capacity in units	50,000	300,000	100,000	200,000
Number of units now being sold to outside customers	50,000	300,000	75,000	200,000
Selling price per unit to outside customers	$100	$40	$60	$45
Variable costs per unit	$63	$19	$35	$30
Fixed costs per unit (based on capacity)	$25	$8	$17	$6
Division B:				
Number of units needed annually	10,000	70,000	20,000	60,000
Purchase price now being paid to an outside supplier*	$92	$39	$60	—

*Before any purchase discount.

Required:

1. Refer to case 1. A study has indicated that Division A can avoid $5 per unit in variable costs on any sales to Division B. Will the managers agree to a transfer, and if so, within what range will the transfer price be? Explain.

2. Refer to case 2. Assume that Division A can avoid $4 per unit in variable costs on any sales to Division B.
   a. Would you expect any disagreement between the two divisional managers over what the transfer price should be? Explain.
   b. Assume that Division A offers to sell 70,000 units to Division B for $38 per unit and that Division B refuses this price. What will be the loss in potential profits for the company as a whole?
3. Refer to case 3. Assume that Division B is now receiving a 5% price discount from the outside supplier.
   a. Will the managers agree to a transfer? If so, within what range will the transfer price be?
   b. Assume that Division B offers to purchase 20,000 units from Division A at $52 per unit. If Division A accepts this price, would you expect its ROI to increase, decrease, or remain unchanged? Why?
4. Refer to case 4. Assume that Division B wants Division A to provide it with 60,000 units of a *different* product from the one that Division A is now producing. The new product would require $25 per unit in variable costs and would require that Division A cut back production of its present product by 30,000 units annually. What is the lowest acceptable transfer price from Division A's perspective?

PROBLEM 11A–6 Transfer Pricing with an Outside Market [LO5]

Galati Products, Inc., has just purchased a small company that specializes in the manufacture of electronic tuners that are used as a component part of TV sets. Galati Products, Inc., is a decentralized company, and it will treat the newly acquired company as an autonomous division with full profit responsibility. The new division, called the Tuner Division, has the following revenue and costs associated with each tuner that it manufactures and sells:

Selling price		$20
Expenses:		
Variable	$11	
Fixed (based on a capacity of 100,000 tuners per year)	6	17
Net operating income		$ 3

Galati Products also has an Assembly Division that assembles TV sets. This division is currently purchasing 30,000 tuners per year from an overseas supplier at a cost of $20 per tuner, less a 10% purchase discount. The president of Galati Products is anxious to have the Assembly Division begin purchasing its tuners from the newly acquired Tuner Division in order to "keep the profits within the corporate family."

Required:

For (1) and (2) below, assume that the Tuner Division can sell all of its output to outside TV manufacturers at the normal $20 price.

1. Are the managers of the Tuner and Assembly Divisions likely to voluntarily agree to a transfer price for 30,000 tuners each year? Why or why not?
2. If the Tuner Division meets the price that the Assembly Division is currently paying to its overseas supplier and sells 30,000 tuners to the Assembly Division each year, what will be the effect on the profits of the Tuner Division, the Assembly Division, and the company as a whole?

For (3) through (6), assume that the Tuner Division is currently selling only 60,000 tuners each year to outside TV manufacturers at the stated $20 price.

3. Are the managers of the Tuner and Assembly Divisions likely to voluntarily agree to a transfer price for 30,000 tuners each year? Why or why not?
4. Suppose that the Assembly Division's overseas supplier drops its price (net of the purchase discount) to only $16 per tuner. Should the Tuner Division meet this price? Explain. If the Tuner Division does *not* meet this price, what will be the effect on the profits of the company as a whole?
5. Refer to (4) above. If the Tuner Division refuses to meet the $16 price, should the Assembly Division be required to purchase from the Tuner Division at a higher price for the good of the company as a whole? Explain.

6. Refer to (4) on the previous page. Assume that due to inflexible management policies, the Assembly Division is required to purchase 30,000 tuners each year from the Tuner Division at \$20 per tuner. What will be the effect on the profits of the company as a whole?

Case

All applicable cases are available with McGraw-Hill's *Connect™ Accounting.*

CASE 11A–7 Transfer Pricing; Divisional Performance [LO5]

Stanco, Inc., is a decentralized organization with five divisions. The company's Electronics Division produces a variety of electronics items, including an XL5 circuit board. The division (which is operating at capacity) sells the XL5 circuit board to regular customers for \$12.50 each. The circuit boards have a variable production cost of \$8.25 each.

The company's Clock Division has asked the Electronics Division to supply it with a large quantity of XL5 circuit boards for only \$9 each. The Clock Division, which is operating at only 60% of capacity, will put the circuit boards into a timing device that it will produce and sell to a large oven manufacturer. The cost of the timing device being manufactured by the Clock Division follows:

XL5 circuit board (desired cost)	\$ 9.00
Other purchased parts (from outside vendors)	30.00
Other variable costs	20.75
Fixed overhead and administrative costs	10.00
Total cost per timing device	\$69.75

The manager of the Clock Division feels that she can't quote a price greater than \$70 per timing device to the oven manufacturer if her division is to get the job. As shown above, in order to keep the price at \$70 or less, she can't pay more than \$9 per unit to the Electronics Division for the XL5 circuit boards. Although the \$9 price for the XL5 circuit boards represents a substantial discount from the normal \$12.50 price, she feels that the price concession is necessary for her division to get the oven manufacturer contract and thereby keep its core of highly trained people.

The company uses return on investment (ROI) to measure divisional performance.

Required:

1. Assume that you are the manager of the Electronics Division. Would you recommend that your division supply the XL5 circuit boards to the Clock Division for \$9 each as requested? Why or why not? Show all computations.
2. Would it be profitable for the company as a whole for the Electronics Division to supply the Clock Division with the circuit boards for \$9 each? Explain your answer.
3. In principle, should it be possible for the two managers to agree to a transfer price in this particular situation? If so, within what range would that transfer price lie?
4. Discuss the organizational and manager behavior problems, if any, inherent in this situation. What would you advise the company's president to do in this situation?

(CMA, adapted)

Appendix 11B: Service Department Charges

LEARNING OBJECTIVE 6
Charge operating departments for services provided by service departments.

Most large organizations have both *operating departments* and *service departments.* The central purposes of the organization are carried out in the **operating departments.** In contrast, **service departments** do not directly engage in operating activities. Instead, they provide services or assistance to the operating departments. Examples of service departments include Cafeteria, Internal Auditing, Human Resources, Cost Accounting, and Purchasing.

Service department costs are charged to operating departments for a variety of reasons, including:

- To encourage operating departments to make wise use of service department resources. If the services were provided for free, operating managers would be inclined to waste these resources.
- To provide operating departments with more complete cost data for making decisions. Actions taken by operating departments have impacts on service department costs. For example, hiring another employee will increase costs in the human resources department. Such service department costs should be charged to the operating departments, otherwise the operating departments will not take them into account when making decisions.
- To help measure the profitability of operating departments. Charging service department costs to operating departments provides a more complete accounting of the costs incurred as a consequence of activities in the operating departments.
- To create an incentive for service departments to operate efficiently. Charging service department costs to operating departments provides a system of checks and balances in the sense that cost-conscious operating departments will take an active interest in keeping service department costs low.

In Appendix 11A, we discussed *transfer prices* that are charged within an organization when one part of an organization provides a product to another part of the organization. The service department charges considered in this appendix can be viewed as transfer prices that are charged for services provided by service departments to operating departments.

Charging Costs by Behavior

Whenever possible, variable and fixed service department costs should be charged to operating departments separately to provide more useful data for planning and control of departmental operations.

Variable Costs

Variable costs vary in total in proportion to changes in the level of service provided. For example, the cost of food in a cafeteria is a variable cost that varies in proportion to the number of persons using the cafeteria or the number of meals served.

A variable cost should be charged to consuming departments according to whatever activity causes the incurrence of the cost. For example, variable costs of a maintenance department that are caused by the number of machine-hours worked in the operating departments should be charged to the operating departments on the basis of machine-hours. This will ensure that these costs are properly traced to departments, products, and customers.

Fixed Costs

The fixed costs of service departments represent the costs of making capacity available for use. These costs should be charged to consuming departments in *predetermined lump-sum amounts* that are determined in advance and do not change. The lump-sum amount charged to a department can be based either on the department's peak-period or long-run average servicing needs.

The logic behind lump-sum charges of this type is as follows: When a service department is first established, its capacity will be determined by the needs of the departments that it will serve. This capacity may reflect the peak-period needs of the other departments, or it may reflect their long-run average or "normal" servicing needs. Depending on how much servicing capacity is provided for, it will be necessary to make a commitment of resources, which will be reflected in the service department's fixed costs. These fixed costs should be borne by the consuming departments in proportion to the amount of capacity each consuming department requires. That is, if available capacity in the service department has been provided to meet the peak-period needs of consuming departments, then the fixed costs of the service department should be charged in predetermined lump-sum amounts to consuming departments on that basis. If available capacity has been provided only to meet "normal" or long-run average needs, then the fixed costs should be charged on that basis.

Once set, charges should not vary from period to period, because they represent the cost of having a certain level of service capacity available and on line for each operating department. The fact that an operating department does not need the peak level or even the "normal" level of service every period is immaterial; the capacity to deliver this level of service must be available. The operating departments should bear the cost of that availability.

Should Actual or Budgeted Costs Be Charged?

The *budgeted,* rather than actual, costs of a service department should be charged to operating departments. This ensures that service departments remain solely responsible for explaining any differences between their actual and budgeted costs. If service departments could base their charges on actual costs, then operating departments would be unfairly held accountable for cost overruns in the service departments.

Guidelines for Service Department Charges

The following summarizes how service department costs should be charged to operating departments:

- Variable and fixed service department costs should be charged separately.
- Variable service department costs should be charged using a predetermined rate applied to the actual services consumed.
- Fixed costs represent the costs of having service capacity available. These costs should be charged in lump sums to each operating department in proportion to their peak-period needs or long-run average needs. The lump-sum amounts should be based on budgeted fixed costs, not actual fixed costs.

Example

Seaboard Airlines has two operating divisions: a Freight Division and a Passenger Division. The company has a Maintenance Department that services both divisions. Variable servicing costs are budgeted at $10 per flight-hour. The department's fixed costs are budgeted at $750,000 for the year. The fixed costs of the Maintenance Department are budgeted based on the peak-period demand, which occurs during the Thanksgiving to New Year's holiday period. The airline wants to make sure that none of its aircraft are grounded during this key period due to unavailability of maintenance facilities. Approximately 40% of the maintenance during this period is performed on the Freight Division's equipment, and 60% is performed on the Passenger Division's equipment. These figures and the budgeted flight-hours for the coming year are as follows:

	Percent of Peak Period Capacity Required	Budgeted Flight-Hours
Freight Division	40%	9,000
Passenger Division	60	15,000
Total	100%	24,000

Year-end records show that actual variable and fixed costs in the aircraft Maintenance Department for the year were $260,000 and $780,000, respectively. One division logged more flight-hours during the year than planned, and the other division logged fewer flight-hours than planned, as shown below:

	Flight-Hours	
	Budgeted	Actual
Freight Division	9,000	8,000
Passenger Division	15,000	17,000
Total flight-hours	24,000	25,000

The amount of Maintenance Department cost charged to each division for the year would be as follows:

			Actual activity	Division	
				Freight	Passenger
	Variable cost charges:				
Budgeted variable rate →	$10 per flight-hour	×	8,000 flight-hours	$ 80,000	
	$10 per flight-hour	×	17,000 flight-hours		$170,000
	Fixed cost charges:				
Peak-period capacity required →	40%	×	$750,000	300,000	
	60%	×	$750,000		450,000
	Total charges			$380,000	$620,000
			Budgeted fixed cost		

Notice that variable servicing costs are charged to the operating divisions based on the budgeted rate ($10 per hour) and the *actual activity* for the year. In contrast, the charges for fixed costs are based entirely on budgeted data. Also note that the two operating divisions are *not* charged for the actual costs of the service department, which are influenced by how well the service department is managed. Instead, the service department is held responsible for the actual costs not charged to other departments as shown below:

	Variable	Fixed
Total actual costs incurred	$260,000	$780,000
Total charges (above)	250,000*	750,000
Spending variance—responsibility of the Maintenance Department	$ 10,000	$ 30,000

*$10 per flight-hour × 25,000 actual flight-hours = $250,000.

Some Cautions in Allocating Service Department Costs

Pitfalls in Allocating Fixed Costs

Rather than charge fixed costs to operating departments in predetermined lump-sum amounts, some companies allocate them using a *variable* allocation base that fluctuates from period to period. This practice can distort decisions and create serious inequities between departments. The inequities arise from the fact that the fixed costs allocated to one department are heavily influenced by what happens in *other* departments.

Sales dollars is an example of a variable allocation base that is often used to allocate fixed costs from service departments to operating departments. Using sales dollars as a base is simple, straightforward, and easy to work with. Furthermore, people tend to view sales dollars as a measure of ability to pay, and, hence, as a measure of how readily costs can be absorbed from other parts of the organization.

Unfortunately, sales dollars are often a very poor base for allocating or charging costs because sales dollars vary from period to period, whereas the costs are often largely *fixed.* Therefore, a letup in sales effort in one department will shift allocated costs from that department to other, more successful departments. In effect, the departments putting forth the best sales efforts are penalized in the form of higher allocations. The result is often bitterness and resentment on the part of the managers of the better departments.

For example, let's assume that a large men's clothing store has one service department and three sales departments—Suits, Shoes, and Accessories. The service department's costs total $60,000 per period and are allocated to the three sales departments according to sales dollars. A recent period showed the following allocation:

	Departments			
	Suits	Shoes	Accessories	Total
Sales by department	$260,000	$40,000	$100,000	$400,000
Percentage of total sales	65%	10%	25%	100%
Allocation of service department costs, based on percentage of total sales	$39,000	$6,000	$15,000	$60,000

In the following period, let's assume the manager of the Suits Department launched a successful program to expand sales in his department by $100,000. Furthermore, let's assume that sales in the other two departments remained unchanged, total service department costs remained unchanged, and the sales departments' expected usage of service department resources remained unchanged. Given these assumptions, the service department cost allocations to the sales departments would change as shown below:

	Departments			
	Suits	Shoes	Accessories	Total
Sales by department	$360,000	$40,000	$100,000	$500,000
Percentage of total sales	72%	8%	20%	100%
Allocation of service department costs, based on percentage of total sales	$43,200	$4,800	$12,000	$60,000
Increase (or decrease) from prior allocation	$4,200	$(1,200)	$(3,000)	$0

After seeing these allocations, the manager of the Suits Department is likely to complain, because by growing sales in his department, he is being forced to carry a larger share of the service department costs. In essence, this manager is being punished for his outstanding performance by being saddled with a greater proportion of service department costs. On the other hand, the managers of the departments that showed no sales growth are being relieved of a portion of the costs they had been carrying. Yet, there was no change in the amount of services provided for any department across the two periods.

This example shows why a variable allocation base such as sales dollars should only be used as a base for allocating or charging costs in those cases where service department costs actually vary with the chosen allocation base. When service department costs are fixed, they should be charged to operating departments according to the guidelines mentioned earlier.

Glossary (Appendix 11B)

Operating department A department in which the central purposes of the organization are carried out. (p. 519)

Service department A department that does not directly engage in operating activities; rather, it provides services or assistance to the operating departments. (p. 519)

Appendix 11B Exercises and Problems

connect ACCOUNTING

All applicable exercises and problems are available with McGraw-Hill's *Connect™ Accounting*.

EXERCISE 11B–1 Service Department Charges [LO6]

Reed Corporation operates a Medical Services Department for its employees. Charges to the company's operating departments for the variable costs of the Medical Services Department are based on the actual number of employees in each department. Charges for the fixed costs of the Medical Services Department are based on the long-run average number of employees in each operating department.

Variable Medical Services Department costs are budgeted at $60 per employee. Fixed Medical Services Department costs are budgeted at $600,000 per year. Actual Medical Services Department costs for the most recent year were $105,400 for variable costs and $605,000 for fixed costs. Data concerning employees in the three operating departments follow:

	Cutting	Milling	Assembly
Budgeted number of employees	600	300	900
Actual number of employees for the most recent year	500	400	800
Long-run average number of employees	600	400	1,000

Required:

1. Determine the Medical Services Department charges for the year to each of the operating departments—Cutting, Milling, and Assembly.
2. How much, if any, of the actual Medical Services Department costs for the year should not be allocated to the operating departments?

EXERCISE 11B–2 Sales Dollars as an Allocation Base for Fixed Costs [LO6]

Lacey's Department Store allocates its fixed administrative expenses to its four operating departments on the basis of sales dollars. During 2009, the fixed administrative expenses totaled $900,000. These expenses were allocated as follows:

	Men's	Women's	Shoes	Housewares	Total
Total sales—2009	$600,000	$1,500,000	$2,100,000	$1,800,000	$6,000,000
Percentage of total sales	10%	25%	35%	30%	100%
Allocation (based on the above percentages)	$90,000	$225,000	$315,000	$270,000	$900,000

During 2010, the following year, the Women's Department doubled its sales. The sales levels in the other three departments remained unchanged. The company's 2010 sales data were as follows:

	Department				
	Men's	Women's	Shoes	Housewares	Total
Total sales—2010	$600,000	$3,000,000	$2,100,000	$1,800,000	$7,500,000
Percent of total sales	8%	40%	28%	24%	100%

Required:

1. Using sales dollars as an allocation base, show the allocation of the fixed administrative expenses among the four departments for 2010.
2. Compare your allocation from (1) above to the allocation for 2009. As the manager of the Women's Department, how would you feel about the administrative expenses that have been charged to you for 2010?
3. Comment on the usefulness of sales dollars as an allocation base.

EXERCISE 11B–3 Service Department Charges [LO6]

Gutherie Oil Company has a Transport Services Department that provides trucks to transport crude oil from docks to the company's Arbon Refinery and Beck Refinery. Budgeted costs for the transport services consist of $0.30 per gallon variable cost and $200,000 fixed cost. The level of fixed cost is determined by peak-period requirements. During the peak period, Arbon Refinery requires 60% of the capacity and the Beck Refinery requires 40%.

During the year, the Transport Services Department actually hauled the following amounts of crude oil for the two refineries: Arbon Refinery, 260,000 gallons; and Beck Refinery, 140,000 gallons. The Transport Services Department incurred $365,000 in cost during the year, of which $148,000 was variable cost and $217,000 was fixed cost.

Required:

1. Determine how much of the $148,000 in variable cost should be charged to each refinery.
2. Determine how much of the $217,000 in fixed cost should be charged to each refinery.
3. Will any of the $365,000 in the Transport Services Department cost not be charged to the refineries? Explain.

PROBLEM 11B–4 Service Department Charges [LO6]

eXcel

Northstar Company has two operating divisions—Machine Tools and Special Products. The company has a maintenance department that services the equipment in both divisions. The costs of operating the maintenance department are budgeted at $80,000 per month plus $0.50 per machine-hour. The fixed costs of the maintenance department are determined by peak-period requirements. The Machine Tools Division requires 65% of the peak-period capacity, and the Special Products Division requires 35%.

For October, the Machine Tools Division estimated that it would operate at 90,000 machine-hours of activity and the Special Products Division estimated that it would operate at 60,000 machine-hours of activity. However, due to labor unrest and an unexpected strike, the Machine Tools Division worked only 60,000 machine-hours during the month. The Special Products Division worked 60,000 machine-hours as planned.

Cost records in the maintenance department show that actual fixed costs for October totaled $85,000 and that actual variable costs totaled $78,000.

Required:

1. How much maintenance department cost should be charged to each division for October?
2. Assume that the company follows the practice of allocating *all* maintenance department costs incurred each month to the divisions in proportion to the actual machine-hours recorded in each division for the month. On this basis, how much cost would be allocated to each division for October?
3. What criticisms can you make of the allocation method used in part (2) above?
4. If managers of operating departments know that fixed service costs are going to be allocated on the basis of peak-period requirements, what will be their probable strategy as they report their estimate of peak-period requirements to the company's budget committee? As a member of top management, what would you do to neutralize any such strategies?

PROBLEM 11B-5 Service Department Charges [LO6]

Björnson A/S of Norway has only one service department—a cafeteria, in which meals are provided for employees in the company's Milling and Finishing departments. The costs of the cafeteria are all paid by the company as a fringe benefit to its employees. These costs are charged to the Milling and Finishing departments on the basis of meals served to employees in each department. Cost and other data relating to the Cafeteria and to the Milling and Finishing departments for the most recent year are provided below. (The Norwegian unit of currency is the krone, which is indicated below by K.)

Cafeteria:

	Budget	Actual
Variable costs for food	300,000K*	384,000K
Fixed costs	200,000K	215,000K

*Budgeted at 20K per meal served.

Milling and Finishing departments:

	Percent of Peak-Period Capacity Required	Number of Meals Served	
		Budget	Actual
Milling Department	70%	10,000	12,000
Finishing Department	30%	5,000	4,000
Total	100%	15,000	16,000

The level of fixed costs in the Cafeteria is determined by peak-period requirements.

Required:

Management would like data to assist in comparing actual performance to planned performance in the Cafeteria and in the other departments.

1. How much Cafeteria cost should be charged to the Milling Department and to the Finishing Department?
2. Should any portion of the actual Cafeteria costs not be charged to the other departments? If so, compute the amount that should not be charged, and explain why it should not be charged.

Chapter 12

Differential Analysis: The Key to Decision Making

Massaging the Numbers

Building and expanding convention centers appears to be an obsession with politicians. Indeed, billions of dollars are being spent to build or expand convention centers in numerous cities across the United States. Given that trade show attendance across the country has been steadily declining, how do politicians justify these enormous investments? Politicians frequently rely on consultants who produce studies that purport to show a favorable economic impact on the area of a new convention center.

These economic impact studies are bogus in two respects. First, a large portion of the so-called favorable economic impact would be realized by a city even if it did not invest in a new or expanded convention center. For example, Portland, Oregon, voters overwhelmingly opposed spending $82 million to expand their city's convention center. Nonetheless, local politicians proceeded with the project. After completing the expansion, more than 70% of the people spending money at trade shows in Portland were from the Portland area. How much of the money spent by these locals would have been spent in Portland anyway if the convention center had not been expanded? We don't know, but in all likelihood much of this money would have been spent at the zoo, the art museum, the theater, local restaurants, and so on. This portion of the "favorable" economic impact cited by consultants and used by politicians to justify expanding convention centers should be ignored. Second, because the supply of convention centers throughout the United States substantially exceeds demand, convention centers must offer substantial economic incentives, such as waiving rental fees, to attract trade shows. The cost of these concessions, although often excluded from consultants' projections, further erodes the genuine economic viability of building or expanding a convention center. ■

BUSINESS FOCUS

Source: Victoria Murphy, "The Answer Is Always Yes," *Forbes*, February 28, 2005, pp. 82–84.

LEARNING OBJECTIVES

After studying Chapter 12, you should be able to:

LO1 Identify relevant and irrelevant costs and benefits in a decision.

LO2 Prepare an analysis showing whether a product line or other business segment should be added or dropped.

LO3 Prepare a make or buy analysis.

LO4 Prepare an analysis showing whether a special order should be accepted.

LO5 Determine the most profitable use of a constrained resource.

LO6 Determine the value of obtaining more of the constrained resource.

LO7 Prepare an analysis showing whether joint products should be sold at the split-off point or processed further.

Managers must decide what products to sell, whether to make or buy component parts, what prices to charge, what channels of distribution to use, whether to accept special orders at special prices, and so forth. Making such decisions is often a difficult task that is complicated by numerous alternatives and massive amounts of data, only some of which may be relevant.

Every decision involves choosing from among at least two alternatives. In making a decision, the costs and benefits of one alternative must be compared to the costs and benefits of other alternatives. The key to making such comparisons is *differential analysis*—focusing on the costs and benefits that *differ* between the alternatives. Costs that differ between alternatives are called **relevant costs.** Benefits that differ between alternatives are called **relevant benefits.** Distinguishing between relevant and irrelevant costs and benefits is critical for two reasons. First, irrelevant data can be ignored—saving decision makers tremendous amounts of time and effort. Second, bad decisions can easily result from erroneously including irrelevant costs and benefits when analyzing alternatives. To be successful in decision making, managers must be able to tell the difference between relevant and irrelevant data and must be able to correctly use the relevant data in analyzing alternatives. The purpose of this chapter is to develop these skills by illustrating their use in a wide range of decision-making situations. These decision-making skills are as important in your personal life as they are to managers. After completing your study of this chapter, you should be able to think more clearly about decisions in many facets of your life.

Cost Concepts for Decision Making

Identifying Relevant Costs and Benefits

LEARNING OBJECTIVE 1
Identify relevant and irrelevant costs and benefits in a decision.

Only those costs and benefits that differ in total between alternatives are relevant in a decision. If the total amount of a cost will be the same regardless of the alternative selected, then the decision has no effect on the cost, so the cost can be ignored. For example, if you are trying to decide whether to go to a movie or rent a DVD for the evening, the rent on your apartment is irrelevant. Whether you go to a movie or rent a DVD, the rent on your apartment will be exactly the same and is therefore irrelevant to the decision. On the other hand, the cost of the movie ticket and the cost of renting the DVD would be relevant in the decision because they are *avoidable costs.*

An **avoidable cost** is a cost that can be eliminated by choosing one alternative over another. By choosing the alternative of going to the movie, the cost of renting the DVD can be avoided. By choosing the alternative of renting the DVD, the cost of the movie ticket can be avoided. Therefore, the cost of the movie ticket and the cost of renting the DVD are both avoidable costs. On the other hand, the rent on your apartment is not an avoidable cost of either alternative. You would continue to rent your apartment under either alternative. Avoidable costs are relevant costs. Unavoidable costs are irrelevant costs.

To refine the notion of relevant costs a little further, two broad categories of costs are never relevant in decisions—sunk costs and future costs that do not differ between the alternatives. As we learned in Chapter 2, a **sunk cost** is a cost that has already been incurred and cannot be avoided regardless of what a manager decides to do. For example, suppose a used car dealer purchased a five-year-old Toyota Camry for $12,000. The amount paid for the Camry is a sunk cost because it has already been incurred and the transaction cannot be undone. Even though it is perhaps counterintuitive, the amount the dealership paid for the Camry is irrelevant in making decisions such as how much to sell the car for. Sunk costs are always the same no matter what alternatives are being considered; therefore, they are irrelevant and should be ignored when making decisions.

Future costs that do not differ between alternatives should also be ignored. Continuing with the example discussed earlier, suppose you plan to order a pizza after you go to the movie theater or you rent a DVD. If you are going to buy the same pizza regardless of your choice of entertainment, the cost of the pizza is irrelevant to the choice of whether you go to the movie theater or rent a DVD. Notice, the cost of the pizza is not a sunk cost because it has not yet been incurred. Nonetheless, the cost of the pizza is irrelevant to the entertainment decision because it is a future cost that does not differ between the alternatives.

To summarize, only those costs and benefits that differ between alternatives are relevant in a decision. Relevant costs are often called *avoidable costs.* The key to successful decision making is to focus on just these relevant costs and benefits and to ignore everything else—including the sunk costs and future costs and benefits that do not differ between the alternatives.

IN BUSINESS

THE RELEVANT COST OF EXECUTIVE PERKS

The Securities and Exchange Commission is concerned about CEOs who use company-owned airplanes for personal travel. For example, consider a CEO who uses his employers' Gulfstream V luxury airplane to transport his family on a 2,000 mile roundtrip vacation from New York City to Orlando, Florida. The standard practice among companies with personal travel reimbursement policies would be to charge their CEO $1,500 for this flight based on a per-mile reimbursement rate established by the Internal Revenue Service (the IRS rates are meant to approximate the per-mile cost of a first-class ticket on a commercial airline). However, critics argue that using IRS reimbursement rates grossly understates the flight costs that are borne by shareholders. Some of these critics claim that the $11,000 incremental cost of the flight, including fuel, landing fees, and crew hotel charges, should be reimbursed by the CEO. Still others argue that even basing reimbursements on incremental costs understates the true cost of a flight because fixed costs such as the cost of the airplane, crew salaries, and insurance should be included. These costs are relevant because the excessive amount of personal travel by corporate executives essentially requires their companies to purchase, insure, and staff additional airplanes. This latter group of critics argues that the relevant cost of the trip from New York City to Orlando is $43,000—the market price that would have to be paid to charter a comparable size airplane for this flight. What is the relevant cost of this flight? Should shareholders expect their CEO to reimburse $0 (as is the practice at some companies), $1,500, $11,000, or $43,000? Or, should all companies disallow personal use of corporate assets?

Source: Mark Maremont, "Amid Crackdown, the Jet Perk Suddenly Looks a Lot Pricier," *The Wall Street Journal,* May 25, 2005, pp. A1 and A8.

Different Costs for Different Purposes

We need to recognize a fundamental concept from the outset of our discussion—costs that are relevant in one decision situation are not necessarily relevant in another. This means that *managers need different costs for different purposes.* For one purpose, a particular group of costs may be relevant; for another purpose, an entirely different group of costs may be relevant. Thus, *each* decision situation must be carefully analyzed to isolate the relevant costs. Otherwise, irrelevant data may cloud the situation and lead to a bad decision.

The concept of "different costs for different purposes" is basic to managerial accounting; we shall frequently see its application in the pages that follow.

An Example of Identifying Relevant Costs and Benefits

Cynthia is currently a student in an MBA program in Boston and would like to visit a friend in New York City over the weekend. She is trying to decide whether to drive or take the train. Because she is on a tight budget, she wants to carefully consider the costs of the two alternatives. If one alternative is far less expensive than the other, that may be decisive in her choice. By car, the distance between her apartment in Boston and her friend's apartment in New York City is 230 miles. Cynthia has compiled the following list of items to consider:

Automobile Costs

	Item	Annual Cost of Fixed Items	Cost per Mile (based on 10,000 miles per year)
(a)	Annual straight-line depreciation on car [($24,000 original cost − $10,000 estimated resale value in 5 years)/5 years]	$2,800	$0.280
(b)	Cost of gasoline ($2.70 per gallon ÷ 27 miles per gallon)		0.100
(c)	Annual cost of auto insurance and license	$1,380	0.138
(d)	Maintenance and repairs		0.065
(e)	Parking fees at school ($45 per month × 8 months)	$360	0.036
(f)	Total average cost per mile		$0.619

Additional Data

	Item	
(g)	Reduction in the resale value of car due solely to wear and tear	$0.026 per mile
(h)	Cost of round-trip train ticket from Boston to New York City	$104
(i)	Benefit of relaxing and being able to study during the train ride rather than having to drive	?
(j)	Cost of putting the dog in a kennel while gone	$40
(k)	Benefit of having a car available in New York City	?
(l)	Hassle of parking the car in New York City	?
(m)	Cost of parking the car in New York City	$25 per day

Which costs and benefits are relevant in this decision? Remember, only those costs and benefits that differ between alternatives are relevant. Everything else is irrelevant and can be ignored.

Start at the top of the list with item (a): the original cost of the car is a sunk cost. This cost has already been incurred and therefore can never differ between alternatives. Consequently, it is irrelevant and should be ignored. The same is true of the accounting depreciation of $2,800 per year, which simply spreads the sunk cost across five years.

Item (b), the cost of gasoline consumed by driving to New York City, is a relevant cost. If Cynthia takes the train, this cost would not be incurred. Hence, the cost differs between alternatives and is therefore relevant.

Item (c), the annual cost of auto insurance and license, is not relevant. Whether Cynthia takes the train or drives on this particular trip, her annual auto insurance premium and her auto license fee will remain the same.[1]

[1] If Cynthia has an accident while driving to New York City or back, this might affect her insurance premium when the policy is renewed. The increase in the insurance premium would be a relevant cost of this particular trip, but the normal amount of the insurance premium is not relevant in any case.

Item (d), the cost of maintenance and repairs, is relevant. While maintenance and repair costs have a large random component, over the long run they should be more or less proportional to the number of miles the car is driven. Thus, the average cost of $0.065 per mile is a reasonable estimate to use.

Item (e), the monthly fee that Cynthia pays to park at her school during the academic year is not relevant. Regardless of which alternative she selects—driving or taking the train—she will still need to pay for parking at school.

Item (f) is the total average cost of $0.619 per mile. As discussed above, some elements of this total are relevant, but some are not relevant. Because it contains some irrelevant costs, it would be incorrect to estimate the cost of driving to New York City and back by simply multiplying the $0.619 by 460 miles (230 miles each way × 2). This erroneous approach would yield a cost of driving of $284.74. Unfortunately, such mistakes are often made in both personal life and in business. Because the total cost is stated on a per-mile basis, people are easily misled. Often people think that if the cost is stated as $0.619 per mile, the cost of driving 100 miles is $61.90. But it is not. Many of the costs included in the $0.619 cost per mile are sunk and/or fixed and will not increase if the car is driven another 100 miles. The $0.619 is an average cost, not an incremental cost. Beware of such unitized costs (i.e., costs stated in terms of a dollar amount per unit, per mile, per direct labor-hour, per machine-hour, and so on)—they are often misleading.

Item (g), the decline in the resale value of the car that occurs as a consequence of driving more miles, is relevant in the decision. Because she uses the car, its resale value declines, which is a real cost of using the car that should be taken into account. Cynthia estimated this cost by accessing the *Kelly Blue Book* website at www.kbb.com. The reduction in resale value of an asset through use or over time is often called *real* or *economic depreciation.* This is different from accounting depreciation, which attempts to match the sunk cost of an asset with the periods that benefit from that cost.

Item (h), the $104 cost of a round-trip ticket on the train, is relevant in this decision. If she drives, she would not have to buy the ticket.

Item (i) is relevant to the decision, even if it is difficult to put a dollar value on relaxing and being able to study while on the train. It is relevant because it is a benefit that is available under one alternative but not under the other.

Item (j), the cost of putting Cynthia's dog in the kennel while she is gone, is irrelevant in this decision. Whether she takes the train or drives to New York City, she will still need to put her dog in a kennel.

Like item (i), items (k) and (l) are relevant to the decision even if it is difficult to measure their dollar impacts.

Item (m), the cost of parking in New York City, is relevant to the decision.

Bringing together all of the relevant data, Cynthia would estimate the relevant costs of driving and taking the train as follows:

Relevant financial cost of driving to New York City:	
Gasoline (460 miles × $0.100 per mile)	$ 46.00
Maintenance and repairs (460 miles × $0.065 per mile)	29.90
Reduction in the resale value of car due solely to wear and tear (460 miles × $0.026 per mile)	11.96
Cost of parking the car in New York City (2 days × $25 per day)	50.00
Total	$137.86
Relevant financial cost of taking the train to New York City:	
Cost of round-trip train ticket from Boston to New York City	$104.00

What should Cynthia do? From a purely financial standpoint, it would be cheaper by $33.86 ($137.86 − $104.00) to take the train than to drive. Cynthia has to decide if the convenience of having a car in New York City outweighs the additional cost and the disadvantages of being unable to relax and study on the train and the hassle of finding parking in the city.

In this example, we focused on identifying the relevant costs and benefits—everything else was ignored. In the next example, we include all of the costs and benefits—relevant or not. Nonetheless, we'll still get the correct answer because the irrelevant costs and benefits will cancel out when we compare the alternatives.

IN BUSINESS

DELL STUMBLES DUE TO POOR CUSTOMER SERVICE

Dell Inc. decided to cut customer service costs by shifting most of its call centers overseas and staffing them with temporary workers who were rewarded for minimizing the length of customer calls. The unintended consequences of Dell's choices were predictable—the number of angry repeat callers skyrocketed and the company's customer satisfaction and "likely to repurchase" survey scores plummeted.

Fearful that unhappy customers would take their business elsewhere, Dell spent $150 million to hire thousands of full-time call center employees in North America. The company also began rewarding these employees based on how well they solved callers' problems. These changes paid off as Dell began receiving two million fewer customer service calls per quarter. Customer satisfaction and "likely to repurchase" scores rose substantially.

Dell's experience highlights the danger of overemphasizing cost cutting while overlooking the revenues that may be lost due to customer dissatisfaction.

Source: David Kirkpatrick, "Dell in the Penalty Box," *Fortune*, September 18, 2006, pp. 70–78.

Reconciling the Total and Differential Approaches

Oak Harbor Woodworks is considering a new labor-saving machine that rents for $3,000 per year. The machine will be used on the company's butcher block production line. Data concerning the company's annual sales and costs of butcher blocks with and without the new machine are shown below:

	Current Situation	Situation with the New Machine
Units produced and sold	5,000	5,000
Selling price per unit	$40	$40
Direct materials cost per unit	$14	$14
Direct labor cost per unit	$8	$5
Variable overhead cost per unit	$2	$2
Fixed costs, other	$62,000	$62,000
Fixed costs, rental of new machine	—	$3,000

Given the data above, the net operating income for the product under the two alternatives can be computed as shown in Exhibit 12–1.

Note that the net operating income is $12,000 higher with the new machine, so that is the better alternative. Note also that the $12,000 advantage for the new machine can be obtained in two different ways. It is the difference between the $30,000 net operating income with the new machine and the $18,000 net operating income for the current situation. It is also the sum of the differential costs and benefits as shown in the last column of Exhibit 12–1. A positive number in the Differential Costs and Benefits column indicates that the difference between the alternatives favors the new machine; a negative number indicates that the difference favors the current situation. A zero in that column simply means that the total amount for the item is exactly the same for both alternatives. Thus, because the difference in the net operating incomes equals the sum of the differences for the individual items, any cost or benefit that is the same for both alternatives will have no impact on which alternative is preferred. This is the reason that costs and benefits that do not differ between alternatives are irrelevant and can be ignored. If we properly account for them, they will cancel out when we compare the alternatives.

EXHIBIT 12–1
Total and Differential Costs

	Current Situation	Situation with New Machine	Differential Costs and Benefits
Sales (5,000 units × $40 per unit)	$200,000	$200,000	$ 0
Variable expenses:			
Direct materials (5,000 units × $14 per unit)	70,000	70,000	0
Direct labor (5,000 units × $8 per unit; 5,000 units × $5 per unit)	40,000	25,000	15,000
Variable overhead (5,000 units × $2 per unit)	10,000	10,000	0
Total variable expenses	120,000	105,000	
Contribution margin	80,000	95,000	
Fixed expenses:			
Other	62,000	62,000	0
Rental of new machine	0	3,000	(3,000)
Total fixed expenses	62,000	65,000	
Net operating income	$ 18,000	$ 30,000	$12,000

We could have arrived at the same solution much more quickly by completely ignoring the irrelevant costs and benefits.

- The selling price per unit and the number of units sold do not differ between the alternatives. Therefore, the total sales revenues are exactly the same for the two alternatives as shown in Exhibit 12–1. Because the sales revenues are exactly the same, they have no effect on the difference in net operating income between the two alternatives. That is shown in the last column in Exhibit 12–1, which shows a $0 differential benefit.
- The direct materials cost per unit, the variable overhead cost per unit, and the number of units produced and sold do not differ between the alternatives. Consequently, the total direct materials cost and the total variable overhead cost are the same for the two alternatives and can be ignored.
- The "other" fixed expenses do not differ between the alternatives, so they can be ignored as well.

Indeed, the only costs that do differ between the alternatives are direct labor costs and the fixed rental cost of the new machine. Hence, the two alternatives can be compared based only on these relevant costs:

Net Advantage of Renting the New Machine	
Decrease in direct labor costs (5,000 units at a cost savings of $3 per unit)	$15,000
Increase in fixed expenses	(3,000)
Net annual cost savings from renting the new machine	$12,000

If we focus on just the relevant costs and benefits, we get exactly the same answer as when we listed all of the costs and benefits—including those that do not differ between the alternatives and, hence, are irrelevant. We get the same answer because the only costs and benefits that matter in the final comparison of the net operating incomes are those that differ between the two alternatives and, hence, are not zero in the last column of Exhibit 12–1. Those two relevant costs are both listed in the above analysis showing the net advantage of renting the new machine.

Why Isolate Relevant Costs?

In the preceding example, we used two different approaches to analyze the alternatives. First, we considered all costs, both those that were relevant and those that were not; and second, we considered only the relevant costs. We obtained the same answer under both approaches. It would be natural to ask, "Why bother to isolate relevant costs when total costs will do the job just as well?" Isolating relevant costs is desirable for at least two reasons.

First, only rarely will enough information be available to prepare a detailed income statement for both alternatives. Assume, for example, that you are called on to make a decision relating to a portion of a single business process in a multidepartmental, multiproduct company. Under these circumstances, it would be virtually impossible to prepare an income statement of any type. You would have to rely on your ability to recognize which costs are relevant and which are not in order to assemble the data necessary to make a decision.

Second, mingling irrelevant costs with relevant costs may cause confusion and distract attention from the information that is really critical. Furthermore, the danger always exists that an irrelevant piece of data may be used improperly, resulting in an incorrect decision. The best approach is to ignore irrelevant data and base the decision entirely on relevant data.

Relevant cost analysis, combined with the contribution approach to the income statement, provides a powerful tool for making decisions. We will investigate various uses of this tool in the remaining sections of this chapter.

IN BUSINESS

ENVIRONMENTAL COSTS ADD UP

A decision analysis can be flawed by incorrectly including irrelevant costs such as sunk costs and future costs that do not differ between alternatives. It can also be flawed by omitting future costs that *do* differ between alternatives. This is a problem particularly with environmental costs because they have dramatically increased in recent years and are often overlooked by managers.

Consider the environmental complications posed by a decision of whether to install a solvent-based or powder-based system for spray-painting parts. In a solvent painting system, parts are sprayed as they move along a conveyor. The paint that misses the part is swept away by a wall of water, called a water curtain. The excess paint accumulates in a pit as sludge that must be removed each month. Environmental regulations classify this sludge as hazardous waste. As a result, a permit must be obtained to produce the waste and meticulous records must be maintained of how the waste is transported, stored, and disposed of. The annual costs of complying with these regulations can easily exceed $140,000 in total for a painting facility that initially costs only $400,000 to build. The costs of complying with environmental regulations include the following:

- The waste sludge must be hauled to a special disposal site. The typical disposal fee is about $55,000 per year for a modest solvent-based painting system.
- Workers must be specially trained to handle the paint sludge.
- The company must carry special insurance.
- The company must pay substantial fees to the state for releasing pollutants (i.e., the solvent) into the air.
- The water in the water curtain must be specially treated to remove contaminants. This can cost tens of thousands of dollars per year.

In contrast, a powder-based painting system avoids almost all of these environmental costs. Excess powder used in the painting process can be recovered and reused without creating hazardous waste. Additionally, the powder-based system does not release contaminants into the atmosphere. Therefore, even though the cost of building a powder-based system may be higher than the cost of building a solvent-based system, over the long run the costs of the powder-based system may be far lower due to the high environmental costs of a solvent-based system. Managers need to be aware of such environmental costs and take them fully into account when making decisions.

Source: Germain Böer, Margaret Curtin, and Louis Hoyt, "Environmental Cost Management," *Management Accounting*, volume 80, issue 3, pp. 28–38.

Adding and Dropping Product Lines and Other Segments

LEARNING OBJECTIVE 2
Prepare an analysis showing whether a product line or other business segment should be added or dropped.

Decisions relating to whether product lines or other segments of a company should be dropped and new ones added are among the most difficult that a manager has to make. In such decisions, many qualitative and quantitative factors must be considered. Ultimately, however, any final decision to drop a business segment or to add a new one hinges primarily on the impact the decision will have on net operating income. To assess this impact, costs must be carefully analyzed.

An Illustration of Cost Analysis

Exhibit 12–2 provides sales and cost information for the preceding month for the Discount Drug Company and its three major product lines—drugs, cosmetics, and housewares. A quick review of this exhibit suggests that dropping the housewares segment would increase the company's overall net operating income by $8,000. However, this would be a flawed conclusion because the data in Exhibit 12–2 do not distinguish between fixed expenses that can be avoided if a product line is dropped and common fixed expenses that cannot be avoided by dropping any particular product line.

In this scenario, the two alternatives under consideration are keeping the housewares product line and dropping the housewares product line. Therefore, only those costs that differ between these two alternatives (i.e., that can be avoided by dropping the housewares product line) are relevant. In deciding whether to drop housewares, it is crucial to identify which costs can be avoided, and hence are relevant to the decision, and which costs cannot be avoided, and hence are irrelevant. The decision should be analyzed as follows.

If the housewares line is dropped, then the company will lose $20,000 per month in contribution margin, but by dropping the line it may be possible to avoid some fixed costs such as salaries or advertising costs. If dropping the housewares line enables the company to avoid more in fixed costs than it loses in contribution margin, then its overall net operating income will improve by eliminating the product line. On the other hand, if the company is not able to avoid as much in fixed costs as it loses in contribution margin, then the housewares line should be kept. In short, the manager should ask, "What costs can I avoid if I drop this product line?"

As we have seen from our earlier discussion, not all costs are avoidable. For example, some of the costs associated with a product line may be sunk costs. Other costs may be allocated fixed costs that will not differ in total regardless of whether the product line is dropped or retained.

EXHIBIT 12–2
Discount Drug Company Product Lines

		Product Line		
	Total	Drugs	Cosmetics	Housewares
Sales	$250,000	$125,000	$75,000	$50,000
Variable expenses	105,000	50,000	25,000	30,000
Contribution margin	145,000	75,000	50,000	20,000
Fixed expenses:				
Salaries	50,000	29,500	12,500	8,000
Advertising	15,000	1,000	7,500	6,500
Utilities	2,000	500	500	1,000
Depreciation—fixtures	5,000	1,000	2,000	2,000
Rent	20,000	10,000	6,000	4,000
Insurance	3,000	2,000	500	500
General administrative	30,000	15,000	9,000	6,000
Total fixed expenses	125,000	59,000	38,000	28,000
Net operating income (loss)	$ 20,000	$ 16,000	$12,000	$ (8,000)

To show how to proceed in a product-line analysis, suppose that Discount Drug Company has analyzed the fixed costs being charged to the three product lines and determined the following:

1. The salaries expense represents salaries paid to employees working directly on the product. All of the employees working in housewares would be discharged if the product line is dropped.
2. The advertising expense represents advertisements that are specific to each product line and are avoidable if the line is dropped.
3. The utilities expense represents utilities costs for the entire company. The amount charged to each product line is an allocation based on space occupied and is not avoidable if the product line is dropped.
4. The depreciation expense represents depreciation on fixtures used to display the various product lines. Although the fixtures are nearly new, they are custom-built and will have no resale value if the housewares line is dropped.
5. The rent expense represents rent on the entire building housing the company; it is allocated to the product lines on the basis of sales dollars. The monthly rent of $20,000 is fixed under a long-term lease agreement.
6. The insurance expense is for insurance carried on inventories within each of the three product lines. If housewares is dropped, the related inventories will be liquidated and the insurance premiums will decrease proportionately.
7. The general administrative expense represents the costs of accounting, purchasing, and general management, which are allocated to the product lines on the basis of sales dollars. These costs will not change if the housewares line is dropped.

With this information, management can determine that $15,000 of the fixed expenses associated with the housewares product line are avoidable and $13,000 are not:

Fixed Expenses	Total Cost Assigned to Housewares	Not Avoidable*	Avoidable
Salaries	$ 8,000		$ 8,000
Advertising	6,500		6,500
Utilities	1,000	$ 1,000	
Depreciation—fixtures	2,000	2,000	
Rent	4,000	4,000	
Insurance	500		500
General administrative	6,000	6,000	
Total	$28,000	$13,000	$15,000

*These fixed costs represent either sunk costs or future costs that will not change whether the housewares line is retained or discontinued.

As stated earlier, if the housewares product line were dropped, the company would lose the product's contribution margin of $20,000, but would save its associated avoidable fixed expenses. We now know that those avoidable fixed expenses total $15,000. Therefore, dropping the housewares product line would result in a $5,000 *reduction* in net operating income as shown below:

Contribution margin lost if the housewares line is discontinued (see Exhibit 12–2)	$(20,000)
Less fixed costs that can be avoided if the housewares line is discontinued (see above)	15,000
Decrease in overall company net operating income	$ (5,000)

EXHIBIT 12–3
A Comparative Format for Product-Line Analysis

	Keep Housewares	Drop Housewares	Difference: Net Operating Income Increase (or Decrease)
Sales	$50,000	$ 0	$(50,000)
Variable expenses	30,000	0	30,000
Contribution margin	20,000	0	(20,000)
Fixed expenses:			
Salaries	8,000	0	8,000
Advertising	6,500	0	6,500
Utilities	1,000	1,000	0
Depreciation—fixtures	2,000	2,000	0
Rent	4,000	4,000	0
Insurance	500	0	500
General administrative	6,000	6,000	0
Total fixed expenses	28,000	13,000	15,000
Net operating loss	$ (8,000)	$(13,000)	$ (5,000)

In this case, the fixed costs that can be avoided by dropping the housewares product line ($15,000) are less than the contribution margin that will be lost ($20,000). Therefore, based on the data given, the housewares line should not be discontinued unless a more profitable use can be found for the floor and counter space that it is occupying.

A Comparative Format

This decision can also be approached by preparing comparative income statements showing the effects of either keeping or dropping the product line. Exhibit 12–3 contains such an analysis for the Discount Drug Company. As shown in the last column of the exhibit, if the housewares line is dropped, then overall company net operating income will decrease by $5,000 each period. This is the same answer, of course, as we obtained when we focused just on the lost contribution margin and avoidable fixed costs.

Beware of Allocated Fixed Costs

Go back to Exhibit 12–2. Does this exhibit suggest that the housewares product line should be kept—as we have just concluded? No, it does not. Exhibit 12–2 suggests that the housewares product line is losing money. Why keep a product line that is showing a loss? The explanation for this apparent inconsistency lies in part with the common fixed costs that are being allocated to the product lines. As we observed in Chapter 6, one of the great dangers in allocating common fixed costs is that such allocations can make a product line (or other business segment) look less profitable than it really is. In this instance, allocating the common fixed costs among all product lines makes the housewares product line appear to be unprofitable. However, as we have shown above, dropping the product line would result in a decrease in the company's overall net operating income. This point can be seen clearly if we redo Exhibit 12–2 by eliminating the allocation of the common fixed costs. Exhibit 12–4 uses the segmented approach from Chapter 6 to estimate the profitability of the product lines.

Exhibit 12–4 gives us a much different perspective of the housewares line than does Exhibit 12–2. As shown in Exhibit 12–4, the housewares line is covering all of its own traceable fixed costs and generating a $3,000 segment margin toward covering the common fixed costs of the company. Unless another product line can be found that will generate a segment margin greater than $3,000, the company would be better off keeping the housewares line. By keeping the product line, the company's overall net operating income will be higher than if the product line were dropped.

EXHIBIT 12–4
Discount Drug Company Product Lines—Recast in Contribution Format (from Exhibit 12–2)

		Product Line		
	Total	Drugs	Cosmetics	House-wares
Sales	$250,000	$125,000	$75,000	$50,000
Variable expenses	105,000	50,000	25,000	30,000
Contribution margin	145,000	75,000	50,000	20,000
Traceable fixed expenses:				
Salaries	50,000	29,500	12,500	8,000
Advertising	15,000	1,000	7,500	6,500
Depreciation—fixtures	5,000	1,000	2,000	2,000
Insurance	3,000	2,000	500	500
Total traceable fixed expenses	73,000	33,500	22,500	17,000
Product-line segment margin	72,000	$ 41,500	$27,500	$ 3,000*
Common fixed expenses:				
Utilities	2,000			
Rent	20,000			
General administrative	30,000			
Total common fixed expenses	52,000			
Net operating income	$ 20,000			

*If the housewares line is dropped, the company will lose the $3,000 segment margin generated by this product line. In addition, we have seen that the $2,000 depreciation on the fixtures is a sunk cost that cannot be avoided. The sum of these two figures ($3,000 + $2,000 = $5,000) would be the decrease in the company's overall profits if the housewares line were discontinued. Of course, the company may later choose to drop the product if circumstances change—such as a pending decision to replace the fixtures.

Additionally, managers may choose to retain an unprofitable product line if the line helps sell other products, or if it serves as a "magnet" to attract customers. Bread, for example, may not be an especially profitable line in some food stores, but customers expect it to be available, and many of them would undoubtedly shift their buying elsewhere if a particular store decided to stop carrying it.

IN BUSINESS

POOR ECONOMY LEADS TO SEGMENT DISCONTINUATIONS

When the economy declines, many companies must decide whether to retain or discontinue struggling products and services. For example, Condé Nast Publications reacted to a steep drop in advertising revenues by cutting 180 jobs and discontinuing four magazines—*Gourmet, Modern Bride, Elegant Bride,* and *Cookie.* It also cut the budgets of its remaining magazines by 20–25%. Pioneer Corp.'s annual plasma television sales dropped from 460,000 units to 290,000 units. The company responded to its shrinking customer demand by cutting thousands of jobs and withdrawing from the plasma television business.

Sources: Russell Adams, "Ax Falls on Four Condé Nast Titles," *The Wall Street Journal,* October 6, 2009, p. B1; and Daisuke Wakabayashi, "Pioneer Unplugs Its TV Business," *The Wall Street Journal,* February 13, 2009, p. B1.

The Make or Buy Decision

LEARNING OBJECTIVE 3
Prepare a make or buy analysis.

Providing a product or service to a customer involves many steps. For example, consider all of the steps that are necessary to develop and sell a product such as tax preparation software in retail stores. First the software must be developed, which involves highly skilled software engineers and a great deal of project management effort. Then the product must be put into a form that can be delivered to customers. This involves burning the application onto a blank CD or DVD, applying a label, and packaging the result in an attractive box. Then the product must be distributed to retail stores. Then the product must be sold. And finally, help lines and other forms of after-sale service may have to be provided. And we should not forget that the blank CD or DVD, the label, and the box must of course be made by someone before any of this can happen. All of these activities, from development, to production, to after-sales service are called a *value chain.*

Separate companies may carry out each of the activities in the value chain or a single company may carry out several. When a company is involved in more than one activity in the entire value chain, it is **vertically integrated.** Some companies control all of the activities in the value chain from producing basic raw materials right up to the final distribution of finished goods and provision of after-sales service. Other companies are content to integrate on a smaller scale by purchasing many of the parts and materials that go into their finished products. A decision to carry out one of the activities in the value chain internally, rather than to buy externally from a supplier, is called a **make or buy decision.** Quite often these decisions involve whether to buy a particular part or to make it internally. Make or buy decisions also involve decisions concerning whether to outsource development tasks, after-sales service, or other activities.

Strategic Aspects of the Make or Buy Decision

Vertical integration provides certain advantages. An integrated company is less dependent on its suppliers and may be able to ensure a smoother flow of parts and materials for production than a nonintegrated company. For example, a strike against a major parts supplier can interrupt the operations of a nonintegrated company for many months, whereas an integrated company that is producing its own parts would be able to continue operations. Also, some companies feel that they can control quality better by producing their own parts and materials, rather than by relying on the quality control standards of outside suppliers. In addition, an integrated company realizes profits from the parts and materials that it is "making" rather than "buying," as well as profits from its regular operations.

The advantages of vertical integration are counterbalanced by the advantages of using external suppliers. By pooling demand from a number of companies, a supplier may be able to enjoy economies of scale. These economies of scale can result in higher quality and lower costs than would be possible if the company were to attempt to make the parts or provide the service on its own. A company must be careful, however, to retain control over activities that are essential to maintaining its competitive position. For example, Hewlett-Packard controls the software for laser printers that it makes in cooperation with Canon Inc. of Japan. The present trend appears to be toward less vertical integration, with companies like Sun Microsystems and Hewlett-Packard concentrating on hardware and software design and relying on outside suppliers for almost everything else in the value chain. These factors suggest that the make or buy decision should be weighed very carefully.

IN BUSINESS

CESSNA OUTSOURCES AIRPLANE CONSTRUCTION TO CHINA

Cessna Aircraft Company hired China's state-owned Shenyang Aircraft Corporation to produce its new 162 SkyCatcher aircraft. While Boeing and Airbus have used Chinese manufacturers for component parts, Cessna is the first company to turn over the complete production of an airplane to a Chinese company. Cessna hopes that buying the planes from a Chinese partner will provide cost savings that enable it to sell the plane for $71,000 less than if the plane were made at its plant in Wichita, Kansas. Cessna expects to sell the first 1,000 SkyCatchers for $109,500, whereas the company's least expensive model manufactured in Wichita sells for $219,500. What are some of the risks that accompany Cessna's decision to outsource production to China?

Source: J. Lynn Lunsford, "Cessna's New Plane to Be Built in China," *The Wall Street Journal*, November 28, 2007, p. A14.

An Example of Make or Buy

To provide an illustration of a make or buy decision, consider Mountain Goat Cycles. The company is now producing the heavy-duty gear shifters used in its most popular line of mountain bikes. The company's Accounting Department reports the following costs of producing 8,000 units of the shifter internally each year:

	Per Unit	8,000 Units
Direct materials	$ 6	$ 48,000
Direct labor	4	32,000
Variable overhead	1	8,000
Supervisor's salary	3	24,000
Depreciation of special equipment	2	16,000
Allocated general overhead	5	40,000
Total cost	$21	$168,000

An outside supplier has offered to sell 8,000 shifters a year to Mountain Goat Cycles at a price of only $19 each. Should the company stop producing the shifters internally and buy them from the outside supplier? As always, the focus should be on the relevant costs—those that differ between the alternatives. And the costs that differ between the alternatives consist of the costs that could be avoided by purchasing the shifters from the outside supplier. If the costs that can be avoided by purchasing the shifters from the outside supplier total less than $19, then the company should continue to manufacture its own shifters and reject the outside supplier's offer. On the other hand, if the costs that can be avoided by purchasing the shifters from the outside supplier total more than $19, the outside supplier's offer should be accepted.

Note that depreciation of special equipment is listed as one of the costs of producing the shifters internally. Because the equipment has already been purchased, this depreciation is a sunk cost and is therefore irrelevant. If the equipment could be sold, its salvage value would be relevant. Or if the machine could be used to make other products, this could be relevant as well. However, we will assume that the equipment has no salvage value and that it has no other use except making the heavy-duty gear shifters.

Also note that the company is allocating a portion of its general overhead costs to the shifters. Any portion of this general overhead cost that would actually be eliminated if the gear shifters were purchased rather than made would be relevant in the analysis. However, it is likely that the general overhead costs allocated to the gear shifters are in fact common to all items produced in the factory and would continue unchanged even if the shifters were purchased from the outside. Such allocated common costs are not relevant costs (because they do not differ between the make or buy alternatives) and should be eliminated from the analysis along with the sunk costs.

EXHIBIT 12–5
Mountain Goat Cycles Make or Buy Analysis

	Total Relevant Costs—8,000 units	
	Make	Buy
Direct materials (8,000 units × \$6 per unit)	\$ 48,000	
Direct labor (8,000 units × \$4 per unit)	32,000	
Variable overhead (8,000 units × \$1 per unit)	8,000	
Supervisor's salary	24,000	
Depreciation of special equipment (not relevant)		
Allocated general overhead (not relevant)		
Outside purchase price		\$152,000
Total cost	\$112,000	\$152,000
Difference in favor of continuing to make	\$40,000	

The variable costs of producing the shifters can be avoided by buying the shifters from the outside supplier so they are relevant costs. We will assume in this case that the variable costs include direct materials, direct labor, and variable overhead. The supervisor's salary is also relevant if it could be avoided by buying the shifters. Exhibit 12–5 contains the relevant cost analysis of the make or buy decision assuming that the supervisor's salary can indeed be avoided.

Because it costs \$40,000 less to make the shifters internally than to buy them from the outside supplier, Mountain Goat Cycles should reject the outside supplier's offer. However, the company may wish to consider one additional factor before coming to a final decision—the opportunity cost of the space now being used to produce the shifters.

IN BUSINESS

OUTSOURCING TASKS RATHER THAN JOBS

Pfizer saved 4,000 of its managers 66,500 hours of work by enabling them to outsource their tedious, time-consuming tasks to companies in India. With the click of a mouse the managers go to a website called PfizerWorks to prepare online work orders for services such as Powerpoint slide preparation, spreadsheet preparation, or basic market research. The requests are sent overseas and completed by a services-outsourcing firm. This outsourcing enables Pfizer's managers to spend their time on higher value work such as motivating teams, creating new products, and strategy formulation.

Source: Jena McGregor, "The Chore Goes Offshore," *BusinessWeek*, March 23 & 30, 2009, p. 50–51.

Opportunity Cost

If the space now being used to produce the shifters *would otherwise be idle*, then Mountain Goat Cycles should continue to produce its own shifters and the supplier's offer should be rejected, as stated above. Idle space that has no alternative use has an opportunity cost of zero.

But what if the space now being used to produce shifters could be used for some other purpose? In that case, the space would have an opportunity cost equal to the segment margin that could be derived from the best alternative use of the space.

To illustrate, assume that the space now being used to produce shifters could be used to produce a new cross-country bike that would generate a segment margin of \$60,000 per year. Under these conditions, Mountain Goat Cycles should accept the supplier's offer and use the available space to produce the new product line:

	Make	Buy
Total annual cost (see Exhibit 12–5)	$112,000	$152,000
Opportunity cost—segment margin forgone on a potential new product line	60,000	
Total cost	$172,000	$152,000
Difference in favor of purchasing from the outside supplier	$20,000	

Opportunity costs are not recorded in the organization's general ledger because they do not represent actual dollar outlays. Rather, they represent economic benefits that are *forgone* as a result of pursuing some course of action. The opportunity cost for Mountain Goat Cycles is sufficiently large in this case to change the decision.

IN BUSINESS

TOUGH CHOICES

Brad and Carole Karafil own and operate White Grizzly Adventures, a snowcat skiing and snowboarding company in Meadow Creek, British Columbia. While rare, it does sometimes happen that the company is unable to operate due to bad weather. Guests are housed and fed, but no one can ski. The contract signed by each guest stipulates that no refund is given in the case of an unavoidable cancellation that is beyond the control of the operators. So technically, Brad and Carole are not obligated to provide any refund if they must cancel operations due to bad weather. However, 70% of their guests are repeat customers and a guest who has paid roughly $300 a day to ski is likely to be unhappy if skiing is canceled even though it is no fault of White Grizzly.

What costs, if any, are saved if skiing is cancelled and the snowcat does not operate? Not much. Guests are still housed and fed and the guides, who are independent contractors, are still paid. Some snowcat operating costs are avoided, but little else. Therefore, there would be little cost savings to pass on to guests.

Brad and Carole could issue a credit to be used for one day of skiing at another time. If a customer with such a credit occupied a seat on a snowcat that would otherwise be empty, the only significant cost to Brad and Carole would be the cost of feeding the customer. However, an empty seat basically doesn't exist—the demand for seats far exceeds the supply and the schedule is generally fully booked far in advance of the ski season. Consequently, the real cost of issuing a credit for one day of skiing is high. Brad and Carole would be giving up $300 from a paying customer for every guest they issue a credit voucher to. Issuing a credit voucher involves an opportunity cost of $300 in forgone sales revenues.

What would you do if you had to cancel skiing due to bad weather? Would you issue a refund or a credit voucher, losing money in the process, or would you risk losing customers? It's a tough choice.

Source: Brad and Carole Karafil, owners and operators of White Grizzly Adventures, www.whitegrizzly.com.

Special Orders

LEARNING OBJECTIVE 4
Prepare an analysis showing whether a special order should be accepted.

Managers must often evaluate whether a *special order* should be accepted, and if the order is accepted, the price that should be charged. A **special order** is a one-time order that is not considered part of the company's normal ongoing business. To illustrate, Mountain Goat Cycles has just received a request from the Seattle Police Department to produce 100 specially modified mountain bikes at a price of $558 each. The bikes would be used to patrol some of the more densely populated residential sections of the city. Mountain Goat Cycles can easily modify its City Cruiser model to fit the specifications of the Seattle Police. The normal selling price of the City Cruiser bike is $698, and its unit product cost is $564 as shown below:

Direct materials	$372
Direct labor	90
Manufacturing overhead	102
Unit product cost	$564

The variable portion of the above manufacturing overhead is $12 per unit. The order would have no effect on the company's total fixed manufacturing overhead costs.

The modifications requested by the Seattle Police Department consist of welded brackets to hold radios, nightsticks, and other gear. These modifications would require $34 in incremental variable costs. In addition, the company would have to pay a graphics design studio $2,400 to design and cut stencils that would be used for spray painting the Seattle Police Department's logo and other identifying marks on the bikes.

This order should have no effect on the company's other sales. The production manager says that she can handle the special order without disrupting any of the company's regular scheduled production.

What effect would accepting this order have on the company's net operating income?

Only the incremental costs and benefits are relevant. Because the existing fixed manufacturing overhead costs would not be affected by the order, they are not relevant. The incremental net operating income can be computed as follows:

	Per Unit	Total 100 Bikes
Incremental revenue	$558	$55,800
Less incremental costs:		
Variable costs:		
Direct materials	372	37,200
Direct labor	90	9,000
Variable manufacturing overhead	12	1,200
Special modifications	34	3,400
Total variable cost	$508	50,800
Fixed cost:		
Purchase of stencils		2,400
Total incremental cost		53,200
Incremental net operating income		$ 2,600

Therefore, even though the $558 price on the special order is below the normal $564 unit product cost and the order would require additional costs, the order would increase net operating income. In general, a special order is profitable if the incremental revenue from the special order exceeds the incremental costs of the order. However, it is important to make sure that there is indeed idle capacity and that the special order does not cut into normal unit sales or undercut prices on normal sales. For example, if the company was operating at capacity, opportunity costs would have to be taken into account, as well as the incremental costs that have already been detailed above.

Utilization of a Constrained Resource

LEARNING OBJECTIVE 5
Determine the most profitable use of a constrained resource.

Managers routinely face the problem of deciding how constrained resources are going to be used. A department store, for example, has a limited amount of floor space and therefore cannot stock every product that may be available. A manufacturer has a limited number of machine-hours and a limited number of direct labor-hours at its disposal. When a limited resource of some type restricts the company's ability to satisfy demand, the company has a **constraint.** Because the company cannot fully satisfy demand, managers must decide which products or services should be cut back. In other words, managers must decide which products or services make the best use of the constrained resource. Fixed costs are usually unaffected by such choices, so the course of action that will maximize the company's total contribution margin should ordinarily be selected.

Contribution Margin per Unit of the Constrained Resource

If some products must be cut back because of a constraint, the key to maximizing the total contribution margin may seem obvious—favor the products with the highest unit contribution margins. Unfortunately, that is not quite correct. Rather, the correct solution is to favor the products that provide the highest *contribution margin per unit of the constrained resource.* To illustrate, in addition to its other products, Mountain Goat Cycles makes saddlebags for bicycles called *panniers.* These panniers come in two models—a touring model and a mountain model. Cost and revenue data for the two models of panniers follow:

	Mountain Pannier	Touring Pannier
Selling price per unit	$25	$30
Variable cost per unit	10	18
Contribution margin per unit	$15	$12
Contribution margin (CM) ratio	60%	40%

The mountain pannier appears to be much more profitable than the touring pannier. It has a $15 per unit contribution margin as compared to only $12 per unit for the touring model, and it has a 60% CM ratio as compared to only 40% for the touring model.

But now let us add one more piece of information—the plant that makes the panniers is operating at capacity. This does not mean that every machine and every person in the plant is working at the maximum possible rate. Because machines have different capacities, some machines will be operating at less than 100% of capacity. However, if the plant as a whole cannot produce any more units, some machine or process must be operating at capacity. The machine or process that is limiting overall output is called the **bottleneck**—it is the constraint.

At Mountain Goat Cycles, the bottleneck (i.e., constraint) is a stitching machine. The mountain pannier requires two minutes of stitching time per unit, and the touring pannier requires one minute of stitching time per unit. The stitching machine is available for 12,000 minutes per month, and the company can sell up to 4,000 mountain panniers and 7,000 touring panniers per month. Producing up to this demand for both products would require 15,000 minutes, as shown below:

	Mountain Pannier	Touring Pannier	Total
Monthly demand (a)	4,000 units	7,000 units	
Stitching machine time required to produce one unit (b)	2 minutes	1 minute	
Total stitching time required (a) × (b)	8,000 minutes	7,000 minutes	15,000 minutes

Producing up to demand would require 15,000 minutes, but only 12,000 minutes are available. This simply confirms that the stitching machine is the bottleneck. By definition, because the stitching machine is a bottleneck, the stitching machine does not have enough capacity to satisfy the existing demand for mountain panniers and touring panniers Therefore, some orders for the products will have to be turned down. Naturally, managers will want to know which product is less profitable. To answer this question, they should focus on the contribution margin per unit of the constrained resource. This figure is computed by dividing a product's contribution margin per unit by the amount of the constrained resource required to make a unit of that product. These calculations are carried out below for the mountain and touring panniers:

	Mountain Pannier	Touring Pannier
Contribution margin per unit (a)	$15.00	$12.00
Stitching machine time required to produce one unit (b)	2 minutes	1 minute
Contribution margin per unit of the constrained resource, (a) ÷ (b)	$7.50 per minute	$12.00 per minute

It is now easy to decide which product is less profitable and should be deemphasized. Each minute on the stitching machine that is devoted to the touring pannier results in an increase of $12.00 in contribution margin and profits. The comparable figure for the mountain pannier is only $7.50 per minute. Therefore, the touring model should be emphasized. Even though the mountain model has the larger contribution margin per unit and the larger CM ratio, the touring model provides the larger contribution margin in relation to the constrained resource.

To verify that the touring model is indeed the more profitable product, suppose an hour of additional stitching time is available and that unfilled orders exist for both products. The additional hour on the stitching machine could be used to make either 30 mountain panniers (60 minutes ÷ 2 minutes per mountain pannier) or 60 touring panniers (60 minutes ÷ 1 minute per touring pannier), with the following profit implications:

	Mountain Pannier	Touring Pannier
Contribution margin per unit	$ 15	$ 12
Additional units that can be processed in one hour	× 30	× 60
Additional contribution margin	$450	$720

Because the additional contribution margin would be $720 for the touring panniers and only $450 for the mountain panniers, the touring panniers make the most profitable use of the company's constrained resource—the stitching machine.

The stitching machine is available for 12,000 minutes per month, and producing the touring panniers is the most profitable use of the stitching machine. Therefore, to maximize profits, the company should produce all of the touring panniers the market will demand (7,000 units) and use any remaining capacity to produce mountain panniers. The computations to determine how many mountain panniers can be produced are as follows:

Monthly demand for touring panniers (a)	7,000 units
Stitching machine time required to produce one touring pannier (b)	1 minute
Total stitching time required to produce touring panniers (a) × (b)	7,000 minutes
Remaining stitching time available (12,000 minutes − 7,000 minutes) (c)	5,000 minutes
Stitching machine time required to produce one mountain pannier (d)	2 minutes
Production of mountain panniers (c) ÷ (d)	2,500 units

Therefore, profit would be maximized by producing 7,000 touring panniers and then using the remaining capacity to produce 2,500 mountain panniers.

This example clearly shows that looking at unit contribution margins alone is not enough; the contribution margin must be viewed in relation to the amount of the constrained resource each product requires.

IN BUSINESS

BOEING IS CONSTRAINED BY A SUPPLIER

Boeing Co. had to delay delivery of its model 777 airplanes to Emirates airline because the German supplier Sell GmbH could not provide the equipment for cooking galleys to Boeing on time. The production bottleneck forced Emirates to repeatedly postpone its planned expansion into the U.S. west coast. It also forced Boeing to accept payment delays for airplanes that sell for more than $200 million apiece. In response, Sell GmbH hired 250 more employees and invested millions of euros in new machine tools and factory space to expand its production capacity.

Source: Daniel Michaels and J. Lynn Lunsford, "Lack of Seats, Galleys Stalls Boeing, Airbus," *The Wall Street Journal*, August 8, 2008, pp. B1 and B4.

LEARNING OBJECTIVE 6
Determine the value of obtaining more of the constrained resource.

Managing Constraints

Effectively managing an organization's constraints is a key to increased profits. As discussed above, when a constraint exists in the production process, managers can increase profits by producing the products with the highest contribution margin per unit of the constrained resource. However, they can also increase profits by increasing the capacity of the bottleneck operation.

When a manager increases the capacity of the bottleneck, it is called **relaxing (or elevating) the constraint.** In the case of Mountain Goat Cycles, the company is currently working one eight-hour shift. To relax the constraint, the stitching machine operator could be asked to work overtime. No one else would have to work overtime. Because all of the other operations involved in producing panniers have excess capacity, up to a point, the additional panniers processed through the stitching machine during overtime could be finished during normal working hours in the other operations.

The benefits from relaxing the constraint are often enormous and can be easily quantified—the key is the contribution margin per unit of the constrained resource that we have already computed. This number, which was originally stated in terms of minutes in the Mountain Goat Cycles example, is restated below in terms of hours for easier interpretation:

	Mountain Pannier	Touring Pannier
Contribution margin per unit of the constrained resource (in minutes) . . .	\$7.50 per minute	\$12.00 per minute
	× 60 minutes per hour	× 60 minutes per hour
Contribution margin per unit of the constrained resource (in hours) . . .	= \$450 per hour	= \$720 per hour

So what is the value of relaxing the constraint—the time on the stitching machine? The manager should first ask, "What would I do with additional capacity at the bottleneck if it were available?" If the time were to be used to make additional mountain panniers, it would be worth \$450 per hour. If the time were to be used to make additional touring panniers, it would be worth \$720 per hour. In this latter case, the company should be willing to pay an overtime *premium* to the stitching machine operator of up to \$720 per hour! Suppose, for example, that the stitching machine operator is paid \$20 per hour during normal working hours and time-and-a-half, or \$30 per hour, for overtime. In this case, the premium for overtime is only \$10 per hour, whereas in principle, the company should be willing to pay a premium of up to \$720 per hour. The difference between what the company should be willing to pay as a premium, \$720 per hour, and what it would actually have to pay, \$10 per hour, is pure profit of \$710 per hour.

To reinforce this concept, suppose that there are only unfilled orders for the mountain pannier. How much would it be worth to the company to run the stitching machine overtime in this situation? Because the additional capacity would be used to make the mountain pannier, the value of that additional capacity would drop to \$7.50 per minute or \$450 per hour. Nevertheless, the value of relaxing the constraint would still be quite high and the company should be willing to pay an overtime premium of up to \$450 per hour.

These calculations indicate that managers should pay great attention to the bottleneck operation. If a bottleneck machine breaks down or is ineffectively utilized, the losses to the company can be quite large. In our example, for every minute the stitching machine is down due to breakdowns or setups, the company loses between \$7.50 and \$12.00.[2] The losses on an hourly basis are between \$450 and \$720! In contrast, there is no such loss of contribution margin if time is lost on a machine that is not a bottleneck—such machines have excess capacity anyway.

The implications are clear. Managers should focus much of their attention on managing the bottleneck. As we have discussed, managers should emphasize products that most profitably utilize the constrained resource. They should also make sure that products are processed smoothly through the bottleneck, with minimal lost time due to breakdowns and setups. And they should try to find ways to increase the capacity at the bottleneck.

[2] Setups are required when production switches from one product to another. For example, consider a company that makes automobile side panels. The panels are painted before shipping them to an automobile manufacturer for final assembly. The customer might require 100 blue panels, 50 black panels, and 20 yellow panels. Each time the color is changed, the painting equipment must be purged of the old paint color, cleaned with solvents, and refilled with the new paint color. This takes time. In fact, some equipment may require such lengthy and frequent setups that it is unavailable for actual production more often than not.

The capacity of a bottleneck can be effectively increased in a number of ways, including:

- Working overtime on the bottleneck.
- Subcontracting some of the processing that would be done at the bottleneck.
- Investing in additional machines at the bottleneck.
- Shifting workers from processes that are not bottlenecks to the process that is the bottleneck.
- Focusing business process improvement efforts on the bottleneck.
- Reducing defective units. Each defective unit that is processed through the bottleneck and subsequently scrapped takes the place of a good unit that could have been sold.

The last three methods of increasing the capacity of the bottleneck are particularly attractive because they are essentially free and may even yield additional cost savings.

The methods and ideas discussed in this section are all part of the Theory of Constraints, which was introduced in Chapter 1. A number of organizations have successfully used the Theory of Constraints to improve their performance, including Avery Dennison, Bethlehem Steel, Binney & Smith, Boeing, Champion International, Ford Motor Company, General Motors, ITT, Monster Cable, National Semiconductor, Pratt and Whitney Canada, Pretoria Academic Hospital, Procter and Gamble, Texas Instruments, United Airlines, United Electrical Controls, the United States Air Force Logistics Command, and the United States Navy Transportation Corps.

IN BUSINESS

ELEVATING A CONSTRAINT

The Odessa Texas Police Department was having trouble hiring new employees. Its eight-step hiring process was taking 117 days to complete and the best-qualified job applicants were accepting other employment offers before the Odessa Police Department could finish evaluating their candidacy. The constraint in the eight-step hiring process was the background investigation that required an average of 104 days. The other seven steps—filling out an application and completing a written exam, an oral interview, a polygraph exam, a medical exam, a psychological exam, and a drug screen—took a combined total of only 13 days. The Odessa Police Department elevated its constraint by hiring additional background checkers. This resulted in slashing its application processing time from 117 days to 16 days.

Source: Lloyd J. Taylor III, Brian J. Moersch, and Geralyn McClure Franklin, "Applying the Theory of Constraints to a Public Safety Hiring Process," *Public Personnel Management*, Fall 2003, pp. 367–382.

The Problem of Multiple Constraints

What does a company do if it has more than one potential constraint? For example, a company may have limited raw materials, limited direct labor-hours available, limited floor space, and limited advertising dollars to spend on product promotion. How would it determine the right combination of products to produce? The proper combination or "mix" of products can be found by use of a quantitative method known as *linear programming,* which is covered in quantitative methods and operations management courses.

Joint Product Costs and the Contribution Approach

LEARNING OBJECTIVE 7
Prepare an analysis showing whether joint products should be sold at the split-off point or processed further.

In some industries, a number of end products are produced from a single raw material input. For example, in the petroleum refining industry a large number of products are extracted from crude oil, including gasoline, jet fuel, home heating oil, lubricants, asphalt, and various organic chemicals. Another example is provided by the Santa Maria Wool Cooperative of New Mexico. The company buys raw wool from local sheepherders, separates the wool into three grades—coarse, fine, and superfine—and then dyes the

EXHIBIT 12–6
Santa Maria Wool Cooperative

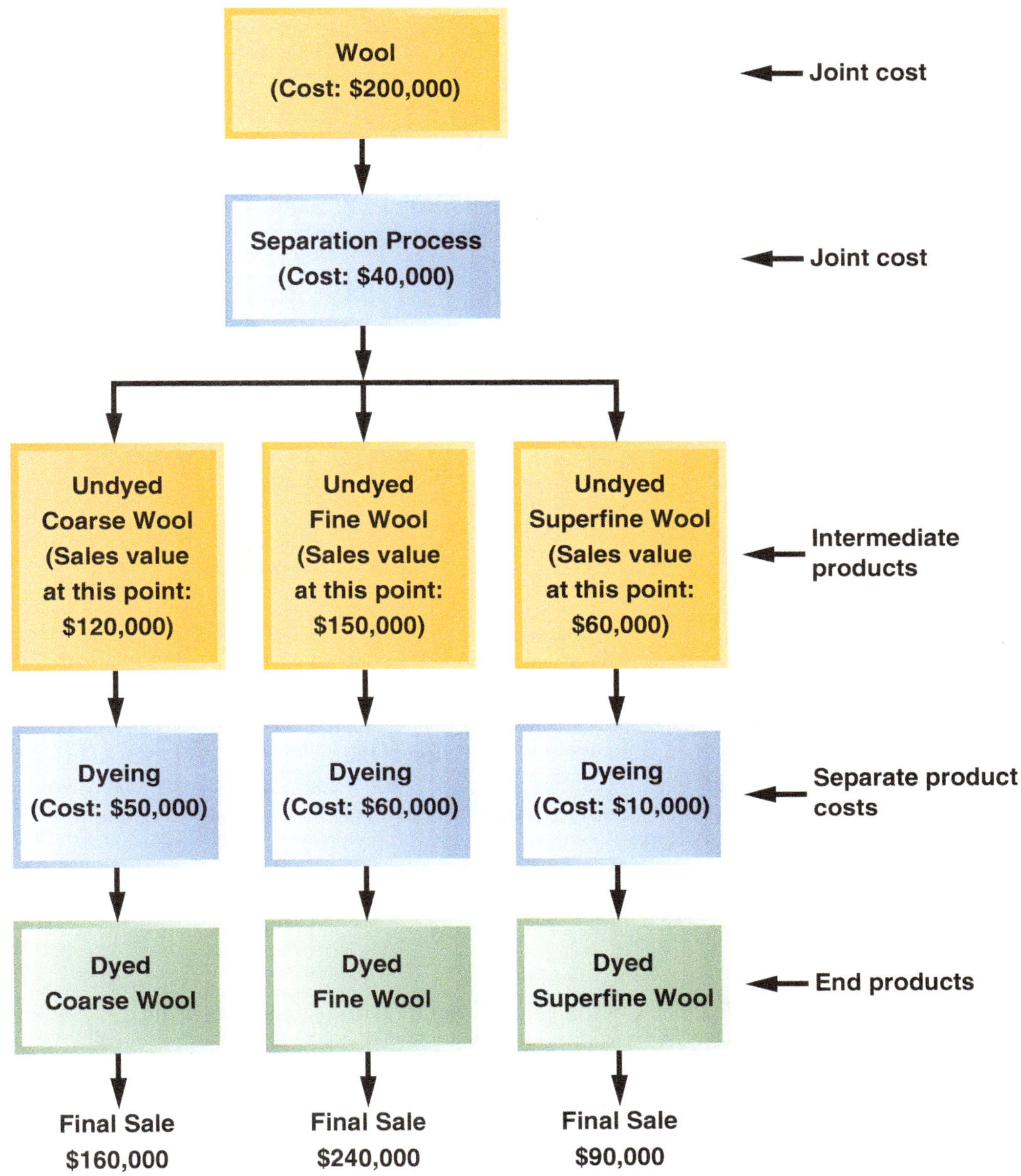

wool using traditional methods that rely on pigments from local materials. Exhibit 12–6 contains a diagram of the production process.

At Santa Maria Wool Cooperative, coarse wool, fine wool, and superfine wool are produced from one input—raw wool. Two or more products that are produced from a common input are known as **joint products.** The **split-off point** is the point in the manufacturing process at which the joint products can be recognized as separate products. This does not occur at Santa Maria Wool Cooperative until the raw wool has gone through the separating process. The term **joint cost** is used to describe the costs incurred up to the split-off point. At Santa Maria Wool Cooperative, the joint costs are the $200,000 cost of the raw wool and the $40,000 cost of separating the wool. The undyed wool is called an *intermediate product* because it is not finished at this point. Nevertheless, a market does exist for undyed wool—although at a significantly lower price than finished, dyed wool.

The Pitfalls of Allocation

Joint costs are common costs that are incurred to simultaneously produce a variety of end products. These joint costs are traditionally allocated among the different products at the split-off point. A typical approach is to allocate the joint costs according to the relative sales value of the end products.

Although allocation of joint product costs is needed for some purposes, such as balance sheet inventory valuation, allocations of this kind are extremely misleading for decision making. The In Business box "Getting It All Wrong" (see below) illustrates an incorrect decision that resulted from using such an allocated joint cost. You should stop now and read that box before proceeding further.

IN BUSINESS

GETTING IT ALL WRONG

A company located on the Gulf of Mexico produces soap products. Its six main soap product lines are produced from common inputs. Joint product costs up to the split-off point constitute the bulk of the production costs for all six product lines. These joint product costs are allocated to the six product lines on the basis of the relative sales value of each line at the split-off point.

A waste product results from the production of the six main product lines. The company loaded the waste onto barges and dumped it into the Gulf of Mexico because the waste was thought to have no commercial value. The dumping was stopped, however, when the company's research division discovered that with some further processing the waste could be sold as a fertilizer ingredient. The further processing costs $175,000 per year. The waste was then sold to fertilizer manufacturers for $300,000.

The accountants responsible for allocating manufacturing costs included the sales value of the waste product along with the sales value of the six main product lines in their allocation of the joint product costs at the split-off point. This allocation resulted in the waste product being allocated $150,000 in joint product cost. This $150,000 allocation, when added to the further processing costs of $175,000 for the waste, made it appear that the waste product was unprofitable—as shown in the table below. When presented with this analysis, the company's management decided that further processing of the waste should be stopped. The company went back to dumping the waste in the Gulf.

Sales value of the waste product after further processing	$300,000
Less costs assigned to the waste product	325,000
Net loss	$ (25,000)

Sell or Process Further Decisions

Joint costs are irrelevant in decisions regarding what to do with a product from the split-off point forward. Once the split-off point is reached, the joint costs have already been incurred and nothing can be done to avoid them. Furthermore, even if the product were disposed of in a landfill without any further processing, all of the joint costs must be incurred to obtain the other products that come out of the joint process. None of the joint costs are avoidable by disposing of any one of the products that emerge from the split-off point. Therefore, none of the joint costs are economically attributable to any one of the intermediate or end products. The joint costs are a common cost of all of the intermediate and end products and should not be allocated to them for purposes of making decisions about the individual products. In the case of the soap company in the accompanying

In Business box "Getting It All Wrong," the $150,000 in allocated joint costs should not have influenced what was done with the waste product from the split-off point forward. Even ignoring the negative environmental impact of dumping the waste in the Gulf of Mexico, a correct analysis would have shown that the company was making money by further processing the waste into a fertilizer ingredient. The analysis should have been done as follows:

	Dump in Gulf	Process Further
Sales value of fertilizer ingredient	0	$300,000
Additional processing costs.	0	175,000
Contribution margin.	0	$125,000
Advantage of processing further	$125,000	

Decisions of this type are known as **sell or process further decisions.** It is profitable to continue processing a joint product after the split-off point *so long as the incremental revenue from such processing exceeds the incremental processing cost incurred after the split-off point.* Joint costs that have already been incurred up to the split-off point are always irrelevant in decisions concerning what to do from the split-off point forward.

To provide a detailed example of the sell or process further decision, return to the data for Santa Maria Wool Cooperative in Exhibit 12–6. We can answer several important questions using this data. First, is the company making money if it runs the entire process from beginning to end? Assuming there are no costs other than those displayed in Exhibit 12–6, the company is indeed making money as follows:

Analysis of the profitability of the overall operation:		
Combined final sales value		
($160,000 + $240,000 + $90,000)		$490,000
Less costs of producing the end products:		
Cost of wool	$200,000	
Cost of separating wool	40,000	
Combined costs of dyeing		
($50,000 + $60,000 + $10,000)	120,000	360,000
Profit		$130,000

Note that the joint costs of buying the wool and separating the wool *are* relevant when considering the profitability of the entire operation. This is because these joint costs *could* be avoided if the entire operation were shut down. However, these joint costs are *not* relevant when considering the profitability of any one product. As long as the process is being run to make the other products, no additional joint costs are incurred to make the specific product in question.

Even though the company is making money overall, it may be losing money on one or more of the products. If the company buys wool and runs the separation process, it will get all three intermediate products. Nothing can be done about that. However, each of these products can be sold *as is* without further processing. It may be that the company would be better off selling one or more of the products prior to dyeing to avoid the dyeing costs. The appropriate way to make this choice is to compare the incremental revenues to the incremental costs from further processing as follows:

Analysis of sell or process further:

	Coarse Wool	Fine Wool	Superfine Wool
Final sales value after further processing	$160,000	$240,000	$90,000
Less sales value at the split-off point	120,000	150,000	60,000
Incremental revenue from further processing	40,000	90,000	30,000
Less cost of further processing (dyeing)	50,000	60,000	10,000
Profit (loss) from further processing	$ (10,000)	$ 30,000	$20,000

As this analysis shows, the company would be better off selling the undyed coarse wool as is rather than processing it further. The other two products should be processed further and dyed before selling them.

Note that the joint costs of the wool ($200,000) and of the wool separation process ($40,000) play no role in the decision to sell or further process the intermediate products. These joint costs are relevant in a decision of whether to buy wool and to run the wool separation process, but they are not relevant in decisions about what to do with the intermediate products once they have been separated.

Activity-Based Costing and Relevant Costs

As discussed in Chapter 7, activity-based costing can be used to help identify potentially relevant costs for decision-making purposes. Activity-based costing improves the traceability of costs by focusing on the activities caused by a product or other segment. However, managers should exercise caution against reading more into this "traceability" than really exists. People have a tendency to assume that if a cost is traceable to a segment, then the cost is automatically an avoidable cost. That is not true. As emphasized in Chapter 7, the costs provided by a well-designed activity-based costing system are only *potentially* relevant. Before making a decision, managers must still decide which of the potentially relevant costs are actually avoidable. Only those costs that are avoidable are relevant and the others should be ignored.

To illustrate, refer again to the data relating to the housewares line in Exhibit 12–4. The $2,000 fixtures depreciation is a traceable cost of the housewares lines because it directly relates to activities in that department. We found, however, that the $2,000 is not avoidable if the housewares line is dropped. The key lesson here is that the method used to assign a cost to a product or other segment does not change the basic nature of the cost. A sunk cost such as depreciation of old equipment is still a sunk cost regardless of whether it is traced directly to a particular segment on an activity basis, allocated to all segments on the basis of labor-hours, or treated in some other way in the costing process. Regardless of the method used to assign costs to products or other segments, the principles discussed in this chapter must be applied to determine the costs that are avoidable in each situation.

Summary

Everything in this chapter consists of applications of one simple but powerful idea. Only those costs and benefits that differ between alternatives are relevant in a decision. All other costs and benefits are irrelevant and should be ignored. In particular, sunk costs are irrelevant as are future costs that do not differ between alternatives.

This simple idea was applied in a variety of situations including decisions that involve adding or dropping a product line, making or buying a component, accepting or rejecting a special order, using a constrained resource, and processing a joint product further. This list includes only a small sample of the possible applications of the relevant cost concept. Indeed, any decision involving costs hinges on the proper identification and analysis of the costs that are relevant. We will continue to focus on the concept of relevant costs in the following chapter where long-term investment decisions are considered.

Review Problem: Relevant Costs

Charter Sports Equipment manufactures round, rectangular, and octagonal trampolines. Sales and expense data for the past month follow:

		Trampoline		
	Total	Round	Rectangular	Octagonal
Sales	$1,000,000	$140,000	$500,000	$360,000
Variable expenses	410,000	60,000	200,000	150,000
Contribution margin	590,000	80,000	300,000	210,000
Fixed expenses:				
Advertising—traceable	216,000	41,000	110,000	65,000
Depreciation of special equipment	95,000	20,000	40,000	35,000
Line supervisors' salaries	19,000	6,000	7,000	6,000
General factory overhead*	200,000	28,000	100,000	72,000
Total fixed expenses	530,000	95,000	257,000	178,000
Net operating income (loss)	$ 60,000	$ (15,000)	$ 43,000	$ 32,000

*A common fixed cost that is allocated on the basis of sales dollars.

Management is concerned about the continued losses shown by the round trampolines and wants a recommendation as to whether or not the line should be discontinued. The special equipment used to produce the trampolines has no resale value. If the round trampoline model is dropped, the two line supervisors assigned to the model would be discharged.

Required:

1. Should production and sale of the round trampolines be discontinued? The company has no other use for the capacity now being used to produce the round trampolines. Show computations to support your answer.
2. Recast the above data in a format that would be more useful to management in assessing the profitability of the various product lines.

Solution to Review Problem

1. No, production and sale of the round trampolines should not be discontinued. Computations to support this answer follow:

Contribution margin lost if the round trampolines are discontinued		$(80,000)
Less fixed costs that can be avoided:		
Advertising—traceable	$41,000	
Line supervisors' salaries	6,000	47,000
Decrease in net operating income for the company as a whole		$(33,000)

The depreciation of the special equipment is a sunk cost, and therefore, it is not relevant to the decision. The general factory overhead is allocated and will presumably continue regardless of whether or not the round trampolines are discontinued; thus, it is not relevant.

2. If management wants a clearer picture of the profitability of the segments, the general factory overhead should not be allocated. It is a common cost and, therefore, should be deducted from

the total product-line segment margin, as shown in Chapter 6. A more useful income statement format would be as follows:

		Trampoline		
	Total	Round	Rectangular	Octagonal
Sales	$1,000,000	$140,000	$500,000	$360,000
Variable expenses	410,000	60,000	200,000	150,000
Contribution margin	590,000	80,000	300,000	210,000
Traceable fixed expenses:				
Advertising—traceable	216,000	41,000	110,000	65,000
Depreciation of special equipment	95,000	20,000	40,000	35,000
Line supervisors' salaries	19,000	6,000	7,000	6,000
Total traceable fixed expenses	330,000	67,000	157,000	106,000
Product-line segment margin	260,000	$ 13,000	$143,000	$104,000
Common fixed expenses	200,000			
Net operating income	$ 60,000			

Glossary

Avoidable cost A cost that can be eliminated by choosing one alternative over another in a decision. This term is synonymous with *relevant cost.* (p. 528)

Bottleneck A machine or some other part of a process that limits the total output of the entire system. (p. 544)

Constraint A limitation under which a company must operate, such as limited available machine time or raw materials, that restricts the company's ability to satisfy demand. (p. 544)

Joint costs Costs that are incurred up to the split-off point in a process that produces joint products. (p. 549)

Joint products Two or more products that are produced from a common input. (p. 549)

Make or buy decision A decision concerning whether an item should be produced internally or purchased from an outside supplier. (p. 539)

Relaxing (or elevating) the constraint An action that increases the amount of a constrained resource. Equivalently, an action that increases the capacity of the bottleneck. (p. 546)

Relevant benefit A benefit that differs between alternatives in a decision. Synonyms are *differential benefit* and *incremental benefit.* (p. 528)

Relevant cost A cost that differs between alternatives in a decision. Synonyms are *avoidable cost, differential cost,* and *incremental cost.* (p. 528)

Sell or process further decision A decision as to whether a joint product should be sold at the split-off point or sold after further processing. (p. 551)

Special order A one-time order that is not considered part of the company's normal ongoing business. (p. 542)

Split-off point That point in the manufacturing process where some or all of the joint products can be recognized as individual products. (p. 549)

Sunk cost Any cost that has already been incurred and that cannot be changed by any decision made now or in the future. (p. 528)

Vertical integration The involvement by a company in more than one of the activities in the entire value chain from development through production, distribution, sales, and after-sales service. (p. 539)

Questions

12–1 What is a *relevant cost?*

12–2 Define the following terms: *incremental cost, opportunity cost,* and *sunk cost.*

12–3 Are variable costs always relevant costs? Explain.

12–4 "Sunk costs are easy to spot—they're the fixed costs associated with a decision." Do you agree? Explain.

12–5 "Variable costs and differential costs mean the same thing." Do you agree? Explain.

12–6 "All future costs are relevant in decision making." Do you agree? Why?

12–7 Prentice Company is considering dropping one of its product lines. What costs of the product line would be relevant to this decision? What costs would be irrelevant?

12–8 "If a product is generating a loss, then it should be discontinued." Do you agree? Explain.

12–9 What is the danger in allocating common fixed costs among products or other segments of an organization?

12–10 How does opportunity cost enter into a make or buy decision?

12–11 Give at least four examples of possible constraints.

12–12 How will relating product contribution margins to the amount of the constrained resource they consume help a company maximize its profits?

12–13 Define the following terms: *joint products, joint costs,* and *split-off point.*

12–14 From a decision-making point of view, should joint costs be allocated among joint products?

12–15 What guideline should be used in determining whether a joint product should be sold at the split-off point or processed further?

12–16 Airlines sometimes offer reduced rates during certain times of the week to members of a businessperson's family if they accompany him or her on trips. How does the concept of relevant costs enter into the decision by the airline to offer reduced rates of this type?

Multiple-choice questions are provided on the text website at www.mhhe.com/garrison14e.

connect ACCOUNTING Applying Excel

LEARNING OBJECTIVE 7

Available with McGraw-Hill's *Connect™ Accounting*.

The Excel worksheet form that appears below is to be used to recreate the example in the text on pages 548–552. Download the workbook containing this form from the Online Learning Center at www.mhhe.com/garrison14e. *On the website you will also receive instructions about how to use this worksheet form.*

	A	B	C	D	E
1	Chapter 12: Applying Excel				
2					
3	**Data**				
4	**Exhibit 12-6 Santa Maria Wool Cooperative**				
5	Cost of wool	$200,000			
6	Cost of separation process	$40,000			
7	Sales value of intermediate products at split-off point:				
8	Undyed coarse wool	$120,000			
9	Undyed fine wool	$150,000			
10	Undyed superfine wool	$60,000			
11	Costs of further processing (dyeing) intermediate products:				
12	Undyed coarse wool	$50,000			
13	Undyed fine wool	$60,000			
14	Undyed superfine wool	$10,000			
15	Sales value of end products:				
16	Dyed coarse wool	$160,000			
17	Dyed fine wool	$240,000			
18	Dyed superfine wool	$90,000			
19					
20	*Enter a formula into each of the cells marked with a ? below*				
21	**Example: Joint Product Costs and the Contribution Approach**				
22					
23	***Analysis of the profitability of the overall operation:***				
24	Combined final sales value		?		
25	Less costs of producing the end products:				
26	Cost of wool	?			
27	Cost of separation process	?			
28	Combined costs of dyeing	?	?		
29	Profit		?		
30					
31	***Analysis of sell or process further:***				
32		*Coarse*	*Fine*	*Superfine*	
33		*Wool*	*Wool*	*Wool*	
34	Final sales value after further processing	?	?	?	
35	Less sales value at the split-off point	?	?	?	
36	Incremental revenue from further processing	?	?	?	
37	Less cost of further processing (dyeing)	?	?	?	
38	Profit (loss) from further processing	?	?	?	
39					

Chapter 12 Form | Filled in Chapter 12 Form | Chapter

You should proceed to the requirements below only after completing your worksheet.

Required:

1. Check your worksheet by changing the cost of further processing undyed coarse wool in cell B12 to $30,000. The overall profit from processing all intermediate products into final products should now be $150,000 and the profit from further processing coarse wool should now be $10,000. If you do not get these answers, find the errors in your worksheet and correct them.
   How should operations change in response to this change in cost?
2. In industries that process joint products, the costs of the raw materials inputs and the sales values of intermediate and final products are often volatile. Change the data area of your worksheet to match the following:

Data Exhibit 12–6 Santa Maria Wool Cooperative	
Cost of wool	$290,000
Cost of separation process	$40,000
Sales value of intermediate products at split-off point:	
Undyed coarse wool	$100,000
Undyed fine wool	$110,000
Undyed superfine wool	$90,000
Costs of further processing (dyeing) intermediate products:	
Undyed coarse wool	$50,000
Undyed fine wool	$60,000
Undyed superfine wool	$10,000
Sales value of end products:	
Dyed coarse wool	$180,000
Dyed fine wool	$210,000
Dyed superfine wool	$90,000

a. What is the overall profit if all intermediate products are processed into final products?
b. What is the profit from further processing each of the intermediate products?
c. With these new costs and selling prices, what recommendations would you make concerning the company's operations? If your recommendation is followed, what should be the overall profit of the company?

Exercises connect ACCOUNTING

All applicable exercises are available with McGraw-Hill's *Connect™ Accounting.*

EXERCISE 12–1 Identifying Relevant Costs [LO1]

A number of costs are listed below that may be relevant in decisions faced by the management of Poulsen & Sonner A/S, a Danish furniture manufacturer:

	Case 1		Case 2	
Item	Relevant	Not Relevant	Relevant	Not Relevant
a. Sales revenue				
b. Direct materials				
c. Direct labor				
d. Variable manufacturing overhead				
e. Book value—Model A3000 machine				
f. Disposal value—Model A3000 machine				
g. Depreciation—Model A3000 machine				
h. Market value—Model B3800 machine (cost)				
i. Fixed manufacturing overhead (general)				
j. Variable selling expense				
k. Fixed selling expense				
l. General administrative overhead				

Required:

Copy the information from the previous page onto your answer sheet and place an X in the appropriate column to indicate whether each item is relevant or not relevant in the following situations. Requirement 1 relates to Case 1, and requirement 2 relates to Case 2. Consider the two cases independently.

1. The company chronically runs at capacity and the old Model A3000 machine is the company's constraint. Management is considering the purchase of a new Model B3800 machine to use in addition to the company's present Model A3000 machine. The old Model A3000 machine will continue to be used to capacity as before, with the new Model B3800 being used to expand production. The increase in volume will be large enough to require increases in fixed selling expenses and in general administrative overhead, but not in the general fixed manufacturing overhead.
2. The old Model A3000 machine is not the company's constraint, but management is considering replacing it with a new Model B3800 machine because of the potential savings in direct materials cost with the new machine. The Model A3000 machine would be sold. This change will have no effect on production or sales, other than some savings in direct materials costs due to less waste.

EXERCISE 12–2 Dropping or Retaining a Segment [LO2]

Jackson County Senior Services is a nonprofit organization devoted to providing essential services to seniors who live in their own homes within the Jackson County area. Three services are provided for seniors—home nursing, Meals On Wheels, and housekeeping. In the home nursing program, nurses visit seniors on a regular basis to check on their general health and to perform tests ordered by their physicians. The Meals On Wheels program delivers a hot meal once a day to each senior enrolled in the program. The housekeeping service provides weekly housecleaning and maintenance services. Data on revenue and expenses for the past year follow:

	Total	Home Nursing	Meals On Wheels	House-keeping
Revenues	$900,000	$260,000	$400,000	$240,000
Variable expenses	490,000	120,000	210,000	160,000
Contribution margin	410,000	140,000	190,000	80,000
Fixed expenses:				
Depreciation	68,000	8,000	40,000	20,000
Liability insurance	42,000	20,000	7,000	15,000
Program administrators' salaries	115,000	40,000	38,000	37,000
General administrative overhead*	180,000	52,000	80,000	48,000
Total fixed expenses	405,000	120,000	165,000	120,000
Net operating income (loss)	$ 5,000	$ 20,000	$ 25,000	$ (40,000)

*Allocated on the basis of program revenues.

The head administrator of Jackson County Senior Services, Judith Miyama, is concerned about the organization's finances and considers the net operating income of $5,000 last year to be too small. (Last year's results were very similar to the results for previous years and are representative of what would be expected in the future.) She feels that the organization should be building its financial reserves at a more rapid rate in order to prepare for the next inevitable recession. After seeing the above report, Ms. Miyama asked for more information about the financial advisability of discontinuing the housekeeping program.

The depreciation in housekeeping is for a small van that is used to carry the housekeepers and their equipment from job to job. If the program were discontinued, the van would be donated to a charitable organization. Depreciation charges assume zero salvage value. None of the general administrative overhead would be avoided if the housekeeping program were dropped, but the liability insurance and the salary of the program administrator would be avoided.

Required:

1. Should the housekeeping program be discontinued? Explain. Show computations to support your answer.
2. Recast the above data in a format that would be more useful to management in assessing the long-run financial viability of the various services.

EXERCISE 12–3 Make or Buy a Component [LO3]

Climate-Control, Inc., manufactures a variety of heating and air-conditioning units. The company is currently manufacturing all of its own component parts. An outside supplier has offered to sell a thermostat to Climate-Control for $20 per unit. To evaluate this offer, Climate-Control, Inc., has gathered the following information relating to its own cost of producing the thermostat internally:

	Per Unit	15,000 Units per Year
Direct materials	$ 6	$ 90,000
Direct labor	8	120,000
Variable manufacturing overhead	1	15,000
Fixed manufacturing overhead, traceable	5*	75,000
Fixed manufacturing overhead, common, but allocated	10	150,000
Total cost	$30	$450,000

*40% supervisory salaries; 60% depreciation of special equipment (no resale value).

Required:

1. Assuming that the company has no alternative use for the facilities now being used to produce the thermostat, should the outside supplier's offer be accepted? Show all computations.
2. Suppose that if the thermostats were purchased, Climate-Control, Inc., could use the freed capacity to launch a new product. The segment margin of the new product would be $65,000 per year. Should Climate-Control, Inc., accept the offer to buy the thermostats from the outside supplier for $20 each? Show computations.

EXERCISE 12–4 Evaluating a Special Order [LO4]

Miyamoto Jewelers is considering a special order for 10 handcrafted gold bracelets to be given as gifts to members of a wedding party. The normal selling price of a gold bracelet is $389.95 and its unit product cost is $264.00 as shown below:

Direct materials	$143.00
Direct labor	86.00
Manufacturing overhead	35.00
Unit product cost	$264.00

Most of the manufacturing overhead is fixed and unaffected by variations in how much jewelry is produced in any given period. However, $7 of the overhead is variable with respect to the number of bracelets produced. The customer who is interested in the special bracelet order would like special filigree applied to the bracelets. This filigree would require additional materials costing $6 per bracelet and would also require acquisition of a special tool costing $465 that would have no other use once the special order is completed. This order would have no effect on the company's regular sales and the order could be fulfilled using the company's existing capacity without affecting any other order.

Required:

What effect would accepting this order have on the company's net operating income if a special price of $349.95 is offered per bracelet for this order? Should the special order be accepted at this price?

EXERCISE 12–5 Utilizing a Constrained Resource [LO5]

Sport Luggage Inc. makes high-end hard-sided luggage for sports equipment. Data concerning three of the company's most popular models appear below.

	Ski Vault	Golf Caddy	Fishing Quiver
Selling price per unit	$220	$300	$175
Variable cost per unit	$60	$120	$55
Plastic injection molding machine processing time required to produce one unit	4 minutes	5 minutes	2 minutes
Pounds of plastic pellets per unit	5 pounds	6 pounds	5 pounds

Required:

1. The total time available on the plastic injection molding machine is the constraint in the production process. Which product would be the most profitable use of this constraint? Which product would be the least profitable use of this constraint?

2. A severe shortage of plastic pellets has required the company to cut back its production so much that the plastic injection molding machine is no longer the bottleneck. Instead, the constraint is the total available pounds of plastic pellets. Which product would be the most profitable use of this constraint? Which product would be the least profitable use of this constraint?
3. Which product has the largest unit contribution margin? Why wouldn't this product be the most profitable use of the constrained resource in either case?

EXERCISE 12–6 Managing a Constrained Resource [LO6]

Georgian Ambience Ltd. makes fine colonial reproduction furniture. Upholstered furniture is one of its major product lines and the bottleneck on this production line is time in the upholstery shop. Upholstering is a craft that takes years of experience to master and the demand for upholstered furniture far exceeds the company's capacity in the upholstering shop. Information concerning three of the company's upholstered chairs appears below:

	Gainsborough Armchair	Leather Library Chair	Chippendale Fabric Armchair
Selling price per unit	$1,300	$1,800	$1,400
Variable cost per unit	$800	$1,200	$1,000
Upholstery shop time required to produce one unit	8 hours	12 hours	5 hours

Required:

1. More time could be made available in the upholstery shop by asking the employees who work in this shop to work overtime. Assuming that this extra time would be used to produce Leather Library Chairs, up to how much should the company be willing to pay per hour to keep the upholstery shop open after normal working hours?
2. A small nearby upholstering company has offered to upholster furniture for Georgian Ambience at a fixed charge of $45 per hour. The management of Georgian Ambience is confident that this upholstering company's work is high quality and their craftsmen should be able to work about as quickly as Georgian Ambience's own craftsmen on the simpler upholstering jobs such as the Chippendale Fabric Armchair. Should management accept this offer? Explain.

EXERCISE 12–7 Sell or Process Further [LO7]

Solex Company manufactures three products from a common input in a joint processing operation. Joint processing costs up to the split-off point total $100,000 per year. The company allocates these costs to the joint products on the basis of their total sales value at the split-off point. These sales values are as follows: product X, $50,000; product Y, $90,000; and product Z, $60,000.

Each product may be sold at the split-off point or processed further. Additional processing requires no special facilities. The additional processing costs and the sales value after further processing for each product (on an annual basis) are shown below:

Product	Additional Processing Costs	Sales Value after Further Processing
X	$35,000	$80,000
Y	$40,000	$150,000
Z	$12,000	$75,000

Required:

Which product or products should be sold at the split-off point, and which product or products should be processed further? Show computations.

EXERCISE 12–8 Sell or Process Further [LO7]

Morrell Company produces several products from processing krypton, a rare mineral. Material and processing costs total $30,000 per ton, one-third of which are allocated to the product merifulon. The merifulon produced from a ton of krypton can either be sold at the split-off point, or processed further at a cost of $13,000 and then sold for $60,000. The sales value of merifulon at the split-off point is $40,000.

Required:

Should merifulon be processed further or sold at the split-off point?

EXERCISE 12–9 Utilization of a Constrained Resource [LO5]
Shelby Company produces three products: product X, product Y, and product Z. Data concerning the three products follow (per unit):

	Product X	Product Y	Product Z
Selling price	$80	$56	$70
Variable expenses:			
Direct materials	24	15	9
Labor and overhead	24	27	40
Total variable expenses	48	42	49
Contribution margin	$32	$14	$21
Contribution margin ratio	40%	25%	30%

Demand for the company's products is very strong, with far more orders each month than the company can produce with the available raw materials. The same material is used in each product. The material costs $3 per pound, with a maximum of 5,000 pounds available each month.

Required:
Which orders would you advise the company to accept first, those for product X, for product Y, or for product Z? Which orders second? Third?

EXERCISE 12–10 Dropping or Retaining a Segment [LO2]
Dexter Products, Inc., manufactures and sells a number of items, including an overnight case. The company has been experiencing losses on the overnight case for some time, as shown on the following contribution format income statement:

Dexter Products, Inc. Income Statement—Overnight Cases For the Quarter Ended June 30		
Sales		$450,000
Variable expenses:		
Variable manufacturing expenses	$130,000	
Sales commissions	48,000	
Shipping	12,000	
Total variable expenses		190,000
Contribution margin		260,000
Fixed expenses:		
Salary of product-line manager	21,000	
General factory overhead	104,000*	
Depreciation of equipment (no resale value)	36,000	
Advertising—traceable	110,000	
Insurance on inventories	9,000	
Purchasing department	50,000†	
Total fixed expenses		330,000
Net operating loss		$ (70,000)

*Allocated on the basis of machine-hours.
†Allocated on the basis of sales dollars.

Discontinuing the overnight cases would not affect the company's sales of its other product lines, its total general factory overhead, or its total purchasing department expenses.

Required:

Would you recommend that the company discontinue the manufacture and sale of overnight cases? Support your answer with appropriate computations.

EXERCISE 12–11 Identification of Relevant Costs [LO1]

Samantha Ringer purchased a used automobile for $10,000 at the beginning of last year and incurred the following operating costs:

Depreciation ($10,000 ÷ 5 years)	$2,000
Insurance	$960
Garage rent	$480
Automobile tax and license	$60
Variable operating cost	8¢ per mile

The variable operating costs consist of gasoline, oil, tires, maintenance, and repairs. Samantha estimates that at her current rate of usage the car will have zero resale value in five years, so the annual straight-line depreciation is $2,000. The car is kept in a garage for a monthly fee.

Required:

1. Samantha drove the car 10,000 miles last year. Compute the average cost per mile of owning and operating the car.
2. Samantha is unsure about whether she should use her own car or rent a car to go on an extended cross-country trip for two weeks during spring break. What costs above are relevant in this decision? Explain.
3. Samantha is thinking about buying an expensive sports car to replace the car she bought last year. She would drive the same number of miles regardless of which car she owns and would rent the same parking space. The sports car's variable operating costs would be roughly the same as the variable operating costs of her old car. However, her insurance and automobile tax and license costs would go up. What costs are relevant in estimating the incremental cost of owning the more expensive car? Explain.

EXERCISE 12–12 Make or Buy a Component [LO3]

Royal Company manufactures 20,000 units of part R-3 each year for use on its production line. At this level of activity, the cost per unit for part R-3 is:

Direct materials	$ 4.80
Direct labor	7.00
Variable manufacturing overhead	3.20
Fixed manufacturing overhead	10.00
Total cost per part	$25.00

An outside supplier has offered to sell 20,000 units of part R-3 each year to Royal Company for $23.50 per part. If Royal Company accepts this offer, the facilities now being used to manufacture part R-3 could be rented to another company at an annual rental of $150,000. However, Royal Company has determined that $6 of the fixed manufacturing overhead being applied to part R-3 would continue even if part R-3 were purchased from the outside supplier.

Required:

Prepare computations showing how much profits will increase or decrease if the outside supplier's offer is accepted.

EXERCISE 12–13 Utilization of a Constrained Resource [LO5, LO6]

Banner Company produces three products: A, B, and C. The selling price, variable costs, and contribution margin for one unit of each product follow:

	Product		
	A	B	C
Selling price	$60	$90	$80
Variable costs:			
Direct materials	27	14	40
Direct labor	12	32	16
Variable manufacturing overhead	3	8	4
Total variable cost	42	54	60
Contribution margin	$18	$36	$20
Contribution margin ratio	30%	40%	25%

Due to a strike in the plant of one of its competitors, demand for the company's products far exceeds its capacity to produce. Management is trying to determine which product(s) to concentrate on next week in filling its backlog of orders. The direct labor rate is $8 per hour, and only 3,000 hours of labor time are available each week.

Required:

1. Compute the amount of contribution margin that will be obtained per hour of labor time spent on each product.
2. Which orders would you recommend that the company work on next week—the orders for product A, product B, or product C? Show computations.
3. By paying overtime wages, more than 3,000 hours of direct labor time can be made available next week. Up to how much should the company be willing to pay per hour in overtime wages as long as there is unfilled demand for the three products? Explain.

EXERCISE 12–14 Special Order [LO4]

Glade Company produces a single product. The costs of producing and selling a single unit of this product at the company's current activity level of 8,000 units per month are:

Direct materials	$2.50
Direct labor	$3.00
Variable manufacturing overhead	$0.50
Fixed manufacturing overhead	$4.25
Variable selling and administrative expenses	$1.50
Fixed selling and administrative expenses	$2.00

The normal selling price is $15 per unit. The company's capacity is 10,000 units per month. An order has been received from a potential customer overseas for 2,000 units at a price of $12.00 per unit. This order would not affect regular sales.

Required:

1. If the order is accepted, by how much will monthly profits increase or decrease? (The order would not change the company's total fixed costs.)
2. Assume the company has 500 units of this product left over from last year that are inferior to the current model. The units must be sold through regular channels at reduced prices. What unit cost is relevant for establishing a minimum selling price for these units? Explain.

EXERCISE 12–15 Dropping or Retaining a Segment [LO2]

Boyle's Home Center, a retailing company, has two departments, Bath and Kitchen. The company's most recent monthly contribution format income statement follows:

		Department	
	Total	Bath	Kitchen
Sales	$5,000,000	$1,000,000	$4,000,000
Variable expenses	1,900,000	300,000	1,600,000
Contribution margin	3,100,000	700,000	2,400,000
Fixed expenses	2,700,000	900,000	1,800,000
Net operating income (loss)	$ 400,000	$ (200,000)	$ 600,000

A study indicates that $370,000 of the fixed expenses being charged to the Bath Department are sunk costs or allocated costs that will continue even if the Bath Department is dropped. In addition, the elimination of the Bath Department would result in a 10% decrease in the sales of the Kitchen Department.

Required:

If the Bath Department is dropped, what will be the effect on the net operating income of the company as a whole?

EXERCISE 12–16 Make or Buy a Component [LO3]

For many years, Diehl Company has produced a small electrical part that it uses in the production of its standard line of diesel tractors. The company's unit product cost for the part, based on a production level of 60,000 parts per year, is as follows:

	Per Part	Total
Direct materials	$ 4.00	
Direct labor	2.75	
Variable manufacturing overhead	0.50	
Fixed manufacturing overhead, traceable	3.00	$180,000
Fixed manufacturing overhead, common (allocated on the basis of labor-hours)	2.25	$135,000
Unit product cost	$12.50	

An outside supplier has offered to supply the electrical parts to the Diehl Company for only $10.00 per part. One-third of the traceable fixed manufacturing cost is supervisory salaries and other costs that can be eliminated if the parts are purchased. The other two-thirds of the traceable fixed manufacturing costs consist of depreciation of special equipment that has no resale value. Economic depreciation on this equipment is due to obsolescence rather than wear and tear. The decision to buy the parts from the outside supplier would have no effect on the common fixed costs of the company, and the space being used to produce the parts would otherwise be idle.

Required:

Prepare computations showing how much profits would increase or decrease as a result of purchasing the parts from the outside supplier rather than making them inside the company.

EXERCISE 12–17 Identification of Relevant Costs [LO1]

Steve has just returned from salmon fishing. He was lucky on this trip and brought home two salmon. Steve's wife, Wendy, disapproves of fishing, and to discourage Steve from further fishing trips, she has presented him with the following cost data. The cost per fishing trip is based on an average of 10 fishing trips per year.

Cost per fishing trip:	
Depreciation on fishing boat* (annual depreciation of $1,500 ÷ 10 trips)	$150
Boat storage fees (annual rental of $1,200 ÷ 10 trips)	120
Expenditures on fishing gear, except for snagged lures (annual expenditures of $200 ÷ 10 trips)	20
Snagged fishing lures	7
Fishing license (yearly license of $40 ÷ 10 trips)	4
Fuel and upkeep on boat per trip	25
Junk food consumed during trip	8
Total cost per fishing trip	$334
Cost per salmon ($334 ÷ 2 salmon)	$167

*The original cost of the boat was $15,000. It has an estimated useful life of 10 years, after which it will have no resale value. The boat does not wear out through use, but it does become less desirable for resale as it becomes older.

Required:

1. Assuming that the salmon fishing trip Steve has just completed is typical, what costs are relevant to a decision as to whether he should go on another trip this year?
2. Suppose that on Steve's next fishing trip he gets lucky and catches three salmon in the amount of time it took him to catch two salmon on his last trip. How much would the third salmon have cost him to catch? Explain.
3. Discuss the costs that are relevant in a decision of whether Steve should give up fishing.

Problems

All applicable problems are available with McGraw-Hill's *Connect™ Accounting.*

PROBLEM 12–18 Dropping or Retaining a Tour [LO2]

Blueline Tours, Inc., operates tours throughout the United States. A study has indicated that some of the tours are not profitable, and consideration is being given to dropping these tours to improve the company's overall operating performance.

One such tour is a two-day Historic Mansions bus tour conducted in the southern states. An income statement from a typical Historic Mansions tour is given below:

Ticket revenue (100 seat capacity × 40% occupancy × $75 ticket price per person)	$3,000	100%
Variable expenses ($22.50 per person)	900	30
Contribution margin	2,100	70%
Tour expenses:		
Tour promotion	$600	
Salary of bus driver	350	
Fee, tour guide	700	
Fuel for bus	125	
Depreciation of bus	450	
Liability insurance, bus	200	
Overnight parking fee, bus	50	
Room and meals, bus driver and tour guide	175	
Bus maintenance and preparation	300	
Total tour expenses	2,950	
Net operating loss	$ (850)	

The following additional information is available about the tour:

a. Bus drivers are paid fixed annual salaries; tour guides are paid for each tour conducted.
b. The "Bus maintenance and preparation" cost on the previous page is an allocation of the salaries of mechanics and other service personnel who are responsible for keeping the company's fleet of buses in good operating condition.
c. Depreciation of buses is due to obsolescence. Depreciation due to wear and tear is negligible.
d. Liability insurance premiums are based on the number of buses in the company's fleet.
e. Dropping the Historic Mansions bus tour would not allow Blueline Tours to reduce the number of buses in its fleet, the number of bus drivers on the payroll, or the size of the maintenance and preparation staff.

Required:

1. Prepare an analysis showing what the impact will be on the company's profits if this tour is discontinued.
2. The company's tour director has been criticized because only about 50% of the seats on Blueline's tours are being filled as compared to an industry average of 60%. The tour director has explained that Blueline's average seat occupancy could be improved considerably by eliminating about 10% of its tours, but that doing so would reduce profits. Explain how this could happen.

PROBLEM 12–19 Sell or Process Further [LO7]

(Prepared from a situation suggested by Professor John W. Hardy.) Abilene Meat Processing Corporation is a major processor of beef and other meat products. The company has a large amount of T-bone steak on hand, and it is trying to decide whether to sell the T-bone steaks as is or to process them further into filet mignon and New York cut steaks.

Management believes that a 1-pound T-bone steak would yield the following profit:

Wholesale selling price ($2.25 per pound)	$2.25
Less joint costs incurred up to the split-off point where T-bone steak can be identified as a separate product	1.70
Profit per pound	$0.55

As mentioned above, instead of being sold as is, the T-bone steaks could be further processed into filet mignon and New York cut steaks. Cutting one side of a T-bone steak provides the filet mignon, and cutting the other side provides the New York cut. One 16-ounce T-bone steak cut in this way will yield one 6-ounce filet mignon and one 8-ounce New York cut; the remaining ounces are waste. The cost of processing the T-bone steaks into these cuts is $0.20 per pound. The filet mignon can be sold for $3.60 per pound, and the New York cut can be sold wholesale for $2.90 per pound.

Required:

1. Determine the profit per pound from processing the T-bone steaks further into filet mignon and New York cut steaks.
2. Would you recommend that the T-bone steaks be sold as is or processed further? Why?

PROBLEM 12–20 Shutting Down or Continuing to Operate a Plant [LO2]

(Note: This type of decision is similar to dropping a product line.)

Hallas Company manufactures a fast-bonding glue in its Northwest plant. The company normally produces and sells 40,000 gallons of the glue each month. This glue, which is known as MJ-7, is used in the wood industry to manufacture plywood. The selling price of MJ-7 is $35 per gallon, variable costs are $21 per gallon, fixed manufacturing overhead costs in the plant total $230,000 per month, and the fixed selling costs total $310,000 per month.

Strikes in the mills that purchase the bulk of the MJ-7 glue have caused Hallas Company's sales to temporarily drop to only 11,000 gallons per month. Hallas Company's management estimates that the strikes will last for two months, after which sales of MJ-7 should return to normal. Due to the current low level of sales, Hallas Company's management is thinking about closing down the Northwest plant during the strike.

If Hallas Company does close down the Northwest plant, fixed manufacturing overhead costs can be reduced by $60,000 per month and fixed selling costs can be reduced by 10%. Start-up costs at the end of the shutdown period would total $14,000. Because Hallas Company uses Lean Production methods, no inventories are on hand.

Required:

1. Assuming that the strikes continue for two months, would you recommend that Hallas Company close the Northwest plant? Explain. Show computations to support your answer.
2. At what level of sales (in gallons) for the two-month period should Hallas Company be indifferent between closing the plant or keeping it open? Show computations. (Hint: This is a type of break-even analysis, except that the fixed cost portion of your break-even computation should include only those fixed costs that are relevant [i.e., avoidable] over the two-month period.)

eXcel

PROBLEM 12–21 Accept or Reject a Special Order [LO4]

Pietarsaari Oy, a Finnish company, produces cross-country ski poles that it sells for €32 a pair. (The Finnish unit of currency, the euro, is denoted by €.) Operating at capacity, the company can produce 50,000 pairs of ski poles a year. Costs associated with this level of production and sales are given below:

	Per Pair	Total
Direct materials	€12	€ 600,000
Direct labor	3	150,000
Variable manufacturing overhead	1	50,000
Fixed manufacturing overhead	5	250,000
Variable selling expenses	2	100,000
Fixed selling expenses	4	200,000
Total cost	€27	€1,350,000

Required:

1. The Finnish army would like to make a one-time-only purchase of 10,000 pairs of ski poles for its mountain troops. The army would pay a fixed fee of €4 per pair, and in addition it would reimburse the Pietarsaari Oy company for its unit manufacturing costs (both fixed and variable). Due to a recession, the company would otherwise produce and sell only 40,000 pairs of ski poles this year. (Total fixed manufacturing overhead cost would be the same whether 40,000 pairs or 50,000 pairs of ski poles were produced.) The company would not incur its usual variable selling expenses with this special order.

   If the Pietarsaari Oy company accepts the army's offer, by how much would net operating income increase or decrease from what it would be if only 40,000 pairs of ski poles were produced and sold during the year?
2. Assume the same situation as described in (1) above, except that the company is already operating at capacity and could sell 50,000 pairs of ski poles through regular channels. Thus, accepting the army's offer would require giving up sales of 10,000 pairs at the normal price of €32 a pair. If the army's offer is accepted, by how much will net operating income increase or decrease from what it would be if the 10,000 pairs were sold through regular channels?

PROBLEM 12–22 Make or Buy Decision [LO3]

Bronson Company manufactures a variety of ballpoint pens. The company has just received an offer from an outside supplier to provide the ink cartridge for the company's Zippo pen line, at a price of $0.48 per dozen cartridges. The company is interested in this offer because its own production of cartridges is at capacity.

Bronson Company estimates that if the supplier's offer were accepted, the direct labor and variable manufacturing overhead costs of the Zippo pen line would be reduced by 10% and the direct materials cost would be reduced by 20%.

Under present operations, Bronson Company manufactures all of its own pens from start to finish. The Zippo pens are sold through wholesalers at $4 per box. Each box contains one dozen pens. Fixed manufacturing overhead costs charged to the Zippo pen line total $50,000 each year. (The same equipment and facilities are used to produce several pen lines.) The present cost of producing one dozen Zippo pens (one box) is given below:

Direct materials	$1.50
Direct labor	1.00
Manufacturing overhead	0.80*
Total cost	$3.30

*Includes both variable and fixed manufacturing overhead, based on production of 100,000 boxes of pens each year.

Required:

1. Should Bronson Company accept the outside supplier's offer? Show computations.
2. What is the maximum price that Bronson Company should be willing to pay the outside supplier per dozen cartridges? Explain.
3. Due to the bankruptcy of a competitor, Bronson Company expects to sell 150,000 boxes of Zippo pens next year. As previously stated, the company presently has enough capacity to produce the cartridges for only 100,000 boxes of Zippo pens annually. By incurring $30,000 in added fixed cost each year, the company could expand its production of cartridges to satisfy the anticipated demand for Zippo pens. The variable cost per unit to produce the additional cartridges would be the same as at present. Under these circumstances, how many boxes of cartridges should be purchased from the outside supplier and how many should be made by Bronson? Show computations to support your answer.
4. What qualitative factors should Bronson Company consider in determining whether it should make or buy the ink cartridges?

(CMA, adapted)

PROBLEM 12–23 Close or Retain a Store [LO2]

Thrifty Markets, Inc., operates three stores in a large metropolitan area. The company's segmented absorption costing income statement for the last quarter is given below:

Thrifty Markets, Inc.
Income Statement
For the Quarter Ended March 31

	Total	Uptown Store	Downtown Store	Westpark Store
Sales	$2,500,000	$900,000	$600,000	$1,000,000
Cost of goods sold	1,450,000	513,000	372,000	565,000
Gross margin	1,050,000	387,000	228,000	435,000
Selling and administrative expenses:				
Selling expenses:				
Direct advertising	118,500	40,000	36,000	42,500
General advertising*	20,000	7,200	4,800	8,000
Sales salaries	157,000	52,000	45,000	60,000
Delivery salaries	30,000	10,000	10,000	10,000
Store rent	215,000	70,000	65,000	80,000
Depreciation of store fixtures	46,950	18,300	8,800	19,850
Depreciation of delivery equipment	27,000	9,000	9,000	9,000
Total selling expenses	614,450	206,500	178,600	229,350
Administrative expenses:				
Store management salaries	63,000	20,000	18,000	25,000
General office salaries*	50,000	18,000	12,000	20,000
Utilities	89,800	31,000	27,200	31,600
Insurance on fixtures and inventory	25,500	8,000	9,000	8,500
Employment taxes	36,000	12,000	10,200	13,800
General office expenses—other*	25,000	9,000	6,000	10,000
Total administrative expenses	289,300	98,000	82,400	108,900
Total operating expenses	903,750	304,500	261,000	338,250
Net operating income (loss)	$ 146,250	$ 82,500	$ (33,000)	$ 96,750

*Allocated on the basis of sales dollars.

Management is very concerned about the Downtown Store's inability to show a profit, and consideration is being given to closing the store. The company has asked you to make a recommendation as to what course of action should be taken. The following additional information is available about the store:

a. The manager of the store has been with the company for many years; he would be retained and transferred to another position in the company if the store were closed. His salary is

$6,000 per month, or $18,000 per quarter. If the store were not closed, a new employee would be hired to fill the other position at a salary of $5,000 per month.

b. The lease on the building housing the Downtown Store can be broken with no penalty.

c. The fixtures being used in the Downtown Store would be transferred to the other two stores if the Downtown Store were closed.

d. The company's employment taxes are 12% of salaries.

e. A single delivery crew serves all three stores. One delivery person could be discharged if the Downtown Store were closed; this person's salary amounts to $7,000 per quarter. The delivery equipment would be distributed to the other stores. The equipment does not wear out through use, but it does eventually become obsolete.

f. One-third of the Downtown Store's insurance relates to its fixtures.

g. The general office salaries and other expenses relate to the general management of Thrifty Markets, Inc. The employee in the general office who is responsible for the Downtown Store would be discharged if the store were closed. This employee's compensation amounts to $8,000 per quarter.

Required:

1. Prepare a schedule showing the change in revenues and expenses and the impact on the overall company net operating income that would result if the Downtown Store were closed.
2. Based on your computations in (1) above, what recommendation would you make to the management of Thrifty Markets, Inc.?
3. Assume that if the Downtown Store were closed, sales in the Uptown Store would increase by $200,000 per quarter due to loyal customers shifting their buying to the Uptown Store. The Uptown Store has ample capacity to handle the increased sales, and its gross margin is 43% of sales. What effect would these factors have on your recommendation concerning the Downtown Store? Show computations.

PROBLEM 12–24 Relevant Cost Analysis in a Variety of Situations [LO2, LO3, LO4]

Barker Company has a single product called a Zet. The company normally produces and sells 80,000 Zets each year at a selling price of $40 per unit. The company's unit costs at this level of activity are given below:

Direct materials	$ 9.50
Direct labor	10.00
Variable manufacturing overhead	2.80
Fixed manufacturing overhead	5.00 ($400,000 total)
Variable selling expenses	1.70
Fixed selling expenses	4.50 ($360,000 total)
Total cost per unit	$33.50

A number of questions relating to the production and sale of Zets are given below. Each question is independent.

Required:

1. Assume that Barker Company has sufficient capacity to produce 100,000 Zets each year without any increase in fixed manufacturing overhead costs. The company could increase sales by 25% above the present 80,000 units each year if it were willing to increase the fixed selling expenses by $150,000. Would the increased fixed selling expenses be justified?
2. Assume again that Barker Company has sufficient capacity to produce 100,000 Zets each year. The company has an opportunity to sell 20,000 units in an overseas market. Import duties, foreign permits, and other special costs associated with the order would total $14,000. The only selling costs that would be associated with the order would be $1.50 per unit shipping cost. Compute the per unit break-even price on this order.
3. One of the materials used in the production of Zets is obtained from a foreign supplier. Civil unrest in the supplier's country has caused a cutoff in material shipments that is expected to last for three months. Barker Company has enough material on hand to operate at 25% of normal levels for the three-month period. As an alternative, the company could close the plant down entirely for the three months. Closing the plant would reduce fixed manufacturing

overhead costs by 40% during the three-month period and the fixed selling expenses would continue at two-thirds of their normal level. What would be the impact on profits of closing the plant for the three-month period?

4. The company has 500 Zets on hand that were produced last month and have small blemishes. Due to the blemishes, it will be impossible to sell these units at the normal price. If the company wishes to sell them through regular distribution channels, what unit cost figure is relevant for setting a minimum selling price? Explain.
5. An outside manufacturer has offered to produce Zets and ship them directly to Barker's customers. If Barker Company accepts this offer, the facilities that it uses to produce Zets would be idle; however, fixed manufacturing overhead costs would continue at 30%. Because the outside manufacturer would pay for all shipping costs, the variable selling expenses would be reduced by 60%. Compute the unit cost that is relevant for comparison to the price quoted by the outside manufacturer.

PROBLEM 12–25 Make or Buy Analysis [LO3]

"That old equipment for producing subassemblies is worn out," said Paul Taylor, president of Timkin Company. "We need to make a decision quickly." The company is trying to decide whether it should rent new equipment and continue to make its subassemblies internally, or whether it should discontinue production of its subassemblies and purchase them from an outside supplier. The alternatives follow:

Alternative 1: Rent new equipment for producing the subassemblies for $60,000 per year.
Alternative 2: Purchase subassemblies from an outside supplier for $8 each.

Timkin Company's current costs per unit of producing the subassemblies internally (with the old equipment) are given below. These costs are based on a current activity level of 40,000 subassemblies per year:

Direct materials	$ 2.75
Direct labor	4.00
Variable overhead	0.60
Fixed overhead ($0.75 supervision, $0.90 depreciation, and $2 general company overhead)	3.65
Total cost per unit	$11.00

The new equipment would be more efficient and, according to the manufacturer, would reduce direct labor costs and variable overhead costs by 25%. Supervision cost ($30,000 per year) and direct materials cost per unit would not be affected by the new equipment. The new equipment's capacity would be 60,000 subassemblies per year.

The total general company overhead would be unaffected by this decision.

Required:

1. The president is unsure what the company should do and would like an analysis showing the unit costs and total costs for each of the two alternatives given above. Assume that 40,000 subassemblies are needed each year. Which course of action would you recommend to the president?
2. Would your recommendation in (1) above be the same if the company's needs were (*a*) 50,000 subassemblies per year, or (*b*) 60,000 subassemblies per year?
3. What other factors would you recommend that the company consider before making a decision?

PROBLEM 12–26 Dropping or Retaining a Product [LO2]

Tracey Douglas is the owner and managing director of Heritage Garden Furniture, Ltd., a South African company that makes museum-quality reproductions of antique outdoor furniture. Ms. Douglas would like advice concerning the advisability of eliminating the model C3 lawnchair. These lawnchairs have been among the company's best-selling products, but they seem to be unprofitable.

A condensed absorption costing income statement for the company and for the model C3 lawnchair for the quarter ended June 30 follows:

	All Products	Model C3 Lawnchair
Sales	R2,900,000	R300,000
Cost of goods sold:		
Direct materials	759,000	122,000
Direct labor	680,000	72,000
Fringe benefits (20% of direct labor)	136,000	14,400
Variable manufacturing overhead	28,000	3,600
Building rent and maintenance	30,000	4,000
Depreciation	75,000	19,100
Total cost of goods sold	1,708,000	235,100
Gross margin	1,192,000	64,900
Selling and administrative expenses:		
Product managers' salaries	75,000	10,000
Sales commissions (5% of sales)	145,000	15,000
Fringe benefits (20% of salaries and commissions)	44,000	5,000
Shipping	120,000	10,000
General administrative expenses	464,000	48,000
Total selling and administrative expenses	848,000	88,000
Net operating income (loss)	R 344,000	R (23,100)

The currency in South Africa is the rand, denoted here by R.

The following additional data have been supplied by the company:

a. Direct labor is a variable cost.

b. All of the company's products are manufactured in the same facility and use the same equipment. Building rent and maintenance and depreciation are allocated to products using various bases. The equipment does not wear out through use; it eventually becomes obsolete.

c. There is ample capacity to fill all orders.

d. Dropping the model C3 lawnchair would have no effect on sales of other product lines.

e. Work in process and finished goods inventories are insignificant.

f. Shipping costs are traced directly to products.

g. General administrative expenses are allocated to products on the basis of sales. There would be no effect on the total general administrative expenses if the model C3 lawnchair were dropped.

h. If the model C3 lawnchair were dropped, the product manager would be laid off.

Required:

1. Given the current level of sales, would you recommend that the model C3 lawnchair be dropped? Prepare appropriate computations to support your answer.
2. What would sales of the model C3 lawnchair have to be, at minimum, in order to justify retaining the product? Explain. (Hint: Set this up as a break-even problem but include only the relevant costs.)

PROBLEM 12–27 Utilization of a Constrained Resource [LO5, LO6]

The Brandilyn Toy Company manufactures a line of dolls and a doll dress sewing kit. Demand for the dolls is increasing, and management requests assistance from you in determining the best sales and production mix for the coming year. The company has provided the following data:

	A	B	C	D	E
1	Product	Demand Next Year (units)	Selling Price Per Unit	Direct Materials	Direct Labor
2	Marcy	26,000	$35.00	$3.50	$4.80
3	Tina	42,000	$24.00	$2.30	$3.00
4	Cari	40,000	$22.00	$4.50	$8.40
5	Lenny	46,000	$18.00	$3.10	$6.00
6	Sewing kit	450,000	$14.00	$1.50	$2.40
7					

Sheet1 Sheet2 Sheet3

The following additional information is available:

a. The company's plant has a capacity of 150,000 direct labor-hours per year on a single-shift basis. The company's present employees and equipment can produce all five products.
b. The direct labor rate of $12.00 per hour is expected to remain unchanged during the coming year.
c. Fixed costs total $356,000 per year. Variable overhead costs are $4.00 per direct labor-hour.
d. All of the company's nonmanufacturing costs are fixed.
e. The company's finished goods inventory is negligible and can be ignored.

Required:

1. Determine the contribution margin per direct labor-hour expended on each product.
2. Prepare a schedule showing the total direct labor-hours that will be required to produce the units estimated to be sold during the coming year.
3. Examine the data you have computed in (1) and (2) above. How would you allocate the 150,000 direct labor-hours of capacity to Brandilyn Toy Company's various products?
4. What is the highest price, in terms of a rate per hour, that Brandilyn Toy Company should be willing to pay for additional capacity (that is, for added direct labor time)?
5. Identify ways in which the company might be able to obtain additional output so that it would not have to leave some demand for its products unsatisfied.

(CMA, adapted)

PROBLEM 12–28 Sell or Process Further [LO7]

The Heather Honey Company purchases honeycombs from beekeepers for $2.00 a pound. The company produces two main products from the honeycombs—honey and beeswax. Honey is drained from the honeycombs, and then the honeycombs are melted down to form cubes of beeswax. The beeswax is sold for $1.50 a pound.

The honey can be sold in raw form for $3.00 a pound. However, some of the raw honey is used by the company to make honey drop candies. The candies are packed in a decorative container and are sold in gift and specialty shops. A container of honey drop candies sells for $4.40.

Each container of honey drop candies contains three quarters of a pound of honey. The other variable costs associated with making the candies are as follows:

Decorative container	$0.40
Other ingredients	0.25
Direct labor	0.20
Variable manufacturing overhead	0.10
Total variable manufacturing cost	$0.95

The monthly fixed manufacturing overhead costs associated with making the candies follow:

Master candy maker's salary	$3,880
Depreciation of candy making equipment	400
Total fixed manufacturing cost	$4,280

The master candy maker has no duties other than to oversee production of the honey drop candies. The candy making equipment is special-purpose equipment that was constructed specifically to make this particular candy. The equipment has no resale value and does not wear out through use.

A salesperson is paid $2,000 per month plus a commission of 5% of sales to market the honey drop candies.

The company had enjoyed robust sales of the candies for several years, but the recent entrance of a competing product into the marketplace has depressed sales of the candies. The management of the company is now wondering whether it would be more profitable to sell all of the honey rather than converting some of it into candies.

Required:

1. What is the incremental contribution margin per container from further processing the honey into candies?
2. What is the minimum number of containers of candy that must be sold each month to justify the continued processing of honey into candies? Explain. Show all computations.

(CMA, adapted)

Cases connect ACCOUNTING

All applicable cases are available with McGraw-Hill's *Connect™ Accounting.*

CASE 12–29 Make or Buy; Utilization of a Constrained Resource [LO1, LO3, LO5]
Storage Systems, Inc., sells a wide range of drums, bins, boxes, and other containers that are used in the chemical industry. One of the company's products is a heavy-duty corrosion-resistant metal drum, called the XSX drum, used to store toxic wastes. Production is constrained by the capacity of an automated welding machine that is used to make precision welds. A total of 2,000 hours of welding time are available annually on the machine. Because each drum requires 0.8 hours of welding time, annual production is limited to 2,500 drums. At present, the welding machine is used exclusively to make the XSX drums. The accounting department has provided the following financial data concerning the XSX drums:

		XSX Drums
Selling price per drum		$154.00
Cost per drum:		
Direct materials	$44.50	
Direct labor ($18 per hour)	4.50	
Manufacturing overhead	3.15	
Selling and administrative expense	15.40	67.55
Margin per drum		$ 86.45

Management believes 3,000 XSX drums could be sold each year if the company had sufficient manufacturing capacity. As an alternative to adding another welding machine, management has looked into the possibility of buying additional drums from an outside supplier. Metal Products, Inc., a supplier of quality products, would be able to provide up to 1,800 XSX-type drums per year at a price of $120 per drum, which Storage Systems would resell to its customers at its normal selling price after appropriate relabeling.

Jasmine Morita, Storage Systems' production manager, has suggested that the company could make better use of the welding machine by manufacturing premium mountain bike frames, which would require only 0.2 hours of welding time per frame. Jasmine believes that Storage Systems could sell up to 3,500 mountain bike frames per year to mountain bike manufacturers at a price of $65 per frame. The accounting department has provided the following data concerning the proposed new product:

Mountain Bike Frames		
Selling price per frame		$65.00
Cost per frame:		
Direct materials	$17.50	
Direct labor ($18 per hour)	22.50	
Manufacturing overhead	15.75	
Selling and administrative expense	6.50	62.25
Margin per frame		$ 2.75

The mountain bike frames could be produced with existing equipment and personnel. Manufacturing overhead is allocated to products on the basis of direct labor-hours. Most of the manufacturing overhead consists of fixed common costs such as rent on the factory building, but some of it is variable. The variable manufacturing overhead has been estimated at $1.05 per XSX drum and $0.60 per mountain bike frame. The variable manufacturing overhead cost would not be incurred on drums acquired from the outside supplier.

Selling and administrative expenses are allocated to products on the basis of revenues. Almost all of the selling and administrative expenses are fixed common costs, but it has been estimated that variable selling and administrative expenses amount to $0.85 per XSX drum and would be $0.40 per mountain bike frame. The variable selling and administrative expenses of $0.85 per drum would be incurred when drums acquired from the outside supplier are sold to the company's customers.

All of the company's employees—direct and indirect—are paid for full 40-hour workweeks and the company has a policy of laying off workers only in major recessions.

Required:

1. Given the margins of the two products as indicated in the reports submitted by the accounting department, does it make any sense to even consider producing the mountain bike frames? Explain.
2. Compute the contribution margin per unit for:
   a. Purchased XSX drums.
   b. Manufactured XSX drums.
   c. Manufactured mountain bike frames.
3. Determine the number of XSX drums (if any) that should be purchased and the number of XSX drums and/or mountain bike frames (if any) that should be manufactured. What is the improvement in net income that would result from this plan over current operations?

As soon as your analysis was shown to the top management team at Storage Systems, several managers got into an argument concerning how direct labor costs should be treated when making this decision. One manager argued that direct labor is always treated as a variable cost in textbooks and in practice and has always been considered a variable cost at Storage Systems. After all, "direct" means you can directly trace the cost to products. If direct labor is not a variable cost, what is? Another manager argued just as strenuously that direct labor should be considered a fixed cost at Storage Systems. No one had been laid off in over a decade, and for all practical purposes, everyone at the plant is on a monthly salary. Everyone classified as direct labor works a regular 40-hour workweek and overtime has not been necessary since the company adopted Lean Production techniques. Whether the welding machine is used to make drums or frames, the total payroll would be exactly the same. There is enough slack, in the form of idle time, to accommodate any increase in total direct labor time that the mountain bike frames would require.

4. Redo requirements (2) and (3) above, making the opposite assumption about direct labor from the one you originally made. In other words, if you treated direct labor as a variable cost, redo the analysis treating it as a fixed cost. If you treated direct labor as a fixed cost, redo the analysis treating it as a variable cost.
5. What do you think is the correct way to treat direct labor in this situation—as a variable cost or as a fixed cost? Explain.

CASE 12–30 Plant Closing Decision [LO1, LO2]

Mobile Seating Corporation manufactures seats for automobiles, vans, trucks, and boats. The company has a number of plants, including the Greenville Cover Plant, which makes seat covers.

Miriam Restin is the plant manager at the Greenville Cover Plant but also serves as the regional production manager for the company. Her budget as the regional manager is charged to the Greenville Cover Plant.

Restin has just heard that Mobile Seating has received a bid from an outside vendor to supply the equivalent of the entire annual output of the Greenville Cover Plant for $21 million. Restin was astonished at the low outside bid because the budget for the Greenville Cover Plant's operating costs for the coming year was set at $24.3 million. If this bid is accepted, the Greenville Cover Plant will be closed down.

The budget for the Greenville Cover Plant's operating costs for the coming year is presented on the following page. Additional facts regarding the plant's operations are as follows:

a. Due to the Greenville Cover Plant's commitment to use high-quality fabrics in all of its products, the Purchasing Department was instructed to place blanket purchase orders with major suppliers to ensure the receipt of sufficient materials for the coming year. If these orders are canceled as a consequence of the plant closing, termination charges would amount to 25% of the cost of direct materials.
b. Approximately 350 employees will lose their jobs if the plant is closed. This includes all of the direct laborers and supervisors, management and staff, and the plumbers, electricians, and other skilled workers classified as indirect plant workers. Some of these workers would have difficulty finding new jobs. Nearly all the production workers would have difficulty matching the Greenville Cover Plant's base pay of $12.50 per hour, which is the highest in the area. A clause in Greenville Cover's contract with the union may help some employees; the company must provide employment assistance and job training to its former employees for 12 months after a plant closing. The estimated cost to administer this service would be $0.8 million.
c. Some employees would probably choose early retirement because Mobile Seating Corporation has an excellent pension plan. In fact, $0.7 million of the annual pension expense would continue whether the Greenville Cover Plant is open or not.

d. Restin and her regional staff would not be affected by the closing of the Greenville Cover Plant. They would still be responsible for running three other area plants.
e. If the Greenville Cover Plant were closed, the company would realize about $2 million salvage value for the equipment in the plant. If the plant remains open, there are no plans to make any significant investments in new equipment or buildings. The old equipment is adequate for the job and should last indefinitely.

Greenville Cover Plant Annual Budget for Operating Costs		
Materials		$ 8,000,000
Labor:		
Direct	$6,700,000	
Supervision	400,000	
Indirect plant	1,900,000	9,000,000
Overhead:		
Depreciation—equipment	1,300,000	
Depreciation—building	2,100,000	
Pension expense	1,600,000	
Plant manager and staff	600,000	
Corporate expenses*	1,700,000	7,300,000
Total budgeted costs		$24,300,000

*Fixed corporate expenses allocated to plants and other operating units based on total budgeted wage and salary costs.

Required:
1. Without regard to costs, identify the advantages to Mobile Seating Corporation of continuing to obtain covers from its own Greenville Cover Plant.
2. Mobile Seating Corporation plans to prepare a financial analysis that will be used in deciding whether or not to close the Greenville Cover Plant. Management has asked you to identify:
   a. The annual budgeted costs that are relevant to the decision regarding closing the plant (show the dollar amounts).
   b. The annual budgeted costs that are not relevant to the decision regarding closing the plant and explain why they are not relevant (again show the dollar amounts).
   c. Any nonrecurring costs that would arise due to the closing of the plant and explain how they would affect the decision (again show any dollar amounts).
3. Looking at the data you have prepared in (2) above, should the plant be closed? Show computations and explain your answer.
4. Identify any revenues or costs not specifically mentioned in the problem that Mobile Seating Corporation should consider before making a decision.

(CMA, adapted)

CASE 12–31 Integrative Case: Relevant Costs; Pricing [LO1, LO4]

Jenco Incorporated's only product is a combination fertilizer-weed killer called Fertikil. Fertikil is sold nationwide through normal marketing channels to retail nurseries and garden stores.

Taylor Nursery plans to sell a similar fertilizer weed killer compound through its regional nursery chain under its own private label. Taylor does not have manufacturing facilities of its own, so it has asked Jenco (and several other companies) to submit a bid for manufacturing and delivering a 25,000 pound order of the private brand compound to Taylor. While the chemical composition of the Taylor compound differs from that of Fertikil, the manufacturing processes are very similar.

The Taylor compound would be produced in 1,000 pound lots. Each lot would require 30 direct labor-hours and the following chemicals:

Chemicals	Quantity in Pounds
CW-3	400
JX-6	300
MZ-8	200
BE-7	100

The first three chemicals (CW–3, JX–6, and MZ–8) are all used in the production of Fertikil. BE–7 was used in another compound that Jenco discontinued several months ago. The supply of BE–7 that Jenco had on hand when the other compound was discontinued was not discarded. Jenco could sell its supply of BE–7 at the prevailing market price less $0.10 per pound selling and handling expenses.

Jenco also has on hand a chemical called CN–5, which was manufactured for use in another product that is no longer produced. CN–5, which cannot be used in Fertikil, can be substituted for CW–3 on a one-for-one basis without affecting the quality of the Taylor compound. The CN–5 in inventory has a salvage value of $500.

Inventory and cost data for the chemicals that can be used to produce the Taylor compound are as shown below:

Raw Material	Pounds in Inventory	Actual Price per Pound When Purchased	Current Market Price per Pound
CW-3	22,000	$0.80	$0.90
JX-6	5,000	0.55	0.60
MZ-8	8,000	1.40	1.60
BE-7	4,000	0.60	0.65
CN-5	5,500	0.75	(Salvage)

The current direct labor rate is $14 per hour. The predetermined overhead rate is based on direct labor-hours (DLH). The predetermined overhead rate for the current year, based on a two-shift capacity of 400,000 total DLH with no overtime, is as follows:

Variable manufacturing overhead	$ 4.50 per DLH
Fixed manufacturing overhead	7.50 per DLH
Combined rate	$12.00 per DLH

Jenco's production manager reports that the present equipment and facilities are adequate to manufacture the Taylor compound. Therefore, the order would have no effect on total fixed manufacturing overhead costs. However, Jenco is within 400 hours of its two-shift capacity this month. Any additional hours beyond 400 hours must be done in overtime. If need be, the Taylor compound could be produced on regular time by shifting a portion of Fertikil production to overtime. Jenco's rate for overtime hours is 1½ times the regular pay rate, or $21 per hour. There is no allowance for any overtime premium in the predetermined overhead rate.

Required:

1. Jenco, has decided to submit a bid for a 25,000 pound order of Taylor Nursery's new compound. The order must be delivered by the end of the current month. Taylor Nursery has indicated that this is a one-time order that will not be repeated. Calculate the lowest price that Jenco could bid for the order without reducing its net operating income.
2. Refer to the original data. Assume that Taylor Nursery plans to place regular orders for 25,000 pound lots of the new compound during the coming year. Jenco expects the demand for Fertikil to remain strong. Therefore, the recurring orders from Taylor Nursery would put Jenco over its two-shift capacity. However, production could be scheduled so that 60% of each Taylor Nursery order could be completed during regular hours. As another option, some Fertikil production could be shifted temporarily to overtime so that the Taylor Nursery orders could be produced on regular time. Current market prices are the best available estimates of future market prices.

   Jenco's standard markup policy for new products is 40% of the full manufacturing cost, including fixed manufacturing overhead. Calculate the price that Jenco would quote Taylor Nursery for each 25,000 pound lot of the new compound, assuming that it is to be treated as a new product and this pricing policy is followed.

(CMA, adapted)

CASE 12–32 Ethics and the Manager; Shut Down or Continue Operations [LO2]

Marvin Braun had just been appointed vice president of the Great Basin Region of the Financial Services Corporation (FSC). The company provides check processing services for small banks. The banks send checks presented for deposit or payment to FSC, which then records the data on each check in a computerized database. FSC sends the data electronically to the nearest Federal Reserve Bank check-clearing center where the appropriate transfers of funds are made between banks. The Great Basin Region consists of three check processing centers in Eastern Idaho—Pocatello, Idaho Falls, and Ashton. Prior to his promotion to vice president, Mr. Braun had been manager of a check processing center in Indiana.

Immediately upon assuming his new position, Mr. Braun requested a complete financial report for the just-ended fiscal year from the region's controller, Lance Whiting. Mr. Braun specified that the financial report should follow the standardized format required by corporate headquarters for all regional performance reports. That report appears below:

Financial Performance
Great Basin Region

		Check Processing Centers		
	Total	Pocatello	Idaho Falls	Ashton
Revenues	$20,000,000	$7,000,000	$8,000,000	$5,000,000
Operating expenses:				
Direct labor	12,200,000	4,400,000	4,700,000	3,100,000
Variable overhead	400,000	150,000	160,000	90,000
Equipment depreciation	2,100,000	700,000	800,000	600,000
Facility expenses	2,000,000	600,000	500,000	900,000
Local administrative expenses*	450,000	150,000	180,000	120,000
Regional administrative expenses†	400,000	140,000	160,000	100,000
Corporate administrative expenses‡	1,600,000	560,000	640,000	400,000
Total operating expense	19,150,000	6,700,000	7,140,000	5,310,000
Net operating income (loss)	$ 850,000	$ 300,000	$ 860,000	$ (310,000)

*Local administrative expenses are the administrative expenses incurred at the check processing centers.
†Regional administrative expenses are allocated to the check processing centers based on revenues.
‡Corporate administrative expenses represent a standard 8% charge against revenues.

Upon seeing this report, Mr. Braun summoned Lance Whiting for an explanation.

Braun: What's the story on Ashton? It didn't have a loss the previous year, did it?

Whiting: No, the Ashton facility has had a nice profit every year since it was opened six years ago, but Ashton lost a big contract this year.

Braun: Why?

Whiting: One of our national competitors entered the local market and bid very aggressively on the contract. We couldn't afford to meet the bid. Ashton's costs—particularly their facility expenses—are just too high. When Ashton lost the contract, we had to lay off a lot of employees, but we could not reduce the fixed costs of the Ashton facility.

Braun: Why is Ashton's facility expense so high? It's a smaller facility than either Pocatello or Idaho Falls and yet its facility expense is higher.

Whiting: The problem is that we are able to rent suitable facilities very cheaply at Pocatello and Idaho Falls. No such facilities were available at Ashton, so we had them built. Unfortunately, there were big cost overruns. The contractor we hired was inexperienced at this kind of work and in fact went bankrupt before the project was completed. After hiring another contractor to finish the work, we were way over budget. The large depreciation charges on the facility didn't matter at first because we didn't have much competition at the time and could charge premium prices.

Braun: Well, we can't do that anymore. The Ashton facility will obviously have to be shut down. Its business can be shifted to the other two check processing centers in the region.

Whiting: I would advise against that. The $900,000 in depreciation charges at the Ashton facility are misleading. That facility should last indefinitely with proper maintenance. And it has no resale value; there is no other commercial activity around Ashton.

Braun: What about the other costs at Ashton?

Whiting: If we shifted Ashton's business over to the other two processing centers in the region, we wouldn't save anything on direct labor or variable overhead costs. We might save $60,000 or so in local administrative expenses, but we would not save any regional administrative expense. And corporate headquarters would still charge us 8% of our revenues as corporate administrative expenses.

In addition, we would have to rent more space in Pocatello and Idaho Falls to handle the work transferred from Ashton; that would probably cost us at least $400,000 a year. And don't forget that it will cost us something to move the equipment from Ashton to Pocatello and Idaho Falls. And the move will disrupt service to customers.

Braun: I understand all of that, but a money-losing processing center on my performance report is completely unacceptable.

Whiting: And if you do shut down Ashton, you are going to throw some loyal employees out of work.

Braun: That's unfortunate, but we have to face hard business realities.

Whiting: And you would have to write off the investment in the facilities at Ashton.

Braun: I can explain a write-off to corporate headquarters; hiring an inexperienced contractor to build the Ashton facility was my predecessor's mistake. But they'll have my head at headquarters if I show operating losses every year at one of my processing centers. Ashton has to go. At the next corporate board meeting, I am going to recommend that the Ashton facility be closed.

Required:

1. From the standpoint of the company as a whole, should the Ashton processing center be shut down and its work redistributed to the other processing centers in the region? Explain.
2. Do you think Marvin Braun's decision to shut down the Ashton facility is ethical? Explain.
3. What influence should the depreciation on the facilities at Ashton have on prices charged by Ashton for its services?

CASE 12–33 Sell or Process Further Decision [LO7]

Midwest Mills has a plant that can mill wheat grain into a cracked wheat cereal and then further mill the cracked wheat into flour. The company can sell all the cracked wheat cereal that it can produce at a selling price of $490 per ton. In the past, the company has sold only part of its cracked wheat as cereal and has retained the rest for further milling into flour. The flour has been selling for $700 per ton, but recently the price has become unstable and has dropped to $625 per ton. The costs and revenues associated with a ton of flour follow:

		Per Ton of Flour
Selling price		$625
Cost to manufacture:		
Raw materials:		
Enrichment materials	$ 80	
Cracked wheat	470	
Total raw materials	550	
Direct labor	20	
Manufacturing overhead	60	630
Manufacturing profit (loss)		$ (5)

Because of the weak price for flour, the sales manager believes that the company should discontinue milling flour and use its entire milling capacity to produce cracked wheat to sell as cereal.

The same milling equipment is used for both products. Milling one ton of cracked wheat into one ton of flour requires the same capacity as milling one ton of wheat grain into one ton of cracked wheat. Hence, the choice is between one ton of flour and two tons of cracked wheat. Current cost and revenue data on the cracked wheat cereal follow:

		Per Ton of Cracked Wheat
Selling price		$490
Cost to manufacture:		
Wheat grain	$390	
Direct labor	20	
Manufacturing overhead	60	470
Manufacturing profit		$ 20

The sales manager argues that because the present $625 per ton price for the flour results in a $5 per ton loss, the milling of flour should not be resumed until the price per ton rises above $630.

The company assigns manufacturing overhead cost to the two products on the basis of milling hours. The same amount of time is required to mill either a ton of cracked wheat or a ton of flour. Virtually all manufacturing overhead costs are fixed. Materials and labor costs are variable.

The company can sell all of the cracked wheat and flour it can produce at the current market prices.

Required:

1. Do you agree with the sales manager that the company should discontinue milling flour and use the entire milling capacity to mill cracked wheat if the price of flour remains at $625 per ton? Support your answer with computations and explanations.
2. What is the lowest price that the company should accept for a ton of flour? Again support your answer with computations and explanations.

Chapter 13

Capital Budgeting Decisions

Capital Investments: A Key to Profitable Growth

BUSINESS FOCUS

Cintas Corporation, headquartered in Cincinnati, Ohio, provides highly specialized services to businesses of all types throughout North America. The backbone of its success is providing corporate identity uniforms to more than five million North American workers. Cintas has 419 uniform rental facilities, 6 manufacturing plants, and eight distribution centers across North America. The challenge for Cintas is choosing among competing capital expansion opportunities.

At Cintas, each capital investment proposal must be accompanied by a financial analysis that estimates the project's cash inflows and outflows. The job of the Controller of Cintas' Rental Division, is to challenge the validity of the assumptions underlying the financial estimates. Is the cost to build the new facility underestimated? Are future revenue growth rates overly optimistic? Is it necessary to build a new facility, or could an existing facility be refurbished or expanded? Asking these types of constructive questions helps Cintas channel its limited investment funds to the most profitable opportunities. ■

Source: Author's conversation with Paul Carmichael, Senior Controller, Cintas Corporation.

LEARNING OBJECTIVES

After studying Chapter 13, you should be able to:

LO1 Evaluate the acceptability of an investment project using the net present value method.

LO2 Evaluate the acceptability of an investment project using the internal rate of return method.

LO3 Evaluate an investment project that has uncertain cash flows.

LO4 Rank investment projects in order of preference.

LO5 Determine the payback period for an investment.

LO6 Compute the simple rate of return for an investment.

LO7 (Appendix 13A) Understand present value concepts and the use of present value tables.

LO8 (Appendix 13C) Include income taxes in a capital budgeting analysis.

Managers often consider decisions that involve an investment today in the hope of realizing future profits. For example, Tri-Con Global Restaurants, Inc., makes an investment when it opens a new Pizza Hut restaurant. L. L. Bean makes an investment when it installs a new computer to handle customer billing. Chrysler makes an investment when it redesigns a product such as the Jeep Eagle. Merck & Co. invests in medical research. Amazon.com makes an investment when it redesigns its website. All of these investments require spending now with the expectation of additional future net cash flows.

The term **capital budgeting** is used to describe how managers plan significant investments in projects that have long-term implications such as the purchase of new equipment or the introduction of new products. Most companies have many more potential projects than can actually be funded. Hence, managers must carefully select those projects that promise the greatest future return. How well managers make these capital budgeting decisions is a critical factor in the long-run financial health of the organization.

Capital Budgeting—Planning Investments

Typical Capital Budgeting Decisions

Any decision that involves an outlay now in order to obtain a future return is a capital budgeting decision. Typical capital budgeting decisions include:

1. Cost reduction decisions. Should new equipment be purchased to reduce costs?
2. Expansion decisions. Should a new plant, warehouse, or other facility be acquired to increase capacity and sales?
3. Equipment selection decisions. Which of several available machines should be purchased?
4. Lease or buy decisions. Should new equipment be leased or purchased?
5. Equipment replacement decisions. Should old equipment be replaced now or later?

Capital budgeting decisions fall into two broad categories—*screening decisions* and *preference decisions.* **Screening decisions** relate to whether a proposed project is acceptable—whether it passes a preset hurdle. For example, a company may have a policy of accepting projects only if they provide a return of at least 20% on the investment. The required rate of return is the minimum rate of return a project must yield to be acceptable. **Preference decisions,** by contrast, relate to selecting from among several acceptable alternatives. To illustrate, a company may be considering several different machines to replace an existing machine on the assembly line. The choice of which machine to purchase is a preference decision. In this chapter, we first discuss screening decisions and then move on to preference decisions toward the end of the chapter.

The Time Value of Money

Capital investments usually earn returns that extend over fairly long periods of time. Consequently, it is important to recognize *the time value of money* when evaluating investment proposals. A dollar today is worth more than a dollar a year from now if for no other reason than you could put a dollar in a bank today and have more than a dollar a year from now. Therefore, projects that promise earlier returns are preferable to those that promise later returns.

Capital budgeting techniques that recognize the time value of money involve *discounting cash flows.* We will spend most of this chapter showing how to use discounted cash flow methods in making capital budgeting decisions. If you are not already familiar with discounting and the use of present value tables, you should read Appendix 13A: The Concept of Present Value, at the end of this chapter, before proceeding any further.

IN BUSINESS

CHOOSING A CAT

Sometimes a long-term decision does not have to involve present value calculations or any other sophisticated analytical technique. White Grizzly Adventures of Meadow Creek, British Columbia, needs two snowcats for its powder skiing operations—one for shuttling guests to the top of the mountain and one to be held in reserve in case of mechanical problems with the first. Bombardier of Canada sells new snowcats for $250,000 and used, reconditioned snowcats for $150,000. In either case, the snowcats are good for about 5,000 hours of operation before they need to be reconditioned. From White Grizzly's perspective, the choice is clear. Because both new and reconditioned snowcats last about 5,000 hours, but the reconditioned snowcats cost $100,000 less, the reconditioned snowcats are the obvious choice. They may not have all of the latest bells and whistles, but they get the job done at a price a small company can afford.

Bombardier snowcats do not have passenger cabs as standard equipment. To save money, White Grizzly builds its own custom-designed passenger cab for about $15,000, using recycled Ford Escort seats and industrial-strength aluminum for the frame and siding. If purchased at retail, a passenger cab would cost about twice as much and would not be as well-suited for snowcat skiing.

Source: Brad & Carole Karafil, owners and operators of White Grizzly Adventures, www.whitegrizzly.com.

Discounted Cash Flows—The Net Present Value Method

LEARNING OBJECTIVE 1
Evaluate the acceptability of an investment project using the net present value method.

Two approaches to making capital budgeting decisions use discounted cash flows. One is the *net present value method,* and the other is the *internal rate of return method.* The net present value method is discussed in this section followed by a discussion of the internal rate of return method.

The Net Present Value Method Illustrated

Under the net present value method, the present value of a project's cash inflows is compared to the present value of the project's cash outflows. The difference between the present value of these cash flows, called the **net present value,** determines whether or not the project is an acceptable investment. To illustrate, consider the following data:

Example A: Harper Company is contemplating the purchase of a machine capable of performing some operations that are now performed manually. The machine will cost $50,000, and it will last for five years. At the end of the five-year period, the machine will have a zero scrap value. Use of the machine will reduce labor costs by $18,000 per year. Harper Company requires a minimum pretax return of 20% on all investment projects.[1]

Should the machine be purchased? Harper Company must determine whether a cash investment now of $50,000 can be justified if it will result in an $18,000 reduction in cost in each of the next five years. It may appear that the answer is obvious because the total cost savings is $90,000 ($18,000 per year × 5 years). However, the company can earn a 20% return by investing its money elsewhere. It is not enough that the cost reductions cover just the original cost of the machine; they must also yield a return of at least 20% or the company would be better off investing the money elsewhere.

[1] For simplicity, we ignore inflation and taxes. The impact of income taxes on capital budgeting decisions is discussed in Appendix 13C.

EXHIBIT 13–1
Net Present Value Analysis of a Proposed Project

Initial cost	$50,000
Life of the project	5 years
Annual cost savings	$18,000
Salvage value	$0
Required rate of return	20%

Item	Year(s)	Amount of Cash Flow	20% Factor	Present Value of Cash Flows
Annual cost savings	1–5	$18,000	2.991*	$53,838
Initial investment	Now	$(50,000)	1.000	(50,000)
Net present value				$ 3,838

*From Exhibit 13B–2 in Appendix 13B at the end of this chapter.

To determine whether the investment is desirable, the stream of annual $18,000 cost savings should be discounted to its present value and then compared to the cost of the new machine. Harper Company's minimum required return of 20% is used as the *discount rate* in the discounting process. Exhibit 13–1 illustrates the computation of the net present value of this proposed project. The annual cost savings of $18,000 is multiplied by 2.991, the present value factor of a five-year annuity at the discount rate of 20%, to obtain $53,838.[2] This is the present value of the annual cost savings. The present value of the initial investment is computed by multiplying the investment amount of $50,000 by 1.000, the present value factor for any cash flow that occurs immediately.

According to the analysis, Harper Company should purchase the new machine. The present value of the cost savings is $53,838, whereas the present value of the required investment (cost of the machine) is only $50,000. Deducting the present value of the required investment from the present value of the cost savings yields the *net present value* of $3,838. Whenever the net present value is zero or greater, as in our example, an investment project is acceptable. Whenever the net present value is negative (the present value of the cash outflows exceeds the present value of the cash inflows), an investment project is not acceptable. In sum:

If the Net Present Value Is . . .	Then the Project Is . . .
Positive	Acceptable because its return is greater than the required rate of return.
Zero	Acceptable because its return is equal to the required rate of return.
Negative	Not acceptable because its return is less than the required rate of return.

There is another way to interpret the net present value. Harper Company could spend up to $53,838 for the new machine and still obtain the minimum required 20% rate of return. The net present value of $3,838, therefore, shows the amount of "cushion" or "margin of error." One way to look at this is that the company could underestimate the cost of the new machine by up to $3,838, or overestimate the net present value of the future cash savings by up to $3,838, and the project would still be financially attractive.

[2] Unless otherwise stated, for the sake of simplicity we will assume in this chapter that all cash flows other than the initial investment occur at the ends of years.

Emphasis on Cash Flows

Accounting net income is based on accruals that ignore when cash flows occur. However, in capital budgeting, the timing of cash flows is critical. The present value of a cash flow depends on when it occurs. For that reason, cash flow rather than accounting net income is the focus in capital budgeting.[3] Examples of cash outflows and cash inflows that are often relevant to capital investment decisions are described below.

Typical Cash Outflows Most projects have at least three types of cash outflows. First, they often require an immediate cash outflow in the form of an initial investment in equipment, other assets, and installation costs. Any salvage value realized from the sale of old equipment can be recognized as a reduction in the initial investment or as a cash inflow. Second, some projects require a company to expand its working capital. **Working capital** is current assets (e.g., cash, accounts receivable, and inventory) less current liabilities. When a company takes on a new project, the balances in the current asset accounts often increase. For example, opening a new Nordstrom's department store requires additional cash in sales registers and more inventory. These additional working capital needs are treated as part of the initial investment in a project. Third, many projects require periodic outlays for repairs and maintenance and additional operating costs.

Typical Cash Inflows Most projects also have at least three types of cash inflows. First, a project will normally increase revenues or reduce costs. Either way, the amount involved should be treated as a cash inflow for capital budgeting purposes. Notice that from a cash flow standpoint, a reduction in costs is equivalent to an increase in revenues. Second, cash inflows are also frequently realized from selling equipment for its salvage value when a project ends, although the company may actually have to pay to dispose of some low-value or hazardous items. Third, any working capital that was tied up in the project can be released for use elsewhere at the end of the project and should be treated as a cash inflow at that time. Working capital is released, for example, when a company sells off its inventory or collects its accounts receivable.

IN BUSINESS

BEST BUY'S BIG GAMBLE

Best Buy is overhauling hundreds of its stores in an effort to tailor merchandise offerings and employee skills to meet the needs of each store's target customers. The cost to revamp one department of one store can easily exceed $600,000 for lighting and fixtures, plus additional costs for employee training. While these initial cash outflows are readily quantifiable, the future cash inflows that they will generate are highly uncertain.

The first few dozen stores overhauled by Best Buy recorded sales growth that was three times greater than nonrenovated stores. Best Buy reacted to these initial results by hastily renovating 154 more stores over the next three months. Shortly after completing these expensive renovations, the company had the misfortune of informing Wall Street that the newly revamped stores' growth rates were only slightly higher than nonrenovated stores. This disappointing news apparently caused the market value of Best Buy's common stock to plummet by almost $3 billion in one day. Clearly, Wall Street analysts had serious concerns about the future cash flow generating ability of this capital investment project. Despite the "bump in the road," Best Buy remains committed to its course of action; however, the company has decided to slow down the pace of its implementation.

Source: Matthew Boyle, "Best Buy's Giant Gamble," *Fortune*, April, 3, 2006, pp. 69–75.

[3] Under certain conditions, capital budgeting decisions can be correctly made by discounting appropriately defined accounting net income. However, this approach requires advanced techniques that are beyond the scope of this book.

In summary, the following types of cash flows are common in business investment projects:

Cash outflows:
- Initial investment (including installation costs).
- Increased working capital needs.
- Repairs and maintenance.
- Incremental operating costs.

Cash inflows:
- Incremental revenues.
- Reduction in costs.
- Salvage value.
- Release of working capital.

Recovery of the Original Investment

The net present value method automatically provides for return of the original investment. Whenever the net present value of a project is positive, the project will recover the original cost of the investment plus sufficient excess cash inflows to compensate the organization for tying up funds in the project. To demonstrate this point, consider the following situation:

Example B: Carver Hospital is considering the purchase of an attachment for its X-ray machine that will cost $3,170. The attachment will be usable for four years, after which time it will have no salvage value. It will increase net cash inflows by $1,000 per year in the X-ray department. The hospital's board of directors requires a rate of return of at least 10% on such investments.

A net present value analysis of the desirability of purchasing the X-ray attachment is presented in Exhibit 13–2. Notice that the attachment has exactly a 10% return on the original investment because the net present value is zero at a 10% discount rate.

Each annual $1,000 cash inflow arising from use of the attachment is made up of two parts. One part represents a recovery of a portion *of* the original $3,170 paid for the attachment, and the other part represents a return *on* this investment. The breakdown of each year's $1,000 cash inflow between recovery *of* investment and return *on* investment is shown in Exhibit 13–3.

The first year's $1,000 cash inflow consists of a return *on* investment of $317 (a 10% return *on* the $3,170 original investment), plus a $683 return *of* that investment. Because

EXHIBIT 13–2
Carver Hospital—Net Present Value Analysis of X-Ray Attachment

Initial cost	$3,170
Life of the project	4 years
Annual net cash inflow	$1,000
Salvage value	$0
Required rate of return	10%

Item	Year(s)	Amount of Cash Flow	10% Factor	Present Value of Cash Flows
Annual net cash inflow . . .	1–4	$1,000	3.170*	$ 3,170
Initial investment	Now	$(3,170)	1.000	(3,170)
Net present value				$ 0

*From Exhibit 13B–2 in Appendix 13B.

EXHIBIT 13–3
Carver Hospital—Breakdown of Annual Cash Inflows

Year	(1) Investment Outstanding during the Year	(2) Cash Inflow	(3) Return on Investment (1) × 10%	(4) Recovery of Investment during the Year (2) − (3)	(5) Unrecovered Investment at the End of the Year (1) − (4)
1	$3,170	$1,000	$317	$ 683	$2,487
2	$2,487	$1,000	$249	751	$1,736
3	$1,736	$1,000	$173	827	$909
4	$909	$1,000	$91	909	$0
Total investment recovered				$3,170	

the amount of the unrecovered investment decreases each year, the dollar amount of the return on investment also decreases each year. By the end of the fourth year, all $3,170 of the original investment has been recovered.

Simplifying Assumptions

Two simplifying assumptions are usually made in net present value analysis.

The first assumption is that all cash flows other than the initial investment occur at the end of periods. This is somewhat unrealistic in that cash flows typically occur *throughout* a period rather than just at its end. The purpose of this assumption is to simplify computations.

The second assumption is that all cash flows generated by an investment project are immediately reinvested at a rate of return equal to the discount rate. Unless these conditions are met, the net present value computed for the project will not be accurate. We used a discount rate of 10% for Carver Hospital in Exhibit 13–2. Unless the cash flows in each period are immediately reinvested at a 10% return, the net present value computed for the X-ray attachment will be misstated.

Choosing a Discount Rate

A positive net present value indicates that the project's return exceeds the discount rate. A negative net present value indicates that the project's return is less than the discount rate. Therefore, if the company's minimum required rate of return is used as the discount rate, a project with a positive net present value has a return that exceeds the minimum required rate of return and is acceptable. Contrarily, a project with a negative net present value has a return that is less than the minimum required rate of return and is unacceptable.

What is a company's minimum required rate of return? The company's *cost of capital* is usually regarded as the minimum required rate of return. The **cost of capital** is the average rate of return the company must pay to its long-term creditors and its shareholders for the use of their funds. If a project's rate of return is less than the cost of capital, the company does not earn enough to compensate its creditors and shareholders. Therefore, any project with a rate of return less than the cost of capital should be rejected.

The cost of capital serves as a *screening device.* When the cost of capital is used as the discount rate in net present value analysis, any project with a negative net present value does not cover the company's cost of capital and should be discarded as unacceptable.

IN BUSINESS

BUCK KNIVES PACKS ITS BAGS

Buck Knives was losing money at its plant in San Diego, California. The company responded by loading its entire factory into a caravan of tractor-trailers and moving to Post Falls, Idaho. The relocation cost \$6.5 million, but Buck Knives justified the move based on the annual cost savings summarized below.

	San Diego	Post Falls
Electricity (cost per kilowatt hour)	\$0.118	\$0.031
Workers' compensation (cost per employee per year)	\$2,095	\$210
Median hourly wage	\$15.15	\$12.40
State business tax	8.84%	7.6%
Health insurance (per family per year)	\$9,091	\$8,563
Office space (cost per square foot)	\$34.20	\$1.50
Sales tax	7.75%	5%

How would you analyze the financial viability of this decision? The first step would be to convert the data in the above table into annual lump sum savings. Then, net present value analysis could be used to compare the discounted value of the annual cost savings to the initial cash outlay associated with the relocation.

Source: Chris Lydgate, "The Buck Stopped Here," *Inc.* magazine, May 2006, pp. 86–95.

An Extended Example of the Net Present Value Method

Example C provides an extended example of how the net present value method is used to analyze a proposed project. This example helps tie together and reinforce many of the ideas discussed thus far.

Example C: Under a special licensing arrangement, Swinyard Corporation has an opportunity to market a new product for a five-year period. The product would be purchased from the manufacturer, with Swinyard responsible for promotion and distribution costs. The licensing arrangement could be renewed at the end of the five-year period. After careful study, Swinyard estimated the following costs and revenues for the new product:

Cost of equipment needed	\$60,000
Working capital needed	\$100,000
Overhaul of the equipment in four years	\$5,000
Salvage value of the equipment in five years	\$10,000
Annual revenues and costs:	
Sales revenues	\$200,000
Cost of goods sold	\$125,000
Out-of-pocket operating costs (for salaries, advertising, and other direct costs)	\$35,000

At the end of the five-year period, if Swinyard decides not to renew the licensing arrangement the working capital would be released for investment elsewhere. Swinyard uses a 14% discount rate. Would you recommend that the new product be introduced?

This example involves a variety of cash inflows and cash outflows. The solution is given in Exhibit 13–4.

Notice how the working capital is handled in this exhibit. It is counted as a cash outflow at the beginning of the project and as a cash inflow when it is released at the end of the project. Also notice how the sales revenues, cost of goods sold, and out-of-pocket costs are handled. **Out-of-pocket costs** are actual cash outlays for salaries, advertising, and other operating expenses.

Because the net present value of the proposal is positive, the new product is acceptable.

EXHIBIT 13–4
The Net Present Value Method—An Extended Example

Sales revenues	$200,000
Less cost of goods sold	125,000
Less out-of-pocket costs for salaries, advertising, etc.	35,000
Annual net cash inflows	$ 40,000

Item	Year(s)	Amount of Cash Flow	14% Factor	Present Value of Cash Flows
Purchase of equipment	Now	$(60,000)	1.000	$ (60,000)
Working capital needed	Now	$(100,000)	1.000	(100,000)
Overhaul of equipment	4	$(5,000)	0.592*	(2,960)
Annual net cash inflows from sales of the product line	1–5	$40,000	3.433†	137,320
Salvage value of the equipment	5	$10,000	0.519*	5,190
Working capital released	5	$100,000	0.519*	51,900
Net present value				$ 31,450

*From Exhibit 13B–1 in Appendix 13B.
†From Exhibit 13B–2 in Appendix 13B.

IN BUSINESS

ECONOMIC WOES SHRINK CAPITAL BUDGETS

When the health of the economy is uncertain, capital spending declines. Rite Aid CEO Mary Sammons cut her company's capital budget by $50 million due to uncertain economic conditions. PetroHawk Energy responded to a weak economy by slashing its $1.5 billion capital budget by one-third. Estee Lauder tightened its belt by challenging managers to defend what they must have and define what they can give up. YUM! Brands (owner of Pizza Hut, KFC, and Taco Bell) navigated the difficult economy by abandoning projects that "might come true" in favor of a "must have" capital budgeting mentality.

Source: Matthew Boyle, "The Budget Knives Come Out," *BusinessWeek*, October 13, 2008, p. 30.

Discounted Cash Flows—The Internal Rate of Return Method

LEARNING OBJECTIVE 2
Evaluate the acceptability of an investment project using the internal rate of return method.

The **internal rate of return** is the rate of return of an investment project over its useful life. The internal rate of return is computed by finding the discount rate that equates the present value of a project's cash outflows with the present value of its cash inflows. In other words, the internal rate of return is the discount rate that results in a net present value of zero.

The Internal Rate of Return Method Illustrated

To illustrate the internal rate of return method, consider the following data:

Example D: Glendale School District is considering the purchase of a large tractor-pulled lawn mower. At present, the lawn is mowed using a small hand-pushed gas mower. The large, tractor-pulled mower will cost $16,950 and will have a useful life of 10 years. It will have a negligible scrap value, which can be ignored. The tractor-pulled mower would do the job faster than the old mower, resulting in labor savings of $3,000 per year.

To compute the internal rate of return of the new mower, we must find the discount rate that will result in a zero net present value. How do we do this? The simplest and most direct approach *when the net cash inflow is the same every year* is to divide the investment in the project by the expected annual net cash inflow. This computation yields a factor from which the internal rate of return can be determined. The formula is as follows:

$$\text{Factor of the internal rate of return} = \frac{\text{Investment required}}{\text{Annual net cash inflow}} \qquad (1)$$

The factor derived from formula (1) is then located in the present value tables to see what rate of return it represents. Using formula (1) and the data for the Glendale School District's proposed project, we get:

$$\frac{\text{Investment required}}{\text{Annual net cash inflow}} = \frac{\$16{,}950}{\$3{,}000} = 5.650$$

Thus, the discount factor that will equate a series of $3,000 cash inflows with a present investment of $16,950 is 5.650. Now we need to find this factor in Exhibit 13B–2 in Appendix 13B to see what rate of return it represents. We should use the 10-period line in Exhibit 13B–2 because the cash flows for the project continue for 10 years. If we scan along the 10-period line, we find that a factor of 5.650 represents a 12% rate of return. Therefore, the internal rate of return of the mower project is 12%. We can verify this by computing the project's net present value using a 12% discount rate as shown in Exhibit 13–5.

Notice from Exhibit 13–5 that using a 12% discount rate equates the present value of the annual net cash inflows with the present value of the investment required for the project, leaving a zero net present value. The 12% rate therefore represents the internal rate of return of the project.

Salvage Value and Other Cash Flows

The technique just demonstrated works if a project's cash flows are identical every year. But what if they are not? For example, what if a project will have some salvage value at the end of its life in addition to the annual cash inflows? Under these circumstances, a trial-and-error process may be used to find the rate of return that will result in a zero net present value. The trial-and-error process can be carried out by hand; however, computer software programs such as spreadsheets can perform the necessary computations in seconds. Erratic or uneven cash flows should not prevent an analyst from determining a project's internal rate of return.

EXHIBIT 13–5
Evaluation of the Mower Using a 12% Discount Rate

Initial cost	$16,950
Life of the project	10 years
Annual cost savings	$3,000
Salvage value	$0

Item	Year(s)	Amount of Cash Flow	12% Factor	Present Value of Cash Flows
Annual cost savings	1–10	$3,000	5.650*	$16,950
Initial investment	Now	$(16,950)	1.000	(16,950)
Net present value				$ 0

*From Exhibit 13B–2 in Appendix 13B.

Using the Internal Rate of Return

To evaluate a project, the internal rate of return is compared to the company's minimum required rate of return, which is usually the company's cost of capital. If the internal rate of return is equal to or greater than the required rate of return, then the project is acceptable. If the internal rate of return is less than the required rate of return, then the project is rejected.

In the case of the Glendale School District example, let us assume that the district has set a minimum required rate of return of 15% on all projects. Because the large mower's internal rate of return is only 12%, the project does not clear the 15% hurdle and should be rejected.

The Cost of Capital as a Screening Tool

As we have seen in preceding examples, the cost of capital is often used to screen out undesirable investment projects. This screening is accomplished in different ways, depending on whether the company is using the internal rate of return method or the net present value method.

When the internal rate of return method is used, the cost of capital is used as the *hurdle rate* that a project must clear for acceptance. If the internal rate of return of a project is not high enough to clear the cost of capital hurdle, then the project is ordinarily rejected. We saw the application of this idea in the Glendale School District example, where the hurdle rate was set at 15%.

When the net present value method is used, the cost of capital is the *discount rate* used to compute the net present value of a proposed project. Any project yielding a negative net present value is rejected unless other factors are significant enough to warrant its acceptance.

The use of the cost of capital as a screening tool is summarized in Exhibit 13–6.

Comparison of the Net Present Value and Internal Rate of Return Methods

The net present value method has several important advantages over the internal rate of return method.

First, the net present value method is often simpler to use than the internal rate of return method. As mentioned earlier, the internal rate of return method may require hunting for the discount rate that results in a net present value of zero. This can be a very laborious trial-and-error process, although it can be automated using a computer.

EXHIBIT 13–6
Capital Budgeting Screening Decisions

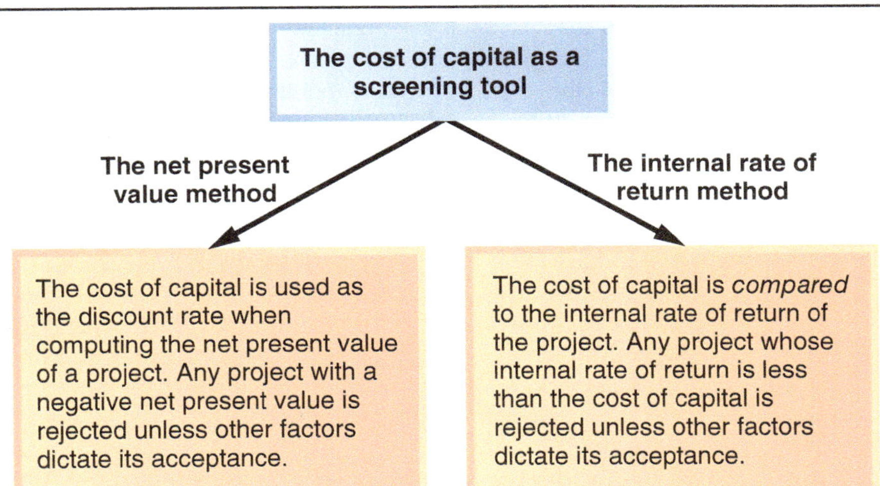

Second, the internal rate of return method makes a questionable assumption. Both methods assume that cash flows generated by a project during its useful life are immediately reinvested elsewhere. However, the two methods make different assumptions concerning the rate of return that is earned on those cash flows. The net present value method assumes the rate of return is the discount rate, whereas the internal rate of return method assumes the rate of return earned on cash flows is the internal rate of return on the project. Specifically, if the internal rate of return of the project is high, this assumption may not be realistic. It is generally more realistic to assume that cash inflows can be reinvested at a rate of return equal to the discount rate—particularly if the discount rate is the company's cost of capital or an opportunity rate of return. For example, if the discount rate is the company's cost of capital, this rate of return can be actually realized by paying off the company's creditors and buying back the company's stock with cash flows from the project. In short, when the net present value method and the internal rate of return method do not agree concerning the attractiveness of a project, it is best to go with the net present value method. Of the two methods, it makes the more realistic assumption about the rate of return that can be earned on cash flows from the project.

Expanding the Net Present Value Method

So far, all of our examples have involved an evaluation of a single investment project. In the following section we expand the discussion of the net present value method to include evaluation of two alternative projects. In addition, we integrate relevant cost concepts into the discounted cash flow analysis. We use two approaches to compare competing investment projects—the *total-cost approach* and the *incremental-cost approach.* Each approach is illustrated in the next few pages.

The Total-Cost Approach

The total-cost approach is the most flexible method for comparing competing projects. To illustrate the mechanics of the approach, consider the following data:

Example E: Harper Ferry Company operates a high-speed passenger ferry service across the Mississippi River. One of its ferryboats is in poor condition. This ferry can be renovated at an immediate cost of $200,000. Further repairs and an overhaul of the motor will be needed five years from now at a cost of $80,000. In all, the ferry will be usable for 10 years if this work is done. At the end of 10 years, the ferry will have to be scrapped at a salvage value of $60,000. The scrap value of the ferry right now is $70,000. It will cost $300,000 each year to operate the ferry, and revenues will total $400,000 annually.

As an alternative, Harper Ferry Company can purchase a new ferryboat at a cost of $360,000. The new ferry will have a life of 10 years, but it will require some repairs costing $30,000 at the end of 5 years. At the end of 10 years, the ferry will have a scrap value of $60,000. It will cost $210,000 each year to operate the ferry, and revenues will total $400,000 annually.

Harper Ferry Company requires a return of at least 14% on all investment projects.

Should the company purchase the new ferry or renovate the old ferry? Exhibit 13–7 shows the solution using the total-cost approach.

Two points should be noted from the exhibit. First, *all* cash inflows and *all* cash outflows are included in the solution under each alternative. No effort has been made to isolate those cash flows that are relevant to the decision and those that are not relevant. The inclusion of all cash flows associated with each alternative gives the approach its name—the *total-cost* approach.

Second, notice that a net present value is computed for each alternative. This is a distinct advantage of the total-cost approach because an unlimited number of alternatives can be compared side by side to determine the best option. For example, another

EXHIBIT 13–7
The Total-Cost Approach to Project Selection

	New Ferry	Old Ferry
Annual revenues	$400,000	$400,000
Annual cash operating costs	210,000	300,000
Annual net cash inflows	$190,000	$100,000

Item	Year(s)	Amount of Cash Flows	14% Factor*	Present Value of Cash Flows
Buy the new ferry:				
Initial investment	Now	$(360,000)	1.000	$(360,000)
Salvage value of the old ferry	Now	$70,000	1.000	70,000
Repairs in five years	5	$(30,000)	0.519	(15,570)
Annual net cash inflows	1–10	$190,000	5.216	991,040
Salvage value of the new ferry	10	$60,000	0.270	16,200
Net present value				701,670
Keep the old ferry:				
Renovation	Now	$(200,000)	1.000	(200,000)
Repairs in five years	5	$(80,000)	0.519	(41,520)
Annual net cash inflows	1–10	$100,000	5.216	521,600
Salvage value of the old ferry	10	$60,000	0.270	16,200
Net present value				296,280
Net present value in favor of buying the new ferry				$ 405,390

*All present value factors are from Exhibits 13B–1 and 13B–2 in Appendix 13B.

alternative for Harper Ferry Company would be to get out of the ferry business entirely. If management desired, the net present value of this alternative could be computed to compare with the alternatives shown in Exhibit 13–7. Still other alternatives might be open to the company. In the case at hand, given only two alternatives, the data indicate that the most profitable choice is to purchase the new ferry.[4]

The Incremental-Cost Approach

When only two alternatives are being considered, the incremental-cost approach offers a simpler and more direct route to a decision. In the incremental-cost approach, only those costs and revenues that *differ* between the two alternatives are included in the analysis. To illustrate, refer again to the data in Example E relating to Harper Ferry Company. The solution using only differential costs is presented in Exhibit 13–8.[5]

Two things should be noted from the data in this exhibit. First, the net present value in favor of buying the new ferry of $405,390 shown in Exhibit 13–8 agrees with the net present value shown under the total-cost approach in Exhibit 13–7. The two approaches are equivalent.

[4] The alternative with the highest net present value is not always the best choice, although it is the best choice in this case. For further discussion, see the section Preference Decisions—The Ranking of Investment Projects.

[5] Technically, the incremental-cost approach is misnamed because it focuses on differential costs (that is, on both cost increases and decreases) rather than just on incremental costs. As used here, the term *incremental costs* should be interpreted broadly to include both cost increases and cost decreases.

EXHIBIT 13–8
The Incremental-Cost Approach to Project Selection

Item	Year(s)	Amount of Cash Flows	14% Factor*	Present Value of Cash Flows
Incremental investment to buy the new ferry	Now	$(160,000)	1.000	$(160,000)
Salvage value of the old ferry now	Now	$70,000	1.000	70,000
Difference in repair costs in five years	5	$50,000	0.519	25,950
Increase in annual net cash inflows	1–10	$90,000	5.216	469,440
Difference in salvage value in 10 years	10	$0	0.270	0
Net present value in favor of buying the new ferry				$ 405,390

*All present value factors are from Exhibits 13B–1 and 13B–2 in Appendix 13B.

Second, the costs used in Exhibit 13–8 are just the differences between the costs shown for the two alternatives in the prior exhibit. For example, the $160,000 incremental investment required to purchase the new ferry in Exhibit 13–8 is the difference between the $360,000 cost of the new ferry and the $200,000 cost required to renovate the old ferry from Exhibit 13–7. The other numbers in Exhibit 13–8 have been computed in the same way.

Least-Cost Decisions

Some decisions do not involve any revenues. For example, a company may be trying to decide whether to buy or lease an executive jet. The choice would be made on the basis of which alternative—buying or leasing—would be least costly. In situations such as these, where no revenues are involved, the most desirable alternative is the one with the *least total cost* from a present value perspective. Hence, these are known as least-cost decisions. To illustrate a least-cost decision, consider the following data:

Example F: Val-Tek Company is considering replacing an old threading machine with a new threading machine that would substantially reduce annual operating costs. Selected data relating to the old and new machines are presented below:

	Old Machine	New Machine
Purchase cost when new	$200,000	$250,000
Salvage value now	$30,000	—
Annual cash operating costs	$150,000	$90,000
Overhaul needed immediately	$40,000	—
Salvage value in six years	$0	$50,000
Remaining life	6 years	6 years

Val-Tek Company uses a 10% discount rate.

Exhibit 13–9 analyzes the alternatives using the total-cost approach. Because this is a least-cost decision, the present values are negative for both alternatives. However, the present value of the alternative of buying the new machine is $109,500 higher than the other alternative. Therefore, buying the new machine is the less costly alternative.

Exhibit 13–10 presents an analysis of the same alternatives using the incremental-cost approach. Once again, when done correctly, the total-cost and incremental-cost approaches arrive at the same answer.

EXHIBIT 13–9
The Total-Cost Approach (Least-Cost Decision)

Item	Year(s)	Amount of Cash Flows	10% Factor*	Present Value of Cash Flows
Buy the new machine:				
Initial investment	Now	$(250,000)	1.000	$(250,000)†
Salvage value of the old machine	Now	$30,000	1.000	30,000 †
Annual cash operating costs	1–6	$(90,000)	4.355	(391,950)
Salvage value of the new machine	6	$50,000	0.564	28,200
Present value of net cash outflows				(583,750)
Keep the old machine:				
Overhaul needed now	Now	$(40,000)	1.000	$ (40,000)
Annual cash operating costs	1–6	$(150,000)	4.355	(653,250)
Present value of net cash outflows				(693,250)
Net present value in favor of buying the new machine				$ 109,500

*All factors are from Exhibits 13B–1 and 13B–2 in Appendix 13B.
†These two items could be netted into a single $220,000 incremental-cost figure ($250,000 − $30,000 = $220,000).

EXHIBIT 13–10
The Incremental-Cost Approach (Least-Cost Decision)

Item	Year(s)	Amount of Cash Flows	10% Factor*	Present Value of Cash Flows
Incremental investment required to purchase the new machine	Now	$(210,000)	1.000	$(210,000)†
Salvage value of the old machine	Now	$30,000	1.000	30,000†
Savings in annual cash operating costs	1–6	$60,000	4.355	261,300
Difference in salvage value in six years	6	$50,000	0.564	28,200
Net present value in favor of buying the new machine				$ 109,500

*All factors are from Exhibits 13B–1 and 13B–2 in Appendix 13B.
†These two items could be netted into a single $180,000 incremental-cost figure ($210,000 − $30,000 = $180,000).

IN BUSINESS

HOME CONSTRUCTION GOES GREEN—OR DOES IT?

Many homebuyers like the idea of building environmentally friendly homes until they get the bill. Specpan, an Indianapolis research firm, estimates a "green" home costs 10%–19% more than a comparable conventional home. For example, installing solar-electric glass-faced tiles on a roof costs $15,000 per 100 square feet compared to $1,200 per 100 square feet for standard fiber-cement tiles. Environmentally friendly interior paint costs $35–$42 per gallon compared to $20–$32 per gallon for standard latex paint. To further complicate this least-cost decision, the average homeowner lives in a house only seven years before moving. Within this time frame, many green investments appear to be financially unattractive. Nonetheless, the American Institute of Architects reports that 63% of their clients expressed an interest in renewable flooring materials such as cork and bamboo, up from 53% a year earlier.

Source: June Fletcher, "The Price of Going Green," *The Wall Street Journal*, February 29, 2008, p. W8.

Uncertain Cash Flows

LEARNING OBJECTIVE 3
Evaluate an investment project that has uncertain cash flows.

Thus far, we have assumed that all future cash flows are known with certainty. However, future cash flows are often uncertain or difficult to estimate. A number of techniques are available for handling this complication. Some of these techniques are quite technical—involving computer simulations or advanced mathematical skills—and are beyond the scope of this book. However, we can provide some very useful information to managers without getting too technical.

An Example

As an example of difficult-to-estimate future cash flows, consider the case of investments in automated equipment. The up-front costs of automated equipment and the tangible benefits, such as reductions in operating costs and waste, tend to be relatively easy to estimate. However, the intangible benefits, such as greater reliability, greater speed, and higher quality, are more difficult to quantify in terms of future cash flows. These intangible benefits certainly impact future cash flows—particularly in terms of increased sales and perhaps higher selling prices—but the cash flow effects are difficult to estimate. What can be done?

A fairly simple procedure can be followed when the intangible benefits are likely to be significant. Suppose, for example, that a company with a 12% discount rate is considering purchasing automated equipment that would have a 10-year useful life. Also suppose that a discounted cash flow analysis of just the tangible costs and benefits shows a negative net present value of $226,000. Clearly, if the intangible benefits are large enough, they could turn this negative net present value into a positive net present value. In this case, the amount of additional cash flow per year from the intangible benefits that would be needed to make the project financially attractive can be computed as follows:

Net present value excluding the intangible benefits (negative)	$(226,000)
Present value factor for an annuity at 12% for 10 periods (from Exhibit 13B–2 in Appendix 13B)	5.650

$$\frac{\text{Negative net present value to be offset, \$226,000}}{\text{Present value factor, 5.650}} = \$40,000$$

Thus, if the intangible benefits of the automated equipment are worth at least $40,000 a year to the company, then the automated equipment should be purchased. If, in the judgment of management, these intangible benefits are not worth $40,000 a year, then the automated equipment should not be purchased.

This technique can be used in other situations in which future cash flows are difficult to estimate. For example, this technique can be used when the salvage value is difficult to estimate. To illustrate, suppose that all of the cash flows from an investment in a supertanker have been estimated—other than its salvage value in 20 years. Using a discount rate of 12%, management has determined that the net present value of all of these cash flows is a negative $1.04 million. This negative net present value would be offset by the salvage value of the supertanker. How large would the salvage value have to be to make this investment attractive?

Net present value excluding salvage value (negative)	$(1,040,000)
Present value factor at 12% for 20 periods (from Exhibit 13B–1 in Appendix 13B)	0.104

$$\frac{\text{Negative net present value to be offset, \$1,040,000}}{\text{Present value factor, 0.104}} = \$10,000,000$$

Thus, if the salvage value of the tanker in 20 years is at least $10 million, its net present value would be positive and the investment would be made. However, if management believes the salvage value is unlikely to be as large as $10 million, the investment should not be made.

Real Options

The analysis in this chapter has assumed that an investment cannot be postponed and that, once started, nothing can be done to alter the course of the project. In reality, investments can often be postponed. Postponement is a particularly attractive option when the net present value of a project is modest using current estimates of future cash flows and the future cash flows involve a great deal of uncertainty that may be resolved over time. Similarly, once an investment is made, management can often exploit changes in the business environment and take actions that enhance future cash flows. For example, buying a supertanker provides management with a number of options, some of which may become more attractive as time unfolds. Instead of operating the supertanker itself, the company may decide to lease it to another operator if the rental rates become high enough. Or, if a supertanker shortage develops, management may decide to sell the supertanker and take a gain. In the case of an investment in automated equipment, management may initially buy only the basic model without costly add-ons, but keep the option open to add more capacity and capability later. The ability to delay the start of a project, to expand it if conditions are favorable, to cut losses if they are unfavorable, and to otherwise modify plans as business conditions change adds value to many investments. These advantages can be quantified using what is called *real options* analysis, but the techniques are beyond the scope of this book.

Preference Decisions—The Ranking of Investment Projects

LEARNING OBJECTIVE 4
Rank investment projects in order of preference.

Recall that when considering investment opportunities, managers must make two types of decisions—screening decisions and preference decisions. Screening decisions, which come first, pertain to whether or not a proposed investment is acceptable. Preference decisions come *after* screening decisions and attempt to answer the following question: "How do the remaining investment proposals, all of which have been screened and provide an acceptable rate of return, rank in terms of preference? That is, which one(s) would be *best* for the company to accept?"

Sometimes preference decisions are called rationing decisions, or ranking decisions. Limited investment funds must be rationed among many competing alternatives. Hence, the alternatives must be ranked. Either the internal rate of return method or the net present value method can be used in making preference decisions. However, as discussed earlier, if the two methods are in conflict, it is best to use the net present value method, which is more reliable.

Internal Rate of Return Method

When using the internal rate of return method to rank competing investment projects, the preference rule is: *The higher the internal rate of return, the more desirable the project.* An investment project with an internal rate of return of 18% is usually considered preferable to another project that has a return of only 15%. Internal rate of return is widely used to rank projects.

Net Present Value Method

The net present value of one project cannot be directly compared to the net present value of another project unless the initial investments are equal. For example, assume that a company is considering two competing investments, as shown below:

	Investment A	Investment B
Investment required	$(10,000)	$(5,000)
Present value of cash inflows	11,000	6,000
Net present value	$ 1,000	$ 1,000

Although each project has a net present value of $1,000, the projects are not equally desirable if the funds available for investment are limited. The project requiring an investment of only $5,000 is much more desirable than the project requiring an investment of $10,000. This fact can be highlighted by dividing the net present value of the project by the investment required. The result, shown below in equation form, is called the **project profitability index.**

$$\text{Project profitability index} = \frac{\text{Net present value of the project}}{\text{Investment required}} \qquad (2)$$

The project profitability indexes for the two investments above would be computed as follows:

	Investment A	Investment B
Net present value (a)	$1,000	$1,000
Investment required (b)	$10,000	$5,000
Project profitability index, (a) ÷ (b)	0.10	0.20

When using the project profitability index to rank competing investments projects, the preference rule is: *The higher the project profitability index, the more desirable the project.*[6] Applying this rule to the two investments above, investment B should be chosen over investment A.

The project profitability index is an application of the techniques for utilizing constrained resources discussed in an earlier chapter. In this case, the constrained resource is the limited funds available for investment, and the project profitability index is similar to the contribution margin per unit of the constrained resource.

A few details should be clarified with respect to the computation of the project profitability index. The "Investment required" refers to any cash outflows that occur at the beginning of the project, reduced by any salvage value recovered from the sale of old equipment. The "Investment required" also includes any investment in working capital that the project may need.

---

[6] Because of the "lumpiness" of projects, the project profitability index ranking may not be perfect. Nevertheless, it is a good starting point. For further details, see the Profitability Analysis Appendix at the end of the book.

IN BUSINESS

FEDEX GOES GREEN—WELL, NOT EXACTLY!

In 2003, FedEx announced a 10-year plan to replace 3,000 delivery trucks per year with environmentally friendly hybrid vehicles, thereby eliminating 250,000 tons of greenhouse gases per year. The hybrid vehicles cost 75% more than conventional trucks, but over 10 years they generate fuel savings that offset the higher cost. By 2007, FedEx had purchased less than 100 hybrid vehicles because management decided that the eco-friendly investment was not the most profitable use of the company's resources. FedEx's environmental director justified the company's actions by saying "we do have a fiduciary responsibility to our shareholders . . . we can't subsidize the development of this technology for our competitors."

This example illustrates the challenges that companies face when attempting to satisfy the expectations of various stakeholders. Perhaps FedEx shareholders would applaud the company's decision to retreat from its 10-year plan, whereas environmentally conscious customers may criticize the company's actions. What do you think?

Source: Ben Elgin, "Little Green Lies," *BusinessWeek*, October 29, 2007, pp. 45–52.

Other Approaches to Capital Budgeting Decisions

The net present value and internal rate of return methods are widely used as decision-making tools. However, some managers also use the payback method and simple rate of return method to make capital budgeting decisions. Each of these methods will be discussed in turn.

The Payback Method

LEARNING OBJECTIVE 5
Determine the payback period for an investment.

The payback method focuses on the *payback period.* The **payback period** is the length of time that it takes for a project to recover its initial cost from the net cash inflows that it generates. This period is sometimes referred to as "the time that it takes for an investment to pay for itself." The basic premise of the payback method is that the more quickly the cost of an investment can be recovered, the more desirable is the investment.

The payback period is expressed in years. *When the annual net cash inflow is the same every year,* the following formula can be used to compute the payback period:

$$\text{Payback period} = \frac{\text{Investment required}}{\text{Annual net cash inflow}} \tag{3}$$

To illustrate the payback method, consider the following data:

Example G: York Company needs a new milling machine. The company is considering two machines: machine A and machine B. Machine A costs $15,000, has a useful life of ten years, and will reduce operating costs by $5,000 per year. Machine B costs only $12,000, will also reduce operating costs by $5,000 per year, but has a useful life of only five years.

Required:
Which machine should be purchased according to the payback method?

$$\text{Machine A payback period} = \frac{\$15{,}000}{\$5{,}000} = 3.0 \text{ years}$$

$$\text{Machine B payback period} = \frac{\$12{,}000}{\$5{,}000} = 2.4 \text{ years}$$

According to the payback calculations, York Company should purchase machine B because it has a shorter payback period than machine A.

IN BUSINESS

ENTREPRENEURIAL INGENUITY AT ITS BEST

Jonathan Pratt owns two Ümani Cafés in Westchester County, New York. He used to pay $200 a month to dispose of the vegetable oil that is used to fry foods in his restaurants. Plus, he bought $700 of gas every month to operate his company's pick-up truck. Then Pratt got an idea. He purchased a diesel-powered Ford F250 on eBay for $11,000 and paid $1,500 to haul the truck from Arizona to New York. Next, he installed an $850 conversion kit on his new truck to enable it to run on vegetable oil. Because he no longer has to pay to dispose of vegetable oil or buy gasoline, Pratt figures that his investment will pay for itself in about 15 months ($13,350 ÷ $900 = 14.83 months). Furthermore, he now has the best smelling car in town—it smells like french fries when he drives down the road.

Source: Jean Chatzky, "Out of the Frying Pan, Into the Ford," *Money*, October, 2004, p. 28.

Evaluation of the Payback Method

The payback method is not a true measure of the profitability of an investment. Rather, it simply tells a manager how many years are required to recover the original investment. Unfortunately, a shorter payback period does not always mean that one investment is more desirable than another.

To illustrate, refer back to Example G on the previous page. Machine B has a shorter payback period than machine A, but it has a useful life of only 5 years rather than 10 years for machine A. Machine B would have to be purchased twice—once immediately and then again after the fifth year—to provide the same service as just one machine A. Under these circumstances, machine A would probably be a better investment than machine B, even though machine B has a shorter payback period. Unfortunately, the payback method ignores all cash flows that occur after the payback period.

A further criticism of the payback method is that it does not consider the time value of money. A cash inflow to be received several years in the future is weighed the same as a cash inflow received right now. To illustrate, assume that for an investment of $8,000 you can purchase either of the two following streams of cash inflows:

Year	0	1	2	3	4	5	6	7	8
Stream 1 . . .					$8,000	$2,000	$2,000	$2,000	$2,000
Stream 2 . . .		$2,000	$2,000	$2,000	$2,000	$8,000			

Which stream of cash inflows would you prefer to receive in return for your $8,000 investment? Each stream has a payback period of 4.0 years. Therefore, if payback alone is used to make the decision, the streams would be considered equally desirable. However, from a time value of money perspective, stream 2 is much more desirable than stream 1.

On the other hand, under certain conditions the payback method can be very useful. For one thing, it can help identify which investment proposals are in the "ballpark." That is, it can be used as a screening tool to help answer the question, "Should I consider this proposal further?" If a proposal doesn't provide a payback within some specified period, then there may be no need to consider it further. In addition, the payback period is often important to new companies that are "cash poor." When a company is cash poor, a project with a short payback period but a low rate of return might be preferred over another project with a high rate of return but a long payback period. The reason is that the company may simply need a faster return of its cash investment. And finally, the payback method is sometimes used in industries where products become obsolete very rapidly—such as consumer electronics. Because products may last only a year or two, the payback period on investments must be very short.

IN BUSINESS

THE ECONOMICS OF HYBRID VEHICLES

The table below shows the price premiums (after tax credits) that customers must pay to buy four types of hybrid vehicles. It also depicts the annual gas savings that customers realize by driving a hybrid version of the vehicle instead of a standard model of the same vehicle (assuming the vehicles are driven 15,000 miles per year and gas costs $2.79 a gallon). Dividing the price premium by the annual gas savings yields the payback period when purchasing the hybrid version of the vehicle.

Make and Model	Price Premium	Annual Gas Savings	Payback Period
Ford Escape	$1,364	$438	3.1
Honda Civic	$1,482	$317	4.7
Toyota Camry	$3,763	$310	12.1
Toyota Highlander	$4,372	$388	11.3

The above payback figures highlight the dilemma faced by customers who want to make environmentally friendly purchases, but are constrained by limited financial resources.

Source: Mike Spector, "The Economics of Hybrids," *The Wall Street Journal,* October 29, 2007, pp. R5–R6.

An Extended Example of Payback

As shown by formula (3) on page 597, the payback period is computed by dividing the investment in a project by the project's annual net cash inflows. If new equipment is replacing old equipment, then any salvage value to be received when disposing of the old equipment should be deducted from the cost of the new equipment, and only the *incremental* investment should be used in the payback computation. In addition, any depreciation deducted in arriving at the project's net operating income must be added back to obtain the project's expected annual net cash inflow. To illustrate, consider the following data:

Example H: Goodtime Fun Centers, Inc., operates amusement parks. Some of the vending machines in one of its parks provide very little revenue, so the company is considering removing the machines and installing equipment to dispense soft ice cream. The equipment would cost $80,000 and have an eight-year useful life with no salvage value. Incremental annual revenues and costs associated with the sale of ice cream would be as follows:

Sales	$150,000
Variable expenses	90,000
Contribution margin	60,000
Fixed expenses:	
Salaries	27,000
Maintenance	3,000
Depreciation	10,000
Total fixed expenses	40,000
Net operating income	$ 20,000

The vending machines can be sold for a $5,000 scrap value. The company will not purchase equipment unless it has a payback period of three years or less. Does the ice cream dispenser pass this hurdle?

Exhibit 13–11 computes the payback period for the ice cream dispenser. Several things should be noted. First, depreciation is added back to net operating income to obtain

EXHIBIT 13–11
Computation of the Payback Period

Step 1: *Compute the annual net cash inflow.* Because the annual net cash inflow is not given, it must be computed before the payback period can be determined:

Net operating income	$20,000
Add: Noncash deduction for depreciation	10,000
Annual net cash inflow	$30,000

Step 2: *Compute the payback period.* Using the annual net cash inflow from above, the payback period can be determined as follows:

Cost of the new equipment	$80,000
Less salvage value of old equipment	5,000
Investment required	$75,000

$$\text{Payback period} = \frac{\text{Investment required}}{\text{Annual net cash inflow}}$$

$$= \frac{\$75{,}000}{\$30{,}000} = 2.5 \text{ years}$$

the annual net cash inflow from the new equipment. Depreciation is not a cash outlay; thus, it must be added back to adjust net operating income to a cash basis. Second, the payback computation deducts the salvage value of the old machines from the cost of the new equipment so that only the incremental investment is used in computing the payback period.

Because the proposed equipment has a payback period of less than three years, the company's payback requirement has been met.

Payback and Uneven Cash Flows

When the cash flows associated with an investment project change from year to year, the simple payback formula that we outlined earlier cannot be used. Consider the following data:

Year	Investment	Cash Inflow
1	$4,000	$1,000
2		$0
3		$2,000
4	$2,000	$1,000
5		$500
6		$3,000
7		$2,000

What is the payback period on this investment? The answer is 5.5 years, but to obtain this figure it is necessary to track the unrecovered investment year by year. The steps involved in this process are shown in Exhibit 13–12. By the middle of the sixth year, sufficient cash inflows will have been realized to recover the entire investment of $6,000 ($4,000 + $2,000).

EXHIBIT 13–12
Payback and Uneven Cash Flows

Year	Investment	Cash Inflow	Unrecovered Investment*
1	$4,000	$1,000	$3,000
2		$0	$3,000
3		$2,000	$1,000
4	$2,000	$1,000	$2,000
5		$500	$1,500
6		$3,000	$0
7		$2,000	$0

*Year X unrecovered investment = Year X-1 unrecovered investment + Year X investment − Year X cash inflow

The Simple Rate of Return Method

LEARNING OBJECTIVE 6
Compute the simple rate of return for an investment.

The **simple rate of return** method is another capital budgeting technique that does not involve discounting cash flows. The simple rate of return is also known as the accounting rate of return or the unadjusted rate of return.

Unlike the other capital budgeting methods that we have discussed, the simple rate of return method focuses on accounting net operating income rather than cash flows. To obtain the simple rate of return, the annual incremental net operating income generated by a project is divided by the initial investment in the project, as shown below.

$$\text{Simple rate of return} = \frac{\text{Annual incremental net operating income}}{\text{Initial investment}} \quad (4)$$

Two additional points should be made. First, depreciation charges that result from making the investment should be deducted when determining the annual incremental net operating income. Second, the initial investment should be reduced by any salvage value realized from the sale of old equipment.

Example I: Brigham Tea, Inc., is a processor of low-acid tea. The company is contemplating purchasing equipment for an additional processing line that would increase revenues by $90,000 per year. Incremental cash operating expenses would be $40,000 per year. The equipment would cost $180,000 and have a nine-year life with no salvage value.

To apply the formula for the simple rate of return, we must first determine the annual incremental net operating income from the project:

Annual incremental revenues		$90,000
Annual incremental cash operating expenses	$40,000	
Annual depreciation ($180,000 − $0)/9	20,000	
Annual incremental expenses		60,000
Annual incremental net operating income		$30,000

Given that the annual incremental net operating income from the project is $30,000 and the initial investment is $180,000, the simple rate of return is 16.7% as shown below:

$$\begin{aligned}\text{Simple rate of return} &= \frac{\text{Annual incremental net operating income}}{\text{Initial investment}}\\ &= \frac{\$30{,}000}{\$180{,}000}\\ &= 16.7\%\end{aligned}$$

Example J: Midwest Farms, Inc., hires people on a part-time basis to sort eggs. The cost of hand sorting is $30,000 per year. The company is investigating an egg-sorting machine that would cost $90,000 and have a 15-year useful life. The machine would have negligible salvage value, and it would cost $10,000 per year to operate and maintain. The egg-sorting equipment currently being used could be sold now for a scrap value of $2,500.

This project is slightly different from the preceding project because it involves cost reductions with no additional revenues. Nevertheless, the annual incremental net operating income can be computed by treating the annual cost savings as if it were incremental revenues as follows:

Annual incremental cost savings		$30,000
Annual incremental cash operating expenses	$10,000	
Annual depreciation ($90,000 − $0)/15	6,000	
Annual incremental expenses		16,000
Annual incremental net operating income		$14,000

Thus, even though the new equipment would not generate any additional revenues, it would reduce costs by $14,000 a year. This would have the effect of increasing net operating income by $14,000 a year.

Finally, the salvage value of the old equipment offsets the initial cost of the new equipment as follows:

Cost of the new equipment	$90,000
Less salvage value of the old equipment	2,500
Initial investment	$87,500

Given the annual incremental net operating income of $14,000 and the initial investment of $87,500, the simple rate of return is 16.0% computed as follows:

$$\text{Simple rate of return} = \frac{\text{Annual incremental net operating income}}{\text{Initial investment}}$$

$$= \frac{\$14{,}000}{\$87{,}500}$$

$$= 16.0\%$$

Criticisms of the Simple Rate of Return

The simple rate of return method ignores the time value of money. It considers a dollar received 10 years from now to be as valuable as a dollar received today. Thus, the simple rate of return method can be misleading if the alternatives have different cash flow patterns. Additionally, many projects do not have constant incremental revenues and expenses over their useful lives. As a result, the simple rate of return will fluctuate from year to year, with the possibility that a project may appear to be desirable in some years and undesirable in others. In contrast, the net present value method provides a single number that summarizes all of the cash flows over the entire useful life of the project.

Postaudit of Investment Projects

After an investment project has been approved and implemented, a *postaudit* should be conducted. A **postaudit** involves checking whether or not expected results are actually realized. This is a key part of the capital budgeting process because it helps keep managers honest in their investment proposals. Any tendency to inflate the benefits or downplay the costs in a proposal should become evident after a few postaudits have been conducted. The postaudit also provides an opportunity to reinforce and possibly expand successful projects and to cut losses on floundering projects.

The same capital budgeting method should be used in the postaudit as was used in the original approval process. That is, if a project was approved on the basis of a net present value analysis, then the same procedure should be used in performing the postaudit. However, the data used in the postaudit analysis should be *actual observed data* rather than estimated data. This gives management an opportunity to make a side-by-side comparison to see how well the project has succeeded. It also helps assure that estimated data received on future proposals will be carefully prepared because the persons submitting the data knows that their estimates will be compared to actual results in the postaudit process. Actual results that are far out of line with original estimates should be carefully reviewed.

IN BUSINESS

ROYAL CARIBBEAN CRUISES LAUNCHES *OASIS OF THE SEAS*

Royal Caribbean Cruises invested $1.4 billion to build the *Oasis of the Seas,* a cruise ship that carries 5,400 passengers and stands 20 stories above the sea. The vessel is a third larger than any other cruise ship and contains 21 pools, 24 restaurants, 13 retail shops, and 300-foot water slides. The company hopes the ship's extraordinary amenities will attract large numbers of customers willing to pay premium prices. However, the economic downturn has caused many customers to refrain from spending on lavish vacations.

Source: Mike Esterl, "Huge Cruise Ships Prepare for Launch but Face Uncertain Waters," *The Wall Street Journal,* December 4, 2009, pp. B1–B2.

Summary

Investment decisions should take into account the time value of money because a dollar today is more valuable than a dollar received in the future. The net present value and internal rate of return methods both reflect this fact. In the net present value method, future cash flows are discounted to their present value. The difference between the present value of the cash inflows and the present value of the cash outflows is called a project's net present value. If the net present value of a project is negative, the project is rejected. The discount rate in the net present value method is usually based on a minimum required rate of return such as a company's cost of capital.

The internal rate of return is the rate of return that equates the present value of the cash inflows and the present value of the cash outflows, resulting in a zero net present value. If the internal rate of return is less than a company's minimum required rate of return, the project is rejected.

After rejecting projects whose net present values are negative or whose internal rates of return are less than the minimum required rate of return, more projects may remain than can be supported with available funds. The remaining projects can be ranked using either the project profitability index or internal rate of return. The project profitability index is computed by dividing the net present value of the project by the required initial investment.

Some companies prefer to use either the payback method or the simple rate of return to evaluate investment proposals. The payback period is the number of periods that are required to fully recover the initial investment in a project. The simple rate of return is determined by dividing a project's accounting net operating income by the initial investment in the project.

Review Problem: Comparison of Capital Budgeting Methods

Lamar Company is considering a project that would have an eight-year life and require a $2,400,000 investment in equipment. At the end of eight years, the project would terminate and the equipment would have no salvage value. The project would provide net operating income each year as follows:

Sales		$3,000,000
Variable expenses		1,800,000
Contribution margin		1,200,000
Fixed expenses:		
Advertising, salaries, and other fixed out-of-pocket costs	$700,000	
Depreciation	300,000	
Total fixed expenses		1,000,000
Net operating income		$ 200,000

The company's discount rate is 12%.

Required:

1. Compute the annual net cash inflow from the project.
2. Compute the project's net present value. Is the project acceptable?
3. Find the project's internal rate of return to the nearest whole percent.
4. Compute the project's payback period.
5. Compute the project's simple rate of return.

Solution to Review Problem

1. The annual net cash inflow can be computed by deducting the cash expenses from sales:

Sales	$3,000,000
Variable expenses	1,800,000
Contribution margin	1,200,000
Advertising, salaries, and other fixed out-of-pocket costs	700,000
Annual net cash inflow	$ 500,000

Or the annual net cash inflow can be computed by adding depreciation back to net operating income:

Net operating income	$200,000
Add: Noncash deduction for depreciation	300,000
Annual net cash inflow	$500,000

2. The net present value is computed as follows:

Item	Year(s)	Amount of Cash Flows	12% Factor	Present Value of Cash Flows
Cost of new equipment	Now	$(2,400,000)	1.000	$(2,400,000)
Annual net cash inflow	1–8	$500,000	4.968	2,484,000
Net present value				$ 84,000

Yes, the project is acceptable because it has a positive net present value.

3. The formula for computing the factor of the internal rate of return is:

$$\text{Factor of the internal rate of return} = \frac{\text{Investment required}}{\text{Annual net cash inflow}}$$

$$= \frac{\$2{,}400{,}000}{\$500{,}000} = 4.800$$

Looking in Exhibit 13B–2 in Appendix 13B at the end of the chapter and scanning along the 8-period line, we find that a factor of 4.800 represents a rate of return of about 13%.

4. The formula for the payback period is:

$$\text{Payback period} = \frac{\text{Investment required}}{\text{Annual net cash flow}}$$

$$= \frac{\$2{,}400{,}000}{\$500{,}000}$$

$$= 4.8 \text{ years}$$

5. The formula for the simple rate of return is:

$$\text{Simple rate of return} = \frac{\text{Annual incremental net operating income}}{\text{Initial investment}}$$

$$= \frac{\$200{,}000}{\$2{,}400{,}000}$$

$$= 8.3\%$$

Glossary

Capital budgeting The process of planning significant investments in projects that have long-term implications such as the purchase of new equipment or the introduction of a new product. (p. 580)

Cost of capital The average rate of return a company must pay to its long-term creditors and shareholders for the use of their funds. (p. 585)

Internal rate of return The discount rate at which the net present value of an investment project is zero; the rate of return of a project over its useful life. (p. 587)

Net present value The difference between the present value of an investment project's cash inflows and the present value of its cash outflows. (p. 581)

Out-of-pocket costs Actual cash outlays for salaries, advertising, repairs, and similar costs. (p. 586)

Payback period The length of time that it takes for a project to fully recover its initial cost out of the net cash inflows that it generates. (p. 597)

Postaudit The follow-up after a project has been approved and implemented to determine whether expected results were actually realized. (p. 602)

Preference decision A decision in which the alternatives must be ranked. (p. 580)

Project profitability index The ratio of the net present value of a project's cash flows to the investment required. (p. 596)

Screening decision A decision as to whether a proposed investment project is acceptable. (p. 580)

Simple rate of return The rate of return computed by dividing a project's annual incremental accounting net operating income by the initial investment required. (p. 601)

Working capital Current assets less current liabilities. (p. 583)

Questions

13–1 What is the difference between capital budgeting screening decisions and capital budgeting preference decisions?

13–2 What is meant by the term *time value of money?*

13–3 What is meant by the term *discounting?*

13–4 Why isn't accounting net income used in the net present value and internal rate of return methods of making capital budgeting decisions?

13–5 Why are discounted cash flow methods of making capital budgeting decisions superior to other methods?

13–6 What is net present value? Can it ever be negative? Explain.

13–7 Identify two simplifying assumptions associated with discounted cash flow methods of making capital budgeting decisions.

13–8 If a company has to pay interest of 14% on long-term debt, then its cost of capital is 14%. Do you agree? Explain.

13–9 What is meant by an investment project's internal rate of return? How is the internal rate of return computed?

13–10 Explain how the cost of capital serves as a screening tool when using (*a*) the net present value method and (*b*) the internal rate of return method.

13–11 As the discount rate increases, the present value of a given future cash flow also increases. Do you agree? Explain.

13–12 Refer to Exhibit 13–4. Is the return on this investment proposal exactly 14%, more than 14%, or less than 14%? Explain.

13–13 How is the project profitability index computed, and what does it measure?

13–14 What is meant by the term *payback period?* How is the payback period determined? How can the payback method be useful?

13–15 What is the major criticism of the payback and simple rate of return methods of making capital budgeting decisions?

Multiple-choice questions are provided on the text website at www.mhhe.com/garrison14e.

Applying Excel

connect ACCOUNTING

LEARNING OBJECTIVES 1, 3

Available with McGraw-Hill's *Connect™ Accounting.*

The Excel worksheet form that appears below is to be used to recreate Example C and Exhibit 13–4 on pages 586–587. Download the workbook containing this form from the Online Learning Center at www.mhhe.com/garrison14e. *On the website you will also receive instructions about how to use this worksheet form.*

	A	B	C	D	E	F	G
1	Chapter 13: Applying Excel						
2							
3	**Data**						
4	**Example C**						
5	Cost of equipment needed			$60,000			
6	Working capital needed			$100,000			
7	Overhaul of equipment in	4	years	$5,000			
8	Salvage value of the equipment in	5	years	$10,000			
9	Annual revenues and costs:						
10	Sales revenues			$200,000			
11	Cost of goods sold			$125,000			
12	Out-of-pocket operating costs			$35,000			
13	Discount rate			14%			
14							
15	*Enter a formula into each of the cells marked with a ? below*						
16	**Exhibit 13-4**						
17							
18	Sales revenues			?			
19	Less cost of goods sold			?			
20	Less out-of-pocket costs			?			
21	Annual net cash inflows			?			
22							
23				*Amount of*	?	*Present Value*	
24		*Year(s)*		*Cash Flow*	*Factor**	*of Cash Flows*	
25	Purchase of equipment	Now		?	1.000	?	
26	Working capital needed	Now		?	1.000	?	
27	Overhaul of equipment	?		?	?	?	
28	Annual net cash inflows from sales of the product line	1- ?		?	?	?	
29	Salvage value of equipment	?		?	?	?	
30	Working capital released	?		?	?	?	
31	Net present value					?	
32							
33	*Use the formulas from Appendix 13B:						
34	Present value of $1 = 1/(1+r)^n						
35	Present value of an annuity of $1 = (1/r)*(1-(1/(1+r)^n))						
36	where n is the number of years and r is the discount rate						
37							

Chapter 13 Form / Filled in Chapter 13 Form / Chapter 13 Form

You should proceed to the requirements below only after completing your worksheet.

Required:

1. Check your worksheet by changing the discount rate to 10%. The net present value should now be between $56,518 and $56,535—depending on the precision of the calculations. If you do not get an answer in this range, find the errors in your worksheet and correct them.

   Explain why the net present value has fallen as a result of reducing the discount rate from 14% to 10%.
2. The company is considering another project involving the purchase of new equipment. Change the data area of your worksheet to match the following:

Data		
Example C		
Cost of equipment needed		$120,000
Working capital needed		$80,000
Overhaul of equipment in	5 years	$40,000
Salvage of the equipment in	10 years	$20,000
Annual revenues and costs:		
Sales revenues		$245,000
Cost of goods sold		$160,000
Out-of-pocket operating costs		$50,000
Discount rate		14%

   a. What is the net present value of the project?

   b. Experiment with changing the discount rate in one percent increments (e.g., 13%, 12%, 15%, etc.). At what interest rate does the net present value turn from negative to positive?

   c. The internal rate of return is between what two whole discount rates (e.g., between 10% and 11%, between 11% and 12%, between 12% and 13%, between 13% and 14%, etc.)?

   d. Reset the discount rate to 14%. Suppose the salvage value is uncertain. How large would the salvage value have to be to result in a positive net present value?

connect ACCOUNTING Exercises

All applicable exercises are available with McGraw-Hill's *Connect™ Accounting*.

EXERCISE 13–1 Net Present Value Method [LO1]

The management of Opry Company, a wholesale distributor of suntan products, is considering the purchase of a $25,000 machine that would reduce operating costs in its warehouse by $4,000 per year. At the end of the machine's 10-year useful life, it will have no scrap value. The company's required rate of return is 12%.

Required:

(Ignore income taxes.)

1. Determine the net present value of the investment in the machine.
2. What is the difference between the total, undiscounted cash inflows and cash outflows over the entire life of the machine?

EXERCISE 13–2 Internal Rate of Return [LO2]

Pisa Pizza Parlor is investigating the purchase of a new $45,000 delivery truck that would contain specially designed warming racks. The new truck would have a six-year useful life. It would save $5,400 per year over the present method of delivering pizzas. In addition, it would result in the sale of 1,800 more pizzas each year. The company realizes a contribution margin of $2 per pizza.

Required:

(Ignore income taxes.)

1. What would be the total annual cash inflows associated with the new truck for capital budgeting purposes?
2. Find the internal rate of return promised by the new truck to the nearest whole percent.

3. In addition to the data already provided, assume that due to the unique warming racks, the truck will have a $13,000 salvage value at the end of six years. Under these conditions, compute the internal rate of return to the nearest whole percent. (Hint: You may find it helpful to use the net present value approach; find the discount rate that will cause the net present value to be closest to zero. Use the format shown in Exhibit 13–4.)

EXERCISE 13–3 Uncertain Future Cash Flows [LO3]

Union Bay Plastics is investigating the purchase of automated equipment that would save $100,000 each year in direct labor and inventory carrying costs. This equipment costs $750,000 and is expected to have a 10-year useful life with no salvage value. The company's required rate of return is 15% on all equipment purchases. This equipment would provide intangible benefits such as greater flexibility and higher-quality output that are difficult to estimate and yet are quite significant.

Required:

(Ignore income taxes.)

What dollar value per year would the intangible benefits have to have in order to make the equipment an acceptable investment?

EXERCISE 13–4 Preference Ranking [LO4]

Information on four investment proposals is given below:

	Investment Proposal			
	A	B	C	D
Investment required	$(85,000)	$(200,000)	$(90,000)	$(170,000)
Present value of cash inflows	119,000	250,000	135,000	221,000
Net present value	$ 34,000	$ 50,000	$ 45,000	$ 51,000
Life of the project	5 years	7 years	6 years	6 years

Required:

1. Compute the project profitability index for each investment proposal.
2. Rank the proposals in terms of preference.

EXERCISE 13–5 Payback Method [LO5]

The management of Weimar, Inc., a civil engineering design company, is considering an investment in a high-quality blueprint printer with the following cash flows:

Year	Investment	Cash Inflow
1	$38,000	$2,000
2	$6,000	$4,000
3		$8,000
4		$9,000
5		$12,000
6		$10,000
7		$8,000
8		$6,000
9		$5,000
10		$5,000

Required:

1. Determine the payback period of the investment.
2. Would the payback period be affected if the cash inflow in the last year were several times larger?

EXERCISE 13–6 Simple Rate of Return Method [LO6]

The management of Wallingford MicroBrew is considering the purchase of an automated bottling machine for $80,000. The machine would replace an old piece of equipment that costs $33,000 per year to operate. The new machine would cost $10,000 per year to operate. The old machine currently in use could be sold now for a scrap value of $5,000. The new machine would have a useful life of 10 years with no salvage value.

Required:

Compute the simple rate of return on the new automated bottling machine.

EXERCISE 13–7 Payback Period and Simple Rate of Return [LO5, LO6]

The Heritage Amusement Park would like to construct a new ride called the Sonic Boom, which the park management feels would be very popular. The ride would cost $450,000 to construct, and it would have a 10% salvage value at the end of its 15-year useful life. The company estimates that the following annual costs and revenues would be associated with the ride:

Ticket revenues		$250,000
Less operating expenses:		
Maintenance	$40,000	
Salaries	90,000	
Depreciation	27,000	
Insurance	30,000	
Total operating expenses		187,000
Net operating income		$ 63,000

Required:

(Ignore income taxes.)

1. Assume that the Heritage Amusement Park will not construct a new ride unless the ride provides a payback period of six years or less. Does the Sonic Boom ride satisfy this requirement?
2. Compute the simple rate of return promised by the new ride. If Heritage Amusement Park requires a simple rate of return of at least 12%, does the Sonic Boom ride meet this criterion?

EXERCISE 13–8 Working With Net Present Value [LO3]

Mountain View Hospital has purchased new lab equipment for $134,650. The equipment is expected to last for three years and to provide cash inflows as follows:

Year 1	$45,000
Year 2	$60,000
Year 3	?

Required:

(Ignore income taxes.) Assuming that the equipment will yield exactly a 16% rate of return, what is the expected cash inflow for Year 3?

EXERCISE 13–9 Basic Net Present Value and Internal Rate of Return Analysis [LO1, LO2]

(Ignore income taxes.) Consider each case below independently.

1. Minden Company's required rate of return is 15%. The company can purchase a new machine at a cost of $40,350. The new machine would generate cash inflows of $15,000 per year and have a four-year life with no salvage value. Compute the machine's net present value. (Use the format shown in Exhibit 13–1.) Is the machine an acceptable investment? Explain.
2. Leven Products, Inc., is investigating the purchase of a new grinding machine that has a projected life of 15 years. It is estimated that the machine will save $20,000 per year in cash operating costs. What is the machine's internal rate of return if it costs $111,500 new?
3. Sunset Press has just purchased a new trimming machine that cost $14,125. The machine is expected to save $2,500 per year in cash operating costs and to have a 10-year life. Compute the machine's internal rate of return. If the company's required rate of return is 16%, did it make a wise investment? Explain.

EXERCISE 13–10 Internal Rate of Return and Net Present Value [LO1, LO2]

Scalia's Cleaning Service is investigating the purchase of an ultrasound machine for cleaning window blinds. The machine would cost $136,700, including invoice cost, freight, and training of employees to operate it. Scalia's has estimated that the new machine would increase the company's cash flows, net of expenses, by $25,000 per year. The machine would have a 14-year useful life with no expected salvage value.

Required:

(Ignore income taxes.)

1. Compute the machine's internal rate of return to the nearest whole percent.
2. Compute the machine's net present value. Use a discount rate of 16%. Why do you have a zero net present value?
3. Suppose that the new machine would increase the company's annual cash flows, net of expenses, by only $20,000 per year. Under these conditions, compute the internal rate of return to the nearest whole percent.

EXERCISE 13–11 Comparison of Projects Using Net Present Value [LO1]

Sharp Company has $15,000 to invest. The company is trying to decide between two alternative uses of the funds as follows:

	Invest in Project A	Invest in Project B
Investment required	$15,000	$15,000
Annual cash inflows	$4,000	$0
Single cash inflow at the end of 10 years		$60,000
Life of the project	10 years	10 years

Sharp Company uses a 16% discount rate.

Required:

(Ignore income taxes.) Which investment would you recommend that the company accept? Show all computations using net present value. Prepare separate computations for each investment.

EXERCISE 13–12 Basic Payback Period and Simple Rate of Return Computations [LO5, LO6]

Martin Company is considering the purchase of a new piece of equipment. Relevant information concerning the equipment follows:

Purchase cost	$180,000
Annual cost savings that will be provided by the equipment	$37,500
Life of the equipment	12 years

Required:

(Ignore income taxes.)

1. Compute the payback period for the equipment. If the company rejects all proposals with a payback period of more than four years, would the equipment be purchased?
2. Compute the simple rate of return on the equipment. Use straight-line depreciation based on the equipment's useful life. Would the equipment be purchased if the company's required rate of return is 14%?

EXERCISE 13–13 Uncertain Future Life [LO3]

Worldwide Travel Service has made an investment in certain equipment that cost the company $307,100. The equipment is expected to generate cash inflows of $50,000 each year.

Required:

How many years will the equipment have to be used in order to provide the company with a 14% return on its investment?

EXERCISE 13–14 Net Present Value Analysis of Two Alternatives [LO1]

Wriston Company has $300,000 to invest. The company is trying to decide between two alternative uses of the funds. The alternatives are as follows:

	A	B
Cost of equipment required	$300,000	$0
Working capital investment required	$0	$300,000
Annual cash inflows	$80,000	$60,000
Salvage value of equipment in seven years	$20,000	$0
Life of the project	7 years	7 years

The working capital needed for project B will be released for investment elsewhere at the end of seven years. Wriston Company uses a 20% discount rate.

Required:

(Ignore income taxes.) Which investment alternative (if either) would you recommend that the company accept? Show all computations using the net present value format. Prepare separate computations for each project.

EXERCISE 13–15 Basic Net Present Value Analysis [LO1]

On January 2, Fred Critchfield paid $18,000 for 900 shares of the common stock of Acme Company. Mr. Critchfield received an $0.80 per share dividend on the stock at the end of each year for four years. At the end of four years, he sold the stock for $22,500. Mr. Critchfield has a goal of earning a minimum return of 12% on all of his investments.

Required:

(Ignore income taxes.) Did Mr. Critchfield earn a 12% return on the stock? Use the net present value method and the general format shown in Exhibit 13–4. Round all computations to the nearest whole dollar.

connect ACCOUNTING Problems

All applicable problems are available with McGraw-Hill's *Connect™ Accounting*.

PROBLEM 13–16 Basic Net Present Value Analysis [LO1]

Renfree Mines, Inc., owns the mining rights to a large tract of land in a mountainous area. The tract contains a mineral deposit that the company believes might be commercially attractive to mine and sell. An engineering and cost analysis has been made, and it is expected that the following cash flows would be associated with opening and operating a mine in the area:

Cost of equipment required	$850,000
Annual net cash receipts	$230,000*
Working capital required	$100,000
Cost of road repairs in three years	$60,000
Salvage value of equipment in five years	$200,000

*Receipts from sales of ore, less out-of-pocket costs for salaries, utilities, insurance, and so forth.

The mineral deposit would be exhausted after five years of mining. At that point, the working capital would be released for reinvestment elsewhere. The company's required rate of return is 14%.

Required:

(Ignore income taxes.) Determine the net present value of the proposed mining project. Should the project be accepted? Explain.

PROBLEM 13–17 Preference Ranking of Investment Projects [LO4]

Austin Company is investigating four different investment opportunities. Information on the four projects under study is given below:

	Project Number			
	1	2	3	4
Investment required	$(480,000)	$(360,000)	$(270,000)	$(450,000)
Present value of cash inflows at a 10% discount rate.	567,270	433,400	336,140	522,970
Net present value.	$ 87,270	$ 73,400	$ 66,140	$ 72,970
Life of the project	6 years	12 years	6 years	3 years
Internal rate of return	16%	14%	18%	19%

Because the company's required rate of return is 10%, a 10% discount rate has been used in the present value computations on the prior page. Limited funds are available for investment, so the company can't accept all of the available projects.

Required:

1. Compute the project profitability index for each investment project.
2. Rank the four projects according to preference, in terms of:
   a. Net present value.
   b. Project profitability index.
   c. Internal rate of return.
3. Which ranking do you prefer? Why?

PROBLEM 13–18 Preference Ranking of Investment Projects [LO4]

Yancey Company has limited funds available for investment and must ration the funds among four competing projects. Selected information on the four projects follows:

Project	Investment Required	Net Present Value	Life of the Project (years)	Internal Rate of Return
A	$800,000	$221,615	7	18%
B	$675,000	$210,000	12	16%
C	$500,000	$175,175	7	20%
D	$700,000	$152,544	3	22%

The net present values above have been computed using a 10% discount rate. The company wants your assistance in determining which project to accept first, which to accept second, and so forth. The company's investment funds are limited.

Required:

1. Compute the project profitability index for each project.
2. In order of preference, rank the four projects in terms of:
   a. Net present value.
   b. Project profitability index.
   c. Internal rate of return.
3. Which ranking do you prefer? Why?

PROBLEM 13–19 Net Present Value Analysis; Uncertain Cash Flows [LO1, LO3]

Tiger Computers, Inc., of Singapore is considering the purchase of an automated etching machine for use in the production of its circuit boards. The machine would cost $900,000. (All currency amounts are in Singapore dollars.) An additional $650,000 would be required for installation costs and for software. Management believes that the automated machine would provide substantial annual reductions in costs, as shown below:

	Annual Reduction in Costs
Labor costs	$240,000
Material costs	$96,000

The new machine would require considerable maintenance work to keep it properly adjusted. The company's engineers estimate that maintenance costs would increase by $4,250 per month if the machine were purchased. In addition, the machine would require a $90,000 overhaul at the end of the sixth year.

The new etching machine would be usable for 10 years, after which it would be sold for its scrap value of $210,000. It would replace an old etching machine that can be sold now for its scrap value of $70,000. Tiger Computers, Inc., requires a return of at least 18% on investments of this type.

Required:

(Ignore income taxes.)

1. Compute the annual net cost savings promised by the new etching machine.

2. Using the data from requirement (1) and other data from the problem, compute the new machine's net present value. (Use the incremental-cost approach.) Would you recommend that the machine be purchased? Explain.
3. Assume that management can identify several intangible benefits associated with the new machine, including greater flexibility in shifting from one type of circuit board to another, improved quality of output, and faster delivery as a result of reduced throughput time. What dollar value per year would management have to attach to these intangible benefits in order to make the new etching machine an acceptable investment?

PROBLEM 13–20 Simple Rate of Return; Payback [LO5, LO6]

Lugano's Pizza Parlor is considering the purchase of a large oven and related equipment for mixing and baking "crazy bread." The oven and equipment would cost $120,000 delivered and installed. It would be usable for about 15 years, after which it would have a 10% scrap value. The following additional information is available:

a. Mr. Lugano estimates that purchase of the oven and equipment would allow the pizza parlor to bake and sell 72,000 loaves of crazy bread each year. The bread sells for $1.25 per loaf.
b. The cost of the ingredients in a loaf of bread is 40% of the selling price. Mr. Lugano estimates that other costs each year associated with the bread would be as follows: salaries, $18,000; utilities, $9,000; and insurance, $3,000.
c. The pizza parlor uses straight-line depreciation on all assets, deducting salvage value from original cost.

Required:

(Ignore income taxes.)

1. Prepare a contribution format income statement showing the net operating income each year from production and sale of the crazy bread.
2. Compute the simple rate of return for the new oven and equipment. If a simple rate of return above 12% is acceptable to Mr. Lugano, will he purchase the oven and equipment?
3. Compute the payback period on the oven and equipment. If Mr. Lugano purchases any equipment with less than a six-year payback, will he purchase this equipment?

PROBLEM 13–21 Basic Net Present Value Analysis [LO1]

Doughboy Bakery would like to buy a new machine for putting icing and other toppings on pastries. These are now put on by hand. The machine that the bakery is considering costs $90,000 new. It would last the bakery for eight years but would require a $7,500 overhaul at the end of the fifth year. After eight years, the machine could be sold for $6,000.

The bakery estimates that it will cost $14,000 per year to operate the new machine. The present manual method of putting toppings on the pastries costs $35,000 per year. In addition to reducing operating costs, the new machine will allow the bakery to increase its production of pastries by 5,000 packages per year. The bakery realizes a contribution margin of $0.60 per package. The bakery requires a 16% return on all investments in equipment.

Required:

(Ignore income taxes.)

1. What are the annual net cash inflows that will be provided by the new machine?
2. Compute the new machine's net present value. Use the incremental cost approach, and round all dollar amounts to the nearest whole dollar.

PROBLEM 13–22 Net Present Value Analysis of a Lease or Buy Decision [LO1]

Blinko Products wants an airplane for use by its corporate staff. The airplane that the company wishes to acquire, a Zephyr II, can be either purchased or leased from the manufacturer. The company has made the following evaluation of the two alternatives:

Purchase alternative. If the Zephyr II is purchased, then the costs incurred by the company would be as follows:

Purchase cost of the plane	$850,000
Annual cost of servicing, licenses, and taxes	$9,000
Repairs:	
First three years, per year	$3,000
Fourth year	$5,000
Fifth year	$10,000

The plane would be sold after five years. Based on current resale values, the company would be able to sell it for about one-half of its original cost at the end of the five-year period.

Lease alternative. If the Zephyr II is leased, then the company would have to make an immediate deposit of $50,000 to cover any damage during use. The lease would run for five years, at the end of which time the deposit would be refunded. The lease would require an annual rental payment of $200,000 (the first payment is due at the end of Year 1). As part of this lease cost, the manufacturer would provide all servicing and repairs, license the plane, and pay all taxes. At the end of the five-year period, the plane would revert to the manufacturer, as owner.

Blinko Products' required rate of return is 18%.

Required:

(Ignore income taxes.)

1. Use the total-cost approach to determine the present value of the cash flows associated with each alternative.
2. Which alternative would you recommend that the company accept? Why?

PROBLEM 13–23 Simple Rate of Return and Payback Analysis of Two Machines [LO5, LO6]

Blue Ridge Furniture is considering the purchase of two different items of equipment, as described below:

Machine A. A machine has just come onto the market that compresses sawdust into various shelving products. Currently, the sawdust is disposed of as a waste product. The following information is available about the machine:

a. The machine would cost $780,000 and would have a 25% salvage value at the end of its 10-year useful life. The company uses straight-line depreciation and considers salvage value in computing depreciation deductions.
b. The shelving products produced by the machine would generate revenues of $350,000 per year. Variable manufacturing costs would be 20% of sales.
c. Fixed annual expenses associated with the new shelving products would be: advertising, $42,000; salaries, $86,000; utilities, $9,000; and insurance, $13,000.

Machine B. A second machine has come onto the market that would automate a sanding process that is now done largely by hand. The following information is available about this machine:

a. The new sanding machine would cost $220,000 and would have no salvage value at the end of its 10-year useful life. The company would use straight-line depreciation.
b. Several old pieces of sanding equipment that are fully depreciated would be disposed of at a scrap value of $7,200.
c. The new sanding machine would provide substantial annual savings in cash operating costs. It would require an operator at an annual salary of $26,000 and $3,000 in annual maintenance costs. The current, hand-operated sanding procedure costs the company $85,000 per year.

Blue Ridge Furniture requires a simple rate of return of 16% on all equipment purchases. Also, the company will not purchase equipment unless the equipment has a payback period of four years or less.

Required:

(Ignore income taxes.)

1. For machine A:
   a. Prepare an income statement showing the expected net operating income each year from the new shelving products. Use the contribution format.
   b. Compute the simple rate of return.
   c. Compute the payback period.
2. For machine B:
   a. Compute the simple rate of return.
   b. Compute the payback period.
3. According to the company's criteria, which machine, if either, should the company purchase?

PROBLEM 13–24 Simple Rate of Return; Payback [LO5, LO6]

Nagoya Amusements Corporation places electronic games and other amusement devices in supermarkets and similar outlets throughout Japan. Nagoya Amusements is investigating the purchase of a new electronic game called Mystic Invaders. The manufacturer will sell 20 games to Nagoya Amusements for a total price of ¥180,000. (The Japanese currency is the yen, which is denoted by the symbol ¥.) Nagoya Amusements has determined the following additional information about the game:

a. The game would have a five-year useful life and a negligible salvage value. The company uses straight-line depreciation.
b. The game would replace other games that are unpopular and generating little revenue. These other games would be sold for a total of ¥30,000.
c. Nagoya Amusements estimates that Mystic Invaders would generate annual incremental revenues of ¥200,000 (total for all 20 games). Annual incremental out-of-pocket costs would be (in total): maintenance, ¥50,000; and insurance, ¥10,000. In addition, Nagoya Amusements would have to pay a commission of 40% of total revenues to the supermarkets and other outlets in which the games were placed.

Required:
(Ignore income taxes.)

1. Prepare a contribution format income statement showing the net operating income each year from Mystic Invaders.
2. Compute the simple rate of return on Mystic Invaders. Will the game be purchased if Nagoya Amusements accepts any project with a simple rate of return greater than 14%?
3. Compute the payback period on Mystic Invaders. If the company accepts any investment with a payback period of less than three years, will the game be purchased?

PROBLEM: 13–25 Net Present Value; Total and Incremental Approaches [LO1]
Eastbay Hospital has an auxiliary generator that is used when power failures occur. The generator is worn out and must be either overhauled or replaced with a new generator. The hospital has assembled the following information:

	A	B	C
1		*Present Generator*	*New Generator*
2	Purchase cost new	$16,000	$20,000
3	Remaining book value	$9,000	-
4	Overhaul needed now	$8,000	-
5	Annual cash operating costs	$12,500	$7,500
6	Salvage value-now	$4,000	-
7	Salvage value-eight years from now	$3,000	$6,000
8			

Sheet1 Sheet2 Sheet3

If the company keeps and overhauls its present generator, then the generator will be usable for eight more years. If a new generator is purchased, it will be used for eight years, after which it will be replaced. The new generator would be diesel-powered, resulting in a substantial reduction in annual operating costs, as shown above.

The hospital computes depreciation on a straight-line basis. All equipment purchases are evaluated using a 16% discount rate.

Required:
(Ignore income taxes.)

1. Should Eastbay Hospital keep the old generator or purchase the new one? Use the total-cost approach to net present value in making your decision.
2. Redo (1) above, this time using the incremental-cost approach.

PROBLEM 13–26 Simple Rate of Return; Payback; Internal Rate of Return [LO2, LO5, LO6]

Chateau Beaune is a family-owned winery located in the Burgundy region of France, which is headed by Gerard Despinoy. The harvesting season in early fall is the busiest part of the year for the winery, and many part-time workers are hired to help pick and process grapes. Mr. Despinoy is investigating the purchase of a harvesting machine that would significantly reduce the amount of labor required in the picking process. The harvesting machine is built to straddle grapevines, which are laid out in lowlying rows. Two workers are carried on the machine just above ground level, one on each side of the vine. As the machine slowly crawls through the vineyard, the workers cut bunches of grapes from the vines, which then fall into a hopper. The machine separates the grapes from the stems and other woody debris. The debris are then pulverized and spread behind the machine as a rich ground mulch. Mr. Despinoy has gathered the following information relating to the decision of whether to purchase the machine:

a. The winery would save €190,000 per year in labor costs with the new harvesting machine. In addition, the company would no longer have to purchase and spread ground mulch—at an annual savings of €10,000. (The French currency is the euro, which is denoted by the symbol €.)
b. The harvesting machine would cost €480,000. It would have an estimated 12-year useful life and zero salvage value. The winery uses straight-line depreciation.
c. Annual out-of-pocket costs associated with the harvesting machine would be insurance, €1,000; fuel, €9,000; and a maintenance contract, €12,000. In addition, two operators would be hired and trained for the machine, and they would be paid a total of €70,000 per year, including all benefits.
d. Mr. Despinoy feels that the investment in the harvesting machine should earn at least a 16% rate of return.

Required:
(Ignore income taxes.)
1. Determine the annual net savings in cash operating costs that would be realized if the harvesting machine were purchased.
2. Compute the simple rate of return expected from the harvesting machine.
3. Compute the payback period on the harvesting machine. Mr. Despinoy will not purchase equipment unless it has a payback period of five years or less. Under this criterion, should the harvesting machine be purchased?
4. Compute (to the nearest whole percent) the internal rate of return promised by the harvesting machine. Based on this computation, does it appear that the simple rate of return is an accurate guide in investment decisions?

PROBLEM 13–27 Net Present Value Analysis of a New Product [LO1]
Atwood Company has an opportunity to produce and sell a revolutionary new smoke detector for homes. To determine whether this would be a profitable venture, the company has gathered the following data on probable costs and market potential:

a. New equipment would have to be acquired to produce the smoke detector. The equipment would cost $100,000 and be usable for 12 years. After 12 years, it would have a salvage value equal to 10% of the original cost.
b. Production and sales of the smoke detector would require a working capital investment of $40,000 to finance accounts receivable, inventories, and day-to-day cash needs. This working capital would be released for use elsewhere after 12 years.
c. An extensive marketing study projects sales in units over the next 12 years as follows:

Year	Sales in Units
1	4,000
2	7,000
3	10,000
4–12	12,000

d. The smoke detectors would sell for $45 each; variable costs for production, administration, and sales would be $25 per unit.
e. To gain entry into the market, the company would have to advertise heavily in the early years of sales. The advertising program follows:

Year	Amount of Yearly Advertising
1–2	$70,000
3	$50,000
4–12	$40,000

f. Other fixed costs for salaries, insurance, maintenance, and straight-line depreciation on equipment would total $127,500 per year. (Depreciation is based on cost less salvage value.)
g. The company's required rate of return is 20%.

Required:

(Ignore income taxes.)

1. Compute the net cash inflow (cash receipts less yearly cash operating expenses) anticipated from sale of the smoke detectors for each year over the next 12 years.
2. Using the data computed in (1) above and other data provided in the problem, determine the net present value of the proposed investment. Would you recommend that Atwood Company accept the smoke detector as a new product?

PROBLEM 13–28 Internal Rate of Return; Sensitivity Analysis [LO2]

Dr. Heidi Black is the managing partner of the Crestwood Dental Clinic. Dr. Black is trying to determine whether or not the clinic should move patient files and other items out of a spare room in the clinic and use the room for dental work. She has determined that it would require an investment of $142,950 for equipment and related costs of getting the room ready for use. Based on receipts being generated from other rooms in the clinic, Dr. Black estimates that the new room would generate a net cash inflow of $37,500 per year. The equipment purchased for the room would have a seven-year estimated useful life.

Required:

(Ignore income taxes.)

1. Compute the internal rate of return on the equipment for the new room to the nearest whole percent. Verify your answer by computing the net present value of the equipment using the internal rate of return you have computed as the discount rate.
2. Assume that Dr. Black will not purchase the new equipment unless it promises a return of at least 14%. Compute the amount of annual cash inflow that would provide this return on the $142,950 investment.
3. Although seven years is the average life for dental equipment, Dr. Black knows that due to changing technology this life can vary substantially. Compute the internal rate of return to the nearest whole percent if the life of the equipment were (*a*) five years and (*b*) nine years, rather than seven years. Is there any information provided by these computations that you would be particularly anxious to show Dr. Black?
4. Dr. Black is unsure about the estimated $37,500 annual cash inflow from the room. She thinks that the actual cash inflow could be as much as 20% greater or less than this figure.
   a. Assume that the actual cash inflow each year is 20% greater than estimated. Recompute the internal rate of return to the nearest whole percent.
   b. Assume that the actual cash inflow each year is 20% less than estimated. Recompute the internal rate of return to the nearest whole percent.
5. Refer to the original data. Assume that the equipment is purchased and that the room is opened for dental use. However, due to an increasing number of dentists in the area, the clinic is able to generate only $30,000 per year in net cash receipts from the new room. At the end of five years, the clinic closes the room and sells the equipment to a newly licensed dentist for a cash price of $61,375. Compute the internal rate of return to the nearest whole percent that the clinic earned on its investment over the five-year period. Round all dollar amounts to the nearest whole dollar. (Hint: A useful way to proceed is to find the discount rate that will cause the net present value of the investment to be equal to, or near, zero).

PROBLEM 13–29 Net Present Value; Uncertain Future Cash Flows; Postaudit [LO1, LO3]

"If we can get that new robot to combine with our other automated equipment, we'll have a complete flexible manufacturing system (FMS) in place in our Northridge plant," said Hal Swain, production manager for Diller Products.

"Let's just hope that reduced labor and inventory costs can justify its acquisition," replied Linda Wycoff, the controller. "Otherwise, we'll never get it. You know how the president feels about equipment paying for itself out of reduced costs."

Selected data relating to the robot are provided below:

Cost of the robot	$1,600,000
Software and installation	$700,000
Annual savings in labor costs	?
Annual savings in inventory carrying costs	$190,000
Monthly increase in power and maintenance costs	$2,500
Salvage value in 12 years	$90,000
Useful life	12 years

Engineering studies suggest that use of the robot will result in a savings of 20,000 direct labor-hours each year. The labor rate is $16 per hour. Also, the smoother work flow made possible by the FMS will allow the company to reduce the amount of inventory on hand by $300,000. The released funds will be available for use elsewhere in the company. This inventory reduction will take place in the first year of operation. The company's required rate of return is 20%.

Required:
(Ignore income taxes.)

1. Determine the net *annual* cost savings if the robot is purchased. (Do not include the $300,000 inventory reduction or the salvage value in this computation.)
2. Compute the net present value of the proposed investment in the robot. Based on these data, would you recommend that the robot be purchased? Explain.
3. Assume that the robot is purchased. At the end of the first year, Linda Wycoff has found that some items didn't work out as planned. Due to unforeseen problems, software and installation costs were $125,000 more than estimated, and direct labor has been reduced by only 17,500 hours per year, rather than by 20,000 hours. Assuming that all other cost data were accurate, does it appear that the company made a wise investment? Show computations, using the net present value format as in (2) above. (Hint: It might be helpful to place yourself back at the beginning of the first year, with the new data.)
4. Upon seeing your analysis in (3) above, the president stated, "That robot is the worst investment we've ever made. And here we'll be stuck with it for years."
   a. Explain to the president what benefits other than cost savings might accrue from using the new robot and FMS.
   b. Compute for the president the dollar amount of cash inflow that would be needed each year from the benefits in (*a*) above in order for the equipment to yield a 20% rate of return.

PROBLEM 13–30 Net Present Value Analysis [LO1]

Frank White will retire in six years. He wants to open some type of small business operation that can be managed in the free time he has available from his regular occupation, but that can be closed easily when he retires. He is considering several investment alternatives, one of which is to open a laundromat. After careful study, Mr. White has determined the following:

a. Washers, dryers, and other equipment needed to open the laundromat would cost $194,000. In addition, $6,000 in working capital would be required to purchase an inventory of soap, bleaches, and related items and to provide change for change machines. (The soap, bleaches, and related items would be sold to customers at cost.) After six years, the working capital would be released for investment elsewhere.
b. The laundromat would charge $1.50 per use for the washers and $0.75 per use for the dryers. Mr. White expects the laundromat to gross $1,800 each week from the washers and $1,125 each week from the dryers.
c. The only variable costs in the laundromat would be 7½ cents per use for water and electricity for the washers and 9 cents per use for gas and electricity for the dryers.
d. Fixed costs would be $3,000 per month for rent, $1,500 per month for cleaning, and $1,875 per month for maintenance, insurance, and other items.
e. The equipment would have a 10% disposal value in six years.

Mr. White will not open the laundromat unless it provides at least a 12% return.

Required:
(Ignore income taxes.)

1. Assuming that the laundromat would be open 52 weeks a year, compute the expected annual net cash receipts from its operation (gross cash receipts less cash disbursements). (Do not include the cost of the equipment, the working capital, or the salvage values in these computations.)
2. Would you advise Mr. White to open the laundromat? Show computations using the net present value method of investment analysis. Round all dollar amounts to the nearest whole dollar.

PROBLEM 13–31 Net Present Value Analysis of Securities [LO1]

Anita Vasquez received $160,000 from her mother's estate. She placed the funds into the hands of a broker, who purchased the following securities on Anita's behalf:

a. Common stock was purchased at a cost of $80,000. The stock paid no dividends, but it was sold for $180,000 at the end of four years.

b. Preferred stock was purchased at its par value of $30,000. The stock paid a 6% dividend (based on par value) each year for four years. At the end of four years, the stock was sold for $24,000.

c. Bonds were purchased at a cost of $50,000. The bonds paid $3,000 in interest every six months. After four years, the bonds were sold for $58,500. (Note: In discounting a cash flow that occurs semiannually, the procedure is to halve the discount rate and double the number of periods. Use the same procedure in discounting the proceeds from the sale.)

The securities were all sold at the end of four years so that Anita would have funds available to start a new business venture. The broker stated that the investments had earned more than a 20% return, and he gave Anita the following computation to support his statement:

Common stock:	
Gain on sale ($180,000 − $80,000)	$100,000
Preferred stock:	
Dividends paid (6% × $30,000 × 4 years) . . .	7,200
Loss on sale ($24,000 − $30,000)	(6,000)
Bonds:	
Interest paid ($3,000 × 8 periods)	24,000
Gain on sale ($58,500 − $50,000)	8,500
Net gain on all investments	$133,700

$$\frac{\$133{,}700 \div 4 \text{ years}}{\$160{,}000} = 20.9\%$$

Required:

(Ignore income taxes.)

1. Using a 20% discount rate, compute the net present value of each of the three investments. On which investment(s) did Anita earn a 20% rate of return? (Round computations to the nearest whole dollar.)
2. Considering all three investments together, did Anita earn a 20% rate of return? Explain.
3. Anita wants to use the $262,500 proceeds ($180,000 + $24,000 + $58,500 = $262,500) from sale of the securities to open a fast-food franchise under a 10-year contract. What net annual cash inflow must the store generate for Anita to earn a 16% return over the 10-year period? Anita will not receive back her original investment at the end of the contract. (Round computations to the nearest whole dollar.)

PROBLEM 13–32 Keep or Sell Property [LO1]

Ben Ryatt, professor of languages at a southern university, owns a small office building adjacent to the university campus. He acquired the property 12 years ago at a total cost of $560,000—$52,000 for the land and $508,000 for the building. He has just received an offer from a realty company that wants to purchase the property; however, the property has been a good source of income over the years, so Professor Ryatt is unsure whether he should keep it or sell it. His alternatives are:

Keep the property. Professor Ryatt's accountant has kept careful records of the income realized from the property over the past 10 years. These records indicate the following annual revenues and expenses:

Rental receipts		$150,000
Less building expenses:		
Utilities	$28,600	
Depreciation of building	17,800	
Property taxes and insurance	19,500	
Repairs and maintenance	10,500	
Custodial help and supplies	43,500	119,900
Net operating income		$ 30,100

Professor Ryatt makes a $12,600 mortgage payment each year on the property. The mortgage will be paid off in 10 more years. He has been depreciating the building by the straight-line method, assuming a salvage value of $9,600 for the building, which he still thinks is an appropriate figure. He feels sure that the building can be rented for another 16 years. He also feels sure that 16 years from now the land will be worth 2.5 times what he paid for it.

Sell the property. A realty company has offered to purchase the property by paying $150,000 immediately and $23,000 per year for the next 16 years. Control of the property would go to the realty company immediately. To sell the property, Professor Ryatt would need to pay the mortgage off, which could be done by making a lump-sum payment of $71,000.

Required:

(Ignore income taxes.) Professor Ryatt requires a 14% rate of return. Would you recommend he keep or sell the property? Show computations using the total-cost approach to net present value.

Cases

connect ACCOUNTING

All applicable cases are available with McGraw-Hill's *Connect™ Accounting.*

CASE 13–33 Comparison of Alternatives Using Net Present Value Analysis [LO1]

Woolrich Company's market research division has projected a substantial increase in demand over the next several years for one of the company's products. To meet this demand, the company will need to produce units as follows:

Year	Production in Units
1	20,000
2	30,000
3	40,000
4–10	45,000

At present, the company is using a single model 2600 machine to manufacture this product. To increase its productive capacity, the company is considering two alternatives:

Alternative 1. The company could purchase another model 2600 machine that would operate along with the one it now owns. The following information is available on this alternative:

a. The model 2600 machine now in use was purchased for $165,000 four years ago. Its present book value is $99,000, and its present market value is $90,000.

b. A new model 2600 machine costs $180,000 now. The old model 2600 machine will have to be replaced in six years at a cost of $200,000. The replacement machine will have a market value of about $100,000 when it is four years old.

c. The variable cost required to produce one unit of product using the model 2600 machine is given under the "general information" on the next page.

d. Repairs and maintenance costs each year on a single model 2600 machine total $3,000.

Alternative 2. The company could purchase a model 5200 machine and use the old model 2600 machine as standby equipment. The model 5200 machine is a high-speed unit with double the capacity of the model 2600 machine. The following information is available on this alternative:

a. The cost of a new model 5200 machine is $250,000.

b. The variable cost required to produce one unit of product using the model 5200 machine is given under the "general information" on the next page.

c. The model 5200 machine is more costly to maintain than the model 2600 machine. Repairs and maintenance on a model 5200 machine and on a model 2600 machine used as a standby would total $4,600 per year.

The following general information is available on the two alternatives:

a. Both the model 2600 machine and the model 5200 machine have a 10-year life from the time they are first used in production. The scrap value of both machines is negligible and can be ignored. Straight-line depreciation is used by the company.

b. The two machine models are not equally efficient. Comparative variable costs per unit of product are as follows:

	Model 2600	Model 5200
Direct materials per unit	$0.36	$0.40
Direct labor per unit	0.50	0.22
Supplies and lubricants per unit	0.04	0.08
Total variable cost per unit	$0.90	$0.70

c. No other factory costs would change as a result of the decision between the two machines.
d. Woolrich Company uses an 18% discount rate.

Required:
(Ignore income taxes.)
1. Which alternative should the company choose? Use the net present value approach. (Round to the nearest whole dollar.)
2. Suppose that the cost of direct materials increases by 50%. Would this make the model 5200 machine more or less desirable? Explain. No computations are needed.
3. Suppose that the cost of direct labor increases by 25%. Would this make the model 5200 machine more or less desirable? Explain. No computations are needed.

CASE 13–34 Ethics and the Manager; Postaudit

After five years with a national CPA firm with mostly large manufacturing clients, Amy Kimbell joined Hi-Quality Productions Inc. (Hi-Q) as manager of Manufacturing Accounting. Amy has both CPA and CMA credentials.

Hi-Q is a publicly held company producing automotive components. One operation in the Alpha Division requires a highly automated process. Hi-Q's top management and board of directors had outsourced this particular high-tech operation to another company to avoid making a large investment in technology they viewed as constantly changing.

Each operating division of Hi-Q has a budget committee. Two years ago, the Alpha Division budget committee presented to the board its proposal to bring the high-tech operation in house. This would require a capital investment of approximately $4 million but would lead to more than enough cost savings to justify this expenditure. The board approved the proposal, and the investment was made. Later the same year, Amy Kimbell was promoted to assistant corporate controller. In this position, she sits on the budget committee of all divisions.

A little more than a year after the high-tech process was put into operation, the board requested a postaudit review of the actual cost savings. When the board requests such a review, the data are supplied by the management of the affected division and are reviewed by the division's budget committee. When the data were sent to the budget committee for review, Amy Kimbell noted that several of the projections in the original proposal were very aggressive. These included a very high salvage value for the equipment as well as a very long useful life over which cost savings were projected to occur. If more realistic projections had been used, Amy doubted that the board would have agreed to make the investment.

Also in the postaudit review, Amy noted that substantial amounts of incremental service department operating costs directly caused by the new investment were not being attributed to the high-tech operation. Instead, these costs were being allocated as general overhead to all departments. In addition, she noted that the estimated rate for spoiled and defective work contained in the proposal was being used in the review rather than the actual rate, which was considerably higher.

When Amy Kimbell brought these points to the attention of the division's budget committee, she was told that as a new member of the committee she would not be held responsible for decisions, such as the investment in the high-tech operation, that were made prior to her arrival. Accordingly, she should let the seasoned members of the committee handle this particular review. When Amy continued to express her concerns, she was firmly informed that it had been the unanimous decision of the committee to approve the original proposal because it was thought to be in the best long-run interest of the company. And given this consensus, it was felt that certain "adjustments and exceptions" to the postaudit review were justified to ensure the overall long-run well-being of the company.

Required:
1. What should Amy do? (Refer to the IMA's Statement of Ethical Professional Practice for guidance.)

2. Do you have any suggestions for revising the way in which postaudits are conducted at Hi-Q?

(Adapted from Roland L. Madison and Curtis C. Verschoor, "New Position Brings Ethical Dilemma," *Strategic Finance,* December 2000, pp. 22, 24. Used with permission from the IMA, Montvale, NJ, USA, www.imanet.org.)

CASE 13–35 Net Present Value Analysis of a Lease or Buy Decision [LO1]

Wyndham Stores operates a regional chain of upscale department stores. The company is going to open another store soon in a prosperous and growing suburban area. In discussing how the company can acquire the desired building and other facilities needed to open the new store, Harry Wilson, the company's marketing vice president, stated, "I know most of our competitors are starting to lease facilities, rather than buy, but I just can't see the economics of it. Our development people tell me that we can buy the building site, put a building on it, and get all the store fixtures we need for $14 million. They also say that property taxes, insurance, maintenance, and repairs would run $200,000 a year. When you figure that we plan to keep a site for 20 years, that's a total cost of $18 million. But then when you realize that the building and property will be worth at least $5 million in 20 years, that's a net cost to us of only $13 million. Leasing costs a lot more than that."

"I'm not so sure," replied Erin Reilley, the company's executive vice president. "Guardian Insurance Company is willing to purchase the building site, construct a building and install fixtures to our specifications, and then lease the facility to us for 20 years for an annual lease payment of only $1 million."

"That's just my point," said Harry. "At $1 million a year, it would cost us $20 million over the 20 years instead of just $13 million. And what would we have left at the end? Nothing! The building would belong to the insurance company! I'll bet they would even want the first lease payment in advance."

"That's right," replied Erin. "We would have to make the first payment immediately and then one payment at the beginning of each of the following 19 years. However, you're overlooking a few things. For one thing, we would have to tie up a lot of our funds for 20 years under the purchase alternative. We would have to put $6 million down immediately if we buy the property, and then we would have to pay the other $8 million off over four years at $2 million a year."

"But that cost is nothing compared to $20 million for leasing," said Harry. "Also, if we lease, I understand we would have to put up a $400,000 security deposit that we wouldn't get back until the end. And besides that, we would still have to pay all the repair and maintenance costs just like we owned the property. No wonder those insurance companies are so rich if they can swing deals like this."

"Well, I'll admit that I don't have all the figures sorted out yet," replied Erin. "But I do have the operating cost breakdown for the building, which includes $90,000 annually for property taxes, $60,000 for insurance, and $50,000 for repairs and maintenance. If we lease, Guardian will handle its own insurance costs and will pay the property taxes, but we'll have to pay for the repairs and maintenance. I need to put all this together and see if leasing makes any sense with our 12% before-tax required rate of return. The president wants a presentation and recommendation in the executive committee meeting tomorrow."

Required:

(Ignore income taxes.)

1. Using the net present value approach, determine whether Wyndham Stores should lease or buy the new store. Assume that you will be making your presentation before the company's executive committee.
2. How will you reply in the meeting if Harry Wilson brings up the issue of the building's future sales value?

Appendix 13A: The Concept of Present Value

LEARNING OBJECTIVE 7
Understand present value concepts and the use of present value tables.

A dollar received today is more valuable than a dollar received a year from now for the simple reason that if you have a dollar today, you can put it in the bank and have more than a dollar a year from now. Because dollars today are worth more than dollars in the future, cash flows that are received at different times must be valued differently.

The Mathematics of Interest

If a bank pays 5% interest, then a deposit of \$100 today will be worth \$105 one year from now. This can be expressed as follows:

$$F_1 = P(1 + r) \qquad (1)$$

where F_1 = the balance at the end of one period, P = the amount invested now, and r = the rate of interest per period.

In the case where \$100 is deposited in a savings account that earns 5% interest, P = \$100 and r = 0.05. Under these conditions, F_1 = \$105.

The \$100 present outlay is called the **present value** of the \$105 amount to be received in one year. It is also known as the *discounted value* of the future \$105 receipt. The \$100 represents the value in present terms of \$105 to be received a year from now when the interest rate is 5%.

Compound Interest

What if the \$105 is left in the bank for a second year? In that case, by the end of the second year the original \$100 deposit will have grown to \$110.25:

Original deposit	\$100.00
Interest for the first year:	
\$100 × 0.05	5.00
Balance at the end of the first year	105.00
Interest for the second year:	
\$105 × 0.05	5.25
Balance at the end of the second year	\$110.25

Notice that the interest for the second year is \$5.25, as compared to only \$5.00 for the first year. This difference arises because interest is being paid on interest during the second year. That is, the \$5.00 interest earned during the first year has been left in the account and has been added to the original \$100 deposit when computing interest for the second year. This is known as **compound interest.** In this case, the compounding is annual. Interest can be compounded on a semiannual, quarterly, monthly, or even more frequent basis. The more frequently compounding is done, the more rapidly the balance will grow.

We can determine the balance in an account after n periods of compounding using the following equation:

$$F_n = P(1 + r)^n \qquad (2)$$

where n = the number of periods of compounding.

If n = 2 years and the interest rate is 5% per year, then the balance in two years will be computed as follows:

$$F_2 = \$100(1 + 0.05)^2$$

$$F_2 = \$110.25$$

Present Value and Future Value

Exhibit 13A–1 shows the relationship between present value and future value. As shown in the exhibit, if \$100 is deposited in a bank at 5% interest compounded annually, it will grow to \$127.63 by the end of five years.

Computation of Present Value

An investment can be viewed in two ways—either in terms of its future value or in terms of its present value. We have seen from our computations above that if we know the present value of a sum (such as our \$100 deposit), the future value in n years can be computed

EXHIBIT 13A–1
The Relationship between Present Value and Future Value

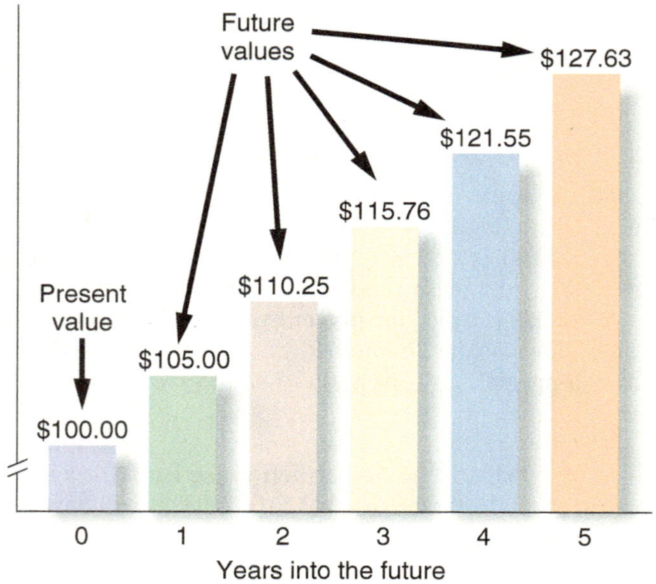

by using equation (2). But what if the situation is reversed and we know the *future* value of some amount but we do not know its present value?

For example, assume that you are to receive $200 two years from now. You know that the future value of this sum is $200 because this is the amount that you will be receiving in two years. But what is the sum's present value—what is it worth *right now?* The present value of any sum to be received in the future can be computed by turning equation (2) around and solving for *P:*

$$P = \frac{F_n}{(1 + r)^n} \tag{3}$$

In our example, F_n = $200 (the amount to be received in the future), $r = 0.05$ (the annual rate of interest), and $n = 2$ (the number of years in the future that the amount will be received).

$$P = \frac{\$200}{(1 + 0.05)^2}$$

$$P = \frac{\$200}{1.1025}$$

$$P = \$181.40$$

As shown by the computation above, the present value of a $200 amount to be received two years from now is $181.40 if the interest rate is 5%. In effect, $181.40 received *right now* is equivalent to $200 received two years from now.

The process of finding the present value of a future cash flow, which we have just completed, is called **discounting.** We have *discounted* the $200 to its present value of $181.40. The 5% interest that we have used to find this present value is called the **discount rate.** Discounting future sums to their present value is a common practice in business, particularly in capital budgeting decisions.

If you have a power key (y^x) on your calculator, the above calculations are fairly easy. However, some of the present value formulas we will be using are more complex. Fortunately, tables are available in which many of the calculations have already been done. For example, Exhibit 13B–1 in Appendix 13B shows the discounted present value of $1 to be received at various periods in the future at various interest rates. The table indicates that the present value of $1 to be received two periods from now at 5% is 0.907. Because in our example we want to know the present value of $200 rather than just $1, we need to multiply the factor in the table by $200:

$$\$200 \times 0.907 = \$181.40$$

This answer is the same as we obtained earlier using the formula in equation (3).

Present Value of a Series of Cash Flows

Although some investments involve a single sum to be received (or paid) at a single point in the future, other investments involve a *series* of cash flows. A series of identical cash flows is known as an **annuity**. To provide an example, assume that a company has just purchased some government bonds. The bonds will yield interest of $15,000 each year and will be held for five years. What is the present value of the stream of interest receipts from the bonds? As shown in Exhibit 13A–2, if the discount rate is 12%, the present value of this stream is $54,075. The discount factors used in this exhibit were taken from Exhibit 13B–1 in Appendix 13B.

EXHIBIT 13A–2
Present Value of a Series of Cash Receipts

Year	Factor at 12% (Exhibit 13B–1)	Interest Received	Present Value
1	0.893	$15,000	$13,395
2	0.797	$15,000	11,955
3	0.712	$15,000	10,680
4	0.636	$15,000	9,540
5	0.567	$15,000	8,505
			$54,075

Exhibit 13A–2 illustrates two important points. First, the present value of the $15,000 interest declines the further it is into the future. The present value of $15,000 received a year from now is $13,395, as compared to only $8,505 if received five years from now. This point underscores the time value of money.

The second point is that the computations used in Exhibit 13A–2 involved unnecessary work. The same present value of $54,075 could have been obtained more easily by referring to Exhibit 13B–2 in Appendix 13B. Exhibit 13B–2 contains the present value of $1 to be received each year over a *series* of years at various interest rates. Exhibit 13B–2 has been derived by simply adding together the factors from Exhibit 13B–1, as follows:

Year	Factors at 12% (from Exhibit 13B–1)
1	0.893
2	0.797
3	0.712
4	0.636
5	0.567
	3.605

The sum of these five factors is 3.605. Notice from Exhibit 13B–2 that the factor for \$1 to be received each year for five years at 12% is also 3.605. If we use this factor and multiply it by the \$15,000 annual cash inflow, then we get the same \$54,075 present value that we obtained earlier in Exhibit 13A–2.

$$\$15,000 \times 3.605 = \$54,075$$

Therefore, when computing the present value of a series of equal cash flows that begins at the end of period 1, Exhibit 13B–2 should be used.

To summarize, the present value tables in Appendix 13B should be used as follows:

Exhibit 13B–1: This table should be used to find the present value of a single cash flow (such as a single payment or receipt) occurring in the future.

Exhibit 13B–2: This table should be used to find the present value of a series of identical cash flows beginning at the end of the current period and continuing into the future.

The use of both of these tables is illustrated in various exhibits in the main body of the chapter. *When a present value factor appears in an exhibit, you should take the time to trace it back into either Exhibit 13B–1 or Exhibit 13B–2 to get acquainted with the tables and how they work.*

Review Problem: Basic Present Value Computations

Each of the following situations is independent. Work out your own solution to each situation, and then check it against the solution provided.

1. John plans to retire in 12 years. Upon retiring, he would like to take an extended vacation, which he expects will cost at least \$40,000. What lump-sum amount must he invest now to have \$40,000 at the end of 12 years if the rate of return is:
   a. Eight percent?
   b. Twelve percent?
2. The Morgans would like to send their daughter to a music camp at the end of each of the next five years. The camp costs \$1,000 a year. What lump-sum amount would have to be invested now to have \$1,000 at the end of each year if the rate of return is:
   a. Eight percent?
   b. Twelve percent?
3. You have just received an inheritance from a relative. You can either receive a \$200,000 lump-sum amount at the end of 10 years or receive \$14,000 at the end of each year for the next 10 years. If your discount rate is 12%, which alternative would you prefer?

Solution to Review Problem

1. *a.* The amount that must be invested now would be the present value of the \$40,000, using a discount rate of 8%. From Exhibit 13B–1 in Appendix 13B, the factor for a discount rate of 8% for 12 periods is 0.397. Multiplying this discount factor by the \$40,000 needed in 12 years will give the amount of the present investment required: \$40,000 × 0.397 = \$15,880.
   b. We will proceed as we did in (*a*) above, but this time we will use a discount rate of 12%. From Exhibit 13B–1 in Appendix 13B, the factor for a discount rate of 12% for 12 periods is 0.257. Multiplying this discount factor by the \$40,000 needed in 12 years will give the amount of the present investment required: \$40,000 × 0.257 = \$10,280.
   Notice that as the discount rate (desired rate of return) increases, the present value decreases.
2. This part differs from (1) above in that we are now dealing with an annuity rather than with a single future sum. The amount that must be invested now is the present value of the \$1,000 needed at the end of each year for five years. Because we are dealing with an annuity, or a

series of annual cash flows, we must refer to Exhibit 13B–2 in Appendix 13B for the appropriate discount factor.

a. From Exhibit 13B–2 in Appendix 13B, the discount factor for 8% for five periods is 3.993. Therefore, the amount that must be invested now to have $1,000 available at the end of each year for five years is $1,000 × 3.993 = $3,993.

b. From Exhibit 13B–2 in Appendix 13B, the discount factor for 12% for five periods is 3.605. Therefore, the amount that must be invested now to have $1,000 available at the end of each year for five years is $1,000 × 3.605 = $3,605.

Again, notice that as the discount rate increases, the present value decreases. When the rate of return increases, less must be invested today to yield a given amount in the future.

3. For this part we will need to refer to both Exhibits 13B–1 and 13B–2 in Appendix 13B. From Exhibit 13B–1, we will need to find the discount factor for 12% for 10 periods, then apply it to the $200,000 lump sum to be received in 10 years. From Exhibit 13B–2, we will need to find the discount factor for 12% for 10 periods, then apply it to the series of $14,000 payments to be received over the 10-year period. Whichever alternative has the higher present value is the one that should be selected.

$$\$200,000 \times 0.322 = \$64,400$$

$$\$14,000 \times 5.650 = \$79,100$$

Thus, you should prefer to receive the $14,000 per year for 10 years rather than the $200,000 lump sum. This means that you could invest the $14,000 received at the end of each year at 12% and have *more* than $200,000 at the end of 10 years.

Glossary (Appendix 13A)

Annuity A series of identical cash flows. (p. 625)
Compound interest The process of paying interest on interest in an investment. (p. 623)
Discount rate The rate of return that is used to find the present value of a future cash flow. (p. 624)
Discounting The process of finding the present value of a future cash flow. (p. 624)
Present value The value now of an amount that will be received in some future period. (p. 623)

connect ACCOUNTING Appendix 13A Exercises

All applicable exercises are available with McGraw-Hill's *Connect™ Accounting*.

EXERCISE 13A–1 Basic Present Value Concepts [LO7]

Largo Freightlines plans to build a new garage in three years to have more space for repairing its trucks. The garage will cost $400,000.

Required:

What lump-sum amount should the company invest now to have the $400,000 available at the end of the three-year period? Assume that the company can invest money at:

a. Eight percent.
b. Twelve percent.

EXERCISE 13A–2 Basic Present Value Concepts [LO7]

You have just learned that you are a beneficiary in the will of your late Aunt Susan. The executrix of her estate has given you three options as to how you may receive your inheritance:

a. You may receive $50,000 immediately.
b. You may receive $75,000 at the end of six years.
c. You may receive $12,000 at the end of each year for six years (a total of $72,000).

Required:
If you can invest money at a 12% return, which option would you prefer?

EXERCISE 13A–3 Basic Present Value Concepts [LO7]
At the end of three years, when you graduate from college, your father has promised to give you a used car that will cost $12,000.

Required:
What lump sum must he invest now to have the $12,000 at the end of three years if he can invest money at:
a. Six percent?
b. Ten percent?

EXERCISE 13A–4 Basic Present Value Concepts [LO7]
Sally has just won the million-dollar Big Slam jackpot at a gambling casino. The casino will pay her $50,000 per year for 20 years as the payoff.

Required:
If Sally can invest money at a 10% rate of return, what is the present value of her winnings? Did she really win a million dollars? Explain.

EXERCISE 13A–5 Basic Present Value Concepts [LO7]
Annual cash inflows from two competing investment opportunities are given below. Each investment opportunity will require the same initial investment.

	Investment X	Investment Y
Year 1	$ 1,000	$ 4,000
Year 2	2,000	3,000
Year 3	3,000	2,000
Year 4	4,000	1,000
Total	$10,000	$10,000

Required:
Compute the present value of the cash inflows for each investment using a 20% discount rate.

EXERCISE 13A–6 Basic Present Value Concepts [LO7]
Martell Products Inc. can purchase a new copier that will save $5,000 per year in copying costs. The copier will last for six years and have no salvage value.

Required:
What is the maximum purchase price that Martell Products should be willing to pay for the copier if the company's required rate of return is:
a. Ten percent?
b. Sixteen percent?

Appendix 13B: Present Value Tables

EXHIBIT 13B-1

Present Value of $1; $\frac{1}{(1+r)^n}$

Periods	4%	5%	6%	7%	8%	9%	10%	11%	12%	13%	14%	15%	16%	17%	18%	19%	20%	21%	22%	23%	24%	25%
1	0.962	0.952	0.943	0.935	0.926	0.917	0.909	0.901	0.893	0.885	0.877	0.870	0.862	0.855	0.847	0.840	0.833	0.826	0.820	0.813	0.806	0.800
2	0.925	0.907	0.890	0.873	0.857	0.842	0.826	0.812	0.797	0.783	0.769	0.756	0.743	0.731	0.718	0.706	0.694	0.683	0.672	0.661	0.650	0.640
3	0.889	0.864	0.840	0.816	0.794	0.772	0.751	0.731	0.712	0.693	0.675	0.658	0.641	0.624	0.609	0.593	0.579	0.564	0.551	0.537	0.524	0.512
4	0.855	0.823	0.792	0.763	0.735	0.708	0.683	0.659	0.636	0.613	0.592	0.572	0.552	0.534	0.516	0.499	0.482	0.467	0.451	0.437	0.423	0.410
5	0.822	0.784	0.747	0.713	0.681	0.650	0.621	0.593	0.567	0.543	0.519	0.497	0.476	0.456	0.437	0.419	0.402	0.386	0.370	0.355	0.341	0.328
6	0.790	0.746	0.705	0.666	0.630	0.596	0.564	0.535	0.507	0.480	0.456	0.432	0.410	0.390	0.370	0.352	0.335	0.319	0.303	0.289	0.275	0.262
7	0.760	0.711	0.665	0.623	0.583	0.547	0.513	0.482	0.452	0.425	0.400	0.376	0.354	0.333	0.314	0.296	0.279	0.263	0.249	0.235	0.222	0.210
8	0.731	0.677	0.627	0.582	0.540	0.502	0.467	0.434	0.404	0.376	0.351	0.327	0.305	0.285	0.266	0.249	0.233	0.218	0.204	0.191	0.179	0.168
9	0.703	0.645	0.592	0.544	0.500	0.460	0.424	0.391	0.361	0.333	0.308	0.284	0.263	0.243	0.225	0.209	0.194	0.180	0.167	0.155	0.144	0.134
10	0.676	0.614	0.558	0.508	0.463	0.422	0.386	0.352	0.322	0.295	0.270	0.247	0.227	0.208	0.191	0.176	0.162	0.149	0.137	0.126	0.116	0.107
11	0.650	0.585	0.527	0.475	0.429	0.388	0.350	0.317	0.287	0.261	0.237	0.215	0.195	0.178	0.162	0.148	0.135	0.123	0.112	0.103	0.094	0.086
12	0.625	0.557	0.497	0.444	0.397	0.356	0.319	0.286	0.257	0.231	0.208	0.187	0.168	0.152	0.137	0.124	0.112	0.102	0.092	0.083	0.076	0.069
13	0.601	0.530	0.469	0.415	0.368	0.326	0.290	0.258	0.229	0.204	0.182	0.163	0.145	0.130	0.116	0.104	0.093	0.084	0.075	0.068	0.061	0.055
14	0.577	0.505	0.442	0.388	0.340	0.299	0.263	0.232	0.205	0.181	0.160	0.141	0.125	0.111	0.099	0.088	0.078	0.069	0.062	0.055	0.049	0.044
15	0.555	0.481	0.417	0.362	0.315	0.275	0.239	0.209	0.183	0.160	0.140	0.123	0.108	0.095	0.084	0.074	0.065	0.057	0.051	0.045	0.040	0.035
16	0.534	0.458	0.394	0.339	0.292	0.252	0.218	0.188	0.163	0.141	0.123	0.107	0.093	0.081	0.071	0.062	0.054	0.047	0.042	0.036	0.032	0.028
17	0.513	0.436	0.371	0.317	0.270	0.231	0.198	0.170	0.146	0.125	0.108	0.093	0.080	0.069	0.060	0.052	0.045	0.039	0.034	0.030	0.026	0.023
18	0.494	0.416	0.350	0.296	0.250	0.212	0.180	0.153	0.130	0.111	0.095	0.081	0.069	0.059	0.051	0.044	0.038	0.032	0.028	0.024	0.021	0.018
19	0.475	0.396	0.331	0.277	0.232	0.194	0.164	0.138	0.116	0.098	0.083	0.070	0.060	0.051	0.043	0.037	0.031	0.027	0.023	0.020	0.017	0.014
20	0.456	0.377	0.312	0.258	0.215	0.178	0.149	0.124	0.104	0.087	0.073	0.061	0.051	0.043	0.037	0.031	0.026	0.022	0.019	0.016	0.014	0.012
21	0.439	0.359	0.294	0.242	0.199	0.164	0.135	0.112	0.093	0.077	0.064	0.053	0.044	0.037	0.031	0.026	0.022	0.018	0.015	0.013	0.011	0.009
22	0.422	0.342	0.278	0.226	0.184	0.150	0.123	0.101	0.083	0.068	0.056	0.046	0.038	0.032	0.026	0.022	0.018	0.015	0.013	0.011	0.009	0.007
23	0.406	0.326	0.262	0.211	0.170	0.138	0.112	0.091	0.074	0.060	0.049	0.040	0.033	0.027	0.022	0.018	0.015	0.012	0.010	0.009	0.007	0.006
24	0.390	0.310	0.247	0.197	0.158	0.126	0.102	0.082	0.066	0.053	0.043	0.035	0.028	0.023	0.019	0.015	0.013	0.010	0.008	0.007	0.006	0.005
25	0.375	0.295	0.233	0.184	0.146	0.116	0.092	0.074	0.059	0.047	0.038	0.030	0.024	0.020	0.016	0.013	0.010	0.009	0.007	0.006	0.005	0.004
26	0.361	0.281	0.220	0.172	0.135	0.106	0.084	0.066	0.053	0.042	0.033	0.026	0.021	0.017	0.014	0.011	0.009	0.007	0.006	0.005	0.004	0.003
27	0.347	0.268	0.207	0.161	0.125	0.098	0.076	0.060	0.047	0.037	0.029	0.023	0.018	0.014	0.011	0.009	0.007	0.006	0.005	0.004	0.003	0.002
28	0.333	0.255	0.196	0.150	0.116	0.090	0.069	0.054	0.042	0.033	0.026	0.020	0.016	0.012	0.010	0.008	0.006	0.005	0.004	0.003	0.002	0.002
29	0.321	0.243	0.185	0.141	0.107	0.082	0.063	0.048	0.037	0.029	0.022	0.017	0.014	0.011	0.008	0.006	0.005	0.004	0.003	0.002	0.002	0.002
30	0.308	0.231	0.174	0.131	0.099	0.075	0.057	0.044	0.033	0.026	0.020	0.015	0.012	0.009	0.007	0.005	0.004	0.003	0.003	0.002	0.002	0.001
40	0.208	0.142	0.097	0.067	0.046	0.032	0.022	0.015	0.011	0.008	0.005	0.004	0.003	0.002	0.001	0.001	0.001	0.000	0.000	0.000	0.000	0.000

EXHIBIT 13B–2

Present Value of an Annuity of $1 in Arrears; $\frac{1}{r}\left[1 - \frac{1}{(1+r)^n}\right]$

Periods	4%	5%	6%	7%	8%	9%	10%	11%	12%	13%	14%	15%	16%	17%	18%	19%	20%	21%	22%	23%	24%	25%
1	0.962	0.952	0.943	0.935	0.926	0.917	0.909	0.901	0.893	0.885	0.877	0.870	0.862	0.855	0.847	0.840	0.833	0.826	0.820	0.813	0.806	0.800
2	1.886	1.859	1.833	1.808	1.783	1.759	1.736	1.713	1.690	1.668	1.647	1.626	1.605	1.585	1.566	1.547	1.528	1.509	1.492	1.474	1.457	1.440
3	2.775	2.723	2.673	2.624	2.577	2.531	2.487	2.444	2.402	2.361	2.322	2.283	2.246	2.210	2.174	2.140	2.106	2.074	2.042	2.011	1.981	1.952
4	3.630	3.546	3.465	3.387	3.312	3.240	3.170	3.102	3.037	2.974	2.914	2.855	2.798	2.743	2.690	2.639	2.589	2.540	2.494	2.448	2.404	2.362
5	4.452	4.329	4.212	4.100	3.993	3.890	3.791	3.696	3.605	3.517	3.433	3.352	3.274	3.199	3.127	3.058	2.991	2.926	2.864	2.803	2.745	2.689
6	5.242	5.076	4.917	4.767	4.623	4.486	4.355	4.231	4.111	3.998	3.889	3.784	3.685	3.589	3.498	3.410	3.326	3.245	3.167	3.092	3.020	2.951
7	6.002	5.786	5.582	5.389	5.206	5.033	4.868	4.712	4.564	4.423	4.288	4.160	4.039	3.922	3.812	3.706	3.605	3.508	3.416	3.327	3.242	3.161
8	6.733	6.463	6.210	5.971	5.747	5.535	5.335	5.146	4.968	4.799	4.639	4.487	4.344	4.207	4.078	3.954	3.837	3.726	3.619	3.518	3.421	3.329
9	7.435	7.108	6.802	6.515	6.247	5.995	5.759	5.537	5.328	5.132	4.946	4.772	4.607	4.451	4.303	4.163	4.031	3.905	3.786	3.673	3.566	3.463
10	8.111	7.722	7.360	7.024	6.710	6.418	6.145	5.889	5.650	5.426	5.216	5.019	4.833	4.659	4.494	4.339	4.192	4.054	3.923	3.799	3.682	3.571
11	8.760	8.306	7.887	7.499	7.139	6.805	6.495	6.207	5.938	5.687	5.453	5.234	5.029	4.836	4.656	4.486	4.327	4.177	4.035	3.902	3.776	3.656
12	9.385	8.863	8.384	7.943	7.536	7.161	6.814	6.492	6.194	5.918	5.660	5.421	5.197	4.988	4.793	4.611	4.439	4.278	4.127	3.985	3.851	3.725
13	9.986	9.394	8.853	8.358	7.904	7.487	7.103	6.750	6.424	6.122	5.842	5.583	5.342	5.118	4.910	4.715	4.533	4.362	4.203	4.053	3.912	3.780
14	10.563	9.899	9.295	8.745	8.244	7.786	7.367	6.982	6.628	6.302	6.002	5.724	5.468	5.229	5.008	4.802	4.611	4.432	4.265	4.108	3.962	3.824
15	11.118	10.380	9.712	9.108	8.559	8.061	7.606	7.191	6.811	6.462	6.142	5.847	5.575	5.324	5.092	4.876	4.675	4.489	4.315	4.153	4.001	3.859
16	11.652	10.838	10.106	9.447	8.851	8.313	7.824	7.379	6.974	6.604	6.265	5.954	5.668	5.405	5.162	4.938	4.730	4.536	4.357	4.189	4.033	3.887
17	12.166	11.274	10.477	9.763	9.122	8.544	8.022	7.549	7.120	6.729	6.373	6.047	5.749	5.475	5.222	4.990	4.775	4.576	4.391	4.219	4.059	3.910
18	12.659	11.690	10.828	10.059	9.372	8.756	8.201	7.702	7.250	6.840	6.467	6.128	5.818	5.534	5.273	5.033	4.812	4.608	4.419	4.243	4.080	3.928
19	13.134	12.085	11.158	10.336	9.604	8.950	8.365	7.839	7.366	6.938	6.550	6.198	5.877	5.584	5.316	5.070	4.843	4.635	4.442	4.263	4.097	3.942
20	13.590	12.462	11.470	10.594	9.818	9.129	8.514	7.963	7.469	7.025	6.623	6.259	5.929	5.628	5.353	5.101	4.870	4.657	4.460	4.279	4.110	3.954
21	14.029	12.821	11.764	10.836	10.017	9.292	8.649	8.075	7.562	7.102	6.687	6.312	5.973	5.665	5.384	5.127	4.891	4.675	4.476	4.292	4.121	3.963
22	14.451	13.163	12.042	11.061	10.201	9.442	8.772	8.176	7.645	7.170	6.743	6.359	6.011	5.696	5.410	5.149	4.909	4.690	4.488	4.302	4.130	3.970
23	14.857	13.489	12.303	11.272	10.371	9.580	8.883	8.266	7.718	7.230	6.792	6.399	6.044	5.723	5.432	5.167	4.925	4.703	4.499	4.311	4.137	3.976
24	15.247	13.799	12.550	11.469	10.529	9.707	8.985	8.348	7.784	7.283	6.835	6.434	6.073	5.746	5.451	5.182	4.937	4.713	4.507	4.318	4.143	3.981
25	15.622	14.094	12.783	11.654	10.675	9.823	9.077	8.422	7.843	7.330	6.873	6.464	6.097	5.766	5.467	5.195	4.948	4.721	4.514	4.323	4.147	3.985
26	15.983	14.375	13.003	11.826	10.810	9.929	9.161	8.488	7.896	7.372	6.906	6.491	6.118	5.783	5.480	5.206	4.956	4.728	4.520	4.328	4.151	3.988
27	16.330	14.643	13.211	11.987	10.935	10.027	9.237	8.548	7.943	7.409	6.935	6.514	6.136	5.798	5.492	5.215	4.964	4.734	4.524	4.332	4.154	3.990
28	16.663	14.898	13.406	12.137	11.051	10.116	9.307	8.602	7.984	7.441	6.961	6.534	6.152	5.810	5.502	5.223	4.970	4.739	4.528	4.335	4.157	3.992
29	16.984	15.141	13.591	12.278	11.158	10.198	9.370	8.650	8.022	7.470	6.983	6.551	6.166	5.820	5.510	5.229	4.975	4.743	4.531	4.337	4.159	3.994
30	17.292	15.372	13.765	12.409	11.258	10.274	9.427	8.694	8.055	7.496	7.003	6.566	6.177	5.829	5.517	5.235	4.979	4.746	4.534	4.339	4.160	3.995
40	19.793	17.159	15.046	13.332	11.925	10.757	9.779	8.951	8.244	7.634	7.105	6.642	6.233	5.871	5.548	5.258	4.997	4.760	4.544	4.347	4.166	3.999

Appendix 13C: Income Taxes in Capital Budgeting Decisions

LEARNING OBJECTIVE 8
Include income taxes in a capital budgeting analysis.

We ignored income taxes in this chapter for two reasons. First, many organizations do not pay income taxes. Not-for-profit organizations, such as hospitals and charitable foundations, and governmental agencies are exempt from income taxes. Second, capital budgeting is complex and is best absorbed in small doses. Now that we have a solid foundation in the concepts of present value and discounting, we can explore the effects of income taxes on capital budgeting decisions.

The U.S. income tax code is enormously complex. We only scratch the surface here. To keep the subject within reasonable bounds, we have made many simplifying assumptions about the tax code. Among the most important of these assumptions are: (1) taxable income equals net income as computed for financial reports; and (2) the tax rate is a flat percentage of taxable income. The actual tax code is far more complex than this; indeed, experts acknowledge that no one person knows or can know it all. However, the simplifications that we make throughout this appendix allow us to cover the most important implications of income taxes for capital budgeting without getting bogged down in details.

The Concept of After-Tax Cost

Businesses, like individuals, must pay income taxes. In the case of businesses, the amount of income tax that must be paid is determined by the company's net taxable income. Tax deductible expenses (tax deductions) decrease the company's net taxable income and, hence, reduce the taxes the company must pay. For this reason, expenses are often stated on an *after-tax* basis. For example, if a company pays rent of $10 million a year but this expense results in a reduction in income taxes of $3 million, the after-tax cost of the rent is $7 million. An expenditure net of its tax effect is known as **after-tax cost.**

To illustrate, assume that a company with a tax rate of 30% is contemplating a training program that costs $60,000. What impact will this have on the company's taxes? To keep matters simple, let's suppose the training program has no immediate effect on sales. How much does the company actually pay for the training program after taking into account the impact of this expense on taxes? The answer is $42,000 as shown in Exhibit 13C–1. While the training program costs $60,000 before taxes, it would reduce the company's taxes by $18,000, so its *after-tax* cost would be only $42,000.

EXHIBIT 13C–1
The Computation of After-Tax Cost

	Without Training Program		With Training Program
Sales	$850,000		$850,000
Less tax deductible expenses:			
Salaries, insurance, and other	700,000		700,000
New training program			60,000
Total expenses	700,000		760,000
Taxable income	$150,000		$ 90,000
Income taxes (30%)	$ 45,000		$ 27,000
Cost of new training program		$60,000	
Less: Reduction in income taxes ($45,000 − $27,000)		18,000	
After-tax cost of the new training program		$42,000	

The after-tax cost of any tax-deductible cash expense can be determined using the following formula:[1]

$$\frac{\text{After-tax cost}}{\text{(net cash outflow)}} = (1 - \text{Tax rate}) \times \text{Tax-deductible cash expense} \qquad (1)$$

We can verify the accuracy of this formula by applying it to the \$60,000 training program expenditure:

$$(1 - 0.30) \times \$60{,}000 = \$42{,}000 \text{ after-tax cost of the training program}$$

This formula is very useful because it provides the actual amount of cash a company must pay after considering tax effects. It is this actual, after-tax, cash outflow that should be used in capital budgeting decisions.

Similar reasoning applies to revenues and other *taxable* cash inflows. Because these cash receipts are taxable, the company must pay out a portion of them in taxes. The **after-tax benefit,** or net cash inflow, realized from a particular cash receipt can be obtained by applying a simple variation of the cash expenditure formula used above:

$$\frac{\text{After-tax benefit}}{\text{(net cash outflow)}} = (1 - \text{Tax rate}) \times \text{Taxable cash receipt} \qquad (2)$$

We emphasize the term *taxable cash receipts* because not all cash inflows are taxable. For example, the release of working capital at the end of an investment project would not be a taxable cash inflow. It is not counted as income for either financial accounting or income tax reporting purposes because it is simply a recovery of the initial investment.

Depreciation Tax Shield

Depreciation is not a cash flow. For this reason, depreciation was ignored in Chapter 13 in all discounted cash flow computations. However, depreciation does affect the taxes that must be paid and, therefore, has an effect on a company's cash flows.

To illustrate the effect of depreciation deductions on tax payments, consider a company with annual cash sales of \$500,000 and cash operating expenses of \$310,000. In addition, the company has a depreciable asset on which the depreciation deduction is \$90,000 per year. The tax rate is 30%. As shown in Exhibit 13C–2, the depreciation deduction reduces the company's taxes by \$27,000. In effect, the depreciation deduction of \$90,000 *shields* \$90,000 in revenues from taxation and thereby *reduces* the amount of taxes that the company must pay. Because depreciation deductions shield revenues from taxation, they are generally referred to as a **depreciation tax shield.**[2] The reduction in tax payments made possible by the depreciation tax shield is equal to the amount of the depreciation deduction, multiplied by the tax rate as follows:

$$\frac{\text{Tax savings from the}}{\text{depreciation tax shield}} = \text{Tax rate} \times \text{Depreciation deduction} \qquad (3)$$

We can verify this formula by applying it to the \$90,000 depreciation deduction in our example:

$$0.30 \times \$90{,}000 = \$27{,}000 \text{ reduction in tax payments}$$

---

[1] This formula assumes that a company is operating at a profit; if it is operating at a loss, the tax situation can be very complex. For simplicity, we assume in all examples, exercises, and problems that the company is operating at a profit.

[2] The term *depreciation tax shield* may convey the impression that there is something underhanded about depreciation deductions—that companies are getting some sort of a special tax break. However, to use the depreciation deduction, a company must have already acquired a depreciable asset—which typically requires a cash outflow. Essentially, the tax code requires companies to delay recognizing the cash outflow as an expense until depreciation charges are recorded.

EXHIBIT 13C–2
The Impact of Depreciation Deductions on Tax Payments

	Without Depreciation Deduction	With Depreciation Deduction
Sales	$500,000	$500,000
Cash operating expenses	310,000	310,000
Cash flow from operations	190,000	190,000
Depreciation expense	—	90,000
Taxable income	$190,000	$100,000
Income taxes (30%)	$ 57,000	$ 30,000

$27,000 lower taxes with the depreciation deduction

Cash flow comparison:		
Cash flow from operations (above)	$190,000	$190,000
Income taxes (above)	57,000	30,000
Net cash flow	$133,000	$160,000

$27,000 greater cash flow with the depreciation deduction

In this appendix, when we estimate after-tax cash flows for capital budgeting decisions, we will include the tax savings provided by the depreciation tax shield.

To keep matters simple, we will assume in all of our examples and problem materials that depreciation reported for tax purposes is straight-line depreciation, with no deduction for salvage value. In other words, we will assume that the entire original cost of the asset is written off evenly over its useful life. Because the net book value of the asset at the end of its useful life will be zero under this depreciation method, we will assume that any proceeds received on disposal of the asset at the end of its useful life will be taxed as ordinary income.

In actuality, the rules for depreciation are more complex than this and most companies take advantage of accelerated depreciation methods allowed under the tax code. These accelerated methods usually result in a reduction in current taxes and an offsetting increase in future taxes. This shifting of part of the tax burden from the current year to future years is advantageous from a present value point of view because a dollar today is worth more than a dollar in the future. A summary of the concepts we have introduced so far is given in Exhibit 13C–3.

EXHIBIT 13C–3
Tax Adjustments Required in a Capital Budgeting Analysis

Item	Treatment
Tax-deductible cash expense*	Multiply by (1 − Tax rate) to get after-tax cost.
Taxable cash receipt*	Multiply by (1 − Tax rate) to get after-tax cash inflow.
Depreciation deduction	Multiply by the tax rate to get the tax savings from the depreciation tax shield.

*Cash expenses can be deducted from the cash receipts and the difference multiplied by (1 − Tax rate). See the example at the top of Exhibit 13C–4.

Example of Income Taxes and Capital Budgeting

Armed with an understanding of after-tax cost, after-tax revenue, and the depreciation tax shield, we are now prepared to examine a comprehensive example of income taxes and capital budgeting.

Holland Company owns the mineral rights to land that has a deposit of ore. The company is uncertain if it should purchase equipment and open a mine on the property. After careful study, the company assembled the following data.

Cost of equipment needed	$300,000
Working capital needed	$75,000
Estimated annual cash receipts from sales of ore	$250,000
Estimated annual cash expenses for salaries, insurance, utilities, and other cash expenses of mining the ore	$170,000
Cost of road repairs needed in 6 years	$40,000
Salvage value of the equipment in 10 years	$100,000

The ore in the mine would be exhausted after 10 years of mining activity, at which time the mine would be closed. The equipment would then be sold for its salvage value. Holland Company uses the straight-line method, assuming no salvage value, to compute depreciation deductions for tax purposes. The company's after-tax cost of capital is 12% and its tax rate is 30%. To be consistent, when we take the net present value of after-tax cash flows, we use the *after-tax* cost of capital as the discount rate.

Should Holland Company purchase the equipment and open a mine on the property? The solution to the problem is given in Exhibit 13C–4. We suggest that you go through this solution item by item and note the following points:

Cost of new equipment. The initial investment of $300,000 in the new equipment is included in full with no reductions for taxes. This represents an *investment,*

EXHIBIT 13C–4
Example of Income Taxes and Capital Budgeting

	Per Year
Cash receipts from sales of ore	$250,000
Less payments for salaries, insurance, utilities, and other cash expenses	170,000
Net cash receipts	$ 80,000

Items and Computations	Year(s)	(1) Amount	(2) Tax Effect*	After-Tax Cash Flows (1) × (2)	12% Factor	Present Value of Cash Flows
Cost of new equipment	Now	$(300,000)	—	$(300,000)	1.000	$(300,000)
Working capital needed	Now	$(75,000)	—	$(75,000)	1.000	(75,000)
Annual net cash receipts (above)	1–10	$80,000	1 − 0.30	$56,000	5.650	316,400
Road repairs	6	$(40,000)	1 − 0.30	$(28,000)	0.507	(14,196)
Annual depreciation deductions	1–10	$30,000	0.30	$9,000	5.650	50,850
Salvage value of equipment	10	$100,000	1 − 0.30	$70,000	0.322	22,540
Release of working capital	10	$75,000	—	$75,000	0.322	24,150
Net present value						$ 24,744

*Taxable cash receipts and tax-deductible cash expenses are multiplied by (1 − Tax rate) to determine the after-tax cash flow. Depreciation deductions are multiplied by the tax rate itself to determine the after-tax cash flow (i.e., tax savings from the depreciation tax shield).

not an expense, so no tax adjustment is made. (Only revenues and expenses are adjusted for the effects of taxes.) However, this investment does affect taxes through the depreciation deductions that are considered below.

Working capital. Observe that the working capital needed for the project is included in full with no reductions for taxes. Like the cost of new equipment, working capital is an investment and not an expense, so no tax adjustment is made. Also observe that no tax adjustment is made when the working capital is released at the end of the project's life. The release of working capital is not a taxable cash flow because it is a return of investment funds back to the company.

Annual net cash receipts. The annual net cash receipts from sales of ore are adjusted for the effects of income taxes, as discussed earlier in the chapter. Note at the top of Exhibit 13C–4 that the annual cash expenses are deducted from the annual cash receipts to obtain the net cash receipts. This simplifies computations.

Road repairs. Because the road repairs occur just once (in the sixth year), they are treated separately from other expenses. Road repairs would be a tax-deductible cash expense, and, therefore, they are adjusted for the effects of income taxes, as discussed earlier in the chapter.

Depreciation deductions. The tax savings provided by depreciation deductions is essentially an annuity that is included in the present value computations in the same way as other cash flows.

Salvage value of equipment. Because the company does not consider salvage value when computing depreciation deductions, book value will be zero at the end of the life of an asset. Thus, any salvage value received is taxable as income to the company. The after-tax benefit is determined by multiplying the salvage value by (1 – Tax rate).

Because the net present value of the proposed mining project is positive, the equipment should be purchased and the mine opened. Study Exhibit 13C–4 thoroughly. *Exhibit 13C–4 is the key exhibit!*

Summary (Appendix 13C)

Unless a company is a tax-exempt organization, such as a not-for-profit school or a governmental unit, income taxes should be considered in making capital budgeting decisions. Tax-deductible cash expenditures and taxable cash receipts are placed on an after-tax basis by multiplying them by (1 − Tax rate). Only the after-tax amount should be used in determining the desirability of an investment proposal.

Although depreciation is not a cash outflow, it is a valid deduction for tax purposes and as such affects income tax payments. The depreciation tax shield—computed by multiplying the depreciation deduction by the tax rate itself—also results in savings in income taxes.

Glossary (Appendix 13C)

After-tax benefit The amount of net cash inflow realized from a taxable cash receipt after income tax effects have been considered. The amount is determined by multiplying the taxable cash receipt by (1 − Tax rate). (p. 632)

After-tax cost The amount of net cash outflow resulting from a tax-deductible cash expense after income tax effects have been considered. The amount is determined by multiplying the tax-deductible cash expense by (1 − Tax rate). (p. 631)

Depreciation tax shield A reduction in tax that results from depreciation deductions. The reduction in tax is computed by multiplying the depreciation deduction by the tax rate. (p. 632)

Appendix 13C Exercises and Problems

All applicable exercises and problems are available with McGraw-Hill's *Connect*™ *Accounting*.

EXERCISE 13C–1 After-Tax Cash Flows in Net Present Value Analysis [LO8]

Kramer Corporation is considering two investment projects, each of which would require $50,000. Cost and cash flow data concerning the two projects are given below:

	Project A	Project B
Investment in high-speed photocopier	$50,000	
Investment in working capital		$50,000
Annual net cash inflows	$9,000	$9,000
Life of the project	8 years	8 years

The high-speed photocopier would have a salvage value of $5,000 in eight years. For tax purposes, the company computes depreciation deductions assuming zero salvage value and uses straight-line depreciation. The photocopier would be depreciated over eight years. At the end of eight years, the investment in working capital would be released for use elsewhere. The company requires an after-tax return of 10% on all investments. The tax rate is 30%.

Required:

Compute the net present value of each investment project. (Round to the nearest whole dollar.)

EXERCISE 13C–2 Net Present Value Analysis Including Income Taxes [LO8]

Press Publishing Company hires students from the local university to collate pages on various printing jobs. This collating is all done by hand, at a cost of $60,000 per year. A collating machine has just come onto the market that could be used in place of the student help. The machine would cost $140,000 and have a 10-year useful life. It would require an operator at an annual cost of $18,000 and have annual maintenance costs of $7,000. New roller pads would be needed on the machine in five years at a total cost of $20,000. The salvage value of the machine in 10 years would be $40,000.

For tax purposes, the company computes depreciation deductions assuming zero salvage value and uses straight-line depreciation. The collating machine would be depreciated over 10 years. Management requires a 14% after-tax return on all equipment purchases. The company's tax rate is 30%.

Required:

1. Determine the before-tax annual net cost savings that the new collating machine will provide.
2. Using the data from (1) above and other data from the exercise, compute the collating machine's net present value. (Round all dollar amounts to the nearest whole dollar.) Would you recommend that the machine be purchased?

EXERCISE 13C–3 After-Tax Costs [LO8]

Solve each of the following parts independently:

1. Stoffer Company has hired a management consulting firm to review and make recommendations concerning Stoffer's organizational structure. The consulting firm's fee will be $100,000. What will be the after-tax cost of the consulting firm's fee if Stoffer's tax rate is 30%?
2. The Green Hills Riding Club has redirected its advertising toward a different sector of the market. As a result of this change in advertising, the club's annual revenues have increased by $40,000. If the club's tax rate is 30%, what is the after-tax benefit from the increased revenues?
3. The Golden Eagles Basketball Team has just installed an electronic scoreboard in its playing arena at a cost of $210,000. For tax purposes, the entire original cost of the electronic scoreboard will be depreciated over seven years, using the straight-line method. Determine the yearly tax savings from the depreciation tax shield. Assume that the income tax rate is 30%.

PROBLEM 13C–4 Basic Net Present Value Analysis Including Income Taxes [LO8]

Rapid Parcel Service has been offered an eight-year contract to deliver mail and small parcels between army installations. To accept the contract, the company would have to purchase several new delivery trucks at a total cost of $450,000. Other data relating to the contract follow:

Annual net cash receipts (before taxes) from the contract	$108,000
Cost of overhauling the motors in the trucks in five years	$45,000
Salvage value of the trucks at termination of the contract	$20,000

If the contract were accepted, several old, fully depreciated trucks would be sold at a total price of $30,000. These funds would be used to help purchase the new trucks. For tax purposes, the company computes depreciation deductions assuming zero salvage value and uses straight-line depreciation. The trucks would be depreciated over eight years. The company requires a 12% after-tax return on all equipment purchases. The tax rate is 30%.

Required:

Compute the net present value of this investment opportunity. Round all dollar amounts to the nearest whole dollar. Would you recommend that the contract be accepted?

PROBLEM: 13C–5 A Comparison of Investment Alternatives Including Income Taxes [LO8]

Ms. Keri Lee, an expert in retrofitting buildings to meet seismic safety standards, has just received a $200,000 after-tax bonus for the successful completion of a project on time and under budget. Business has been so good that she is planning to retire in 12 years, spending her time relaxing in the sun, skiing, and doing charitable work. Ms. Lee is considering two alternatives for investing her bonus.

Alternative 1. Municipal bonds can be purchased that mature in 12 years and that bear interest at 8%. This interest would be tax-free and paid annually.

Alternative 2. A small discount perfume shop is available for sale at a nearby factory outlet center. The business can be purchased from its current owner for $200,000. The following information relates to this alternative:

a. Of the purchase price, $80,000 would be for fixtures and other depreciable items. The remainder would be for the company's working capital (inventory, accounts receivable, and cash). The fixtures and other depreciable items would have a remaining useful life of at least 12 years but would be depreciated for tax reporting purposes over eight years using the following allowances published by the Internal Revenue Service:

Year	Percentage of Original Cost Depreciated
1.	14.3%
2.	24.5
3.	17.5
4.	12.5
5.	8.9
6.	8.9
7.	8.9
8.	4.5
	100.0%

Salvage value is not deducted when computing depreciation for tax purposes. At any rate, at the end of 12 years, these depreciable items would have a negligible salvage value; however, the working capital would be released for reinvestment elsewhere.

b. Store records indicate that sales have averaged $400,000 per year, and out-of-pocket costs have averaged $370,000 per year (*not* including income taxes). These out-of-pocket costs include rent on the building, cost of goods sold, utilities, and wages and salaries for the sales staff and the store manager. Ms. Lee plans to entrust the day-to-day operations of the store to the manager.

c. Ms. Lee's tax rate is 40%.

Required:

Advise Ms. Lee as to which alternative should be selected. Use the total-cost approach to discounted cash flows in your analysis and a discount rate of 8%. (Round all dollar amounts to the nearest whole dollar.)

PROBLEM: 13C–6 Net Present Value Analysis Including Income Taxes [LO8]

The Crescent Drilling Company owns the drilling rights to several tracts of land on which natural gas has been found. The amount of gas on some of the tracts is somewhat marginal, and the company is unsure whether it would be profitable to extract and sell the gas that these tracts contain. One such tract is tract 410, on which the following information has been gathered:

Investment in equipment needed for extraction work	$600,000
Working capital investment needed	$85,000
Annual cash receipts from sale of gas, net of related cash operating expenses (before taxes)	$110,000
Cost of restoring land at completion of extraction work	$70,000

The natural gas in tract 410 would be exhausted after 10 years of extraction work. The equipment would have a useful life of 15 years, but it could be sold for only 15% of its original cost when extraction was completed. For tax purposes, the company would depreciate the equipment over 10 years using straight-line depreciation and assuming zero salvage value. The tax rate is 30%, and the company's after-tax discount rate is 10%. The working capital would be released for use elsewhere at the completion of the project.

Required:

1. Compute the net present value of tract 410. Round all dollar amounts to the nearest whole dollar.
2. Would you recommend that the investment project be undertaken?

Chapter 14

Statement of Cash Flows

BUSINESS FOCUS

Understanding Cash Flows

In 2009, The Kroger Company, the largest food and drug retailer in the United States, reported net income of $57 million. During the same year the company spent $2.3 billion for plant and equipment, paid dividends totaling $238 million, paid off $432 million of long-term debt, and spent $218 million to purchase shares of its own common stock. At first glance, these figures may seem confusing because Kroger is spending amounts of money that far exceed its net income. In this chapter you'll learn about the statement of cash flows that explains the relationship between a company's net income and its cash inflows and outflows. ■

Source: The Kroger Company, 2009 Form 10-K Annual Report, www.sec.gov/edgar/searchedgar/companysearch.html.

LEARNING OBJECTIVES

After studying Chapter 14, you should be able to:

LO1 Classify cash inflows and outflows as relating to operating, investing, or financing activities.

LO2 Prepare a statement of cash flows using the indirect method to determine the net cash provided by operating activities.

LO3 Compute free cash flow.

LO4 (Appendix 14A) Use the direct method to determine the net cash provided by operating activities.

Three major financial statements are required for external reports—an income statement, a balance sheet, and a statement of cash flows. The **statement of cash flows** highlights the major activities that impact cash flows and, hence, affect the overall cash balance. Managers focus on cash for a very good reason—without sufficient cash at the right times, a company may miss golden investment opportunities or may even go bankrupt.

The statement of cash flows answers questions that cannot be easily answered by looking at the income statement and balance sheet. For example, where did Delta Airlines get the cash to pay a dividend of nearly \$140 million in a year in which, according to its income statement, it lost more than \$1 billion? How was The Walt Disney Company able to invest nearly \$800 million to expand and renovate its theme parks despite a loss of more than \$500 million on its investment in EuroDisney? Where did The Kroger Company get \$2.3 billion to invest in plant and equipment in a year when its net income was only \$57 million? The answers to such questions can be found on the statement of cash flows.

The statement of cash flows is a valuable analytical tool for managers as well as for investors and creditors, although managers tend to be more concerned with forecasted statements of cash flows that are prepared as part of the budgeting process. The statement of cash flows can be used to answer crucial questions such as:

1. Is the company generating sufficient positive cash flows from its ongoing operations to remain viable?
2. Will the company be able to repay its debts?
3. Will the company be able to pay its usual dividend?
4. Why do net income and net cash flow differ?
5. To what extent will the company have to borrow money in order to make needed investments?

Managers prepare the statement of cash flows by applying a fundamental principle of double-entry bookkeeping—the change in the cash balance must equal the changes in all other balance sheet accounts besides cash.[1] This principle ensures that properly analyzing the changes in all noncash balance sheet accounts always quantifies the cash inflows and outflows that explain the change in the cash balance. Our goal in this chapter is to translate this fairly complex principle into a small number of concepts and steps that simplify the process of preparing and interpreting a statement of cash flows.

Before delving into the specifics of how to prepare the statement of cash flows, we need to review two basic equations that apply to all asset, contra-asset, liability, and stockholders' equity accounts:

Basic Equation for Asset Accounts

Beginning balance + Debits − Credits = Ending balance

Basic Equation for Contra-Asset, Liability, and Stockholders' Equity Accounts

Beginning balance − Debits + Credits = Ending balance

These equations will help you compute various cash inflows and outflows that are reported in the statement of cash flows and they'll be referred to throughout the chapter.

---

[1] The statement of cash flows is based on the following fundamental balance sheet and income statement equations.

(1) Change in cash + Changes in noncash assets = Changes in liabilities + Changes in stockholders' equity

(2) Net cash flow = Change in cash

(3) Changes in stockholders' equity = Net income − Dividends + Changes in capital stock

These three equations can be used to derive the following equation.

(4) Net cash flow = Net income − Changes in noncash assets + Changes in liabilities − Dividends + Changes in capital stock

Essentially, the statement of cash flows, which explains net cash flow, is constructed by starting with net income and then adjusting it for changes in noncash balance sheet accounts.

The Statement of Cash Flows: Key Concepts

The statement of cash flows summarizes all of a company's cash inflows and outflows during a period, thereby explaining the change in its cash balance. In a statement of cash flows, cash is broadly defined to include both cash and cash equivalents. **Cash equivalents** consist of short-term, highly liquid investments such as Treasury bills, commercial paper, and money market funds that are made solely for the purpose of generating a return on temporarily idle funds. Most companies invest their excess cash reserves in these types of interest-bearing assets that can be easily converted into cash. Because such assets are equivalent to cash, they are included with cash in a statement of cash flows.

The remainder of this section discusses four key concepts that you'll need to understand to prepare a statement of cash flows. These four concepts include organizing the statement of cash flows, distinguishing between the direct and indirect methods of preparing a portion of the statement of cash flows, completing the three-step process underlying the indirect method, and recording gross cash flows where appropriate within a statement of cash flows.[2]

IN BUSINESS

APPLE'S CASH STASH

Apple Inc. accumulated $20.8 billion in cash and short-term investments. Its investors had a variety of opinions about how the company should use this money. Some investors wanted Apple to explore acquisition targets in the music industry. Others believed Apple should invest in start-up companies that are developing emerging technologies, such as improved batteries for the iPhone. Still others felt the company should stockpile raw materials in the face of looming price hikes.

This example illustrates the never-ending cycle of managing a business. Once a company succeeds in generating positive cash flows, it immediately raises another question in the minds of investors—what are you planning to do for me now?

Source: Peter Burrows, "Apple's Cash Conundrum," *BusinessWeek*, August 11, 2008, p. 32.

Organizing the Statement of Cash Flows

LEARNING OBJECTIVE 1
Classify cash inflows and outflows as relating to operating, investing, or financing activities.

To make it easier to compare data from different companies, U.S. generally accepted accounting principles (GAAP) and International Financial Reporting Standards (IFRS) require companies to follow prescribed rules when preparing the statement of cash flows. One of these rules requires organizing the statement into three sections that report cash flows resulting from *operating activities, investing activities,* and *financing activities.* **Operating activities** generate cash inflows and outflows related to revenue and expense

[2] Another concept that relates to the statement of cash flows is direct exchange transactions, which refer to transactions where noncurrent balance sheet items are swapped. For example, a company might issue common stock in a direct exchange for property. Direct exchange transactions are not reported on the statement of cash flows; however, they are disclosed in a separate schedule that accompanies the statement. More advanced accounting courses cover this topic in greater detail. We will not include direct exchange transactions in this chapter.

EXHIBIT 14–1
Cash Inflows and Outflows Resulting from Operating, Investing, and Financing Activities

	Cash Inflow	Cash Outflow
Operating activities		
Collecting cash from customers	√	
Paying suppliers for inventory purchases		√
Paying bills to insurers, utility providers, etc		√
Paying wages and salaries to employees		√
Paying taxes to governmental bodies		√
Paying interest to lenders		√
Investing activities		
Buying property, plant, and equipment		√
Selling property, plant, and equipment	√	
Buying stocks and bonds as a long-term investment		√
Selling stocks and bonds held for long-term investment	√	
Lending money to another entity		√
Collecting the principal on a loan to another entity	√	
Financing activities		
Borrowing money from a creditor	√	
Repaying the principal amount of a debt		√
Collecting cash from the sale of common stock	√	
Paying cash to repurchase your own common stock		√
Paying a dividend to stockholders		√

transactions that affect net income. **Investing activities** generate cash inflows and outflows related to acquiring or disposing of noncurrent assets such as property, plant, and equipment, long-term investments, and loans to another entity. **Financing activities** generate cash inflows and outflows related to borrowing from and repaying principal to creditors and completing transactions with the company's owners, such as selling or repurchasing shares of common stock and paying dividends. The most common types of cash inflows and outflows resulting from these three activities are summarized in Exhibit 14–1.[3]

Operating Activities: Direct or Indirect Method?

U.S. GAAP and IFRS allow companies to compute the net amount of cash inflows and outflows resulting from operating activities, which is known formally as the **net cash provided by operating activities,** using either the *direct* or *indirect* method. Both of these methods have the same purpose, which is to translate accrual-based net income to a cash basis. However, they approach this task in two different ways.

Under the **direct method,** the income statement is reconstructed on a cash basis from top to bottom. For example, cash collected from customers is listed instead of revenue, and payments to suppliers is listed instead of cost of goods sold. In essence, cash receipts are counted as revenues and cash disbursements pertaining to operating activities are counted as expenses. The difference between the cash receipts and cash disbursements is the net cash provided by operating activities.

Under the **indirect method,** net income is adjusted to a cash basis. That is, rather than directly computing cash sales, cash expenses, and so forth, these amounts are derived *indirectly* by removing from net income any items that do not affect cash flows. The indirect method has an advantage over the direct method because it shows the reasons for any differences between net income and net cash provided by operating activities.

[3] Operating cash inflows can also include interest income and dividend income; however, in this chapter we will limit our scope to cash receipts from sales to customers.

Although both methods result in the same amount of net cash provided by operating activities, only about 1% of companies use the direct method and the remaining 99% use the indirect method.[4] If a company uses the direct method to prepare its statement of cash flows, then it must also provide a supplementary report that uses the indirect method. However, if a company chooses to use the indirect method, there is no requirement that it also report results using the direct method. Because the direct method requires more work, very few companies choose this approach. Therefore, we will explain the direct method in Appendix 14A, and we will cover the indirect method in the main body of the chapter.

The Indirect Method: A Three-Step Process

The indirect method adjusts net income to net cash provided by operating activities using a three-step process.

Step 1 The first step is to *add depreciation charges* to net income. Depreciation charges are the credits to the Accumulated Depreciation account during the period—the sum total of the entries that have increased Accumulated Depreciation. Why do we do this? Because Accumulated Depreciation is a noncash balance sheet account and we must adjust net income for all of the changes in the noncash balance sheet accounts that have occurred during the period.

To compute the credits to the Accumulated Depreciation account we use the equation for contra-assets that was mentioned earlier:

Basic Equation for Contra-Asset Accounts

Beginning balance − Debits + Credits = Ending balance

For example, assume the Accumulated Depreciation account had beginning and ending balances of $300 and $500, respectively. Also, assume that the company sold equipment with accumulated depreciation of $70 during the period. Given that we use debits to the Accumulated Depreciation account to record accumulated depreciation on assets that have been sold or retired, the depreciation that needs to be added to net income is computed as follows:

Beginning balance − Debits + Credits = Ending balance

$300 − $70 + Credits = $500

Credits = $500 − $300 + $70

Credits = $270

The same logic can be depicted using an Accumulated Depreciation T-account. Given that we know the account's beginning and ending balances and the amount of the debit that would have been recorded for the sale of equipment, the credit side of the T-account must equal $270.

Accumulated Depreciation

		Beg. Bal.	$300
Sale of equipment	70		270
		End. Bal.	$500

For service and merchandising companies, the credits to the Accumulated Depreciation T-account equal the debits to the Depreciation Expense account. For these companies,

---

[4] American Institute of Certified Public Accountants, *Accounting Trends and Techniques: 2007* (Jersey City, NJ, 2007), p. 503.

the adjustment in step one consists of adding depreciation expense to net income. However, for manufacturing companies, some of the credits to the Accumulated Depreciation T-account relate to depreciation on production assets that are debited to work in process inventories rather than depreciation expense. For these companies, the depreciation charges do not simply equal depreciation expense.

Because depreciation is added back to net income on the statement of cash flows, some people erroneously conclude that a company can increase its cash flow by simply increasing its depreciation expense. This is false; a company cannot increase its net cash provided by operating activities by increasing its depreciation expense. If it increases its depreciation expense by X dollars, then net income will decline by X dollars and the amount of the adjustment in step one of this process will increase by X dollars. The decline in net income and the increase in the amount of the adjustment in step one exactly offset each other, resulting in zero impact on the net cash provided by operating activities.

Step 2 The second step is to *analyze net changes in noncash balance sheet accounts* that impact net income. Exhibit 14–2 provides general guidelines for how to analyze current asset and current liability accounts.[5] For each account shown in the exhibit, you'll begin by referring to the balance sheet to compute the change in the account balance from the beginning to the end of the period. Then, you will either add each of these amounts to net income or subtract them from net income as shown in Exhibit 14–2. Notice that changes in all current asset accounts (Accounts Receivable, Inventory, and Prepaid Expenses) result in the same type of adjustment to net income. If an asset account balance increases during the period, then the amount of the increase is subtracted from net income. If an asset balance decreases during the period, then the amount of the decrease is added to net income. The current liability accounts (Accounts Payable, Accrued Liabilities, and Income Taxes Payable) are handled in the opposite fashion. If a liability account balance increases, then the amount of the increase is added to net income. If a liability account balance decreases, then the amount of the decrease is subtracted from net income.

Keep in mind that the purpose of these adjustments is to translate net income to a cash basis. For example, the change in the accounts receivable balance measures the difference between credit sales and cash collections from customers who purchased on account. When the accounts receivable balance increases it means that the amount of credit sales exceeds the amount of cash collected from customers. In this case, the change in the accounts receivable balance is subtracted from net income because it reflects the amount by which credit sales exceeds cash collections from customers. When the accounts receivable balance decreases it means that cash collected from customers exceeds credit sales. In this case, the change in the accounts receivable balance is added

EXHIBIT 14–2
General Guidelines for Analyzing How Changes in Noncash Balance Sheet Accounts Affect Net Income on the Statement of Cash Flows

	Increase in Account Balance	Decrease in Account Balance
Current Assets		
Accounts receivable	Subtract	Add
Inventory.	Subtract	Add
Prepaid expenses.	Subtract	Add
Current Liabilities		
Accounts payable	Add	Subtract
Accrued liabilities	Add	Subtract
Income taxes payable	Add	Subtract

[5] Other accounts such as Interest Payable can impact these computations. However, for simplicity, in this chapter we will focus on the accounts shown in Exhibit 14–2.

to net income because it reflects the amount by which cash collections from customers exceeds credit sales.

The other accounts shown in Exhibit 14–2 have a similar underlying logic. The inventory and accounts payable adjustments translate cost of goods sold to cash paid for inventory purchases. The prepaid expenses and accrued liabilities adjustments translate selling and administrative expenses to a cash basis. The income taxes payable adjustment translates income tax expense to a cash basis.

Step 3 The third step in computing the net cash provided by operating activities is to *adjust for gains/losses* included in the income statement. Under U.S. GAAP and IFRS rules, gains and losses must be included in the investing activities section of the statement of cash flows. Because gains and losses are already in net income, which is in the operating activities section, they must be removed from net income before they can be shown in the investing activities section. To make this adjustment, subtract gains from net income and add losses to net income in the operating activities section.

IN BUSINESS

SLOW PAYMENTS SQUEEZE SMALL BUSINESSES

When the California real estate market crashed, Artisan Shutter Company encountered severe cash flow problems. Half of the company's customers started making late payments. Eventually, the company had to lay off 15% of its employees due to insufficient cash inflows. This problem would be evident from the statement of cash flows, which would show that the late payments increased Artisan's accounts receivable balance and, hence, decreased its net cash provided by operating activities. The company's owners had to raid their retirement accounts and rack up huge credit card debts just to pay their bills and avoid bankruptcy.

Take a moment to contrast this In Business box with the box titled "Amazon.com Boosts Cash Flows" on page 658. What are your thoughts?

Source: Kelly K. Spors and Simona Covel, "Slow Payments Squeeze Small-Business Owners," *The Wall Street Journal*, October 31, 2008, pp. B1 and B6.

Investing and Financing Activities: Gross Cash Flows

U.S. GAAP and IFRS require that the investing and financing sections of the statement of cash flows disclose gross cash flows. To illustrate, suppose Macy's Department Stores purchases $50 million in property during the year and sells other property for $30 million. Instead of showing the net change of $20 million, the company must show the gross amounts of both the purchases and sales. The $50 million purchase would be disclosed as a cash outflow and the $30 million sale would be reported as a cash inflow in the investing section of the statement of cash flows. Similarly, if Alcoa receives $80 million from selling long-term bonds and then pays out $30 million to retire other bonds, the two transactions must be reported separately in the financing section of the statement of cash flows rather than being netted against each other.

The gross method of reporting cash flows is not used in the operating activities section of the statement of cash flows, where debits and credits are netted against each other. For example, if Sears adds $600 million to its accounts receivable as a result of

EXHIBIT 14–3
General Guidelines for Analyzing How Changes in Noncash Balance Sheet Accounts Affect the Investing and Financing Sections of the Statement of Cash Flows

	Increase in Account Balance	Decrease in Account Balance
Noncurrent Assets (Investing activities)		
Property, plant, and equipment	Subtract	Add
Long-term investments	Subtract	Add
Loans to other entities	Subtract	Add
Liabilities and Stockholders' Equity (Financing activities)		
Bonds payable	Add	Subtract
Common stock	Add	Subtract
Retained earnings	*	*

*Requires further analysis to quantify cash dividends paid.

sales during the year and $520 million of accounts receivable are collected, only the net increase of $80 million is reported on the statement of cash flows.

To compute gross cash flows for the investing and financing activities sections of the statement of cash flows, you'll begin by calculating the changes in the balance of each applicable balance sheet account. As with the current assets, when a noncurrent asset account balance (including Property, Plant, and Equipment; Long-Term Investments; and Loans to Other Entities) increases, it signals the need to subtract cash outflows in the investing activities section of the statement of cash flows. If the balance in a noncurrent asset account decreases during the period, then it signals the need to add cash inflows. The liability and equity accounts (Bonds Payable and Common Stock) are handled in the opposite fashion. If a liability or equity account balance increases, then it signals a need to add cash inflows to the financing activities section of the statement of cash flows. If a liability or equity account balance decreases, then it signals a need to subtract cash outflows. Exhibit 14–3 summarizes these general guidelines.

While these guidelines provide a helpful starting point, to properly calculate each account's *gross* cash inflows and outflows you'll need to analyze the transactions that occurred within that account during the period. We will illustrate how to do this using Property, Plant, and Equipment and Retained Earnings.

Property, Plant, and Equipment When a company purchases property, plant, or equipment it debits the Property, Plant, and Equipment account for the amount of the purchase. When it sells or disposes of these kinds of assets, it credits the Property, Plant, and Equipment account for the original cost of the asset. To compute the cash outflows related to Property, Plant, and Equipment we use the basic equation for assets mentioned earlier:

Basic Equation for Asset Accounts
Beginning balance + Debits − Credits = Ending balance

For example, assume that a company's beginning and ending balances in its Property, Plant, and Equipment account are $1,000 and $1,800, respectively. In addition, during the period the company sold a piece of equipment for $40 cash that originally cost $100 and had accumulated depreciation of $70. The company recorded a gain on the sale of $10, which had been included in net income.

We start by calculating the $800 increase in the Property, Plant, and Equipment account. This increase signals the need to subtract cash outflows in the investing activities section of the statement of cash flows. In fact, it may be tempting to conclude that the proper way to analyze Property, Plant, and Equipment in this instance is to record an $800 cash outflow corresponding with the $800 increase in the account balance. However, that would only be correct if the company did not sell any property, plant, and equipment during the year. Because the company did sell equipment, we must use the basic equation for asset accounts to compute the cash outflows as follows:

$$\text{Beginning balance} + \text{Debits} - \text{Credits} = \text{Ending balance}$$
$$\$1{,}000 + \text{Debits} - \$100 = \$1{,}800$$
$$\text{Debits} = \$1{,}800 - \$1{,}000 + \$100$$
$$\text{Debits} = \$900$$

The same logic can be depicted using a Property, Plant, and Equipment T-account. Given that we know the account's beginning and ending balances and the amount of the credit that would have been recorded to write off the *original cost* of the equipment that was sold, the additions to the account, as summarized on the debit side of the T-account, must equal $900.

Property, Plant, and Equipment

Beg. Bal.	$1,000		
Additions	900	Sale of equipment	100
End. Bal.	$1,800		

So, instead of reporting an $800 cash outflow pertaining to Property, Plant, and Equipment in the investing activities section of the statement of cash flows, the proper accounting requires subtracting the $10 gain on the sale of equipment from net income in the operating activities section of the statement. It also requires disclosing a $40 cash inflow from the sale of equipment and a $900 cash outflow for additions to Property, Plant and Equipment in the investing activities section of the statement.

Retained Earnings When a company earns net income it credits the Retained Earnings account and when it pays a dividend it debits the Retained Earnings account. To compute the amount of a cash dividend payment we use the basic equation for stockholders' equity accounts mentioned earlier:

Basic Equation for Stockholders' Equity Accounts

$$\text{Beginning balance} - \text{Debits} + \text{Credits} = \text{Ending balance}$$

For example, assume that a company's beginning and ending balances in its Retained Earnings account are $2,000 and 3,000, respectively. In addition, the company reported net income of $1,200 and paid a cash dividend, but we don't know how much. We start by calculating the $1,000 increase in the Retained Earnings account. However, this amount reflects the net income earned during the period as well as the amount of the dividend payment. Therefore, we must use the equation above to calculate the amount of the dividend payment as follows:

$$\text{Beginning balance} - \text{Debits} + \text{Credits} = \text{Ending balance}$$
$$\$2{,}000 - \text{Debits} + \$1{,}200 = \$3{,}000$$
$$\$3{,}200 = \$3{,}000 + \text{Debits}$$
$$\text{Debits} = \$200$$

The same logic can be depicted using a Retained Earnings T-account. Given that we know the account's beginning and ending balances and the net income that would have been recorded on the credit side of the T-account, the dividend, as reported on the debit side of the T-account, must equal $200.

Retained Earnings

		Beg. Bal.	$2,000
Dividend	200	Net income	1,200
		End. Bal.	$3,000

So, instead of erroneously reporting a $1,000 cash flow pertaining to the overall change in Retained Earnings, the proper accounting requires disclosing net income of $1,200 within the operating activities section of the statement of cash flows and a $200 cash dividend in the financing activities section of the statement.

IN BUSINESS

DELTA PETROLEUM SELLS STOCK TO FUND EXPANSION

Delta Petroleum Corporation wanted to increase its drilling for natural gas and oil in Colorado and Utah. However, the company's capital budget for 2008 exceeded its cash flow. To make up the difference, Delta sold 36 million new shares of its common stock to Tracinda Corporation for $684 million. Delta is confident that the cash inflow from this transaction will increase its reserve of natural resources and ultimately drive up its stock price; however, the transaction gave Tracinda a 35% ownership stake in Delta and allows Tracinda to appoint one-third of Delta's board of directors.

When companies cannot finance their expansion plans with internally generated cash, they usually pursue one of two options for gaining access to cash. They can either borrow money from lenders or sell common stock to buyers who take an ownership stake in their company.

Source: Russell Gold, "Delta Petroleum's Stake Sale Eases Need for Cash," *The Wall Street Journal*, January 2, 2008, p. A3.

Summary of Key Concepts

Exhibit 14–4 summarizes the four key concepts just discussed. The first key concept is that the statement of cash flows is divided into three sections: operating activities, investing activities, and financing activities. The net cash used or provided by these three types of activities is combined to derive the net increase/decrease in cash and cash equivalents, which explains the change in the cash balance. The second key concept is that the operating activities section of the statement of cash flows can be prepared using the direct or indirect method. The direct method translates sales, cost of goods sold, selling and administrative expenses, and income tax expense to a cash basis. The indirect method begins with accrual-based net income and adjusts it to a cash basis. The third key concept is that the indirect method requires three steps to compute net cash provided by operating activities. The first step is to add back depreciation to net income. The second step is to analyze net changes in noncash balance sheet accounts that impact net income. The third step is to adjust for gains or losses included in the income statement. The fourth key concept is to record gross cash inflows and outflows in the investing and financing activities sections of the statement of cash flows.

EXHIBIT 14–4
Summary of Key Concepts Needed to Prepare a Statement of Cash Flows

Key Concept #1

The statement of cash flows is divided into three sections:

Operating activities	
Net cash provided by (used in) operating activities	$xx
Investing activities	
Net cash provided by (used in) investing activities	xx
Financing activities	
Net cash provided by (used in) financing activities	xx
Net increase/decrease in cash and cash equivalents	xx
Cash and cash equivalents, beginning balance	xx
Cash and cash equivalents, ending balance	$xx

Key Concept #2

U.S. GAAP and IFRS allow two methods for preparing the operating activities section of the statement of cash flows:

Direct Method (Appendix 14A)	
Cash receipts from customers	$ xx
Cash paid for inventory purchases	(xx)
Cash paid for selling and administrative expenses	(xx)
Cash paid for income taxes	(xx)
Net cash provided by (used in) operating activities	$ xx
Indirect Method	
Net income	$ xx
Various adjustments (+/−)	xx
Net cash provided by (used in) operating activities	$ xx

Key Concept #3

Computing the net cash provided by operating activities using the indirect method is a three step process:

	Operating Activities	
	Net income	$xx
	Adjustments to convert net income to a cash basis:	
Step 1	Add: Depreciation	xx
Step 2	Analyze net changes in noncash balance sheet accounts:	
	Increase in current asset accounts	(xx)
	Decrease in current asset accounts	xx
	Increase in current liability accounts	xx
	Decrease in current liability accounts	(xx)
Step 3	Adjust for gains/losses:	
	Gain on sale	(xx)
	Loss on sale	xx
	Net cash provided by (used in) operating activities	$xx

Key Concept #4

The investing and financing sections of the statement of cash flows must report gross cash flows:

Net cash provided by (used in) operating activities	$xx
Investing Activities	
Purchase of property, plant, and equipment	(xx)
Sale of property, plant, and equipment	xx
Purchase of long-term investments	(xx)
Sale of long-term investments	xx
Net cash provided by (used in) investing activities	(xx)
Financing Activities	
Issuance of bonds payable	xx
Repaying principal on bonds payable	(xx)
Issuance of common stock	xx
Purchase own shares of common stock	(xx)
Paying a dividend	(xx)
Net cash provided by (used in) financing activities	xx
Net increase/decrease in cash and cash equivalents	xx
Cash and cash equivalents, beginning balance	xx
Cash and cash equivalents, ending balance	$xx

An Example of a Statement of Cash Flows

LEARNING OBJECTIVE 2
Prepare a statement of cash flows using the indirect method to determine the net cash provided by operating activities.

To illustrate the ideas introduced in the preceding section, we will now construct a statement of cash flows for a merchandising company called Apparel, Inc. The company's income statement and balance sheet are shown in Exhibits 14–5 and 14–6.

EXHIBIT 14–5
Apparel, Inc., Income Statement

Apparel, Inc.
Income Statement
(dollars in millions)

Sales	$3,638
Cost of goods sold	2,469
Gross margin	1,169
Selling and administrative expenses	941
Net operating income	228
Nonoperating items: Gain on sale of store	3
Income before taxes	231
Income taxes	91
Net income	$ 140

EXHIBIT 14–6
Apparel, Inc., Balance Sheet

Apparel, Inc.
Comparative Balance Sheet
(dollars in millions)

	Ending Balance	Beginning Balance	Change
Assets			
Current assets:			
Cash and cash equivalents	$ 91	$ 29	+62
Accounts receivable	637	654	−17
Inventory	586	537	+49
Total current assets	1,314	1,220	
Property, plant, and equipment	1,517	1,394	+123
Less accumulated depreciation	654	561	+93
Net property, plant, and equipment	863	833	
Total assets	$2,177	$2,053	
Liabilities and Stockholders' Equity			
Current liabilities:			
Accounts payable	$ 264	$ 220	+44
Accrued liabilities	193	190	+3
Income taxes payable	75	71	+4
Total current liabilities	532	481	
Bonds payable	479	520	−41
Total liabilities	1,011	1,001	
Stockholders' equity:			
Common stock	157	155	+2
Retained earnings	1,009	897	+112
Total stockholders' equity	1,166	1,052	
Total liabilities and stockholders' equity	$2,177	$2,053	

Let's also assume the following facts with respect to Apparel, Inc.:

1. The company sold a store that had an original cost of $15 million and accumulated depreciation of $10 million. The cash proceeds from the sale were $8 million. The gain on the sale was $3 million.
2. The company did not issue any new bonds during the year.
3. The company did not repurchase any of its own common stock during the year.
4. The company paid a cash dividend during the year.

Notice that the balance sheet in Exhibit 14–6 includes the amount of the change in each balance sheet account. For example, the beginning and ending balances in Cash and Cash Equivalents are $29 million and $91 million, respectively. This is a $62 million increase in the account balance. A similar computation is performed for all other balance sheet accounts. Study the changes in these account balances because we will be referring to them in the forthcoming pages. For example, keep in mind that the purpose of Apparel's statement of cash flows is to disclose the operating, investing, and financing cash flows underlying the $62 million increase in Cash and Cash Equivalents shown in Exhibit 14–6. *Also, please be advised that although the changes in account balances are computed for you in Exhibit 14–6, you'll ordinarily need to compute these amounts yourself before attempting to construct the statement of cash flows.*

Operating Activities

This section uses the three-step process explained earlier to construct Apparel's operating activities section of the statement of cash flows.

Step 1 The first step in computing Apparel's net cash provided by operating activities is to *add depreciation* to net income. The balance sheet in Exhibit 14–6 shows Apparel's Accumulated Depreciation account had beginning and ending balances of $561 million and $654 million, respectively. We also know from the assumptions listed above that Apparel sold a store during the year that had $10 million of accumulated depreciation. Given these facts, we can use the basic equation for contra-assets (introduced on page 640) to determine that Apparel needs to add $103 million of depreciation to its net income:

$$\text{Beginning balance} - \text{Debits} + \text{Credits} = \text{Ending balance}$$
$$\$561 \text{ million} - \$10 \text{ million} + \text{Credits} = \$654 \text{ million}$$
$$\text{Credits} = \$654 \text{ million} - \$561 \text{ million} + \$10 \text{ million}$$
$$\text{Credits} = \$103 \text{ million}$$

Step 2 The second step in computing net cash provided by operating activities is to *analyze net changes in noncash balance sheet accounts* that impact net income. Exhibit 14–7 explains the five adjustments Apparel needs to make to complete this step. For your ease of reference, the top half of Exhibit 14–7 reproduces an excerpt of the general guidelines for completing this step that were previously summarized in Exhibit 14–2. The bottom half of Exhibit 14–7 applies the general guidelines from the top half of the exhibit to Apparel's balance sheet. For example, Exhibit 14–6 shows that Apparel's Accounts Receivable balance decreased by $17 million. The top half of Exhibit 14–7 says that decreases in accounts receivable are added to net income. This explains why the bottom half of Exhibit 14–7 includes a plus sign in front of Apparel's $17 million decrease in Accounts Receivable. Similarly, Exhibit 14–6 shows that Apparel's Inventory balance increased by $49 million. When inventory increases, the amount of the increase is subtracted from net income. This explains why the bottom half of Exhibit 14–7 includes a minus sign in front of Apparel's $49 million increase in Inventory. Similar logic can be used to explain why the increases from Exhibit 14–6 in Accounts Payable (+44), Accrued Liabilities (+3), and Income Taxes Payable (+4) all result in the additions to Apparel's net income that are shown in the bottom half of Exhibit 14–7.

EXHIBIT 14–7
Apparel, Inc.: Analyzing How Net Changes in Noncash Balance Sheet Accounts Affect Net Income on the Statement of Cash Flows

	Increase in Account Balance	Decrease in Account Balance
General Guidelines from Exhibit 14–2		
Current Assets		
Accounts receivable	Subtract	Add
Inventory	Subtract	Add
Current Liabilities		
Accounts payable	Add	Subtract
Accrued liabilities	Add	Subtract
Income taxes payable	Add	Subtract
	Increase in Account Balance	**Decrease in Account Balance**
Apparel's Account Analysis		
Current Assets		
Accounts receivable		+17
Inventory	−49	
Current Liabilities		
Accounts payable	+44	
Accrued liabilities	+3	
Income taxes payable	+4	

Step 3 The third step in computing the net cash provided by operating activities is to *adjust for gains/losses* included in the income statement. Apparel reported a $3 million gain on its income statement in Exhibit 14–5; therefore, this amount needs to be subtracted from net income. Subtracting the gain on sale removes the gain from the operating activities section of the statement of cash flows. The entire amount of the proceeds related to this sale will be recorded in the investing activities section of the statement.

Exhibit 14–8 shows the operating activities section of Apparel's statement of cash flows. Take a moment to trace each of the numbers that we just computed to this exhibit. The total amount of the adjustments to net income is $119 million, which results in net cash provided by operating activities of $259 million.

EXHIBIT 14–8
Apparel, Inc.: Operating Activities Section of the Statement of Cash Flows

Apparel, Inc.
(dollars in millions)

	Operating Activities		
	Net income		$140
	Adjustments to convert net income to a cash basis:		
Step 1 →	Depreciation	103	
Step 2 →	Decrease in accounts receivable	17	
	Increase in inventory	(49)	
	Increase in accounts payable	44	
	Increase in accrued liabilities	3	
	Increase in income taxes payable	4	
Step 3 →	Gain on sale of store	(3)	119
	Net cash provided by operating activities		$259

Investing Activities

Apparel's investing cash flows pertain to its Property, Plant, and Equipment account, which according to Exhibit 14–6 had beginning and ending balances of $1,394 million and $1,517 million, respectively, for an increase of $123 million. This increase suggests that Apparel purchased equipment; however, it does not capture the gross cash flows that need to be reported in the statement of cash flows.

The assumptions on page 651 says that Apparel sold a store that had an original cost of \$15 million for \$8 million in cash. The cash inflow from this sale needs to be recorded in the investing activities section of the statement of cash flows. To compute the cash outflows related to purchases of property, plant, and equipment we use the basic equation for assets that was mentioned in the beginning of the chapter:

$$\text{Beginning balance} + \text{Debits} - \text{Credits} = \text{Ending balance}$$

$$\$1{,}394 \text{ million} + \text{Debits} - \$15 \text{ million} = \$1{,}517 \text{ million}$$

$$\text{Debits} = \$1{,}517 \text{ million} - \$1{,}394 \text{ million} + \$15 \text{ million}$$

$$\text{Debits} = \$138 \text{ million}$$

Notice the credits in the equation above include the original cost of the store that was sold. When the cash outflows of \$138 million are combined with the \$8 million of cash proceeds from the sale of the store, Apparel's net cash used in investing activities is \$130 million.

Financing Activities

Exhibit 14–9 explains how to compute Apparel's financing cash flows related to its Bonds Payable and Common Stock balance sheet accounts. The top half of the exhibit reproduces an excerpt of the general guidelines for analyzing financing cash flows that was previously summarized in Exhibit 14–3. The bottom half of Exhibit 14–9 applies the general guidelines from the top half of the exhibit to these two accounts from Apparel's balance sheet. We will analyze each account in turn.

Exhibit 14–6 shows that Apparel's Bonds Payable balance decreased by \$41 million. Because, as stated on page 651, Apparel did not issue any bonds during the year, we can conclude that the \$41 million decrease in the account is due solely to retiring bonds payable. The top half of Exhibit 14–9 says that a decrease in Bonds Payable signals the need to subtract cash outflows in the investing activities section of the statement of cash flows. This explains why the bottom half of the exhibit includes a minus sign in front of Apparel's \$41 million decrease in Bonds Payable. Similarly, Exhibit 14–6 shows that Apparel's Common Stock balance increased by \$2 million. Because, as stated on page 651, Apparel did not repurchase any of its own stock during the year, we can conclude that the \$2 million increase in the account is due solely to issuing common stock. The top half of Exhibit 14–9 says that increases in common stock signal the need to add cash inflows in the investing activities section of the statement of cash flows. This explains why the bottom half of the exhibit includes a plus sign in front of Apparel's \$2 million increase in Common Stock.

EXHIBIT 14–9
Apparel, Inc.: Analyzing How Changes in Noncash Balance Sheet Accounts Affect Financing Cash Flows on the Statement of Cash Flows

	Increase in Account Balance	Decrease in Account Balance
General Guidelines from Exhibit 14–3		
Liabilities and Stockholders' Equity		
Bonds payable	Add	Subtract
Common stock	Add	Subtract
	Increase in Account Balance	**Decrease in Account Balance**
Apparel's Account Analysis		
Liabilities and Stockholders' Equity		
Bonds payable		−41
Common stock	+2	

EXHIBIT 14–10
Apparel, Inc. Statement of Cash Flows

Apparel, Inc.
Statement of Cash Flows—Indirect Method
(dollars in millions)

Operating Activities		
Net income		$140
Adjustments to convert net income to a cash basis:		
Depreciation	103	
Decrease in accounts receivable	17	
Increase in inventory	(49)	
Increase in accounts payable	44	
Increase in accrued liabilities	3	
Increase in income taxes payable	4	
Gain on sale of store	(3)	119
Net cash provided by operating activities		259
Investing Activities		
Additions to property, plant, and equipment	(138)	
Proceeds from sale of store	8	
Net cash used in investing activities		(130)
Financing Activities		
Retirement of bonds payable	(41)	
Issuance of common stock	2	
Cash dividends paid	(28)	
Net cash used in financing activities		(67)
Net increase in cash and cash equivalents		62
Cash and cash equivalents, beginning balance		29
Cash and cash equivalents, ending balance		$ 91

The final financing cash outflow for Apparel is its dividend payment to common stockholders. The dividend payment can be computed using the basic equation for stockholders' equity accounts mentioned at the beginning of the chapter:

$$\text{Beginning balance} - \text{Debits} + \text{Credits} = \text{Ending balance}$$
$$\$897 \text{ million} - \text{Debits} + \$140 \text{ million} = \$1{,}009 \text{ million}$$
$$\$1{,}037 \text{ million} = \$1{,}009 \text{ million} + \text{Debits}$$
$$\text{Debits} = \$28 \text{ million}$$

When the cash outflows of \$69 million (= \$41 million + \$28 million) are combined with the cash inflows of \$2 million, Apparel's net cash used in financing activities is \$67 million.

Exhibit 14–10 shows Apparel's statement of cash flows. The operating activities section of this statement is carried over from Exhibit 14–8. Take a moment to trace the investing and financing cash flows just discussed to Exhibit 14–10. Notice, the net increase in cash and cash equivalents is \$62 million (= \$259 million − \$130 million − \$67 million), which agrees with the change in the Cash and Cash Equivalents account shown on the balance sheet in Exhibit 14–6.

Seeing the Big Picture

In the beginning of the chapter, we mentioned that a statement of cash flows is prepared by analyzing the changes in noncash balance sheet accounts. We then presented a method of preparing a statement of cash flows. This method simplified the process of creating the statement of cash flows, and now we will show that it is equivalent to analyzing the changes in noncash balance sheet accounts.

EXHIBIT 14–11
T-Accounts after Posting of Account Changes—Apparel, Inc. (in millions)

Cash

		Debit	Credit		
Net income	(1)	140	49	(4)	Increase in inventory
Depreciation	(2)	103	3	(12)	Gain on sale of store
Decrease in accounts receivable	(3)	17			
Increase in accounts payable	(5)	44			
Increase in accrued liabilities	(6)	3			
Increase in income taxes payable	(7)	4			
Net cash provided by operating activities		259			
Proceeds from sale of store	(12)	8	138	(8)	Additions to property, plant, and equipment
Increase in common stock	(11)	2	41	(9)	Decrease in bonds payable
			28	(10)	Cash dividends paid
Net increase in cash and cash equivalents		62			

Accounts Receivable

Debit	Credit
Bal. 654	
	17 (3)
Bal. 637	

Inventory

Debit	Credit
Bal. 537	
(4) 49	
Bal. 586	

Property, Plant, and Equipment

Debit	Credit
Bal. 1,394	
(8) 138	15 (12)
Bal. 1,517	

Accumulated Depreciation

Debit	Credit
	561 Bal.
(12) 10	103 (2)
	654 Bal.

Accounts Payable

Debit	Credit
	220 Bal.
	44 (5)
	264 Bal.

Accrued Liabilities

Debit	Credit
	190 Bal.
	3 (6)
	193 Bal.

Income Taxes Payable

Debit	Credit
	71 Bal.
	4 (7)
	75 Bal.

Bonds Payable

Debit	Credit
	520 Bal.
(9) 41	
	479 Bal.

Common Stock

Debit	Credit
	155 Bal.
	2 (11)
	157 Bal.

Retained Earnings

Debit	Credit
	897 Bal.
(10) 28	140 (1)
	1,009 Bal.

Exhibit 14–11 uses T-accounts to summarize how the changes in Apparel Inc.'s noncash balance sheet accounts quantify the cash inflows and outflows that explain the change in its cash balance. The top portion of the exhibit is Apparel's Cash T-account and the bottom portion provides T-accounts for the company's remaining balance sheet accounts. Notice that the net cash provided by operating activities ($259 million) and the net increase in cash and cash equivalents ($62) shown in the Cash T-account agree with the corresponding figures in the statement of cash flows shown in Exhibit 14–10.

We will explain Exhibit 14–11 in five steps. Entry (1) records Apparel's net income ($140 million) in the credit side of the Retained Earnings account and the debit side of the Cash account. The net income of $140 million shown in the Cash T-account will be adjusted until it reflects the $62 million net increase in cash and cash equivalents. Entry (2) adds the depreciation of $103 million to net income. Entries (3) through (7) adjust net income for the

IN BUSINESS

SEC REQUIRES CATERPILLAR TO RESTATE CASH FLOWS

The Securities and Exchange Commission (SEC) required Caterpillar to restate its cash flows for 2002 and 2003 as follows (amounts are in millions):

	2002	2003
Cash flows as originally reported by Caterpillar:		
Net cash provided by operating activities	$ 2,366	$ 2,066
Net cash used for investing activities	(2,708)	(2,793)
Total	$ (342)	$ (727)
Catepillar's restated cash flows:		
Net cash used for operating activities	$(3,962)	$(5,611)
Net cash provided by investing activities.	3,620	4,884
Total.	$ (342)	$ (727)

The restatement resulted in a dramatic drop in Caterpillar's net cash provided by operating activities in both 2002 and 2003, although the overall change in the company's cash and short-term investments remained the same after the restatement. Why do you think the SEC required Caterpillar to report the reclassifications summarized above?

Source: Ghostwriter, "SEC Acts to Curb Cash Flow Shenanigans," *Inc.*, June 2005, p. 26, and Caterpillar's 10-K forms's for 2002, 2003, and 2004.

changes in the current asset and current liability accounts. Entries (8) through (11) summarize the cash outflows and inflows related to the additions to property, plant, and equipment, the retirement of bonds payable, the payment of the cash dividend, and the issuance of common stock. Entry (12) records the sale of the store. Notice that the gain on the sale ($3 million) is recorded in the credit side of the Cash T-account. This is equivalent to subtracting the gain from net income so that the entire amount of the cash proceeds from the sale ($8 million) can be recorded in the investing activities section of the statement of cash flows.

Interpreting the Statement of Cash Flows

Managers can derive many useful insights by studying the statement of cash flows. In this section, we will discuss two guidelines managers should use when interpreting the statement of cash flows.

Consider a Company's Specific Circumstances

A statement of cash flows should be evaluated in the context of a company's specific circumstances. To illustrate this point, let's consider two examples related to start-up companies and companies with growing versus declining sales. Start-up companies are usually unable to generate positive cash flows from operations; therefore, they rely on issuing stock and taking out loans to fund investing activities. This means that start-up companies often have negative net cash provided by operating activities and large spikes in net cash used for investing activities and net cash provided by financing activities. However, as a start-up company matures, it should begin generating enough cash to sustain day-to-day operations and maintain its plant and equipment without issuing additional stock or borrowing money. This means the net cash provided by operating activities should swing from a negative to a positive number. The net cash used for investing activities should decline somewhat and stabilize and the net cash provided by financing activities should decrease.

A company with growing sales would understandably have an increase in its accounts receivable, inventory, and accounts payable balances. On the other hand, if a company with declining sales has increases in these account balances, it could signal trouble. Perhaps accounts receivable is increasing because the company is attempting to boost sales by selling to customers who can't pay their bills. Perhaps the increase in inventory suggests the company is stuck with large amounts of obsolete inventory. Accounts payable may be increasing because the company is deferring payments to suppliers in an effort to inflate its net cash provided by operating activities. Notice that the plausible interpretations of these changes in account balances depend on the company's circumstances.

Consider the Relationships among Numbers

While each number in a statement of cash flows provides useful information, managers derive the most meaningful insights by examining the relationships among numbers.

For example, some managers study their company's trends in cash flow margins by comparing the net cash provided by operating activities to sales. The goal is to continuously increase the operating cash flows earned per sales dollar. If we refer back to Apparel's income statement in Exhibit 14–5 and its statement of cash flows in Exhibit 14–10, we can determine that its cash flow margin is about $0.07 per dollar of sales (= $259 ÷ $3,638). Managers also compare the net cash provided by operating activities to the ending balance of current liabilities. If the net cash provided by operating activities is greater than (less than) the current liabilities, it indicates the company did (did not) generate enough operating cash flow to pay its bills at the end of the period. Apparel's net cash provided by operating activities of $259 million (see Exhibit 14–10) was not enough to pay its year-end current liabilities of $481 million (see Exhibit 14–6).

As a third example, managers compare the additions to property, plant, and equipment in the investing activities section of the statement of cash flows to the depreciation included in the operating activities section of the statement. If the additions to property, plant, and equipment are consistently less than depreciation, it suggests the company is not investing enough money to maintain its noncurrent assets. If we refer back to Apparel's statement of cash flows in Exhibit 14–10, its additions to property, plant, and equipment ($138 million) are greater than its depreciation ($103 million). This suggests that Apparel is investing more than enough money to maintain its noncurrent assets.

LEARNING OBJECTIVE 3
Compute free cash flow.

Free Cash Flow

Free cash flow is a measure used by managers to look at the relationship among three numbers from the statement of cash flows—net cash provided by operating activities, additions to property, plant, and equipment (also called capital expenditures), and dividends. **Free cash flow** measures a company's ability to fund its capital expenditures for property, plant, and equipment and its dividends from its net cash provided by operating activities.[6] The equation for computing free cash flow is as follows:

$$\text{Free cash flow} = \text{Net cash provided by operating activities} - \text{Capital expenditures} - \text{Dividends}$$

Using this equation and the statement of cash flows shown in Exhibit 14–10, we can compute Apparel's free cash flow (in millions) as follows:

$$\text{Free cash flow} = \$259 - \$138 - \$28$$
$$\text{Free cash flow} = \$93$$

[6] For a summary of alternative definitions of free cash flow, see John Mills, Lynn Bible, and Richard Mason, "Defining Free Cash Flow," *CPA Journal*, January 2002, pp. 36–42.

The interpretation of free cash flow is straightforward. A positive number indicates that the company generated enough cash flow from its operating activities to fund its capital expenditures and dividend payments. A negative number suggests that the company needed to obtain cash from other sources, such as borrowing money from lenders or issuing shares of common stock, to fund its investments in property, plant, and equipment and its dividend payments. Negative free cash flow does not automatically signal poor performance. As previously discussed, a new company with enormous growth prospects would be expected to have negative free cash flow during its start-up phase. However, even new companies will eventually need to generate positive free cash flow to survive.

Earnings Quality Managers and investors often look at the relationship between net income and net cash provided by operating activities to help assess the extent to which a company's earnings truly reflects operational performance. Managers generally perceive that earnings are of higher quality, or more indicative of operational performance, when the earnings (1) are not unduly influenced by inflation, (2) are computed using conservative accounting principles and estimates, and (3) are correlated with net cash provided by operating activities. When a company's net income and net cash provided by operating activities move in tandem with one another (in other words, are correlated with one another), it suggests that earnings result from changes in sales and operating expenses. Conversely, if a company's net income is steadily increasing and its net cash provided by operating activities is declining, it suggests that net income is being influenced by factors unrelated to operational performance, such as nonrecurring transactions or aggressive accounting principles and estimates.

IN BUSINESS

AMAZON.COM BOOSTS CASH FLOWS

Amazon.com immediately receives cash from its customers when sales occur on its website. When the company stretched the number of days taken to pay its suppliers from 63 to 72 days, this created a huge jump in the company's accounts payable balance, which helped increase free cash flow from $346 million to $1.36 billion. In one quarter, Amazon.com's sales increased 28%, but its accounts payable nearly doubled, causing a 116% increase in free cash flow. Do you think managers should increase cash flows by delaying payments to suppliers? Would it promote a cooperative relationship with suppliers?

Source: Martin Peers, "Amazon's Astute Timing," *The Wall Street Journal,* October 30, 2009, p. C10.

Summary

The statement of cash flows is one of three major financial statements prepared by organizations. It explains how cash was generated and how it was used during a period. The statement of cash flows is widely used as a tool for assessing the financial health of organizations.

For external reporting purposes, the statement of cash flows must be organized in terms of operating, investing, and financing activities. The net cash provided by operating activities is an important measure because it indicates how successful a company is in generating cash on a continuing basis. The indirect method of computing the net cash provided by operating activities is a three-step process. The first step is to add depreciation to net income. The second step is to analyze net changes in noncash balance sheet accounts that impact net income. The third step is to adjust for gains or losses included in the income statement.

The investing and financing sections of the statement of cash flows must report gross cash flows. The statement of cash flows summarizes the net increase/decrease in cash and cash equivalents during the period, which explains the change in the cash balance.

Review Problem

Rockford Company's comparative balance sheet for 2011 and the company's income statement for the year follow:

Rockford Company Comparative Balance Sheet (dollars in millions)	2011	2010
Assets		
Current assets:		
Cash and cash equivalents	$ 26	$ 10
Accounts receivable	180	270
Inventory	205	160
Prepaid expenses	17	20
Total current assets	428	460
Property, plant, and equipment	430	309
Less accumulated depreciation	218	194
Net property, plant, and equipment	212	115
Long-term investments	60	75
Total assets	$700	$650
Liabilities and Stockholders' Equity		
Current liabilities:		
Accounts payable	$230	$310
Accrued liabilities	70	60
Income taxes payable	15	8
Total current liabilities	315	378
Bonds payable	135	40
Total liabilities	450	418
Stockholders' equity:		
Common stock	140	140
Retained earnings	110	92
Total stockholders' equity	250	232
Total liabilities and stockholders' equity	$700	$650

Rockford Company Income Statement For the Year Ended December 31, 2011 (dollars in millions)	
Sales	$1,000
Cost of goods sold	530
Gross margin	470
Selling and administrative expenses	352
Net operating income	118
Nonoperating items:	
Loss on sale of equipment	4
Income before taxes	114
Income taxes	48
Net income	$ 66

Additional data:

1. Rockford paid a cash dividend in 2011.
2. The $4 million loss on sale of equipment reflects a transaction in which equipment with an original cost of $12 million and accumulated depreciation of $5 million was sold for $3 million in cash.
3. Rockford did not purchase any long-term investments during the year. There was no gain or loss on the sale of long-term investments.
4. Rockford did not retire any bonds payable during 2011, or issue or repurchase any common stock.

Required:

1. Using the indirect method, determine the net cash provided by operating activities for 2011.
2. Construct a statement of cash flows for 2011.

Solution to Review Problem

The first task you should complete before turning your attention to the problem's specific requirements is to compute the changes in each balance sheet account as shown below (all amounts are in millions):

Rockford Company
Comparative Balance Sheet
(dollars in millions)

	2011	2010	Change
Assets			
Current assets:			
Cash and cash equivalents	$ 26	$ 10	−16
Accounts receivable	180	270	−90
Inventory	205	160	+45
Prepaid expenses	17	20	−3
Total current assets	428	460	
Property, plant, and equipment	430	309	+121
Less accumulated depreciation	218	194	+24
Net property, plant, and equipment	212	115	
Long-term investments	60	75	−15
Total assets	$700	$650	
Liabilities and Stockholders' Equity			
Current liabilities:			
Accounts payable	$230	$310	−80
Accrued liabilities	70	60	+10
Income taxes payable	15	8	−7
Total current liabilities	315	378	
Bonds payable	135	40	+95
Total liabilities	450	418	
Stockholders' equity:			
Common stock	140	140	+0
Retained earnings	110	92	+18
Total stockholders' equity	250	232	
Total liabilities and stockholders' equity	$700	$650	

Requirement 1:

You should perform three steps to compute the net cash provided by operating activities.

Step 1: Add depreciation to net income.

To complete this step, apply the equation on page 640 as follows:

$$\text{Beginning balance} - \text{Debits} + \text{Credits} = \text{Ending balance}$$

$$\$194 \text{ million} - \$5 \text{ million} + \text{Credits} = \$218 \text{ million}$$

$$\text{Credits} = \$218 \text{ million} - \$194 \text{ million} + \$5 \text{ million}$$

$$\text{Credits} = \$29 \text{ million}$$

Step 2: Analyze net changes in noncash balance sheet accounts that affect net income.
To complete this step, apply the logic from Exhibit 14–2 as follows:

	Increase in Account Balance	Decrease in Account Balance
Current Assets		
Accounts receivable		+90
Inventory	−45	
Prepaid expenses		+3
Current Liabilities		
Accounts payable		−80
Accrued liabilities	+10	
Income taxes payable	+7	

Step 3: Adjust for gains/losses included in the income statement.
Rockford's $4 million loss on the sale of equipment must be added to net income.

Having completed these three steps, the operating activities section of the statement of cash flows would appear as follows:

Rockford Company Statement of Cash Flows—Indirect Method For the Year Ended December 31, 2011 (dollars in millions)		
Operating Activities		
Net income		$66
Adjustments to convert net income to a cash basis:		
Depreciation	$29	
Decrease in accounts receivable	90	
Increase in inventory	(45)	
Decrease in prepaid expenses	3	
Decrease in accounts payable	(80)	
Increase in accrued liabilities	10	
Increase in income taxes payable	7	
Loss on sale of equipment	4	18
Net cash provided by operating activities		$84

Requirement 2:
To finalize the statement of cash flows, we must complete the investing and financing sections of the statement. This requires analyzing the Property, Plant, and Equipment, Long-Term Investments, Bonds Payable, Common Stock and Retained Earnings accounts. The table below is based on Exhibit 14–3 and it captures the changes in four account balances for Rockford.

	Increase in Account Balance	Decrease in Account Balance
Noncurrent Assets (Investing activities)		
Property, plant, and equipment	−121	
Long-term investments		+15
Liabilities and Stockholders' Equity (Financing activities)		
Bonds payable	+95	
Common stock	No change	No change
Retained earnings	*	*

*Requires further analysis to quantify cash dividends paid.

The data at the beginning of the problem state that Rockford did not purchase any long-term investments during the year and that there was no gain or loss on the sale of long-term investments. This means that the $15 million decrease in Long-Term Investments corresponds with a $15 million cash inflow from the sale of long-term investments that is recorded in the investing section of the statement of cash flows. The data also state that Rockford did not retire any bonds payable during the year; therefore, the $95 million increase in Bonds Payable must be due to issuing bonds payable. This cash inflow is recorded in the financing section of the statement of cash flows.

The Common Stock account had no activity during the period, so it does not impact the statement of cash flows. This leaves two accounts that require further analysis—Property, Plant, and Equipment and Retained Earnings.

The company sold equipment that had an original cost of $12 million for $3 million in cash. The cash proceeds from the sale need to be recorded in the investing activities section of the statement of cash flows. The cash outflows related to Rockford's investing activities can be computed using the basic equation for assets mentioned on page 640:

$$\text{Beginning balance} + \text{Debits} - \text{Credits} = \text{Ending balance}$$

$$\$309 \text{ million} + \text{Debits} - \$12 \text{ million} = \$430 \text{ million}$$

$$\text{Debits} = \$430 \text{ million} - \$309 \text{ million} + \$12 \text{ million}$$

$$\text{Debits} = \$133 \text{ million}$$

Rockford's Retained Earnings account and the basic equation for stockholders' equity (introduced on page 640) can be used to compute the company's dividend payment as follows:

$$\text{Beginning balance} - \text{Debits} + \text{Credits} = \text{Ending balance}$$

$$\$92 \text{ million} - \text{Debits} + \$66 \text{ million} = \$110 \text{ million}$$

$$\$158 \text{ million} = \$110 \text{ million} + \text{Debits}$$

$$\text{Debits} = \$48 \text{ million}$$

The company's complete statement of cash flows is shown below. Notice that the net increase in cash and cash equivalents ($16 million) equals the change in the Cash and Cash Equivalents account balance.

Rockford Company
Statement of Cash Flows—Indirect Method
For the Year Ended December 31, 2011
(dollars in millions)

Operating Activities:		
Net income		$ 66
Adjustments to convert net income to a cash basis:		
Depreciation	$ 29	
Decrease in accounts receivable	90	
Increase in inventory	(45)	
Decrease in prepaid expenses	3	
Decrease in accounts payable	(80)	
Increase in accrued liabilities	10	
Increase in income taxes payable	7	
Loss on sale of equipment	4	18
Net cash provided by operating activities		84
Investing Activities:		
Additions to property, plant, and equipment	(133)	
Decrease in long-term investments	15	
Proceeds from sale of equipment	3	
Net cash used in investing activities		(115)
Financing Activities:		
Increase in bonds payable	95	
Cash dividends paid	(48)	
Net cash provided by financing activities		47
Net increase in cash and cash equivalents		16
Cash and cash equivalents at beginning of year		10
Cash and cash equivalents at end of year		$ 26

Glossary

Cash equivalents Short-term, highly liquid investments such as Treasury bills, commercial paper, and money market funds, that are made solely for the purpose of generating a return on temporarily idle funds. (p. 641)

Direct method A method of computing the net cash provided by operating activities in which the income statement is reconstructed on a cash basis from top to bottom. (p. 642)

Financing activities These activities generate cash inflows and outflows related to borrowing from and repaying principal to creditors and completing transactions with the company's owners, such as selling or repurchasing shares of common stock and paying dividends. (p. 642)

Free cash flow A measure that assesses a company's ability to fund its capital expenditures and dividends from its net cash provided by operating activities. (p. 657)

Indirect method A method of computing the net cash provided by operating activities that starts with net income and adjusts it to a cash basis. (p. 642)

Investing activities These activities generate cash inflows and outflows related to acquiring or disposing of noncurrent assets such as property, plant, and equipment, long-term investments, and loans to another entity. (p. 642)

Net cash provided by operating activities The net result of the cash inflows and outflows arising from day-to-day operations. (p. 642)

Operating activities These activities generate cash inflows and outflows related to revenue and expense transactions that affect net income. (p. 641)

Statement of cash flows A financial statement that highlights the major activities that impact cash flows and, hence, affect the overall cash balance. (p. 640)

Questions

14–1 What is the purpose of a statement of cash flows?

14–2 What are *cash equivalents,* and why are they included with cash on a statement of cash flows?

14–3 What are the three major sections on a statement of cash flows, and what type of cash inflows and outflows should be included in each section?

14–4 What general guidelines can you provide for interpreting the statement of cash flows?

14–5 If an asset is sold at a gain, why is the gain subtracted from net income when computing the net cash provided by operating activities under the indirect method?

14–6 Why aren't transactions involving accounts payable considered to be financing activities?

14–7 Assume that a company repays a $300,000 loan from its bank and then later in the same year borrows $500,000. What amount(s) would appear on the statement of cash flows?

14–8 How do the direct and the indirect methods differ in their approach to computing the net cash provided by operating activities?

14–9 A business executive once stated, "Depreciation is one of our biggest operating cash inflows." Do you agree? Explain.

14–10 If the Accounts Receivable balance increases during a period, how will this increase be recognized using the indirect method of computing the net cash provided by operating activities?

14–11 Would a sale of equipment for cash be considered a financing activity or an investing activity? Why?

14–12 What is the difference between net cash provided by operating activities and free cash flow?

Multiple-choice questions are provided on the text website at www.mhhe.com/garrison14e.

Exercises

connect | ACCOUNTING

All applicable exercises are available with McGraw-Hill's *Connect™ Accounting*.

EXERCISE 14–1 Classifying Transactions [LO1]

Below are certain events that took place at Hazzard, Inc., last year:

a. Paid bills to insurers and utility providers.
b. Purchased equipment with cash.
c. Paid wages and salaries to employees.
d. Paid taxes to the government.
e. Loaned money to another entity.
f. Sold common stock.
g. Paid a cash dividend to stockholders.
h. Paid interest to lenders.
i. Repaid the principal amount of a debt.
j. Paid suppliers for inventory purchases.
k. Borrowed money from a creditor.
l. Paid cash to repurchase its own stock.
m. Collected cash from customers.

Required:

Prepare an answer sheet with the following headings:

	Activity		
Transaction	Operating	Investing	Financing
a.			
b.			
Etc.			

Enter the cash inflows and outflows above on your answer sheet and indicate how each of them would be classified on a statement of cash flows. Place an X in the Operating, Investing, or Financing column as appropriate.

EXERCISE 14–2 Net Cash Provided by Operating Activities [LO2]

For the just completed year, Strident Company had net income of $84,000. Balances in the company's current asset and current liability accounts at the beginning and end of the year were as follows:

	December 31	
	End of Year	Beginning of Year
Current assets:		
Cash	$60,000	$80,000
Accounts receivable	$165,000	$190,000
Inventory	$437,000	$360,000
Prepaid expenses	$12,000	$14,000
Current liabilities:		
Accounts payable	$370,000	$390,000
Accrued liabilities	$8,000	$12,000
Income taxes payable	$36,000	$30,000

The Accumulated Depreciation account had total credits of $50,000 during the year.

Required:

Using the indirect method, determine the net cash provided by operating activities for the year.

EXERCISE 14–3 Calculating Free Cash Flow [LO3]
Paisley Company prepared the following statement of cash flows for the current year:

Paisley Company Statement of Cash Flows—Indirect Method		
Operating activities:		
Net income		$ 40,000
Adjustments to convert net income to cash basis:		
Depreciation	$ 22,000	
Increase in accounts receivable	(50,000)	
Increase in inventory	(35,000)	
Decrease in prepaid expenses	6,000	
Increase in accounts payable	60,000	
Decrease in accrued liabilities	(12,000)	
Increase in income taxes payable	5,000	(4,000)
Net cash provided by operating activities		36,000
Investing activities:		
Proceeds from the sale of equipment	24,000	
Loan to Allen Company	(30,000)	
Additions to plant and equipment	(120,000)	
Net cash used for investing activities		(126,000)
Financing activities:		
Increase in bonds payable	80,000	
Increase in common stock	50,000	
Cash dividends	(20,000)	
Net cash provided by financing activities		110,000
Net increase in cash		(20,000)
Cash balance, beginning of year		27,000
Cash balance, end of year		$ 47,000

Required:
Compute Paisley Company's free cash flow for the current year.

EXERCISE 14–4 Prepare a Statement of Cash Flows; Free Cash Flow [LO1, LO2, LO3]
Comparative financial statement data for Holly Company are given below:

	December 31	
	This Year	Last Year
Assets		
Cash	$ 4	$ 7
Accounts receivable	36	29
Inventory	75	61
Total current assets	115	97
Property, plant, and equipment	210	180
Less accumulated depreciation	40	30
Net property, plant, and equipment	170	150
Total assets	$285	$247
Liabilities and Stockholders' Equity		
Accounts payable	$ 45	$ 39
Common stock	90	70
Retained earnings	150	138
Total liabilities and stockholders' equity	$285	$247

For this year, the company reported net income as follows:

Sales	$500
Cost of goods sold	300
Gross margin	200
Selling and administrative expenses	180
Net income	$ 20

This year Holly declared and paid a cash dividend. There were no sales of plant and equipment during this year. The company did not repurchase any of its own stock this year.

Required:
1. Using the indirect method, prepare a statement of cash flows for this year.
2. Compute Holly's free cash flow for this year.

EXERCISE 14–5 Prepare a Statement of Cash Flows [LO1, LO2]
The following changes took place last year in Herald Company's balance sheet accounts:

Asset and Contra-Asset Accounts			Liabilities and Equity Accounts		
Cash	$20	I	Accounts payable	$20	I
Accounts receivable	$10	D	Accrued liabilities	$10	D
Inventory	$30	I	Income taxes payable	$15	I
Prepaid expenses	$5	D	Bonds payable	$20	D
Long-term investments	$30	D	Common stock	$40	I
Property, plant, and equipment	$120	I	Retained earnings	$40	I
Accumulated depreciation	$40	I			

D = Decrease; I = Increase.

Long-term investments that had cost the company $50 were sold during the year for $45, and land that had cost $30 was sold for $70. In addition, the company declared and paid $35 in cash dividends during the year. Besides the sale of land, no other sales or retirements of plant and equipment took place during the year. Herald did not issue any bonds during the year or repurchase any of its own stock.

The company's income statement for the year follows:

Sales		$600
Cost of goods sold		250
Gross margin		350
Selling and administrative expenses		280
Net operating income		70
Nonoperating items:		
Loss on sale of investments	$(5)	
Gain on sale of land	40	35
Income before taxes		105
Income taxes		30
Net income		$ 75

The company's beginning cash balance was $100 and its ending balance was $120.

Required:
1. Use the indirect method to determine the net cash provided by operating activities for the year.
2. Prepare a statement of cash flows for the year.

EXERCISE 14–6 Net Cash Provided by Operating Activities [LO2]
Changes in various accounts and gains and losses on the sale of assets during the year for Weston Company are given at the top of the next page.

Item	Amount
Accounts receivable	$70,000 decrease
Inventory	$110,000 increase
Prepaid expenses	$3,000 decrease
Accounts payable	$40,000 decrease
Accrued liabilities	$9,000 increase
Income taxes payable	$15,000 increase
Sale of equipment	$8,000 gain
Sale of long-term investments	$12,000 loss

Required:

For each item, place an X in the Add or Subtract column to indicate whether the dollar amount should be added to or subtracted from net income under the indirect method when computing the net cash provided by operating activities for the year. Use the following column headings in preparing your answers:

Item	Amount	Add	Subtract

Connect Accounting Problems

All applicable problems are available with McGraw-Hill's *Connect™ Accounting*.

PROBLEM 14–7 Understanding a Statement of Cash Flows [LO1, LO2]

Logan Company is a merchandiser that prepared the statement of cash flows and income statement provided below:

Logan Company Statement of Cash Flows—Indirect Method		
Operating Activities		
Net income		$175
Adjustments to convert net income to cash basis:		
Depreciation	$108	
Decrease in accounts receivable	21	
Decrease in inventory	39	
Decrease in accounts payable	(50)	
Decrease in accrued liabilities	(6)	
Increase in income taxes payable	5	
Loss on sale of equipment	3	120
Net cash provided by operating activities		295
Investing Activities		
Additions to property, plant, and equipment	(110)	
Proceeds from sale of equipment	9	
Net cash used in investing activities		(101)
Financing Activities		
Retirement of bonds payable	(31)	
Issuance of common stock	4	
Cash dividends paid	(35)	
Net cash used in financing activities		(62)
Net increase in cash and cash equivalents		132
Cash and cash equivalents, beginning balance		70
Cash and cash equivalents, ending balance		$202

Logan Company Income Statement	
Sales	$4,120
Cost of goods sold	2,890
Gross margin	1,230
Selling and administrative expenses	835
Net operating income	395
Nonoperating items: Loss on sale of equipment	(3)
Income before taxes	392
Income taxes	217
Net income	$ 175

Required:

Assume that you have been asked to teach a workshop to the employees within Logan Company's Marketing Department. The purpose of your workshop is to explain how the statement of cash flows differs from the income statement. Your audience is expecting you to explain the logic underlying each number included in the statement of cash flows. Prepare a memo that explains the format of the statement of cash flows and the rationale for each number included in Logan's statement of cash flows.

eXcel

PROBLEM 14–8 Prepare a Statement of Cash Flows [LO1, LO2]

A comparative balance sheet and income statement for Eaton Company follow:

Eaton Company Comparative Balance Sheet December 31, 2011 and 2010	2011	2010
Assets		
Cash	$ 4	$ 11
Accounts receivable	310	230
Inventory	160	195
Prepaid expenses	8	6
Total current assets	482	442
Property, plant, and equipment	500	420
Less accumulated depreciation	85	70
Net property, plant, and equipment	415	350
Long-term investments	31	38
Total assets	$928	$830
Liabilities and Stockholders' Equity		
Accounts payable	$300	$225
Accrued liabilities	70	80
Income taxes payable	71	63
Total current liabilities	441	368
Bonds payable	195	170
Total liabilities	636	538
Common stock	160	200
Retained earnings	132	92
Total stockholders' equity	292	292
Total liabilities and stockholders' equity	$928	$830

Eaton Company Income Statement For the Year Ended December 31, 2011		
Sales		$750
Cost of goods sold		450
Gross margin		300
Selling and administrative expenses		223
Net operating income		77
Nonoperating items:		
Gain on sale of investments	$5	
Loss on sale of equipment	(2)	3
Income before taxes		80
Income taxes		24
Net income		$ 56

During 2011, Eaton sold some equipment for $18 that had cost $30 and on which there was accumulated depreciation of $10. In addition, the company sold long-term investments for $12 that had cost $7 when purchased several years ago. A cash dividend was paid during 2011 and the company, repurchased $40 of its own stock. Eaton did not retire any bonds during 2011.

Required:

1. Using the indirect method, determine the net cash provided by operating activities for 2011.
2. Using the information in (1) above, along with an analysis of the remaining balance sheet accounts, prepare a statement of cash flows for 2011.

PROBLEM 14–9 Prepare a Statement of Cash Flows; Free Cash Flow [LO1, LO2, LO3]
Foxboro Company's income statement for Year 2 follows:

Sales	$700,000
Cost of goods sold	400,000
Gross margin	300,000
Selling and administrative expenses	216,000
Net operating income	84,000
Gain on sale of equipment	6,000
Income before taxes	90,000
Income taxes	27,000
Net income	$ 63,000

Its balance sheet amounts at the end of Years 1 and 2 are as follows:

	A	B	C
1		*Year 2*	*Year 1*
2	*Assets*		
3	Cash	$ 11,000	$ 19,000
4	Accounts receivable	250,000	180,000
5	Inventory	318,000	270,000
6	Prepaid expenses	7,000	16,000
7	Total current assets	586,000	485,000
8	Plant and equipment	620,000	500,000
9	Accumulated depreciation	165,000	130,000
10	Net plant and equipment	455,000	370,000
11	Loan to Harker Company	40,000	-
12	Total assets	$ 1,081,000	$ 855,000
13			
14	*Liabilities and Stockholders' Equity*		
15	Accounts payable	$ 310,000	$ 260,000
16	Accrued liabilities	42,000	50,000
17	Income taxes payable	84,000	80,000
18	Total current liabilities	436,000	390,000
19	Bonds payable	190,000	100,000
20	Total liabilities	626,000	490,000
21	Common stock	335,000	275,000
22	Retained earnings	120,000	90,000
23	Total stockholders' equity	455,000	365,000
24	Total liabilities and stockholders' equity	$ 1,081,000	$ 855,000

Equipment that had cost $30,000 and on which there was accumulated depreciation of $10,000 was sold during Year 2 for $26,000. The company declared and paid a cash dividend during Year 2. It did not retire any bonds or repurchase any of its own stock.

Required:

1. Using the indirect method, compute the net cash provided by operating activities for Year 2.
2. Prepare a statement of cash flows for Year 2.
3. Compute the free cash flow for Year 2.
4. Briefly explain why cash declined so sharply during the year.

PROBLEM 14–10 Classification of Transactions [LO1]

Below are several transactions that took place in Mohawk Company last year:

a. Bonds were retired by paying the principal amount due.
b. Interest was paid to a lender.
c. Income taxes were paid to the government.
d. A long-term loan was made to a supplier.
e. Cash dividends were declared and paid.
f. Common stock was sold for cash to investors.
g. Equipment was sold for cash.
h. Paid wages to employees.
i. Collected cash from customers.
j. Paid cash to repurchase its own stock.
k. Bought equipment for cash.
l. Paid suppliers for inventory purchases.

Required:

Prepare an answer sheet with the following headings:

	Activity				
Transaction	Operating	Investing	Financing	Cash Inflow	Cash Outflow
a.					
b.					
Etc.					

Enter the transactions above on your answer sheet and indicate how each of them would be classified on a statement of cash flows. As appropriate, place an X in the Operating, Investing, or Financing column. Also, place on X in the Cash Inflow or Cash Outflow column.

PROBLEM 14–11 Prepare a Statement of Cash Flows [LO1, LO2]

A comparative balance sheet and an income statement for Blankley Company are given below:

Blankley Company
Comparative Balance Sheet
(dollars in millions)

	Ending Balance	Beginning Balance
Assets		
Current assets:		
Cash and cash equivalents	$ 39	$ 81
Accounts receivable	640	588
Inventory	650	610
Total current assets	1,329	1,279
Property, plant, and equipment	1,505	1,484
Less accumulated depreciation	770	651
Net property, plant, and equipment	735	833
Total assets	$2,064	$2,112

Liabilities and Stockholders' Equity		
Current liabilities:		
Accounts payable	$ 260	$ 160
Accrued liabilities	180	170
Income taxes payable	77	72
Total current liabilities	517	402
Bonds payable	415	600
Total liabilities	932	1,002
Stockholders' equity:		
Common stock	145	145
Retained earnings	987	965
Total stockholders' equity	1,132	1,110
Total liabilities and stockholders' equity	$2,064	$2,112

Blankley Company
Income Statement
(dollars in millions)

Sales	$3,700
Cost of goods sold	2,540
Gross margin	1,160
Selling and administrative expenses	880
Net operating income	280
Nonoperating items: Gain on sale of equipment	2
Income before taxes	282
Income taxes	112
Net income	$ 170

Blankley also provided the following information:

1. The company sold equipment that had an original cost of $12 million and accumulated depreciation of $7 million. The cash proceeds from the sale were $7 million. The gain on the sale was $2 million.
2. The company did not issue any new bonds during the year.
3. The company paid a cash dividend during the year.
4. The company did not complete any common stock transactions during the year.

Required:

1. Using the indirect method, prepare a statement of cash flows for the year.
2. Assume that Blankley had sales of $3,900, net income of $190, and net cash provided by operating activities of $160 in the prior year (all numbers are stated in millions). Prepare a memo that summarizes your interpretations of Blankley's financial performance.

PROBLEM 14–12 Missing Data; Statement of Cash Flows [LO1, LO2]
Estes Company listed the *net changes* in its balance sheet accounts for the past year as follows:

	Debits > Credits by:	Credits > Debits by:
Cash	$ 51,000	
Accounts receivable	170,000	
Inventory		$ 63,000
Prepaid expenses	4,000	
Long-term loans to subsidiaries		80,000
Long-term investments	90,000	
Plant and equipment	340,000	
Accumulated depreciation		65,000
Accounts payable		48,000
Accrued liabilities	5,000	
Income taxes payable		9,000
Bonds payable		200,000
Common stock		120,000
Retained earnings		75,000
	$660,000	$660,000

The following additional information is available about last year's activities:

a. Net income for the year was $_?_.
b. The company sold equipment during the year for $35,000. The equipment originally cost the company $160,000, and it had $145,000 in accumulated depreciation at the time of sale.
c. The company declared and paid $10,000 in cash dividends during the year.
d. The beginning and ending balances in the Plant and Equipment and Accumulated Depreciation accounts are given below:

	Beginning	Ending
Plant and equipment	$2,850,000	$3,190,000
Accumulated depreciation	$975,000	$1,040,000

e. The balance in the Cash account at the beginning of the year was $109,000; the balance at the end of the year was $_?_.
f. If data are not given explaining the change in an account, make the most reasonable assumption as to the cause of the change.

Required:
Using the indirect method, prepare a statement of cash flows for the year.

PROBLEM 14–13 Prepare and Interpret a Statement of Cash Flows [LO1, LO2]
A comparative balance sheet for Alcorn Company containing data for the last two years is as follows:

Alcorn Company Comparative Balance Sheet	This Year	Last Year
Assets		
Current assets:		
Cash and cash equivalents	$ 71,000	$ 50,000
Accounts receivable	590,000	610,000
Inventory	608,000	420,000
Prepaid expenses	10,000	5,000
Total current assets	1,279,000	1,085,000
Property, plant, and equipment	2,370,000	1,800,000
Less accumulated depreciation	615,000	560,000
Net property, plant, and equipment	1,755,000	1,240,000
Long-term investments	80,000	130,000
Loans to subsidiaries	120,000	70,000
Total assets	$3,234,000	$2,525,000

Liabilities and Stockholders' Equity		
Current liabilities:		
Accounts payable	$ 870,000	$ 570,000
Accrued liabilities	25,000	42,000
Income taxes payable	133,000	118,000
Total current liabilities	1,028,000	730,000
Bonds payable	620,000	400,000
Total liabilities	1,648,000	1,130,000
Stockholders' equity:		
Common stock	1,090,000	1,000,000
Retained earnings	496,000	395,000
Total stockholders' equity	1,586,000	1,395,000
Total liabilities and stockholders' equity	$3,234,000	$2,525,000

The following additional information is available about the company's activities during this year:

a. The company declared and paid a cash dividend this year.
b. Bonds with a principal balance of $380,000 were repaid during this year.
c. Equipment was sold during this year for $70,000. The equipment had cost $130,000 and had $40,000 in accumulated depreciation on the date of sale.
d. Long-term investments were sold during the year for $110,000. These investments had cost $50,000 when purchased several years ago.
e. The subsidiaries did not repay any outstanding loans during the year.
f. Alcorn did not repurchase any of its own stock during the year.

The company reported net income this year as follows:

Sales		$3,000,000
Cost of goods sold		1,860,000
Gross margin		1,140,000
Selling and administrative expenses		930,000
Net operating income		210,000
Nonoperating items:		
Gain on sale of investments	$60,000	
Loss on sale of equipment	20,000	40,000
Income before taxes		250,000
Income taxes		80,000
Net income		$ 170,000

Required:

1. Using the indirect method, prepare a statement of cash flows for this year.
2. What problems relating to the company's activities are revealed by the statement of cash flows that you have prepared?

PROBLEM 14–14 Prepare and Interpret a Statement of Cash Flows; Free Cash Flow [LO1, LO2, LO3]

eXcel

Sharon Feldman, president of Allied Company, considers $20,000 to be a minimum cash balance for operating purposes. As can be seen from the following statements, only $15,000 in cash was available at the end of 2011. Because the company reported a large net income for the year, and also issued bonds and sold some long-term investments, the sharp decline in cash is puzzling to Ms. Feldman.

Allied Company Comparative Balance Sheet December 31, 2011, and 2010	2011	2010
Assets		
Current assets:		
Cash	$ 15,000	$ 33,000
Accounts receivable	200,000	210,000
Inventory	250,000	196,000
Prepaid expenses	7,000	15,000
Total current assets	472,000	454,000
Long-term investments	90,000	120,000
Plant and equipment	860,000	750,000
Less accumulated depreciation	210,000	190,000
Net plant and equipment	650,000	560,000
Total assets	$1,212,000	$1,134,000
Liabilities and Stockholders' Equity		
Current liabilities:		
Accounts payable	$ 175,000	$ 230,000
Accrued liabilities	8,000	15,000
Income taxes payable	42,000	39,000
Total current liabilities	225,000	284,000
Bonds payable	200,000	100,000
Total liabilities	425,000	384,000
Stockholders' equity:		
Common stock	595,000	600,000
Retained earnings	192,000	150,000
Total stockholders' equity	787,000	750,000
Total liabilities and stockholders' equity	$1,212,000	$1,134,000

Allied Company Income Statement For the Year Ended December 31, 2011		
Sales		$800,000
Cost of goods sold		500,000
Gross margin		300,000
Selling and administrative expenses		214,000
Net operating income		86,000
Nonoperating items:		
Gain on sale of investments	$20,000	
Loss on sale of equipment	(6,000)	14,000
Income before taxes		100,000
Income taxes		30,000
Net income		$ 70,000

The following additional information is available for the year 2011:

a. The company sold long-term investments with an original cost of $30,000 for $50,000 during the year.

b. Equipment that had cost $90,000 and on which there was $40,000 in accumulated depreciation was sold during the year for $44,000.

c. The company declared and paid a cash dividend during the year.

d. The stock of a dissident stockholder was repurchased for cash and retired during the year. No issues of stock were made.

e. The company did not retire any bonds during the year.

Required:

1. Using the indirect method, compute the net cash provided by operating activities for 2011.
2. Prepare a statement of cash flows for 2011.
3. Compute free cash flow for 2011.
4. Explain the major reasons for the decline in the company's cash balance.

Appendix 14A: The Direct Method of Determining the Net Cash Provided by Operating Activities

LEARNING OBJECTIVE 4
Use the direct method to determine the net cash provided by operating activities.

To compute the net cash provided by operating activities under the direct method, we must reconstruct the income statement on a cash basis from top to bottom. Exhibit 14A–1 shows the adjustments that must be made to adjust sales, expenses, and so forth, to a cash basis. To illustrate, we have included in the exhibit the Apparel, Inc., data from the chapter.

Note that the net cash provided by operating activities of $259 million agrees with the amount computed in the chapter by the indirect method. The two amounts agree because the direct and indirect methods are just different roads to the same destination. The investing and financing activities sections of the statement will be exactly the same as shown for the indirect method in Exhibit 14–10. The only difference between the indirect and direct methods is in the operating activities section.

Similarities and Differences in the Handling of Data

Although we arrive at the same destination under either the direct or indirect method, not all data are handled the same way in the two adjustment processes. Stop for a moment, flip back to the bottom half of Exhibit 14–7 on page 652 and compare the adjustments described in that exhibit to the adjustments made for the direct method in Exhibit 14A–1.

EXHIBIT 14A–1
General Model: Direct Method of Determining the Net Cash Provided by Operating Activities

Revenue or Expense Item	Add (+) or Deduct (−) to Adjust to a Cash Basis	Illustration—Apparel, Inc. (in millions)	
Sales (as reported)		$3,638	
Adjustments to a cash basis:			
Increase in accounts receivable	−		
Decrease in accounts receivable	+	+17	$3,655
Cost of goods sold (as reported)		2,469	
Adjustments to a cash basis:			
Increase in inventory	+	+49	
Decrease in inventory	−		
Increase in accounts payable	−	−44	
Decrease in accounts payable	+		2,474
Selling and administrative expenses (as reported)		941	
Adjustments to a cash basis:			
Increase in prepaid expenses	+		
Decrease in prepaid expenses	−		
Increase in accrued liabilities	−	−3	
Decrease in accrued liabilities	+		
Depreciation	−	−103	835
Income tax expense (as reported)		91	
Adjustments to a cash basis:			
Increase in income taxes payable	−	−4	
Decrease in income taxes payable	+		87
Net cash provided by operating activities			$ 259

The adjustments for accounts that affect revenue (which includes only accounts receivable in our example) are handled the same way in the two methods. In either case, increases in the accounts are subtracted and decreases are added. However, the adjustments for accounts that affect expenses (which include all remaining accounts in Exhibit 14–7) are handled in opposite ways in the indirect and direct methods. This is because under the indirect method the adjustments are made to *net income,* whereas under the direct method the adjustments are made to the *expense accounts* themselves.

To illustrate this difference, note the handling of inventory and depreciation in the indirect and direct methods. Under the indirect method (Exhibit 14–7 on page 652), an increase in the Inventory account ($49) is *subtracted* from net income in computing the amount of net cash provided by operating activities. Under the direct method (Exhibit 14A–1), an increase in inventory is *added* to cost of goods sold. The reason for the difference can be explained as follows: An increase in inventory means that the period's inventory purchases exceeded the cost of goods sold included in the income statement. Therefore, to adjust net income to a cash basis, we must either subtract this increase from net income (indirect method) or we must add this increase to cost of goods sold (direct method). Either way, we will end up with the same figure for net cash provided by operating activities. Similarly, depreciation is added to net income under the indirect method to cancel out its effect (Exhibit 14–8), whereas it is subtracted from selling and administrative expenses under the direct method to cancel out its effect (Exhibit 14A–1). These differences in the handling of data are true for all other expense items in the two methods.

In the matter of gains and losses on sale of assets, no adjustments are needed under the direct method. These gains and losses are simply ignored because they are not part of sales, cost of goods sold, selling and administrative expenses, or income taxes. Observe that in Exhibit 14A–1, Apparel's $3 million gain on the sale of the store is not listed as an adjustment in the operating activities section.

Special Rules—Direct and Indirect Methods

As stated earlier, when the direct method is used, U.S. GAAP and IFRS require a reconciliation between net income and the net cash provided by operating activities, as determined by the indirect method. Thus, *when a company elects to use the direct method, it must also present the indirect method* in a separate schedule accompanying the statement of cash flows.

On the other hand, if a company elects to use the indirect method to compute the net cash provided by operating activities, then it must also provide a special breakdown of data. The company must provide a separate disclosure of the amount of interest and the amount of income taxes paid during the year. This separate disclosure is required so that users can take the data provided by the indirect method and make estimates of what the amounts for sales, income taxes, and so forth, would have been if the direct method had been used instead.

Appendix 14A Exercises and Problems

All applicable exercises and problems are available with McGraw-Hill's *Connect™ Accounting*.

EXERCISE 14A–1 Net Cash Provided by Operating Activities [LO4]

Refer to the data for Strident Company in Exercise 14–2. The company's income statement for the most recent year was:

Sales	$1,000,000
Cost of goods sold	580,000
Gross margin	420,000
Selling and administrative expenses	300,000
Income before taxes	120,000
Income taxes	36,000
Net income	$ 84,000

Required:

Using the direct method (and the data from Exercise 14–2), convert the company's income statement to a cash basis.

EXERCISE 14A–2 Net Cash Provided by Operating Activities [LO4]

Refer to the data for Holly Company in Exercise 14–4.

Required:

Using the direct method, convert the company's income statement to a cash basis.

EXERCISE 14A–3 Adjust Net Income to a Cash Basis [LO4]

Refer to the data for Herald Company in Exercise 14–5.

Required:

Use the direct method to convert the company's income statement to a cash basis.

EXERCISE 14A–4 Net Cash Provided by Operating Activities [LO4]

Jones Company is a merchandiser whose income statement for Year 2 follows:

Sales	$2,000
Cost of goods sold	1,200
Gross margin	800
Selling and administrative expenses	500
Income before taxes	300
Income taxes	120
Net income	$ 180

The company's selling and administrative expense for Year 2 includes $80 of depreciation expense. Selected balance sheet accounts for Jones at the end of Years 1 and 2 are as shown on next page:

	Year 2	Year 1
Current Assets		
Accounts receivable	200	230
Inventory	160	180
Prepaid expenses	40	36
Current Liabilities		
Accounts payable	100	80
Accrued liabilities	15	20
Income taxes payable	90	70

Required:

1. Using the direct method, convert the company's income statement to a cash basis.
2. Assume that during Year 2 Jones has a $7,000 gain on the sale of investments and a $2,000 loss on the sale of equipment. Explain how these two transactions would affect your computations in (1) above.

PROBLEM 14A–5 Prepare a Statement of Cash Flows [LO1, LO4]
Refer to the financial statement data for Eaton Company in Problem 14–8.

Required:

1. Using the direct method, adjust the company's income statement for 2011 to a cash basis.
2. Using the information obtained in (1) above, along with an analysis of the remaining balance sheet accounts, prepare a statement of cash flows for 2011.

PROBLEM 14A–6 Prepare and Interpret a Statement of Cash Flows [LO1, LO4]
Refer to the financial statement data for Foxboro Company in Problem 14–9. Mike Perry, president of the company, considers $15,000 to be the minimum cash balance for operating purposes. As can be seen from the balance sheet data, only $11,000 in cash was available at the end of the current year. The sharp decline is puzzling to Mr. Perry, particularly because sales and profits are at a record high.

Required:

1. Using the direct method, adjust the company's income statement to a cash basis for Year 2.
2. Using the data from (1) above and other data from the problem as needed, prepare a statement of cash flows for Year 2.
3. Explain why cash declined so sharply during the year.

PROBLEM 14A–7 Prepare and Interpret a Statement of Cash Flows [LO1, LO4]
Refer to the financial statements for Allied Company in Problem 14–14. Because the Cash account decreased substantially during 2011, the company's executive committee is anxious to see how the income statement would appear on a cash basis.

Required:

1. Using the direct method, adjust the company's income statement for 2011 to a cash basis.
2. Using the data from (1) above and other data from the problem as needed, prepare a statement of cash flows for 2011.

Chapter 15

Financial Statement Analysis

Keeping an Eye on Dividends

BUSINESS FOCUS

When the economy sours, investors look closely at a company's ability to pay dividends. In 2008, 36 of the Standard & Poor's 500 companies suspended $33.3 billion of dividend payments. Citigroup sliced its dividend 41%, Washington Mutual (now part of JPMorgan Chase) reduced its quarterly dividend per share from 15 cents to a penny, and CIT Group slashed its dividend by 60%. Some companies increase their market appeal during difficult economic times by remaining committed to generous dividend payments. For example, in 2008 Adrian Darley, of Ignis Asset Management, recommended investing in Vivendi, France Telecom, and Deutsche Telekom because these companies committed to making scheduled dividend payments that ranged from 4.9% to 7.2% of their respective stock prices. ■

Sources: Andrea Tryphonides, "Dividends Replace P/Es as Stock Guides," *The Wall Street Journal,* November 24, 2008, p. C2; Tom Lauricella, "Keeping the Cash: Slowdown Triggers Stingy Dividends," *The Wall Street Journal,* April 21, 2008, p. C1; and Annelena Lobb, "Investors Lick Wounds from Dividend Cuts," *The Wall Street Journal,* November 7, 2008, p. C1.

LEARNING OBJECTIVES

After studying Chapter 15, you should be able to:

LO1 Prepare and interpret financial statements in comparative and common-size form.

LO2 Compute and interpret financial ratios that would be useful to a common stockholder.

LO3 Compute and interpret financial ratios that would be useful to a short-term creditor.

LO4 Compute and interpret financial ratios that would be useful to a long-term creditor.

All financial statements are historical documents. They summarize what *has happened* during a particular period. However, most users of financial statements are concerned with what *will happen* in the future. For example, stockholders are concerned with future earnings and dividends and creditors are concerned with the company's future ability to repay its debts. While financial statements are historical in nature, they can still provide users with valuable insights. These users rely on *financial statement analysis,* which involves examining trends in key financial data, comparing financial data across companies, and analyzing financial ratios to assess the financial health and future prospects of a company. In this chapter, we focus our attention on the most important ratios and other analytical tools that financial analysts use.

In addition to stockholders and creditors, managers are also vitally concerned with the financial ratios discussed in this chapter. First, the ratios provide indicators of how well the company and its business units are performing. Some of these ratios might be used in a balanced scorecard approach as discussed in an earlier chapter. The specific ratios selected depend on the company's strategy. For example, a company that wants to emphasize responsiveness to customers may closely monitor the inventory turnover ratio discussed later in this chapter. Second, because managers must report to stockholders and may want to raise funds from external sources, managers must pay attention to the financial ratios used by external investors.

Limitations of Financial Statement Analysis

This section discusses two limitations of financial statement analysis related to comparing financial data across companies and looking beyond ratios when formulating conclusions.

Comparing Financial Data across Companies

Comparisons of one company with another can provide valuable clues about the financial health of an organization. Unfortunately, differences in accounting methods between companies sometimes make it difficult to compare their financial data. For example, if one company values its inventories by the LIFO method and another company by the average cost method, then direct comparisons of their financial data such as inventory valuations and cost of goods sold may be misleading. Sometimes enough data are presented in footnotes to the financial statements to restate data to a comparable basis. Otherwise, the analyst should keep in mind any lack of comparability. Even with this limitation in mind, comparisons of key ratios with other companies and with industry averages often suggest avenues for further investigation.

Looking beyond Ratios

Ratios should not be viewed as an end, but rather as a *starting point.* They raise many questions and point to opportunities for further analysis, but they rarely answer any questions by themselves. In addition to ratios, analysts should evaluate industry trends, technological changes, changes in consumer tastes, changes in broad economic factors, and changes within the company itself.

Statements in Comparative and Common-Size Form

LEARNING OBJECTIVE 1
Prepare and interpret financial statements in comparative and common-size form.

An item on a balance sheet or income statement has little meaning by itself. Suppose a company's sales for a year were $250 million. In isolation, that is not particularly useful information. How does that stack up against last year's sales? How do the sales relate to the cost of goods sold? In making these kinds of comparisons, three analytical techniques are widely used:

1. Dollar and percentage changes on statements (*horizontal analysis*).
2. Common-size statements (*vertical analysis*).
3. Ratios.

The first and second techniques are discussed in this section; the third technique is discussed in the remainder of the chapter. Throughout the chapter, we will illustrate these analytical techniques using the financial statements of Brickey Electronics, a producer of specialized electronic components.

Dollar and Percentage Changes on Statements

Horizontal analysis (also known as **trend analysis**) involves analyzing financial data over time, such as computing year-to-year dollar and percentage changes within a set of financial statements. Exhibits 15–1 and 15–2 show Brickey Electronics' financial

EXHIBIT 15–1

Brickey Electronics
Comparative Balance Sheet
(dollars in thousands)

	This Year	Last Year	Increase (Decrease) Amount	Increase (Decrease) Percent
Assets				
Current assets:				
Cash	$ 1,200	$ 2,350	$(1,150)	(48.9)%*
Accounts receivable, net	6,000	4,000	2,000	50.0%
Inventory	8,000	10,000	(2,000)	(20.0)%
Prepaid expenses	300	120	180	150.0%
Total current assets	15,500	16,470	(970)	(5.9)%
Property and equipment:				
Land	4,000	4,000	0	0.0%
Buildings and equipment, net	12,000	8,500	3,500	41.2%
Total property and equipment	16,000	12,500	3,500	28.0%
Total assets	$31,500	$28,970	$ 2,530	8.7%
Liabilities and Stockholders' Equity				
Current liabilities:				
Accounts payable	$ 5,800	$ 4,000	$ 1,800	45.0%
Accrued payables	900	400	500	125.0%
Notes payable, short term	300	600	(300)	(50.0)%
Total current liabilities	7,000	5,000	2,000	40.0%
Long-term liabilities:				
Bonds payable, 8%	7,500	8,000	(500)	(6.3)%
Total liabilities	14,500	13,000	1,500	11.5%
Stockholders' equity:				
Preferred stock, $100 par, 6%	2,000	2,000	0	0.0%
Common stock, $12 par	6,000	6,000	0	0.0%
Additional paid-in capital	1,000	1,000	0	0.0%
Total paid-in capital	9,000	9,000	0	0.0%
Retained earnings	8,000	6,970	1,030	14.8%
Total stockholders' equity	17,000	15,970	1,030	6.4%
Total liabilities and stockholders' equity	$31,500	$28,970	$ 2,530	8.7%

*The changes between this year and last year are expressed as a percentage of the dollar amount for last year. For example, Cash decreased by $1,150 between this year and last year. This decrease expressed in percentage form is computed as follows: $1,150 ÷ $2,350 = 48.9%. Other percentage figures in this exhibit and Exhibit 15–2 are computed in the same way.

EXHIBIT 15–2

Brickey Electronics
Comparative Income Statement and Reconciliation of Retained Earnings
(dollars in thousands)

	This Year	Last Year	Increase (Decrease) Amount	Increase (Decrease) Percent
Sales	$52,000	$48,000	$4,000	8.3%
Cost of goods sold	36,000	31,500	4,500	14.3%
Gross margin	16,000	16,500	(500)	(3.0)%
Selling and administrative expenses:				
Selling expenses	7,000	6,500	500	7.7%
Administrative expenses	5,860	6,100	(240)	(3.9)%
Total selling and administrative expenses	12,860	12,600	260	2.1%
Net operating income	3,140	3,900	(760)	(19.5)%
Interest expense	640	700	(60)	(8.6)%
Net income before taxes	2,500	3,200	(700)	(21.9)%
Income taxes (30%)	750	960	(210)	(21.9)%
Net income	1,750	2,240	$ (490)	(21.9)%
Dividends to preferred stockholders, $6 per share (see Exhibit 15–1)	120	120		
Net income remaining for common stockholders	1,630	2,120		
Dividends to common stockholders, $1.20 per share	600	600		
Net income added to retained earnings	1,030	1,520		
Retained earnings, beginning of year	6,970	5,450		
Retained earnings, end of year	$ 8,000	$ 6,970		

statements in this *comparative form.* The dollar changes highlight the changes that are the most important economically; the percentage changes highlight the changes that are the most unusual.

Horizontal analysis can be even more useful when data from a number of years are used to compute *trend percentages.* To compute **trend percentages,** a base year is selected and the data for all years are stated as a percentage of that base year. To illustrate, consider the sales and net income of McDonald's Corporation, the world's largest food service retailer, with more than 31,000 restaurants worldwide:

	2008	2007	2006	2005	2004	2003	2002	2001	2000	1999
Sales (millions)	$23,522	$22,787	$20,895	$19,117	$17,889	$16,154	$14,527	$14,074	$13,794	$13,251
Net income (millions)	$4,313	$2,395	$3,544	$2,602	$2,279	$1,471	$893	$1,637	$1,977	$1,948

Be careful to note that the above data have been arranged with the most recent year on the left. This may be the opposite of what you are used to, but it is the way financial data are commonly displayed in annual reports and other sources. By simply looking at these data, you can see that sales increased every year, but the net income has not. However, recasting these data into trend percentages aids interpretation:

	2008	2007	2006	2005	2004	2003	2002	2001	2000	1999
Sales	176%	172%	158%	144%	135%	122%	110%	106%	104%	100%
Net income . . .	221%	123%	182%	134%	117%	76%	46%	84%	101%	100%

In the above table, both sales and net income have been restated as a percentage of the 1999 sales and net income. For example, the 2008 sales of $23,522 are 221% of the 1999 sales of $13,251. This trend analysis is particularly striking when the data are plotted as in Exhibit 15–3. McDonald's sales growth was impressive throughout the 10-year period, but net income was far more erratic. Notice that net income plummeted in 2001 and 2002, fully recovered by 2004, and then plummeted again in 2007. In 2008, McDonald's earned record sales and profits.

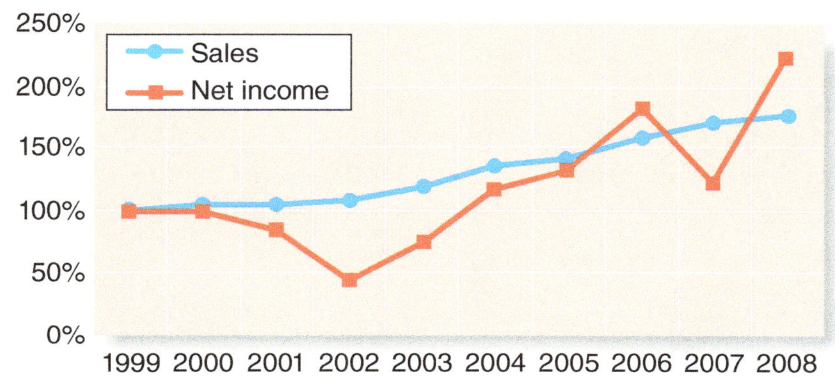

EXHIBIT 15–3
McDonald's Corporation: Trend Analysis of Sales and Net Income

Common-Size Statements

Horizontal analysis, which was discussed in the previous section, examines changes in financial statement accounts over time. **Vertical analysis** focuses on the relations among financial statement accounts at a given point in time. A **common-size financial statement** is a vertical analysis in which each financial statement account is expressed as a percentage. In income statements, all items are usually expressed as a percentage of sales. In balance sheets, all items are usually expressed as a percentage of total assets. Exhibit 15–4 contains Brickey Electronics' common-size balance sheet and Exhibit 15–5 contains its common-size income statement.

Notice from Exhibit 15–4 that placing all assets in common-size form clearly shows the relative importance of the current assets as compared to the noncurrent assets. It also shows that significant changes have taken place in the composition of the current assets over the last year. For example, accounts receivable have increased in relative importance and both cash and inventory have declined in relative importance. Judging from the sharp increase in accounts receivable, the deterioration in the cash balance may be a result of an inability to collect from customers.

Shifting now to the income statement, in Exhibit 15–5 the cost of goods sold as a percentage of sales increased from 65.6% last year to 69.2% this year. Or looking at this from a different viewpoint, the *gross margin percentage* declined from 34.4% last year to 30.8% this year. Managers and investment analysts often pay close attention to this measure of profitability. The **gross margin percentage** is computed as follows:

$$\text{Gross margin percentage} = \frac{\text{Gross margin}}{\text{Sales}}$$

The gross margin percentage should be more stable for retailing companies than for other companies because the cost of goods sold in retailing excludes fixed costs. When

EXHIBIT 15–4

Brickey Electronics
Common-Size Comparative Balance Sheet
(dollars in thousands)

	This Year	Last Year	Common-Size Percentages This Year	Common-Size Percentages Last Year
Assets				
Current assets:				
Cash	$ 1,200	$ 2,350	3.8%*	8.1%
Accounts receivable, net	6,000	4,000	19.0%	13.8%
Inventory	8,000	10,000	25.4%	34.5%
Prepaid expenses	300	120	1.0%	0.4%
Total current assets	15,500	16,470	49.2%	56.9%
Property and equipment:				
Land	4,000	4,000	12.7%	13.8%
Buildings and equipment, net	12,000	8,500	38.1%	29.3%
Total property and equipment	16,000	12,500	50.8%	43.1%
Total assets	$31,500	$28,970	100.0%	100.0%
Liabilities and Stockholders' Equity				
Current liabilities:				
Accounts payable	$ 5,800	$ 4,000	18.4%	13.8%
Accrued payables	900	400	2.9%	1.4%
Notes payable, short term	300	600	1.0%	2.1%
Total current liabilities	7,000	5,000	22.2%	17.3%
Long-term liabilities:				
Bonds payable, 8%	7,500	8,000	23.8%	27.6%
Total liabilities	14,500	13,000	46.0%	44.9%
Stockholders' equity:				
Preferred stock, $100, 6%	2,000	2,000	6.3%	6.9%
Common stock, $12 par	6,000	6,000	19.0%	20.7%
Additional paid-in capital	1,000	1,000	3.2%	3.5%
Total paid-in capital	9,000	9,000	28.6%	31.1%
Retained earnings	8,000	6,970	25.4%	24.0%
Total stockholders' equity	17,000	15,970	54.0%	55.1%
Total liabilities and stockholders' equity	$31,500	$28,970	100.0%	100.0%

*Each asset account on a common-size statement is expressed as a percentage of total assets, and each liability and equity account is expressed as a percentage of total liabilities and stockholders' equity. For example, the percentage figure above for this year's Cash balance is computed as follows: $1,200 ÷ $31,500 = 3.8%.

fixed costs are included in the cost of goods sold, the gross margin percentage should increase and decrease with sales volume. With increases in sales volume, fixed costs are spread across more units and the gross margin percentage should improve.

Common-size statements are particularly useful when comparing the performance of different companies. For example, in 2008 Burger King's net income was $190 million and McDonald's was $4,313 million. It would be naïve to look at these two numbers and conclude that McDonald's outperformed Burger King. McDonald's is much larger than Burger King, so its higher net income may be due solely to its larger size rather than its

EXHIBIT 15–5

Brickey Electronics
Common-Size Comparative Income Statement
(dollars in thousands)

	This Year	Last Year	Common-Size Percentages* This Year	Common-Size Percentages* Last Year
Sales	$52,000	$48,000	100.0%	100.0%
Cost of goods sold	36,000	31,500	69.2%	65.6%
Gross margin	16,000	16,500	30.8%	34.4%
Selling and administrative expenses:				
Selling expenses	7,000	6,500	13.5%	13.5%
Administrative expenses	5,860	6,100	11.3%	12.7%
Total selling and administrative expenses	12,860	12,600	24.7%	26.3%
Net operating income	3,140	3,900	6.0%	8.1%
Interest expense	640	700	1.2%	1.5%
Net income before taxes	2,500	3,200	4.8%	6.7%
Income taxes (30%)	750	960	1.4%	2.0%
Net income	$ 1,750	$ 2,240	3.4%	4.7%

*Note that the percentage figures for each year are expressed as a percentage of total sales for the year. For example, the percentage figure for this year's cost of goods sold is computed as follows: $36,000 ÷ $52,000 = 69.2%

managerial performance. To control for their different sizes, each company's net income can be expressed as a percentage of its sales revenues. Given that Burger King's sales revenues were $2,455 million and McDonald's were $23,522 million, Burger King's net income as a percentage of sales was 7.7% and McDonald's was 18.3%. These common-size percentages support the more informed conclusion that McDonald's performance compares favorably with Burger King's performance.

Ratio Analysis—The Common Stockholder

LEARNING OBJECTIVE 2
Compute and interpret financial ratios that would be useful to a common stockholder.

Common stockholders use financial ratios related to net income, dividends, and stockholders' equity to assess a company's financial performance. This section describes seven of those ratios. *All calculations will be performed for this year.*

Earnings per Share

An investor buys a stock in the hope of realizing a return in the form of either dividends or future increases in the value of the stock. Because earnings form the basis for dividend payments and future increases in the value of shares, investors are interested in a company's *earnings per share.*

Earnings per share is computed by dividing net income available for common stockholders by the average number of common shares outstanding during the year. "Net income available for common stockholders" is net income minus dividends paid to preferred stockholders.

$$\text{Earnings per share} = \frac{\text{Net income} - \text{Preferred dividends}}{\text{Average number of common shares outstanding}}$$

Using the data in Exhibits 15–1 and 15–2, Brickey Electronics' earnings per share would be computed as follows:

$$\text{Earnings per share} = \frac{\$1{,}750{,}000 - \$120{,}000}{(500{,}000 \text{ shares*} + 500{,}000 \text{ shares})/2} = \$3.26 \text{ per share}$$

*$6,000,000 total par value ÷ $12 par value per share = 500,000 shares.

IN BUSINESS

PENNIES MATTER!

In January 2005, on-line auctioneer eBay announced that its fourth quarter earnings for 2004 rose 44% compared to the same quarter from the prior year. While eBay's fourth quarter earnings of 30 cents per share matched the company's own forecast, it came up short of Wall Street analysts' forecasts by an average of four cents per share. Consequently, eBay's stock price tumbled $15.36 in less than 24 hours. Given that eBay had about 662 million shares of common stock outstanding at the time, the company's stockholders saw more than $10 billion of wealth evaporate in one day.

EBay's experience clearly illustrates how Wall Street investors exert pressure on publicly traded companies to deliver quarterly earnings that meet expectations. Critics often urge managers to take a more long-run point of view when making decisions, but managers face the cold, hard reality that if their quarterly earnings fall short of Wall Street's expectations, their stock price will probably take a beating.

Source: Mylene Mangalindan, "EBay Posts 44% Jump in Profit; Forecast Is Tepid," *The Wall Street Journal*, January 20, 2005, p. A3.

IN BUSINESS

DO ANALYSTS BIAS THEIR EARNINGS FORECASTS?

Research from Penn State University suggests that Wall Street analysts' earnings per share (EPS) forecasts are intentionally overstated. The study examined analysts' long-term (three to five years) and short-term (one year) EPS forecasts from 1984 through 2006. Over this 22-year period, the analysts' average estimated long-term EPS growth rate was 14.7% compared to an actual average long-term growth rate of 9.1%. The analysts' average short-term EPS projection was 13.8% compared with an actual annual EPS growth rate of 9.8%. The professors who conducted the study claim that "analysts are rewarded for biased forecasts by their employers, who want them to hype stocks so that the brokerage house can garner trading commissions and win underwriting deals."

Source: Andrew Edwards, "Study Suggests Bias in Analysts' Rosy Forecasts," *The Wall Street Journal*, March 21, 2008, p. C6.

Price-Earnings Ratio

The **price-earnings ratio** expresses the relationship between a stock's market price per share and its earnings per share. If we assume that Brickey Electronics' stock has a market price of $40 per share at the end of this year, then its price-earnings ratio would be computed as follows:

$$\text{Price-earnings ratio} = \frac{\text{Market price per share}}{\text{Earnings per share}}$$

$$= \frac{\$40 \text{ per share}}{\$3.26 \text{ per share}} = 12.3$$

The price-earnings ratio is 12.3; that is, the stock is selling for about 12.3 times its current earnings per share.

A high price-earnings ratio means that investors are willing to pay a premium for the company's stock—presumably because the company is expected to have higher than average future earnings growth. Conversely, if investors believe a company's future earnings growth prospects are limited, the company's price-earnings ratio would be relatively low. In the late 1990s, the stock prices of some dot.com companies—particularly those with little or no earnings—were selling at levels that resulted in huge and nearly unprecedented price-earnings ratios. Many commentators cautioned that these price-earnings ratios were unsustainable in the long run—and they were right. The stock prices of almost all dot.com companies subsequently crashed.

Dividend Payout and Yield Ratios

Investors in a company's stock make money in two ways—increases in the market value of the stock and dividends. In general, earnings should be retained in a company and not paid out in dividends as long as the rate of return on funds invested inside the company exceeds the rate of return that stockholders could earn on alternative investments outside the company. Therefore, companies with excellent prospects of profitable growth often pay little or no dividend. Companies with little opportunity for profitable growth, but with steady, dependable earnings, tend to pay out a higher percentage of their cash flow from operations as dividends.

The Dividend Payout Ratio

The **dividend payout ratio** quantifies the percentage of current earnings being paid out in dividends. This ratio is computed by dividing the dividends per share by the earnings per share for common stock:

$$\text{Dividend payout ratio} = \frac{\text{Dividends per share}}{\text{Earnings per share}}$$

For Brickey Electronics, the dividend payout ratio is computed as follows:

$$\text{Dividend payout ratio} = \frac{\$1.20 \text{ per share (see Exhibit 15–2)}}{\$3.26 \text{ per share}} = 36.8\%$$

There is no such thing as a "right" dividend payout ratio, although the ratio tends to be similar for companies within the same industry. As noted above, companies with ample growth opportunities at high rates of return tend to have low payout ratios, whereas companies with limited reinvestment opportunities tend to have higher payout ratios.

The Dividend Yield Ratio

The **dividend yield ratio** is computed by dividing the current dividends per share by the current market price per share:

$$\text{Dividend yield ratio} = \frac{\text{Dividends per share}}{\text{Market price per share}}$$

Because the market price for Brickey Electronics' stock is $40 per share, the dividend yield is computed as follows:

$$\text{Dividend yield ratio} = \frac{\$1.20 \text{ per share}}{\$40 \text{ per share}} = 3.0\%$$

The dividend yield ratio measures the rate of return (in the form of cash dividends only) that would be earned by an investor who buys common stock at the current market price. A low dividend yield ratio is neither bad nor good by itself.

IN BUSINESS

IBM RAISES ITS DIVIDEND BY 25%

In the early 1990s, IBM nearly collapsed and was forced to slash its dividend payout. However, since then the company has rebounded nicely. In 2008, IBM raised its quarterly dividend per share by 25%, thereby increasing the company's annual payout to about $2.5 billion. The 25% increase marked the 13th straight year that IBM has increased its dividend per share. The company also plans to spend $12 billion to buy back shares of its own stock. This transaction will reduce the number of shares of stock outstanding and increase the company's earnings per share.

Source: William M. Bulkeley, "IBM, Flush with Cash, Raises Dividend 25%," *The Wall Street Journal,* April 30, 2008, p. B7.

Return on Total Assets

The **return on total assets** is a measure of operating performance that is defined as follows:

$$\text{Return on total assets} = \frac{\text{Net income} + [\text{Interest expense} \times (1 - \text{Tax rate})]}{\text{Average total assets}}$$

Interest expense is added back to net income to show what earnings would have been if the company had no debt. With this adjustment, the return on total assets can be compared for companies with differing amounts of debt, or for a single company that has changed its mix of debt and equity over time. Notice that the interest expense is placed on an after-tax basis by multiplying it by the factor (1 − Tax rate).

The return on total assets for Brickey Electronics is computed as follows (from Exhibits 15–1 and 15–2):

$$\text{Return on total assets} = \frac{\$1,750,000 + [\$640,000 \times (1 - 0.30)]}{(\$31,500,000 + \$28,970,000)/2} = 7.3\%$$

Brickey Electronics has earned a return of 7.3% on average total assets employed over the last year.

Return on Common Stockholders' Equity

The **return on common stockholders' equity** is based on the book value of common stockholders' equity. It is computed as follows:

$$\begin{array}{c}\text{Return on common}\\ \text{stockholders' equity}\end{array} = \frac{\text{Net income} - \text{Preferred dividends}}{\text{Average common stockholders' equity}}$$

where

$$\begin{array}{c}\text{Average common}\\ \text{stockholders' equity}\end{array} = \begin{array}{c}\text{Average total stockholders' equity}\\ - \text{Average preferred stock}\end{array}$$

For Brickey Electronics, the return on common stockholders' equity is computed as follows:

$$\text{Average total stockholders' equity} = \frac{(\$17{,}000{,}000 + \$15{,}970{,}000)}{2} = \$16{,}485{,}000$$

$$\text{Average preferred stock} = \frac{(\$2{,}000{,}000 + \$2{,}000{,}000)}{2} = \$2{,}000{,}000$$

$$\text{Average common stockholders' equity} = \$16{,}485{,}000 - \$2{,}000{,}000 = \$14{,}485{,}000$$

$$\text{Return on common stockholders' equity} = \frac{\$1{,}750{,}000 - \$120{,}000}{\$14{,}485{,}000} = 11.3\%$$

Compare the return on common stockholders' equity above (11.3%) with the return on total assets computed in the preceding section (7.3%). Why is the return on common stockholders' equity so much higher? The answer lies in *financial leverage.*

Financial Leverage

Financial leverage results from the difference between the rate of return the company earns on investments in its own assets and the rate of return that the company must pay its creditors. If the company's rate of return on total assets exceeds the rate of return the company pays its creditors, *financial leverage is positive.* If the rate of return on total assets is less than the rate of return the company pays its creditors, *financial leverage is negative.*

We can see financial leverage in operation in the case of Brickey Electronics. Notice from Exhibit 15–1 that the company pays 8% interest on its bonds payable. The after-tax interest cost of these bonds is only 5.6% [8% interest rate × (1 − 0.30) = 5.6%]. As shown earlier, the company's after-tax return on total assets is 7.3%. Because the return on total assets of 7.3% is greater than the 5.6% after-tax interest cost of the bonds, leverage is positive, and the difference goes to the common stockholders. This explains in part why the return on common stockholders' equity of 11.3% is greater than the return on total assets of 7.3%. If financial leverage is positive, having some debt in the capital structure can substantially benefit common stockholders. For this reason, companies often try to maintain a level of debt that is considered to be normal within their industry.

Unfortunately, leverage is a two-edged sword. If assets do not earn a high enough return to cover the interest costs of debt and preferred stock dividends, then the common stockholder suffers. In that case, financial leverage is negative.

Book Value per Share

Book value per share measures the amount that would be distributed to holders of each share of common stock if all assets were sold at their balance sheet carrying amounts (i.e., book values) and if all creditors were paid off. Book value per share is based entirely on historical costs. The formula for computing it is:

$$\text{Book value per share} = \frac{\text{Total stockholders' equity} - \text{Preferred stock}}{\text{Number of common shares outstanding}}$$

The book value per share of Brickey Electronics' common stock is computed as follows:

$$\text{Book value per share} = \frac{\$17{,}000{,}000 - \$2{,}000{,}000}{500{,}000 \text{ shares}} = \$30 \text{ per share}$$

If this book value is compared with the $40 market value of Brickey Electronics' stock, then the stock may appear to be overpriced. However, as we discussed earlier, market prices reflect expectations about future earnings and dividends, whereas book value largely reflects the results of events that have occurred in the past. Ordinarily, the market value of a stock exceeds its book value. For example, in one year, Microsoft's common stock often traded at over 4 times its book value, and Coca-Cola's market value was over 17 times its book value.

Ratio Analysis—The Short-Term Creditor

LEARNING OBJECTIVE 3
Compute and interpret financial ratios that would be useful to a short-term creditor.

Short-term creditors, such as suppliers, want to be repaid on time. Therefore, they focus on the company's cash flows and on its *working capital* because these are the company's short-term primary sources of cash. *All calculations in this section will be performed for this year.*

Working Capital

The excess of current assets over current liabilities is known as **working capital.**

$$\text{Working capital} = \text{Current assets} - \text{Current liabilities}$$

The working capital for Brickey Electronics is computed as follows:

$$\text{Working capital} = \$15{,}500{,}000 - \$7{,}000{,}000 = \$8{,}500{,}000$$

Ample working capital provides some assurance to short-term creditors that they will be paid by the company. However, maintaining large amounts of working capital isn't free. Working capital must be financed with long-term debt and equity—both of which are expensive. Therefore, managers often want to minimize working capital.

A large and growing working capital balance may not be a good sign. For example, it could be the result of unwarranted growth in inventories. To put working capital into proper perspective, it should be supplemented with the following four ratios—the current ratio, the acid-test ratio, the accounts receivable turnover, and the inventory turnover—each of which will be discussed in turn.

Current Ratio

A company's working capital is frequently expressed in ratio form. A company's current assets divided by its current liabilities is known as the **current ratio:**

$$\text{Current ratio} = \frac{\text{Current assets}}{\text{Current liabilities}}$$

For Brickey Electronics, the current ratio is computed as follows:

$$\text{Current ratio} = \frac{\$15{,}500{,}000}{\$7{,}000{,}000} = 2.21$$

Although widely regarded as a measure of short-term debt-paying ability, the current ratio must be interpreted with great care. A *declining* ratio might be a sign of a deteriorating financial condition, or it might be the result of eliminating obsolete inventories or other stagnant current assets. An *improving* ratio might be the result of stockpiling inventory, or it might indicate an improving financial situation. In short, the current ratio is useful, but tricky to interpret.

The general rule of thumb calls for a current ratio of at least 2. However, many companies successfully operate with a current ratio below 2. The adequacy of a current ratio depends heavily on the *composition* of the assets. For example, as we see in the table on the next page, both Worthington Corporation and Greystone, Inc., have current ratios of 2. However, they are not in comparable financial condition. Greystone is more likely to have difficulty meeting its current financial obligations because almost all of its current assets consist of inventory rather than more liquid assets such as cash and accounts receivable.

	Worthington Corporation	Greystone, Inc.
Current assets:		
Cash	$ 25,000	$ 2,000
Accounts receivable, net	60,000	8,000
Inventory	85,000	160,000
Prepaid expenses	5,000	5,000
Total current assets (a)	$175,000	$175,000
Current liabilities (b)	$ 87,500	$ 87,500
Current ratio, (a) ÷ (b)	2	2

Acid-Test (Quick) Ratio

The **acid-test (quick) ratio** is a more rigorous test of a company's ability to meet its short-term debts than the current ratio. Inventories and prepaid expenses are excluded from total current assets, leaving only the more liquid (or "quick") assets to be divided by current liabilities.

$$\text{Acid-test ratio} = \frac{\text{Cash + Marketable securities + Accounts receivable + Short-term notes receivable}}{\text{Current liabilities}}$$

The acid-test ratio measures how well a company can meet its obligations without having to liquidate or depend too heavily on its inventory. Ideally, each dollar of liabilities should be backed by at least $1 of quick assets. However, acid-test ratios as low as 0.3 are common.

The acid-test ratio for Brickey Electronics is computed below:

$$\text{Acid-test ratio} = \frac{\$1{,}200{,}000 + \$0 + \$6{,}000{,}000 + \$0}{\$7{,}000{,}000} = 1.03$$

Although Brickey Electronics' acid-test ratio is within the acceptable range, an analyst might be concerned about several trends revealed in the company's balance sheet. Notice in Exhibit 15–1 that short-term debts are rising, while the cash balance is declining. Perhaps the lower cash balance is a result of the substantial increase in accounts receivable. In short, as with the current ratio, the acid-test ratio should be interpreted with one eye on its basic components.

Accounts Receivable Turnover

The *accounts receivable turnover* and *average collection period* ratios measure how quickly credit sales are converted into cash. The **accounts receivable turnover** is computed by dividing sales on account (i.e., credit sales) by the average accounts receivable balance for the year:

$$\text{Accounts receivable turnover} = \frac{\text{Sales on account}}{\text{Average accounts receivable balance}}$$

Assuming that all of Brickey Electronics' sales were on account, its accounts receivable turnover is computed as follows:

$$\text{Accounts receivable turnover} = \frac{\$52{,}000{,}000}{(\$6{,}000{,}000 + \$4{,}000{,}000)/2} = 10.4$$

The accounts receivable turnover can then be divided into 365 days to determine the average number of days required to collect an account (known as the **average collection period**).

$$\text{Average collection period} = \frac{365 \text{ days}}{\text{Accounts receivable turnover}}$$

The average collection period for Brickey Electronics is computed as follows:

$$\text{Average collection period} = \frac{365 \text{ days}}{10.4} = 35 \text{ days}$$

This means that on average it takes 35 days to collect a credit sale. Whether this is good or bad depends on the credit terms Brickey Electronics is offering its customers. Many customers will tend to withhold payment for as long as the credit terms allow. If the credit terms are 30 days, then a 35-day average collection period would usually be viewed as very good. On the other hand, if the company's credit terms are 10 days, then a 35-day average collection period is worrisome. A long collection period may result from having too many old uncollectible accounts, failing to bill promptly or follow up on late accounts, lax credit checks, and so on. In practice, average collection periods ranging all the way from 10 days to 180 days are common, depending on the industry.

Inventory Turnover

The **inventory turnover ratio** measures how many times a company's inventory has been sold and replaced during the year. It is computed by dividing the cost of goods sold by the average level of inventory [(Beginning inventory balance + Ending inventory balance) ÷ 2]:

$$\text{Inventory turnover} = \frac{\text{Cost of goods sold}}{\text{Average inventory balance}}$$

Brickey's inventory turnover is computed as follows:

$$\text{Inventory turnover} = \frac{\$36{,}000{,}000}{(\$8{,}000{,}000 + \$10{,}000{,}000)/2} = 4.0$$

The number of days needed on average to sell the entire inventory (called the **average sale period)** can be computed by dividing 365 by the inventory turnover:

$$\text{Average sale period} = \frac{365 \text{ days}}{\text{Inventory turnover}}$$

$$= \frac{365 \text{ days}}{4 \text{ times}} = 91\tfrac{1}{4} \text{ days}$$

The average sale period varies from industry to industry. Grocery stores, with significant perishable stocks, tend to turn over their inventory quickly. On the other hand, jewelry stores tend to turn over their inventory slowly. In practice, average sales periods of 10 days to 90 days are common, depending on the industry.

A company whose inventory turnover ratio is much slower than the average for its industry may have too much inventory or the wrong sorts of inventory. Some managers argue that they must buy in large quantities to take advantage of quantity discounts. But these discounts must be compared to the added costs of insurance, taxes, financing, and risks of obsolescence and deterioration that result from carrying added inventories.

Inventory turnover should increase in companies that adopt Lean Production. If properly implemented, Lean Production should result in both a decrease in inventories and an increase in sales due to better customer service.

Ratio Analysis—The Long-Term Creditor

LEARNING OBJECTIVE 4
Compute and interpret financial ratios that would be useful to a long-term creditor.

Long-term creditors are concerned with a company's ability to repay its loans over the long run. For example, if a company paid out all of its available cash in the form of dividends, then nothing would be left to pay back creditors. Consequently, creditors often seek protection by requiring that borrowers agree to various restrictive covenants, or rules. These restrictive covenants typically include restrictions on dividend payments as well as rules stating that the company must maintain certain financial ratios at specified levels. Although restrictive covenants are widely used, they do not ensure that creditors will be paid when loans come due. The company still must generate sufficient earnings to cover payments.

Times Interest Earned Ratio

The most common measure of a company's ability to provide protection to its long-term creditors is the **times interest earned ratio.** It is computed by dividing earnings before interest expense and income taxes (i.e., net operating income) by interest expense:

$$\text{Times interest earned} = \frac{\text{Earnings before interest expense and income taxes}}{\text{Interest expense}}$$

For Brickey Electronics, the times interest earned ratio for this year is computed as follows:

$$\text{Times interest earned} = \frac{\$3{,}140{,}000}{\$640{,}000} = 4.9$$

The times interest earned ratio is based on earnings before interest expense and income taxes because that is the amount of earnings that is available for making interest payments. Interest expenses are deducted *before* income taxes are determined; creditors have first claim on the earnings before taxes are paid.

A times interest earned ratio of less than 1 is inadequate because interest expense exceeds the earnings that are available for paying that interest. In contrast, a times interest earned ratio of 2 or more may be considered sufficient to protect long-term creditors.

IN BUSINESS

HOME BUILDERS FACE A LIQUIDITY CRISIS

The economic downturn took a toll on the home building industry. Many builders, who borrowed large amounts of money to buy land during the earlier housing boom, slashed home prices in an attempt to generate cash to make their interest payments. The share prices of home builders Tousa, Standard Pacific, and WCI Communities, Inc., dropped 98%, 88%, and 82%, respectively. WCI, a high-rise condominium builder in coastal Florida, failed to maintain the minimum times interest earned ratio required in its loan agreement. The uncertainty surrounding the Florida condo market made it unclear if WCI would be able to pay its $120 million of interest expense in the coming year.

Source: Michael Corkery, "Beware of Liquidity Traps in Builders," *The Wall Street Journal,* November 29, 2007, pp. C1–C2.

Debt-to-Equity Ratio

Long-term creditors are also concerned with a company's ability to keep a reasonable balance between its debt and equity. This balance is measured by the **debt-to-equity ratio**:

$$\text{Debt-to-equity ratio} = \frac{\text{Total liabilties}}{\text{Stockholders' equity}}$$

Brickey's debt-to-equity ratio for this year is computed as follows:

$$\text{Debt-to-equity ratio} = \frac{\$14{,}500{,}000}{\$17{,}000{,}000} = 0.85$$

The debt-to-equity ratio indicates the relative proportions of debt and equity on the company's balance sheet. At the end of this year, Brickey Electronics' creditors were providing 85 cents for each \$1 being provided by stockholders.

Creditors and stockholders have different views about the optimal debt-to-equity ratio. Ordinarily, stockholders would like a lot of debt to take advantage of positive financial leverage. On the other hand, because equity represents the excess of total assets over total liabilities, and hence a buffer of protection for the creditors, creditors would like to see less debt and more equity.

In practice, debt-to-equity ratios from 0.0 (no debt) to 3.0 are common. Generally speaking, in industries with little financial risk, creditors tolerate high debt-to-equity ratios. In industries with more financial risk, creditors demand lower debt-to-equity ratios.

IN BUSINESS

SMALL BUSINESS STRUGGLES TO MANAGE ITS DEBT

Chuck Bidwell and Jennifer Guarino bought J.W. Hulme Company to expand the business into luxury briefcases, backpacks, and handbags. The co-owners planned to grow the company's catalog mailing list tenfold to 10,000 households while doubling its product assortment to 250 items. To finance this growth strategy, the company borrowed more than \$2 million, causing its debt-to-equity ratio to jump from 2.94 to 5.53. When the company subsequently sought \$250,000 in additional loans to finance its next round of catalogs, lenders were apprehensive. The company's most recent annual sales of \$1.5 million fell \$500,000 short of the owners' projections. Furthermore, inventory levels had ballooned to \$1 million signaling declining demand for the company's products.

Source: Julie Jargon, "On Front Lines of Debt Crisis, Luggage Maker Fights for Life," *The Wall Street Journal*, January 9, 2009, pp. A1 and A8.

Summary of Ratios and Sources of Comparative Ratio Data

Exhibit 15–6 (on the next page) contains a summary of the ratios discussed in this chapter. The formula for each ratio and a summary comment on each ratio's significance are included in the exhibit.

Exhibit 15–7 (page 696) contains a listing of public sources that provide comparative ratio data organized by industry. These sources are used extensively by managers, investors, and analysts. The EDGAR database listed in Exhibit 15–7 is a particularly rich source of data. It contains copies of all reports filed by companies with the SEC since about 1995—including annual reports filed as Form 10-K.

EXHIBIT 15–6
Summary of Ratios

Ratio	Formula	Significance
Gross margin percentage	Gross margin ÷ Sales	A broad measure of profitability
Earnings per share (of common stock)	(Net income − Preferred dividends) ÷ Average number of common shares outstanding	Affects the market price per share, as reflected in the price-earnings ratio
Price-earnings ratio	Market price per share ÷ Earnings per share	An index of whether a stock is relatively cheap or relatively expensive in relation to current earnings
Dividend payout ratio	Dividends per share ÷ Earnings per share	An index showing whether a company pays out most of its earnings in dividends or reinvests the earnings internally
Dividend yield ratio	Dividends per share ÷ Market price per share	Shows the return in terms of cash dividends being provided by a stock
Return on total assets	{Net income + [Interest expense × (1 − Tax rate)]} ÷ Average total assets	Measures how well assets have been employed by management
Return on common stockholders' equity	(Net income − Preferred dividends) ÷ (Average total stockholders' equity − Average preferred stock)	When compared to the return on total assets, measures the extent to which financial leverage is working for or against common stockholders
Book value per share	(Total stockholders' equity − Preferred stock) ÷ Number of common shares outstanding	Measures the amount that would be distributed to common stockholders if all assets were sold at their balance sheet carrying amounts and if all creditors were paid off
Working capital	Current assets − Current liabilities	Measures the company's ability to repay current liabilities using only current assets
Current ratio	Current assets ÷ Current liabilities	Test of short-term debt-paying ability
Acid-test ratio	(Cash + Marketable securities + Accounts receivable + Short-term notes receivable) ÷ Current liabilities	Test of short-term debt-paying ability without having to rely on inventory
Accounts receivable turnover	Sales on account ÷ Average accounts receivable balance	Measures how many times a company's accounts receivable have been turned into cash during the year
Average collection period	365 days ÷ Accounts receivable turnover	Measures the average number of days taken to collect an account receivable
Inventory turnover	Cost of goods sold ÷ Average inventory balance	Measures how many times a company's inventory has been sold during the year
Average sale period	365 days ÷ Inventory turnover	Measures the average number of days taken to sell the inventory one time
Times interest earned	Earnings before interest expense and income taxes ÷ Interest expense	Measures the company's ability to make interest payments
Debt-to-equity ratio	Total liabilities ÷ Stockholders' equity	Measures the amount of assets being provided by creditors for each dollar of assets being provided by the stockholders

EXHIBIT 15–7
Sources of Financial Ratios

Source	Content
Almanac of Business and Industrial Financial Ratios, Aspen Publishers; published annually	An exhaustive source that contains common-size income statements and financial ratios by industry and by the size of companies within each industry.
AMA Annual Statement Studies, Risk Management Association; published annually.	A widely used publication that contains common-size statements and financial ratios on individual companies; the companies are arranged by industry.
EDGAR, Securities and Exchange Commission; website that is continually updated; www.sec.gov	An exhaustive Internet database that contains reports filed by companies with the SEC; these reports can be downloaded.
FreeEdgar, EDGAR Online, Inc.; website that is continually updated; www.freeedgar.com	A site that allows you to search SEC filings; financial information can be downloaded directly into Excel worksheets.
Hoover's Online, Hoovers, Inc.; website that is continually updated; www.hoovers.com	A site that provides capsule profiles for 10,000 U.S. companies with links to company websites, annual reports, stock charts, news articles, and industry information.
Industry Norms & Key Business Ratios, Dun & Bradstreet; published annually	Fourteen commonly used financial ratios are computed for over 800 major industry groupings.
Mergent Industrial Manual and Mergent Bank and Finance Manual; published annually	An exhaustive source that contains financial ratios on all companies listed on the New York Stock Exchange, the American Stock Exchange, and regional American exchanges.
Standard & Poor's Industry Survey, Standard & Poor's; published annually	Various statistics, including some financial ratios, are given by industry and for leading companies within each industry grouping.

IN BUSINESS

XBRL: THE NEXT GENERATION OF FINANCIAL REPORTING

The Securities and Exchange Commission (SEC) encourages companies to submit financial reports using a computer code known as Extensible Business Reporting Language, or XBRL for short. XBRL is a "financial reporting derivation of Extensible Markup Language, or XML—a framework that establishes individual 'tags' for elements in structured documents, allowing specific elements to be immediately accessed and aggregated."

XBRL dramatically improves the financial reporting process in two ways. First, data are tagged in accordance with a generally accepted framework. This simplifies the process of making apples-to-apples comparisons of financial results across companies. For example, "many of the components of a 'property, plant, and equipment' listing on a balance sheet . . . may be described differently by different companies, but when tagged in XBRL, a straight comparison becomes much simpler."

Second, XBRL simplifies the exchange of financial data. Without XBRL, a company's financial data are typically stored in a format that is unique to that company's specific financial software application and that cannot be easily read by other financial software. This problem is overcome with XBRL because the tagged data become "independent of the originating application and can readily be shared with any application that recognizes XBRL. This feature of XBRL makes the markup language very attractive for government regulators and financial analysts."

Sources: Glenn Cheney, "U.S. gets its XBRL in gear: SEC, FDIC OK tagged data," *Accounting Today,* March 14–April 3, 2005, pp. 26–27; Neal Hannon, "XBRL Fundamentals," *Strategic Finance,* April 2005, pp. 57–58; and Ghostwriter, "From Tags to Riches," *CFO-IT,* Spring 2005, pp. 13–14.

Summary

The data contained in financial statements represent a quantitative summary of a company's operations and activities. Someone who is skillful at analyzing these statements can learn much about a company's strengths, weaknesses, emerging problems, operating efficiency, profitability, and so forth.

Many techniques are available to analyze financial statements and to assess the direction and importance of trends and changes. In this chapter, we have discussed three such analytical techniques—dollar and percentage changes in statements (horizontal analysis), common-size statements (vertical analysis), and ratio analysis. Refer to Exhibit 15–6 for a detailed listing of the ratios.

Review Problem: Selected Ratios and Financial Leverage

Starbucks Corporation is the leading retailer and roaster of specialty coffee in North America, selling freshly brewed coffee, pastries, and coffee beans. Data (slightly modified) from the company's financial statements are as follows:

Starbucks Corporation
Comparative Balance Sheet
(dollars in millions)

	This Year	Last Year
Assets		
Current assets:		
Cash	$ 281	$ 313
Marketable securities	157	141
Accounts receivable	288	224
Inventories	692	636
Other current assets	278	216
Total current assets	1,696	1,530
Property and equipment, net	2,890	2,288
Other assets	758	611
Total assets	$5,344	$4,429
Liabilities and Stockholders' Equity		
Current liabilities:		
Accounts payable	$391	$341
Short-term bank loans	710	700
Accrued payables	757	662
Other current liabilities	298	233
Total current liabilities	2,156	1,936
Long-term liabilities	904	265
Total liabilities	3,060	2,201
Stockholders' equity:		
Preferred stock	0	0
Common stock and additional paid-in capital	40	40
Retained earnings	2,244	2,188
Total stockholders' equity	2,284	2,228
Total liabilities and stockholders' equity	$5,344	$4,429

Starbucks Corporation Income Statement (dollars in millions)	This Year
Sales	$9,411
Cost of goods sold	3,999
Gross margin	5,412
Selling and administrative expenses:	
Store operating expenses	3,216
Other operating expenses	294
Depreciation and amortization	467
General and administrative expenses	489
Total selling and administrative expenses	4,466
Net operating income	946
Plus interest and other income	110
Interest expense	0
Net income before taxes	1,056
Income taxes (about 36%)	384
Net income	$ 672

Required:

1. Compute the return on total assets.
2. Compute the return on common stockholders' equity.
3. Is Starbucks' financial leverage positive or negative? Explain.
4. Compute the current ratio.
5. Compute the acid-test ratio.
6. Compute the inventory turnover.
7. Compute the average sale period.
8. Compute the debt-to-equity ratio.

Solution to Review Problem

1. Return on total assets:

$$\text{Return on total assets} = \frac{\text{Net income} + [\text{Interest expense} \times (1 - \text{Tax rate})]}{\text{Average total assets}}$$

$$= \frac{\$672 + [\$0 \times (1 - 0.36)]}{(\$5{,}344 + \$4{,}429)/2} = 13.8\% \text{ (rounded)}$$

2. Return on common stockholders' equity:

$$\text{Return on common stockholders' equity} = \frac{\text{Net income} - \text{Preferred dividends}}{\text{Average common stockholders' equity}}$$

$$= \frac{\$672 - \$0}{(\$2{,}284 + \$2{,}228)/2} = 29.8\% \text{ (rounded)}$$

3. The company has positive financial leverage because the return on common stockholders' equity of 29.8% is greater than the return on total assets of 13.8%. The positive financial leverage was obtained from current and long-term liabilities.
4. Current ratio:

$$\text{Current ratio} = \frac{\text{Current assets}}{\text{Current liabilities}}$$

$$= \frac{\$1{,}696}{\$2{,}156} = 0.79 \text{ (rounded)}$$

5. Acid-test ratio:

$$\text{Acid-test ratio} = \frac{\text{Cash} + \text{Marketable securities} + \text{Accounts receivable} + \text{Short-term notes receivable}}{\text{Current liabilities}}$$

$$= \frac{\$281 + \$157 + \$288 + \$0}{\$2{,}156} = 0.34 \text{ (rounded)}$$

6. Inventory turnover:

$$\text{Inventory turnover} = \frac{\text{Cost of goods sold}}{\text{Average inventory balance}}$$

$$= \frac{\$3{,}999}{(\$692 + \$636)/2} = 6.02 \text{ (rounded)}$$

7. Average sale period:

$$\text{Average sale period} = \frac{365 \text{ days}}{\text{Inventory turnover}}$$

$$= \frac{365 \text{ days}}{6.02} = 61 \text{ days (rounded)}$$

8. Debt-to-equity ratio:

$$\text{Debt-to-equity ratio} = \frac{\text{Total liabilities}}{\text{Stockholders' equity}}$$

$$= \frac{\$2{,}156 + \$904}{\$2{,}284} = 1.34 \text{ (rounded)}$$

Glossary

(Note: Definitions and formulas for all financial ratios are shown in Exhibit 15–6. These definitions and formulas are not repeated here.)

Common-size financial statements A statement that shows the items appearing on it in percentage form as well as in dollar form. On the income statement, the percentages are based on total sales revenue; on the balance sheet, the percentages are based on total assets. (p. 683)

Financial leverage A difference between the rate of return on assets and the rate paid to creditors. (p. 689)

Horizontal analysis A side-by-side comparison of two or more years' financial statements. (p. 681)

Trend analysis See *Horizontal analysis.* (p. 681)

Trend percentages Several years of financial data expressed as a percentage of performance in a base year. (p. 682)

Vertical analysis The presentation of a company's financial statements in common-size form. (p. 683)

Questions

15–1 Distinguish between horizontal and vertical analysis of financial statement data.

15–2 What is the basic purpose for examining trends in a company's financial ratios and other data? What other kinds of comparisons might an analyst make?

15–3 Assume that two companies in the same industry have equal earnings. Why might these companies have different price-earnings ratios? If a company has a price-earnings ratio of 20 and reports earnings per share for the current year of $4, at what price would you expect to find the stock selling on the market?

15–4 Would you expect a company in a rapidly growing technological industry to have a high or low dividend payout ratio?

15–5 What is meant by the dividend yield on a common stock investment?

15–6 What is meant by the term financial leverage?

15–7 The president of a plastics company was quoted in a business journal as stating, "We haven't had a dollar of interest-paying debt in over 10 years. Not many companies can say that." As a stockholder in this company, how would you feel about its policy of not taking on debt?

15–8 If a stock's market value exceeds its book value, then the stock is overpriced. Do you agree? Explain.

15–9 A company seeking a line of credit at a bank was turned down. Among other things, the bank stated that the company's 2 to 1 current ratio was not adequate. Give reasons why a 2 to 1 current ratio might not be adequate.

Multiple-choice questions are provided on the text website at www.mhhe.com/garrison14e.

Exercises

connect ACCOUNTING

All applicable exercises are available with McGraw-Hill's *Connect™ Accounting.*

EXERCISE 15–1 Common-Size Income Statement [LO1]

A comparative income statement is given below for Ryder Company:

Ryder Company Comparative Income Statement	This Year	Last Year
Sales	$5,000,000	$4,000,000
Cost of goods sold	3,160,000	2,400,000
Gross margin	1,840,000	1,600,000
Selling and administrative expenses:		
Selling expenses	900,000	700,000
Administrative expenses	680,000	584,000
Total selling and administrative expenses	1,580,000	1,284,000
Net operating income	260,000	316,000
Interest expense	70,000	40,000
Net income before taxes	$ 190,000	$ 276,000

The president is concerned that net income is down even though sales have increased during the year. The president is also concerned that administrative expenses have increased because the company made a concerted effort to cut waste out of the organization.

Required:

1. Express each year's income statement in common-size percentages. Carry computations to one decimal place.
2. Comment briefly on the changes between the two years.

EXERCISE 15–2 Financial Ratios for Common Stockholders [LO2]

Comparative financial statements for Heritage Antiquing Services for the fiscal year ending December 31 appear on the following page. The company did not issue any new common or preferred stock during the year. A total of 600 thousand shares of common stock were outstanding. The interest rate on the bond payable was 14%, the income tax rate was 40%, and the dividend per share of common stock was $0.75. The market value of the company's common stock at the end of the year was $26. All of the company's sales are on account.

Heritage Antiquing Services Comparative Balance Sheet (dollars in thousands)	This Year	Last Year
Assets		
Current assets:		
Cash	$ 1,080	$ 1,210
Accounts receivable, net	9,000	6,500
Inventory	12,000	10,600
Prepaid expenses	600	500
Total current assets	22,680	18,810
Property and equipment:		
Land	9,000	9,000
Buildings and equipment, net	36,800	38,000
Total property and equipment	45,800	47,000
Total assets	$68,480	$65,810
Liabilities and Stockholders' Equity		
Current liabilities:		
Accounts payable	$18,500	$17,400
Accrued payables	900	700
Notes payable, short term	—	100
Total current liabilities	19,400	18,200
Long-term liabilities:		
Bonds payable	8,000	8,000
Total liabilities	27,400	26,200
Stockholders' equity:		
Preferred stock	1,000	1,000
Common stock	2,000	2,000
Additional paid-in capital	4,000	4,000
Total paid-in capital	7,000	7,000
Retained earnings	34,080	32,610
Total stockholders' equity	41,080	39,610
Total liabilities and stockholders' equity	$68,480	$65,810

Heritage Antiquing Services Comparative Income Statement and Reconciliation (dollars in thousands)	This Year	Last Year
Sales	$66,000	$64,000
Cost of goods sold	43,000	42,000
Gross margin	23,000	22,000
Selling and administrative expenses:		
Selling expenses	11,500	11,000
Administrative expenses	7,400	7,000
Total selling and administrative expenses	18,900	18,000
Net operating income	4,100	4,000
Interest expense	800	800
Net income before taxes	3,300	3,200
Income taxes	1,320	1,280
Net income	1,980	1,920
Dividends to preferred stockholders	60	400
Net income remaining for common stockholders	1,920	1,520
Dividends to common stockholders	450	450
Net income added to retained earnings	1,470	1,070
Retained earnings, beginning of year	32,610	31,540
Retained earnings, end of year	$34,080	$32,610

Required:
Compute the following financial ratios for common stockholders for this year:
1. Gross margin percentage.
2. Earnings per share of common stock.
3. Price-earnings ratio.
4. Dividend payout ratio.
5. Dividend yield ratio.
6. Return on total assets.
7. Return on common stockholders' equity.
8. Book value per share.

EXERCISE 15–3 Financial Ratios for Short-Term Creditors [LO3]
Refer to the data in Exercise 15–2 for Heritage Antiquing Services.

Required:
Compute the following financial data for short-term creditors for this year:
1. Working capital.
2. Current ratio.
3. Acid-test ratio.
4. Accounts receivable turnover.
5. Average collection period.
6. Inventory turnover.
7. Average sale period.

EXERCISE 15–4 Financial Ratios for Long-Term Creditors [LO4]
Refer to the data in Exercise 15–2 for Heritage Antiquing Services.

Required:
Compute the following financial ratios for long-term creditors for this year:
1. Times interest earned ratio.
2. Debt-to-equity ratio.

EXERCISE 15–5 Selected Financial Measures for Short-Term Creditors [LO3]
Rightway Products had a current ratio of 2.5 on June 30 of the current year. On that date, the company's assets were as follows:

Cash	$ 80,000
Accounts receivable, net	460,000
Inventory	750,000
Prepaid expenses	10,000
Plant and equipment, net	1,900,000
Total assets	$3,200,000

Required:
1. What was the company's working capital on June 30?
2. What was the company's acid-test ratio on June 30?
3. The company paid an account payable of $100,000 immediately after June 30.
   a. What effect did this transaction have on working capital? Show computations.
   b. What effect did this transaction have on the current ratio? Show computations.

EXERCISE 15–6 Selected Financial Ratios [LO3, LO4]
Recent financial statements for Madison Company follow:

Madison Company Balance Sheet June 30		
Assets		
Current assets:		
Cash		$ 21,000
Accounts receivable, net		160,000
Merchandise inventory		300,000
Prepaid expenses		9,000
Total current assets		490,000
Plant and equipment, net		810,000
Total assets		$1,300,000
Liabilities and Stockholders' Equity		
Liabilities:		
Current liabilities		$ 200,000
Bonds payable, 10%		300,000
Total liabilities		500,000
Stockholders' equity:		
Common stock, $5 par value	$100,000	
Retained earnings	700,000	
Total stockholders' equity		800,000
Total liabilities and stockholders' equity		$1,300,000

Madison Company Income Statement For the Year Ended June 30	
Sales	$2,100,000
Cost of goods sold	1,260,000
Gross margin	840,000
Selling and administrative expenses	660,000
Net operating income	180,000
Interest expense	30,000
Net income before taxes	150,000
Income taxes	45,000
Net income	$ 105,000

Account balances at the beginning of the company's fiscal year were: accounts receivable, $140,000; and inventory, $260,000. All sales were on account.

Required:

Compute financial ratios as follows:

1. Gross margin percentage.
2. Current ratio.
3. Acid-test ratio.
4. Average collection period.
5. Average sale period.
6. Debt-to-equity ratio.
7. Times interest earned.
8. Book value per share.

EXERCISE 15–7 Selected Financial Ratios for Common Stockholders [LO2]

Refer to the financial statements for Madison Company in Exercise 15–6. In addition to the data in these statements, assume that Madison Company paid dividends of $3.15 per share during the year. Also assume that the company's common stock had a market price of $63 per share on June 30 and that there was no change in the number of outstanding shares of common stock during the fiscal year.

Required:

Compute the following:

1. Earnings per share.
2. Dividend payout ratio.
3. Dividend yield ratio.
4. Price-earnings ratio.

EXERCISE 15–8 Selected Financial Ratios for Common Stockholders [LO2]

Refer to the financial statements for Madison Company in Exercise 15–6. Assets at the beginning of the year totaled $1,100,000, and the stockholders' equity totaled $725,000.

Required:

Compute the following:

1. Return on total assets.
2. Return on common stockholders' equity.
3. Was financial leverage positive or negative for the year? Explain.

EXERCISE 15–9 Selected Financial Ratios for Common Stockholders [LO2]

Selected financial data from the September 30 year-end statements of Kosanka Company are given below:

Total assets	$5,000,000
Long-term debt (12% interest rate)	$750,000
Preferred stock, $100 par, 7%	$800,000
Total stockholders' equity	$3,100,000
Interest paid on long-term debt	$90,000
Net income	$470,000

Total assets at the beginning of the year were $4,800,000; total stockholders' equity was $2,900,000. There has been no change in preferred stock during the year. The company's tax rate is 30%.

Required:

1. Compute the return on total assets.
2. Compute the return on common stockholders' equity.
3. Is the company's financial leverage positive or negative? Explain.

EXERCISE 15–10 Trend Percentages [LO1]

Starkey Company's sales, current assets, and current liabilities (all in thousands of dollars) have been reported as follows over the last five years (Year 5 is the most recent year):

	Year 5	Year 4	Year 3	Year 2	Year 1
Sales	$5,625	$5,400	$4,950	$4,725	$4,500
Current assets:					
Cash	$ 64	$ 72	$ 84	$ 88	$ 80
Accounts receivable	560	496	432	416	400
Inventory	896	880	816	864	800
Total current assets	$1,520	$1,448	$1,332	$1,368	$1,280
Current liabilities	$ 390	$ 318	$ 324	$ 330	$ 300

Required:

1. Express all of the asset, liability, and sales data in trend percentages. (Show percentages for each item.) Use Year 1 as the base year, and carry computations to one decimal place.
2. Comment on the results of your analysis.

Problems

All applicable problems are available with McGraw-Hill's *Connect™ Accounting*.

PROBLEM 15–11 Common-Size Statements and Financial Ratios for Creditors [LO1, LO3, LO4]
Modern Building Supply sells various building materials to retail outlets. The company has just approached Linden State Bank requesting a $300,000 loan to strengthen the Cash account and to pay certain pressing short-term obligations. The company's financial statements for the most recent two years follow:

eXcel

Modern Building Supply Comparative Balance Sheet	This Year	Last Year
Assets		
Current assets:		
Cash	$ 90,000	$ 200,000
Marketable securities	0	50,000
Accounts receivable, net	650,000	400,000
Inventory	1,300,000	800,000
Prepaid expenses	20,000	20,000
Total current assets	2,060,000	1,470,000
Plant and equipment, net	1,940,000	1,830,000
Total assets	$4,000,000	$3,300,000
Liabilities and Stockholders' Equity		
Liabilities:		
Current liabilities	$1,100,000	$ 600,000
Bonds payable, 12%	750,000	750,000
Total liabilities	1,850,000	1,350,000
Stockholders' equity:		
Preferred stock, $50 par, 8%	200,000	200,000
Common stock, $10 par	500,000	500,000
Retained earnings	1,450,000	1,250,000
Total stockholders' equity	2,150,000	1,950,000
Total liabilities and stockholder's equity	$4,000,000	$3,300,000

Modern Building Supply Comparative Income Statement and Reconciliation	This Year	Last Year
Sales	$7,000,000	$6,000,000
Cost of goods sold	5,400,000	4,800,000
Gross margin	1,600,000	1,200,000
Selling and administrative expenses	970,000	710,000
Net operating income	630,000	490,000
Interest expense	90,000	90,000
Net income before taxes	540,000	400,000
Income taxes (40%)	216,000	160,000
Net income	324,000	240,000
Dividends paid:		
Preferred dividends	16,000	16,000
Common dividends	108,000	60,000
Total dividends paid	124,000	76,000
Net income retained	200,000	164,000
Retained earnings, beginning of year	1,250,000	1,086,000
Retained earnings, end of year	$1,450,000	$1,250,000

During the past year, the company has expanded the number of lines that it carries in order to stimulate sales and increase profits. It has also moved aggressively to acquire new customers. Sales terms are 2/10, n/30. All sales are on account.

Assume that the following ratios are typical of companies in the building supply industry:

Current ratio	2.5
Acid-test ratio	1.2
Average collection period	18 days
Average sale period	50 days
Debt-to-equity ratio	0.75
Times interest earned	6.0
Return on total assets	10%
Price-earnings ratio	9

Required:

1. Linden State Bank is uncertain whether the loan should be made. To assist it in making a decision, you have been asked to compute the following amounts and ratios for both this year and last year:
   a. Working capital.
   b. Current ratio.
   c. Acid-test ratio.
   d. Average collection period. (The accounts receivable at the beginning of last year totaled $350,000.)
   e. Average sale period. (The inventory at the beginning of last year totaled $720,000.)
   f. Debt-to-equity ratio.
   g. Times interest earned.
2. For both this year and last year (carry computations to one decimal place):
   a. Present the balance sheet in common-size form.
   b. Present the income statement in common-size form down through net income.
3. From your analysis in (1) and (2) above, what problems or strengths do you see for Modern Building Supply? Make a recommendation as to whether the loan should be approved.

PROBLEM 15–12 Financial Ratios for Common Stockholders [LO2]

Refer to the financial statements and other data in Problem 15–11. Assume that you have just inherited several hundred shares of Modern Building Supply stock. Not being acquainted with the company, you decide to do some analytical work before making a decision about whether to retain or sell the stock you have inherited.

Required:

1. You decide first to assess the well-being of the common stockholders. For both this year and last year, compute the following:
   a. The earnings per share.
   b. The dividend yield ratio for common stock. The company's common stock is currently selling for $45 per share; last year it sold for $36 per share.
   c. The dividend payout ratio for common stock.
   d. The price-earnings ratio. How do investors regard Modern Building Supply as compared to other companies in the industry? Explain.
   e. The book value per share of common stock. Does the difference between market value and book value suggest that the stock at its current price is too high? Explain.
2. You decide next to assess the company's rate of return. Compute the following for both this year and last year:
   a. The return on total assets. (Total assets at the beginning of last year were $2,700,000.)
   b. The return on common stockholders' equity. (Stockholders' equity at the beginning of last year was $1,786,000.)
   c. Is the company's financial leverage positive or negative? Explain.
3. Based on your analytical work (and assuming that you have no immediate need for cash), would you retain or sell the stock you have inherited? Explain.

PROBLEM 15–13 Interpretation of Financial Ratios [LO2, LO3]

Being a prudent investor, Sally Perkins always investigates a company thoroughly before purchasing shares of its stock for investment. Ms. Perkins is interested in the common stock of Plunge Enterprises. The following data are available for the company:

	Year 3	Year 2	Year 1
Current ratio	2.8	2.5	2.0
Acid-test ratio	0.7	0.9	1.2
Accounts receivable turnover	8.6	9.5	10.4
Inventory turnover	5.0	5.7	6.8
Sales trend	130.0	118.0	100.0
Dividends paid per share*	$2.50	$2.50	$2.50
Dividend yield ratio	5%	4%	3%
Dividend payout ratio	40%	50%	60%
Return on total assets	13.0%	11.8%	10.4%
Return on common stockholders' equity	16.2%	14.5%	9.0%

*There were no changes in common stock outstanding over the three-year period.

Ms. Perkins would like answers to a number of questions about the trend of events over the last three years in Plunge Enterprises. Her questions are as follows:

a. Is the market price of the company's stock going up or down?
b. Is the earnings per share increasing or decreasing?
c. Is the price-earnings ratio going up or down?
d. Is the company employing financial leverage to the advantage of the common stockholders?
e. Is it becoming easier for the company to pay its bills as they come due?
f. Are customers paying their bills at least as fast now as they did in Year 1?
g. Is the total of the accounts receivable increasing, decreasing, or remaining constant?
h. Is the level of inventory increasing, decreasing, or remaining constant?

Required:

Answer each of Ms. Perkins's questions and explain how you arrived at your answer.

PROBLEM 15–14 Effects of Transactions on Various Ratios [LO3]

Selected amounts from Reingold Company's balance sheet from the beginning of the year follow:

	A	B
1	Cash	$70,000
2	Marketable Securities	$12,000
3	Accounts receivable, net	$350,000
4	Inventory	$460,000
5	Prepaid expenses	$8,000
6	Plant and equipment, net	$950,000
7	Accounts payable	$200,000
8	Accrued liabilities	$60,000
9	Notes due within one year	$100,000
10	Bonds payable in five years	$140,000
11		

During the year, the company completed the following transactions:

x. Purchased inventory on account, $50,000.
a. Declared a cash dividend, $30,000.
b. Paid accounts payable, $100,000.
c. Collected cash on accounts receivable, $80,000.
d. Purchased equipment for cash, $75,000.
e. Paid a cash dividend previously declared, $30,000.
f. Borrowed cash on a short-term note with the bank, $60,000.
g. Sold inventory costing $70,000 for $100,000, on account.
h. Wrote off uncollectible accounts in the amount of $10,000 reducing the accounts receivable balance accordingly.

i. Sold marketable securities costing $12,000 for cash, $9,000.
j. Issued additional shares of common stock for cash, $200,000.
k. Paid off all short-term notes due, $160,000.

Required:

1. Compute the following amounts and ratios as of the beginning of the year:
   a. Working capital.
   b. Current ratio.
   c. Acid-test ratio.
2. Indicate the effect of each of the transactions given above on working capital, the current ratio, and the acid-test ratio. Give the effect in terms of increase, decrease, or none. Item (x) is given as an example of the format to use:

	The Effect on		
Transaction	Working Capital	Current Ratio	Acid-Test Ratio
(x) Purchased inventory on account	None	Decrease	Decrease

PROBLEM 15–15 Effects of Transactions on Various Financial Ratios [LO2, LO3, LO4]

In the right-hand column below, certain financial ratios are listed. To the left of each ratio is a business transaction or event relating to the operating activities of Graham Company.

Business Transaction or Event	Ratio
1. Inventory was sold for cash at a profit.	Debt-to-equity ratio
2. Land was purchased for cash.	Earnings per share
3. Inventory was sold on account at cost.	Acid-test ratio
4. Some accounts payable were paid off.	Working capital
5. A customer paid an overdue bill.	Average collection period
6. A cash dividend was declared, but not yet paid.	Current ratio
7. A previously declared cash dividend was paid.	Current ratio
8. The company's common stock price increased.	Book value per share
9. The company's common stock price increased and earnings per share remained unchanged.	Dividend yield ratio
10. Property was sold for a profit.	Return on total assets
11. Obsolete inventory was written off as a loss.	Inventory turnover ratio
12. Bonds were sold with an interest rate less than the company's return on assets.	Return on common stockholders' equity
13. The company's common stock price decreased and the dividend paid per share remained the same.	Dividend payout ratio
14. The company's net income decreased, but long-term debt remained unchanged.	Times interest earned
15. An uncollectible account was written off against the Allowance for Bad Debts.	Current ratio
16. Inventory was purchased on credit.	Acid-test ratio
17. The company's common stock price increased and earnings per share remained unchanged.	Price-earnings ratio
18. The company paid off some accounts payable.	Debt-to-equity ratio

Required:

Indicate the effect that each transaction or event would have on the ratio listed opposite to it. State the effect in terms of increase, decrease, or no effect on the ratio involved, and give the reason for your choice. In all cases, assume that the current assets exceed current liabilities both before and after the event or transaction. Use the following format for your answers:

	Effect on Ratio	Reason for Increase, Decrease, or No Effect
1.		
2.		
Etc.		

PROBLEM 15–16 Comprehensive Ratio Analysis [LO2, LO3, LO4]

You have just been hired as a loan officer at Fairfield State Bank. Your supervisor has given you a file containing a request from Hedrick Company, a manufacturer of auto components, for a $1,000,000 five-year loan. Financial statement data on the company for the last two years are given below:

Hedrick Company
Comparative Balance Sheet

	This Year	Last Year
Assets		
Current assets:		
Cash	$ 320,000	$ 420,000
Marketable securities	0	100,000
Accounts receivable, net	900,000	600,000
Inventory	1,300,000	800,000
Prepaid expenses	80,000	60,000
Total current assets	2,600,000	1,980,000
Plant and equipment, net	3,100,000	2,980,000
Total assets	$5,700,000	$4,960,000
Liabilities and Stockholders' Equity		
Liabilities:		
Current liabilities	$1,300,000	$ 920,000
Bonds payable, 10%	1,200,000	1,000,000
Total liabilities	2,500,000	1,920,000
Stockholders' equity:		
Preferred stock, 8%, $30 par value	600,000	600,000
Common stock, $40 par value	2,000,000	2,000,000
Retained earnings	600,000	440,000
Total stockholders' equity	3,200,000	3,040,000
Total liabilities and stockholders' equity	$5,700,000	$4,960,000

Hedrick Company
Comparative Income Statement and Reconciliation

	This Year	Last Year
Sales (all on account)	$5,250,000	$4,160,000
Cost of goods sold	4,200,000	3,300,000
Gross margin	1,050,000	860,000
Selling and administrative expenses	530,000	520,000
Net operating income	520,000	340,000
Interest expense	120,000	100,000
Net income before taxes	400,000	240,000
Income taxes (30%)	120,000	72,000
Net income	280,000	168,000
Dividends paid:		
Preferred stock	48,000	48,000
Common stock	72,000	36,000
Total dividends paid	120,000	84,000
Net income retained	160,000	84,000
Retained earnings, beginning of year	440,000	356,000
Retained earnings, end of year	$ 600,000	$ 440,000

Marva Rossen, who just two years ago was appointed president of Hedrick Company, admits that the company has been "inconsistent" in its performance over the past several years. But Rossen argues that the company has its costs under control and is now experiencing strong sales growth, as evidenced by the more than 25% increase in sales over the last year. Rossen also argues that investors have recognized the improving situation at Hedrick Company, as shown by the jump in the price of its common stock from $20 per share last year to $36 per share this year. Rossen believes that with strong leadership and with the modernized equipment that the $1,000,000 loan will enable the company to buy, profits will be even stronger in the future.

Anxious to impress your supervisor, you decide to generate all the information you can about the company. You determine that the following ratios are typical of companies in Hedrick's industry:

Current ratio	2.3
Acid-test ratio	1.2
Average collection period	31 days
Average sale period	60 days
Return on assets	9.5%
Debt-to-equity ratio	0.65
Times interest earned	5.7
Price-earnings ratio	10

Required:

1. You decide first to assess the rate of return that the company is generating. Compute the following for both this year and last year:
   a. The return on total assets. (Total assets at the beginning of last year were $4,320,000.)
   b. The return on common stockholders' equity. (Stockholders' equity at the beginning of last year totaled $3,016,000. There has been no change in preferred or common stock over the last two years.)
   c. Is the company's financial leverage positive or negative? Explain.
2. You decide next to assess the well-being of the common stockholders. For both this year and last year, compute:
   a. The earnings per share.
   b. The dividend yield ratio for common stock.
   c. The dividend payout ratio for common stock.
   d. The price-earnings ratio. How do investors regard Hedrick Company as compared to other companies in the industry? Explain.
   e. The book value per share of common stock. Does the difference between market value per share and book value per share suggest that the stock at its current price is a bargain? Explain.
   f. The gross margin percentage.
3. You decide, finally, to assess creditor ratios to determine both short-term and long-term debt paying ability. For both this year and last year, compute:
   a. Working capital.
   b. The current ratio.
   c. The acid-test ratio.
   d. The average collection period. (The accounts receivable at the beginning of last year totaled $520,000.)
   e. The average sale period. (The inventory at the beginning of last year totaled $640,000.)
   f. The debt-to-equity ratio.
   g. The times interest earned.
4. Make a recommendation to your supervisor as to whether the loan should be approved.

PROBLEM 15–17 Common-Size Financial Statements [LO1]

Refer to the financial statement data for Hedrick Company given in Problem 15–16.

Required:

For both this year and last year:

1. Present the balance sheet in common-size format.
2. Present the income statement in common-size format down through net income.
3. Comment on the results of your analysis.

PROBLEM 15–18 Ethics and the Manager [LO3]

Mountain Aerosport was founded by Jurgen Prinz to produce a ski he had designed for doing aerial tricks. Up to this point, Jurgen has financed the company with his own savings and with cash generated by his business. However, Jurgen now faces a cash crisis. In the year just ended, an acute shortage of a vital tungsten steel alloy arose just as the company was beginning production for the Christmas season. Jurgen had been assured by his suppliers that the steel would be delivered in time to make Christmas shipments, but the suppliers had been unable to fully deliver on this promise. As a consequence, Mountain Aerosport had large stocks of unfinished skis at the end of the year and had been unable to fill all of the orders that had come in from retailers for the Christmas season. Consequently, sales were below expectations for the year, and Jurgen does not have enough cash to pay his creditors.

Well before the accounts payable were due, Jurgen visited a local bank and inquired about obtaining a loan. The loan officer at the bank assured Jurgen that there should not be any problem getting a loan to pay off his accounts payable—providing that on his most recent financial statements the current ratio was above 2.0, the acid-test ratio was above 1.0, and net operating income was at least four times the interest on the proposed loan. Jurgen promised to return later with a copy of his financial statements.

Jurgen would like to apply for a $120 thousand six-month loan bearing an interest rate of 10% per year. The unaudited financial reports of the company appear below.

Mountain Aerosport
Comparative Balance Sheet
As of December 31, This Year and Last Year
(in thousands of dollars)

	This Year	Last Year
Assets		
Current assets:		
Cash	$105	$225
Accounts receivable, net	75	60
Inventory	240	150
Prepaid expenses	15	18
Total current assets	435	453
Property and equipment	405	270
Total assets	$840	$723
Liabilities and Stockholders' Equity		
Current liabilities:		
Accounts payable	$231	$135
Accrued payables	15	15
Total current liabilities	246	150
Long-term liabilities	0	0
Total liabilities	246	150
Stockholders' equity:		
Common stock and additional paid-in capital	150	150
Retained earnings	444	423
Total stockholders' equity	594	573
Total liabilities and stockholders' equity	$840	$723

Mountain Aerosport Income Statement For the Year Ended December 31, This Year (in thousands of dollars)	
Sales (all on account)	$630
Cost of goods sold	435
Gross margin	195
Selling and administrative expenses:	
Selling expenses	63
Administrative expenses	102
Total selling and administrative expenses	165
Net operating income	30
Interest expense	0
Net income before taxes	30
Income taxes (30%)	9
Net income	$ 21

Required:

1. Based on the above unaudited financial statements and the statement made by the loan officer, would the company qualify for the loan?
2. Last year Jurgen purchased and installed new, more efficient equipment to replace an older heat-treating furnace. Jurgen had originally planned to sell the old equipment, but found that it is still needed whenever the heat-treating process is a bottleneck. When Jurgen discussed his cash flow problems with his brother-in-law, he suggested to Jurgen that the old equipment be sold or at least reclassified as inventory on the balance sheet because it could be readily sold. At present, the equipment is carried in the Property and Equipment account and could be sold for its net book value of $68,000. The bank does not require audited financial statements. What advice would you give to Jurgen concerning the machine?

eXcel

PROBLEM 15–19 Incomplete Statements; Analysis of Ratios [LO2, LO3, LO4]

Incomplete financial statements for Tanner Company are given below:

Tanner Company Income Statement For the Year Ended December 31	
Sales	$2,700,000
Cost of goods sold	?
Gross margin	?
Selling and administrative expenses	?
Net operating income	?
Interest expense	45,000
Net income before taxes	?
Income taxes (40%)	?
Net income	$?

Tanner Company Balance Sheet December 31	
Current assets:	
Cash	$?
Accounts receivable, net	?
Inventory	?
Total current assets	?
Plant and equipment, net	?
Total assets	$?
Current liabilities	$250,000
Bonds payable, 10%	?
Total liabilities	?
Stockholders' equity:	
Common stock, $2.50 par value	?
Retained earnings	?
Total stockholders' equity	?
Total liabilities and stockholders' equity	$?

The following additional information is available about the company:

a. Selected financial ratios computed from the statements above are given below:

Current ratio	2.40
Acid-test ratio	1.12
Accounts receivable turnover	15.0
Inventory turnover	6.0
Debt-to-equity ratio	0.875
Times interest earned	7.0
Earnings per share	$4.05
Return on total assets	14%

b. All sales during the year were on account.

c. The interest expense on the income statement relates to the bonds payable; the amount of bonds outstanding did not change throughout the year.

d. There were no changes in the number of shares of common stock outstanding during the year.

e. Selected balances at the *beginning* of the current year (January 1) were as follows:

Accounts receivable	$160,000
Inventory	$280,000
Total assets	$1,200,000

Required:

Compute the missing amounts on the company's financial statements. (Hint: You may find it helpful to think about the difference between the current ratio and the acid-test ratio.)

Appendix A

Pricing Products and Services

LEARNING OBJECTIVES

After studying this appendix, you should be able to:

LO1 Compute the profit-maximizing price of a product or service using the price elasticity of demand and variable cost.

LO2 Compute the selling price of a product using the absorption costing approach.

LO3 Compute the target cost for a new product or service.

Introduction

Some products have an established market price. Consumers will not pay more than this price and there is no reason for a supplier to charge less—the supplier can sell all that it produces at this price. Under these circumstances, the supplier simply charges the prevailing market price for the product. Markets for basic raw materials such as farm products and minerals follow this pattern.

In this appendix, we are concerned with the more common situation in which a business is faced with the problem of setting its own prices. Clearly, the pricing decision can be critical. If the price is set too high, customers won't buy the company's products. If the price is set too low, the company's costs won't be covered.

The usual approach in pricing is to *mark up* cost.[1] A product's **markup** is the difference between its selling price and its cost and is usually expressed as a percentage of cost.

$$\text{Selling price} = (1 + \text{Markup percentage}) \times \text{Cost}$$

For example, a company that uses a markup of 50% adds 50% to the costs of its products to determine selling prices. If a product costs $10, then the company would charge $15 for the product. This approach is called **cost-plus pricing** because a predetermined markup percentage is applied to a cost base to determine the selling price.

Two key issues must be addressed with the cost-plus approach to pricing. First, what cost should be used? Second, how should the markup be determined? Several alternative approaches are considered in this appendix, starting with the approach generally favored by economists.

IN BUSINESS

THE BUSINESS OF ART SCULPTURE

Shidoni Foundry, located in Tesuque, New Mexico, is a fine art casting and fabrication facility. The process of creating a bronze or other metal sculpture is complex. The artist creates the sculpture using modeling clay and then hires a foundry such as Shidoni to produce the actual metal sculpture. Shidoni craftspeople make a rubber mold from the clay model then use that mold to make a wax version of the original. The wax is in turn used to make a ceramic casting mold, and finally the bronze version is cast. Both the wax and the ceramic casting mold are destroyed in the process of making the metal casting, but the rubber mold is not and can be reused to make additional castings.

The surface of the metal sculpture can be treated with various patinas. One of the accompanying photos shows Harry Gold, the shop's patina artist, applying a patina to a metal sculpture with brush and blowtorch. The other photo shows a finished sculpture with patinas applied.

The artist is faced with a difficult business decision. The rubber mold for a small figure such as the seated Indian in the accompanying photo costs roughly $500; the mold for a life-size figure such as the cowboy costs $3,800 to $5,000. This is just for the mold! Fortunately, as discussed above, a number of metal castings can be made from each mold. However, each life-size casting costs $8,500 to $11,000. In contrast, a casting of the much smaller Indian sculpture would cost about $750. Given the fixed costs of the mold and variable costs of the casting, finish treatments, and bases, the artist must decide how many castings to produce and how to price them. The fewer the castings, the greater the rarity factor, and hence the higher the price that can be charged to art lovers. However, in that case, the fixed costs of making the mold must be spread across fewer items. The artist must make sure not to price the sculptures so high that the investment in molds and in the castings cannot be recovered.

Source: Conversations with Shidoni personnel, including Bill Rogers and Harry Gold, and Shidoni literature. See www.shidoni.com for more information concerning the company.

---

[1] There are some legal restrictions on prices. Antitrust laws prohibit "predatory" prices, which are generally interpreted by the courts to mean a price below average variable cost. "Price discrimination"—charging different prices to customers in the same market for the same product or service—is also prohibited by the law.

The Economists' Approach to Pricing

If a company raises the price of a product, unit sales ordinarily fall. Because of this, pricing is a delicate balancing act in which the benefits of higher revenues per unit are traded off against the lower volume that results from charging a higher price. The sensitivity of unit sales to changes in price is called the *price elasticity of demand.*

LEARNING OBJECTIVE 1
Compute the profit-maximizing price of a product or service using the price elasticity of demand and variable cost.

Elasticity of Demand

A product's price elasticity should be a key element in setting its price. The **price elasticity of demand** measures the degree to which a change in price affects the unit sales of a product or service. Demand for a product is said to be *inelastic* if a change in price has little effect on the number of units sold. The demand for designer perfumes sold by trained personnel at cosmetic counters in department stores is relatively inelastic. Raising or lowering prices on these luxury goods has little effect on unit sales. On the other hand, demand for a product is *elastic* if a change in price has a substantial effect on the volume of units sold. An example of a product whose demand is elastic is gasoline. If a gas station raises its price for gasoline, unit sales will drop as customers seek lower prices elsewhere.

Price elasticity is very important in determining prices. Managers should set higher markups over cost when customers are relatively insensitive to price (i.e., demand is inelastic) and lower markups when customers are relatively sensitive to price (i.e., demand is elastic). This principle is followed in department stores. Merchandise sold in the bargain basement has a much lower markup than merchandise sold elsewhere in the store because customers who shop in the bargain basement are much more sensitive to price (i.e., demand is elastic).

The price elasticity of demand for a product or service, ϵ_d, can be estimated using the following formula.[2,3]

$$\epsilon_d = \frac{\ln(1 + \%\text{ change in quantity sold})}{\ln(1 + \%\text{ change in price})}$$

For example, suppose that the managers of Nature's Garden believe that a 10% increase in the selling price of their apple-almond shampoo would result in a 15% decrease in the number of bottles of shampoo sold.[4] The price elasticity of demand for this product would be computed as follows:

$$\epsilon_d = \frac{\ln[1 + (-0.15)]}{\ln[1 + (0.10)]} = \frac{\ln(0.85)}{\ln(1.10)} = -1.71$$

For comparison purposes, the managers of Nature's Garden believe that another product, strawberry glycerin soap, would experience a 20% drop in unit sales if its price is increased by 10%. (Purchasers of this product are more sensitive to price than the purchasers of the apple-almond shampoo.) The price elasticity of demand for the strawberry glycerin soap is:

$$\epsilon_d = \frac{\ln[1 + (-0.20)]}{\ln[1 + (0.10)]} = \frac{\ln(0.80)}{\ln(1.10)} = -2.34$$

Both of these products, like other normal products, have a price elasticity that is less than −1.

---

[2] The term "ln( )" is the natural log function. You can compute the natural log of any number using the LN or ln$x$ key on your calculator. For example, ln(0.85) = −0.1625.

[3] This formula assumes that the price elasticity of demand is constant. This occurs when the relation between the selling price, p, and the unit sales, q, can be expressed in the following form: $\ln(q) = a + \epsilon_d \ln(p)$. Even if this is not precisely true, the formula provides a useful way to estimate a product's price elasticity.

[4] The estimated change in unit sales should take into account competitors' responses to a price change.

Note that the price elasticity of demand for the strawberry glycerin soap is larger (in absolute value) than the price elasticity of demand for the apple-almond shampoo. This indicates that the demand for strawberry glycerin soap is more elastic than the demand for apple-almond shampoo.

In the next subsection, the price elasticity of demand will be used to compute the selling price that maximizes the profits of the company.

The Profit-Maximizing Price

Under certain conditions, the profit-maximizing price can be determined by marking up *variable cost* using the following formula:[5]

$$\text{Profit-maximizing markup on variable cost} = \frac{-1}{1 + \epsilon_d}$$

Using the above markup, the selling price would be set using the formula:

$$\text{Profit-maximizing price} = (1 + \text{Profit-maximizing markup on variable cost}) \times \text{Variable cost per unit}$$

The profit-maximizing prices for the two Nature's Garden products are computed below using these formulas:

Apple-Almond Shampoo

$$\text{Profit-maximizing markup on variable cost} = \left(\frac{-1}{1 + (-1.71)}\right) = 1.41$$

$$\text{Profit-maximizing price} = (1 + 1.41)\$2.00 = \$4.82$$

Strawberry Glycerin Soap

$$\text{Profit-maximizing markup on variable cost} = \left(\frac{-1}{1 + (-2.34)}\right) = 0.75$$

$$\text{Profit-maximizing price} = (1 + 0.75)\$0.40 = \$0.70$$

Note that the 75% markup for the strawberry glycerin soap is lower than the 141% markup for the apple-almond shampoo. The reason for this is that the purchasers of strawberry glycerin soap are more sensitive to price than the purchasers of apple-almond shampoo. Strawberry glycerin soap is a relatively common product with close substitutes available in nearly every grocery store.

Exhibit A–1 shows how the profit-maximizing markup is generally affected by how sensitive unit sales are to price. For example, if a 10% increase in price leads to a 20% decrease in unit sales, then the optimal markup on variable cost according to the exhibit is 75%—the figure computed above for the strawberry glycerin soap. Note that the optimal markup drops as unit sales become more sensitive to price.

Caution is advised when using these formulas to establish a selling price. The formulas rely on simplifying assumptions and the estimate of the percentage change in unit sales that would result from a given percentage change in price is likely to be inexact. Nevertheless, the formulas can provide valuable clues regarding whether prices should be increased or decreased. Suppose, for example, that the strawberry glycerin soap is currently being sold for $0.60 per bar. The formula indicates that the profit-maximizing

[5] The formula assumes that (a) the price elasticity of demand is constant; (b) Total cost = Total fixed cost + Variable cost per unit × Quantity sold; and (c) the price of the product has no effect on the sales or costs of any other product. The formula can be derived using calculus.

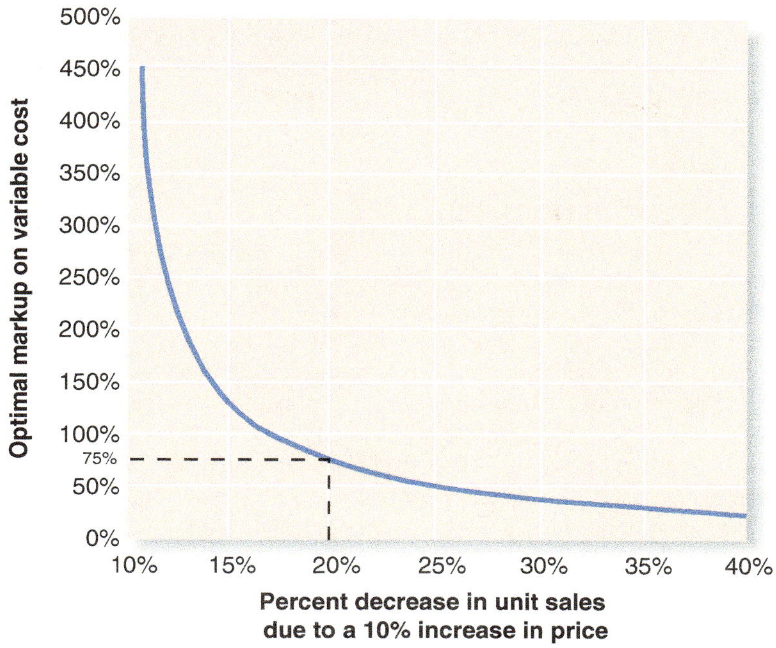

EXHIBIT A–1
The Optimal Markup on Variable Cost as a Function of the Sensitivity of Unit Sales to Price

price is \$0.70 per bar. Rather than increasing the price by \$0.10, it would be prudent to increase the price by a more modest amount to observe what happens to unit sales and to profits.

The formula for the profit-maximizing price conveys a very important lesson. If the total fixed costs are the same whether the company charges \$0.60 or \$0.70, they cannot be relevant in the decision of which price to charge for the soap. The optimal selling price should depend on two factors—the variable cost per unit and how sensitive unit sales are to changes in price. Fixed costs play no role in setting the optimal price. Fixed costs are relevant when deciding whether to offer a product but are not relevant when deciding how much to charge for the product.

We can directly verify that an increase in selling price for the strawberry glycerin soap from the current price of \$0.60 per bar is warranted, based just on the forecast that a 10% increase in selling price would lead to a 20% decrease in unit sales. Suppose, for example, that Nature's Garden is currently selling 200,000 bars of the soap per year at the price of \$0.60 a bar. If the change in price has no effect on the company's fixed costs or on other products, the effect on profits of increasing the price by 10% can be computed as follows:

	Present Price	Higher Price
Selling price (a)	\$0.60	\$0.60 + (0.10 × \$0.60) = \$0.66
Unit sales (b)	200,000	200,000 − (0.20 × 200,000) = 160,000
Sales (a) × (b)	\$120,000	\$105,600
Variable cost (\$0.40 per unit)	80,000	64,000
Contribution margin	\$ 40,000	\$ 41,600

Despite the apparent optimality of prices based on marking up variable costs according to the price elasticity of demand, surveys consistently reveal that most managers approach the pricing problem from a completely different perspective.[6] They prefer to mark up some version of full, not variable, costs, and the markup is based on desired profits rather than on factors related to demand. This approach is called the *absorption costing approach to cost-plus pricing.*

IN BUSINESS

COMPETITION INFLUENCES PRICES

The Department of Transportation says Cincinnati has the most expensive airport in the United States. Cincinnati passengers pay an average fare of 20.63¢ per mile while more than 20 airports, such as Buffalo, Oakland, Reno, and Tampa, offer flights at less than 12¢ per mile. Why the higher prices in Cincinnati? Delta Airlines controls more than 80% of the Cincinnati market so the lack of competition enables it to charge higher fares. For example, Delta charges $529 to fly direct from Cincinnati to Las Vegas because it is the only airline to offer nonstop service on this route. However, Delta can only charge $258 to fly direct from Atlanta to Las Vegas because AirTran Airways also flies nonstop on this route. Of course, Delta must balance the desire to raise prices at the Cincinnati airport with the realization that its customers can defect to competing airline departures from nearby airports in Dayton, Columbus, Louisville, Lexington, and Indianapolis.

Source: Scott McCartney, "The Most Expensive City to Leave: Cincinnati," *The Wall Street Journal,* December 11, 2007, pp. B9–B10.

The Absorption Costing Approach to Cost-Plus Pricing

LEARNING OBJECTIVE 2
Compute the selling price of a product using the absorption costing approach.

The absorption costing approach to cost-plus pricing differs from the economists' approach both in what costs are marked up and in how the markup is determined. Under the absorption approach to cost-plus pricing, the cost base is the absorption costing unit product cost, as defined in Chapter 3, rather than variable cost.

Setting a Target Selling Price Using the Absorption Costing Approach

To illustrate, assume that the management of Ritter Company wants to set the selling price on a product that has just undergone some design modifications. The accounting department has provided cost estimates for the redesigned product as shown below:

	Per Unit	Total
Direct materials	$6	
Direct labor	$4	
Variable manufacturing overhead	$3	
Fixed manufacturing overhead		$70,000
Variable selling and administrative expenses	$2	
Fixed selling and administrative expenses		$60,000

[6] One study found that 83% of the 504 large manufacturing companies surveyed used some form of full cost (either absorption cost or absorption cost plus selling and administrative expenses) as the basis for pricing. The remaining 17% used only variable costs as a basis for pricing decisions. See V. Govindarajan and Robert N. Anthony, "How Firms Use Cost Data in Pricing Decisions," *Management Accounting,* July 1983, pp. 30–36. A less extensive survey by Eunsup Shim and Ephraim F. Sudit, "How Manufacturers Price Products," *Management Accounting,* February 1995, pp. 37–39, found similar results.

On the other hand, a survey of small-company executives summarized in *Inc.* magazine, November 1996, p. 84, revealed that only 41% set prices based on cost. The others charge what they think customers are willing to pay or what the market demands.

The first step in the absorption costing approach to cost-plus pricing is to compute the unit product cost. For Ritter Company, this amounts to $20 per unit at a volume of 10,000 units, as computed below:

Direct materials	$ 6
Direct labor	4
Variable manufacturing overhead	3
Fixed manufacturing overhead ($70,000 ÷ 10,000 units)	7
Unit product cost	$20

Ritter Company has a general policy of marking up unit product costs by 50%. A price quotation sheet for the company prepared using the absorption approach is presented in Exhibit A–2. Note that selling and administrative expenses are not included in the cost base. Instead, the markup is supposed to cover these expenses.

EXHIBIT A–2
Price Quotation Sheet—Absorption Basis (10,000 Units)

Direct materials	$ 6
Direct labor	4
Variable manufacturing overhead	3
Fixed manufacturing overhead (based on 10,000 units)	7
Unit product cost	20
Markup to cover selling and administrative expenses and desired profit—50% of unit manufacturing cost	10
Target selling price	$30

Determining the Markup Percentage

Ritter Company's markup percentage of 50% could be a widely used rule of thumb in the industry or just a company tradition that seems to work. The markup percentage may also be the result of an explicit computation. As we have discussed, the markup over cost should be largely determined by market conditions. However, many companies base their markup on cost and desired profit. The reasoning goes like this. The markup must be large enough to cover selling and administrative expenses and provide an adequate return on investment (ROI). Given the forecasted unit sales, the markup can be computed as follows:

$$\text{Markup percentage on absorption cost} = \frac{(\text{Required ROI} \times \text{Investment}) + \text{Selling and administrative expenses}}{\text{Unit product cost} \times \text{Unit sales}}$$

To show how this formula is applied, assume Ritter Company invests $100,000 in operating assets such as equipment to produce and market 10,000 units of the product each year. If Ritter Company requires a 20% ROI, then the markup for the product would be determined as follows:

$$\text{Markup percentage on absorption cost} = \frac{(20\% \times \$100{,}000) + (\$2 \text{ per unit} \times 10{,}000 \text{ units} + \$60{,}000)}{\$20 \text{ per unit} \times 10{,}000 \text{ units}}$$

$$= \frac{(\$20{,}000) + (\$80{,}000)}{\$200{,}000} = 50\%$$

As shown earlier, this markup of 50% leads to a target selling price of $30 for Ritter Company. *If the company actually sells 10,000 units* of the product at this price, the company's ROI on this product will indeed be 20%. This is verified in Exhibit A–3. However,

EXHIBIT A–3
Income Statement and ROI Analysis—Ritter Company
Actual Unit Sales = 10,000 Units; Selling Price = $30

Direct materials	$ 6
Direct labor	4
Variable manufacturing overhead	3
Fixed manufacturing overhead ($70,000 ÷ 10,000 units)	7
Unit product cost	$20

Ritter Company
Absorption Costing Income Statement

Sales ($30 per unit × 10,000 units)	$300,000
Cost of goods sold ($20 per unit × 10,000 units)	200,000
Gross margin	100,000
Selling and administrative expenses ($2 per unit × 10,000 units + $60,000)	80,000
Net operating income	$ 20,000

ROI

$$\text{ROI} = \frac{\text{Net operating income}}{\text{Average operating assets}}$$

$$= \frac{\$20{,}000}{\$100{,}000}$$

$$= 20\%$$

if it turns out that more than 10,000 units are sold at this price, the ROI will be greater than 20%. If less than 10,000 units are sold, the ROI will be less than 20%. *The required ROI will be attained only if the forecasted unit sales volume is attained.*

IN BUSINESS

THE LIMITATIONS OF COST-PLUS PRICING

The invention of flat-panel televisions has destroyed customer demand for the entertainment armoires that used to house the bulky televisions of yesteryear. Hotel chains have dumped more than 40,000 armoires helping create a huge supply of obsolete units that practically nobody wants to buy. From a cost-plus pricing perspective, the cost to manufacture an armoire has probably increased in recent years as lumber prices have climbed. However, this cost-focused perspective is irrelevant in a marketplace where demand for armoires has all but disappeared.

Source: Juliet Chung, "Au Revoir, Armoire," *The Wall Street Journal,* November 10–11, 2007, pp. W1 and W3.

Problems with the Absorption Costing Approach

The absorption costing approach makes pricing decisions look deceptively simple. All a company needs to do is compute its unit product cost, decide how much profit it wants, and then set its price. It appears that a company can ignore demand and arrive at a price that will safely yield whatever profit it wants. However, as noted above, the absorption costing approach relies on a forecast of unit sales. Neither the markup nor the unit product cost can be computed without such a forecast.

The absorption costing approach essentially assumes that customers *need* the forecasted unit sales and will pay whatever price the company decides to charge. However, customers have a choice. If the price is too high, they can buy from a competitor or they may choose not to buy at all. Suppose, for example, that when Ritter Company sets its

EXHIBIT A–4
Income Statement and ROI Analysis—Ritter Company Actual Unit Sales = 7,000 Units; Selling Price = $30

Direct materials	$ 6
Direct labor	4
Variable manufacturing overhead	3
Fixed manufacturing overhead ($70,000 ÷ 7,000 units)	10
Unit product cost	$23

Ritter Company
Absorption Costing Income Statement

Sales ($30 per unit × 7,000 units)	$210,000
Cost of goods sold ($23 per unit × 7,000 units)	161,000
Gross margin	49,000
Selling and administrative expenses ($2 per unit × 7,000 units + $60,000)	74,000
Net operating loss	$ (25,000)

ROI

$$\text{ROI} = \frac{\text{Net operating income}}{\text{Average operating assets}}$$

$$= \frac{-\$25{,}000}{\$100{,}000}$$

$$= -25\%$$

price at $30, it sells only 7,000 units rather than the 10,000 units forecasted. As shown in Exhibit A–4, the company would then have a loss of $25,000 on the product instead of a profit of $20,000.[7] Some managers believe that the absorption costing approach to pricing is safe. This is an illusion. The absorption costing approach is safe only if customers choose to buy at least as many units as managers forecasted they would buy.

Target Costing

LEARNING OBJECTIVE 3
Compute the target cost for a new product or service.

Our discussion thus far has presumed that a product has already been developed, has been costed, and is ready to be marketed as soon as a price is set. In many cases, the sequence of events is just the reverse. That is, the company already *knows* what price should be charged, and the problem is to *develop* a product that can be marketed profitably at the desired price. Even in this situation, where the normal sequence of events is reversed, cost is still a crucial factor. The company can use an approach called *target costing*. **Target costing** is the process of determining the maximum allowable cost for a new product and then developing a prototype that can be profitably made for that maximum target cost figure. A number of companies have used target costing, including Compaq, Culp, Cummins Engine, Daihatsu Motors, Chrysler, Ford, Isuzu Motors, ITT Automotive, Komatsu, Matsushita Electric, Mitsubishi Kasei, NEC, Nippodenso, Nissan, Olympus, Sharp, Texas Instruments, and Toyota.

[7] It may be *impossible* to break even using an absorption costing approach when the company has more than one product—even when it would be possible to make substantial profits using the economists' approach to pricing. For details, see Eric Noreen and David Burgstahler, "Full Cost Pricing and the Illusion of Satisficing," *Journal of Management Accounting Research* 9 (1997).

The target cost for a product is computed by starting with the product's anticipated selling price and then deducting the desired profit, as follows:

$$\text{Target cost} = \text{Anticipated selling price} - \text{Desired profit}$$

The product development team is then given the responsibility of designing the product so that it can be made for no more than the target cost.

Reasons for Using Target Costing

The target costing approach was developed in recognition of two important characteristics of markets and costs. The first is that many companies have less control over price than they would like to think. The market (i.e., supply and demand) really determines price, and a company that attempts to ignore this does so at its peril. Therefore, the anticipated market price is taken as a given in target costing. The second observation is that most of a product's cost is determined in the design stage. Once a product has been designed and has gone into production, not much can be done to significantly reduce its cost. Most of the opportunities to reduce cost come from designing the product so that it is simple to make, uses inexpensive parts, and is robust and reliable. If the company has little control over market price and little control over cost once the product has gone into production, then it follows that the major opportunities for affecting profit come in the design stage where valuable features that customers are willing to pay for can be added and where most of the costs are really determined. So that is where the effort is concentrated—in designing and developing the product. The difference between target costing and other approaches to product development is profound. Instead of designing the product and then finding out how much it costs, the target cost is set first and then the product is designed so that the target cost is attained.

IN BUSINESS

MANAGING COSTS IN THE PRODUCT DESIGN STAGE

The Boeing Company is building the airframe of its 787 Dreamliner jet using carbon fiber-reinforced plastic. While this type of plastic has been used in golf club shafts and tennis rackets, it has never been used to construct the exterior of an airplane. Boeing is excited about this innovative raw material because it allows enormous cost savings. For example, Boeing's Dreamliner should be 20% more fuel efficient than the Boeing 767 or Airbus A330, its maintenance costs should be 30% less than aluminum planes, and the number of fasteners needed to assemble its fuselage should be 80% less than conventional airplanes. In addition, aluminum airplanes require costly corrosion inspections after 6 years of service, while the Dreamliner can fly 12 years before it would need a comparable inspection. To Boeing's delight, the Dreamliner's sales have "taken off" because "customers get tremendous bang for their bucks. For $120 million—about what they paid for the comparable Boeing 767-300 back in the 1980s—airlines get an all-new aircraft that flies faster than the competition and costs substantially less to operate."

Source: Stanley Holmes, "A Plastic Dream Machine," *BusinessWeek*, June 20, 2005, pp. 32–36.

An Example of Target Costing

To provide a simple example of target costing, assume the following situation: Handy Company wishes to invest $2,000,000 to design, develop, and produce a new hand mixer. The company's Marketing Department surveyed the features and prices of competing products and determined that a price of $30 would enable Handy to sell an estimated

40,000 hand mixers per year. Because the company desires a 15% ROI, the target cost to manufacture, sell, distribute, and service one mixer is $22.50 as computed below:

Projected sales (40,000 mixers × $30 per mixer)	$1,200,000
Less desired profit (15% × $2,000,000)	300,000
Target cost for 40,000 mixers	$ 900,000
Target cost per mixer ($900,000 ÷ 40,000 mixers)	$22.50

This $22.50 target cost would be broken down into target costs for the various functions: manufacturing, marketing, distribution, after-sales service, and so on. Each functional area would be responsible for keeping its actual costs within target.

Summary

Pricing involves a delicate balancing act. Higher prices result in more revenue per unit but drive down unit sales. Exactly where to set prices to maximize profit is a difficult problem, but, in general, the markup over cost should be highest for those products where customers are least sensitive to price. The demand for such products is said to be price inelastic.

Managers often rely on cost-plus formulas to set target prices. From the economists' point of view, the cost base for the markup should be variable cost. In contrast, in the absorption costing approach the cost base is the absorption costing unit product cost and the markup is computed to cover both nonmanufacturing costs and to provide an adequate return on investment. With the absorption approach, costs will not be covered and return on investment will not be adequate unless the unit sales forecast used in the cost-plus formula is accurate. If applying the cost-plus formula results in a price that is too high, the unit sales forecast will not be attained.

Some companies take a different approach to pricing. Instead of starting with costs and then determining prices, they start with prices and then determine allowable costs. Companies that use target costing estimate what a new product's market price is likely to be based on its anticipated features and prices of products already on the market. They subtract desired profit from the estimated market price to arrive at the product's target cost. The design and development team is then given the responsibility of ensuring that the actual cost of the new product does not exceed the target cost.

Glossary

Cost-plus pricing A pricing method in which a predetermined markup is applied to a cost base to determine the target selling price. (p. 716)

Markup The difference between the selling price of a product or service and its cost. The markup is usually expressed as a percentage of cost. (p. 716)

Price elasticity of demand A measure of the degree to which a change in price affects the unit sales of a product or service. (p. 717)

Target costing The process of determining the maximum allowable cost for a new product and then developing a prototype that can be profitably made for that maximum target cost figure. (p. 723)

Questions

A–1 What is cost-plus pricing?

A–2 What does the price elasticity of demand measure? What is inelastic demand? What is elastic demand?

A–3 According to the economists' approach to setting prices, the profit-maximizing price should depend on what two factors?

A–4 Which product should have a larger markup over variable cost, a product whose demand is elastic or a product whose demand is inelastic?

A–5 When the absorption costing approach to cost-plus pricing is used, what is the markup supposed to cover?

A–6 What assumption does the absorption costing approach make about how consumers react to prices?

A–7 Discuss the following statement: "Full cost can be viewed as a floor of protection. If a company always sets its prices above full cost, it will never have to worry about operating at a loss."

A–8 What is target costing? How do target costs enter into the pricing decision?

Multiple-choice questions are provided on the text website at www.mhhe.com/garrison14e.

Exercises

All applicable exercises are available with McGraw-Hill's *Connect™ Accounting*.

EXERCISE A–1 The Economists' Approach to Pricing [LO1]

Kimio Nakimura owns an ice cream stand that she operates during the summer months in Jackson Hole, Wyoming. Her store caters primarily to tourists passing through town on their way to Yellowstone National Park.

Kimio is unsure of how she should price her ice cream cones and has experimented with two prices in successive weeks during the busy August season. The number of people who entered the store was roughly the same each week. During the first week, she priced the cones at $1.79 and 860 cones were sold. During the second week, she priced the cones at $1.39 and 1,340 cones were sold. The variable cost of a cone is $0.41 and consists solely of the costs of the ice cream and of the cone itself. The fixed expenses of the ice cream stand are $425 per week.

Required:

1. Did Kimio make more money selling the cones for $1.79 or for $1.39?
2. Estimate the price elasticity of demand for the ice cream cones.
3. Estimate the profit-maximizing price for ice cream cones.

EXERCISE A–2 Absorption Costing Approach to Setting a Selling Price [LO2]

Naylor Company is considering the introduction of a new product. Management has gathered the following information:

Number of units to be produced and sold each year	12,500
Unit product cost	$30
Projected annual selling and administrative expenses	$60,000
Estimated investment required by the company	$500,000
Desired return on investment (ROI)	18%

The company uses the absorption costing approach to cost-plus pricing.

Required:

1. Compute the markup required to achieve the desired ROI.
2. Compute the target selling price per unit.

EXERCISE A–3 Target Costing [LO3]

Eastern Auto Supply, Inc., produces and distributes auto supplies. The company is anxious to enter the rapidly growing market for long-life batteries that is based on lithium technology. Management believes that to be fully competitive, the price of the new battery that the company is developing cannot exceed $65. At this price, management is confident that the company can sell 50,000 batteries per year. The batteries would require an investment of $2,500,000, and the desired ROI is 20%.

Required:

Compute the target cost of one battery.

connect ACCOUNTING **Problems**

All applicable problems are available with McGraw-Hill's *Connect™ Accounting*.

PROBLEM A–4 The Economists' Approach to Pricing [LO1]

The postal service of St. Lucia, an island in the West Indies, obtains a significant portion of its revenues from sales of special souvenir sheets to stamp collectors. The souvenir sheets usually contain several high-value St. Lucia stamps depicting a common theme, such as the anniversary of Princess Diana's funeral. The souvenir sheets are designed and printed for the postal service by Imperial Printing, a stamp agency service company in the United Kingdom. The souvenir sheets cost the postal service $0.60 each. (The currency in St. Lucia is the East Caribbean dollar.) St. Lucia has been selling these souvenir sheets for $5.00 each and ordinarily sells 50,000 units. To test the market, the postal service recently priced a new souvenir sheet at $6.00 and sales dropped to 40,000 units.

Required:

1. Does the postal service of St. Lucia make more money selling souvenir sheets for $5.00 each or $6.00 each?
2. Estimate the price elasticity of demand for the souvenir sheets.
3. Estimate the profit-maximizing price for souvenir sheets.
4. If Imperial Printing increases the price it charges to the St. Lucia postal service for souvenir sheets to $0.70 each, how much should the St. Lucia postal service charge its customers for the souvenir sheets?

PROBLEM A–5 Standard Costs; Absorption Costing Approach to Setting Prices [LO2]

Euclid Fashions, Inc., is introducing a sports jacket. A standard cost card has been prepared for the new jacket, as shown below:

	Standard Quantity or Hours	Standard Price or Rate	Standard Cost
Direct materials	2.0 yards	$4.60 per yard	$ 9.20
Direct labor	1.4 hours	$10.00 per hour	14.00
Manufacturing overhead (1/6 variable)	1.4 hours	$12.00 per hour	16.80
Total standard cost per jacket			$40.00

The following additional information relating to the new jacket is available:

a. The only variable selling and administrative cost will be $4 per jacket for shipping. Fixed selling and administrative costs will be (per year):

Salaries	$ 90,000
Advertising and other	384,000
Total	$474,000

b. Because the company manufactures many products, no more than 21,000 direct labor-hours per year can be devoted to production of the new jackets.

c. An investment of $900,000 will be necessary to carry inventories and accounts receivable and to purchase some new equipment. The company's required rate of return is 24%.

d. Manufacturing overhead costs are allocated to products on the basis of direct labor-hours.

Required:

1. Assume that the company uses the absorption approach to cost-plus pricing.
   a. Compute the markup that the company needs on the jackets to achieve a 24% ROI if it sells all of the jackets it can produce using 21,000 hours of labor time.

b. Using the markup you have computed, prepare a price quote sheet for a single jacket.
c. Assume that the company is able to sell all of the jackets that it can produce. Prepare an income statement for the first year of activity, and compute the company's ROI for the year on the jackets, using the ROI formula from Chapter 11.

2. After marketing the jackets for several years, the company is experiencing a falloff in demand due to an economic recession. A large retail outlet will make a bulk purchase of jackets if its label is sewn in and if an acceptable price can be worked out. What is the minimum acceptable price for this order?

PROBLEM A–6 Missing Data; Markup Computations; Return on Investment; Pricing [LO2]

Rest Easy, Inc., has designed a new puncture-proof, self-inflating sleeping pad that is unlike anything on the market. Because of the unique properties of the new sleeping pad, the company anticipates that it will be able to sell all the pads that it can produce. On this basis, the following budgeted income statement for the first year of activity is available:

Sales (__?__ pads at __?__ per pad)	$?
Cost of goods sold (__?__ pads at __?__ per pad)	4,000,000
Gross margin	?
Selling and administrative expenses	2,160,000
Net operating income	$?

Additional information on the new sleeping pad is given below:

a. The company will hire enough workers to commit 100,000 direct labor-hours to the manufacture of the pads.

b. A partially completed standard cost card for the new sleeping pad follows:

	Standard Quantity or Hours	Standard Price or Rate	Standard Cost
Direct materials	5 yards	$6 per yard	$30
Direct labor	2 hours	$? per hour	?
Manufacturing overhead	? hours	$? per hour	?
Total standard cost per sleeping pad			$?

c. An investment of $3,500,000 will be necessary to carry inventories and accounts receivable and to purchase some new equipment. Management has decided that the design of the new pad is unique enough that the company should set a selling price that will yield a 24% return on investment (ROI).

d. Other information relating to production and costs follows:

Variable manufacturing overhead cost (per pad)	$7
Variable selling expense (per pad)	$5
Fixed manufacturing overhead cost (total)	$1,750,000
Fixed selling and administrative expense (total)	$?
Number of pads produced and sold (per year)	?

e. Manufacturing overhead costs are allocated to production on the basis of direct labor-hours.

Required:

1. Complete the standard cost card for a single pad.
2. Assume that the company uses the absorption approach to cost-plus pricing.
   a. Compute the markup that the company needs on the pads to achieve a 24% return on investment (ROI).
   b. Using the markup you have computed, prepare a price quotation sheet for a single pad.

   c. Assume, as stated, that the company can sell all the pads that it can produce. Complete the income statement for the first year of activity, and then compute the company's ROI for the year.

3. Assume that direct labor is a variable cost. How many units would the company have to sell at the price you computed in requirement (2) to achieve the 24% ROI? How many units would have to be produced and sold to just break even?

PROBLEM A–7 Target Costing [LO3]

Choice Culinary Supply, Inc., sells restaurant equipment and supplies throughout most of the United States. Management is considering adding a gelato machine to its line of ice cream making machines. Management will negotiate the price of the gelato machine with its Italian manufacturer.

Management of Choice Culinary Supply believes the gelato machines can be sold to its customers in the United States for $3,795 each. At that price, annual sales of the gelato machine should be 80 units. If the gelato machine is added to Choice Culinary Supply's product lines, the company will have to invest $50,000 in inventories and special warehouse fixtures. The variable cost of selling the gelato machines would be $350 per machine.

Required:

1. If Choice Culinary Supply requires a 20% return on investment (ROI), what is the maximum amount the company would be willing to pay the Italian manufacturer for the gelato machines?
2. Management would like to know how the purchase price of the machines would affect Choice Culinary Supply's ROI. Construct a graph that shows Choice Culinary Supply's ROI as a function of the purchase price of the gelato machine. Put the purchase price on the *X*-axis and the resulting ROI on the *Y*-axis. Plot the ROI for purchase prices between $2,400 and $3,400 per machine.
3. After many hours of negotiations, management has concluded that the Italian manufacturer is unwilling to sell the gelato machine at a low enough price for Choice Culinary Supply to earn its 20% required ROI. Apart from simply giving up on the idea of adding the gelato machine to Choice Culinary Supply's product lines, what could management do?

PROBLEM A–8 The Economists' Approach to Pricing; Absorption Costing Approach to Cost-Plus Pricing [LO1, LO2]

Softway, Inc., was started by two young software engineers to market AdBlocker, a software application they had written that blocks ads when surfing the Internet. Sales of the software have been good at 20,000 units a month, but the company has been losing money as shown below:

Sales (20,000 units × $18.95 per unit)	$379,000
Variable cost (20,000 units × $5.90 per unit)	118,000
Contribution margin	261,000
Fixed expenses	264,000
Net operating income (loss)	$ (3,000)

The company's only variable cost is the $5.90 fee it pays to another company to reproduce the software on CDs, print manuals, and package the result in an attractive box for sale to consumers. Monthly fixed selling and administrative expenses are $264,000.

The company's marketing manager has been arguing for some time that the software is priced too high. She estimates that every 10% decrease in price will yield a 20% increase in unit sales. The marketing manager would like your help in preparing a presentation to the company's owners concerning the pricing issue.

Required:

1. To help the marketing manager prepare for her presentation, she has asked you to fill in the blanks in the following table. The selling prices in the table were computed by successively decreasing the selling price by 10%. The estimated unit sales were computed by successively increasing the unit sales by 20%. For example, $17.06 is 10% less than $18.95 and 24,000 units are 20% more than 20,000 units.

Selling Price	Unit Sales	Sales	Variable Cost	Fixed Cost	Operating Income
$18.95	20,000	$379,000	$118,000	$264,000	$(3,000)
$17.06	24,000	$409,440	$141,600	$264,000	$ 3,840
$15.35	28,800	?	?	?	?
$13.82	34,560	?	?	?	?
$12.44	41,472	?	?	?	?
$11.20	49,766	?	?	?	?
$10.08	59,719	?	?	?	?
$9.07	71,663	?	?	?	?
$8.16	85,996	?	?	?	?
$7.34	103,195	?	?	?	?

2. Using the data from the table, construct a graph that shows the net operating income as a function of the selling price. Put the selling price on the *X*-axis and the net operating income on the *Y*-axis. Using the graph, estimate the approximate selling price at which net operating income is maximized.
3. Compute the price elasticity of demand for the AdBlocker software. Based on this calculation, what is the profit-maximizing price?
4. The owners have invested $120,000 in the company and feel that they should be earning at least 2% per month on these funds. If the absorption costing approach to pricing were used, what would be the target selling price based on the current sales of 20,000 units? What do you think would happen to the net operating income of the company if this price were charged?
5. If the owners of the company are dissatisfied with the net operating income and return on investment at the selling price you computed in (3) above, should they increase the selling price? Explain.

Appendix B

Profitability Analysis

LEARNING OBJECTIVES

After studying this appendix, you should be able to:

LO1 Compute the profitability index and use it to select from among possible actions.

LO2 Compute and use the profitability index in volume trade-off decisions.

LO3 Compute and use the profitability index in other business decisions.

Introduction

Perhaps more than any other information, managers would like to know the profitability of their products, customers, and other business segments. They want this information so that they know what segments to drop and add and which to emphasize. This appendix provides a coherent framework for measuring profitability, bringing together relevant materials from several chapters. After studying this appendix you should have a firm grasp of the principles underlying profitability analysis. The first step is to distinguish between *absolute profitability* and *relative profitability.*

IN BUSINESS

PIONEER PULLS THE PLUG ON ITS TV BUSINESS

Pioneer Corporation exited the plasma television business because it was *absolutely* unprofitable. The company only made 50-inch and 60-inch plasma-display models, so when the economy tanked, demand for these luxury models plummeted. Pioneer attempted to cut costs by buying its plasma-display panels from Panasonic rather than making them, but it was not enough to overcome a 37% drop in annual unit sales coupled with intense price competition from larger rivals.

Source: Daisuke Wakabayashi, "Pioneer Unplugs Its TV Business," *The Wall Street Journal,* February 13, 2009, p. B1.

Absolute Profitability

Absolute profitability is concerned with the impact on the organization's overall profits of adding or dropping a particular segment such as a product or customer—without making any other changes. For example, if Coca-Cola were considering closing down its operations in the African country of Zimbabwe, managers would be interested in the absolute profitability of those operations. Measuring the absolute profitability of an existing segment is conceptually straightforward—compare the revenues that would be lost from dropping the segment to the costs that would be avoided. When considering a new potential segment, compare the additional revenues from adding the segment to the additional costs that would be incurred. In each case, include only the additional costs that would actually be avoided or incurred. All other costs are irrelevant and should be ignored.

In practice, figuring out what costs would change and what costs would not change if a segment were dropped (or added) can be very difficult. Activity-based costing can help in identifying such costs, but all costs should be carefully analyzed to determine whether they would really change. For example, an activity-based costing study of Coca-Cola's Zimbabwe operations might include charges for staff support provided to the Zimbabwe operations by Coca-Cola's corporate headquarters in Atlanta. However, if eliminating the Zimbabwe operations would have no impact on actual costs in Atlanta, then these costs are not relevant and should be excluded when measuring the absolute profitability of the Zimbabwe operations.

For examples of the measurement of absolute profitability, see "Appendix 7A: ABC Action Analysis," the section "Segmented Income Statements and the Contribution Approach" in Chapter 6, and the section "Adding and Dropping Product Lines and Other Segments" in Chapter 12.

Relative Profitability

LEARNING OBJECTIVE 1
Compute the profitability index and use it to select from among possible actions.

Even when every segment is *absolutely* profitable, managers often want to know which segments are most and least profitable. **Relative profitability** is concerned with ranking products, customers, and other business segments to determine which should be emphasized.

Why are managers interested in ranking segments or determining the relative profitability of segments? The answer to this deceptively simple question provides the key to measuring relative profitability. The only reason to rank segments is if something forces you to make trade-offs among them. If trade-offs are not necessary, the solution is simple—keep every segment that is absolutely profitable. What would force a manager to make trade-offs among profitable segments? There is only one answer—a *constraint.* In the absence of a constraint, all segments that are absolutely profitable should be pursued. On the other hand, if a constraint is present, then by definition the company cannot pursue every profitable opportunity. Choices have to be made. Thus, measuring relative profitability makes sense only when a constraint exists that forces trade-offs. This point cannot be overemphasized; constraints are fundamental to understanding and measuring relative profitability.

How should relative profitability be measured? Divide each segment's measure of absolute profitability, which is the incremental profit from that segment, by the amount of the constraint required by the segment. For example, refer to the data below for two of the many segments within a company:

	Segment A	Segment B
Incremental profit	$100,000	$200,000
Amount of constrained resource required	100 hours	400 hours

Segment B may seem more attractive than Segment A because its incremental profit is twice as large, but it requires four times as much of the constrained resource. In fact, Segment B would not be the best use of the constrained resource because it generates only $500 of incremental profit per hour ($200,000 ÷ 400 hours), whereas Segment A generates $1,000 of incremental profit per hour ($100,000 ÷ 100 hours). Another way to look at this is to suppose that 400 hours of the constrained resource are available. Would you rather use the hours on four segments like Segment A, generating a total incremental profit of $400,000, or on one segment like Segment B, which generates $200,000 in incremental profit?

In general, the relative profitability of segments should be measured by the **profitability index** as defined below:

$$\text{Profitability index} = \frac{\text{Incremental profit from the segment}}{\text{Amount of the constrained resource required by the segment}}$$

The profitability index is computed below for the two segments in the example:

	Segment A	Segment B
Incremental profit (a)	$100,000	$200,000
Amount of constrained resource required (b)	100 hours	400 hours
Profitability index (a) ÷ (b)	$1,000 per hour	$500 per hour

We have already encountered several examples of the profitability index in previous chapters. For example, in Chapter 13 the project profitability index was defined as:

$$\text{Project profitability index} = \frac{\text{Net present value of the project}}{\text{Amount of investment required by the project}}$$

The project profitability index is used when a company has more long-term projects with positive net present values than it can fund. In this case, the incremental profit from the segment is the net present value of the project. And because the investment funds are the constraint, the amount of the constrained resource required by the segment is the amount of investment required by the project.

As an example of the use of the profitability index, consider the case of Quality Kitchen Design, a small company specializing in designing kitchens for upscale homes. Management is considering the 10 short-term projects listed in Panel A of Exhibit B–1. The incremental profit from each project is listed in the second column. For example, the incremental profit from Project A is \$9,180. This incremental profit consists of the revenues from the project less any costs that would be incurred by the company as a consequence of accepting the project. The company's constraint is the lead designer's time. Project A would require 17 hours of the lead designer's time. If all of the projects were accepted, they would require a total of 100 hours. Unfortunately, only 46 hours are available. Consequently, management will have to turn down some projects. The profitability index will be used in deciding which projects to accept and which to turn down. The profitability index for a project is computed by dividing its incremental profit by the amount of the lead designer's time required for the project. In the case of Project A, the profitability index is \$540 per hour.

The projects are ranked in order of the profitability index in Panel B of Exhibit B–1. The last column in that panel shows the cumulative amount of the constrained resource (i.e., lead designer's time) required to do the projects at that point in the list and higher. For example, the 7 hours listed to the right of Project J in the cumulative column represents the sum of the 4 hours required for Project F plus the 3 hours required for Project J.

To find the best combination of projects within the limits of the constrained resource, go down the list in Panel B to the point where all of the available constrained resource is used. In this case, because 46 hours of lead designer time are available, that would be the point above the solid line drawn in Panel B of Exhibit B–1. Projects F, J, B, I, D, and A lie above that line and would require a total of exactly 46 hours of lead designer time. The optimal plan consists of accepting these six projects and turning down the others. The total incremental profit from accepting these projects would be \$32,930 as shown in Panel C of Exhibit B–1. No other feasible combination of projects would yield a higher total incremental profit.[1]

[1] In this example, the top projects exactly consumed all of the available constrained resource. That won't always happen. For example, assume that only 45 hours of lead designer time are available. This small change complicates matters considerably. Because of the "lumpiness" of the projects, the optimal plan isn't necessarily to do projects F, J, B, I, and D—stopping at Project D on the list and a cumulative requirement of 29 hours. That would leave 16 hours of unused lead designer time. The best use of this time may be Project C, which has an incremental profit of \$7,040. However, other possibilities exist too. Finding and evaluating all of the most likely possibilities can take a lot of time and ingenuity. When the constrained resource is not completely exhausted by the top projects on the list, some tinkering with the solution may be necessary. For this reason, the list generated by ranking based on the profitability index should be viewed as a starting point rather than as a definitive solution when the projects are "lumpy" and take big chunks of the constrained resource.

EXHIBIT B–1
Ranking Segments Based on the Profitability Index

Panel A: Computation of the Profitability Index

	Incremental Profit (A)	Amount of the Constrained Resource Required (B)	Profitability Index (A) ÷ (B)
Project A	$9,180	17 hours	$540 per hour
Project B	$7,200	9 hours	$800 per hour
Project C	$7,040	16 hours	$440 per hour
Project D	$5,680	8 hours	$710 per hour
Project E	$5,330	13 hours	$410 per hour
Project F	$4,280	4 hours	$1,070 per hour
Project G	$4,160	13 hours	$320 per hour
Project H	$3,720	12 hours	$310 per hour
Project I	$3,650	5 hours	$730 per hour
Project J	$2,940	3 hours	$980 per hour
		100 hours	

Panel B: Ranking Based on the Profitability Index

	Profitability Index	Amount of the Constrained Resource Required	Cumulative Amount of the Constrained Resource Used
Project F	$1,070 per hour	4 hours	4 hours
Project J	$980 per hour	3 hours	7 hours
Project B	$800 per hour	9 hours	16 hours
Project I	$730 per hour	5 hours	21 hours
Project D	$710 per hour	8 hours	29 hours
Project A	$540 per hour	17 hours	46 hours
Project C	$440 per hour	16 hours	62 hours
Project E	$410 per hour	13 hours	75 hours
Project G	$320 per hour	13 hours	88 hours
Project H	$310 per hour	12 hours	100 hours

Panel C: The Optimal Plan

	Incremental Profit
Project F	$ 4,280
Project J	2,940
Project B	7,200
Project I	3,650
Project D	5,680
Project A	9,180
	$32,930

We should reinforce a very important point that may be forgotten in the midst of these details. The profitability index is based on *incremental* profit. When computing the incremental profit for a segment such as a product, customer, or project, only the *incremental* costs of the segment should be included. Those are the costs that could be avoided—whether fixed or variable—if the segment is eliminated. All other costs are not relevant and should be ignored—including allocations of common costs.

IN BUSINESS

KRAFT BULKS UP AND THEN SLIMS DOWN

In 2000, Kraft Foods Inc. acquired Nabisco for $19 billion. This acquisition, coupled with nine others, pushed Kraft's annual sales above $32 billion. Indeed, Kraft had assembled an impressive portfolio of brands including Oreo cookies, Oscar Mayer meats, Post cereals, Maxwell House coffees, and DiGiorno pizzas, to name a few. However, Kraft's CEO, Roger K. Deromedi, has decided that it is time to slim down the company a bit. In 2004, Kraft sold its Life Savers and Altoids brands to Wm. Wrigley Jr. Co. for $1.5 billion in cash. Deromedi sold these laggard brands to enable Kraft to "concentrate on the blockbuster brands that can be tops in their categories worldwide." Presumably, Kraft considered Life Savers and Altoids to be relatively unprofitable compared to the other brands within the organization that were competing for scarce investment funds.

Source: Michael Arndt, "Why Kraft Is on a Crash Diet," *BusinessWeek,* November 29, 2004, p. 46.

Volume Trade-Off Decisions

LEARNING OBJECTIVE 2
Compute and use the profitability index in volume trade-off decisions.

Earlier we stated that you have already encountered several examples of the profitability index in this book. One was the project profitability index in Chapter 13. The other example of the profitability index is in the section "Utilization of a Constrained Resource" in Chapter 12. That section deals with situations in which a company does not have enough capacity to satisfy demand for all of its products. Therefore, the company must produce less than the market demands of some products. This is called a volume trade-off decision because the decision, at the margin, consists of trading off units of one product for units of another. Fixed costs are typically unaffected by such decisions—capacity will be fully utilized, it is just a question of how it will be utilized. In volume trade-off decisions where fixed costs are irrelevant, the profitability index takes the special form:

$$\text{Profitability index for a volume trade-off decision} = \frac{\text{Unit contribution margin}}{\text{Amount of the constrained resource required by one unit}}$$

This profitability index is identical to the "contribution margin per unit of the constrained resource" that was used in Chapter 12 to decide which products should be emphasized. An example of a volume trade-off decision is presented in Exhibit B–2. In this example, the company makes three products that use the constrained resource—a machine that is available 2,200 minutes per week. As shown in Panel B of Exhibit B–2, producing all three products up to demand would require 2,700 minutes per week—500 more minutes than are available. Consequently, the company cannot fully satisfy demand for these three products and some product or products must be cut back.

The profitability index for this decision is computed in Panel C of Exhibit B–2. For example, the profitability index for product RX200 is $3 per minute. The comparable figure for product VB30 is $5 per minute and for product SQ500 is $4 per minute. Consequently, the correct ranking of the products is VB30 followed by SQ500, then followed by RX200.

The optimal production plan is laid out in Panel D of Exhibit B–2. The most profitable products, VB30 and SQ500, are produced up to demand and the remaining time on the constraint is used to make 200 units of RX200 (1,000 available minutes ÷ 5 minutes per unit).

The total contribution margin from following this plan is computed in Panel E of Exhibit B–2. The total contribution margin of $8,600 is higher than the contribution margin that could be realized from following any other feasible plan. Assuming that fixed costs are not affected by the decision of which products to emphasize, this plan will also yield a higher total profit than any other feasible plan.

EXHIBIT B–2
Using the Profitability Index in a Volume Trade-Off Decision

Panel A: Product Data

	Products		
	RX200	VB30	SQ500
Unit contribution margin	$15 per unit	$10 per unit	$16 per unit
Demand per week	300 units	400 units	100 units
Amount of the constrained resource required	5 minutes per unit	2 minutes per unit	4 minutes per unit

Panel B: Total Demand on the Constrained Resource

	Products			
	RX200	VB30	SQ500	Total
Demand per week (a)	300 units	400 units	100 units	
Amount of the constrained resource required (b)	5 minutes per unit	2 minutes per unit	4 minutes per unit	
Total amount of the constraint required per week to meet demand (a) × (b)	1,500 minutes	800 minutes	400 minutes	2,700 minutes

Panel C: Computation of the Profitability Index

	Products		
	RX200	VB30	SQ500
Unit contribution margin (a)	$15 per unit	$10 per unit	$16 per unit
Amount of the constrained resource required (b)	5 minutes per unit	2 minutes per unit	4 minutes per unit
Profitability index (contribution margin per unit of the constrained resource) (a) ÷ (b)	$3 per minute	$5 per minute	$4 per minute

Panel D: The Optimal Plan

Amount of constrained resource available	2,200 minutes
Less: Constrained resource required for production of 400 units of VB30	800 minutes
Remaining constrained resource available	1,400 minutes
Less: Constrained resource required for production of 100 units of SQ500	400 minutes
Remaining constrained resource available	1,000 minutes
Less: Constrained resource required for production of 200 units of RX200*	1,000 minutes
Remaining constrained resource available	0 minutes

*1,000 minutes available ÷ 5 minutes per unit of RX200 = 200 units of RX200.

Panel E: The Total Contribution Margin under the Optimal Plan

	Products			
	RX200	VB30	SQ500	Total
Unit contribution margin (a)	$15 per unit	$10 per unit	$16 per unit	
Optimal production plan (b)	200 units	400 units	100 units	
Contribution margin (a) × (b)	$3,000	$4,000	$1,600	$8,600

Managerial Implications

LEARNING OBJECTIVE 3
Compute and use the profitability index in other business decisions.

In addition to the add-or-drop and volume trade-off decisions discussed above, the profitability index can be used in other ways. For example, which products would you rather have your salespersons emphasize—those with a low profitability index or those with a high profitability index? The answer is, of course, that salespersons should be encouraged to emphasize sales of the products with the highest profitability indexes. However, if salespersons are paid commissions based on sales, what products will they try to sell? The selling prices of products RX200, VB30, and SQ500 appear below:

	Products		
	RX200	VB30	SQ500
Unit selling price	$40	$30	$35

If salespersons are paid a commission based on gross sales, they will prefer to sell product RX200, which has the highest selling price. But that is the *least* profitable product given the current constraint. It has a profitability index of only $3 per minute compared to $5 per minute for VB30 and $4 per minute for SQ500.

This suggests that salespersons should be paid commissions based on the profitability index and the amount of constraint time sold rather than on sales revenue. This would encourage them to sell the most profitable products, rather than the products with the highest selling prices. How would such a compensation system work? Prior to making a sales call, a salesperson would receive an up-to-date report indicating how much of the constrained resource is currently available and a listing of all products showing the amount of the constraint each requires and the profitability index. Such a report would appear as follows:

Marketing Data Report

	Products		
	RX200	VB30	SQ500
Unit selling price	$40	$30	$35
Unit variable cost	25	20	19
Unit contribution margin (a)	$15	$10	$16
Amount of the constrained resource required per unit (b)	5 minutes	2 minutes	4 minutes
Profitability index (a) ÷ (b)	$3 per minute	$5 per minute	$4 per minute

Total available time on the constrained resource: 100 minutes

The key here is to realize that the salesperson is, in essence, selling time on the constraint. A salesperson who is paid based on the profitability index will prefer to sell product VB30 because the salesperson would get credit for sales of $500 if all 100 minutes are used on product VB30 ($5 per minute × 100 minutes), whereas the credit would be only $300 for product RX200 or $400 for product SQ500.[2]

[2] Equivalent incentives would be provided by commissions based on total contribution margin. If all 100 available minutes are used to make product VB30, 50 units could be produced (100 minutes ÷ 2 minutes per unit), for which the total contribution margin would be $500 ($10 per unit × 50 units). Likewise, the total contribution margin for products RX200 and SQ500 would be $300 and $400, respectively, if all available minutes were used to make just those products.

The profitability index also has implications for pricing new products. Suppose that the company has designed a new product, WR6000, whose variable cost is \$30 per unit and that requires 6 minutes of the constrained resource per unit. Because the company is currently using all of its capacity, the new product would necessarily displace production of existing products. Consequently, the price of the new product should cover not only its variable cost, but it should also cover the opportunity cost of displacing existing products. What product would be displaced? Production of RX200 should be cut first because it is the least profitable existing product. And how much is a minute of the constrained resource worth if it would otherwise be used to make product RX200? A minute of the constrained resource is worth \$3 per minute, the profitability index of product RX200. Therefore, the selling price of the new product should at least cover the costs laid out below:[3]

$$\begin{matrix}\text{Selling price of}\\ \text{new product}\end{matrix} \geq \begin{matrix}\text{Variable cost of}\\ \text{the new product}\end{matrix} + \left(\begin{matrix}\text{Opportunity}\\ \text{cost per unit of}\\ \text{the constrained}\\ \text{resource}\end{matrix} \times \begin{matrix}\text{Amount of the}\\ \text{constrained resource}\\ \text{required by a unit of}\\ \text{the new product}\end{matrix}\right)$$

In the case of the new product WR6000, the calculations would be:

$$\begin{matrix}\text{Selling price of}\\ \text{WR6000}\end{matrix} \geq \$30 + (\$3 \text{ per minute} \times 6 \text{ minutes}) = \$30 + \$18 = \$48$$

WR6000 should sell for at least \$48 or the company would be better off continuing to use the available capacity to produce RX200.[4]

IN BUSINESS

DEALING WITH UNPROFITABLE CUSTOMERS

One retailer discovered that many of the biggest spending customers in their "loyalty" program were unprofitable because they bought only sale items and returned lots of items. The company stopped sending these customers notices of upcoming "private" sales.

Source: Larry Selden and Geoffrey Colvin, "Will this Customer Sink Your Stock?" *Fortune*, September 30, 2002, pp. 127–132.

Summary

A strong distinction should be made between absolute profitability and relative profitability. A segment is considered profitable in an absolute sense if dropping it would result in lower overall profits. Absolute profitability is measured by the segment's incremental profit, which is the difference between the revenues from the segment and the costs that could be avoided by dropping the segment.

A relative profitability measure is used to rank segments. Such rankings are necessary only if a constraint forces the organization to make trade-offs among segments. To appropriately measure relative profitability, three things must be known. First, the constraint must be identified. Second, the incremental profit associated with each segment must be computed. Third, the amount of the

[3] In addition, the selling price of a new product should cover any avoidable fixed costs of the product. This is easier said than done, however, because achieving this goal involves estimating how many units will be sold—which in turn depends on the selling price.

[4] If production of WR6000 eventually completely displaces production of RX200, the opportunity cost would change. It would increase to \$4 per minute, the profitability index of the next product in line to be cut back.

constrained resource required by each segment must be determined. Relative profitability is measured by the profitability index, which is the incremental profit from the segment divided by the amount of the constrained resource required by the segment. The profitability index can be used in a variety of situations, including selections of projects and volume trade-off decisions.

Glossary

Absolute profitability The impact on the organization's overall profits of adding or dropping a particular segment such as a product or customer—without making any other changes. (p. 732)

Profitability index The measure of relative profitability, which is computed by dividing the incremental profit from a segment by the amount of the constrained resource required by the segment. (p. 733)

Relative profitability A ranking of products, customers, or other business segments for purposes of making trade-offs among segments. This is necessary when a constraint exists. (p. 733)

Questions

B–1 What is meant by *absolute* profitability?

B–2 What is meant by *relative* profitability?

B–3 A successful owner of a small business stated: "We have the best technology, the best products, and the best people in the world. We have no constraints." Do you agree?

B–4 What information is needed to measure the *absolute* profitability of a segment?

B–5 What information is needed to measure the *relative* profitability of a product?

B–6 How should the relative profitability of products be determined in a volume trade-off decision?

B–7 What costs should be covered by the selling price of a new product?

Multiple-choice questions are provided on the text website at www.mhhe.com/garrison14e.

Exercises connect ACCOUNTING

All applicable exercises are available with McGraw-Hill's *Connect™ Accounting*.

EXERCISE B–1 Ranking Projects Based on the Profitability Index [LO1]

Atlantic Amusements is in the process of reviewing proposals for new rides at its theme parks in cities scattered throughout the Atlantic coast. The company's only experienced safety engineer must carefully review plans and monitor construction on each and every project—this constraint makes it impossible to build all of the new rides this year. The net present values and the amount of safety engineer time required for the proposed rides are listed below:

Proposed Ride	Net Present Value	Safety Engineer Time Required (hours)
Ride 1	$ 741,400	220
Ride 2	382,500	150
Ride 3	850,500	350
Ride 4	450,500	170
Ride 5	620,400	220
Ride 6	1,004,400	310
Ride 7	953,800	380
Ride 8	332,500	190
Ride 9	385,500	150
Ride 10	680,400	270
Total	$6,401,900	2,410

Required:

1. The safety engineer is available to work on new rides for 1,220 hours during the year. Which of the proposed rides should the company build this year? (Note: The incremental profit of a long-term project such as constructing a new ride is its net present value.)
2. What would be the total net present value of the rides built under your plan?

EXERCISE B–2 Volume Trade-Off Decision [LO2]

Bateaux du Bois, Ltd., makes reproductions of classic wooden boats. The bottleneck in the production process is fitting wooden planks to build up the curved sections of the hull. This process requires the attention of the shop's most experienced craftsman. A total of 1,800 hours are available per year in this bottleneck operation. Data concerning the company's four products appear below:

	Trader	Trapper	Quebec	Runner
Unit contribution margin	$444	$464	$312	$462
Annual demand (units)	80	80	70	120
Hours required in the bottleneck operation per unit	6	8	4	7

No fixed costs could be avoided by modifying how many units are produced of any product or even by dropping any one of the products.

Required:

1. Is there sufficient capacity in the bottleneck operation to satisfy demand for all products?
2. What is the optimal production plan for the year?
3. What would be the total contribution margin for the optimal production plan you have proposed?

EXERCISE B–3 Pricing a New Product [LO3]

Java Stop owns and operates a chain of popular coffee stands that serve over 30 different coffee-based beverages. The constraint at the coffee stands is the amount of time required to fill an order, which can be considerable for the more complex beverages. Sales are often lost because customers leave after seeing a long waiting line to place an order. Careful analysis of the company's existing products has revealed that the opportunity cost of order-filling time is $3.40 per minute.

The company is considering introducing a new product, amaretto cappuccino, to be made with almond extract and double-fine sugar. The variable cost of the standard size amaretto cappuccino would be $0.46 and the time required to fill an order for the beverage would be 45 seconds.

Required:

What is the minimum acceptable selling price for the new amaretto cappuccino product?

connect ACCOUNTING **Problems**

All applicable problems are available with McGraw-Hill's *Connect™ Accounting*.

PROBLEM B–4 Ranking Alternatives and Managing with a Constraint [LO1, LO3]

Terri's Baking Company has developed a reputation for producing superb, one-of-a-kind wedding cakes in addition to its normal fare of breads and pastries. While the wedding cake business is a major moneymaker, it creates some problems for the bakery's owner, Terri Chavez—particularly in June. The company's reputation for wedding cakes is largely based on the skills of Megan Easterling, who decorates all of the cakes. Unfortunately, last year the company accepted too many cake orders for some June weekends, with the result that Megan was worked to a frazzle and almost quit. To prevent a recurrence, Terri has promised Megan that she will have to work no more than 33 hours in any week to prepare the wedding cakes for the upcoming weekend. (Megan also has other duties at the bakery, so even with the 33-hour limitation, she would be working more than full time in June.)

A number of reservations for wedding cakes for the first weekend in June had already been received from customers by early May. When a customer makes a reservation, Ms. Chavez gets enough information concerning the size of the wedding party and the desires of the customer to determine the cake's price, the cost to make it, and the amount of time that Megan will need to spend decorating it. The reservations for the first weekend in June are listed below:

Customer	Incremental Profit	Megan's Time Required (hours)
Audet	$ 140	4
Boyer	124	4
Comfort	160	5
Donaghe	96	3
Due.	190	5
Dupuy.	288	8
Ebberts	93	3
Imm	136	4
Mulgrew	234	6
Paulding	204	6
Total	$1,665	48

For example, the Audet cake would require 4 hours of Megan's time and would generate a profit of $140 for the bakery. Following industry practice, pricing for the cakes is based on their size and standard formulas and does not reflect how much decorating would be required.

Required:

1. Ms. Chavez feels that she must cancel enough cake reservations to reduce Megan's workload to the promised level. She knows that customers whose reservations have been canceled will be disappointed, but she intends to refer all of those customers to an excellent bakery across town. If the sole objective is to maximize the company's total profit, which reservations should be canceled?
2. What would be the total profit if your recommendation in part (1) above is followed?
3. Assume that for competitive reasons it would not be practical for Terri's Baking Company to change the pricing of its wedding cakes. What recommendations would you make to Ms. Chavez concerning taking reservations in the future?
4. Assume that Terri's Baking Company could change the way it prices its wedding cakes. What recommendations would you make to Ms. Chavez concerning how she should set the prices of wedding cakes in the future?
5. What might Ms. Chavez be able to do to keep both Megan and her customers happy while increasing her profits? Be creative. (Hint: Review the section on managing constraints in Chapter 12.)

PROBLEM B–5 Customer Profitability and Managerial Decisions [LO1, LO3]

FirstLine Pharmaceuticals, Inc., is a wholesale distributor of prescription drugs to independent retail and hospital-based pharmacies. Management believes that top-notch customer representatives are the key factor in determining whether the company will be successful in the future. Customer representatives serve as the company's liaison with customers—helping pharmacies monitor their stocks, delivering drugs when customer stocks run low, and providing up-to-date information on drugs from many different companies. Customer representatives must be ultra-reliable and are highly trained. Good customer representatives are hard to come by and are not easily replaced.

Customer representatives routinely record the amount of time they spend serving each pharmacy. This time includes travel time to and from the company's central warehouse as well as time spent replenishing stocks, dealing with complaints, answering questions about drugs, informing pharmacists of the latest developments and newest products, reviewing bills, explaining procedures, and so on. Some pharmacies require more hand-holding and attention than others and consequently they consume more of the representatives' time.

Recently, customer representatives have increasingly complained that it is impossible to do their jobs without working well beyond normal working hours. This has led to an alarming increase in the number of customer representatives quitting for jobs in other organizations. As a consequence, management is considering dropping some customers to reduce the workload on customer representatives. Data concerning a representative sample of the company's customers appears below:

	Willows Pharmacy	Swedish Hospital Pharmacy	Georgetown Clinic Pharmacy	Kristen Pharmacy
Total revenues	$344,880	$1,995,200	$1,414,170	$154,800
Cost of drugs sold	$263,340	$1,446,520	$1,047,660	$120,960
Customer service costs	$12,240	$62,640	$39,900	$4,500
Customer representative time	180	1,160	570	90

Customer service costs include all of the costs—other than the costs of the drugs themselves—that could be avoided by dropping the customer. These costs include the hourly wages of the customer representatives, their sales commissions, the mileage-related costs of the customer representatives' company-provided vehicles, and so on.

Required:

1. Rank the four customers in terms of their profitability.
2. Customer representatives are currently paid $25 per hour plus a commission of 1% of sales revenues. If these four pharmacies are indeed representative of the company's customers, could the company afford to pay its customer representatives more in order to attract and retain customer representatives?

PROBLEM B–6 Volume Trade-Off Decision; Managing the Constraint [LO2, LO3]

Enumclaw Brick, Inc., manufactures bricks using clay deposits on the company's property. Raw clays are blended and then extruded into molds to form unfired bricks. The unfired bricks are then stacked onto movable metal platforms and rolled into the kiln where they are fired until dry. The dried bricks are then packaged and shipped to retail outlets and contractors. The bottleneck in the production process is the kiln, which is available for 2,000 hours per year. Data concerning the company's four main products appear below. Products are sold by the pallet.

	Traditional Brick	Textured Facing	Cinder Block	Roman Brick
Gross revenue per pallet	$789	$1,264	$569	$836
Contribution margin per pallet	$370	$497	$328	$390
Annual demand (pallets)	120	80	180	70
Hours required in the kiln per pallet	5	7	4	6

No fixed costs could be avoided by modifying how much is produced of any product.

Required:

1. Is there sufficient capacity in the kiln to satisfy demand for all products?
2. What is the production plan for the year that would maximize the company's profit?
3. What would be the total contribution margin for the production plan you have proposed?
4. The kiln could be operated for more than 2,000 hours per year by running it after normal working hours. Up to how much per hour should the company be willing to pay in overtime wages, energy costs, and other incremental costs to operate the kiln additional hours?
5. The company is considering introducing a new product, glazed Venetian bricks, that would have a variable cost of $530 per pallet and would require 11 hours in the kiln. What is the minimum acceptable selling price for this new product?
6. Salespersons are currently paid a commission of 5% of gross revenues. Will this motivate the salespersons to make the right choices concerning which products to sell most aggressively?

PROBLEM B–7 Interpreting Common Practice [LO1]

In practice, many organizations measure the relative profitability of their segments by dividing the segments' margins by their revenues. The segment margin for this purpose is the segment's revenue less its fully allocated costs—including allocations of fixed common costs. For example, a hospital might compute the relative profitability of its major segments as follows:

Memorial Hospital Profitability Report (in thousands of dollars)	Emergency Room	Surgery	Acute Care	Total
Revenue	$8,650	$14,870	$12,120	$35,640
Fully allocated cost	8,360	14,490	11,760	34,610
Margin	$ 290	$ 380	$ 360	$ 1,030
Profitability (Margin ÷ Revenue)	3.4%	2.6%	3.0%	2.9%

The hospital's net operating income for this period was $1,030,000.

Required:

1. Evaluate the use of the margin, as defined above, in the numerator of the profitability measure.
2. Evaluate the use of revenue in the denominator of the profitability measure.

Case

connect ACCOUNTING

All applicable cases are available with McGraw-Hill's *Connect™ Accounting*.

CASE B-8 Redirecting Effort [LO2]

Prevala Corporation recently suffered from its fourth straight decline in quarterly earnings—despite modest increases in sales. Unfortunately, Prevala's industry is highly competitive, so the company is reluctant to increase its prices. However, management believes that profits would improve if the efforts of its sales force were redirected toward the more profitable products in its offerings.

Several years ago Prevala decided that its core competencies were strategy, design, and marketing and that production should be outsourced. Consequently, Prevala subcontracts all of its production.

Prevala's salespersons are paid salaries and commissions. All of the company's salespersons sell the company's full line of products. The commissions are 6% of the revenue generated by a salesperson and average about 70% of a salesperson's total compensation. There has been some discussion of increasing the size of the sales force, but management prefers for the present to redirect the efforts of salespersons towards the more profitable products. While management is reluctant to tinker with the sales compensation scheme, revenue targets for the various products will be set for the regional sales managers based on the products that management wants to push most aggressively. The regional sales managers will be paid a bonus if the sales targets are met.

The company computes product margins for all of its products using the following formula:

Selling price
Less: Sales commissions
Less: Cost of sales
Less: Operating expenses
= Product margin

The cost of sales in the product margin formula is the amount Prevala pays to its production subcontractors. The operating expenses represent fixed costs. Each product is charged a fair share of those costs, calculated this year as 37.2% of the product's selling price.

Management is convinced that the best way to improve overall profits is to redirect the efforts of the company's salespersons. There are no plans to add or drop any products.

Required:

How would you measure the relative profitability of the company's products in this situation? Assume that it is not feasible to change the way salespersons are compensated. Also assume that the only data you have available are the selling price, the sales commissions, the cost of sales, the operating expenses, and the product margin for each product.

Photo Credits

Page 1 © Tom Grill/Corbis
Page 9 © Imagestate Media (John Foxx)
Page 17 © Author's Image/Punchstock
Page 24 © Mark Graham/The New York Times/Redux
Page 28 © Moodboard/Corbis
Page 31 © Sandee Noreen
Page 42 © Getty Images/flickr RF
Page 83 Courtesy of University Tees, Inc.
Page 85 © Sandee Noreen
Page 85 © Sandee Noreen
Page 92 © Keith Brofsky/Getty Images
Page 141 © Lester Lefkowitz/Corbis
Page 144 © AP Photo/Yves Logghe
Page 146 © Mark Ralston/AFP/Getty Images
Page 183 © Comstock Images
Page 196 © Yellow Dog Productions/Getty Images
Page 199 © Bloomberg via Getty Images
Page 203 © Royalty-Free/CORBIS
Page 229 © Tetra Images/Jupiter Images
Page 238 © Photodisc Collection/Getty Images
Page 241 © TRBfoto/Getty Images
Page 248 © Duncan Smith/Getty Images
Page 272 © Royalty-Free/CORBIS
Page 275 © Sandee Noreen
Page 275 © Sandee Noreen
Page 276 © Sandee Noreen
Page 286 © Ryan McVay/Getty Images
Page 335 © Sandee Noreen
Page 349 © Ryan McVay/Getty Images
Page 352 © Brand X Pictures/PunchStock
Page 353 © Eric Noreen
Page 356 © AP Photo/Stew Milne
Page 383 © AFP/Getty Images
Page 390 © Getty Images
Page 393 © Janis Christie/Getty Images
Page 395 © 2005 Comstock Images, JupiterImages Corporation
Page 418 © Bloomberg via Getty Images
Page 422 © Getty Images/Digital Vision
Page 427 © Royalty-Free/CORBIS
Page 432 © Rob Melnychuk/Getty Images
Page 472 © Getty Images
Page 477 © AP Photo/Marcio Jose Sanchez
Page 487 © TongRo Image Stock/Alamy
Page 490 © Ryan McVay/Getty Images
Page 527 © Royalty-Free/Corbis
Page 541 © Getty Images/PictureIndia RF
Page 546 © The McGraw-Hill Companies, Inc./Andy Resek, photographer
Page 579 Courtesy of Cintas Corporation.
Page 593 © Ingram Publishing/SuperStock
Page 597 © The McGraw-Hill Companies, Inc./Jill Braaten, photographer
Page 603 © PRNewsFoto/Royal Caribbean International
Page 639 © Bloomberg via Getty Images
Page 641 © The McGraw-Hill Companies, Inc./Jill Braaten, photographer
Page 645 © Steve Mason/Getty Images
Page 658 © Randy Allbritton/Getty Images
Page 679 © AP Photo/Mary Altaffer
Page 686 © Doug Menuez/Getty Images
Page 694 © Jack Hollingsworth/Getty Images
Page 716 © Eric Noreen
Page 716 © Eric Noreen

Index

Page numbers followed by n refer to notes.